Fostering Children's Mathematical Power:

An Investigative Approach to K-8 Mathematics Instruction

Arthur J. Baroody
University of Illinois at Urbana-Champaign

with

Ronald T. Coslick
Niskayuna (New York) Middle School (retired)

 LAWRENCE ERLBAUM ASSOCIATES, PUBLISHERS

1998   Mahwah, New Jersey   London

Lawrence Erlbaum Associates, Inc., Publishers
10 Industrial Avenue
Mahwah, New Jersey 07430

Library of Congress Cataloging-in-Publication Data

Baroody, Arthur J., 1947-
    Fostering children's mathematical power : an investigative
approach to K-8 mathematics instruction / Arthur J. Baroody with
Ronald T. Coslick.
        p.   cm.
    Includes bibliographical references (p.   -   ) and index.
    ISBN 0-8058-3105-3 (pbk. : acid-free paper)
    1. Mathematics--Study and teaching (Elementary) I. Coslick,
Ronald T. II. Title.
QA135.5.B2847 1998
372.7'044--dc21   98-24187
                                                       CIP

Books published by Lawrence Erlbaum Associates are printed
on acid-free paper, and their bindings are chosen
for strength and durability.

Printed in the United States of America

10 9 8 7 6 5 4 3

ACKNOWLEDGMENTS

This guide builds on the research and writing of numerous mathematics educators and psychologists, only some of whom are cited in the text. We are particularly grateful to the following colleagues for their invaluable comments and suggestions on earlier drafts of this guidebook: Thomasenia Lott Adams (University of Florida), Bobbye Bartels (Christopher Newport University), Nadine Bezuk (San Diego State University), Randall Charles (San Jose State), Clarence Dockweiler (Texas A & M), Peter Glidden (West Chester University), Sheryl A. Maxwell (University of Memphis), Don Peck (University of Utah), Janet M. Sharp (Iowa State University), Dorothy Jo Stevens (University of Nebraska), Lynda R. Wiest (University of Nevada at Reno), and Linda Zech (University of Nevada). Thanks are also due to Sharon C. Baroody, Joan Campagnolo, Colleen Harvey, Anisha Jogee, Carol McGehe, Lauren Mlade, Linda Peterson, Ellen Satom, Linda Scharp, Barbara Rudell, Nicole Tempia, and Jay Wilkins for carefully reading the text and their many suggestions. Special thanks are due to the following people who diligently prepared the typed text and some graphics: June Chambliss, Donna Auble, Lana Bates, Selena Douglass, Teri Frerichs, and Debra Gough of the Word Processing Unit in the UIUC College of Education. I am particularly grateful to Selena Douglass for preparing the camera-ready copy of this book. Much thanks also to Alexi A. Baroody for preparing many of the graphics and serving as my technology advisor. We are grateful to the many classroom teachers who contributed their ideas, particularly Melinda Ostergren and Patti Stoffel of the Urbana (Illinois) School District. We are indebted to Jo Lynn Baldwin, Diane Dutton, Linda Moore, and Carol Sweeney of the Mahomet (Illinois) School District for sharing their classrooms with us so that we could try out instructional ideas described in this text. Last but not least, we want to express our appreciation to the many elementary- and college-level students whose questions and strategies were a constant source of amazement and edification. We are particularly grateful for the opportunity to learn from Alison, Alexi, and Arianne.

DEDICATION

For all the students we have taught and learned from, particularly Alexi, Alison, and Arianne, and for all the students our readers will teach and learn from.

TABLE OF CONTENTS

END MATTER

PREFACE

Dear Reader:

As a teacher, you will have the awesome responsibility of helping *all* of your students construct the disposition and knowledge needed to live successfully in a complex and rapidly changing world. To meet the challenges of the twenty-first century, students will especially need *mathematical power*: a positive disposition toward mathematics (e.g., curiosity and self confidence), facility with the processes of mathematical inquiry (e.g., problem solving, reasoning, and communicating), and well-connected mathematical knowledge (an understanding of mathematical concepts, procedures, and formulas). Imagine having the power to foster children's mathematical power—the ability to excite them about mathematics, to help them see that it makes sense, and to enable them to harness its might for solving everyday and extraordinary problems. The aim of this teaching guide is to help you achieve this power so that your students can achieve the mathematical power they will need.

Your journey toward empowerment may require you to rethink what and how mathematics should be taught. Unfortunately, the mathematics curriculum, the instructional practices, and assessment methods that you might be accustomed to (e.g., a focus on written arithmetic procedures, lectures and work sheets, and timed tests) are generally not effective in promoting children's mathematical power. "Improving mathematics education is not a matter of adding a little spice to a dull subject or of making a few minor changes in content or approach. It requires no less than a redefinition of . . . mathematics [instruction] and an understanding that [its] goal . . . must be the development of mathematical power in all students" (Parker, 1993, p. xi). To further these aims, the National Council of Teachers of Mathematics, or NCTM for short, has issued the *Curriculum and Evaluation Standards for School Mathematics (Curriculum Standards)* in 1989, the *Professional Standards for School Mathematics (Professional Standards)* in 1991, and the *Assessment Standards for School Mathematics (Assessment Standards)* in 1995. These *Standards* do not recommend a band-aid approach to reform (i.e., supplementing existing practices with some new techniques to better accomplish the same old goals)—an approach that has characterized some efforts to improve mathematics instruction in the past. Instead, the *Standards* propose radical surgery—profound changes in what and how mathematics is taught and assessed.

The heart of the NCTM's proposed reforms is a new way of teaching mathematics, which we will call the investigative approach. Past efforts to reform mathematics instruction have focused on only one or two of the following aims: making mathematics instruction (a) relevant to the everyday life of students, (b) process-based (e.g., problem-solving or reasoning based), or (c) understandable.* The investigative approach attempts to foster mathematical power by accomplishing all three of these aims. By teaching content in a purposeful context, an inquiry-based fashion, and a meaningful manner, this approach promotes children's mathematical learning in an interesting, thought-provoking, and comprehensible way. This teaching guide is designed to help you appreciate the need for the investigative approach and to provide practical advice on how you can make this approach really happen in your classroom.

Your journey toward empowerment will require you to learn more about mathematics, children's mathematical learning, and mathematics teaching. As in any domain, powerful knowledge is actively constructed, not passively absorbed by a learner. So we designed this guide not only to dispense a wealth of information but to serve as a catalyst for exploring, conjecturing about, dis-

---

* For example, proponents of the Social Utility Movement proposed to eliminate from the arithmetic curriculum any subject matter that had no "life value"—that had "little direct use in the life of the child" (Caldwell & Courtis, 1925, p. 68). Proponents of Progressive Education went even further by advocating incidental learning—learning mathematics naturally through personal experience (cf. John Dewey, 1963). William Brownell (1935) agreed that mathematics instruction should not be taught in isolation or without purpose but felt that incidental learning did not adequately develop the meaningful concepts and thinking processes needed for real arithmetical ability. Unfortunately, Brownell's Meaningful Approach focused primarily on making arithmetic instruction understandable and did little to promote mathematical inquiry. In the 1960s, advocates of the New Math suggested making mathematics understandable by helping children reason out mathematical conclusions. However, this reform movement did not take into account children's interests, needs, or thinking and, unhappily, often promoted the rote memorization it was designed to avoid (Kline, 1974).

cussing, and contemplating the teaching and learning of mathematics.

To help you actively construct the knowledge necessary to foster children's mathematical power, this teaching guide has a unique format, one that requires you to interact with the text material. To prompt wonder, speculation, debate, and reflection—the keys for advancing understanding—we have included *reader inquiries*. These inquiries encourage readers to explore key ideas about mathematics, children's mathematical learning, and mathematics teaching in a way that models the investigative approach to elementary mathematics instruction recommended by the NCTM (1989, 1991). Thus, we not only discuss how to teach problem solving, but invite you to enhance your own problem-solving ability by solving genuine problems. We not only discuss how to promote understanding, but encourage you to deepen your own understanding of mathematics by employing recommended procedures (e.g., using manipulatives, playing math games, or engaging in discovery-learning activities). We not only discuss teaching philosophies, practices, and methods but prompt you to critically examine your own philosophy, to try out teaching techniques yourself, and to critically analyze curricula materials. We not only suggest integrating technology into mathematics instruction but ask you to undertake activities that involve calculators or computers. Reader inquiries, then, are not a secondary feature of this guide but its core. Our hope is that they will help you become a more reflective and capable mathematical and pedagogical problem solver and, thus, a more effective mathematics teacher than you might have been if you simply read a textbook. Reader inquiries can also serve to illustrate the investigative approach and provide a basis for implementing it in your own classroom.

The process of constructing a deeper understanding of mathematics, how children learn it, and how it can be taught effectively can be greatly aided by discussing these topics with others. Particularly as you tackle the reader inquiries, we encourage you to collaborate with a small group of your peers. This should be helpful in answering the questions or the problems posed and in constructing an understanding of the guide's content. It will also give you a better understanding of the value of—and the difficulties with—small-group cooperative learning.

Your journey toward empowerment will be ongoing. To accommodate this fact, this guide has another unique feature. Its pages are prepunched to fit a three-ring binder. This feature will allow you to add additional material provided by your instructor, as well as that obtained from sources (e.g., colleagues, books for teachers, workshops, conferences). Moreover, this format permits you to organize and reorganize the material in any way you wish. Some readers may want, for example, to select certain material and fashion it into a plan for a lesson, a unit, or even their own teacher-made curriculum. The notebook format will also enable you to bring only what you need to class or school as opposed to lugging around a weighty reference book. If you tutor a child, it will allow you to pull out a reader inquiry to serve as a basis for a lesson.

To help you get started on your journey to becoming an effective mathematics teacher, we first discuss further the purposes and features of this teaching guide and then explore the critical role a student's frame of mind plays in the teaching-learning process (chapter 0). In chapters 1, 2, and 3, we provide a rationale and general framework for the rest of the guide. In chapters 4 to 16, we explore mathematical content areas now recommended for K-8 instruction by the NCTM. In chapter 17, we close the guide with some thoughts on organizing instruction and teacher professional development.

It took 8 years to write, rewrite, revise, and re-revise this guide. This process was guided by extensive field testing. We regularly tried out teaching tips and classroom activities with elementary classes or small groups of elementary-age children. Throughout the writing phase, we piloted the reader inquiries and other aspects of this guide with preservice teachers in elementary mathematics method courses.

Nevertheless, as teaching is an ongoing building process, we would greatly appreciate your suggestions for making this learning tool more informative, more readable, and easier to use. You can communicate your ideas in writing to Art Baroody, College of Education, University of Illinois, Champaign, IL 61820, by phone (217-333-4791), by FAX (217-244-4572), or by e-mail (baroody@uiuc.edu).

Art Baroody and Ron Coslick

0 PROLOGUE: UNDERSTANDING THIS TEACHING GUIDE AND THE ROLE OF AFFECT IN THE TEACHING-LEARNING PROCESS

To me math is

To me math is scaree. I get nevous when we have time tests. *Bay*	To me math is boring. I hate doing worksheets. *Cey*	To me math is knowing how to add and stuff. *Dey*	To me math is fun. I like to solve problems and puzzles. *Fay*
To me math is like stepping in cow dung. I can't stand it. *Gay*	To me math is thinking hard. Miss DeJesus gave us hard problems. And we could usually figure them out if we worked together. *Hay*	To me math is looking for patterns so that I can solv problems *Jay*	To me math is knowing facts like 2 + 2 = 4 *Kay*

✐ The *To-Me-Math-Is* bulletin board above can be an interesting way for a class to share their thoughts and feelings about mathematics. (Note that publicly sharing such personal information should be voluntary.) Students could then include the *To-Me-Math-Is* writing assignment in their math journals. Such an assignment at the beginning of the school year can help you assess each child's writing ability and disposition toward mathematics. Repeating the assignment at the end of the school year could provide students and teacher alike a sense of how class members' views of mathematics and their feelings about the subject have changed.

THIS CHAPTER

𝓜any students find learning mathematics stressful or at least unpleasant—something they would gladly forgo if given the chance. Not coincidentally, many prospective and practicing teachers feel much the same way about teaching mathematics. Subsequent chapters of this guidebook describe a new way of teaching mathematics—one that both student and teacher can find enjoyable and rewarding. To prepare you for your exploration of this new approach, we first describe the guidebook (Unit 0•1). To help you understand better the need for a new teaching approach and how to help your students (and perhaps yourself) develop a positive disposition toward mathematics, we then explore the role of affect in the teaching-learning process, including why many people dislike or even dread the subject (Unit 0•2).

☞ Complete the phrase: To me math is . . .

0•1 UNDERSTANDING THIS TEACHING GUIDE

Figure 0.1: What's the Real Point of Education Anyway?

YOUNG ONES' VIEW

What do you hope to gain from your elementary mathematics methods course and this teaching guide anyway? Unlike Steven in Figure 0.1, farsighted readers will recognize that the real purpose is not simply getting a grade, course credit, or a diploma, but preparing for a most important and challenging task—teaching children mathematics. Although working through this guide will require time and effort, the rewards can be greater confidence and personal satisfaction in teaching mathematics—a most worthwhile return on your investment. In Subunit 0•1•1, we describe the rationale for this teaching guide; in Subunit 0•1•2, we discuss the key features found in each chapter.

0•1•1 RATIONALE FOR THIS TEACHING GUIDE

In this subunit, we consider what is required to be a good teacher in general and an effective teacher of mathematics in particular and how this teaching guide can help you achieve these goals.

The Art of Teaching

When Adele Brill announced to her parents her intention to major in elementary education, their reaction surprised her. She thought that, as elementary teachers themselves, they would be delighted by her decision, rather than speechless and apparently concerned. When Adele pressed them for a response, her mother finally said weakly, "With your academic record, we thought you might go into a profession—something prestigious and financially rewarding. Why do you want to go into teaching Adele?"

Adele suddenly felt that she didn't really know her parents. Were these aliens before her the people who—for as long as she could remember—cherished knowledge, self-fulfillment, and service—had encouraged her to learn for learning's sake, to be anything *she* wanted to be, to find satisfaction in helping others? Although the answers to her mother's question seemed obvious to her, a distraught Adele could only manage to say, "*I* care deeply about children and enjoy working with them."

This section addresses three interrelated questions: *What is a professional? Can teaching really be considered a profession? Is caring for children enough to be a good teacher?*

Characteristics of a Professional. Webster's Dictionary defines a professional as engaging in a learned profession—a calling requiring specialized knowledge and often long and intensive academic preparation. A large knowledge base is essential because a professional typically must be an independent decision maker. In contrast, technicians require a much smaller knowledge base because—by and large—they simply follow the instructions of others.

Teachers—Professionals or Technicians? Particularly when it comes to teaching mathematics, many teachers operate like technicians—blindly following the prescriptions set down in the teacher's edition of their textbooks or other authoritative sources. The following vignette suggests why good teaching requires teachers to rise to the level of a true professional—as educators who draw on a vast store of knowledge to make their own decisions.

After completing her course registration, Adele Brill returned to her living quarters. Marcie, a roommate in pre-med, asked, "What courses are you taking this semester Adele?"

"I'm taking several courses on the methods of teaching," replied Adele.

"Methods of teaching?" choked Marcie in genuine disbelief. "What's to know about teaching?"

Something snapped in the normally mild-mannered Adele, "You don't think teaching is very important or challenging, do you Marcie?"

Snooty and unaccustomed to being challenged, Marcie responded testily, "Well dear, it doesn't take a rocket scientist to follow the curriculum outlined in a teacher's manual and to tell or show kids the simplest things they need to know."

With unaccustomed anger, Adele shot back, "I bet you didn't know that Clara Barton quit teaching because she had a nervous breakdown. She then undertook the less stressful job of attending wounded soldiers on battlefronts under hostile fire."

Surprised by her own anger and the shocked expression on her roommate's face, Adele composed herself and started over, "Marcie, it's not true that just anyone can be a *good* teacher. Last semester, I observed Mrs. Jones, a second-grade teacher, who really made a difference in her students' lives. They loved coming to school and learning about things. It was exciting to watch those children become thrilled about new ideas and new ways of thinking about things. I know it won't make me rich or famous, but I want to be that special kind of person like Mrs. Jones who can fire up children's curiosity and make a classroom come alive."

Still defensive, Marcie countered, "But you can't possibly equate a teacher with a doctor. Medicine is a profession. Doctors must think for themselves in order to solve complicated medical problems and make life-and-death decisions."

Adele had to think before responding, "Although some teachers are merely followers, good teachers must regularly draw on their knowledge of the subject matter, children, and teaching techniques to make decisions. Good teachers don't simply teach material, they teach *children*." Echoing what she had learned from her courses, Adele continued, "Focusing on whether children are learning is much more complicated than focusing on what to teach. Each class—each child—is different, and so there are no cookbook recipes that will work for all situations. Good teachers are problem solvers. Obviously, a teacher's mistakes won't physically harm anyone, but they can damage children's interest in learning or harm their self-esteem and confidence."

Caring and Competence. Still not entirely convinced that teaching qualified as a profession, Marcie added, "It's not the same. A doctor needs to know a tremendous amount of information."

Adele, who herself did not have a good sense of how much a good teacher really needed to know, could not counter Marcie's argument. But her roommate's comment did cause her to think about how she was unable to help one of Mrs. Jones' children because of her lack of knowledge.

Adele had been asked to tutor Alfie, who was having difficulty with mathematics. More specifically, he still often wrote numerals backwards, had trouble remembering the basic addition and subtraction facts such as $8 + 5 = 13$ and $9 - 5 = 4$, and regularly came up with incorrect answers such as $53 - 27 = 34$ on his arithmetic worksheets. Adele really liked Alfie and wanted to help him. But the extra worksheets she provided only made a bad situation worse.

After one particularly fruitless session, Alfie tried to comfort his frustrated tutor, "It's not your fault Miss Brill, I'm just stupid."

Adele saw the sadness, the fatigue, the defeat in the boy's eyes and wanted desperately to dispel the boy's pain. "No you're not Alfie," she comforted gently.

"You can't help me Miss Brill. I can't be helped," Alfie countered with moist eyes.

Caring is not enough, Adele now thought to herself. Maybe I could have helped, Alfie—if I had only known more. She hated feeling helpless and the vague guilt that her ignorance may have contributed to Alfie's difficulty and pain. Adele hoped that her math methods course would give her some clues to solving Alfie's difficulties so that she would do a better job next time.

Aims of This Teaching Guide

The purpose of this teaching guide is to help prepare you as a professional—to help you construct the knowledge needed to confidently make independent decisions. To make informed decisions about teaching mathematics, teachers need to be knowledgeable about (a) the subject matter (mathematics), (b) the learner (child psychology), and (c) instructional techniques (pedagogy) (e.g., Ball, 1991; Peterson, Fennema, & Carpenter, 1991). Thus, this book has three general aims:

(1) further the reader's own mathematical knowledge and ability to engage in mathematical inquiry;

(2) foster an understanding of how children's mathematical knowledge and thinking develops; and

(3) promote understanding and reflection about methods of K-8 mathematics instruction.

Mathematics. Teachers should (a) *understand* the mathematics they teach and (b) be capable of thinking and communicating mathematically themselves (e.g., Ball, 1991).

Why is it important to understand the mathematics you will teach? You probably would have no difficulty determining the answer to the expression $\frac{1}{2} \div \frac{1}{8}$. More than likely, you would invert the divisor $\frac{1}{8}$ and multiply. The point is that you probably have mastered the mechanics of elementary arithmetic—you know *how* to add with renaming (carrying or borrowing), *how* to multiply with decimals, *how* to divide with fractions, and so forth. But after more than a decade of formal schooling, most preservice teachers do not understand *why* these procedures work (see, e.g., Ball, 1990; Fennema & Franke, 1992; and Simon, 1993). Do you?

Confronted with this question, Debbie complained, "Why do I have to understand these procedures? I don't know why you invert and multiply, but I can divide with fractions. One-half divided by one-fourth is one-eighth [sic]." Five reasons for understanding the mathematics you will teach are listed below.

- You will be less likely to get confused yourself, make errors, and confuse your students. For example, if Debbie *understood* fraction division, she may have recognized that her answer did not make sense.

- You will be in a better position to help students make sense of mathematics and construct an understanding of it. As John Holt (1970) put it, "If we, unlike so many . . . teachers, know what *we* are doing when [for instance] we [divide] fractions, . . . we will have a much better chance of finding things to do or say, or materials and projects for the children to work with, that will help them make sense of [mathematics]" (p. 158). Moreover, only if you know how mathematical ideas are related to each other and to real-world examples, can you help children see these connections.

- You will be in a better position to help students explore the questions they frequently ask such as, "Why does one-half divided by one-eighth equal four? Isn't division suppose to make things smaller?" and "Why do I need to know this?"

- You will have a better idea of the task confronting children. A comprehension of the complexity of mathematical ideas can help you better grasp why it takes time to construct a solid understanding of mathematical concepts and where children may experience difficulties.

- You need to be comfortably knowledgeable about mathematics so that you can respond flexibly and creatively to students' insights as well as their difficulties.

- You will be better able to select or devise problems for exploring and practicing mathematical content in a purposeful and stimulating manner.

A key aim of this guide, then, is to help you understand the whys behind elementary mathematics—why procedures or formulas work and why it is important to learn various aspects of mathematics.

Why is it important for you to develop proficiency with such mathematical processes as problem-solving, reasoning, conjecture-making and -testing, and communicating? Despite many years of formal mathematical training, you may have had little or no experience solving challenging mathematical problems. Although you may have some experience solving word problems, this experience may have left you unprepared or unsure about tackling genuine problems. Moreover, you may have had little opportunity to engage in mathematical reasoning; making, testing, or justifying mathematical conjectures; or communicating mathematical ideas to others.

This guide provides opportunities to develop and to practice such processes of inquiry as problem-solving, reasoning, conjecturing, and communicating. This is important if you are to model these processes and to guide the development of children's mathematical thinking. Moreover, actually solving problems yourself can give you a better idea of what difficulties children may encounter and how you can help them.

Child Psychology. Teachers need to understand how children think and learn. Research shows that as teachers better comprehend how children construct mathematical ideas, they can better make instructional decisions and organize their classrooms in ways that foster meaningful learning and mathematical achievement (e.g., Campbell, 1997).

Yet another major aim of this guide, then, is to help the reader better understand the development of children's mathematical knowledge. An appreciation of their informal strengths and the ways in which their knowledge is incomplete can better help you extend their knowledge. A grasp of how their thinking develops can help you understand where and why children commonly encounter difficulty and how to help them. For example, it can help you understand why children have such a difficult time understanding division with fractions and make such errors as $\frac{1}{2} + \frac{1}{8} = \frac{1}{4}$. It can also help you appreciate why they are puzzled when $\frac{1}{2} + \frac{1}{8}$ results in an answer of four, not an answer smaller than one-half.

It is particularly important to understand children's thinking when it differs from adult thinking. This can help a teacher see that unexpected answers make sense from a child's point of view. It can also better enable a teacher to help children bridge the gulf between their thinking and adults' thinking. For example, why does an answer 34 for the expression 53 - 27 make perfect sense to many children? How can a teacher help such children see that the difference must be less than 34?

Pedagogy. Teachers must (a) know effective methods for teaching mathematics and (b) *understand* their rationale. Moreover, you need to become a reflective practitioner who can autonomously make instructional decisions.

What is there to learn about teaching mathematics? Teachers typically teach the way they were taught. If taught by the lecture-drill method themselves, they tend to equate teaching with telling students information and grading their worksheets. Was this how you were taught mathematics? Was mathematics interesting, thought provoking, and meaningful to you? Do you want to teach your students mathematics in the same way you were taught? A basic aim of this guide is to illustrate *how* to teach elementary mathematics in a new way that promotes interest, thinking, and understanding.

Why is it important to understand the rationale for teaching methods? Oftentimes, teachers are given instructional recommendations but not their underlying rationale or theory. However, they need more than a basket of tricks (e.g., how to use manipulatives to teach division with fractions meaningfully). Teachers need to understand the *why*, as well as the how, of effective instructional techniques. They need sufficient theoretical background to understand why a general teaching recommendation or a particular instructional method may be useful. Without this understanding, they may implement the recommendation or method ineffectively or incorrectly. For instance, they may fail to adapt the method to their particular circumstances or to the particular needs of their students. Moreover, when given conflicting advice, they cannot evaluate for themselves which recommendation makes more sense. In this guide, we make a concerted effort to explain the why, as well as the how, of instructional techniques. That is, we explain the mathematical, psychological, and pedagogical rationale for teaching practices as well as provide practical teaching tips. The aim is to help you construct a realistic and powerful theoretical framework for making informed educational decisions (e.g., to guide your choice and use of specific instructional methods).

Why is it necessary for a teacher to prepare as a decision maker? Teachers are often prepared as technicians, programmed to implement others' instructional decisions. However, teaching is too complex for simple prescriptions. Each class, each child, comes with its own set of challenges. It would be impossible for this guide, or any amount of training, to prepare you for every situation you will face as a teacher. Moreover, it is important as a teacher to evaluate critically the methods suggested by textbooks and curriculum guides to ensure they are psychologically and pedagogically sound. An aim of this teaching guide is to help you appreciate the importance of being a reflective teacher and practice pedagogical problem solving. To these ends, we will regularly ask you to evaluate instructional suggestions or the instructional needs of a child.

0•1•2 SOME FEATURES OF THIS GUIDE

To help you better appreciate and understand the investigative approach, this guide contains numerous reader inquiries, which provides opportunities to engage in purposeful and meaningful inquiry into mathematical and pedagogical content. Firsthand experience conjecturing, reasoning, and communicating about issues and solving mathematical and pedagogical problems should help you see that active, inquiry-based learning can be enjoyable and effective. It should also help you construct the broad base of knowledge necessary to teach mathematics effectively. An example of a reader inquiry is illustrated by Investigation 0.1.

☞ Try Investigation 0.1 (pages 0-7 and 0-8).

To help you better appreciate the investigative approach, we describe *why* such an approach is important to use. The rationale for using this approach is discussed in chapter 1 and throughout the guide. Note that these reasons can be used to justify this approach to students, parents, school administrators, and colleagues.

To help you get off to a good *start* on the challenging and exciting task of fostering children's mathematical power, we also describe and illustrate the investigative approach and suggest general recommendations for implementing it. In particular, we show again and again how to provide a purposeful context for mathematics instruction by integrating it with the instruction of other content areas such as science and language arts, relating it to everyday situations, or developing it through interesting activities or games.

Throughout the guide, we provide ideas for or examples of lessons and units that can involve students in mathematical inquiry, many of which show how technology can be an integral aspect of mathematics instruction. We regularly indicate how mathematics can build on what children already know to make it meaningful to them. Some tips and ideas for teaching specific content are also included.

Boxes throughout the guide include: (a) example lessons of the investigative approach; (b) illustrations of teaching ideas or aids; (c) case studies illustrating children's often surprising mathematical strengths or their learning difficulties; or (d) dialogues that raise issues, prompt questions about instructional practices, or illustrate common teaching difficulties or effective teaching techniques.

Samples from a fictional textbook, *The Math Book From Hell*, illustrate ineffective materials. These samples are not intended as a general condemnation of textbooks. They serve to underscore—we hope humorously—the need for teachers to be reflective. Although textbook publishers are making earnest efforts to meet the spirit of the *Curriculum Standards* proposed by the National Council of Teachers of Mathematics (NCTM, 1989), the extent to which new textbook series embody the NCTM's recommendations and make use of the most recent psychological and educational research varies. As Ohanian (1992) observed, "publishers stake out different territories" (p. 93). While one offers challenges and explorations, another offers cookbook recipes and planning charts "that 'itemizes the objectives of the chapter lessons . . . and shows you exactly how . . . the text meets the NCTM *Standards*,' thus transmogrifying the *Standards* into nothing more than a skills chart" (Ohanian, 1992, p. 93). Moreover, although aspects of recently published textbooks have changed considerably and for the better, market forces and other factors prompt some publishers to retain many traditional features (e.g., sterile practice exercises) or to disguise traditional features with misleading labels (e.g., labeling practice exercises as "Problem Solving") (Ginsburg, Klein, & Starkey, 1998).

Throughout the guide, you will encounter installments about the adventures of various teachers including Mrs. MeChokemchild, an implacable believer in traditional methods, Ms. Socrates, an advocate of the new (continued on page 0-9)

✿ Investigation 0.1: A Graphic Introduction[†]

◆ Types of data and graphs ◆ K-8 ◆ Whole class

This graphing activity can serve as a way of sharing personal information and introducing classmates to each other. In the process, students can learn much about types of data and the graphs used to picture them.

Answer the questions listed in the *Data Sheet* on the next page. (You or your instructor may wish to add questions to the list. Note also that the questions can be adapted to the grade level of the students. For example, useful questions for primary-level children might be: How do you get to school—walk, ride a school bus, ride in a car, or other? What is the number of the bus you take? What is your favorite animal?).

For each item, compile the data for your group and consider how it could be best displayed in a graph. Afterward, share your group's data with the class, discuss graphing options, and construct graphs that summarize the class data.

Questions for Reflection

1. (a) How did your answers for Questions 1 to 5 on the *Data Sheet* differ from those for Questions 7 to 10? (b) How did your answers for Questions 7 and 8 differ from those for Question 9 and 10?

2. (a) What types of graphs could you use to picture the class data for (i) Questions 1 to 5, (ii) Questions 7 and 8, and (iii) Questions 9 and 10? (b) In what ways are the graphs for Questions 1 to 5, Questions 7 and 8, and Questions 9 and 10 different?

3. Could a pie graph be used to picture any of the data? If so, how? If not, why not?

4. (a) If your college status was represented by a number (e.g., junior = 3 and grad = 5), would this change how the data were graphed? Why or why not? (b) If the question asked, "How many years have you attended college?" would this change how the data were graphed? Why or why not?

5. Is your answer to Question 6 (grade level) more like the data for Questions 1 to 5, that for Questions 7 and 8, or that for Questions 9 and 10?

☞ **Teaching Tip. Initial lessons on collecting data should focus on helping children recognize that there are two types of information—categorical and numerical data** (Kennedy & Tipps, 1994). **It is crucial that children recognize the distinction between categorical data (name or word answers) and numerical data (answers involving a number or a scale), because the type of data affects how the information is organized, described, and analyzed. Graphing activities such as this investigation can prompt students to make this distinction implicitly or explicitly.**

[†] Based on an in-service teacher workshop described in "Experiential Statistics and Probability for Elementary Teachers" by W. A. Juraschek & N. S. Angle in *Teaching Statistics and Probability* (pp. 8-18, 1981 Yearbook), edited by A. P. Schulte and © 1981 by the National Council of Teachers of Mathematics.

Investigation 0.1 continued

Enter your data in the *Your data* column. Enter the names and the data of people in your group under the columns titled *Your group's data*.

Data Sheet

Item	Your data	Your group's data				
1. Gender						
2. College status (e.g., junior, grad)						
3. Area of specialization (e.g., early childhood, middle school math)						
4. Favorite hobby						
5. Favorite TV program						
6. Grade level you (hope to) teach						
7. Number of college math courses taken						
8. Number of siblings						
9. Age in years (e.g., $20\frac{1}{2}$ or 21)						
10. Height in inches						
11.						
12.						

investigative approach, and Miss Brill, a first-year teacher.* Although the characters are fictional, the situations described are often based on real classroom events and dialogues. Moreover, the problems Miss Brill encounters, the feelings she expresses, and the questions she asks might be those of any teacher.

*Mrs. MeChokemchild was inspired by Charles Dickens' character Mr. M'Choakumchild, who focused on memorizing facts by rote at the expense of all else (*Hard Times* edited by G. Ford and S. Monod and © 1966 by W. W. Norton & Company, Inc.). Ms. Socrates is based on the Greek philosopher who is credited with originating the Socratic method. Miss Brill was chosen for reasons that will become apparent after reading the guide.

0•2 GETTING INTO THE RIGHT FRAME OF MIND TO LEARN—THE CRITICAL ROLE OF AFFECT IN THE TEACHING-LEARNING PROCESS

Figure 0.2: For Many Students (and Teachers), Math Is a Stressful Subject

SHOE Reprinted by permission of the Tribune Media Service.

Given a problem, Opal eagerly tried different ideas to solve it, openly shared her suggestions (even though some turned out to be off track), and came to a better understanding of the problem and mathematics involved. Fearfully shrinking from the task, Rochelle didn't even consider solving the problem. Afraid of humiliating herself, she offered nothing to her group's discussion. And having made no effort to understand the problem or her group's discussion of it, she had no better grasp of mathematics at the end of the period.

Why did Opal and Rochelle respond in such different ways? Both girls were, in fact, equally bright, had similar home backgrounds, and previously had similar success in math. The reason for their different reactions is that the students approached the learning situation with very different frames of mind. Simply put, like many students, Rochelle had a bad attitude toward mathematics.

Because a bad attitude (negative disposition) toward mathematics can be a serious barrier to learning mathematics (see Figure 0.2)—or learn

ing about teaching mathematics—we address up front why so many people dislike or even fear mathematics and what can be done about it. In Subunit 0•2•1, we discuss a vicious cycle that operates at the social level; in Subunit 0•2•2, we describe another that operates at the level of the individual personality. The first vicious cycle helps explain why so many students—including Skyler in Figure 0.2—do not like mathematics and blow it off; the second helps explain why some children suffer from math anxiety.

0•2•1 THE EFFECTS OF CULTURAL AND CLASSROOM CLIMATE ON STUDENT AFFECT

☞ Consider Probe 0.1 (pages 0-10 to 0-13).

In this subunit, we dissect why Miss Brill, the new teacher described in Part III of Probe 0.1, got off to such a terrible start.

Teaching the Whole Child

A key reason for Miss Brill's dismal lesson was that in planning and implementing it, she focused exclusively (text continued on page 0-14)

➤ Probe 0.1: Your Mathematical Frame of Mind

As you begin your exploration of teaching mathematics, it is worth reflecting on your own experiences as a mathematics student and your attitudes toward mathematics and teaching it. After completing the questionnaire (Part I) below, discuss your responses with your group or class and complete the analysis described in Part II. Then consider and discuss the *Questions for Reflection*. Next, read the vignette in Part III, answer the questions that follow, and discuss your responses with your group or class.

Part I: Some Personal Questions

1. Overall, evaluate the mathematics instruction you have received to date.

2. What was one of your best experiences in a mathematics class as a student? What made it so positive and memorable?

3. What was one of your worst experiences in a mathematics class as a student? What made it so negative and memorable?

4. Imagine you are at a social gathering talking with an engaging person. You casually ask what the person does and the response is, "Why I'm a mathematician." How does this response make you feel?

5. On a scale of 1 to 5, rate how you feel about the prospect of teaching mathematics: 5 = wildly enthusiastic (my favorite subject) to 1 = dread the thought (would avoid if I could).

Part II: Affective Aspect of Learning

Students are not merely cognitive (intellectual) beings. They have beliefs, attitudes, interests, needs, and feelings. These affective factors play a crucial role in learning mathematics.

Indeed, to get a sense of the tremendous importance of affective factors, ask teachers or students about their mathematics classes. They are just as likely to make comments about affective issues (e.g., how much math is liked or hated, and whether it makes them feel accomplished or stupid) as they are cognitive issues (e.g., the particular mathematical ideas covered or achievement levels) (McLeod, 1992).

How did you and your classmates respond to Question 1 of the questionnaire in Part I above? Analyze and classify your responses as *primarily cognitive* or *primarily affective*. Note that some responses may be difficult to pigeonhole. Decide as a class how you want to handle ambiguous responses. After counting the number of responses involving cognitive issues and those involving affective issues, consider how you could summarize and display the data.

Questions for Reflection

1. Compile the class' responses to Question 5. Do most people in your class have a basically positive disposition toward teaching mathematics (responded 4 or 5), seem indifferent (responded 3), or have a basically negative disposition toward teaching mathematics (responded 1 or 2)? What are the implications of these results?

2. Many people freely admit that they were failures in school mathematics or that they don't have "a mind for math." Yet people seldom admit that they are illiterate. Why are people more likely—even eager—to proclaim their ignorance of mathematics (McLeod, 1992)?

Probe 0.1 continued

3. Complete the following statement, compile the responses of your class, and discuss the implications of your results. *Mathematical ability is—*

   a. largely determined by innate factors.
   b. mostly determined by innate factors.
   c. mostly determined by effort.
   d. largely determined by effort.

Part III: A Math Clash or the Case of a Cultural Vicious Cycle

For Miss Brill, the prospect of teaching mathematics was one of the least enticing aspects of her chosen career, ranking well below cleaning up after a sick child. No one had ever related mathematics to her personal life or her career goals, and—aside from a few obvious applications—she did not really appreciate its usefulness. To make matters worse, she had never understood school mathematics or done well in it. Miss Brill had always assumed her difficulties in understanding mathematics were her fault—that she simply didn't have much math ability. Mathematics made her feel inadequate, and she developed a strong dislike for it. As she proceeded through school and the mathematics became more difficult, Miss Brill put forth less and less effort to learn it and stopped taking mathematics courses as soon as she could.

Asked during her job interview, if she felt comfortable teaching fifth-grade math, Miss Brill broke out in a cold sweat, choked, and considered for less than a nanosecond a truthful answer, "Actually, I feel terrified about the prospect of teaching fifth-grade mathematics. Unlike language arts, I have always felt incompetent about mathematics." Miss Brill desperately wanted to teach, and she doubted that a forthcoming response would help her job prospects. So she searched her mind for a quasi-truthful answer and was greatly relieved when the principal's air-conditioning unit broke loose from its moorings, prematurely ending the interview.

After getting the job, Miss Brill eagerly prepared interesting language arts and social studies lessons for the first few weeks of school. She kept putting off making plans for math. The day before school, she sought the advice of an experienced colleague Mrs. MeChokemchild.

The veteran teacher informed her, "Some teachers I know start the school year by playing math games or posing math puzzles—by playing around with mathematics. This gives kids the wrong idea. Learning mathematics is hard work and requires mental discipline. So even before I review last year's material, I hit my students with something really challenging—fraction division. This shows them I really mean business and gets them off on the right foot."

Because Miss Brill didn't have the foggiest idea herself what dividing with fractions meant, she desperately read through the relevant section of the teacher's edition for her textbook. This did not help her understand division with fractions any better, but it did give her some ideas about how to proceed. Using the tips from the teacher's edition, Miss Brill devised a plan. Unbeknown to her, the plan was almost identical to one Mrs. Crude had used 12 years earlier to teach Miss Brill fraction division.

In fact, Miss Brill's whole approach to teaching mathematics would be remarkably similar to Mrs. Crude's. She would follow the textbook page for page, fearing to deviate from this prescribed course. She would rely heavily on telling students exactly what to do and then having them practice it. Indeed, like Mrs. Crude before her, Miss Brill would routinely assign enormous doses of seatwork. This kept the class quiet and busy for long periods of time and permitted Miss Brill to focus attention on her real interest: small-group reading. She would rationalize this marvelous control device with the belief that "practice makes perfect." After all, how else can mathematical knowledge be impressed on the minds of students? Miss Brill would so fervently assigned math seatwork that her class nicknamed her *Miss "Drill-and-Kill" Brill.*

Probe 0.1 continued

The next day, Miss Brill summoned her courage and launched into her meticulously well-organized math lesson. "It's time for math," she noted without enthusiasm, "Please take out your math books."

Several students immediately slumped down in their seats; several others put their heads down on their desks and buried their faces as if to prepare themselves for the inevitable and overwhelming ennui of another math lesson. There were audible groans and complaints such as, "Do we really have-ta?" "It's the first week of school. I don't think my brain is ready for this yet." This was followed by a volley of snide remarks including, "Your brain will never be ready Rodney."

Miss Brill felt what little enthusiasm she had for teaching the math lesson drain out of her. She woodenly explained to the class that to divide with fractions you invert and multiply. To illustrate this point, she wrote the expression $\frac{1}{4} \div \frac{1}{8} = \frac{1}{4} \times \frac{8}{1} = 2$ on the chalkboard.

After a minute of stunned silence, the classroom broke into a buzz of whispering.

Hector: "It didn't take long for this one to flip out."

Jose: "No, she's a new teacher. She's probably just a little confused."

Yuri: "It's got to be a joke. Is this April 1st?"

Disconcerted by all the noise, Miss Brill asked for silence, consulted the textbook for another example, demonstrated the procedure again, and then asked for a volunteer to do the procedure.

Victor whispered to his neighbor, "Why do you invert and multiply?"

A number of students noticed something peculiar about the answer. "How did the answer get bigger?" marveled Winnie, "I thought division is supposed to make things smaller?"

"It's math magic," Hi Jung responded, "You're not supposed to understand it."

"I think you have to be a genius or something to understand math," replied Winnie.

Unable to contain his curiosity any longer, LeMar—one of the bolder children—finally asked the questions many others were wondering about, "Miss Brill, why do you invert and multiply and why does the answer get bigger?"

Taken back by LeMar's questions, Miss Brill fought to maintain her composure and responded authoritatively, "You won't be tested on such questions. All you have to know is the procedure." Miss Brill hoped this would put an end to the embarrassing questions she could not answer.

However, LeMar persisted, "But *why* does it work, Miss Brill?"

Frustrated by her inability to answer and fearful that her mathematical ineptitude would be revealed, Miss Brill chastised LeMar, "If you had been listening carefully, you would have heard me say you do not have to know that. We don't have time to waste."

Frustrated, LeMar said under his breath a bit too loudly, "A good teacher could explain things instead of wasting our time talking junk."

After sending LeMar to the principal's office for insubordination, Miss Brill mechanically completed the lesson. The remaining students unenthusiastically did what was required of them. After finishing guided practice at the board, Miss Brill assigned what seemed like a zillion computations for seatwork. "Practice makes perfect," she said in a saccharin tone when the class groaned in pain.

Miss Brill sensed that little was learned, even by those who stayed "on task." She could barely stand the humiliation of teaching mathematics. Moreover, she could not stand the obvious pain mathematics caused her students. At heart, Miss Brill was a decent and dedicated teacher. She wanted to help children to learn and to be happy. Miss Brill secretly vowed that she would do as little math as possible. She sensed this was not a good solution, but—at that moment—she just did not know what else to do.

Probe 0.1 continued

After sending LeMar to the office for speaking his mind, Miss Brill felt very badly. The novice teacher realized that the boy was frustrated with how she was teaching mathematics. She realized that he was essentially correct—she did not do a good job.

The next day she cleared LeMar's name with the principal and apologized to him before the class. Even LeMar felt a morsel of respect for the new teacher. As he commented to his friends later, "At least she's got some guts—I give her that much credit."

Miss Brill also realized that avoiding mathematics as much as possible was no real solution to her problem. She needed to do something about becoming a better teacher of mathematics. For advice, she went to Ms. Socrates because her class actually seemed to enjoy mathematics. "What can I do to improve my math instruction?" Miss Brill asked of the more experienced teacher.

Ms. Socrates seemed surprised by the question. In all her years of teaching, none of her colleagues, new or otherwise, had ever asked such a question. She was genuinely pleased that this new teacher was concerned about teaching mathematics well. "I think one of the most important things," Ms. Socrates began, "is that *you* have a positive disposition toward math and math instruction—to exhibit curiosity about the subject and excitement about teaching it."

Miss Brill found the advice hard to swallow, "Easier said than done. How do you do that when you don't like math—when you're down right afraid of it? Fake it? How do you fake curiosity and excitement about something you view as dull and dreadful?"

"No, faking it won't do," replied the ever patient Ms. Socrates. "You need to examine why you feel the way you do. Why do you dislike math?"

"That's easy," answered Miss Brill, "I'm not good at it."

"And why's that?" inquired Ms. Socrates.

The answer seemed obvious to Miss Brill, "I don't have a mind for math." When she saw Ms. Socrates's look of disbelief, she vehemently added, "I'm a math moron, okay."

Ms. Socrates added gently, "You'll have to forgive me, but I have a hard time believing that's the case. My guess is that your lack of mathematical expertise can be blamed on poor instruction and the lack of encouragement, not on a lack of ability on your part."

Memories suddenly started to flood back into Miss Brill's conscious. She remembered how senseless math seemed to her. She remembered Mrs. Crude pushing the boys to do well in math, but not the girls. Miss Brill remembered when both she and Benji Silver got "0s" on an arithmetic worksheet. Mrs. Crude made Benji do it over; the teacher had told her, "Don't worry your pretty head about things like this." She remembered in junior high school a counselor advising her not to take the demanding math courses because she didn't need that stuff. After blaming herself for so many years, it suddenly seemed like a burden had been lifted from her shoulders. She asked for reassurance, "You're saying that I was *made* a math moron, not born that way?"

"My guess," affirmed Ms. Socrates. "Whether or not you have the potential for mathematical genius, you undoubtedly have much more mathematical ability than you have been credited for or that you have given yourself credit for. Why you probably have a whole bunch of mathematical ability just waiting to be used and developed."

1. What concerns, if any, do you have about teaching mathematics?

2. Is Miss Brill's bad attitude toward mathematics common among elementary teachers?

3. Why does Miss Brill feel the way she does? What is the cause of her attitude?

4. What possible consequences could Miss Brill's negative attitude have for her students?

on the cognitive or intellectual aspects of the teaching-learning process. She considered what content to cover, what she would say and do, how she would say and do it, and what she wanted the students to do. She completely overlooked the affective aspects of the teaching-learning process.

Affect—broadly defined as beliefs, attitudes, interests, needs, and feelings—plays a crucial role in mathematics teaching and learning (Hart & Walker, 1993; McLeod, 1992). It energizes or motivates our behavior and, hence, has a profound impact on how effectively we teach or learn mathematics (e.g., Reyes, 1984). It stands to reason that if teachers and students enjoy mathematics and have a positive attitude toward it, learning will be facilitated (Renga & Dalla, 1993). Affect, then, is intricately and inseparably interwoven into the intellectual aspects of the teaching-learning process and has a major impact on the success or failure of school mathematics. This is why we begin this text with a discussion of affective issues and why reform efforts such as the NCTM's (1989) *Curriculum Standards* place special importance on them (McLeod, 1992). Indeed, the first two of five general educational goals for precollege students listed in the *Curriculum Standards* (NCTM, 1989, pp. 5-6) are affective goals—

1. "Learning to value mathematics" and

2. "Becoming confident in one's own ability."

As the case of Miss Brill illustrates, students who do not see the importance of mathematics in their current or future lives are unlikely to dedicate themselves to the task of learning it. Confidence is one of the "dominant forces in shaping" students' mathematical behavior (Lester, Garofalo, & Kroll, 1989, p. 85) and strongly related to their mathematical achievement (Hart & Walker, 1993; McLeod, 1992; Renga & Dalla, 1993; Reyes, 1984).

Our Mathematical Frame of Mind—A National Crisis

Children typically begin school eager to learn. Research such as the National Assessment of Educational Progress or NAEP (Dossey, Mullis, Lindquist, & Chambers, 1988) reveals that chil-

dren "become less positive about mathematics as they proceed through school" (McLeod, 1992, p. 576). Their enjoyment of mathematics and self-confidence dwindle rather than increase. By adulthood, many people feel helpless, inadequate, and anxious about mathematics (e.g., Hughes, 1986). Overall, women and minorities are less likely than white males to appreciate the value of mathematics or to have faith in their mathematical ability (Hart & Walker, 1993).

Prospective and practicing elementary teachers tend to reflect our culture's attitude toward mathematics. Like Miss Brill, many feel uncomfortable about mathematics and teaching it. As Donna, a preservice teacher, put it, "The thought of teaching math scares me. In fact, I think it scares a lot of elementary school teachers" (Civil, 1990, p. 297).

Causes of a Negative Disposition

Why do many children lose faith in their ability to do mathematics and interest in this vitally important subject? How do many prospective and practicing elementary teachers acquire their bad attitude toward teaching mathematics? This section describes three key reasons for why a negative disposition towards mathematics is so pervasive—the nature of instruction, cultural beliefs, and teacher affect.

The Nature of Instruction. A negative disposition is learned, in large part, from *how* mathematics is taught in school. For example, children may learn to mistrust their mathematical ability when their teachers imply or announce that there is only one correct way—the school-taught procedure—for doing a mathematical task and that informal (self-invented) strategies, such as finger counting, are unwelcomed. Recall from Probe 0.1 that Miss Brill did not encourage her students to consider informal strategies for dividing fractions, but tried to force feed them the standard invert-and-multiply procedure. (See chapter 10 for a discussion of informal fraction-division strategies and how instruction can build on this informal knowledge.) Moreover, when school mathematics is incomprehensible to children, they are more than likely to lose interest in it. Recall the lack of interest in Miss Brill's unintelligible lesson on fraction division.

Cultural Beliefs About Mathematical Ability. *Why is mathematical ignorance—unlike illiteracy—socially acceptable?* In our culture, it is widely believed that mathematical ability has more to do with innate endowment than effort (McLeod, 1992). Girls and minority students, in particular, are encouraged by the actions and words of teachers, counselors, parents, and peers to believe that they lack the innate gift of mathematical ability. Recall from Probe 0.1 that Miss Brill believed her difficulties in comprehending and learning mathematics were due to her being a math moron, not the ineffective instruction of her teachers such as Mrs. Crude.

The Effect of Teacher Affect. A teacher's disposition toward mathematics can greatly influence how it is taught. Teachers who have little interest in mathematics or who feel insecure about it can shortchange the subject and their students in many ways. Like Miss Brill in Probe 0.1, they may approach mathematics instruction unenthusiastically or mechanically. As Donna, a preservice teacher, noted "[A lack of confidence leads] many teachers [to] rely on textbooks with the answers printed in black and white. Let us face the facts, most teachers teach this way because it is less scary for [them]. I think textbook teaching is boring for both the teacher and learner" (Civil, 1990, p. 297). And like Miss Brill was tempted to do, some spend as little time as possible on math.

If a teacher is uninterested in mathematics, feels intimidated by it, or believes that math ability is largely innate, he or she can convey such affect to children either consciously or nonconsciously. In effect, a teacher's negative disposition toward mathematics can prejudice his or her students. These students then grow up to be parents and teachers with a negative disposition toward mathematics and can prejudice the next generation of children. In effect, a teacher's negative disposition toward mathematics can feed a cultural vicious cycle of disinterest, insecurity, and anxiety about it.

Miss Brill was not consciously aware of this vicious cycle—that she was a victim of poor instruction and that her lack of understanding and her feelings of inadequacy were due to the way she was taught. Now she was teaching the way she had been taught with—much to her horror—the same results. The victim was now victimizing

others. How many children would leave her class not comprehending and fearing mathematics? How many of her students would become teachers like her and Mrs. Crude?

Breaking the Cultural Vicious Cycle

How can teachers, particularly those with a negative disposition toward mathematics, break the cultural vicious cycle and help their students develop a positive disposition toward mathematics? In this section, we discuss some tips that you can consider now and some that can be useful later when teaching.

Reflecting on Your Beliefs About Teaching Mathematics. The first step in breaking the cultural vicious cycle is becoming aware of it. The second step is to change the disposition that feeds the vicious cycle. Changing one's disposition entails examining and changing one's beliefs.

Contrary to conventional wisdom and, perhaps your own experience, teaching *mathematics can be enjoyable* for both students and teachers. From reading this guide, you will discover the powerful informal mathematical knowledge you and children have at your disposal. You will find that mathematics can actually make sense. You will learn new ways of teaching mathematics that can make it interesting and challenging to children. In brief, the aim of this guide is to help you construct sufficient knowledge about mathematics, children, and teaching so that—unlike Miss Brill—you can approach the task of teaching mathematics with a sense of confidence and joy.

Affective Considerations in the Classroom. Six ways teachers can foster a positive disposition toward mathematics are listed below and illustrated in Box 0.1 on pages 0-16 and 0-17.

☞ **When planning or implementing mathematics instruction, take into account both cognitive and affective factors.** To have a complete picture of school mathematics, teachers need to consider their students' beliefs, attitudes, interests, needs, and feelings (Cobb, Yackel, & Wood, 1989). They should assess students' affect and use this information to adjust their teaching, the learning environment, and the program (Shaughnessy, Haladyna, & Shaughnessy, 1983). To gauge student affect, a teacher can hold a class

Box 0.1: Getting Off to a Good Start—Focusing First on Affective Issues

Vignette (Brief Story)	Comments
"Would someone like to play me in a game of *Equal Nim*?" announced Mr. Yant to his surprised class. After coaxing a volunteer to come forward, he drew two rows of seven circles and explained, "On each turn, a player must cross out one or more circles in just one of the rows. The player who crosses out the last remaining circle or circles wins." After several demonstrations of the game, he had the students pair up and challenged the class to find a winning strategy. When some of the students became frustrated, he suggested looking at simpler cases (e.g., games involving one, two, or three items per row).	To help his eighth-grade students get into the right frame of mind to learn mathematics, a teacher began each school year by playing a math game and discussing affective issues. The game demonstrated that mathematics can be challenging but fun. It also provided an opportunity to teach the class a problem-solving strategy (examine simpler cases).
After discussing the students' solution to the *Nim* problem, Mr. Yant shifted gears, commenting, "Many people readily proclaim their ignorance of mathematics. It is even fashionable to do so—a badge of honor. Would anyone readily admit or proudly boast, 'I could never read'? Why is it acceptable, even desirable, to be innumerate and shameful to be illiterate? Is it because mathematics is not a very useful tool?" At this point, Mr. Yant's students offered a variety of reasons and examples of mathematics importance.	The teacher immediately addressed cultural beliefs that might impede effort and learning. The teacher's comment created an opportunity for students to reflect on the value of mathematics.
"If mathematics is such an important tool," continued Mr. Yant, "why is innumeracy socially acceptable?" After some soul searching, students offered, "Many people can't understand mathematics, so they put it down"; "Mathematics makes people feel stupid, so they 'dis' it"; and "Mathematics is so dense it makes people uncomfortable."	The teacher prompted students to analyze the sources of our culture's attitude toward mathematics.
"Why don't many students understand mathematics?" asked Mr. Yant. "Most people aren't born with math minds," offered Pat.	The teacher attempted to build students' confidence by encouraging them to consider the real reasons for why mathematics seems dense and even overwhelming to many people.
"Like any field," replied Mr. Yant, "there may be only a few mathematical geniuses—people of remarkable talent. However, we are all capable of learning some pretty impressive mathematics." At this juncture, the teacher	The teacher attempted to foster students' sense of mathematical power by underscoring the importance of effort and using a historical frame of reference to help them appreciate the power of their existing mathematical knowl-

Box 0.1 continued

delighted in pointing out some powerful mathematics his students knew but took for granted. He noted, for example, that their efficient multidigit algorithms for calculating written sums or differences have been in wide use for only about 500 years.*

"I've had good and bad teachers," offered Galen. "The good ones have helped me understand math. So it doesn't have to be a fog."

edge. Note also that the teacher exhibits enthusiasm and interest about mathematics.

The teacher's comments prompted students to recognize that mathematical difficulties typically do not arise from a lack of mathematical ability.

*An algorithm is a step-by-step procedure. This term is derived from the name of an Arabian mathematician Al-Khowarizmi, who wrote a book in 820 describing the Arabic numerals and how they could be used in arithmetic calculations (Bunt, Jones, & Bedient, 1976). These number and computational systems were not quickly adopted in Western Europe. After the year 1000, "algorists" (supporters of this new system) struggled many years with "abacists" (supporters of the traditional Roman numeral system in which calculation was done using an abacus). Not until the middle of the 16th century was the clear advantages of arabic numerals generally recognized.

vote (e.g., Who would like to pursue this question further?), assign a writing exercise (e.g., the *To Me Math Is* activity described on page 0-1), or use a questionnaire (e.g., How much do you like working in a group? 1 = It's super 2 = A lot 3 = So, so 4 = Not much 5 = I hate it).

☞ **Help children to appreciate the value of mathematics.** Help them explore how mathematics has been used throughout history to solve practical problems (e.g., see *Historical Topics for the Mathematics Classroom*, © 1989 by the NCTM). Present real or realistic problems to solve. Help them see how mathematics is used in a wide variety of careers. Particularly for primary-level students, discuss how your pupils and their families use mathematics in everyday life (Renga & Dalla, 1993). Illustrate how mathematics can increase their personal power when playing games, shopping, or other personally important activities. A writing assignment *Why Do We Study Mathematics?* can help you assess students' perceived usefulness of mathematics (see the bulletin board on page 1-1 of chapter 1) and provide a basis for discussing the value of mathematics.

☞ **Foster students' confidence in their mathematical ability.** This can be achieved by ensuring that mathematics instruction makes sense, encouraging children's intuitive reasoning and use of informal strategies, choosing experiences carefully so that students can succeed, and withholding judgmental feedback. IT IS IMPORTANT THAT TEACHERS EXPLICITLY ESPOUSE A BELIEF THAT ALL CHILDREN ARE CAPABLE OF SIGNIFICANT MATHEMAT-

ICAL POWER. Help those who already feel inadequate about their mathematical prowess to see that differences in ability can often be traced to differences in the opportunity to learn.

☞ **Help students to see that effort, rather than innate ability, is central to becoming more proficient in mathematics.** In fact, although mathematical genius *may* be largely predetermined by genetics, mathematical achievement in school is largely dependent on effort. In all probability, even students who have never done well have hidden mathematical talent and the potential for considerable mathematical development.

☞ **Model excitement and curiosity about mathematics.** Children's interests are molded by their social environment and, in the social environment of the classroom, the teacher sets the tone. A positive attitude toward mathematics on the part of the teacher can have a profound impact on the students' disposition toward learning and doing mathematics. If a teacher exhibits interest in the subject, it greatly increases the chances that students will also take an interest.

☞ **Have fun with mathematics.** Having fun and learning mathematics are not incompatible, as Mrs. MeChokemchild announced in Probe 0.1. If children enjoy an activity, they are more likely to stay with it and to learn from it. In addition to being educational, playing math games, figuring out math puzzles, and experimenting with ideas can help build a positive disposition toward mathematics. Children may conclude, for instance, that mathematics can be exciting (rather than a drudgery) and can involve creativity (not merely memorization). Indeed, a series of enjoyable activities are—contrary to Mrs. McChokemchild's advice—a particularly good way to start off the school year. For specific ideas, see, for example, the resources listed on pages 0-22 and 0-23.

0•2•2 MATH ANXIETY: A PERSONAL VICIOUS CYCLE

Math anxiety involves an intellectually and emotionally paralyzing fear of mathematics. How can a teacher or a child with math anxiety possibly overcome this malady and develop a positive disposition toward mathematics? In this subunit, we first describe a key cause of math anxiety and then outline what you can do to help someone overcome this paralyzing fear.

Unreasonable Beliefs: The Engine of Math Anxiety

Beliefs help explain why some children eagerly undertake the challenge of learning mathematics or solving a mathematical problem while others shrink from such tasks (Schoenfeld, 1982, 1985).

A Model of Math Anxiety. The basic assumption of the *Anxiety Model* is that our emotional responses are not determined by objective reality but by our *interpretation* of events—by our subjective reality (Ellis & Harper, 1975). Consider the cases of Opal and Rochelle described at the beginning of this unit. Opal's reasonable beliefs allowed her to see the situation in perspective. This girl viewed the problem as a challenge and an opportunity to learn. Realistically recognizing that no one knows everything, Opal accepted the fact that she might make mistakes or might not be able to solve the problem without the input of others. Rochelle's unreasonable beliefs prevented her from seeing the situation in perspective and responding effectively to it. Indeed, her beliefs were so extreme they led to a self-defeating, self-perpetuating cycle called math anxiety.

•**Unreasonable beliefs.** Unreasonable beliefs can lead children to overexaggerate greatly the importance of, say, answering correctly and to underestimate their own self worth. Rochelle, in particular, believed that smart kids *always*

answer correctly and that only children who are smart are worthy of others' admiration and love. These beliefs led her to view the problem as a *threat* to her well being. That is, the girl told herself that if she could not solve the problem, everyone would discover that she's not smart, worthy, and lovable.

•**Anxiety.** Although fear is an appropriate response to real dangers, unreasonable beliefs can create imagined dangers so intense they prompt panic. In Rochelle's case, the threat of not being able to solve the problem led to an anxiety attack.

•**Protective behaviors**. To control anxiety, children may resort to protective behaviors. The *short-term advantage* of a protective behavior is that it minimizes anxiety. Unfortunately, the *long-term disadvantage* of a protective behavior is that it does nothing to dispel the unreasonable beliefs and, indeed, can *reinforce* these beliefs. For instance, Rochelle fell back on not trying. This provided an excuse for avoiding the anxiety-provoking situation (answering incorrectly): "Who can blame me for not solving a problem for which I have no interest." However, irritated by Rochelle's unwillingness to help, several group mates expressed their dissatisfaction with her, verbally or nonverbally. Rochelle took this criticism as further evidence of her lack of smartness and worth. Because her unreasonable beliefs were reinforced, her next effort to solve a problem will be even more threatening and anxiety provoking. In effect, a protective behavior can become a bad habit.

☞ To apply and check your understanding of the *Anxiety Model*, try Probe 0.2 (pages 0-19 and 0-20).

Traditional Schooling—A Key Source of Unreasonable Beliefs. Traditional instruction fosters distorted beliefs about mathematics and mathematical ability—distortions that can inhibit mathematical thinking and learning (see, e.g., Box 0.2 on page 0-21). For instance, when quickly responding with *the* correct answer is emphasized and rewarded, children may conclude that mathematics and being a good student involve rapidly spouting the right answer—not thinking carefully, trying to understand, or explaining ideas with carefully crafted reasoning. (Continued on page 0-21.)

→ Probe 0.2: The *Anxiety Model*—A Model of Math Anxiety

According to the *Anxiety Model*, math anxiety can be viewed as a personal vicious cycle of unreasonable beliefs, anxiety, and protective behaviors. The case of Paul (Baroody, 1987) below illustrates this practical model of math anxiety. After reading it, answer the questions about the model on the next two pages.

The Case of Paul

Despite his mother's efforts to help him, Paul was more than a year behind his third-grade peers, and the situation appeared to be getting worse. Reluctance to do mathematics had become resistance to do mathematics. Moreover, the boy had begun to break out in hives. In brief, Paul had both psychological and physical symptoms of math anxiety.

A key problem became evident during Paul's first session with a mathematics learning specialist. The boy was extremely anxious about using his fingers to compute sums, differences, and products. He would hold his fingers under the table and move them as little as possible. At school and at home, Paul had been told not to use his fingers as a crutch. He had come to believe that smart children did arithmetic in their heads—that only stupid children had to count on their fingers. Because of this belief, doing arithmetic assignments had become threatening and anxiety-provoking situations (see the figure below). Paul's protective behavior—his way of quelling his anxiety or panic—was to avoid doing the assignment. This protective behavior had the short-term advantage of eliminating the need to count on his fingers, forestalling any chance of getting caught in this terrible act, and thus extinguishing his anxiety. In the long-term, however, it resulted in Paul falling further behind, subjecting him to more criticism. In effect, the protective behavior backfired: Paul's suspicions that he was not smart, worthy, and lovable were confirmed. Moreover, opportunities to demonstrate his considerable intelligence were lost.

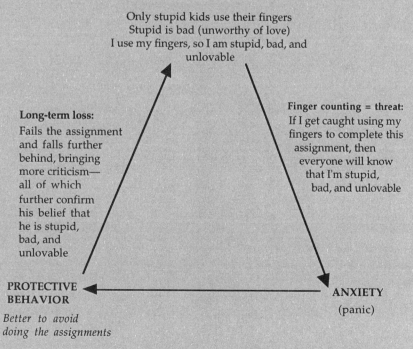

Probe 0.2 continued

Questions Regarding the *Anxiety Model*

1. (a) The *Anxiety Model* implies that a teacher should do what to counter math anxiety?
(b) Consider the case of Paul described above. What specifically should a teacher do to help Paul overcome his debilitating anxiety. (Hint: A common answer is to ensure that Paul has successful experiences with mathematics. Unfortunately, like many math-anxious children, Paul had become too afraid to even try.)

2. After studying the model of math anxiety described on the previous page, Chloe concluded, "Some people respond well to math because they have confidence; others become anxious because they lack confidence. These differences have nothing to do with what people believe." (a) Do you agree or disagree with Chloe's view? Why? (b) Are confidence and beliefs related? Why or why not?

3. Mr. Beast had a reputation for being very hard on student teachers. Heeran went for a classroom visit before starting her student-teaching stint. Mr. Beast greeted her with, "So you're the new know-it-all from the great University come to show me how mathematics should be taught." Heeran, who was already somewhat anxious about student teaching, became extremely agitated and changed the subject, "Nice day we're having." Despite the fact that Mr. Beast grew increasingly abrasive during her stay in his class, Heeran never replied directly to his derogatory comments. Instead, she pretended not to hear what he said and pursued another line of conversation. The next semester, Gwen was assigned to Mr. Beast for student teaching. On her initial visit to his classroom Gwen also was greeted with the line, "So you're the new know-it-all . . ." Unperturbed by this obvious assault, Gwen replied, "Well, I know a few things that may be of interest to you, and I'd be happy to share what I know. But frankly, I'm here because I was hoping that you would have a lot to show me about teaching mathematics." According to the *Anxiety Model*, why did Gwen respond to Mr. Beast differently than did Heeran?

4. (a) Diagram how Heeran's behavior fits the *Anxiety Model*. Circle what starts the vicious emotional cycle. Indicate the short- and long-term effects of the cycle. (b) According to the *Anxiety Model*, how could Heeran's supervisor help her? Give a specific example of what the supervisor could say to help Heeran counteract her overwhelming anxiety.

5. Apply the same instructions in Question 4 to the three cases below:

The Case of Leigh. In previous years, Leigh had never been a good mathematics student, but she had always been fairly conscientious about completing her work. But Mr. Rosini noticed that since the beginning of the year, Leigh's homework grades had steadily gone downhill. When he asked her about this, Leigh explained she was very busy and just didn't have enough time. In fact, Leigh would keep putting off doing her work until the very last minute. Then she would rush through it and, of course, not do well. As time went along she found more and more reasons for procrastinating.

The Case of the Nervous Public Speaker. Two equally intelligent and accomplished teachers Mrs. Positive and Mrs. Negative had to address the parents and guardians of their students for their school's *Get-Acquainted Night*. Each spent the same amount of time preparing her 10-minute talk about the goals for her class. Both had the same goals for their class and were equally committed to accomplishing these goals. Yet Mrs. Positive was energetic and thrived on parents' questions, while Mrs. Negative was a nervous wreck and intimidated by parents' questions. Why did one teacher enjoy public speaking while the other dreaded it?

The Case of Peach and Ozzie. When new material was introduced that she did not understand, Peach raised her hand and asked questions, while Ozzie—no less puzzled or motivated to learn—remained silent. Why did Peach and Ozzie respond so differently?

Box 0.2: Harmful Beliefs Can Develop Early

From how they are taught mathematics, children learn quickly what is valued and what is not. The development of unhelpful beliefs can begin as early as kindergarten (and even earlier depending on a child's preschool experience and parents). Consider the cases of Lane and Margot, who participated in a study investigating children's use of basic arithmetic principles.[†]

First- and second-graders were shown a card with an expression such as $7 + 5$ and asked to determine the answer. After counting out the sum, a child recorded the answer. The card with the expression and its answer was then placed to the side in full view of the child and a new expression such as $5 + 7$ was placed before the child. If the child understood the commutative property of addition (the order in which addends are added does not affect their sum), then there was no need to compute the sum of $5 + 7$.

_____

[†]For details, see "Children's Use of Mathematical Structure" by A. J. Baroody, H. P. Ginsburg, and B. Waxman in the _Journal for Research in Mathematics Education, Vol. 14_ (May 1983), pp. 156-168.

Although told they could figure out the answers _any_ way they wished, some children apparently felt that looking at the previous expression was "naughty." Lane furtively looked at his previous answers and provided the cover story, "I didn't look. I just remembered that one." While surreptitiously looking at her previous answer, Margot realized that her tester was watching her. Sinking down in her seat, she confessed, "I cheated on that one. I looked at the [previously computed sum]." Even though the tester reassured her that she could determine the answers any way she wished, Margot continued her surreptitious behavior.

Why did Lane and Margot behave the way they did? From their worksheet-based instruction that focused on practicing computation and recall, these children had come to believe that looking for patterns and using regularities to reason out answers was cheating, not intelligent problem solving. These primary-grade children had already learned beliefs detrimental to mathematical thinking.

Preventing or Overcoming Math Anxiety

Math anxiety is learned, and so it can be prevented or unlearned. In addition to the tips listed earlier on pages 0-15 to 0-18), teachers can do the following to avoid or overcome math anxiety:

☞ **Minimize fear and anxiety.** To do so, a teacher can:

• emphasize understanding and thinking rather than memorizing and quickly regurgitating the correct answer;
• encourage a variety of strategies, including children's informal methods, instead of requiring children to learn a single school-taught procedure;
• treat questions and errors as learning opportunities and as signs of active intelligence, not as interruptions or signs of stupidity;
• choose experiences carefully so that children generally experience success; and
• encourage children to work in groups.

☞ **To prevent or break the vicious cycle of math anxiety, encourage reasonable and construc-**

tive beliefs. Foster beliefs that promote curiosity and a desire to learn rather than anxiety and protective behaviors. For students already afflicted with math anxiety, the _Anxiety Model_ suggests encouraging them to examine and _refute_ debilitating beliefs and to _replace_ them with constructive beliefs. Indeed, it may be necessary to change entrenched and debilitating beliefs _before_ efforts are made to remedy academic deficiencies. Math anxious students may be so afraid of mathematics, they will not even try. Thus, it is difficult for them to experience success or for teachers praise their effort or progress. In brief, to break the emotional freeze produced by math anxiety, a teacher must attack the source of the problem—the unreasonable beliefs causing the anxiety.

Consider the case of Paul described on page 0-19 of Probe 0.2. This boy believed that counting on his fingers to compute answers was a shameful sign of stupidity. To help Paul overcome the resulting math anxiety, he, his teacher, and his parents had to be convinced that finger counting was a sensible strategy that practically all children use. With this new perspective, the boy felt better about his informal strategies, stopped breaking out in hives, and began to make significant progress.

Perfectionistic beliefs, in particular, are common among children and disable many. Help them see the fallacies of such beliefs and develop perspective. Avoid stressing the need to always get the right answer. John Holt (1964) described several analogies useful in constructing more realistic beliefs. For instance, in the major leagues, batters are doing very well if they obtain a batting average of .300. This means that even really good hitters *fail* to get a hit 7 out of every 10 times at bat.

Many students don't ask questions out of fear of appearing stupid. To counter this fear, Holt (1964) suggested the following analogy: If you are on a trip and leave your luggage at a motel, it's going to be easier if you turn back sooner rather than later. In other words, it is better to ask about puzzling material immediately—rather than maintain appearances, only to become more confused as the material becomes more complicated.

 ↪ ✐ **Invite math autobiographies.** This can encourage students to reflect on the origins of their anxiety (e.g., a critical incident when they were publicly humiliated or a disabling belief espoused by a teacher, parent, or peer). Writing and perhaps discussing their autobiography may help them gain perspective.

PARTING THOUGHTS

"Teachers are the key figures in changing how mathematics is learned and understood by . . . children. The kind of teaching envisioned by the NCTM [1991] *Professional Standards for Teaching Mathematics* . . . is significantly different from what many teachers themselves have personally experienced" (Thornton & Wilson, 1993, p. 273). It will require truly professional teachers—teachers well versed in mathematics, the psychology of mathematical learning, and a variety of teaching techniques. In many cases, it will also require teachers to change their attitudes toward mathematics so that the next generation of students has the chance to develop a positive disposition toward mathematics and their enormous mathematical potential. A key aspect of building a positive disposition toward mathematics is fostering constructive and reason-

able beliefs about mathematics and mathematics learning.

RESOURCES

SOME INSTRUCTIONAL RESOURCES

Making Mathematics Interesting & Fun

Primary-level teachers should find the Anno books listed below helpful. Intermediate-level teachers, particularly, should find portions of the second and fifth to seventh references useful. The third and fourth references are rich sources of interesting instructional ideas for all teachers.

☛ **Anno's Math Games** (© 1987) and **Anno's Math Games III** (© 1991) written by Mitsumasa Anno. Published by Philomel Books and distributed by Dale Seymour Publications. *Anno's Math Games* describes games that involve comparing and classifying, adding and subtracting, and measuring and graphing. *Anno's Math Games III* encourages children to look at situations from various perspectives.

☛ **Beyond Numeracy** by John Allen Paulos, © 1991 by Alfred A. Knopf. This reference provides tidbits of history and interesting examples that can be helpful in understanding a variety of topics including Arabic numerals, prime numbers, rational and irrational numbers, averages (means, medians, and modes), probability, geometry (topology, area, and volume), algebra, and functions.

☛ **Enhance Chance** by Jan Becker, Mary Laycock, and Genevieve Waring, © 1973 by Activity Resources Company, Inc. This valuable resource describes 45 dice games that involve such topics as sets, place-value, whole-number arithmetic operations, fractions, decimals, percents, coordinates, probability, and logic.

☛ **The Joy of Mathematics: Discovering Mathematics All Around You** by Theoni Pappas, © 1989 by Wide World Publishing/Tetra. This book includes over 100 activities, problems, puzzles, and games. One example is:

■ **Gaining Grains** (◆ 5-8). If one grain of wheat is placed on the first square of a chessboard, two on the second, four on the third, eight on the fourth, and this doubling process was continued to the last or sixty-fourth square, how many grains of wheat would you need?

☞ **Mathematical Bafflers** compiled and edited by Angela Dunn, © 1964 by Litton Industries, Inc. and published by McGraw-Hill Book Company. This book is a collection of interesting puzzles and problems of various levels of difficulty.

☞ **Mathematicians Delight** by W. W. Sawyer, © 1943 and published by Penguin Books. This book describes key ideas about arithmetic, graphs, and algebra in easy to read terms.

☞ **Mathematics Games for Fun and Practice** by Alan Barson, © 1992 by Addison-Wesley. This resource describes 38 games for practicing grade 4-8 level math skills involving computation, geometry, and measurement.

Math Anxiety

☞ Three references that include ideas for combating math anxiety are: **Fear of Math: How to Get Over It and Get on with Your Life** by Claudia Zaslavsky (© 1994 and published by Rutgers University Press and distributed by Dale Seymour Publications), **Math Panic** by Laurie Buxton (© 1991, Heinemann), and **Overcoming Math Anxiety** by Shiela Tobias (© 1978, Norton). Tobias writes, "People remember math as being taught in an atmosphere of tension created by the emphasis on right answers and especially by the demands of timed test" (p. 24). (What can you as a teacher do to reduce this tension?) "More than any other aspect of elementary arithmetic, except perhaps fractions, word problems cause panic among the math anxious . . . . Their attitudes, not their math ability, gets in the way" (p. 129). (According to this teaching guide, how could a teacher help minimize this panic?) "[Many people assume] that if it is in [their] head it has to be wrong . . . . They do not trust their intuitions. Either they remember the 'right formula' immediately or they give up" (p. 58). How can a teacher counter such beliefs?

A SAMPLE OF CHILDREN'S LITERATURE

☞ **Mathematical Games for One or Two** by Mannis Charosh, © 1972 by Thomas Y. Crowell Company. Playing games and analyzing magic tricks are enjoyable ways for students of all ages to learn problem-solving strategies and mathematical concepts and skills. This resource describes a number of games that can be played by one child or pairs of children (see, e.g., the *Nim* game described on page 0-16).

☞ **The $1.00 Word Riddle Book** by Marilyn Burns, © 1990 by Math Solutions Publication and distributed by Cuisenaire Company of America, Inc. This book of riddles can help build vocabulary while providing practice adding decimals. To solve a picture riddle, children must come up with a word that *adds up to $1.00*, assuming that a = $.01, b = $.02, c = $.03, and so forth.

TIPS ON USING TECHNOLOGY

Calculators and computers can provide an entertaining way to explore mathematical ideas and practice mathematical skills (see, e.g., Activity File 0.1 and Box 0.3 on the next page). The first resource listed below includes hundreds of calculator-based activities for exploring a variety of content areas. The second reference includes a review on the educational impact of computer games as well as other math games.

▦ **CAMP-LA** (Calculators and Mathematics Project, Los Angeles), edited by D. Pagni (©1991, Cal State Fullerton Press), includes volumes for K-2, 3&4, 5&6, and 7&8.

▯ **Learning and Mathematics Games** (*Journal for Research in Mathematics Monograph, Vol. 1*) by G. Bright, J. Harvey, and M. Wheeler, © 1985 by NCTM.

Advice and support for new (and experienced) teachers can be found on the internet (see, e.g., "Ask Dr. Math" at http://forum.swarthmore.edu/dr.math/drmath.elem.html and "Teachers Helping Teachers" at http://www.pacificnet.net/~mandel/). "Terri Santi's Homepage: A Homepage for New Math Teachers" (http://www.clarityconnect.com/webpages/terri/terri.html), for example, includes information on How to Start Making Connections, Multicultural Mathematics, Resources for New Math Teachers, Classroom

---

▦ 🍎 Activity File 0.1: Calculator Explorations

◆ Operation sense ◆ 2-8 ◆ Any number

Activity I: What are the Limits?

It may surprise children to learn that some calculations are too hard for a calculator. Encourage them to explore the limits of their calculators for each of the operations. For example, what is the largest addend that can be added on a Texas Instruments (TI) *Math Explorer*? What is the largest addend that can be added to 100? What is the largest number from which you can subtract 100? What is the largest factor that can be multiplied? What is the largest factor that can be multiplied by 100? Us-

ing whole numbers, what is the largest difference you can obtain? Are your answers above the same for a different calculator?

Activity II: Getting Around a Limit

Challenge students to figure out a way to make a computation that exceeds the limits of a calculator. For example, how could you add 6,420,000,000 and 5,390,000,586 on a TI *Math Explorer*? How could you multiply 1,250 and 444,444? Further challenge students to devise the *most efficient* alternative method.

🖥 Box 0.3: Computer Fun Can Equal Serious Learning

At lunch Ms. Socrates excitedly described her new software. Mrs. MeChokemchild, who kept her computer unplugged in her supply closet, was unimpressed. "Computers are just another educational fad," she snorted. "It makes little sense to waste time on them."

"In fact, computers are used in nearly all businesses and government offices and in many homes," replied Ms. Socrates, more for Miss Brill's benefit than for that of the obstinate Mrs. MeChokemchild. "'Unlike other educational innovations, computers are in schools' . . . because educators, employers, government officials, and parents recognize their importance for everyday life and insist that children become computer literate. 'Because of these pressures, computers are not going to be a fad that is here today and gone tomorrow; they are going to remain a part of the teaching environment from now on'" (Bright, 1987, p. x).

"I'm really nervous about using computers," commented Miss Brill. "I'm computer illiterate. How can I use them as a teaching tool?"

"Fortunately, computer applications are becoming more user friendly—easier to use—all the time," reassured Ms. Socrates. "Besides, there is no reason why you can't learn along with your students. Let me show you several computer games that you and your students will find interesting and challenging."

"Games!" hooted Mrs. MeChokemchild. "That's all kids need—sitting stone-faced in front of a screen playing mindless games. I'm sure that will go over big with the principal, parents, and the board of education."

"Actually," answered Ms. Socrates, "computer games are a highly motivating way to introduce elementary children to computers, to familiarize them with this technology, and to foster a positive disposition toward them. Moreover, computer games can be used instructionally for two purposes: (a) to teach subject matter ('content games') and (b) to encourage problem solving, reasoning and other thinking skills ('process games')" (Olds, Schwartz, & Willie, 1980, cited in Kaput, 1992)."

Management, Other Professional Suggestions, and Great Sites for Math Teachers. Information about efforts to reshape students' attitudes about mathematics is available at www.terc.edu. Students may enjoy the following web sites: "Kids-Web Mathematics" (http://www.npac.syr.edu/textbook/ kidsweb/math.html) and "Just

for Middle School Kids" (http://www.westnet.com/~rickd/Kids.html). Those who enjoy mathematical puzzles can visit "The Aims Puzzle Corner" (http://204.161.33.100/Puzzle/PuzzleList.html) or "The University of Idaho Mathematics Department's Internet Math Challenge" (www.uidaho.edu/LS/Math/imc).

1 | FOSTERING MATHEMATICAL POWER: THE NEED FOR PURPOSEFUL, INQUIRY-BASED, AND MEANINGFUL INSTRUCTION

Why Do We Study Mathematics?

Y do we study Math JACOB
To get good grads

Y da We study ~~Math~~ Math
To get good grades Steven

Jamie
① To work with money and how much to find
of something you have.

Andrew
Why do we study Math
because we use it when
we buy things we need
to know how much it cost
too make shure there not
riping us off and to make
sure that we have enough

Why do we study math?
By Alexis Baroody 4-19-95
We study math so that we can navigate a course or to tell who has the most CD's. In a world of numbers it's crucial to under stand them. Basically we study math to become problem solvers.

Arianne
1. To help us solve problems.
2. We study math to find short cuts so we do not hafe to do it over again.

Alison
1. To help us solve problem
2. To find patterns
3. To make our lifes easier
4. To make sovling problems easier
5. To help us understand things

☞ In writing, answer the following question: *Why do we study mathematics?*

✐ The *Why do we study mathematics?* question can serve as the basis for a useful writing exercise. In addition to practicing language arts skills, such an exercise can provide teachers insight into their students' view of the importance of mathematics and their reasons for studying it. Some children may think of mathematics as a tool for solving problems or for accomplishing everyday tasks. Others may see learning mathematics as a way of getting a grade. Yet others may see no purpose in studying it. The student essays could provide a basis for a class discussion, a bulletin board (as shown above), or both.

THIS CHAPTER

*O*n the second day of class, Mr. Yant underscored the importance of mathematics by explaining, "Education is a journey in which you can acquire the tools to control more and more of your life. Mathematics is one of those tools. This tool becomes more and more useful by building an ever larger repertoire of concepts and strategies. This construction of mathematical knowledge occurs gradually through curiosity, desire, practice, and perseverance. After all, one does not become an accomplished athlete, musician, or artist overnight either." Mr. Yant concluded by inviting his students to turn up their mathematical power. His students liked the idea of sharing in the power of mathematics.

Mathematical power implies the capacity to apply mathematical knowledge to new or unfamiliar tasks. This requires:

1. *a positive disposition to learn and use mathematics* (e.g., the self confidence and willingness to seek, evaluate, and apply quantitative and spatial information to solve problems and make decisions);

2. the ability *to engage in the processes of mathematical inquiry* (to explore, conjecture, reason logically, solve challenging problems, and communicate about and through mathematics); and

3. *a deep understanding of mathematics* (mathematical ideas that are well connected to other mathematical content, other subject areas, and everyday life).

Elementary-level instruction is crucial for laying a foundation for mathematical power. Experiences in these early grades shape and, in many cases, forever fix a child's disposition toward learning and using mathematics. Early educational experiences mold and often cement habits of mathematical thinking. K-8 instruction can also help children construct a fundamental understanding of mathematical ideas needed to tackle more advanced mathematics and everyday tasks. Whether or not instruction fosters mathematical power depends on what mathematics is taught and, perhaps more importantly, on how mathematics is taught. Unfortunately, traditional instruction all too often leaves children mathematically powerless (e.g., Trafton & Shulte, 1989).

Along with chapters 0, 2, and 3, this chapter provides a general framework for the rest of the book. We examine different ways of thinking about mathematics education (Unit 1•1) and discuss a new way of teaching mathematics—an approach that can foster mathematical power (Unit 1•2). The chapter expands on the discussion of fostering a positive disposition toward mathematics begun in chapter 0. Chapter 2 will consider further the importance of focusing on the processes of mathematical inquiry such as problem solving; chapter 3, the importance of focusing on understanding. Chapters 4 through 16 will examine how the general framework can be applied to teaching specific content areas.

WHAT THE NCTM *STANDARDS* SAY

Founded in 1920, the National Council of Teachers of Mathematics (NCTM) is a professional association of teachers, administrators, teacher educators, and researchers dedicated to improving mathematics teaching and learning. A summary of the changes in content and emphasis suggested by NCTM (1989) are listed on pages 1-3 and 1-4.

1•1 DIFFERENT VIEWS OF MATHEMATICS EDUCATION

Figure 1.1: Many Children Believe That Math Must be Taken on Faith

SUMMARY OF CHANGES IN CONTENT AND EMPHASIS†

K-4 MATHEMATICS

INCREASED ATTENTION

Number
- Number sense
- Place-value concepts
- Meaning of fractions and decimals
- Estimation of quantities

Operations and Computation
- Meaning of operations
- Operation sense
- Mental computation
- Estimation and the reasonableness of answers
- Selection of an appropriate computational method
- Use of calculators for complex computation
- Thinking strategies for basic facts

Geometry and Measurement
- Properties of geometric figures
- Geometric relationships
- Spatial sense
- Process of measuring
- Concepts related to units of measurement
- Actual measuring
- Estimation of measurements
- Use of measurement and geometry ideas throughout the curriculum

Probability and Statistics
- Collection and organization of data
- Exploration of chance

Patterns and Relationships
- Pattern recognition and description
- Use of variables to express relationships

Problem Solving
- Word problems with a variety of structures
- Use of everyday problems
- Applications
- Study of patterns and relationships
- Problem-solving strategies

Instructional Practices
- Use of manipulative materials
- Cooperative work
- Discussion of mathematics
- Questioning
- Justification of thinking
- Writing about mathematics
- Problem-solving [based] instruction
- Content integration
- Use of calculators and computers

DECREASED ATTENTION

Number
- Early attention to reading, writing, and ordering numbers symbolically

Operations and Computation
- Complex paper-and-pencil computations
- Isolated treatment of paper-and-pencil computations
- Addition and subtraction without renaming
- Isolated treatment of division facts
- Long division
- Long division without remainders
- Paper-and-pencil fraction computation
- Use of rounding to estimate

Geometry and Measurement
- Primary focus on naming geometric figures
- Memorization of equivalencies between units of measurement

Problem Solving
- Use of clue words to determine which operation to use

Instructional Practices
- Rote practice
- Rote memorization of rules
- One answer and one method
- Use of worksheets
- Written practice
- Teaching by telling

---

† Reprinted from pages 20-21 and 70-73 of the *Curriculum and Evaluations for School Mathematics*, © 1989 by the NCTM, with the permission of the National Council of Teachers of Mathematics.

To get more information about the *Standards*, contact the NCTM at 703-620-9840 (extension 113), e-mail infocentral@nctm.org, or visit the NCTM website at http://www.nctm.org. NCTM documents and information can also be obtained through its fax service: 800-220-8483.

5-8 MATHEMATICS

INCREASED ATTENTION	DECREASED ATTENTION

Problem Solving, Reasoning, and Communicating

INCREASED ATTENTION
- Pursuing open-ended problems and extended problem-solving projects
- Investigating and formulating questions from problem situations
- Representing situations verbally, numerically, graphically, geometrically, or symbolically
- Reasoning in spatial contexts
- Reasoning with proportions
- Reasoning from graphs
- Reasoning inductively and deductively
- Discussing, writing, reading, and listening to mathematical ideas

DECREASED ATTENTION
- Practicing routine, one-step problems
- Practicing problems categorized by types (e.g., coin problems, age problems)
- Relying on outside authority (teacher or an answer key)
- Doing fill-in-the-blank worksheets
- Answering questions that require only yes, no, or a number as responses

Connections

INCREASED ATTENTION
- Connecting mathematics to other subjects and to the world outside the classroom
- Connecting topics within mathematics
- Applying mathematics

DECREASED ATTENTION
- Learning isolated topics
- Developing skills out of context

Number/Operations/Computation

INCREASED ATTENTION
- Developing number sense
- Developing operation sense
- Creating algorithms and procedures
- Using estimation both in solving problems and in checking the reasonableness of results
- Exploring relationships among representations of, and operations on, whole numbers, fractions, decimals, integers, and rational numbers
- Developing an understanding of ratio, proportion, and percent

DECREASED ATTENTION
- Memorizing rules and algorithms
- Practicing tedious paper-and-pencil computations
- Finding exact forms of answers
- Memorizing procedures, such as cross-multiplication, without understanding
- Practicing rounding numbers out of context

Algebra, Patterns, and Functions

INCREASED ATTENTION
- Developing an understanding of variables, expressions, and equations
- Using a variety of methods to solve linear equations and informally investigate inequalities and nonlinear equations
- Identifying and using functional relationships
- Developing and using tables, graphs, and rules to describe situations
- Interpreting among different mathematical representations

DECREASED ATTENTION
- Manipulating symbols
- Memorizing procedures and drilling on equation solving

Statistics and Probability

INCREASED ATTENTION
- Using statistical methods to describe, analyze, evaluate, and make decisions
- Creating experimental and theoretical models of situations involving probabilities

DECREASED ATTENTION
- Memorizing formulas

Geometry and Measurement

INCREASED ATTENTION
- Developing an understanding of geometric objects and relationships
- Using geometry and measurement to solve problems
- Estimating measurements

DECREASED ATTENTION
- Memorizing geometric vocabulary
- Memorizing facts and relationships
- Memorizing and manipulating formulas
- Converting within and between measurement systems

Instructional Practices

INCREASED ATTENTION
- Actively involving students individually and in groups in exploring, conjecturing, analyzing, and applying mathematics in both a mathematical and a real-world context
- Using appropriate technology for computation and exploration
- Using concrete materials
- Being a facilitator of learning
- Assessing learning as an integral part of instruction

DECREASED ATTENTION
- Teaching computations out of context
- Drilling on paper-and-pencil algorithms
- Teaching topics in isolation
- Stressing memorization
- Being the dispenser of knowledge
- Testing for the sole purpose of assigning grades

In Figure 1.1 on page 1-2, Calvin believes that mathematics is magical (and not worth doing). Indeed, many students believe that mathematics is something you simply accept on faith. Consider the following journal entry of a preservice teacher: *To me math is a bunch of numbers and formulas that somehow, when put together, work out.—Jennifer Drew*

Teachers' beliefs about mathematics, how children learn it, and what constitutes good teaching affect the mathematics they choose to teach and the way they choose to teach it (Dossey, 1992; Fennema et al., 1996; Hersh, 1986; Koehler & Grouws, 1992; Peterson, Fennema, Carpenter, & Loef, 1989; A. Thompson, 1992). These choices, in turn, can profoundly affect students' view of mathematics and their learning of it. For these reasons, we begin our discussion of how to teach mathematics by examining different views of mathematics (Subunit 1•1•1), mathematical learning (Subunit 1•1•2), and mathematics instruction (Subunit 1•1•3).

☞ Fill out Probe 1.1 (pages 1-6 to 1-8).

1•1•1 MATHEMATICS

In this subunit, we examine different beliefs that teachers hold about mathematics and the true nature of mathematics.

Different Views of Mathematics

Three different views of mathematics have been identified among teachers—(a) mathematics as a collection of unrelated basic skills, (b) mathematics as a coherent network of skills and concepts, and (c) mathematics as a way of thinking (Ernest, 1988).

Mathematics as Skills (Meaningless, Unrelated Content). Mrs. MeChokemchild, the traditional teacher described in Part I of Probe 1.1, holds the conventional view of math as stuff (see Figure 1.2)—as a jumble of "rules without reason" carved in stone (Skemp, 1978, p. 9). In her view, understanding why is unimportant to achieving proficiency with the isolated how-to skills that make up the prescribed curriculum. In brief, math is seen as a set of socially useful—but largely incomprehensible, unconnected, and fixed—facts, rules, formulas, and procedures.

Mathematics as a Network of Skills and Concepts (*Meaningful, Related* Content). Some teachers believe that mathematics in-

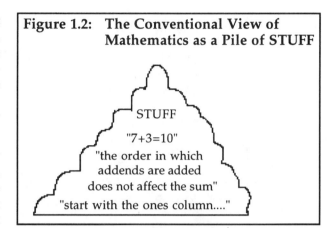

Figure 1.2: The Conventional View of Mathematics as a Pile of STUFF

STUFF

"7+3=10"

"the order in which addends are added does not affect the sum"

"start with the ones column...."

volves "knowing both what to do and why" (Skemp, 1978, p. 9). Recognizing that understanding can facilitate mastery of basic skills, they foster meaningful learning by helping students learn concepts and then relating facts, rules, formulas, and procedures to these concepts. Like educators with conventional beliefs, though, these teachers assume that mathematics is a static body of knowledge and that students can discover its immutable truths but not create or improve on them (Ernest, 1988).

Mathematics as a Way of Thinking (A *Process of Inquiry*). Some teachers view mathematics as a *process of inquiry*—an effort to understand our world and to extend our knowledge of it. That is, they view the discipline as an effort to solve problems, which entails thinking creatively, finding patterns, reasoning logically, and communicating clearly. These teachers view mathematics as a dynamic field—as a way of adding to our ever-growing understanding.

The Nature of Mathematics

☞ Investigation 1.1 (pages 1-9 and 1-10).

Contrary to the conventional view, mathematics is not simply a collection of isolated pieces of information. As a science, it is a field of inquiry that builds on a network of interrelated ideas. As a means of inquiry, mathematics is an invaluable tool for exploring and characterizing the order we perceive in our world. As illustrated by Investigation 1.1, it is, at heart, an ongoing effort to solve problems by finding patterns (Steen, 1990a, p. iii). As an open-ended search for patterns, mathematics continues to grow (Steen, 1990b). Indeed, as a result of computer technology, it is growing at a tremendous rate (Lindquist, 1989). (Continued on page 1-11.)

➤ Probe 1.1: Examining Beliefs About Mathematics, Learning, and Teaching

Whether conscious or not, your beliefs about mathematics, how it is learned, and how it should be taught strongly influence your instructional decisions. And your decisions can profoundly affect the level of mathematical power achieved by your students. For these reasons, it is essential that you *consciously* examine your beliefs about mathematics, learning, and teaching. To help you examine these beliefs, complete Parts I and II.

Part I: One View of Teaching Mathematics

Although eager to begin her first year of teaching, Miss Brill harbored deep reservations about teaching mathematics.

"The formula for success—pardon the pun—is really quite simple," announced the veteran teacher Mrs. MeChokemchild. "Just follow the textbook. If you don't get to the last few chapters, don't worry about it. The year-end achievement test has almost no questions on stuff like ratios, statistics, and probability anyway. Focus on the important things—whole number-, fraction-, and decimal-arithmetic procedures."

Mrs. MeChokemchild paused and looked around to see if anyone else might be listening. Then in a conspiratorial tone, she added, "You appear to be the down-to-earth type, not like some of those radical weirdos normal schools [teachers' colleges] turn out these days. Our colleague Ms. Socrates went back to get her master's degree some years ago. They filled her head with all sorts of nonsense, and she's been off the wall ever since. Be aware, she'll talk your ear off about helping children understand mathematics and solve problems. Nonsense! Elementary school children don't need to understand math to master basic skills. Theirs is not to reason why but to know how. Besides most of them don't know enough to understand math or solve problems anyway. They just get all muddled up, and the result is confusion. Next thing you know you have an angry principal and teed-off parents on your back."

"Believe me," continued Mrs. MeChokemchild who was now clearly overexcited, "It's just easier to teach them *how* to do it. If kids don't know something, don't mess around. Tell and show them what they need to know. Then have them practice, practice, practice. If kids are ever going to memorize basic facts and procedures, they need plenty of seatwork and homework. Believe me, it's the only way they will do well on achievement tests. And anyone with a lick of sense will tell you high achievement-test scores are *the* sign of a quality education. Remember, high test scores mean happy parents and school administrators."

"One other thing," added Mrs. MeChokemchild, "Review. It seems that no matter how much they practice, many children forget anyway. Kids today are so lazy, and a lot of them are just plain stupid." You'll have to spend the first part of the year reviewing everything they were taught last year. Summer vacation produces the fall vacuum, if you know what I mean. Moreover, make sure you review newly-taught material after each unit and especially before the standardized test in the spring." Miss Brill was beginning to understand why she might not get to the last chapters in the textbook.

1. Mrs. MeChokemchild's advice is based on what implicit assumptions about mathematics, children, and teaching?

2. With which assumptions do you agree, with which do you disagree, and with which are you undecided about?

3. Try re-analyzing Mrs. MeChokemchild's advice after you read the chapter. List her assumptions that the reading has helped you detect.

Probe 1.1 continued

Part II: A Questionnaire

Complete Questions 1, 2, and 3 of the Questionnaire. Discuss your responses with your group or class. After finishing this chapter (or the entire guidebook), complete the Questionnaire again. What, if any, of your beliefs changed?

1. For each item, if you strongly agree with the statement on the left, circle 1. If you agree with the statement on the left more than you do the statement on the right, circle 2. If you are undecided, circle 3. If you agree more with the statement on the right than you do the statement on the left, circle 4. If you strongly agree with the statement on the right, circle 5.

Mathematics is essentially a body of information (socially useful facts, rules, formulas, and procedures).	1 2 3 4 5	Mathematics is essentially a way of thinking about and solving problems.
The main goal of elementary mathematics education is ensuring mastery of basic facts, rules, formulas, and procedures.	1 2 3 4 5	The main goal of elementary mathematics education is cultivating mathematical understanding and thinking.
The growth of knowledge involves accumulating information to become more informed.	1 2 3 4 5	The growth of knowledge involves gaining new insights and reorganizing one's thinking.
Learning is essentially a receptive and passive process of memorizing information.	1 2 3 4 5	Learning is essentially an active process of constructing understanding and strategies.
The accurate memorization of facts and procedures requires children to stay on task: listen carefully and practice diligently what has been taught.	1 2 3 4 5	The active construction of knowledge entails doing mathematics (e.g., discovering patterns, making and testing conjectures, and solving problems).
Direct instruction and practice are the most effective way to transmit information to children.	1 2 3 4 5	Actively involving students in discovery learning and solving problems is the most effective way to encourage insight and thinking.
Teaching is telling—a teacher is principally an information transmitter.	1 2 3 4 5	Teaching is guiding—a teacher serves principally to facilitate discovery and thinking.
Because children do not have a natural interest in learning mathematics, it is essential for educators to find ways to prompt learning.	1 2 3 4 5	Because children have a natural interest in exploring and making sense of things, mathematics can be inherently interesting.

Probe 1.1 continued

2. Answer the following questions about mathematics. For each statement below, circle SA if you strong agree, A if you agree, N if you are neutral, D if you disagree, and SD if you strongly disagree.

   a. Mathematics is not supposed to make sense. SA A N D SD

   b. Mathematics mainly involves memorizing and following rules (e.g., the carrying procedure for doing addition). SA A N D SD

   c. Mathematical proficiency or expertise is characterized by an ability to cite arithmetic facts or to do computations quickly. SA A N D SD

   d. Mathematical knowledge is essentially fixed and unchanging. SA A N D SD

   e. Mathematics is well defined; it is not open to questions, arguments, or personal interpretations. SA A N D SD

   f. Mathematical ability is essentially something you are born with or without. SA A N D SD

   g. Mathematicians typically work in isolation. SA A N D SD

3. Answer the following questions about mathematical teaching and learning. For each statement below, circle SA if you strongly agree, A if you agree, N if you are neutral, D if you disagree, and SD if you strongly disagree.

   a. Nonstandard procedures should be discouraged because they can interfere with learning the correct procedure. SA A N D SD

   b. Mathematics instruction should begin with teaching basic skills and move toward fostering higher-order thinking. SA A N D SD

   c. When introducing a mathematical topic, a teacher should adhere to the KISS principle (*Keep it simple and straightforward*) and only later introduce complex problems. SA A N D SD

   d. Elementary-age children are mathematically helpless. That is, they are typically unable to solve even elementary mathematical problems because they lack the prerequisite experience and knowledge. SA A N D SD

   e. To understand elementary mathematics, children must be lead through a systematic sequence of well-organized lessons. SA A N D SD

   f. A teacher must serve as the judge of what is or is not correct. SA A N D SD

   g. A teacher should always give feedback (e.g., praise students' correct answers and immediately correct their incorrect answers). SA A N D SD

   h. A teacher should act quickly to eliminate disagreements because they are disruptive and may cause unnecessary confusion. SA A N D SD

   i. To foster independence, students should work alone to complete assignments. SA A N D SD

✿ Investigation 1.1: The Nature of Mathematics[†]

◆ Looking for patterns and drawing conclusions ◆ Any number

Many people equate mathematics with arithmetic—with memorizing and following rules for doing written calculations (McLeod, 1992). Arithmetic, though, is merely a finger (a small branch of) mathematics, not its heart (essence). Indeed, mathematics has little to do with manipulating written symbols and everything to do with creating and exploring ideas. The essence of mathematics is finding patterns in order to solve problems. To get a flavor of what mathematics is really about, try Parts I and II of this investigation. Working with others in a small group or as a class can be helpful.

Part I: Deciphering a Space Message (◆ 3-8)

There is probably intelligent life on other worlds in the universe. How might we try to communicate with them? Scientists involved with the *Explorer* project faced just such a question. They concluded that using natural languages such as Chinese, English, French, Spanish, Russian, or Yiddish was not a good choice, because it seemed unlikely that aliens would comprehend them. The project scientists decided to start communications effort with a mathematical message, because mathematics is considered a universal language.

Below are radio signals as they might appear on an oscilloscope. Each line represents a mathematical expression. Can you decipher the patterns in these messages and determine what each expression says?

[†]Adapted from pages 2 and 3 of *Mathematics: A Human Endeavor* by C. Jacobs (1982) with the permission of the publisher: W. H. Freeman, San Francisco.

Investigation 1.1 continued

Part II: Deciphering an Ancient Message (♦ 4-8)

Archeologists confront a similar task when they try to decipher ancient languages. The Babylonians, who dated back to 4000 B.C., were active mathematicians and recorded information about their number system, algebra, and geometry on clay tablets. They wrote on wet clay with a stylus to create the wedge-shaped forms called cuneiforms (kyü-ne- ə -forms). The following is a pictorial representation of clay tablets that dates back to about 1800 B.C.

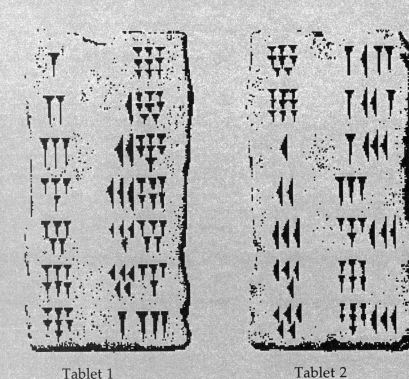

Tablet 1   Tablet 2

1. Can you decipher the cuneiform symbols? It may help to translate the symbols on the left-hand side of each tablet first.

2. a. What do you notice about the first six entries of the right-hand column on Tablet 1?

   b. What would you predict the seventh entry of this column would represent? That is, what must ![symbols] represent?

3. a. What is the relationship between the left- and right-hand column of Tablet 1?

   b. Given this relationship and what you know about the left-hand column of Tablet 2, what do the entries on the right-hand side of Tablet 2 represent?

4. What other patterns or relationships can you detect in the tablets?

1•1•2 LEARNING

In this subunit, we outline three different views of the learning process and then explore what recent research reveals about the nature of children's mathematical learning.

Different Views of Learning

Mathematical learning can be viewed primarily as a process of (a) memorizing content by rote, (b) understanding content, or (c) developing mathematical thinking.

Mathematics Learning as Memorizing Content by Rote. Mrs. MeChokemchild holds the conventional view of children as stuffless stuffees who must be stuffed with stuff (see Figure 1.3). If mathematics is a collection of isolated, meaningless, and fixed facts, procedures, rules, and formulas and children are uninformed and helpless, then mathematical learning must entail *memorizing* prescribed information *by rote*.

Figure 1.3: The Conventional View of Children as STUFFEES

STUFF

Empty head lacks stuff

Mathematics Learning as Understanding Content (Meaningful Memorization). If mathematics is a network of skills and concepts, then mathematical learning should encompass *understanding* the conceptual basis or rationale for facts, procedures, rules, and formulas. Like the conventional view, then, learning is seen as *internalizing prescribed content*. Unlike the conventional view, however, learning is accomplished by *meaningful memorization* rather than memorization by rote.

Mathematics Learning as the Development of Mathematical Thinking. If mathematics is a process of inquiry, then mathematical learning should involve developing the thinking processes—the problem-solving strate-

gies and reasoning ability—necessary to conduct mathematical inquiry. In contrast to the two views just discussed, learning is envisioned as a process of expanding thinking, "not as a process of internalizing carefully packaged knowledge" (Cobb, Wood, & Yackel, 1991, p. 5).

The Nature of Children's Learning

☞ Try Probe 1.2 (pages 1-12).

Contrary to conventional beliefs, constructivist theory and research suggests that children don't begin school as empty vessels, meaningful learning isn't simply a matter of passively absorbing information, and children are not naturally disinterested in learning (e.g., Putnam, Lampert, & Peterson, 1990; Steffe & Wood, 1990).

Children's Surprising Informal Knowledge. As Vignette 1 in Probe 1.2 illustrates, the development of mathematical knowledge begins before school (e.g., Court, 1920; Ginsburg, 1989). Children engage in all sorts of everyday activities that involve mathematics and, as a result, develop a considerable body of informal knowledge. As Vignettes 1 to 3 in Probe 1.2 illustrate, children can draw on their everyday knowledge to informally solve significant mathematical problems. For example, 5-year-old Alison exploited her informally learned knowledge of the counting sequence to solve the problem of finding out her new score after earning two more points. Furthermore, as we will see again and again in this book, such informal mathematical knowledge is a key basis for understanding formal (symbolic, school-taught) mathematics.

Active Construction of Knowledge. Children actively construct meaningful mathematical knowledge (e.g., Koehler & Grouws, 1992). Substantive learning is an *active problem-solving process* in that children try to make sense of (personally important) tasks and to devise solutions for them (e.g., Cobb et al., 1991). It entails *reorganizing our thinking*—broadening our perspective—rather than merely accumulating information (e.g., Cobb et al., 1991).

A clear sign that children are active learners is that they spontaneously invent their own strategies. For example, in Vignette 1 of Probe 1.2, no one had shown Alison how to compute sums mentally by counting. She used her informal knowledge to intuitively (continued on page 1-13)

➤ Probe 1.2: Reflecting on Children's Mathematical Learning

Teachers' beliefs about the learning process can profoundly affect the way they teach. The aim of this probe is to help you reflect on how children learn and what this means for teaching mathematics. After reading Box 1.1 and Vignettes 1 to 4 below, answer the following questions: (1) Is each vignette consistent with the conventional views described in Box 1.1? Why or why not? (2) What enabled the children in Vignettes 1 to 3 to devise solutions to the the mathematical problem each confronted? (3) In Vignette 3, what does Violet's error of *twenty-ten* imply about children's learning? (4) In Vignette 4, Miss Brill's observation of the children at the activity center clearly conflicted with Ms. Maple's advice. What conclusion reconciles this conflict? Discuss your conclusions with your group or class.

Box 1.1: The Conventional View of the Learner and the Learning Process

Children are uninformed and helpless. They begin school as blank slates—with essentially little or no useful mathematical knowledge and, thus, are helpless to tackle new learning tasks or problems themselves. In brief, children must be spoonfed.

Learning is a passive, receptive process. Learning is simply a process of absorbing (memorizing) information presented by teachers or textbooks. Thus, children must be good listeners but need not think about or understand what is presented to them.

Children have little desire to learn mathematics. Because children have little or no natural interest in mathematics, they must be bribed or threatened to learn.

Vignette 1: Creative Score Keeper. Alison, just 5-years-old and about to enter kindergarten, was playing a basketball-like game with her father. After each score, he announced, "That's two." After making five baskets, Alison got another two points and decided to keep track of her score. She concluded that her previous total was 11 and counted, "One, two, three, four, five, six, seven, eight, nine, ten, eleven," paused and continued, "fourteen, seventeen." Following another basket, she gleefully began tallying her score again, "One, two, three, four, five, six, seven, eight, nine, ten, eleven (pause), fourteen, seventeen." After a moment's reflection, she remarked, "*No, that's what I had.*" She then proceeded to correct herself, "One, two, three, four, five, six, seven, eight, nine, ten, eleven, fourteen, seventeen—sixteen, nineteen."

Vignette 2: Fracturing Fraction. While engaged in a project, a group of fourth- and fifth-graders encountered the following problem: What's two-thirds of 90? As the class had not yet studied how to multiply a fraction and a whole number, the students did not have a ready way of solving the problem. Ten-year-old Arianne said, "Let's see, half. No, you have to divide the 90 into three parts, and you have two [of the three] parts. Thirty, Sixty." She went on to prove her answer by using the smaller example two-thirds of nine and by drawing the picture shown to the right.

Vignette 3: Preschool Counter. Without instruction, 4-year-old Violet continued her count past *twenty-five*: "Twenty-six, twenty-seven, twenty-eight, twenty-nine, *twenty-ten.*"

Vignette 4: A Short Attention Span? Young children are often accused of having a short attention span. Ms. Maple, for example, told her student teacher Miss Brill not to plan any lesson for more than 10 minutes. "These kindergartners are just too immature; they just can't concentrate," she explained. Miss Brill watched Ms. Maple's math lesson, which largely consisted of completing worksheets. Sure enough, the children quickly became distracted. Miss Brill noted that during play time, a number of children were engaged by a mathematical puzzle that Ms. Maple had put in an activity center. The children tried solving the puzzle for *half an hour.* Indeed, they would have worked on it longer if Ms. Maple had not dragged them away from the activity center.

reason that seventeen points and two more points had to be two numbers past *seventeen*. Likewise, Arianne in Vignette 2 used her informally learned knowledge to invent strategies to solve a fraction multiplication problem. When engaged by problems important to them, children do not wait passively for someone to tell or show them what to do, they actively make an effort to use what they know to solve it.

Another clear sign that children actively construct knowledge, rather than passively absorb it, is their spontaneous systematic errors (Ginsburg, 1989). For example, in Vignette 3 of Probe 1.2, Violet counted, "Twenty-eight, twenty-nine, *twenty-ten*." This common counting error is neither taught nor rewarded by others. Children make such a systematic error because they notice patterns in the count sequence and actively construct rules (e.g., the twenties are formed by combining the term *twenty* with each number in the counting series *one, two, three...nine*) but then overextend these rules.

Children as Naturally Curious. Children have an inherent need to make sense of the world and to master it. They have an intrinsic desire to search for patterns, explanations, and solutions. As their knowledge grows, children spontaneously seek out increasingly difficult challenges. For example, in Vignette 1 of Probe 1.2, Alison decided herself to keep score and to devise a mental counting strategy for doing so. Although this required considerable effort, the girl kept at it—even laboriously recalculating when she realized an error had been made. As Vignette 4 in Probe 1.2 illustrates, children are often accused of having short attention spans. In fact, they act much like adults do: spending considerable time and effort on interesting tasks and avoiding uninteresting ones.

1•1•3 TEACHING

Mathematics teaching can be viewed primarily as a process of transmitting information (a skills approach), guiding meaningful learning (a conceptual approach), or facilitating mathematical thinking (a problem-solving approach).

Skills Approach: Teaching for Skill Mastery. Traditionalists such as Mrs. MeChokemchild take the overly simplistic view of teaching as a process of stuffing stuff into stuffees (see Figure 1.4). To foster mastery of the

Figure 1.4: The Conventional View of Teaching as a STUFFING Process

Direct instruction + practice = STUFFERS

basic skills necessary for higher level mathematics or everyday life, they believe that the prescribed curriculum, which largely consists of *how* to do basic arithmetic and geometry procedures (procedural content), must be imposed on children. To ensure the accurate rote memorization of facts, rules, formulas, and procedures, the teacher must authoritatively transmit this information to largely passive children and then ensure they practice it adequately. Student input is seen as unnecessary because mathematical knowledge is assumed to be well defined, not open to personal interpretation, or improveable—particularly by children (Resnick, 1989).

Conceptual Approach: Teaching for Understanding. In this approach, teaching involves helping children to understand prescribed material—why, for instance, procedures work (conceptual content). The teacher serves as a guide, ensuring that instruction fits the readiness and interest of students and that it is meaningfully memorized by them (Ausubel, 1968). Although there is more student participation in a conceptual approach, it still entails imposing knowledge on children.

Problem-Solving Approach: Teaching for Mathematical Thinking. In this approach, teaching focuses on fostering problem-solving and reasoning—the thinking processes necessary to conduct mathematical inquiry. A teacher serves as a consultant, helping students to choose issues to explore, to devise solution strategies, and to reach consensus. In this approach, children construct their own understandings and procedures.

1•2 NEW DIRECTIONS IN MATHEMATICS EDUCATION

Figure 1.5: Imposing Knowledge on Children is Difficult to Do

As Figure 1.5 implies, the traditional skills approach is often uninspiring and unpleasant for students and teachers alike. In Subunit 1•2•1, we discuss the need to reform mathematics instruction. In Subunit 1•2•2, we outline the changes recommended by the National Council of Teachers of Mathematics (1989, 1991). In Subunit 1•2•3, we describe the investigation approach, which embodies the NCTM's recommendations.

1•2•1 THE NEED FOR REFORM

A Growing Need for Mathematical Power

Business, governmental, and educational leaders now recognize that schooling must foster children's mathematical power (e.g., Carnegie Forum on Education and the Economy, 1986; National Commission on Excellence in Education, 1983). Two reasons for this consensus are:

1. **Our society is rapidly changing.** Today, quantitative methods are needed in nearly all aspects of our personal and professional lives. Furthermore, our information-based and technology-oriented society requires different mathematical competencies than those needed for an industrial society of just 30 years ago (Davis, 1984; Fuson, 1992b; Lindquist, 1989). Mathematical literacy now entails comprehending novel situations and thinking creatively and logically about them (e.g., deciding what data are needed), knowing what to do with data (e.g., organizing, manipulating, and interpreting quantitative information), and communicating results succinctly and clearly (Fey, 1990).

The widespread use of electronic devices such as computers, calculators, and price scanners also put a premium on understanding and problem solving and reduces the importance of memorized computational facts and procedures (e.g., Coburn, 1989). With these electronic aids, proficiency with arithmetic skills is no longer necessary for the effective use of mathematics (Fey, 1990). Today mathematical literacy involves knowing how to use technology to process data and determining when calculated results are reasonable.

2. **Our economy faces increasingly stiff international competition.** To be competitive in a world-wide economy, our students must be on a par with those from other industrialized nations. However, cross-cultural research indicates that the mathematical achievement of schoolchildren in the United States is relatively low (e.g., McKnight et al., 1987; Stevenson, Lee, & Stigler, 1986). For example, Japanese children outperform U.S. children on word problems and real world applications of mathematics over all topics in the curriculum—as well as on computational skills (see Fuson, 1992a). Some factors that may contribute to this difference are listed in Box 1.2 on the next page.

The Effects of the Traditional Skills Approach: Mathematical Powerlessness

The traditional skills approach robs children's mathematical power in three ways:

1. It fosters a negative disposition toward mathematics by (a) cultivating counterproductive

---

Box 1.2: A Cross-Cultural Comparison

Japan	United States
• Teachers, parents, and children typically attribute mathematical success to effort.	• Many teachers, parents, and children believe that mathematical ability is essentially innate.
• Parents support of and involvement in children's education is extensive.	• Parental support and involvement varies considerably.
• Much class time is spent working on and discussing one or two difficult problems.	• Much class time is spent on individual seatwork consisting of numerous routine computations.

---

beliefs (e.g., focusing on the rote memorization of facts and procedures can lead children to believe that mathematics isn't supposed to make sense), (b) fostering dependence (e.g., relying on the feedback of teachers can undermine children's confidence in their own resources), and (c) failing to generate interest in and curiosity about mathematics (e.g., imposing instruction and practice for which children see no purpose can lead them to believe that math is boring).

2. It does not give children an adequate opportunity to engage in problem solving (e.g., devising solution strategies themselves), reasoning (e.g., evaluating the validity of a claim themselves), and communicating (e.g. sharing, defending, and debating ideas) and, thus, most do not adequately develop these competencies.

3. It promotes *routine expertise (knowledge that can be quickly and accurately applied to familiar tasks only)* rather than *adaptive expertise (knowledge that is understood and thus can be applied or adapted to a new task)* (Hatano, 1988). Routine expertise promotes helplessness in two critical ways: (a) Without understanding, transfer is unlikely and students must be spoonfed even slightly new material (Wertheimer, 1959). For example, students who have successfully memorized by rote a renaming (borrowing) algorithm for subtracting three-digit numbers such as 326 - 78 typically cannot figure out for themselves how to subtract when borrowing from the tens place is not possible (e.g., 306 - 78). (b) Without understanding, students cannot effectively use what they know to solve problems (Davis, 1984; Kilpatrick, 1985a). For example, 13-year-olds were given the following problem on an NAEP test:

■ **Thirty-One Buses Plus** (◆ 5-8). An Army bus holds 36 soldiers. If 1128 soldiers are being bused to their training site, how many buses are needed?

Nearly a third mechanically answered 31.33. [Imagine 31.33 buses.] Nearly a quarter of the children ignored the remainder and thoughtlessly answered 31.

1•2•2 FOSTERING MATHEMATICAL POWER

To foster the mathematical power of students, what mathematics is taught and how it is taught must change (NCTM, 1989, 1991) (see Box 1.3). In this subunit, we consider how instruction can encourage (a) a positive disposition toward mathematics, (b) the processes of mathematical inquiry, and (c) an understanding of mathematical content.

A Positive Disposition Toward Mathematics

Box 1.3: Major Changes in Current Practices Needed to Empower Students

The NCTM (1991, p. 3) recommends a shift:

1. "toward connecting mathematics, its ideas, and its applications—away from treating mathematics as a body of isolated concepts and procedures";
2. "toward conjecturing, inventing, and problem solving—away from an emphasis on mechanistic answer-finding";
3. "toward mathematical reasoning—away from merely memorizing procedures";
4. "toward logic and mathematical evidence as verification—away from the teacher as the sole authority for right answers";
5. "toward classrooms as mathematical communities—away from classrooms as simply a collection of individuals."

Appendix H delineates the type of questions that can promote mathematical power.

To promote children's willingness to learn and to use mathematics, cultivate (a) accurate beliefs about mathematics, (b) student autonomy, and (c) interest about mathematics.

Foster Accurate Beliefs About Mathematics. Beliefs about mathematics and one's mathematical ability are forged in the elementary grades (e.g., Cobb, 1985).

↪ To support and enhance children's sense of mathematical power, foster by word and—more importantly—by deed accurate beliefs about mathematics. How we teach mathematics "tells" children how we view this subject and how they should view it. Thus, the most powerful way to foster accurate beliefs about mathematics is to involve children in meaningful, inquiry-based instruction. Teachers also need to *explicitly* advocate accurate beliefs, particularly when students announce conventional beliefs. For example, if a student notes, "I've never been able to understand math because I don't have a math mind," a teacher might initiate a discussion that underscores that, with the right kind of help, mathematics can make sense to everyone. Accurate beliefs about mathematics include:

• **Mathematics makes sense.** Emphasizing connections and understanding is essential to creating this impression (NCTM, 1989; Lappan & Briars, 1995). Children need to see that mathematical knowledge does fit together in logical ways and that there are reasons for mathematical procedures and formulas. That is, they need to understand that a fact such as 6 + 6 = 12 is related to other facts such as 12 - 6 = 6 or 2 x 6 = 12; that a procedure such as that for dividing fractions (invert and multiply) has a rationale, and that a formula such as A = $\frac{1}{2}$b•h (the area of a triangle) actually has a common-sense basis.

• **Mathematics involves *inquiry* into a broad range of ideas.** To help children understand that arithmetic is but one branch of mathematics, mathematics instruction should include content areas that are often not found in traditional curricula (e.g., patterns, functions, proportional reasoning, statistics, and probability). To help children recognize that mathematics is not merely content, but a *way of thinking* about the world and organizing our experience, regularly involve them in mathematical inquiry (reasoning about and solving problems and precisely communicating ideas). Immersion in the processes of inquiry

can help them to see that "mathematics deals with ideas. Not pencil marks or chalk marks, not physical triangles or physical sets, but ideas (which may be represented or suggested by physical objects)" (Hersh, 1986, p. 22).

• **Real mathematical proficiency involves finding patterns and solving problems.** "Seeing and revealing patterns are what mathematicians do best" (Steen, 1990b, p. 1). Real mathematical competence is gauged by problem-solving ability, not calculational proficiency. To help children understand the true nature of mathematical proficiency, emphasize searching for patterns and solving problems, not quick and mindless computing.

• **Mathematics is a dynamic discipline**. Unlike its stereotypic image, mathematics is an ever growing field. Often, it is invented and adopted out of practical need. For example, the Egyptians invented simple arithmetic and geometry so that they could reset the boundary markers of their fields that the Nile flooded each spring (Bunt et al., 1976). As it is still needed to solve new problems, mathematical knowledge continues to grow. Although most of this new mathematics is not appropriate for elementary instruction, it is important to teach mathematics in way that children see it as a dynamic and evolving body of knowledge. Exploring its history can help children understand that mathematics is a dynamic field (see the Mathematics section of SOME INSTRUCTIONAL RESOURCES on page 1-36).

• **Mathematics is for everyone.** Although only a few are capable of mathematical genius, everyone is capable of developing significant mathematical competence (NCTM, 1989). Children must understand that mathematics is not simply for a few genius but is needed by everyone (see Activity File 1.1 on the next page). For example, everyone needs to recognize how data can be misused by government, business, legal, educational, and other officials to justify self-serving or meaningless statements. Students also need to appreciate that their own mathematical competence can—with experience and effort—grow.

• **Mathematics is a social activity**. Unlike the stereotypic image, mathematicians often work together or as part of an interdisciplinary

---

◀ Activity File 1.1: *Who Needs It?*[†]

◆ Fostering an appreciation of mathematics ◆ 1-8 ◆ Any number

At the top of a chalkboard or handout, pose a question such as: *Geometry, Who Needs It?* (A similar question can be posed for other areas such as Problem Solving or Probability.) Individually, in groups, or as a class, encourage students to list as many occupations that use geometry (or some other aspect of mathematics). As a class, discuss how the mathematics is used and create a master list. (✎ Encourage students to write an essay justifying a listed item.)

[†] Based on an idea suggested by Ruth E. Parker (1993) in *Mathematical Power.*

---

team to solve problems. Moreover, the construction of mathematical knowledge is very much a community effort. Mathematicians build on the ideas of others, share their findings, and test each others' ideas to build a consensus about new advances. To help children appreciate the social nature of mathematics, use cooperative-learning groups, encourage whole-class dialogues, and promote small-group and whole-class efforts to reach consensus.

Promote Autonomy. Teachers can enhance children's autonomy and, hence, their mathematical power in the following ways:

☞ **Encourage the use and development of students' informal knowledge.** Teachers should help students unlock the wealth and power of the informal knowledge they bring to school (e.g., Carey, Fennema, Carpenter, & Franke, 1995). Often understanding new material or solving new problems is simply a matter of applying what is already known. Many students would have a much greater capacity to solve challenging mathematical problems *if only* they would think to tap their informal knowledge. For example, when the division problem nine cookies shared among four children spontaneously arose in a second-grade class, children with no formal training in division drew on their everyday knowledge of fair sharing and informally solved the problem by divvying up cookies. Malik concluded the answer was 2 with one leftover; Ashley two and one-third. Note these informal solutions can later provide a basis for recognizing that 2r1 and $2\frac{1}{3}$ are equivalent answers for the expression $9 \div 4$. (See also Vignettes 1 and 2 of Probe 1.2 on page 1-12 for additional examples.)

☞ **Actively involve students in constructing mathematical knowledge by promoting interaction with their physical and social environ-**

ments (e.g., Kamii, 1985; Yackel, Cobb, Wood, Wheatley, & Merkel, 1990). Active involvement here implies interaction that require students to be *mentally* active—to think. Instructional activities should engender reflection and problem solving (Cobb et al., 1991). Indeed, as significant learning is essentially an active problem-solving process, "one of . . . teachers' primary responsibilities should be to engage students in activities that give rise to genuine mathematical problems for them" (Cobb, 1988, p. 95).

☞ **Foster self-reliance by encouraging children to *discover* facts and rules and to *invent* their own procedures and formulas.** Instead of imposing definitions, say, encourage a class to discover and to refine the meaning of mathematical terms. Instead of imposing algorithms or problem solutions, encourage students to invent their own strategies. Keep in mind that, at first, anything that works is good. Refinement and efficiency can come later. In time, children can be prompted to reinvent standard algorithms or procedures.

☞ **Foster autonomy by encouraging children to determine for themselves if answers are correct and by using class consensus and indirect intervention to establish mathematical truths.** Instead of imposing mathematical facts, rules, procedures, solutions, and so forth by fiat, encourage the class to debate alternative suggestions and to vote for the most reasonable case. *If the class deadlocks or agrees on a formulation that is incomplete or inaccurate, should a teacher ever intervene and, if so, when?* A guideline we find helpful is: IF STUDENTS ARE NOT READY TO UNDERSTAND A CONCEPT, LET THEIR ERROR STAND. (After all, children can't be expected to understand everything at once.) On the other hand, IF STUDENTS ARE READY TO UNDERSTAND A CONCEPT, TRY TO POSE A TASK, PROBLEM, OR QUESTION THAT WILL PROMPT REFLECTION AND HELP THEM REFORMULATE THEIR IDEAS (see, e.g., Box 1.4 on the next page).

Box 1.4: Indirect Instruction—Encouraging Reflection by Posing Questions

Mr. Bradley, an avid stamp collector, explained to his class that the U.S. Postal Service was going to conduct a lottery to distribute 150,000 panes of stamps that contained an error. He noted that the Postal Service had received about 450,000 orders for the panes and asked what his chances were of getting a pane if he submitted only one order. After some discussion, the class concluded that his chances of getting a pane was about $\frac{150,000}{450,000}$ or $\frac{1}{3}$.

Mr. Bradley then asked what his chances of getting *at least* one order filled if he sent in two orders. Todd's group concluded that Mr. B's chances would double—would be $\frac{2}{3}$. Holly's group argued that the probability would still be $\frac{1}{3}$ because each order stood a 1 in 3 chance of being chosen. Mari's group suggested that it might be between $\frac{2}{3}$ and $\frac{1}{3}$ but could not explain their intuition. After debating the solutions, Todd won over the dissidents and the class agreed on a solution of $\frac{2}{3}$.

To prompt further reflection, Mr. Bradley then asked the class what his chances would be if he sent in three orders. Todd reasoned that Mr. B. was certain to get at least one order filled. Others agreed noting that the probability would now be $\frac{3}{3}$ or 1.

At this point, Mr. Bradley asked the class how they could prove their answer. Karilynne suggested using a model. Mr. Bradley encouraged the class to consider how they could model getting at least one order filled if each order had a one in three chance of being chosen. Most groups decided to use a spinner divided in three equal parts; one group decided on using a die and equated a roll of 1 or 2 with a filled order. Each group then spun a spinner or rolled a die three times to simulate three orders. Four groups found that at least one order was filled; two groups found that they did not get a single order filled. From this evidence, the class concluded that, with three orders, Mr. B. could not be entirely certain of getting at least one order filled. To underscore the class' finding, Mr. Bradley asked what his chances of getting at least one order filled if he sent in four orders. The class recognized that his chances could not quadruple to $\frac{4}{3}$ because this was beyond certainty. The contrary evidence prompted the class to reconsider the two-order problem and to devise a new and correct solution to it.

Invite Interest. Teachers should focus on making mathematics instruction interesting, rather than relying on rewards and punishment to motivate students. It can be made inviting in the following ways:

☞ **Strive for authentic or *purposeful* instruction—that is, create a *real need* to introduce or practice mathematics.** CHILDREN LEARN BEST WHEN THERE IS A REAL REASON TO KNOW SOMETHING. Three ways to create a real need for learning and practicing mathematics are listed below:

1. **Take advantage of questions, conjectures, or problems that arise naturally in the classroom.** If teachers listen, children ask many mathematically rich questions and make many conjectures worth pursuing. Box 1.5 (on page 1-19) illustrates how one teacher exploited a real problem for instructional purposes.

2. **Use a project-based approach to instruction.** Mathematics classrooms that embody the NCTM *Standards* are alive with activity, and instruction is often organized around rich and important mathematical investigations, units that extend for many days, weeks, or even months (Parker, 1993). Box 1.6 (on page 1-20) illustrates one mathematically rich, long-term project. New "nontextbook" series, such as *Everyday Mathematics K-6*, published by Everyday Learning Corporation, and *MathLand* published by Creative Publications (© 1995), and *Investigations in Number, Data, and Space* published by Dale Seymour (© 1996-97) provide many project ideas. (See pages 1-37 and 1-38 for a description of these and other project-rich resources.)

3. **Playing and inventing games are excellent ways to prompt mathematical exploration, to introduce content, and practice mathematical skills in a purposeful way.** As Investigation 1.2 (on pages 1-22 and 1-23) illustrates, playing a game can lead to intriguing problems, raise interesting questions, or provide hours of entertaining computational practice. Activities 1 and 2 of Activity File 1.2 (page 1-20) (text continued on page 1-21)

Box 1.5: Taking Advantage of an Everyday Situation

■ **Reclaiming the Playground** (◆ 3-8). It was unbearable to go out on the school playground; hungry mosquitoes swarmed over anyone who came near. An advertisement Mr. Bostic received in his mail offered a promising solution. A seed company was offering mosquito plants, a geranium with a citronella-like fragrance. (Citronella is a southern Asian grass, which produces the sharp-smelling citronella oil used in perfume, soap, and *insect repellent*.) According to the ad, a mosquito plant could provide mosquito protection for *up to* 100 square feet. Mr. Bostic wondered how many plants it would take to keep the playground mosquito-free. He had his class measure the playground and make a scale drawing (shown to the right). Assuming each plant actually protects an area of 100 square feet, how many plants would be needed to protect the playground from insect invaders?

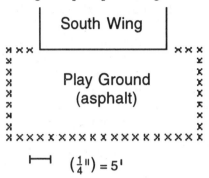

Note that this problem involves measurement, proportions (making a scale drawing), and geometry (area). Using 1-inch x 1-inch square tiles, Mr. Bostic used this opportunity to introduce the concept of area and how it was measured. He had groups of students determine how many square tiles were needed to cover a rectangle 2" x 1", 5" x 2", and 6" x 3", and 4" x 4". The children quickly recognized that the number of square tiles (the area in square inches) could be determined by multiplying the length and the width of the rectangle. The class then discussed what dimensions a 100 square-foot rectangle might have. The children agreed that one solution was a 10' x 10' square. (More advanced children might recognize that the effective mosquito-repelling area around a plant would actually be circular. This could lead to a discussion of how the area of a circle can be estimated and ultimately to the invention of the formula $A = \pi r^2$. Solving the expression 100 square feet $= \pi r^2$ could serve as an algebra problem.)

Mr. Bostic then had the class consider how a 10' x 10' square would be represented on the scale drawing of the playground. First, he had students draw what a 5' x 5' square would look like on the map. Nearly all groups drew a $\frac{1}{4}$" by $\frac{1}{4}$" rectangle like Figure A below. Next, Mr. Bostic asked them to represent 50 square feet. Alvin's group drew a rectangle $1\frac{1}{4}$" long and $\frac{1}{4}$" wide (Figure B below). Asked to evaluate this representation, Amelia's group noted that "50 square feet was twice 25 square feet so it should be just two ($\frac{1}{4}$" x $\frac{1}{4}$") squares" (see Figure C). Mr. Bostic then asked the class how 100 square feet would be represented on the map. The class concluded a $\frac{1}{2}$" x $\frac{1}{2}$" square was needed (see Figure D).

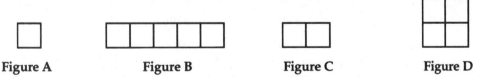

| **Figure A** | **Figure B** | **Figure C** | **Figure D** |

Note that this realistic problem requires students to make decisions. One decision is where to place the plants: Is it necessary to cover the entire area of the playground or would it be enough to create a protective barrier around the perimeter of the playground? (The answer depends on what conditions are assumed such as the location of the pests' breeding grounds: Are areas of standing water entirely outside the playground?) Another decision is how to use the scale map to solve the problem. One way is to draw a $\frac{1}{2}$" x $\frac{1}{2}$" square on a wax paper. This template can then be placed over the map.

Note also that the problem situation could serve as an English and Consumer Education lesson. Specifically, the class could analyze the advertisement's claim of *up to* 100 square feet of protection. Does it mean a minimum of 100 square feet of protection or a maximum of 100 square feet of protection? That is, does it mean *at least* 100 square feet of protection or 0 *to* 100 square feet of protection? From this discussion, students should recognize that *up to* can be a misleading advertising ploy.

🖳 🍎 Box 1.6: An Example of an Extended Class Project[1]

A long-term class project can provide numerous opportunities to engage the processes of mathematical inquiry, learn new content, and practice skills. Mrs. Crittendon's eighth-grade needed money for the annual class trip to Washington, D.C. As tourism was an important industry to their community, she proposed setting up a touring business for visiting school children. Teams of students researched and planned how to conduct a tour of their community. This entailed gathering, organizing, and comparing data on bus rentals and admission fees (statistics), gauging a total cost and settling on a reasonable charge (estimating and calculating with decimals), considering discounts for larger-sized groups (percents), planning tour routes (map reading and problem solving). The class also explored how to set up a web site and advertised the tours over the internet. When a Canadian group inquired about the tours, Mrs. C. noted that many countries used the metric system rather than the English system. This led the class to translate their information (e.g., the height of key landmarks, distances between landmarks) into metric units (measurement).

🍎 Activity File 1.2: *Dice Baseball*

Activity 1: *Basic Dice Baseball—Addition* (◆ Practice counting out, reasoning out, or recalling sums to 12 ◆ 1-4 ◆ Pairs or two small teams)

The basic game requires two six-sided numeral dice numbered 1 to 6, a board with baseball diamond, and at least four tokens to represent a batter and base runners. (A teacher may wish to begin with dot dice.) Two teams of one or more children can play. The child "at bat" throws the dice. After determining the value (sum) of the throw, the outcome is determined by the key below. Have the children keep score and keep track of the number of outs. After three outs, the "side" is retired, and the other team takes their turn at bat.

Throw = Outcome

2 = triple (batter goes to third base)
3 = out
4 = walk (batter goes to first base)
5 = out
6 = out
7 = out
8 = single (batter goes to first base; any base runners advance one base)
9 = out
10 = double (batter goes to second base; any base runners advance two bases)
11 = out
12 = home run

Activity 2: *Advanced Dice Baseball—Addition* (◆ Practice counting out, reasoning out, and recalling sums of 8 to 18 ◆ 1-4 ◆ Pairs or two small teams)

This version is played with numeral dice each numbered 4 to 9. The outcome chart above can be changed by adding 6 to each entry (e.g., 2 + 6 or an 8 = a triple and 3 + 6 or a 9 = an out).

Activity 3: *Devising a Dice Baseball Game—Addition* (◆ Informally or formally explore probability + practice recalling sums to 18 + statistics ◆ 3-8 ◆ Small groups of four)

Begin by asking students to devise their own dice baseball game. This should lead to questions about the relative frequency (probability) of different hitting outcomes (outs, singles, doubles, triples, and home runs) and the relative frequency of different dice outcomes (e.g., How often do sums of 7 occur?). Perhaps after doing Activity 1 or 2, distribute two 10-sided (0 to 9) dice to each group. Challenge students to devise as realistic a dice baseball game as they can. Encourage the groups to share their game simulations and their justifications for their designs. After a satisfactory simulation has been devised, encourage the class to set up leagues, plan a schedule, play the games, and keep appropriate records (statistics).

illustrate one way to practice basic addition combinations in a personally meaningful way to children. Devising their own games can involve students in extended activities that require a variety of mathematics in personally interesting and rewarding ways. Activity 3 of Activity File 1.2, for example, illustrates how creating a game can prompt mathematical inquiry and exploration of new content (probability and statistics) as well as provide practice of a basic skill (mastery of single-digit addition combinations).

☞ Try Investigations 1.2 (pages 1-22 and 1-23) and 1.3 (page 1-24).

∞ **To motivate inquiry, promote doubt, surprise, and conflict.** Doubt drives us to inquire—to seek understanding (e.g., Dewey, 1933). Surprise and conflict create doubt and, thus, are important tools for fostering curiosity and learning. The problems in Investigation 1.3, for example, can cause doubt, surprise, and conflict—all of which spark curiosity and exploration (see Box 1.7).

Processes of Mathematical Inquiry

To foster problem-solving, reasoning, and communicating abilities, instruction must actively involve children in (a) doing mathematics and (b) participating in a "mathematical community."

Children Actively Doing Mathematics. Doing mathematics is important for fostering mathematical power, but—as Figure 1.6 implies—it does not mean mechanically reciting facts or completing worksheets. Doing mathematics entails searching for patterns, formulating and testing conjectures, reasoning about data,

Figure 1.6: Mathematics Is Something Children Should Do, Not Something That Should Be Done To Them

---

Box 1.7: The Role of Conflict in Motivating Inquiry

Miss Brill's students—and Miss Brill herself—were surprised by the outcome of Problems A and B on page 1-24 of Investigation 1.3. For *Rectangular Patios* (Problem A), they found that 12 square patio blocks could be arranged to make 6 different rectangles (1 x 12, 2 x 6, 3 x 4, 4 x 3, 6 x 2 and 12 x 1). For *Rectangular Patios Revisited* (Problem B), they were astounded that the 16 blocks made fewer rectangles. "Gee," marveled Andy, you would expect that more blocks would give you more possibilities."

"How can this be?" asked Michelle. The unexpected result led the class to examine the situations more closely. One group finally proposed the conjecture, 12 has more factors than 16. They proceeded to test this conjecture by checking other examples.

Moreover, this inquiry led to conflict and debate about the relationship between squares and rectangles. Although most students and Miss Brill thought squares did not count as rectangles, Judi's group argued that square patios should be considered in the count of rectangular patios. When challenged to prove their conjecture, the group looked up the definition of rectangle in a textbook. Much to the surprise of nearly everyone, a square fit the definition of a rectangle. (Like a rectangle, a square is a parallelogram—a four-sided figure with opposite sides parallel—but with right angles.)

Rodney summarized the confusion most class members felt when he said, "I was taught that a square and a rectangle are different shapes—they even have different names, for crying out loud. Now you're telling me a square is a rectangle. How can a square not be a rectangle and be a rectangle at the same time? This is very confusing."

Andy announced excitedly, "I think I know how. A square is a *special* kind of rectangle."

---

solving problems, and clearly communicating ideas and results (e.g., Lappan & Briars, 1995; Lappan & Schram, 1989; Resnick, 1989).

∞ **In addition to learning mathematical content, children should regularly engage in the *processes* of mathematical inquiry** (NCTM, 1989). Actively solving prob- (continued on page 1-25)

♧ Investigation 1.2: *Totolospi*[†]

◆ Whole-number, fraction, or decimal ordering + probability
◆ K-8 ◆ Two teams of two children each or four individual players

Games can be excellent ways to prompt mathematical inquiry, introduce concepts or skills, or practice computational skills purposefully. The following game can be used in all three ways. It is based on *Totolospi* (to-to'-los-pi), a game of chance played by Hopi children and adults.

Rule 1. In the team version, teammates place their markers on an end circle at opposite sides of a board (see, e.g., Figure A). The team that exchanges places first is the winner. In the individual version, each player places a marker on a circle and the winner is the first player to get to the opposite circle.

A. Totolospi Board

B. Skill Stick

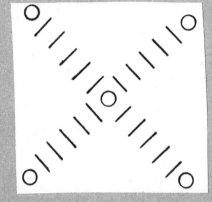
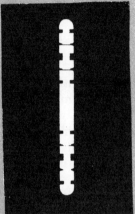

Rule 2. To determine *how far* (how many lines or circles) a team can advance on its turn, a player drops two skill sticks (see Figure B) or Popsicle™ sticks—each with one painted side—on end.

Both painted sides up = move 3
Both unpainted sides up = move 2
A painted and an unpainted side up = move 1

Rule 3. To determine *if* a team can advance the prescribed distance, a player must answer correctly a number-order question. The question is determined by rolling a 10-sided die, spinning a spinner, or drawing a card. The digits are recorded in order on the team's score pad. The type of number-order question can be varied with the developmental level of the children (see the chart to the right for suggested levels of difficulty). After a player places the correct *greater than* or *less than* symbol (or, alternatively, circles the larger number), the other players vote on its correctness. If the vote is not unanimous, disagreements can be resolved by class discussion.

Grade	Type of Comparison	Players score card
K-1	Single-digit whole numbers	8 ▷ 6
1-2	2- or 3-digit whole numbers	2 9 5 ◁ 8 3 3
3-5	4- or 5-digit whole numbers	_ _,_ _ _ □ _ _,_ _ _
2-5	Simple fractions	- □ -
4-8	Fractions involving 2 digits	= = □ = = — — □ — —
2-4	Decimals to tenths	_ . _ □ _ . _
3-5	Decimals to hundredths	_ . _ _ □ _ . _ _
4-6	Decimals to thousandths	. _ _ _ □ . _ _ _
4-6	Uneven decimals	. _ _ □ . _ _ _ . _ _ _ □ . _ _ . _ □ . _ _ _ . _ □ _ . _ _ 0. _ _ □ 0. _ . _ _ □ . 0 _ _

[†]For details, see *Multicultural Mathematics Materials* by Marina C. Krause, © 1983 by NCTM.

*Skill sticks are sold in craft stores and can also be used for geometry projects (e.g., to build model buildings or make patterns).

Investigation 1.2 continued

Rule 4. More than one player may occupy a line or a circle.

Rule 5. To finish, a player must score the exact number of points needed to move to the finish circle (e.g., if one space away from finishing, a player must toss one painted and one unpainted stick.) Otherwise, the turn is forfeited.

Questions for Reflection

Playing *Totolospi* can raise a number of challenging questions and lead to the exploration of such content as probability and fractions. Questions 1 to 3 can be explored empirically (by performing repeated experiments) by even primary-level students or theoretically (by reasoning logically) by intermediate-level students. Questions 4 to 7 could be a basis for group or class discussion by intermediate-level students. Question 8 would be appropriate for either elementary- or intermediate-level students.

1. (a) What are the chances that two *Totolospi* sticks will both land with the painted side up? (b) What is the probability that both will land with the unpainted side up? (c) How likely is it that one stick will land with the painted side up and the other will land with the unpainted side up?

2. Lanny's group concluded that the answer to each part of Question 1 was $\frac{1}{3}$. They argued, "There are three possible outcomes, so each has a one in three chance of coming up." Do you agree or disagree? Briefly explain why.

3. (a) Assuming a child always answered correctly (as required by Rule 3), what is the minimum number of turns it would take to cross the *Totolospi* board? (b) What is the probability of this happening? (c) *If* on average a child answered correctly one half of the time, what then is the probability of getting across the Totolospi board in the minimum number of turns?

4. The students in Ms. Socrates's class played *Totolospi* a total of 1,000 times, and never once did anyone complete the game in the minimum number turns they had predicted for Question 3a above. (a) Does this mean it is impossible to do so? Why or why not? (b) In theory, what is the advantage of answering Question 3b above theoretically (by using logical reasoning) rather than empirically (actually performing experiments)?

5. (a) Assuming a child answered every question correctly, what is the maximum number of turns it would take to cross the *Totolospi* board? Why? (b) Gina's group concluded that the maximum number of turns would be 12 because, they reasoned, the smallest move was one space and there are 12 spaces. Do you agree or disagree with Gina's group? Why?

6. (a) Assuming a child answered every question correctly, what is the most probable number of turns it would take to cross the *Totolospi* board? Why? (b) Gina's group concluded that the most probable number of turns would be 12 because, they reasoned, it was more likely to move one space each turn than it was to move any other number of spaces. Do you agree or disagree with Gina's group? Why?

7. While playing Totolospi, players came up with the following comparisons: (a) $\frac{0}{8}$ or $\frac{1}{9}$, (b) $\frac{7}{0}$ or $\frac{6}{1}$, and (c) $\frac{5}{0}$ or $\frac{0}{9}$. In each case, which fraction—if either—is larger? Justify each answer.

8. The fraction version of *Totolospi* can raise the issues: *How can we tell which fraction is larger?* This can lead to a discussion of informal strategies for comparing fractions or to introducing a comparison strategy such as the *rectangular cake-cutting analogy* (see Activity IV of Investigation 9.3 on page 9-22 of chapter 9). Consider what questions the other versions of *Totolospi* could raise and how they could serve as the basis for an inquiry-based approach for other content areas.

♻ Investigation 1.3: The Role of Conflict in Learning[†]

◆ Problem solving + multiplication (factors) + geometry (definition of rectangles) ◆ 3-8
◆ Individual students + group or class discussion

Surprise and conflict can create doubt, which in turn, can motivate a search for understanding. As Ms. Socrates asked Miss Brill rhetorically, "When have you been really driven to explore and to understand something? Probably when something unexpected happens or when confronted with two incompatible explanations." She then recommended two problems that could serve these purposes (Problems A and B below). Solve these problems and answer Questions 1 and 2 on your own. Then address Question 3 with your group or class.

■ **Problem A: Rectangular Patios.** To expand his garden, Mr. Wilson dug up the 12 1-yard by 1-yard patio blocks bordering the garden. He offered his neighbor Mr. Ullom the blocks to make a patio. How many different ways could Mr. Ullom arrange 12 square patio blocks to make a *rectangular* patio with an edge parallel to the backside of his house?[*][**]

■ **Problem B: Rectangular Patios Revisited.** Mr. Wilson found an additional 4 patio blocks under his porch and offered these to Mr. Ullom. How many different ways could Mr. Ullom arrange 16 square patio blocks to make a *rectangular* patio with an edge parallel to the backside of his house?

1. (a) Using square tiles or a drawing, solve the two problems above and compare the results. Was Mr. Ullom able to make more, the same number of, or fewer rectangles with 16 square blocks as he could with 12 square blocks? (b) Did this result surprise you?

2. Nearly everyone in the class agreed that in Problem B, Mr. Ullom could make only four rectangles with 16 tiles—1 row of 16 blocks (1 x 16) 16 rows of 1 blocks (16 x 1), 2 rows of 8 blocks (2 x 8), and 8 rows of 2 blocks (8 x 2). Much to the surprise of Miss Brill and the other students, Judi's group claimed that Mr. Ullom could a make a fifth rectangle—four rows of 4 blocks (4 x 4). (a) Who do you think is correct? (b) What other number of square patio blocks will make an odd number of rectangles?

3. Compare your answers to Questions 1 and 2 to those of others in your group or class. (a) What consensus did you arrive at? (b) How can the results of Question 1a be explained? (c) How can the disagreement noted in Question 2 be resolved?

◆ **Extension.** What number or numbers of tiles make the fewest rectangles and why?

[†]Inspired by a vignette (on pages 11 to 15) of the *Professional Standards,* published in 1991 by the NCTM, Reston, VA.

[*]A question that often arises is, *Are a 12 x 1 and a 1 x 12 patio the same*? If Mr. Wilson looks out his patio door, will a patio 12-yards long by 1-yard wide appear different than a patio 1-yard long by 12-yards wide?

[**]Problem A underscores the careful use of language. Note that the problem specifies that the patio is parallel to the backside of the house. This constraint eliminates turning a 12 x 1 rectangle any number of degrees to create any number of solutions.

lems, making and testing conjectures, reasoning, and communicating ideas is the best way to develop these abilities.

Why is it so important to focus on the processes of mathematical inquiry? There are at least three reasons: (a) In a complex and ever-changing world in which calculators and computers are readily available, problem solving, reasoning, and communicating have become as, if not more, important than calculational skill. (b) Solving problems can be an effective way of introducing and practicing subject-matter content. (c) Testing is changing to include problem solving, reasoning, and communicating.

Children Actively Participating in a Mathematical Community. Simulating a mathematical community not only involves students in the processes of mathematical inquiry, it is probably the most effective way of fostering accurate beliefs about mathematics.

☞ **Use small groups on a regular basis, particularly when solving challenging problems.** Cooperative learning groups of about four children each is a key way of building a mathematical community. It underscores that doing mathematics is a social endeavor. Other advantages of group work are delineated in chapter 2.

☞ **Recognize and build on students' informal contributions.** This is important for fostering a mathematical community, children's confidence, and their disposition to think mathematically. One way of recognizing student contributions is giving them the opportunity to present and defend their ideas. Another is illustrated in Box 1.8. Note that such techniques also underscore key beliefs about mathematics and mathematical learning listed on pages 1-16 and 1-17.

Understanding

To promote adaptive expertise, instruction should foster meaningful learning—help students construct an understanding of mathematical content (NCTM, 1989).

☞ Try Probe 1.3 (page 1-26).

☞ **To foster understanding, help children to see connections.** Help them relate skills to concepts and to everyday applications. Help them link a concept to other concepts and to familiar everyday situations. As Probe 1.3 underscores, in-

---

Box 1.8: A Technique for Building a Mathematical Community

Mrs. Perez wanted to help her students see that mathematics is a way of thinking, that it is a dynamic discipline, and that mathematics was something everyone—including elementary-level students—can do. So she encouraged students to use their own informal techniques to solve problems or do other mathematical tasks. When a student (or a group) suggested a new conjecture or method to the class and the rest of the class understood and accepted the idea, the teacher named it after the student (or the group). Thereafter, the class referred to the idea by the student's (or group's) name.

For example, Mrs. Perez's class was carrying out a project that involved multiplying numbers with two or more digits by 10. Russo, who had been using a calculator, noticed a pattern. "Whenever I multiply a number by 10," he explained to the class, "all you have to do is add a zero to it. Like 10 x 453 is 4530." Although Mrs. Perez was familiar with this computational shortcut herself, she was excited that one of her students had discovered it for himself. She dubbed the shortcut *Russo's Rule*, which filled Russo with pride. By referring to *Russo's Rule*, Mrs. Perez's students saw that one of their own could discover a shortcut and that the contributions of students were valued.

---

struction that fosters understanding (meaningful memorization) is more effective than instruction that focuses on memorization by rote in four ways:

1. *Better disposition*. Students are less threatened by and more interested in learning comprehensible material—making it even more likely they will learn it.

2. *Easier learning*. It takes less time and effort to learn comprehensible or related information than to memorize incomprehensible or isolated pieces of information by rote.

3. *Better retention*. Children who see how symbols and procedures are connected to concepts and how concepts are connected with each other are more likely to understand and to remember school mathematics (e.g., Hiebert & Carpenter, 1992). This greatly reduces the amount of practice and review required. (Continued on page 1-27.)

✒ Probe 1.3: Two Learning Exercises

Common questions about meaningful instruction include: *Isn't meaningful learning harder to achieve than rote learning? How will I ever get through the curriculum if I take the time to help children understand mathematics? In brief, is fostering understanding really practical?* The aim of this probe is to help you compare and contrast memorizing by rote and meaningful memorization (memorization with understanding).

Part I: Learning Mathematics is Like Learning Chinese

There are over 50,000 Chinese words. To read a newspaper requires knowledge of only 7,000 characters. Even so, memorizing 7,000 separate characters can seem like an overwhelming task. Shown below are only 18 characters.

Consider the time and effort it would require to memorize all of these characters separately. As you examine the Chinese characters above, is there anything you notice? Is it really necessary to memorize 18 isolated bits of information? How is learning mathematics like learning Chinese?

Part II: A Number Lesson

Give yourself a minute to learn the following "body of knowledge": 481216202428

Now cover up the number. Can you remember it? What strategy did you use to learn this number? Compare your strategy with others in your group or class. What strategy would be most effective if the body of knowledge above doubled or tripled in size? What strategy would best enable you to remember this information tomorrow or next year?

Questions for Reflection

1. Which is more likely to foster a positive disposition toward mathematics: memorizing unrelated facts by rote or looking for relationships and meaningful memorization?

2. Which is easier to do—memorizing by rote or meaningful memorization?

3. Which is more likely to foster retention in the long run and, thus, minimize the need for repeated review—memorization by rote or meaningful memorization?

4. Which is more likely to facilitate the learning of new material in the future—memorization by rote or meaningful memorization?

4. *Better transfer*. Pupils are far more likely to apply meaningful knowledge when learning new content, making the construction of new concepts and procedures easier.

1•2•3 AN INVESTIGATIVE APPROACH

An investigative approach involves purposeful, inquiry-based, and meaningful instruction and, thus, can foster all aspects of mathematical power: a positive disposition, the processes of mathematical inquiry, and understanding.

Characteristics

How is the investigative approach different from the traditional skills approach? How is it similar to, and different from, the conceptual approach or the problem-solving approach?

A Broad Focus. The investigative approach is based on the premises that basic skills, concepts, and inquiry processes are all necessary for mathematical power—for learning more advanced mathematics and applying school mathematics to everyday problems. *Teachers teach for skill mastery, understanding, and mathematical thinking.* Unlike the skills approach and like the conceptual approach, the investigative approach attempts to achieve content goals (teach skills and concepts) in a meaningful fashion. Unlike the conceptual approach and like the problem-solving approach, though, it is inquiry-based and, therefore, attempts to promote such processes as problem solving and reasoning.

☞ Consider Probe 1.4 (pages 1-28 to 1-32) and Investigation 1.4 (page 1-33).

A Relatively Democratic Role for Teachers. Traditionally, teachers have played an authoritarian role and tried to directly transmit (teach) knowledge to students. Mr. Ordin (Vignette 1 of Probe 1.4) typifies the skills approach. Although caring, he tried to control all aspects of the learning situation. Moreover, with lectures, demonstrations, and worksheets, he tried—with little success—to impose mathematical knowledge on his students. While teachers who use the conceptual approach tend to be somewhat more democratic, they too *try* to impose knowledge (albeit understanding as well as skills) on their students. For instance, such teachers might use a meaningful example and demonstrate with manipulatives why division of fractions can result in an answer larger than the dividend, or they might explain and illustrate why you invert and multiply when dividing fractions.

Unlike either the skills or conceptual approach and like the problem-solving approach, the investigative approach requires a different role for teachers. To enhance the mathematical power of their students, teachers must step back and—like Mrs. Perez in Vignette 2 of Probe 1.4—give them more freedom to participate actively in the learning process. As Mrs. Perez explained to Miss Brill, "You can't teach mathematics. No matter how hard you try, you can't make children's brains understand concepts or think mathematically. Understanding and mathematical thinking aren't things you can impose on them. A teacher must serve as a 'guide on the side, not as a sage on the stage.'"

Creating a learning environment that actively involves students does not mean that teachers should adopt a passive or laissez faire (hands-off) style of teaching. Quite the contrary, the new learning environment necessary for developing all students' mathematical power requires even more of teachers than the traditional skills approach. "Teachers must structure, monitor, and adjust activities for students to engage in" (Koehler & Grouws, 1992, p. 119). In the investigative approach, teachers serve as intermediaries who *indirectly prompt* learning. That is, they create opportunities for students to construct an understanding of mathematical ideas and to reorganize their thinking." As noted in *Everybody Counts* (National Research Council, 1989, p. 58), "Effective teachers are those who can stimulate students to learn mathematics." In brief, a teacher serves as an instigator of reflection, conflict, and discussion.

A Relatively Autonomous Role for Children. "Educational research offers compelling evidence that students learn mathematics well only when they *construct* their own mathematical understanding. To understand what they learn, [students] must . . . themselves . . . 'examine,' 'represent,' 'transform,' 'solve,' 'apply,' 'prove,' 'communicate.' This happens most readily when students work in groups, engage in discussion, make presentations, and in other ways take charge of their own learning" (National Research Council, 1989, pp. 58-59). (Continued on page 1-34.)

➤ Probe 1.4: The Investigative Approach

The investigative approach involves purposeful, inquiry-based, and meaningful instruction and does not exactly fit the mold of the skills, the conceptual, or the problem-solving approach. The aim of this probe is to help you understand the rationale and implication of this fourth approach.

Part I: A Comparison of Two Approaches

Vignettes 1 and 2 below illustrate the skills approach and the investigative approach, respectively. Compare and contrast the teaching styles and practices of the two teachers depicted.

☞ Before reading the vignettes, try to solve the *Alternative Payment Plans* problem described on the next page. Discuss your solution strategy and solution with your group or class.

Miss Brill's principal Mrs. Dew-Wright thought it would be a good idea for her new teachers to visit some exemplary classrooms in the districts. She arranged for a substitute one day and scheduled Miss Brill to visit Mr. Ordin and Mrs. Perez's fourth-grade classes in the Peak School on the east side of town. When Miss Brill questioned how useful visiting fourth-grade classes would be for her, Mrs. Dew-Wright commented, "Watch *how* they teach."

Vignette 1: The Case of Orderly Mr. Ordin (The Skills Approach). Miss Brill reported to the office of Peak School and was told she would visit Mr. Ordin first. The secretary offered that he was considered one of the best teachers in the district. Miss Brill was greeted enthusiastically by Mr. Ordin. He proudly produced a plan book so meticulous and detailed it nearly took Miss Brill's breath away. Mr. Ordin also provided her a textbook and indicated the pages of the day's math lesson. Miss Brill took a seat in the back of the room and watched carefully as the lesson unfolded.

Mr. Ordin began by checking the previous day's assignment—a worksheet on two-digit multiplication. The students exchanged papers, and Mr. Ordin read off the answers. Because many students had missed items that involved renaming, he wrote the expression to the right on the board and patiently redemonstrated the algorithm.

$$\begin{array}{r} 67 \\ \times 2 \\ \hline \end{array}$$

Next, Mr. Ordin introduced new material by saying, "Today we are going to extend our knowledge of multiplication by learning how to multi ply with an even bigger factor—with a three-digit factor." After a brief explanation and a demonstration at the chalkboard, he had the class examine another example illustrated in the textbook with base-ten blocks. He then called on a student to do another example at the chalkboard. The student recorded the results of the ones-digit multiplication as shown to the right.

$$\begin{array}{r} 158 \\ \times 3 \\ \hline 24 \end{array}$$

Pointing to the 2 in the partial product 24, Mr. Ordin asked, "Is that where the two goes?" When the student placed the 2 over the 1, he patiently explained that it went over the 5—the tens place.

Next, Mr. Ordin gave the class their new assignment—a textbook page consisting of 20 practice items such as 136 x 4 and two rate problems involving multidigit multiplication. He showed the class how to solve a similar word problem on the chalkboard. The class spent the rest of math time working on the assignment. While the students worked quietly, Mr. Ordin moved around the room stopping to correct mistakes, praise correct answers, and answer questions.

Miss Brill heard Kim sitting nearby whisper to her neighbor, "What are you supposed to do when the answer to these first numbers is too big?" When advised to carry the tens digit [of the partial product] to the tens place, the bewildered girl asked, "Why carry it to the tens place rather than the hundreds place?"

"No talking ladies and gentlemen. Everyone is to do their own work," announced Mr. Ordin.

When two boys began to argue, Mr. Ordin quickly intervened by calmly but firmly asking what the problem was. One student responded, "Roger said I was doing it wrong."

Mr. Ordin examined the student's paper and commented matter-of-factly, "Roger is right." He then went on to point out the student's mistake and how to correct it.

Miss Brill was impressed by Mr. Ordin's organization, efficiency, and control. No wonder,

Probe 1.4 continued

she thought to herself, he's considered such a good teacher.

Vignette 2: The Case of Shockingly Different Instruction (The Investigative Approach). In the afternoon, Miss Brill visited Mrs. Perez's class. Invited to sit at the teacher's desk, her attention was drawn to the following notation in the plan book on the desk: *Science + Math: Population growth + pay-rate prob-lem. Math process goals: Review make a table + look for patterns. Math content goals: Geometric sequences + Multidigit multiplication*

Mrs. Perez did not begin the lesson with a lecture as Miss Brill expected. Instead, she briefly commented, "We're going to start studying population growth tomorrow. To help us understand how populations grow, let's examine an interesting problem about a related idea—a growing amount of money." Mrs. Perez then read the following problem written on the chalkboard:

■ **Alternative Payment Plans (◆ 4-8).** Mrs. Twist was going on vacation for 12 days and asked Aileen to feed her cat. She offered to pay Aileen a dollar a day *or*—if Aileen preferred—a penny the first day and double the previous day's amount on each successive day. Which payment plan should Aileen choose and why?

Mrs. Perez then encouraged the class to work together in their groups. How can she expect these children to solve this problem? wondered Miss Brill. She has not shown them how to do it yet. The children worked in groups of four. They *talked*; they talked a lot; they talked loudly. Such commotion, thought Miss Brill. How does any learning take place in such a classroom? Mrs. Perez seemed immune to the noise. This teacher isn't teaching; this is just chaos, thought Miss Brill. They want me to teach like this?

If the hubbub was not evidence enough that Mrs. Perez should be stripped of her teaching license, this teacher didn't provide feedback to her students. One group excitedly concluded that the correct choice had to be taking a dollar a day. However, instead of indicating they were wrong and helping them determine the correct answer, Mrs. Perez asked, "Why do you think so? How could you convince others your answer is correct?"

"It's obvious," one student offered. "A dollar is a lot more than a penny, so a dollar a day has got to be a lot more than the other way."

To this intuitive explanation, Mrs. Perez responded, "Does everyone agree?"

One student indicated that she wasn't sure. "How could the rest of you convince Becca here that your solution is correct?" prompted Mrs. Perez. The group began to consider more deeply how to compare the two payment plans.

Another group seemed puzzled about how to proceed. Instead of telling them what to do, Mrs. Perez ask, "What problem-solving strategy have we used in the past to help us?"

"Making a table might help," replied a student. Now with a focus, the group got busy working on the problem again.

Yet another group was actually arguing. Mrs. Perez just kept on chatting with other students. Why doesn't Mrs. Perez put a stop to it? Either she is irresponsible or she has gone deaf with all this noise she allows, thought Miss Brill. She approached the older teacher and commented, "Mrs. Perez, I thought you might want to know that the group over here is having an argument."

"Wonderful!" exclaimed Mrs. Perez.

Wonderful? thought a completely astounded Miss Brill. The constant chaos must have addled her too, she mused to herself.

Mrs. Perez could tell from the horrified expression of Miss Brill's face that an explanation was needed. "I was taught as a child that polite people never argued—that conflict was bad and to be avoided. I believed that for a long time and discouraged my students from arguing. When I went back to get my masters degree, I took a great social studies education course. It made clear to me that this country was founded on debate—reasoned arguments. I took a good mathematics education course too. In that class, I learned that teachers should encourage children to discuss their ideas and engage in reasoned arguments. Conflict and argument are themselves neither good nor bad. After all, some things are worth arguing about. How we resolve conflicts and how we argue can be good or bad. What we as teachers

Probe 1.4 continued

need to do is help students learn how to argue and resolve conflicts in socially acceptable ways," added Mrs. Perez. "It's okay to disagree and even get angry as long as you express your thoughts and feelings in a manner that respects others' thoughts and feelings. By keeping this in mind, I found that it was easier to speak my mind. And believe me there are plenty of times as a teacher, wife, and mother when you need to take a stand."

By the time Miss Brill and Mrs. Perez got to the group, the arguing had stopped. "What were you debating?" asked Mrs. Perez.

"Merl thinks Aileen should take one cent the first day," commented Elise, "and we all thought he was crazy until we looked at his table."

Later, Mrs. Perez had the groups share their solution strategies with the whole class. To explain the first payment plan, Ava Marie noted that a dollar was 100 cents and 100 cents a day for 12 days could be figured out by multiplying 100 by 12. To explain the second payment plan, Elise noted that the payment for the second day could be figured by multiplying one cent by 2, the payment for the third day, by multiplying previous day's payment by 2, and so forth. Merl noted that to fill out his table (shown below), he used a calculator to add 100 12 times and to carry out the doubling process (e.g., 64 doubled → press 64, press +, press 64, press +).

Day	1	2	3	4	5
100¢/day	100	200	300	400	500
double each day	1	2	4	8	16

6	7	8	9	10	11	12
600	700	800	900	1000	1100	1200
32	64	128	256	512	1024	2048

Mrs. Perez noted that Ava Marie had multiplied 100 by 12 and Merl had added 100 12 times and asked why these two different methods gave the same answer.

Hui-Min replied, "Times is just repeated addition; it's just easier to write [12 x 100 than it is 100 + 100 + 100 + 100 + 100 + 100 + 100 + 100 + 100 + 100 + 100 + 100]."

Mrs. Perez then asked Ava Marie how she multiplied 100 by 12. The girl charged to the chalkboard and explained, "My older sister taught me a shortcut for multiplying with zero. See [pointing to Figure A to the right]. Just put the zeros over here to the right, write them down in the answer, and then multiply as usual."

$$\begin{array}{r} \text{A.} \quad 12 \\ \times\ 100 \\ \hline 1200 \end{array}$$

"It works," Sherika shrieked. "I thought of twelve times one hundred as ten groups of one hundred, which is a thousand and two groups of one hundred which is two hundred. So together the answer *is* one thousand two hundred.

Napoleon added, "I did something like Sherika," and wrote on the chalkboard the expression illustrated in Figure B to the right. "I started with the two—two groups of one hundred is two hundred," he continued. "Ten groups of one hundred is a thousand."

$$\begin{array}{r} \text{B.} \quad 100 \\ 12 \\ \hline 200 \\ 1000 \\ \hline 1200 \end{array}$$

"How did you figure out two times one hundred twenty eight?" asked Mrs. Perez.

"The same way," replied Napoleon as he wrote Figure C on the chalkboard.

"See two groups of eight is sixteen," he clarified. "Two groups of twenty is forty, and two groups of one hundred is two hundred."

$$\begin{array}{r} \text{C.} \quad 128 \\ 2 \\ \hline 16 \\ 40 \\ 200 \\ \hline 256 \end{array}$$

Miss Brill was impressed by the children's informal solutions but worried that they were not learning the standard multidigit multiplication algorithm taught in Mr. Ordin's class.

When asked about this, Mrs. Perez answered, "It's more important right now that they understand what they are doing. In due time, they will discover—themselves or with my guidance—shortcuts for Napoleon's informal strategy, including the standard algorithm. In the end, my students will be able to do multidigit multiplication as well, if not better, than students who are simply told the standard algorithm."

Mrs. Perez concluded with an interesting comment, "Real teaching is a subversive activity. As real learning involves constructing a broader

Probe 1.4 continued

perspective—new ways to think about things—my primary job is to get my students to reflect on, rethink, and reorganize what they know. That is why I start with challenging problems and encourage, or even incite, conflict and argument."

Miss Brill suddenly felt very uncomfortable. The contrast of Mr. Ordin's and Mrs. Perez's classes caused her to question what she believed constituted good teaching. She recalled that Mr. Ordin's students had little understanding about what they were taught and that many seem to have difficulty doing multidigit multiplication calculations. Moreover, in contrast to the enthusiasm and mental energy of Mrs. Perez's class, Mr. Ordin's students seem apathetic and intellectually dead. Miss Brill was beginning to appreciate the value of the investigative approach, but her visit raised a host of troubling questions.

1. (a) How does the investigative approach differ from the skills approach? (b) How does it differ from either the conceptual approach or the problem-solving approach?

2. (a) Why do you suppose Mr. Ordin was re-puted to be one of the best teachers in the district? (b) Do you suppose most principals would favor Mr. Ordin's or Mrs. Perez's approach? Why?

3. Why do you suppose Miss Brill was initially put off by Mrs. Perez's instruction?

4. Which teacher, Mr. Ordin or Mrs. Perez, is more likely to enhance the mathematical power of students? Why?

Part II: Reflecting on Different Approaches

Consider the following questions. Discuss your reactions with your group or class.

1. After examining Chart A below, answer the following questions:

   a. Mr. Ordin, who used the skills approach, felt it was his responsibility to help children master the multidigit multiplication algorithm specified by their text as quickly as possible. What view of knowledge and authority did Mr. Ordin apparently take?

Chart A: Teachers' Beliefs About Mathematics Instruction[†]

View	Knowledge	Authority
Dualism	Right or wrong with no shades of grey: There is *one* correct procedure or answer.	Absolute external authority: As the expert, the teacher is *the* judge of correctness. Procedures or answers that differ from those advocated by the teacher are wrong and not tolerated.
Pluralism	Continuum from right to wrong: There is a choice of possible but not equally valid procedures or answers. Objectively, there is one best possibility.	Tolerant external authority: Teacher accepts diverse procedures and answers but strives for perfection: learning of the best procedure or answer.
Extreme Relativism	No right or wrong: There are many possible, equally valid possibilities.	No external authority: Teacher and each student define his or her own truth.
Instrumentalism	Many right choices: There is a choice if possible if procedures or answers and many are good.	Open internal authority: Teacher or student remains committed to a method or viewpoint as long as it is effective.

[†]Based on the work of Perry (1970) and Dewey (1958).

Probe 1.4 continued

b. Mrs. Perez, who used the investigative approach, encouraged her students to consider informal strategies and shortcuts as well as the formal multidigit multiplication procedure. She helped students to reconsider incorrect procedures by creating conflict (e.g., checking their answer against that determined by others or a calculator). Her view is what?

c. Ms. Brill was impressed by the children's informal procedures but worried they weren't learning the standard multidigit multiplication algorithm. What view did she take?

d. To wean his students from their overdependence on authorities, Mr. Bunion let his students devise their solutions to word problems involving multidigit multiplication. When an argument broke out because different methods resulted in different answers, Mr. Bunion did not intervene. Class ended with the conflict unresolved. What approach to teaching mathematics did Mr. Bunion take and on what view of knowledge and authority is it based?

e. To help her students understand, the formal multidigit multiplication procedure taught in their textbook, Ms. Block modeled the procedure with a manipulative (base-ten blocks) and had them imitate both the written and manipulative procedure. What approach to teaching mathematics did Ms. Block take and on what view of knowledge and authority is it based?

f. Which of the four views of knowledge and authority do you feel most comfortable with?

2. There are three main teaching styles—authoritarian, democratic, and laissez-faire. An authoritarian teacher uses a hands-on approach with a very tight grip (teaches by imposition). A democratic teacher uses a hands-on approach with a light touch—actively guides students (teaches by negotiation). A laissez-faire teacher uses a hands-off style—gives students little or no direction, guidance, or feedback. Each of these teaching styles could in theory he coupled with instruction that focuses on skill learning, understanding, or thinking. These two continua are summarized in Chart B below.

For each of the following teachers, indicate the letter or letters in Chart B that best represents his or her approach to teaching (e.g., if an approach focused on both understanding and thinking and fell between highly and somewhat authoritarian, it would be designated D-I). (a) Mr. Ordin (the skills approach), (b) Mrs. Perez's (the investigative approach), (c) Mr. Bunion (an unguided problem-solving approach), (d) Ms. Block (the conceptual approach).

Chart B: Teaching Focus and Teaching Styles

Laissez faire (hands-off)	U	V	W	X	Y
	P	Q	R	S	T
Democratic (teaching by negotiation)	K	L	M	N	O
	F	G	H	I	J
Authoritarian (teaching by imposition)	A	B	C	D	E
	Focus on memorizing skills		Focus on understanding concepts		Focus on thinking

⌣ Investigation 1.4: *Zork Odd or Even*

◆ Problem solving + odd-even concept + division involving 0 + statistics + probability
◆ K-8 ◆ Pairs of students + class discussion

The investigative approach begins with a worthwhile task. Part I of this investigation illustrate how playing a game can naturally raise questions that lead to the exploration of significant content. Part II illustrates how a problem can serve as a vehicle for introducing content. To see how, try both parts.

Part I: The Game *Zork Odd or Even*

Zork Odd or Even is similar to the children's game *Odd or Even*, except that Zorkians (inhabitants of the planet Zork) have two fingers on each of their hands instead of five.

The Rules. By flipping a coin, tossing a die, or by some other means, two players decide who is the *even player* and who is the *odd player*. Then one player announces, "One, two, three, shoot," and *each* player extends zero, one, *or* two fingers. (Note that either the even or the odd player may extend an even or an odd number of fingers.) If the *total number* of fingers displayed is even, the even player is awarded a point. Otherwise, the odd player is awarded the point. With a partner, play the game *Zork Odd or Even*. Then discuss the content issues raised by playing this game with your group or class.

☞ **Teaching Tips.** This activity could be used to introduce or to elaborate on the concepts of *even* and *odd*. Frequently, playing the game raises the following questions:

1. What is an even number, and what is an odd number? (How are these concepts formally defined for intermediate-level students? How can these concepts be informally defined so that primary-level children could understand them?)

2. What if both players put out no fingers? Is *zero* an even number, an odd number, or neither—and why? What is *zero* according to the formal definitions of *even* and *odd*? What content issue does the previous question raise? Consider how primary-level children could decide the status of *zero*.

3. Can zero be divided by two? That is, is $0 \div 2$ equal to zero or is it undefined? Is $2 \div 0$ zero

or undefined? How could you prove which was which?

Part II: A Problem of Fairness

The Problem. Try solving the problem below. Then discuss the content issues raised by this problem with your group or class.

■ **The Fairness of *Zork Odd or Even*.** After introducing the game *Zork Odd and Even*, a teacher can ask, "When is a game fair? Is this game fair?" "How could we find out?"

☞ **Teaching Tips.** A game is fair if each player has an equal chance of winning. Note that such a view of fairness involves probabilistic thinking. By playing the game a number of times and keeping track of who wins, students can determine the empirical probability of a player winning (the number of wins by that player compared to the total number of games played). Note that solving the problem creates a real need for collecting and organizing data in a table. By combining their data with others in their class, students might informally learn that the larger the sample, the more reliable the result.

◆ Extensions

Theoretical Probability (◆ 5-8). More advanced students can also be encouraged to analyze the game at a theoretical level. How can you logically determine if the game is fair—if it is equally probable that each player has a chance to win? (✚ Hint: To identify all the possible combinations in *Zork Odd or Even*, consider making a list or drawing a table. That is, consider what plays one player can make and what plays an opponent can make. What are the total number of possibilities? Of that number, how many does the even player win?)

■ **Beating the Odds (◆ 3-8).** If you are the odd player, how can you maximize your chances of winning—at least until your opponent discovers your strategy?

Moreover, to become good mathematical problem solvers, children must learn to think mathematically—develop a disposition, for instance, to notice patterns, to find similarities across situations, and to see real-world situations in quantitative terms (e.g., analyzing music in terms of the number of beats per minute). Such a disposition cannot be imposed by direct instruction. Learning to think mathematically—like learning to make wise moral decisions—requires a socialization process. It requires an apprenticeship in which they learn by actually doing and by making mistakes. In brief, children must have the opportunity to engage in mathematical reasoning and to solve problems themselves.

Top-Down Instruction. Instruction in both the skills and the conceptual approach is bottom up: Basic skills are introduced before complex skills, problems, or applications. Like the problem-solving approach, though, the investigative approach is top-down. That is, the instruction of basic skills and concepts is embedded in and follows from tackling complex tasks or problems. In Probe 1.4, for example, Mrs. Perez did *not* teach her class about geometric progressions or show them how to perform multidigit multiplication before posing a problem involving this content. She posed the problem as a way of getting students to explore these content areas. Unlike the problem-solving approach in which content instruction is essentially accidental, teachers using the investigative approach typically begin planning a lesson by deciding on the content aims. They then try to find or devise a project, game, problem, or other rich task that naturally leads to an exploration of the content desired.

More Open-Ended, Inquiry-Based Methods of Instruction. The instructional practices of the investigative approach differ from those of the traditional skills approach in the following ways:

• In contrast to the mathematically sterile and uninspiring skills approach, the investigative approach begins with a *worthwhile task* (see Box 1.9). In Probe 1.4, whereas Mr. Ordin introduced multidigit multiplication in a purposeless fashion, Mrs. Perez created a context where there was a real need for the skill. Whereas Mr. Ordin began each day by reviewing old material and lecturing on new material, Mrs. Perez began with an interesting and thought-provoking problem. She then let the lesson evolve, reacting as

---

Box 1.9: Worthwhile Mathematical Tasks

A *worthwhile task* does "not separate mathematical thinking from mathematical concepts or skills," but "captures students' curiosity and [invites] them to speculate and to pursue their hunches" (NCTM, 1991, p. 25). Such tasks can typically be approached in different ways and, thus, naturally lead to discussion. They can consist of a problem, a question, a project, or a game—anything that can prompt the exploration of mathematical ideas or the use of mathematical knowledge (see, e.g., Investigation 1.4 on page 1-33). Tasks can stem from students' conjectures or questions, a real classroom situation, or any of a wide variety of instructional resources such as a textbook, a book of problems, computer software (NCTM, 1991).

---

needed to guide students' thinking and learning. Whereas Mr. Ordin had his students do numerous practice items, Mrs. Perez had her class focus on a single challenging problem.

• **In contrast to the insular lessons of the skills approach, the lessons of the investigative approach are mathematically rich.** Whereas Mr. Ordin's lesson had a single, isolated aim of limited scope (memorization of a multidigit multiplication algorithm), Mrs. Perez's lesson had multiple, interconnected aims. Her lesson involved using mathematics to understand a science concept (population growth), solving a mathematically challenging problem, using problem-solving strategies (make a table and look for a pattern), exploring an important mathematical concept (geometric sequences), and understanding the meaning of multidigit multiplication.

• **In contrast to the skills approach that requires little faith in children, the investigative approach requires trusting them.** Whereas, Mr. Ordin viewed his students as helpless sheep that needed to be lead each step of the way, Mrs. Perez believed that her students could use their informal knowledge to solve problems and, thus, did not begin her class by demonstrating a solution strategy.

• **In contrast to the skills approach in which students work in isolation, group work is a regular and important aspect of the investigative approach.** Whereas Mr. Ordin did not allow students to discuss their assigned work or help each other, cooperative learning was in integral aspect of Mrs. Perez's class. In her class, other children were seen as an essential element of challenging a student's thinking, and constructing a more effective strategy or a more complete understanding.

• **In contrast to the skills approach where disagreements are viewed as disruptive, conflict and argument are an essential aspect of the investigative approach and are encouraged.** Whereas Mr. Ordin felt uncomfortable about arguments and put a stop to them as quickly as possible, Mrs. Perez welcomed disagreements and even promoted them. She recognized that disagreements can create the cognitive conflict necessary to advance mathematical understanding.

• **In contrast to the skills approach in which a teacher serves as the final judge of truth, in the investigative approach, a teacher encourages students to evaluate their own solutions.** Whereas Mr. Ordin was judgmental and quickly pointed out errors and provided praise for correct answers, Mrs. Perez tended to withhold judgment. Instead, she tried to encourage children to depend on themselves for gauging the reasonableness of their solutions.

• **In contrast to the skills approach that focuses exclusively on the school-taught algorithm, the investigative approach encourages multiple strategies—particularly children's informal or self-invented strategies.** Whereas, Mr. Ordin insisted that his students do multidigit multiplication using the standard written algorithm, Mrs. Perez encouraged her students' self-invented procedures. She recognized that there are various way of determining an answer and that the student's informal procedures made sense.

• **In contrast to the skills approach that relies on written mathematics, the investigative approach encourages mental math and the use of calculators and computers as well as written math.** Whereas Mr. Ordin's class focused on doing written work on the chalkboard and on paper, Mrs. Perez's students used mental calculation and calculators, as well as written calculations.

• **In contrast to the skills approach that relies on textbooks and workbooks, the investigative approach uses a wide range of resources to involve students actively in learning.** Whereas Mr. Ordin followed the textbook and used it as a basis for his lesson and assignments, Mrs. Perez drew problems, activities, and assignments from various resources, including references on projects (see, e.g., pages 1-37 and 1-38) and children's literature (see, e.g., the *Math Curse* described on page 1-38). Her class used textbooks as a reference to answer questions raised in their discussions and as a source of problems.

Some Tips on Implementing the Investigative Approach

When Miss Brill returned from her visit to the Peak School, the new teacher had many more questions about teaching than she did before. Ms. Socrates was pleased, "Questions are a good sign. That means the visit got you thinking. What's on your mind?"

A Variety of Methods. Miss Brill responded, "I can see where children are more likely to master basic skills with the investigative approach because they have a real purpose for learning the material and do so meaningfully. *But is that the only way I should teach?*

"There is no one correct way to teach mathematics" (e.g., Rowen & Cetorelli, 1990), commented Ms. Socrates emphatically. "I usually use the investigative approach, but sometimes I use other approaches. Moreover, there is no one correct way to implement the investigative approach. Effective teachers use a variety of methods to enhance the mathematical power of their students" (National Research Council, 1987, cited in Thornton & Wilson, 1993).

Growing into a New Role. "The investigative approach intrigues me," interjected Miss Brill, "but *won't my students go wild with so much freedom?* I'm afraid to give up as much control over my lessons and class as Mrs. Perez does."

Ms. Socrates explained sympathetically, "It is hard adopting a more democratic approach. When I started teaching and was still unsure of my teaching ability, I most feared discipline problems. I wanted to maintain a tight control over everything my class did to prevent pandemonium. I soon recognized that children were the least disruptive when they were really engaged by interesting and challenging work. Even then I had trouble giving up control. As I experimented with problem solving, I realized that children have impressive informal strengths and I did not need to lead them every step of the way. As my trust in children grew, I was able to step back more and more."

"But can an inexperienced teacher like myself really develop and carry out a nontraditional, inquiry-based program?" asked Miss Brill. "I don't think I know enough about mathematics to help my students understand it or to find interesting and appropriate problems. Even if I had the mathematical knowledge, I don't have the time —given everything else I have to do—to create a whole inquiry-based program on my own."

"The wonderful thing about the investigative approach is that you can learn along with your students," replied Ms. Socrates. "Not knowing everything can even be an advantage because you may be less likely to act as the final authority and may be more likely to listen to students. Let me add that as my own understanding of mathematics, children, and teaching slowly grew, I *gradually* became a better advisor. I was in a better position to help my students see connections and to choose interesting and challenging problems. A fairly democratic investigative approach is an ideal toward which you can aspire. Don't view it as an all-or-nothing proposition. Implement as much inquiry-based instruction as you can your first year and then keep building on what you've done."

Reflective Teaching. "*How do you know when to introduce a concept or when should you help?*" asked Miss Brill.

Ms. Socrates answered, "The role of the traditional teacher was easier, because it involved following clear-cut recipes. The new role for teachers envisioned by the NCTM *Standards* is more challenging (e.g., Even & Lappan, 1994; Simon, 1995; Stein, Silver, & Smith, in press), because there aren't definitive prescriptions for teaching every topic to every child in every situation. I can give you some general guidelines (see, e.g., the text in caps on page 1-17), but ultimately you will have to make your own decisions."

PARTING THOUGHTS

Miss Brill was beginning to understand what her mathematics professor had meant by, "When are you going to stop trying to remember and start trying to think" (NCTM, 1992, p. 70). "Mathematics is not merely content to be memorized", he noted, "but a way of making sense of things that requires such processes as looking for patterns, reasoning, and making and testing conjectures." The new teacher was also beginning to understand

what Ms. Socrates had meant by, "You must set aside two fundamental assumptions about teaching and learning. One is that telling is teaching, and listening is learning (NCTM, 1992, p. 71). The other is 'that basic skills develop before *higher order skills* and must be taught first'" (Holmes Group, 1988, cited in Madsen & Baker, 1993). Mathematical understanding and thinking cannot be imposed but must be constructed by learners. And this requires their active involvement with ideas. Active engagement depends on teachers posing rich "worthwhile mathematical tasks," rather than stripped down and sterile ones (NCTM, 1991). In brief, "children are not vessels to be filled but lamps to be lighted" (Henry Steele Commager). "To foster mathematical power, teachers should strive to meld interesting and challenging tasks, a learning environment that fosters exploration and knowledge construction, and student discourse" (NCTM, 1991). Moreover, keep in mind that "how we teach mathematics is every bit as important as what mathematics we teach" (Parker, 1993, p. 16).

RESOURCES

SOME INSTRUCTIONAL RESOURCES

Mathematics

Four informative and readable references on the history of mathematics are listed below.

☞ **Classic Math: History Topics for the Classroom** (by Art Johnson, Dale Seymour Publications) has 24 history-based problems and activities.

☞ **The Historical Roots of Elementary Mathematics** (by Lucas N. H. Bunt, Philip S. Jones, and Jack D. Bedient, © 1976 by Prentice-Hall) recounts how ancient societies contributed to the construction of our number and arithmetic systems, algebra, and geometry.

☞ **Historical Topics for the Mathematics Classroom**, © 1989 by NCTM. Chapters include using the history of mathematics as a teaching tool and the history of numbers, computation, geometry, and algebra.

☞ **Mathematics** by David Bergammi and the editors of LIFE, © 1963 by Time Inc. This readable overview of mathematics includes history and everyday applications.

Children's Mathematical Development

☙ **Children's Arithmetic (2nd ed.)** by Herbert P. Ginsburg, © 1989 by Pro-Ed.

Teaching Mathematics

☙ Resources that further outline the rationale and methods of the investigative approach include: **Curriculum and Evaluation Standards for School Mathematics** (© 1989 by NCTM), **Everybody Counts: A Report on the Future of Mathematics Education** by the National Research Council (© 1989, National Academy Press), **Garbage Pizza, Patchwork Quilts, and Math Magic: Stories about Teachers Who Love to Teach and Children Who Love to Learn** by Susan Ohanian (© 1992, W. H. Freeman and Company), **How Big Is the Moon? Whole Maths in Action** by Dave Baker, Cheryl Semple, and Tony Stend (© 1990, Heinemann), **Mathematical Power: Lessons from a Classroom** by Ruth E. Parker (© 1993, Heinemann), **New Directions for Elementary School Mathematics (1989 Yearbook)** edited by P. R. Trafton and A. P. Shulte (© 1989, NCTM), **Professional Standards for Teaching Mathematics** (© 1991, NCTM), **Reshaping School Mathematics: A Philosophy and Framework for Curriculum** (published by the National Research Council and © 1990 by the National Academy Press), and **Teaching and Learning Mathematics in the 1990s (1990 Yearbook)** edited by T. J. Cooney & C. R. Hirsch (© 1990, NCTM).

The following resources describe projects for making instruction purposeful:

☙ **Encyclopedia of Math Topics and References: A Resource for Projects and Explorations** (compiled by Dale Seymour, © 1996 by Dale Seymour Publications) includes hundreds of ideas for projects appropriate for grades 6 to 8.

☙ **Everyday Mathematics K-6** published by the Everyday Learning Corporation and **Transition Mathematics (2nd Edition)** published by Scott Foresman. Both programs were developed by the University of Chicago School Mathematics Project. *Everyday Mathematics K-6* is an activity-based curriculum, which embodies the ideals of the investigative approach. It also includes such features as "Minute Math" (brief activities) and "Home Link" (suggestions for parents or guardians for involving children with mathematics in the home). Each chapter in *Transition*

Mathematics describes projects, including small-group projects, for exploring mathematical concepts. Other features include hands-on activities, graphs that use real-world data, an introduction to using spreadsheets, and an emphasis on probability.

☙ **Investigations in Number, Data and Space** by TERC, © 1997, and distributed by Dale Seymour. This activity-based curriculum for grades K-5 explores whole number and rational number concepts and operations, statistics and probability, and geometry and measurement through hands-on investigations. Lesson plans include class questions and tips for the linguistically diverse classroom. Assessment segments include discussions of, for example, embedded assessment, portfolios, and observation. Blackline masters include game boards and family letters.

☙ **Math Excursion K (1, or 2): Project-Based Mathematics for Kindergartners (First Graders or Second Graders)** by Donna Burk, Adlyn Snider, and Paula Symonds, © 1991-2 by Heinemann and distributed by Dale Seymour. Three volumes describe classroom-tested projects for grades K to 2.

☙ **MathLand: Journeys Through Mathematics** by Linda Charles, Micaelia R. Brummett, Heather McDonald, and Joan Westley, © 1995 by Creative Publications (website: http://www.mathland.com). "In MathLand teachers create mathematical environments and encourage students to think, to invent, to investigate, and to make connections. Teachers ask questions and set up challenges, then observe, question, and listen as students get busy building meaning for themselves" (p. T1). The program includes *Daily Tune-Ups* to practice skills developed in each unit and needed for later investigations; *Ongoing Projects* to prompt purposeful exploration and learning; *Thinking Games* to stimulate interest, social interaction, and thinking; *Calculator* activities to foster looking for patterns and thinking; and *Math Journals* to promote reflection and communicating skills. The third-grade edition has the following units: (1) Free Play (manipulative familiarization), (2) Skip Counting Patterns (finding patterns and solving problems using skip counting), (3) strategies (building a network of number-fact relationships), (4) Equal

Groups (using multiplication and division), (5) Numbers Beyond (making sense of 4-digit numbers and fractions), (6) Approximations (measuring perimeter, area, and volume), (7) Getting Squared Away (exploring geometry), (8) Animals, Animals (applying mathematics to real-world situations), and (9) A Fair Shake (exploring probability through games).

☞ **Mathematics Projects Handbook** by Adrien I. Hess, Glenn D. Allinger, and Lyle E. Anderson, © 1989 by NCTM. Provides practical tips for developing and looking for projects and includes general project topics for grades 6 to 8 and lists of resources.

☞ **Math Projects: Organization, Implementation, and Assessment** by Katie DeMeulemeester, © 1995 by Dale Seymour Publications. This resource includes specific examples involving skits, games, or videos appropriate for grades 6 to 12.

☞ **MathScape: Seeing and Thinking Mathematically**, Creative Publications, includes 21 units for grades 6 to 8, such as *The Language of Numbers: Inventing and Comparing Number Systems, Gulliver's World: Measuring and Scaling*, and *Patterns in Numbers and Shapes: Using Algebraic Thinking*.

☞ **MEGA Projects** by Carole Greenes, Linda Schulman, Rika Spungin, Suzanne Chapin, Carol Findell, and Art Johnson, © 1996 by Dale Seymour Publications. This resource consists of three guides for grades 6, 7, and 8. Each guide describes 50 projects.

☞ **101 Mathematics Projects** by Brian Bolt and David Hobbs, © 1989, Carolina Biological Supply. Projects, appropriate for grades 7 and 8, connect mathematics with art, science, and other real-world situations.

☞ **Teaching Through Projects: Creating Effective Learning Environments** (by H. Goodrich, T. Hatch, G. Wiatrowski, and C. Unger, © 1996 by Addison-Wesley) includes everyday-life projects for grades 3 to 6.

A SAMPLE OF CHILDREN'S LITERATURE

☜ **Math Curse** by Jan Scieszka and published by Viking (© 1995). When Mrs. Fibonacci announces in math class that "you can think of almost everything as a math problem," a student develops math anxiety. Suddenly, the child see every aspect of everyday life as a word problem. This "math curse" drives the child to despair. All seems lost until the child discovers a way of breaking the curse and concludes, "I can solve any problem." This delightful book provides a humorous forum for pointing out the applications of mathematics to everyday life, discussing math anxiety, and the nature and importance of mathematical power. The book is full of mathematical problems appropriate for elementary-level children and covering a wide range of topics. Some (facetious) problems do not have sufficient information to be solved and can be used to underscore that not all problems can be solved.

TIPS ON USING TECHNOLOGY

Internet sources on the history of mathematics include "MacTutor History of Mathematics Archive" (http://www-groups.des. st-and.ac.uk/~history/index.html). An IBM web site (http://www.solutions./bm.com/k12/ teacher/96jul.html) details activities that involve using Internet resources to research the history of mathematics and real-world uses of math skills. A suggested class project is participating in the "Global Grocery List" at http:// www.landmark-project.com/ggl.html. More information about mathematics can be obtained at "Frequently Asked Questions about Mathematics" (http://daisy.uwaterloo.ca/~alopez-o/ math-faq/). Two resources are listed below:

🖳 **The Guide to Math & Science Reform** (5th edition), © 1996 by The Annenberg/CPB Math and Science Project (1-800-965-7373; FAX: 1-802-864-9846). This interactive resource for teachers, curriculum coordinators, and administrators provides up-to-date information on reform initiatives, resources, and organizations. Available on disk in Macintosh or Windows format or through the Internet (http://www.learner.org/k12). A resource catalog (**Building Better Math & Science**) is also available in hard copy.

🖳 **MathFinder™ CD-ROM** created by Education Development Center and published by The Learning Team (1-800-793-TEAM). This data base describes over 1,000 lessons for implementing the NCTM *Standards*.

2 PROCESSES OF MATHEMATICAL INQUIRY: PROBLEM SOLVING, REASONING, AND COMMUNICATING

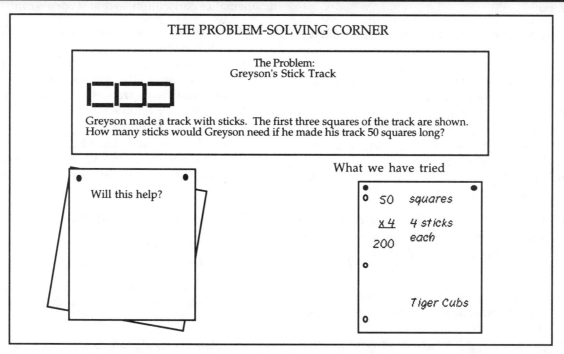

THE PROBLEM-SOLVING CORNER

The Problem:
Greyson's Stick Track

Greyson made a track with sticks. The first three squares of the track are shown. How many sticks would Greyson need if he made his track 50 squares long?

Will this help?

What we have tried

50 squares
x4 4 sticks each
200

Tiger Cubs

A problem-solving bulletin board can consist of (a) a problem (*The Problem*); (b) some tips on understanding the problem or developing a solution, such as "Look for a pattern" (*Will this help?*); and (c) a place for individuals or groups to display their solution attempts (*What we have tried*) (Jacobson, Lester, & Stengel, 1980). A display of different solutions can prompt debate, discussion, and further inquiry.

☞ With your group, solve the problem above. Discuss your solution strategy and solution with your class.

THIS CHAPTER

*I*n our information- and technology-based society, business, industry, and government increasingly need workers capable of using the power of mathematics to solve problems—people who can analyze and think logically about new situations, devise unspecified solution procedures, and communicate their solution clearly and convincingly to others (Lappan & Schram, 1989). Computation is typically done by machines. What is needed are people who can tell the machines what to do and check whether the results are sensible.

In our increasingly complex and rapidly changing world, we cannot prepare children in advance to solve all the problems they will encounter. We need to arm them with general problem-solving strategies and the disposition to tackle problems.

In chapter 1, we made a case for the inquiry-based investigative approach to elementary mathematics instruction. In this chapter, we focus on the basic processes of mathematical inquiry: problem solving (Unit 2•1), reasoning (Unit 2•2), and communicating (Unit 2•3). These are the basic tools of a mathematician or any user of mathematics. This and subsequent chapters illustrate how problem solving, reasoning, and communicating can be integral aspects of the investigative approach to content instruction.

WHAT THE NCTM *STANDARDS* SAY[†]

Mathematics as Problem Solving

Standard 1 for both grades K to 4 and grades 5 to 8 is *Mathematics as Problem Solving*.

Grades K-4. "The study of mathematics should emphasize problem solving so that students can:

- use problem-solving approaches to investigate and understand mathematical content;
- formulate problems from everyday and mathematical situations;
- develop and apply strategies to solve a wide variety of problems;
- verify and interpret results with respect to the original problem;
- acquire confidence in using mathematics meaningfully" (p. 23).

Grades 5-8. "The mathematics curriculum should include numerous and varied experiences with problem solving as a method of inquiry and application so that students can:

- use problem-solving approaches to investigate and understand mathematical content;
- formulate problems from situations within and outside mathematics;
- develop and apply a variety of strategies to solve problems, with emphasis on multistep and nonroutine problems;
- verify and interpret results with respect to the original problem situation;
- generalize solutions and strategies to new problem situations;
- acquire confidence in using mathematics meaningfully" (p. 75).

Mathematics as Reasoning

Standard 3 for both grades K to 4 and grades 5 to 8 is *Mathematics as Reasoning*.

Grades K-4. "The study of mathematics should emphasize reasoning so that students can:

- draw logical conclusions . . .;

[†]The standards above and in subsequent chapters are reprinted with permission of the National Council of Teachers of Mathematics (NCTM), Reston, VA.

- use models, known facts, properties, and relationships to explain their thinking;
- justify their answers and solution processes;
- use patterns and relationships to analyze mathematical situations;
- believe mathematics makes sense" (p. 29).

Grades 5-8. "Reasoning shall permeate the mathematics curriculum so that students can:

- recognize and apply deductive and inductive reasoning;
- understand and apply reasoning processes, especially spatial reasoning and reasoning with proportions and graphs;
- make and evaluate mathematical conjectures and arguments;
- validate their own thinking;
- appreciate the pervasive use and power of reasoning as a part of mathematics" (p. 81).

Mathematics as Communicating

Standard 2 for both grades K to 4 and grades 5 to 8 is *Mathematics as Communicating*.

Grades K-4. "The study of mathematics should include numerous opportunities for communication so that students can:

- relate physical materials, pictures, and diagrams to mathematical ideas;
- reflect on and clarify their thinking about mathematical ideas and situations;
- relate their everyday language to mathematical language and symbols;
- realize that representing, discussing, reading, writing, and listening to mathematics are a vital part of learning and using mathematics" (p. 26).

Grades 5-8. "The study of mathematics should include opportunities to communicate so that students can:

- model situations using oral, written, concrete, pictorial, graphical, and algebraic methods;
- reflect on and clarify their own thinking about mathematical ideas and situations;
- develop common understandings of mathematical ideas, including the role of definitions;
- use reading, listening, and viewing to interpret and evaluate mathematical ideas;

◆ discuss mathematical ideas and make conjectures and convincing arguments;

◆ appreciate the value of mathematical notation and its role in the development of mathematical ideas" (p. 78).

2•1 MATHEMATICS AS PROBLEM SOLVING

Many students and teachers equate problem solving with determining the answers to story or word problems. As Figure 2.1 suggests, many people view word problems as dense, difficult, discouraging, deflating, disturbing, debilitating, disgusting, deadening, demonic, and/or damnable—to mention a few of the more polite adjectives. Asked how she was doing in mathematics, one first-grade girl summarized her dislike for word problems by saying, "I'm doing well, except I don't like those *problem words!*"[1]

In this unit, we examine the nature of problem solving (Subunit 2•1•1), explore children's learning of problem-solving strategies—including why so many hate word problems—(Subunit 2•1•2), and then offer tips on how to make problem-solving instruction inviting and profitable (Subunit 2•1•3).

2•1•1 MATHEMATICS: UNDERSTANDING PROBLEM SOLVING

In this subunit, we define problem solving, outline what it takes to be a successful problem solver, and examine general problem-solving strategies.

The Case of the Loosely Used Term

What is problem solving? Miss Brill examined the *District's Curriculum Guide for Mathematics*, which had recently been revised in light of the NCTM (1989) *Curriculum Standards*. The guide noted that mathematics educators have long advised putting more emphasis on problem solving and that the National Council of Teachers of Mathematics had recommended making problem solving a focus of mathematics instruction.

Although emphasizing problem solving seemed like a good idea, Miss Brill had only a hazy notion of what this entailed. An examination of her textbook did not clarify the matter. Nearly everything in the textbook was labeled a problem,

Figure 2.1: A Common Reaction to Story Problems

THE FAR SIDE copyright 1987 UNIVERSAL PRESS SYNDICATE. Reprinted with permission. All rights reserved.

Hell's library

including drill items for practicing basic computational facts and procedures, such as $5 + 3 = \square$ and $76 + 48 = ?$. Miss Brill went next door to get some advice. Ms. Socrates nodded sympathetically and noted, "There is a great deal of confusion about what constitutes a problem. Even my Webster's (New Twentieth Century Unabridged) Dictionary (2nd ed.) suggests two different definitions for this term: (1) 'In mathematics, a problem is anything required to be done . . . .' (2) 'A problem is a question . . . that is perplexing or difficult.'"

Exercises. "The dictionary's first definition," noted Ms. Socrates, "equates a problem with any assignment as in: 'For your seatwork, do Problems 1 to 50 on page 8 of your workbook.' However, many mathematics educators prefer to call a *task for which a person already has a strategy for finding the solution an exercise.* Because a way of determining the answer is known, an exercise can be done automatically or even thoughtlessly."

Problems. "The dictionary's second definition," continued Ms. Socrates, "better captures what mathematicians mean by the term *problem*: a puzzling task for which a person does not have a readily available solution strategy. Because it is useful to distinguish between puzzles that do and do not motivate interest and action, let's agree that a *problem entails (a) the lack of an obvious way to find a solution and (b) an interest in finding the solution* (Charles & Lester, 1982). Problems, then, require a thoughtful analysis and, perhaps, an extended effort."

Enigmas. "Let's agree to call *a task a person simply ignores or accepts as unsolvable an enigma*," concluded Ms. Socrates. "Because a person has no interest in finding an answer or is convinced it cannot be found, enigmas typically are not given a second thought and are quickly dismissed."

☞ Consider Probe 2.1 (page 2-5).

The Task Confronting Children

The chances of solving genuine problems are affected by three sets of factors: (a) cognitive, (b) affective, and (c) metacognitive factors (cf. Charles & Lester, 1982). Cognitive factors include conceptual understanding (adaptive expertise) and strategies for applying existing knowledge to new situations (general problem-solving strategies). Affective factors (e.g., interest and confidence) influence children's disposition to solve problems (e.g., Lester, 1980; Schoenfeld, 1982, 1985, 1992). Metacognition includes self-monitoring (e.g., self-checking whether a strategy or a solution makes sense) (Garofalo, 1987). Effective problem solvers typically have another characteristic: flexibility.

General Problem-Solving Strategies

☞ Tackle Investigation 2.1 (pages 2-6 to 2-8).

This subunit discusses general problem-solving strategies: a four-phase approach for attacking genuine problems and some aids (heuristics) for facilitating problem-solving efforts.

A Four-Phase Approach. Although there are various ways of solving problems, George Polya (1973) proposed a now popular four-phase scheme for approaching problems in a systematic fashion.

• **Phase 1: Understand the problem.** The first step in solving a challenging problem, such as those in Part I of Investigation 2.1, is to understand what is being asked. A clear understanding of the question and the unknown is essential for decid-ing what information is needed, which solution strategies are appropriate, and what answers are reasonable. Understanding a problem also entails recognizing what constraints do and do not apply to a problem (see, e.g., Part II of Investigation 2.1).

• **Phase 2: Devise a plan.** Once a problem is understood, it is time to consider how to determine the solution(s). Ideally, a thoughtful analysis will lead to considering alternative solution strategies and picking the most appropriate plan.

• **Phase 3: Carry out the plan.** The third phase entails carrying out the plan devised in Phase 2 and carefully monitoring the solution procedure. Monitoring is important not merely to check whether the procedure is executed accurately but to gauge whether the plan is doing the job intended. Sometimes it becomes clear there are unanticipated complications or that more data are needed.

• **Phase 4: Look back.** As Part III of Investigation 2.1 illustrates, once a solution is determined, it is important to check the results. Does the solution make sense? Does it answer the original question? Is there any other way the problem could be solved and, if so, do alternative strategies produce the same solution?

Some Problem-Solving Heuristics. Box 2.1 (on page 2-9) lists some general problem-solving aids or heuristics that can helpful in carrying out each of Polya's four phases.

2•1•2 LEARNING: A CASE OF STUNTED GROWTH

This subunit examines children's informal problem-solving ability and schoolchildren's problem-solving performance.

Informal Strategies

Conventional wisdom holds that children are not capable of analyzing and solving word problems before they receive formal arithmetic instruction. Indeed, because word problems are considered so difficult, they are often not introduced until after students learn basic skills and concepts. In fact, research indicates that even before formal arithmetic training begins, children can use their informal knowledge to analyze and solve simple arithmetic word problems (e.g., Carpenter, 1986). (Continued on page 2-9.)

➤ Probe 2.1: Exercises, Problems, and Enigmas

The aim of this probe is to help you distinguish among *exercises, problems,* and *enigmas* and to recognize some of the difficulties of doing so. Complete Parts I and II on your own. Then discuss your answers with your group or class.

Part I: Analyzing Some Tasks

Examine the following tasks. For each, note whether you consider it an exercise, a problem, or an enigma. Compile your and your group's or class' responses. Did everyone agree with your classifications? Why or why not? What does this suggest about classifying a task as an exercise, a problem, or an enigma?

Task 1. What is the product of 316,742,850,192 x 28?

Task 2. What is the largest amount you can have in change that does *not* equal $1.00 and still not be able to give change for a dollar?

Task 3. According to a coding system, Annabelle, Elberta, and Marina are each 6. Eartha, Hunter, and Maxine are 4. Anne, Holt, and Steve are 2. How much is Cinderella in this system?

Part II: Analyzing Problem-Solving Activities in a Textbook

1. (a) Does the task on workbook page 18 below qualify as a problem? Why or why not? (b) Would the task on worksheet page 27 below be an exercise, a problem, or an enigma for all first graders? Why or why not?

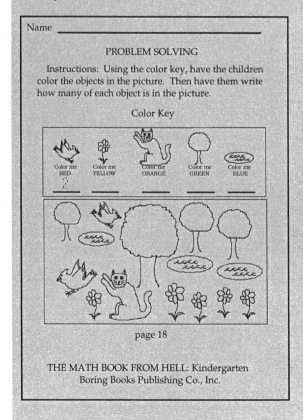

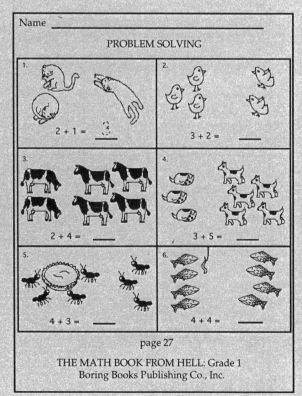

2. Miss Brill commented to Ms. Socrates that their textbook had numerous word problems, which should provide students ample problem-solving experience. Can word problems be considered genuine problems? Why or why not?

⌘ Investigation 2.1: Sample Problems

◆ Practice problem solving + creating a need for problem-solving heuristics
◆ Groups of about four + whole-class discussion

In the investigative approach, problem-solving strategies—like other subject content—are introduced purposefully. Regularly posing challenging problems can create opportunities to introduce problem-solving strategies. For example, while trying to solve challenging problems, students may become stuck (blocked). This can generate a real need and interest in problem-solving strategies.

Part I: Some Challenging Problems

To hone your problem-solving skills, try solving the problems below. Working in a group may be particularly helpful. Solve as many problems as you can. Some problems may be too difficult for you to solve. In some cases you may not even know where to begin. This is to be expected. If you become blocked, discuss with your group or class what heuristics might be helpful, consider Box 2.1 on page 2-9. After completing this part of the investigation, discuss with your group or class what heuristics were useful in solving each problem. This process should help you appreciate better the value of heuristics.

■ **Problem 1: Rhythmic Drops**[†] (◆ 4-8). Maggie was trying desperately to study for her final exams. Unfortunately, the faucet in her apartment kitchen leaked making a dripping sound. Worse, her roof leaked making a binging sound as the water dripped into a pan placed under the leak. The noise was about to drive Maggie crazy when she noticed the soothing rhythm made by the drips and bings. The drips and bings were each evenly spaced with the former occurring 3 times a minute and the latter, 5 times a minute. If the drips and bings started at exactly the same time, what was the order in which Maggie heard the drips and bings?

■ **Problem 2: The Inexperienced Carpenter** (◆ 4-8). A do-it-yourself carpenter wanted to build a stairway from ground level to an existing house porch. The height between ground level and the porch floor was 10 feet 8 inches (128 inches). The height of each step was supposed to be 8 inches. How many steps must the carpenter build to have a staircase that reaches from the ground to the porch floor?

■ **Problem 3: Rapid Rabbits**[†] (◆ 4-8). Ralphie the Rapid Rabbit bet Quickie Karl Rabbit that he (Ralphie) was the faster in the 50-yard dash. Ralphie won the race by 5 yards. Ralphie then bet Karl "double or nothing" that he could beat Karl in the 50-yard dash even if he started 5 yards behind the starting line and Karl started at the starting line. "If we tie," added Ralphie, "I'll give back what you lost in the first race."

"You're a real sport, Ralphie," replied Karl.

Is Ralphie a sport? Did he get carried away and make a bad bet? Who, if anyone, would win the second race? Assume the rabbits were tireless and both ran the second race at the same rate of speed they ran the first race.

■ **Problem 4: An Unhappy Couple**[†] (◆ 4-8). Abby and Bartheleme were a military couple. Abby had every third day off; Bartheleme had every sixth day off. If Abby had Sunday (January 1) off and Bartheleme had Monday (January 2) off, how often during the course of a year would the couple get the same day off?

[†]This problem was inspired by a problem described in *Mathematician's Delight* by W. W. Sawyer, © 1971 by Penguin, Middlesex, England.

■ **Problem 5: Won't-Come-Out-Even Problem** (◆ 3-8). Nyugen decided to count the pennies he had in his piggy bank. He decided it would be quicker to count by fives. However, he ended with two uncounted pennies. So he tried counting by twos but ended up with a remainder of one. He then tried counting by threes and finally by fours. In each of these cases, there was one remaining penny. Nyugen concluded that sometimes it just isn't worth taking shortcuts. Although he knew he had less than $1.00 worth of pennies, he still did not have an exact count. How many pennies did Nyugen have in his bank?

■ **Problem 6: Sum of An Arithmetic Series** (◆ 3-8). Miss Brill decided to challenge her class with the following problem: *What is the sum of the numbers from 1 to 100?* LeMar began to write out the problem but soon tired and simply noted:
$$1 + 2 + 3 + 4 + 5 + 6 + 7 + 8 + 9 + 10 \ldots 98 + 99 + 100$$
If writing out the problem made him feel tired, the prospect of adding the 100 numbers was downright depressing. Noticing LeMar's reaction, Miss Brill coaxed, "Is there an easier way to solve the problem?"

■ **Problem 7: A Staircase Problem** (◆ 3-8). Two children were building a staircase from wooden cubes. The first step consisted of one cube; the second step, two stacked cubes; the third step, three stacked cubes; and so forth. One of the children asked, "If we had 50 steps, I wonder how many blocks we'd need?" How many blocks would the children need?

■ **Problem 8: Sum of Three Consecutive Numbers** (◆ 4-8). The sum of three consecutive whole numbers is 534. What are the three numbers?

■ **Problem 9: Golf Balls** (◆ 4-8). Marcus spent an afternoon in the woods near a golf course collecting golf balls. On his way home, he was stopped by a Fleadirt gang member, who demanded half his golf balls plus two. After paying off the gang member, Marcus encountered a second Fleadirt associate who made the same demand. After paying off the second gang member, he encountered a third Fleadirt thug who also demanded half his golf balls plus two. After paying off the last gang member, Marcus had two golf balls left. How many golf balls did he begin with?

Part II: Problems with a Twist

A major barrier to solving problems is inferring constraints that do not really exist. Try solving the problems below. What unwarranted constraints may hamper solving each?

■ **Problem 10: The Nine-Dot, Four-Line Problem** (◆ 4-8). Connect all the dots in Figure A with only four straight lines. Constraint: Once started, you may not lift your pencil or retrace a line.

Figure A: • • •
       • • •
       • • •

■ **Problem 11: Equal Pennies** (◆ 4-8). Arrange six pennies as shown in Figure B. Moving a single penny once, create an arrangement where the number of pennies in the column of pennies is the same as the number of pennies in the row of pennies. You must use all the pennies, and you cannot create a new row or column. Note that there are multiple solutions.

Figure B: •
       •
       •
       • • •

Investigation 2.1 continued

■ **Problem 12: The Checkboard Problem** (◆ 4-8). How many squares does the checkboard shown in Figure C have?

Figure C:

■ **Problem 13: The Utilities Problem** (◆ 4-8). Three new houses (A, B, and C) each needed electric (e), water (w), and sewage (s) service. In Figure D, connect each house to each utility. Constraint: You may not cross utility lines.

Figure D:

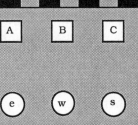

Part III: Problems Worth Reconsidering

Looking back can be an invaluable heuristic. Checking a solution is essential, even when it seems obvious. Students should get in the habit of asking themselves such questions as: Does the solution make sense? Does it answer the problem posed? Is there another way of solving the problem and, if so, do the alternative strategies produce the same solution? Are there other solutions to the problem? Try solving the following problems. Check your solution and then discuss it with your group or class.

■ **Problem 14: A Hamburger-Hungry Dieter** (◆ 5-8). Hammond loved hamburger and ate $\frac{5}{8}$ pounds of the meat a day. After testing revealed that his blood consisted mostly of cholesterol, he decided to alter his eating habits by cutting his hamburger consumption by $\frac{3}{4}$ (75%). How many pounds of hamburger a day did Hammond eat on his new "low-cholesterol" diet?

■ **Problem 15: A Problematic Sports Problem** (◆ 5-8). If $\frac{2}{3}$ of the boys in the seventh grade of Raucous Middle School played football only and $\frac{1}{2}$ played baseball only, what fraction of the seventh-grade children played neither?

■ **Problem 16: Waiting for the Bus** (◆ 5-8). Rosalie arrived at Campus Bus Stop Number 1 just as a bus was pulling away. Adding to her frustration, she saw a total of 72 people—including students, visitors, demonstrators, dope pushers, or whatever in line in front of her waiting to take the next bus. If the maximum capacity of a campus bus was 24, and a bus left the stop every 10 minutes, how long before Rosalie could board a bus and leave for campus? Assume that all arriving buses are empty, that Rosalie doesn't butt ahead, that no one leaves the bus stop, and that no one else arrives at the bus stop before Rosalie leaves.

■ **Problem 17: How Far the House?** (◆ 5-8). Larry, Marv, and Philippe all lived on the same straight road. Larry's house and Marv's house were 3 miles apart, and Marv's house and Philippe's house were 4 miles apart. How far apart were Larry's house and Philippe's house? Assume that the boys live on the same side of the street or that the width of their houses is not a factor.

How do young children informally solve simple arithmetic word problems? Initially try to concretely model the meaning of a problem with fingers or other objects. That is, they represent the quantities mentioned in the problem, imitate the action implied by the problem, and count to determine the answer (Carpenter, 1986). To solve an addition problem such as Problem 2.1 below, for example, young children: (a) first count out five blocks, fingers, or other objects to represent the amount Ruffus began with; (b) then count out another three items to represent how much was added; and (c) lastly, count all the items to determine the total. In brief, without training, children often use their everyday knowledge, concrete materials, and common sense to solve simple, but novel arithmetic problems.

■ **Problem 2.1: Ruffus' Bones (◆ K-1).** Ruffus the dog had five bones. He tipped Mr. Purdy's garbage can over and got three more bones. How many bones does Ruffus have altogether now?

Schoolchildren's Problem-Solving Ability

Performance on Routine and Nonroutine Problems. Results from the National Assessment of Educational Progress (NAEP) show that, generally, students at all ages successfully solve the one-step simple translation word problems prevalent in older textbooks (routine problems) but have difficulty with word problems that require some analysis or thinking (nonroutine problems) (Carpenter, Matthews, Lindquist, & Silver, 1984; Kouba, Carpenter, & Swafford, 1989). (A one-step simple translation problem involves translating the word language of an oral or written word problem involving a single operation into a number sentence. For example, Problem 2.1 above can be translated into the equation $5 + 3 = ?$) For two-step (two-operation) word problems such as Problem 2.2 below, for example, less than a third of the third graders participating in the Fourth NAEP correctly determined the answer was 6 cents.

■ **Problem 2.2: A Two-Step Problem (◆ 3-6).** Chris buys a pencil for 35 cents and a soda for 59 cents. How much change does she get back from $1.00?

Effects of the Skills Approach. Perplexed, Miss Brill asked, *"If young children gladly and effec-*

Box 2.1: Problem-Solving Heuristics for Each of Polya's Four Problem Solving Phases

Some Problem-Solving Hints

PHASE 1: UNDERSTANDING THE PROBLEM. Did you try the following?

✦ State the problem in your own words.

✦ Decide what the unknown is.

✦ Decide what information is needed.

PHASE 2: DEVISE A PLAN. Might the following help?

✦ Draw a picture.

✦ Examine some examples and look for patterns.

✦ Organize the data in a list, table, or chart and look for patterns.

✦ Simplify the problem and look for patterns.

✦ Relate the problem to familiar problems.

✦ Write a number sentence.

✦ Work backwards.

✦ Use logical reasoning to eliminate possibilities.

✦ Try and adjust.

PHASE 3: CARRY OUT THE PLAN. Did you do the following?

✦ Decide whether or not the plan is working.

PHASE 4: LOOK BACK. Did you consider the following questions?

✦ Is the solution reasonable?

✦ Does the solution answer the question?

✦ Are there other solutions?

✦ Are there other ways to solve the problem and, if so, do they result in the same solution?

tively solve problems, why do my students hate problem solving so and have so much difficulty with it?

☞ Try Probe 2.2 (page 2-10). (Text continued on page 2-11.)

↗ Probe 2.2: Problems with the Traditional Skills Approach to Problem Solving

The aim of this probe is to prompt reflection about the conventional way of teaching problem solving. Complete the questions below. Then discuss your answers with your group or class.

1. A key-word approach involves telling children to look for key words in word problems to help them decide what operation to choose. For example, in the worksheet illustrated to the right, children are supposed to remember that *and* or *in all* means *add* and *left* means *subtract*.

    a. Consider the three problems below. What are the dangers of using the key-word approach?

    ■ **Problem A: Disappearing Biscuits** (◆ 1-2). Mary baked 12 biscuits. Ruffus her dog ate 3 of them. How many biscuits could Mary serve for supper?

    ■ **Problem B: An Early Retirement Program for Mail Carriers** (◆ 2-4). Ruffus had forced 5 mailmen to retire, *and* Bruno the Beagle had forced 2 to retire. How many more mailmen had Ruffus forced to retire than Bruno?

    ■ **Problem C: The Case of the Unwelcomed Deposits** (◆ 1-2). Ruffus *left* 3 messes in Mr. Purdy's yard. Bruno *left* 2. How many messes did the two dogs leave in Mr. Purdy's yard?

    b. Obviously the wording of a problem is important, and children need to pay careful attention to it. How might a teacher help children understand this point without falling into the trap of the key-word approach?

> Name:
>
> ### PROBLEM-SOLVING STRATEGY
>
> Directions: Read the following story problems to the class. Have the students decide whether they should add or subtract. Remind them to look for the words *and*, *in all*, or *left* to help them decide what they should do. Have them circle the correct sign.
>
> 1. Three little chickens were eating corn. Two more little chickens joined them. How many little chickens are there in all?
>
>
>
> + or -
>
> 2. Five little chickens were eating corn. Four little chickens went into the barn. How many chickens were left eating corn?
>
>
>
> + or -
>
> page 88
>
> THE MATH BOOK FROM HELL: Grade 1
> Boring Books Publishing Co., Inc.

2. a. Based on your experience, were mathematics problems used primarily as routine practice exercises (a way of practicing previous content), a vehicle for raising questions and exploring content, or a means for promoting mathematical thinking?

    b. What effect did this have on your disposition and ability to solve problems?

3. a. Below is a classic type of problem. Were you encouraged to use your informal knowledge to solve it or were you shown a specific solution technique?

    ■ **A Train Problem** (◆ 7-8). The *City of New Orleans* leaves Chicago and a freight train leaves Champaign at the same time. The two trains head toward each other on the same track. If the trains begin 120 miles apart, the *City of New Orleans* travels at an average speed of 40 miles per hour, and the freight train travels at 20 miles per hour, how far outside Chicago would they crash?

    b. What effect did this have on your disposition and ability to solve problems?

"A key reason why children have little interest in problem solving or have difficulty with it," replied Ms. Socrates sadly, "is how math is usually taught. The traditional skills approach does not foster the adaptive expertise necessary to understand and think critically about nonroutine problems. Instruction on problem solving is frequently limited to the key-word approach, which is often inadequate to solve nonroutine problems. Moreover, problems are merely used as routine exercises to practice previously taught facts, formulas, or procedures, a practice that undercuts interest in problem solving and discourages thoughtful analysis of problems (Davis, 1992). Indeed requiring children to use 'the prescribed' procedure instead of encouraging their own informal solutions undermines the self confidence, autonomy, and flexibility needed to solve nonroutine problems" (e.g., Underhill, 1988).

2•1•3 TEACHING: FOSTERING MATHEMATICAL PROBLEM-SOLVING

In this subunit, we examine the different ways problem solving can be incorporated into instruction and how a teacher can help children become better problem solvers.

Approaches to Using Problems

How should problem solving be incorporated into instruction?

Three Different Approaches. Instructionally, problems can be used in three very different ways (Schroeder & Lester, 1989; Stanic & Kilpatrick, 1989).

1. **Teaching *about* problem solving.** This approach involves direct instruction about general problem-solving strategies. It commonly entails explaining and illustrating Polya's (1973) four-phase model of problem solving (or some variation of it) and specific heuristics for implementing the four phases. In effect, problem-solving techniques such as the heuristic of drawing a picture are treated as subject-matter content. This is how problem solving would be taught in the traditional skills approach to mathematics instruction.

2. **Teaching *via* problem solving.** This approach focuses on using problem solving as a means for teaching subject-matter content. In ad-

dition to serving as a vehicle for practicing basic computational skills, problems are often used to show how content relates to the real world. They are also used to introduce and provoke discussion about a topic. Problems are sometimes used to motivate students to study and master content. One way this is done is to present a problem at the beginning of a unit to show students what they will be able to accomplish by studying the unit. Another way is to use recreational problems to show how school-learned skills can be used in entertaining ways. Such uses of problem solving are consistent with the conceptual approach.

3. **Teaching *for* problem solving.** This approach focuses on teaching general problem-solving strategies by actually giving children the opportunity to solve challenging problems and to use Polya's four-phase approach and problem-solving heuristics. This is how problem solving would be taught in the problem-solving approach.

An Integrated Approach. In practice, teaching about, via, and for problem solving often overlap (Schroeder & Lester, 1989). Indeed, it makes sense to combine content instruction about problem-solving strategies and other subject matter with process-oriented instruction that focuses on how to solve genuine problems. This is how problem solving would be taught in the investigative approach (see Box 2.2 on the next page).

Extending Children's Problem-Solving Ability

How is problem solving learned? "Slowly and with difficulty" (Kilpatrick, 1985b, p. 8). Becoming a better problem solver is a gradual building process that requires taking on challenging and sometimes frustrating problems. An important part of this building process is promoting adaptive expertise; how to help children construct a conceptual understanding of mathematics will be addressed in the next chapter. Other tips for fostering children's problem-solving competence are discussed below.

☞ **Provide students regular problem-solving practice with a variety of problems.** Helping students become good problem solvers is like helping them learn how to ride a bicycle; tips can be helpful, but it's impossible to master the process without actually trying it (see Box 2.3 on the next page). CHILDREN NEED TO TACKLE CHALLENGING

Box 2.2: The Investigative Approach to Teaching Problem Solving

The investigative approach can integrate problem solving and content instruction in a purposeful way. As Ms. Socrates explained to the parents of her students at her first open house, "I use the investigative approach to mathematics instruction. Most of our time is spent solving problems. Typically, I begin a unit of instruction with a challenging problem. I don't show the children how to solve the problem. Instead, they usually work in small groups to devise their solution procedures and solutions. The discussion of our different solution procedures and solutions then provides a basis for introducing new content and problem-solving strategies. Additional problems are given to extend and practice the new material. Working on genuine problems creates a real need to learn new concepts, computational strategies, and problem-solving strategies and, thus, helps children see why these things are important to learn. Moreover, working on problems gives them the opportunity to apply and to practice concepts, skills, and strategies in interesting, meaningful, purposeful, and creative ways."

PROBLEMS ON A WEEKLY, IF NOT ON A DAILY, BASIS. Besides using problems as a basis for class instruction, regularly pose optional problems ("The Daily Challenge" or "The Weekly Challenge") in a "Problem-Solving Corner" on a bulletin board or in an activity center. Both routine and nonroutine problems can be used for class instruction and optional challenges. Nonroutine problems include complex (multistep) translation problems, problems with too little or too much information, problems with multiple solutions, nongoal-specific problems (open-ended problems that do not have a prescribed solution or solutions), applied (real or realistic), or theoretical (e.g., contrived or fanciful) problems.

Problems can come from various sources including textbooks, other printed teacher resources, computer software, the internet, or teachers themselves. Students should also be encouraged to pose their own problems (NCTM, 1991). Teachers should include problems that require an extended (multiday, -week, or -month) effort such as planning an excursion, investigating why some things float and other things sink, making furniture for the classroom, or how to save water in the school (Baker, Semple, & Stead, 1990). Teachers should

Box 2.3: The Case of the Problematic Problem-Solving Instruction

Although not sure how to proceed, Miss Brill was convinced her class needed problem-solving instruction. She checked her text and the *District Curriculum Guide for Mathematics*. Outlined in both was an explanation of Polya's four-phase problem-solving approach and a number of problem-solving heuristics. She concluded it would be a good idea for her students to learn these general problem-solving strategies and described them to her class in detail. To reinforce these ideas, she asked the class to read the section in their textbook about problem-solving strategies and to answer the questions at the end of the section. At the end of the week, she tested the class. One question entailed listing the four steps in Polya's model. The results of the test were very depressing.

Deeply disappointed that her students did not share her enthusiasm about learning problem-solving strategies, Miss Brill sought Ms. Socrates' advice. Her co-worker allowed that children needed to learn about such strategies. She noted, however, "It's a mistake to treat Polya's four-phase problem-solving approach and problem-solving heuristics merely as 'stuff' (content) to be memorized. It's not enough for kids to learn about general problem-solving strategies; they need practice using them to solve genuine problems. In brief, the best way to learn about problem solving is to engage in problem solving."

also include "problems that will enable students of varying abilities to invent a variety of [solution] strategies" (Ohanian, 1992, p. 71).

∞ **Make practice more profitable by (a) helping children learn problem-solving strategies, and (b) discussing problem strategies and solutions** (Charles & Lester, 1982). However important, practice alone will probably not help them to develop a wide array of strategies needed to tackle a variety of genuine problems (Kilpatrick, 1985b). Primary-level children can begin with a few strategies such as drawing a picture, organizing data in a table and looking for a pattern, or trying and adjusting. Strategies can be gradually added until intermediate-level students are familiar with all the heuristics listed in Box 2.1 on page 2-9.

☞ Try Investigation 2.2 (pages 2-13 and 2-14). (Text continued on page 2-15.)

✿ Investigation 2.2: Problems to Practice Using Heuristics

◆ Guided practice of heuristics ◆ Groups of four + class discussion

After students have been introduced to a heuristic, solving problems where the problem-solving aid may be helpful can reinforce its value. With the help of your group try solving the following problems. When need be, consider the hints. With your group or class, discuss your solutions and which heuristics were helpful and how.

■ **Problem 1: The Long Elevator Ride** (◆ 4-8). Absent-minded Professor Trumble got on the elevator at the first floor of his hotel. Unfortunately, he forgot to push the button for the 14th floor. The elevator went up 12 floors, went up another 5 floors, went yet another 6 floors, down 9 floors, up 4 floors, up 7 floors, and down 8 floors. Sensing something had gone awry, and thoroughly confused, Professor Trumble got off the elevator. How many floors away from the 14th floor was he? Assume that the ground floor is the first floor and that the building has a 13th floor.
✚ Hints: Drawing a picture might be helpful. Look back: What's wrong with an answer of 3?

■ **Problem 2: Sluggish Progress** (◆ 4-8). A slug fell into a ditch 18 inches deep. Each day the slug moved 6 inches up the wall of the ditch, only to slip back 3 inches at night. How many days will it take the sluggish slug to reach the top of the ditch wall? Assume that the slug will get out if it reaches the lip of the ditch.
✚ Hints: Although the answer seems readily apparent, draw a picture. Is there anything you overlooked?

■ **Problem 3: Costly Cuts** (◆ 4-8). Mr. Tilden needed a board cut into 8 equal lengths. When he had a board cut into 4 equal lengths, the lumber yard had charged him $1.20. How much could Mr. Tilden expect to pay now? Assume that all cuts are in one direction (parallel).
✚ Hints: Although the answer may seem obvious, try drawing a picture. What does a picture reveal?

■ **Problem 4: Stamp Tetrominoes** (◆ 2-8). Mr. Ki, the new postmaster, wanted very much to please his customers. When Mrs. Vogel asked for four stamps, Mr. Ki surprised her by asking, "Attached or unattached." Not wanting lose stamps in her handbag, Mrs. Vogel indicated attached. Mr. Ki's next question was even more surprising, "In what shape do you want your four attached stamps?" Mrs. Vogel wondered—with some irritation—how many shapes could four attached stamps have? Assume that Mr. K. is viewing the back or featureless side of the stamps and that the attached stamps are square shaped. Not counting examples created by turning or flipping an arrangement, how many tetrominos (four squares joined at a side) are there? Consider the example and nonexample shown to the right.
✚ Hint: Try to draw all of the possibilities in a systematic fashion.

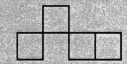

A tetromino

Not a tetromino

■ **Problem 5: A Train of Toothpick Triangles** (◆ 2-8). If toothpicks are arranged as a row of triangles as shown below, how many toothpicks will be needed to make a row of 100 triangles?
✚ Hints: Examine simpler cases of the problem (e.g., the number of toothpicks needed for 1, 2, and 3 triangles). Organize the data in a table, and look for a pattern.

Investigation 2.2 continued

■ **Problem 6: Inverting a 36 Penny Triangle** (◆ 7-8). Thirty-six pennies are arranged in the form of a triangle. The first three rows are shown in the figure to the right. What is the fewest number of moves it would take to turn the triangle upside down? Constraint: Only one penny may be moved per turn.

✚ Hints: Examine simpler cases (e.g., triangles made of 3, 6, and 10 pennies). Organize the data in a table and look for a pattern. Actually manipulating concrete objects can be immeasurably useful in solving this problem.

■ **Problem 7: Spoke Addition** (◆ 2-8). Write the numerals 1 to 19 in the 19 circles to the right so that any three numbers in a row (on the opposite ends of a spoke plus the center number) have the same sum.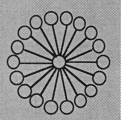

✚ Hints: Solve a simpler problem (e.g., fill in a 5-circle version with the numbers 1 to 5) and look for a pattern.

■ **Problem 8: An Uneven Effort** (◆ 4-8). Three friends, Gif, Harvey, and Iagnacio earned $320 for a trip. Gif earned eight times the amount Harvey earned. Iagnacio's earned the difference between Gif and Harvey. How much did each earn?

✚ Hint: Express the information given as a number sentence.

■ **Problem 9: The Big Loser** (◆ 6-8). A gambler took his paycheck (all the money he had) for a weekend fling at the race track. On each day, he had to pay $3 for parking and another $10 for lunch. On Saturday morning he lost one-fourth of his money left after paying for the parking. On Saturday afternoon he lost one-fourth of his money left after paying for lunch. The same thing happened Sunday morning and afternoon. By the time he got home Sunday night, the gambler had only $60. How big was the gambler's paycheck?

✚ Hints: Draw a picture and work backward.

■ **Problem 10: Poison** (◆ 3-8). *Poison* is a two-person game, in which any number of objects (e.g., blocks) are put out (or drawn). A player may take (cross out) one or two items on his or her turn. The object of the game is not to be the player who takes (crosses out) the last item. Determine the winning strategy for playing *Poison* with 26 objects.

✚ Hints: Examine particular examples of the game with small numbers of items. Organize the data in a table and look for a pattern.

■ **Problem 11: A Homework Mystery** (◆ 6-8). Three of Miss Su's students did not put a name on their homework. The grades on the papers were A, B, and C. Joy, Kiwane, and Lola were the only children for whom Miss Su had not recorded a grade. The next day, Joy and Kiwane were absent, and so the teacher asked Lola about her paper. Lola noted she had written about her skiing adventure with Kiwane's sisters. After the teacher handed Lola her paper, she complained, "Rats, my paper was twice as long as anyone's, and I still didn't get an A." If the B paper, the shortest of the three, was an intriguing autobiographical account of the advantages and disadvantages of being an only child, which paper belonged to which student?

✚ Hints: Make a table and use logical reasoning to eliminate possibilities.

■ **Problem 12: Misleading Labels** (◆ 7-8). Little Feather put two nickels in a box, a nickel and a dime in another, and two dimes in a third box. She then applied labels 10 cents, 15 cents, and 20 cents to the wrong boxes and challenged her friend Javier to correctly identify the contents of all three boxes by taking a single coin from one of the boxes.

✚ Hints: Make a table and use logical reasoning to eliminate possibilities.

A three-step process for helping children learn problem-solving heuristics is outlined below.

- **Step 1: Introduce heuristics *purposefully* by creating a situation where students feel a genuine need for a strategy.** As illustrated by Investigation 2.1, the investigative approach to teaching heuristics begins by posing a challenging problem, giving students a free hand to tackle the problem, waiting until they become stumped ("blocked"), and then introducing the heuristic as a tool for overcoming the blockage. In a follow-up discussion, have someone illustrate how the heuristic was helpful. In this way, students can clearly see its value.

- **Step 2: Follow-up with *guided practice.*** Providing additional challenging problems with the hint that a recently introduced

heuristic might be helpful can help students master heuristics in a purposeful manner (see, e.g., Investigation 2.2).

- **Step 3: In time, provide *unguided practice.*** Having students decide for themselves which of the previously introduced heuristics is useful is important for achieving the ultimate aim of independent or autonomous problem solving.

∞ **Promote a positive disposition toward problem solving by creating a spirit of inquiry.** Creating a climate conducive to problem solving should be a key aim of mathematics instruction at all levels. As Box 2.4 illustrates, this may not be easy for either students or teachers accustomed to the traditional skills approach. Not only may students have to break old habits and learn new ones, but so may teachers. Not only may students have to overcome entrenched beliefs and learn new ones, but so may teachers.

Box 2.4: The Case of the Tight Teacher and Tutees

Miss Brill was eager to introduce her class to genuine problem solving. She decided to give her students problems on a regular basis, using problems to introduce and practice content and problem-solving strategies whenever she could. However, the beginning teacher recognized that she would have to devote every waking moment and more to math to pull off a program like that of Ms. Socrates. Even with the more experienced teacher's help, it was going to take time to collect or devise suitable problems for the required content. Considering the other demands on her time such as preparing a reading program for four different levels of students, house chores, and a desperate need for rest, Miss Brill needed a stopgap measure for the near term. She decided to start by devoting one math class a week to problem solving. She dubbed this session: "The Freewheeling Friday Function."

Miss Brill was pleased with the idea of the Freewheeling Friday Function. It allowed her to quickly put more emphasis on problem solving while not overwhelming her. Miss Brill was reasonably sure she could come up with one challenging problem a week. The stopgap measure also gave her a comfortable way of beginning the new challenge of teaching problem solving. She felt secure devoting one day a week to her experiment. If things didn't work out, she

still had four days to accomplish what was outlined in the textbook. Moreover, Miss Brill sensed that it would take time for her to adjust to a more open approach to teaching. She thought she could handle the uncertainties of an unaccustomed approach one day a week.

Although some students such as LeMar eagerly embraced the challenge of solving difficult problems, Miss Brill was disappointed that most students greeted the Freewheeling Friday Function with reluctance or even resistance. She was often greeted with panic-motivated questions like: "Will we have problems like this on our test?" Frequently, students complained, "Why can't you just tell us how to do this?"

Miss Brill was disappointed, moreover, by their problem-solving efforts. Frequently students raced to shout out an answer before group discussions had even begun. Many students tried to solve problems by blindly applying the mathematical procedure they had most recently learned—even when it should have been clear that the procedure was not relevant. When Miss Brill asked them if using the procedure made sense, students often looked confused or even betrayed. "That's what we learned about this week," was a common reply. (Box continued on page 2-16.)

Box 2.4 continued

Reading the disappointment in Miss Brill's face, students would then launch into a barrage of questions in an effort to identify which previously studied procedure was appropriate. They scrutinized her face, gestures, and comments for clues as to the correct procedure. From a wince here, a smile there, students attempted to divine the correct method. Seldom did they analyze the problem as carefully as they did their teacher's reactions.

The students were not the only reason why the Friday Freewheeling Function did not live up to its name. Miss Brill could not resist a deeply ingrained impulse to control what her students were doing. When students asked for help, Miss Brill took control and dutifully showed the students how to solve the problem. When students asked if their answer was right, she instinctively praised them if they were right and often gave them the correct answer otherwise.

Miss Brill was stunned that her students seemed to be becoming even more passive. Exasperated, she went back to Ms. Socrates.

Ms. Socrates observed, "Unfortunately, your children have not had much instruction on problem-solving strategies or opportunities to solve genuine problems before. They are used to being spoonfed and not thinking for themselves. They have become 'grade grubbers'; interest in getting grades has supplanted interest in learning and thinking for many. Their previous schooling encourages them to be impulsive.

They've learned that the goal in mathematics is to respond quickly with something—anything [Kilpatrick, 1985b]. From past experiences, they assume that there is only one correct way to solve a problem and that way is most likely the procedure they have learned last. When that doesn't work, they turn to you—the authority—for the solution."

"I've tried giving them problems for a month now," complained Miss Brill, "and they don't show any signs of improving. Is there any hope for them?"

"Patience. All is not lost, even at this late stage of the game," counseled Ms. Socrates. "You have to remember, they have been exposed to a very different way of teaching for many years now. It will not be easy breaking old habits and changing the whole way they view mathematics and mathematics instruction." The older teacher confided that it usually took her at least several months before most of her students felt comfortable with an approach that focused on understanding and problem solving instead of memorizing facts and routines: "It takes time to help them regenerate their curiosity and to get hooked on problem solving. I expect that as the primary teachers do more and more problem solving in the early grades, it will take less and less time for our students to become accustomed to the demands of problem solving."

"But what can I do now?" pleaded Miss Brill.

Although easier to accomplish if efforts begin early, it is never too late to create a spirit of inquiry. A teacher must be patient, though, because change and progress will often be slow and uneven. A teacher must also actively work to create a climate conducive to problem solving. In Box 2.5 (page 2-17), we describe some actions a teacher can take before, during, and after students solve a problem. In Box 2.6 (pages 2-18 to 2-21), we illustrate these actions. Note that in each case, the teacher acts as a facilitator, not an information dispenser. In effect, these actions model heuristics for each of the four phases of problem solving you hope your students will internalize and use on their own eventually.

One way of creating a spirit of inquiry and making problems more meaningful and interesting is through *problem posing: encouraging children to write their own problems, which are then presented to their peers* (English, 1997; Silver, 1994). To introduce word-processing skills and the advantages of using word processing (e.g., the relative ease of making revisions and the spellcheck function to check for spelling errors), have students compose their problems on a computer. Sharing problems with peers can provide authors with valuable feedback about a problem's clarity and entertainment value as well as provide their critics with problem-solving practice (English, Cudmore, & Tilley, in press).

Box 2.5: Teacher Actions Before, During, and After Students Solve Problems†

TEACHER ACTIONS BEFORE: UNDERSTANDING THE PROBLEM

1. To underscore the importance of reading problems carefully, read, or have a student read, the problem to the class. This is particularly important for children who may have trouble reading. Discuss words that have special meanings in mathematics, other unfamiliar vocabulary, and the problem setting so that children can accurately comprehend the problem.

2. To help children focus on key data and to clarify the problem, ask them what they think the unknown is, and what data are needed to determine it. Encourage students to state the problem in their own words. It can be helpful to write out specific questions and hints before class begins.

TEACHER ACTIONS DURING: DEVISING AND CARRYING OUT A PLAN

3. (Optional.) To help students consider possible solution strategies, encourage brainstorming. Do not criticize any suggestions or suggest there is one correct way to do the problem.

4. To evaluate students' progress and difficulties, monitor their work on the problem and ask them to justify their efforts.

5. To help students overcome blocks, give them hints, not a solution strategy. Hints can be in the form of a heuristic such as: "Consider a simpler problem," or "Is this like any problems you have solved before?" In some cases, it may be necessary to help students reanalyze the problem (see Teacher Actions 1 and 2 above). Keep in mind that the goal

is to have your students do as much thinking for themselves as possible.

TEACHER ACTIONS AFTER: LOOKING BACK

6. To encourage students to evaluate their solutions, ask them to justify it (e.g., whether or not a solution is reasonable and answers the original question).

7. To challenge those who finish early and to help children generalize their solution strategies to new problems, pose extensions of the problem. For example, have students consider what would happen if one of the components in a problem had a different value. It is probably best to consider how you will pose extensions before class begins.

8. To illustrate the variety of possible solution methods, have students discuss their solution strategies with the whole class. Encourage students to justify their strategies and solutions, to evaluate others' suggestions, and to arrive at a conclusion themselves. To foster autonomy, refrain from serving as the final judge.

9. To demonstrate the generality of solution methods, discuss how the problem relates to other problems or situations: How is it similar and different from problems solved previously? How might a similar problem arise in different situations?

10. To help students consider the impact of special features, have them discuss important aspects of the problem. For example, was anyone misled by an accompanying picture (not an uncommon difficulty), a "key word," or extra information?

†This box is based on the Teacher Actions outlined on pages 42 and 43 of *Teaching Problem Solving: What, Why, and How* by R. I. Charles and F. K. Lester, © 1982 by Dale Seymour. Reprinted by permission.

☞ **Foster autonomy by encouraging children to use their informal knowledge and to discover as much for themselves as possible** (Polya, 1981). Instead of imposing strategies and solutions on children, give them the opportunity to devise, share, and reformulate their own. Instead of always serving as the final authority, encourage children to evaluate their strategies and solutions themselves by asking, for example, "Does your solution make sense?" "Can you justify your solution?" "Does everyone agree on the solution?" (Text continued on page 2-21.)

Box 2.6: Teacher Actions in an Example of the Investigative Approach

Vignette[2]	Comments
Mrs. Stein, a third-grade teacher, handed out a sheet of paper with the following problem:	The lesson begins with a single challenging problem.

■ **Rosa's Outfits** (◆ 1-8). Rosa had four different-colored blouses: pink, yellow, green, and blue. She had three different-colored skirts: white, navy, and brown. In how many ways could Rosa combine four blouses and three shirts?

☞ Before reading on, try solving this problem yourself or with the help of a group. Discuss your solution with your group or class.

TEACHER ACTIONS BEFORE: UNDERSTANDING THE PROBLEM

Mrs. Stein asked Luis to read the problem out loud. Several students indicated they did not understand the question, particularly, the word *combine*. After a brief discussion, Luis rephrased the question: "How many different outfits could Rosa make with four blouses and three dresses?" Maxine corrected, "Three skirts, not three dresses." Because the boys in the class seemed bewildered by this distinction, Maxine noted that dresses have a top and a bottom, whereas a skirt is just a bottom and needs a top.	To underscore the importance of reading problems carefully and thoughtfully, the teacher had the problem read to the class (Teacher Action 1). The terms *combine* and *skirts* were defined so that everyone would understand the context. Moreover, the children were encouraged to rephrase the problem in their own words.
Mrs. Stein asked the class if there were any questions before they began. Argus who had already misplaced his paper, asked, "What color were the blouses again?" Deter pointed out that knowing the specific colors was not important. All one needed to know was that Rosa had four different blouses and three different skirts.	The teacher used a whole-class discussion to help students better understand the problem (Teacher Action 2). Note that this helped to define what information was relevant to the problem (number of different blouses and skirts) and what information was irrelevant (e.g., the color of blouses).
Mrs. Stein then asked the class, "What is it you're trying to figure out?"	The teacher asked specific clarifying questions such as, "What is the unknown?"

TEACHER ACTIONS DURING: DEVISING AND CARRYING OUT A PLAN

Mrs. Stein circulated among the groups to monitor their progress. At the first group, Sherard complained, "We don't know what to do."	Skipping a whole-class discussion of possible solution strategies (Teacher Action 3), the teacher gauged her students' difficulties and progress by observing and questioning them (Teacher Action 4).
"Might drawing a picture help?" suggested Mrs. Stein. The four members of the group then busily set about trying to represent the problem.	The teacher provided a hint, but not a specific solution strategy (Teacher Action 5).
At the next group Abdullah noted, "There are probably more [combinations] but, so far, we have found six different outfits":	

P+W   Y+N   G+Br   B+N   Y+W   G+N

Box 2.6 continued

"Why do you think that?" asked Mrs. Stein.

"We keep coming up with more ways," offered Claiborne, "It's so hard to know when we've got them all."

"Is there any way you could list the possibilities in a systematic way?" hinted Mrs. Stein.

One group excitedly called Mrs. Stein over. "Is the answer three?" they asked with eager anticipation.

Resisting the temptation to dismiss this apparently ridiculous answer and to take over the discussion, Mrs. Stein asked, "Why do you think it's three?"

Shanti explained, "Look [pointing to the diagram below], these three blouses match up with these four skirts to make three outfits. The last blouse doesn't have a shirt to match up with, so Rosa can only make three outfits. Is that right?"

Mrs. Stein responded, "What do you think? Does everyone agree?"

With a smile Shanti remarked, "I should have known by now, she always answers a question with a question."

Sandy seized the opportunity to press her doubts, "I guess I don't understand the problem."

"Can you state the problem in your own words?" suggested Mrs. Stein.

Sandy offered, "How many ways could Rosa mix her blouses and skirts to make different outfits." At this point, the other members of the group insisted their original solution of three had to be right. Sandy was still unconvinced but could not offer an alternative solution.

Pointing at their diagram, Mrs. Stein then asked, "Is there another way the blouses and skirts can be combined?" Grant drew a new diagram:

The teacher encouraged the students to monitor their own progress by asking them to justify their conclusion (Teacher Action 4).

Note that the teacher again gave the children a hint but not a specific solution strategy or solution (Teacher Action 5).

The teacher encouraged the students to evaluate their solution themselves (Teacher Action 6). Note that she did not criticize the students' solution but, instead, asked them to justify it.

Note that the teacher again resisted passing judgment. She responded to the common "Is this right?" question with questions of her own. Although students may find this disconcerting at first, they often become accustomed to it, particularly if they understand its purpose.

A student experienced blockage. At this critical juncture, the teacher provided a hint (Teacher Action 5) by asking students to rephrase the question in more familiar terms (Teacher Action 1 again).

Because the teacher sensed that the group could go no further, she offered another hint in the form of a question (Teacher Action 5 again). Note that

Box 2.6 continued

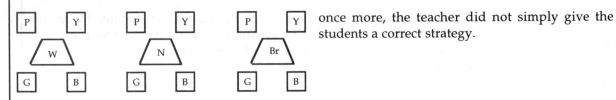

once more, the teacher did not simply give the students a correct strategy.

"So, four and four is eight, and four more is twelve," beamed Grant.

TEACHER ACTIONS AFTER: LOOKING BACK (CHECKING)

Julie proudly showed Mrs. Stein the chart her group had developed.

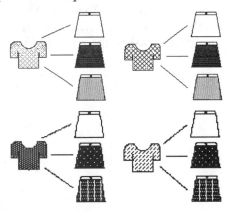

After the group explained its solution, Mrs. Stein presented two new problems and the following challenge: "See if you can figure out a shortcut for determining the total number of combinations."

After the teacher had the group justify its solution (Teacher Action 6), she provided extension problems (Teacher Action 7).

■ For his party, Alexander had 5 flavors of ice cream and 3 toppings. How many different kinds of ice cream treats could be made if a child could choose combinations of one flavor and one topping?

■ Alina had 5 different-shaped cookie cutters and 4 different colors of icing. How many different-looking cookies could Alina make?

Mrs. Stein had the groups represent their solutions on the board. In addition to Shanti's and Julie's solutions already shown, two other methods were illustrated. Abdullah's group hit on the following solution:

The teacher then encouraged the groups to share their solution strategies and answers with the whole class (Teacher Action 8).

Pi + W	Y + W	G + W	B + W
Pi + N	Y + N	G + N	B + N
Pi + Br	Y + Br	G + Br	B + Br

Box 2.6 continued

Gilberto's group drew: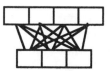

Pointing to a drawing of four blouses and three skirts, Shadawn noted that her group had arrived at a different answer: Seven. Mrs. Stein asked the class what they thought. Stuart commented that seven had to be wrong because nobody else got it. After Mrs. Stein asked if Stuart's conclusion was necessarily true, and the class agreed that it was not, she asked, "Why do you think it's seven, Shadawn?"

"Because four and three is seven altogether," responded Shadawn.

"Why did you add?" asked Izzie.

"Adding doesn't make sense," commented Sreka. "That tells how many pieces of clothing Rosa had altogether, not how many outfits she can make."

Shadawn remarked brightly, "Okay, I see now."

Next, Mrs. Stein asked the class how this problem was similar and different to other problems they had solved. Stuart offered that unlike previous problems that involved combining things, this problem did not involve adding the two numbers.

Note that the teacher did not act as the final judge but encouraged the class to evaluate each group's solution (Teacher Action 8). Explanations from peers are often less threatening and more intelligible to children. Also note that the teacher encouraged reasoned arguments, because an opinion held by a majority does not make it correct.

The teacher encouraged the children to relate the problem to other problems (Teacher Action 9).

☞ What is the shortcut for determining the number of possible combinations?

☞ **To encourage flexibility, prompt students to consider carefully the conditions (the constraints) of problems.** To encourage flexibility, regularly present students with tasks that require them to overcome unwarranted constraints (see, e.g., the problems in Part II of Investigation 2.1).

Moreover, explicitly discuss the need to consider all the constraints of a problem, the danger of reading into a problem constraints that don't exist, and how a problem can have very different solutions depending on what conditions are assumed (see, e.g., Box 2.7).

Box 2.7: A Case of Different Conditions and Different Solutions

Children need to consider the conditions or constraints of a problem (e.g., not read in constraints that are not there) and to recognize that a problem can have different solutions depending on the conditions that are assumed. The following vignette illustrates how a teacher guided students to consider the actual constraints of a problem and to recognize that assuming different conditions can lead to different solutions. Note that this lesson also provides an intuitive intro-

duction to advanced counting techniques such as combinations and permutations.

As part of a social studies lesson on Easter, Mrs. Stein proposed making decorative Easter eggs. "Using flip-top molds," the teacher suggested, "we can make eggs made of JELL-O® called Egg Jigglers® (to order molds call 1-800-535-5666) and proposed the following problem:

Box 2.7 continued

■ **Egg Colors** (◆ 1-8). With the molds, it is possible to make a JELL-O® egg that is half one color and half another. If we can make red (R), yellow (Y), and blue (B) JELL-O®, how many different types of eggs can we make?

The children had no sooner set about trying to solve the problem, when Beth asked, "Can we have eggs of just one color?"

"Does the problem prohibit other possibilities?" replied Mrs. Stein.

"No," answered Beth. The class then informally determine that there were nine possibilities (RR, RY, RB, YR, YY, YB, BR, BY, BB). Katie noted that the problem *Egg Colors* was like the problem (*Rosa's Outfits* on page 2-18) they had solved the day before.

Jim voiced his reservation, "But is an egg that is half blue and half red really different from one that is half red and half blue? Shouldn't the answer be less than nine?" Lara countered that the top half of the egg was smaller than the bottom half and so their answer made sense.

Mrs. Stein next asked, "What if the top and bottom halves of the egg were identical, how many different types of eggs are possible?"

After the class agreed the solution was six, Katie Lee asked, "But what if we only wanted two-color eggs?"

Grace interjected, "Should we assume that the top and bottom of an egg are different?"

"What difference does it make?" prompted Mrs. Stein. The class soon agreed that assuming the top and bottom were different led to solution of six but assuming they weren't led to a solution of three.

2•2 MATHEMATICS AS REASONING

Figure 2.2: A Case of Unreliable Reasoning

PEANUTS reprinted by permission of UFS, Inc.

Reasoning is essential for solving mathematical and everyday problems. Indeed, the ability to critically examine our own and others' conclusions is a basic survival skill. For example, if Charlie Brown in Figure 2.2 had not made the groundless conclusion that reading a book necessarily made Lucy more trustworthy, then he could have avoided the pain of being tricked by her again. In Subunit 2•2•1, we examine reasoning itself. In Subunit 2•2•2, we describe how instruction can foster mathematical reasoning in developmentally appropriate and interesting ways.

2•2•1 MATHEMATICS: UNDERSTANDING MATHEMATICAL REASONING

In this subunit, we explore why reasoning is important to study and its limits or misuses.

☞ Complete Investigation 2.3 (page 2-24), Probe 2.3 (page 2-25), and Investigation 2.4 (pages 2-26 to 2-29) before reading on.

Reasons for Focusing Reasoning

The Reasoning Needed to Do Mathematics. Because mathematics involves an exploratory side as well as a logical side, intuitive and inductive reasoning as well as deductive reasoning play an important role in the development and application of mathematics.

• **Conjectures.** The creation of mathematics normally begins with a problem (Clements & Battista, 1992). The exploration of a problem typically starts by making conjectures—claims or conclusions drawn from intuitive or inductive reasoning. More specifically, *a conjecture is a guess, inference, theory, or prediction based on untested or unproven—and, hence, uncertain or incomplete—evidence*. Conjectures can be tested empirically or logically.

• **Empirical tests.** A key way of empirically testing a conjecture is to search for *counterexamples—examples that contradict or are inconsistent with the conjecture*. A counterexample necessitates revising the conjecture or proposing a new one. Another valuable way of empirically testing a conjecture is to construct a model (e.g., a computer simulation).

• **Logical tests.** Mathematical truth is ultimately established by a logical proof—deductive reasoning based on axioms (premises accepted as true by the mathematical community) (Clements & Battista, 1992). Deductive reasoning, then, is a means for checking and evaluating conjectures.

The Need for Reasoning in School Mathematics. Reasoning should be an essential aspect of elementary mathematics because:

1. A focus on reasoning can promote mathematical power by helping children see that mathematics is logical and makes sense. ACTUAL EXPERIENCES IN LOOKING FOR PATTERNS AND FORMULATING AND EVALUATING CONJECTURES CAN HELP THEM BETTER UNDERSTAND THE IMPORTANCE AND MECHANICS OF BOTH THE EXPLORATORY AND THE LOGICAL SIDES OF MATHEMATICS (Silver, Kilpatrick, & Schlesinger, 1990).

2. Reasoning is a critical tool for many aspects of school and everyday life. Finding patterns and using if-then (deductive) reasoning can be central to science and other content areas. Critically evaluating the arguments of lawyers, advertisers, politicians, journalists, or others' is essential to make many everyday decisions and to avoid being hoodwinked.

Limitations and Misuses

To evaluate their own and others' conclusions effectively, students need to know the limitations and pitfalls of each type of reasoning (see Part I on page 2-26 of Investigation 2.4).

2•2•2 TEACHING: FOSTERING MATHEMATICAL REASONING

Broad guidelines are outlined below.

☞ **Intuitive, inductive, and deductive reasoning and conjecturing should be an integral part of mathematics instruction at all grade levels.** Children should be regularly encouraged to use intuitive and inductive reasoning to make conjectures. Moreover, even primary-level children should be encouraged to make simple deductions such as using if-then reasoning to eliminate possibilities (e.g., Donaldson, 1978). Investigation 2.3 (on page 2-24) and Probe 2.3 (on page 2-25) describe a number of activities and games that can be used with elementary-age children to examine and practice reasoning.

☞ **Help children to see they are surrounded by a wide variety of patterns.** There are regularities in events (e.g., the class eats lunch at 12:15 P.M. every day), everyday things (e.g., designs in wall paper, rugs, or quilts), space (e.g., things "grow" smaller with distance), and numbers (e.g., four groups of three and three groups of four both make twelve). Visual patterns are a good place to begin with primary children. Auditory patterns (e.g., rhythmic beats or music) and motion patterns (e.g., stand, squat, sit patterns) are also appropriate for young children. Number and arithmetic patterns can be introduced in time. (Continued on page 2-30)

☾ Investigation 2.3: Types of Reasoning[†]

◆ Intuitive, inductive, and deductive reasoning ◆ 2-8 ◆ Any number

The aims of this investigation are (a) to engage elementary-level pupils in mathematical reasoning and (b) to help intermediate-level students identify the types of reasoning in an engaging way. To see how and to deepen your own understanding of mathematical reasoning, answer the following questions yourself. Discuss your answers with your group or class.

1. In 1514, Albrecht Dürer made an engraving titled "Melancholy." In the background of this depiction of a depressed woman is the interesting grid of numbers shown at the right. Two cells appear to be missing numbers. Can you determine what number goes in each blank cell?

16	3	2	13
5	10	11	8
9	6		12
4	15	14	

2. Conclusions can stem from intuitive, inductive, or deductive reasoning.

   Intuitive reasoning involves *playing a hunch*. Frequently we do not have all the information necessary to make a decision and so we base our decision on what is obvious (appearances) or what feels right (an assumption). The following is an example of a child's (accidentally correct) intuitive reasoning: "If I multiply 5 and 3, I guess the product would be odd because 5 and 3 are odd."

   Inductive reasoning involves looking for a pattern and perceiving a regularity. (The heuristic of looking for a pattern discussed in Unit 2•1 involves this type of reasoning.) Inductive reasoning entails observing specific examples and discerning (inducing) a rule (a general conclusion). The following is an example of inductive reasoning: "When I multiplied the odd numbers 1 and 9, 3 and 3, 5 and 9, 7 and 3, and 9 and 7, all the products were odd [observation about particular instances]; therefore, the product of any two odd numbers is odd [general inference]."

   Deductive reasoning entails drawing a logical conclusion—one that necessarily follows from given information. It allows us to use what we know to figure what we don't know. Deductive reasoning begins with a premise (general proposition) and leads inescapably to a conclusion about a particular instance. Consider the following example: "Multiplying two odd numbers always results in an odd product [general premise]; 5 and 3 are odd numbers [other given]; therefore, the product of 5 and 3 *must* be odd [conclusion about a specific case]."

Intuitive reasoning:	I bet that white bird in the distance is a swan.
Inductive reasoning:	Every swan I have ever seen is white (observation of a pattern among examples), so all swans are white (general rule).
Deductive reasoning:	All swans are white (general rule) and the bird being shipped to us is a swan (other given); therefore, the bird is white (conclusion about a specific case that necessarily follows from the givens).

   a. What kind of reasoning was involved when you concluded that it was possible to determine what the missing numbers were?

   b. What kind of reasoning was involved when you determined a rule for figuring out the numbers?

   c. What kind of reasoning was involved when you used the rule to figure out the missing numbers?

3. There are a number of interesting patterns in Dürer's number grid (Jamski, 1989). Consider the four numbers in the corners. What do you notice about them? Does this four-number pattern appear elsewhere in the number grid?

[†]Questions 1 to 3 of this investigation were adapted from page 44 of *Mathematics: A Human Endeavor* by H. R. Jacobs, © 1982. The adaptation is used with permission of the publisher: W. H. Freeman, San Francisco.

➤ Probe 2.3: Drawing Conclusions and Identifying Types of Reasoning

According to the NCTM (1989) *Curriculum Standards*, looking for patterns and drawing logical conclusions should be integral aspects of elementary mathematics instruction. One aim of this probe is to give you a sense of what problems, games, and activities could be used to foster children's reasoning abilities. Moreover, if you are to help children develop their reasoning ability and intermediate-level students recognize different types of reasoning, then you must be able to distinguish among intuitive, inductive, and deductive reasoning. This probe provides an opportunity to do so.

Word Problems

Word problems can be an entertaining way to practice reasoning and to encourage reflection about it. Consider the problem below.

■ **Tom, Dick, and Harry** (◆ 4-8).† Three golfers named Tom, Dick, and Harry are walking to the clubhouse. Tom, the best golfer of the three, always tells the truth. Dick sometimes tells the truth, while Harry, the worst golfer, never does. (1) Can you figure out who is who? Explain how you know. (Hint: First, figure out which one is Tom.) (2) What type of reasoning did you use to identify the characters above? Briefly justify your answer.

Some Games and Activities That Involve Reasoning

Clue (Parker Brothers), *Mastermind* (Pressman Toy Co.), and *20 Questions* all entail reasoning. Analyze each of these games and the following activities and indicate the type or types of reasoning involved. Justify your answer. (➪ **Teaching Tip:** Note that a teacher could have intermediate-level students do the same after they have tried an activity or played a game.)

 Guess My Rule. In this game, children are shown some examples of a pattern (see Example A below) or a relationship (see Example B below) and must decipher the underlying rule. Children can be asked to describe the rule and/or to make a prediction based on the rule. Does figuring out the rule involve the same kind of reasoning as making the prediction?

Example A: Can you tell what comes next? Why? ΔOΔΔOΔΔOΔ__

Example B: What function is represented by the following pairs of numbers and what is the value of
              x?   (-1,-1)(0,0)(1,1)(2,8)(3,*x*)

 In-Out (Function) Machines. A function machine is another *Guess-My-Rule* activity. It takes an input and uses a particular rule to translate it into an output. Does determining the rule of a function machine involve the same kind of reasoning as filling in the blank spaces in the table?

INPUT ⟶ ⟶ OUTPUT

IN	OUT
2	1
6	5
9	8
4	
8	
5	

 Am I? This activity involves starting with a definition and asking children to identify whether specific examples fit this definition. The following example involves two definitions:

An even number is an integer that is divisible by 2; an odd number is an integer that is not even. (a) Is 0 an even number? (b) Is -4 an even number? (c) Is -3 an odd number?

---

†This problem is based on a problem appearing on page 45 of *Mathematics: A Human Endeavor* by H. R. Jacobs, © 1982. The problem and accompanying graphic are used with the permission of the publisher: W. H. Freeman, San Francisco.

✿ Investigation 2.4: Evaluating Reasoning

◆ Reflecting on the limits of reasoning + informally evaluating conclusions ◆ Whole class

An ability to evaluate their own and others' conclusion is an essential skill for everyday life as well as mathematics. The questions of Part I are designed to prompt reflection about the limitations of intuitive, inductive, and deductive reasoning. Parts II to IV illustrate informal methods for evaluating a conjecture or a logical conclusion.

Part I: Limitations of Reasoning (◆ 5-8)

1. (a) Which straight line to the right is longer? (b) What kind of reasoning would children probably use to draw their conclusion? (c) How could they evaluate (check) their conclusion? (d) What point can this activity demonstrate?

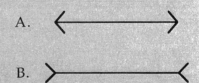

2. (a) Can you guess the rule used to choose the following numbers: 3, 5, 7? (b) What kind of reasoning was involved in drawing your conclusion? (c) Compare your conclusion to those of your group or class. Did everyone come to the same conclusion? (d) Even if everyone came to the same conclusion, is it necessarily true? Why or why not? (e) What point can this activity demonstrate?

3. Consider deductive arguments A and B below. (a) Is each valid (logical)? (b) Is the conclusion of each true (reasonable)? (c) What point about deductive reasoning does this activity demonstrate?

Argument A:
Teachers are grossly overpaid. (Premise 1)
Winnie is a teacher. (Premise 2)
Winnie is grossly overpaid. (Conclusion)

Argument B:
Teachers are slaves. (Premise 1)
Slaves are underpaid. (Premise 2)
Teachers are underpaid. (Conclusion)

4. Deductive reasoning is powerful in that it allows us to use what we know to draw conclusions about what we don't know. However, it leads to conclusions that are necessarily true if and only if (a) what is given (the premise) is true (see Question 3 above) and (b) the argument is valid or logical. (a) Which of the following arguments is logical—leads to a conclusion that necessarily follows from the premise that *all rhombuses have equal sides*? (Put differently, assuming that the premise is true, what conclusions are necessarily true?) (b) Which of the following is not logical—leads to a conclusion that does not necessarily follow from the premise? (c) If an argument is not logical, is the conclusion possibly true or necessarily false?

   A. Figure A has equal sides; therefore, it is a rhombus.
   B. Figure B does not have equal sides; therefore, it cannot be a rhombus.
   C. Figure C is a rhombus; therefore, all sides of Figure C must be equal.
   D. Figure D is not a rhombus; therefore, all the sides of Figure D must not be equal.

5. (a) The theorems below are commonly taught in plane geometry. Are each of these deductions true in all possible situations? (b) What does this imply about logical deductions?

   Theorem A: The shortest distance between two points is a straight line.
   Theorem B: If two lines are each perpendicular to a third line, then the two lines are parallel to each other.

☞ **Teaching Tip**. A teacher could introduce Question 4 above with a question such as, *"Do you think it is easy to distinguish between logical arguments and illogical arguments?"* Students could individually evaluate the four arguments listed in Question 4. The teacher could anonymously tally how the students responded on each item. The class could then discuss the results. Try this with your own group or class. Is there consensus on which arguments are logical and which are not? Disagreements about whether or not an argument is logical can be resolved by using the informal techniques described in Parts III and IV on the next two pages.

Investigation 2.4 continued

Part II: Using Counterexamples to Evaluate Conjectures (◆ 1-8)

A counterexample is an example that shows a statement is false. Even primary-level children can use counterexamples to evaluate *conjectures—educated guesses that stem from intuitive or inductive reasoning and that have neither been proven nor disproven.* For example, a first-grader might make the conjecture, "The largest number with two numbers [digits] in it is 90." Instead of correcting the child, a teacher could ask the class if they can think of any counterexamples (e.g., *91*). Can you come up with a counterexample to disprove each of the following four conjectures? Revise any false statements to make them true.

1. The sum of any four whole numbers is even.

2. The sum of any two whole numbers can be evenly divided by two.

3. The sum of any four whole numbers can be evenly divided by two.

4. The sum of any three whole numbers can be evenly divided by two.

Part III: Using Counterexamples to Evaluate Deductive Arguments (◆ 5-8)

Counterexamples can also serve as an informal means for identifying logical or valid arguments (conclusions that necessarily follow from a premise) and illogical or invalid arguments (conclusions that do not necessarily follow from a premise). Consider the following example.

Premise: If George makes his sister cry, then he is sent to his room.
Argument: George was sent to his room (condition), so he must have made his sister cry (conclusion).

Are there any other reasons why George might have been sent to his room? You bet. Some other reasons are (a) he made his mother cry, (b) he didn't finish his homework, or (c) he talked back to his father. Note that students need find only one counterexample to bring the validity of an argument into question. After you answer the following questions, discuss your answers with your group or class.

1. (a) Indicate whether each of the following arguments is valid or not. (b) For an invalid argument, cite a counterexample to prove that it is not necessarily true.

   A. If Gia studies, then she does well on tests. Gia did not study for her math test. Thus, she must not have done well on her math test.

   B. If a restaurant fails its health inspection, then it is closed down. Stu's Septic Diner is closed down; therefore, it must have failed its health inspection.

   C. If it rains, then Lorraine takes the bus. Lorraine is taking the bus; therefore, it must be raining.

   D. If Hank gets an A on his report card, then he gets a dollar. Hank did not get a dollar, so he must not have gotten an A on his report card.

2. The two arguments below are based on the following premise: If two triangles are congruent, then a side and an adjacent angle of each triangle must be equal. (a) Indicate whether each argument is valid or invalid. (b) For an invalid argument, cite a counterexample to prove that it is not necessarily true.

   A. Triangles A and B are not congruent; therefore, no side and its adjacent angle of each triangle is equal.

   B. Triangles C and D have a side and an adjacent angle that is equal; therefore, Triangles C and D are congruent.

Investigation 2.4 continued

Part IV: Using Euler (pronounced "oiler") Diagrams to Evaluate Deductive Arguments

Euler diagrams are another way of informally identifying valid and invalid arguments. To see how, let's consider an everyday example before tackling some more abstract examples.

Step 1: Represent the premises by setting up the Euler diagram.

Premise: If George makes his sister cry, then he is sent to his room. An Euler diagram represents a class with a large circle and a subclass with a small circle inside the large circle. As making his sister cry is but one reason for being sent to his room, it is represented by the inner circle.

Step 2: Locate the position of the argument's condition in the diagram and evaluate its conclusion.

Valid Argument About an Example. Does the conclusion of the following argument necessarily follow from what has been given: *George made his sister cry* (condition), *so he was sent to his room* (conclusion)? The condition of the argument can be located in only *one* place in the diagram—inside the small circle (designated by point p). Note that point p is also inside the large circle. Thus it necessarily follows from the diagram that George must have been sent to his room. The argument, then, is logical (valid).

Valid Argument About a Nonexample. (A nonexample here refers to *the negation of a statement.* For example, "George was not sent to his room" is the negation of the statement "George was sent to his room.") Does the conclusion of the following argument necessarily follow from the premise and the condition: *George was not sent to his room* (condition), *so he did not make his sister cry* (conclusion)? The condition of the argument can be located in only *one* place in the diagram—outside the large circle (designated by point q). Note that point q is also outside the small circle. Thus it necessarily follows from the diagram that George was not sent to his room. The argument, then, is logical (valid).

Invalid Argument About an Example. Now consider the following argument: *George was sent to his room* (condition), *so he made his sister cry* (conclusion). Unfortunately, the condition of the argument can be located in *two* places in the diagram—inside the small circle (designated by point r) or outside the small circle but inside the large circle (designated by point s). Note that point r implies that the conclusion is true—that George was sent to his room because he made his sister cry. However, point s implies that the conclusion is not true—that George may have been sent to his room for some other reason. In brief, the argument is invalid or not logical, because the conclusion that *George made his sister cry* does not *necessarily* follow from the premise and condition.

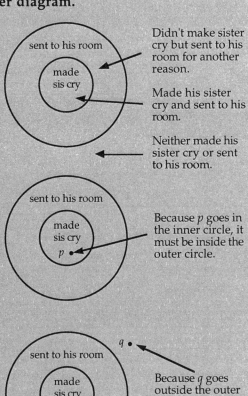

Didn't make sister cry but sent to his room for another reason.

Made his sister cry and sent to his room.

Neither made his sister cry or sent to his room.

Because p goes in the inner circle, it must be inside the outer circle.

Because q goes outside the outer circle, it must be outside the inner circle.

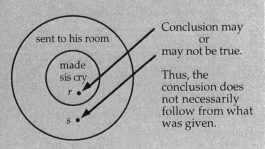

Conclusion may or may not be true.

Thus, the conclusion does not necessarily follow from what was given.

Investigation 2.4 continued

Invalid Argument About a Nonexample. Does the conclusion of the following argument necessarily follow from what has been given: *George did not make his sister cry* (condition), *so he was not sent to his room* (conclusion)? Unfortunately, the condition of the argument can again be located in *two* places in the diagram—outside the small circle but inside the large one (designated by point *t*) *or* outside both the small and large circles (designated by point *u*). Note that point *u* implies that the conclusion is true—that George was not sent to his room. However, point *t* implies that the conclusion is not true—that George may have been sent to his room for some other reason. In brief, the argument is invalid or not logical, because the conclusion that *he was not sent to his room does* not *necessarily* follow from the premise and condition—it may or may not be true.

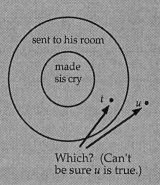

Which? (Can't be sure *u* is true.)

1. (a) Draw an Euler diagram to represent the premises of Question 4 of Part I (*All rhombuses have equal sides*). (b) Illustrate how the diagram can be used to evaluate the validity of each of the arguments a, b, c, and d listed in Question 4 of Part I.

2. One of the biggest difficulties students have in using Euler diagrams is setting up the diagram properly. (a) Evaluate each of the following Euler diagrams. Is it set up correctly? That is, does the outer circle represent the larger class? (b) If not, draw a correct Euler diagram. (c) Illustrate how the diagram can be used to evaluate each conclusion in Question 1 of Part III.

A. Premise: If Gia studies, then she does well on tests.

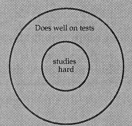

B. Premise: If a restaurant fails its health inspection, then it is closed down.

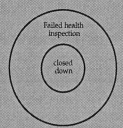

C. Premise: If it rains, then Lorraine takes the bus.

D. Premise: If Hank gets an A on his report card, then he gets a dollar.

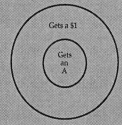

3. After examining several examples of Euler diagrams, Jennifer noted, "The *if*-part of a premise is always represented by the inner circle; the *then*-part of the premise, by the outer circle" Is Jennifer's observation always correct, sometimes correct, or never correct? Why?

4. (a) Draw an Euler diagram to represent the premise posed in Question 2 of Part III. (b) Illustrate how it can be used to identify whether each of the conclusions (A and B) is valid or not.

5. Show how an Euler diagram could be used to evaluate the following argument: If a number is a multiple of 8, then it is a multiple of 4 (premise). The product of 2980 and 15 is not a multiple of 8 (condition). Therefore, this product is not a multiple of 4 (conclusion).

⧠ **Introduce sorting and classifying activities concretely and early.** Such activities can be used to involve even primary-level children in logical (deductive) reasoning (e.g., *if* the block is red, *then* it goes in the pile with the fire truck and the apple). Ideally, such activities would be done in a purposeful manner (see, e.g., Activity File 2.1 to the right and Activity File 2.2 below).

⧠ **Encourage children to informally evaluate conjectures (intuitive and inductive conclusions) and deductions** (see, e.g., Box 2.8 on the next page). Throughout the elementary years, students should be prompted to consider additional examples (see, e.g., Box 2.9 on page 2-32) and to look for counterexamples (see, e.g., Parts II and III of Investigation 2.4 on page 2-27). This can lead them to reject a conjecture altogether or amend a general conclusion by making it more specific. For example, if a child conjectures that "multiplying with an odd number must results in an odd product," a teacher could ask the class, "Does this

---

🍎 **Activity File 2.1: The Investigative Approach to Sorting and Classifying**

◆ Sorting + classifying ◆ K-8 ◆ Any number

There are numerous opportunities in other content areas to sort and classify. In science, students might sort things into two categories, such as living and nonliving things, things that roll or don't roll, magnetic or nonmagnetic items, objects that float or sink, or foods high in (> 3 grams) cholesterol foods or low in cholesterol. Examples with three or more categories include classifying rocks as igneous, sedimentary, or metamorphic, and sorting foods into food groups. In language arts, students could sort characters into heroes and villains; words into nouns and verbs; or grammatical examples into those requiring a comma, those where a comma is optional, and those where a comma should not be used. In Social Studies, countries could be classified as democratic or not, predominantly Muslim or not, etc.

🍎 **Activity File 2.2:** *Classifying and Diagramming Our Class*[†]

◆ Sorting + classifying + using Venn diagrams ◆ K-4 ◆ Whole group

Ask a class, "How could we split the class up into two groups?" Students may offer various criteria such as girls or boys, left-handed or right-handed, and tall or short. The last example leads naturally to a discussion of "What is tall?" and underscores the importance of defining a criterion clearly. Some students may suggest criteria such as 9-years-old or *not* 9-years-old. Note that criteria such as tall or short can also be expressed in the same manner: tall or *not* tall.

Sort the class according to a criterion. For example, have hot-lunch children go to one side of the room; cold-lunch children, to the other. Note that *all* the children eat either a hot lunch *or* a cold lunch, that *some* eat a hot lunch and those who do *not* eat a cold lunch, and that *none* of the children remain in their seats. This demonstrates that a set is the sum of its subsets and that, in the case of a concept and its negation, every element in a set must be in one subset or the other.

Have the class consider other criteria. Do two mutually exclusive characteristics always completely partition the class? Consider the following criteria: Youngest in the family or oldest in the family; has brown hair or blond hair; and walked to school this morning or rode the bus to school this morning. Have the class consider, for example, whether all children who did not walk to school this morning rode the bus. Are two characteristics always mutually exclusive? Consider the following criteria: Have a cat or have a dog; have a brother or have a sister; walk to school or take the bus. Does having a cat necessarily mean a child does not have a dog?

Teams of children can then each choose a criterion, use construction paper to devise a Venn diagam, and canvas the class to see where each class member fits into the diagram. With primary-age children, particularly, it can be helpful to discuss how to set up each Venn diagram, including how many loops are necessary and whether or not the loops interlock or are concentric. Each team could also summarize their findings to the class. The diagrams then could be hung up as a display: "Our Class." This would be ideal before a Parents' Visitation Night.

[†]Based on a lesson in the Nuffield Mathematics Project described in *Logic*, © 1972 and published for the Nuffield Foundation in the U.S. by John Wiley and Sons, New York.

apply to all examples of multiplication with an odd number?" Students should find instances where the conjecture makes sense (e.g., 3 x 5 and 9 x 7) and others where it doesn't (e.g., 3 x 4 and 9 x 8). This could lead the class to revise the conjecture: "Multiplying two odd numbers results in an odd product." Moreover, children need to recognize that even if a conjecture holds up over a wide range of examples, there is always the possibility of finding an exception. Thus, conjectures must be justified by more certain means, such as by deductive reasoning. For instance, after considering numerous examples, a class concluded, "All prime numbers are odd." A teacher could encourage students to apply logical reasoning: "If our conjecture is true, what must we conclude about 2? [It can't be prime because its even.] Does this conclusion make sense. [No, because 2 fits the definition of prime: It has only two factors, 1 and itself.] Elementary-level students can use Venn diagrams to informally assess conjectures (see Box 2.10 on page 2-32). Intermediate-level students can also use Euler diagrams to informally evaluate the validity of deductive arguments (see, e.g., Part IV of Investigation 2.4 on pages 2-28 and 2-29).

Box 2.8: Helping Students Evaluate Their Conjectures[3]

Mrs. Song presented her third-grade class with the following problem on the chalkboard:

■ **The Tallest Child (◆ 3-5).** Alton is taller than Brittney, who is taller than Cameron or Dot. Of these four children, who is the tallest and who is the shortest?

Vignette	Comments
Akiko commented, "I can tell just by looking that it can't be answered."	A student made a conjecture based on what appeared to be intuitive reasoning.
Mrs. Song responded, "Are you saying there is insufficient information to answer either question? How could you convince others? Would drawing a picture help?"	The teacher encouraged the child to reflect on her conjecture and consider how she could defend it.
The class reached a consensus that Alton was the tallest child. Davis added enthusiastically, "Oh, I know who the shortest is: It's Brittney." Asked to justify his conclusion, Davis answered, "Because Alton is taller than Brittney."	After using the heuristic of drawing a picture, the class correctly deduced who is the tallest child. Another child overlooked one of the constraints specified by the problem and jumped to a conclusion about who is the shortest child.
"Does that by itself make Brittney the smallest?" questioned Mrs. Song. After Davis answered *no*, Mrs. Song followed up with, "What other information in the problem either supports or refutes your conclusion?"	The teacher helped the child to consider whether his answer fit all the facts.
"Wait," retorted Davis, "Brittney is taller than Cameron or Dot, so she can't be the smallest."	Quickly assessing that his conjecture was ill-founded, the child adjusted his reasoning.
Avraham offered, "Dot must be the smallest."	Perhaps accustomed to questions that can always be answered, a student made a guess. The teacher then asked the child to consider the implications of his answer and whether the information given was consistent with it.
"If so, what else does this imply, and does the problem support your claim?" asked Mrs. Song.	
Avraham reasoned, "If Dot was the smallest, then Cameron would be bigger than her. The problem doesn't really say. I guess we can't tell who is smallest."	

Box 2.9: Encouraging Children to Evaluate Additional Examples

Mr. Adams challenged his third-grade class to find a winning strategy for the game *Poison* (see Problem 10 of Investigation 2.2 on page 2-14). He encouraged them to work with relatively simple cases (small numbers of items), to make a table, and to look for a pattern.

Number of items	1	2	3	4	5	6	7	8
Player who wins			1	2	1			

From their partially completed tables, such as the one shown above, several groups concluded that if there were an even number of items, then a player should choose to go second; if there were an odd number of items, then a player should choose to go first. Instead of indicating that this conjecture was right or wrong, Mr. Adams asked, "Who do you think will win if there are six items?" The students predicted that the second player should win. Mr. Adams then encouraged them to check out their prediction and systematically examine other cases.

Questions for Reflection

1. Was the students' prediction correct?

2. What lessons about conjectures based on inductive reasoning was Mr. Adams trying to make by prompting his students to make a prediction and check it?

3. Evaluate Tara's description of the pattern her group found[4]:

> Nuber Pattern — Tara
>
> The number pattern that we got is 2 1 2 1 2 1 2, from one to ten. If you want to be first, 2 you want to be second and so on. I figured it out with some wonderful friends.

4. For a 20-item game, should you choose to go first or second?

Box 2.10: Using a Venn Diagram to Sort and Evaluate Data and Address Conjectures†

After Pet Day, in which the class tallied and graphed their favorite pets, several students wondered if their preferences were generally shared. Cherish, a cat lover, conjectured that perhaps dogs weren't the most popular pet in every school. Sakina conjectured that perhaps cats would be more popular in rural areas than suburban. Chanmi proposed that birds might be more popular than either cats or dogs in urban areas. To test these conjectures, the class devised a simple questionnaire and posted it on an electronic bulletin board. Responses were recorded by sticking animal icons on a Venn diagram consisting of two interlocking circles labeled Urban and Rural. The intersection of the circles represented Surburban. The class analyzed the display for patterns and found that while horses were relatively popular in rural areas only, cats were quite popular in all areas but particularly in the suburbs.

† Based on *Mining Mathematics through the Internet* by Kristine Lynes, *Teaching Children Mathematics*, Vol. 3, No. 7, pp. 394-396.

2•3 MATHEMATICS AS COMMUNICATING

Figure 2.3: What We Have Here is a Failure to Communicate

PEANUTS reprinted by permission of UFS, Inc.

In a traditional skills approach, communication is largely a one-way affair. Teachers provide information; students listen quietly. Because they receive only a small fraction of their teachers' attention and sporadic feedback and because they are not allowed to talk with their peers, children learn mathematics essentially in isolation. As Figure 2.3 illustrates, attempting to make sense of (abstract) lectures and assigned work alone can often be frustrating. In Subunit 2•3•1, we consider why opening the channels of communication in the classroom is important. In Subunit 2•3•2, we discuss how this can be accomplished.

2•3•1 MATHEMATICS AND LEARNING: REASONS FOR FOCUSING ON COMMUNICATING

Why should mathematics instruction focus on communicating? Both mathematics and mathematical learning are, at heart, social activities (Schoenfeld, 1992).

Mathematics as a Social Activity

Mathematical Proofs and Theorems. Mathematicians first test their conjectures themselves by developing a formal proof (usually a logical or deductive proof). After finding convincing evidence for a conjecture, they submit the generalization and proof to the review and criticism of other mathematicians (e.g., Bell, 1976). An idea accepted as proven by the mathematical community at large is called a (formal) theorem. To provide a basis for understanding the roles of formal proofs and theorems in high school, an elementary teacher can help students recognize the social nature of knowledge—the need for public verification of ideas (Clements & Battista, 1992). This can probably be best achieved by encouraging them to propose, defend, and evaluate conjectures and proofs themselves.

Mathematics as a Language. Mathematics provides an invaluable tool for communicating a variety of ideas clearly, precisely, and succinctly. Indeed, it has been called the "language of science" (Dantzig, 1954) and serves as the language of engineering and commerce as well. Because people the world over can use it to communicate despite differences in their native tongues, it has even been called "the universal language" (Jacobs, 1982). Success, then, in a wide variety of fields depends on mastering the "second" language of mathematics. As in learning any second language, mastering the language of mathematics can be facilitated by actually using it in purposeful efforts to communicate ideas.

Mathematics Learning as a Social Activity

Although teacher-to-pupil communication is important, pupil-to-teacher and pupil-to-pupil interactions are crucial for a number of reasons. It gives children the opportunity to propose ideas and to test their own and others' ideas. This is essential for the development of mathematical thinking and understanding. As Piaget (1928) noted, "Surely it must be the shock of our thought coming into contact with that of others [that] produces doubt and the desire to prove . . . . Proof is the outcome of argument" (p. 204). THE OPPORTUNITY TO EXCHANGE IDEAS IS NECESSARY FOR CHILDREN TO DEVELOP THE DISPOSITION AND STRATEGIES NECESSARY TO THINK CRITICALLY FOR THEMSELVES AND TO ANALYZE OTHERS' IDEAS CRITICALLY.

Note that peer-to-peer interactions fostered by small-group collaboration greatly increases children's opportunities to be actively involved in a discussion. In traditional instruction, only one child at a time has a chance to address the class, and relatively few members of the class may have a chance to express their reactions. With small groups, many children can speak simultaneously, and practically everyone can be involved in providing feedback.

2•3•2 TEACHING: OPENING CHANNELS OF COMMUNICATION

Build A Mathematical Community

To open up communications, teachers need to build a mathematical community. This can be promoted by encouraging informal justifications and group consensus, developing a communal language, and using cooperative-learning groups.

Foster Informal Justifications and Group Consensus. Encourage students to provide informal proofs and to agree on informal theorems (Balacheff, 1988). *An informal proof is an informal justification of a conjecture and can take the form of examples, explanations, demonstrations, or informal deductive arguments. An informal theorem is an informal proof accepted by a group or class.*

∞ **Regularly ask children to informally justify their conjectures and answers**. Habitually follow up students' contributions with responses such as "Prove it," "What makes you think so?" "What's your evidence?" or simply "Why?" This can help them see that a justification is at least as important as an answer. Moreover, encouraging children to explain their thinking verbally or in writing can prompt reflection (NCTM, 1989), and this can help them see connections or discern gaps in their understanding.

∞ **Involve the whole class in evaluating conjectures and informal proofs**. Regularly ask, for example, "Does everyone agree?" In the give-and-take of an open discussion, it should quickly become evident that not just any explanation or informal proof will do. A justification must be plausible—it must be convincing to others. All children need experience in fashioning arguments that are convincing to others (Silver et al., 1990).

∞ **As children increase in age and experience, use stricter standards for what is a convincing argument**. Whereas young children should be helped to see that one or two examples are not sufficient to prove a rule and should be encouraged to find additional examples, older children should be helped to see that even numerous examples do not constitute an iron-clad proof. For instance, 50, 100, or 1,000 examples do not prove that whole-number multiplication always results in a product that is larger than the factors. Such a rule can be disproved by such counterexamples as 0 x 8 or 3 x 0. Intermediate-level students can be helped to see that mathematical arguments begin with agreed-on principles (premises) and must follow specific rules (the rules of logic). They might even be encouraged to spell out an informal deductive argument with the challenge: "How can you prove that logically?"

Develop a Communal Language. For children to adopt mathematics as a communal language and use it effectively, this language needs to be introduced carefully.

∞ **Introduce formal definitions and notations purposefully**. Personalized and experience-based lessons such as carrying out projects, preparing for a field trip, or keeping track of team scores can forge a genuine purpose for communicating mathematical ideas (Curcio, 1990). This, in turn, can create a real need for using (introducing, learning, and practicing) mathematical terms and symbols.

∞ **Introduce definitions and notations by building on children's informal or existing knowledge**. Introduce mathematical and symbolic language gradually. Children can be encouraged to move through four stages of describing real mathematical situations listed and illustrated in Box 2.10 on the next page (Irons & Irons, 1989).

Use Cooperative Learning Groups. Small-group work gives children a chance to share questions, insights, and strategies. The result can be greater understanding (e.g., Cobb, 1985), higher mathematical achievement (e.g., Davidson, 1990; Johnson & Johnson, 1989; Slavin, 1983), better problem solving (Noddings, 1985), greater confidence (e.g., Cobb et al., 1991), and more effective social and communications skills. However, simply putting students together in small groups does not guarantee cooperation or success (Lester, 1989) (see Probe 2.4 on page 2-37). Teachers need to help children learn how to work together so that all members benefit. To maximize success, keep groups small (to about four), help students address problems directly and rationally, foster mutual effort and social skills, and use journals to monitor individual progress and group difficulties.

Foster All Aspects of Communicating

Help children to communicate mathematical ideas in a variety of ways: by representing (e.g., creating a concrete model or a symbolic expression), listening, reading, discussing, and writing. Box 2.11 (on pages 2-35 and 2-36) describes a game that can be used at any grade level to foster more precise mathematical communication. Investigation 2.5 (page 2-38) illustrates another entertaining game that can serve to introduce geometric terms purposefully and can create a real need for listening, discussing, and recording.

✐ In the past, writing in particular was not considered a natural part of mathematics or included in mathematics instruction (Wilde, 1991). The NCTM (1989), however, recommend putting more emphasis on expressing mathematical ideas in writing. Writing activities can focus on the process of communicating ideas (the communicative approach) or on writing to learn (the reflective approach). The latter can be thought of as "thinking aloud on paper" (Rose, 1989) and involves using writing to foster reflection and understanding (Connolly, 1989). Math autobiogra-

Box 2.10: Four Stages of Introducing a Concept Using Multiplication as an Example

1. *Natural-Language Stage* entails using children's own language: *Ricardo's father gave him a block of stamps with Elvis' picture on it. The block had 4 stamps in each row and there were 3 rows. So Ricardo had 12 Elvis stamps altogether. I love stamps even without Elvis.*

2. *Material-Language Stage* involves using the terminology of a concrete or a pictorial model: Three rows of 4 cubes makes 12 cubes altogether, which after trading is 1 long (ten) and 2 cubes (ones).

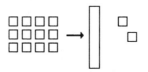

3. *Shorthand Stage* entails using a few words to summarize mathematical situations: *3 rows of 4 → 12*

4. *Symbolic-Language Stage* involves using mathematical terminology or symbols as an even more economical way to record mathematical situations: *3 × 4 = 12*

Box 2.11: *Talking Math*

Reflecting on her students' inability to use mathematical language precisely, Miss Brill suddenly had an inspiration. She took a stack of plain paper and wrote a single mathematical term on each piece. In class, she chose a page and announce the term. Then Miss Brill allowed each student to make a statement containing and/or describing the word. Each statement had to be a complete sentence. One word or phrase would not be acceptable. When a word had been adequately described, Miss Brill would move on to a new word. To the word "triangle," class members made such responses as, "A triangle is a kind of shape"; "A triangle has three sides"; "Connect three points and you get a triangle"; and "A right triangle has a 90 degree angle."

Often the students' statements provided opportunities for further investigation and learning. "Try to draw three points that when connected will *not* result in a triangle," Miss Brill said as she wrote the challenge on the chalkboard. During spare moments that day, a number of students tackled the challenge, and some were successful. Before dismissal, students displayed their efforts and concluded that, indeed, three connected points sometimes did not result in a triangle. Miss Brill introduced a new word, "collinear," which was written on paper and added to the stack of math words.

An excited Lakesha asked, "Miss Brill, can we make our math words into a game show? We could have a host and teams of four. The host would hold up a word that one team member and the class could see. The other team members would have their backs to the host so that they could not see the word. The first team member would have to give clues so that the other team members could guess the word. If the 'guessers' got stuck, the 'clue-giver' could decide to 'pass' and proceed with the next word. The team would have one minute to try up to five words."

Miss Brill accepted the role of first host, shuffled the papers, and took the top five words for the first game. Lakesha served as the first clue-giver and her teammates Jessica, Cheryl, and Kisha, served as the first guessers. Tom served as the timekeeper. Miss Brill held up the first word so that Lakesha and the class could see it, and Tom started a stopwatch.

Lakesha: "A dot."

Jessica: "A point."

Lakesha: "A number with a dot in it."

Cheryl: "A decimal?"

Miss Brill: "Right." The teacher then displayed the second word.

Lakesha: "What do you get when you divide?"

Jessica: "The answer."

Lakesha: "The name for that answer."

Box 2.11 continued

Jessica: "Oh, the remainder."

Lakesha: "No, the name for the answer to eight divided by two?"

Jessica: "Four?"

Lakesha: "The answer to any division. [After it was clear the guessers weren't going to respond, Lakesha decided to pass, and Miss Brill displayed the third word.] A round shape."

Kisha: "A circle."

Miss Brill announced, "Right," and held up the fourth word.

Lakesha: "Three, five, seven."

Cheryl: "Odd numbers."

Lakesha: "No. Two, eleven, and thirteen."

"Primes," Jessica adduced just before Tom pronounced that time was up.

Miss Brill: "Primes is right. Lakesha's team had three words correct."

The game was dubbed *Talking Math* and became a regular activity in Miss Brill's class. Whenever there were a few extra minutes, a student would suggest, "Let's play *Talking*

Math!" When a team of students were stuck on a word and ran out of time, their classmates were eager to suggest clues that could have been used. As new terms were introduced, Miss Brill wrote each on a piece of paper, laminated it, and placed it in the pile. Multiple packs were made for small group use.

Some students invented a competitive variation of *Talking Math* that could be played by three to nine children. In this variation, the host chose the words and gave the clues. The first team (one to four children) to raise a hand could respond. Ties were handled by flipping a coin. If the first team was wrong, the second team was given an opportunity to respond. The team that identified the most words within a specified time or number of words won.

✐ In time, several students proposed a more challenging variation of the game they called *Talking and Writing Math*. To score points, a contestant not only had to specify the correct term but write it correctly.

▣ In addition to using their textbook, class members began to search out and use other references as a source of terms and definitions. Judi found a web site titled "Mathematics Dictionary" (http://www.mathpro.com/math/glossary/glossary.html).

phies and math journals can entail communicative, reflective, or both types of writing. For example, with "Divided Page" journals, students can record their problem solutions, drawings, and calculations on the righthand side of the page and think aloud, expressing whatever thoughts and feelings they wish, on the lefthand side of the page (Tobias, 1989).

☞ Try Probe 2.4 (page 2-37) and Investigation 2.5 (page 2-38).

PARTING THOUGHTS

"The first duty of [teachers] of mathematics is to do . . . everything in [their] power to develop [their] students' ability to solve problems" (Polya, 1949, p. 2). "A teacher of mathematics has a great opportunity. If [she] fills [her] allot-

ted time with drilling [her] students in routine operations, [she] kills their interest, hampers their intellectual development, and misuses [her] opportunity. But if [she] challenges the curiosity of [her] students by setting them problems proportionate to their knowledge, and helps them to solve their problems with stimulating questions, [she] may give them a taste for, and some means of independent thinking" (Polya, 1957, p. v). "Problem solving [then] should be a central focus of the mathematics curriculum . . . . [It] is not a distinct topic but a process that should permeate the entire program and provide the context in which concepts and skills can be learned" (NCTM, 1989, p. 23).

Reasoning and communicating are also critical processes in mathematical sense making. "If we want to help our stu- (continued on page 2-39)

➤ Probe 2.4: Some Common Difficulties with Small-Group Work

The aim of this probe is to familiarize you with some common difficulties that students of all ages—including college-level students—experience with group work. Read the vignettes below and answer the accompanying questions.

Vignette I: A Lack of Consensus

Ms. Socrates had her groups decide answers and solutions by consensus (unanimous agreement) rather than by majority vote. Miss Brill adopted this policy when she started experimenting with cooperative learning. However, she quickly ran into a problem. Most of the groups had trouble getting all members to agree on a decision. After one particularly emotional battle, Andy complained, "We've been arguing all period and everyone agrees with me except LeMar. Can our group turn in two solutions that will each be graded separately? That way we will get the grade we deserve and LeMar will get what he deserves."

1. (a) What are the advantages of requiring groups to reach a unanimous agreement rather than using majority rule? (b) What are the advantages of using majority rule? (c) By what means do juries decide on a verdict and why?

2. Aside from the logistical consideration of having more work to correct, what are the disadvantages of Andy's proposal?

3. Miss Brill agreed to Andy's proposal with the following amendment. The grades for the two factions would be *averaged*. (a) Miss Brill's method of grading the group's factions more or less fair than Andy's recommendation? (b) Why might Miss Brill have suggested this grading scheme?

4. How else might a group resolve differences of opinion?

Vignette II: Different Paces

The next time the class worked in groups, Miss Brill noticed that Andy, Rodney, and Jose looked glum. "How are things going boys?" she inquired.

"LeMar gets the answer too quickly," answered Rodney.

"He tells us the answer before we even have a chance to finish reading the problem," amplified Andy.

"Not only that," added Jose, "he goes on to solve the next problem without bothering to explain to us how he got the answer to the first problem."

1. What might Miss Brill suggest to remedy this situation?

2. Challenging the speedier LeMar with extensions of problems while his groupmates worked at their own pace would have what advantages and what disadvantages?

Vignette III: The Buddy System

A short time later, Miss Brill checked on LeMar's group again and asked if they reached agreement on the solution to a problem. Because LeMar and Andy disagreed, she asked the others in the group what they thought.

Rodney answered, "I agree with Andy."

To probe his reasoning, Miss Brill asked, "Why?"

"Because he's my friend!" retorted Rodney.

"Do you always agree with your friends?" commented a surprised Miss Brill.

"You do if you don't want to lose them," answered Rodney.

1. Do you suppose social factors often play the deciding role in how children vote in their groups?

2. Miss Brill knew it was time for a serious talk about the rules of evidence. What could she say and do to address this issue?

Vignete IV: A Group Meltdown

Miss Brill had been using cooperative-learning groups for several weeks when she noticed that no one in LeMar's group, except LeMar, was working on the problem. "How about getting together to discuss this problem?" she suggested.

"Hey, I'm not going to say anything," responded Andy. "The last time I did, my answer was wrong and everyone blamed me."

"Well, it wasn't fair," snapped LeMar. "I had the right answer. We would have gotten it right if you had listened to me."

"Mr. Show Boat here thinks he's always right and always wants to do things his way," interjected Rodney. "What's the point of trying?"

"Well, I wouldn't have to do everything if you weren't such a veggie," retorted LeMar.

1. Many students, such as Andy, feel threatened when openly challenged. What can a teacher say and do to help them feel more comfortable with this crucial aspect of learning?

2. How could a teacher respond to a child such as LeMar, who feels cheated because his group did not accept his correct solution?

3. How can a teacher deal with a group's complaint that one of its members is a freeloader?

4. What can a teacher say or do to help a low-achieving child feel comfortable about participating in a group?

5. How can a teacher help students learn the social skills (e.g., resolving conflicts amiably) necessary for effective group work?

⟡ Investigation 2.5: Communication Games

Activity I: *Guess the Figure* (◆ Geometric thinking + reasoning + communication skills ◆ 1-8 ◆ Class partitioned into groups of four). *Guess the Figure* is an excellent game for introducing and practicing geometric terminology, exercising spatial and deductive reasoning, and sharpening communication skills. Distribute a geoboard and rubber bands to each group and to a master of ceremonies (MC). (The teacher can serve as the MC or choose a student to do so.) If geoboards are unavailable, dot-matrix paper could be substituted. Without showing the class, the MC creates a geometric shape on a geoboard such as the one shown to the right.

Two versions of the game can be played. The objective of the *Congruent Version* is to be the first group to create a *congruent* shape on its geoboard—*create a design of the same shape and size*, irrespective of orientation. The objective of the *Similar Version* is to be the first group to create a *similar* shape—*create a design of the same shape* but not necessarily of the same size or orientation. On their turn, a group may ask a question that can be answered yes or no. For example, does the figure contain a right angle? A group may use their turn to show the MC (and the rest of the class) their educated guess. If incorrect, the MC announces, "No," and play continues with the next group's turn.

Note that initially, the range of designs can be limited to a single polygon. With sophisticated players, the limits can be eased to include open as well as closed figures and multiple polygons. Limits on designs are important because if children serve as the MC, some will be tempted to devise designs so complex that it will be extremely difficult, if not nearly impossible, for players to identify them.

Questions for Reflection

1. How might playing the game promote learning of geometric content (concepts)?

2. What type of reasoning does the game entail? Justify your answer.

3. (a) Young children, particularly, create a design and ask if it is the correct figure on their first turn. Is this a good idea? Why or why not? (b) When trying to narrow down possibilities, should initial questions be specific or general? Why?

4. What lessons about communicating might be learned by playing this game?

5. How might the game foster a positive disposition toward mathematics?

Activity II: *Design Teaching* (◆ Communication and social skills + geometry terminology ◆ K-8 ◆ Small groups). The aim of *Design Teaching* is for a "teacher" to communicate verbally a description of a design so that a "student" or small group of "students" can reproduce it. The design can be drawn (see Figure A) or made of manipulative materials such as pattern blocks (see Figure B) or geoboards and rubberbands (see Figure C). The "teacher" can create his or her own design or a design can be provided. The complexity of the design can be tailored to the developmental level of the students.

The rules specify that the "teacher" may verbally describe the design but may not gesture or picture the design. To ensure that only verbal communication is used, the teacher could sit on one side of a barrier with the design and the "student(s)" could sit on the other side. The students may ask questions at any time. Indeed, a wise teacher encourages questions. The teacher should be given an opportunity to prepare a "lesson" on the design—to organize his or her thoughts about how to best communicate about the design. The activity can be played with a time limit, which can create pressure to communicate efficiently and add an element of excitement. The teacher's success can be gauged by whether or not the student reproduced the design. If there are a group of students, then success can be gauged by how many could accurately reproduce the design.

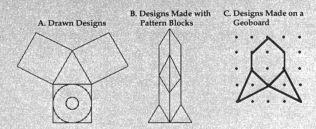

A. Drawn Designs   B. Designs Made with Pattern Blocks   C. Designs Made on a Geoboard

dents to value mathematics, to develop mathematical power, and to have the confidence to tackle new solutions, we must pose interesting, challenging problem situations and give our students time to explore, to formulate problems, to develop strategies, to make conjectures, to reason about the validity of these conjectures, to discuss, to argue, to predict, and, of course, to raise more questions!" (Lappan & Schram, 1989, p. 30). "Any mathematics lesson can incorporate opportunities to reason and to communicate ideas" (Lappan & Schram, 1989, p. 29).

RESOURCES

SOME INSTRUCTIONAL RESOURCES

☞ Valuable resources on *problem solving, reasoning,* and *communicating* include: **About Teaching Mathematics: A K-8 Resource** by Marilyn Burns (© 1992 by Math Solutions Publications, distributed by the Cuisenaire Company of America, Inc.), **Activities with Attributes: Experiences in Logical Problem Solving** by Maria Marolda (© 1993, Dale Seymour Publications), **Cooperative Learning in Mathematics** edited by Neil Davidson (© 1990, Addison-Wesley), **The Elementary Mathematician** published by COMAP (57 Bedford St., Suite 210, Lexington, MA 02173. Phone: 617-862-7878. FAX: 617-863-1202), **From Puzzles to Projects: Solving Problems All the Way** by Johnny and Ann Baker (© 1993, Heinemann), **How to Evaluate Progress in Problem Solving** by Randall Charles, Frank Lester, and Phares O'Daffer (© 1987, NCTM), **Language in Mathematics** edited by Jennie Bickmore-Brand (© 1993, Heinemann), **Language in the Mathematics Classroom: Talking, Representing, Recording** by Rachel Griffiths and Margaret Clyne (© 1994, Heinemann), **Make It Simpler** by Carol Meyer and Tom Sallee (© 1983, Addison-Wesley), **The Middle Grades Mathematics Project** by Glenda Lappan and others (© 1986, Addison-Wesley), **The Pattern Factory: Elementary Problem Solving Through Patterning** by Ann Roper and Linda Harvey (© 1980, Creative Publications), **The Problem Solver 3: Activities for Learning Problem Solving Strategies** by Shirley Hoogeboom and Judy Goodnow (© 1987, Creative Publications), **Problem-Solving Experiences in Mathematics** by Randall I. Charles, Robert P. Mason, Joan M. Nofsinger, and Catherine A. White (© 1985-1996, Addison-Wesley), **Teaching Problem Solving: What Why & How** by Randall Charles and

Frank Lester (© 1989, Dale Seymour Publications), **ThinkAbility** by Marco Meirovitz (© 1995, LEARNING Inc.), **30 Wild and Wonderful Math Stories to Develop Problem-Solving Skills, Grades 4-8** by Dan Greenberg (© 1992, Scholastic Inc.), **What's Your Problem? Posing and Solving Mathematical Problems, K-2** by Penny Skinner (© 1991, Heinemann), and **Writing to Learn Mathematics: Strategies that Work, K-12** by Joan Countryman (© 1992, Heinemann).

A SAMPLE OF CHILDREN'S LITERATURE

🐾 **The I Hate Mathematics! Book** by Marilyn Burns, © 1975 by Little, Brown and Company, Boston. After listing examples of disparaging comments made by children about mathematics (e.g., "Mathematicians have little pig eyes"), readers are encouraged to vent their own feelings about mathematics. The book suddenly changes tack, noting it will use fun and games to change mathematical weaklings into mathematical heavyweights. The secret, it announces, is that "YOU ARE A MATHEMATICAL GENIUS IN DISGUISE!" and that all it takes is to reorganize what is already in the reader's head (p. 9). In other words, it advances the belief that anyone can develop mathematical aptitude by learning to exploit their existing knowledge more effectively. Burns goes on to note that "the password of mathematics is patterns" (p. 9). Written for intermediate-level students, this book is a rich source of problems involving combinations and permutations, ratios, large numbers, primes, and probability.

TIPS ON USING TECHNOLOGY

Calculators

▦ **Cooperative Problem Solving with Calculators** by Ann Roper, Shirley Hoogeboom, and Judy Goodnow, © 1991, and **The Problem Solver with Calculators** by Terrence G. Coburn, Shirley Hoogeboom, and Judy Goodnow, © 1989, both published by Creative Publications.

▦ **Problem Solving Using the Calculator** by Joan Duea, George Immerzeek, Earl Ockenga, and John Tarr. Chapter 12 (pp. 117-126) in *Problem Solving in School Mathematics: 1980*

Yearbook, edited by Stephen Krulik and Robert E. Reys and published by the NCTM.

Computers

The Internet is a rich source of problems. For example, Terri Santi's Homepage for New Math Teachers (http://www.clarityconnect.com/webpages/terri/terri.html) includes a "Best Problem of the Month" (e.g., What is the remainder when 2^{50} is divided by 3?). Accompanying the problem is a teaching tip ("Tell students that when a problem seems to be impossible or overwhelming, it usually has a simpler solution that can be found by using a pattern") and the solution. See also the "Internet Center for Mathematics Problems" (http://www.mathpro.com/math/mathCenter.html). Examples of problem-solving and reasoning software include:

The Adventures of Jasper Woodbury video-disk problem-solving series created by the Cognition and Technology Group, Peabody College of Vanderbilt University, © 1993-1996 and distributed by LEARNING, Inc. This series uses a humorous story format to present challenging and realistic (applied) problems that require grades 5-8 students to use a variety of mathematical concepts, skills, and strategies. The series is predicated on the investigative approach: presenting a single complex problem before children have been introduced to subject-matter content. In one episode, for example, children are confronted with the problem of calculating the rate at which an airplane travels. Research on the materials indicates that intermediate-level students working in groups can intuitively discover that distance traveled is a function of the rate of travel multiplied by the time. (It is probably a good idea for teachers to help student summarize such intuitive discoveries as a formula: in this case, that D = R x T). Calculating rates leads students into the area of partial units, creating a need to explore decimals. The episode also gets into other subject matter domains such as science, specifically aerodynamics. The videodisk allows students to go back to any part of the story and access information needed to solve the problem. The problems are open-ended in the sense that there is no one correct solution. Extension of the original problem is provided by asking students "what if?" questions (e.g., What if the plane only carried 5 gallons of gas?) Research indicates that students generally respond enthusiastically to the rich problems (Pellegrino et al., 1991).

Blockers and Finders and **Blockers and Finders II** designed by Thomas C. O'Brien and published by Sunburst. Both programs involve making and testing conjectures in an entertaining situation. The original program is appropriate for children in grades 2 to 8 and is available on Apple, IBM, or Macintosh disks. The II version is appropriate for students in grades 4 to 8 and is available on Apple and IBM disks only. Network versions of both programs are also available.

The King's Rule by Thomas C. O'Brien, © 1984 by Sunburst. Appropriate for grades 4 to 8, this program involves inductive reasoning and is available on Apple, IBM, or Macintosh disks. Appleshare, IBM ICLAS and Tandy SchoolMate Network versions are also available. The aim is to advance into the heart of a castle and confront a king. To advance beyond the first level (the Castle Gate), a student must solve three relatively transparent number riddles: number patterns involving small upward or downward jumps. A riddle is posed as three numbers, which are related by a "secret" rule. Consider the example: 29 24 19. Players can then check their hunch (conjecture) about the secret rule by posing their own set of numbers. For our example, posing 30 25 20 or 38 33 28 would elicit the response from the computer: It fits the rule. When the player feels ready, the computer poses a five-question quiz. After successfully completing this diagnostic test, the players go on to the next riddle.

Videotape/Laserdisk

Becoming Successful Problem Solvers available from HRM Video. Sets 1 and 2 are appropriate for students in grades 4-7; Set 3, for students in grades 5-8. Each set illustrates nonroutine problems.

The Garage Dump Dilemma available from HRM Video. This program is appropriate for students in grades 5-8, presents a problem that mimics real-world problems.

3 FOSTERING AND EVALUATING MEANINGFUL LEARNING: MAKING CONNECTIONS AND ASSESSING UNDERSTANDING

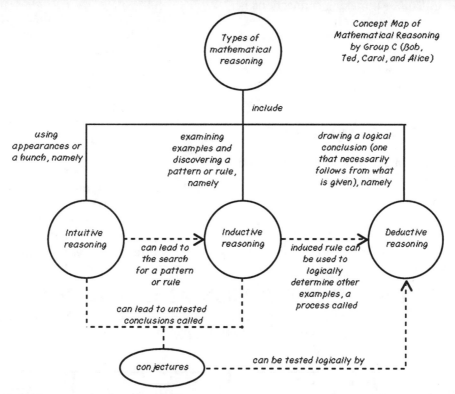

Concept Map of Mathematical Reasoning by Group C (Bob, Ted, Carol, and Alice)

Concept mapping involves diagramming how concepts are thought to be related to each other. The concept map in the bulletin board above was devised by preservice teachers to illustrate the connections among the types of reasoning discussed in chapter 2. (How concept maps can be used at the elementary level is discussed further in Unit 3•3 of this chapter.)

Each group can post its concept map on a bulletin board. There will probably be differences among the maps. This should prompt discussion. In many cases, there may, in fact, be more than one way of drawing a concept map—that is, there may be different ways of thinking about the relationships among concepts. At other times, the class can work toward a consensus about what the concept map should look like.

Concept maps of a domain can be posted early and again late in the year. This would allow class members and visitors to see how the students' knowledge grew. As new topics are introduced, additional panels can be added. This would give students the opportunity to discuss and to draw in the connections between new and previously studied topics. In any case, surrounding children with their concept maps can be a way of encouraging them to think about connections and driving home the important point that studying mathematics involves making connections.

THIS CHAPTER

*I*n chapter 1, we noted that meaningful learning is actually easier than learning by rote, because remembering related ideas is easier than remembering numerous isolated facts. We also noted that the skills approach does not help students make connections (e.g., link school mathematics to their everyday life). Not surprisingly, many children have little understanding of mathematics.

In chapter 2, we examined the processes involved in mathematical inquiry. In this chapter, we focus on another process—making connections. As we will see in Unit 3•1, making connections is at the heart of meaningful learning. In Unit 3•2, we examine how to assess the connectedness of students' knowledge (the degree of their understanding). In Unit 3•3, we address a key proposal of the NCTM's (1995) *Assessment Standards*—integrating instruction and evaluation.

WHAT THE NCTM *STANDARDS* SAY

Standard 4 for both grades K to 4 and grades 5 to 8 is *Mathematical Connections*.

Grades K-4

"In grades K-4, the study of mathematics should include opportunities to make connections so that students can:

- link conceptual (why) and procedural (how-to) knowledge;
- relate various representations of concepts or procedures to one another;
- recognize relationships among different topics in mathematics;
- use mathematics in other [content] areas [and] their daily lives" (p. 32).

Grades 5-8

"In grades 5-8, the mathematics curriculum should include the investigation of mathematical connections so that students can:

- see mathematics as an integrated whole;
- explore problems and describe results using graphical, numerical, physical, algebraic, and verbal mathematical models or representations;
- use . . . [ideas] to further their understanding of other mathematical ideas;
- apply mathematical thinking and modeling to solve problems that arise in other disciplines, such as art, music, psychology, science, and business;
- value the role of mathematics in our culture and society" (p. 84).

3•1 MEANINGFUL INSTRUCTION AND LEARNING

Figure 3.1: Many Children Just Don't Understand Math

PEANUTS reprinted by permission of UFS, Inc.

In Subunit 3•1•1, we describe the nature and development of understanding. In Subunit 3•1•2, we examine why instruction often fails to help children understand mathematics (see Figure 3.1) and discuss what teachers can do to foster meaningful learning.

3•1•1 LEARNING: UNDERSTANDING UNDERSTANDING

The Nature of Understanding

The NCTM (1989) *Curriculum Standards* recommend focusing on meaningful learning, because understanding underlies adaptive expertise. *But what is understanding and how does it develop?*

Understanding as Connections. Recent research suggests a clear-cut way of thinking about understanding: It involves "seeing" a *connection* between pieces of information (e.g., Ginsburg, 1989; Hiebert & Carpenter, 1992). Understanding *decimals*, for instance, can involve connecting symbolic decimal notation to familiar experiences (e.g., 12.75 is analogous to one $10 bill; two $1 bills; 7 dimes, which are seven-tenths of a $1; and 5 pennies, which are five-hundredths of a $1) or concrete models (e.g., 12.75 can be represented by base-ten blocks: 1 large cube = 10, 2 flats = 2, 7 longs = .7, and 5 cubes = .05).

"The degree of understanding is determined by the number and the strength of the connections" (Hiebert & Carpenter, 1992, p. 67). A concept, fact, formula, procedure, or rule is well (deeply) understood if it has many strong links to other aspects of knowledge. For example, although decimals can be understood without knowing how they are related to fractions, a *deep* understanding of decimals entails connections to fraction knowledge. One link is that decimals are a way of writing fractions as base-ten, place-value numerals (e.g., 0.8 is an alternative representation for $\frac{4}{5}$, $\frac{8}{10}$, and other equivalent fractions). Another link is that a fraction such as $\frac{4}{5}$ can be converted into a decimal by dividing the numerator (top digit) by the denominator (bottom digit). In brief, constructing a deep understanding of mathematics involves building a well connected network of ideas.

As children's knowledge becomes progressively more complete and well connected, their adaptive expertise grows in two important ways: (a) reasoning and problem solving become more flexible and effective (e.g., Davis, 1983) and (b) meaningful learning snowballs (i.e., learning new material becomes increasingly easier).

Building Connections. There are basically two ways to build connections or understanding: (a) relate new experiences or information to what is already known (assimilation) and (b) discover a relationship between existing pieces of knowledge (integration). Both assimilating new ideas and integrating existing ideas cause a reorganization in thinking. Thus, meaningful learning is not merely a process of adding information but a process that transforms our thinking (DeRuiter & Wansart, 1982).

• **Assimilation**. *Assimilation involves making sense of what is not known by connecting it to what is known.* Consider the case of Fazle. Because this first-grader did not know what the minus sign represented, he responded to subtraction expressions such as 5 - 3 and 8 - 4 by adding the digits. Recognizing this problem, his teacher re-lated the expression 5 - 3 to a familiar everyday situation: If you had five marbles and your younger brother took away three, how many marbles would you have left? With this connection, Fazle understood the minus sign and had no further difficulty determining the answers to subtraction expressions.

• **Integration**. *Integration essentially entails an insight into how previously unrelated pieces of information fit together.* Consider the case of Amber. This third-grader knew that 5 + 5 was 10 and that 2 x 5 could represent *two groups of five.* But she did not realize that these two facts were related or that 2 x 5 was 10. After her class discussed how multiplication was simply a short-cut for repeated addition (e.g., 4 + 4 + 4 = 3 x 4), Amber realized that 2 x 5 and 5 + 5 were equal and that the answer to 2 x 5 must also be 10.

☞ Try Probe 3.1 (pages 3-4 to 3-5).

Readiness Is a Key Factor in Learning. Perhaps you have heard comments such as, "This child is ready for more challenging work!" or "This child is not ready yet for first-grade math." *What determines readiness?* It follows from Piaget's principle of assimilation that "the most important single factor influencing learning is what the learner already knows" (Ausubel, 1968, p. vi). Two key implications of the principle of assimilation are noted below:

• **Gradual learning.** Because of the process of assimilation, most things worth knowing take a long time to learn (Duckworth, 1982). Even with highly effective instruction, it is unlikely that children will construct an entirely complete and accurate understanding all at once (Resnick & Ford, 1981). "We must recognize that partially grasped ideas and periods of confusion are a natural part of the process of developing understanding. When a student does not reach the anticipated conclusion, we must resist giving an explanation and try to ask a question or pose a new problem that will give the student the opportunity to contemplate evidence not previously considered" (Parker, 1993, p. 17).

• **Individual differences.** Differences in background knowledge may mean that not everyone in a class may be ready to assimilate the same material at the same time. "Nor can we expect all students to get the same thing out of the same experience . . . . (Continued on page 3-6.)

↱ Probe 3.1: An Assimilation Demonstration

Meaningful learning involves assimilating, not absorbing, new information (Piaget, 1964). *Assimilation involves filtering, interpreting, and remembering new information in terms of what is already understood.* The following probe is designed to illustrate the importance of connecting school instruction to students' existing knowledge—thus facilitating assimilation and meaningful learning.

Part I: A Lesson on Alien Numbers

One day a space force of giant aliens landed on the earth. They wanted everyone on earth to enjoy the benefits of their advanced culture, and so they instituted compulsory education. Listen, your Giant-Alien instructor CON FUSE is about to address your class:

"Greetings non-intergalactic-space traveling beings called *earthlings*. Our first lesson together concerns the Giant-Alien Numeration System, or GANS for short. Listen carefully as I explain. GANS is a base-ten, positional-notation system. This numeral (•) is the symbol for the number called 'uw.' Uw is the set of all equivalent sets with the property of a unitary element (nonplurality) in any given exemplar."

"As you can see, the representation for uw has a quasi-conic feature. [Don't you just hate it when someone says, "As you can see," and you don't.] Indeed, all the numerals you earthlings call *one*, *two*, *three*, *four*, and *five* pictographically represent their class properties. Moreover, pictographic aspects of the GANS orthography carries over to the numerals that you call *six*, *seven*, *eight*, and *nine*. These combinatory symbols reflect the fact that like you earthlings, we Giant Aliens have five fingers on our hands. Is that some coincidence or what?"

"It is important to remember that a numeral is but one name for a number. Consider the number represented by ∧. We call this numeral 'ue.' Another name for the number designated by the numeral ue is: Vv vanish Uo. This is written 大–¦– — This should make much clearer our concept of ue, no?"

"Now, if you have listened carefully and you can think logically, you will have no problem with Workbook Assignments 1 and 2. You will not be allowed to go to recess or to the Pete, no that's not right, the . . . uh . . . John until you finish your assignment."

It is important to note that the Giant Aliens react with extreme prejudice to students who fail to complete their assignments successfully. They take incomplete or incorrect work as a sign of indolence. The Giant Aliens have no patience with lazy people. Because they have found that many of their provincial students are indolent, the Giant Aliens severely punish incomplete or incorrect work. Under the assumption that severe punishment will motivate students to work harder, any student not correctly completing its assignments is placed in a vaporizing chamber, nervously referred to by human students as the tanning salon. You may not talk to anyone about your assignment. Giant Aliens do not like for their students to talk—they consider it a distraction from serious efforts to learn. After completing Exercises 1 and 2, assess your chances of being sent to the irridation chamber and then read on.

Exercise 1 on the Giant Alien Numeration System

Instructions: Circle the correct Giant-Alien number symbol for each pictorial representation of earth things.

Exercise 2 on the Giant Alien Numeration System

Instructions: Write the Giant-Alien number symbol for each collection of earthly things.

Probe 3.1 continued

Part II: A Revised Lesson on the Giant-Alien Number System

How did you think you did on Lessons 1 and 2? Did you learn much about GANS from CON FUSE's technically correct, but highly verbal and abstract lesson? If you are like most readers, you are probably on your way to the irridation chamber for a less than sterling performance.

Fortunately for you and the human race, the report by the Giant Alien Commission on Educational Practices for Less-Advanced Civilizations (GACEPFLAC for short) arrived by AXE (audio x-ray emission). After eliminating more than a few civilizations, the Commission concluded that Giant Alien teachers were mistaken in their efforts to impose knowledge upon the minds of less-advanced creatures. The Commission concluded that it was essential to relate new information to the less-advanced students' existing knowledge. This should help said students understand their lessons. Taking into account this novel educational principle (Piaget, 1964, called this principle the *principle of assimilation*), CON FUSE and other giant alien teachers set about the task of revising their instruction.

Revised Lesson 1 (shown below) was designed so that groups of human students could discover for themselves the connection between their own number system and the GANS. (They could have made the task of connecting the two systems simpler by writing, for example, the Hindu-Arabic numbers below the Giant Alien numerals. However, CON FUSE and other alien teachers wanted the human students to get into the habit of thinking.) To foster the discovery of how the Giant Alien and Hindu-Arabic number systems are connected, they encouraged human students to examine the number line shown below and to discuss their ideas with other students.

Try Revised Lesson 1 yourself. What patterns do you see? Discuss your conclusions with your group or class.

Revised Lesson 1 on the Giant-Alien Numeration System

Instructions: Shown below is a number line with Giant-Alien Numerals. Draw upon your experiences with number lines representing your own earthling numbers. Can you decode the Giant Alien Numeration system? Justify your answer.

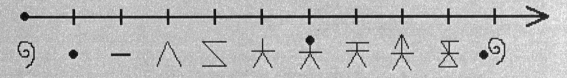

☞ Teaching Tips

🍎 The revised lesson above can make for an interesting pattern-detection activity for pupils in grades 3 to 8. Encourage them to explain why each symbol represents the number it does.

Questions for Reflection

1. (a) What visual patterns might help you remember the GANS symbols for 1 to 5? (b) How might knowing the GANS symbols for 1 to 5 help you remember the GANS numerals for 6 to 9?

2. (a) Understanding can be defined as seeing connections. Assimilation can be thought of as learning new information with understanding. How does assimilation involve making a connection? (b) Why is fostering assimilation in particular and connection-making in general crucial for teaching elementary mathematics?

We should try to provide activities that have the potential for being understood at many different levels" (Parker, 1993, p. 16).

Moving From Concrete to Abstract

Regardless of age or content, understanding frequently begins with *personal knowledge of specific examples (concrete knowledge)* and then broadens to include *general* or *theoretical knowledge (abstract concepts)*.

Direct Perception: Concrete Knowledge Based on Appearances. Our first understandings of a mathematical domain are typically intuitions based on the apparent. For example, a 5-year old announced that 5 + 3 and 4 + 4 must have different sums "because they look different."

☞ Consider Probe 3.2 (page 3-7).

Informal Knowledge: Concrete Knowledge Based on Everyday Experiences. From everyday activities, children can construct an impressive amount of informal knowledge. For instance, by counting on his fingers, 6-year-old Andre discovered that 5 + 3 and 4 + 4 actually have the same sum. Figure 3.2 on page 3-7 illustrates the following points about children's informal knowledge:

1. Children have their own way of thinking about and doing mathematics. Regardless of their curriculum or nationality, young children frequently rely on counting to solve mathematical problems. Without instruction, they use informal knowledge to invent their own ingenious counting-based strategies. Peppermint Patty, for example, added 7 + 3 by counting-on from seven until she had counted all the points on the 3 (*eight*, top point; *nine*, middle point; *ten*, bottom point).

2. Informal knowledge has limitations. For example, children may not be able to use it effectively with larger collections or numbers. That is essentially what Peppermint Patty means by, "No one can be expected to answer a problem with 'twelve' in it."

3. Children feel confident when they use their informal knowledge but often lose confidence when they can't (e.g., compare the last two frames of Figure 3.2).

Formal Knowledge: School-Taught,

Symbolic Knowledge. In school, children learn symbolic mathematics (e.g., how to write numerals such as 7 and 8). This symbolic mathematics is more abstract and powerful than children's concrete knowledge. For example, shown the equation 6 + 6 = 8 + 4 a 7-year old knows—without counting—that both 6 + 6 and 8 + 4 must have the same sum and that, if 6 + 6 = 12, then 8 + 4 must be 12 also. Algebra represents an even greater step toward abstract knowledge than formal arithmetic. For instance, the algebraic equation a + b = 12 implies that there are an infinite number of numbers that sum to 12.

3•1•2 TEACHING

Limitations of the Traditional Skills Approach

Although making connections is crucial to understanding mathematics, the pace and focus of traditional instruction prompts disconnected learning. Efforts to "cover the curriculum" usually require a swift, lockstep instructional pace that does not give most students a chance to construct connections and, as a result, many feel lost (Fuys & Liebov, 1993). To make matters worse, the skills approach focuses on memorizing *isolated* facts, definitions, formulas, and procedures. Leinhardt and Smith (1985) found that inexperienced teachers, particularly, failed to help students make connections. Even when connections are made by teachers, they are often implicit rather than explicit and, thus, may escape the notice of students (Lampert, 1986).

When instruction fails to help students make a connection, the result is a *gap* in knowledge (Ginsburg, 1989; Hiebert, 1984). Gaps can occur:

1. between symbolic instruction and children's existing (informal) knowledge (e.g., not knowing that formal multiplication expressions such as 3 x 4 represent familiar repeated-addition situations such as combining three bags of four marbles each),

2. between procedures or *how*-to knowledge and concepts or an understanding of *why* (e.g., memorizing by rote the invert-and-multiply procedure for fraction division but not understanding why the algorithm works or why it sometimes results in answers larger than the dividend), (continued on page 3-8)

➡ Probe 3.2: The Importance of Informal Mathematical Knowledge

Informal knowledge evolves largely from everyday experiences. Such experiences can provide a wealth of concrete mathematical knowledge—personally significant knowledge of specific concepts, examples, strategies, and so forth. The recent realization that mathematical knowledge can be acquired outside school has important educational implications (Nunes, 1992). The aim of this probe is to help consider some of these implications. After reading the cartoon below, answer the questions that follow.

Figure 3.2: Peppermint Patty's Thoughts on Mathematics reprinted by permission of UFS, Inc.

1. What does the cartoon in Figure 3.2 illustrate about children's informal knowledge?

2. (a) How does Peppermint Patty react when she can't connect formal mathematics to what she already understands (her informal knowledge)? (b) How does she react when she can engage her informal knowledge?

3. How does the fact that children come to school with a wealth of informal mathematical knowledge change the way teachers should plan and carry out school instruction?

3. among various representations of concepts or procedures (e.g., not knowing how to relate a symbolic equation such as $\frac{1}{2} \times \frac{3}{5} = \frac{3}{10}$ to a real-world example or how to use manipulatives to translate it into a concrete model),

4. among mathematical topics (e.g., not making the link that $\frac{1}{4} = 1 \div 4 = 0.25$), or

5. between mathematics and its applications to other curricular areas, such as science, or everyday life (e.g., not recognizing that graphs are a useful tool for comparing data and discovering relationships in many endeavors).

Designing Meaningful Instruction

To foster meaningful learning, adaptive expertise, and mathematical power, focus on helping children make connections and move from the concrete (specific and familiar) to the abstract (general and symbolic).

☞ Try Investigation 3.1 (page 3-9) and Probe 3.3 (page 3-10).

Making Connections. TO PROMOTE UNDER-STANDING, FOCUS ON FOSTERING CONNECTIONS (A) BETWEEN FORMAL MATHEMATICS AND CHILDREN'S EXISTING KNOWLEDGE, (B) BETWEEN PROCEDURES AND CONCEPTS, (C) AMONG VARIOUS REPRESENTA-TIONS OR MODELS, (D) AMONG DIFFERENT MATHE-MATICAL TOPICS, AND (E) WITH ITS APPLICATIONS TO OTHER CONTENT AREAS AND EVERYDAY LIFE.

• **Connecting formal symbols and procedures to children's existing (informal) knowledge.** The developmental principle of assimilation has the following important educational implications:

☞ **Build on children's existing knowledge, particularly their informal knowledge.** To facilitate the assimilation of formal mathematics, it is important to help children connect symbols and procedures to their existing understanding. Especially for children just beginning school, informal knowledge—what they have already learned from everyday experiences—is a key basis for understanding what is taught in school. At all grade levels, exploiting informal strengths can have important cognitive and affective consequences. In addition to helping make school mathematics meaningful and interesting, it can foster success and a feeling of competence—a sense of mathematical power.

☞ **New information, problems, and tasks should be** *moderately novel*—**neither too familiar or too unfamiliar.** According to Piaget's *moderate novelty principle, only somewhat new (moderately novel) information can be understood (assimilated) and pique interest.* If information is too unfamiliar, students cannot use what they know to make sense of it and quickly lose interest in trying to learn this incomprehensible material. On the other hand, if information is highly familiar, children will understand it but—like adults—will have little interest in exploring the obvious. Thus new information, problems, and tasks children encounter should be just beyond their existing knowledge.

☞ **Because constructing meaningful knowledge is a gradual process, do not hurry instruction.** Plan for meaningful learning to take a long time. In the long run, a patient teacher will help children construct a more solid understanding of mathematics.

☞ **In general, instruction should proceed through three phases: the conceptual phase, the connecting phase, and the symbolic phase** (e.g., Baratta-Lorton, 1976).

1. *Conceptual phase.* Initially, give children the opportunity to explore a topic in personally meaningful ways so that they can construct a basic and intuitive understanding of it. Encourage them to exploit and to extend their informal knowledge. For example, prompt students to use what they know to devise their own solutions to problems with manipulatives or drawings.

2. *Connecting phase.* Once children have a solid conceptual understanding of the mathematics, help them to *link* it to written symbols and procedures. That is, help them discover that written symbols and procedures are convenient ways to represent concrete (familiar) experiences, examples, analogies, and models.

3. *Symbolic phase.* Once children understand the formal mathematics (e.g., the connection between a procedure and its underlying rationale), then they can operate exclusively with the abstract symbols. (Continued on page 3-11.)

⌘ Investigation 3.1: The *Fundamental Counting Property*

◆ Probability + problem solving + inductive reasoning ◆ 4-8 ◆ Groups of four + class discussion

This investigation illustrates how students can be helped to rediscover the *Fundamental Counting Property* and its application to probability in a meaningful way.

Part I: Groundwork

Rediscovering the *Multiplication Principle.* By informally solving combination problems, recording the data, and looking for a pattern, children as early as third grade can discover a key basis for the *Fundamental Counting Property*. Solve the following combination problems *informally* and summarize the data in the table below. What shortcut could be used to determine the number of combinations in each problem?

■ **Combination Problem A** (◆ 3-8). Johanna designed a birthday-party invitation on her computer. If she could print out the invitation in one of four colors and use one of three borders, how many different types of invitations could she print out?

■ **Combination Problem B** (◆ 3-8). Donato's offered a choice of four different pizzas (small with thin or thick crust and large with thin or thick crust) and five toppings (cheese, sausage, pepperoni, all three, or cheese and pepperoni). How many different combinations of pizza and toppings did Donato's offer?

	Number of choices— first item	Number of choices— second item	Number of combinations
Problem A			
Problem B			

Other Groundwork. To further set the stage for this investigation, students should be familiar with operations on fractions such as $\frac{1}{2} + \frac{1}{3} = \frac{5}{6}$ and $\frac{1}{2} \times \frac{3}{4} = \frac{3}{8}$. (See chapter 10 for how children can be helped to discover fraction-arithmetic procedures.) They should also be familiar with basic probability notation—that probability can be represented as a fraction: Number of events of interest/Total number of events possible.

Part II: Rediscovering *Fundamental Counting Property*

1. Try solving the following problem *informally*—as elementary students might:

■ **Chancy Dresser** (◆ 4-8). Katarina was late getting ready for an awards dinner. She set out a red, a yellow, and a green blouse on her bed along with a black and a white skirt. While washing up, she decided that the green blouse and black skirt would be the best combination. Unfortunately, just as Katarina was leaving her bathroom to get dressed, there was a blackout in her apartment building. "I've worked too long and hard," she thought, "to let some silly blackout keep me from getting my award tonight. In the darkness, Katarina grabbed a blouse and a skirt. How likely is it she grabbed the green blouse and black skirt she wanted to wear? (✚ Summarizing the data in a table can be an invaluable aid in solving *Chancy Dresser*. What is the probability of picking the green blouse from the blouses on the table? What is the probability of picking the black skirt from the skirts on the bed? What is the probability of choosing the desired combination of green blouse and black skirt?)

2. To help intermediate-level students see a pattern, a teacher could follow up *Chancy Dresser* with other similar problems such as those below. Encourage students to solve each problem informally (e.g., by using a table), to summarize the data in the table below, and to look for a solution shortcut. What shortcut could be used to solve such problems?

■ **Chancy Dresser Revised** (◆ 4-8). Assume Katarina had put out five different blouses (red, yellow, green, blue, and violet) and three different skirts (black, white, and gray). Now what are the chances of her picking the desired combination of green blouse and black skirt?

■ **Chancy Dresser Part II** (◆ 4-8). If Katarina put out six scarves (pink, chiffon, light green, light blue, beige, and purple) and four brooches (gold, silver, copper and green), what is the likelihood she would pick the combination of light green scarf and green brooch in the dark?

	Probability of choosing first item	Probability of choosing second item	Probability of choosing both items
Chancy Dresser			
Chancy Dresser Revised			
Chancy Dresser Part II			

◆ **Extension: Chancy Dresser—The Grand Finale** (◆ 5-8). With 5 blouses, 3 skirts, 6 scarves, and 4 brooches to pick from, what are the chances that in the dark, Katarina will pick the following coordinated outfit: the combination of green blouse, black skirt, light-green scarf, and green brooch?

→ Probe 3.3: Reflecting on the Value of Concrete Models

Part I: Using Base-Ten Blocks to Explore Our Decimal Numeration System. Size embodiments like base-ten blocks can be useful in helping children to construct multidigit concepts and to connect written symbols to these concepts (Fuson, 1992b). The aim of this part of the probe is to help you think how base-ten blocks can be used to model our number system and how this might help students discover key features of it. Consider the chart at the bottom of the page. Then answer the questions that follow.

1. ■ **Model for a Million** (♦ 3-8). Base-ten blocks include cubes (which can represent ones), longs (which can represent tens), flats (which can represent hundreds), and large cubes (which can represent thousands) (see the chart below). What do you suppose the base-ten block for representing one million would look like? (✚ What would base-ten block models of 10,000 and 100,000 look like? ✦ What would the base-ten block models for 10,000,000 and 100,000,000 look like?)

2. (a) How do the base-ten block models for one thousand, ten thousand, and hundred thousand parallel those for ones, tens, and hundreds? (b) What might be an appropriate model *name* for the base-ten block models of 10,000, and 100,000?

3. Base-ten blocks can underscore grouping by ten because they require 10-for-1 trades (e.g., it takes one such trade to exchange 10 cubes for a long). (a) How many 10-for-1 trades does it take to exchange cubes for a flat, a large cube, and a 10,000 cube? (b) In each case, what are the various ways in which these exchanges could be represented formally?

Part II: Cure-All? *If a teacher uses manipulatives, does it guarantee meaningful learning?* Consider the following example. By reassigning values, base-ten blocks can be used to model decimals (e.g., let a flat = 1, a long = .01, and a cube = 0.01) and operation on decimals, including decimal division.

Task: Find the quotient of 1.82 ÷ 1.4. (For purposes of this demonstration, assume that you do not know how to use the written algorithm for dividing decimals or how to use a calculator to determine the answer. That is, put yourself in the shoes of a fifth-grader who has only the blocks to determine the answer.)

Step 1: Represent the dividend 1.82 with blocks: one flat, eight longs, and two cubes.

Step 2: Arrange the blocks into a rectangle with a side of 1.4. Note that this requires trading in a long for 10 cubes. The other side of the rectangle indicates the quotient.

Divisor = 1.4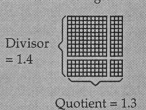

Quotient = 1.3

1. Use base-ten blocks (or a drawing of such blocks) to find the quotient for the following expressions: (a) 1.82 ÷ 1.3, (b) 1.82 ÷ 2.6, (c) 1.82 ÷ .02, and (d) 1.12 ÷ 1.4.

2. Did you successfully complete Question 1? Why or why not? What lessons about using manipulatives did you learn?

Chart of How Base-Ten Blocks Model Our Decimal Numeration System

Count name	Hundred thousand	Ten thousand	Thousand	Hundred	Ten	Ones
Numeral	100,000	10,000	1,000	100	10	1
Concrete model	(not shown)	(not shown)				
model name			large cube	flat	long	cube

• **Connecting procedures and concepts.**
Children should understand the rationale of procedures they learn and use. By tying procedures to conceptual understanding, they "will not perceive mathematics as an arbitrary set of rules; will not need to . . . memorize as many procedures; and will have the foundation to apply, recreate, and invent new ones when needed" (NCTM, 1989, p. 32). The following guidelines can help ensure that children's procedural knowledge is connected to conceptual knowledge:

☞ **During the conceptual phase, encourage children to solve problems (particularly real ones) informally and to discuss such strategies in their own terms (using natural language).** For example, keeping score of a game can be a genuinely challenging and important problem for young primary-level children. It can create a real opportunity for them to devise and share informal strategies and to construct the concepts that underlie the written renaming algorithm for multidigit addition. For instance, by using blocks or tally marks to keep score, children may recognize that grouping "markers" by ten can make keeping track or totaling large scores easier. The conceptual phase should last as long as it takes to understand the underlying concepts for a procedure.

☞ **During the connecting phase, encourage children—for the sake of convenience—to devise written procedures that parallel their informal strategies.** For example, after inventing or learning a concrete addition procedure (e.g., see Figure A below), prompt them to invent written procedures as a less cumbersome way to do game-score computations. Direct them to develop a written procedure that models each step of their concrete procedure. Figures B, C, and D below are examples of such child-invented procedures (Fuson & Burghardt, 1993). Note that these informal procedures are at least as efficient as the standard school-taught algorithm (Figure E).

☞ **Ideally, formal written procedures would evolve as shortcuts for informal procedures.** For example, challenged to devise a written scoring procedure that parallels their informal tallying strategy (Figure A below), some children may actually reinvent the standard U.S. algorithm (Figure E). If not, a teacher can always introduce it as another way of adding multidigit numbers. Investigation 3.1 illustrates how children can reinvent a key probability procedure by looking for a shortcut to an informal procedure.

• **Connecting various representations of concepts and procedures.** Mathematical ideas and processes can be represented in various ways—in everyday terms (natural language), by an *assortment* of concrete and pictorial models, by model (material) terms, as mathematical symbols, and by formal terminology (language) (see, e.g., Figure 3.3 on the next page).

☞ **Help children relate real cases and everyday descriptions, concrete models and material terms, and mathematical symbols and formal language** (again see Figure 3.3 on page 3-12). For example, while using base-ten blocks to model multidigit addition, encourage children to describe their actions in their own terms (e.g., "I had 14, so I made a ten group"), in model terms (e.g., "I had 14 cubes, so I traded 10 cubes for a long"), and formal terms ("I renamed *fourteen ones* as *one ten and four ones*"). To help reinforce these links, a teacher should also use the various terms interchangeably.

☞ **Introduce children to a wide range of concrete and pictorial models and help them to relate one to another** (see Figure 3.4 on page 3-12). Clearly, children should have the opportunity to thoroughly explore and become comfortable with a particular model. However, there are three reasons why using a variety of models can be helpful: (a) Children are less likely to identify

Figure A	Figure B	Figure C	Figure D	Figure E
	$$\begin{array}{r} 37 \\ +28 \\ \hline 65 \end{array}$$	$$\begin{array}{r} 4 \\ \cancel{3}7 \\ +28 \\ \hline 65 \end{array}$$	$$\begin{array}{r} 37 \\ +28 \\ \hline \end{array}$$ $$\begin{array}{r} 1 \\ 65 \end{array}$$	$$\begin{array}{r} 1 \\ 37 \\ +28 \\ \hline 65 \end{array}$$
8 cubes and 7 cubes is 15 cubes; but 10 of these cubes can be traded for a long (a group of 10)	7 + 8 = 15; *mentally* add the 1 to a tens digit	7 + 8 = 15; *physically* add the 1 to a tens digit	7 + 8 = 15; record 1 below tens digits	7 + 8 = 15; record the 1 above tens digits

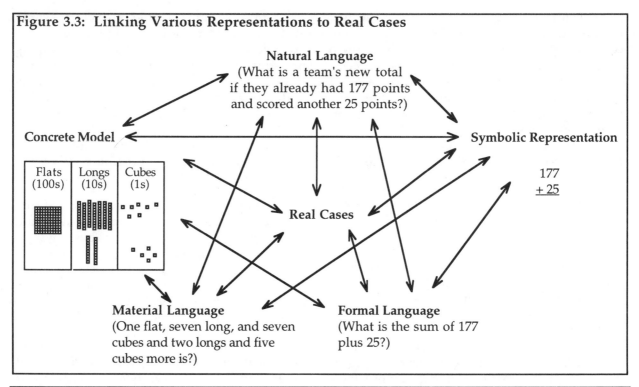

Figure 3.3: Linking Various Representations to Real Cases

Natural Language
(What is a team's new total
if they already had 177 points
and scored another 25 points?)

Concrete Model

Symbolic Representation

Flats (100s)	Longs (10s)	Cubes (1s)

177
+ 25

Real Cases

Material Language
(One flat, seven long, and seven
cubes and two longs and five
cubes more is?)

Formal Language
(What is the sum of 177
plus 25?)

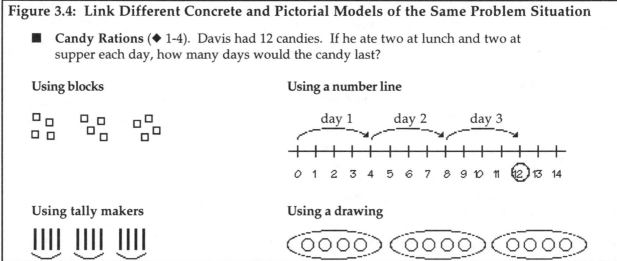

Figure 3.4: Link Different Concrete and Pictorial Models of the Same Problem Situation

■ **Candy Rations** (◆ 1-4). Davis had 12 candies. If he ate two at lunch and two at supper each day, how many days would the candy last?

Using blocks

Using a number line

day 1   day 2   day 3

0 1 2 3 4 5 6 7 8 9 10 11 12 13 14

Using tally makers

Using a drawing

a concept or procedure narrowly with a particular embodi-ment and, thus, are more likely to develop a broad understanding of it. (b) Discussing the similarities and differences of various models may help children discern the defining or critical attributes of a concept or the essential elements of a procedure.[*] (c) Different children may find different models meaningful.

☞ ✓ **Encourage students to translate symbolic**

representations into realistic examples or models, as well as translate realistic examples or models into symbolic representations. Although it is important for children to translate real examples or concrete models into symbols, understanding can be deepened if they are asked to reverse the process—to translate symbolic expressions into real examples or concrete models. Indeed, this is an excellent way of gauging understanding of a symbol or procedure.

• **Connecting mathematical topics.** Mathematical topics are interconnected and should

[*] According to Dienes' (1960) principle of perceptual variability, a variety of models is important for abstraction—developing a general or abstract understanding.

be taught in a way that highlights these connections.

↩ **Teach mathematics in an integrated fashion rather than topic by topic.** Note that even the newest elementary textbooks typically take a topical approach. Providing more integrated instruction may require a teacher to sometimes go beyond the textbook. Using a project- or problem-based investigative approach is an ideal way to raise diverse issues and introduce mathematical content in an integrated and purposeful manner.

• **Connecting mathematics and its applications to other content areas and everyday life.** Ideally, a teacher would integrate the instruction of mathematics with that of other content areas (see, e.g., Box 3.1 below) and help children understand how it is useful in everyday life.

↩ **To connect mathematics with other content areas and everyday life, use a project-based approach to instruction.** Instead of always having discrete periods for mathematics, sciences, social studies, reading, and so forth, at least some of the time substitute long project periods, where the class tackles large complex projects that involve a range of content areas. For example, as part of a project on Native-Americans, the class could explore their counting systems (see Activity File 3.1 on the next page) or devise scale models of different tribal habitats (see Activity File 3.2 on page 3-14). The latter activity could provide a basis for discussing differences in the tribes' housings and life styles as well as a basis for exploring ratios and proportions.

Moving from Concrete to Abstract Instruction. Instruction should help students move from an implicit and disconnected understanding of a concept to an explicit and logically coherent understanding. In this section, we discuss what role concrete manipulatives can play in this process and how to help children construct an *explicit understanding of mathematics—the ability to explain concepts and procedures.*

• **The role of manipulatives.** Misconceptions about concrete instruction, in general, and the usefulness of manipulatives, in particular, abound.

What is concrete? Many educators have in-

🖎 **Box 3.1: Using Children's Literature as a Basis for the Investigative Approach to Mathematics Instruction**

In *Math and Literature (K-3)* (© 1992 by Math Solutions Publications), Marilyn Burns noted: "Children's books are effective classroom vehicles for motivating students to think and reason mathematically. . . . Incorporating children's books into math instruction helps students experience the wonder possible in mathematical problem solving and . . . see a connection between mathematics and the imaginative ideas in books" (p. 1).

Using children's literature as a basis for the investigative approach to mathematics instruction may require teachers to modify how they read a book to a class. Normally, a book is read from beginning to end with a focus on comprehending the story line. When a mathematical problem or question is posed, the teacher simply reads on and supplies the answer. Children sometimes memorize the answer by rote through repeated readings of the story. In the investigative approach, if teachers encountered a question or problem, they would interrupt the story to give children the opportunity to answer the question or problem themselves. Moreover, they would look for mathematical situations in the story and use them to pose their own questions or problems.

Consider, for example, *The Doorbell Rang* by Pat Hutchins (published in 1986 by Greenwillow Books). The first page illustrates a mother presenting a plate of cookies to a brother and a sister and saying, "Share them between yourselves." Before reading on, a primary-level teacher could pose the problem (e.g., "How many cookies should each child get?") and ask students to devise their own solution strategies. This problem should raise the question of how many cookies are pictured on the plate. For kindergartners and first graders, this raises the issue of how do you accurately count a pictured collection of items. Once the class agreed on how many cookies each child should get, the teacher could proceed to the next page, which indicates the answer. (If the class' answer and the books' answer were different, the teacher could then engage the class in a discussion of why and guide them to resolving the difference.)

🍎 Activity File 3.1: Exploring Counting in Other Cultures

◆ Integrated mathematics (oral counting & grouping concept) and social studies lesson ◆ 1-3 ◆ Any number

Exploring the counting systems of North American Indians could provide a basis for discussing native cultures and the concepts underlying our number system. (For more information, see *Native American Mathematics* edited by Michael P. Closs, © 1986 by the University of Texas Press.) In *The World of Mathematics*, Conant (1956) noted that some American Indian tribes used fingers and hand claps to indicate a number. For example, counting to twelve involved raising successive fingers until all ten were up, clapping to represent a group of 10, and then raising two more fingers. Children could be encouraged to consider how this system parallels our counting and written-number systems.

📖 African counting systems and cultures can be explored simultaneously with the aid of such children's books as *Count on Your Fingers African Style* (by Claudia Zaslavsky, © 1980 by Thomas Y. Crowell), *Mojo Means One: A Swahili Counting Book* (by Muriel Feelings, © 1971 by Dial), and *Count Your Way through Africa* (by Jim Haskins, © 1989 by Carolrhoda Books). Other counting systems and cultures can be introduced with other books in the *Count Your Way Through* series: Arab World (Egyptian count), Canada (French), China, Japan, Korea, Mexico (Spanish), and Russia.

🍎 Activity File 3.2: Modeling Native-American Habitats

◆ Integrated and extended mathematics (proportions and measurement) and social studies lesson ◆ 4-8 ◆ Any number

Using library books and references, the world wide web, and other resources, have the class collect information about and pictures of the types of housing and village layout used by a native American tribe. Have students use graph paper to draw floor plans of houses or villages. This can entail deciding on a convenient scale. Students can then use cloth, balsa wood, toothpicks, twigs and so forth to construct models to scale.

---

terpreted Piaget's work as implying that elementary-level children must actively manipulate real objects to construct mathematical concepts. That is, concrete is often used to imply a touchable object (a manipulative). Although this text often uses the term *concrete* in this way, the reader should keep in mind that concrete instruction really implies something broader—examples, terms, analogies, and experiences that are *familiar* to children. The particular medium (e.g., real objects, pictures of objects, or video displays of pictured objects) is probably less important than using experiences that are personally meaningful to children.

Are manipulatives helpful? Are they appropriate for children beyond kindergarten or

first grade? Many teachers believe that although manipulatives may be fine for really young children or slow students, they are not important to use with pupils past first or second grade. Research indicates that using manipulatives can help students of *all* ages construct a deeper understanding of mathematics. Students who use manipulatives usually outachieve those who do not (e.g., Sowell, 1989, Suydam, 1984). As Part I of Probe 3.3 (page 3-10) illustrates, manipulatives can be seen, touched, and moved and, thus, they provide children something real to reflect on. As a result, they can help students construct mathematical concepts or devise informal procedures. Because they can promote meaningful learning, manipulatives can improve retention and problem solving (Clements & McMillen, 1996) and foster a positive disposition toward mathematics (Sowell, 1989).

Do manipulatives guarantee meaningful learning? How should manipulatives be used? Some teachers assume that all they have to do is provide students with manipulatives and show them how to use the materials. And magically, the students will *understand* what they are doing. For several reasons, manipulatives by themselves do not assure understanding. For one thing, children can learn to use manipulatives by rote just as they learn to manipulate symbols by rote. For another, manipulatives—no matter how well designed—are not inherently meaningful and cannot impose understanding on the user. For example, although base-ten blocks are designed to underscore the concepts underlying our base-ten numeration system, children may not recognize this and may use the blocks inappropriately

(Nunes & Moreno, in press). For example, asked what number eight longs represent, they may treat the longs merely as objects, count by ones, and conclude they represent *eight*. As Part II of Probe 3.3 (page 3-10) illustrates, without at least some conceptual understanding, a child cannot use a manipulative adaptively. In brief, a teacher cannot simply give children manipulatives or show them how to use them and expect to promote meaningful learning. Manipulatives are a tool and—like any tool—must be used carefully and thoughtfully to be effective. Some tips on using manipulatives follow:

↬ **Students of *all* ages should be encouraged to consider the use of a concrete model when tackling new ideas or problems.** A variety of manipulatives should be available in all K-8 classrooms. Instruction should help students understand that constructing concrete models and experimenting with them is a good problem-solving heuristic.

↬ **Encourage children to use their existing informal knowledge to invent their own manipulative models.** In the skills approach, manipulatives typically are not used. In the conceptual approach, teachers typically use manipulatives to concretely model and explain a prescribed procedure. They show students the manipulative procedure and then encourage them to *imitate* it. In the investigative or the problem-solving approach, teachers do not attempt to impose concrete models on students with the hope that this will result in understanding. Instead, they prompt children to draw on real-life experiences to make sense of a problem and to devise their own solutions using manipulatives. Teachers may also ask students to use manipulatives to justify their reasoning, informal procedure, or answer (Peck & Jencks, 1988). By using manipulatives in a personally meaningful manner, children may discover patterns or relationships that further deepen their understanding.

✓ **To evaluate understanding, ask children to solve a task using a new manipulative.** For example, if a class has been using *Fraction Circles* and *Cuisenaire rods* to model fraction division, ask them to use *Fraction Tiles* to do so. If children *understand* fraction division, they should be able to figure out how to use the new manipulative. If they have simply memorized a manipulative procedure by rote, they probably will not.

↬ **Children need to be actively engaged with manipulatives *mentally* as well as physically.** Put differently, it is not enough to do, it is important that children reflect on what they are doing (see Figure 3.5). To ensure this, children should be asked to explain what they are doing with the manipulative and to justify their answers.

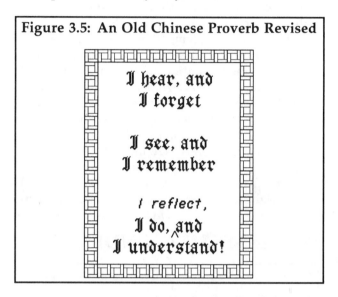

Figure 3.5: An Old Chinese Proverb Revised

• **Fostering explicit understanding.** Children have an *implicit understanding* of many things. Because *this knowledge is nonconscious or unanalyzed, they cannot explain it.* For example, Chomsky's work suggests that children come to school with an implicit knowledge of their native language. English-speaking children implicitly understand that plurals are formed by adding an s, use this rule, and may even recognize that the expression *the three boy went home* is not right. Ask why, they may respond, "I don't know" and really mean it. Informal knowledge often consists of implicit understandings.

In contrast, *explicit understanding involves knowledge that a child is consciously aware of, can analyze, and can—at least to some extent— explain.* Because it is conscious and can be analyzed, children are more likely to recognize logical inconsistencies and gaps. Moreover, as chapter 2 implied, trying to explain an idea or process can be an aid in clarifying and furthering understanding. As Parker (1993) observed, "We need to recognize the importance of verbalization. Putting thoughts into words requires students to organize their thinking and to confront their incomplete understanding" (p. 17). Formal mathematical knowledge is an effort to describe explicitly our mathematical understandings. One goal of instruction, then, is to help children make their implicit mathematical knowledge explicit so that it can more readily evolve into a complete and coherent system of knowledge.

∓ **Encourage students to analyze others' answers and justifications critically and, when applicable, to disagree respectfully.** It is through conflict and by having their ideas challenged that children will construct a more complete and coherent understanding of mathematics. *But won't conflict and disagreement crush children's confidence and otherwise harm them?* Whether the effect is positive or negative depends largely on the classroom atmosphere. If a teacher creates an open atmosphere where individuals and their differences are respected, conflict will be seen as way for all to construct a better understanding and being right will be considered less important than trying to think. In brief, in an atmosphere of mu-

tual respect, conflict and disagreement are not political tools used to bolster oneself at the expense of another but are learning tools that enable everyone to benefit.

∓ **Use a variety of examples and nonexamples to help clarify concepts.** Students need to see various representative items, because a single example is frequently not enough to form a well-defined concept. Furthermore, to help them define the boundaries of a concept, they need to see *nonexamples* (items not representative of a concept). By examining what is common to various examples of a concept and how they differ from nonexamples, children can induce the defining or critical attributes of a concept. Investigation 3.2 illustrates discovery-learning exercises that use examples and nonexamples in two different ways to define a mathematical concept.

☞ Try Investigation 3.2 (page 3-17).

3•2 ASSESSING UNDERSTANDING

Figure 3.6: Evaluating Understanding is Often Not Easy

YOUNG ONES' VIEW

In Subunit 3•2•1, we compare the traditional view of assessment with that outlined in the NCTM's (1995) *Assessment Standards*. These standards suggest, for example, that conventional testing methods such as true-false tests (see Figure 3.6) are not adequate to gauge students' understandings. In Subunit 3•2•2, we outline what teachers need to look for in order to achieve accurate assessment. In Subunit 3•2•3, we describe specific assessment methods.

3•2•1 TWO DIFFERENT VIEWS OF ASSESSMENT

Miss Brill had no sooner sat down in the teacher's lounge to eat her lunch, when Mrs. MeChokemchild asked, "Have you started thinking about assessment yet Missy?"

"Assessment?" Miss Brill responded incredulously, "This is still September—I've only started to think about what and how I was going to teach. Isn't assessment something you worry about at the end of the year when the standardized tests and grades are given?"

"Oh, no Missy," Mrs. MeChokemchild retorted. "Assessment is an on-going process."

Hoping for a dissenting opinion, Miss Brill turned to Ms. Socrates, who added, "I agree with Mrs. MeChokemchild's point but disagree with her about the nature of this process. In my opinion, 'Traditional assessment practices . . . are inconsistent with . . . new views of [how to teach mathematics] and how learning progresses' (NCTM, 1995, p. 3). Improving mathematics instruction requires 'funda- (continued on page 3-18)

✿ Investigation 3.2: Math Detective—Using Examples and Nonexamples

♦ Concepts of an *arithmetic sequence* and a *rhomboid* ♦ 7-8 ♦ Whole class

Presenting students with a variety of examples and nonexamples can enable them to induce the *critical attributes* of a concept (*the characteristics common to all examples of the concept*) and to defining the concept explicitly. This investigation illustrates two ways this can be done.

Activity I: An Open-Ended and Discussion-Based Discovery-Learning Approach.
Many students do not have a clear understanding of what an arithmetic sequence is. Do the following activity with your group or class. Elect a guide, who should check the answer key in the *Instructor's Guide* for the answers to the clues below. The clues are in the form of questions. Record your educated guess for each question below. Do not proceed to the next question until you discuss your answers and get your feedback from the guide.

1. a. This is an example of an arithmetic sequence: 2, 4, 6, 8, 10.
    b. This is also: 1, 7, 13, 19, 25.
    c. This is not an arithmetic sequence: 6, 10, 2, 8, 4.
    d. Neither is this: 2, 14, 10, 18, 6.

2. Is 5, 7, 1, 9, 3 an example of an arithmetic sequence?

3. Is 1, 3, 5, 7, 9 an example of an arithmetic sequence?

4. Is 1, 4, 7, 10, 13 an example?

5. Is 2, 5, 8, 11, 14 an example?

6. Is 1, 3, 6, 10, 15 an example?

7. Is 2, 4, 7, 11, 16 an example?

8. Is 1, 2, 3, 4, 5 an example of an arithmetic sequence?

9. Is 1, 2, 4, 8, 16 an example of an arithmetic sequence?

10. Define an arithmetic sequence.

11. Is 11, 8, 5, 2, -1, -4 an example?

Activity II: A Direct Discovery-Learning Approach Using *Best Examples*.
Activity I provided a few clues at a time. Another way to help children construct accurate concepts is to begin with "best examples"—"clear cases demonstrating the variation of the concept's attributes" (Tennyson, Youngers, & Suebsonthi, 1983, p. 281). This activity illustrates how this approach can be used to clarify the concept of *rhomboid*—a concept that most people do not fully or accurately understand. After examining the best examples and nonexamples, answer the questions below.

Examples   Nonexamples

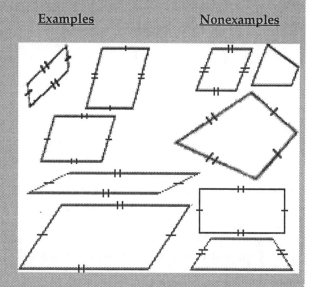

1. Define a *rhomboid*.

2. Are squares and diamonds rhomboids? Why or why not?

3. What is the difference between a rhomboid and a parallelogram?

Questions for Reflection

1. Roseann complained that she did not like Activity I because she didn't like being wrong. How might you respond to her?

2. In Mr. Brandon's class, about half the students argued that the sequence 1, 3, 6, 10, 15 (Question 6 of Activity I) was an arithmetic sequence. For example, Gwen explained, "But see the numbers go in order—they each get bigger." Other students such as Kelli argued that the numbers had to go up by the same amount each time. (a) Are the examples and nonexamples presented in Activity I sufficient to determine who is correct? (b) How could Mr. Brandon help his class resolve this debate?

3. (a) What are the advantages of using examples and nonexamples in a more open-ended way, as Activity I illustrates? (b) What are the advantages of using best examples and nonexamples, as Activity II illustrates? (c) Which approach more accurately reflect how concepts are formed in everyday life. Why?

mental changes in the way mathematical knowledge is evaluated—different in content, in format, and particularly in spirit' (Mathematical Sciences Education Board, National Research Council, 1993, p. 3)."

Purposes of Assessment

Traditional View. "Oh, fiddlesticks," pronounced Mrs. MeChokemchild sternly. "The primary aim of assessment has always been and will always be to give grades. You have to give tests after every unit to find out if pupils mastered the material. Those who have should be rewarded with high grades; those who haven't should be punished with low grades. I give laggards who fail a test an extra large dose of additional practice and retest them. This extra punishment makes them think twice about goofing off again."

Assessment Standards. "The whole spirit of assessment needs to change," countered Ms. Socrates. "Although recognizing student achievement is important, assessment needs to be much more than a way of dispensing rewards and punishment in the form of grades. At its heart, it should be a means for helping teachers better understand their students so that they can effectively guide learning."

The NCTM (1995) *Assessment Standards* outline four broad purposes of assessment.

1. **Monitor student progress in order to promote student growth.** Assessment should be viewed as an integral aspect of instruction and should be an ongoing process. To foster meaningful learning, teachers must regularly assess students' readiness and progress. Even *before* instruction begins, they should gauge students' preexisting knowledge, including their informal concepts and strategies. This is necessary to determine what problems and concepts will be moderately novel to children. It is also important to gauge in what ways children's knowledge is incomplete so as to provide them the experience they need to grow. As Ausubel (1968) put it, "ascertain [what the learner already knows] and teach him accordingly" (p. vi). During the course of instruction, it is important to monitor students' performance to ensure they are making satisfactory progress toward the goals set for them. In effect, monitoring progress is an on-going process.

2. **Make instructional decisions to improve instruction.** "When students don't learn," commented Ms. Socrates to Mrs. MeChokemchild, "some teachers blame the pupils and never consider that the difficulties may stem from what is taught and how it is taught. When monitoring indicates that students aren't making satisfactory progress, more often than not teachers need to adjust or modify their instruction to better facilitate learning."

3. **Evaluate students' achievement in order to recognize accomplishment.** Periodically, it is essential to gauge whether students have achieved expected goals and report the results to parents, administrators, and the students themselves.

4. **Evaluate programs in order to modify them.** Achievement and other data should be used to consider whether or not the mathematics program overall is helping students achieve set goals and to modify the expectations. Should the pace of instruction be slowed down or speeded up? Do the students need additional examples or more opportunities to apply the material? Do they need more challenging applications or material?

The Nature of Errors

The dramatic change in the spirit of assessment suggested by the NCTM (1995) *Assessment Standards* is illustrated by the profoundly different view of errors emerging from cognitive research.

☞ Try Probe 3.4 (page 3-19).

Traditional View. Traditionally, errors have been viewed as shameful deficiency—as evidence of a character or mental defect. As Mrs. MeChokemchild put it, "If I see errors on a test, then I know a kid hasn't absorbed the material. Errors are a sure sign of carelessness, inattentiveness, laziness, or just plain stupidity."

Assessment Standards. "Many teachers," Ms. Socrates noted, "believe that children's errors are random—due to carelessness or incorrect recall. Undoubtedly, children do make slips—particularly when confronted with long, tedious assignments. However, their errors are frequently systematic (e.g., Ashlock, 1998; Buswell & Judd, 1925). Such errors arise when children use their incomplete knowledge to make sense of tasks as best they can. (Continued on page 3-20.)

➤ Probe 3.4: Reflecting on Assessment

In Part I of this probe, you are asked to consider: *Why do children make errors? What is the educational importance of errors?* In Part II, you are asked to reflect on: *What can a teacher conclude about children's understanding from their answers to an assessment item?*

Part I: The Nature of Children's Errors[1]

1. In the traditional skills approach, (a) what would be the primary aim of evaluating the homework or test questions illustrated below? (b) How would errors be viewed? (c) What would remedial instruction focus on?

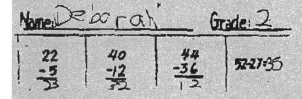

2. In each case above, analyze the child's answers. Are the child's errors systematic (i.e., did the child make the same kind of error for each item)? If so, what systematic error does the child appear to be making?

3. Why would examining children's work for systematic errors make more sense than simply grading an assignment or test in terms of the number of correct answers?

Part II: The Need to Examine Process

1. In each of the following cases, evaluate the student's answer. Can you conclude whether or not the child understood the concept tested?

   a. A researcher posed the following question: In Figure A (to the right), what is the length of the bottom line?[2] Milenko answered, "Six." Can you be sure he correctly deduced the length of the unknown side from what was given? Why or why not?

   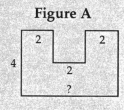

   Figure A

   b. To practice mental addition, Miss Brill gave her class the word problem below. Andy answered 33, LeMar said 55, and Judi said 693. Who answered correctly?

   ■ **Pet Day** (◆ 2-6). For Pet Day, Mr. Bing's 21 students brought: 6 gerbils, 2 mice, 7 fish, 3 birds, 4 hamsters, 5 dogs, and 6 cats. How many animals are there altogether in Mr. Bing's class?

   c. Arturo's response to a quiz question is shown below. Is he right or wrong?

   $$2 + 4 = \partial$$

   d. An achievement test posed the following question: In the picture to the right which duck is *FIRST*? Betty Bellow opted for A. Is Betty's answer right or wrong?

   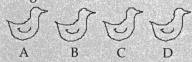

2. Is examining *product (the answers children produce)* enough to evaluate underlying understanding? Why or why not? Why should a teacher examine *process (how the child arrived at the answers)*?

3. Dr. Tek, the superintendent of the Rosie Scenerio School District, reported in a PTA meeting that the third-grade classes in the district's elementary schools scored well above average on an achievement test. Is this good evidence that the third-graders *understand* the mathematics tested? Why or why not?

4. Why must teachers guard against summarily dismissing as incorrect a child's answer that does not agree with the answer they have in mind?

In a sense, errors are a window to a child's mind—they provide a teacher an opportunity to learn how the child is thinking." Systematic errors can take the following two forms:

• **Invented-but-incorrect procedures.** Particularly when children do not understand a procedure, they may forget all or some of the steps. As a result, they may be forced to improvise their own procedures to determine an answer. Consider the first two cases in Part I of Probe 3.4 on page 3-19. Cassie knew she had to rename but could not remember the standard procedure. So for 53 - 24, for example, she "borrowed" 1 (not a ten) from the tens place and added this to the 3 to make 4. Now she could subtract 4 from 4. The case of Deborah illustrates a common incorrect invention. Unable to recall what to do with 22 - 5, for example, she subtracted the smaller ones digit from the larger ones digit (5 - 2 = 3).

• **Incomplete procedures.** Particularly when children do not understand a procedure, they may forget one or more steps in an algorithm. Consider the case of Pam in Part I of Probe 3.4. The standard algorithm specifies that you deduct the largest multiple of the divisor *that is less than the dividend digits being considered.* Pam remembered all but the critical (italicized) qualifying phrase. As result, when confronted with 263 ÷ 9, she appeared to think: The closest multiple of 9 to 26 is 27, so 9 goes into 26 three times. That takes care of the 26. Now the closest multiple of 9 to 3 is 0, so 9 goes into 3 zero times.

✓ ∽ **Teachers should view errors as a natural part of learning and encourage children to do the same.** They should help students recognize that the construction of meaningful knowledge is a gradual process—that the construction of a relatively complete and accurate understanding takes time (Resnick & Ford, 1981). Systematic errors are the *natural* result of children's partially successful efforts to construct knowledge (Resnick, Nesher, Leonard, Magone, Omanson, & Peled, 1989). In brief, errors should be viewed as *incomplete responses* rather than *wrong responses* (DeReuiter & Wansart, 1982)—as a sign of incomplete understanding rather than moral turpitude or intellectual dullness.

Process of Assessment

Traditional View. For Mrs. MeChokemchild, the process of assessment was straightfor-

ward and required little thought on her part. After completing a unit, she duplicated the unit test provided in the teaching materials accompanying her textbook. She used the answer key provided to mark wrong answers and then computed the percent correct.

Assessment Standards. For Ms. Socrates, assessment was an intricate process that required reflection. For her, assessment included:

1. **planning** (asking, e.g., "What needs to be assessed? What methods can be used to perform the assessment? What criteria for judging performance make sense? How can the results be best summarized and reported?);

2. **gathering evidence** (ensuring, e.g., that students understood the tasks and that appropriate manipulatives and materials are available);

3. **interpreting evidence** (considering, e.g., whether the evidence accurately represents a child's understanding or whether the criteria were appropriately applied); and

4. **using the results** (e.g., contemplating what actions need to be taken next to adjust instruction and remedy incomplete understanding or to build on students' new knowledge).

As Figure 3.7 illustrates, though, this four-phase sequence is not necessarily linear or sequential. That is, it doesn't always begin with Phase 1 and end with Phase 4. Instead, the phases are interactive. For example, while administering a

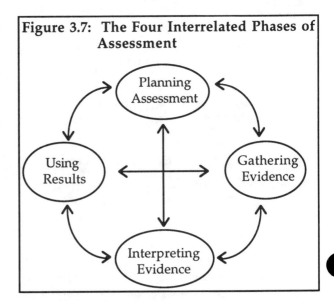

Figure 3.7: The Four Interrelated Phases of Assessment

task (gathering evidence), Ms. Socrates noticed that the wording of a problem was ambiguous (interpreting evidence) and decided to add a constraint to clarify the problem (using the results and planning future assessment). She also made a note to recognize the child who spotted the ambiguity for her thoughtful reading of the problem (both interpreting evidence and using the results).

The Nature of Assessment

Key changes in assessment emphasis recommended by the NCTM are outlined below and summarized in Box 3.2.

The Mathematics and Coherence Standards. The unit tests that Mrs. MeChokemchild administered throughout the school year and the standardized achievement test she administered in the spring consisted entirely of "objective-style" questions that could readily be marked right or wrong. Unfortunately, such questions generally are best suited for assessing knowledge of facts and procedures but not key aspects of mathematical power such as problem solving or conceptual understanding. The net result is that objective-style test typically focus on gauging a narrow band of mathematical knowledge. When such test are the sole criterion for assessing mathematical knowledge, they reinforce or foster instruction that focuses on the rote memorization of facts and procedures. In effect, they become the

tail that wags the dog—they establish the instructional goals rather than simply measure them.

In contrast, in the *Assessment Standards*, the NCTM (1995) suggests that teachers first need to establish their goals and use these goals to choose assessment measures. More specifically, the *mathematics standard* specifies that "assessment should reflect the mathematics all students need to know and be able to do" (NCTM, 1995, p. 11). The *coherence standard* notes that assessment methods should match or be appropriate for the kind of mathematical knowledge being gauged. A clear implication of these two standards is that teachers need to use a wide variety of assessment tools.

The Equity Standard. Mrs. MeChokemchild did not care that different children had different background experiences or might not be able to demonstrate their understanding on objective-style tests. The *equity standard* suggests that assessment promote equity by taking into account children's readiness and remaining open to alternative ways of gauging understanding. Probing students' thinking and considering their interpretation of task is essential to accurately assessing what students know.

The Openness Standard. Mrs. MeChokemchild didn't inform her students about her expectations or how they would be tested because it never dawned on her that it was important to

---

✓ **Box 3.2: Changes in Assessment Emphases**[†]

Decreased Attention	Increased Attention
• Simply counting correct answers on tests for the sole purpose of assigning grades	• Having assessment be an integral part of teaching
• Assessing what students do not know	• Assessing what students know and how they think about mathematics
• Focusing on a large number of specific and isolated skills organized [hierarchically]	• Focusing on a broad range of . . . tasks and taking a holistic view of mathematics
• Using exercises or word problems requiring one or two skills	• Developing problem situations that require the applications of a number of mathematical ideas
• Excluding calculators, computers, and manipulatives from the assessment process	• Using calculators, computers, and manipulatives in assessment
• Using only written tests	• Using multiple assessment techniques, including written, oral, and demonstration formats

[†]Source: page 191 of the *Curriculum and Evaluation Standards for School Mathematics*, © 1989 by NCTM.

do so. Neither did she provide immediate feedback to students and parents about the results of assessment. She felt that the less they knew about her test results, the better. After all, if student or parents were uninformed, they couldn't whine and complain.

According to *openness standard*, teachers should inform students about what they are expected to know and how they are expected to demonstrate competence before assessment takes place. They should share assessment information promptly with students and parents and welcome scrutiny, for this might lead to improvements in both assessing and teaching.

The Learning Standard. Mrs. McChokemchild and her students viewed the unit test as something that marked the end of learning cycle. They viewed the standardized test simply as an interruption to the learning process. According to the *learning standard*, "assessment should enhance mathematics learning" (NCTM, 1995, p. 13). Not only should assessment be an integral part of instruction, it should provide students opportunities to learn as well as to demonstrate what they know. This implies that teachers need to include challenging problems and other rich and interesting tasks in assessment.

The Inference Standard. For Mrs. McChokemchild, judging what students knew was a simple process: determine the percent correct on a test. Unfortunately, such a crude approach can be misleading, particularly when trying to assess higher level competencies such as problem-solving ability or conceptual understanding.

Because children's knowledge cannot be observed directly, teachers must make inferences about what they know. According to the *inference standard*, assessment then is a process of gathering evidence and using it to make valid inferences about student knowledge. Consistent with the coherence standard, "a valid inference requires appropriate and adequate evidence" (NCTM, 1995, p. 19). That is, it requires evidence tailored to a particular aspect of mathematical knowledge and drawn from multiple sources. The importance of the inference standard is discussed further in the next subunit.

3•2•2 WHAT TO LOOK FOR

For accurate assessment, teachers should focus on evidence of *mathematical power*, not merely the mechanics of arithmetic. Such evidence can best be gathered by examining the *processes* by which students determine their answers.

Key Aspects of Mathematical Power

For well rounded assessment, teachers should examine students' (a) disposition toward mathematics, (b) ability to conduct mathematical inquiry (e.g., solve problems, analyze and reason, and communicate effectively), and (c) understanding of concepts and procedures (NCTM, 1989). Two tips for assessing understanding are noted below.

✓ **If understanding is defined in terms of connections, then it follows that the degree of understanding can be gauged by the number, accuracy, and the strength of a student's connections.** Teachers need to consider whether or not students can, for example, relate their knowledge of procedures to concrete models (e.g., represent a formal procedure with manipulatives), to other mathematical topics (e.g., recognize that a division can be used to translate fractions into decimals), and to real-world examples (e.g., can write a word problem to represent an equation such as $3 \times 6 = 18$).

✓ **Transfer (application of existing knowledge to a new task) provides strong evidence of understanding** (adaptive expertise). For instance, can children apply their understanding of fraction multiplication effectively by modeling their procedures with a new manipulative or apply what they have learned about subtracting two-digit numbers to subtracting three-digit numbers?

The Need to Examine Process

To make valid inferences about students' learning, "we must be interested in what students are really thinking and understanding" (Parker, 1993, p. 17). In other words, TO ASSESS HIGHER-ORDER THINKING (PROBLEM-SOLVING AND REASONING), COMMUNICATION FACILITY, UNDERSTANDING, AND DISPOSITION, IT IS ESSENTIAL TO EXAMINE *PROCESS (HOW CHILDREN ARRIVE AT ANSWERS)* AS WELL AS PRODUCT (THEIR ANSWERS).

True and False Indications of Understanding. *Does correctly answering a test question indicate understanding? Does incorrectly answering a test question indicate a lack of understanding?* The answer to these questions is: No! A teacher must take care to distinguish between true and false success and between true and false shortfalls (Peck, Jencks, & Connell, 1989).

• **True success.** *A true success occurs when a child who understands the underlying concept of a test question answers correctly.*

• **False success.** *A false success occurs when a child who does not understand the underlying mathematics of a test question nevertheless answers correctly.* Although it is tempting to conclude that a correct answer indicates understanding, recall from chapter 1 that students can blindly use procedures memorized by rote to calculate correct answers. Moreover, students can obtain the correct answer for the wrong reasons. Consider the case of Milenko (Question 1a in Part II of Probe 3.4 on page 3-19) who concluded that the unknown side in the figure was six. After the interviewer responded, "Great, how did you get it?" the child responded, "Four and two is six." Instead of recognizing that the unknown side had to equal the sum of the parallel sides (2 + 2 + 2), he accidentally produced the correct answer by adding 4 + 2. A false success can also occur because of a lucky guess. For example, on a true-false test, a child has a 50-50 chance of guessing the correct answer.

• **True shortfall.** *A true shortfall occurs when a child who does not understand the mathematics does not correctly answer a test question.*

• **False shortfall.** *A false shortfall occurs when a child who really understands the concept measured by the test item responds incorrectly.* This can occur because the child, for example, misinterpreted the test item or was distracted for a moment. In such cases, the test does not accurately reflect a true understanding or competence. A false shortfall can also occur when a teacher fails to see that an ambiguous question can be interpreted in more than one way.

Product Versus Process. In the traditional skills approach, assessment focuses on *product*—on what a child produces. More bluntly, standardized, textbook, and teacher-made tests often concentrate on the number of correct answers. Unfortunately, a focus on product may not accurately reflect a students' understanding of mathematics (e.g., Kamii, 1990a; Peck et al., 1989). More specifically, it can result in many false successes and false shortfalls and, thus, can be misleading or unhelpful.

✓ **Assessment should focus on *process*.** Mathematics educators have long recognized that the evaluation of learners should focus on their underlying understanding, not merely on whether or not they answered correctly (e.g., Davis, 1984; Erlwanger, 1975; Ginsburg, 1989). To avoid overestimating or underestimating understanding, a teacher needs to concentrate on *how* children arrive at the answers they do. Moreover, a focus on process may be the best—and sometimes only—way to gauge problem-solving, reasoning, communicating competence; metacognitive functioning (e.g., self-monitoring); and disposition.

✓ **Assessment should be an ongoing process conducted primarily by teachers, not with written tests.** "Teachers are . . . in the best position to [examine process and] to judge the development of students' progress and, hence, must be . . . the primary assessors of students (NCTM, 1995, p. 1). "Observing, listening, and questioning are the most common methods for gathering evidence of learning during instruction" (NCTM, 1995, p. 46).

3•2•3 ASSESSMENT METHODS

In this section, we discuss rubric scoring and outline three methods for examining process (performance, oral, and written assessments). We also touch on an invaluable but often overlooked source of assessment information—student input.

Rubric Scoring

Definition and Rationale. *Rubric scoring is a set of authoritative rules that provides direction in the scoring of an assessment task or activity* (NCTM, 1995). A useful rubric is based on a careful analysis of children operating at various levels. Rubric scoring is consistent with the NCTM's philosophy that to gauge achievement, teachers need to compare students' performance with valid performance criteria rather than that of other students. It is also consistent with the psychological perspective that there are levels of understanding rather than the view that understanding is an all-or-nothing phenomenon. When rubrics are shared with students, they can serve as learning guides by helping students understand clearly what constitutes a good performance.

☞ Try Probe 3.5 (pages 3-24 to 3-26). (Text continued on page 3-27.)

➤ Probe 3.5: Techniques for Assessing Mathematical Understanding

The aim of this probe is to familiarize you with four techniques for examining process.

Part I: Rubric Scoring. After reading the example of a general rubric and the example of task-specific rubric, evaluate the samples of student work below for the following task:

✓ *What does $\frac{3}{4}$ mean to me?*

Level	General Rubric	Task-Specific Rubric
Complete	Explicit understanding of all defining criteria of a concept.	Recognizes that $\frac{3}{4}$ can represent three of four <u>equal</u> parts of a whole.
Fairly complete	Explicit understanding of some defining criteria of a concept.	Recognizes that $\frac{3}{4}$ can represent three of four parts of a whole.
Somewhat complete	Intuitive (implicit) understanding of some aspect of the concept.	Recognizes that $\frac{3}{4}$ can represent a part of the whole.
Incomplete	No explicit or implicit understanding of the defining criteria of a concept.	No sensible meaning of $\frac{3}{4}$ given.

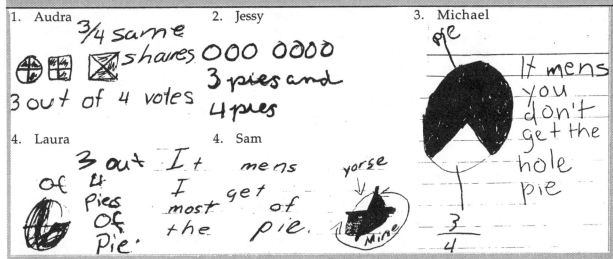

Part II: Interviewing Children. Interviewing individuals or small groups of children is one way of conducting performance assessment and can provide invaluable process information for diagnostic purposes (e.g., Does a child have the counting skills necessary to solve addition problems informally?), instructional feedback (e.g., Does a child *understand* how to use rods to add unlike fractions—as opposed to simply using a procedure memorized by rote?), and grading (e.g., Does a child *understand* the connection between fractions and decimals?). Even brief interviews of a few minutes can provide rich insights into a child's thinking, strategy, understanding, or disposition (Peck et al., 1989). Individual interviews can be an integral part of other assessment techniques such as open-ended tasks and authentic assessment. Interviewing children is a real art. Read the interviewing tips below and then analyze the transcript of an interview with a 5-year-old child on page 3-26.

1. **Establish rapport with a child before beginning the interview.** Some children may feel uneasy talking to a new teacher or adult. To help them feel at ease, ask about personal things such as their age, whether they have any brothers or sisters, what they like to do after school, their favorite animal, and so forth. Playing a game first can be helpful—particularly for kindergarten screening.

2. **Use an engaging task or format.** For children of any age, presenting an interview task as a *game* can be motivating. For younger children, especially, using puppets or muppets

may also make an interview more enjoyable. Note that speaking through a muppet, for example, can provide shy or nonconfident children, in particular, a relatively safe way to advance their ideas.

3. **Whenever appropriate, consider performance with materials as well as verbal responses.** Offering manipulative responses instead of, or in addition to, verbal response can minimize false shortfalls due to weak verbal skills. Make sure all needed materials are ready for use. It is distracting for an interviewer to search for needed material or to figure out what should be used.

4. **Talk at the child's level.** Use vocabulary a child understands. For example, a young child may understand "take-away" but not "subtract," "as big as" but not "same size," "as many as," but not "same number," etc. On the other hand, don't "talk down" to the child or use "baby talk." Sentence structure should also be suited to the child. Long and complex sentences and questions should be avoided.

5. **Refrain from leading questions.** Leading questions (e.g., "It's more than five isn't it?" "Don't you think $\frac{1}{3}$ is larger than $\frac{1}{4}$?" "Did you conclude that 7 + 9 was 16 because we figured out that 9 + 7 was 16 earlier?" or "You probably don't like word problems?") suggest an answer. Some children are more interested in pleasing adults than speaking their mind frankly and may simply confirm the answer the interviewer appears to desire.

6. **Strike a balance between being too directive and too nondirective.** If an interviewer is too pushy, a child may become anxious, reticent, or even hostile. On the other hand, if an interviewer is too passive, the interview may not be informative.

7. **Encourage explanations rather than single-word answers or other evasions.** For example, "How do you know 12 is even?" is a better question than "Is 12 even?" Single-word answers such as "yes" or "no" are often not informative and may be just a guess. For the same reasons, use requests such as "Show me how to multiply 7 x 9" rather than questions such as "*Can* you multiply 7 x 9." The latter

invites the evasive answer "yes" (or "no"), which is often followed by a stony silence. Explanations such as "I don't know" or "My daddy told me" may also be evasions—requiring, perhaps, a new tack to your questioning.

8. **Respond in an accepting but neutral manner.** An interviewer's verbal responses or body language should not provide cues to correctness. Verbal responses such as "Is that what you really mean?" "Are you sure that . . . ?" "Look at what the problem says" imply that the child is wrong and should change answers. Body language such as tone of voice, frowning, or lifting an eyebrow can likewise relay expectations. Verbal responses such as "Good" and body language such as smiles clue correctness and encourage guessing rather than thoughtful responses. Note that many teachers want their students to be successful and consciously or nonconsciously act in ways to "coax" the correct answer from children. Moreover, children—particularly those who are least certain—look for clues and try to answer in a way that will please the interviewer. Remember that the aim of the interview is to gauge what the child understands, not teaching. Keep phrasing, facial expressions, gestures, voice tone nondirective.

9. **Ask children to explain or justify both correct and incorrect answers.** If you follow-up on only incorrect answers, this will cue a child that her answer is wrong and may lead her to change her answer.

10. **Give a child ample opportunity to respond and to complete an answer.** Wait patiently after asking a question and again after the child responds. These wait times are important for encouraging thoughtful reflection and complete answers.

11. **Sidestep request for feedback.** Children often ask if their answer is correct. Respond with encouraging but neutral comments such as, "I see you are thinking hard about this" or "That's an interesting answer."

Analyze the following transcript in terms of the interviewing technique discussed above and evaluate the interviewer's conclusion.

Probe 3.5 continued

Interviewer (I): How much are three and two? [No response from the child.] If you had three candies and I gave two more, how many candies would you have altogether?

Child (C): Six.

I: What did you say? Did you say six?

C: I think it's five.

I: Okay! Now what's two and three more altogether?

C [nervously]: One, two, three, four, five . . .

I: Good!

I: Let's try four and three.

C [after a moment]: Seven.

I: Right again. How did you figure that out? Did you know three and three was six and this [pointing to 4 + 3] had to be one more?

C: Yah.

I: Quickly, what's three and four?

C: I'd have to figure it out.

The interviewer concluded that the child did not know the principle of commutativity (the order in which addends are added does not affect the sum).

Part III: Questioning Students with Open-Ended Questions. Box 3.3 below compares close-ended questions with open-ended, process-oriented questions. (1) Interview several children using one or more of the open-ended questions below, assess the children's understanding, and report your results to your group or class. (2) Devise your open-ended question.

Part IV: Error Analyses. Analyzing children's systematic errors is a type of written assessment that can help reveal their conceptual level. Consider the following two examples:

1. Asked to indicate what fraction of each pie illustrated below had been eaten (dark portion), Plato wrote $\frac{1}{3}$, $\frac{1}{4}$, $\frac{1}{2}$, and $\frac{1}{4}$, and Tess wrote $\frac{1}{2}$, $\frac{1}{3}$, $\frac{1}{2}$, and $\frac{1}{3}$ for Examples a, b, c, and d, respectively. What can you conclude about each child's understanding of fractions?

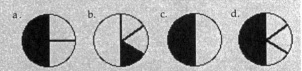

a.   b.   c.   d.

2. Mr. Roxbury included the following item on a test: Which of the following decimals represents the largest number: 0.2, 0.38, or .178? Reggie chose 0.2 and Vedia chose .178. (a) Why might each of these children answer as they did? (b) Which child has a more complete understanding of decimals? Why?

Part V: Write a Story Problem. ✓ Write a story that would fit the equation $\frac{1}{4} \times \frac{2}{3} = \frac{2}{12} = \frac{1}{6}$. Share your story with your group or class. With the help of your peers, evaluate your effort.

✓ Box 3.3: Examples of Two Types of Oral Questions	
Closed-Ended Questions	**More Open-Ended, Process-Oriented Questions**
What is the sum of 8 + 7?	What are some ways you can get the answer to 8 + 7?
What is the formula for the area of a rectangle?	How could we figure out how much space this rectangle covers?
What is 2 x 9?	How can you use what you already know to figure out 2 x 9?
A child has written: 37 + 28 = 515.	A child has written: 37 + 28 = 515.
After adding 7 and 8 to get 15, should you put the one where he did?	Do you think this answer makes sense? Why or why not?
What is the difference of 162 - 65?	What is the first thing you did to find the difference of 162 - 65?
Is that where the decimal goes?	Why did you put the decimal there?

Two Types of Rubrics. *A general rubric is "an outline for creating task-specific rubrics or guiding expert judgment"; a task-specific rubric is a description of performance levels on a particular task* (NCTM, 1995, p. 90). See Part I of Probe 3.5 for an example of each.

Two Types of Scoring. Rubric scoring distinguishes among levels of understanding—levels of completeness, accuracy and/or integration of knowledge. *Holistic scoring entails assigning a single level of performance for a task* (e.g., again see Part I of Probe 3.5). Analytic scoring involves assigning separate scores for several fundamentally different dimensions of task performance (see, e.g., Box 3.4). Because this type of scoring is more involved than holistic scoring, it can be more informative.

Methods for Assessing Process

Performance Assessment. Performance assessment provides a key way to examine process. It involves gauging children's dispositions, strategies, or understandings by actually *observing* them performing a task and by *analyzing* their performance. Performance assessment can include (a) *open-ended test items* (see Box 3.5 on the next page), (b) *informal observations* of ongoing classroom activities (see Box 3.6 on pages 3-28 and 3-29), (c) *authentic assessment* (see Box 3.7 on page 3-29), and (d) *individual interviews* (see Part II on pages 3-24 to 3-26 of Probe 3.5). Open-ended test items can provide structured (preplanned) performance assessment, whereas informal observation can provide spontaneous performance assessment (Stiggins & Bridgeford, 1985). Authentic assessment and individual interviews can provide either structured or spontaneous assessment.

✓ Box 3.4: An Example of Analytic Rubric Scoring

The following task and task-specific rubric are intended for children who have not yet been introduced to the formal (cross-products) procedure for solving proportion problems.

■ **A Bigger Scale Drawing (◆ 4-6).** Mattias figured out his classroom could be represented by floor plan consisting of a rectangle 6 inches long and 4 inches wide. However, he realized that this scale drawing would be too small. So he decided to draw a rectangle with the same shape but 9 inches long. How long should the width of this larger rectangle be?

Affect	Inquiry Processes	Content (Understanding of Proportions)
3 = Highly positive (e.g., focused on solving the problem and persevered despite setbacks or an inability to solve the problem).	3 = Diligently solved the problem (e.g., understood problem, devised a workable plan, obtained the correct solution, looked back, clearly justified solution).	3 = Uses multiplicative reasoning (i.e., recognized that 9 is $1\frac{1}{2}$ times larger than 6, so the width must be 1 times larger than 3).
2 = Somewhat positive.	1-2 = Some successes (e.g., misinterpreted part of the problem, used a partially correct procedure, looking back did not help, did not clearly justify solution).	2 = Uses additive or other informal reasoning correctly (e.g., reasons that there are 3" of length for every 2" of width so 3 + 3 + 3 or 9 would be matched by 2 + 2 + 2 or 6).
1 = Somewhat negative.		
0 = Highly negative (e.g., avoided solving the problem or readily gave up).	0 = No success (i.e., completely misunderstood problem, no attempt or inappropriate plan, incorrect solution, did not look back or justify solution).	1 = Uses additive reasoning incorrectly (i.e., reasons because 9 is 3 more than 6, the new width must be 3 more than 4 or 7) or other incorrect reasoning.
		0 = No understanding.

✓ Box 3.5: Examples of Open-Ended Questions and Problems

Unlike traditional test items that required using *the* school-taught procedure, open-ended tasks invite the use of *various* strategies.

Item 1: Understanding of Place Value (◆ 1-3). Mrs. Martin taught her class how to add with written numbers. One of the students wondered if the answer to $\begin{array}{r} 36 \\ +28 \\ \hline \end{array}$ could be 514. How should Mrs. Martin answer? Explain or illustrate how she could help the child understand why this answer is right or wrong.

Item 2: Flexibility of Mental Subtraction (◆ 2-6). Describe two ways you can subtract 53 - 26 in your head. Which is easier to do? Would you subtract 74 - 39 in your head the same way you would subtract 53 - 26? Explain why or why not.

Item 3: Understanding of Fraction Size (◆ 2-6). Evangela pointed out that $\frac{2}{5}$ was larger than $\frac{2}{7}$. Brother Evangelos said that $\frac{2}{7}$ had to be larger than $\frac{2}{5}$. Who do you think was right? Why?

Item 4: Geometry (◆ 5-8). School Street and Commerce Street meet at a right angle. From this corner to Bethany's house at the end of Commerce Street is 2 miles. The turn from Commerce Street to the path between Bethany's house and the school is half of a right angle. Tell what you can about Bethany's neighborhood.

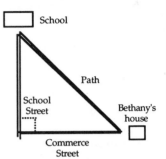

Item 5: Higher-Order Thinking—Problem Solving and Reasoning (◆ 2-6)[†]. Alessandra heard that 50% of the students who applied to the new magnet school were accepted and that 50% of the students who applied to the technology program were accepted. Alessandra concluded that by applying to both, she stood a 100% chance of getting out of the boring school she was in. Evaluate Alessandra's conclusion. Does it make sense or not? Justify your answer.

[†]Based on an item from the California State Department of Education (*A Question of Thinking*, published in 1989).

✓ Box 3.6: Observation Techniques

Teachers can learn much about children by carefully observing them and listening to them as they participate in class, toil individually, or work in a group. From such firsthand experiences, teachers can more readily spot true success, what children are doing wrong, how their knowledge is incomplete, what strengths (informal and otherwise) they have, and so forth. Indeed, some learning goals (e.g., an ability to work with others without becoming overly defensive or slavish, an ability to take a listener's viewpoint, a tendency to check whether an answer makes sense) can only be assessed by observation.

Comment Cards. Anecdotal information can be recorded on 3-inch x 5-inch index cards and then filed in a child's folder. This can provide a rich source of information for planning, grading, or conferencing with parents later. Particularly at first, it may help to look for just a couple of things to record. Some teachers may prefer to make notes during class; others, after class or school each day, and yet others, at the end of each week.

Geoff   *4-29*

Solved 43 - 17 using negative numbers: 3 - 7 → -4, 40 - 10 → 30, 30 - 4 = 26. Wow. Had trouble explaining this to others → became frustrated. Better at listening to other's thoughts. Still needs to take the time to check accuracy of his answers.

Checklists. Checklists can focus a teacher's attention of specific goals and provide a convenient way of recording large amounts of data. Illustrated on the next page is an example of a general checklist and a specific checklist. Teachers should tailor their checklists to the particular goals they wish to emphasize.

Box 3.6 continued

WEEK OF 4/25	Aldrich	Hakeem	GROUP: B Mario	Orti3
Looked back	W			M Th
Looked for counterexample			Th F	
Patiently explained ideas	M	W Th		
Acknowledged an error				T
Used model appropriately	T	T	T Th	T
Related symbols to model	M W Th	M W	W Th	M
Justified procedure	T		Th	
Willing to explain strategy		F		W
Perseveres	M Th	M	M	Th
Showed interest (e.g., visited math center, did bonus problem)	M–W	M–W	M, Th	M–W, Th

(General checklist)

Date: April 25–29 NAME	GROUP	OK	Relates multiplication equation to area model Comments
Evaugh	A	√	
Nalin		√	Struggled to model 3 x 4
Sabrina			Had trouble finding area with blocks
Winette			Did not recognize that 3 in 3 x 4 represents the length of one side
Aldrich	B	√	

(Specific Checklist)

✓ Box 3.7: Authentic Assessment

Authentic assessment entails a rich, real-life, open-ended task (e.g., Lesh & Lamon, 1992). It can involve problems, projects, or investigations—which can be preplanned or can arise spontaneously from other classroom activities. Two examples of authentic assessment follow.

■ **Flower Petals** (◆ 2-8). For her art project, Daneka decided to paint a field of spring flowers she had seen the previous day. To help her reflect on her proposed effort, Mr. Arkin asked, "What kinds of flowers will you paint? How many petals do these flowers have?" Daneka seemed unsure about these things. "A good artist is a careful observer," Mr. Arkin commented. "Before you paint, examine the flowers in the field. Do all flowers of the same type have the same number of petals? Petals frequently come in what number or numbers? Petals seldom or never occur in what number or numbers?" Consider how Daneka could answer these questions. What answers did you find?

■ **Baseball Diamond** (◆ 4-8). A regulation baseball diamond is 90 feet from base to base, 60 feet 6 inches from the pitcher's mound to home plate, and about 127 feet $3\frac{3}{8}$ inches from second base to home plate. Youth play on a shortened diamond. Lay out a baseball diamond that is $\frac{2}{3}$ as large as a regulation field. Include a drawing.

Oral Assessment. There are two reasons why oral assessment is important in trying to construct an understanding of children's knowledge. One is that many students can often explain their mathematical ideas, reasoning, strategies, and so forth better verbally than they can by writing. Another is that students' verbal explanations can more readily reveal process (their thinking, reasoning, and underlying understanding) than can traditional paper-and-pencil tests. Consider, for example, Arturo's response to 2 + 4 (Question 1c in Part II of Probe 3.4 on page 3-19). Is his written answer a backward 6 and thus correct or, perhaps, an upside-down 9 and thus incorrect? The only way a teacher could know for sure is to ask the boy. Four techniques for performing an oral assessment are briefly described below.

1. **Questioning students.** Asking questions to evaluate students' knowledge can be an integral part of ongoing instruction (Cazden, 1986). It can also be a key way of following up on performance and written assessment. If done effectively, asking students questions can be an invaluable way of assessing process and higher-order knowledge. To do so, a teacher should ask more *open-ended, process-oriented* questions. In contrast to closed-ended questions that request a specific answer, such questions ask students to focus on solution methods and reasons for their answers (see Box 3.7 in Part III of Probe 3.5 on page 3-26). Open-ended, process-oriented questions can help them to see that mathematics involves more than getting correct answers. Effective questioning depends on a teacher: (a) responding in an accepting but neutral manner (e.g., "So you are saying . . . ," "I understand your point," or simply listening intently without speaking); (b) asking children to explain or justify both correct and incorrect answers (e.g., "How do you know that?" "How can you convince the rest of us of your answer?"); (c) waiting for students to answer or complete their answer; and (d) asking for alternatives (e.g., "Does anyone disagree?" "Are there any other answers?" "What do the rest of you think?").

2. **Student justifications.** Asking students to justify their reasoning, strategies, or answers to the class can quickly reveal their depth of understanding. Perhaps, as importantly, it can help students recognize for themselves how well they understand what they are doing.

3. **Peer-group exchanges.** Listening to a group of students as they discuss a task can provide invaluable insight into their higher-order thinking processes, their communication ability, level of understanding, and disposition.

4. **Debates or panel discussions.** Both debates and panel discussions provide rich opportunities to gauge children's ability to reason and communicate ideas effectively as well as their level of understanding. These activities can be planned events or the spontaneous outgrowth of disagreements. These forums also provide an opportunity for a teacher to discuss such issues as weighing substance against style, does a majority vote guarantee truth, and what constitutes a convincing case?

Written Assessment. Written assessment can and should involve much more than counting the number of correct or incorrect answers. It can entail:

1. **Student portfolios.** For many occupations, people compile portfolios so that prospective employers can evaluate their work. Encouraging students to create portfolios of their mathematical efforts can (a) help them to learn how to construct a portfolio (a useful real-world skill), (b) provide a way of emphasizing their strengths (e.g., personal discoveries or inventions, original contributions to the classroom community, elegant strategies, and interesting questions), and (c) foster mathematical power (e.g., ownership of mathematical ideas and pride in their mathematical ability including their informal knowledge). Note that student portfolios (a) create an authentic need to communicate ideas in writing and with drawings, (b) require students to explain explicitly their mathematical ideas, and (c) provide a record of growth that students, teacher, and parents can see. Note also that if portfolios are used for grading purposes, clear (though flexible) criteria are important (e.g., what may be an outstanding portfolio for a second grader may not be satisfactory for a fourth grader).

2. **Journals.** In chapter 2, we discussed journals as a learning tool. Journals can also serve to evaluate students progress. Journals can be open-ended (where students are free to discuss what they wish), highly structured (where students respond to specific questions or request of the teacher), or some combination of the two. Journals provide a relatively safe way for students to voice their thoughts and feelings—particularly

about things that are troubling them. Entries can include questions about course content; describe difficulties with a student's group or course content; or note thoughts and feelings about a classroom activity, a problem, or a discussion. Particularly if structured questions are used, journals provide an effective way to monitor student understanding and affect on an ongoing basis. Keeping journals in a loose leaf notebook can facilitate examining entries, because a student can submit just the entry instead of the entire journal. How journal entries are evaluated depends on the particular purpose of the entry. Some entries, such as those involving students' opinions or feelings, can be scored simply as *entry made* or *entry not made*. Sometimes, such as when students are asked to write a word problem that can be represented by 2 x 5, a teacher may simply write comments or provide other helpful feedback. On other occasions, a teacher may wish to develop a specific scoring rubric.

3. **Other methods** include (a) analyzing the errors, particularly the systematic errors, in students' written work (see Part IV of Probe 3.5); (b) examining students' written responses to open-ended questions; (c) asking students to record their answers on, for instance, mini-slates; (d) evaluating students' written stories or word problems; (e) considering students' written responses to open-ended prompts such as "Tell me what you think about . . ."; and (f) asking students to write stories or word problems (see, e.g., Part V of Probe 3.5).

Student Input

Assessment should include self-review and peer review (NCTM, 1992). Students' reflections about their progress, difficulties, and disposition can provide teachers invaluable diagnostic information and instructional feedback. It can also foster self-monitoring and -control. Students' input about their peers can give a teacher valuable insight into a child's contribution to a group.

3•3 INTEGRATING INSTRUCTION AND ASSESSMENT

Figure 3.7: Feedback or Fear

SHOE reprinted by permission of the Tribune Media Service.

☞ Try Probe 3.6 (pages 3-32 to 3-35).

Good teachers have long used assessment for diagnosis and instructional feedback as well as grading. One technique for accomplishing this is to write *See me* on a test or paper—to request an individual interview (see Figure 3.7). The interview can then be used to gauge more clearly how a child's understanding is incomplete and how to help him or her fill in the gap. For example, in Vignette 1 on page 3-32 of Probe 3.6, David's teacher did not simply correct the seatwork and record a grade for grading purposes. Instead, the teacher set about trying to find out the source of his difficulty so that she was in a position to help the boy. After interviewing David for a couple of minutes, the teacher discovered he did not understand the symbols for addition and subtraction. Once she related the plus sign (+) to his informal knowledge of *adding more* and the minus sign (-) to his informal knowledge of *taking away*, David had no further difficulty with the written representations of addition and subtraction. (Continued on page 3-36.)

↱ Probe 3.6: Integrating Assessment and Instruction

Daily instruction and assessment should go hand in hand. As Vignette 1 below illustrates, teachers must continually assess their students' mathematical knowledge and progress in order to plan and adjust instruction. This probe illustrates three techniques that can simultaneously serve instructional and assessment aims: using errors (Part I), student-generated tests (Part II), and concept maps (Part III).

Vignette 1: The Case of David[3]. David, a first-grader, did poorly on Worksheet 4 shown below. His teacher first conjectured that he could not read the numerals and so was just guessing. She collected data on this educated guess by testing David's numeral-reading skill. The results did not support her conjecture. The teacher then conjectured that David did not understand the concepts of addition and subtraction.

1. How could you evaluate this conjecture?

2. Analyze David's work. What conjectures can you come up with to explain his performance? Note that your explanation should account for all of David's answers.

David		Worksheet 4
$1 + 1 = 0$ ✓		$3 + 2 = 1$ ✓
$2 - 1 = 3$ ✓		$4 - 1 = 5$ ✓
$2 + 2 = 0$ ✓		$1 + 3 = 2$ ✓
$4 - 2 = 2$ C		$4 - 3 = 1$ C
$1 + 4 = 3$ ✓		$2 + 1 = 1$ ✓
$5 - 4 = 1$ C		$3 - 1 = 4$ ✓

Part I: Using Errors as a Springboard to Inquiry. Errors can have important instructional, as well as diagnostic, uses (Borasi, 1994).

Vignette 2: A Case of Mishandled Errors. Miss Brill's class was discussing a problem that involved adding the decimals 3.2 and .58. "What did you come up with?" asked Miss Brill. Rodney answered nine-tenths. Without comment, she called on Georgina.

"Three hundred seventy-eight," the girl responded enthusiastically.

Again, without comment, Miss Brill turned to the next student. After LeMar answered, "Three point seven eight," she commented, "good."

1. What beliefs about errors might Miss Brill have conveyed to her class?

2. How could she have responded to Rodney's and Georgina's incorrect answers in a way that would have promoted their and other students' learning? That is, how could Miss Brill have used the situation described in Vignette 2 as a springboard to inquiry?

Vignette 3: A Case of Error, Conflict, and Insight. Although a class had previously discussed an area meaning of multiplication and multiplying fractions less than one, it had not yet encountered a problem like the one below:

■ **Area with Mixed Numbers (◆ 4-8).** The floor of Archie's tree house was $3\frac{1}{2}$-meters long and $2\frac{1}{3}$-meters wide. What was its area?

Alexi commented, "Oh easy," and proceeded to write:

$$\begin{array}{r} 3\frac{1}{2} \\ \times\ 2\frac{1}{3} \\ \hline 6\frac{1}{6} \end{array}$$

Some students were puzzled by the task and so the teacher prompted, "What could you do to help you solve this problem?"

Alison noted that drawing a picture might help. With minimal help, Arianne proceeded to make the drawing below:

She then reasoned that the area of the six 1 x 1 squares was 6, that the area of the two 1 x $\frac{1}{2}$ rectangles totaled another 1 and that the three 1 x $\frac{1}{3}$ rectangles added yet another whole. This left the area of the small corner. After prompting, Arianne next concluded that the area of this $\frac{1}{3}$ x $\frac{1}{2}$ corner had to be another $\frac{1}{6}$-square units. Adding each of the separate areas, she concluded that the total area was $8\frac{1}{6}$-square units.

Probe 3.6 continued

The teacher encouraged Alexi, who meanwhile had been trying unsuccessfully to use Cuisenaire rods to check his answer, to compare his answer with that of his neighbors. Noticing the discrepancy with Arianne's answer, he set out to make his own drawing to discover what Arianne had done wrong. (In this case, the *perceived* error of another student motivated the inquiry.)

After using a picture to work out the solution of $8\frac{1}{6}$-square units, Alexi noted that his initial answer had to be wrong. The teacher asked, "Why didn't your procedure work?"

Alexi responded, "I multiplied them separately"—meaning that he had multiplied 2 x 3 and $\frac{1}{3}$ x $\frac{1}{2}$ but not $\frac{1}{3}$ x 3 (the area of the 3-by-$\frac{1}{2}$ rectangle) or 2 x $\frac{1}{2}$ (the area of 2-by-$\frac{1}{2}$ rectangle).

The teacher then prompted, "How could you multiply them to get the correct answer?"

Alexi responded, "I don't know. Wait . . . Like this." In writing (see the figure to the right), he proceeded to reinvent and demonstrate a standard algorithm for multiplying mixed numbers.

$$
\begin{array}{r}
3 \quad\ \frac{1}{2} \\
\times 2 \quad \frac{1}{3} \\
\hline
6 \\
1 \\
1 \ \frac{1}{6} \\
\hline
\end{array}
$$

"[Based on my correct answer] I figured I'd have to do something more." (Note that the students' computational error served as a prompt to explore his invented procedure and repair it.)

The teacher then encouraged Alexi to share his shortcut for multiplying mixed numbers.

1. The vignette above illustrates what instructional uses of errors?

2. What role did the teacher play in Vignette 3, and how was it different from that played by Miss Brill in Vignette 2?

Part II: Student-Generated Test

Develop a test that could be used to evaluate students' understanding of Unit 3•2. Provide an answer key. How well do you need to understand material to write a test about it?

Part III: Concept Maps

What is a concept map? A concept map pictures and describes mathematical connections. More specifically, it is a drawing of how an individual or a group think concepts are related.

Concepts maps have three elements:

1. Concept labels written inside loops, circles, or polygons (e.g., rectangles) represent concepts.

2. Linking lines (as in webbing activities or flow charts) or arrows (as in arrow diagrams) show connections between two concepts.

3. Linking phrases, which label linking lines, specify the relationship between two concepts.

A concept map can illustrate the hierarchical relationship among ideas. In hierarchical maps, the most general concepts are placed at the top. More and more specific concepts are placed at successively lower levels. Examples, which are highly specific pieces of information, are placed at the bottom.

1. The hierarchical concept map below illustrates some geometric concepts and their relationships. Evaluate this map. Does it accurately reflect the relationships among the concepts? Why or why not? Discuss your conclusions with your group or class.

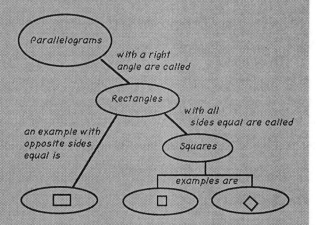

2. (a) Show how the concept of *quadrilaterals* could be represented on this map. (b) Now represent the following concepts: *geometric figures, plane (two-dimensional) figures, polygons,* and *triangles.* (Hints: Identify the most general concept and place it at the top of your map. Then locate the next most general

Probe 3.6 continued

concept and place it under the most general concept. Continue in this way until you have used all the concepts listed. Label the connections with linking phrases that clearly describe the relationships between concepts.

3. Show where *trapezoids* would fit in the concept map above. How should this concept be connected to other concepts such as *quadrilaterals* and *parallelograms*? Why?

4. (a) Questions 2 and 3 above raise what questions? What did you learn about your understanding of geometry as a result of attempting to answer Questions 2 and 3?

5. As Vignette 4 below illustrates, concept mapping can serve as a source of conflict, discussion, and doubt—and, thus, as an invaluable instructional tool. (a) Which definition of isosceles triangle is mathematically correct? (b) Both Andy's and Pedro's group indicated that isosceles triangles, but not equilateral triangle, could be right triangles. Were they correct? Why or why? What does this indicate about the student's understanding of triangles?

Vignette 4: Conflicting Concept Maps

 On the advice of Ms. Socrates, Miss Brill tried the following concept-mapping activity: Draw a cgoncept map that includes the following concepts: *Equilateral Triangles, Isosceles Triangles, Right Triangles,* and *Types of Triangles*. Label the connections between concepts by describing how the concepts are related.

Andy's group drew Concept Map A below; Pedro's group, Concept Map B.

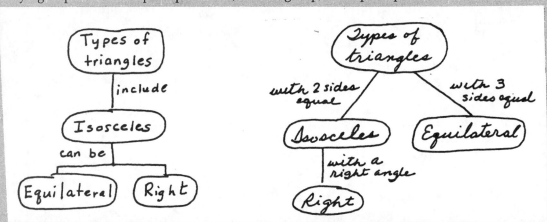

Figure A: Andy's Group   Figure B: Pedro's Group

Andy explained that it made sense that an equilateral triangle was just a special type of isosceles triangle, "If you've got three sides equal, then you've got two sides equal."

Pedro justified his group's map by noting their math books always discussed and depicted isosceles and equilateral triangles separately. From what they had learned previously, they assumed that there was no connection between isosceles and equilateral triangles.

"Our group agrees with Pedro's," interjected Judi "We looked *isosceles* up in the dictionary and it said, *having two equal sides as in an isosceles triangle*. We thought this meant *just two equal sides* rather than *at least two equal sides* because you never hear anyone refer to a square as an isosceles rectangle.

Michelle disagreed, "Our group's diagram is like Andy's, except we said that isosceles was *a triangle with two or three sides equal*. We got this definition from our math textbook."

Probe 3.6 continued

6. Consider how concept mapping could be used as an assessment tool. Discuss your ideas with your group or class.

7. (a) Evaluate the following concept maps. What does each say about the map maker's understanding of the figures depicted? (b) In Rod and Cal's concept maps, is the linking phrase *includes* the best way to define the relationship between two concepts? Why or why not?

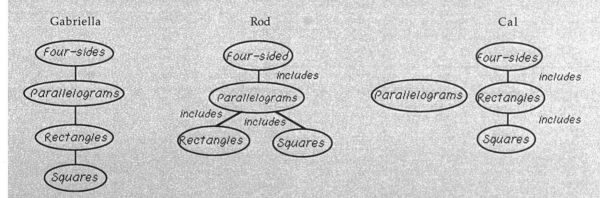

8. A class was asked to draw a concept map representing the following concepts: *decimals, fractions,* and *names for one-tenth.* They were also supposed to illustrate their concepts with examples. Collette's map, shown below, was typical and illustrates a common difficulty children have with concept maps. (a) How could the map be simplified and still accurately represent the relationships illustrated? (b) Why might, children be prone to make overelaborate maps such as Collette's?

9. Aristotle added *whole divided into 10 parts* to his concept map. Is there any way he could simplify his map and still accurately represent the relationships among the concepts?

Colette's Map   Aristotle's Map

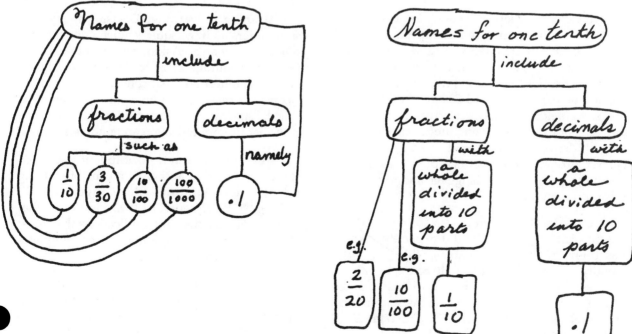

Unfortunately, as Figure 3.7 (page 3-31) implies, many students view assessment as a system for distributing rewards and punishment, not as an opportunity to learn. Helping students see that feedback is a natural part of learning is a key reason why assessment should be an integral aspect of ongoing instruction. In this unit, we describe three practical techniques for actively involving students in learning and simultaneously providing an indication of their level of understanding: student analyses of errors (Subunit 3•3•1), student-generated tests (Subunit 3•3•2), and concept mapping (Subunit 3•3•3).

3•3•1 STUDENT ANALYSES OF ERRORS

Rationale

Source of Doubt and Conflict. In the traditional skills approach, errors are *not* viewed positively by teachers or students (Borasi, 1994). Teachers typically reward correct answers and punish incorrect answers. They often reject or ignore answers until a student announces the correct answer. For example, instead of exploring Rodney's and Georgina's incorrect responses (Vignette 2 on page 3-32 of Probe 3.6), Miss Brill quickly dismissed their errors. Some teachers even believe that discussing an error may interfere with learning because students may inadvertently remember the incorrect answer.

However, as chapter 1 noted, inquiry is motivated by doubt, and the unexpected creates doubt. Children are often surprised to find they are wrong. Thus, their errors are a natural stimulus for reflection and exploration (see, e.g., Vignette 3 on pages 3-32 and 3-33 of Probe 3.6). Note that some fields routinely use errors as a teaching device. For example, in computer sciences, beginning students are encouraged to analyze and to correct programming errors ("bugs") as a way learning a programming language and improving their programming skill.

Benefits. Using errors as a springboard for inquiry can help students: (a) explicitly verbalize their mathematical ideas; (b) explicitly identify incomplete or inaccurate concepts or procedures; (c) actively explore and discuss mathematical ideas with others; (d) see the importance of careful reasoning and coherent understanding; and (e) view mathematics and learning as a dynamic, social process.

Instructional Recommendations

☞ **Encourage students to use their own errors and those of others as *"springboards to inquiry"*** (Borasi, 1992). That is, they should encourage students to view errors as an opportunity to learn. Encouraging students to analyze and to reflect on their own errors and those of others can actively involve them in constructing a more complete understanding of mathematics.

☞ **Where a child believes an error is correct, foster conflict and doubt.** For various reasons (e.g., incomplete knowledge, the opinion of the majority or a trusted peer), children often believe their errors make sense. In these cases, conflict and doubt can be created by asking students to compare their answers to the answers of others (as was done in Vignette 3 on pages 3-32 and 3-33 of Probe 3.6) or to compare their answers from different methods (e.g., compare their answer determined by a symbolic procedure with that determined by manipulatives or a calculator).

3•3•2 STUDENT-GENERATED TEST

As Part II on page 3-33 of Probe 3.6 illustrates, asking students to construct a test can accomplish two aims: (a) help them construct a deeper understanding of assigned content and (b) indicate the depth of their understanding of it.

• **Meaningful learning.** Devising an effective test of understanding requires a deep understanding of a content area. Asking students to generate a test can encourage them to delve into assigned content—to reflect on what concepts are key, how concepts are related, and how concepts might be applied. Asking them to include an answer key can further prompt reflection and understanding.

• **Authentic evaluation.** Student-generated tests can serve as an authentic means of gauging student understanding (de Lange, Burrill, Romberg, & Van Reeuwijk, 1993); indicate what concepts, connections, and applications they view as key; and provide a glimpse at the completeness of their understanding.

Students will need guidance about constructing tests. Some students may not recognize, for example, that a test serves to *sample*—more or less systematically—all the key concepts, not just the simplest or the most difficult concepts. They may not recognize that a test should gauge understanding as well as computational skill. Moreover, they may not recognize that the test format (e.g., true-false, essay, constructing a concrete model, solve a problem) is dictated by the aims of the test rather than vice versa. Modeling ideal tests can be a key way of helping students understand the goals of test construction and constructing effective tests. Students should also be given the time necessary to construct a solid understanding before they must turn in their constructed tests. Moreover, because different personalities may favor different types of tests, a mix of personalities may help in the construction of a balanced test (Jacobs & Lajoie, 1994).

3•3•3 CONCEPT MAPPING

Given that understanding can be viewed as connections and that drawing a concept mapping requires *explicitly* defining connections, concept mapping seems ideally suited for fostering and assessing conceptual learning (Bartels, 1995) (see Part III of Probe 3.6 on pages 3-33 to 3-35).

PARTING THOUGHTS

"One of the most widely accepted ideas within the mathematics education community is . . . that students should understand mathematics" (Hiebert & Carpenter, 1992, p. 65). "Understanding involves recognizing relationships between pieces of information (Hiebert & Carpenter, 1992, p. 67)—making connections. Mathematics instruction should focus on helping children see how school mathematics is related to their informal knowledge. Moreover, procedures should be connected to meaningful concepts (a comprehensible rationale). Symbolic expressions should be linked to various real-life examples and concrete models. It should also help them "see how mathematical ideas are related . . . . Once introduced, a topic [should be] used throughout the mathematics program. Teachers [should] seize opportunities that arise from classroom situations to relate different areas and uses of mathematics" (NCTM, 1989, p. 32). Mathematics should be related to applications in everyday life and other content areas. "Traditionally, a lesson was considered successful when all or most of the students got the anticipated and correct outcome. In the [investigative approach], a lesson is successful when children's thinking and understanding is revealed. Confusion is seen as a natural part of

the process of learning " (Parker, 1993, p. 47). To gauge understanding, assessment should focus on how well students have constructed connections.

RESOURCES

SOME INSTRUCTIONAL RESOURCES

Meaningful and Purposeful Instruction

☞ **Baseball Math** by Christopher Jennison and **Basketball Math** and **Football Math** by Jack and David Coffland, © 1995 and distributed by Carolina Biological Supply Company.

☞ **Bringing the NCTM Standards to Life: Best Practices from Elementary Educators** by Lisa B. Owen and Charles E. Lamb, © 1996 by Eye on Education, Inc.

☞ **The Challenge of the Unknown Teaching Guide** (which accompanies **The Challenge of the Unknown Film Series**), by Debrah A. Hudson and Joshua G. Miller, © 1986 by J.C. Crimmins & Company and published in the U.S. by W.W. Norton & Company.

☞ **Connected Mathematics** (Grades 6-8) by G. Lappan, W. Fitzgerald, S. Friel, J. Fey, and E. Phillips, © 1995-1997, Dale Seymour Publications.

☞ **Connecting Mathematics Across the Curriculum (1995 Yearbook)**, edited by Peggy A. House, © 1995 by the NCTM.

☞ **Connections: Linking Manipulatives to Mathematics (Grades 1-8)** by Micaelia Randolph Brummett and Linda Holden Charles, © 1989 by Creative Publications.

☞ **EQUALS Investigation Set** developed by the Lawrence Hall of Science, University of California at Berkeley, © 1994-1995 and distributed by, for example, Carolina Biological Supply Company and Dale Seymour Publications.

☞ **Exploring Everyday Math: Ideas for Students, Teachers, and Parents** by Maja Apelman and Julie King, © 1993, Heinemann. Distributed by Dale Seymour Publications.

☞ **Hands-On Math!: Ready-to-Use Games & Activities for Grades 4-8** by Frances M.

Thompson, © 1994 by The Center for Applied Research in Education.

☞ **Making Integrated Curriculum Work: Teachers, Students, and the Quest for Coherent Curriculum** by Elizabeth P. Pate, Elaine R. Homestead, and Karen L. McGinnis, © 1997, Teachers College Press.

☞ **Making Sense: Teaching and Learning Mathematics with Understanding** (by James Hiebert, Thomas P. Carpenter, Elizabeth Fennema, Karen Fuson, Diana Wearne, Hanlie Murray, Alwyn Oliver, and Piet Human, © 1997, Heinemann) provides a theory- and research-based framework for teaching with understanding. It includes a long-term case study of an urban Latino classroom and illustrates Cognitively-Guided Instruction.

☞ **Math and Music** by Trudi Hammel Garland and Charity Vaughan Kahn, © 1995 by Dale Seymour Publications.

☞ **Maths in Context: A Thematic Approach** by Deidre Edwards, © 1990, Heinemann.

☞ **The Multicultural Math Classroom: Bringing in the World** (by Claudia Zaslavsky, © 1995, Heinemann) includes discussions of a multicultural mathematics curriculum, mathematics-literature connections, and multicultural games. Topics include counting and numbers, calculating, geometry, and statistics.

☞ **Math Makes Sense: Teaching and Learning in Contexts** by Rachel Griffiths and Margaret Clyne, © 1994, Heinemann.

☞ **Multicultural Mathematics Materials** by Marina C. Krause, © 1983 by the NCTM.

☞ **Multicultural Science and Math Connections: Middle School Projects and Activities** by Beatrice Lumpkin and Dorothy Strong, © 1995 and distributed by Carolina Biological Supply Company.

☞ **Realistic Mathematics Education in Primary School** edited by Leen Streefland, © 1991 Freudenthal Institute (Center for Science and Mathematics Education, Utrecht University, P.O. Box 80008, 3508 TA Utrecht, The Netherlands).

☞ **Real-World Mathematics through Science Series** developed by University of Washington MESA (Mathematics, Engineering, Science Achievement Group), © 1994-1996, and distributed by Carolina Biological Supply Company and Dale Seymour Publications.

☞ **Teaching Mathematics Through Children's Art** by Doug Williams, © 1995, Heinemann.

☞ **Thinking like Mathematicians: Putting the K-4 NCTM *Standards* into Practice** by Thomas Rowan and Barbara Bourne, © 1994, Heinemann.

Assessment

☞ **Assessment in the Mathematics Classroom (1993 Yearbook)**, edited by N. L. Webb & A. F. Coxford, © 1993, NCTM. In Part 1, general guidelines on assessment are offered, including a chapter on integrating assessment and instruction. Discussions of K-4 and 5-8 assessment can be found in Parts 2 and 3, respectively. General issues, including a chapter on student self-assessment, can be found in Part 5.

☞ **Assessment Standards for School Mathematics**, © 1995, NCTM. This resource outlines the latest thinking about assessment, including equity.

☞ **Authentic Assessment** by Diane Hart, © 1994, Addison-Wesley. This valuable reference describes the limitations of standardized testing, describes authentic assessment, and provides practical tips on observing students, evaluating student portfolios, conducting performance grading, and more.

☞ **Authentic Assessment: Grades K through 8**, published in 1995 by Silver Burdett Ginn. This series of booklets describes interview activities for assessing various aspects of elementary instruction.

☞ **A Collection of Performance Tasks and Rubrics: Upper Elementary School Mathematics** and **Middle School Mathematics** both by Charlotte Danielson, © 1997, Eye On Education. This series illustrates how to use realistic problems to assess concepts and skills.

☞ **How to Evaluate Progress in Problem Solving** by Randall Charles, Frank Lester, and

Phares O'Daffer, © 1987 by NCTM. This valuable 85-page reference addresses the following questions: What are you trying to evaluate? What are some evaluation techniques? How do you organize and manage an evaluation program? and How do you use evaluation results?

☞ **Mathematics Assessment: Myths, Models, Good Questions, and Practical Suggestions** (edited by J. K. Stenmark, © 1992, NCTM), a product of the Student Assessment Mathematics Project, contains many practical suggestions about assessment, including how to focus on student thinking. Chapters cover interviewing, performance assessment, observation, and student portfolios.

☞ **Mathematics Assessment: What Works in the Classroom** by Gerald Kulm, © 1994, Jossey-Bass. This resource provides practical advice on assessing understanding of procedures, concepts, and problem solving.

☞ **Measure for Measure: Using Portfolios in K-8 Mathematics** by Therese M. Kuhs, © 1997, Heinemann.

☞ **Measuring Up: Prototypes for Mathematics Assessment** by the Mathematical Sciences Education Board and the National Research Council, © 1993 by the National Academy Press. This book outlines a rationale for new approaches to assessment based on the NCTM (1989) *Curriculum and Evaluation Standards*. It describes 13 assessment prototypes that exemplify the changes recommended by these standards. The prototypes are written in both English and Spanish and can be copied for classroom use as either an assessment or an instructional tool. For each prototype, there is a protorubric (scoring key) for gauging high, medium, and low responses.

☞ **Test of Early Mathematics Ability—Second Edition** (TEMA-2) by H. P. Ginsburg & A. J. Baroody, © 1990 by Pro-Ed. This test was designed to gauge key aspects of *informal*, as well as formal, knowledge for children ranging in age from 3 to 9 years. It can be used for either performance assessment (e.g., identifying a developmental level or diagnosing a gap in knowledge) or written assessment (i.e., gauging achievement).

A SAMPLE OF CHILDREN'S LITERATURE

The following resources provide a wealth of information for teachers who wish connect mathematics to literature.

🕮 **Books You Can Count On: Linking Mathematics and Literature** by Rachel Griffths and Margaret Clyne, © 1991, Heinemann.

🕮 **How to Use Children's Literature to Teach Mathematics** by Rosamond Welchman-Tischler, © 1992 by the NCTM. This book begins with a rationale for integrating literature and mathematics instruction and a summary chart of children's books. In addition to grade level, the chart indicates what mathematical topics each listed book involves and how a book can be used (e.g., providing a context, introducing a manipulative, modeling a creative experience, posing a problem, or developing a concept). For instance, *The Twelve Days of Christmas* leads to interesting problems for second to sixth graders. In the story, a boy brings his girlfriend a partridge in a pear tree the first day, this item again and two turtle doves the second day, both previous items and three French hens the third day, and so forth. Children might be asked how many presents will the boy bring on the seventh day ($1 + 2 + 3 + 4 + 5 + 6 + 7$) or the twelfth day ($1 + 2 + 3 \ldots + 10 + 11 + 12$). They might also be asked what the total number of gifts the girlfriend has accumulated on the seventh or twelfth day. (Note that after three days, she has three partridges, four turtle doves and three French hens.)

🕮 **Integrating Children's Literature and Mathematics in the Classroom: Children as Meaning Makers, Problem Solvers, and Literary Critics** by Michael Schiro, © 1997, Teachers College Press. This reference uses, for example, *The Doorbell Rang* to illustrate how children's literature can be used to teach mathematical concepts.

🕮 **Math and Literature (K-3)** by Marilyn Burns, © 1992; **Math and Literature (K-3): Book Two** by Stephanie Sheffield, © 1995; and **Math and Literature (Grades 4-6)** by Rusty Bresser, © 1995; all published by Math Solutions Publications and distributed by, for example, Dale Seymour Publications. These references provide invaluable information for integrating mathematics and literature instruction. Part 1 of the Burns' reference, for instance, includes 10 detailed lessons that build on children's books. Part 2 includes a brief description of 21 children's stories including *Anno's Mysterious Multiplying Jar*, *The Doorbell Rang*, *The Shapes Games*, and *What Comes in 2's, 3's, and 4's?*

🖝 **Read Any Good Math Lately? Children's Books for Mathematics Learning K-6**, © 1992, and **It's the Story That Counts: More Children's Books for Mathematical Learning**, © 1995. Both written by David J. Whitin and Sandra Wilde, published by Heinemann, and also distributed by Dale Seymour Publications. This reference includes sample scenarios of how each story can serve to prompt investigation into such topics as arithmetic operations, place value, estimation, fractions, geometry, and measurement.

🖝 **Storytime Mathtime: Math Explorations in Children's Literature** by Patricia Satariano, © 1994 by Dale Seymour. This resource describes how 18 children's books can be used to help primary-level students explore mathematics. Stories include *Corduroy* by Don Freeman, *Who Sank the Boat* by Pamela Allen, *Cloudy with a Chance of Meatballs* by Judi Barrett and *Curious George Rides a Bike* by H. A. Rey. For *Millions of Cats* by Wanda Gág, for instance, children can be asked to picture different situations (e.g., one cat joined by two others) and summarize the situation as an arithmetic equation (1 + 2 = 3). Another activity involves finding half of 4 cats, 6 cats, 8 cats and so forth. Another activity involves constructing a picture graph (though there does not seem to be a real purpose for doing so).

🖝 **The Wonderful World of Mathematics** edited by Dianne Thiessen and Margaret Mathias, © 1992 by the National Council of Teachers of Mathematics. This excellent reference provides a critically annotated list of children's books about mathematics. Part 1 covers early number concepts including counting to ten, rhymes, numbers in other cultures, larger numbers and place value, and beginning addition and subtraction. Part 2 describes books that involve number extensions and connections, number patterns, number

theory, arithmetic operations, statistics and probability, reasoning and technology. Part 3 focuses on measurement including time and money. Part 4 lists books on geometry and spatial sense. This reference provides a brief overview of each book and a rating (highly recommended, recommended, acceptable, and not recommended for mathematics concepts).

TIPS ON USING TECHNOLOGY

Computers

The following web sites describe *lesson ideas*: "Busy Teachers' Web Site K-12 (mathematics section)" (http://www.ceismc.gatech.edu/BusyT/math.html), "Math Archives K-12" (http://archives.math.utk.edu/K12.html), "Math Classroom Materials" (http://forum.swarthmore.edu/major.providers/lesson.plans.html), and "More Math Lessons K-12" (http://www.mste.uiuc.edu/mathed/lessontitles.html). "*USA Today* Classline Online" (classline.usatoday.com) provides curriculum ideas based on current news stories. Information on the National Assessment of Educational Progress (NAEP) *Mathematics Report Cards* can be obtained at www.ed.gov/NCES/naep.

The following are examples of software that can help build connections:

🖥 **Hot Dog Stand: The Works** published by Sunburst. Appropriate for grades 5-8, program simulates running a hot dog stand and, thus, helps connect a wide variety of mathematics to everyday applications. In addition to practicing problem-solving and communicating strategies, students are involved in practicing arithmetic operations, making estimates, gathering data, creating and interpreting graphs, recognizing patterns, choosing appropriate tools, and translating information into different forms. Available on a Macintosh or Windows CD.

🖥 **SemNet** developed by SemNet Research Group, Suite 215, 1043 University Avenue, San Diego, CA 92103-9334. This application for Macintosh personal computers allows users to construct, save, and revise concept maps. By examining each saved version of a user's concept map, it is possible for a teacher to track and to analyze a student's conceptual development.

4 BASIC MATHEMATICAL TOOLS: NUMBERS AND NUMERALS

We Use Numbers in Different Ways

We use numbers in many different situations and in some very different ways. Illustrated below are some ways numbers are used. For each picture below, can you tell whether the numbers are used in the same way or in a different way? Can you explain how numbers are used differently?

Are the numbers announced by Gavin and Yankel used in the same or a different way?

Is *four* identifying the number of bone-crushing linemen used in the same way as *300* identifying their weight?

Is the number identifying Alejandro's address (36) used in the same way as the number (2nd) locating the position of his house on East Avenue?

Horse	Place
27	1
3	2
12	3

Are the numbers used to identify the horses used in the same way as the numbers that identify the place in which the horses finished?

 Consider the bulletin board above. Can you identify the various ways numbers are used in the examples illustrated?

THIS CHAPTER

𝒩umbers and numerals (written representations of numbers) are basic and indispensable tools for mathematics and everyday life. Humankind devised a concept of number before recorded history began. It is conceivably one of the earliest and most important abstractions made by our ancient ancestors (Gundlach, 1989). Numbers allow us to quantify and to communicate about many things, including our environment, finances, and feelings. To get a sense of our sweeping dependence on numbers, consider Activity File 4.1.

Typically, children learn number concepts and counting skills before they learn how to interpret, make, and use written representations of numbers (Ginsburg, 1989). So, in this chapter, we focus first on number concepts and counting skills (Unit 4•1) and then on reading and writing the numerals to 9 (Unit 4•2). The number knowledge discussed in this chapter provide a basis for learning whole-number arithmetic discussed in chapter 5. In chapter 6, we extend this chapter's discussion of numerals to multidigit numerals. In chapters 7 and 8, we explore further the discussion of number patterns and a number sense (an intuitive feel for numbers) begun in this chapter.

🍎 Activity File 4.1: *Life Without Numbers*

◆ Importance of numbers ◆ K-8 ◆ Whole class

Read *Numbers* (by Henry Pluckrose, © 1988, Franklin Watts), which asks, "Can you imagine a world without numbers?" Challenge pupils to try to carry out their normal affairs for several hours or even half an hour without any numerical references or concepts. Encourage them to monitor each other and note "violations." Discuss violations with the class. Conduct a public trial for violators, where monitors could explain their case and the class could vote on guilt or innocence.

☞ Try this activity with your own class.

WHAT THE NCTM *STANDARDS* SAY

In grades K-4, the mathematics curriculum should include whole-number concepts and skills so that students can:

- ◆ construct number meanings through real-world experiences and the use of physical materials;
- ◆ develop number sense;
- ◆ interpret the multiple uses of numbers encountered in the real world.

4•1 NUMBER CONCEPTS AND COUNTING SKILLS

Figure 4.1: And You Thought Counting was a Simple Task?

PEANUTS reprinted by permission of UFS, Inc.

Although we use numbers in a wide variety of ways, most of us are not consciously aware that numbers can have an assortment of meanings. We use numbers so automatically that it is difficult for us to imagine the enormous challenge learning number concepts and counting skills poses for children. As Figure 4.1 illustrates, this learning is not something that can be imposed on them. (Note that Linus' explanation of the mechanics of counting is so involved, it overwhelms Sally.)

One aim of this unit is to encourage reflection and a clear understanding of the various meanings of numbers (Subunit 4•1•1). A second aim is to foster an understanding of how number concepts and counting skills develop and common difficulties encountered during this development (Subunit 4•1•2). A third aim is to outline how children can be helped to construct number concepts and to master counting skills in an interesting and purposeful fashion (Subunit 4•1•3).

4•1•1 MATHEMATICS: UNDERSTANDING THE MEANINGS OF NUMBER

Numbers can have four distinct meanings.

Cardinal Meaning

Numbers can be used to *quantify*—to describe how many items are in a collection (e.g., five pennies). In a sense, a cardinal number "classifies" a collection (e.g., ^Oo_O, $*^*_*$, and ❑ ❑ ❑ all belong to the same number class called "three"). On the bulletin board (page 4-1), for example, both Gavin and Yankel are using a cardinal meaning.

Measurement Meaning

Numbers can be used to *measure*—to describe measurements. Some quantities (discrete quantities), such as a collection of baseball cards or a group of people, can be counted. Other quantities (continuous quantities) such as length, area, volume, weight, time, and so forth must be measured rather than counted. (The distinction between discrete and continuous quantities is discussed further in Chapter 9.) For instance, on page 4-1, while the number of tacklers (4) involves a cardinal meaning, the weight of the tacklers (300 pounds) involves a measurement meaning.

Ordinal Meaning

Numbers can be used to *locate*—to indicate the relative position or the order of items. Ordinal numbers, such as *first, second, third*, are one way to indicate this ordering meaning. For example, on page 4-1, specifying that Alejandro's house is the *second* house after the East Avenue sign involves an ordinal meaning. Because house numbers are typically in order so that an address can be located, Alejandro's house number (36) also has an ordinal meaning.

Nominal Meaning

Numbers can be used in a nonquantitative manner to *label*—to name items so as to distinguish among them. That is, they are essentially used to code or categorize items. For instance, on page 4-1, numbers are assigned to horses merely for the purpose of identification.

☞ Try Probe 4.1 (pages 4-4 and 4-5).

4•1•2 LEARNING: UNDERSTANDING THE TASK CONFRONTING CHILDREN

Counting is children's primary vehicle for constructing a concept of number and the basis of much of their informal mathematics. Difficulties with counting can seriously hamper a child's mathematical progress in school. Thus, it is important for schooling to foster and to further children's counting competencies. In this subunit, we focus on the development of three key counting skills: oral counting, object counting, and comparing quantities.

Oral Counting

In this section, we discuss how children learn the *forward counting sequence* ("one, two, three . . .") and use it in increasingly flexible ways.

☞ Consider Probe 4.2 (pages 4-6 and 4-7).

Forward Counting Sequence. Oral counting is sometimes inaccurately called *rote counting*. Although English-speaking children must memorize the first twelve or so terms by rote, learning the forward counting sequence largely entails discovering patterns (e.g., Ginsburg, 1989). Specifically, counting to *one hundred* requires:

- memorizing by rote the single-digit sequence *one* to *nine*;
- recognizing the pattern that a *nine* signals the end of a series and the need to begin a new one (e.g., *nineteen* marks the end of the teens);
- learning the decade term that begins each new series (e.g., *twenty* follows *nineteen*)— a process which involves both memorizing terms such as *ten*, *twenty*, and *thirty* by rote and recognizing a pattern: "add *-ty* to the single-digit sequence" (e.g., *six+ty*, *seven +ty*, *eight+ty*, *nine+ty*;)
- recognizing the pattern that each new series involves combining a decade and the single-digit sequence, such as *twenty*, *twenty + one, twenty + two . . . .*

By the beginning of kindergarten, children typically have mastered the forward counting sequence to at least 12 (Fuson, 1988). Learning to count beyond this point is (continued on page 4-8)

➤ Probe 4.1: Meanings of Numbers and Uses of Counting

Part I: Meanings of Number

The aim of Part I is to help you construct an explicit understanding of the meanings of number.

1. Fuson and Hall (1983) noted that adults can readily shift among meanings of numbers: "The statement that 'Despite a seventy-eight yard run by number thirty-four, the Bears lost by two touchdowns and dropped into sixth place' may bring consternation, but not confusion [to Chicago Bears' football fans]" (p. 49). For each of the following numbers, indicate whether it has a cardinal meaning (indicates how many), a measurement meaning (describes a measurement), an ordinal meaning (locates a position or order), or a nominal meaning (labels or names an item):

   (a) 78 yards; (b) Player number 34; (c) 2 touchdowns; (d) 6th place.

2. In a stamp catalog, each distinct stamp is identified by a unique number. For example, the U.S. stamp commemorating the 50th anniversary of the first transatlantic flight by Charles Lindbergh has a *Scott's Stamp Catalogue* number of 1710. What number meaning(s) might this number have?

Part II: Counting Skills

As adults, we use a variety of counting skills without even thinking. We execute these skills so automatically, we take them for granted. The aim of this part is to help you construct an explicit understanding of key counting skills and what is required to perform—what may seem to us—trivial tasks. This is important because teachers need to be able to take the perspective of their students. Putting yourself in the shoes of children—understanding the challenges that confront them—will put you in a better position to guide their learning. Consider the following vignette:

Without pointing to objects, Anabelle, a toddler, counts "one, two, three, four" over and over again as she plays with the sand in a sandbox. Ben-Zion, a 5-year old, counts "one, two, three, four" as he points, in turn, to each of his marbles and announces, "I have four marbles." Consuela comments, "I'll get four marbles from my bag of marbles too." She then counts out four marbles, "One, two, three, four." Diedre counts her marbles, "One, two, three, four, five," and concludes she has more marbles than Ben or Consuela. Each of these children is using different number skills.

Oral Counting. For Anabelle, *oral counting (saying the counting sequence "one, two, three, four")* was merely a sing-song or meaningless chant (Ginsburg, 1989). Only gradually do preschoolers see that counting words are associated with quantity—can be used to count collections, identify the size of a collection, and compare the sizes of collections. Although it may not indicate any understanding of numbers, oral counting is an important first step toward constructing number concepts and skills.

Object Counting. Object counting includes *counting a collection to determine the number of items in it (enumeration)* and *counting out a specified number of items (set production)*.

• **Enumeration**. In contrast to Anabelle, Ben-Zion used numbers in a meaningful and, hence, a qualitatively different way. He counted his collection of marbles to specify how many it had.

• **Set production**. Consuela used numbers in an even more sophisticated manner. In contrast with enumeration that begins with a collection and results in a number, *set production* begins with a number and involves creating a collection. For example, Consuela decided she needed "four" marbles and so counted out four from a bag of marbles.

Comparing Quantities. *Comparing quantities entails determining whether two (or more) collections are equal* and, if not, *ordering them (deciding which is larger)*. Diedre used numbers in this relatively sophisticated manner.

Probe 4.1 continued

1. For each of the following situations, indicate whether it involves:
   (i) oral counting, (ii) enumeration, (iii) set production, or (iv) comparing quantities.

   _____ a. A child counts the number of children at a table to determine the number of children present.

   _____ b. Because there are seven children at a table, a child counts out seven pieces of drawing paper from the stack of paper she is carrying.

   _____ c. A child is chosen as "it" for a game of hide-n-seek and counts out loud up to twenty, while the other children hide.

   _____ d. A child who is five concludes he is older than his friend who is four.

   _____ e. While playing a board game, a child rolls a die and counts the six dots.

   _____ f. Because she rolled a six, the child moves her marker six spaces on the game board.

2. Compare the collections below. Are there more triangles or more squares?

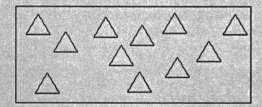 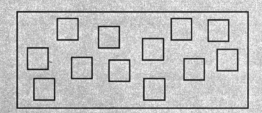

   A common solution strategy is to count the collections. Analyze what is involved in using such a strategy to make the decision above. Suggestion: Work backwards.

   a. How would someone decide which collection is larger? A common answer is: "Well, I know that twelve is bigger than eleven." But how do you know that twelve is bigger than eleven? How could you prove it to a child who does not know that twelve is bigger than eleven?

   b. Adults typically compare *twelve* with *eleven* rather than their actual counts ("one, two, three, four, five, six, seven, eight, nine, ten, eleven, twelve" with "one, two, three, four, five, six, seven, eight, nine, ten, eleven"). Why do we compare two numbers (*twelve* and *eleven* in this case) rather than use two actual counts? What knowledge enables you to do this? In other words, in this case, what makes *twelve* and *eleven* special?

   c. What was involved in counting a collection? That is, what governs how to count a collection?

3. Sirpa, Hellevi, and Carrie Anne were playing *Bean-Bag Toss.* On her turn, Sirpa tossed a bean bag onto the 8 ring of the target. To note her score, she counted and took eight cubes from a large box of cubes. To check her score, Hellevi counted the six blocks she had taken earlier and concluded, "You're winning Sirpa." Carrie Anne then threw the bean bag, which landed on the 7 ring. "Oh good," she concluded, "seven beats eight—I'm ahead." She proceeded to count out seven blocks from the larger box of blocks. (a) In the vignette above, which children used oral counting? (b) Which enumerated a collection? (c) Which produced a collection? (d) Which compared quantities correctly? (e) Which compared quantities incorrectly and what might account for this difficulty?

➤ Probe 4.2: An Analysis of Oral-Counting Skills

Part I: A Comparison of Three Number Systems

The aim of Part I is to help you reflect on your knowledge of the counting sequence. How far can you count? Probably further than you care to try. This raises the questions, *What enables you to know so many counting numbers? Have you memorized them all by rote?* Without patterns, our capacity to memorize ordered lists is severely limited and our knowledge of counting numbers would be lamentably restricted. We have the capacity to count on indefinitely because counting sequences have a structure. Now different cultures have arrived at different solutions for making the production of counting numbers easy (Nunes, 1992). Some languages have clear-cut patterns and clues to these patterns; others have less clear-cut patterns and clues. The chart on the next page compares Hindu-Arabic (written) numerals, the English (oral) counting sequence, and the Korean (oral) counting sequence. After examining it, answer the questions below.

1. Compare our written number system with our oral-counting system. Is the written-number system utterly irregular, somewhat regular, highly regular, or completely regular? Is the same true of our oral-counting system? Why or why not?

2. Compare our English oral-counting system with a Korean oral-counting system. What do you notice about the Korean system?

3. (a) What do you suppose the Korean term for *sixteen* is? (b) How about *sixty*? (c) *Eighty-five*?

4. (a) What kind of reasoning was involved in deciphering the patterns of the Korean oral counting sequence? (b) What kind of reasoning was involved in answering Question 3?

5. (a) What patterns underlie our English oral counting sequence? (b) What counting terms, then, should be relatively difficult for children to learn and why?

6. Consider Box 4.1 below. (a) What must a child know to count to 100? (b) Which aspects of this knowledge did Katie know? (c) What skill did she need to master in order to count to 100 efficiently? (c) At which numbers will children encounter the most difficulty when counting to 100?

Box 4.1: The Case of the Determined Counter

Asked to count as high as she could, Katie—a child labeled "mildly mentally handicapped"—counted up to *thirty-nine* and paused. She counted to herself, "One, two, three, four" and then announced, "Forty." Next, Katie quickly listed off *forty-one* to *forty-nine* and paused again. She counted to herself, "One, two, three, four, five," announced, "Fifty," quickly listed off *fifty-one* to *fifty-nine*, and again determined the next decade by counting by ones. She repeated this process until she got to *one hundred*.

Part II: Extensions of Orally Counting by One

Once children learn the forward counting sequence, they begin to build on this knowledge in many useful ways. This part of the probe raises some questions regarding three of these extensions.

1. Asked by her father, "What comes after *nine*?" Alison a preschooler could not respond. Asked by her mother, "What comes after one, two, three, four, five, six, seven, eight, nine?" the girl immediately responded, "Ten." What does the vignette suggest about children's ability to determine the number after a given term?

2. Do you think a child would find indicating the number before a term to be easier than, more difficult than, or equally easy as indicating the number after a term? Why?

3. Which do children learn first: counting by ones to one hundred or counting by tens to one hundred (the decade sequence: "ten, twenty, thirty, forty. . . ")? Why?

Probe 4.2 continued

Arabic (Written) Numerals	English Oral Count	Korean Oral Count	Arabic (Written) Numerals	English Oral Count	Korean Oral Count
1	One	Eel	51	Fifty-one	
2	Two	Ee	52	Fifty-two	
3	Three	Sahm	53	Fifty-three	
4	Four	Sah	54	Fifty-four	
5	Five	Oh	55	Fifty-five	
6	Six	Yook	56	Fifty-six	
7	Seven	Chil	57	Fifty-seven	
8	Eight	Pal	58	Fifty-eight	
9	Nine	Goo	59	Fifty-nine	
10	Ten	Sip	60	Sixty	
11	Eleven	Sip-eel	61	Sixty-one	
12	Twelve	Sip-ee	62	Sixty-two	
13	Thirteen	Sip-sahm	63	Sixty-three	
14	Fourteen	Sip-sah	64	Sixty-four	
15	Fifteen	Sip-oh	65	Sixty-five	
16	Sixteen		66	Sixty-six	
17	Seventeen		67	Sixty-seven	
18	Eighteen		68	Sixty-eight	
19	Nineteen	Sip-goo	69	Sixty-nine	
20	Twenty	Ee-sip	70	Seventy	
21	Twenty-one	Ee-sip-eel	71	Seventy-one	
22	Twenty-two		72	Seventy-two	
23	Twenty-three		73	Seventy-three	
24	Twenty-four		74	Seventy-four	
25	Twenty-five		75	Seventy-five	
26	Twenty-six		76	Seventy-six	
27	Twenty-seven		77	Seventy-seven	
28	Twenty-eight		78	Seventy-eight	
29	Twenty-nine		79	Seventy-nine	
30	Thirty	Sahm-sip	80	Eighty	
31	Thirty-one		81	Eighty-one	
32	Thirty-two		82	Eighty-two	
33	Thirty-three		83	Eighty-three	
34	Thirty-four		84	Eighty-four	
35	Thirty-five		85	Eighty-five	
36	Thirty-six		86	Eighty-six	
37	Thirty-seven		87	Eighty-seven	
38	Thirty-eight		88	Eighty-eight	
39	Thirty-nine		89	Eighty-nine	
40	Forty	Sah-sip	90	Ninety	
41	Forty-one		91	Ninety-one	
42	Forty-two		92	Ninety-two	
43	Forty-three		93	Ninety-three	
44	Forty-four		94	Ninety-four	
45	Forty-five		95	Ninety-five	
46	Forty-six		96	Ninety-six	
47	Forty-seven		97	Ninety-seven	
48	Forty-eight		98	Ninety-eight	
49	Forty-nine		99	Ninety-nine	
50	Fifty	Oh-sip	100	One-hundred	Baek

complicated by the fact the English counting sequence—unlike the Korean and some other counting sequences—is not entirely regular. For example, *thirteen* and *fifteen* often cause difficulties because they are exceptions to the teen rule: "add *teen* to the single-digit sequence of numbers (e.g., six + *teen*, seven + *teen*).

Extensions. By the time they enter kindergarten, most children can automatically cite the *number after a term* without a running start (without counting from one). For example, asked "What comes after *six*?" they can immediately respond *seven* instead of counting: "One, two, three, four, five, six—seven." In time, children become so familiar with the counting sequence, they can quickly determine the *number before a term*. This sets the stage for *counting backward* from any given number.

Children also gradually master skip counting. They typically learn counting by twos (*Two, four, six . . .*), fives (*Five, ten, fifteen . . .*), and tens (*ten, twenty, thirty . . .*) first because of their utility in counting larger collections. The *decade-after* skill entails automatically knowing, for instance, that *sixty* follows *fifty*.

Object Counting

In this section, we discuss what is involved in key object-counting competencies.

Enumeration. To enumerate a collection of objects correctly, a child must (a) know the relevant portion of the counting sequence, (b) assign a single number word to an object, and (c) keep track of which objects have been counted and which need to be counted (Gelman & Gallistel, 1978). Most children entering kindergarten can successfully enumerate collections of at least five items. Difficulties with larger, particularly haphazard, collections most often stem from not knowing keeping-track strategies (e.g., systematically going from top to bottom and left to right) (Fuson, 1988).

Cardinality Principle. This principle provides a shortcut for labeling a collection. Instead of using the entire sequence of counting words used in enumerating a collection, only the last term is used to represent the whole collection. For instance, instead of calling a collection of 12 blocks "One, two, three, four, five, six, seven, eight, nine, ten, eleven, twelve," we refer to it simply as, "Twelve." *The cardinality principle implies that the last term in the enumeration process has special significance because it not only locates the last item enumerated but it represents the total number of items in the collection.* Nearly all preschoolers spontaneously construct an understanding of the cardinality principle through their everyday counting activities (e.g., Fuson, 1988).

Set Production. Counting out a collection of a given size is more difficult than enumeration, because it requires the child to *remember* how many objects have been requested and to stop counting objects when that many objects have been reached (Resnick & Ford, 1981). Children beginning school typically have little difficulty producing collections of up to five items, but some kindergartners may have difficulty accurately counting out larger collections.

Comparing Quantities (Numerical Relations)

In this section, we discuss two aspects of numerical relations that are fundamental to understanding number and operations on number: a concept of (a) *equivalence and inequivalence* and (b) *ordering numbers* (Piaget, 1965). Unlike object counting that involves a single collection, numerical relationships involve two or more collections (or numbers). Not surprisingly the ability to compare quantities develops later than object-counting and seems to depend largely on counting experiences.

With small sets of up to four or five, even young children can quickly see whether two collections are equal and, if not, which is larger. Direct perception, however, is not reliable with larger collections, particularly when they are about the same size and haphazardly arranged. From counting and comparing small collections, children discover two important relationships:

1. the *same number-name principle*: *Two collections are equal if they share the same number name* (e.g., although the collections • • • • • • and • • • look different, they are equal because both have *six* items).

2. *ordering-numbers principle*: *the later a number word appears in the counting sequence, the larger the collection it represents* (e.g., *four*

represents a larger collection than *three* because it follows *three*).

The ordering-numbers principle allows children to mentally make *distant-number comparisons—determine which of two spoken or written "far-apart" numbers is larger* (e.g., *ten* is more than *three* because it comes much later when we count). Once children can automatically determine the number after a term, they can use the principle to mentally make *next-number comparisons—determine which of two spoken or written number neighbors is larger* (e.g., 8 is more than 7 because *eight* comes after *seven* when we count). Except for those with little informal experience, children beginning school typically can make such comparisons up to five. Many kindergartners, though, need to learn next-number comparisons for numbers larger than five.

4•1•3 TEACHING

In this subunit, we consider how to help children construct number meanings, what role counting should play in number-concept instruction, and the meaningful learning of oral-counting, object-counting, and comparing quantities.

Meanings of Number

Instruction should foster an intuitive sense and then an explicit understanding of number uses.

☞ **Use real-world experiences (e.g., everyday classroom activities and games) to expose children to all the meanings of number** (cardinal, measurement, ordinal, and nominal uses). That is, actively involve them in concrete activities that require the use of numbers to (a) quantify collections (e.g., determine how many pupils are in a group), (b) measure (e.g., gauge the length of objects), (c) locate the relative position or order of items (e.g., list games in the order of preference), and (d) label (e.g., name storage boxes). Forming a class in line; assigning winners in athletic, academic, or artistic competitions (first place, second place . . .); and giving direction (e.g., Get the third box from the pencil sharpener), for instance, all involve the ordinal meaning. The game *High Die*, for example, can involve deciding who goes first, second, and so forth (ordinal use) as well as determining how many dots each players' (oversized) die shows and who got the largest roll (cardinal uses). *Numbers* (by Henry Pluckrose) offers many real-world examples of the uses of numbers.

☞ **In time, help children distinguish explicitly among the different meanings of number.** After children are comfortable using numbers in different ways, encourage them to consciously distinguish among cardinal (telling how many items), measurement (telling what extent), ordinal (locating or ordering an item), and nominal (labeling or naming) meanings (see, e.g., the bulletin board on page 4-1). Older children can be challenged to puzzle over ambiguous cases such as street address numbers (again see the bulletin board on page 4-1). (A persuasive argument could be made that a house number serves both an ordinal role or locating function and a nominal role or labeling function.)

The Role of Counting in Number Development

It may be surprising to learn that there has been considerable debate about what role counting plays in the development of a number concept and, thus, what role it should play in initial mathematics instruction (e.g., Brainerd, 1973).

Logical-Prerequisites View. Piaget (1965) believed that counting skills were learned by rote and did not play a key role in helping children understand number. He argued that the construction of a number concept depended on the development of the logical thinking abilities necessary for classifying, ordering, and matching (e.g., Gibb & Castaneda, 1975). Piaget considered *number-pattern recognition (e.g., immediately seeing that • • • is "three")*, for instance, a rotely learned skill, unimportant to number-concept development. Moreover, he believed that children should be encouraged to use matching to establish equivalence and inequivalence, not counting.

Counting View. Counting, particularly finger-counting, probably played a crucial role in the development of human kind's concept of number (Dantzig, 1954). So, it is not surprising that recent research has found that counting experiences are key to the development of children's understanding of number and arithmetic. Children gradually construct basic number and arithmetic concepts from real experiences that largely involve counting (e.g., Fuson, 1988; Gelman & Gallistel, 1978). In fact, there is little evidence that logical training is necessary for developing a concept of number (e.g., Clements & Callahan, 1983), but there is considerable evidence that counting experiences are related to the richness of a number sense (e.g., Baroody, 1987). Indeed, research suggests that practice on meaningful counting activities leads to improved performance on logical tasks as well as number tasks (Payne & Huinker, 1993). The key instructional implications stemming from the Counting View are listed below.

☞ **Counting, particularly finger counting, should be an integral component of school mathematics from the beginning.** ORAL- AND OBJECT-COUNTING SHOULD BE A KEY FEATURE OF PRESCHOOL AND KINDERGARTEN MATHEMATICS INSTRUCTION.

☞ **Number-pattern recognition, particularly finger patterns, should be a focus of early mathematics instruction.** Many children entering kindergarten can already use finger patterns to represent numbers up to five (e.g., quickly and simultaneously putting up four fingers to indicate "four"). Finger patterns up to 10 provide children with concrete models of these numbers and their relative size. These models can make informally calculating sums, differences, and products immeasurably easier (Steffe, von Glasersfeld, Richards, & Cobb, 1983). Thus, children should be encouraged to produce and to recognize finger patterns up to 10 (e.g., five fingers on one hand and four on another is nine). Games involving dot dice and dominoes can foster pattern recognition. Five and Ten Frames, shown in Box 4.2, are useful in encouraging children to think of numbers in terms of groups of five and ten (Flexer, 1986; Thompson & Van de Walle, 1984; Van de Walle & Watkins, 1993).

☞ **To establish the equality or inequality of larger collections, children initially should be encouraged to use their preferred informal method for comparing quantities—counting.** (When children want to be sure about comparing two collections of more than five items that are not clearly different, they generally count rather than match the collections.)

Oral Counting

First, help children to become familiar with the forward counting sequence. Then, build on this foundation to help them master next-number, counting-backward, and skip-counting skills.

Forward Counting Sequence. For the minority of kindergartners unable to count to at least *twelve*, intensive efforts should be made to

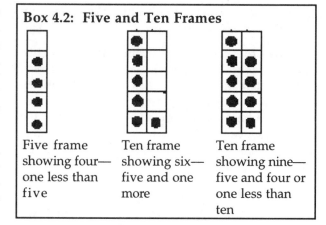

Box 4.2: Five and Ten Frames

| Five frame showing four—one less than five | Ten frame showing six—five and one more | Ten frame showing nine—five and four or one less than ten |

help them to memorize this rote sequence. For most, initial instruction should focus on learning the teens and beyond.

☞ **Practice oral counting purposefully.** Activity File 4.2 illustrates the investigative approach to oral-counting instruction. Games that involve counting objects can be a particularly effective and entertaining way to provide practice (see Activity Files 4.3 and 4.4 on page 4-11).

 Activity File 4.2: *Hide-n-Seek*

◆ Oral counting to 12, 20, or beyond
◆ K-2 ◆ Any number

Preparing to play *Hide-n-Seek* during recess can provide a pretext for discussing and practicing the counting sequence. Explain that the game involves one player who is "it" and who must try to find the other players who are hiding. To give the other players a chance to hide, the player who is "it" starts the game by covering his or her eyes and counting to *twenty*.

☞ **Teaching Tips**

• Note the endpoint of the count and even the type of the count can be changed to fit the developmental needs of your students. For those who need to work on the rote portion of counting sequence, the end point can be *twelve*; for advanced counters, *one hundred*. This game can also provide an opportunity to discuss and practice skip counts (e.g., the player who is "it" must count to *one hundred* by fives) or counting backward.

• After describing the rules of the game, a teacher can encourage children to discuss and to rehearse the count needed for the game. Focus on patterns and exceptions to these patterns.

Activity File 4.3: *Balloon Afloat*

◆ Oral and object counting to 100⁺ ◆ K-1
◆ Groups of three to twelve

A balloon is tossed up in the air amid a small group of children standing in a circle. Without moving, the players try to keep the balloon afloat by tapping it up with their hands. The object of the game is to see how long the group can keep the balloon off the ground. Because the players must work together, this is an excellent game for promoting cooperation.

After playing the game several times to familiarize children with the rules, have them consider how they can keep score. With any luck, someone will suggest counting the number of hits. Add the rule that the player hitting the balloon must cite the count (e.g., the player hitting the balloon the fourth time must say, "*Four*").

To gauge how high players may have to count, have them estimate the total number of hits in previous games. Choose a target number somewhat larger than consensus estimate. To prepare for the game, encourage students to discuss counting to the target. In particular, have them focus on patterns, decades (transitions to new series), and exceptions. Students may even want to practice counting to the target once or twice before starting the game.

To promote participation, use the rule that a player may not hit the balloon twice in a row. To maximize participation, implement the rule that players can move but that they must hit the balloon in a predetermined order. A group can compete against other groups or against their own high count.

Activity File 4.4: *Dominoes Just After*

◆ Oral and object counting and number after up to 10 ◆ K-1 ◆ Groups of two to four

This game from the *Wynroth* (1986) *Math Program* is played like *Dominoes* except that the added domino must be the number after the end item, rather than the same number. This is a good game for introducing the number-after-a-term skill, because counting the end domino gives children a running start (e.g., "The end domino has one, two, three, four dots, so I've got to look for a five").

☞ **For children who have learned the number sequence to *twelve*, instruction should focus on finding the following counting patterns:**

• Most teens are formed by combining a single-digit term and teen (e.g., *seven + teen*);
• nine always ends a series;
• the decade sequence *ten* to *ninety* parallels the *one*-to-*nine* sequence; and,
• new (nonteen) series consist of the decade combined with the *one*-to-*nine* sequence.

☞ **Encourage children to note and discuss exceptions to counting-sequence patterns.** Error-detection activities can provide an enjoyable forum for discussing patterns and exceptions (see Box 4.3 on the next page).

Extensions. As with the forward counting sequence, a teacher should take advantage of real situations to discuss and to practice counting extensions. Next-number (number-after and -before) knowledge can be helpful, for example, when trying to locate a room or a locker (see Box 4.4 on page 4-13). Counting backward can be used, for instance, to mark off the time (e.g., "Each of you has 15 seconds at the drinking fountain. Rosella will go first. Those waiting for a turn count with me, 'Fifteen, fourteen, thirteen . . .'." or "It's five days before our pageant, tomorrow there will be how many days? On Saturday there will be? On Sunday? On Monday?"). Skip counting can be encouraged as a shortcut for counting large collections. Games can also create a real need for discussing and practicing counting extensions (see, e.g., Activity File 4.2 on page 4-10).

Object Counting

In this section, we discuss teaching tips on enumeration, the cardinality principle, the production of sets, and finger patterns.

Enumeration. Although most children should have little trouble counting small collections, many may need help enumerating collections larger than five.

☞ **Enumeration practice should be done in a purposeful and interesting manner.** There are numerous everyday opportunities to use and, thus, discuss and practice counting collections. To ensure that the required number items is available, students can be asked to count pieces of paper, ribbon, cloth, or other items needed for an assignment or an art project. They can be asked to help

---

🍎 Box 4.3: An Example of an Error-Detection Activity

Passing Cora Conway's kindergarten room, Miss Brill heard shrieks of joy, laughter, and much commotion. She quickly concluded that Mrs. Conway had slipped out for a moment and that her class had taken advantage of the situation to go wild. Ready to put an end to the nonsense, Miss Brill moved briskly to the open door. She was startled to find Mrs. Conway present.

"Oh look class," intoned Mrs. Conway cheerfully, "we have a visitor, Miss Brill our new fifth-grade teacher. We're playing *Cora Gets Confused*, Would you like to join us?" Miss Brill managed a smile and took a seat, a very low seat. Mrs. Conway explained, "Sometimes I have trouble remembering how to count correctly, and the class is trying very hard to help me. They listen very carefully and try to catch any mistakes I make. Then they have to tell me why I am wrong and how I can correct myself." In an aside directed at Miss Brill, Mrs. Conway whispered, "It provides a basis for discussing the patterns in the counting sequence, the exceptions, and some common counting errors."

Mrs. Conway turned to the class and continued, "What if Cora counted up to 'thirteen' and then said, 'fourteen, *fourteen*, sixteen'?"

Nearly everyone in class roared with glee, "You can't say the same number again."

Another child added, "Each number has to be different when we count so that different amounts get different numbers."

Mrs. Conway then said, "Well, Cora wants to try again: 'Thirteen, fourteen, *fiveteen*, sixteen'." Many of the children giggled. When asked what was wrong, one child noted that the correct term was *fifteen*, not fiveteen. Mrs. Conway, who knew that several children in the class who had difficulty with fifteen, added, "It would make a lot of sense if our number after fourteen were fiveteen, but it's not. So Cora will have to make a special effort to remember fifteen, because it does not fit the teen pattern exactly."

When Cora later counted *ten-teen*, the class discussed recognizing nine as a signal for ending a series and switching to a new series. When Cora left out *twenty-four*, the class discussed how each new series was a repetition of the *one*-through-*nine* sequence.

Questions for Reflection

1. (a) For preschoolers learning the rote portion of the sequence up to 12, consider what types of errors you might wish to illustrate. (b) For first and second graders learning the number sequence to 1000, what errors might you wish to illustrate?

2. Note that the error-detection activity above was fun because an adult was pretending to slip up and children could pretend to correct an adult (for a change). Consider how a teacher could help children understand that difference between this game and making fun of real mistakes.

---

with a head count for hot lunch, a class vote, attendance, and so forth. Counting the number of cans collected for a food drive or a recycling project or counting the number of days on a calendar until a special event can also provide real contexts for enumerating collections. Games, such as *Balloons Afloat* and *Dominoes Just After* (see Activity Files 4.3 and 4.4 on page 4-11) and *Soccer* (Activity File 4.5 on page 4-14) can also provide enumeration practice in a purposeful and entertaining fashion.

☞ **For most children, enumeration instruction should focus on learning keeping-track strategies.** As keeping-track difficulties are the most common source of enumeration errors for kindergarteners, help them devise strategies for sorting counted items from uncounted items. For moveable objects, for instance, have them place counted items aside in a pile clearly separated from uncounted items.

Cardinality Principle. For the few who need it, games such as *Dominoes Just After* (Activity File 4.4 on page 4-11) can be used to discuss, model, and practice this principle.

Production of Sets. Everyday situations, such as distributing school supplies (e.g., give each person five sheets of paper), art supplies

⚜ Box 4.4: An Investigative Approach to Teaching Number After and Number Before

Vignette	Comments
Mr. McCarty announced to his kindergarten class, "Today is our first visit to the Music Room, and, being new to this school, I need your help finding it. Our room is Room 7, and the Music Room is Room 28. Is there anyway we can use this information to find the Music Room?"	Note that children are encouraged to think mathematically about the everyday situation of locating a room. Not only does this encourage them to use quantitative knowledge and reasoning to solve an everyday problem, they see usefulness of mathematics.
Vera offered, "The rooms go 'One, two, three'" (go in order).	The teacher allowed the students to use their informal observations to offer a solution.
Mr. McCarty asked, "If we go out our door and turn right toward the Office and front doors, we first pass Miss Bogan's room. What's her room number?"	
Jonathan remarked, "I think that's Room 6."	
Lori quickly concluded, "Don't go that way."	
Asked to justify her conclusion, Lori noted cryptically, "Because it's getting smaller and we want bigger."	Because not all students may have followed Lori's line of deductive reasoning, the teacher asked her to justify her conclusion.
After Mr. McCarty clarified Lori's explanations, he asked what room number Mrs. Carmean to the left would have. A number of students surmised it would be Room 8 and that they should turn left to get to the Music Room.	
As the class proceeded through the hall, Mr. McCarty would stop occasionally and ask questions such as, "This is Room 24. What room should come next?" As some students seemed puzzled by the class' responses, McCarty asked, "Why twenty-five?" On the way back to their classroom, he again quizzed the class about what room would come next.	The teacher takes the opportunity of going to and from the Music Room to practice number-after and number-before skills. To help developmentally less advanced children, he encouraged other children to explain their answers.

(e.g., put eight buttons on each desk), food (e.g., give each person three cookies), and so forth can create a real need for discussing and practicing set production. Games such as *Soccer* (Activity File 4.5 on page 4-14) can also provide a real context for learning and practicing counting out small collections (if needed) or larger ones.

Comparing Numbers

In this section, we discuss tips on helping children learn to compare two (or more) collections or numbers.

☞ **Instruction and practice on comparing numbers should be purposeful.** Games can provide a purposeful context for promoting an explicit discussion of number-comparison principles, encouraging children to devise strategies for comparing numbers, and practicing number-comparison skills (e.g., see Activity File 4.6 and Box 4.5 on the next page).

☞ **Instruction on *same number as*, *more*, and *less* should build on children's informal experiences and counting knowledge.** If a child has not already discovered the same number-name or

● Activity File 4.5: *Soccer*

◆ Practice enumerating and producing collections of 1 to 20 ◆ K-1 ◆ Two children

In the *Advanced Game* (sets of 11 to 20), the players decide who "kicks" first. The first kicker places the soccer ball (e.g., a plastic disk) in her goal and picks a card from a deck of cards with 11 to 20 dots. The player counts the dots on the drawn card and advances the soccer ball that

number of spaces. The other player then draws a card and advances the ball in the opposite direction. A point is scored when a player can advance the ball into (or beyond) the opponent's goal. After a score, the opponent restarts play by placing the ball in his or her goal.

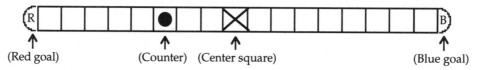

(Red goal)   (Counter) (Center square)   (Blue goal)

The *Intermediate Game* (sets of 6 to 10) is played on a field with 9 spaces between the goal and with a deck of cards with 6 to 10 dots on a card. The *Basic Game* (sets 0 to 5) is played on a

field with 7 spaces between the goal and a deck of cards (or die) with 0 to 5 dots on a card. In this version, the play starts with the ball placed at center field.

● Activity File 4.6: *War*

◆ Order numbers of any size mentally ◆ K-4 ◆ Two to five children

By using 3 x 5 cards to create your own decks of cards, this classic card game can involve children in comparing numbers of any size. Less advanced children can play with the numbers 1 to 10 or even just 1 to 5. More advanced children can play with larger numbers. To make the game more concrete, each card could depict a collection of shapes.

The game is played by dealing out all of the cards to the players face down. Players then turn over the top card of their pile; the player with the highest number wins. If two or more players share the highest number, they put a second card down and a third card up. The player with the higher third card wins all the cards played. The aim is to collect every card.

Box 4.5: A Great Aid for Making Number Comparisons

During the card game *War*, 5-year-old Arianne drew an 8 and her father drew a 6. Unsure which number was larger, the girl got up and went to the channel selector of the VCR. She looked up each number on the channel selector and concluded, "Eight *is* higher than six." Soon after, a 7 and 8 came up. She again went to the channel changer to determine the

larger number. Later, a 9 and 8 came up. "Which is bigger Daddy?" she asked. Asked what she thought, Arianne returned to the channel selector and concluded, "Nine is much bigger." Several plays later a 9 and 8 came up again. This time Arianne counted the spades on her 9 card and took the cards because nine followed eight when she counted.

the ordering-numbers principle, provide concrete experiences comparing small collections (1 to 5 items). Comparing ages can also provide a personally important and meaningful analogy for these principles. To order larger collections, encourage children to count each collection to see which requires the longer count. As Box 4.5 illustrates, using a number line can be helpful when

children begin to try ordering numbers, particularly numbers larger than *five*. In time, encourage them to use their number-after knowledge (e.g., "Seven is more than six because when we count it comes after six").

☞ Try Probe 4.3 (on page 4-15). (Text continued on page 4-16.)

➦ Probe 4.3: An Analysis of the Number Instruction in the *Mathematics Their Way* (*MTW*) Curriculum

MTW (Baratta-Lorton, 1976) is an outstanding early childhood (K-2) mathematics curriculum. Its stated goal is to develop an understanding of the patterns of mathematics. The format is a series of child-centered activities designed to help children see relationships among mathematical ideas. The program exploits counting activities to teach number and arithmetic concepts. Strong emphasis is given to using real and familiar materials that can be concretely manipulated. A concerted effort is made to link the concrete to the abstract through "connecting-level" exercises. For example, children start by working with sets of objects (the concept level), next match sets with written numbers (the connecting level), and only then proceed to using numerals alone to represent sets (the symbolic level). Similarly, concrete experiences with combining sets is followed by experiences in which this concrete process is labeled with symbols, and only then do children work with just symbolic addition expressions.

Because teachers need to use even outstanding curricula thoughtfully, this probe asks you to evaluate key aspects of *MTW*.

1. *MTW* introduces activities that involve sorting and classifying materials by such attributes as size, shape, and color before activities that involve counting and numbers. What view of early number development discussed in this chapter is this approach based on? Given the available research evidence, does it make sense to delay counting-based number activities?

2. According to *MTW*, children must *memorize* the "arbitrary order which makes up the sequence of number words," and so counting instruction consists of numerous counting-in-unison activities to "reinforce the auditory pattern of the counting order" (Baratta-Lorton, 1976, p. 90). Evaluate this recommendation in light of those suggested by this chapter.

3. In *MTW*, enumeration instruction is combined with physical activities such as hand-clapping, foot stomping, and finger snapping to "provide experience saying one number with one motion" (Baratta-Lorton, 1976, p. 90). Which of the three component(s) of the enumeration process do such activities practice? Which do they not practice? According to this chapter, does this activity make sense for the typical kindergartner?

4. Comparison activities in *MTW* involve matching, not counting, because "numbers are too abstract" (Baratta-Lorton, 1976, p. 116). For example, for *Things in the Room,* children determine if there are, say, more pencils or more windows by *visually* matching these sets. "When it is not obvious visually that there is more of one item than another, match *Unifix* cubes one to one with the objects being compared and use the stacks of cubes to help determine which is more and which is less. *This enables children to compare large numbers of objects which cannot be brought into one-to-one correspondence with another. If asked to make this comparison without cubes, the child would have to count and compare numbers, a very abstract skill which few children at this stage would understand or find relevant*" (Baratta-Lorton, 1976, p. 117). In the *Handsful Activity,* two players each grab a handful of differently colored blocks, and then one player predicts whether his or her blocks are less than the opponent's. The players check the prediction by placing one set of blocks on one side of an egg carton and the second set on the other side. The row of blocks that is shorter has less. (a) Evaluate the procedure for comparing collections suggested for *Things in the Room* in light of the research on children's informal knowledge of number discussed in this chapter. (b) Evaluate the value of the *Handsful Activity* for enhancing a typical kindergarten-age child's understanding of "more."

5. *MTW* stresses the use of familiar materials but makes no mention of using fingers or finger patterns. Many educators avoid encouraging the use of fingers because they fear children will become dependent upon it and will be unable to develop more efficient means of working with numbers. Is this view consistent with that taken by this teaching guide?

4•2 NUMERAL LITERACY

Figure 4.2: A Nose for Numerals

PEANUTS reprinted by permission of UFS, Inc.

Sally in Figure 4.2 above has informally discovered a helpful strategy for writing the numeral 6 correctly. Like Sally, most young children master numeral-reading and writing skills with little help. Many children, however, encounter difficulty reading and writing numerals, and some experience unbearable frustration with these skills. Children with learning difficulties often continue to have numeral-writing difficulties past the primary grades. In Subunit 4•2•1, we explore what is required to read and write numerals correctly and the underlying reasons for common difficulties, such as confusing sixes with nines and reversing numerals (e.g., writing seven as Γ). In Subunit 4•2•2, we explain how to help children master numeral-reading and -writing skills with a minimum of difficulty and frustration.

4•2•1 LEARNING: UNDERSTANDING NUMERAL LITERACY

To help children avoid or overcome difficulties with reading and writing numerals, teachers need to understand what these skills involve.

Key Terms

Children learn to recognize and read numerals before they learn to copy and write them. The distinctions among these terms are defined below.

Numeral Recognition. *Numeral recognition involves identifying the written form of a spoken number.* It can be tested by reading a corresponding number to a child and asking the child to pick the numeral from several choices (e.g., Which of the following is *seven*: 3 7 2 9 5?).

Numeral Reading. *Numeral reading entails naming a written numeral* (e.g., showing a child a numeral such as 7 and asking: "What number is this?"*).

Copying Numerals. *Copying numerals involves drawing the likeness of a model numeral* (e.g., showing a child a numeral such as 7 and saying: "Write this number").

Writing Numerals. *Writing a numeral entails drawing a numeral from memory* (e.g., with no 7s visible, asking: "Draw a seven").

The Task Confronting Children

☞ Try Probe 4.4 (pages 4-17 to 4-19).

Why do some children confuse 6s and 9s? Why do some persist in writing numerals backwards? Why can copying numerals be so difficult? (Continued on page 4-20.)

---

* Technically, the symbol 7 is a numeral, *not* a number. The numeral 7 is a label or name for representing the number—an abstract concept—called *seven*. Other names for (representations of) seven are | | | | | | |, 5 + 2, 8 - 1, 14 ÷ 2, and $\sqrt{49}$. *Should teachers refer to a written number as a number or a numeral?* Purists might insist that they use the technically correct terminology numeral to refer to written numbers. Others (e.g., Ginsburg, 1989) dismiss the distinction as unimportant. After all, children will tend to call written numerals *numbers* any way. We recommend that teachers make an effort to use the terms number and numeral correctly so that children might learn from their example. However, for the sake of clear communication (e.g., if a child were puzzled by the term numeral), it would make sense to call a numeral such as 8 a number. In testing young children, for example, it may be preferable to use the term *number* rather than *numeral*. Moreover, teachers need not insist that children call written numbers *numerals* rather than numbers or correct them if they do.

➤ Probe 4.4: Understanding Numeral Skills

Part I: Some Common Difficulties with Numerals.

There is considerable confusion and misinformation about numeral skills. Test your own knowledge by considering the case studies of common difficulties described below. Reassess your answers after completing Subunit 4•2•1.

1. **A Case of Mistaken Identity.** Aberdeen, a first grader, confuses some numerals. For example, she reads 6 sometimes as "six" and other times as "nine." Mr. Warren, the special-education teacher, recommended work on reading 6s first and then 9s later, so as not to confuse her. Mrs. Garcia, the reading specialist, suggested that it might help to work on such easily confused numerals simultaneously. Who—if either—is right?

2. **A Case of Scribbles.** Even after 8 months of kindergarten, 5-year-old Bart was still having tremendous difficulty writing the numerals to 9. Except for 1, most numerals were not recognizable. Miss Skeen, who has taught kindergarten for 30 years, noted that Bart probably lacks the fine-motor control to hold a pencil and control its movements properly. She recommended delaying writing instruction until first grade when Bart should develop small-muscle control. Ms. Green, who recently graduated from a teacher's college, suggested tracing and copying activities to help Bart develop a kinesthetic sense of how the numerals are formed (e.g., tracing a finger over sandpaper numerals or making clay copies of numerals). In time, the cues could be slowly withdrawn to help the boy make the transition from copying to writing numerals. An example of a "fade-out" exercise is shown below. Who—if either—is right?

3. **A Case of Write and Wrong.** Che, a third grader labeled learning disabled, still has problems reversing numerals. For example, as often as not, he writes "seven" as Г . Mrs. Weinstein, the school psychologist, suggested that Che had perceptual-motor difficulties and suggested remedying these difficulties first. She suggested activities to enhance, for example, figure-ground perception, fine-motor control, and visual-motor coordination. Mrs. Yo suggested giving Che extensive practice copying the numerals so that he would overlearn how to form them. Who—if either—is right?

Part II: Questions About the Traditional Skills Approach to Numeral Difficulties.

This part of the probe asks you to critically examine the assumptions of the traditional approach to remedying difficulties with numeral skills.

Recognizing and Reading Numerals. The skills approach is based on the assumption that children learn to recognize and read numerals by a rote associative process. Association are imprinted on children's brains by repeated demonstrations (e.g., a teacher might say, "Six," while pointing to the numeral 6) and practice. It follows from this view that to minimize the possibility of associative confusions, easily confused numerals such as 2 and 5 or 6 and 9 should be learned separately.

Copying and Writing Numerals. According to the conventional wisdom, copying numerals is a relatively easy task. The only requirements are (a) fine-motor control and (b) accurate perception. Many educators, such as Miss Skeen in Part I, believe that kindergartners lack the small-muscle control to copy numerals. Writing numerals is viewed as a relatively difficult task, because children have to learn motor habits. The formation of these habits depends on practice. In the skills approach, numeral-writing practice often begins with tracing activities (e.g., using chalk, crayons, finger paint, or magic markers to trace over a numeral). A common exercise involves repeatedly tracing a finger over felt or sandpaper numerals. Practice then moves on to copying numerals (e.g., making clay copies or making copies in sand or with finger paints). In time, fade-out exercises, in which clues are gradually removed, are introduced to help children make the transition from copying to writing.

Special Children. Children with learning difficulties often have great difficulty reading, recognizing, copying, and writing numerals. These difficulties have often been attributed to perceptual-motor deficits (e.g., Meyers & Burton, 1989). Remedial instruction for such children has

Probe 4.4 continued

often focused on (a) perceptual-motor training to develop fine-motor skills, visual ability, or visual-motor coordination and (b) massive practice to achieve "overlearning." Consider, though, the following case study:

The Case of Joey. A primary-grade teacher asked Joey to write a numeral on the chalkboard. He wrote ⌐ and indicated that it was backward. Asked to try again, the boy wrote another backward seven and grimaced. Already frustrated, he tried once more, failed again, and asked, "How do you make a seven?" The teacher drew a seven on the chalkboard. After examining the model for a moment, Joey—much to his horror—copied it backwards.

1. Evaluate the conclusion that Joey's writing difficulty was due to perceptual confusion— sometimes seeing numerals backward.

2. Evaluate the conclusion that Joey's writing difficulty was due to a motor difficulty. Consider whether he could have written a backward 7 if he lacked small-muscle control.

3. Why didn't the model help Joey? In other words, why isn't copying a numeral much easier than writing it?

Part III: A New, Research-Based Analysis of Learning to Write Numerals. Recent research suggests that to write a numeral correctly, a child must have (a) an accurate mental image of the numeral and (b) a motor plan for translating the mental image into motor actions. The aim of this part of the probe is to help you construct an explicit understanding of this new model so that you can analyze and remedy numeral-copying and -writing difficulties.

Mental Image. An accurate mental image of a numeral such as 6 consists of knowing (a) what *parts* make up the numeral; (b) how the parts fit together (the *part-whole relationships*); and (c) the correct *left-right orientation* of the numeral.

   1. **Parts.** A six consists of two parts: a ball (loop) and stick (curved line). Knowing these parts helps a child distinguish a 6 from what other numerals? Put differently, how many other numerals consist of a curved line and a loop?

   2. **Part-Whole Relationships.** The parts of a 6 fit together in a particular way: the loop of a 6 joins the *lower* side of the curved line. This unique part-whole relationship distinguishes 6s from what other numeral?

   3. **Left-Right Orientation.** The loop of a 6 is attached to the right-hand side of the curved line, not the left-hand side (δ). Left-right orientation further distinguishes a 6 from a 9. Many young children have difficulty with left-right orientation. Consider whether it is necessary to distinguish a 6 from a 9. Does a child need a completely accurate mental image to distinguish among and identify the numerals 1 to 9?

Motor Plan. A motor plan is a step-by-step plan of execution. It specifies where to start, what direction to go, where to stop, how to change direction, and so forth.

Why is copying not significantly easier than writing numerals? Consider an analogous situation: Try copying Figure A below with a continuous motion (without picking up and repositioning your pencil) and without retracing an existing line. For example, the solution shown in Figure B below is *not* acceptable because line 7 (the dotted line) retraces line 4.

Figure A: 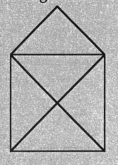   **Figure B:**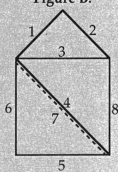

1. Were you able to find the solution? Were others in your group or class readily able to find a solution? If you found this a relatively difficult task, how did it make you feel?

2. Compare this task to the task confronting children when learning how to copy numerals. Successfully completing both tasks depends on what? How do you suppose children

Probe 4.4 continued

feel when they cannot find the key to copying a numeral correctly and keep making errors?

Part IV: Evaluating Numeral-Recognition Assessment Tasks.

This part of the probe asks you to apply the new model of numeral skills to the task of assessing numeral recognition.

1. To test whether or not her kindergartners could recognize numerals, Ms. Sunshine individually asked each child to point out the numbers one to nine on a number line as they were called out in random order. Nearly everyone in Ms. Sunshine's class had a perfect score. Mrs. Blossom, another kindergarten teacher, found these results hard to believe, because many children in her class had difficulty recognizing a few numerals and some had difficulty with more than a few. Evaluate Ms. Sunshine's numeral-recognition task.

2. Mrs. Blossom asked about each numeral in random order *and* presented the choices in random order. If she used only correctly formed numerals and a child accurately identified all nine numerals, would this imply knowledge of (a) the parts, (b) the part-whole relationships, and/or (c) the left-right orientation for each numeral? That is, can she conclude that the child has a completely accurate mental image? Why or why not?

Part V: Evaluating Cases of Numeral Difficulties.

This part of the probe asks you to analyze cases of numeral difficulties in terms of the new model of numeral skills. For each case described below, gauge the source of the child's difficulty and decide whether remedial efforts should be directed at learning (a) the parts, (b) the part-whole relationships, (c) the left-right orientation, or (d) the motor plan of each numeral. Your analysis should address the following questions:

- Does the child have at least a partially accurate mental image of each numeral? That is, can the child distinguish among (*identify or read*) the standard numerals, a skill that requires knowing the parts and part-whole relationships?
- Does the child have a completely accurate mental image? That is, can the child distinguish between standard numerals and back ward numerals, a skill that requires knowing the correct left-right orientation of a numeral?
- Does the child have a complete and accurate motor plan (a step-by-step plan of execution that translates a mental image into motor actions)? That is, does the child have difficulty writing the numerals, or even copying them with a model present?

1. **The Case of Zelda Zero.** Zelda, a first grader, was not completing her arithmetic assignments. Her teacher discovered that although Zelda could compute sums when given word problems, the girl had difficulty reading symbolic problems in the textbook and could not record sums she could compute. Testing revealed the following strengths and weaknesses:

	1	2	3	4	5	6	7	8	9
Recognizes	+	+	+	+	+	–	–	–	–
Distinguishes from backward numeral	+	+	–	+	–	–	–	–	–
Reads	+	+	+	+	–	–	–	–	–
Copies	+	–	–	+	–	–	–	–	–
Writes	+	–	–	–	–	–	–	–	–

2. **The Case of Kurt Confused**. Sometimes Kurt, a first grader, wrote numerals correctly but about half the time he reversed them. When he made an error, he tried to correct it.

3. **The Case of Wright Wrongway**. It was February, and first grader Wright Wrongway still regularly reversed 5, 6, and 9 (ᒣ, ϱ, ꟼ). When this happened, he noted, "That's not right." Efforts to rewrite a 5, 6, or 9 inevitably resulted in the same error, making Wright overwrought.

4. **The Case of Dianne Dyslexic**. Dianne, a second grader, could read simple addition expressions such as 5 + 3, 2 + 6, and 9 + 7. She also had no difficulty identifying page numbers in books (e.g., asked to turn to page seven, the girl could readily locate page 7). Dianne, however, often had difficulty writing the numerals 2, 3, 4, 5, 6, 7, and 9. More specifically, she often reversed these numerals. Do you have enough information to specify what her difficulty is? If so, how does the evidence support your conclusion? If not, what additional information do you need to collect?

Recognizing and Reading Numerals. To recognize or read a numeral such as 6, children must be able to distinguish it from other numerals such as 7 and 9 (and other symbols such as the letter b). To do so, they must have a partially complete mental image—must know the parts of a numeral and how the parts fit together to make a whole numeral (the part-whole relationships). Knowing that a 6 consists of a curved line and a loop distinguishes it from all other numerals except 9. Knowing the relationship between these parts (that the loop of a 6 joins the lower side of the curved line) distinguishes it from a 9.

Writing a Numeral. To write a numeral correctly from memory, children must have (a) a *completely* correct mental image of the numeral and (b) a motor plan (a step-by-step plan of execution for translating this mental image into motor actions) (Baroody, 1989). That is, children must know the correct left-right orientation of the numeral as well as its parts and part-whole relationships.* Moreover, they need a pre-planned course of action that specifies where to start (e.g., at the top of a line or just below it), in what direction to head (left, right, up, down, diagonally), what needs to be drawn (e.g., a straight line, an arc), when to stop a given step, how to change directions, how to begin the next step, and where to stop (Goodnow & Levine, 1973).

---

* Technically, the left-right orientation of a numeral is an aspect of its part-whole relationships. However, for pedagogical purposes, it will be discussed separately from other aspects of a numeral's part-whole relationships.

Unless children have an accurate motor plan in mind *before* they start writing a numeral, they will probably make a mistake. Indeed, they may make the same mistake time and time again. Joey (described in Part II of Probe 4.4 on pages 4-17 and 4-18), for example, began his 7s by heading from right to left—a process that resulted in backward 7s. Until their motor plan is corrected, children may make such errors repeatedly, despite the fact they can see they are writing the numeral incorrectly.

Copying Numerals. Copying numerals likewise requires a motor plan. To copy Figure A in Part III of Probe 4.4 (page 4-18), you needed to know what you were going to do before you started out. Without a motor plan, once you set out on an incorrect course, you could not complete the task. The same is true of copying a numeral. If children start off in the wrong direction—even with a model numeral in front of them—they will—in all likelihood—reverse the numeral.

4•2•2 TEACHING

Two general guidelines for fostering numeral-literacy skills are noted below:

☞ **Ensure a solid foundation for numeral-writing instruction.** In general, children should master (a) oral- and object-counting skills to 9 first, (b) then recognizing numerals to 9, and (c) finally, writing the numerals. This teaching progression is summarized in Figure 4.3.

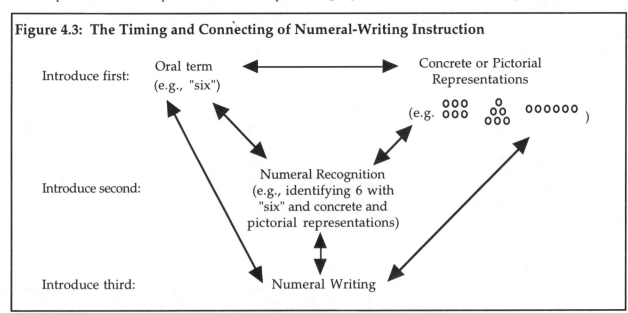

Figure 4.3: The Timing and Connecting of Numeral-Writing Instruction

↬ Numeration instruction and practice should flow out of experiences where children *need* to identify, read, or record numbers. THERE ARE NUMEROUS EVERYDAY OPPORTUNITIES FOR LEARNING ABOUT AND PRACTICING NUMERAL-RECOGNITION, -READING, AND -WRITING IN A PURPOSEFUL MANNER (e.g., identifying room or bus numbers; reading the date on a calendar or the age on a birthday card; and recording personal information such as a home telephone number, street address, and bus number on a personal identification necklace). Playing games such as *BINGO* (see Activity File 4.7) can also create a genuine need for recognizing and reading numerals. Creating a game board to play a game (see Activity File 4.8) or keeping score of a game such as *Pick-Up* (Activity File 4.9) can create a real purpose for numeral writing. Various extended projects can do the same (see, e.g., Activity File 4.10 on the next page).

Three specific guidelines for fostering numeral-recognition and reading skills are:

↬ **For children who can't recognize a numeral, help them construct the following aspects of its mental image: (a) the parts that make up the numeral and (b) how these parts fit together (the part-whole relationships).** Encourage them to analyze numerals and to discuss their distinguishing characteristics. This can be done, for example, in the context of tracing activities.

↬ **To highlight their differences, introduce easily confused numerals such as 2 and 5 or 6 and 9 together.** Encourage children to explicitly consider what distinguishes a 2 from a 5 and a 6 from a 9.

↬ **Use analogies to help children form a mental image.** For example, as Sally noted in Figure 4.2 (page 4-16), a 6 looks like a nose.

Two specific guidelines for fostering numeral-copying and writing skills are noted below:

↬ **Ensure that children have a completely accurate mental image, including left-right orientation.** Before children can construct a motor plan for copying or writing numerals, they need a completely accurate mental image of each numeral—something that can be translated into motor actions. If a child cannot recognize a numeral, a teacher should first focus on helping him or her learn its parts and part-whole relationships. To further prepare the child for numeral writing, instruction can next focus on left-right orientation.

Activity File 4.7: *BINGO*

◆ Identification of numerals 1 to 9
◆ K ◆ Two or more players or teams

This is a relatively difficult numeral-identification activity because the numerals used on the Bingo boards are not in order. Call off numbers in random order by drawing cards with a numeral from 1 to 9 from a deck of numeral cards. Players place a marker on the appropriate square of their board. Note that each three-column by three-row board should have a different arrangement of numerals. The first player to get three markers in a row wins. In an alternative version, two or more children can play on their own by drawing a card with up to 9 dots on it from a deck of cards. After counting the dots, the players place a marker on the appropriate space of their Bingo cards. Note that this version of the game can help children connect numerals with pictorial representations of sets as well as verbal numbers.

Activity File 4.8: Preparing to Play *BINGO*

◆ Purposeful practice of numeral writing
◆ K-2 ◆ Class as individuals

Using a BINGO card to illustrate your points, explain the rules of *BINGO*. Then have the children make up their own BINGO cards to play the game. With kindergartners you may wish to pass out paper with a 3 x 3 grid (9 grids) and have them write in haphazard order the numerals 0 to 9 or 1 to 10. To practice writing two-digit numerals, specify a range (e.g., 0 to 20, 11 to 29, 11 to 50, or 11 to 99). With more experienced players, use paper with a 4 x 4 grid (16 grids) or a 5 x 5 gird (25 grids). Note that in successive games, children can make up new BINGO cards.

Activity File 4.9: *Pick Up*

◆ Practice enumeration and numeral writing to 9
◆ K-1 ◆ Two to six children

On their turn, a player turns over a card from a deck of cards with 1 to 9 dots. The number of dots on the card is the number of points scored that turn. The player then records his or her score. After, say, four rounds, the players can use a hand-held calculator to tally their score.

Activity File 4.10: Gift Calendars

◆ Purposeful practice of numeral writing to 31
+ calendar instruction + spatial problem solving
◆ K-2 ◆ Individual or small-group project

To create a useful holiday gift for a parent or guardian, children can make a calendar like the one below. Note that in addition to practicing numeral writing, this extended project involves discussing the spelling and the order of days of the week and months of the year, the number of days in each month, and significant events associated with each month (e.g., spring begins in March). It also involves art and careful planning. Provide the children with twelve 5 x 7 grids, each with spaces to write in the names of the month, names of the days of the week (Sunday, Monday . . .), and the dates (1, 2, . . .) Discuss where to record the first day of each month. One way the completed calendar can be bound together is by punching holes in the paper and tying the pages together with yarn. A challenging problem for primary-age children is how to design the calendar so that it all fits together properly (e.g., where should the holes be punched so that the picture and the days of the month are both right-side up). This is not a trivial task. Encourage children to experiment with mock-ups to figure out the best design.

☞ Encourage children to construct their own motor plans for numerals; for those who ask or are having difficulty, *explicitly* point out a motor plan. Purposeful numeral-writing activities can prompt children to ask questions such as, "How do you write a six?" This indicates that they have a felt need to learn a motor plan. Take this opportunity to help them construct an accurate and a complete motor plan (see Box 4.6 on the next page). After describing and demonstrating a motor plan, it may help some to define the starting point with a dot. As children practice tracing, copying, or writing a numeral, talk them through the motor plan and, if necessary, have them verbally rehearse their plan of action.

☞ To check your understanding of this subunit, try Probe 4.5 (page 4-24).

PARTING THOUGHTS

Questions such as How many marbles do you have? How old will you be on your next birthday? When is it my turn to be first in line? What's my bus number? illustrate children's personal need for understanding the various meanings of numbers. Questions such as How far should I count before I chase you? How many presents did I get? How many spaces can I move? Who has more—you or me? reveal children's personal need for the various uses of number words and symbols (Payne & Rathmell, 1975). "Children come to understand number meanings [and uses] gradually. To encourage these understandings, teachers can offer classroom experiences in which students first manipulate physical objects and then use their own language to explain their thinking" (NCTM, 1989, p. 38). Perhaps just as important is taking advantage of unplanned or everyday opportunities to use numbers. In either case, "emphasizing exploratory experiences with numbers that capitalize on the natural insights of children enhances their sense of mathematical competency, enables them to build and extend number relationships, and helps them to develop a link between their world and the world of mathematics" (NCTM, 1989, p. 38).

RESOURCES

SOME INSTRUCTIONAL RESOURCES

☞ **Wynroth Math Programs**, 521 Bradford Parkway, Syracuse, (continued on page 4-25)

Box 4.6: Motor Plans for the Numerals 1 to 9

The numerals are presented in the order below so that instruction builds on previous learning. Note that easily confused numerals, such as 5 and 2 or 6 and 9 are taught one after the other so that differences in their execution can be highlighted. The motor plans below are rather detailed. Many children will *not* need such elaborate instructions. As long as the child has enough guidance to make the numeral accurately, the simpler the motor plan the better. To facilitate direction-giving, particularly for children who don't know their left from their right, use the writing paper with directional clues such as that shown to the right.

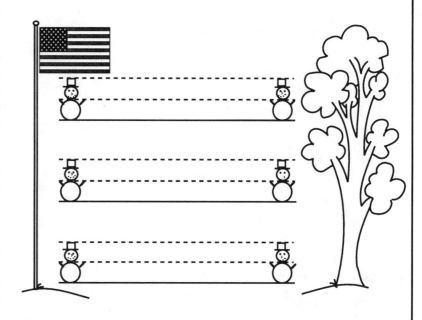

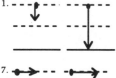 1. Start at the top line and drop straight down to the bottom line (ground).

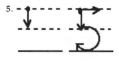 7. Start at the top line, move along the top line toward the tree side, <u>stop</u>, and then slide down to the bottom line and back toward the flag side.

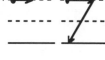 4. (1) Start at the top line, drop straight down to the middle line, <u>stop</u>, then walk along the middle line toward the tree side, and stop. (2) Then start another line at the top line and drop straight down to the ground, crossing the first line that goes along the middle."

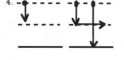 5. 1) Start at the top line, drop straight down to the middle line, stop (like the four), and then make a big tummy towards the tree side that ends up on the ground. (2) Five also has a hat. Go back to the top line where you started, walk along the top line toward the tree side, and stop.

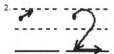 2. Start below the top line (at the rim of the hat); now make an ear by traveling up to the top line toward the tree side, curving around all the way down to the bottom line, stopping underneath where you began; and then add a tail by walking along the bottom line toward the tree side.

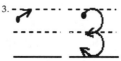 3. Start below the top line (at the rim of the hat like the number two) and travel up to the top line toward the tree side, touch the top line, make a tummy that rests on the middle line, make a bigger tummy toward the tree side that touches the bottom line (ground) and curls up toward the flag side.

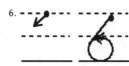 6. Start at the top line, curve down toward the flag side until reaching the middle line, continue to curve down but now toward the tree side until you reach the bottom line, and then make a ball at the bottom that touches the middle line before it closes.

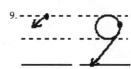 9. Start below the top line (at the rim of the hat), make a ball above the middle line that first goes toward the flag side and returns to the start, and then curves down toward the tree side until you reach the bottom line (ground). So six has a ball at the bottom that faces the tree side, and nine has a ball at the top that faces the flag side.

 8. Start at the top line and make a capital S. Without lifting your pencil, connect the two ends of the S.

↗ Probe 4.5: Analyzing Numeral-Writing Instruction

This probe asks you to apply the new model of numeral skills to the task of analyzing numeral-writing instruction methods.

Part I: *Mathematics Their Way*

Evaluate the following suggestions by *Mathematics Their Way* for teaching numeral writing:

1. Numeral-writing training is done as an art lesson, "long before the children need to use the numbers" (Baratta-Lorton, 1976, p. 43). Should such skill instruction be separated from application?

2. Except for one, each numeral is drawn in two parts: the first part in purple, the second part in green. (Some teachers use green, implying "go," to draw the first part and red, implying "stop" to draw the second part.) Will drawing the numerals 2 to 9 in two parts (colors) help children learn to *recognize* these numerals?

3. The purple-and-green model is recommended as a way of minimizing or remedying reversals. Will it help children construct an accurate motor plan and thus deal effectively with the reversal problem?

4. Initially, children copy a numeral with finger motions in the air or in the palm of their hand, as they view its purple-and-green model. Is this an effective approach to fostering numeral-writing competency?

5. The copying activity just described is followed by activities such as tracing templates, making clay models, and copying numerals on a geoboard or in fingerpaint. How effective are these activities?

6. Writing Papers provides practice copying the numerals. The writing paper for 4, for instance, uses an arrow to indicate the starting point and outlines the first part of the numeral as shown below:

Would this help children master writing the numeral 4?

Part II: Rhymes for Writing Numerals[1]

Evaluate whether or not the following rhymes for writing numerals provide explicit motor plans.

1. A straight line down just for fun, is how you make the number 1.
2. Around, down and over to tie your shoe, this is how to make the number 2.
3. Around the tree, around the tree, will make a perfect number 3.
4. Down and over and down once more, now you've made the number 4.
5. Old fat 5 is down and around, put a flag on top and see what you've found.
6. A stick and a ball are good for tricks, they also make the number 6.
7. Across the sky and down from heaven, will make an excellent number 7.
8. Make an "S" but do not wait, climb back up for number 8.
9. Draw a leaky balloon on a line, this is also the number 9.

Part III: An Example of Textbook Instruction

The *Math Book from Hell: Grade 1* provides the following advice for correcting the common error of writing a 2 backwards: "Provide dot models ∴ for the children to trace." Evaluate this method for correcting reversals. Is it likely to work? Why or why not?

NY 13224 (1-315-449-0125). This program is based on the following three principles:

1. Conceptual instruction precedes symbolic instruction. For example, a preworksheet phase entails learning number concepts in a concrete fashion. Only after this phase is completed are worksheets on number skills introduced (e.g., using the equal, greater-than, and less-than signs).

2. Concepts are introduced purposefully in the context of games. For example, *Animal Spots* requires players to throw a die with 0 to 5 dots to determine how many pegs ("spots") they can take for their leopard or giraffe (an animal figure cut out of wood with holes drilled for pegs). (The game can also be played with 0- to 10-dot die or cards.) The first child to fill his or her animal with spots is the winner. Playing *Animal Spots* entails oral counting, enumeration, the cardinality principle, and production of sets. To ensure accurate set production, have children count their pegs into a dish before placing them in their animal. By learning the rules of a game, a child learns a key mathematical concept such as equivalence ("same number as"). Thus, games are used to teach concepts as well as practice skills.

3. Number and arithmetic concepts are introduced meaningfully in terms of counting. For example, the concept of equivalence is taught in the context of playing *Dominoes Same Number*. This game is like regular dominoes except that the dominoes have varied, even haphazard, arrangements of dots. After the dominoes are evenly distributed to the (2 to 6) players, the player with the "double two" begins. The next player then must find a domino with the same number. Initially, children are encouraged to count the dots in a trial-and-error fashion. If a child counts two dots then he or she may match it to one of the ends of the double-two domino. Play continues in this fashion until one player uses all his or her dominoes or no player can find a match. In the latter case, the player with the fewest dominoes wins.

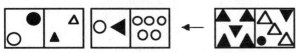

Note that equivalence (*same number as*) in *Dominoes Same Number* is defined as counting two collections and arriving at the same cardinal designation, not in terms of matching and one-to-one correspondence.

A SAMPLE OF CHILDREN'S LITERATURE[2]

The following is a sample of a variety of counting stories which enhance early math concepts and a brief description of how the book might be used:

- **Anno's Counting Book** by M. Anno, © 1977, Thomas Y. Crowell. This picture book starts with counts of 0 and extends to those with 12. The pictures include variously arranged collections of people and can be used to practice oral counting to 12 and enumeration (including keeping-track strategies).

- **Brian Wildsmith's 1, 2, 3's** by B. Wildsmith, © 1965, Franklin Watts. This book uses colorful geometric shapes to introduce children to oral and object counting to 10.

- **Counting Penguins** by C. W. Howe, © 1983, Harper & Row. This picture book starts the count sequence with 0 and ends with 9. Because of the nature of the pictures, this book encourages the understanding that a number coming later in the count sequence represents a larger quantity.

- **Counting Wildflowers** by B. McMillan, © 1986, Lothrop, Lee, & Shepard Books (William Morrow & Company, Inc.). The numbered illustrations of beautiful flowers can provide an opportunity to practice the count sequence to 20, enumeration, cardinality, and numeral recognition. The last picture shows a field of flowers and notes, "Too many to count."

- **A Farmer's Dozen** by S. J. Russell, © 1982, Harper & Row. A farmer who starts out as one lone person and through additions (e.g., marriage, the birth of a child, the adoption of a stray dog) ends up with a dozen people and animals. The story illustrates number sequence to 12 and how these numbers are built up by adding one more. An added feature is the introduction and meaning of the vocabulary term "dozen."

🐝 **Over in the Meadow** by J. Langstaff & F. Rojankovsky, © 1957, Harcourt. This book offers practice of the oral count sequence 1 to 10, via poetic rhyme and text. It can be particularly effective in a preschool setting for group story listening and fingerplays.

🐝 **Ten Cats and Their Tales** by M. Lehman, ©1981, Holt, Rinehart & Winston. This picture book offers practice of the oral count sequence to 10, with its primary focus on the order of the number terms in poetic verse.

🐝 **Up to Ten and Down Again** by L. C. Ernst, © 1986, William Morrow & Company, Inc. This book can be an effective tool for practicing both forward and backward oral count sequences. The pictures of objects become increasingly cluttered, which makes keeping-track and enumeration increasingly difficult. However, at the end of the book there is a chart of the pictured objects, arranged in a row and labeled with a corresponding numeral. This can be used as a basis for work on enumeration, cardinality, number comparisons, and numeral recognition—as well as oral counting.

🐝 **The Very Hungry Caterpillar** by E. Carle, © 1969, Putnam Publishing Group. This book is appropriate for practicing oral and object counting to 5 with preschool children. The linear arrays of pictured objects minimizes the effort needed to keep track.

Additional books regarding *counting* and *numbers* include: **Handtalk Zoo** by G. Ancona & M. B. Miller, © 1989, Macmillan; **I Can Count the Petals of a Flower** by J. & S. Wahl, © 1985, NCTM; **M&Ms Brand Chocolate Candies Counting Book** by B. B. McGrath, © 1994, Charlesbridge Publishing; **The Marcel Marceau Counting Book** by G. Mendoza, © 1971, Doubleday; **The Most Amazing Hide-and-Seek Counting Book** by R. Crowther, © 1981, Viking Penguin; **Nessa's Fish** by N. Luenn, © 1990, Macmillan/McGraw-Hill; **One Hundred Hungry Ants** by E. J. Pinczes, © 1993, Scholastic; **Sesame Street One, Two, Three Story Book** by E. P. Kingsley, J. Moss, N. Stiles, & D. Wilcox, © 1973, Random House; **10 Bears in My Bed** by S. Mack, © 1974, Pantheon;

Ten, Nine, Eight by M. Bang, © 1983, William Morrow & Company, Inc.; and **Up The Down Elevator** by N. Farber & A. Gusman, © 1979, Addison-Wesley.

TIPS ON USING TECHNOLOGY

Calculators

▦ **Keystrokes: Calculator Activities for Young Students: Counting and Place Value,** by R. E. Reys and others, © 1980 by Creative Publications. For grades 2 and 3, this resource describes a variety of activities for using calculators to explore counting patterns and to practice other mathematical skills. Activity Card 2-1, for example, instructs children how to count by ones: Using a Texas Instrument (TI) *Math Explorer*, for example, press +, 1, =. Then by repeatedly pressing the = key, the calculator counts. The activity card poses the question: How long did it take to count from 1 to 100? Next, it asks children to estimate how long it will take to count from 1 to 1000 and then to determine the actual time it takes. What do you suppose you have to enter to have a calculator count by twos? Activity Card 2-2 introduces counting backwards and includes the following two questions: (a) What do you suppose you have to enter to have a calculator count backwards from 10? (b) What happens if you do not stop at 0? Consider to what question this might lead. Activity Card 2-3 introduces skipping around and includes the following four questions: (a) What do you suppose you have to enter to have a calculator count by twos starting with five? (b) What do you suppose has to be entered to count by fives starting with 55? (c) What do you suppose has to be entered to count by tens beginning with 100? (d) What do you suppose has to be entered to count by threes beginning with 10?

Computers

▢ **Millie's Math House** published by Edmark and distributed by Sunburst. Appropriate for grades K to 2 and available on disk or CD-ROM for IBM or Macintosh format. Six activities involve counting, sequencing, patterns, and identifying numerals and collections.

5 INTRODUCING ARITHMETIC: UNDERSTANDING THE WHOLE-NUMBER OPERATIONS AND MASTERING THE BASIC NUMBER COMBINATIONS

The Number Sentence 5 − 3 = ? Could be Used to Describe Which of the Following Word Problems?

A. Mary had five dolls. Ruffus her dog buried three of them. How many dolls does Mary have left?

B. Five pests make their home on Ruffus' stomach. Three were fleas, and the rest were ticks. How many ticks camped out on Ruffus' stomach?

C. Ruffus crushed five flowers in the garden. Bruno the Beagle crushed three. How many more flowers did Ruffus crush than Bruno?

D. Ruffus had scratched and ruined five pieces of furniture. Bruno the Beagle had scratched and ruined only three. How many more pieces of furniture must Bruno ruin to catch up to Ruffus in the Most Destructive Dog of the Day Contest?

E. Bruno the Beagle ate five hamburgers off Mr. Smith's grill; Ruffus ate three. Ruffus stole how many hamburgers fewer than Bruno?

☞ The aim of the bulletin board above is to prompt reflection and discussion about what real-life situations the symbolic subtraction expression 5 - 3 = ☐ can represent. Which word problems above do you think 5 - 3 = ☐ can represent? Which do you think can be represented by 3 + ☐ = 5?

THIS CHAPTER

*R*ushing into symbolic arithmetic (e.g., introducing equations such as 5 + 3 = ☐ or 5 + ☐ = 8) and pushing the memorization of basic number facts (e.g., reciting 7 + 5 = 12 quickly) can undermine children's critical thinking and their disposition to learn mathematics and to solve problems. For example, asked her opinion about mathematics, Emily a first grader responded, "I don't understand and can't do problems on papers, I'm too young for it." If required to work with symbols they do not understand, children cannot think logically or creatively. If rewarded for regurgitating basic number facts quickly and mindlessly, they have little incentive to engage in critical thinking (Kouba & Franklin, 1993). When their own thinking is devalued, many children lose confidence in their mathematical ability and interest in doing mathematics.

A key to fostering mathematical power is helping children value their own informal thinking and knowledge. This chapter explores children's surprising informal arithmetic strengths, which build on the counting concepts and skills described in Chapter 4. From their concrete, everyday counting experiences, children construct a fundamental understanding of arithmetic and devise sophisticated, counting-based arithmetic strategies. In this chapter, we also examine how a teacher can build on children's informal knowledge and introduce formal arithmetic concepts and skills in a meaningful manner. In Unit 5•1, we explore single-digit addition and subtraction; in Unit 5•2, single-digit multiplication and division. In Unit 5•3, we examine one of schoolchildren's biggest bugaboos—learning the basic number facts—and how instruction can foster mastery of combinations with addends or factors up to 9 without frustrating both students and teachers. Learning basic arithmetic concepts and skills provides a firm foundation for multidigit arithmetic, which is explored in the next chapter. Developing a number sense about the arithmetic operation is explored further in chapter 7.

WHAT THE NCTM *STANDARDS* SAY

Grades K-4

"In grades K-4, the mathematics curriculum should include concepts of addition, subtraction, multiplication, and division of whole numbers so that students can:

◆ develop meaning for the operations by modeling and discussing a rich variety of problem situations;
◆ relate the mathematical language and symbolism of operations to problem situations and informal language;
◆ recognize that a wide variety of problem structures can be represented by a single operation;
◆ develop operation sense" (p. 41).

"In grades K-4, the mathematics curriculum should develop whole-number computation so that students can:

◆ model, explain, and develop reasonable proficiency with basic facts . . . ;
◆ use calculators in appropriate computational situations;
◆ select and use computation techniques appropriate to specific problems and determine whether the results are reasonable" (p. 44).

Grades 5-8

"In grades 5-8, the mathematics curriculum should develop the concepts underlying computation . . . in various contexts so that students can:

◆ compute with whole numbers . . . ;
◆ develop, analyze, and explain procedures for computation [with whole numbers]. . . ;
◆ use computation [with whole numbers] . . . to solve problems" (p. 94).

5•1 ADDITION AND SUBTRACTION

Figure 5.1: Counting is Children's Informal Means of Adding and Subtracting

As noted in chapter 3, children have their own way of adding and subtracting. They count using fingers, objects, marks, or whatever is available. Even when teachers try to discourage informal methods and encourage more efficient methods, many children continue to use what makes sense to them—just more surreptitiously (see Figure 5.1). In this unit, we consider how addition and subtraction instruction can build on what children know. In Subunit 5•1•1, we examine the meanings of addition and subtraction. In Subunit 5•1•2, we describe the informal foundations that enable children to solve problems concretely. In Subunit 5•1•3, we examine adding and subtracting with symbols.

5•1•1 MATHEMATICS: UNDERSTANDING ADDITION AND SUBTRACTION

You may be surprised to learn that a *variety* of addition and subtraction situations exist in the real world. The aim of this subunit is to help you construct an explicit understanding of these different meanings so that you are in a position to help your students do the same.

Types of Addition and Subtraction Situations Involving Objects

In this section, we focus on adding and subtracting collections of things (discrete quantities), because children can readily apply their informal number and counting knowledge to such situations. (Problems involving operations on continuous quantities such as length, area, weight, and time can be introduced later as a basis for learning about measurement concepts and skills.)

Addition. An addition expression such as 5 + 3 can represent two different situations.

• **Change add-to situations.** Some situations imply a physical action. They begin with a certain number of items, and then some *more* items are added, *increasing* the original amount. Such active situations can be called *change add-to* problems, because something is literally added to a preexisting amount and *changes* it by making the amount larger. For example, a child has five candies. After incessant pleading, his mother caves in and gives him three more candies. The sum of the original amount and the added amount specifies the size of the new, larger amount.

• **Part-part-whole situations.** Other situations do not imply physical action. In passive situations, a collection of things is subdivided into two (or more) parts, and the whole is the sum of its parts. For instance, a boy has some candies in his left pants pocket (Part 1) and the rest in his right pants pocket (Part 2). The addition of the two parts specifies his total candies (the whole).

Subtraction. A subtraction expression such as 8 - 5 can represent a change situation or two types of "difference" situations.

• **Change take-away situations.** Some situations begin with a certain number of items and then some items are removed (taken away), *decreasing* (changing) the original amount. Problem A in the bulletin board on page 5-1 is an example of a *change take-away* situation.

• **Equalize situations.** In some difference situations, an effort is made to eliminate the discrepancy between two amounts. That is, the task involves determining how much must be added to the smaller amount to make it equal to the larger amount (or subtracted from the larger amount to make it equal to the smaller amount). Problem D in the bulletin board on the first page is an *equalize* situation.

• **Compare situations.** Other difference situations simply focus on determining the size of the discrepancy—specifying by how much a smaller and a larger amount differ. Problems C and E in the bulletin board on page 5-1 are *compare* situations.

Types of Word Problems

The taxonomy illustrated in Figure 5.2 (on page 5-4) summarizes one way of classifying word problems. There are five main types of word problems, which parallel the five meanings of addition and subtraction described earlier. For each of the five main types of problems, the unknown can be the sum or difference (a + b = ? or a - b = ?), the second addend (a + ? = c or a - ? = c), or the first addend (? + b = c or ? - b = c). Note that a word problem is classified as addition or subtraction according to its semantics, not the operation that is used to solve it.

Teachers should be familiar with the various types of problems that exist in the real world in order to ensure that their students encounter a

Figure 5.2: A Taxonomy of Addition and Subtraction Word Problems

Problem Type [a]	Missing Sum or Difference (a + b = ? or a - b = ?)	Missing 2nd Addend (a + ? = c or a - ? = c)	Missing 1st Addend (? + b = c or ? - b = c)
CHANGE ADD-TO with	...UNKNOWN OUTCOME	...UNKNOWN CHANGE	...UNKNOWN START
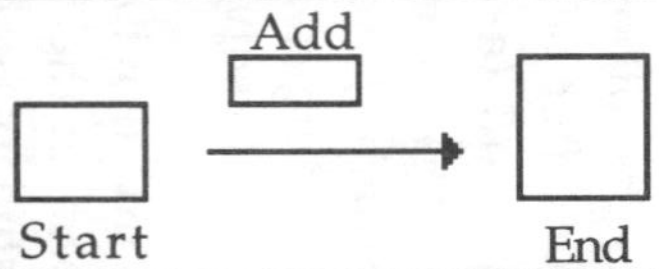	Alexi had 5 candies. Barb gave him 3 more. How many candies does he have altogether now?	Alexi had 5 candies. Barb gave him some more. Now he has 8 altogether. How many candies did Barb give him?	Alexi had some candies. Barb gave him 3 more. Now he has 8 altogether. How many candies did he start with?
CHANGE TAKE-AWAY with	...UNKNOWN OUTCOME	...UNKNOWN CHANGE	...UNKNOWN START
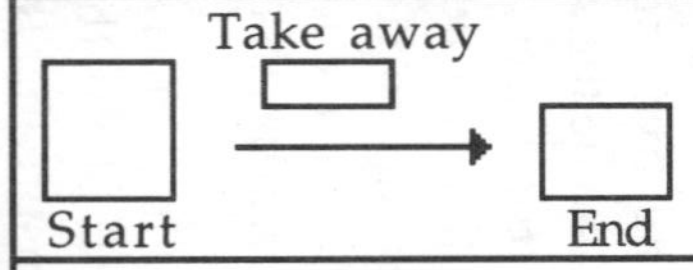	Alexi had 8 candies. He gave 5 to Barb. How many candies does he have left?	Alexi had 8 candies. He gave some to Barb. Now he has 3 left. How many candies did he give to Barb?	Alexi had some candies. He gave 5 to Barb. Now he has 3 left. How many candies did he start with?
PART-PART-WHOLE with	...UNKNOWN WHOLE [b]	...UNKNOWN SECOND PART	...UNKNOWN FIRST PART
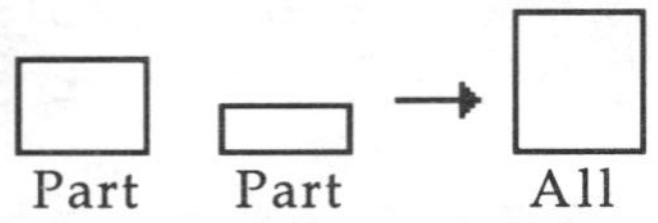	Alexi had 5 fireballs and 3 lollipops. How much candy did he have altogether?	Alexi had 5 fireballs and some lollipops. He had 8 candies altogether. How many were lollipops?	Alexi had some fireballs and 3 lollipops. He had 8 candies altogether. How many were fireballs?
EQUALIZE with	...UNKNOWN DIFFERENCE	...UNKNOWN SECOND PART	...UNKNOWN FIRST PART
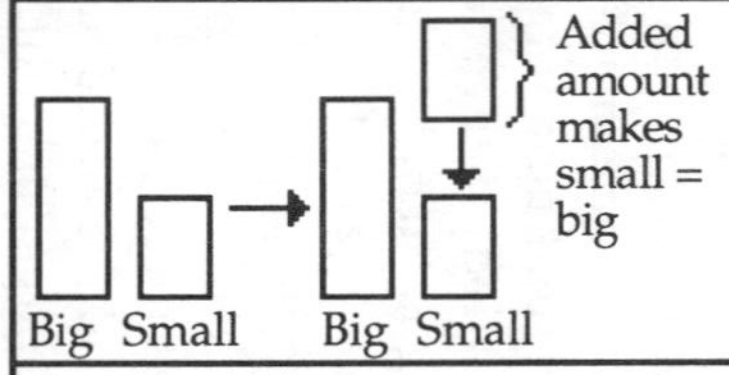	Alexi had 8 candies. Barb had 5. How many more does Barb have to buy to have as many as Alexi?	Alexi had 8 candies. Barb had some. If she got 3 more candies, she'd have the same number as Alexi. How many candies did Barb have already?	Alexi had some candies. Barb, who had 5 candies, had to get 3 more to have the same number as Alexi. How many candies did Alexi have?
COMPARE with	...UNKNOWN DIFFERENCE	...UNKNOWN SECOND PART	...UNKNOWN FIRST PART
	Alexi had 8 candies. Barb had 5. How many more candies did Alexi have than Barb?	Alexi had 8 candies. He had 3 more than Barb. How many candies did Barb have?	Alexi had some candies. He had 3 more than Barb who had 5. How many candies did Alexi have?

[a] The diagrams depicting the various situations are based on those presented in Fuson (1992b). [b] *All* may make more sense than *whole* for many children.

Note. The examples of equalize and compare problems all involve a *more* relationship. These difference problems could be reworded to involve a *less* relationship. For example, the equalize unknown-difference problem could be reworded: Alexi had 8 candies, Barb had 5. How many does *Alexi have to give up to have as many as Barb?*

5-4

wide variety of problem situations. Although publishers are making an effort to include more types of addition and subtraction in textbooks and curriculum materials, teachers need to analyze the problems available in their instructional materials and, if necessary, supplement them with inadequately represented problems.

☞ Try Probe 5.1 (pages 5-6 and 5-7).

5•1•2 ADDING AND SUBTRACTING WITH OBJECTS

Learning

Children can learn to distinguish among different types of addition and subtraction word problems (e.g., complete Part I of Probe 5.1 on page 5-6) and can learn to solve them, albeit, not all at once (Carpenter, Fennema, Peterson, Chiang, & Loef, 1989; Fuson, 1992b).

Informal Strategies for Solving Addition and Subtraction Problems. Children construct a basic concept of addition and subtraction during the preschool years (Ginsburg et al., 1998). Before formal arithmetic instruction, they can use this informal knowledge to comprehend simple addition and subtraction problems and to *model their meaning* (e.g., Carpenter & Moser, 1984; DeCorte & Verschaffel, 1987). For instance, to solve a problem involving five take-away three, a child might employ a *concrete take-away strategy*: Count out five blocks, remove three, and count the remaining two blocks (see the description and figure on page 5-6 of Probe 5.1). In time, children spontaneously invent increasingly efficient counting strategies to determine sums and differences (e.g., Resnick & Ford, 1981). For example, to solve "five take away three," many invent a *counting-down strategy*: Count backwards three times from the starting amount five ("Five, four [is one less], three [is two less], two [is three less]—so the answer is two").

Relative Difficulty of Word Problems. Because teachers need to take into account developmental readiness when posing problems, they should have some sense of the relative difficulty of problems. Problems in which the outcome, whole, or difference is unknown are relatively easy. Of these situations, equalize and compare problems may be more difficult to model than change and part-part-whole problems. Because of their informal change view of addition and subtraction, it is even more difficult for children to model a problem in which the change or a part is unknown. Unknown start or unknown first-part problems may be especially confusing, because children are accustomed to knowing the starting amount.

Teaching: Four Guidelines

☙ **Word problems should be used to** *introduce* **arithmetic operations with whole numbers.** BECAUSE WORD PROBLEMS CAN BE MORE MEANINGFUL TO CHILDREN THAN SYMBOLIC EXPRESSIONS, THEY SHOULD BE AN INTEGRAL ASPECT OF INSTRUCTION FROM THE START (see, e.g., Feinberg, 1988).

☙ **Exploit everyday situations to introduce and to discuss addition and subtraction.** Numerous situations in the classroom, playground, or home involve adding and subtracting (see, e.g., Activity File 5.1 on page 5-8). By taking advantage of such everyday opportunities, teachers can help children apply or extend their informal arithmetic knowledge in a purposeful and meaningful way.

☙ **To foster a broad and well-connected understanding of addition and subtraction, use a variety of problem situations** (see, e.g., *The Thinking Story Books*, © 1985 by Open Court). Encountering a variety of problems can challenge children's thinking, improve their problem-solving performance on even more difficult types of problems, and help them construct a more complete understanding of arithmetic operations (e.g., Fuson, 1992b; Stigler, Fuson, Ham, & Kim, 1986).

☙ **Hearten children to solve addition and subtraction problems informally and to share their informal strategies.** Encourage their counting strategies (Folsom, 1975; Ginsburg, 1989). Allow children to use fingers or other objects, make tally marks, or draw pictures (e.g., to model change add-to missing-change problems with the *concrete counting-all strategy* described on page 5-6 of Probe 5.1). Support children's natural graduation to more sophisticated counting strategies by encouraging them to demonstrate or otherwise share their invented shortcuts. Box 5.1 on page 5-9 illustrates several ways of indirectly prompting children to invent the relatively elegant strategy of *counting-on* (described earlier on page 3-6 and again on page 5-7). (Continued on page 5-9.)

➤ Probe 5.1: Addition and Subtraction Word Problems

Part I: Identifying Addition and Subtraction Word Problems

The aim of Part I is to help you construct an explicit understanding of the variety of real-world addition and subtraction situations. Use the taxonomy of addition and subtraction word problems on page 5-4 (Figure 5.2) to answer the questions below. You may find it helpful to work with others. Share your answers with your group or class.

1. For each problem below, indicate the problem type and the unknown term.

   ■ **Problem 1 (◆ K-1):** Georgia had 6 cookies. She ate 4. How many does she have left?

   ■ **Problem 2 (◆ K-1):** Georgia had 4 cookies. She got 2 more out of the cookie jar. How many does she have now?

   ■ **Problem 3 (◆ K-3):** Georgia has 4 chocolate chip cookies and 2 ginger snaps. How many cookies does she have altogether?

   ■ **Problem 4 (◆ 1-3):** Georgia scored 6 points and Helga scored 4. Georgia won by how many points?

   ■ **Problem 5 (◆ 1-3):** Georgia scored 6 points and Helga scored 4. How many points must Helga score to catch up to Georgia?

   ■ **Problem 6 (◆ 1-3):** Georgia had 6 dresses. Her mother bought her some more. Georgia found 9 dresses hanging in closet. How many new dresses did Georgia's mom buy?

   ■ **Problem 7 (◆ 1-3):** Of Georgia's 9 dresses, 5 were pink, and the rest were different colors. How many dresses did Georgia have that were not pink?

2. (a) Which of the five main types of word problems in the taxonomy on page 5-4 (Figure 5.2) involve starting with a single collection and increasing or decreasing this amount to create a new amount? (b) Which involve beginning with two numbers, which are then added or subtracted to find the whole, the difference, or one of the parts?

3. (a) Which of the problems above describe physical actions or "active" situations? (b) Which describe static situations (i.e., do not involve physical actions)?

4. (a) Describe the difference between a change-add-to and a part-part-whole addition prob-

lem. (b) Describe the difference between a compare and an equalize situation.

5. We purposely placed Problem 3 immediately after Problem 2 and Problem 5 immediately after Problem 4. Why?

Part II: Identifying Informal Strategies

Without instruction, children invent a variety of impressive counting-based strategies to solve addition and subtraction problems. The aim of Part II of this probe is to help you better appreciate such feats.

1. Put yourself in the place of a young child who does not know the basic addition and subtraction facts. Consider how the child might concretely model the meaning of Problems 1 to 5 above with blocks?

2. Described and illustrated below are four informal strategies for directly or concretely modeling an addition or subtraction problem situation. For each, identify whether it models the meaning of Problem 1, 2, 3, 4, or 5.

a. *Concrete counting all:*
(1) Count out objects to represent an amount;

(2) produce objects to represent another amount;

(3) count all the objects put out to determine the answer.

b. *Concrete taking away:*
(1) Count out objects to represent the starting amount;

(2) remove the number that the problem specifies were taken away;

(3) count the remaining objects to determine the amount left.

c. *Concrete equalizing:*
(1) Create two parallel rows of objects to represent each amount;

(2) add objects to the smaller row until it is equal to the other row;

(3) count the number of objects added to the smaller row.

Probe 5.1 continued

d. *Matching*:
(1) Create two parallel rows of objects to represent each amount; □□□□□□□□ □□□□□

(2) count the number of unmatched objects in the larger row. □□□□□¹□²□³□ □□□□□

3. In time, children devise more sophisticated strategies (e.g., Resnick & Ford, 1981). Described below are four such strategies. For each, identify which problem (Problem 1, 2, 3, 4, or 5) it most closely models.

   a. *Abstract counting-all*: (1) Starting with one, count up to the cardinal value of the first addend (e.g., 2 + 4: "One, two, . . ."), (2) continue the count by the number indicated by the second addend ("three is one more, four is two more, five is three more, six is four more—the sum is six").

   b. *Abstract counting-on from larger*: (1) Start with the cardinal value of the larger addend (e.g., 2 + 4: "Four, . . .") and count-on a number of times equal to the smaller addend ("five is one more, six is two more—so the sum is six").

   c. *Abstract counting down*: (1) Start with the minuend (e.g., 5 - 3: "Five . . .") and (2) count backwards the number of times specified by the subtrahend ("four is one less, three is two less, two is three less—the answer is two").

   d. *Abstract counting up*: (1) Start with the subtrahend (e.g., 5 - 3: "Three . . .") and (2) count up to the minuend while counting the counts ("four is one, five is two—so the answer is two").

Part III: Analyzing the Use of Word Problems in Curricula

Traditionally, word problems have been introduced after symbolic arithmetic, partly because they were deemed to be relatively difficult for children. Answer the following questions in terms of what you have learned about children's problem solving.

1. A first-grade teacher screened her children at the beginning of the year. The screening included the following three tasks:

   Task A. Determining the sum to the written expression 5 + 3 = □.

   Task B. Mentally calculating (counting out) the sum of the following word problem read by the teacher: "Joyce has 5 candies. She buys 3 more. How many candies does she have altogether?"

   Task C. Using available objects such as blocks to solve the following word problem read by the teacher: "Garth has 5 marbles. He wins 3 more. How many marbles does he have altogether?"

   a. On which task above would the most children be successful?

   b. On which task above would the fewest be successful?

   c. Your answers to Questions a and b above imply what about when and how word problems should be used in instruction?

2. MTW (Baratta-Lorton, 1976) suggests introducing addition and subtraction word problems *after* introducing these operations with concrete activities and games but *before* introducing symbolic arithmetic.* According to the *Guide to Facilitate Classroom Planning*, these operations are introduced in Lesson 40; word problems, in Lesson 55; and symbolic addition and subtraction in Lesson 56. Evaluate this use of word problems. (a) In what way is the curriculum consistent with the developmental approach advocated by this guidebook? (b) In what way is it inconsistent?

3. All the examples of subtraction word problems in MTW describe a situation like that illustrated by the following problem:

   ■ **Dog Gone (◆ K-2).** Mary had five cookies. Ruffus the dog ate three of them. How many cookies does Mary have left?

   (a) What meaning of subtraction does the problem *Dog Gone* illustrate? (b) What other meanings involving subtraction would be appropriate for primary-level children?

---

* Because of Mary Baratta-Lorton's death, the original *MTW* text cannot be revised. However, much to its credit, the *MTW* program is constantly evolving. Thus, the recommendations of the original text may be different than the recommendations made in current *MTW* workshops and newsletters.

🍎 Activity File 5.1: Everyday Situations Involving Addition and Subtraction

◆ Purposeful addition and subtraction ◆ K-3 ◆ Any number

The following situations can provide kindergartners and first graders the opportunity to consider the *addition or subtraction of one*:

- Ask who has a birthday this week. Asked the children how old they are now and how old they will be on their next birthday.

- Routinely keep track of the day of the month. For example, say, "Let's update our calendar. Yesterday was October eighth. So today is October . . . ?

- Count down the days to a special event such as a class picnic, class trip, a school play, a holiday, or summer vacation.

- As part of the introduction of a new child to a class, a teacher can say, for example, "We had 23 students in our class. With the addition of Moira, how many do we have now?" Similarly, the departure of a child can provide an opportunity to subtract.

The following situations involve the *change add-to* meaning with numbers larger than one:

- Keep a running score of a game.

- On a daily, weekly, monthly, or semester basis, determine how many teeth were lost, books were read, absences incurred, weight gained, or height (in cm) grown by individuals, groups, or the whole class. Add the amount to the total for the day, week, month, semester, or year.

- Keep a running total of how many cans of food (or other items) the class has collected for a charity drive (or other activities).

- Have students help with the lunch count. For example, have them tally how many students want hot lunch and how many have a cold lunch. Have them add the tallies to ensure all are accounted for. (Note that these situations can also be used to create compare problems. For example, ask the class how many more hot-lunch people are there than cold-lunch people.)

The following situations involve the *change take-away* meaning of subtraction with numbers larger than one:

- Keep track of school supplies as they are used up (e.g., Our box of chalk has eight pieces of chalk. If we use two pieces of chalk this week, how many will be left?)

- To keep track of a team's strength during a game (e.g., Your team had 12 players, 3 were "captured." How many players are left and do you still have more players than the other team?).

The following situations entail determining a *difference*:

- Compare the number of days in a week that will be spent in school as opposed to out of school. For example, this week we are in school for four days. How many days are we out of school?" After the class determines that the answer is three, ask, "How many more days are we in school this week than out?"

- In passing out school supplies, food, and so forth, take advantage of students' complaints that they got short changed. For example, "Everyone is supposed to have five sheets of construction paper. Ivor got only three sheets. How many more sheets of construction paper should Ivor get?

Box 5.1: Four Methods for Prompting the Invention of Counting-On

Method 1: Building on Children's Knowledge of *n* + 1 Combinations

Help children master *n* + 1 combinations (see Box 5.4 on page 5-31). This can serve as a scaffold for counting-on (e.g., if the sum of 5 + 1 is the number after 5 or six, then 5 + 2 must be two numbers after 5: Six, seven—seven") (Baroody, 1995).

Method 2: Solving Problems Involving Larger Numbers

Asking children to solve problems with larger numbers (e.g., 17 + 5 or 24 + 7) can sometimes prompt children to invent more sophisticated strategies (Carpenter & Moser, 1982).

Method 3: Using a Numeral and a Dot Die

Wynroth (1986) suggests playing addition games with a numeral and a dot die. This may prompt children to begin with the cardinal value indicated by the numeral die and the count-on using the dots of the dot die.

Method 4: The Hiding Method

After a child has represented each addend of a problem with objects, a teacher can cover the objects representing the first addend and ask, "How many are there?" With any luck, the child will recall the cardinal value and start counting the sum from this number.

5•1•3 ADDING AND SUBTRACTING WITH SYMBOLS

☞ Try Investigation 5.1 (page 5-10).

Learning: Informal Knowledge

Foundation for Formal Knowledge. Informal arithmetic knowledge is a key basis for understanding formal arithmetic (e.g., Ginsburg, 1989; Hiebert, 1984). Consider two examples:

• **Example 1: Understanding of symbolic addition and subtraction.** Children tend to assimilate addition and subtraction expressions in terms of their informal arithmetic knowledge. More specifically, they tend to interpret formal addition expressions such as 5 + 3 = ? in terms of

their informal change add-to view of addition: How much are five things and three *more* altogether? Children tend to interpret symbolic subtraction expressions such as 8 - 5 = ? in terms of their informal change take-away concept: Eight things take away three leaves what?

• **Example 2: Inverse relationship between addition and subtraction.** Even before school, children have some sense that addition and subtraction are related. Specifically, they realize that adding one to a set can be undone by taking one away or vice versa (Gelman & Gallistel, 1978). About kindergarten or first grade, children recognize that adding any number can be undone by subtracting that number (Bisanz, Lefevre, Scott, & Champion, 1984).

Learning Difficulties. Two key reasons for difficulties with formal arithmetic are:

1. **Gaps between formal arithmetic instruction and children's informal knowledge.** Consider the following three examples: (a) When subtraction expressions such as 5 - 3 are not related to their informal take-away view of subtraction, children may not understand the minus sign and simply guess or confuse it with a plus sign and add the numbers. (b) When missing-addend expressions such as 4 + □ = 7 are not related to children's informal change add-to view of addition, they have difficulty understanding such expressions and often simply add the numbers (4 + 7 is 11). (c) When the add-back checking procedure for subtraction is not related to their informal understanding of the inverse principle, children either apply the procedure blindly or forget it.

2. **Blind spots due to children's incomplete knowledge.** Consider four examples: (a) Children initially view the various addition and subtraction situations as conceptually different and unconnected. For instance, they may relate the symbolic expressions such as 5 - 3 to take-away situations but not to equalize or compare situations and fail to realize that the operation of subtraction is applicable to these latter two situations (Fischbein, Deri, Nello, & Marino, 1985). This tendency is reinforced by teachers who refer to subtraction expressions such as 5 - 3 exclusively as "take away." (b) Children's informal change add-to view of addition leads them to believe that addition is not commutative (e.g., to view 5 + 3 as *five and three more* and 3 + 5 as *three and five more*—(continued on page 5-11)

⌘ Investigation 5.1: Using Concept Maps to Explore Arithmetic Concepts

◆ Reflecting on the connections among arithmetic concepts ◆ 1-8
◆ Whole class, small groups, or individually

To check the connectedness of your own knowledge, construct a concept map using the following list of concepts. Make sure the links between concepts are clearly and specifically defined.

addition
arithmetic operations
associativity
change add-to unknown-outcome problems
change take-away unknown-outcome problems
commutativity

compare unknown-difference problems
equalize unknown-difference problems
part-part-whole unknown-whole problems
properties
subtraction

Questions for Reflection

1. The concept-mapping activity above is probably more appropriate for intermediate-level students than primary-level students. How could this activity be adapted so that it would be appropriate for primary-level children?

2. How are the operations of addition and subtraction connected? Represent these links on your concept map above. Make sure you use clear and specific linking phrases.

3. A student asks, "What's the difference between the commutative principle of addition and the associative principle of addition?" What could you say or do to help the student understand the difference between these two arithmetic concepts?

4. Illustrated below is the "add-back" method for checking subtraction. As Box 5.2 below illustrates, many students do not understand the underlying rationale for this procedure and, hence, forget or mechanically (and perhaps ineffectively) apply it. Note also that without understanding the conceptual basis for this procedure, the students described in the vignette were unable to devise an analogous checking procedure for division. (a) What arithmetic principle provides the underlying rationale for the *add-back* checking procedure for subtraction illustrated below? (b) How could a teacher help students understand why you add to check subtraction?

```
  9  ← first addend
- 2  ← number subtracted
  7  ← difference
+ 2  ← add the number subtracted to the difference
  9  ← a match between the sum and the first addend
       indicates the subtraction was done correctly
```

Box 5.2: Checked Out

Miss Brill found that her class had no idea how division could be checked. In an effort to relate the topic to something her students might know, Miss Brill asked, "Well, how do you check subtraction?" The blank stares from most of the class were not reassuring. Finally, a few students dimly recalled that they had to add something.

After some discussion, Judi concluded "You have to add your answer to what you subtracted and that should give you the big number." Then she asked a question Miss Brill had never considered, "Why does checking your subtraction by adding work?"

as different situations with different outcomes). (c) Children tend to interpret the equal sign as meaning *makes* or *produces* (an operator view), not the *same number as* (a relational view) (e.g., viewing 5 + 3 = 8 as five and three *adds up to* eight) (Behr, Erlwanger, & Nichols, 1980). (d) Children's understanding of part-part-whole relationships may be incomplete (e.g., Resnick, 1983). For example, not recognizing that a whole can be created or decomposed in various ways, they may assume that expressions with different addends (e.g., 5 + 2, 6 + 1, and 4 + 3) have different sums.

Teaching

Instruction should build on and extend children's informal knowledge.

☞ **Connect formal addition and subtraction terms such as *plus*, formal expressions or equations such as 5 + 3, 8 - 5 = □, or 5 + □ = 8, and formal procedures such as the "add back" checking procedure for subtracting to children's informal knowledge.** (a) Introduce symbolic representations as a shorthand for communicating about informal models and ideas that children already understand (see, e.g., Activity Files 5.2 and 5.3).

 Activity File 5.2: Using Egyptian Hieroglyphics as a Link Between Informal and Formal Addition

Conceptual Phase. A kindergarten or first-grade teacher can begin by having students solve word problems, such as the one below, by using Egyptian hieroglyphics. Using Egyptian hieroglyphics to represent and to solve such word problems is easy (I I   I I I) and consistent with children's own informal method of using tally marks and a concrete counting-all strategy.

■ **New Additions (◆ K-1).** A pharaoh of ancient Egypt had two adult cats, which he considered sacred. Much to his delight, his adult cats had three kittens. How many cats does the pharaoh have now?

Connecting Phase. A teacher can later have children solve word problems such as the one above using Egyptian hieroglyphics and then use a formal number sentence as a summary. Children should readily see that our system for representing addition is more compact.

$$\underset{2}{||} \; \underset{+}{+} \; \underset{3}{|||} \; \rightarrow \; \underset{5}{||||}$$

 Activity File 5.3: Creating a Need for Writing Symbolic Equations

In her teacher workshop, the math coordinator Mrs. Bryce recommended introducing and practicing addition and subtraction with word problems. *"But, what if students are having trouble with reading?"* asked Mr. Zar, a first-grade teacher. "Won't reading difficulties interfere with or prevent solving word problems?"

"Good question," responded Mrs. Bryce. "There are a couple of ways of dealing with reading problems. One is to integrate your reading and math instruction. Use word problems to create a real need for reading instruction and practice. Another method is to read the problems to the class. This creates a real need to record key information contained in a problem in an easily understood but shorthand form. Children quickly recognize that writing out a problem verbatim is a lot of work and hard to do. Encourage them to consider how they can make their task easier."

"For example," continued Mrs. Bryce, "I use

to read *A Bag Full of Pups* by Dick Gackenback (© 1981; Clarion) to my first graders. The story entails various people taking a pup or two from a litter that originally numbered 12. With each take-away situation, I encouraged my students to record on their minislates what they needed to solve the problem and their solution. Our discussion focused on *how to represent* the problem and solution, as well as the solution itself."

"I also used children's books to introduce missing-addend situations and their representations," added Mrs. Bryce. "At the beginning of the year, we did a *Who Am I* unit, which included counting and recording the number of teeth in each child's mouth. In the spring, I read *Little Rabbit's Loose Tooth* by Lucy Bate (© 1975, Crown). Invariably, students offer that they have loose or missing teeth. A typical problem is 'Selena had 20 teeth; she lost some; now she has 18. How many permanent teeth must grow in so that she has 20 again?'" (Whitin & Wilde, 1992).

A connecting-level activity can first involve encouraging children to solve word problems concretely and then asking them to record with symbols what they have done. You may wish to first allow children to devise and to discuss their own recording systems and then introduce the conventional symbolism. To foster and to check understanding, ask students to reverse the process—to translate a formal expression such as 7 + 3 = □ into word problems or concrete models. (b) To introduce symbolic missing-addend equations, encourage students to represent change-add-to, missing-change, and part-part-whole missing-parts problems (Carpenter, Moser, & Bebout, 1988) (e.g., Activity File 5.2). Next, prompt them to write word problems or create models for symbolic equations such as 7 + □ = 10. Playing games such as *Fill In* (Activity File 5.4 on the next page) can provide an entertaining means of practicing informal solution strategies and linking formal representations to informal knowledge. (c) Explicitly relate the "add-back" checking procedure for subtraction to children's informal understanding of the inverse principle. Once children recognize that, for example, adding three can undo subtracting three (and vice versa), guide them to discover that this knowledge can be used to check subtracting by three. It may be helpful to concretely model taking three from the seven and then adding three back to restore the original amount.

☞ **Help children to construct relatively broad concepts of addition and subtraction.** (a) Relate symbolic expressions to *various* types of problem situations. After children have identi-

fied and solved equalize and compare problems, for instance, help them explicitly link these difference situations to symbolic subtraction expressions (see, e.g., the bulletin-board activity illustrated on page 5-1). Seeing that these situations can be represented by the same number sentences that represent change take-away situations can help children recognize that these three conceptually different scenarios are all related to the same operation, subtraction. (b) Box 5.3 below illustrates how the investigative approach can help children to construct a relational view of the equals sign as "*the same number as.*" (c) The commutative and associative properties of addition are ideally suited for guided discovery learning. For example, solving successive word problems with commuted numbers or playing games such as *Fill In* (Activity File 5.4 on page 5-13) can create an opportunity for children to discover that addend order does not affect the sum. (d) Activity File 5.4 also illustrates a conceptual-level activity designed to help children see that a whole can be created by or decomposed into component parts in various ways. (e) Help children see that a numeral such as 7 is but one name for a number with, for example, the *Names-for-a-Number Game* (see Part I of Probe 13.1 on page 13-9) or *Other Names for the Date*. In the latter activity, the teacher notes that the date is, say, October 7 and asks children for other ways of describing 7 (e.g., 5 + 2, 7 + 0, 3 + 3 + 1, 1 + 1 + 1 + 1 + 1 + 1, number of days in a week, 8 - 1, 5 + 4 - 2, | | | | | | | (tallies or Egyptian hieroglyphics), VII, seven, siete (in Spanish), 7 x 1, 56 ÷ 8, (15 + 3) + 2, $\sqrt{49}$, $3^2 - 2$, -5 + 12, 13 (in base four).

Box 5.3: Using Cognitive Conflict to Foster a Relational View of the Equals Sign[1]

To help his second graders construct a relational meaning of the equals sign (*the same as*), Mr. Adams encouraged them to use the symbol in a variety of contexts, including tied game scores (e.g., 12 points = 12 points), *Cuisenaire rod* equivalents (e.g., 2 white rods = 1 red rod, or 6 white rods = 2 light green rods = 1 dark green rod), money equivalents (e.g., 5 pennies = 1 nickel, or 100 pennies = 20 nickels = 10 dimes = 4 quarters = 2 half dollars = 1 dollar), and measurement equivalents (e.g., 12 inches = 1 foot, 36 inches = 3 feet = 1 yard, or 1 inch = 2.54 centimeters).

✎ Several months later, Mr. Adams gave his class the following writing assignment: *(1) What does = mean to you? (2) What does*

= mean in the number sentence 5 + 3 = 8? (3) What does it mean in the math sentence 2 white rods = 1 red rod? What does it mean in the math sentence 5 pennies = 1 nickel? He then had the students share and discuss their answers. Nearly everyone agreed that the = sign in Questions 1 and 2 meant *makes*. Most students agreed, though, that it meant something different in Questions 3 and 4—that it meant *can be traded for, is as much as,* or *is the same as.* A number of students were confused that the = sign could mean different things. This led to a debate that was finally resolved when Quinto suggested that = means *the same as* in all situations. Callie added, "It makes sense even when you got something like 5 = 5 or 5 = 3 + 2."

🍎 Activity File 5.4: *Fill In*

◆ Familiarization with the number sentences representing various arithmetic concepts
◆ 1-3 ◆ Groups of two to six

Games, such as *Fill-In* described below, can provide a purposeful and interesting way of extending children's informal arithmetic knowledge. Note that this game, particularly the conceptual- and connecting-level versions, builds on children's informal counting-based knowledge.

Conceptual Level. In the *Basic Version of Fill In*, each player receives a mat of (incomplete) dot equations like the one illustrated in Example A below. (Each mat should have a different set of number sentences.) Play begins with each player blindly choosing five squares from a pile of squares with various numbers and arrangements of dots, including no or "zero" dots. On their turn, players see if they can use one of their squares to complete a number sentence. For instance, Example A below illustrates a player using a square with two dots to complete Number Sentence 2.

Initially, children can be encouraged to use a try-and-adjust strategy. For example, to solve Number Sentence 2 in Example A below, a child could start by filling in the blank with a one-dot square. Because counting the dots on each side of the equation does not result in the same number ("five is not the same number as six"), the child could then try filling in the blank with a square with two dots, which—in this case—would result in the same number on each side of the equation.

The number sentences in Example A concretely illustrate missing-addend equations (e.g., Number Sentence 1 is a more concrete version of the symbolic equation $3 + \square = 4$). Note that the missing part is relatively small—one, two, or three—and easy to determine. After children become adept at completing such equations, mats with more difficult missing-addend equations can be introduced. Completing equations such as those in Example B below can help children consolidate the inverse principle. Completing equations such as those in Example C can help them discover commutativity. Example D can serve to illustrate that a whole can be decomposed into parts in different ways. All the examples, particularly Examples D, E, and F, reinforce the other-name-for a number concept.

Connecting Level. To help children connect concrete and symbolic representations, have them play the *Intermediate Version of Fill In,* which involves using squares that have both dots and numerals (see, e.g., the figure to the right).

Symbolic Level. In time, introduce the *Advanced Version of Fill In*—use mats with numerical equations, such as $\boxed{3} + \square = \boxed{5}$.

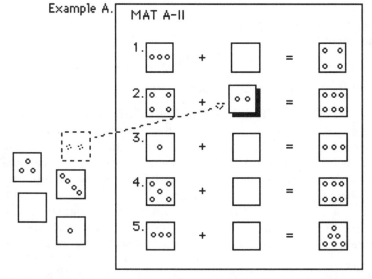

5•2 MULTIPLICATION AND DIVISION

Figure 5.3: Sharing Provides an Informal Basis for Understanding Division, *If* Done Fairly

PEANUTS reprinted by permission of UFS, Inc.

As with addition and subtraction, children have informal bases for understanding and solving simple multiplication and division problems. For example, although perverted by Lucy in Figure 5.3, experiences sharing things fairly provide children with a basis for understanding division before it is formally introduced in school. In Subunit 5•2•1, we address how a teacher can help children make sense of multiplication, and in Subunit 5•2•2, we do the same for division.

5•2•1 MAKING SENSE OF MULTIPLICATION

In this subunit, we explore various meanings of multiplication, the process of learning about this operation, and how multiplication can be introduced meaningfully.

Mathematics: Types of Multiplication Situations

Symbolic multiplication can represent a variety of real-world situations. In asymmetrical situations, the factors play different roles. For example, in the situation *How many oranges does Rohana have if she has three boxes of 12 oranges each?* (which can be represented by 3 x 12), the 3 specifies the number of groups and 12 specifies the number in each group. In symmetrical situations, the factors play the same and, hence, interchangeable roles (Kouba & Franklin, 1993). For

instance, in the situation *What is the area of a rectangle with one side of 5 inches and another side of 3 inches?* (which can be represented by 5 x 3), both the 5 and the 3 specify *lengths*, sizes of the same type of measure. Groups-of, rate, and comparison meanings involve asymmetrical situations (and apply to measures or continuous quantities as well as collections or discrete quantities); combinations and area meanings, symmetrical situations (see Probe 5.3 for a definition and examples of each of these meanings).

☞ Consider Probes 5.2 (page 5-15) and 5.3 (page 5-16).

Learning

In this section, we outline the relative difficulty of problem types, children's informal strategies, and some common learning difficulties.

Relative Difficulty of Problem Types. Research indicates that the types of multiplication word problems are not equally easy (Kouba & Franklin, 1993). Groups-of problems are relatively easy and can be solved by some first graders. Combinations and area problems are more difficult but, with a little guidance, can be solved by third graders. Rate and comparison problems are relatively difficult. Many children have no clear idea what, for instance, *four times as many* means. (Continued on page 5-17.)

➤ Probe 5.2: Meanings of Multiplication

The aim of this probe is to help you construct an explicit understanding of the various multiplication meanings and how they are related to other arithmetic concepts.

Part I: Identifying Multiplication Word Problems.

After reading the description of the six meanings of multiplication below, analyze the word problems that follow. For each word problem, (a) use the letter A, B, C, D, E, or F, to identify which of the meaning of multiplication fits best and (b) consider how a child might informally model and solve it.

Groups-Of. *Groups-of* situations involve joining a number of equal collections—so many *groups-of* a quantity.

■ **Problem A** (◆ 1-3). On a candy hunt, Mileva found 3 bags of candies with 5 candies in each bag. How many candies did Mileva find altogether?

Rectangular-array situations, which involve joining *rows* of equal collections, are a special case of groups-of situations. The orderly rows of items make it clear that each collection is equal.

■ **Problem B** (◆ 1-3). In the parade, Raul saw 3 rows of 5 soldiers march by. How many soldiers did Raul see in the parade?

Rate. *Rate* problems involve finding a total given a number of items and a rate affecting them.

■ **Problem C** (◆ 3-4). Gwen sold 3 boxes of light bulbs at $5 per box. What was the total amount of Gwen's sales?

Comparison. *Comparison* situations involve determining the size of a set, given the size of another set and how many times larger the unknown is. (Such problems do not necessarily include the "key words" *times larger*.)

■ **Problem D** (◆ 3-6). Abraham scored 3 points. Menachem scored 5 *times as many*. How many points did Menachem score?

Combinations. A *combinations* problem involves finding all the ways of combining the items of one type with those of another.

■ **Problem E** (◆ 3-6). Wendy had 3 different blouses and 5 different pants. How many different blouse-pant combinations did she have to choose from?

Area. *Area* situations entail finding the area (in square units) of a rectangle given its length and width. (Mention of the words *area*, *square feet*, and so forth does not necessarily make a word problem an area problem.)

■ **Problem F** (◆ 3-6). A rectangular garden 3 feet long and 5 feet wide has an area of how many square feet?

____ 1. ■ **Out Boned** (◆ 4-6). Bruno the Beagle was depressed. He had collected 23 bones. But Ruffus—having discovered a Pet Cemetery—collected three-fold that. How many bones had Ruffus collected?

____ 2. ■ **Ruffus Revamped** (◆ 3-6). Mary decided to dress up Ruffus. She had 4 ribbons and 3 hats. Using a ribbon and a hat, how many different ways could Mary dress up Ruffus?

____ 3. ■ **Ruffus on the Rampage** (◆ 3-6). Ruffus the dog knocked over 3 garbage pails at each of the five houses on his street. How many garbage pails did Ruffus spill altogether?

____ 4. ■ **Ruffus the Earth Mover** (◆ 3-6). Ruffus dug up an area of 3 square feet in Mr. Purdy's garden on each of seven days. How many square feet of Mr. Purdy's garden had Ruffus dug up by week's end?

____ 5. ■ **Doesn't Neatness Count?** (◆ 2-4). Ruffus the dog very neatly buried Mary's dolls in 3 rows of 6 dolls each. Unimpressed by the orderly burial of her dolls, Mary was furious and insisted that her father replace the dolls. How many dolls would Mary's dad have to replace?

____ 6. ■ **Eliminating a Safety Hazard** (◆ 3-6). Ruffus had dug a deep 4-feet by 3-feet hole in Mr. Purdy's garden path. To cover this hole, Mr. Purdy should cut a piece of plywood with an area no smaller than what?

Part II: Mapping Multiplication Meanings.

Add the following concepts to the concept map you began in Investigation 5.1 (page 5-10): *area meaning, asymmetrical situations, combinations meaning, comparison meaning, groups-of meaning, multiplication, rate meaning, rectangular-array meaning,* and *symmetrical situations*. Specify clearly the links among these concepts and their links with addition and subtraction concepts and arithmetic principles already on the map.

➤Probe 5.3: Modeling the Various Meanings of Multiplication

The aim of this probe is to help you develop an explicit understanding of some of the ways students can concretely model the various multiplication meanings. Answer the following questions either by yourself or with the help of your group. Then share your ideas with your group or class.

1. Illustrated on the next page are 13 models of 3 x 4. For each, identify which of the following meanings of multiplication is illustrated: groups-of, rectangular-array variation of groups-of, rate, combinations, and area. In several cases, a model could be interpreted in different ways. For these models, identify all applicable meanings.

2. Evelyn argued that the number-sticks example (Example B) could be considered a rectangular-array model of 3 x 4 because you have three even groups of four that form a rectangle. Evaluate her claim.

3. Children are often puzzled by multiplication involving zero. (a) Which models below could be *modified* to represent 3 x 0 so as to help them discover why multiplying zero three times is zero? (b) Which could be *modified* to represent 0 x 3 so as to help children see why multiplying three zero times is zero? (c) Illustrate how each can be done.

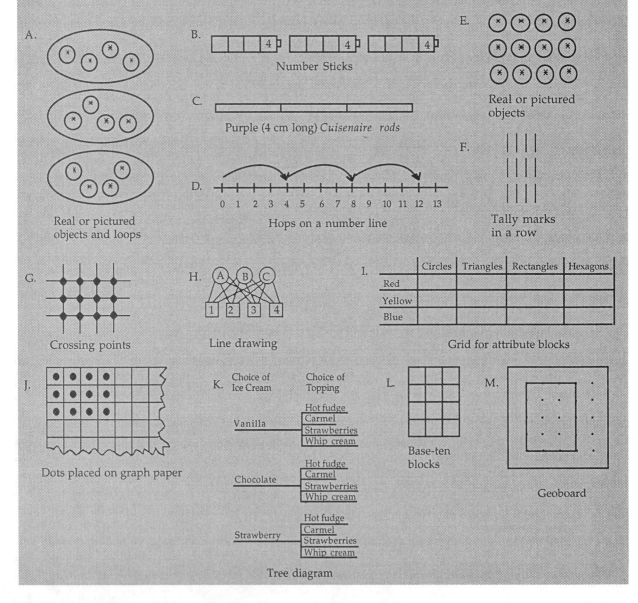

A. Real or pictured objects and loops

B. Number Sticks

C. Purple (4 cm long) *Cuisenaire rods*

D. Hops on a number line

E. Real or pictured objects

F. Tally marks in a row

G. Crossing points

H. Line drawing

I. Grid for attribute blocks

J. Dots placed on graph paper

K. Tree diagram

L. Base-ten blocks

M. Geoboard

Informal Strategies. As with addition and subtraction, children initially try to model the meaning of a multiplication problem directly. For a problem involving "three groups of four," for instance, children as early as first grade will—without instruction—count out three collections of four items each and then count all the items in the collection to determine the product *twelve* (see, e.g., Model A on page 5-16) (Kouba, 1989). They might model a rate problem involving $3 for every 4 items, for instance, by matching three blocks (to represent the $3) with a triangle (to represent an item) and then repeat this process a second, a third, and a fourth time. (Models B, C, and D on page 5-16 could serve as rate model as well as a groups-of model.) On page 5-16, Model H illustrates one way of informally solving combinations problems; Models L and M, two ways of informally solving area problems.

In time, children devise more sophisticated counting and reasoning strategies such as (a) counting a single group repeatedly (e.g., 3 groups of 4: raise four fingers and, without restarting, count them three times: "1, 2, 3, 4; 5, 6, 7, 8; 9, 10, 11, 12"), (b) skip counting (e.g., 3 groups of 4: verbally counting, "Four [is one group], eight [is two groups], twelve [is three groups]"), or (c) using known addition or multiplication combinations (e.g., 3 groups of 4: "Two times four is eight and four more is twelve").

Difficulties. Difficulties learning multiplication are typically caused by instruction that (a) does not connect formal symbolism to informal knowledge, (b) overlooks children's informal knowledge, or (c) fosters an overly narrow conception of multiplication (e.g., viewing 3 x 5 exclusively as *three counted five times* or *three added five times*).

Teaching

IN THE INVESTIGATIVE APPROACH, THE MEANINGFUL LEARNING OF MULTIPLICATION WOULD STEM FROM CHILDREN'S EXPLORATIONS INTO BROAD ISSUES. The Marilyn Burn's multiplication replacement unit (see page 5-34 for details), for instance, integrates the study multiplication with that of probability, statistics, patterns, and functions. Additional teaching tips are noted below.

☞ **Begin multiplication instruction with problems involving repeated addition and introduce symbolic multiplication as a *shortcut* for representing repeated-addition problems.** This builds on children's existing knowledge of addition. Ideally, the problems would stem from real issues facing children. Word problems can be used to supplement these real problems. Children can be encouraged to first represent repeated-addition problems as an addition number sentence and to then devise a shorthand for such symbolic expressions. Finally, the formal symbolism can be introduced as the standard (socially agreed on) shortcut for multiplication.

☞ **Relate multiplication symbolism to a variety of real-world examples, problem situations, and models** (see, e.g., Probe 5.3 on page 5-16). Although repeated addition provides a natural basis for introducing whole-number multiplication, it is important to accustom children to interpreting symbolic multiplication as *"groups of"* (e.g., thinking of 3 x 5 as *three groups of five*). This interpretation is broader than children's informal interpretation of repeated addition and can be useful in interpreting fraction and decimal multiplication. Instruction should also help children see that symbolic multiplication can also represent combinations, area, and comparison situations (Greer, 1992).

☞ **Encourage children to invent, share, and improve on their own informal multiplication strategies.** Prompt them to look for shortcuts to direct-modeling and to discuss more advanced strategies such as skip counting.

☞ **Help children discover the commutative and associative properties of multiplication.** As with addition, these principles are well suited for guided discovery learning.

5•2•2 MAKING SENSE OF DIVISION

In this subunit, we describe types of division problems, the learning process, and guidelines for meaningful instruction.

☞ Try Investigation 5.2 (pages 5-18 and 5-19).

Mathematics: Types of Division Situations

Asymmetrical Situations: Divvy Up and Measure Out. Because division can be thought of as forming groups and because the factors in groups-of situations play different roles, it follows that there are two different ways to form groups: (1) form a specified number of groups, or (2) form groups of a speci- (continued on page 5-20)

♻ Investigation 5.2: Explicitly Relating Division to Multiplication Meanings

◆ Types of division situations ◆ 3-5 ◆ Any number

Because multiplication and division are related operations (e.g., *18 ÷ 6 = what?* can be thought of as *6 x what? = 18*) and multiplication can involve asymmetrical or symmetrical situations, it follows that division can likewise involve asymmetrical or symmetrical situations. The aim of the activity is to help you construct an explicit understanding of the various division meanings by building on your knowledge of multiplication meanings. Answer the following questions either by yourself or with the help of your group. Then share your thoughts with your group or class.

Part I: Relating Division to Asymmetric Multiplication Situations

1. (a) Represent Problem A below and its solution as a multiplication number sentence. (b) Label which number represents the number of groups, which represents the size of the groups, and which represents the total amount. (c) Is one factor clearly the multiplier? Why or why not?

   ■ **Problem A: Bags of Candy Apples** (◆ 2-4). Kiwe's mom gave him three bags. If she put two candy apples in each bag, how many candy apples did Kiwe have?

2. (a) Represent Problem B below as a multiplication number sentence. Use □ to show the unknown. Label which element represents the number of groups, which represents the size of the groups, and which represents the total. (b) Rewrite the number sentence you recorded for Question 2a as a division number sentence and label each element again. What does the divisor represent? What does the quotient (answer) represent? (c) Using a □ to represent the unknown, represent Problem C below as a multiplication number sentence and label each element. (d) Rewrite the number sentence you recorded for Question 2c as a division number sentence and label each number again. What does the divisor represent? What does the quotient represent? Are the divisor and the quotient the same as those you noted for Question 2b? Why or why not?

   ■ **Problem B: Bags of Candy Apples II** (◆ 3-5). Kiwe's mom gave him three bags. If she put the same number of apples in each and he had a total of six candy apples, how many were in each bag?

   ■ **Problem C: Bags of Candy Apples III** (◆ 3-5). Kiwe's mom gave him some bags with two candy apples each. If he had a total of six candy apples, how many bags did he have?

3. Problem D below is called a *divvy-up* division problem because a total amount is divided into (divvied up among) a specified number of groups. (a) Write a division number sentence for this divvy-up problem. Use a □ to represent the unknown. Label each element in the number sentence. (b) Is this word problem more akin to Problem B or Problem C? Why?

   ■ **Problem D: Shared Candy Apples** (◆ 3-5). Kiwe had six candy apples. If he shared them fairly among three people, how many candy apples did each person get?

4. Problem E below is called a *measure-out* division problem because a total amount is separated into groups of a specific size (literally measured out). (a) Write a division number sentence for this measure-out problem. Use a □ to represent the unknown. Label each element in the number sentence. (b) Is this word problem more akin to Problem B or Problem C? Why?

   ■ **Problem E: Candy Apple Shares** (◆ 3-5). Kiwe had six apples, if he made shares of two apples each, how many people could share his apples?

Investigation 5.2 continued

Part II: Relating Division to Symmetrical Multiplication Situations

1. (a) Represent the area problem below and its solution as a multiplication number sentence. (b) Label what each number represents. (c) Is one factor clearly the multiplier? Why or why not?

    ■ **Problem F: King-Size Corral** (◆ 3-4). Madra made a rectangular toy corral that was three feet on one side and two feet on the other. What was the area of Madra's corral?

2. (a) Using a □ to show the unknown, represent Problem G below as a multiplication number sentence. (b) Label what each element represents. (c) Rewrite the multiplication equation as a division equation. (d) Would the label of the □ (quotient) be different if the problem had specified the known side was two feet and the area was six square feet? Why or why not?

    ■ **Problem G: King-Size Corral II** (◆ 3-4). Madra made a rectangular toy corral that was three feet on one side. If the area was six square feet, what was the length of the other side?

Questions for Reflection

1. (a) What type of division problem is Problem H below? (b) Put yourself in the shoes of a primary-age child who has not been taught division and does not know the division combinations. How would you concretely model Problem H with objects or tally marks? (c) What type of division problem is Problem I below? (d) How do you suppose a young child might concretely model the meaning of this problem with objects or tally marks?

    ■ **Problem H:** Doreen bought a bag containing 32 candies. She split the candy up into 4 equal piles to make special treats for her four best friends. How many candies were in each pile (special treat)?

    ■ **Problem I:** Doreen bought a bag of 32 candies. She decided to wrap 4 candies together as a Halloween treat. How many trick or treaters could she give this special treat to?

2. A number line might be used to solve which problem, Problem H or Problem I? Illustrate how.

3. Repeated subtraction would be a solution strategy most closely associated with which, Problem H or Problem I?

    0   32

4. Arianne ($8\frac{1}{2}$-years-old) was asked to solve the following problem:

    ■ **Problem J: Bags of Candy** (◆ 2-4). If you had 8 candies and put 2 candies in a bag, how many bags of candies could you make up for your friends?

    Her first response was to ask, "How many bags?" After being told "That's the question" and a rereading of the problem, Arianne drew Figure A. "The answer is four, I think." Asked why, she noted, that if one bag had two candies, two would have four, "and four and four is eight." To check whether her answer was correct she completed the diagram (Figure B). (a) What type of problem is *Bags of Candy*? (b) Initially, Arianne seemed confused by the problem. What might account for this confusion and her question, "How many bags?" (c) The diagram she drew to check her initial answer suggests what informal strategy for solving the problem?

    A.

    B.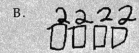

fied size. The first is referred to as a partitive division; the second, as a quotitive or measurement division. In terms that make sense to children, the first can be called "divvy up"; the second, "measure out" (Laycock, 1977). In terms of familiar fair-sharing situations, divvy-up problems begin with a quantity to be shared (the amount) and a *number of shares* (people) the amount is divided among. The answer or quotient specifies the size of the shares. In contrast, measure-out problems begin with an amount and *the size of the shares*. The quotient specifies the number of shares (people served). These two meanings of division are illustrated in Figure 5.4.

Symmetrical Situations: Missing Factor. With area and combination multiplication problems neither factor is clearly the multiplier. Thus, these situations are related to only one type of division—missing-factor division.

Learning

Informal Strategies. Children as young as kindergarten age can understand and solve division word problems. As with the other operations, they can devise informal strategies that model the meaning of divvy-up and measure-out word problems (e.g., Hiebert & Tonnesen, 1978).

• **Divvy-up problems**. Children often use the following two concrete strategies to model and to solve divvy-up problems:

1. *Divvying-Up*: This strategy entails dealing out items into groups. To solve a problem involving "8 items shared fairly among 4 people," for instance, a child might (1) count out eight blocks, (2) deal out one block to each of four piles, (3) re-

peat Step 2 until all the blocks were distributed, and (4) then count the number of blocks in one of the piles (two).

2. *Trial-and-error grouping*: This strategy involves estimating how many items each person gets and then making the appropriate adjustments. To solve 8 shared fairly among 4, for instance, a child might estimate 3 each. After making two piles of 3, the child would realize there is not enough to make the last two piles and would then try making piles of two each.

• **Measure-out problems**. Two informal strategies for solving measure-out problems are:

1. *Measuring-out*. A measuring-out strategy involves making groups of a specified size. To solve a problem involving "8 items divided into shares of two each," for instance, a child might (1) count out eight blocks, (2) form a pile of two, (3) repeat Step 2 until all the blocks were grouped, and (4) then count the number of piles (four).

2. *Repeated subtraction*. Some children may discover a repeated-subtraction strategy. For example, to determine the number of shares when 18 items are divided into shares of 3, a child would in effect, do the following: 18 - 3 = 15, 15 - 3 = 12, 12 - 3 = 9, 9 - 3 = 6, 6 - 3 = 3, 3 - 3 = 0. This might be noted 1̸8̸, 1̸5̸, 1̸2̸, 9̸, 6̸, 3̸, 0. The answer would be determined by counting the number of times 3 was subtracted: six.

Common Difficulties with Formal Instruction. Often symbolic division, division

Figure 5.4: Asymmetric Types of Division Word Problems

	Divvy Up	Measure Out
General case	Amount ÷ number of groups = number in each group	Amount ÷ number in each group = number of groups
Fair-sharing situations	Amount ÷ number of shares = size of the shares	Amount ÷ size of the shares = number of shares
Sample word problem	If Arianna had 8 stickers and wanted to give an equal number to her 4 party guests, how many stickers could she give each party guest?	If Arianna had 8 stickers and wanted to give friends 2 stickers each, how many friends could Arianna give stickers to?

facts, and division procedures are introduced in a disembodied fashion. As a result, many children do not connect this formal mathematics to what they already know—to anything meaningful. For example, they are clueless as to what the $r2$ in the expression $14 \div 3 = 4\ r2$ means. To make matters worse, students are frequently not helped to construct measure-out and area meanings of division—alternative interpretations of division that are important for understanding division with fractions and decimals.

Teaching

As with the other operations, instruction should begin at a concrete level. Formal instruction should build on this basis and help children to see that school-taught mathematics is simply a more efficient way of representing what they already know or doing what they can already figure out.

Conceptual Phase. Children should have ample experience solving real problems and word problems involving division before symbolic division is introduced. Such experiences can begin as early as kindergarten.

☞ **Children should be introduced to measure-out problems as well as divvy-up problems.** Our observations suggests that many students, including preservice teachers, are not familiar with a measure-out meaning of division. As we will find out later in Chapters 10 and 11, this is a severe handicap in trying to make sense of division with rational numbers.

☞ **Encourage children to invent, discuss, and share their own informal strategies for solving division problems.** Activity File 5.5 illustrates how the investigative approach can promote reflection and discussion of divvying up and measuring out among primary-level children.

🍎 Activity File 5.5: Everyday Classroom Situations Involving Division

◆ Informal whole-number division ◆ 1-3 ◆ Whole class

On the first day of class, Mr. Jagger (Mr. J.) involved his class in a number of projects that served a practical purpose (e.g., an interesting welcome to school) and engage his students' mathematical thinking.

🖎 Activity I: Using Children's Literature as a Source of Divvying-Up Problems

To begin school in an entertaining way and to explore division informally, Mr. J. had his class assemble on "The Reading Rug" and read the story *The Doorbell Rang* by Pat Hutchins. In this story two children consider sharing 12 cookies between themselves. Before reading on, Mr. J. posed the problem, "How many cookies will each child get?"

Jesus observed, "That's hard." A number of children nodded their heads in agreement.

"How can we make solving a hard problem easier?" asked Mr. J. He led the class to consider working together in groups and the problem-solving heuristic of using a model. He then had the students pair up and gave each pair a bag of wooden cubes, a miniature chalkboard, and a piece of chalk. He observed the children as they worked to see who had trouble counting out

12 blocks and who intuitively knew a divvying-up strategy and who did not. Mr. J. had each pair record its answer on a miniature chalkboard. After sharing and discussing strategies and answers, Mr. J. continued with the story. (For a more complete description of *The Doorbell Rang*, see page 5-36.)

Activity II: Preparing for a Crafts Project—Divvying Up with a Real Purpose

To prepare for a crafts project and to further practice an informal divvying-up strategy, Mr. J. proposed to divide the class equally into four groups—one each for the four project centers he had prepared. After completing *The Doorbell Rang*, he commented, "I'm having trouble remembering everyone's name. It would really help me if each of you had a head band with your name on it. (Note that the headbands could also be worn on days in which a substitute teacher was in.) Let's make a headband. Now I have four stations set up to make headbands."

■ **Problem 1: Divvying Up the Class.** "If we have 24 students and we want the same number of children at each station, how many children should we send to each of the four stations?"

Activity File 5.5 continued

Once the class had informally determined that six children should go to each station, Mr. J. handed each child a precut strip of construction paper on which the child's name had been preprinted and assigned the child to a station. With all the children at a station, Mr. J. continued his instructions, "We're going to make Indian headbands. To decorate your headbands, I want you to cut out shapes from the construction paper provided and paste them on your band. Make sure you don't cover your name." The class then discussed some possible shapes they could cut out, thus, involving geometry instruction. Mr. J. then pointed out that each station had 18 feathers (precut from white construction paper) and posed the following problem:

■ **Problem 2: Divvying Up a Craft Supply.** "If you share 18 feathers fairly among six children, how many feathers should each child get?"

The students then colored the feathers with crayons and stapled them to the headband, Mr. J. and four fifth-grade volunteers helped the children fit the headbands to their heads and staple them.

Mr. J. also had his students make bracelets out of string and beads.

■ **Problem 3: Divvy Up a Group of Children**. "At each station," the teacher noted, "there are two bags of beads. How many children should share a bag?"

After the students shared their solutions and agreed that three children should share a bag, Mr. J. posed the following problem:

■ **Problem 4: Divvying Up Another Craft Supply.** "There are 36 beads in each bag. If the beads are shared fairly among three children, how many beads should each child get?"

Activity III: Reorganizing the Classroom—Measuring Out with a Real Purpose

Later in the day, Mr. J. announced, "This year I want to try something new. I think it would be a good idea if we continued to work in groups instead of by ourselves. So instead of having rows of desks, let's put our desks together to make tables for our groups." He proceeded to pose the following problem:

■ **Problem 5: Measuring Out Desks.** "We have 24 desks in our classroom. If we put four desks together to make a table, how many tables can we make?"

✦ To make solving the problem easier, he encouraged pupils to model the problem with square tiles. ✦ Mr. J. could have posed the following more open-ended problem:

✦ **Problem 6: A Desks' Problem with Multiple Answers.**[†] "We have 24 desks in our classroom. If we put desks together to make tables and each table has the same number of desks, how many tables can we make? How many different answers can you find?"

[†]Based on a lesson "Divvying Desks" in the *Everyday Mathematics* curriculum (© 1995), developed by the *University of Chicago School Mathematic Project* and published by the Everyday Learning Corporation, and a lesson plan by Mary Beth Foxglover, Gina Koyer, Aniela Peronto, Judy Sayre, Margie Taucher, and Karen Vaicaitis—all teachers in the Chicago, IL area.

Connecting Phase. Linking symbolic division to existing knowledge can demystify it.

☞ Consider Probe 5.4 (page 5-23).

∞ **Help children connect symbolic division to both divvy-up and measure-out situations and a variety of models.** Formal division symbolism such as $6 \div 3$, $3\overline{)6}$, and $\frac{6}{3}$ should be introduced as a shorthand for representing problem situations. To further cement these links, encourage children to reverse the process—to illustrate a division

equation such as $18 \div 3 = 6$ by writing a divvy-up or measure-out word problem. By connecting symbolic division to concrete divvy-up situations, for instance, children can readily see that the *r2* in $14 \div 3 = 4\ r2$ means that "all but two items can be shared fairly." (All of the above should help Garth described in Question 1 of Probe 5.4.) Symbolic division can also be connected to an area meaning of division (see Question 3 of Probe 5.4) and to a paper-folding or a measurement model (see Question 4 of Probe 5.4). To help children (continued on page 5-24)

➤ Probe 5.4: Helping to Make Division Meaningful

This probe explores some ways to help make symbolic division more concrete and meaningful to children. Answer the following questions on your own or with your group. Then discuss your answers with your group or class.

1. Garth was having trouble understanding symbolic division expressions such as $14 \div 3 = 4\ r2$. In particular, he did not understand the $r2$ notation. (a) How might a teacher help a student like Garth? (b) How could a teacher introduce the idea of remainders informally so that expression above would make sense to children?

2. (a) What is atypical about the following nonroutine division word problem? (b) Why might it be important to include such problems in division instruction?

   ■ **Diana's Leftovers.** Diana the Dinosaur had 22 bones. If she gave each of her four baby dinosaurs the same amount, how many bones would that leave for Diana's midnight snack?[2] (Assume that Diana gave her babies as many of the bones as possible.)

3. How can the expression $12 \div 3$ be represented by an area model? Hint: Division is the *inverse* of multiplication and, thus, $12 \div 3$ is related to $3 \times \square = 12$ (or $\square \times 3 = 12$). How could you construct an area model of $3 \times 4 = 12$? How could you modify this model to illustrate the inverse operation of division?

4. Paper strips and a number line can be used to represent expressions such as $6 \div 2 = 3$.

   A. How many 2-unit parts can a 6-unit strip be divided into? Cut a strip 6 units long. Then fold the strip so that each part is 2 units long. Count the number of resulting parts to determine the answer.

   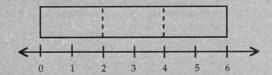

   B. What size will the parts be if a 6-unit strip is divided into 2 equal parts? Cut a strip 6 units long. Then fold the strips into 2 equal parts. Measure the length of each strip to determine the answer.

   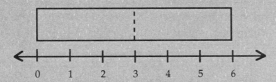

   a. Model A models which meaning of division, divvy up or measure out?

   b. Model B models has which meaning?

5. Many students are confused by division involving zero. They can't remember whether $0 \div n$ or $n \div 0$ is 0 and which is undefined. To help you decide, make up a divvy-up word problem for each of the following: (a) $6 \div 3 = ?$, (b) $0 \div 6 = ?$, and (c) $6 \div 0 = ?$

6. (a) Key in $\boxed{0}\ \boxed{\div}\ \boxed{6}\ \boxed{=}$ into a calculator. What is the outcome? (b) Key in $\boxed{6}\ \boxed{\div}\ \boxed{0}\ \boxed{=}$ into the calculator. What is the outcome? (c) From Questions 6a and 6b, what do you conclude about division involving zero?

determine whether 0 can be divided by a number or a number can be divided by 0, encourage them to consider a meaningful analogy such as divvy-up situations (see Question 5 of Probe 5.4) or to use a calculator (see Question 6 of Probe 5.4).

☞ **Help children sort out the properties of division and the connections between division and** **the other operations**. Help intermediate-level students see that both a divvy-up and a measure-out interpretation of division can be related to multiplication. The first can be thought of as a missing-number-in-each-group multiplication problem (e.g., 3 x ? = 12); the latter, as a missing-number-of-groups multiplication problem (e.g., ? x 4 = 12).

5•3 MASTERING THE BASIC NUMBER COMBINATIONS

Figure 5.5: Many Children Have Little Interest in Memorizing Number Facts by Rote

PEANUTS reprinted by permission of UPS, Inc.

Mastery of the basic number combinations involves quickly and correctly generating the answer for a single-digit addition or a multiplication combination such as 8 + 5 or 7 x 6 or for a related subtraction and division combination such as 13 - 8 and 42 ÷ 6. This basic proficiency has been a central goal of elementary instruction since the start of public schools in the U.S. Unfortunately, most children—like Sally in Figure 5.5—are less than enthusiastic about achieving this proficiency. Indeed, for many children, memorizing basic facts is a difficult and dreadful task, and for a surprising number of students, one that is never completely accomplished.

In Subunit 5•3•1, we explore how children master the basic combinations and why so many have such difficulty learning this basic knowledge. In Subunit 5•3•2, we outline general suggestions for helping children to master basic addition, subtraction, multiplication, and division combinations in an interesting and meaningful manner.

☞ Consider Probe 5.5 (page 5-25) and then read on.

5•3•1 LEARNING: UNDERSTANDING HOW CHILDREN MASTER THE BASIC COMBINATIONS*

In this subunit, we explore two different views on how to foster the mastery of the basic number combinations, what psychological research suggests about this process, and the difficulties caused by overlooking these developmental facts.

Two Views: Memorization by Rote Versus Meaningful Memorization

Miss Brill was worried. Many of her fifth graders did not know their basic multiplication and division facts, and some didn't know their basic addition and subtraction facts. *"Shouldn't they have mastered these basic facts already?"* she asked Ms. Socrates. *"Isn't it important to memorize the basic facts? And how do I get them to memorize this stuff?"* (Continued on page 5-26.)

* In general, *number facts* will imply automatic knowledge of sums, differences, products, and quotients learned mechanically by rote memorization, and *number combinations* will imply automatic knowledge of arithmetic equations learned in a meaningful manner.

➥ Probe 5.5: Mastering the Basic Number Combinations

To help you reflect on the process of mastering the basic number combinations, do Parts I to III below and then discuss your answers with your group or class.

Part I: How Children Master the Basic Number Combinations

1. Mastery (quick and accurate production of a correct answer to basic number combinations) involves (circle any of the following)—

   a. Fact recall—retrieving a discrete arithmetic fact
   b. Reasoning—using relationships to reason out answers
   c. Counting—computing answers mentally by counting

2. Quickly write down the sum or difference for each of the following combinations. Reflect on how you generated each answer. How did you efficiently generate the answers? Compare your reflections to those of others in your group or class.

a. 7 + 0	e. 7 + 6	i. 7 - 6
b. 7562 + 0	f. 9 + 7	j. 654 - 653
c. 5 + 1	g. 8 - 0	k. 4 - 4
d. 4366 + 1	h. 6 - 1	l. 462 - 462

Part II: Thinking Strategies That Build On What Children Know

1. (a) How could a teacher build on children's existing counting knowledge to help them master $n + 1$ combinations such as 7 + 1? Hint: What counting knowledge do first-graders typically have that could be applied to $n + 1$ combinations such as 7 + 1? (b) How could a teacher build on children's existing counting knowledge to help them master $n - 1$ combinations such as 7 - 1?

2. Children often learn the addition doubles such as 5 + 5 and 6 + 6 early. How could children use this knowledge to reason out other combinations?

3. Children often learn large-addend-first combinations such a 6 + 3 or 9 + 7 before they do small-addend-first combinations such as 2 + 7 or 6 + 8. How could they use their knowledge of the former to reason out the sums of the latter?

4. What other patterns or regularities could children use to reason out sums?

5. How could children use existing knowledge to reason out differences such as 5 - 2, 6 - 4, 7 - 3, or 9 - 7?

● Part III: Product Patterns (◆ Discovering and sharing thinking strategies + inductive reasoning ◆ 3-8 ◆ Individually, in small groups, or as a class).

The basic number combinations provide a rich opportunity to look for patterns and relationships. One group of third graders found over 30 different patterns in the multiplication table below. How many can you find? Note which may help in the meaningful memorization of the 100 single-digit multiplication combinations.

First Factor

x	0	1	2	3	4	5	6	7	8	9
0	0	0	0	0	0	0	0	0	0	0
1	0	1	2	3	4	5	6	7	8	9
2	0	2	4	6	8	10	12	14	16	18
3	0	3	6	9	12	15	18	21	24	27
4	0	4	8	12	16	20	24	28	32	36
5	0	5	10	15	20	25	30	35	40	45
6	0	6	12	18	24	30	36	42	48	54
7	0	7	14	21	28	35	42	49	56	63
8	0	8	16	24	32	40	48	56	64	72
9	0	9	18	27	36	45	54	63	72	81

Second Factor

Questions for Reflection

1. Other than using their knowledge of counting by twos, how could children build on what they already know to reason out quickly the products of $2 \times n$ (and $n \times 2$) combinations?

2. How could children build on their knowledge of $2 \times n$ (and $n \times 2$) combinations to reason out the products of (a) $4 \times n$ (and $n \times 4$) combinations, and (b) $8 \times n$ (and $n \times 8$) combinations?

3. What are two ways children could intuitively determine the products of $n \times 5$ (and $5 \times n$) combinations.

4. What reasoning strategy could children use to figure out the products of $n \times 9$ and $9 \times n$ combinations?

5. How could children build on what they know to reason out the division combinations?

The Traditional Skills Approach: Focus on Memorizing by Rote. "Everyone agrees that mastery of the basic number combinations is essential for performing more complex skills such as multidigit arithmetic and everyday tasks such as balancing a checkbook," answered Ms. Socrates. "However, there are two schools of thought about how to best foster this mastery. Traditional teachers such as Mrs. MeChokemchild—and many parents and school administrators—view the basic combinations as a collection of isolated facts that can be quickly memorized by rote. Understanding, finding patterns and relationships, and reasoning are *not* seen as relevant to the process of mastering the basic combinations. What is considered crucial for memorizing these separate, senseless facts is practice and more practice. Because memorizing several hundred basic combinations by rote is viewed as a simple-minded task, traditional teachers assume that—with sufficient practice—children can memorize the basic combinations in short order."

"Many traditional teachers," continued Ms. Socrates, "seem willing to sacrifice all on the great altar of instant skill mastery." Noticing the puzzled look on Miss Brill's face, she said more simply, "They seem willing to achieve mastery of the basic combinations quickly at any cost—including children's interest in mathematics and their self-esteem. It appears that most children—like any intelligent and sensible adult—have little interest in memorizing hundreds of pointless facts by rote. As a result, traditional teachers have to find ways to motivate this essential learning. Mrs. MeChokemchild told me that she found fear to be a wonderful motivator. She lights a blowtorch and makes veiled threats like, 'Those who don't master the basic facts get burned.' "[*]

"That seems a little extreme," interjected an incredulous Miss Brill.

"Indeed," commented Ms. Socrates sadly. "But in their single-minded pursuit of fact mastery, many teachers are just *more subtle* about using fear than Mrs. MeChokemchild."

The Investigative Approach: Focus on Patterns, Connections, and Meaningful Memorization. "Another position is that instruction should focus on making sense of arithmetic and discovering patterns and relationships among basic combinations," continued Ms. Socrates. "In an age of calculators and computers, understanding arithmetic is more important than being able to perform it quickly but blindly. After all, machines can do the number crunching quickly. What we need are people who can make sense of data, tell the machines what to do, and then be able to check whether the machine's results make sense."

"But there are times when we must do arithmetic without the help of a machine," protested Miss Brill. "You can't effectively estimate the sums of larger numbers, for example, without readily recalling basic addition facts."

"I agree that children need *some* efficient means of determining the answers to basic combinations," countered Ms. Socrates. "But recalling basic facts learned by rote is only *one* strategy for doing so."

"I'm confused. What do you mean by that?" asked a perplexed Miss Brill.

"Even adults use a rich variety of strategies to determine the answers to basic number combinations quickly and accurately" (Baroody, 1994; LeFevre, Sadesky, & Bisanz, 1996), began Ms. Socrates. "In addition to recall, some do so by rapidly counting. Many also use what they know to efficiently reason out the answers of unknown combinations. Nearly all also use automatic or near-automatic rules based on patterns or relationships. For example, what is the sum of these expressions?" asked Ms. Socrates writing $9{,}765 + 0$ and $9{,}828 + 1$ on the chalkboard.

"Why, *nine thousand seven hundred sixty-five* and *nine thousand eight hundred twenty-nine*," responded Miss Brill immediately. "But what does this have to do with our discussion?"

"Did you spend hours practicing $9{,}765 + 0 = 9{,}765$ and $9{,}828 + 1 = 9{,}829$ until you memorized them by rote?" asked Ms. Socrates.

"No, of course not," answered Miss Brill. "I rather doubt that I have ever done those particular sums before."

"How did you come up with these sums so quickly then?" countered Ms. Socrates.

Miss Brill thought for a moment and responded hesitantly, "Rules and reasoning?"

[*] Based on a true account. The name of the source has been withheld to protect the innocent.

"Exactly," confirmed Ms. Socrates. "You learned that adding zero does not change a number—a rule that can be applied to an infinite number of cases including those you have never encountered before. For 9,828 + 1, you used your knowledge of the counting sequence—that the number after 9,828 is 9,829—and the number-after relationship—that the sum of a number and one is the next number—to instantly deduce that 9,828 + 1 is 9,829. The basic number combinations have many other patterns and relationships that children and adults can use to *quickly* reason out answers."

"The *meaningful memorization* of basic number combinations is a *gradual* process," continued Ms. Socrates. "It builds on children's informal understanding and reasoning. And it takes time for this understanding and reasoning to develop—for children to see relationships and understand how they can be used to reason out unknown combinations. Moreover, using rules or relationships to reason out answers quickly takes practice."

Phases of Development

The *meaningful* memorization of basic number combinations involves the following three phases of development: (l) counting, (2) reasoning, and (3) mastery (e.g., Rathmell, 1978; Steinberg, 1985).

Counting Phase. Children first use counting strategies to compute answers to symbolic arithmetic expressions. As with word problems, they invent increasingly sophisticated and efficient counting strategies.

Reasoning Phase. Children incorporate the relationships and patterns they discover into *thinking strategies*—into *clever ways of using what they know to reason out the answer to unknown combinations*. For example, children who know the addition doubles such as 6 + 6 may reason out near doubles such as 7 + 6 (e.g., if 6 + 6 = 12 and 7 is 1 more than 6, then 7 + 6 must be 1 more than 12, or 13).

Mastery Phase. Research indicates that children typically do not memorize the basic combinations quickly and that the mastery phase typically involves automatic reasoning processes as well as automatic recall of specific facts (Baroody, 1987, 1994).

Difficulties with the Traditional Skills Approach

Traditional instruction frequently overlooks children's need for a prolonged period of informal exploration (e.g., Carpenter, Fennema, Peterson, & Carey, 1988; Carpenter & Moser, 1984; Fuson, 1992b). Indeed, many teachers actively discourage informal counting and reasoning strategies. Research suggests that introducing drill before children understand symbolic arithmetic or before they devise their own ways to compute or reason out answers can hinder mastery (Suydam & Weaver, 1975).

A focus on memorizing the basic number facts by rote causes many learning difficulties because it (1) does not encourage the informal experiences needed to develop efficient counting strategies, making it less likely children will notice patterns and relationships; (2) does not invite children to discover mathematical patterns and relationships that can facilitate the mastery of basic number combinations; and (3) fosters a negative disposition toward mathematics, including math anxiety.

5•3•2 TEACHING: MEANINGFUL MASTERY OF BASIC COMBINATIONS

Instruction should focus on *meaningful memorization* of basic combinations. In this section, we discuss the advantages of such an approach and some tips for implementing it.

Advantages of the Investigative Approach. *"Won't instruction that focuses on meaningful memorization take too much time?"* asked Miss Brill. *"Is it really practical?"*

"In fact," Ms. Socrates replied, "such an approach is practical and has at least three advantages over traditional instruction that focuses on memorizing the basic facts by rote:

1. **For children of all abilities, an approach that focuses on the meaningful memorization of basic combinations is more effective and efficient than drill alone in fostering retention and transfer to unpracticed combinations** (Rathmell, 1978; Suydam & Weaver, 1975; Thornton & Smith, 1988; Thorton & Toohey, 1985). Why don't most of our students know their basic

number facts after four years of drill and practice? They either forgot them over the summer or never bothered to learn them in the first place. So, each new school year, a tremendous amount of time must be spent reviewing and repracticing basic number combinations. By focusing on meaningful memorization, most children learn the basic combinations more quickly and with less need for drill and review. Moreover, they can apply the number patterns and relationships they learn to other tasks including multidigit computation and estimation.

2. **An approach that emphasizes thinking strategies also involves both inductive and deductive reasoning.** Encourage children to look for patterns and using relationships to figure out number combination involves mathematical reasoning.

3. **It is more likely to create a positive disposition toward mathematics.** Learning the basic combinations by discovering patterns and relationships can be exciting and intellectually stimulating rather than something dull and done out of fear. Moreover, instruction that focuses on relationships can broaden children's view and appreciation of mathematics. For example, it is more likely to foster the beliefs that the essence of mathematics is searching for patterns and thinking, not the mindless memorization and recitation of facts" (e.g., Cobb & Merkel, 1989).

Teaching Tips. PRACTICE WITH THE BASIC COMBINATIONS APPEARS MOST EFFECTIVE WHEN DONE PURPOSEFULLY AND AFTER A PERIOD OF INFORMAL EXPLORATION. Key teaching tips are outlined below.

☞ **Create a real need for using and learning the basic number combinations.** During *all* phases of development, practice with the basic number combinations should be done for a reason. Solving word problems can provide one source of purposeful practice for encouraging efficient counting and reasoning strategies and for fostering combination mastery (e.g., Bebout & Carpenter, 1989) (see Box 5.4). Playing games can be another, and one that is entertaining as well. For example, Activity File 5.6 (on the next page) illustrates an authentic way of practicing subtraction combinations; Activity File 5.7 (on page 5-29), an entertaining and thought-provoking way of practicing the combinations of any operation.

☞ **Give children ample opportunity to invent, share, and use informal counting methods for determining sums, differences, products, or quotients.** The counting phase provides the conceptual foundation for subsequent phases and the opportunity to discover relationships (see, e.g., Activity 5.8 on the next page). The use of informal calculational procedures should be recognized as evidence of understanding and strongly encouraged (see, e.g., Box 5.5 on page 5-30).

☞ **Encourage children to devise and share thinking strategies** (e.g., Bebout & Carpenter, 1989). During the reasoning phase, instruction should encourage the search for and discussion of patterns and relationships (see Box 5.6 on pages 5-31 to 5-33). It is particularly important to encourage children to build on what they already know to reason out unknown combinations.

☞ **Practice should focus on using thinking strategies, not on recalling isolated facts.** Once children discover patterns and relationships and use these discoveries to devise thinking strategies, practice is essential for making these reasoning processes automatic.

Box 5.4: The Advantages of a Problem-Based Approach to Basic Arithmetic Instruction

Many teachers are reluctant to sacrifice time devoted to teaching computational skills to spend more time on developing understanding and solving problems. The results of an in-service program (Carpenter et al., 1989), called "Cognitively Guided Instruction" (or CGI for short), indicate that a meaningful problem-based approach to basic arithmetic instruction can have a positive effect on disposition at no cost to achievement (Fuson, 1992a). Such an ap-

proach can foster mastery of basic skills as well as, if not better than, the traditional skills approach. Although CGI teachers spent significantly more time on problem solving and significantly less time on drilling the basic combinations than did teachers not participating in the program, children in the CGI classes mastered significantly *more* combinations than did children of nonparticipating, traditionally-oriented teachers.

♬ Activity File 5.6: *Difference Game*

◆ Practice counting out, reasoning out, or recalling single-digit differences ◆ 1-4 ◆ Pairs of students

The aims of this game include (a) introducing or reviewing a difference meaning of subtraction; (b) practicing the computations of difference informally; and (c) mastering basic subtraction combinations. Dice with 0 to 5 or 1 to 6 dots are needed for the most basic game; dice with numerals 0 to 5 or 1 to 6 are needed for children ready to count up mentally; and a spinner with 10 sections of 1 to 10 dots or 10 cards numbered 1 to 10 are needed for more advanced players. Each player obtains a number (by rolling a die, spinning a spinner, or drawing a card). The player with the larger number wins. The number of points the winner gets is determined by how much the player's number beat his/her opponent's. For beginners, the difference can be computed by a concrete matching strategy. For example, if Jason's card has five dots and Karen's card has three, Jason could count out five blocks to represent his number and three blocks to represent Karen's. He could then line up the three blocks under the line of five blocks and count the number of unmatched blocks (two) to determine the difference. More advanced children use a counting-up strategy: Begin with the smaller number ("Three") and count up to the larger number ("Four [is one apart], five [is two apart]—so the answer is two").

♬ Activity File 5.7: *Crypto*

◆ Basic arithmetic combinations ◆ 3-8 ◆ Any number

Crypto is an entertaining way to practice the basic addition, subtraction, multiplication, and division combinations and to foster a number sense. The game is essentially a challenging puzzle. It is played by picking five numbers from 1 to 20 (e.g., by drawing five cards from a deck of cards numbered 1 to 20). A sixth card is then picked. The aim of the activity is to add, subtract, multiply, or divide the first five numbers so that the result is the sixth number. Each of the first five numbers can be used once and only once. Examples are illustrated below:

First five numbers	Sixth	Solution
7, 8, 15, 2, 11	9	15 - 7 - 8 + 11 - 2
5, 9, 11, 19, 3	10	(11 x 3) - (19 + 9) + 5

First five numbers	Sixth	Solution
7, 18, 2, 13, 5	9	7 + 2 - 18 + 13 + 5
2, 3, 5, 7, 11	19	[(2 x 3) - 5] + 7 + 11

♬ Activity File 5.8: Wynroth's Vertical Keeping-Track Method

◆ Aid in the computation and meaningful memorization of multiplication combinations, particularly larger combinations ◆ 2-4 ◆ Individually or by groups

Encourage children to summarize the results of their informal multiplication computations in a table. For example, suppose a child needs to multiply 7 x 7. She could hold up 7 fingers, count the fingers, and record the result (7) on the line below the ⑦. She could repeat this process a second time (to represent two sevens) and write 14 on the next line. The child could continue this process until she counted her fingers a seventh time to represent seven groups of seven and recorded the answer 49. This written record could then be used later to compute the product of 8 x 7

	①	②	③	④	⑤	⑥	⑦	⑧	⑨
1	1	2	3	4	5	6	7	8	9
2	2	4	6	8	10	12	14	16	18
3	3	6	9	12	15	18	21	24	27
4	4	8	12	16	20	24	28	32	36
5	5	10	15	20	25	30	35	40	45
6	6	12	18	24	30	36	42	48	
7	7	14	21	28	35	42	49	56	
8	8	16	24	32	40	48			
9	9	18	27		45				

(eight groups of seven). The child would just count down the list until she comes to the product for 7 x 7 (1 seven is 7, 2 sevens is 14 . . . 7 sevens is 49) and count on seven more (50, 51, 52, 53, 54, 55, *56*).

Box 5.5: Some "Handy" Methods for Computing Products

Method 1: Multiplying with Factors Greater Than Five Using 8 x 7 as an Example

1. Turn the palms of your hands to face you.

2. Point your fingers toward each other.

3. Label your fingers with numbers as shown in the diagram below:

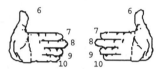

4. To solve a multiplication problem such as 8 x 7, touch the "8" finger of your left hand to the "7" finger of your right hand.

5. Count your touching fingers and all those above them by tens. For example:

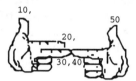

6. Multiply the remaining fingers on your left hand by the remainder on your right hand. For example:

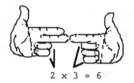

2 x 3 = 6

7. Now add the two figures to get your answer. For example: 50 + 6 = 56. So, 8 x 7 = 56!

Method 2: Determining the Products of Nine Using 4 x 9 (or 9 x 4) as an Example

1. Extend the fingers of both hands, with the palms facing away. Beginning with the left-most finger, count the fingers until the term multiplied by nine is reached. For example, with the palms facing away, the product of four times nine can be determined by beginning with the little finger of the left hand and counting this finger and the next three (see Figure A below).

2. Fold down the last finger counted in Step 1

(e.g., for 4 x 9, fold down the fourth finger from the left as shown in Figure B).

3. The number of fingers to the left of the folded finger specifies the tens digit of the product. The number of fingers to the right of the folder finger specifies the ones digit. For 4 x 9, for instance, this process yields three fingers to the left and six to the right or "36" (see Figure C).

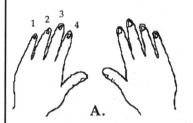

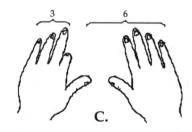

A.   B.   C.

∽ **Teaching Tips.** A teacher might demonstrate the interesting finger-based strategies above after students have shared their own informal strategies. This can underscore that there are a variety of procedures and that even finger-counting strategies are acceptable. The latter belief is important for building confidence in informal procedures. Children may or may not find these strategies useful and adopt them. If they do, reflecting on the results of these strategies may help them discover patterns (e.g., Method 2 may help children discover that the tens digit and ones digit in the product of a nines-times combination always sums to nine).

☞ Use Method 1 to compute the product of (a) 7 x 9, (b) 6 x 8, (c) 9 x 10, (d) 6 x 6, and (e) 6 x 7.

Box 5.6: Thinking Strategies for Basic Number Combinations

Addition and Subtraction

+ 0 or - 0 combinations: The zero rule. Adding zero to a number or subtracting zero from a number does not change the number (e.g., 6 + 0 = 6, 0 + 7 = 7, 6 - 0 = 6). Typically, children quickly discover this rule for themselves.

+ 1 or - 1 combinations: The number-after or -before rule. The sum of an addend and one is the number after the addend in the counting sequence (e.g., 6 + 1 is the counting number after *six*— *seven*). Similarly, the difference of an addend and one is the number before the addend in the counting sequence (e.g., 6 - 1 is the counting number before *six—five*). Recall that children entering first grade typically know both the number after and the number before the numbers up to 18 or so. Once children make the connection between this existing knowledge and adding or subtracting by one, they can quickly respond to such combinations. In effect, the work of memorizing these combinations has already been done when they learned the next-number relationships in the counting sequence. This helps explain why *n* + 1 and *n* - 1 combinations are among the first to be mastered.

+ 2 or - 2 combinations: Skip the next-number rule. The sum of an addend and two is the number after the next number after the addend. Once children recognize, for example, that the sum of 7 + 1 is the number after *seven*, then they can reason that 7 + 2 must be the number after *eight*—that is, *nine*. In effect, children can exploit their well-established mental representation of the counting sequence in the service an efficient skip-the-next-number rule.

***a* + *b* and *b* + *a* combinations: Commutativity principle.** Addend order does not affect the sum (e.g., if 6 + 4 = 10, then 4 + 6 also equals 10). Typically, children quickly discover this principle themselves. If a child has already mastered 6 + 4 = 10, she can quickly reason that 4 + 6 must also be 10—without ever having practiced the combination.

Doubles. The sums of doubles such as 4 + 4 and 7 + 7 are all even, and each successive sum increases by two. Thus, these sums parallel the skip-count-by-two sequence ("Two, four, six, . . . eighteen"), which children learn relatively early. An even or odd number added to itself is even, and the double 5 + 5 is two more than 4 + 4 because each five is one more than a four. This pattern and the fact that addition doubles have special psychological significance (i.e., represent the repetition of a collection or an event such as two pairs of two hands [2 + 2], two hands of five fingers each [5 + 5], two rows of six eggs each [6 + 6], two weeks of seven days each [7 + 7]) may help to account for why these combinations are learned relatively early.

Near doubles: Doubles plus or minus one. The near double 6 + 5 can be thought of as the double 5 + 5 plus one or the double 6 + 6 minus one. Once children have memorized the doubles, then they can use this knowledge as a basis for reasoning out near doubles such as 7 + 8. Given that 7 + 7 = 14 and 8 is one more than 7, it follows that 7 + 8 must be one more than 14 or 15. Note that such a strategy involves deductive reasoning.

Addends two apart: Make a double. Combinations like 5 + 3 can be converted into doubles by taking away one from the larger term and giving it to the smaller term (e.g., 5 + 3 = [5 - 1] + [3 + 1] = 4 + 4 = 8).

+ 8 or + 9 and - 8 or - 9: Make a 10 combination. A combination such as 9 + 4 can be changed into the easier combination 10 + 4 less one (because 9 is one less than 10). Similarly, the subtraction combinations 17 - 9 can be thought of as the easier combination the 17 - 10 plus one. A variation of this thinking strategy commonly taught in other countries is the "over-ten" method: splitting the smaller addend into parts so that one part can be combined with larger addend to make 10 (e.g., in symbolic terms, 8 + 6 = 8 + [2 + 4] = [8 + 2] + 4 = 10 + 4 = 14) (Fuson, 1992a). Note that this variation requires children to know the sums to 10 and the sums of 10 and a number (Steinberg, 1985).

***n* - *n*: Same-number rule.** A number subtracted from itself leaves nothing (e.g., 6 - 6 = 0).

Differences between number neighbors: The difference-of-one rule. Whenever neighbors in the number sequence (e.g., 6 and 7) are subtracted, the difference is one (7 - 6 = 1).

Any subtraction combination: Related-addition combination. Any subtraction combination

Box 5.6 continued

can be figured out by recalling its related addition combination. For instance, 8 - 5 can be thought of as what do I need to add to five to make 8: three (because 5 + 3 = 8). Note that to implement this strategy, a child must already have mastered the addition combinations and recognized that addition and subtraction are related operations. A teacher needs to foster both of these prerequisites in order for children to figure out differences by recalling related addition combinations.

Multiplication and Division

$2 \times n$ and $n \times 2$ or $n \div 2$: Recall addition doubles. A combination such as 2×7 (two groups of seven) is equivalent to the addition double $7 + 7$. By discovering this connection and exploiting their existing knowledge of the addition doubles, children can readily master the $2 \times n$ and $n \times 2$ with little or no additional practice. Many children discover this connection for themselves—a fact that helps explain why the two-times and times-two combinations are among the easiest combinations for children to master. Division by 2 can be related to halving, which can also draw on knowledge of the addition doubles (e.g., $14 \div 2 \rightarrow$ half of $14 \rightarrow$ What added to itself makes 14? $\rightarrow$ *Seven*).

$n \times 0$ or $0 \times n$ and $0 \div n$ combinations: Zero rules. Any multiplication involving zero is zero ($n \times 0$ or $0 \times n = 0$ rule) and zero divided by any number is zero ($0 \div n = 0$ rule). Children quickly discover these patterns for themselves, particularly if they understand a groups-of meaning of multiplication (e.g., 7×0: seven groups of nothing is nothing) and a divvy-up meaning of division (e.g., $0 \div 7$: no items shared among seven people means everyone gets nothing for their share).

$n \times 1$ or $1 \times n$ and $n \div 1$ combinations: Identity rules. Multiplication involving a number and one always equals the number ($n \times 1$ or $1 \times n = n$). Any number divided by one equals the number ($n \div 1 = n$). Again, children quickly discover these patterns for themselves, particularly if they understand the groups-of meaning of multiplication (e.g., 1×7: one group of seven is seven) and a divvy-up meaning of division (e.g., $7 \div 1$: Seven items shared with one person means the person gets all seven items).

$a \times b$ and $b \times a$ combinations: Commutativity principle. The commutativity principle specifies that factor order does not affect the product (e.g., if $6 \times 3 = 18$, then 3×6 also equals 18). This principle applies to all but the doubles and reduces by half the effort required to master nondouble combinations.

$4 \times n$ or $n \times 4$, $8 \times n$ or $n \times 8$, and $6 \times n$ or $n \times 6$: Doubling known combinations. The product of a $4 \times n$ or $n \times 4$ combination is double that of the corresponding $2 \times n$ or $n \times 2$ combination (e.g., 4×7 is twice the product of 2×7 or $14 + 14$). The same reasoning can be applied to combinations such as 8×7 (double the product of 4×7) or 6×7 (double the product of 3×7).

Two even factors: Half then double. A combination such as 6×8 can first be simplified by halving a factor (e.g., $3 \times 8 = 24$) and then doubling the product ($24 + 24$ or $2 \times 24 = 48$).

$n \times 5$ or $5 \times n$: Make a 10 combination and half. Multiplication combinations involving 5 can be translated into known combinations involving 10 and then halving the product. For example, 8×5 can be translated into 8×10 or 80, halved—40. This strategy is particularly useful in multiplying 5 and multidigit numbers (e.g., $5 \times 180 \rightarrow 10 \times 180 = 1800 \rightarrow 1800 \div 2 = 900$).

Neighbors of known combinations: Add one group. Any unknown combination can be reasoned out quickly by building on a known neighbor. For example, if a child does not know 6×7, but knows that 5×7 is 35, she can add $35 + 7$ to determine the product of 6×7. In effect, the child adds five groups of seven and one group of seven to determine the answer of six groups of seven.

Near doubles: One-less-than-the-double rule. The product of the near double 5×7 is one less than that of the product of 6×6.

$n \times 9$ and $9 \times n$ combinations: Nifty-nine strategies. The product of combinations involving 9 can be figured out in several ways. (a) One is to translate a $9 \times n$ (or $n \times 9$) combination into an easier $10 \times n$ combination and subtract one group of n (e.g., $9 \times 7 = [10 \times 7] - 7 = 70 - 7 = 63$). (b) Another is to form the tens digit of the product by subtracting 1 from n and the ones digit by

Box 5.6 continued

subtracting this difference from 9 (e.g., 9 x 7 → the tens digit equals 7 - 1 or 6, and the ones digit equals 9 - 6 or 3—63).

• **Any division combination: Related-multiplication combination**. Because division and multiplication are related operations, the quotient of a division combination such as 56 ÷ 7 can

be determined by reasoning, "What times seven makes 56?" Many children have difficulty memorizing division combinations meaningfully—particularly larger division combinations—either because they do not realize that their knowledge of multiplication combinations can be used or because they have not memorized the related multiplication combinations.

☜ **The ten frame can help children to visualize sums to 18 in terms of patterns based on five or ten** (Flexer, 1986). Children first explore the patterns for the numbers 1 to 10 (see Box 4.2 on page 4-10). Next, children use the ten-frame to represent addition problems with sums up to 10 like 4 + 2 = ? (see Frame A of Figure 5.6). By transforming 4 + 2 into 5 + 1, children can see that the sum is 6. In time, children can be encouraged to visualize what 4 + 2 would look like on the ten-frame and to transform the problem mentally. For sums greater than 10, a double ten-frame is used. This is especially helpful for teaching the recomposition-to-10 strategy for solving the relatively difficult plus-eight or nine facts (see Frame B of Figure 5.6) (Thompson & Van de Walle, 1984). Note that it also is useful for introducing the base-ten place value idea that, say, 13 represents one group of ten and 3 ones, which is essential for multidigit mental computation.

PARTING THOUGHTS

"The emphasis . . . should be on helping children develop a sound and varied conceptual basis for giving meaning to [arithmetic] situations, rather than on . . . rushing into the memorization of [basic number] facts or using those facts to solve symbolic [expressions] . . . . We need . . . to help children build from their own experiences and un-

derstandings a variety of ways to represent and model [arithmetic] situations" (Kouba & Franklin, 1993, p. 123).

RESOURCES

SOME INSTRUCTIONAL RESOURCES

☞ Numerous commercially available games can provide entertaining and purposeful practice with the basic number combinations. Teachers could suggest to parents that these games be played at home to provide additional practice. For example, *Giant Die* (Discovery Toys, Pleasant Hill, CA 94523) is a Bingo-like game that can be used by two to four players to practice two, three, or all four operations. In the addition-subtraction-multiplication version, players roll two 0 to 6 dice on their turn and determine the sum, difference, and product of the rolled numbers. They may then use a counter to cover any one of these numbers on a 36-number square grid. The first player to complete a row, column, or diagonal is the winner. *Pac-Man* (Milton Bradley Co., Springfield, MA 01101) is a card game for two to four players can be used to practice addition, subtraction, and multiplication. It can highlight adding or multiplying by 0, 1, 5, and 10 and can serve to

Figure 5.6: Using Ten-Frames to Visualize Sums

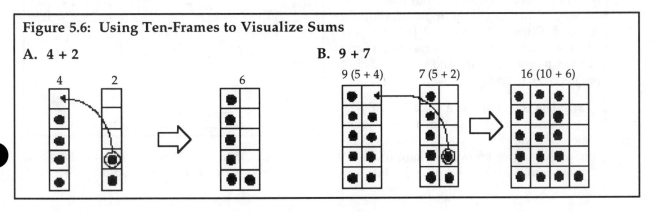

introduce the idea of negative numbers (e.g., 5 - 10 = ?). *Risk* (Parker Brothers, Beverly, MA 01915), a board game for 2 to 6 players, involves dividing by three. To determine the number of new armies for each turn, a player must count the number of territories he or she occupies, divide this number by three and discard any fraction. *Tens* (House of Games, Bramalea, Ontario) is a game for two to four players, who attempt to make combinations adding to 10.

☞ **Math By All Means: Multiplication, Grade 3** by Marilyn Burns, © 1991 by Math Solutions Publications and distributed by Cuisenaire Company of America, Inc. This resource provides a complete unit for helping children construct an understanding of multiplication. This Marilyn Burns replacement unit—like others in the series—includes whole-class lessons for introducing concepts, menu activities for individual and small-group learning experiences, and assessment suggestions.

☞ **MATH BALANCE** made in England by Invicta and distributed in the U.S. by Learning Resources. Activity File 5.9 describes a number of ways a balance beam can be used.

☞ **Young Children Reinvent Arithmetic** by Constance Kamii, © 1985, Teachers College Press. This reference illustrates how children can be encouraged to learn addition and subtraction in a meaningful and purposeful manner. In addition to describing a number of games, it provides many examples of how teachers can exploit real situations in school to encourage arithmetic thinking. As illustrated by the Problem 5.1 below, talking about time is one real way to introduce the topic of addition and subtraction. Problem 5.2 (on the next page) stems from the very real classroom need to collect permission slips and to remind children to return them.

■ **Problem 5.1: Time to a Vacation** (◆ 1-2). A teacher might note that it is 2 weeks before a vacation. Young children commonly want to know how long this is in more familiar terms—days. The teacher

🍎 **Activity File 5.9: Concrete Equations**

◆ Discover or reinforce number, addition, and multiplication concepts ◆ 1-4 ◆ Whole class, small group, or individual exploration

A *Math Balance* can provide (a) a concrete model for the relational (*same number as*) meaning of the = sign, (b) practice finding the sums up to 18*, (c) an opportunity to discover commutativity (e.g., 7 and 3 are balanced by 3 and 7), (d) an intuitive trial-and-error means for solving missing-addend expressions (e.g., what must be added to 8 on the left side of the balance to balance a 10 on the right side), (e) an opportunity to see atypical expressions and to discover other names for a number (e.g., 5 and 4 is balanced by 6 and 3), and (f) a chance to explore part-part-whole relationships (e.g., 8 can be decomposed into—balanced by—6 and 2).

Additionally, the balance can provide practice finding sums to 18. For example, 8 + 8 = 16 can be represented by two weights at the 8 position of the left arm and a weight at the 10 position and one at the 6 position of the right arm. Note that representing the sum involves a grouping-by-ten concept. The balance beam can also be used to explore multiplication (e.g., four weights at the 6 is balanced by two weights at the 10 and one at the 4 position of the right arm).

To highlight the link with symbolic equations, an equal sign can be fixed to the balance point, as the figure below illustrates. To further connect these concrete and symbolic representations of equivalence, ask children to translate a concrete model into a symbolic equation and vice versa (e.g., the symbolic representation for the model below is 7 + 3 = 10).

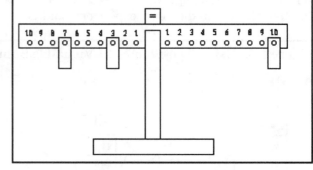

can then note that 1 week is 7 days and ask, "How many days would 2 weeks be?"

■ **Problem 5.2: Missing Permission Slips** (♦ 1-2). A teacher can note, for instance, that 8 of the 10 boys in the class have returned their permission slips. The question can then be posed, "How many more boys need to bring their permission slips in so that all the boys can go on the field trip?"

A SAMPLE OF CHILDREN'S LITERATURE

Numerous children's stories entail arithmetic operations subtraction and can provide a basis for discussing these operations, predicting outcomes, solving problems, and devising informal counting or reasoning strategies.

🕮 **Arithmetic in Verse and Rhyme**, edited by Alan and Leland Jacobs (© 1971, Garrard), includes, for instance, the delightful poem "Using Subtraction" by Lee Blair. The poem begins "I often heard the teachers say, 'Subtraction means less or take away.' And so I'd get great satisfaction if I could only do subtraction on all of them . . ." The poet then lists things she would like removed from her life. After reading the poem, a teacher could ask the class to distinguish between less (compare) and take-away situations and give examples of each. ✍ An interesting writing activity would be to have children rewrite the poem and list the things they would like eliminated from their life (Whitin & Wilde, 1992).

Addition

🕮 **One Elephant Balancing** by Edith Fowke (© 1989 by Harcourt, Brace, Jovanovich), **Pigs Plus** by John Burmingham (© 1983, Viking Press), **So Many Cats** by Beatrice Schenk de Regniers (© 1985, Clarion Books), **There Was an Old Lady Who Swallowed a Fly** by Pam Adams (© 1973, Playspaces), and **Twelve Days of Christmas** by Jack Kent (© 1973, Scholastic) all involve addition.

Subtraction

🕮 **One, Two, Three Going to Sea** by Alain, © 1964 Scholastic. This book begins with,

"If one fisherman meets one fisherman going to sea, that makes . . . two fishermen." One more fisherman is added each time until there are 10. Then four swim home leaving . . . six ($10 - 4 = 6$), three are taken home by a pelican ($6 - 3 = 3$), two ride seals home ($3 - 2 = 1$), and the last is saved by a fishing net ($1 - 1 = 0$).

🕮 **Porwigles** by Julie Holder (in J. Foster [Ed.], *First Poetry Book* (© 1979 by Oxford University Press), **Six Brave Explorers** by Kees Moerbeck and Carla Dijs (© 1988, Price Stern Sloan), and **Take Away Monsters** by Colin Hawkins (© 1983, G. P. Putnam's Sons) all involve taking away one.

Multiplication

🕮 **Building Tables on Tables: A Book about Multiplication** by John V. Trivett, © 1975, Thomas Y. Crowell. This book invites children to consider other names for a number (e.g., $3 \times 5 = 5 + 5 + 5 = 4 + 5 + 6 = 3 + 5 + 7 = (1 + 1 + 1) \times (4 + 1)$).

🕮 **Bunches and Bunches of Bunnies** by Louise Mathews, © 1978 by Scholastic. Using rhymes and pictures, this book lightheartedly illustrates a groups-of meaning of multiplication. For example, on one page, six groups of six bunnies are depicted. Before continuing, children can be encouraged to informally determine the total and represent the problem and solution symbolically. This activity can serve to underscore that multiplication is a shorthand for repeated addition (e.g., $6 \times 6 = 6 + 6 + 6 + 6 + 6 + 6$).

🕮 **Lucy and Tom's 1, 2, 3** by Shirley Hughes, © 1987, Viking. This book illustrates a rectangular-array model with various real-world examples of multiplication.

🕮 **What Comes in 2's, 3's, and 4's** by Suzanne Aker, © 1990, Simon and Schuster. This story can serve as the basis for skip counting by twos, threes, and fours (e.g., "How many eyes were watching if 9 people looked on?"). Moreover, a class can compile their own list of things that come in 2's, 3's, 4's, 5's . . . 10's, 11's, and 12's.

Division

☜ **The Country Bunny and Little Gold Shoes** by DuBose Heyward, © 1939 Houghton Mifflin. This story illustrates a measure-out meaning of division.

☜ **The Doorbell Rang** by Pat Hutchins, © 1986, published by Greenwillow Books and available through Scholastic. This book provides an entertaining way of prompting a discussion of fair sharing among primary-age children and their invention of an informal divvy-up strategy. Victoria and Sam are pleased that their mother has made them cookies. Ma instructs them to share a plateful of cookies. Before continuing the story, a teacher may wish to point out that there are 12 cookies on the plate and have the students try to figure out for themselves how many cookies Victoria and Sam will each get. On the next page, the children determine that each will get six. But before they eat any cookies, the doorbell rings and two neighbor children come in. Ma invites them to share the cookies. Again a teacher may wish to have the class determine that the 4 children will each get 3 cookies. To the growing consternation of Victoria and Sam, the doorbell rings twice more, with 2 and then 6 more children joining the feast. Each time the children find that their share shrinks. Finally with everyone posed to eat only one cookies, the doorbell rings again. Much to the relief of Victoria and Sam, it's their Grandma with a huge batch of cookies.

The story can easily be adapted to challenge older children. Third- and fourth-graders might find it interesting to try to figure out how many cookies each child would get if Grandma's cookies made the total, say, 120.

TIPS ON USING TECHNOLOGY

Calculators

▦ **Keystrokes: Multiplication and Division Calculator Activities for Young Students**, by Robert E. Reys, Barbara J. Bestgen, Terrence G. Coburn, Harold L. Schoen, Richard J. Shumway, Charlotte L. Wheatley, Grayson H. Wheatley, and Arthur L. White, © 1979 by Creative Publications. The first section of

this resource ("SKIP COUNTING") include calculator activities that can help children discover the connection between multiplication and repeated addition or skip counting.

 Activity File 5.10: Jammed Division Key

◆ Connecting division with other operations
◆ 3-8 ◆ Whole class

Pose the following the task to the class: Pretend the division key on your calculator is jammed. How could you use the calculator to determine the answer of 72 ÷ 9? (More advanced students can be asked to determine the answer of a multidigit expression such 408 ÷ 17.)

Computers

▯ **Computational Games** designed by Education Development Center and published by Sunburst. The games involve associativity, commutativity, identities, and inverses as well as place value and order of operations and are appropriate for students grades 4 to 6. The kit includes *How the West Was One + Three x Four* software described below. The program is available on Apple II, IBM, or Macintosh formatted disks, and in AppleShare or Macintosh network versions.

▯ **How the West Was One + Three x Four** designed by Bonnie Seiler and published by Sunburst. Suitable for students in grades 4-8, this program provides entertaining computational practice and involves using parenthesis to construct and determine the solution to expressions such as (3 + 1) x 2. Available on disks formatted for Apple, IBM (DOS or Windows), or Macintosh; CD versions available for Windows or Mac.

▯ **Math Blasters** series produced by Davidson and available through, for example, Scholastic and Soft Ware House. **Math Blaster Jr.** is appropriate for grades K to 2; **Math Blaster I: In Search of Spot**, grades 1 to 6; **Math Blaster 2: Secret of the Lost City**, grades 3 to 8. All are available on CD-ROM. 1 is available on Windows or Macintosh disk; 2, on Windows disk only. Provides practice for all four whole number operations plus number patterns, estimation, fractions, decimals, and percents.

6 UNDERSTANDING BASE-TEN, PLACE-VALUE SKILLS: READING, WRITING, AND ARITHMETIC WITH MULTIDIGIT NUMBERS

Math Detective:
The Egyptian Hieroglyphics

The ancient Egyptians used different number symbols than we do. Shown below are some examples of their numbers called hieroglyphics.

I = 1   ∩II = 12   ∩∩I = 21   ℮∩∩∩IIIII = 135

𝔛℮℮IIII = 1204   ⸮∩ = 10,010

Test your skills as a math detective. Answer the following questions:

1. Can you figure out the number code the ancient Egyptians used? How would they have written (a) 7, (b) 16, (c) 24, (d) 30, (e) 101, (f) 138, (g) 1032, and (h) 12,842?

2. Birthdays can be written in numbers to show the month, date, and year. For example, June 14, 1985 can be written 6-14-85 because June is the sixth month. (a) Use numbers to write your birthday. (b) Now translate this into Egyptian hieroglyphics. (c) How would 1985 be written in Egyptian hieroglyphics?

3. Can you decode the following numbers written in Egyptian hieroglyphics:

   (a) ⸮⸮⸮𝔛℮℮℮∩∩III   (b) ⸮⸮𝔛IIIIII?

4. Our number system is based on making groups of ten—10 ones are grouped to make a ten, 10 tens are grouped to make a hundred, 10 hundreds are grouped to make a thousand, and so forth. Were the Egyptian hieroglyphics based on making groups of 10 also or not? Explain your answer.

5. Many children like to experiment with writing letters and numerals backwards. The ancient Egyptians sometimes wrote their numbers backward too. (a) Try writing the following Egyptian hieroglyphic backward. Check your effort by placing a mirror along the dotted line below:

   ⸮𝔛℮℮℮∩II⦙

(b) Both the Egyptian hieroglyphic above and its mirror image represented the same number. What is that number? (c) Based on what you have learned, do you think the Egyptian hieroglyphics were a place-value system? Why or why not?

☞ Complete the activity sheet above.

A study of the hieroglyphic numbers of ancient Egypt could be an element of an extended and integrated unit involving mathematics, history, and language arts. The activity sheet above could be posted on a bulletin board or in an activity center and could serve as the basis for an enrichment activity or a class discussion. This should prompt questions and reflection on the underlying concepts of our base-ten, place-value numeration system.

THIS CHAPTER

*W*hereas children's counting-based concepts and strategies serve them well when trying to figure out arithmetic problems involving small numbers (see chapter 5), this informal knowledge becomes increasingly less useful as the numbers in problems become larger. Multidigit skills, such as writing 3-digit numerals and renaming (carrying and borrowing) algorithms, are powerful tools for representing and working with larger quantities.

In Unit 6•1, we discuss why reading and writing multidigit numerals can be difficult for children. In Unit 6•2, we describe common difficulties with multidigit arithmetic. In each unit, we also consider how instruction can be comprehensible and interesting. In chapter 7, we discuss further how to develop children's intuitive feel (number sense) for multidigit numbers.

WHAT THE NCTM *STANDARDS* SAY

Grades K-4

Numeration. Standard 6 for grades K-4 specifies that "the mathematics curriculum should include whole number concepts and skills so that students can:

- construct number meanings through real-world experiences and the use of physical materials;

- understand our numeration system by relating counting, grouping, and place-value concepts" (p. 38).

Multidigit Arithmetic. The following goals of Standards 7 and 8 apply to arithmetic with multidigit numbers:

- "develop operation sense" (p. 41);
- "use calculators in appropriate computational situations;
- select and use computational techniques appropriate to specific problems and determine whether the results are reasonable" (p. 44)

Grades 5-8

Numeration. Standard 6 specifies, in part, that the intermediate-level "curriculum should help students:

- "develop and use order relations for whole numbers . . . " (p. 91).

Multidigit Arithmetic. Standard 7 notes that the intermediate-level curriculum should develop the concepts underlying computation . . . in various contexts so that students can:

- compute with whole numbers . . . ;
- develop, analyze, and explain procedures for computation . . . " (p. 94).

6•1 READING AND WRITING MULTIDIGIT NUMBERS

Figure 6.1: Big Trouble With Big Numbers

YOUNG ONES' VIEW

Many adults can't imagine why learning to read and write multidigit numerals is so difficult for young children (e.g., see Figure 6.1). In Subunit 6•1•1, we explore the underlying rationale of our number system so that you can better understand the complex challenge confronting young children. In Subunit 6•1•2, we discuss some common difficulties children have in this area. In Subunit 6•1•3, we consider how teachers can help students construct a solid understanding of multidigit concepts and master reading and writing multidigit numerals in a purposeful and meaningful fashion.

6•1•1 MATHEMATICS: THE MEANING OF WRITTEN MULTIDIGIT NUMBERS

In this subunit, we discuss the grouping and place-value concepts that provide the rationale for our written number system.

Grouping Concept

Rashaan's teacher assigned him the task of inventorying the year's supply of chalk stored in a shoe box and keeping track of the supply over the course of the school year. Examining the contents of the box, the boy estimated that there had to be over 100 pieces of chalk. Good grief, he thought. How am I going to keep track of the chalk stock without counting every piece each time and spending a good part of the school year in the supply closet? After some thought, he devised the following plan: He bundled five pieces of chalk together with a rubber band. (Five made a good-size group. Bundles of pairs would have required a lot of rubber bands and more counting; bundles of ten would have been difficult to distinguish from a bundle when one or two pieces had been taken.) He then wrapped five bundles of five in a piece of construction paper to make a large bundle of 25. Now he could count untampered large bundles by twenty fives, whole small bundles by five, and incomplete small bundles by ones.

Rashaan solved his problem of keeping track of a large amount by grouping by five—combining single items into larger groups of five, and then combining five of these larger groups to make an even larger group of 25. Our written number system is based on grouping by ten—combining single items into a group of ten, combining 10 groups of ten into a larger group of 100, and so forth. *Because we group by ten our number system is called a base-ten or decimal system.* (Decimal is derived from the Latin *decem* meaning *ten*.)

Place-Value Concepts

Our written number system is a positional-notation or place-value system because the position of a digit determines its value. For example, the digit 4 in 4270, 2470, and 2740, and 2704 represents different values by virtue of its position: four one-thousands (4 x 1000 or 4000), four one-hundreds (4 x 100 or 400), four tens (4 x 10 or 40), and four ones (4 x 1 or 4), respectively.

☞ Try Investigation 6.1 (pages 6-4 to 6-6).

6•1•2 LEARNING

In this subunit, we outline the development of the concepts underlying multidigit numeration and why children often have so much difficulty with multidigit numeration skills.

Underlying Concepts

Grouping. Children with a counting-based concept of numbers do not think in terms of grouped items (larger units like tens, hundreds, and so forth) and single items (units). Thus, they view 24, for instance, as a collection of *twenty-four units*, not as two groups of 10 and four ones. To understand the underlying rationale of the decimal numeration system and multidigit arithmetic procedures—particularly those involving renaming (carrying and borrowing)—children must discover the importance of grouping quantities into larger and larger units. Put differently, they must transcend their informal counting-based concept of number and construct a new understanding of number based on a grouping concept (e.g., view 24 as two groups of 10 and four single items).

Place-Value. Children initially do not realize that a digit's position is crucial to its value. They view a numeral such as 12 either as two distinct single-digit numbers ("one" and "two") or as an inseparable whole ("twelve" units). Children need to learn that each place increases in value by a factor of 10 as we move from right to left, because items are repeatedly grouped by ten (e.g., 10 units are grouped to make *a* ten, 10 tens are grouped to make *a* hundred, 10 hundreds are grouped to make *a* thousand, and so forth). In effect, with the numeral 4,325, the 4 represents 4 x 1,000; the 3, 3 x 100; the 2, 2 x 10; and the 5, 5 units. These are foreign and relatively abstract ideas for children. (Continued on page 6-7.)

✿ Investigation 6.1: Analyzing Various Numeration Systems

◆ Foster an explicit understanding of grouping and place-value concepts ◆ 1-8
◆ Small groups + class discussion

Our Hindu-Arabic numerals are a base-ten, place-value numeration system. *Base-ten* refers to grouping by ten; *place-value* means that the position (place) of a digit defines its value. By comparing and contrasting our base-ten, place-value numeration system with other numeration systems, students can develop a better and more explicit understanding of it. To see how, analyze the four numeration systems illustrated below and answer the questions that follow.

🖎 ∽ **Teaching Tip**. Each month introduce a different numeration system by, for example, displaying it on a bulletin board (e.g., see page 6-1) and reading about it in Glory St. John's *How to Count Like a Martian*. To facilitate the comparison with our Hindu-Arabic numeration system, encourage students to translate and to record dates in the new numeration system (Whitin & Wilde, 1992). Analysis of the Babylonian and Mayan systems might be appropriate for intermediate-level students; Roman numerals could be explored as early as second grade; and Egyptian hieroglyphics can be introduced in kindergarten or first grade.

Arabic	Babylonian	Egyptian Hieroglyphics	Roman Numerals
1	▽	I	I
4	▽ ▽ ▽ ▽	IIII	IV
5	▽ ▽ ▽ ▽ ▽		V
9	▽ ▽ ▽ ▽ ▽ ▽ ▽ ▽ ▽		IX
10	◁	∩	X
15	◁ ▽ ▽ ▽ ▽ ▽		XV
50	◁ ◁ ◁ ◁ ◁		L
60	▽		LX
62	▽ ▽▽	∩∩∩∩∩∩ II	LXII
100	▽ ◁ ◁ ◁ ◁	ℓ	C
120	▽▽		CXX
300	▽▽▽▽▽		
500	▽▽▽▽▽▽▽ ◁◁		IↃ
600			
1,000		⚱	M
3,600			
10,000		⅂	M̄

Part I: Babylonian Numeration

1. (a) Was the Babylonian numeration system a place-value system (i.e., use position to indicate magnitude)? (b) Use two examples to illustrate whether this was or was not the case.

2. Represent the following using Babylonian symbols: (a) 195, (b) 267, (c) 371.

Investigation 6.1 continued

3. How do you suppose the Babylonians represented 600, 1,000, 3,600, and 10,000?

4. Our Arabic numeration system is called a base-ten system because we group by 10. For example, when we have collected *ten* $1, we can trade them in for a single $10 bill. After collecting *ten* $10, we can trade them in for a single $100 bill. After collecting *ten* $100, we can trade them in for a single $1000 bill and so forth. Is the Babylonian system a base-ten system? Explain why or why not, using 1547 as an example.

Part II: Egyptian Hieroglyphics[1]

1. (a) Complete column 3 of the table on page 6-4. (b) Is it a base-ten system? Why or why not? (c) Is the Egyptian system a place-value system? Briefly justify your answer. (⇨ **Teaching Tip.** Challenge student to find how many ways the digits 1, 2, and 5 can be combined to form a three-digit numeral. Ask them if 153, 215, 251, 512, and 521 represent the same number as 125 (Whitin & Wilde, 1992). Repeat the challenge with I, ∩, and ℃. Discuss the similarities and differences between our Arabic numerals and Egyptian hieroglyphics.)

2. Alexi, $7\frac{1}{2}$- years old, was shown the Egyptian hieroglyphics for 1, 2, 10, and 100. Asked to represent the number 4, he wrote I I I I. Asked to represent 12, he wrote I I I I I I I I I I I I. (a) Alexi's answer for 12 is a very common error among U.S. children. Why? (b) How could a teacher help children discover the correct method for representing 12 in Egyptian hieroglyphics?

3. A puzzled 7-year-old Arianne wondered how to write 12 in Egyptian hieroglyphics. Her $8\frac{1}{2}$-year-old sister Alison volunteered to help and wrote: ∩ I I. Asked why 12 was written that way, Arianne quickly noted, "Because ten [pointing to the heel], eleven, twelve [pointing to each staff in turn]." (a) What place-value concepts were introduced to Arianne by asking her to translate 12 into Egyptian hieroglyphics? (b) What impact might such a task have on her informal methods for adding?

4. Asked to show 103 with Egyptian hieroglyphics, one third grader inquired, "How did the ancient Egyptians write zero?" (a) How would you answer such a question? (b) The following variation of this question provides a good way to assess an understanding of a key place-value concept: *Why do we have a zero while the ancient Egyptians did not?* What is the answer to this question and what place-value concept does it test?

5. A second-grade class was introduced to the Egyptian hieroglyphics for 1, 2, 10, 100, and 1000 and then asked to represent 9,999 in Egyptian hieroglyphics. About halfway through this task, Julius groaned, "Boy, am I getting tired of writing!" Why do you suppose the class was given the task of translating 9,999 into Egyptian hieroglyphics? Julius' comment sets the stage for making what point about our system? (⇨ **Teaching Tip.** To highlight the contrast between numeration systems, ask half the class to record a number such as *nine thousand eight hundred seventy six* in Arabic numerals. Ask the other half to use Egyptian hieroglyphics. Have children raise a hand when done. Discuss why a performance difference occurs.)

6. Working with Egyptian hieroglyphics can also provide an opportunity to tackle problems in other areas of mathematics. For example, before students complete Question 6 above, a teacher could ask, "How many symbols do you think the ancient Egyptians have to use to represent 9,999?" (a) How many hieroglyphics would it take? (b) Solving the problem entails what mathematics?

Investigation 6.1 continued

Part III: Roman Numerals

1. Are Roman Numerals a place-value system? Justify your answer.

2. Is it a base-ten system? Briefly explain your answer.

Part IV: Mayan Number Symbols*

The ancient Mayas of Central America devised a hieroglyphic number system that involved three symbols. From the examples shown below, can you decode the Mayan number system? What does the symbol ⬭ mean? After examining the first row, Jarek concluded that this symbol meant *multiply by 20*. What reason do you suppose he gave to justify this conjecture? Examine the examples in the other two rows. Note, in particular, the Mayan representation for 21 and 421. Are these consistent with Jarek's conjecture?

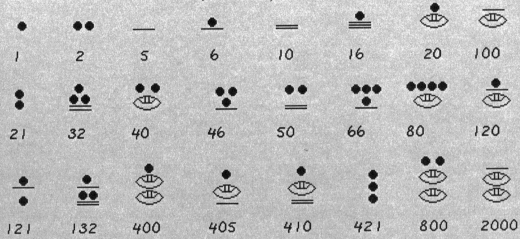

1. Once you think you know the code, try to determine what the following Mayan hieroglyphics show:

(a)   (b)   (c)   (d)

2. How would the Mayans have written the following numbers:

(a) 19   (b) 25   (c) 74   (d) 109   (e) 500   (f) 903?

3. How is the Mayan number system similar to, or different from, our decimal (base-ten, place-value) system?

Part V: Hindu-Arabic Numerals

Read the following numeral: 7,352,468,329. Now reflect on how you went about accomplishing this task. Discuss your observation with your group or class.

---

*The Mayans, in fact, had two types of numeration systems—one that used icons and the more common hieroglyphics system shown here (Byrkit & Sanchez, 1989). This latter hieroglyphic system was used for civic and business purposes, a modified version of this hieroglyphic system involved grouping by 360 and was used for calendar calculations.

Common Difficulties

Children taught in the traditional manner frequently have great difficulty with multidigit numeration concepts and skills (Fuson, 1992a). Three key reasons are outlined below.

1. A major problem with the skills approach is that children are expected to master multidigit numeral-reading and -writing skills before they comprehend the underlying rationale for these skills. As a result, children commonly make such errors as writing numerals as they hear them (e.g., write *forty-two* as 402).

2. U.S. children have difficulty constructing grouping and place-value concepts (a) because the English counting sequence disguises the fact that we group by ten (e.g., *twelve* does not highlight that 12 things make a group of ten and two single items) (Miura, 1987), and (b) because instruction on these concepts too quickly becomes abstract.

3. Reading and writing multidigit numbers is complicated by the fact that written numbers do not correspond directly with spoken counting numbers (e.g., *seventeen* is written in reverse order 17, not 71, and *twenty-five* is written 25, not 205).

6•1•3 TEACHING

It took thousands of years for our ancient ancestors to construct the elegant numeration system we have today. To really understand our numeration system, children need to be given the time and opportunity to reconstruct it for themselves.

Grouping and Place-Value Concepts

Although constructing grouping and place-value concepts is an enormous psychological step, with developmentally appropriate instruction it can begin as early as kindergarten. Teaching tips are outlined below.

⤷ **Introduce and practice grouping and place-value concepts purposefully by taking advantage of problems that arise in everyday situations such as keeping game scores.** Determining and labeling the number of items in large collections—collections of 25 to 100 or even more—can create opportunities for inventing, discussing, and practicing grouping strategies and place-value notation (see Activity File 6.1 below). Any game that involves keeping a running score can do the same (see, e.g., Activity File 6.2 on the next page). For additional ideas about introducing numeration concepts purposely and meaningfully, see the Marilyn Burns place-value replacement unit described on pages 6-29 and 6-30.

🍎 Activity File 6.1: The Investigative Approach to Introduce Numeration Concepts[†]

◆ Introducing base-ten (grouping), place-value concepts ◆ K-1 ◆ Any number

Examples of real classroom situations that require enumerating large sets include:

1. inventoring classroom supplies (might entail counting interlocking blocks, crayons, etc.);

2. making chains for decorations (could involve counting the links to ensure a sufficient supply;

3. preparing for an assembly could encompass counting the chairs to insure sufficient seating for the estimated audience);

4. getting ready for a classroom party (might require counting cookies, candies, or party favors in order to determine fair shares); and

5. conducting a science experiment or an opinion survey (could entail tallying and counting results—e.g., tracking weather patterns over the course of a school year can involve totaling the number of sunny or rainy days each month or totaling the daily amounts of precipitation each week).

Encourage the class to suggest and discuss strategies for counting larger collections efficiently. Children will probably suggest grouping and skip counting by twos, fives, and ten. Two-digit numerals can be introduced as a way of recording groupings by ten (e.g., "four groups of ten and three leftover" can be represented succinctly as 43).

[†]Based on lessons described in "Links Between Teaching and Learning Place Value with Understanding in First Grade" by J. Hiebert and D. Wearne (1992), *Journal for Research in Mathematics Education*, Vol. 23, pp. 98-122.

🍎 Activity File 6.2: Trading Games

◆ Introducing and practicing base-ten (grouping) and place-value concepts ◆ K-4
◆ Groups of two to four

Keeping score for a game, such as those described below, can create purposeful opportunities for inventing, discussing, and practicing grouping and place-value strategies. Once children start to tally scores, particularly large-number scores, they will probably feel a genuine need to move beyond collecting markers or recording tallies that represent a single point each. Encourage them to devise their own concrete or written procedures, such as the one illustrated below—a procedure that involves trading 10 ones for a ten whenever possible.

• *Cumulation.* This game entails accumulating points or play money by throwing two dice, drawing a number card, or spinning a spinner. (If play money is used, limit the bills to multiples of 10: $1, $10, $100, $1000, and so forth). Play continues until a player reaches a predetermined score such as 100 or after a predetermined amount

of time. For more advanced versions of this game, use dice, number cards, or spinners with 2-, 3-, and even 4-digit numbers.

• *Target Game.* This game consists of throwing or sliding a marker at a target consisting of rings with various values. One example would be a table-top shuffleboard game. On their turn players would take one shot and score the value of the "hit." (As with *Cumulation,* the values of the rings can be adjusted.)

• *High Card.* This game is similar to *Cumulation* except that all players draw a card, compare cards, and only the player with the highest card scores points on that turn. If more than one player has the high card, then each scores points that turn. Note that this game also provides practice comparing and ordering multi-digit numbers.

A Concrete Scoring Procedure Using Base-Ten Blocks

A.   Score at the start of a turn

B.   Scored 9 points on the turn

C.   Trading in 10 cubes for a long

D.   Adjusting the written score

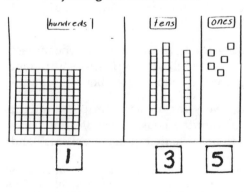

☞ ✓ **Early and ample experiences with concrete and pictorial models can help children construct a solid and broad understanding of grouping and place-value concepts.** Grouping and place-value instruction should gradually build on children's informal counting-based knowledge. The sequence of concrete models illustrated on the left-hand side of page 6-10 can serve this purpose (e.g., Engelhardt, Ashlock, & Wiebe, 1984). By expanding the variety of numeration models children encounter, pictorial models (see the right-hand side of the figure on page 6-10 of Probe 6.1) can help them construct a more general (abstract) understanding of grouping and place value. Although demonstrating manipulative-based or pictorial models may help some students, there is the real danger others will simply memorize the concrete procedure by rote. Ideally, they should be given a variety of manipulatives and drawing materials and encouraged to devise, share, and refine their own grouping strategies and methods for recording multidigit numbers. Encouraging children to devise their own numeration system (see Box 6.1) can prompt discussion and reflection about grouping and place-value ideas or serve as a vehicle for assessing such understanding. These aims can also be accomplished by introducing new manipulatives and asking students to consider how these materials could be used to represent multidigit numbers.

Box 6.1: Inventing New Numeration Systems[2]

Miss Smith used Part II of Investigation 6.1 (page 6-5) to introduce her second-grade class to Egyptian hieroglyphics. The students were so enthralled, they suggested creating their own secret (number) code. They agreed on their own symbols for 1, 10, 100, and so forth, and dubbed their numeration system "The Smith Code." (☞ **Teaching Tip.** If children don't spontaneously suggest it, challenge them to make up their own code.)

☞ Try Probe 6.1 (pages 6-10 and 6-11).

☞ **Help children to *connect* number names, model (e.g., base-ten block) names, and numerals.** For example, encourage children to identify a base-ten block model for 42 as *four longs and two cubes*, as *forty-two*, and as 42.

Reading and Writing Multidigit Numerals

Instruction on multidigit numeration skills can, for the most part, be done as a natural outgrowth of the base-ten, place-value instruction described above. Some additional teaching tips—tips that are particularly important for children having difficulty—are outlined below.

☞ **Help children to identify explicitly the rules for reading multidigit numerals, irregularities (most notably the teens), and differences between written numerals and spoken numbers.** For instance, help them to identify the value each comma in a numeral represents, that the teens are read from right to left and not left to right, and that zeros are not read (e.g., 203 is read *two hundred three*).

☞ **Encourage children to discover the regularities of our written number system.** For example, help them see that each higher level (thousands, millions, and so forth) consist of hundreds, tens, and ones like the first level.

Other Base Systems

Why, when, and how should other bases be introduced?

☞ Try Investigation 6.2 (pages 6-12 and 6-13).

Rationale. Introducing other base systems in conjunction with meaningful instruction on our base-ten system can accomplish the following:

1. help students understand better the grouping and place-value concepts that underlie our numeration system (e.g., Investigation 6.2 can help students understand why *ten* is written 10);

2. engage them in the processes of inquiry (e.g., Investigation 6.2 involves problem solving and looking for patterns); and

3. foster the learning of basic concepts and skills (e.g., working in base 4 may help children recognize that 6 can be thought of as a group of four and two more and help them master the basic number combination 4 + 2 = 6).

Moreover, understanding other bases is important because there are many real-world instances where we need to group by amounts other than 10. For example, computers operate on a base 2 system; cooking can entail grouping by twos (e.g., 2 cups in a pint; 2 pints in a (continued on page 6-14)

➤ Probe 6.1: Analyzing Multidigit Models

Depicted below are increasing abstract models of multidigit numbers using objects or pictures.* The aim of this probe is to help you construct an explicit understanding of the differences among these models so that you will be in a better position to make developmentally appropriate decisions. After analyzing the chart below, answer the questions on the next page. Note that in *proportional models, the item representing a ten is physically 10 times larger than that representing a one.*

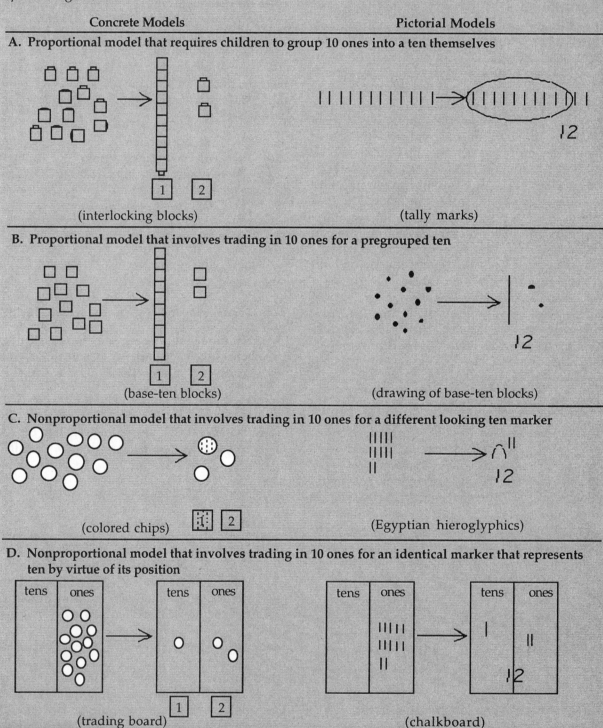

Concrete Models	Pictorial Models

A. Proportional model that requires children to group 10 ones into a ten themselves

(interlocking blocks) (tally marks)

B. Proportional model that involves trading in 10 ones for a pregrouped ten

(base-ten blocks) (drawing of base-ten blocks)

C. Nonproportional model that involves trading in 10 ones for a different looking ten marker

(colored chips) (Egyptian hieroglyphics)

D. Nonproportional model that involves trading in 10 ones for an identical marker that represents ten by virtue of its position

(trading board) (chalkboard)

Probe 6.1 continued

1. Items i to iv below illustrate four different ways the number 132 can be concretely modeled. Item v illustrates a model of 25. Analyze each of these multidigit models, and classify it as a Model A, B, C, D (see page 6-10) or "something-else" model. Briefly justify your classification.

   i. Play Money Using Denominations of $1, $10, and $100.

   ii. Peg and Disk of the Same Color.

   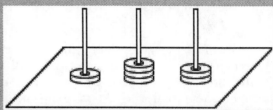

   iii. Colored Chips and Trading Board.

   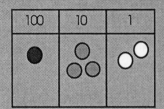

   ● = blue

   ◐ = red

   ○ = white

   iv. Abacus.

   v. A Running Tally of a Bowling Game. Note that the six tallies in Frame 1 are combined with four of the seven tallies in Frame 2 to make a group of 10. Thus the total score for Frame 2 is 1 ten and 3 ones or 13. The ungrouped tallies in Frame 2 were then combined with the seven tallies in Frame 3 to make a total score for Frame 3 of 2 tens and 0 ones or 20.

   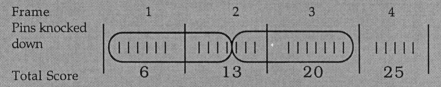

2. (a) Which of the models illustrated on pages 6-10 and 6-11 involve *concrete 10-for-1 trading* (trading 10 ones for a single ten that clearly consist of 10 ones but cannot be decomposed into ones)? (b) Which of the models illustrated in this probe involve *abstract 10-for-1 trading* (trading 10 ones for a single ten that does not clearly consist of 10 ones and cannot be decomposed into ones)?

3. Which model(s) illustrated in this probe would be most appropriate for a child with learning difficulties who was struggling to understand multidigit numeration concepts? That is, which model is the most concrete? Justify your answer.

4. Which models illustrated in this probe involve a place-value concept?

---

* Note that the concrete and pictorial models shown on page 6-10 could be first introduced without the accompanying written numeral. This might be helpful to do with interlocking blocks at the kindergarten level to accustom children to grouping. Otherwise, it is probably unnecessary.

✆ Investigation 6.2: Thinking About Other Bases

◆ Grouping and place-value concepts + inductive and deductive reasoning ◆ 3-8 ◆ Any number

Part I: Patterns in Other Base Systems

The aim of this structured discovery-learning activity is to provide an opportunity for discovering patterns across the numeration systems of various bases and, thus, to deepen students' understanding of our decimal numeration system. To see what is involved and to perhaps deepen your own understanding of numeration systems, try the activity yourself. You may find it helpful to work in a group and share your ideas with others.

1. Base 5 involves grouping by fives: five singles to make a group of five, five groups of five to make a group of 25, five groups of twenty-five to make a group of 125, and so forth. In base 5, note that collections of one to four are represented by the numerals 1 to 4 (as they are in base 10). A collection five, however, is represented 10 (meaning one group of five and no singles or units). A collection of eight is represented as 13_5 (meaning one group of five and three singles); a collection of 36; as 121_5 (meaning one group of twenty-five, two groups of five, and one single—$25 + 2 \bullet 5 + 1 = 36$). Complete the following chart. What patterns do you see? What do you notice about the symbol 10 in the various base systems? What about the symbol 100? In base 10, a 9 signals the transition to a new series. What signals a transition to a new series in base 3, base 4, base 5, base 6, and base 12? Is there anything special or unusual about base 12?

Quantity	Base 3 numerals	Base 4 numerals	Base 5 numerals	Base 6 numerals	Base 10 numerals	Base 12 numerals
•			1		1	
••			2		2	
•••			3		3	
••••			4		4	
•••••			10		5	
••••• •					6	
••••• ••					7	
••••• •••			13		8	
••••• ••••					9	
••••• •••••					10	
••••• ••••• •					11	
••••• ••••• ••					12	
••••• ••••• •••					13	
••••• ••••• ••••					14	
••••• ••••• •••••					15	
••••• ••••• ••••• •					16	

Investigation 6.2 continued

2. How would 25, 36, and 144 be written in (a) Base 3? (b) Base 4? (c) Base 5? (d) Base 6? (e) Base 12?

3. For base systems beyond 10, we do not have enough number symbols to represent all the "basic building blocks" (single-digit numbers). Instead of arbitrarily picking symbols, such as * or # to represent additional building blocks, one convention is to use the letters of the alphabet. In the duodecimal (base 12) system, for example, a set of 10 can be represented as A; a set of 11, as B. Answer the following questions for both base 12 and 5. If not applicable, write NA.

	Base 12	Base 5
a. How many building blocks (single-digit symbols) does the base have?	_____	_____
b. How would a set of thirty-four be represented?	_____	_____
c. How many items are represented by the numeral B2?	_____	_____
d. How would a set of one hundred fifty-four be represented?	_____	_____
e. Would the numeral 12 ever appear in this system? If so, what quantity would it represent?	_____	_____
f. Would the numeral 15 ever appear in this system? If so, what quantity would it represent?	_____	_____

Part II: A Math Detective Exercise on Bases

The following activity entails applying an understanding of grouping and place-value concepts. From Items a, b, and c, figure out the number code (the base system) that is being used. After you decipher the code, complete the remaining items. Note that the same code (base system) is used for all items. After completing the activity, devise your own code and version of the activity.

Number of Items	Code	Number of Items	Code	Number of Items	Code
a. oooooo	6	c. oooooooooo oooooooooo	26	e. oooooooooo oooo	_____
b. oooooooooo ooo	16	d. oooooooooo	_____	f. _____	32

Part III: Applications of Other Bases

✐ 1. Although we often group by tens, sometimes we group by twos, fives, twelves, sixties, or other sizes. List and describe everyday uses in which we group by some number other than ten.

2. To identify the litter and individual pigs, an earnotching system is used.[3] The litter identification can be found on the right ear. This ear is divided into five zones as shown below. The individual identification can be found on the left ear, which is divided into three zones as shown below. (a) What base does this earnotching system use? (b) A notch in the tip of the pig's right ear (Zone 5) would represent what number? (c) How would the ears of pig 2 in litter 15 be notched? (d) How would the ears of pig 7 in litter 24 be notches? (e) How would the ears of pig 9 in litter 149 be notched?

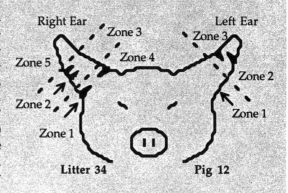

Right Ear   Left Ear

Zone 3   Zone 3

Zone 4

Zone 5   Zone 2

Zone 2   Zone 1

Zone 1

Litter 34   **Pig 12**

quart) and fours (e.g., 4 cups in a quart; 4 quarts in a gallon), the produce industry uses groups of eight (8 quarts per peck), four (4 pecks per bushel), and twelve (12 = dozen; 12 dozens = gross; 12 gross = great gross); and time involves base 60 (60 seconds = 1 minute; 60 minutes = 1 hour).

Instructional Tips. *Won't it confuse children if you introduce other bases?* If done concretely, other bases can be introduced meaningfully as early as kindergarten. In the *Mathemat-* ics *Their Way* program (Baratta-Lorton, 1976), for example, other bases are introduced by counting collections and substituting a nonsense word for *four* (e.g., for six items: "one, two, three, zurkle, zurkle and one, zurkle and two") or some other number. Children are then involved in activities that require grouping by, say, four and constructing numerical labels for them (e.g., ② ③ for two groups of four and 3 ungrouped items or units, a numeral that can also be read "two zurkles and three").

6•2 WRITTEN MULTIDIGIT ARITHMETIC

Figure 6.2: Introducing Algorithms Too Early Can Make Things Unduly Complicated

PEANUTS reprinted by permission of UFS, Inc.

When children do not understand an imposed arithmetic procedure, it can seem very complicated (see Figure 6.2) In this unit, we outline the rationale and key ingredients of the investigative approach to multidigit addition and subtraction (Subunit 6•2•1) and multidigit multiplication and division (Subunit 6•2•2).

6•2•1 ADDITION AND SUBTRACTION

Because children's informal counting-based strategies for adding and subtracting become increasingly time consuming, unwieldy, and error-prone as the numbers involved increase in size (Fuson, 1992a), they need to learn more efficient ways to add and subtract multidigit numbers. In this subunit, we consider the importance of encouraging children to use their existing knowledge to invent both concrete models and symbolic procedures for performing multidigit addition and subtraction and how instruction can achieve this.

Learning

In the traditional skills approach, formal algorithms are imposed on children—often before they have had the opportunity to construct an understanding of foundational (base-ten, place-value) concepts (Ross, 1989). As a result, a good number of children have considerable difficulty understanding and learning formal renaming procedures (Fuson, 1992b). Moreover, the imposition of algorithms can lead to inflexibility. Some children, for example, become resistant to alternative, or even more efficient, methods (e.g., Labinowicz, 1985; Parker, 1993).

Given the opportunity, children can invent their own concrete procedures for doing multidigit addition and subtraction and devise their own efficient written procedures to represent these informal models (e.g., Fuson & Burghardt, 1993; Pengelly, 1988). For example, children who learned meaningfully how to add and subtract without renaming can figure out for themselves how to add and subtract with blocks when re-grouping is necessary or how to add and subtract with symbols when renaming is necessary (Hiebert & Wearne, 1992). Illustrated below are two such child-invented algorithms (see page 3-10 of chapter 3 for additional examples).

$$
\begin{array}{r}
45 \\
+\ 37 \\
\hline
12 \\
70 \\
\hline
82
\end{array}
$$

(Add right to left. Record partial sums. Sum partial sums.)

$$
\begin{array}{r}
45 \\
+\ 37 \\
\hline
72 \\
8
\end{array}
$$

(Add tens digit first and record 7. Add ones digits and adjust [rename] tens digit in sum.)

Teaching

How and when should written multidigit addition and subtraction be introduced?

☞ Consider Probe 6.2 (page 6-16) and Investigation 6.3 (page 6-17).

Conceptual Phase. As early as kindergarten, children should be given the opportunity to solve multidigit addition and subtraction prob-lems with manipulatives and pictorial representations (Baroody, 1987; Engelhardt et al., 1984; Thompson & Van de Walle, 1984). This can help them construct the conceptual basis for inventing and understanding written algorithms later.

☞ **To foster reflection, problem solving, and meaningful use of concrete and pictorial renaming models, create real situations that require multi-digit addition or subtraction and encourage children to invent their own *concrete* renaming procedures.** This is the goal of the *Not Enough Ones* problem from the *Mathematics Their Way* program (Baratta-Lorton, 1976) described in Question 1 of Probe 6.2 (page 6-16). Investigation 6.3 (page 6-17) illustrates how the investigative approach and Egyptian hieroglyphics can be employed to introduce trading-up and trading-down procedures. Activity File 6.3 illustrates how keeping score for a game can create a real need for devising concrete multidigit addition and subtraction procedures. Activity File 6.4 (on page 6-18) illustrates how an exploration of multidigit subtraction can be prompted purposefully through children's literature and science investigations.

☞ *Concrete* **multidigit addition and subtraction instruction should be** (continued on page 6-18)

🍎 Activity File 6.3: *Two-Dice Difference Game*

◆ Place value + ordering two-digit numbers + difference meaning of subtraction + multidigit addition and subtraction ◆ 1-2 ◆ Pairs of students or two teams of two students each + class discussion

Each player or team rolls two 10-sided dice numbered 0 to 9 and arranges them to make the largest two-digit number possible. The player or team with the larger two-digit number wins the round. Note that this aspect of the game involves applying place-value and number-order knowledge. The winner of a round is awarded points equal to the difference of the two two-digit numbers. For example, if Kayla's team rolled a 5 and a 1 and Manuel's team rolled a 3 and 2, Kayla's team would score 51 - 32 or 19 points that round. Note that the game can serve to (a) review a *difference* (compare) meaning of subtraction and (b) raise the issue of how to compute multidigit differences in an authentic way. That is, it could plunge the class into a discussion of how to determine the difference of multidigit terms. Note that in the investigative approach, a teacher would encourage students to draw on their existing knowledge to devise informal strategies for determining the difference. The teacher might ask the class to consider how interlocking cubes or base-ten blocks could be used to do so. Later, the teacher could encourage children to devise a written algorithm that parallels and short-cuts their informal concrete method.

The game can be played until a team achieves a preset total such as 100 points, a preset number of rounds is played, or until a preset time is reached. Note that keeping score raises the issues of how to perform multidigit addition in an authentic manner. Indeed, while a second-grade class was playing the game, one girl whose team's total was 16 and who had just scored 16 more points asks, "How do you add this?"[4] The game had created an opportunity to invent, share, and discuss informal mental multidigit addition strategies (see chapter 7) or concrete (manipulative-based) multidigit addition procedures (see Probe 6.1 on page 6-10).

➤ Probe 6.2: Pedagogical Questions About Using Manipulatives to Teach Multidigit Addition and Subtraction

Conceptual Phase

1. *Mathematics Their Way* (Baratta-Lorton, 1976) includes the following problem:

    ■ ⚫ **Not Enough Ones.** Children represent, for instance, 3 zurkles (groups of four) and 2 on a place-value mat. Then children are asked to subtract one item, then another, and finally another. Teachers are cautioned about the last step, "Don't teach children what to do. Question them until they come up with a method to solve the problem" (p. 285).

Zurkles	Singles
O O O	O O

    (a) With what problem does the last step confront children? (b) Why are children encouraged to solve this problem themselves? (c) Why is the problem introduced in the contexts of other bases before it is introduced in the context of base 10?

2. The models for introducing base-ten, place-value concepts illustrated on page 6-10 of Probe 6.1 can also serve as concrete methods for computing multidigit sums. Which of the models in Probe 6.1 most closely models the written renaming algorithm for multidigit addition? Specifically, which most faithfully models the formal procedure of writing a 1, not a 10 above the tens column? Why?

3. The concrete scoring procedure using base-ten blocks depicted on page 6-8 illustrates trading up, which models the renaming procedure for addition. (a) How could this model be modified to illustrate trading down, which models the renaming procedure for subtraction? (b) Illustrate how your trading-down model could be used to determine the difference to the problem: Asim had 124 baseball cards. He sold 56 cards. How many cards does he have left?

Connecting Phase

1. Adding multidigit numbers such as 157 and 62 entails two crucial principles. The first is that only like units can be combined (e.g., the 7 ones can be combined with 2 ones but not the 6 tens, and the 5 tens can be combined with 6 tens but not 2 ones). The second is that the sum of each position cannot exceed nine. Sums greater than nine require a 10-for-1 trade. How can a teacher help students rediscover these crucial principles for adding multidigit symbols?

2. (a) Delineate in order *each step* of the written algorithm for solving $\begin{array}{r} 503 \\ -47 \\ \hline \end{array}$

    (b) Illustrate how *each* of these steps can be modeled with base-ten blocks.

3. Ms. Sunshine introduced her second grade to the renaming procedure for multidigit subtraction. Thanomporn learned the procedure well— too well it seems. As shown to the right, the child used the renaming procedure even when it was unnecessary. How could Ms. Sunshine help Thanomporn to use the renaming algorithm more selectively?

    $\begin{array}{r} ^4\!\!\not1 \\ \not3 6 \\ -18 \\ \hline 38 \end{array}$ $\begin{array}{r} ^3\!\!\not1 \\ \not4 7 \\ -16 \\ \hline 21 \end{array}$

4. For the expression 38 + 26, Donovan got an answer of 514. How could a teacher create cognitive conflict, which might prompt Donovan to reconsider and self-correct his faulty addition procedure?

☾ Investigation 6.3: Renaming with Egyptian Hieroglyphics

◆ Pictorially representing the renaming algorithms ◆ 2-4 ◆ Whole class

Mr. Adams wanted to create an opportunity for students to invent pictorial or written renaming procedures, including the standard renaming algorithms. His second-grade class had worked with concrete renaming models throughout the previous year. After spending several weeks with such models, he decided it was time to learn written renaming procedures. Instead of encouraging his students to translate their concrete models into written procedures directly, Mr. Adams decided to take an intermediate step. He had them use their knowledge of concrete procedures to devise a pictorial model with Egyptian hieroglyphics and then translate this type of paper-and-pencil model into a written procedure with number symbols.

Mr. Adams began with a social studies lesson on ancient Egypt, showing his class pictures of the Great Pyramids, the Sphinx, and other cultural artifacts of the time. He then introduced the ancient Egyptian numeration system—the Egyptian hieroglyphics (see page 6-5 of Investigation 6.1). After the students felt comfortable with names and symbols of this system, Mr. Adams asked his class how the ancient Egyptians might have solved a word problem involving a herd of 234 cattle and the addition of 155 more cattle. With little or no guidance, the children devised various strategies. Costis' group, for instance, offered the following procedure: (Step 1) represent each addend in Egyptian hieroglyphics; (Step 2) count the number of staffs, arches, and coils; and (Step 3) note the results:

1. Then Mr. Adams posed another problem in which another 155 cattle were added to the herd of 389. He again encouraged the class to work in small groups to figure out how the ancient Egyptians might have solved the problem. Most groups encountered difficulties. For instance, Ato's group proceeded to add the 5 staffs and 7 staffs (ones digits) and recorded 12 staffs in their answer. Mr. Adams prodded, "Is there an easier way to represent 12?" The children quickly recognized that it could be represented as ∩|| (1 group of ten and 2 ones). (a) Invent your own procedure for adding 389 + 155 with Egyptian hieroglyphics. (b) Illustrate how Egyptian hieroglyphics and the procedure devised by Costis' group can be used to determine the sum of 389 + 155.

2. Mr. Adams gave his class several problems that involved renaming so that they could practice and master the Egyptian hieroglyphic method of adding. Illustrate how Egyptian hieroglyphics could be used to determine the total number of gold pieces if a pharaoh owned 956 pieces of gold and obtained another 347 gold pieces.

3. Next Mr. Adams posed a problem below and challenged his class to show how it could be solved using Egyptian hieroglyphics. Illustrate how you think this could be done.

   ■ **Lost Ships.** The pharaoh's navy began a sea battle with 124 ships. In the battle 47 ships were lost. How many ships did the pharaoh's navy have left?

Questions for Reflections

1. In time, Mr. Adams asked his students to show how their procedures with Egyptian hieroglyphic could be done with Arabic numerals. Note that the right-to-left procedures devised by Costis' group translates into the standard written algorithms commonly taught in U.S. schools. What is the advantage of adding the ones digits first, the tens digit next, and so forth?

2. (a) Explain how each step of the procedure for adding Egyptian hieroglyphics devised by Costis' group models a step in the written renaming algorithm for addition standardly taught in the U.S. (b) Do the same for the standard renaming algorithm for subtraction.

✎ 🍎 Activity File 6.4: A Unit on Temperature Drops

◆ Creating a need for multidigit subtraction + compare meaning of subtraction + measurement (temperature & weight) + statistics (data collection and analysis & graphing) ◆ 2-8
◆ Whole-class, group, or individual extended project

Mrs. Maretti read *Clementine's Winter Wardrobe* (by Kate Spohn, © 1989, Orchard Books Watts), which described a wide variety of clothing. This story served as a basis for a sorting activity (classifying clothing by attributes) and estimation (e.g., gauging the number of coats Clementine had). The next day, Mrs. Maretti used the story line to introduce an extended integrated science-mathematics unit: "Do you think all of Clementine's winter coats would keep her equally warm? No? Which coats do you think would be the warmest? After the class agreed that the heaviest coat would be the warmest, Mrs. Maretti asked, "Do you think the type of material would be an important factor? More important than how heavy a coat is? Would you like to do an experiment to find out?"

Mrs. Maretti proposed that they heat large beakers of water to body temperature (99° F), wrap the beakers in different materials (thick down-filled cloth, thick cotton, thick wool, thick corduroy, thick polyester), place them outside, and periodically check the temperature of each. To introduce the measurement of weight and temperature, she read the following children's books: *How Little and How Much: A Book About Scales* by Franklyn M. Branley, *Weighing and Balancing* by Jane Jonas Srivastava, and *Temperature and You* by Giulio Maestro.

To prepare for their experiment, Mrs. Maretti asked the class why it was important to add the same amount of water to each beaker and heat each beaker of water to the same starting temperature. A thermometer was inserted in each beaker, and each beaker was sealed with cellophane wrap and a rubber band. The material was weighed and wrapped around, under, and over the beaker and secured with a rubber band. Most of the thermometer protruded through a crease in the material wrap.

Just before recess, the beakers were prepared and the initial temperatures of each were recorded. During recess, the beakers were brought outside. New readings were recorded every 5 minutes.

Afterward the drop in temperature from 99° F for each material was calculated for each reading. For example, 99° F (base line) - 92° F (reading 5 minutes after recess began), 92° F - 85° F (second reading during recess), and so forth. Note that this analysis involves relating a comparison meaning to the operation of subtraction as well as creating a need for multidigit subtraction. The resulting rate of temperature drop can be more clearly seen if graphed. The children were surprised that the down, the lightest material used, was relatively effective in preventing heat loss. This led to a discussion of types of heat loss, insulation, and animal adaptations to heat loss.

---

introduced *in conjunction* with base-ten, place-value instruction. Concrete or pictorial models for introducing base-ten, place-value concepts, such as those depicted earlier on page 6-10, can also concretely model the renaming algorithm for multidigit addition. Such trading-up models can help children to see that only like multiple units can be added (e.g., tens can only be added to tens, not ones, hundreds, and so forth). Once children are familiar with trading-up models, they should have little difficulty applying this understanding to the task of inventing "trading-down" models to solve multidigit subtraction problems (see, e.g., Question 3 of Probe 6.2).

Connecting Phase. Symbolic multidigit addition and subtraction can be explored after children have constructed an understanding of base-ten, place-value concepts and can efficiently add and subtract multidigit numbers concretely.

☞ **Encourage children to use their knowledge of concrete or pictorial models to invent, share, and refine their own *written* algorithms for adding and subtracting multidigit numbers.** Prompt them to consider explicitly how each step of their concrete or pictorial procedure can be represented symbolically (i.e., translated step by step into a written procedure). By considering how to add with base-ten blocks or Egyptian hieroglyphics, say, children might conclude for themselves that ones must be added to ones, tens must be added to tens, and so forth, that addends must be aligned on the right, and that sums greater than nine require a 10-for-1 trade.

⌦ **Help children to reinvent or rediscover the formal algorithms and to see the connection between each step of these written algorithms and each step of informal concrete or pictorial models.** When encouraged to translate concrete or pictorial models into written procedures, some children may reinvent the standard renaming algorithms (see, e.g., Investigation 6.3 on page 6-17). Another method for *indirectly* introducing a standard algorithm is to present it and other examples of correct and incorrect procedures for student analysis and evaluation (see Box 6.2 on the next page).

⌦ **Encourage students to *check* the results of formal written procedures against the results of conceptually-based strategies.** This is especially important when children are first learning a formal procedure or when they make an error. By comparing their results against those derived from trusted procedures, children can judge *for themselves* whether or not they are using a formal procedure correctly. Moreover, the cognitive conflict caused by mismatching answers may prompt children to *troubleshoot* and *correct* the written procedure *on their own* (see Box 6.3 on the next page).

Symbolic Phase. Children should commence with purely written multidigit arithmetic after *they* no longer feel the need to use concrete or pictorial aids.

☞ Try Investigation 6.4 (page 6-21).

⌦ **Multidigit addition and subtraction instruction and practice should be purposeful.** Solving story problems and keeping score for games such as *Largest-Sum* (see Investigation 6.4) are natural avenues for providing ample practice of written procedures in a consequential and entertaining manner.

⌦ **Underscore that there can be more than one correct procedure.** Children should realize that there are often various ways of calculating sums and differences. Encouraging them to share their

invented procedures can help foster this belief. Parents educated in other countries can also be invited to describe the algorithms they were taught.

⌦ **Children should be encouraged to check their answers for reasonableness and accuracy.** They should be accustomed to checking their computations. Children should be familiar with various ways of checking computations including the use of estimation, calculators, and the inverse principle.

6•2•2 MULTIPLICATION AND DIVISION

In this subunit, we describe how multidigit multiplication and division can be taught in a challenging and meaningful manner. Basically the same suggestions for teaching multidigit addition and subtraction apply to teaching multidigit multiplication and division.

Meaningful Multidigit Multiplication Instruction

☞ Try Investigation 6.5 (pages 6-22 and 6-23).

During the conceptual phase, encourage children to devise their own informal strategies for solving *groups-of* and *area* problems. During the connecting phase, help them see that formal expressions such 3 x 54 or $\frac{54}{x3}$ and 12 x 48 or $\frac{48}{x12}$ can be linked to meaningful *groups-of* and *area* analogies. Encourage the invention and use of informal strategies, such as the expanded partial-products strategy, illustrated in Parts I and II of Investigation 6.5. Prompt children to discover shortcuts—particularly when multiplying by 10 or powers of 10 (see, e.g., Part III of Investigation 6.5). In time, the standard algorithm can be introduced as a shortcut for the informal expanded partial-products procedure. This should help minimize the confusion and errors illustrated in Part IV of Investigation 6.5.

Meaningful Multidigit Division Instruction

Miss Brill examined the division unit in her textbook. The orderly sequence of multidigit algorithms seemed (continued on page 6-24)

Box 6.2: An Example of the Investigative Approach for Introducing the Standard Addition Algorithm—Using Student Analyses of Correct and Incorrect Procedures

After her second graders had invented their own concrete and written multidigit procedures, Ms. Sunshine wanted them to learn the standard algorithm for computing multidigit sums. Instead of describing and showing the class this procedure, she began her lesson with the following problem:

■ **Contrary Sums** (◆ 1-3). Ashon, Bayton, Carrick and Dwight's team amassed 127 points in the first four days of the Second-Grade Olympics. On the fifth day, their team scored another 45 points. To find out how many points they had altogether, each boy tried to add the numbers, but all of their answers were different.

Ashon	Boyton	Carrick	Dwight
127	127	127	127
+ 45	+ 45	+ 45	+ 45
577	1612	172	162

Ms. Prim told the boys they could not enter their score on the class scoreboard until they had decided on the correct answer. Which boy is correct? Use your own procedure to determine the sum of 127 and 45. Explain how the one boy got the correct answer. Explain how the other three boys got their incorrect answers.*

---

* Instead of using a word problem, Ms. Sunshine could have set up her own Second Grade Olympics and encouraged her class to invent written procedures—shortcuts for their manipulative-based method for keeping score. The teacher could then have had the class analyze samples of these invented procedures. If no one reinvented the standard algorithm, the teacher could include for analyses several written procedures (including the standard algorithm) "she had seen in previous years."

Box 6.3: Creating Cognitive Conflict to Encourage Self-Correction of Faulty Procedures

Like many children, Adam had difficulty learning the renaming algorithm for multidigit addition. For the expression to the right, for instance, he forgot to rename.

$$\begin{array}{r} 37 \\ + 8 \\ \hline 315 \end{array}$$

Method 1: Comparison with the Result of an Informal Procedure. When addition expressions were put in the context of a meaningful word problem, Adam had no trouble determining the correct answer by counting-on (e.g., 37; 38, 39, 40, 41, 42, 43, 44, 45). By having him record this answer and compare it to the answer produced by the written algorithm (315), Adam recognized that he was doing something incorrect with the written algorithm. (He trusted his informal counting-on procedure and concluded that 45 was a sensible answer.) Indeed, the mismatch prompted him to retry his written procedure. When he again came up with an answer 315 instead of 45, Adam spontaneously tried to modify the written procedure. He soon realized that the 1 had to be placed in the tens column and added to the other digit (3) there (Baroody, 1987).

Method 2: Comparison with a Meaningful Estimate. Ask children to compare their incorrect sum to an estimate. For example, Adam could have been asked to estimate the sum of, say, 37 stamps and 8 more.

Method 3: Comparison with the Result of a Known Formal Procedure. For instance ask children to compare the results of their incorrect renaming procedure with that of their known procedure for adding multidigit numbers without renaming. Asked to compare the results of the expression to the right, Adam should have concluded that 37 + 8 had to be less than 49 because 41 is greater than 37.

$$\begin{array}{rr} 37 & 41 \\ + 8 & + 8 \\ \hline 315 & 49 \end{array}$$

▣ **Method 4: Comparison with a Calculator-Determined Result.** Ask children to check their computed result on a calculator. By keying 37 + 8 = into a calculator, Adam might have discovered that his answer did not make sense.

⌣ Investigation 6.4: *Largest (Smallest) Sum (Difference)*

◆ Purposeful practice multidigit addition and subtraction ◆ 2-6
◆ Any number of teams of two to four players

This game provides an exciting and purposeful way to practice multidigit addition and subtraction. Illustrated below is the game sheet for practicing 3-digit computations. Game sheets for computations involving 2-digits or 4-digits or more can be made simply by subtracting or adding empty boxes. Using a spinner, cards, or a 10-sided die, a teacher (or other game host) randomly picks a digit from 0 to 9. Instruct the players to begin by focusing on the six boxes labeled A. Each team of players must decide in which box to place the digit so as to make the largest sum. After all teams have recorded the digit in a box in ink (so that changes cannot be made), the process is repeated until all the boxes have been filled. Then the teams compute their sums. The teams with the largest sum are awarded a point. After four rounds, the teams with the largest number of points win the game. An alternative scoring procedure provides additional practice. Each team's sum can serve as their score for a round. The teams with the largest sum over four rounds win the game.

This game has numerous variations. In *Smallest Sum* or *Smallest Difference*, the team(s) with the smallest answer wins. With *Largest Difference*, the aim is to subtract two numbers so as to obtain the largest answer. Note that with Difference versions, negative scores are possible (e.g. 541 - 920 = -379). With younger children, you may wish to make a rule that disqualifies such scores: Scores less than 0 automatically lose. With older students you can play the *Absolute-Value* versions, where -379 would be treated as 379 or the *Integer* versions, where positive and negative scores would be possible. In the *Absolute-Value Version* of the *Smallest Difference* game, the team whose score is closest to zero wins (e.g., -17 beats 23 or -23).

Note also that this game is an excellent way of developing a number sense—an intuitive feel for how numbers and arithmetic work. It also provides a basis for exploring probability at an intuitive level, because it raises the following question: Is it likely that a larger (smaller) digit will come up? (See, e.g., Problem 2 of Investigation 13.8 on page 13-25.)

Try this game with your study group or class. We believe that you will agree it is a very entertaining way to practice multidigit addition or subtraction. Indeed, it makes for a very interesting party game for partygoers of any age.

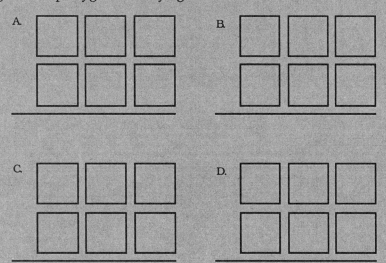

---

* In *Real Math Level 2* (© 1985 by Open Court), this activity is played with a 4-box matrix and called the "Roll a Number Game."

☪ Investigation 6.5: Symbolic Multidigit Multiplication

◆ Meaningful learning of written multidigit multiplication ◆ 4-6 ◆ Any number

After children have had the opportunity to solve multidigit groups-of problems intuitively with manipulatives, drawings, and reasoning (the conceptual phase), encourage them to devise written procedures that parallel and short-cut their informal methods (the connecting phase). Part I of this investigation illustrates this process. Part II illustrates how a symbolic multiplication can also be related to an area meaning. Part III demonstrates a guided-discovery approach to finding shortcuts for multiplying by 10 and powers of 10. Part IV shows how student analyses of correct and incorrect procedures can serve as a vehicle for discussing, making sense of, and learning the formal multidigit algorithm. To understand what is involved and to perhaps deepen your own understanding of multidigit multiplication, work through each part below, either by yourself or with your group. Share your findings with your group or class.

Part I: *Groups-Of* Analogy

1. Mrs. von Friend introduced multidigit multiplication by having her class solve groups-of problems. Below are two examples.

   ■ **Tea Order** (◆ 2-4). Mr. Po ordered three trays of tea, each of which had 72 tea bags. How many tea bags were in Mr. Po's order?

   ■ **Juice Order** (◆ 2-4). Mr. Po ordered four packs of juice boxes. If there were 27 juice boxes in every pack, how many boxes of juice did Mr. Po order?

   (a) Solve the problems above using any informal means you wish. Share your strategy with your group or class. (b) Illustrate how base-ten blocks could be used to model and to determine the products of the two word problems above. (c) One of Mrs. von Friend's groups invented the following strategy: To solve *Tea Order*, Abba's group used base-ten blocks to model three groups of two (3 groups of 2 cubes) and three groups of 70 (3 groups of 7 longs). Summarize the key information in the *Tea Order* problem, the concrete solution strategy used by Abba's group, and their solution as a vertical multiplication equation.

2. Use a groups-of meaning and the concrete strategy devised by Abba's group to determine the product of the following:

   (a) 27   (b) 204   (c) 356   (d) 87
        x 4   x 3   x 2   x 53

3. As shown below, Mr. Blackburg's fourth graders used various strategies to determine the partial products of 53 x 87. What strategies could be used to determine the partial products of 24 x 36?

```
 87
x 53
 21
240
350
4000
```

① *3 groups of 7*: Some children recalled that 3 x 7 is 21, others skip counted or used addition knowledge (e.g., 7 + 7 = 14, and another 7 makes 21).

② *3 groups of 8 tens* or 80: A few children reasoned that if 3 x 8 = 24, then 30 x 8 would be 240.

③ *50 groups of 7*: Although a few students tenaciously tried to add 50 sevens, most recognized the need for a shortcut. What strategies could be employed to make this part of the computation more manageable?

④ *50 groups of 8 tens or 80*: What shortcuts could be used to make this part of the computation more manageable?

Investigation 6.5 continued

Part II: Area Analogy

1. Illustrate how base-ten blocks can be used to model an area meaning of (a) 32 x 14 and (b) 43 x 24.

2. Compare the area model you constructed for 43 x 24 with the expanded partial-products procedure illustrated to the right. What parallels between the components of the area model and the partial products do you notice?

$$
\begin{array}{r}
24 \\
\times\ 43 \\
\hline
\end{array}
$$

partial products $\begin{cases} 3 \times 4 = 12 \\ 3 \times 20 = 60 \\ 40 \times 4 = 160 \\ 40 \times 20 = 800 \end{cases}$

$$\overline{1032}$$

Part III: Discovering Shortcuts

1. Use a calculator to determine the product of the following expressions. Do you see a shortcut for making multiplying by 100 easier?

8	23	123	2,187	13,542	2,668,479
x 100	x 100	x 100	x 100	x 100	x 100

2. (a) What shortcut would make multiplying by 10 easier? (b) By 1000? (c) By a decade such as 30? (d) By hundreds other than 100 such as 300?

Part IV: Making Sense of a Formal Algorithm

1. Miss Brill introduced the multidigit multiplication algorithm and found that a number of students aligned all the partial products on the right (Figure A below), instead of moving them over as she had taught (Figure B below). She encouraged her students to add zeros as shown in Figure C, but some seemed more confused than ever. Rodney, for example asked, "Doesn't adding the zero change the numbers?"(Kennedy, Ball, McDiarmid, & Schmidt, 1991). Miss Brill then tried a method suggested by the textbook—showing the students with grid paper how to move the numbers over (see Figure D below). Unfortunately, her students did not seem to understand the procedure. Michelle spoke for most when she asked, "But why do you move the numbers (partial products) over?" (a) How would you answer Michelle's question? (b) How could you model the procedure concretely with base-ten blocks to show the students why adding zero or moving the partial products over makes sense?

A.
```
  654
 x321
  654
 1308
 1962
 3,924
```

B.
```
   654
  x321
   654
  1308
  1962
 209,934
```

C.
```
   654
  x321
    654
  13080
 196200
 209934
```

D.

		6	5	4
	x	3	2	1
		6	5	4
1	3	0	8	
1	9	6	2	
2	0	9	9	3	4

2. A student teacher noticed that her fifth-grade students were having difficulty with 2-digit multiplication.[5] In particular, many students sometimes multiplied when they should have added. Several samples are shown to the right.

```
  2
  4
  26
 x48
 208
 104
1008
```

```
  85
 x93
  2
 255
 765
8055
```

(a) Why might students make such an error? (b) How could the student teacher help her students realize that the partial products must be added, not added *and* multiplied?

logical. First review 2-digit and then 3-digit numbers divided by 1-digit numbers with no regrouping, next review division that involves regrouping with such numbers, and then review such division with remainders. Introduce 3-digit numbers divided by 2-digits with no regrouping and proceed to division with regrouping and then to division with a remainder, and so forth. Although she should have known by now, Miss Brill was still surprised when Ms. Socrates noted that she did not adhere to the sequence of instruction outlined in the textbook. "What is essential," the experienced teacher added, "is that instruction be meaningful." Miss Brill wondered: Why couldn't Ms. Socrates just once say, "Follow the simple prescriptions in your textbook." With a sigh of resignation, she listened.

Conceptual Phase. *"How should multi-digit division be introduced?"* began Ms. Socrates.

From all their previous conversations, Miss Brill was pretty certain the answer was, "Solving problems informally." "As with basic division," noted Ms. Socrates, "children can be given *divvy-up*, *measure-out*, and *area* problems and encouraged to solve them informally. For example, *measure-out* problems can be solved concretely using blocks and a grouping strategy or more abstractly by using repeated subtraction."

☞ Try Probe 6.3 (pages 6-25 and 6-26).

Connecting Phase. The introduction of formal symbols and procedures should be purposeful and build on children's informal knowledge. Activity File 6.5 illustrates one way to implement the investigative approach to this topic. Some suggestions for meaningful instruction are described on pages 6-27 and 6-28.

🖩 Activity File 6.5: Formulating a Reading Schedule[6]

◆ Purposefully introducing symbolic division + using the calculator to determine quotients
◆ 3-4 ◆ Class discussion + groups of four

Ms. Quarles used a literature-based reading program that involved students reading *chapter books*. (Unlike picture books that are relatively short, have many pictures, and can be read in one sitting, chapter books have many chapters, few pictures, and typically require several sittings to complete.) To assure a successful transition to this type of book, Ms. Quarles had students sign contracts that stipulated they had two weeks to complete a book.

The students formed book clubs (groups of four to six students reading the same book) and were asked to devise a schedule for completing their book on time. This raised questions about setting up the schedule such as, How do you set up a schedule? Do we read only the pages scheduled for that day? Could we read more pages? What if we get behind? It also raised the following mathematical issue: *How many pages a day should we read to complete our book in two weeks?*

What Ms. Quarles did next left many students wide-eyed with disbelief. Instead of providing an answer or telling them how to proceed, the teacher remarked, "That's an interesting problem isn't it? Ms. Quarles then distributed calculators and encouraged each

group to discuss how they could figure out a solution themselves. (Note that solving this practical problem eliminated the need for the teacher to help each time a group started a new book and, thus, fostered autonomy.)

Some groups used a trial-and-error strategy and tried adding or even multiplying the number of pages in their book to the number of days (10 for those who considered only school days; and 14 for those who also included weekends).* Their number sense helped them to see these sums or products did not make sense. Some groups tried subtracting the number of days from the total pages but realized that the resulting number still represented far too many pages for one day's reading. In several groups, someone suggested using that "other thing"—the key for division (÷). Only a few children identified this key as division. (Continued on page 6-27.)

---

* Note that by observing how students approach the problem, a teacher could get a sense of how well they understood the operations. Children who proceed by a trail-and-error basis beginning with addition may not have a good sense of what each operation means. Students who quickly dismissed addition and multiplication probably have a deeper understanding of the operations.

↗ Probe 6.3: Reinventing Multidigit Division Algorithms

The aim of this probe is to help you consider how children could be helped to reinvent the formal multidigit division algorithms (or at least to understand their rationales). On your own or, better yet, with your group, answer the following questions. Share your answers with your group or class.

Part I: The Distributive Long-Division Algorithm

After her class had informally solved multidigit division problems for a while, Ms. Socrates presented the following real problem:

■ **Sharing Computer Time** (◆ 4-6). The computer lab could accommodate seven students at a time and each group of seven had been allotted 406 minutes of computer time to surf the Internet. If the 406 minutes were shared fairly among each of seven students in a group, how many minutes could each student surf the net?

1. *Sharing Computer Time* is what kind of division problem? Why?

2. Assume you do not know a formal division algorithm. Solve the problem above informally. Share your strategy with your group or class.

3. Several groups in Ms. Socrates's class decided to use base-ten blocks to solve the problem above. Illustrate how this could be done.

4. After the whole class had seen how base-ten blocks could be used to solve the problem, Ms. Socrates asked how this concrete procedure could be translated into a written procedure. Show step by step how each step of your concrete procedure could be done with written symbols using the $7\overline{)406}$ format.

5. The formal *distributive long-division algorithm* is illustrated below. Describe how your base-ten block model parallels and explains each step of the algorithm.

Step 1: Determine how many times the divisor is contained in the number represented by the left-hand-most digit of the dividend (e.g., 7 is contained in 4 how many times?). If the divisor is larger than this number, proceed to Step 2.

$$\begin{array}{r} ? \\ 7\overline{)406} \end{array}$$

Step 2: Determine how many times the divisor is contained in the number represented by the two left-hand-most digits of the dividend (e.g., 7 is contained in 40 how many times?).

$$\begin{array}{r} ? \\ 7\overline{)40\underset{\smile}{6}} \end{array}$$

Step 2a: Determine what multiple of the divisor is closest to but smaller than this two-digit number (e.g., 5 times 7 is 35, which is the multiple of 7 closest to but smaller than 40).

$$\begin{array}{r} 5 \\ 7\overline{)406} \end{array}$$

Step 2b: Multiply the divisor by the factor determined in Step 2a and record the product (e.g., multiply 7 by 5 and record the product 35 below 40).

$$\begin{array}{r} 5 \\ 7\overline{)406} \\ \underline{35} \end{array}$$

Step 2c: Subtract the product determined in Step 2b (e.g., subtract 35 from 40).

$$\begin{array}{r} 5 \\ 7\overline{)406} \\ \underline{-35} \\ 5 \end{array}$$

Step 3: Bring down the next digit in the dividend and repeat Step 2.

$$\begin{array}{r} 58 \\ 7\overline{)406} \\ \underline{-35}\downarrow \\ 56 \\ \underline{-56} \\ 0 \end{array}$$

Probe 6.3 continued

Part II: The Subtractive Algorithm

Ms. Socrates also had her class solve problems like the one below.

■ **Long Trip** (◆ 4-6). The trip took 406 days, how many weeks did it take?

1. *Long Trip* is what kind of division problem? Why?

2. How could fourth or fifth graders solve this problem informally?

3. Several groups in Ms. Socrates's class decided to solve the problem using repeated subtraction. They quickly recognized that repeatedly subtracting seven would take a long time. How could the students short-cut their repeated-subtraction strategy?

4. Illustrated below is the *subtractive algorithm*. (a) How does it parallel children's informal repeated-subtraction strategy? (b) How does it short-cut this informal strategy?

Step 1a: Estimate how many times the divisor can fit into the dividend (e.g., approximately how many groups of 7 can fit into 406?).

$$\begin{array}{r} ? \\ 7\overline{)406} \end{array}$$

Step 1b: Record your first estimate, multiply it and the divisor and subtract the product from the dividend.

$$\begin{array}{r} 7\overline{)406} \\ \underline{70} \quad 10 \\ 336 \end{array}$$

Step 2: Repeat Step 1 until no more groups of 7 can be formed.

$$\begin{array}{r} 7\overline{)406} \\ \underline{70} \quad 10 \\ 336 \\ \underline{70} \quad 10 \\ 266 \\ \underline{70} \quad 10 \\ 196 \\ \underline{70} \quad 10 \\ 126 \\ \underline{70} \quad 10 \\ 56 \\ \underline{56} \quad 8 \\ 0 \end{array}$$

Step 3: Sum the estimates.

$10+10+10+10+10+8 = 58$

Questions for Reflection

1. Michelle asked, "*With addition, subtraction, and multiplication, we go from right to left; so with division why do we go the opposite way?*" Why does the distributive division algorithm start with the largest digit in the dividend (proceed from left to right), while the multidigit algorithms for other operations begin with the ones digit?

2. In addition to the concrete models discussed in Parts I and II above, Ms. Wise had her class use base-ten blocks to construct an area model of multidigit division problems. Illustrate how a problem such as 243 ÷ 13 could be modeled in this way.

Activity File 6.5 continued

Ms. Quarles had the class discuss why using the division key made sense. Some children offered, "Because using the other keys don't make sense." The teacher countered, "Does this necessarily mean that the division key is the right one to use? How could you prove that it is the right key? What does this symbol (writing ÷ on the board) mean?"

Students finally agreed that ÷ represented *division*, which was "like sharing a bunch of things fairly." Mr. Quarles asked how that meaning applied to the schedule problem. One child offered, "It's like sharing the pages of a book between (sic) the days." Asked to give an example, the child offered, "If you have 20 pages to read in 10 days, each day would get ... two pages." Ms. Quarles had the class consider other fair-sharing situations with relatively small numbers to confirm that the calculator procedure with the ÷ key gave them the correct answer. For example, she asked the class to figure out how many apples each of 4 children would get if they had a total of 12 apples. The students checked the calculator answer against the answer *three* that they determined informally by divvying blocks or by other means.

The groups refocused on the original problem. One of the groups divided 175 pages by 14 days and got an answer of 12.5.* This raised the issue of what does .5 mean. Some students thought it meant 125 pages. Other students argued that was too many. Ms. Quarles offered, "What does a sign such as $12.50 mean?" The class concluded that .50 represented 50¢ and that was half of a dollar. By using base-ten blocks (see chapter 11) the class discovered that 12.5 and 12.50 meant the same thing.

Some of the children noted that reading half a page might be confusing and that they would rather read a whole page. This naturally lead to a discussion of rounding. The class debated the advantages and disadvantages of reading 12 pages a day versus 13 pages. The group that had raised the question in the first place decided to schedule 13 pages a day so that they had only a few pages left the last day.

"If you read 13 pages a day and your book was 175 pages long, how many pages would you have to read on the last day?" asked Ms. Quarles taking advantage of the teaching moment. Note that this raises the issue of multidigit multiplication and could serve to review multidigit subtraction.

―――――
* To raise the issue of remainders instead of decimals, a teacher could have students use a TI *Math Explorer* and the INT ÷ (integer division) key.

☞ **Even after children recognize that formal representations such as 24 ÷ 3 or 132 ÷ 12 can represent multidigit divvy-up and measure-out situations, continue to encourage informal strategies and shortcuts.** Box 6.4 (on the next page) illustrates one girl's efforts. Note that such informal strategies suggest a real understanding of the numbers and operations involved and some impressive mathematical reasoning.

☞ **Encourage children to reinvent the standard division algorithms, or at least help them connect these formal procedures to meaningful analogies.** The two commonly taught algorithms are the distributive and the subtractive algorithms.

• **The distributive algorithm.** This algorithm (see page 6-25 of Probe 6.3) follows from a divvy-up interpretation of division. (An amount is *distributed* among a certain number of groups to determine the size of each group.) Children could be prompted to reinvent it by asking them to solve divvy-up problems with multidigit dividends. Modeling such problems with base-ten blocks or play money (in denominations of $1, $10, and $100) can lead them to discover that for $406 divvied up among seven people, for instance, four $100 bills cannot be shared fairly and must be traded in 40 $10 bills (Step 1 of the formal algorithm).* By encouraging children to devise a written procedure that parallels each step of

―――――
*Children's self-invented procedures can provide a springboard to reinventing the formal algorithms. Note that the second informal strategy described in Box 6.4 (next page) involves using place value, a key element of the distributive algorithm. By encouraging students to model Arianne's decomposition-into-tens-and-ones strategy with base-ten blocks, a teacher could help them view 26 ÷ 4 as 2 tens and 6 ones shared fairly among four people (instead of 20 and 6 shared among four people as Arianne did).

their concrete model, they can effectively reinvent the formal distributive algorithm (see Figure 6.3 on page 6-29).

• **Subtractive algorithm.** This algorithm (see page 6-26 of Probe 6.3) follows from a measure-out interpretation of division. As with the distributive algorithm, encourage children to devise this algorithm or a facsimile themselves. (Note that the third self-invented informal strategy described in Box 6.4 is analogous to the subtractive algorithm.) As children use the algorithm, they should develop a better sense about estimating the size of a divisor. For example, unlike Janelle, Chu-Chin realized that there were at least 10 sevens (70 units) in 84, reducing the repeated subtractions to 2 instead of 12 steps.

PARTING THOUGHTS

"Understanding place value is [a] critical step in the development of children's comprehension of number concepts . . . . SINCE PLACE-VALUE MEANINGS GROW OUT OF GROUPING EXPERIENCES," INSTRUCTION SHOULD CREATE OPPORTUNITIES (E.G., KEEPING SCORE OF GAMES) WHERE COUNTING ACTIVITIES NATURALLY LEAD TO GROUPING EFFORTS (NCTM, 1989, p. 39). As with single-digit number concepts, help children to use multidigit number ideas fluently by linking written symbols to physical models, model terms, and number-sequence terms (e.g., 142 can be connected to the base-ten block model of *one flat, four longs,* and *two cubes* and the counting term *one hundred forty-two*) (NCTM, 1989).

AT THE ELEMENTARY LEVEL, THE EMPHASIS SHOULD BE ON CHILDREN ACTIVELY DEVISING THEIR OWN PROCEDURES FOR OPERATING ON MULTIDIGIT NUMBERS. "It is exciting as a teacher to watch children use manipulative materials to develop their own algorithms. It's even more exciting to

---

Box 6.4: Self-Invented Multidigit Division Procedures

Ten-year-old Arianne invented a variety of informal procedures to compute quotients.

Decomposition to Simpler Numbers and Divvying Up

For 36 ÷ 2, for example, she simplified the task by decomposing the number dividend into 10, 10, 10, and 6. She then proceeded to divvy up these amounts.

Decomposition into Tens and Ones

To determine the mean average of four scores totaling 26, Arianne wrote $4\overline{)26}$. She then used a variation of the strategy above, reasoning: Twenty shared among four is ... five. Six shared among four is one more. So its six (with two leftover).

For 42 ÷ 5, she similarly reasoned: Each (of the five) person gets two in each 10. There's 4 tens. So each gets eight (with two leftover).

Estimation and Repeated Addition

To figure out $5\overline{)627}$, Arianne estimated the share size for each of five people. Recognizing that an answer of 100 would be too small (5 x 100 = 500) and an answer of 200 would be too large (5 x 200 = 1000), she settled on 125. She then added 125 five times for a sum of 625 and wrote as the quotient *125 R2*.

To determine the solution of a problem involving 346 ÷ 12, Arianne estimated that each share would be 50. After adding only eight 50s, she noted the sum 400 was already more than 346.) Recognizing that the size of the share had to be less than 50, she next tried 25, but found that twelve 25s was close to but less than 346. By using such a try-and-adjust strategy, a child could close in on the answer 28 r10.

Figure 6.3: Connections Among a Fair-Sharing Analogy Using Money, a Base-Ten Model, and the Symbolic Distributive Algorithm

Verbal Explanation	Concrete Model	Symbolic division

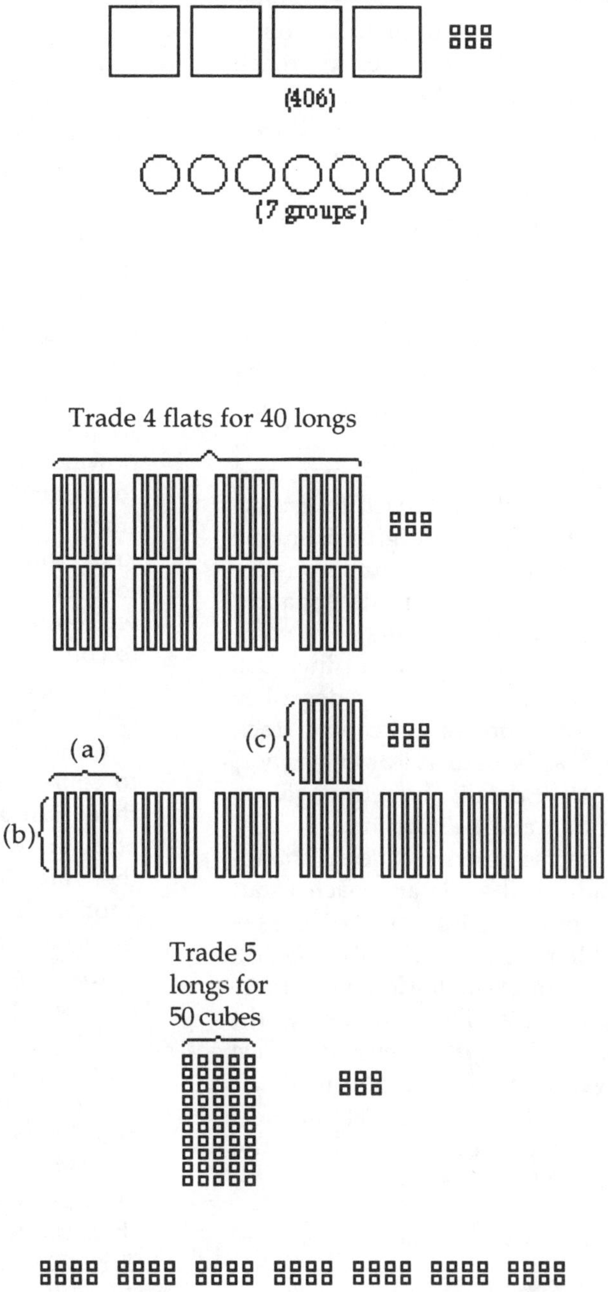

Four hundred six dollars (4 flats and 6 cubes) shared fairly among 7 people will make shares of what size?

(406)

(7 groups)

$7\overline{)406}$

Four $100 bills (4 flats) cannot be divided among 7 people.

1. $7\overline{)406}^{?}$

Trade in each $100 bill (flat) for ten $10 bills (10 longs). Forty $10 bills (40 longs) can be distributed among 7 people.

Trade 4 flats for 40 longs

2. $7\overline{)406}^{?}$

(a) Each person gets five $10 bills (5 longs),
(b) using up 7 groups of 5 or 35 $10 bills (35 longs),
(c) which leaves 5 of the $10 bills (5 longs) undistributed.

(a) (b) (c)

3.
$$7\overline{)406} \\ \underline{35} \\ 5$$

Trade in the 5 remaining $10 bills (5 longs) for fifty $1 (50 cubes) and add these to the six $1 bills (6 cubes) already available, making a total of fifty-six $1 bills (cubes)

(a) Each person then gets eight $1 bills (8 cubes),
(b) using up 7 groups of 8 or fifty-six $1 bills (56 cubes),
(c) leaving none undistributed.

Trade 5 longs for 50 cubes

$$58 \\ 7\overline{)406} \\ \underline{35} \\ 56 \\ \underline{56} \\ 0$$

see the variety of different algorithms children discover when allowed and encouraged to be creative" (Kouba & Franklin, 1993, p. 114). In time, children can be prompted to reinvent the formal algorithms or helped to discover that these written procedures are simply shortcuts for their sensible manipulative-based procedures.

RESOURCES

SOME INSTRUCTIONAL RESOURCES

☞ **Math By All Means: Place Value, Grade 2** by Marilyn Burns, © 1994 by Math Solutions

Publications and distributed by Cuisenaire Company of America, Inc. This replacement unit provides a completely developed 5-week unit for helping children construct an understanding of our base-ten, place-value number system. The intent is to supplant textbook instruction with a student-centered approach that is consistent with the NCTM *Standards*. In addition to experiences with multidigit numbers, the manipulative and literature-based activities involve measurement, geometry, logical reasoning, and data collection, graphing, and interpretation.

☞ **Young Children Continue to Reinvent Arithmetic—2nd Grade—Implications of Piaget's Theory** by Constance Kamii with Linda Leslie Joseph, © 1989 by Teachers College Press. Parts I (chapters 1 to 3) and II (chapters 4 and 5) outline the rationale and aims of a child-centered approach to grouping, place-value, and multidigit-arithmetic instruction. Part III discusses numerous instructional ideas. More specifically, chapter 6 covers teacher-initiated discussions of computational and story problems and includes three example lessons. Chapter 7 describes how everyday situations (e.g., keeping track of lunch money) can be used as learning opportunities. Chapter 8 details numerous games involving addition and subtraction. Part IV discusses one teacher's perspective on changing from a traditional skills approach to an investigative approach. It also discusses evaluating children's progress. Three related videotapes are: (a) *Double-Column Addition: A Teacher Uses Piaget's Theory*; (b) *Multiplication of 2-Digit Numbers: Two Teachers Using Piaget's Theory*, and (c) *Multidigit Division: Two Teachers Using Piaget's Theory*. For information about the videotapes, call (800) 445-6638.

A SAMPLE OF CHILDREN'S LITERATURE

🕮 Ohanian (1992) suggested reading **Anno's Mysterious Multiplying Jar** by Masaichiro and Mitumasa Anno (©1983, published by Philomel) to third graders as way of introducing the concept and representation of factorials (e.g., 3! = 3 x 2 x 1). Determining the factorials of smaller numbers can provide multidigit multiplication practice (e.g., 6! involves 6 x 5 = 30, 30 x 4 =

120, 120 x 3 = 360, 360 x 2 = 720, 720 x 1 = 720). Determining the factorials of larger numbers such as 10 can provide practice using calculators to perform multidigit multiplication. Some additional references are noted below.

🕮 **How to Count Like a Martian** by Glory St. John © 1975 by H. Z. Walck. Various numeration systems, including Egyptian hieroglyphics, are described.

🕮 **The King's Commissioners** (a Marilyn Burns Brainy Day Books) by Aileen Friedman, © 1994 by Marilyn Burns Education Associates and published by Scholastic, Inc. This book addresses the issue of grouping and the value of grouping by ten in particular. The King was confused because he did not know how many commissioners he had. He decided to count them but got distracted and lost track. Fortunately, one of his advisors had kept track with tallies. At this point a teacher could pose the problem: "Although we count by ones, are there any quicker ways to count the tallies?" With any luck, students will suggest counting by twos, fives, and so forth. One way to proceed is to encourage students to use their own grouping method and to count a copy of the tallies distributed to them. Another way is to continue with the story in which one advisor concludes that there are 23 groups of two and one more and another finds nine groups of five and two more–only confusing the King further. At this juncture, a teacher could ask if each of these two solutions made sense and if these different answers were equal. Proceeding with the story, the King's daughter proposes to arrange the Commissioners in rows of 10— and finds there are four rows of 10 and seven left over. A teacher might ask how this arrangement could be counted quickly and then proceed with the daughter's solution: Ten, twenty, thirty, forty, and seven more is 47. Students can then be asked if the daughter's solution is equivalent to the advisors' solutions and why or why not?

🕮 **Take a Number** by Jeanne Bendick and Marcia Levin, © 1961 by Whittlesey House, McGraw-Hill. This interesting book covers a wide range of number topics including basic counting concepts, number theory, and exponents. A central focus, though, is our decimal numeration system and other numeration systems (e.g., Egyptian hieroglyphics) and base systems. It provides a brief history of number and numeration. Numerals may have been invented in the first place because of the difficulty of counting strokes.

🖎 **Zero is Not Nothing** by Mindel and Harry Sitomer, © 1978 by Thomas Y. Crowell. This resource explores the various roles of zero. It can represent nothing (e.g., no points or no more cookies). Zero can also serve as a reference point. In this role, it might represent nothing (e.g., weightless on weight scale or no length on a ruler) or something (e.g., the time of a rocket's blast off or the break-event point in finances and some games). Perhaps most important for the purposes of this chapter, the book explores zero as a place holder. It notes that the term zero is derived from the Indian term *sunya* meaning an empty space (in a counter or abacus) and the Arabic term *zifr*.

TIPS ON USING TECHNOLOGY

Calculators

▦ **Keystrokes—Calculator Activities for Young Students: Counting and Place Value** by Robert E. Reys and others, © 1980 by Creative Publications. In addition to the number activities mentioned in chapter 4, this resource includes two units on place value. Of special note are the activities that help children explore the structure of the number system—specifically, the largest one-digit number, the largest two-digit number, the largest three-digit number, and so forth. By repeatedly adding one, children can discover, for instance, that 9 is the largest one-digit number. By using the add-one test, they can also discover, for instance, that 199 is the largest three-digit number—not as many children think, 109 or 190. In the unit on Place Value and Problem Solving, the resource describes a number of challenging problems for children that can promote discussion and reflection about grouping and place-value concepts. Two examples are shown below.

■ **Problem A.** Key in 736 on a calculator. What would you have to key in to change 736 to 726?

■ **Problem B.** Key in 193 on a calculator. What would you have to key in to change the 9 to a 0? (Activity File 6.6 below is based on this problem.)

▦ 🍎 **Activity File 6.6: Nil**

◆ Place value + operation sense ◆ 1-3
◆ Pairs of students (independent activity) or groups of four (class activity)

In this game, a player or team must reduce a three-digit number to zero by subtracting a three-digit, a two-digit, and a one-digit number. For example, 257 can be reduced to 0 by (1) subtracting 200, (2) subtracting 50, and (3) subtracting 7. Such a solution underscores the place value of each digit. Each successful effort is awarded a point. Note that there are alternative solutions (e.g., for 257: subtract 175, 80, and then 2). Thus, even if a player or team made an error on the first operation, a recovery would be possible (e.g., for 257: subtract 5 → 252, oops, so subtract 200 and then 52). Although such solutions do not necessarily underscore place value, they do promote an operation sense—a sense of how arithmetic works. Even so, to keep the focus on place value a teacher or class can amend the rules to specify that each subtraction must result in replacing a digit with a 0.

▦ **Keystrokes—Calculator Activities for Young Children: Multiplication and Division** by Robert E. Reys and others, © 1979 by Creative Publications. This resource includes a section on multiplying and dividing with multidigit numbers. Of particular interest are the activities geared to discovering patterns (e.g., commutativity, multiplying by 10 and factors of 10.

☞ **Teaching Tip.** To facilitate the discovery of shortcuts for multiplying 10, 100, 1000, and so forth, encourage students to create a table like the one shown below, to use a calculator to determine the products, to record their results in the table, and to look for patterns.

x	10	100	1000	
5				
12				
20				

Computers

Although computers can provide individualized and entertaining practice in using arithmetic algorithms, they have the potential for more important roles. Drill-and-practice programs can help students become efficient algorithm users. However, as implied earlier in the text, this should no longer be the most important goal for elementary mathematics instruction. Indeed, it could even be argued that complex algorithms such as the long-division procedure should *not* be extensively practiced because it damages children's dispositions to think (Clements, 1989). Computers can, perhaps, most usefully be employed to help students develop grouping, place-value, and multidigit arithmetic concepts and to foster the search for patterns.

Computers can provide active pictorial models of grouping and place-value concepts. As with concrete manipulatives (see page 6-10), computer-based models can vary in abstractness. Visual displays of 10, for instance, can be constructed by the child using unit-block displays or come as 10 unit blocks already stuck together. Moreover, the models for 1s, 10s, 100s, and 1000s can be proportional in size or not. As with concrete and other pictorial representations, teachers need to consider whether computer-based models are at the right level of abstractness for a child. Consider, for example, the display of 12 from the program *Hodge Podge*:

What model illustrated on page 6-10 does this representation fit? Would it be appropriate for kindergartners just beginning to explore a grouping concept? Why or why not?

Computer-Based Numeration Instruction by Audrey B. Champagne and Joan Rogalska-Saz, chapter 7 in *Computers in Mathematics Education—1984 Yearbook* (pp. 43-53) edited by V. P. Hansen and M. J. Zweng, © 1984 by the NCTM. This chapter describes some of the advantages of using computer-based models. For example, computer-generated representations can help provide students with multiple representations and can minimize the management problems associated with manipulatives. The chapter also outlines a model program for introducing grouping, place-value, and multidigit addition and subtraction concepts. The program outlined has three important characteristics.

- The pictorial representation clearly underscores a grouping concept. The program allows children to place 10 unit blocks into a "long box" to represent a group of 10 and to place 10 long boxes into a large square box to represent a group of 100.

- The pictorial representation clearly connects written numbers to displays of grouped and ungrouped blocks. Each digit of a multidigit number symbol is linked directly to the pictorial model.

- The program encourages verbalization about the pictured display—a process which can be important for mediating learning. The physical representation is observable and can be manipulated, which encourages students to make decisions about concrete actions. Moreover, students can work on the program in pairs, which can encourage discussions of decisions.

Divide and Conquer designed by David W. Carraher and distributed by Sunburst. This code-cracking program involving division, looking for patterns, and making and testing conjectures is suitable for students in grades 4 to 8+ and is available on IBM or Macintosh formatted disks. A Windows and network versions are also available.

Maya Math designed by Bank Street College of Education and distributed by WINGS *for learning*—Sunburst. Working as math archeologists, students try to decipher the Mayan base-20 system, experiment with Mayan numbers, and convert between Mayan calendar dates to base-ten dates. The program is designed for fourth- through eighth-graders and is available on disks formatted for Apple, IBM, or Macintosh computers. Also available for Windows and on Apple-Share Network.

Unifix® Software, published by Didax, can provide for open-ended or guided exploration using pictorial Unifix® cubes. Work can be saved or printed for portfolios, classroom activities, or take-home explorations. Available in Macintosh or Windows.

7 THINKING WITH WHOLE NUMBERS: NUMBER SENSE, ESTIMATION, AND MENTAL COMPUTATION

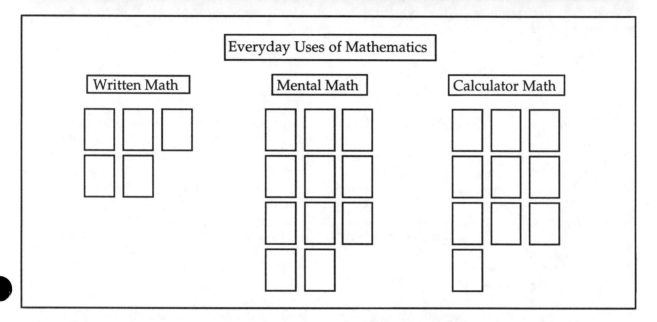

☞ Consider Investigation 7.1 (page 7-2) and then read on.

The bulletin board above can be created after a class has completed the *Math-Uses* activity described in Part I of Investigation 7.1. (To involve writing, encourage students to describe how mathematics is used or to write a story illustrating an example of its use. To involve art, have them illustrate the description or story with a drawing, a picture cut from a magazine, or a computer graphic.) The *Math-Uses* activity and bulletin board could be expanded to underscore the four different methods of computation commonly used in everyday life:

(a) paper-and-pencil algorithm (written math);
(b) electronic device (e.g., computer and calculator math);
(c) mental computation (mental math); and
(d) estimation (also mental math).

Note that the first three uses above involve determining exact answers, whereas the last involves gauging an approximate answer.

THIS CHAPTER

Number sense involves an intuitive feel for numbers and how they work. It includes, for example, a sense that 90 is much larger than 10, almost 100, and much smaller than 1000. It also includes, for instance, a sense that adding 8 + 4 should result in something larger than 8. Both in school and in everyday life, number sense is essential for solving problems or completing routine tasks involving the size of quantities or arithmetic. For example, it is essential for checking the reasonableness of computed answers and detecting computational errors.

Without a well-developed number sense, children do not have a cognitive compass to head them in the right direction when doing school mathematics. The lack of a well-developed number sense is also a severe handicap in the real world. Consider the architects who designed a hillside library but who did not take into account the weight of the books the library would house. The project gave new meaning to the term *mobile library*. (Continued on page 7-3.)

⌖ Investigation 7.1: Uses of Mental Arithmetic

◆ Underscore the value of estimation and mental computation in everyday life
◆ 4-8 ◆ Groups of four + class discussion

The aim of this investigation is to help students reflect on the following questions: *With the widespread use of calculators and computers, is estimation skill more or less important today than in the pre-electronic age? Is mental calculation still an important skill?* Complete Part I on your own and then discuss your answers with your group or class. It may be a good idea to do Part II with your group.

Part I: Math Uses

1. Take a minute or two to list the ways you use mathematics in everyday life.

2. Share your ideas with your group or class. List the suggestions on a piece of paper or chalkboard using the following categories: *written math, mental math,* or *calculator math.* Obviously, there will be disagreements. Many people keep track of their spending for groceries, for instance, by mentally estimating a running total. Many others bring a calculator to the grocery store. Some individuals bring a pad and a pencil to keep track. (Really.) Resolve disagreements by taking a vote—the majority wins. Analyze the distribution of examples among the three categories. (a) What does this *Math-Uses* activity reveal about the everyday uses of mathematics? (b) What are the instructional implications of your results?

Part II: Miscalculating Calculators

As the use of calculators and computers grows, so does the need for estimation to check the reasonableness of answer. After all, if such electronic devices are given incorrect data or instructions, they simply do as they are told. In brief, garbage in, garbage out.

In each of the following cases, a person has used a calculator to determine the answer. Estimate whether each answer is plausible. If an answer is implausible, determine how the miscalculation occurred. Consider how you can "zero in" on the error.

1. 900 eggs put into cartons of a dozen each. How many cartons? Answer: .01333̄

2. Item cost for a remodeling project were $1,027.99, $396.00, $2,333.67, $27.95 for a total of $6,552.66.

3. A business account included expenditures for $100.97, $30.50, $1,230.85, $26.12 and $3,597.19 for a total of $4,962.122.

4. Checks written during a week for $70.27, $125.66, $199.99, $30.52, and $82.50 for a total of $308.95.

5. Receipts for $50.50, $136.95, $88.20, $145.75, and $156.90 for a total of $478.30.

6. A tally of a card game scores of 20, 50, 30, 90, 100 points produced a total of 380 points.

7. A check of grocery charges of $5.25, $1.18, $1.99, $2.05, $9.65, $9.65 resulted in a total of $59.54.

8. Total of 175 yards for a football running back who gained 12 yards, 8 yards, 15 yards, and 5 yards on four runs.

A well developed number sense is particularly important for mental arithmetic—for *estimating (mentally judging approximate answers)* and *mental computation (mentally calculating exact answers)*. Working on estimation and mental computation, in turn, is a key way of developing number sense (Sowder & Kelin, 1993). Moreover, as the bulletin-board activity described on page 7-1 illustrates, "mental math" has numerous practical applications (Reys, 1984; Trafton, 1978) and, indeed, in everyday life is used more often than written math. For example, with the widespread use of calculators and computers, estimation is more important than ever as a means of checking the reasonableness of answers (Hope, 1986). Mental computation is handy, particularly in situations where paper and pencil or calculators are not readily available (e.g., figuring out tips in restaurants or quickly checking the cost of items at the grocery or hardware store). It is also a prerequisite for estimation facility.

Although mental arithmetic has as much, if not more, practical value as any aspect of the elementary mathematics curriculum (Bell, 1974), school mathematics has traditionally focused on paper-and-pencil math and paid little attention to estimation and mental computation. In the *Curriculum Standards*, the NCTM (1989) recommends focusing on the development of number sense, estimating, and mental computing.

In this chapter, we examine number sense, estimation, and mental computation with whole numbers. (Mental arithmetic with fractions, decimals, and percents is discussed later in the chapters 10, 11, and 12.) This chapter first explores number sense (Unit 7•1) and then estimation (Unit 7•2). Although this chapter follows chapters 4, 5, and 6, the cultivation of a number sense and estimation proficiency are actually integral aspects of teaching number, arithmetic, and place-value concepts and skills. Indeed, number-sense and estimation activities should be one of the first things done to introduce number, basic arithmetic, and multidigit arithmetic—should precede efforts to determine exact quantities by counting or exact answers by computing.

In this chapter, we also discuss multidigit mental computation (Unit 7•3). This skill builds on children's knowledge of the number sequence (discussed in chapter 4), addition and subtraction concepts (chapter 5), single-digit combinations (chapter 5), and place-value and base-ten concepts (chapter 6). Our discussion of multidigit mental computation picks up where Unit 5•3 (Basic Number Combinations) in chapter 5 left off. Although this chapter follows the discussion of teaching written multidigit algorithms (chapter 6), instruction on multidigit mental arithmetic should begin before the written algorithms are introduced.

WHAT THE NCTM *STANDARDS* SAY

Grades K-4

Number Sense. Standard 6 notes that "in grades K-4, the mathematics curriculum should include whole number concepts and skills so that students can develop number sense" (NCTM, 1989, p. 38). Standard 8 suggests developing an *operation sense—number sense for arithmetic.*

Estimation. According to Standard 5, "the curriculum should include estimation so students can:

♦ explore estimation strategies;
♦ recognize when an estimate is appropriate;
♦ determine the reasonableness of results;
♦ apply estimation in working with quantities, measurement, computation, and problem solving" (page 36).

Standard 8 notes that students should also be able to:

♦ use a variety of estimation techniques.

Mental Computation. Standard 8 also recommends instruction on whole-number computation that enables students to:

♦ use a variety of mental computation techniques.

Grades 5-8

Standard 7 for grades 5 to 8 specifies that the mathematics curriculum should develop the concepts underlying computation and estimation in various contexts so that students can, in part:

♦ "develop, analyze, and explain . . . techniques for estimation;
♦ . . . select and use an appropriate method for computing from among mental arithmetic; paper-and-pencil, calculator, and

computer methods;

◆ use . . . estimation . . . to solve problems;

◆ use estimation to check the reasonable-ness of results" (page 94).

7•1 NUMBER SENSE

In this unit, we first explore what number sense means (Subunit 7•1•1). We then consider how it develops in children (Subunit 7•1•2). Taking into account the message of Figure 7.1, we conclude with suggestions for effectively fostering number sense (Subunit 7•1•3).

7•1•1 MATHEMATICS: UNDERSTANDING NUMBER SENSE

What is number sense?

Definition

Number sense is an intuitive feel for numbers that guides intelligent and flexible decision making about number uses (e.g., Howden, 1989; Sowder, 1992). It is necessary for such everyday tasks as gauging the reasonableness of estimates or calculated answers (NCTM, 1989). Number sense permits flexibly switching among different representations of numbers and flexibly choosing among estimation or mental-computation strategies (Markovits & Sowder, 1994).

Components

The NCTM (1989) *Curriculum Standards* identify five components of number sense:

1. *Understanding of the various number meanings.* A broad understanding of number in-cludes an intuitive comprehension of the cardi-nal, ordinal, nominal, and measurement meanings of number.

2. *Concrete understanding of number rela-tionships.* Number sense involves intuitions based on actual experiences.

3. *Understanding the relative magnitudes of numbers.* This entails understanding, for exam-ple, that 42 is much larger (about 10 times larger) than 4, about the same size as (but slightly larger than) 39, and considerably smaller than (about half as large as) 90.

4. *Understanding the relative effects of op-erating on numbers.* This involves a sense of what direction an answer should go and roughly about how far (e.g., unlike Calvin in Figure 7.1 above, recognizing that the sum of 8 + 4 must be at least several units larger than eight).

5. *Relating measures to common referents (everyday objects or situations).* This entails un-derstanding, for example, that an inch is about the length of a regular paper clip but not the length of a new pencil.

7•1•2 LEARNING: UNDERSTANDING CHILDREN'S NUMBER SENSE

Number sense develops *gradually* (e.g., Reys et al., 1991; Sowder, 1992). The development of the first two components was discussed in chapters 4 and 5. In this subunit, we focus on the development of a sense of number size (Component 3) and the relative effect of arithmetic operations (Component 4). Relating measures to common referents (Component 5) is discussed in chapter 15.

Sense of Number Size

An important aspect of number sense is a "feel" for how big a number is. This sense of a number's size comes from relating it to personally meaningful experiences.

Fuzziness About Big Numbers. Consider the following exchange between a $4\frac{1}{2}$-year-old and her father on his birthday.

Arianne: "Dada, how old are you today?"
Father: "Forty-two."
Arianne: "Is that close to 100?"
Father (darkly amused): "Not *that* close."

This vignette illustrates an important characteristic of children's number sense. Unlike their sense of small numbers, young people's sense of "large" numbers is not well defined. With small numbers—with numbers they can relate to concrete examples and experiences—children have a well developed sense of number size. For example, one is clearly distinct from—and clearly smaller than—two. With large numbers—with numbers that they cannot relate to concrete examples and experiences—children have little or no sense of number size. As a result, they do not clearly distinguish among such numbers and may have great difficulty ordering them.

Children's Expanding Number Sense. As children's experience with numbers grows, so does their notion of a large number. A big number for many 2-year-olds is anything beyond *two*; for a 3-year-old, anything beyond three. (A 3-year-old may have a clear mental picture *one*, *two*, and *three* but think of *five* and *ten* as basically the same size. This has been referred to as the "one, two, three, beacoup" phenomenon because everything past three is seen as *many*.) A big number for some children just starting school is *ten*; for others, *one hundred*. In time, a *million* and a *billion* are viewed as really big numbers.

The Role of Numerical Benchmarks. *A numerical benchmark is a personally meaningful example of a number's size*. For example, fourth-, sixth-, and eighth-grade students were asked about how many people might attend a rock-and-roll concert and were given the following choices: (a) 65, (b) 300, (c) 40,000, and (d) 5,000,000 (Sowder & Kelin, 1993). Those who could relate this question to what they knew about the capacity of a local stadium correctly chose 40,000.

When children cannot relate numbers to familiar contexts (e.g., informal counting experiences), they have difficulty understanding a number's size. Particularly with really large numbers such as a million and a billion, even many intermediate-level students do not have numerical benchmarks and, thus, do not have any clear sense of their relative magnitude. As one eighth grader put it, "A million, a billion. Big numbers are just big numbers. What's the difference?"

The Consequences of Innumeracy. Without a sense of number size, people cannot evaluate for themselves the information needed to make all sorts of decisions. Paulos (1988) has noted, for example, that "without some appreciation of common large numbers, it's impossible to react with the proper skepticism to terrifying reports that more than a million American kids are kidnapped each year, or with the proper sobriety to a war head carrying a megaton of explosive power—the equivalent of a million tons (or two billion pounds) of TNT" (p. 7).

Operation Sense: Understanding the Relative Effects of Arithmetic Operations

Another important aspect of number sense is an *operation sense, a feeling for how the arithmetic operations affect numbers.*

Addition and Subtraction. Even before children can accurately compute the answers to addition and subtraction word problems, they can use their informal understanding of these operations to determine the correct direction of the answer (Sophian & McCorgray, 1994). Consider Problem 7.1.

■ **Problem 7.1: Spending Spree** (♦ K-2). Vinny got $12 for his birthday. He spent $8 on pet supplies. How much money did Vinny have left?

Although kindergarten-age children may have difficulty determining that the answer to Problem 7.1 is *four*, many could use their informal understanding of take away to reason that the answer had to be less than *twelve*.

Operation sense for symbolic expressions often develops later but in a parallel manner. Asked to estimate the sum of 4 + 5, children with little or no understanding of the symbolism might simply guess a number regardless of its size or try to relate it to what they do know (e.g., answer *five* because they know that it is the larger number). Now consider the case of 5-year-old Aaron who tried but could not compute the sum of 4 + 5. "If I had to guess," he continued, I'd say *four* or *five*. Wait, those are numbers [addends]. Six or Seven" Similarly, several weeks later, the boy responded to 1 + 7 by saying, "Six." Shaking his head no, he then commented, "Seven—no—eight or nine or something." Unlike Calvin in Figure 7.1 (page 7-4), Aaron's number sense told him that the sum must be larger than what he was adding.

Dennis, a mildly mentally handicapped 11-year-old, exhibited an even more well-developed number sense. Asked the sum of 6 + 2, he responded with the answer *seven*. Apparently recognizing that 6 + 2 could not have the same sum as 6 + 1, he added, "No, I know its *eight* cause you add two." Unlike a much younger Aaron, Dennis was beginning to discriminate between adding one and adding more than one and to respond to each with a different strategy.

Multiplication and Division. Operation sense for multiplication is based on children's informal concept of this operation as repeated addition or groups of. Operation sense for division grows out of their informal understanding of divvying up. As with addition and subtraction, operation sense for these operations is probably first evident when solving repeated-addition or divvy-up word problems and only later is applied to symbolic expressions such as 5 x 3 or 12 ÷ 4. As with addition and subtraction, a sense for how multiplication and division affect numbers evolves slowly. Children who see no connection between symbolic expressions such 5 x 3 and their informal knowledge may simply guess, exploit what they know (e.g., interpret the expression as addition or subtraction and answer *eight* or *two*), or devise some other mechanical strategy (e.g., state a factor *five* or *three* or combine the factors and answer *fifty-three*). Once children

see a connection between the symbolism and their intuitive knowledge of multiplication, they began to use more accurate estimation strategies. For example, given 5 x 3, children may recognize that the answer has to be related to the skip count 3, 6, 9, 12, 15, 18 . . . and chose a multiple of three (e.g., *nine*). They may also use their existing knowledge of arithmetic combinations to estimate answers. For example, a child may reason that if 3 x 3 (three groups of three) is 9, then 5 x 3 (five groups of three) must be more than nine—maybe *eleven* or *twelve*. With experience, a child might recognize that eleven or twelve is too low (e.g., reason that 5 x 3 must be two threes past nine or about *fourteen* or *fifteen*).

7•1•3 TEACHING: FOSTERING NUMBER SENSE

Fostering number sense should be a major objective of elementary mathematics instruction (NCTM, 1989; National Research Council, 1989). In this subunit, we discuss how number-sense instruction should be approached and some tips on cultivating a sense of number size and operation sense.

Ineffective and Effective Approaches

To foster number sense, teachers need to teach for adaptive expertise, rather than focus primarily on routine expertise.

Teaching for Routine Expertise. Chapter 1 noted that the traditional skills approach can promote routine expertise—an ability to solve familiar tasks quickly and accurately. Unfortunately, this type of expertise is nonintuitive and inflexible—antithetical to a well-developed number sense. Indeed, "students who have experienced traditional instruction do not exhibit number sense in many numerical situations" (Markovits & Sowder, 1994, p. 5).

Teaching for Adaptive Expertise. Fostering children's "number sense is more . . . a *way of teaching* than a topic to be taught" (Van de Walle & Watkins, 1993, p. 146). It is more a way of thinking about numbers than a set of specific number skills. AN INTUITIVE FEEL FOR NUMBERS AND THEIR FLEXIBLE USE COMES FROM OPPORTUNITIES TO EXPLORE NUMERICAL SITUATIONS AND TO REFLECT ON THESE EXPERIENCES. IT IS NOT SOMETHING THAT CAN BE IMPOSED ON CHILDREN. A teacher's responsibility, then, is to "create a classroom environment that nurtures number sense" (Reys et al., 1991).

☞ **Foster exploration and the construction of informal strategies**. "Providing carefully structured opportunities for discovering rules and inventing algorithms" seems crucial to fostering adaptive expertise—the flexible use of numbers (Markovits & Sowder, 1994, p. 5). Number sense is strengthened when children are encouraged to 'poke around' with numbers, gaining insight into the relative effects certain changes have on their solutions" (Whitin, 1989, p. 28). Supporting and promoting children's informal insights and strategies is essential for creating a climate conducive to the development of number sense (Van de Walle & Watkins, 1993).

☞ **Encourage student-student as well as student-teacher discourse**. Children should regularly be given the opportunity for open-ended verbal *interaction* (Van de Walle & Watkins, 1993). Consider the first graders who spontaneously grappled with the issue of whether infinity is a quality or a quantity while discussing the role of words during a writing lesson.[1]

J.D.: Infinity is just a term like *world* or *blue*.
Samson: It's a number.
J.D.: It can't be because you can't count it. It's just a description like other vocabulary words.
Samson: But infinity means counting forever; so it's a quantity.

☞ **To prompt reflection, pose interesting and purposeful tasks—particularly those involving everyday experiences or concrete materials** (NCTM, 1989). Games and problems are two purposeful ways to promote student reflection. Consider, for example, *Double War*, which is played like the children's card game *War*, except that the players flip over two cards from their decks on each turn. The player whose cards have the largest sum wins; ties are resolved by flipping over two additional cards. While playing this game, children may discover that using more-than or less-than relationships is easier than computing sums (Kamii, 1985). For example, if one child draws five and three and a second child draws nine and two, they may notice nine is four more than five and that two is only one less than three, therefore the second child's 9 + 2 must be

larger than the first child's 5 + 3. Box 7.1 illustrates how concrete materials can help foster an understanding of numerical relationships. Investigations 7.2 to 7.5 illustrate a variety of challenging tasks that can foster an intuitive feel for numbers.

Box 7.1: Japanese Number Tiles

Japanese number tiles consist of square tiles that represent ones and rectangular tiles that represent fives. Like *Five and Ten Frames* (shown earlier on page 4-10), these tiles can help children think about numbers in terms of five and ten.

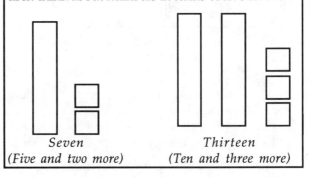

Seven
(Five and two more)

Thirteen
(Ten and three more)

☞ Try Investigations 7.2 (page 7-8), 7.3 (page 7-9), 7.4 (pages 7-10 and 7-11), and 7.5 (page 7-12).

Number Size

Understanding number size encompasses the abilities to order two numbers (e.g., Which is larger 47 or 63?), to find the numbers between two given numbers (e.g., What whole numbers fit between 47 and 63?), and to identify which of two numbers is closer to a third number (e.g., Which is closer to 57—47 or 63?). Instruction should help children construct a sense of number size for increasingly larger numbers. For example, *Missing Digit* (Activity File 7.1 on page 7-8) can be used to foster reflection on two-digit numbers and up.

☞ **With large numbers particularly, encourage children to construct numerical benchmarks—to relate key numbers to familiar contexts or examples** (Sowder & Kelin, 1993). Task III of Investigation 7.2 (on page 7-8) illustrates a structured way of helping students formulate such benchmarks by relating large numbers to the passage of time. Activity 1 of Activity File 7.2 (on page 7-13) illustrates a more open-ended method; Activities 2 and 3 could provide practice using numerical benchmarks. (Continued on page 7-13.)

☝ Investigation 7.2: Thinking About Big Numbers

◆ Number sense for large numbers ◆ 4-8 ◆ Any number

With a ballooning national debt, fattening lottery payoffs, expanding worldwide travel, waxing interest in celestial phenomena of astronomical proportions, and so forth, it is increasingly important that students have an intuitive feel for large—really large—numbers. Besides, it is just plain fun for kids to think about really large numbers. The following tasks can help prompt reflection and discussion about large numbers. Try them yourself. Compare and discuss your answers with your group or class.

Task I: A Number-Sense Activity

Read the following description of *Missing Digit* (Activity File 7.1). Then try the *Seven-Digit Version* below yourself.

🍎 Activity File 7.1: *Missing Digit*

◆ Number (place-value) sense ◆ 1-4 ◆ Any number

Present students with a format such as the following: _ 0 _ 9. (The number of digits used can be adjusted to match the developmental level of students. For instance, with less-advanced students, a teacher might use a two- or three-digit format; with more-advanced students, a five-to ten-digit format.) Have them fill in the blanks to make, for instance, the following:

1. The biggest possible number using any digits.
2. The biggest possible number with no two digits alike.
3. The smallest possible number with no two digits alike.
4. A number between 5000 and 5010.
5. A number between 8000 and 8100.
6. The closest numbers to 6100.

Seven-Digit Version: For __ 0 __ 9 __ __ __, fill in the blanks to make: (1) The biggest possible number less than 5,000,000 with no two digits alike, (2) The smallest possible number larger than 7,000,000 with no two digits alike, and (3) The number closest to (a) 4,100,000 and (b) 5,555,555.

Task II: The Names for Big Numbers

The textbook lesson was supposed to review and explore place names up to millions. But Mr. Ma'kwaganda got a bit carried away and wrote way too many digits: 1,000,000,000,000,000,000. His class was excited about the prospect of considering such a large number.

What are the names of each place past the millions place? Hint: Mr. M. explained that million was derived from the Latin mille meaning a thousand—a million is a *thousand* thousands or 1,000 x 1000. Billion was derived from the Latin bis meaning twice—literally a thousand multiplied twice by a thousand or *1,000 x 1,000* x 1,000). What prefix have you heard that indicates three? Four? Five? Six? Consider the names given to multiple births of three, four, five, and six babies.

🖥 Task III: A Million vs. a Billion

After reading an article about the national debt and discussing it, some of Mrs. Erst-Wyle's students were curious about big numbers. *How big is a billion compared to a million?* Is a million dollars in government debt only a little less than a billion dollars of debt? Is a billionaire only a little wealthier than a millionaire? To help students develop a sense of relative size—to help them differentiate between a million and a billion—analogies to time can be helpful. Consider the following questions.

1. How many days would a million seconds of guaranteed happiness be?
2. How many days would a billion seconds of guaranteed happiness be?
3. What are the answers to Questions 1 and 2 above in years rounded to the nearest tenth?

Ⓒ ✔ **Investigation 7.3: Qualitative Reasoning About Operations on Whole Numbers**

◆ Qualitative and logical reasoning ◆ 2-8
◆ Any number either individually, in groups, or as a class

Unlike quantitative reasoning that involves determining a specific numerical answer for a situation, qualitative reasoning entails thinking about how numbers behave in general. Qualitative reasoning about arithmetic situations, for example, can involve (a) gauging whether or not an answer is even possible, (b) if so, determining what the direction of the answer should be, and/or (c) what range of answers would be reasonable.

Try the following tasks yourself. Compare and discuss your answers with your group or class.

Task I: What Happens? (◆ 2-4)

Letters have been placed over the digits in the subtraction expression to the right. Answer the following questions. Briefly *justify* your answers.

$$\begin{array}{ccc} \boxed{A} & \boxed{B} & \boxed{C} \\ - \boxed{D} & \boxed{E} & \boxed{F} \\ \hline \end{array}$$

1. (a) Could the answer be a 1-digit number? (b) A 2-digit number?
    (c) A 3-digit number? (d) A 4-digit number?

2. What would happen if F were larger than C?

3. (a) What would happen to the answer if the digit under E was replaced by a smaller digit?
    (b) What would happen to the answer if the digits under both B and E were replaced by larger digits?

Task II: Alphabet Arithmetic (◆ 3-8)

Try to decode the alphabet arithmetic to the right. Different letters represents different digits (e.g., *if* Ts = 1, then no other letter can represent 1). The digits 0 to 9 must be assigned so that the expression works out mathematically. Hint: Start by considering what values T might have. Note that there can be more than one correct code (solution). Assume that F is not 0.

$$\begin{array}{r} TWO \\ + TWO \\ \hline FOUR \end{array}$$

Task III: More Alphabet Arithmetic (◆ 2-8)

For the alphabet arithmetic expressions ME + ME = US and NO + GO = NIX, answer the following questions: (a) Is there more than one solution? (b) Could the sum be odd? Why or why not? (c) Could the ones digit of the addends be 0? Why or why not? (d) What is the largest and smallest sum possible? Why?

Task IV: Sizing Up a Word Problem (◆ Any grade level depending on the content)

Ideally, before solving word problems, students should draw on their number sense to gauge the direction and the reasonable limits of an answer. For the word problem below, for example, students should consider the permissible limits of the answer. (1) What would be a reasonable range for the answer? (2) What would a reasonable estimate for the answer? (3) Justify your answers.

■ **An Unaverage Average Problem (◆ 4-8).** If 15 boys contributed an average of 25¢ and 10 girls contributed an average of 35¢, what is the average per student if all contributions are combined?

✒ Investigation 7.4: Whole-Number Operation Sense

Operation sense is an intuitive feel for how operations affect numbers. Conceptual understanding and qualitative reasoning are its foundation. Tackling tasks that involve qualitative reasoning and estimating can foster operation sense. Reflecting on tasks that involve quantitative reasoning and determining exact answers can also promote this sense.

Try the challenging tasks below yourself. You may find it helpful to work in a group. Discuss your answers with your group or class.

Task I: How Many Digits?[†] (◆ Gauging the size of an answer ◆ 1-8 ◆ Any number)

This task can serve as the basis for a class discussion or for a game played by individual contestants or small groups of contestants. The number sentences below would be appropriate for intermediate-level students. By adjusting the difficulty of the number sentence, the task can be made suitable for primary-level students.

Without calculating exact answers, gauge how many digits each of the expressions should have. Justify your estimate.

a. 135 x 1,986	c. 3,466 ÷ 152
b. 1,076 x 50,842	d. 322,385 ÷ 4,865

Task II: What Can You Tell From?[††] (◆ To promote reflection on and discussion about the size of addends or factors + deductive reasoning ◆ 1-8 ◆ Any number)

Example 1. What can you tell about the addends from the following statement: *The sum of three two-digit numbers is less than 90*? For each statement about the addends below, decide whether it is (a) necessarily (always) true, (b) necessarily (always) false, or (c) possibly (sometimes) true. Justify your answer.

a. Each addend is less than 30.

b. One addend is 70.

c. If two addends are each greater than 35, then the third addend must be less than 20.

d. If two addends are each less than 30, then the third addend is greater than 30.

Example 2. What can you tell about the factors from the following statement: *The product of two two-digit factors is less than 1000*. For each statement below, decide whether it is (a) necessarily true, (b) necessarily false, or (c) possibly true. Justify your answer.

a. Each factor is more than 35.

b. One factor is 99.

c. If one factor is greater than 50, the other factor has to be less than 20.

d. Each factor is less than 40.

[†] Source: "Estimation" by Robert E. Reys, *Arithmetic Teacher, Vol. 32*(No. 6) [February 1985], pages 37-41.

[††] Source: "Research into Practice: Number Sense and Nonsense" by Zvia Markovits, Rina Hershkowitz, and Maxim Bruckheimer, *Arithmetic Teacher, Vol. 36*(No. 6) [February 1989], pages 53-55.

Investigation 7.4 continued

Task III: Largest Addend or Factor (◆ Gauging the effects of an addend or factor's digit size ◆ 2-8 ◆ Any number)

Selecting any five digits (e.g., 0, 2, 5, 6, 8). (a) Place the digits in the boxes of the Expression A below to produce the largest product possible. (b) Place the digits in the boxes of Expression B below to produce the smallest product possible. In each case, you may use a digit only once.

☞ **Teaching Tip.** Note that different-size expressions and different operations could be used. For example, a 5-digit addend could be subtracted from a 6-digit addend.

Expression A. □ □ □   Expression B. □ □ □

x □ □   x □ □

Task IV: Missing Digits (◆ Using operation sense to deduce missing addend or factors ◆ 1-8 ◆ Any number)

Use a calculator and any operation to determine the missing digits to the expressions to the right.

□ □   □ □
x □   x □
165   216

Task V: Four Fours[†] (◆ Playing with operations to determine particular outcomes ◆ 4-8 ◆ Any number)

Use four fours in a number sentence to create each of the whole number values from 0 to 25. For example, $\frac{4}{4} \times \frac{4}{4} = 1$. Note that this task can create a need for square roots. Children will discover that they cannot create a number sentence of four fours for all the numbers to 25. An understanding of $\sqrt{4}$ provides students another powerful tool for completing the task. For instance, 18 can now be expressed as $4 \times 4 + 4 - \sqrt{4}$. To provide extension, encourage students to find alternative ways to use four fours to create numbers.

Task VI: Changes[††] (◆ Exploring operations ◆ 3-8 ◆ Any number)

1. a. 39 + 57 = 96. What happens if 1 is added to 39 and 1 is subtracted from 57? Why?
    b. 39 x 57 = 2223. What happens if 1 is added to 39 and 1 is subtracted from 57? Why?
    c. 57 - 39 = 18. What happens if 1 is added to 57 and 1 is subtracted from 39? What happens if 1 is subtracted from 57 and 1 is added to 39? Why?

2. a. 108 + 48 = 156. Would adding 2 to 108 change the sum as much as adding to 2 to 48?
    b. 28 x 58 = 1624. Would adding 2 to 28 change the product as much as adding 2 to 58?

[†] Adapted from *Mathematical Bafflers* by Angela Dunn, © 1964, McGraw-Hill, New York.

[††] Based on a suggestion by Z. Markovits and J. Sowder in "Developing Number Sense: An Intervention Study in Grade 7" appearing in the *Journal for Research in Mathematics Education, Vol 25*, pages 4-29 (1994).

⌘ Investigation 7.5: Choosing an Appropriate Calculation Method

◆ Operation sense ◆ 1-8* ◆ Any number

In the real world, students must be able to decide which of the following computational methods is the most reasonable to use: (a) paper-and-pencil algorithm; (b) calculator math; (c) mental computation, or (d) estimation. The aim of this investigation is to foster student reflection and discussion about which of these calculational strategies would be most appropriate for various everyday situations. Read each of the following situations yourself. Consider whether an approximate answer will do or whether an exact answer is needed. If an exact answer is needed, what is the most practical way of determining it? Discuss your answers with your group or class.

Situation 1. Mary had to take a taxi downtown to retrieve her dog Ruffus, who had snapped his leash and chased after another dog. When she got to the store where Ruffus was being held, the storekeeper handed her a list of items Ruffus had damaged chasing his friend through the store. The costs were: $12.82, $10.99, $5.75, $4.99, and $1.75. Mary asked the storekeeper for the total. What was the total?

Situation 2. After paying the storekeeping for the damaged items with a check, Mary went next door to a pet store and bought a new "heavy duty, steel reinforced" leash—one recommended by "animal trainers of wild animals the world over." The leash cost $17.99. The pet-store owner had to determine the tax (7%) and the total. What was the tax?

Situation 3. After paying for the leash by check, Mary retrieved Ruffus and escorted him to the awaiting taxi. By the time they got back home, the taxi fare was $45.75. Mary wanted to give the taxi driver a big (20%) tip because (a) he had been so patient and helpful and (b) Ruffus had drooled and slobbered all over her back seat. How much was the 20% tip?

Situation 4. With Ruffus securely home again, Mary decided to determine the damage caused by Ruffus' latest misadventure. She took out the check book to determine what she had spent and the new balance. The three checks Mary had written were $36.30, $19.25, and $55. How much had Ruffus' adventure cost and what was the new balance if the old balance was $178.50?

Situation 5. Mary's folks agreed to repay Mary for Ruffus' expenses if she would do extra chores around the house. While pulling weeds in the garden, Mary wondered how long she would have to work at $5 an hour to pay off $110.55? How many hours of work had Ruffus cost Mary?

Situation 6. Perhaps sensing he was on shaky grounds with his master, Ruffus came to the garden and started digging next to Mary. She noticed his big sad eyes, hugged the dog, and said, "I always love you no matter what." Then she noticed that Ruffus had unearthed a diamond ring—lost there apparently before her family had bought the house. A jeweler appraised the ring at $450. After paying off her parents the $110.55 she owed, Mary wondered if she could afford the new coat she wanted for $199 and a set of doggie toys (for Ruffus) for $45. Could she? Briefly justify.

---

*The example illustrated here would be appropriate for intermediate-level students. The problems chosen for this activity could be adapted for any age level.

🍎 Activity File 7.2: Numerical Benchmark Activities

◆ Sense of number size ◆ K-8 ◆ Any number

Activity 1: Establishing Numerical Benchmarks. Depending on grade level and experience, encourage children to relate key numbers such as 5; 10; 20; 50; 100; 1,000; 10,000; 100,000; and 1,000,000 to familiar contexts or experiences. For example, kindergartners might relate 5 to the number of fingers on one hand or the number of birthdays they have had. With children in fourth grade and up, 500,000 might be related to the number of minutes in a year (60 min/hr x 24 hr/day x 30 days/month x 12 months/year ≈ 518,400 minutes/year).

Activity 2: Using Numerical Benchmarks to Make Estimates. Pose questions such as "The number of crayons the school orders each year is about how much?" (benchmark: the number of crayons in the class) or "The population of our state is about how much?" (benchmark: hometown population). Ideally, such questions would arise while solving a problem or investigating issues in a content area—that is, purposefully.

Activity 3: Using Numerical Benchmarks to Evaluate "Facts." A key component of numerical literacy is the ability to gauge whether "facts" appearing in news reports, advertisements, political speeches, and so forth are reasonable. To foster such critical thinking, encourage children to use known references to evaluate the reasonableness of facts such as:

• The school disposes of 1,000 pounds of paper waste a day.
• Over 500 parents attended the school's PTO meeting on changing the mathematics curriculum.
• The school cafeteria sells about 2,000 cartons of milk a day.
• The school averages 100 absences a day.
• The U.S. population is 65% male.

Operation Sense

Cultivating operation sense entails helping children to recognize the effects of arithmetic operations and to choose wisely among the four computational options listed on page 7-1.

The Effects of Arithmetic Operations. During the conceptual and connecting phases, particularly, instruction should focus on fostering operation sense. For example, when introducing symbolic single-digit addition, a teacher could present $5 + 0$, $5 + 1$, $5 + 2$, and $5 + 3$ in sequence and ask the class, a small group, or an individual child to estimate the sum of each. The teacher could encourage a discussion about plausible sums by asking such questions as, "Could the sum of $5 + 2$ be smaller than five, equal to five, or larger than five? Why? Could the sum of $5 + 2$ and $5 + 1$ be the same? Why or why not?"

☞ **Encourage qualitative reasoning as a vehicle for understanding and checking arithmetic procedures.** Qualitative reasoning is the heart of number sense. It involves *general* understandings about how numbers behave (e.g., the number further along in the counting sequence represents the larger quantity). Qualitative reasoning about arithmetic situations involves determining *the direction of change*, rather than the exact amount of change (Behr, Harel, Post, & Lesh, 1992). Task I of Investigation 7.3 (on page 7-9), for example, asks for the relative size of the answer. Qualitative reasoning tasks such as those in Investigation 7.3 are excellent tools for encouraging reflection and discussion while learning about an arithmetic procedure. The solution to Task II, for instance, requires students to recognize that the sum of two digits cannot be larger than 18. That is, because T can be no larger than 9, T + T can be no larger than 18, and so F must be 1. (Note this involves deductive reasoning as well.)

☞ **Encourage a reflective approach to using arithmetic procedures.** When students tackle either a qualitative task or a quantitative task (when determining a numerical solution), encourage them to ask such questions as:

• *What type of number or outcome should be expected?* For example, in Question 1 of Task I in Investigation 7.3, students should recognize that three-digit subtraction expressions can have a one-, two- or three-digit answer only.

• *Is it even possible to determine an answer for the task?* As suggested earlier in chapter 2, not all mathematical tasks can be solved. Thus, it is important to consider whether there is sufficient information to solve a task before proceeding. For example, Question 3a of Task I in Investigation 7.3 is answerable but Question 3b is not. If both digits B and E in the expression $\frac{ABC}{-DEF}$ were replaced by larger digits, it would not be possible to determine the effect on the differences without knowing *how much* B and E were increased. (If B were increased more than E, then the difference would increase. If B were increased less than E, then the difference would decrease. If B and E were increased by the same amount, the difference would remain the same.) A discussion of qualitative reasoning can help children focus on the conceptual basis of a procedure and its key properties. For this reason, such tasks are ideal for assessing *understanding* of procedures.

• *What limits are reasonable?* How large or small could the answer possibly be? For example, with Task IV in Investigation 7.3, the average amount should be between 25¢ and 35¢.

Note that qualitative-reasoning tasks are particularly useful for sensitizing students to the importance of asking reflective questions. Investigation 7.4 (pages 7-10 and 7-11) illustrates some qualitative- and quantitative-reasoning tasks that can be used to foster reflection and an operation sense.

Choosing Wisely. Students accustomed to the traditional skills approach may blindly assume that a written algorithm is the only legitimate way to perform computations. Instruction should help children to see that there are computational choices and to choose wisely among them.

☞ **Encourage children to consider what options are possible when a computation is needed and which option is best suited for the task.** Children should recognize that paper-and-pencil calculation is not the most useful computational method in many, if not most, everyday situations. The activity and bulletin board described on page 7-1 could be used to underscore this point. Investigation 7.5 (page 7-12) illustrates another way of helping children explicitly consider the best computational method for a task.

7•2 ESTIMATION

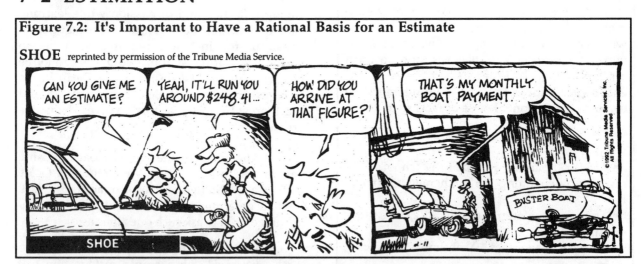

Figure 7.2: It's Important to Have a Rational Basis for an Estimate

Estimation can involve gauging the size of a collection (number estimation), the size of a measurement (measurement estimation), or the outcome of a computation (computational estimation). Estimation is, at heart, a problem-solving activity requiring thoughtful analysis and flexibility (cf. Figure 7.2). Thus, it can also be an important vehicle for encouraging mathematical thinking and problem solving (Driscoll, 1981). In this unit, we compare the skills approach for teaching estimation with the investigative approach, which underscores the true nature of estimation (Subunit 7•2•1). We then examine number and measurement estimation (Subunit 7•2•2) and computational estimation (Subunit 7•2•3).

7•2•1 A TALE OF TWO APPROACHES

Proficient estimators appreciate the importance of estimation and draw on their rich number sense. They have the mental flexibility to choose an appropriate strategy or to adjust their strategy and are willing to risk giving inexact answers.

Unfortunately, many students do not appreciate the value of estimation, do not think to draw on their number sense, assume that there is only one correct way to estimate, or are afraid to estimate. They respond inflexibly and poorly on estimation tasks (Carpenter, Coburn, Reys, & Wilson, 1976). On the Fourth NAEP test, for example, only about half the third graders recognized that 72 - 49 was closer to 70 - 50 than 70 - 40, 80 - 40, or 80 - 50 (Kouba et al., 1989). In this subunit, we outline how the traditional skills approach contributes to children's estimation difficulties and how instruction can help children become effective and confident estimators.

Learning: Difficulties With the Traditional Skills Approach

Why does the skills approach fail to produce proficient and confident estimators? Consider, for example, how rounding has traditionally been taught.

☞ Try Probe 7.1 (page 7-16) and Investigation 7.6 (page 7-17).

Purposeless Instruction. Rounding has traditionally been treated as a prerequisite skill for computational estimation and introduced before it. In effect, the skill was taught out of context and with no real purpose. As a result, children did not see how it was connected to other topics and real-world applications or why it was used (e.g., to make otherwise difficult or impossible computations manageable).

Unconnected to Number Sense. The traditional skills approach focused on *how*, not why. Students were required to memorize by rote specific prescriptions for rounding such as: *When rounding to tens, if the ones digit is less than 5 round down (e.g., 124 → 120); if the ones digit is 5 or more, round up (e.g., 126 → 130).* No effort was made to help children understand the rationale for this prescription. The reason for rounding 124 down to 120, for example, is that it is *closer* to 120

than 130. Unfortunately, the skills approach does not build on such counting knowledge.

Note that without well developed counting knowledge, children will probably have difficulty with rounding. In Part I of Probe 7.1, for example, Amanda could count by tens to 100 and had no difficulty rounding 2-digit numbers to tens. Moreover, she could count by hundreds to 1000 and had no difficulty rounding 3-digit numbers to hundreds. However, she could not count by tens over 100 ("110, 120, 130 . . . "). This prevented her from constructing an appropriate number line and the rounding 3-digit numbers to tens.

Fostering Inflexibility. *How do you round, say, $93.50 off to the nearest dollar?* Products of the traditional skills approach typically assume that there is only *one* correct way to round and mechanically apply their rotely memorized rule: $93.50 should be rounded up to $94. However, there is no one correct way of rounding with a 5. As Part II of Probe 7.1 implies, $93.50 is equally far from $94 as it is from $93. How you resolve this ambiguous case (whether you round $93.50 up or down) depends on your goal—whether you want a liberal or a conservative estimate. Because it is better to undermedicate than overmedicate, medical practitioners are taught to round down (e.g., 93.5 would be rounded to 93). To minimize the effects of rounding errors, scientists sometimes alternate between rounding up and rounding down: When the digit to the left of the 5 is odd, round up (e.g., 3.75 is rounded up to 3.8). When the digit to the left of the 5 is even, round down (e.g., 3.65 is rounded down to 3.6). This minimizes the effects of rounding errors.

Indeed, as Investigation 7.6 suggests, there is *not* one correct way to round with numbers other than 5 either. Although Belinda's rounding-to-the-nearest-decade strategy was the most accurate, Melinda's rounding-up strategy was the most appropriate for ensuring that a limited amount of money was not overspent.

Unfortunately, the traditional skills approach does not encourage children to consider which of a variety of strategies is most appropriate for a particular situation. Because they learn estimation skills out of context and by rote, they do not realize that an estimation strategy is determined by a thoughtful analysis of task goals. (Continued on page 7-18.)

➤ Probe 7.1: Rounding Instruction

The aim of this probe is to help you reflect on how estimation should be taught. The case study in Part I illustrates a common problem with rounding instruction—particularly for children who have been taught using the traditional skills approach. Part II focuses on the rules for rounding. After considering each part yourself, discuss your answers with your group or class.

Part I: The Case of Amanda[2]

A third-grade class was introduced to rounding using a number line. Amanda had no problem constructing a number line with increments of five and ten up to 100 (see Figure A below) and rounding 2-digit numbers to the nearest 10. For example, she believed that 55 or 57 should be rounded to 60 and that 52 or 54 should be rounded to 50. Amanda could also construct a number line with increments of one hundred up to 1000 (see Figure B below) and round 3-digit numbers to the nearest hundred (e.g., round 359 to 400, 507 to 500, and 831 to 800). When asked to round 3-digit numbers to the nearest ten, however, she could *not* construct a number line and became very confused. For example, she rounded 315 to 400. Even more evident of her confusion, Amanda rounded 654 to 554 and 229 to 429.

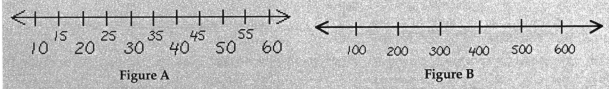

Figure A	**Figure B**

1. What is the basis of Amanda's rounding difficulty? Consider what counting knowledge is needed to round three-digit numbers to the nearest tens—knowledge that the girl apparently had not yet constructed.

2. Consider how you would help Amanda construct the prerequisite knowledge for rounding three-digit numbers to the nearest tens.

Part II: Rounding Rules

1. Consider the following questions:

    a . Items cost $236, $388, and $450. What would these costs be when rounded to the nearest hundred dollars?

    b. A psychologist had the following reaction-time measurements: 3.2 seconds, 3.5 seconds, 3.9 seconds, and 4.5 seconds. She needed to round these measurements off to the nearest unit. How should each of the four reaction-time measurement be rounded off? What are the rounded values?

2. Compare your results with others in your group or class. Is there a general agreement about how rounding should be done? That is, is it obvious how the rounding for Questions 1a and 1b should be done?

3. The vast majority of adults know the following school-taught rule for rounding: With *1 to 4 round down; with 5 to 9, round up.* Thus, in Question 1a, it seem obvious that $450 should be rounded off to $500. Moreover, in Question 1b, it is equally obvious that 3.5 sec. should be rounded off to 4 sec. and that 4.5 sec. should be rounded off to 5 sec. Consider though, the implications of the answer to the following questions: *Is 450 closer to 400 or 500? Is 4.5 closer to 4.0 or 5.0?*

5. Consider whether or not the school-taught rule of rounding up a 5 applies to the following real-world situation: A doctor leaves instructions to give a patient 1.25 gram doses of medication hourly. The nurse can measure the medication accurately to tenths only. Should she give 1.3 grams of medicine or 1.2 grams? Why?

☙ Investigation 7.6: Evaluating Estimates

◆ Discussion of estimation strategies ◆ 1-8 ◆ Any number

This investigation involves presenting students an estimation story problem and then asking them questions to prompt reflection about the estimates in the story. Read through the sample story below and answer the questions posed.

Evaluating Estimates: Holiday Spending

The triplets Belinda, Linda, and Melinda had a total of $105 to spend for holiday presents. Each used a rounding strategy to make sure they did not overspend this money. The prices of the items they selected and their estimates are listed below:

Item	Item Price	Belinda's Estimate	Linda's Estimate	Melinda's Estimate
Dad's present	$34	$30	$30	$40
Mom's present	$42	$40	$40	$50
Brother Linn's Present	$13	$10	$10	$20
Lucinda the dog's present	$17	$20	$10	$20

1. According to Belinda, would they have enough money to buy all the presents they chose?

2. According to Linda, would they have enough money to buy all the items they picked out?

3. According to Melinda, would they have enough money to buy the items selected?

4. What rounding strategy did each triplet use?

5. Whose strategy was the most accurate? That is, whose estimate came closest to the actual total price?

6. Whose strategy do you think the triplets should use in *this* situation? That is, whose strategy would keep them from overspending what they had?

7. In what situations would it be appropriate to use Linda's strategy?

Questions for Reflection

1. What point about rounding does the investigation described above make?

2. What are the disadvantages of teaching children one correct way to round numbers?

3. A useful estimation technique is to determine the range of plausible estimates. (a) Which estimation strategy could be used to identify the maximum reasonable estimate? (b) Which could be used to identify minimum reasonable estimate?

Undermining a Disposition to Estimate. Miss Brill tried some estimation activities but found her students reluctant to give inexact answers. Even after repeated encouragement, most resorted to calculating the exact answer, if they responded at all. Quite discouraged, Miss Brill facetiously confided to Ms. Socrates, "If given the choice of estimating or eating worms, I'm afraid most of my students would choose the latter. Why do they resist estimating, even when I make it clear it's desirable?"

Ms. Socrates smiled with quiet recognition. "You have to understand that your words run counter to all their previous mathematical training.

1. Because little time is spent on estimation, children sense that it is not important (e.g., Driscoll, 1981). I fear that most of our teachers still treat estimation as a secondary or enrichment topic. Practically speaking, that means most of our primary-level teachers don't touch number and measurement estimation or computational estimation with basic number combinations such as 9 + 7 and 15 - 8. The third-grade teachers only briefly touch on estimation when required to teach rounding.

2. Traditional instruction focuses on getting *the* correct answer. As early as first grade, some children become so concerned with this focus, they refuse to make estimates. Many students are so concerned about being correct, they insist on laboriously calculating the exact answer or they surreptitiously compute an exact answer and *then* round (e.g., asked to estimate the sum of 348 + 176, they mentally compute a sum of 524 and round off this answer to nearest tenth for an 'estimate' of 520).

3. Frequently, the primary approach to practicing estimation skills has been a 'guess-and-check' procedure, which further underscores the importance of getting the right (exact) answer, not the importance of estimating."

Teaching: The Investigative Approach

In the investigative approach, a teacher helps children appreciate the purpose of estima-

tion, builds on their existing knowledge, and fosters flexibility. Moreover, to promote a positive disposition toward giving approximate answers, estimation instruction should (a) minimize comparisons to exact answers and (b) begin early.

☞ Consider Investigation 7.7 (page 7-19).

Purposeful Instruction. Students should be helped to see that estimation is an important tool for a variety of everyday situations.

∞ **Underscore the uses of estimation in a variety of topics and situations** (e.g., Trafton, 1986). Highlight everyday opportunities to use estimation in a purposeful manner. Newer textbooks now feature both estimation and mental-computation activities and exercises regularly throughout so as to underscore the relationship between mental mathematics and other areas. However, unless teachers recognize the importance of estimation and mental computation, they may tend to overlook these activities and exercises.

∞ **One of the most important things a teacher can do is model estimation skills for the class by "thinking out loud"** (e.g., Our class will have about 22 at the picnic, and Mrs. Braun's will have about 27, so we need about 20 plus 30—50 cups".) This provides concrete evidence that the teacher values the process of estimation.

∞ **Practice estimation skills using realistic problems under realistic conditions.** To practice computational estimation, for example, present problems involving situations where it makes sense to estimate answers rather than calculate the exact answer. Moreover, place a time limit on estimation efforts. Consider the following tasks:

Task 1. Hope went to an estate sale that was auctioning off a doll collection. She had $100 to spend and had just successfully bid on two dolls. Now she had to determine quickly whether she could afford a bid of $42 on the next doll. Within 5 seconds, write down on your individual minislate whether or not Hope could afford a bid of $42, if she had already promised to pay $37 and $48 for the two other dolls.

Task 2. Within 10 seconds write down on your individual minislate, about how much of her $100 Hope had left if she had already spent $37 and $48. (Continued on page 7-20.)

⚛ Investigation 7.7: Using Everyday Knowledge to Make Estimates[3]

◆ Making connections to formulate estimates ◆ K-8 ◆ Small groups or whole class

We are sometimes asked to make estimates that—at first blush—seem impossible to make. Yet, if we draw reflectively on what we know, we can often make a reasonable estimate. Consider the following tasks. Work with your group to determine an estimate for each. Discuss your estimates with your class.

■ Task 1: A Long Season

A boy asked his mother, "How many baseball games do the Chicago Cubs play during a season?" Not ever having been a baseball fan, the mother's first reaction was: "I don't have the foggiest idea." Perhaps your reaction is similar (How would I know?). If so, try to come up with an estimate by, perhaps, putting your head together with that of others in your group. (Baseball fans should move directly to the next task.)

■ Task 2: A Big Distance

What is the circumference of the earth?

■ Task 3: Oregon Trail

The settlers gathered in St. Louis, headed west along the Missouri River and later northwest along the North Fork of the Platte River, across the Rocky Mountains and finally to Oregon. To get past the Rocky Mountains before winter, they left St. Louis in late March or early April. During traveling hours, about how many miles per hour did the settlers who took the Oregon Trail travel overall?

■ Task 4: Many People

(a) What is the population of the United States? (b) What is the population of the world?

↦ Instructional Tips

The difficulty of problems such as those above will vary greatly with the background knowledge of students. The problems above may quite challenging for most fifth- to eighth-graders. For primary-age children particularly, begin with problems that draw directly on their personal knowledge. For example, the *School Population* problem below would be more concrete than the *Many People* problem above.

■ **School Population** (◆ 2-4). Margo wanted to help the flood victims. If each child in our school gave only a dime, that would be a good start, she thought. If each child in your school gave a dime, about how many dimes could be collected? About how many dollars would this be?

Note that with the tasks above, unlike practice with written worksheets, it makes little sense to compute the exact answer and then round off (as some children are prone to do). An exact answer is hardly necessary to answer Task 1 and computing exact answers and rounding is impractical in light of the time limit imposed by both Tasks 1 and 2.

Build on Existing Knowledge. Estimation instruction should build on what children already know, including their intuitive number sense.

∞ **Rounding instruction, for example, should build on children's existing knowledge of the counting sequence.** The activity *Closer To* (Activity File 7.3 on page 7-21) introduces rounding in the familiar terms of comparing numbers. It also underscores that rounding with 5 is an ambiguous case because, for instance, 45 is as close to 40 as is 50. Moreover, it can prompt children to invent the rules for rounding for themselves.

∞ **When estimating, encourage children to make use of their everyday knowledge, as well as their number, arithmetic, and place-value knowledge.** Investigation 7.7 (page 7-19) illustrates that by using our existing everyday knowledge, it is possible to make reasonable estimates in situations for which an estimate seems difficult, if not impossible. For example, in our experience, the majority of female students do not have any idea of how many games a major-league baseball team plays (Task 1 of Investigation 7.7). Yet many can draw on what they do know to arrive at an answer that is within 20% or even 10% of the correct answer. Problems like those in Investigation 7.7 can underscore the importance of estimating while involving students in mathematical thinking.

Promote Flexibility. It is essential that instruction foster adaptive, rather than routine, expertise.

∞ **Help children see that there are various ways to estimate and that the choice of strategy depends on the task goals** (Leutzinger, Rathmell, & Urbatsch, 1986; Reys, 1986; Trafton, 1986). To underscore that estimation is a problem-solving process, prompt children to consider first the goal of a task and the level of accuracy needed. Help them see that this will determine how the estimation should be done. If a relatively accurate estimate is needed, then round up digits greater than 5 and round down digits less than 5. If a liberal estimate is needed so that, for instance, you do not overspend the money you have, then consistently round up (see, e.g., Investigation 7.6 on page 7-17). If a conservative estimate is needed (e.g., when administering medicine), then consistently round down.

∞ **To further underscore that there are various ways to estimate answers, encourage children to invent and share their own estimation strategies.** Ideally, this would lead children to discover rounding off to the nearest unit of choice, rounding up, and so forth themselves.

∞ **Encourage children to justify their estimation strategies.** Prompt them to *explain the rationale* for their estimation procedure in terms of the goals of a task. Ask, for instance, "Did you need a relatively accurate or crude estimate?" "Would it be a good idea to overestimate or underestimate in this situation?" "What kind of estimate does your strategy provide?"

Focus on Approximate Answers, Not Exact Ones. It is crucial to help students understand that estimation involves gauging approximate answers and that this can be a valuable process in its own right.

∞ **Use language that underscores the need for approximate answers rather than exact answers.** When posing or discussing estimation tasks, use terms such as *about*, *a little more* (or *less*) *than*, *close to*, and *between*.

∞ **Avoid a *guess-and-check* procedure, at least initially.** It is especially important at first to avoid the common practice of asking children to make an estimate, then determine the exact answer, and finally compare the estimate to the exact answer (Carlow, 1986). *Once* children are comfortable with estimation, a guess-and-check procedure can be used to help hone estimation skills.

∞ **Have students define the range of reasonable estimates (the maximum and minimum answers that make sense).** This can underscore that what is important is the reasonableness of estimates, not determining exact answers.

∞ **Accept a range of estimates.** This further underscores that estimation involves gauging a reasonable answer rather than determining a particular answer.

🍎 Activity File 7.3: *Closer To*†

◆ Informal introduction to rounding ◆ 1-3* ◆ Two or more children or several small teams of children

Closer To introduces rounding in the familiar context of comparing numbers. Playing the game naturally raises the question, "What should be done about rounding with five?" This activity can lead children to induce the rules for rounding two-digit numbers to the nearest decade, three-digit numbers to the nearest hundred, three-digit numbers to the nearest decade, and so forth.

The game can be played noncompetitively, students can compete against their own record, or individuals or teams can compete against each other. On a chalkboard, draw a large triangle and, to its right, a large square. Have each student do the same on a piece of paper. For the *Two-Digit Version*, which requires rounding a two-digit number to the nearest ten, have them put the smaller of two consecutive decades (e.g., 40) in the triangle and the larger (e.g., 50) in the square. In the *Basic Three-Digit Version*, which requires rounding three-digit numbers to the nearest hundred, the smaller of two consecutive hundreds (e.g., 400) goes in the triangle and the larger (e.g., 500) goes in the square. In the *Advanced Three-Digit Version*, which requires rounding a three-digit number to the nearest decade, a number such as 450 can be placed in the triangle and the number with next larger decade (460) would go in the square.

Announce, for example, "Is 42 closer to 40 or 50?" (*Two-Digit Version*), Is 452 closer to 400 or 500?" (*Basic Three-Digit Version*), or "Is 452 closer to 450 or 460?" (*Advanced Three-Digit Version*). The child would then record the announced number under the triangle or the square. After all announced numbers are recorded in this fashion, answers could be discussed and checked. How much time is given to record an answer depends on the goals of the lesson and the sophistication of the students.

An *alternative* way to play the *Advanced Three-Digit Version* is to place the smaller of two successive hundreds (e.g., 400) in the triangle and the larger in the square (e.g., 500).

Students would then write the announced number above a hash mark representing the nearest ten. For example, 452 would be written under the middle hash mark because it closer to 450 than to 460 (see the figure below). The game can be extended to four-digit numbers and beyond.

The following vignette illustrates how the game can encourage children to use their knowledge of counting to devise rounding rules for themselves. Playing the *Basic Three-Digit Version* (triangle = 400, square = 500), 9-year-old Arianne listed 441 under the triangle. Asked to justify her answer, the girl pointed to the hundreds digit and said, "Because of the four."

To help Arianne consider the validity of her rule, her teacher next presented 499. Recognizing that the number was closer to 500 and that simply focusing on the hundreds digit was not correct, the girl noted, "No that won't work. So it's the end one."

To encourage Arianne to reflect on her revised rule (If the ones digit is 6, 7, 8, or 9 round up, otherwise round down), her teacher followed up with 491. "Oh you're trying to trick me,"she commented. "It's not the last one, it's the middle one [that matters]."

Her teacher then presented 450, to which Arianne noted, "That's in the middle. Next her teacher tried 452 to which Arianne again applied her "middle-number" rule and announced, "Middle."

To help Arianne refine her rules, her teacher introduced simpler cases. The girl quickly recognized that 50 was in the middle of 0 and 100 but that 51 was closer to 100. Arianne then decided 452 had to be closer to 500. She then spontaneously checked where she had placed her previous answers and noted that 441 did belong under the triangle because it was less than 450.

---

† Based on an activity described in *Elementary School Mathematic:s Teaching Developmentally* (2nd ed) by J. Van de Walle, © 1994 by Longman, New York.

* Depends on readiness. First graders might play with two or more digits, third graders, with four or more digits.

☞ **Encourage students to focus on whether or not an estimate is reasonable.** Particularly, at first, avoid feedback that undermines a disposition to estimate. Rather than asking which estimate is closest to the correct answer, ask, for example, "Does the strategy yield sensible estimates?" "Are the estimates accurate enough to accomplish our intended aim?"

Early and Broad Emphasis. Estimation of all kinds should be an integral part of instruction throughout the elementary curriculum.

☞ **Estimation instruction should begin in kindergarten and continue throughout the elementary grades.** This can help students (a) understand that only some situations require finding the exact answer while others involve making educated guesses, and (b) remain flexible.

☞ **Estimation instruction should include number, measurement, and single-digit computational estimation as well as multidigit computational estimation.** A key component of number sense is the ability to estimate accurately the size of collections (see Subunit 7•2•2), the size of various measurements (see chapter 15), and the answers of single-digit and multidigit computations (see Subunit 7•2•3).

7•2•2 NUMBER ESTIMATION

In this subunit, we touch briefly on the development of children's ability to gauge the size of collections and how to promote this ability.

Learning: Children's Development

Children initially rely on direct perception and only gradually construct a mental framework for estimating the size of collections.

Direct Perception. Most children entering school can quickly and accurately recognize small collections of up to four items. Typically, they can readily see, for instance, that ●●●● is "four" without even counting. However, this direct perception of number is quite limited. Even adults have difficulty specifying the exact number of haphazardly arranged collections larger than five.

Numerical Benchmarks. To gauge the size of larger collections accurately, children need to use a numerical benchmark—a known amount. To estimate the size of a collection of 14 blocks, for instance, a child might use a numerical benchmark of about the same size, such as 10. By comparing the appearance of the unknown collection to that of the known quantity, the child could conclude that the unknown collection was more than 10. A child could also compare a small numerical benchmark such as five to this unknown collection and conclude that it consisted of about three groups of the known amount or about 15.

Teaching

Two instructional implications follow.

☞ **Encourage children to discuss their informal numerical *benchmark* strategies for estimating the size of collections.** Particularly when presented with regular arrays such as those shown in Figures A and B below, even some young children will decompose them into small, easily recognized collections. A child might see that the collection illustrated in Figure B, for example, can be split into two groups of four and therefore, quickly recognize that there are four plus four or eight items in the set. This informal decomposition strategy can provide the basis for using a benchmark to estimate larger quantities (see, e.g., Figure C below). Box 7.2 (on the next page) illustrates a more complex estimation task that involves the same principle.

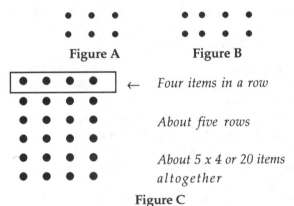

Figure A   Figure B

← *Four items in a row*

About five rows

About 5 x 4 or 20 items altogether

Figure C

☞ **Help children construct *mental* numerical benchmarks.** Children need to remember what key benchmarks such as 5, 10, 20, and 100 look like. Shown six rows of four items each, a child might estimate about 5 rows of four each is about 20 altogether.

7•2•3 COMPUTATIONAL ESTIMATION

Two teaching tips are summarized below.

Box 7.2: Numerical Benchmark Problems

Problem 1. Show students a jar full of marbles and pose the following problem:

■ **Many Marbles** (◆ 2-6). Jimi saw a glass canning jar full of marbles at a garage sale. To see if the price was fair he asked the seller how many marbles were in the jar. The seller indicated that she had no idea because the marbles belonged to her sons. Jimi thought about counting the marbles. He decided, however, that would take a lot of time. Besides the lady looked fussy and probably wouldn't let him anyway for fear of spilling or losing some of the marbles. *How could Jimi estimate the number of marbles in the jar?*

Encourage children to discuss their estimation strategies. One relatively effective strategy would be to use a numerical benchmark: (1) Examine the bottom view of the jar, and count the bottom layer of marbles (e.g., about 15 marbles for a pint-sized canning jar). (2) Examine the side view of the jar, and estimate the numbers of layers of marbles (e.g., about 9 layers for a pint-sized jar). (3) Using repeated addition or multi-

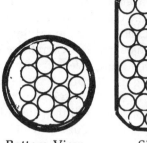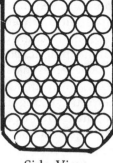

Bottom View   Side View

plication, estimate the number of marbles in the jar (e.g., 9 x 15 or 135 for a pint-sized jar).

Problem 2. As part of a school beautification project, say, take children to a large rectangular or circular garden plot. Ask them, for example, how many tulip bulbs would be needed if the bulbs had to be planted at least 2 inches apart. Again, a relatively effective strategy would be to divide the garden plot into equal size subsections (e.g., square subsections for a rectangular plot or a 30° wedge for a circular plot), determine the number of bulbs needed for a subsection, and multiply this number by the number of subsections.

☞ **After children understand an operation and can model it concretely, mental arithmetic should *begin* with estimating answers.** Cultivating a number sense in this way can facilitate self-monitoring (self-checking) and mastery of basic number combinations later.

☞ **Encourage children to consider a variety of estimation strategies.** Promote such strategies as

a *front-end strategy* (working with just the digits that have the biggest impact—e.g., for 456 + 243 + 175 + 63 + 4, adding only the hundreds-place digits [4 + 2 + 1] for an estimate of *at least seven hundred*), using *compatible numbers* (e.g., 93 - 47 could be changed 95 - 45, which is relatively easy to do mentally), and an *averaging strategy* (e.g., 42 + 39 + 37 + 44 could thought of as roughly 40 + 40 + 40 + 40)—as well as rounding.

7•3 MENTAL CALCULATION

Figure 7.3: A Lack of a Cognitive Compass (Number Sense) Makes Mental Calculation Difficult

PEANUTS reprinted by permission of UFS, Inc.

Mental facility with multidigit arithmetic is important even in the age of calculators. It is an important application of number sense (see Figure 7.3) and a key cornerstone for estimation. Mental arithmetic has many everyday applications and can even be more efficient than using a calculator. In this unit, we explore mental calculation strategies (Subunit 7•3•1), the development of such strategies (Subunit 7•3•2), and how instruction can facilitate flexible and efficient mental calculation (Subunit 7•3•3).

7•3•1 MATHEMATICS: THE NATURE OF SKILLED MENTAL CALCULATION

In this subunit, we explore how skilled calculators perform mental calculation, the relative advantages of different mental-calculation strategies, and the importance of flexibility and inventiveness in skilled mental calculation.

☞ Consider Probe 7.2 (page 7-25).

Characteristics of Skilled Mental Calculators

Most people are amazed by individuals who can effortlessly calculate the answer to multidigit expressions such as 24 x 12 in their head. *How do skilled mental calculators perform such feats? What do they do differently from unskilled mental calculators?*

One study found the following four differences between skilled and unskilled mental calculators (Hope & Sherrill, 1987):

1. Skilled students often worked from left to right, whereas unskilled students frequently used the standard right-to-left algorithm (also see Madell, 1985).

2. Skilled students typically used strategies that avoided renaming, whereas unskilled students don't.

3. Skilled students exploited knowledge about the structure of numbers and kept a running total. For instance, 645 + 123 might be solved by adding 600 and 100, then adding the sum of 40 + 20 to the running total of 700, and finally adding the sum of 5 and 3 to the running total of 760. Unskilled students tended to add isolated digits

without considering place value or other numerical relationships. For 645 + 123, for example, they mechanically combined the ones digit (5 + 3), the tens digit (4 + 2), and the hundreds digit (6 + 1).

4. Skilled students flexibly used a variety of strategies, whereas unskilled students inflexibly applied the standard right-to-left algorithm to all situations.

Skilled mental calculators recognize that there are many different ways to perform a computation. They flexibly choose, or even invent, a strategy that fits the demands of a task. They constantly look for ways to short-cut computational effort. Such flexibility requires understanding and a well developed number sense.

The Advantages of Left-to-Right Strategies

Why do skilled mental calculators tend to choose a left-to-right strategy over the standard right-to-left algorithm? Going from left to right often makes mental calculation easier to do.

7•3•2 LEARNING: UNDERSTANDING CHILDREN'S MULTIDIGIT MENTAL COMPUTING

In this subunit, we consider how children informally do mental computations, what the development of mental-computation proficiency entails, and common difficulties with developing such proficiency.

Children's Informal Strategies

Initially, children may perform multidigit calculations by applying the informal strategies they invented to do single-digit arithmetic. To mentally add 40 + 10, for instance, many first count-on ten from 40: "40; 41 [is one more], 42 [is two more] . . . 49 [is nine more], 50 [is ten more]—so the answer is *fifty*."

Given the opportunity, children can and do invent increasingly efficient mental-arithmetic procedures (see, e.g., Cobb & Wheatley, 1988; Kamii, 1989). They can even invent procedures for mentally handling renaming situations such as 29 + 12 (e.g., Kamii, 1989). Moreover, studies all over the world show that, outside of school, children tend to use their (continued on page 7-26)

➤ Probe 7.2: Strategies for Calculating the Sums and Differences of Multidigit Expressions

What makes some people highly proficient in mentally calculating sums and differences? This probe explores this question so that you can better help your students become proficient mental calculators and, perhaps, extend your own proficiency. Complete each question below and then discuss your answers with your group or class.

1. Mentally calculate the answer to the word problem below. Analyze your strategy and compare it with how others in your group or class determined the sum.

   ■ **Hardware Cost (◆ 2-8).** Gwen spent $157 on tools and $286 on hardware supplies. How much did she spend altogether?

2. The chart below summarizes three mental-addition strategies. Analyze the decomposition strategy and compare it to the standard right-to-left procedure.

   a. What advantage would this strategy have over using the standard (right-to-left) renaming algorithm that is used for written arithmetic?

   b. How would left-to-right strategy be used to compute the sum of 157 + 286 or the difference of 234 - 178? What happens to the difficulty of the left-to-right strategy when renaming is introduced?

A Comparison of Three Mental-Addition Strategies

Standard (Right-to-Left) Renaming Algorithm	Left-Right Decomposition Strategy	Partial-Decomposition Strategy
$\begin{array}{r} 1 \\ 46 \\ +38 \\ \hline 84 \end{array}$	$\begin{array}{l} 46 \rightarrow\ 40+\ 6 \rightarrow \\ +38 \rightarrow\ 30+\ 8 \rightarrow \\ 84\quad 70+14 \rightarrow 84 \end{array}$	$\begin{array}{l} 46 \rightarrow\ 46 \\ +38 \rightarrow\ 30+8 \\ 76+8=84 \end{array}$
Step 1: Add the ones digit (6 + 8 = 14).	Step 1: Decompose the addends and add the digits in the tens place—40 + 30 is 70	Step 1: Decompose one addend only and add its decade to the other addend—38 = 30 + 8 and 46 + 30 is 76
Step 2: Mentally note 4 and "carry" 1 to the tens place.	Step 2: Add the digits in the ones place—6 + 8 is 14.	Step 2: Add the units value of the second addend to this partial sum—76 + 8—and state the sum: *eighty four.*
Step 3: Add the tens digits 1, 4, and 3 and mentally note the sum 8.	Step 3: Mentally note the 4 and readjust the partial sum of the tens place—70 + 10 is 80	
Step 4: State by naming the partial products in the reverse order computed—*eighty-four.*	Step 4: State the sum *eighty-four.*	

---

3. Analyze the partial-decomposition strategy and compare it to the decomposition strategy.

   a. How would such a strategy be used to determine the answers of 157 + 286 and 234 - 178?

   b. How is the strategy easier or more difficult than a left-to-right decomposition strategy?

4. (a) How would you determine a 15% tip for a $32 dinner? (b) Was this strategy self-invented or learned in school? (c) How did most people in your group or class determine the tip?

own invented mental-computation strategies rather than school-taught algorithms (e.g., Carraher, Carraher, & Schliemann, 1987; Ginsburg, Posner, & Russell, 1981; Plunkett, 1979; Saxe, 1988). Like skilled calculators, children's informal strategies for mental addition, subtraction, and multiplication frequently involve operating from *left to right*. Below are typical examples of mental-computation strategies children invent when encouraged to do so (Kamii, 1990b, p. 1):

$$
\begin{array}{ll}
\begin{array}{r} 16 \\ + \underline{17} \end{array} &
\begin{array}{l}
10 + 10 = 20 \\
6 + 7 = 13 \rightarrow 10 + 3 \\
20 + 10 = 30 \\
30 + 3 = 33
\end{array} \\[2em]
\begin{array}{r} 13 \\ \underline{\times 4} \end{array} &
\begin{array}{l}
4 \times 10 = 40 \\
4 \times 3 = 12 \\
40 + 12 = 52
\end{array} \\[2em]
\begin{array}{r} 43 \\ \underline{-15} \end{array} &
\begin{array}{l}
40 - 10 = 30 \\
3 - 5 = 2 \text{ below } 0 \\
30 - 2 = 28
\end{array} \\[2em]
22\overline{)275} &
\begin{array}{l}
22 + 22 + 22... \\
\text{until the total comes close to 275,} \\
\text{or } 10 \times 22 = 220 \text{ and then proceed} \\
\text{by adding successive 22s.}
\end{array}
\end{array}
$$

The Development of Mental-Computation Proficiency

The development of multidigit mental-computation proficiency depends on a well-developed number sense. Like learning the basic number combinations, it entails discovering (a) relationships with existing knowledge and (b) new patterns. Such discoveries depend heavily on understanding grouping and place-value concepts. Consider multidigit mental addition.

Connections with Counting Knowledge. Counting knowledge is a key basis for constructing multidigit addition strategies. For instance, children can learn to add a decade and 10 (e.g., 40 + 10) *automatically* by exploiting their existing decade-after knowledge (Resnick, 1983). Those accustomed to grouping by tens and counting such groups can readily count by tens ("ten, twenty, thirty . . . ") and cite the decade after another (e.g., the decade after *forty* is *fifty*). Once children recognize the link between their extant decade-after knowledge and adding ten (namely, that each successive decade is 10 more than the previous decade), they can formulate the *decade-after rule*: The sum of a decade and 10 is the next decade (e.g., for 40 + 10, state the decade after forty—*fifty*).

Connections with Basic Arithmetic Knowledge. Children can also use their existing knowledge of the basic arithmetic facts to do multidigit mental computations. There are numerous parallels between single-digit arithmetic and multidigit arithmetic. Once discovered, these relationships can greatly increase the efficiency of multidigit mental arithmetic. For example, 40 + 40 and 400 + 400 both parallel 4 + 4 = 8, and 70 + 50 and 700 + 500 both parallel 7 + 5 = 12. Note that the child who thinks of multidigit numbers in terms of ones, groups of ten, groups of a hundred, and so forth are more likely to recognize this parallel. For example, thinking of 40 + 40 as *4 tens plus 4 tens*, increases a child chance of recognizing the parallel with 4 + 4 = 8.

Discovery of Patterns Involving 10 and Powers of 10. Furthermore, skilled calculators discover new multidigit number patterns. One example is the "teen" rule for adding a number to 10—10 + n (or n + 10) is n + *teen* (e.g., 10 + 7 = *seven + teen*). This eliminates the need to, say, count on (e.g., 10 + 7: "10; 11, 12, 13, 14, 15, 16, 17") or apply the standard right-to-left algorithm (e.g., 10 + 7: Zero and seven is seven and one [ten] makes seventeen"). Note that children who view 10 as a group of ten and no ones are more likely to recognize this useful shortcut. A similar shortcut is useful for adding a single-digit number to other decades, hundreds, and so forth (e.g., 40 + 7, 400 + 7), or for adding two-digit number to hundreds, thousands, and so forth (e.g., 100 + 77, 1000 + 77), and so on.

Difficulties

Because they have difficulty with mental computation, many children avoid it. Two main causes of difficulty are (a) an early focus on standard written algorithms and (b) inadequate opportunity to develop a number sense.

Early Focus on Written Algorithms. Children required to memorize the standard right-left algorithm early, often have great difficulty recognizing that other computational approaches are possible or, in some cases, even more desirable. Rather than intuitively thinking how they can use what they know to determine, for example, the sum of 5900 + 1000, 490 + 10, or even 799 + 1, they blindly use the paper-and-pencil algorithm. When encouraged to do such computations mentally, they mechanically rely on the relatively inefficient standard (right-to-left renaming) algorithm. *Why does imposing the standard algorithm on young children undermine their natural disposition to use informal strategies?* Three reasons are outlined below.

1. The standard algorithms operate in the opposite direction of informal strategies.

2. The standard algorithm encourages children to work with isolated digits rather than think in terms of numbers.

3. Use of the standard algorithm—particularly when learned by rote—encourages mechanical calculation rather than reflection.

Inadequate Opportunity to Develop Number Sense. Some children are prevented from inventing informal mental calculation strategies because their knowledge of counting, basic arithmetic facts, grouping, or place-value is incomplete. Many others have such knowledge but do not realize that it can be used to do mental addition. Moreover, many children do not take advantage of the repetitive nature of our number system. As a result of such knowledge gaps, children must resort to less efficient methods of mental calculation such as counting-on or using the standard algorithm.

7•3•3 TEACHING

Instruction should encourage the exploration of mental-computation strategies and foster mental-computation proficiency. Some general guidelines are outlined below.

☞ Consider Probe 7.3 (page 7-28).

∞ **Encourage children's informal mental-calculation strategies *before* instruction on the standard right-to-left algorithm.** This can foster the reflective thinking and flexibility needed for everyday mental-calculation tasks.

∞ **Promote informal left-to-right strategies.** Although the right-to-left algorithm is efficient for performing written calculations, left-to-right strategies are more efficient for performing mental arithmetic. Playing the game *Advanced Grid Race* (Activity File 7.4 on page 7-28) can help children discover and practice the partial-decomposition strategy. In time, players should

recognize that if, for example, their marker is on square 43 and they have to move 25 spaces, they can simply move up two rows to 63 (parallels adding 43 + 20) and then count to the right 5 spaces (parallels adding 63 + 5).

∞ **Prompt children to consider a variety of strategies and shortcuts for mental computation.** Help them to understand that there is not just one correct way of mentally computing sums, differences, products, or quotients. Encourage them to examine different strategies and compare their relative advantages (see, e.g., Probe 7.2 on page 7-25).

∞ **Help children master multidigit combinations by (a) encouraging them to discover the connections between these combinations and their existing counting and arithmetic knowledge and (b) inviting them to discover patterns involving powers of 10.** For example, help children see that a decade plus ten can be determined by using their existing decade-after knowledge (e.g., 70 + 10 is the decade after seventy: *eighty*) and that 40 + 40 can be thought of as 4 tens + 4 tens, which can be solved by recalling the basic number combination 4 + 4. Help them also to discover such patterns as the *teen rule*: $10 + n$ (where n is a single-digit number) = n + teen (e.g., $10 + 7 \rightarrow$ seven + teen).

∞ **Create a real need for mental calculation.** Ideally, the invention, discussion, and practice of informal strategies and shortcuts would flow out of real projects or activities. Likewise, the practice of multidigit combinations should be purposeful. Games such as *Grid Race* (Activity File 7.4) can help children master combinations such as 40 + 10 = 50 in a purposeful and entertaining way.

PARTING THOUGHTS

"Children must understand numbers if they are to make sense of the ways numbers are used in their everyday world" (NCTM, 1989, p. 38). "Number sense is something that 'unfolds' rather than something that is 'taught' directly" (Trafton, 1989, p. 75). "The individual facets of number sense [an intuitive understanding of number, estimation, and mental computation] are intricately connected and rely upon a strong conceptual development" (Van de Walle & Watkins, 1993, p. 46). "No substitute exists for a skillful teacher and an environment that fosters curiosity and exploration at all (continued on page 7-29)

➤ Probe 7.3: Analyzing a Game Involving Mental Computation

Probe 7.2 (on page 7-25) described a partial-decomposition strategy. The game described in Activity File 7.4 below (*Grid Race*) can serve as the basis for discovering, discussing, or practicing this strategy. It can also help children discover patterns for multidigit addition and subtraction. Read through the following description of the various versions of *Grid Race*. Play *Basic Grid Race* with your group or a friend. Reflect on what children might learn while playing the game. Then try answering the following questions:

1. By including a disproportionate number of 10s in the deck used for *Basic Grid Race*, a teacher can ensure ample practice in adding 10 to single- and multidigit numbers. How do you suppose a child initially (informally) determines where to move after drawing a 10 if her marker was already on space 7? On space 36?

2. What rules for adding with 10 might children discover by repeatedly playing this game and using an informal strategy?

3. Using 34 + 25 as an example, consider how the game board below could be used to model the partial-decomposition strategy. How might children discover this strategy by playing *Advanced Grid Race*?

🍎 Activity File 7.4: *Grid Race*

◆ Mental addition and subtraction ◆ Grade 1 and up ◆ Small groups of two to six

Materials needed are a game board (shown to the right), deck of cards, spinner or die, and $\frac{3}{8}$ x $\frac{3}{8}$ x $\frac{3}{8}$-inch colored cubes or other position markers.

90	91	92	93	94	95	96	97	98	99
80	81	82	83	84	85	86	87	88	89
70	71	72	73	74	75	76	77	78	79
60	61	62	63	64	65	66	67	68	69
50	51	52	53	54	55	56	57	58	59
40	41	42	43	44	45	46	47	48	49
30	31	32	33	34	35	36	37	38	39
20	21	22	23	24	25	26	27	28	29
10	11	12	13	14	15	16	17	18	19
0	1	2	3	4	5	6	7	8	9

To start *Basic Grid Race*, players place their marker at 0. On their turn, they draw a card from a deck, spin a spinner, or roll a die and move the number of spaces indicated. (For beginners, a die can include, for example, +1, +2, +3, +5, and two +10s.) The object of the game is to be the first to get to the end—the 99 square. A player need not get the exact amount on her last turn to finish. For example, a player on square 96 could roll a 3 or more to finish. All players finishing on a given turn are winners. *Advanced Grid Race* is played like *Basic Grid Race* except that cards or a spinner include only multidigit numbers, such as +15, +17, +20, +28, and +32, and the winner is the first player to reach 99 and then return to 0.

Basic Backward Grid Race is played like *Basic Grid Race* except that players start at the 99 square and *subtract* the value indicated by a drawn card, spinned number, or die roll.

Advanced Backward Grid Race is played like *Basic Backward Grid Race* except that cards or a spinner include only multidigit numbers and players must go to 0 and return to 99 to win.

grade levels" (Howden, 1989, p. 11). To foster number sense, students should regularly be encouraged to share their ideas and invent their own strategies from the earliest grades on.

RESOURCES

SOME INSTRUCTIONAL RESOURCES

☞ **Learning from Children: New Beginnings for Teaching Numerical Thinking** by Ed Labinowicz, © 1985 by Addison-Wesley, and **Mathematics for the Young Child** edited by Joseph N. Payne, © 1990 by NCTM. These two resources describe how counting activities can be used to help children learn number relationships. In *Mathematics for the Young Child*, see, in particular, the chapter titled *Concepts of Number* (pages 63-87) by John A. Van de Walle.

☞ **Double-Column Addition: A Teacher Uses Piaget's Theory**, © 1989 (20-minute videotape), **Multiplication of 2-Digit Numbers: Two Teachers Using Piaget's Theory**, © 1990 (22-minute videotape), and **Multidigit Division: Two Teachers Using Piaget's Theory**, © 1990 (19-minute videotape), distributed by Teachers College Press, P.O. Box 2032, Colchester, VT 05449 (800-445-6638). These three videotapes by Constance Kamii illustrate a student-centered approach to teaching multidigit arithmetic and a variety of informal strategies for doing mental computation.

☞ **Developing Number Sense** by Barbara J. Reys, Rita Barger, Maxim Bruckheimer, Barbara Dougherty, Jack Hope, Linda Lembke, Zvia Markovits, Andy Parnac, Sue Reehm, Ruthi Sturdevant and Marianne Weber; © 1991 by NCTM. This valuable resource is part of the *Curriculum and Evaluation Standards for School Mathematics Addenda Series for Grades 5-8*. In addition to outlining general guidelines for encouraging number sense, it includes 43 activities. A number of these activities explore the size of large numbers and the effects of whole-number arithmetic. Other activities do the same with fractions and decimals. A number of activities involve estimating and assessing the reasonableness of answers. Activity 8 of this resource encourages children to relate a million to a comprehensible context (numerical benchmark)—to a pile of one thousand (fake) $1 bills. Students

are encouraged to consider whether $1,000,000 dollars would fit in a standard suitcase. How large would a container have to be to hold a million $1 bills? How heavy would a million $1 bills be? What smallest denomination of bills would be required so that a million dollars would fit in a standard suitcase? Activity File 7.5 (on the next page) is based on Activity 13 in this resource.

☞ **Estimation and Mental Computation** (1986 NCTM Yearbook) edited by H. L. Schoen and M. J. Zweng, © 1986 by the NCTM. This is an excellent source of teaching ideas for estimation.

☞ **Number Sense and Operations: Addenda Series, Grades K-6** by Grace M. Burton and others, © 1993, NCTM. This resource includes a compilation of lessons and activities that can prompt explorations of numerical relationships and the effects of operations and that underscore various representations and real-world uses of numbers.

☞📼 **Number Sense Now** directed by Francis "Skip" Fennell, © 1993, NCTM. This set of three videotapes and guidebook outlines teaching strategies for fostering number sense.

☞ **Sideways Arithmetic from Wayside School** (© 1989) and **More Sideways Arithmetic from Wayside School** (© 1994) written by Louis Sachar and published by Scholastic, Inc. *More Sideways Arithmetic from Wayside School*, for instance, contains 50 math puzzles that—like Tasks I, II, and III of Investigation 7.3 on page 7-9 involve students in reasoning qualitatively about multidigit addition, subtraction, and multiplication.

☞ **Thinker Math: Developing Number Sense & Arithmetic Skills** (Volumes 1, 2, and 3) by Carole Greene, Linda Schulman and Rika Spungin, © 1989 by Creative Publications. *Fit-the-Facts* tasks (see Activity File 7.6 on page 7-30) are an interesting, informative, and challenging way to foster number sense. Such a task consists of a short story in which the numerical information has been replaced by a blank. In the basic version, students must fill in the blanks by choosing from a list of numbers so that story makes sense both mathematically *and* contextually. In the

🍎 Activity File 7.5: Comparing Numerical Expressions

◆ Operation sense ◆ 1-8 ◆ Any number

This activity involves qualitative reasoning and can prompt discussion about the effects of arithmetic operations. (Note that this activity can also be used with fractions and decimals to foster an operation sense with rational numbers.) Without calculating, students must compare each side of an expression and gauge whether the <, =, or > sign belongs in the box. Encourage student to justify their answers.

The activity can be used as the basis of a whole-class discussion or as a competitive game involving individuals or groups of students. In

the latter case, give contestants or groups a limited amount of time to record their answer on a piece of paper or a small slate board. After time has run out, the contestants or groups simultaneously display their answers. After a discussion determines the most reasonable answer, each group with that answer is awarded 1 point.

The expressions below are appropriate for fourth graders. Simpler expressions could be substituted for younger primary-level children and more complex expressions could be substituted for intermediate-level students.

1. 504 + 689 + 732 ☐ 732 + 689 + 508

2. 53 + 54 + 55 ☐ 3 x 54

3. 16 x 127 ☐ 15 x 182

4. 364 ÷ 9 ☐ 372 ÷ 8

5. 24 x 10 x 8 ☐ 24 x 10 x 4 x 2

6. 542 - 87 - 43 ☐ 542 - 43 - 87

🍎 Activity File 7.6: Fit the Facts

◆ Using context to determine reasonable values + computational practice + connections
◆ K-8 ◆ Any number

Use the numbers listed in the right to complete the following story. A number may be used just once.

In (A) ____ at the age of (B) ____ , Millard Fillmore was elected Vice President of the United States. The day after President Zachary Taylor died in July (C) _____ he became the (D) _____ th president. Although considered one of the less important presidents, he did send Commodore Perry to Japan in (E) _____ to open trade with this country. (F) _____ years later, he died in Buffalo at the age of (G) _____.

1853

1850

1848

74

48

21

13

advanced (open-ended) version, students must fill in the blanks using their own educated guesses. Note that *Fit-the-Facts* tasks can illustrate different meanings of number (e.g., *the* implies an ordinal use) and encourage the considerations of number relationships (e.g., that 1850 comes after 1848 and, thus, represents a later date). Note also that such tasks could be designed to practice basic arithmetic skills in a purposeful manner. Note further that the *Fit-the-Facts* tasks involve other content areas (e.g., reading

comprehension and Social Studies in the case of Activity File 7.6).

Thinker Math includes numerous examples in the same format shown in Activity File 7.6. Teachers, of course, can make up their own Fit-the-Facts tasks to suit their own instructional needs in mathematics or other content areas. (Take care to carefully check such self-made tasks.) For example, the following science-based segment entails recognizing the appropriateness of different types of numbers.

The atomic number of oxygen is (A)_8_.

Its atomic mass is (B)___15.999_ and

its major oxidation state is (C)_2-_

The atomic number identifies an elements position in the periodic table. For example, oxygen is the eighth most complex element. Thus, a natural number such as 8 is suitable for blank A. The atomic mass specifies the mass of an atom—a measurement of a continuous quantity. Hence, a decimal is appropriate. The oxidation state indicates the number of electrons an element must gain or lose to achieve a chemically stable state. Thus, an integer is needed to indicate how many electrons are required and the direction of change (their gain or loss). For example, oxygen must gain two negatively-charged electrons (+ [-2] or -2) to achieve chemical stability and, hence, its oxidation state is indicated by the integer 2-. Calcium, on the other hand, must give up two negatively-charged electrons (-[-2] or +2) to achieve stability and, thus, its oxidation state is indicated by the integer 2+.

A SAMPLE OF CHILDREN'S LITERATURE

Number Sense

☚ Stories that involve big numbers include *The Doughnuts* from **Homer Price** by Robert McCloskey (© 1943, Viking), **The 500 Hats of Bartholomew Cubbins** by Dr. Seuss (© 1938, Vanguard), **A Million Fish . . . More or Less** by Dena Schutzer (© 1992, Alfred A. Knopf), **Millions of Cats** by Wanda Gág (© 1928, Coward, McCann, and Geoghegan), **The Millionth Egg** by Bernice Myers (© 1991, Lothrop, Lee, & Shepard), and **O n e Watermelon Seed** by Celia B. Lottridge (© 1986, Oxford). Reading such stories can prompt wonderment, discussion, and reflection about big numbers as well as be fun.

☚ Books that explain large numbers include two books both titled **How Much Is a Million?**—one by Steven Kellog (© 1985, Scholastic) and the other by David Schwartz (© 1985, Lothrop, Lee, and Shepard). Whitin and Wilde (1992) noted that the latter version "is probably the best single introduction to big numbers and to developing an intuitive sense

of their magnitude" (p. 130). A companion book by Schwartz is **If You Made a Million** (© 1989).

☚ One way of producing big numbers is repeatedly multiplying a number (powers). Books about doubling include **Binary Numbers** by Clyde Watson (© 1977, Crowell), **Melisande** by Edith Nesbit (© 1989, Harcourt Brace Jovanovich), and **Mirror Mirror** by Rosemary and Calvin Irons (© 1987, Rigby Education). Other books that involve this special kind of geometric progression include **A Grain of Rice** by Helena Pittman (© 1986, Hastings House) and **The King's Chessboard** by David Birch (© 1988, Dial). Box 7.3 illustrates how an extended science-math unit on population (exponential) growth can build on children's literature.

☚ 📖 Box 7.3: An Extended Unit on Population Growth

The day after Mrs. Perez introduced the *Alternative Payment Plans* problem (see page 1-29 of Probe 1.4), she read **Germs Make Me Sick!** by Melvin Berger (© 1985, Crowell). As a follow-up activity, Mrs. Perez had the class diagram the population growth of a bacteria (•, ••, ••••, and so forth) (Whitin & Wilde, 1992). To reinforce the concept of exponential population growth, the teacher read **The Habits of Rabbits** by Virginia Kahl (© 1957, Scribner, Troll Assoc., 1986).

On a subsequent day, Mrs. Perez asked her class, "How many people do you think live on our planet earth?" After students offered various estimates, the class considered how they could find information about the world population. A search of the world wide web turned up a website titled, "World Population" (http://sunsite.unc.edu/lunarbin/worldpop). Mrs. Perez suggested recording the population and date and posting this information on a class "Population Growth" bulletin board. Then, on a monthly basis, students checked the web site to update their information and track the world's population growth. To summarize this information, one group of students devised a graph. Another group calculated the monthly increases in population. This led to a class discussion of percentages and calculating the percentage of monthly increase.

Estimation

🕮 **Estimation** by Charles F. Linn (© 1970, Thomas Y. Crowell) illustrates real-world examples of when estimation is useful. **The Jelly Bean Contest** by Kathy Darling (© 1972, Garrard) and **The Dinosaur Who Lived in My Backyard** by B. G. Hennessy (© 1988, Viking Kestrel) illustrate estimation strategies.

Some interesting books that can serve as the basis for estimation activities and instruction include the following:

🕮 **Counting on Frank** by Gareth Stevens, © 1991 by Children's Books. A dog named Frank and his young master investigate a variety of amusing situations that involve number or measurement estimation. For example, the duo explore how long it takes to fill the bathroom with water (volume and time estimation). Although written for primary-age children, intermediate-level students and adults will enjoy the zany examples and the challenge of estimating their own answers. By the way, how long do you think it would take to fill the nearest bathroom with water? How could you make an estimate without incurring water damage and the resulting expenses? Activity File 7.7 illustrates how another situation described in the book could provide the basis for an entertaining and educational activity.

🕮 **Count and See** by T. Hoban, © 1972 by Macmillan. This book illustrates collections of familiar things. The items pictured in the collection are large and distinct enough to be counted easily. The pictures can be used for estimation activities as well as oral-counting and enumeration practice. There are collections from 1 to 15 items, plus pictures of key benchmarks collections (20 watermelon seeds, 30 bottle caps, 40 peanuts,

---

🕮 🍎 **Activity File 7.7: A Pen Problem**

◆ Measurement estimation ◆ 1-8 ◆ Whole class or small groups

Read *Counting on Frank* to the class. In one situation, Frank and his master examine the question, *How long a line can a ball point pen make before running out of ink?* The book shows a line drawn over walls, furniture and a sleeping dad. Before finishing the story, pose the question above to the class. Encourage them to estimate the distances in inches, feet, yards, centimeters, meters or some combination of these units. Prompt justifications and discussion of the estimates.

Then taking care to underscore the point that writing on walls, furniture, and people is fine for fictional characters but not for responsible children, encourage the class to devise a plan for evaluating their estimates. Someone may suggest drawing the line on butcher paper stretched out down the hallway. Either through actual experimentation or discussion, students should recognize that the paper needed will extend far beyond a single hallway. Perhaps a student will suggest measuring the length of a piece of butcher paper and going back and forth. The length of the paper times the number of lengths drawn would give the total distance.

Sooner or later students recognize that using up all the ink will be a time-consuming matter. Note that if Pilot V ball pens or some other transparent pen is used, the students could measure the length of a full ink cartridge, divide the length into equal-sized parts, use up the ink in one part and then multiply the length of the drawn line by the number of equal parts. For example, if the cartridge was divided into fifths, the students would have to use up only one-fifth of the ink and multiply the length of the drawn line by five. In brief, an investigation of the original problem can lead to devising a numerical-benchmark strategy and using measurement skills in a purposeful manner. (By the way, Frank and his master found that their ball point pen could draw a line 2,300 yards long.)

↪ **Teaching Tip.** Note that instead of a pen, it might be more convenient to use a crayon. (How long a line can a *crayon* make before it is used up?) A regular-sized crayon should be used up more quickly than a pen. Moreover, a crayon makes it easy to use the numerical-benchmark strategy discussed above.

50 nails, and 100 dots). In addition to pictured collections, the text illustrates numbers with organized dot diagrams, which underscore grouping by ten (e.g., •••••••••• •• = 12).

📖 **In One Day** by Tom Parker, © 1984 by Houghton Mifflin Co. This book lists 365 statistics about one day in the life of Americans. The facts and illustrations (e.g., 10,000 and 100,000 are each represented on a page by dots) can provide benchmarks for estimation tasks. Many facts such as Fact 312 ("Americans need 115 million gallons of drinking water . . .") are accompanied by comparisons (". . . Imagine a tumbler of . . . water 500 feet fall and 200 feet in diameter"). By leaving out a piece of information, such comparisons can serve as challenging estimation problems:

■ **Problem 7.3: A Big Container** (◆ 7-8). If all 15 million gallons of water drunk by Americans in one day were put in a drinking glass 200 feet in diameter, about how high would the glass have to be?

◆ **Problem 7.4: Extension of a Big Container.** Note that an open-ended problem could be fashioned by omitting mention of the glass' diameter.

TIPS ON USING TECHNOLOGY

Calculators

Experimenting with calculators can be invaluable for fostering a number or an operation sense. Problem 7.5 (which is a take-off of Task III in Investigation 7.4 on page 7-11), its extension (Problem 7.6), *Calculator Sense* (Activity File 7.8), and *Pushing the Limits* (Activity File 7.9 on the next page) all encourage such playful exploration. Note that the last two activities can be used to explore very small numbers (decimals) as well as very large (whole) numbers.

■ **Problem 7.5: Six Digit** (◆ 2-6, depending on the operation). Use the digits 1 to 6 to form two three-digit numbers, which when added (subtracted, multiplied, or divided) make the largest possible sum (difference, product, or quotient). Each digit may be used only once.

🖩 🍎 **Activity File 7.8: Calculator Sense**

◆ Operation sense with very large and very small numbers + calculator familiarity
◆ 5-8 ◆ Any number

Encourage students to play around with calculators to determine the limits of their operation. Have them consider such questions as, What is the largest numbers that can be keyed into the calculator? How many digits does it have and what is its counting name? What happens when this number is (a) added to 2, (b) subtracted by 2, (c) multiplied by 2, or (d) divided by 2? Which of these calculations result in a curious or nonintuitive answer? Why? Which of these calculations result in an error statement? What is the smallest number that can be keyed into the calculator? How many digits after the decimal point does this number have? What is its counting name? What happens when this number is (a) added to 0.9, (b) subtracted by 0.9, (c) multiplied by 0.9, or (d) divided by 0.9? Which calculation results in a negative integer? Which calculation results in a curious or nonintuitive answer? Why? Which results in an error statement? How is this error statement different from the one observed earlier? What are the possible meanings of these two different error statements? Have students consider the following problem:

■ **What Makes 0.0000001?** Aside from keying the number in directly, how could a *Math Explorer* calculator be used to generate a display of 0.0000001? Limit your answers to a maximum of two terms (e.g., two factors are acceptable, three or more are not).

◆ **Problem 7.6: Extension of Six Digits.** Use the digits 0 to 5 to form two three-digit numbers, which when added (subtracted, multiplied, or divided) make the largest possible sum (difference, product, or quotient). Each digit may be used only once.

Computers

Like calculators, computers can provide numerous opportunities that would be difficult or impossible to explore without a swift calculating machine (see, e.g., Activity File 7.10 on the upper

▦ 🍎 Activity File 7.9: Pushing the Limits

◆ Operation sense with very large or very small numbers ◆ 5-8 ◆ Two to six players or teams

In this game, a judge presents such questions as, "If 900,000 is multiplied by 100 will a calculator be able to determine the product or not" (or will it *overflow*)? "If 10,000 is squared, will the calculator be able to determine the answer or overflow?" (A *Math Explorer*, for example, could calculate the answer to the first question [900,000 x 100 = 90,000,000] but not the second [$10,000^2$ = 100,000,000, which would register as an overflow error].) Note that this game would be useful for estimating the number of digits in an answer. Consider, for example, the following questions: Could a *Math Explorer* calculate the answers to the following:

(a) 50,342,672 + 38,975,111;

(b) 120,000,000 - 18,999,997;

(c) 10 x 10,120,135; and

(d) 180,644,330 ÷ 10?

Note that this game could also be played with decimals as well as whole numbers. For example, with a *Math Explorer*, could you calculate the answer to (a) 0.1 x 999,999,999 or (b) 18,977,843 ÷ 0.1, (c) 0.01 x 0.00006, (d) 0.0000001 ÷ 5.5?

After a question is posed by the game host, players (or teams) record whether an answer can be calculated or not. The players then check the calculation on the calculator. Each player (or team) that responded correctly is awarded a point.

🖥 🍎 Activity File 7.10: Counting to a Million[†]

◆ Sense of size for larger numbers
◆ 5-8 ◆ Small groups of two to six

For those with programming experience, encourage students to write a counting program. A program written in BASIC might look like:

```
10      X = X + 1
20      PRINT X
30      GOTO 10
```

Have the students watch the monitor as the program runs. After a minute, interrupt the program by keying in Control C. Encourage the students to estimate how many minutes it would take the computer to count a million, a billion, a trillion. (With Apple IIe, the program can count to 2,000 in 1 minute. It would take 500 minutes or more than 8 hours to reach one million. Note that, although the computer can count relatively quickly, it takes a relatively long time to print out the count.)

[†]Based on Activity 9 in *Developing Number Sense* (*Addenda Series Grades 5-8*) by Barbara J. Rey, © 1991 by the National Council of Teachers of Mathematics.

right-hand corner of this page). Students may want to check out the "Googalplex" web site at http://www.uni-frankfurt.de/~fp/Tools/Googoal.html. A sample of software follows.

🖥 **Counting on Frank: A Math Adventure Game** produced by Creative Wonders and distributed by Soft Ware House. Appropriate for grades 3 to 8; available on CD ROM disk (Mac requires 68040 or more of memory). In this take off of the book *Counting on Frank*, players gather clues to guess the number of jelly beans.

🖥 **Survival Math** designed by Walter Koetke and published by Sunburst. Appropriate for grades 6 to 8[+]; available on apple disks. Includes four simulations that require applying mathematics to everyday situations.

🖥 **What Do You Do with a Broken Calculator?** designed by Judah L. Schwartz and published by Sunburst. Appropriate for grades 4 to 8; available on Apple, DOS, or Macintosh formatted disks. The program underscores that—without using a calculator—an arithmetic expression such as 25 + 39 can be calculated in various ways.

🖥 **The Whatsit Corporation: Survival Math Skills** designed by The Waterford School District and distributed by Sunburst. In this business simulation, students must run a business, which includes estimating expenses and keeping records. Appropriate for students in grades 6 to 8[+] and available on disks formatted for Apple and IBM.

8 EXPLORING NUMBERS FURTHER: NUMBER THEORY AND INTEGERS & OPERATIONS ON INTEGERS

EVEN AND ODD

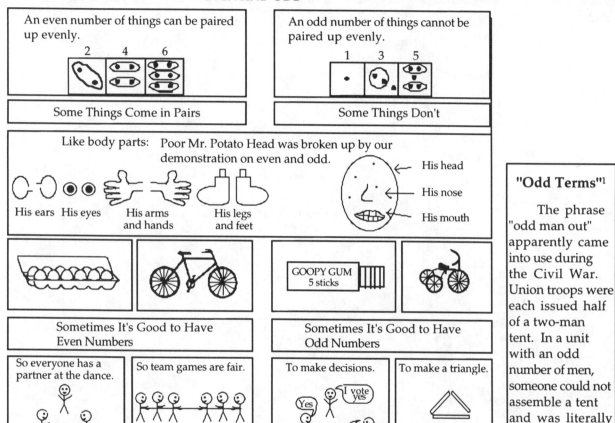

An even number of things can be paired up evenly.

2 4 6

Some Things Come in Pairs

An odd number of things cannot be paired up evenly.

1 3 5

Some Things Don't

Like body parts: Poor Mr. Potato Head was broken up by our demonstration on even and odd.

His ears His eyes His arms and hands His legs and feet

His head ←
His nose ←
His mouth ←

Sometimes It's Good to Have Even Numbers

GOOPY GUM 5 sticks

Sometimes It's Good to Have Odd Numbers

So everyone has a partner at the dance.

So team games are fair.

To make decisions.

Yes / I vote yes / I vote no

To make a triangle.

"Odd Terms"[1]

The phrase "odd man out" apparently came into use during the Civil War. Union troops were each issued half of a two-man tent. In a unit with an odd number of men, someone could not assemble a tent and was literally "left out in the cold."

The bulletin board above illustrates two number patterns that can interest young children—even and odd numbers. A teacher might illustrate each with a few examples and then challenge students to add their own examples. They might draw pictures of their examples or cut out pictures of them. The issue of even and odd numbers naturally leads to the issue of body symmetry and asymmetries. Some parts come in pairs and some don't. This can be illustrated concretely or pictorially with a Mr. Potato Head©, by making puppets, or with drawings of people or animals.[†] Reflecting on the meaning of phrases such as *odd man out* can deepen a child's understanding of odd and even and enrich their vocabulary. A bulletin board for older children can focus on other patterns such as numbers that form triangles. After collecting examples of "triangular numbers" (e.g., 3 dots, 6 acrobats in a human pyramid, 10 bowling pins, and 15 racked pool balls), students can try to extend the sequence and predict successive numbers in the series.

☞ Consider Probe 8.1 (pages 8-2 and 8-3). (Text continued on page 8-4.)

(Text continued on page 8-4.)

[†] Mr. Potato Head, a Playschool toy, is produced and copyrighted by Hasbro, Inc.

➤ Probe 8.1: The Real-Number Hierarchy

In the compartmentalized instruction of the skills approach, students learn about different types of numbers (counting numbers, whole numbers, integers, rational numbers, and real numbers) but not about how they are related. The aim of this probe is to help you explicitly reflect on the connections among these different types of numbers so that you can help your students do the same. (Students should enter high school with an explicit understanding of how various types of numbers listed above are related.) In particular, this probe can help students understand how counting (natural) numbers, which are the focus of number theory, and integers, which are also discussed in this chapter, are related to other categories of numbers. In effect, it provides a context for this chapter and subsequent chapters on rational numbers.

The tree diagram below summarizes the real-number hierarchy and illustrates how its various elements are related. After examining it, answer the questions that follow either on your own or, ideally, with the help of a group. Discuss your answers with your group or class.

Tree Diagram of the Real-Number Hierarchy

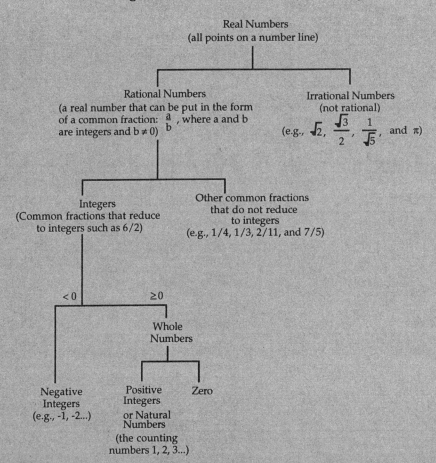

1. "Why can't rational numbers have 0 in the denominator?" asked Khalid. What do you think?

2. Nadia could see why $\frac{3}{5}$ or even $\frac{4}{3}$ were considered rational numbers but wondered about numbers such as 3 and 4. Can an integer such as 3 or 4 be considered a rational number?

   Why or why not?

3. a. Asked to identify which numbers on a test were rational numbers, Eugene excluded 0. He justified his answer by writing: *0 did not meet the definition of a rational number.* Does zero fit the definition of a rational number? Why or why not?

Probe 8.1 continued

b. Mr. Hinkle wanted to check whether his students understood the concept of rational numbers and so posed the following question: Does the number that can be named $\frac{3.5}{2}$ fit the definition of a rational number, an irrational number, and/or a real number? Why?

4. Circle any of the following that is a natural numbers:

    (a) -3 (b) 0 (c) 1 (d) 3 (e) 10 (f) 0.1

5. Draw a Venn diagram to depict the relationships shown in the tree diagram on page 8-2. Caution: A common error is to leave spaces within a ring that are undefined (see Figure A below). The area within the *Real Number* ring should be entirely taken up by the area within the rings for *Rational* and *Irrational* Numbers. Why? Figure B illustrates a common solution to this error. (Note that a Venn diagram does not necessarily have to be composed of circles). Although Figure B is fine, there is another method that would allow you to use just two circles. Can you see how?

Figure A   **Figure B**

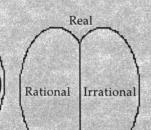

6. (a) Using the tree diagram on page 8-2 as a guide, draw a hierarchical concept map that includes the following concepts: *real numbers, irrational numbers, rational numbers, other common fractions, integers, negative integers, whole numbers, positive integers,* and *zero*. (b) Using linking terms that clearly and precisely define the relationships between two concepts. (c) Consider where the following examples should go in your hierarchical map: -3, 0, 5, 6½, and √47 . (Ideally, each example would appear only once in your map.)

Questions for Reflection

1. Are there numbers that are not real numbers?

2. One student asked an interesting question, "How can irrational numbers be on the number line? Hint: An informal proof using a geometric analogy can help answer this question. Consider a rectangle 2-units long and 1-unit wide. The length of this figure can be placed on a number line. If one end is placed on the 0 position of the number line, the other end can be marked off at the 1-unit position on the number line. Likewise, the rectangle can be turned so that its width spans the number line from 0 to 1. Is there a geometric figure that has a dimension that spans a distance from 0 on the number line to a position that is not rational?

↪ Teaching Tips

Children will more readily understand and use a new type of number if they recognize how it is related to what they already know, how it is connected to other types of numbers, and how it can be used.

↪ **Begin instruction on each type of number with informal explorations.** The instruction of a new type of number should build on children's personal experiences and what they already know.

↪ **Underscore how various types of numbers fit together in a logical and coherent manner.** When exploring a new type of number, encourage children to compare its similarities and differences with other types of numbers and to note the relationships among different types of numbers. They can summarize their discoveries with a Venn diagram, a concept map, or a tree diagram. In time, a tree diagram would grow into the real-number hierarchy illustrated on the previous page.

↪ **Help students understand why we need numbers beyond the whole numbers.** Underscore why each type of number is useful. Insight into how different number systems are used can increase a student's sense of power over numbers.

THIS CHAPTER

$\mathcal{N}$umbers can grow on students. Not only do they encounter larger and larger numbers (as we discussed in chapter 7), children learn more about the individual personalities and behaviors of numbers. Some numbers, for example, can be divided evenly by two; others cannot. Deciphering the similarities and differences of numbers can provide endless hours of intriguing detective work for children. In Unit 8•1, we examine number theory, the branch of mathematics that focuses on describing patterns and relationships among the counting or natural numbers (introduced in chapter 4).

Numbers can grow on students in another sense. As they proceed through the mathematics curriculum, children keep encountering new types of numbers. In addition to the whole numbers (the focus of chapters 4 to 7), they are introduced to the integers, the rational numbers, the irrationals, and the real numbers. *Why do we need so many different types of numbers? What are the differences among them? How are these types of numbers related?* In Unit 8•2, we take our first step beyond the whole-number system and introduce the integers, which include the negative numbers. This chapter lays the groundwork for discussing other number systems (the rational and irrational numbers) in chapters 9 and 11.

WHAT THE NCTM *STANDARDS* SAY

Grades K-4

"From the earliest grades, the curriculum should give students opportunities to focus on regularities . . . in sets of numbers" (p. 60). Moreover, "relating patterns in numbers, geometry, and measurement helps them understand connections among mathematical topics" (p. 60).

Grades 5-8

"The mathematics curriculum should include the study of number systems and number theory so that students can:

◆ understand and appreciate the numbers beyond the whole numbers;
◆ develop and apply . . . concepts [such as] primes, factors, and multiples in real-world and mathematical problem situations" (p. 91).

8•1 NUMBER THEORY

Figure 8.1: What's in a Number Name?

YOUNG ONES' VIEW

The study of number patterns can be traced back to the ancients, who seriously believed in numerology (the study of the magical significance of numbers). The followers of Pythagoreas, for instance, saw a parallel between feminine traits and the even or "feminine" numbers (cf. Figure 8.1). Although we no longer examine numbers in an effort to divine the future, there are at least four reasons for studying number theory: (1) Because the rules governing the natural numbers range from relatively simple to difficult, number theory can be a challenging topic for students at all levels of the elementary program (and beyond). (2) The study of number theory can be an engrossing and rewarding way to involve children in activities that are at the heart of mathematics: looking for patterns and thinking about relationships. It "offers many rich opportunities for explorations that are interesting . . . and . . . have payoffs in problem solving, in understanding . . . other mathematical concepts, in illustrating the beauty of mathematics, and in understanding the human aspects of the historical development of number" (NCTM, 1989, p. 91). (3) It is worth noting that an exploration of number theory also provides numerous opportunities for practicing computational skills in a purposeful and interesting manner. (4) Number theory can be a welcomed departure from arithmetic for many children. They do not have to recall numerous number combinations quickly or compute the sum or differences of multidigit problems accurately to be successful at number theory. In other words, number theory can give children who are not particularly successful with arithmetic a chance to shine.

In this unit, we examine the following topics in number theory: even and odd patterns (Subunit 8•1•1), prime numbers (Subunit 8•1•2), common factors and multiples (Subunit 8•1•3), divisibility (Subunit 8•1•4), unsolved problems (Subunit 8•1•5), and exponents and roots (Subunit 8•1•6).

8•1•1 EVEN AND ODD NUMBERS

Primary-level children can begin an exploration of number theory by examining even and odd patterns.

☞ Try Investigation 8.1 (page 8-6).

Definitions

Why are 2, 4, 6, 8 . . . called even numbers, and why are 1, 3, 5, 7 . . . called odd numbers? Kindergartners and first graders can explore even and odd numbers concretely by counting collections two items at a time and by exploring patterns with square tiles (see, e.g., Activity I in Investigation 8.1). In time, children can be encouraged to define the concept of *even numbers* explicitly but informally as, for example, *a collection where all the items have a partner* and to use their informal definition and patterns to identify larger numbers as even or odd. In the intermediate grades, children can define an *even number* formally as *an integer that is divisible by two.*

Even and Odd Patterns

There are a number of interesting even and odd arithmetic patterns that children can explore (see, e.g., Activity II of Investigation 8.1).

Addition. Encourage children to discover that adding two odd or two even numbers always

results in an even number and that adding an odd number and an even number always results in an odd number. Activity III of Investigation 8.1 can help them understand why these patterns occur.

The Sum of Consecutive Odd Numbers. The solutions to Activity IV of Investigation 8.1 often surprise children and adults. Representing this pattern geometrically can be invaluable in helping children see the relationship underlying the pattern; representing it both geometrically and numerically can help them connect geometry and arithmetic (NCTM, 1989).

Multiplication. As with addition, students can be helped to rediscover even-odd patterns for multiplication and why they occur (see, e.g., Activity V of Investigation 8.1).

8•1•2 PRIME AND COMPOSITE NUMBERS

☞ Try Investigations 8.2 (page 8-7) and 8.3 (page 8-8).

Learning: Informal Knowledge

As children become familiar with multiplication, they may notice that some natural numbers such as 11 have only two factors and others such as 12 have more than two factors. That is, they may recognize that some natural numbers can only be produced by multiplying the number itself and one (e.g., only 11 and 1 can be multiplied to yield the product 11). Other numbers can be produced in various ways (e.g., 12 can be generated by multiplying 12 and 1, 6 and 2, or 4 and 3). Thus, while 11 has only two factors (1 and itself), 12 has six factors: 1, 2, 3, 4, 6, and 12. The number 11 is an example of a prime number; the number 12 is an example of a composite number.

Teaching

Informally Introducing Primes and Composites. The distinction between primes and composites can be introduced concretely by posing a problem such as the *Rows of Stamps* problem (see Activity I of Investigation 8.2) and encouraging children to solve it with manipulatives such as square tiles or base-ten blocks. Activities II and III of Investigation 8.2 illustrate two other concrete ways of distinguishing primes from composites. (Continued on page 8-9.)

☽ Investigation 8.1: Exploring Even-Odd Patterns

◆ Number and arithmetic patterns + inductive reasoning ◆ Any number

Even-odd number and arithmetic patterns provide fertile opportunities to begin the exploration of number theory and to practice inductive reasoning. To see how, and to perhaps deepen your own understanding of even-odd patterns, try the activities below. It might be more valuable to do this with a group and to discuss your answers with your group or class.

Activity I: Geometric Analogies for Even and Odd Numbers (◆ K-4)

1. (a) How could square tiles be used to construct a concrete model of even numbers—a model that distinguishes them from odd numbers? (b) After using square tiles to model 2, 3, 4, 5, 6, and 7, Duena conjectured, "Even numbers can form a rectangle, but odd numbers don't." Evaluate Duena's conjecture. (c) Garey countered that 1, 3, 5, 7, and 9 square tiles all formed boxes (e.g., 5 tiles could be put in a single row of five and 9 could be put in three rows of three). Is there any way to reconcile Duena's conjecture and Garey's observation?

2. An odd number of cubes greater than 1 can be arranged to form what capital letters?

Activity II: Even and Odd Problems (◆ 1-8)

■ 1. (a) Is the Zorkian (base-four) number 12_4 even? (b) Is the Zorkian number 13_4? (c) Is the base-five number 12_5 even? (d) Is the base-five number 13_5?

    ☞ **Teaching Tips.** Primary-age children can also be asked questions about multi-digit base-ten numbers such as 42 and 63. Encourage children to consider how they can prove whether such a "large" number is even or odd and to discuss shortcuts for identifying even and odd numbers.

■ 2. How could you informally prove that zero is an even number, an odd number, or neither?

Activity III: Even-Odd Addition Patterns (◆ 1-8)

1. Miss Brill had her class use a sorting activity to discover even-odd sum patterns. After the class discovered that all the combinations in the *even-sum* pile involved adding two even numbers or two odd numbers and that all the

combinations in the *odd-sum* pile involved adding an odd and an even number (or vice versa), Hosni raised the following questions: *"Why does an odd plus an even make an odd? Why does an odd plus an odd make an even?" "And why does an even plus an even make an even?"* (✚ To address these questions, examine some simple examples concretely).

2. Even and odd numbers can be pictured as dot diagrams (Figure A and B, respectively) or, more simply, as a rectangle and a rectangle with an extension (Figures C and D, respectively) (Sawyer, 1964).

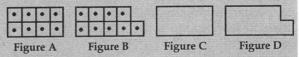

Figure A   Figure B   Figure C   Figure D

Using figures such as Figures A and B or C and D, illustrate why (a) odd + odd = even, (b) odd + even = odd, and (c) even + even = even.

Activity IV: The Sum of Consecutive Odd Numbers (◆ 3-8)

The sum of the first two consecutive odd natural numbers (1 + 3) is 4. Determine the sum of the first three consecutive odd natural numbers. Do the same for the first four and the first five. (a) What do you notice about the sums of these series? (b) Predict what the sum of the first eight consecutive odd natural numbers is. Do the same for the first twelve. (c) Why do the sums of consecutive odd natural numbers work out as they do?

Activity V: Odd-Even Multiplication Patterns (◆ 3-8)

For addition, even + even is even, even + odd is odd, and odd + odd is even. Are there odd-even patterns for multiplication? If so, what are they? Illustrate how could you use blocks and string or pictures to help students answer this question and to explain any patterns you find.

ℭ Investigation 8.2: Square-Tile Models of Primes and Composites

◆ Informal introduction to prime and composite numbers ◆ 2-5 ◆ Any number

Square-tiles can provide a concrete way of introducing and modeling prime and composite numbers. To see how and to perhaps deepen your own understanding of topic, try the following activities either by yourself or with your group. Discuss your findings with your group or class.

■ **Activity I:** *Rows of Stamps* **Problem**

To organize his stamp collection, Rasheed decided to mount his stamps in an album made of graph paper. He had a set of stamps commemorating the National Parks, another set honoring famous inventors, another set illustrating the state flags, and so forth. He wanted to put each set on a separate page in equal *rows*. A set of four stamps, for example, could be arranged three ways: one row of four stamps each, two rows of two stamps each, and four rows of one stamp each. If a set consisted of a single stamp, how many different ways could he arrange the set in equal rows? If a set consisted of two stamps, how many different ways could he arrange the set in equal rows? What about a set of three stamps? What about sets of five to thirteen stamps? (Note that a stamp can be oriented in only one way; it cannot be turned.)

1. (a) What number of stamps would you predict would have the smallest number of possible arrangements? (b) What number of stamps would you predict would have the largest? (c) Would you predict that 11 stamps would have more, no more, or fewer arrangements than 2 stamps would?

2. Use square tiles, blocks, or graph paper to check your predictions. Summarize your results in the table below.

number of stamps	1	2	3	4	5	6	7	8	9	10	11	12	13
number of arrangements													

3. (a) How many arrangements would you predict that 15 stamps would have? (b) 16? (c) 19? (d) 25? (e) 28? (f) 29? (g) 30? (h) 50? (i) 100? (j) 101?

Activity II: Rectangular Numbers

Although any number of square tiles can be arranged in a straight line, only some numbers of square tiles can be arranged to form a rectangle consisting of at least two rows of two or more tiles. Numbers that can form a rectangle involving multiple rows with more than one tile in each row are called *rectangular numbers*.

1. What are the rectangular numbers from 1 to 20?

2. (a) Is 1 a rectangular number? Why or why not? (b) Is 2? Why or why not? (c) Is 3? Why or why not? (d) Is 4? Why, or why not?

Activity III: Rectangular-Area Model

Using a geoboard or dot-matrix paper, determine how many different-looking rectangles with an area of 1-square unit can be made. How many can you make with an area of 2, 3, 4, and so forth?

☼ Investigation 8.3: Counting Distinct Factors

◆ Fostering an explicit understanding of primes and composites ◆ 5-8
◆ Individually, small groups, or as a class

Summarize the results for the *Row of Stamps problem* (Activity I of Investigation 8.2) for 1 to 20 stamps in the chart below and answer the questions that follow it.

Number	Arrays (Factors)	Distinct Factors	Number of Arrays (Distinct Factors)	
1				
2				
3				
4				
5				
6				
7				
8				
9	1 x 9, 9 x 1, 3 x 3	1, 3, 9	3	
10				
11				
12				
13				
14				
15				
16				
17				
18				
19				
20				

1. In terms of the number of distinct factors, what number is unlike any other? How so? Put an X through this number.

2. (a) What do the numbers 2, 3, 5, and 19 have in common? (b) What other numbers share this characteristic? Circle all these numbers.

3. What do the remaining numbers have in common?

Explicitly Defining Primes and Composites. The natural numbers have three subcategories:

1. *One or the unit has only a single distinct factor that is a natural number, namely 1.*

2. *Primes have exactly two distinct factors that are natural numbers: 1 and itself.* For example, there are only two natural numbers (1 and 3) that when multiplied produce 3.

3. *Composites have more than two distinct factors that are natural numbers: 1, itself, and some other natural number(s).* For example, 6 has the factors 1, 2, 3, and 6.

Encourage children to summarize the results of their concrete explorations in a table, look for patterns, and define *the unit, primes,* and *composites* in their own terms. For example, after solving the *Rows of Stamps* problem in Investigation 8.2 (page 8-7) and completing the table in Investigation 8.3 (page 8-8), sixth-grader Alison induced the following definition of prime numbers: "One and that number."

☞ Complete Investigations 8.4 (page 8-10) and 8.5 (page 8-11).

The Fundamental Theorem of Arithmetic. Investigation 8.4 involves an interesting number trick. With any luck, students will wonder how it works, setting the stage for a discussion of prime factors and the Fundamental Theorem of Arithmetic. To help students construct an understanding of this theorem, have them try a discovery-learning activity such as Investigation 8.5. An understanding of the Fundamental Theorem of Arithmetic should demystify the number trick described in Investigation 8.4.

8•1•3 GREATEST COMMON FACTOR AND LOWEST COMMON MULTIPLE

Mathematics

GCF. Some pairs of natural numbers (e.g., 3 and 17, 4 and 9, and 15 and 16) have only 1 as a *common factor.* Others have at least two factors in common. For example, 12 and 16 have three common factors: 1, 2, and 4. The *greatest common factor (abbreviated GCF) is the largest factor common to two (or more) natural numbers.* For in-

stance, the GCF of 12 and 16 is 4. Put differently, the GCF of two or more natural numbers is the largest natural number that will divide into each evenly.*

Greatest Common Factor

LCM. Within the natural-number system, two or more numbers may also have common multiples. (A *multiple* of a number is a product of the number and some other number. For example, 12 is a product of both 4 and 6 and, thus, a multiple of each.) The *least common multiple (abbreviated LCM) is the smallest multiple (greater than 1) common to two or more natural numbers.* For example, 6 is the LCM of 2 and 3. In other words, the least common multiple or divisor of two or more natural numbers is the smallest natural number that is evenly divisible by both of them.

Least Common Multiple

Learning: Children's Difficulties with Formal Terminology

Children who do not really understand the underlying concepts may confuse the terms *greatest common factor* and *least common multiple.* Misled by the adjective "greatest," they may expect the GCF to be larger than the natural numbers given and answer with LCM. Likewise, misled by the adjective "lowest," children may expect the LCM to be smaller than the natural numbers given and answer with GCF. Children with an incomplete understanding of the concept may believe that the LCM of numbers is always the product of the natural numbers given (e.g., 24 for 4 and 6). (Continued on page 8-12.)

---

* Children may be familiar with the terms factors and divisors from previous multiplication and division instruction but may not explicitly understand the connection between these terms. In fact, when working within the natural-number system, factor and divisor mean the same thing and can be used interchangeably. Consider, for instance, 3 x 4 = 12: 3 and 4 are factors of 12 and, because multiplication and division are inverse operations, they are also the divisors of 12. Thus, the GCF is sometimes called the greatest common divisor (GCD).

☕ Investigation 8.4: A Number Trick

◆ Motivating a discussion of prime numbers and a fundamental theorem
◆ 6-8 ◆ Whole class

This investigation illustrates one way the investigative approach can serve to introduce prime factors and a fundamentally important theorem involving them. Read the following description of a number trick and then answer the questions that follow.

Miss Brill's Number Trick

Miss Brill filled a bag with red, orange, yellow, and blue counters. On the board, she put the following key:

$$red = 2, \; orange = 3, \; yellow = 5, \; blue = 7$$

The teacher then asked for a student to choose a number of counters from the bag, multiply the value of the counters, and announce the product. Miss Brill claimed that as Miss Math Magic, she would be able to tell exactly what counters were retrieved from the bag. The class was highly skeptical that Miss Brill, Miss Math Magic, or anyone else would be able to determine the counters chosen.

Michelle noted with a smile, "Oh I get it. Of course, you're going to watch as the person pulls out the counters."

"That wouldn't be much of a trick," replied Miss Brill. "No, I'll turn my back and close my eyes while the counters are drawn. Michelle, why don't you draw first."

Michelle drew two reds and a blue and announced, "The product is 28."

"That's an easy one," replied Miss Brill as she correctly identified the colors.

"Just checking," responded Michelle as she searched for a new set of counters. "How about a total of 210."

Miss Brill paused, checked the key, and announced, "You picked one of each color."

There was an audible collective gasp. "Give her a really hard one," urged Rodney.

"Alright," Michelle said, taking out her calculator, "Try this: 1,260."

Miss Brill sketched a few things on the board and, after about 30 seconds, announced, "Two red, two orange, a yellow, and a blue."

"How do you do that?" asked LeMar for an amazed class.

Questions for Reflection

1. Do you know how Miss Brill was able to determine what blocks were chosen? (If not, complete Investigation 8.5 on the next page and see if that helps.)

2. (a) If you think you understand the basis of the trick, what would Miss Brill's answer be if Michelle had chosen the number 144? (b) Try the trick with some of your friends. Were they baffled by the trick or not?

☼ Investigation 8.5: Prime Factors

◆ Rediscovering a fundamental theorem ◆ 6-8 ◆ Any number

A composite number is a natural number with at least one divisor or factor other than 1 and itself. This investigation explores these other factors of composite numbers. To see what is involved and to perhaps deepen your own understanding of prime factors, answer the questions below yourself. Discuss your answers with your group or class.

1. Other than multiplying 1 and the number itself, only the combination 2 • 2 has the product 4 and—not considering factor order—only 2 • 3 has the product 6. Likewise, 8 can be produced by the combination 2 • 4, which can be further factored into 2 • 2 • 2. The factors other than 1 and the number itself for some composites are summarized below.

4 = 2 • 2	10 = 2 • 5	20 = 2 • 10 = 2 • 2 • 5
6 = 2 • 3	14 = 2 • 7	22 = 2 • 11
8 = 2 • 4 = 2 • 2 • 2	15 = 3 • 5	25 = 5 • 5
	18 = 2 • 9 = 2 • 3 • 3	

   For each case above, what do you notice about the factors when a composite number has been factored as much as possible? That is, what do you notice about the factors inside the rectangles?

2. Some composite numbers can be factored in more than one way. Consider, for example, the cases of 12, 16, and 24 shown below. (a) Complete the factoring for these composites; then factor 32.

   12 = 2 • 6 = [   ]   16 = 2 • 8 = 2 • 2 • 4 = [   ]

   12 = 4 • 3 = [   ]   16 = 4 • 4 = [   ]

   24 = 2 • 12 = 2 • 2 • 6 = [   ]   32 =   = [   ]

   24 = 8 • 3 = 2 • 4 • 3 = [   ]   32 =   = [   ]

   24 = 4 • 6 = [   ]

   (b) For each composite above, what do you notice about the factors inside the rectangles? That is, what do you notice when you compare the results of factoring a composite in different ways?

3. Do the set of factors inside the rectangle for any two *different* composite numbers match?

4. Do your observations from Questions 1 to 3 above hold for all composite numbers? Consider some examples such as 36, 120, and 945. A factor tree is one way of summarizing the results of factoring. The prime-factor trees for 36 are shown below. Complete prime-factor trees for (a) 120 and (b) 945.

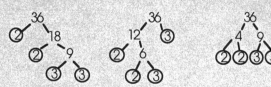

5. Use a factor-tree diagram to determine the prime factors of 320. Compare how you went about factoring 320 with how others in your group did it.

Teaching: Fostering the Conceptual Groundwork for and the Meaningful Instruction of GCF and LCM

Conceptual Groundwork. To lay the conceptual groundwork for GCF and LCM, invite children to solve problems involving common factors and common multiples informally. It may help some children to work with, reflect on, and discuss concrete methods for determining common factors (see, e.g., Figure 8.2) and common multiples (see, e.g., Frame A of Figure 8.3). Others may be helped to construct an explicit understanding of these concepts by using a hundreds chart (e.g., see Frame B of Figure 8.3).

Meaningful Instruction of GCF and LCM. By examining concrete solutions such as that shown in Figure 8.2, students can easily identify the greatest common factor (4 in the case of 12 and 16). By examining concrete or pictorial models such as those shown in Figure 8.3, they can also readily determine the smallest common multiple of numbers (6 in the case of 2 and 3). To minimize confusion between finding the GCF and the LCM, have the children focus on what they need to examine: *common factors* in the case of the GCF and *common multiples* in the case of the LCM.

More abstractly, students can use prime factorization to determine the GCF and LCM of natural numbers. To find the GCF, determine the prime factors of each number, circle the common factors, and then multiply these factors. Consider the pair of numbers 24 and 36:

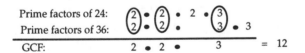

Figure 8.3: Models for Common Multiples (Using 2 and 3 as an Example)

A. Concrete Model Using Number Sticks

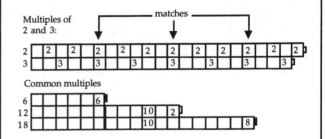

B. More Abstract Model Using a Hundreds Chart

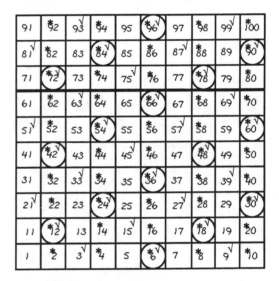

* = multiple of 2

√ = multiple of 3

○ = common multiple

Figure 8.2: A Concrete Model of Common Factors Using Number Sticks

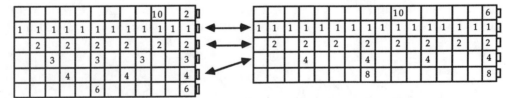

Factors of 12: 1, 2, 3, 4, 6

Factors of 16: 1, 2, 4, 8

Common Factors: 1, 2, 4

*Number sticks are composed of numbered interlocking blocks. For example, one could be represented by a white cube labeled *1*; two, by two red interlocked cubes labeled *2*, and so forth.

To find the LCM, determine the prime factors, circle common and uncommon factors, and then multiply a representative from each circle. For 24 and 36, the process would look like:

Prime factors of 24:
Prime factors of 36:

LCM: 2 • 2 • 2 • 3 • 3 = 72

8•1•4 DIVISIBILITY

☞ Try Investigation 8.6 (pages 8-14 and 8-15).

Mathematics: The Usefulness of Divisibility Rules

Why is knowing divisibility rules even important? There are numerous instances in school and everyday life where it can help to know if one number is divisible by another. For example, divisibility rules can be used to check computation, to determine whether a number is prime, to reduce a fraction such as $\frac{45}{84}$, or to simplify a ratio such as 717:999. They can also be used to solve some real-world problems such as the *Bolt Barren* problem (see Part I of Investigation 8.6).

Some students may wonder why it is important to learn divisibility rules when it is relatively easy to use a calculator to check whether a number is divisible by another. One answer, of course, is that calculators are not always available. Another is that, in some cases, it is actually more efficient to use a divisibility rule than to use a calculator. For example, consider how long it would take to use a calculator and a divisibility rule to determine whether 977,728 is divisible by four. Knowing divisibility rules enhances our number sense and command over numbers.

Teaching: The Investigative Approach

Encourage students to discover or to deduce the divisibility rules themselves (e.g., see Part II of Investigation 8.6). Just as important as knowing the divisibility rules is understanding why they work. A child who understands the underlying rationale of the divisibility rules has taken an important step in constructing a number sense. Challenge students to demonstrate with base-ten blocks why the divisibility rules work (see Part III of Investigation 8.6).

8•1•5 UNSOLVED PROBLEMS

Because many children believe that all mathematical problems have a solution, it is important to introduce them to examples that remain unsolved. In number theory, as in any branch of mathematics, there are many problems that remain unresolved. A sample of such problems that children may find interesting to explore are illustrated in Investigation 8.7.

☞ Try Investigations 8.7 (page 8-16), 8.8 (pages 8-17 and 8-18), and 8.9 (page 8-19).

8•1•6 EXPONENTS AND ROOTS

Mathematics

Basic Meaning of Exponentials. An exponential is a mathematical abbreviation. For example, the exponential form 2^5 is a compact expression for 2 x 2 x 2 x 2 x 2 or 2 • 2 • 2 • 2 • 2. In the expression 2^5, 2 is called the *base* and the superscript 5 is called the *exponent*. An exponential a^n is read *a to the* n^{th} *power* or *the* n^{th} *power of a*. For instance, 5^4 is read *five to the fourth power* or *the fourth power of five*. When 2 or 3 is the exponent, the exponential is typically read in a different fashion. For example, 5^2 is usually read as *five squared* or *the square of five*, and 5^3 is read as *five cubed* or *the cube of five*.

Geometric Models for Square Numbers, Square Roots, Cubes, and Cube Roots. *Why is the exponent 2 called squared and the exponent 3 called cubed?* The exponential 3^2 is called *three squared* because it can be related to the geometric analogy of a square—can be represented by a square with sides of 3 linear units (see Example A in Figure 8.4 on page 8-20). The area of the square (9 square units) represents the square number 9. An equation such as $\sqrt{9} = ?$ can be thought of as: *A square with an area of 9 squares units has sides of what length?* (see Example B in Figure 8.4). The expression 3^3 can be related to a volume model—can be viewed as a cube with sides of 3 linear units (see Example C in Figure 8.4). The volume of this cube (27 cubic units) represents the cube number 27. An equation such as $\sqrt{27} = ?$ can be thought of as: *A cube with a volume of 27 has sides of what length?* (see Example D in Figure 8.4).

Teaching

Squares and Square Roots. Instruction on exponents and roots can (continued on page 8-20)

✿ Investigation 8.6: An Example of the Investigative Approach to Learning the Divisibility Rules

◆ Inducing or deducing the divisibility rules ◆ 5-8 ◆ Individually or small groups

The aim of this investigation is to help students (a) understand the value of divisibility rules, (b) discover or reason out these rules for themselves, and (c) understand why these rules work. To see how and to perhaps deepen your own understanding of the topic, try the following investigations yourself, preferably with the help of your group. Discuss your findings with your group or class.

Part I: A Reason for Divisibility Rules

Mr. Adams presented his combination fifth-sixth grade class the following problem:

■ **Bolt Barren.** El Cheapo Manufacturers produces a children's carseat that requires eight bolts to assemble. Of course, El Cheapo puts exactly eight bolts in a box. The monthly inventories of bolts used for the last quarter of a year is shown. Assuming all the bolts used went into boxes, did the firm meet its objective of not including any extra bolts? What months, if any, did the firm fail to achieve this objective?

Oct	Nov	Dec
1,352,256	1,369,104	1,237,148

After students had a chance to solve the problem in their groups, Mr. Adams asked them to share their solution strategies. There was general agreement that each number had to be divided by eight to see whether or not there was a remainder. Mr. Adams took this opportunity to define *divisibility*, "We say that a number like 1,352,256 is divisible by 8 because dividing it by 8 leaves no remainder." Mr. Adams then asked the class Question 1 below.

1. Is 1,352,256 divisible by 2, 3, 4, 5, 6, or 9?

2. The students quickly concluded that 1,352,256 was divisible by 2, but not divisible by 5. How did they know this? (That is, what are the divisibility rules for 2 and 5?)

3. The class was uncertain about whether 1,352,256 was divisible by 3, 4, 6, or 9. Alex proposed using a calculator to find out. What did the class find out?

Mr. Adams then ask the class how they would figure out whether 1,369,104 was divisible by 2, 3, 4, 5, 6 or 9, if they didn't have calculators available. Serra immediately noted that except for 2 and 5, they would have to long divide by hand. Andrea pointed out that this would be a lot of work. "And what if you needed to know this information quickly?" asked Mr. Adams. "How did you figure out whether a number was divisible by 2 or 5 so quickly?" he prompted The class explicitly summarized their informal ideas as divisibility rules for 2 and 5. Mr. Adams then posed an interesting question, "Are there shortcuts or rules for determining divisibility by 3, 4, 6, 8, and 9?"

Part II: Using Examples and Nonexamples to Induce Divisibility Rules or Logic to Deduce Them

1. Mr. Adams asked the class to give him examples of numbers that were evenly divisible by 3. Some examples were 6, 12, 24, 57, 81, 111, 300, 312, 651, and 777. Some nonexamples were 8, 13, 25, 56, 80, 112, 301, 313, 653, and 778. What do the examples have in common—a commonality not shared by the nonexamples?

Investigation 8.6 continued

2. Mr. Adams next asked the class to give him examples of numbers that were evenly divisible by 4. Some examples were *120, 248, 396, 1016, 3308, 5544,* and *9992.* (☞ **Teaching Tip.** Note that 396 and 9992 are particularly good examples because it would not be obvious to most students that these numbers are divisible by four.) Some nonexamples were *121, 246, 398, 1017, 3306, 5544,* and *9994.* What do the examples have in common—a commonality not shared by the nonexamples? Mr. Adams gave his class the following hint: Note that 248, 396, 3308, and 9992 are divisible by both 2 and 4 but 246, 398, 3306, and 9994 are not.

3. Mr. Adams next asked the class for examples and nonexamples of numbers divisible by 8. List some of each. What do the examples have in common that the nonexamples do not share? Hint: Build on what you know about the divisibility rules for 2 and 4.

4. To reason out the divisibility rule for 6, consider what you know about the number and the divisibility rules you already know about.

5. To determine the divisibility rules for 9, consider what you know about this number and what you already know about divisibility rules.

Questions for Reflection

1. What is the divisibility rules for 16, 32, and 64?

2. What is the divisibility rule for 27?

Part III: Rationales for the Divisibility Rules

Why do the divisibility rules work? With your group, use base-ten blocks to show why the divisibility rules for 2, 3, 4, 5, 8, and 9 work. Illustrate your solutions.

1. Why is a number divisible by 2 if the last digit is even? Hints: Concretely model 1336 with base-ten blocks. Why can we disregard the tens, hundreds, and thousands place in this number and focus only on whether or not the last digit is divisible by two? Consider what happens if you trade in a large cube for units and group these small cubes by two. Do the same for the flats and the longs.

2. Why is a number divisible by 3 if the sum of the digits is divisible by 3? Hints: Create a model of 126 with base-ten blocks. Consider what happens if you trade in a flat for 100 cubes (units) and group them by threes. What happens if you do the same with the longs?

3. Why is a number divisible by 4 if the number formed by the tens and units digit is divisible by 4? Hints: Consider the concrete models for (a) 196, (b) 1,236, and (c) 1,352. Why can we disregard the hundreds and thousands place and simply focus on the last two digits? Is 1300 divisible by 4? Why or why not?

4. Why is a number divisible by 5 if the units digit is 0 or 5? Why can we disregard all but the ones place?

5. Why is a number divisible by 8 if the number formed by the hundreds, tens, and ones digit is divisible by 8? Why can we disregard digits beyond the hundreds place?

6. Why is a number divisible by 9 if the sum of its digits is divisible by 9? Concretely model 126 with base-ten blocks. Adapt and apply the hints given in Question 2.

✂ Investigation 8.7: Enrichment Topics in Number Theory

◆ Inductive reasoning ◆ 5-8 ◆ Individually or in small groups

This investigation can provide students an opportunity to discuss several aspects of number theory and to look for patterns. To see what is involved and to perhaps extend your knowledge of the natural numbers, try the two activities below.

Activity I: Perfect, Deficient, and Abundant Numbers. The natural number 6 is considered perfect because it equals the sum of its proper divisors (all divisors except the number itself): 1, 2, and 3. Unlike a perfect number (P), a deficient number (D) is a natural number that is greater than the sum of its proper divisors, and an abundant number (A) is a natural number that is less than the sum of its proper divisors.

1. Are perfect numbers relatively common or rare? Complete the chart for the numbers up to 30 to get a sense of their frequency.

Natural Number	Proper Divisors	Sum	P, D, or A	Natural Number	Proper Divisors	Sum	P, D, or A	Natural Number	Proper Divisors	Sum	P, D, or A
1				11				21			
2				12				22			
3				13				23			
4				14				24			
5				15				25			
6	1, 2, 3	6	P	16				26			
7				17				27			
8				18				28			
9				19				29			
10				20				30			

2. After hearing the definition of a proper divisor, sixth-grader Alison deduced, "Zero must have an infinite number of proper divisors." Evaluate this deduction. (a) Reconstruct her premises and argument. (b) Was her argument valid? Is her conclusion true?

3. Can 1 be a perfect number? Why or why not?

4. While trying to identify the perfect numbers up to 30, sixth-grader Alison concluded, "Well we can cross out [i.e., discount] all the prime numbers." (a) Is Alison's deduction correct or not? Why? (b) Is a prime number such as 401 a perfect, a deficient, or an abundant number? Why?

5. Is 496 a perfect, a deficient, or an abundant number?

6. Are there odd perfect numbers?

Activity II: Goldbach's Conjectures. Can even natural numbers be written as the sum of two odd primes? Can odd natural numbers be written as the sum of three odd primes? Complete the chart below. What conclusions do you draw?

2		10		18		3		11	3 + 3 + 5	19	
4		12	5 + 7	20		5		13		21	
6		14		22		7		15		23	
8		16		24		9		17		25	

☞ **Teaching Tip.** Note that Activity II could be made more open-ended by posing the questions: Can even natural numbers be written as the sum of two odd primes? Can they be written as the sum of three odd primes? Is the same true of odd natural numbers?

☾ Investigation 8.8: Exploring Squares, Square Roots, Cubes, and Cube Roots Concretely

◆ Exponentials and roots + problem solving and reasoning out square roots ◆ 3-8
◆ Groups of four + class discussion

Square numbers and *cubes* are two examples of polygonal numbers. This investigation involves creating geometric models of these ideas with manipulatives and using these models to make sense of the concepts *square roots* and *cube roots* and to gauge roots such as $\sqrt{20}$ and $\sqrt[3]{20}$. To see what is involved and to perhaps deepen your understanding of the topic, work through the following activities with your group. Discuss your findings with your class.

Activity I: Squares (◆ 3-5)

1. Using up to 100 square tiles, how many different squares can you make and how many square tiles are in each square?

2. A multiplication combination can be represented by an area model. For example, the combination 4 x 3 = 12 can be thought of as a rectangle 4-units long and 3-units wide with an area of 12 squares or square units (see Figures A and B to the right). Using square tiles, base-ten blocks, graph paper, or a geoboard construct an area model of the 25 multiplication expressions from 1 x 1 to 5 x 5. Which of these 25 basic combinations form a square?

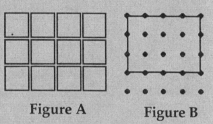

Figure A　　　　**Figure B**

3. What is the area of each square identified in Question 1? Complete the table below.

multiplication combination					
area (number of square tiles)					

Activity II: Square Roots (◆ 5-8)

1. Use square tiles, base-ten blocks, a geoboard, or graph paper to solve the following problem:

   ■ **Unknown Sides.** The area of square patio is 16 square units. How long is a side?

2. (a) Illustrate how you could use an area model to determine the square root of 25 ($\sqrt{25}$). (b) In an area model, what does the 25 represent? (c) In an area model, what does the $\sqrt{25}$ represent?

3. Miss Brill asked her class to concretely determine the square root of the perfect squares 4, 9, 16, and 25. To determine the square root of 25, for example, students counted out 25 chips to represent an area of 25 square units, arranged them in a square (a 5-by-5 array), and counted the number of chips on a side to determine the length of a side: five. The activity prompted an interesting question. Helen noticed that they had skipped over the numbers between the perfect squares, and she wondered if these intermediate numbers had square roots. "Miss Brill," Helen inquired, "We determined the square root of 16 and 25. What about the numbers in between? Do numbers such as 17, 18, and 20 have a square root?" Explain why or why not.

4. By now Helen should have anticipated Miss Brill would answer her question with a question: "What do you think?"

   A moment later, Rodney announced: "No, 20 can't have a square root, because 20 chips can't be arranged as a square."

   To prompt reflection, Miss Brill purposely created cognitive conflict, "Are you telling us that a square can't have an area of 20?"

"It could, but the side won't be a whole [a positive integer] like 4 or 5," answered Helen shortly. A number of students were not entirely convinced by Helen's answers. So, Miss Brill asked if there was any other way to show that 20 had a square root.

▦ Andy suggested using a calculator: "If you punch in 20 and then the square root key, you get 4.472136." Miss Brill recorded the number on the chalkboard.

After Andy explained to the class that $\sqrt{}$ was the square-root function, Miss Brill asked" "How can you be sure 4.472136 is the square root of 20?"

"When I multiplied 4.472136 times 4.472136," LeMar noted, "I got 20."

"It also works if you enter 4.472136 and hit the square key ($\boxed{x^2}$)," observed Andy.

The class concluded the square roots of perfect squares were counting (natural) numbers and that the square roots of other numbers were "decimals."

(a) Illustrate how you could use square tiles, base-ten blocks, or graph paper to model $\sqrt{20}$. (b) What problem did you encounter? (c) What is the square root of 20 to the nearest whole number? Justify your answer.

5. If base-ten blocks are used, defining the cube as 1-square unit does not allow a student to determine the square root of 20 beyond the units place. Illustrate how the base-ten blocks could be used to determine the $\sqrt{20}$ to the tenths place. Hint: Consider defining as 1-square unit a block other than the cube. Assume that large cubes, flats, longs, and cubes, but not chips (tenths of a cube), are available.

6. How could the leftover blocks be used to determine a more accurate estimate of the $\sqrt{20}$?

7. Illustrate how base-ten blocks could be used to determine the square root of 150 accurate to tenths.

▦ **Activity III: Using a Calculator to Estimate Square Roots (◆ 5-8)**

1. Assume that your calculator did not have a square-root function or that you were unaware your calculator had such a function. How could you use a calculator and what you know about the square roots of perfect squares (and an area model) to estimate the square root of (a) 20 and (b) 10 accurate to tenths?

2. Why would it be important for a class to consider such a task even if their calculators had a square-root function?

Activity IV: Cubes and Cube Roots (◆ 6-8)

1. Mr. Ottey asked Lon to make a display of square-shaped boxes. Not particularly industrious, Lon put out one box. Mr. Ottey's response was, "I need a bigger cube." (a) How many square-shaped boxes will it take to build the next larger cube? (◆ Hint: Use blocks to create a model). (b) Mr. Ottey was still dissatisfied with the size of the next larger cube. How many square-shaped boxes will it take to build the next even larger cube?

2. (a) Consider how 1-inch cubes or base-ten blocks could be used to model 2^3. (b) What would the 2 represent in this model? (c) What does 2^3 equal and what would this answer represent in the model?

3. (a) Illustrate how $\sqrt[3]{27}$ could be modeled with base-ten blocks. (b) Illustrate how base-ten blocks could be used to determine the cube root of 20 accurate to tenths.

☪ Investigation 8.9: Exploring Exponents

Part I: Exponent Puzzles (◆ Using patterns to answer questions about the exponent 0 ◆ 6-8 ◆ Whole class). This investigation illustrates how the following questions can be addressed in a meaningful manner: *Why does $10^0 = 1$? What does a negative exponent such as 10^{-3} or 2^{-5} mean? And does any number raised to the 0 power equal 1 and why?* To see how and to perhaps deepen your own understanding of these issues, try the following investigations. Discuss your findings with your group or class.

Activity 1: Why Does $10^0 = 1$? In the intermediate grades, students are introduced to exponents, including the convention that $10^0 = 1$. Typically, students simply memorize this convention. Curious students may wonder why. A relatively straightforward and convincing informal proof is outlined below.

Step 1. Examine column A in the chart to the right.

A		B
10^6	=	1,000,000
10^5	=	100,000
10^4	=	10,000
10^3	=	1,000
10^2	=	100
10^1	=	10
$10^?$	=	?

a. What happens to the successive exponent as you go from the top entry (10^6) to 10^1?

b. Based on the pattern you observed in Step 1a above, what would you predict the exponent in the last entry ($10^?$) would be?

Step 2. Now examine column B. Note that as you go from the top entry (1,000,000) to each successive lower entry, there is one less zero.

a. How does this come about? What must be done to 1,000,000 to get the next entry 100,000? What must be done to 100,000 to get 10,000 and so forth?

b. Based on the pattern you observed in Step 2a, what would you predict the entry in the box should be?

Activity 2: Negative Exponents. The logical extension of the discovery-learning activity outlined in Activity 1 could lead to a discussion of negative exponents and what they mean.

1. Using the pattern discovered in Step 1a of Activity 1, what would you predict would come before the $10^?$ entry in Column A?

2. Using the pattern discovered in Step 2a of Activity 1, what would you predict would come before the ? entry in column B?

Activity 3: Why Does $X^0 = 1$??? After demonstrating why $10^0 = 1$, students sometimes ask, *"Why does any number raised to the 0 power equal 1?"* Why does 3^0, for example, equal 1? How would you help students answer such a question? Hint: Consider how you were helped to see that $10^0 = 1$ in Activity 1. How could this demonstration be adapted to show that 3^0 also equals 1 and that any number raised to the zero power is 1?

Part II: A Discovery-Learning Approach to Operations with Exponents (◆ Inducing the rules for exponent arithmetic ◆ 7-8 ◆ Ideally, small groups). In the traditional skills approach, students are spoon-fed the rules for exponent arithmetic and expected to memorize them. These rules typically make little sense to them and are often quickly forgotten. In fact, students can rediscover the rules for exponent arithmetic for themselves. This underscores the theme that mathematics involves looking for patterns and promotes a sense of mathematical power. Moreover, students know that if they forget a rule, they can always reconstruct it. To see what is involved and to perhaps refresh your memory about the rules regarding exponent arithmetic, try the investigation yourself, preferably with the aid of your group. Discuss your discoveries with your group or class.

1. (a) Devise a rule for multiplying exponentials such as $2^4 \times 2^5$, $3^2 \times 3^3$, $4^2 \times 4^2$, and $5^1 \times 5^2$. Hints: Consider how a teacher could build upon students' existing knowledge of exponents to introduce multiplication with exponents in a meaningful fashion. Consider what 2^4 and 2^5 represent by themselves. (b) Does the rule apply to cases such as $3^1 \times 2^4$ and $2^2 \times 4^3$ or $4^2 \times 3^2$ and $2^3 \times 5^3$? (c) Does the rule apply to cases such as $4^0 \times 4^2$ or $3^3 \times 3^0$?

2. What is $3^6 \div 3^4$? Use an informal approach to devise a rule for dividing with exponents.

3. What is $(2^4)^3$? Use an informal approach to devise a rule for multiplying exponents.

4. What is $2^3 \times 5^3$? Use an informal approach to devise a rule for multiplying two numbers with like exponents.

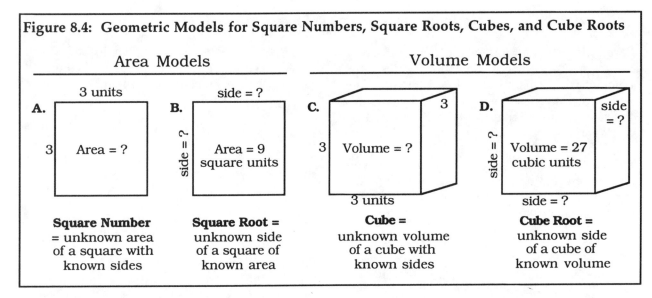

Figure 8.4: Geometric Models for Square Numbers, Square Roots, Cubes, and Cube Roots

begin with a concrete exploration of square numbers. Encourage children to discover that a counting number multiplied by itself can literally form a square. For example, ask them to model various multiplication expressions with square tiles, to sort the models into those that form square arrays and those that do not, and to summarize their findings in a table like that below (see Activity I of Investigation 8.8 on page 8-17):

dimensions that produced a square area	1 x 1	2 x 2	3 x 3	4 x 4	...
(square number)	1	4	9	16	

Square roots can then be explored concretely by posing problems where the area of a square is known but the sides are unknown (see, e.g., Questions 1 and 2 in Activity II of Investigation 8.8). Encourage students to solve such problems informally (e.g., using square tiles or base-ten blocks).

In time, the formal terminology and notation of square numbers and square roots can be explicitly related to the area model (e.g., 3^2 or "three squared" can be related to "What is the area of a 3-unit by 3-unit square?" and $\sqrt{9}$ or the "square root of nine" can be related to "What are the sides of a square with an area of 9 square units?"

Gauging Square Roots: An Exercise in Thinking. *Can numbers such as 20 and 35 have a square root?* As Questions 3 and 4 of Activity II in Investigation 8.8 illustrate, children can be prompted to discover that, while multiplying two natural numbers results in a *perfect square* (represented by a square with whole-number lengths), other integers can be multiplied by themselves to make a square number (represented by a square with nonwhole-number lengths). As Questions 4 to 7 of Activity II (on pages 8-17 and 8-18) illustrate, the square roots of nonperfect squares such as 20 can be estimated concretely. As Activity III on page 8-18 of Investigation 8.8 illustrates, it can also be estimated using a calculator without a square-root function.

Cubes, Cube Roots, and Other Exponentials. Cubes and cube roots can be related to a volume model (see, e.g., Activity IV on page 8-18 of Investigation 8.8). Other exponentials can be introduced as a short cut for the repeated multiplication of the same factor (e.g., 4^5 is an abbreviation for 4 x 4 x 4 x 4 x 4).

Zero as an Exponent. *Why does $10^0 = 1$?* Activity 1 of Investigation 8.9 (on page 8-19) illustrates how encouraging students to look for patterns can address this question. (Activity 2 illustrates how extending the pattern can lead naturally to a discussion of negative exponents and their meaning.)

Why does any number raised to the zero power equal one? As with $10^0 = 1$, this question can be answered by encouraging students to examine patterns (see also Activity 3 of Investigation 8.9). Consider the following charts:

$3^4 = 81$ $4^4 = 256$ $5^4 = 625$
$3^3 = 27$ $4^3 = 64$ $5^3 = 125$
$3^2 = 9$ $4^2 = 16$ $5^2 = 25$
$3^1 = 3$ $4^1 = 4$ $5^1 = 5$
$3^0 =$ $4^0 =$ $5^0 =$

If $3^4 = 81$, $3^3 = 27$, $3^2 = 9$, and $3^1 = 3$, then 3^0 would be 1 because each successive value in both the first and the second column is obtained by dividing the previous value by 3 (e.g., $3^2 \div 3 = 3^1$ and $9 \div 3 = 3$ and, thus, $3^1 \div 3 = 3^0$ and $3 \div 3 = 1$). By showing that this pattern holds true across various examples (e.g., 3^0, 4^0, 5^0, and 10^0), students can discover the general rule that any numbers raised to the zero power is one.

Arithmetic with Exponents. In the traditional skills approach, children are required to memorize the properties of exponents. For example, to multiply $2^4 \times 2^5$, they use the memorized rule: record the common base (2) and add the exponents ($4 + 5 = 9$), which produces the answer 2^9. Devoid of any idea of why such a procedure works, many students simply accept it as more math magic. Quite often, they quickly forget the procedure or fail to use it effectively. In the investigative approach, a teacher can begin by posing a question or problem and then can encourage students to exploit their existing knowledge to construct a rule for multiplying exponentials themselves (see, e.g., Part II of Investigation 8.9 on page 8-19).

8•2 INTEGERS AND OPERATIONS ON INTEGERS

Figure 8.5: A Need for Negative Numbers

☞ Consider Probe 8.2 (page 8-22) before and after reading this unit on integers.

There are some circumstances where the whole numbers are not enough. In this unit, we explore why integers are important (cf. Figure 8.5) and how to help children understand this type of number (Subunit 8•2•1). We then examine integer arithmetic (Subunit 8•2•2).

8•2•1 THE CONCEPT OF INTEGERS

Mathematics: Understanding Integers

Integers, why another set of numbers?

The Role of the Integers. Sometimes it does not make sense to talk about numbers less than zero. For example, the attendance of class cannot drop below zero, even if a community is gripped by a plague or some other disaster. In such cases, the whole numbers do just fine, thank you. Sometimes it does make sense to talk about numbers less than zero. For example, it is cold out when the temperature drops below 0°C; it is very cold out when the temperature drops below 0°F. In the era of plastic credit, it is easier than ever to end up in debt. Bad football teams can end up with negative net yards gained. Some games, such as the television game show *Jeopardy*, entail penalty points and negative scores. In other games, such as the card game *Hearts*, a player is glad to run up a negative score, because the fewer points the better. In discussing elevation, one can go below as well as above sea level.

Put differently, sometimes it is enough to know the size of a quantity; other times it is important to know a quantity's size *and* its location. Whole numbers are fine for indicating a magnitude, but integers are needed to indicate both magnitude *and* direction. With integers, 0 is a reference point, and the (continued on page 8-23)

8-22

→ **Probe 8.2: Some Questions About Integers**

The primary grades focus on whole-number instruction. Traditionally, the integers (positive *and* negative numbers) have been introduced in the intermediate grades, if not later. The aim of this probe is to help you reflect on the need for integers, the nature of integers, and common difficulties in understanding negative numbers and operating on integers. Answer the five questions below. Then discuss your answers with your group or class.

1. In the skills approach, negative numbers are frequently introduced purposelessly and without any explanation as to why they are needed. Considering the following vignette and the answer the questions that follow it.

   The *Pac-Man*™ Incident. The object of *Pac-Man*™ is to be the first player to accumulate 100 points. On their turn, players draw a card, which can be 0, 1, 5, 10, +, -, or x. Players can place the card on their own board or an opponent's board. If the card completes an expression, the card's owner gets the number of points indicated by the expression.

   While playing *Pac-Man*™, Alexi, almost 9-years-old, was confronted with the situation depicted to the right. The boy wanted to interpret the expression 5 - 10 as *10 take away* 5. Told it was 5 minus 10, he asked, "How could that be?" An example of going into debt was used to illustrate the expression. Asked if there were any other places you might encounter negative numbers, Alexi thought a moment and then indicated some math problems. Asked if you would encounter it when measuring temperature, he replied, "Oh yeah, under zero." Six months later, asked where you might encounter a number such as *negative two*, Alexi immediately responded, "In Pac-Man."
   "

   (a) What does Alexi's experience with the *Pac-Man*™ game suggest about introducing children to negative numbers? (b) Other than temperature, accounting (credit and debt), and keeping score in some games, are there other everyday uses of integers? (c) Mathematically, what do integers tell us that whole numbers do not?

2. A student teacher reads the expressions -6 + (+7) as "minus six and plus seven" and 6 - (+7) as "six minus plus seven." Is this good educational practice? Why or why not?

3. April had finally arrived, and a student teacher was preparing to take over a second-grade class. The student teacher proposed a lesson on introducing the addition of negative numbers. What advice should a supervising teacher give this student teacher: Get a new career, get real, or get to it?

4. What is the answer to 5 - (-8) = ? How would you explain to a student the answer you got?

5. What is the answer to -5 x (-8) = ? Why does it have the sign it does?

Pac-Man™ is a Milton Bradley game published by Midway Manufacturing Co., © 1980.

sign of a number serves to indicate the number's direction relative to 0. In brief, integers are useful tools for situations when we need to know *how* big something is and *where* the bigness is.*

Definition and Symbolism. Concretely, the minus sign in front of a number, such as -2, "turns [it] upside down, like the reflection of trees . . . on a river" (Sawyer, 1971, p. 62). Mathematically, negative numbers are defined as the opposites of positive numbers. For example, -2 is defined as the solution to the expression $2 + \square = 0$. For example, +2 and -2 indicate the same magnitude but -2 goes in the opposite direction of +2. A number line provides a clear depiction of this interpretation. For example, +2 can be thought of as two units to the *right* of zero; -2, as two units to the *left* of zero.

Learning: A Common Source of Confusion

The use of a + or - sign to indicate the direction of an integer is *different* from children's customary interpretation of these symbols. More specifically, the sign of a signed number does *not* indicate the arithmetic operation of addition or subtraction as it did in the familiar context of whole numbers. With the introduction of signed numbers, suddenly -2, for instance, does not necessarily mean *take away two*. Confusion about the meaning of an integer's sign may be compounded by everyday references to integers. For example, it is common to refer to temperatures below zero as "minus" so many degrees.

Teaching: Building on Informal Knowledge

At what grade level should negative numbers be introduced and how? Like any topic, when negative numbers should be introduced depends on the readiness of a student. In general, primary-level children can be introduced to negative numbers if done in a developmentally appropriate manner. Some teaching tips for doing so are noted below.

☞ **Ideally, a discussion of negative numbers would arise from a genuine need for such numbers.**

---

*In physics, the distinction between whole numbers and integers is paralleled by the distinction between scalar and vector quantities. Scalar quantities such as mass or time have a magnitude but do not act in a particular direction. Vector quantities such as weight have both magnitude and direction.

For example, as Part I of Probe 8.2 illustrates, certain games can create the opportunity to discuss negative scores.

☞ **Relate negative numbers to real and familiar situations** (e.g., owing money or temperatures below zero).

☞ **Help children understand the need for integers: In some situations we need to know direction as well as magnitude.**

☞ **To avoid confusion and to underscore their real meaning, refer to integers as positive or negative, not as plus or minus** (e.g., -3 should be called *negative three*, not *minus three*).

☞ **A number line can be a useful tool for helping children think about and use integers.** It can be particularly helpful when trying to order integers (e.g., determining whether -2 or -9 is larger).

8•2•2 OPERATIONS ON INTEGERS

In this subunit, we contrast the traditional skills approach with the meaningful investigative approach.

☞ Try Investigation 8.10 (pages 8-24 to 8-27).

Learning: Common Difficulties with the Skills Approach

Frequently, traditional instruction introduces integer arithmetic before students have had a chance to construct an understanding of negative numbers and little or no effort is made to relate the symbolism to everyday situations such as credit and debt. Instead, instruction focuses on fostering the memorization of meaningless rules (e.g., see Box 8.1 on page 8-24).

For instance, like many textbooks, the 8th-grade edition of *The Math Book from Hell* defines subtraction as "*adding the opposite.*" It illustrates this point with the example: 5 - (-2) = 5 + (+2) = 7. It notes that 5 minus a negative two means 5 plus the opposite of negative 2 or 5 plus 2. Unfortunately, many students do not find such an explanation helpful in *understanding* subtraction with integers. Moreover, like some textbooks, *The Math Book from Hell* does not provide any everyday analogies or word problems so that students can attach meaning to this process. For example, an expression such as 5 - (-2) does not make a great deal of (continued on page 8-28)

☪ Investigation 8.10: Meaningful Instruction of Operations on Integers

◆ Informal integer addition, subtraction, multiplication, and division ◆ Any number

Was your instruction similar to that illustrated in Box 8.1 below? *Do you recall how to answer* $5 - (-8) = \Box$ *or* $-5 \times (-8) = \Box$ *? Could you explain to a student why you get the answer you got?* The aim of this activity is to help students relate integer operations to what they know and help them rediscover the rules for such arithmetic procedures. To see what is involved and to perhaps deepen your own understanding of integer operations, try the following activities yourself, preferably with the aid of your group. Discuss your findings with your group or class.

Box 8.1: A Case of What Not to Do When Teaching Operations on Integers

At the beginning of her student-teaching assignment, Miss Brill was sent to Ms. Quick's eighth-grade class to observe. She found her to be highly organized and efficient. The lesson for the day was summarized neatly on the board:

Rules for Multiplying Signed Numbers
 *Determine the value of the product
  by multiplying the factors.
 *If the signs of the factors are the
  same, the product is positive.
 *If the signs of the factors are
  different, the product is negative.

Ms. Quick illustrated the rules with examples such as $(-7)(+5) = -35$ and $(-7)(-5) = +35$, noted that the material would be tested at the end of the week and, to foster the memorization of the rules, assigned a vast amount of homework. Most of the students simply accepted the rules as more math magic and passively began their assignment. But not Janis who asked, "Why does a negative times a negative produce a positive?" Miss Brill found the question disconcerting. Ms. Quick mumbled something, but neither Janis nor Miss Brill understood it.

Activity I: A Credit-and-Debit Analogy for Adding and Subtracting Integers (◆ 3-8)

1. Solve each of the following word problems informally.

  ■ **Problem A.** The balance in Marco's checking account was $12 when he wrote a check for $7 for a calculator he bought from Joe's Jip Joint. If he added a debit of $7 to his balance of $12, what new balance should Marco record in his checkbook?

  ■ **Problem B.** The calculator Marco bought at Joe's Jip Joint acted peculiarly from the start and then died altogether. Marco called Joe's and was told that all he probably needed was a new battery. A new battery did not help, and Marco called the bank to cancel the $7 check he wrote for the calculator. What's Marco's new balance if the debit of $7 is canceled?

  ■ **Problem C.** Marco was so happy that justice was served he went to dinner and wrote a check for $17 to cover the expenses. If he added a debit of $17 to his account, what's Marco's new balance?

  ■ **Problem D.** After dinner, Marco bought some art supplies for $7 and paid for it by check. If this debt is also added to his account, what happens to his balance?

  ■ **Problem E.** The next day Marco got some bad news from the bank. The check for $10 he got from Rocko for his Beatles' *Revolver* Album—and that he had already recorded in his check book— bounced. If Marco canceled out this credit for $10, what is his new balance?

  ■ **Problem F.** It suddenly dawned on Marco he didn't have much money in his checking account. He went to the bank and deposited $20. Adding a credit of $20 does what to his balance?

  ■ **Problem G.** The bank teller completed the transaction and noted Marco's new balance still indicated he was overdrawn. Marco asked to have his last (the $7) check voided, went to the art store, and paid the $7 by—what else—credit card. After the $7 check was canceled, what was his balance?

Investigation 8.10 continued

2. Write a number sentence that summarizes the events of each word problem above using (a) whole-number notation and (b) integer notation.

Activity II: A Charged-Particles Analogy for Adding and Subtracting Integers (◆ 5-8)

Using two differently colored counters such as black and red checkers can provide a useful concrete model for representing operations on integers (Battista, 1983). For example, black checkers can represent credits and red checkers can represent debits. Students should quickly see that one black checker and one red checker or any equal number of black and red checkers neutralize each other.

A particularly useful analogy for guiding the use of counters is the charged-particles analogy. Black checkers can be thought of as positively-charged particles; the red checkers, as negatively-charged particles. Before using this analogy to model operations on integers, it can be helpful to introduce the idea of a net charge. Imagine a box with a number of positive and negative charges such as the examples shown below. What is the net charge of each box? Check your answer with your group or class.

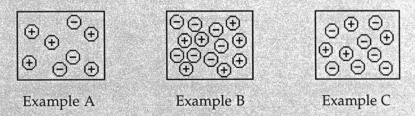

Example A   Example B   Example C

A charged-particles analogy is highly intuitive because it builds on a student's familiar change-add-to interpretation of addition and change take-away meaning of subtraction. Consider what happens to the net charge of the box after some positive or negative charges have been added or taken away. In Example D below, the box starts with a net charge of +2, three negatively-charged particles are added to the box, resulting in a new net charge of -1. In Example E, the box starts with a net charge of -3 and two negatively-charged particles are removed from the box, resulting in a new net charge of -1.

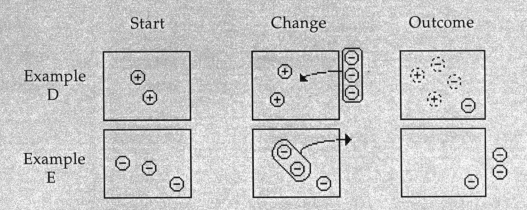

Any model of integer addition and subtraction should clearly distinguish between + and - signs indicating a direction and those indicating an operation. Note that the charged-particle analogy meets this essential criterion. Example D can be illustrated by the expression (+2) + (-3) = -1. Note that the + (positive) sign in +2 represents the *positive charge (the direction of the charge)* and + (plus) sign between +2 and -3 represents *adding* charges to the box (*the operation of addition*). Example E can be illustrated by the expression (-3) - (-2) = (-1). The - (negative)

sign in -3, -2, and -1 each represent a negative charge (the direction of the charge) and - (minus) sign between -3 and -2 represents *taking away* charges from the box *(the operation of subtraction)*.

In addition to the net charge, this model assumes that a box also contains an infinite number of positive charges and an equal number of negative charges. Example E on page 8-25, for instance, shows a net starting charge of -3. Not shown are all the positive and negative charges that neutralize each other. In some cases, it will be necessary to depict neutralized charges as well as the net charge. For each equation below, illustrate how the charged-particle model could be used to determine the answer. In which of the situations below do you need to represent neutralized charges as well as the net charge. Why?

Equation	Start ⟶	Change ⟶	Outcome
(+3) + (+2) = +5			
(+3) + (-2) = + 1			
(-3) + (+2) = -1			
(-3) + (-2) = -5			
(+3) - (+2) = +1			
(+3) - (-2)= +5			
(-3) - (+2) = -5			
(-3) - (-2) = -1			

Investigation 8.10 continued

Activity III: Analyzing a Car Analogy for Integer Addition and Subtraction[2] (◆ 5-8)

The following analogy involves driving a car on a number line.

- A positive integer = drive forward the distance indicated; a negative integer = drive in reverse the distance indicated.

- A plus sign indicates the car continues to face right; a minus sign, the car turns around (does a 180).

1. Does this model clearly and consistently distinguish between the direction and operation meaning of the + and - signs?

2. Does the model work in all possible instances?

Activity IV: A Repeated-Addition Analogy for Integer Multiplication (◆ 6-8)

1. Could 3 x 5 and 3 x (-5) be readily interpreted in terms of a repeated-addition analogy?

2. Is there any way to make sense of -3 x (+5) in terms of a repeated-addition analogy?

3. (a) Is there any way to make sense of -3 x (-5) in terms of a repeated-addition analogy?
   (b) Can this analogy be modified to explain the expression in Question 3a?

Activity V: Charged-Particles Analogy for Multiplying Integers (◆ 6-8)

Assume that you start with a neutral box. Using a *groups-of* interpretation, what would happen to the neutral box in each of the following situations: (a) (+3) x (+2), (b) (+3) x (-2), (c) (-3) x (+2), (d) (-3) x (-2)?

Activity VI: Division of Integers (◆ 7-8)

1. Write a rate problem for the expressions -18 ÷ -3 = ☐ and -18 ÷ 6 = ☐. Assume these two expressions are related to the same multiplication expression -3 x (+6) = -18.

2. If (+2) x (+3) = +6 can be thought of as "Add two groups of three positive charges to a neutral box resulting in a net charge of positive six," then (+6) ÷ (+3) = ? can be thought of as: "How many groups of positive three do I need to add or subtract to a neutral box to give it a net charge of +6?" Clearly, you would need to *add two* groups of +3. Thus, the quotient is +2. Explain how the charged-particle analogy would apply to each of the following equations: (a) -6 ÷ (-3) = ?, (b) (-6) ÷ (+3) = ?, or (c) (+6) ÷ (-3) = ?. Illustrate how counters could be used to determine each quotient.

Activity VII: Rediscovering the Rules for Operating on Integers (◆ 7-8)

1. Consider how the charged-particles analogy illustrated in Activity II could lead students to rediscover (a) the rule for adding integers and (b) the *add-the-opposite* rule for subtracting integers.

2. Consider how the charged-particles analogy could lead students to discover the rules for multiplying integers for themselves.

sense to students because they do not understand how you can take away a negative quantity.

.The result is that although students typically have little trouble adding integers, many have great difficulty with the other operations. For example, when asked to answer (-2) - (-7), some students will guess -9, +9, and -5 before they finally try the correct answer: +5.[3]

Teaching: The Investigative Approach

The investigative approach can avoid the difficulties common to the traditional skills approach. Consider the following general guidelines.

☞ **Introduce and practice operations on integers in a purposeful way.** Creating a real need for integer addition, subtraction, multiplication, and division makes exploring and practicing operations on integers worthwhile and interesting to students. One way this can be done is to set up a classroom economic system where students can accumulate credits and debts (see Activity File 8.1). Another way is to play games that involve positive and negative scores (see, e.g., Activity File 8.2 on the next page).

☞ **Relate operating on integers to children's existing knowledge and help them devise informal strategies for performing operations on integers.** Investigation 8.10 illustrates some meaningful analogies that children can use as the basis for modeling operations on integers with manipulatives or pictures. For example, pose problems tied to familiar analogies such as credit and debit or temperature like Problem 8.1 below.

■ **Problem 8.1: A Drop in Temperature** (◆ 2-6). It's very cold out, only 5° F. It gets colder and the temperature drops 7°. What is the new temperature?

Note that contrary to the warning often heard from primary teachers, in some situations it makes sense to subtract the larger (absolute value) from the smaller (absolute value). It is not possible only if we specify that answers must be a whole number.

☞ **For some children, a number line may help to make operating of integers more concrete.** Children can count on a number line to determine an answer and use it to see where the answer stands relative to zero. For the temperature problem above, for instance, a child could begin at 5 on

---

⚫ Activity File 8.1: Classroom Economy[4]

◆ Operations on integers ◆ 2-8 ◆ Whole class

To introduce operations on integers, keeping track of a checking account, and consumer-education issues, Mrs. Bartels instituted an economic system for her classroom. Each week, the teacher issued each child in the class a paycheck. The paycheck included a base salary plus bonuses for good effort and performing extra class chores. Fines for misconduct levied by the class court were deducted from the paycheck. Children deposited their paychecks in the class bank, managed by students. They could spend money at, for example, a class store and entertainment center—both also managed by students. The class store contained various items including some of Mrs. Bartels' personal memorabilia, items discovered in cleaning out the classroom closet, donated items, and an assortment of school supplies. The entertainment center contained, for example, a computer with computer games and an assortment of board games. Student purchases were recorded by shopkeepers by stamping the amount spent in a buyer's checkbook in red ink. Students could also use their class money as barter among themselves. Transfer of funds had to be recorded at the bank though.

---

the number line, count seven to the left to model the drop of 7°, and see that the answer is less than zero.

☞ **Encourage children to translate integer problem situations into symbolic form and vice versa** (see, e.g., Activity I on pages 8-24 and 8-25 of Investigation 8.10). In time, symbolic representations can be introduced. Initially, Problem 8.1 above could be represented as 5 - 7 = -2. Later, the more formal representation 5 + (-7) = -2 or (+5) + (-7) = -2 could be introduced to represent such a problem.*

---

*The expressions 5 - 7 and 5 + (-7) mean exactly the same thing. Though not written as (+5) + (-7) in practice, this highly stylized format may have the advantage of reminding children that integers are directed magnitudes (indicate direction as well as magnitude). Moreover, because the direction indicators are enclosed in parentheses with the value for magnitude, it may help children to distinguish between + and - signs as direction symbols and these signs as operation symbols. Once children understand these key ideas, the common format of 5 + (-7) can be introduced as a shortcut for writing (+5) + (-7). Indeed, coming full circle, the format 5 - 7 can be viewed as a more compact way of writing 5 + (-7).

🍎 Activity File 8.2: *Golf*

◆ Introduce or practice adding integers ◆ 2-8 ◆ Two to six

Mrs. Kail combined her passion for golf and the investigation approach to introduce the integers and integer addition informally in the form of a game. After a brief discussion of the sport of golf, she noted that a golfer can be par (sink the ball in the prescribed number of strokes), over par (take more than the prescribed number of strokes), or under par (take fewer than the prescribed number of strokes).

The Rules. Mrs. Kail then noted that each group of four would be a foursome. Each group was given a brown paper bag containing a green die and a red die, each labeled 0 to 5. Mrs. Kail explained, "To determine the scores for a hole, each player in turn will reach into the bag and—without looking—pull out one die, roll it, and put it back into the bag. The color of the die and the outcome of the roll dictate a player's score (e.g., a green 3 indicated three *over* par; a green or red 0, par; and a red 1, one *under* par). A player's score for the hole is added to his or her existing score, if any. The player with the *lowest* score after 9 holes is the winner. (For a longer game, have players complete 18 turns.)

The class started to play, and this resulted in a number of questions. For example, Little Bear asked, "My score is one green, and I've rolled a red 2. I am not sure, but I think my score is one red." Mrs. Kail asked if that made sense. Little Bear and his group agreed that it did.

Concrete Scoring Procedure (◆ 2-4).[5] To help the students keep score, Mrs. Kail gave each group a pile of green and red chips and instructed, "If Aziz, for example, rolled a green 5 on his first turn, he would collect five green chips. If he rolled a red 3 on his next turn, he would collect three red chips and add them to the chips he already has. Now what do you think happens

when a red chip and a green chip are placed together? The class agreed that these chips would cancel each other and could be returned to the pot. Mrs. Kail then asked what Aziz's new score would be. There was general agreement it was now two green chips or two over par.

Symbolic Scoring Procedure (◆ 3-8). In time, Kristin's group proposed using number symbols—for example, $\underline{1}$ for a green 1 (one over par) and $\overline{3}$ for a red 3 (three under par)—to keep a running tally as shown to the right.

$$\frac{\begin{array}{r} \underline{1} \\ + \ \ \underline{3} \end{array}}{\underline{2}}$$

Later, Mrs. Kail introduced more conventional symbols for integers and a score sheet, a part of which is shown below.

Particularly for cases such as + 3 - (-5), there was sometimes confusion. For example, Rochester argued that it could not be done. At this juncture, Mrs. Kail encouraged students to think about the green-and-red chip model. She also related such symbolism to a credit-debit analogy (e.g., you combine receiving $3 with spending $5) or temperature analogy (3° C combined with a drop of 5°). Typically, students soon reasoned that the answer had to be a minus two. Mrs. Kail suggested using *negative two* so that people would not be confuse -2 with "subtracting two."

↪ **Encourage children to rediscover the rules for operating on integers.** BY USING MEANINGFUL ANALOGIES TO DETERMINE THE OUTCOME OF AN INTEGER OPERATION, REPRESENTING IT IN A NUMBER SENTENCE, AND LOOKING FOR PATTERNS, STUDENTS CAN DEVISE THE FORMAL RULES FOR OPERATING ON INTEGERS THEMSELVES. For example, by using a charged-particles analogy and colored cubes, children can solve problems involving integer ad-

dition. By summarizing their solutions as equations (e.g., +3 + [+2] = +5, -3 + [-2] = -5, +3 + [-2] = +1, -3 + [+2] = -1) and looking for patterns, they should be able to discover the following shortcuts for their informal procedures: *When adding two integers with like signs, find their sum and keep the same sign. When adding two integers with different signs, find their dif-*

ference and use the sign of the integer with the larger magnitude. Playing a game (see, e.g., Activity File 8.2 on page 8-29) can be a motivating way for encouraging students to find such rules.

PARTING THOUGHTS

"Instruction should help students see the underlying structure of mathematics, which bonds its many individual facets into a useful, interesting, and logical whole . . . . Understanding this structure . . . offers insights into how the whole number system is extended to the rational number system and beyond [and] improves problem-solving capability by providing a [broader] perspective of arithmetic operations . . . . Instruction . . . should employ informal explorations and emphasize the reasons why various kinds of numbers occur, . . . and relationships between number systems" (NCTM, 1989, p. 91).

The study of number theory and integers provide rich opportunities for exploring, conjecturing, problem solving, reasoning, and practicing basic skills. Instruction in these areas should encourage informal understanding and looking for patterns.

RESOURCES

SOME INSTRUCTIONAL RESOURCES

☛ **Number Lines, Functions, and Fundamental Topics** by David A. Page, © 1964 by Macmillan. This text uses a cricket jumping on a number line to illustrate various mathematical concepts including negative numbers. The figures below illustrate counting by threes starting with 0 and counting by threes starting with 2.

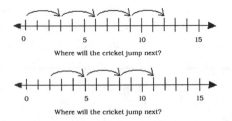

Where will the cricket jump next?

Where will the cricket jump next?

On page 49, the text suggests that a number line can be used to introduce negative numbers: "Negative numbers come up spontaneously when a class considers what to do when they are jumping to the left and they get close to

zero." Page noted that children come up with interesting informal answers (e.g., "under two," "zero minus two" and "good-bye two") as well as more conventional answers (e.g., "two below zero").

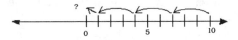

The text offers a number of excellent recommendations for teaching negative numbers. One is using informal symbols to denote negative numbers such as b3 for "three below zero." With an informal number line like that shown below, children can make sense of expressions such as 2 - 3 (answer: b1) or b2 - 1 (answer: b3). Note that with this informal notation, the sign for a position below zero and the sign for subtraction are distinct.

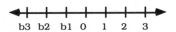

☛ **Problems with Patterns and Numbers,** © 1984 by the Shell Centre for Mathematical Education, University of Nottingham, Nottingham, England. This program is a particularly rich source of instructional ideas on number and arithmetic patterns. It is an excellent example of an inquiry-based program. For example, the activities begin with a challenging problem. Though most of the activities are appropriate for intermediate-grade students, a number of activities can be used, or adapted for use, with primary students. The activity titled *Factors* poses questions such as: What sequence of numbers has, with the exception of 1, only even factors? What sequence of numbers has even numbers for exactly one-half of its factors? For each sequence above, explain why the pattern is true. Another example of an activity from this program is illustrated by Activity I in Investigation 8.11 on page 8-33.

A SAMPLE OF CHILDREN'S LITERATURE

☚ **Charlie and the Great Glass Elevator** by Roald Dahl, © 1972, Alfred A. Knopf. This story involves negative numbers.

☚ **Cosmic View: The Universe in 40 Jumps** by Kees Boeke, © 1957, John Dax. This book takes readers on a journey from the edge of the universe to inside the atom and can provide a jumping off point for discussing huge and tiny numbers. This, in turn, can create a need to discuss powers of ten and scientific notation.

- **Less Than Nothing Is Really Something** by Robert Froman, © 1973 by Thomas Y. Crowell. This book introduces negative numbers in terms of debt (owing money), temperature, elevation below sea level, and a launch count down (e.g., 0 - 3 seconds means 3 seconds *before* blast off, blast off is 0 or the origin, and 0 + 3 seconds means 3 seconds after blast off). It uses a number line and a shuffleboard-like game named P.A.M. to elucidate negative numbers and addition with such numbers. One thing the book does not point out is that, mathematically, the minus sign can have two different meanings. Indeed, it refers to owing one penny as *minus* one, which may obscure the direction connotation of the symbol. (A teacher could point out that the minus sign in a sign number indicates direction, rather than subtraction and, though -1 is commonly referred to as minus one, it might be less confusing to call it negative one.)

- **Number Ideas Through Pictures** by Mannis Charosh, © 1974 by Thomas Y. Crowell. The natural numbers are introduced as "the numbers we count with" and can also *play* with (p. vi). Even and odd numbers are defined in terms of pairing familiar things such as the number of children in your class. The even and odd sequences are then *deduced* from these definitions by encouraging readers to identify which numbers from 1 to 10, represent collections that can be paired up and which that cannot. The odd-even pattern of the counting is then noted.

The reader is then encouraged to discover the even-odd rules for addition by posing questions such as "What kind of numbers do you get if you add two even numbers?" (p. 8). The L-shaped pattern for odd numbers and the square numbers are introduced as a prelude for asking what happens when the L-shaped arrays of consecutive odd numbers are combined (e.g., 1 + 3 + 5 + 7).

Triangular numbers are introduced as a prelude to asking what happens when we add consecutive counting numbers (e.g., 1 + 2 + 3 + 4). Common examples of triangular numbers such as bowling pins and racked pool balls are shown. The reader is then encouraged to think about what happens when two consecutive triangular numbers are added. Answer the following questions based on this book. (1) What shape results from adding a triangular number eight times and then adding one? (2) Adding 3-squared (9) and 4-squared (16) produces another square. Is it true of the sum of any two squared numbers? What pattern do you notice?

- **Number Patterns Make Sense** by Howard Fehr, © 1965, Holt, Rinehart & Winston. Problems can prompt students to rediscover patterns central to number theory.

- **Odds and Evens** by Thomas C. O'Brien, © 1971 by Thomas Y. Crowell. Though even and odd numbers are never explicitly defined, this book is a treasure trove of examples and ideas. Using the analogy of people, the book notes there are "many types of numbers" (p. 4). Even and odd numbers are two types of numbers. Examples of each up to 10 and 9, respectively, are illustrated with various everyday things. The importance of even numbers is underscored by suggesting that team sports usually have an even number of players. For instance, a basketball team may have an odd number of players, but the game involves an even number. The importance of odd numbers is illustrated by the difficulties caused by a split vote in a family with an even number of people.

The even sequence is introduced in an interesting fashion by having the reader touch thumbs (two); then thumbs and first fingers (four); next thumbs, first fingers, and second fingers (six); and so forth. Using the picture of an alien creature, the reader is asked to imagine matching up more than 10 fingers. The reader is then asked what the type of numbers are obtained by matching fingers.

The book then poses a number of problems that are designed to encourage the exploration of the odd and even pattern for addition. It even broaches the odd and even patterns of repeated addition (multiplication) by posing the question: Are there an even number of noses, ears and other body parts in your family?

Some questions:

1. Encouraging children to identify various numbers of matched fingers as even involves what types of reasoning? Recall that the term had previously been associated with two, four, six, eight, and ten things.

2. The odd-even pattern for addition is introduced with a delightful activity. The reader is encouraged to use a pencil to punch three holes through two pieces of paper held together. The child is then encouraged to count the total number of holes in both papers and to determine if there is an even or odd number of holes. The child is encouraged to do the same with four and five pencil punches. Consider how this activity could be used to introduce odd-even multiplication patterns. How could you structure the activity such that children were likely to notice the pattern?

TIPS ON USING TECHNOLOGY

Calculators

As Investigation 8.11 illustrates, there are numerous ways of exploring number patterns with calculators. One resource is described below.

☞ Try Investigation 8.11 (pages 8-33 and 3-34).

▦ **Keystrokes: Calculator Activities for Young Students: Multiplication and Division** by Robert E. Reys, Barbara J. Bestgen, Terrence G. Coburn, Harold L. Schoen, Richard J. Shumway, Charlotte L. Wheatley, Grayson H. Wheatley, and Arthur L. White, © 1979 by Creative Publications. This resource includes activities on factors, primes and composites, prime factorization, and divisibility rules.

Computers

You or your students may wish to visit the following web sites: "The Largest Known Primes" (http://www.utm.edu/research/primes/largest.html), "Fibonacci Numbers and the Golden Section" (http://www.mcs.surrey.ac.uk/Personal /R.Knott/Fibonacci/fib.html), and "Numbers and Units" (http://www.math-science.sfasu.edu/physics101/NUMBERS&UNITS.html). The latter includes information and challenging questions about scientific notation.

▯ 🍎 As part of a project, encourage children to collect data on the Internet and use scientific notation as a shorthand for recording the data totals. The following reference describes programs for generating different types of numbers.

▯ **Mathematics** by Irving Adler, © 1990 by Doubleday. Among other topics, this resource describes in straightforward language and pictorial models even and odd numbers; integers; rectangular numbers (composites); prime numbers; divisors; square numbers; triangular numbers; squares, perfect, amicable, and sociable numbers; and the Fibonacci numbers. It delineates a BASIC program and a flow chart for printing out most of these types of numbers. Importantly for computer novices, it explains why each step of the program is written as it is. The program for printing the first 20 Fibonacci Numbers is show below:

```
20   A=1:B=1:N=2
30   PRINT A:PRINT B
40   C=A+B:N=N+1
50   IF N=21 THEN STOP
60   PRINT C
70   A=B:B=C:GOTO 40
```

In Step 20, N=2 means the first two numbers in the sequence; A and B define the value of the first two terms. Step 30 simply tells the computer to print out the first two numbers: 1 1. What do the two commands in Step 40 tell the computer to do? Why is Step 50 included in the program? What do the first two commands in Step 70 (A=B:B=C) do? What does the third command (GOTO 40) do?

The text also encourages readers how to modify a program to create new programs. How can the program for printing the natural numbers up to 20 (below) be modified to print the even or odd numbers:

```
10   N=1
20   PRINT N
30   N=N+1
35   IF N=21 THEN STOP
40   GO TO 20
```

🖩 ✎ Investigation 8.11: Exploring Number Patterns with a Calculator

◆ Inductive reasoning ◆ Individually, small group or class*

Calculators can be an invaluable aid in looking for patterns because they free students from the tedium of calculating. This investigation illustrates six calculation-based explorations of patterns. To see what is involved and to perhaps deepen your own understanding of numbers, try them yourself. Share your findings with your group or class.

Activity I: *Target*† (◆ 3-8)

Make each number from 1 to 10 using two or more of the following keys in your calculator.

You may use a key more than once. Make sure to clear each time. Is there more than one way to make some of the numbers?

| 3 | 4 | x | - | = |

1:	6:
2:	7:
3:	8:
4:	9:
5:	10:

Activity II: Nines Gone Wild (◆ 4-8)

"Last week I asked you to write a paper on how much money you thought you would need to live the good life," began Miss Brill. "Rodney came up with an interesting answer: nine hundred ninety-nine trillion, nine hundred ninety-nine billion, nine hundred ninety-nine million, nine hundred ninety-nine thousand, nine hundred ninety-nine *times* nine." Writing out each name and digit as it was announced produced:

$$999,999,999,999,999 \times 9$$

The class quickly recognized the repetitive pattern of our spoken number system. Some students were curious about how the terms millions, billions and trillions come about. Miss Brill suggested they check a reference like an unabridged dictionary. (Jane later reported that million comes from the Latin word mille meaning a thousand: A million is a thousand thousands. Billion comes from the French contraction of the Latin word bis meaning twice and million: twice a million. Trillion comes from the French tri and million.)

After a discussion of the spoken number system, Miss Brill asked Rodney why he had settled on the number written on the board. Rodney indicated that he thought of the largest number he knew and—just to be on the safe side—multiplied it by nine. "What is 999,999,999,999,999 times 9?" Miss Brill asked coyly. Several students tried to use their calculators but found they could not enter all 15 digits of the huge number.

"It appears we'll have to use another method to get the answer," commented Miss Brill.

"We could just multiply it out," noted Rodney. "But that would take awhile." Zev started to multiply using the multidigit algorithm anyway.

"You don't need to go through all the work of multiplying it out if you know nine times nine," commented Miss Brill.

"How would that help?" asked Rodney. "This is 15 nines times 9."

---

†This activity is based on a lesson described in *Problems with Patterns and Numbers*, © 1984 by the Shell Centre for Mathematical Education, University of Nottingham, England.

Investigation 8.11 continued

"Well," proceeded Miss Brill, "what's 99 x 9? 999 x 9? 9999 x 9?"

"I don't know," answered Rodney.

"Well, then, our next task is to learn the facts involving 99, 999, or 9,999 and a single-digit number from 0 to 9."

"Great," whispered Rick as he jabbed Rodney in the back. "Because of your stupid essay, we have to memorize a billion new multiplication facts."

"She really has gone too far this time," whispered Rodney as he tried to jab Rick's arm with his elbow.

Rick and Rodney weren't the only ones upset. Indeed, the groaning and complaining were so loud, Miss Brill's next words could not be heard. From the glint in her eye, LeMar figured the teacher had something up her sleeve. "Let her finish," he commanded.

The room fell silent and Miss Brill continued, "You may work in your groups and you may use a calculator to determine the answers."

LeMar, curious what Miss Brill had in mind, began calculating answers. Rodney suggested creating a table to keep track of the answers.

1. Is it as difficult as Miss Brill's class initially thought to learn 99 x 1, 99 x 2, 99 x 3, ...99 x 9; 999 x 1, 999 x 2, 999 x 3, ...999 x 9; and 9,999 x 1, 9,999 x 2, 9,999 x 3, ...9,999 x 9? Why or why not?

2. After the table was completed, Miss Brill challenged the class with: Predict what 999,999,999,999,999 x 9 will be.

3. After the class made their prediction, Zev who had finally finished calculating the product by hand commented: "That's what I got, it makes sense." Try using the multidigit algorithm to find the product of 999,999,999,999,999 x 9. What do you notice?

Activity III: A Square Root Too Far (◆ 5-8)

Enter a small number such as 3 in your calculator, hit the square-root key, and keep hitting this key. What eventually happens? Try another number. Does the same thing happen? Try a third number. What do you predict will happen? Is the twenty-fifth root of 3 really what the calculator says? Why or why not? Try graphing the roots of 3. What problems do you encounter? What does the graph illustrate?

Activity IV: Patterns in the Fibonacci Numbers (◆ 5-8)

The Fibonacci numbers (1, 1, 2, 3, 5, 8 . . .) are formed by adding the previous two terms (e.g., the sixth term is formed by adding the fourth and fifth terms: 3 + 5 = 8). Use a calculator to determine the first 20 Fibonacci Numbers. Examine this list for patterns. How often do multiples of the first five primes come up? Do the multiples of any other numbers reoccur and, if so, is there a pattern?

Activity V: Dividing by Eleven Made Easy[†] (◆ 4-8)

A class was working on converting fractions into decimals by dividing the numerator by the denominator. They found that $\frac{1}{11}$ = .09090909 . . . . Working with other fractions involving elevenths, some students discovered an interesting pattern. (a) Use a calculator to convert other fractions involving elevenths into decimals. What do you notice? (b) Does the pattern hold for improper fractions like $\frac{12}{11}$, $\frac{13}{11}$ or $\frac{14}{11}$?

Activity VI: Multiplying with 12345679[†] (◆ 4-8)

Follow the instructions and answer the questions below.

a. Calculate the product of 12345679 x 9. Is the product in any way surprising or interesting?
b. Now, calculate the product of 12345679 x 18. Is this product in any way surprising or interesting?
c. Try calculating the product of 12345679 x 27. Does there seem to be any pattern?
d. Represent the three expressions above and your calculated products in the form of number sentences. Does there seem to be any pattern?
e. Do you think there is anything that 12345679 can be multiplied by to produce 444444444? Try and see.

[†] Based on the case Study of Paul reported by S.R.A. Court's self-taught arithmetic from the age of five to the age of eight (*Pedagogical Seminary*, 1923, 30, 510-558) described in *Children's Arithmetic* (Ginsburg, 1989).

9 WORKING WITH "PARTS OF A WHOLE" AND OTHER MEANINGS OF RATIONAL NUMBERS AND COMMON FRACTIONS

It's Rational-Number Man. He's different. But he's powerful. He comes in many disguises and can do many things. Can you find him to the right?

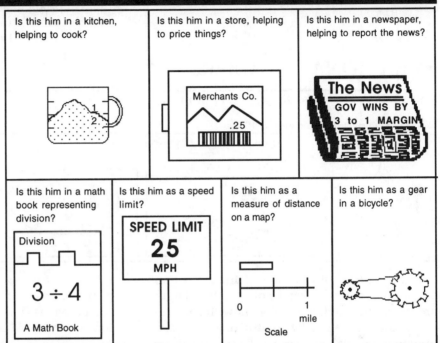

Is this him in a kitchen, helping to cook?

Is this him in a store, helping to price things?

Merchants Co. .25

Is this him in a newspaper, helping to report the news?

The News
GOV WINS BY
3 to 1 MARGIN

Is this him in a math book representing division?

Division

3 ÷ 4

A Math Book

Is this him as a speed limit?

SPEED LIMIT
25
MPH

Is this him as a measure of distance on a map?

0   1
mile
Scale

Is this him as a gear in a bicycle?

☞ Which of the items above illustrate a rational number? To create a "living bulletin board," students could be encouraged to add their own examples of how the rational numbers, in their various guises, are used in everyday life. What examples can you add?

THIS CHAPTER

Rational numbers are, as the bulletin board suggests, an invaluable "beast of burden" but a different kind of animal. (Recall from chapter 8 that a *rational number is a ratio of two integers a and b, where b is not equal to 0.*) In chapters 4 to 7, we examined whole-number concepts and skills, the focus of primary-level mathematics. In chapter 8, we examined patterns involving whole numbers and introduced a new set of numbers called the *integers*, which include the negative numbers. However, there are many situations involving *parts of things*, situations that whole numbers and integers cannot adequately describe. The numbers that can describe parts of things are called the *rational numbers*. Rational numbers can behave quite differently from the familiar whole numbers. In this chapter, we explore why they can seem SO STRANGE to children and can cause them so much fear.

As implied by the bulletin board above, describing parts of things is but one role rational numbers can play. In Unit 9•1, we describe these various roles. In Unit 9•2, we explore common fractions (e.g., $\frac{1}{3}$, $\frac{4}{5}$, and $\frac{9}{7}$), which are one way of representing rational numbers. This chapter lays the foundation for our discussion of operations on fractions (chapter 10), decimals (chapter 11), ratios (chapter 12), probability (chapter 13), measurement (chapter 14), and functions (chapter 16). "What's the connection?" you might ask. Read on.

WHAT THE NCTM *STANDARDS* SAY

Grades K-4

In grades K-4, the mathematics curriculum should include fractions so that students can:

- "develop concepts of fractions [and] mixed numbers . . . ;
- develop number sense for fractions [e.g., an ability to order fractions];
- use models . . . to find equivalent fractions;
- apply fractions . . . to problem situations" (p. 57).

Grades 5-8

9•1 RATIONAL NUMBERS

"In grades 5-8, the . . . curriculum should include the continued development of number and number relationships so that students can:

- understand, represent, and use numbers in a variety of equivalent forms [including fractions] in real-world and mathematical problem situations;
- develop number sense for . . . fractions . . . and rational numbers" (p. 87).

Figure 9.1: A Different Kind of Division

PEANUTS reprinted by permission of UFS, Inc.

In Figure 9.1, Sally is correct. In *some* situations, a smaller number can be divided by a larger number. In this unit, we explore how this is possible (Subunit 9•1•1), why constructing an understanding of rational numbers can be so difficult for children (Subunit 9•1•2), and some suggestions for rational-number instruction (Subunit 9•1•3).

9•1•1 MATHEMATICS

In this subunit, we examine why fractions were invented and why rational numbers are important mathematically. We then outline key meanings of rational numbers and the distinctions among rational numbers, fractions, and common fractions.

The Need for Rational Numbers Then and Now

☞ Consider Probe 9.1 (page 9-3) and Investigation 9.1 (pages 9-4 and 9-5).

Historical Perspective. The growth of agriculture, commerce, and civilization required surveying land, exchanging goods, and collecting taxes. Because these matters required written records and often involved parts of units or wholes, a need arose for symbols that represented parts of something. Fractions were invented to fill this practical need.

How do you specify the number of things when you have a part of something? The ancients solved problems such as those in Part I of Investigation 9.1 by dividing a whole into *equal*-size parts, counting the parts of interest, and comparing this count to the total number of parts. Fractions provided a convenient and compact way of representing parts of a whole.

The fundamentally important concept of *equal partitioning (dividing a quantity into equal size parts)* can be done with either *countable collections (discrete quantities)* or *quantities that must be measured (continuous quantities).* Consider, for example, Part II of Investigation 9.1. A candy stick can be shared fairly among five people by estimating one-fifth of the stick, seeing if this length will fit the stick exactly five times, adjusting the estimate, and so forth.

Mathematical Perspective. *How is division unique among the arithmetic operations on whole numbers and how is this relevant to understanding rational numbers?* When whole numbers are added, subtracted, or multiplied, the outcome is always a whole number. The same is not true for division. In some situations, a quantity can be equally divided and the outcome is a whole number. For Problems A and C in Part III of Investigation 9.1, for example, 12 (continued on page 9-6)

➤ Probe 9.1: Discrete Versus Continuous Quantities

To better understand rational numbers, it is important to understand explicitly the distinction between discrete and continuous quantities. Chapters 4 to 8 focused on topics involving *discrete quantities*: collections consisting of distinct items. Because collections consists of separate, whole items, they have *no "in-betweens."* For example, a family might have two or three children, but not $2\frac{1}{2}$ or $2\frac{3}{4}$ children. Thus, the magnitude of any discrete quantities can, at least in principle, be determined by *counting*.

In contrast, *continuous quantities* involve nondiscrete quantities such as length, area, or volume. Such quantities can involve parts of a unit or *in-betweens*. For example, the length of an object can between 0 and 1 unit (e.g., $\frac{1}{2}$ unit) or between 2 and 3 units (e.g., $2\frac{3}{4}$ units). Such quantities must be *measured*.

To practice distinguishing between discrete and continuous quantities, answer the questions below either on your own or with the help of your group. Discuss your answers with your group or class.

1. Consider the examples below. Label discrete quantities D and continuous quantities C.

    ____ a. time

    ____ b. height

    ____ c. the population of the U.S.

    ____ d. air pressure

    ____ e. elevation above sea level

    ____ f. size of a car inventory

    ____ g. size of the national debt

    ____ h. level of math anxiety

2. Sometimes an object can be viewed as a discrete quantity for some purposes and as a continuous quantity for others. Consider the figure below:

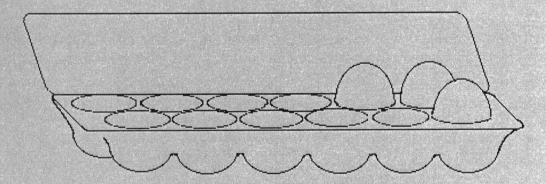

a. The number of eggs in the carton is what kind of quantity?

b. The weight of the eggs is what kind of quantity?

c. The amount of space an egg occupies is what kind of quantity?

d. The number of depressions in the egg carton is what kind of quantity?

e. The volume of air filling the depressions is what kind of quantity?

f. Can you specify whether the egg carton is a discrete quantity or a continuous quantity?

☿ Investigation 9.1: Understanding the Conceptual Basis for Fractions

◆ Equal partitioning of discrete and continuous quantities + proportional reasoning
◆ 4-8 ◆ Groups of four + class discussion

Part I illustrates several problems that involve determining the size of a part of some quantity. Ancient civilizations devised an intriguing solution for such problems—a solution that underlies both fractions and measurement. Part II illustrates an application of this solution to a fair-sharing task. Part III examines a unique operation and how an understanding of this operation can serve as a basis for understanding fractions. Complete each part below with the help of your group. Discuss your solutions with your group or class.

Part I: Problems Involving Parts of Things

What must be done to solve each of the following problems and why?

■ **Problem 1: Land Tax.** Land is taxed at $320 per undeveloped acre in Longgone County. The county agent's map shows that Mr. Bennett owns the part of an acre shown below. How much undeveloped land does Mr. Bennett own? How much tax does he owe?

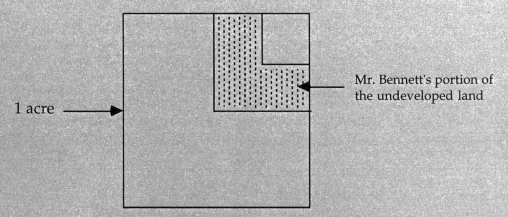

1 acre ⟶

Mr. Bennett's portion of the undeveloped land

■ **Problem 2: The Jail Sentence.** In Yukastan, the penalty for the possession of 1 kilo of cocaine is 100 years in jail. Sian the Smuggler was caught with the following amount of cocaine. How much cocaine did he have in his possession at the time of his apprehension? How many years in jail can Sian expect to spend?

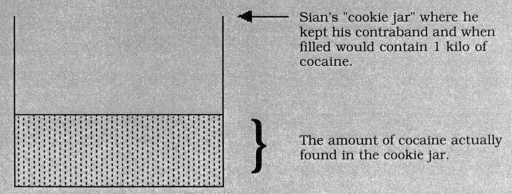

Sian's "cookie jar" where he kept his contraband and when filled would contain 1 kilo of cocaine.

} The amount of cocaine actually found in the cookie jar.

■ **Problem 3: Rope Rip-Off.** Beni needed only the darkened portion of a rope length shown in the figure below. What part of the rope length did he need? If the price for the full rope length was $3.60, how much should Beni be charged for the portion he wanted?

Investigation 9.1 continued

Part II: Sharing (a Continuous) Quantity Fairly[1]

Pretend that a straw is a candy stick. Without folding it, how could you share the straw fairly between two people? How could you determine each person's fair share if there were five people?

Sidelight: Evolution of Fraction Notation

Used by the Babylonians as early as 2000 B.C., fractions appear in the oldest written mathematical records found (Mainville, 1989). Early representations, though, were quite incomplete. For example, the ancient Egyptians represented fractions by placing a special symbol ($\bigcirc$) above the symbol for a counting number. For example, $\frac{1}{3}$ was represented by $\overset{\bigcirc}{\text{III}}$. However, with the exception of $\frac{2}{3}$ and $\frac{3}{4}$, the ancient Egyptians used only unit fractions such as $\frac{1}{2}$, $\frac{1}{3}$, and $\frac{1}{10}$ (Bunt et al., 1976, Davis, 1989). The Hindus either invented or borrowed from the later ancient Greeks the forerunner to modern fraction notation: writing the numerator above the denominator without a fraction bar. The Arabs then introduced the fraction-bar notation ($\frac{a}{b}$) as early as 1000 AD (Mainville, 1989).

1. How would the ancient Egyptians have represented $\frac{1}{10}$?

2. How would they have represented the following situation: A unit of land shared fairly among 21 people?

Part III: Examining a Unique Operation

Consider the following word problems:

- **Problem A:** Mr. Franklin had 12 large steel marbles ("steelies") that he wanted to give to his three sons. Could all the steelies be shared fairly among the sons and, if so, how many would each boy get?

- **Problem B:** While Mr. Franklin was driving home, the bag of steelies fell on the floor of the car and two disappeared through a hole in the floorboard. Could the remaining 10 steelies be shared fairly among his three sons and, if so, how many would each boy get?

- **Problem C:** Sally baked 12 cookies for her party. Including Sally, four children attended the party. Could all the cookies be shared fairly among the four children? If so, how many cookies did each child get?

- **Problem D:** Unfortunately, Ruffus the dog ate two cookies before the party. Can 10 cookies be shared fairly among four children? If so, how many cookies would each child get?

1. (a) Compare Problem A with B and C with D. What do these situations illustrate about division with whole numbers? (b) Now consider how division with whole numbers is different than the other operations with whole numbers.

2. How are Problems B and D similar and how do they differ?

3. In Figure 9.1 (on page 9-2), Charlie Brown told his sister Sally that 50 can't go into 25. (a) Why might he have drawn this conclusion? (b) Are there situations in which he is essentially correct? (c) In what situations is he, in fact, incorrect?

things can be divided evenly among three or four people. In other situations, a quantity cannot be divided evenly and the outcome is not a whole number. In Problems B and D, for instance, 10 whole objects *cannot* be divided fairly among three or four people.

In some of these situations, as in Problem B in Part III of Investigation 9.1, it makes sense to talk about a remainder: 10 marbles fairly shared among three boys would leave one leftover, because it is impossible to divide up the remaining marble. We represent such division situations with a remainder sign (e.g., $10 \div 3 = 3$ r1). In other situations, such as in Problem D in Part III of Investigation 9.1, though, a remaining item can be subdivided. To represent division situations in which the answer is not a whole number and there is no remainder, we need the rational numbers.[*] For example, the solution to Problem D can be represented by $10 \div 4 = 2\frac{1}{2}$.

Rational-Number Concepts and Symbols

Rational-Number Concepts or Meanings. *What meanings can rational numbers have?* Four primary meanings have been identified: part of a whole, ratio, quotient, and operator (Kieren, 1988).[**]

---

[*] For example, though the solutions to Problems A and C in Part III of Investigation 9.1 can be represented by integers, Problems B and D cannot. That is, within the integer number system, 10 cannot be divided equally and exhaustively by 3 or 4 and, thus, solutions to Problems B and D are not possible. (Mathematically, division—like other arithmetic operations—is defined as a binary operation. Because all the terms involved in a binary operation must come from the *same* number system, the division of two integers must have as a quotient an integer. The binary operation of division implies that a quantity being divided up must be shared equally and completely. Cases where division results in a remainder—that cannot be expressed as an integer—are not possible. When, as a practical matter, we represent division with a remainder sign [e.g., $10 \div 3 = 3$ r1], we are actually treating division as a *nonbinary* operation.) With only the integers, expressions such as $10 \div 4 = \square$ or $4 \times \square = 10$ cannot be completed. In some situations, such as Problem B in Part II of Investigation 9.1, it makes sense to dismiss the problem as unsolvable: If the 10 marbles must be shared fairly among three children and all the marbles must be shared, then a solution is not possible. In other situations, such as Problem D, a practical solution exists and it can be useful to model or represent these situations. Mathematicians accepted the rational numbers, then, because they needed a new number system to complete expressions such as $10 \div 4 = \square$ or $4 \times \square = 10$.

• **Part of a Whole.** The term *fraction* comes from the Latin *fractio* (a derivative of *frangere* meaning *to break*) and, thus, can refer to something broken into parts. More specifically, common fractions can represent a part-whole relationship: a number of parts (represented by the top term or the *numerator*) of a whole divided into equal-sized parts (the bottom term or the *denominator*).[***] What is involved in learning this meaning of fractions is developed further in this chapter.

• **Quotient.** A fraction can also represent division or a quotient meaning. For instance, $\frac{3}{4}$, can be used to represent three dollars divided fairly among four people. A quotient meaning of fractions is explored further in this chapter.

• **Ratio.** A fraction such as $\frac{4}{5}$ can also represent a ratio. A ratio can be represented in other ways such as 4:5. It describes a relationship between two quantities, which may or may not be a part-whole relationship. For example, the ratio 4:5 can represent either (a) four of the five marbles were blue (a part-whole relationship) or (b) there were four blue marbles for every five white marbles (not a part-whole relationship). Chapter 12 discusses various ways ratios can be used to compare quantities.

• **Operator.** An operator meaning can be thought of as a function that involves multiplying by a fraction. For example, an in-out machine with the rule *multiply by two-fifths* would transform an input of 15 into an output of 6. The ordered pairs (5, 2), (10, 4), (15, 6), and so forth could be used to graph this function.

Symbols for Rational Numbers: Common Fractions. *A common fraction is a fraction*

[**] Various other analyses of rational numbers have been offered (see Ohlsson, 1988). The Rational Number Project (Behr, Lesh, Post, & Silver, 1983), for example, included decimals (a special type of part-whole relationship in which the whole is equally divided into a number of parts that are a power of 10) and rate (a new quantity that is defined by the relationship between two other quantities—e.g., speed is the quotient of distance and time).

[***] Although the terms *numerator* and *denominator* are truly descriptive of only part-of-a-whole situations, they will be used to describe the top digit and bottom digit of a fraction representing the other rational number meanings as well.

in which both the terms are integers. For example, the fraction $\frac{3}{4}$ is a common fraction; the fraction $\frac{\sqrt{3}}{4}$ is not. Common fractions represent (are *names* for) rational numbers. At the elementary level, it is not particularly important to stress the distinctions between a concept and a symbol for the concept. What is important is that children understand that common fractions can have various meanings.

A *unit fraction* such as $\frac{1}{3}$ or $\frac{1}{10}$ has a numerator of 1; a *nonunit fraction* such as $\frac{2}{3}$ or $\frac{11}{10}$ has a numerator greater than 1. Unlike proper fractions, *improper fractions* such as $\frac{4}{3}$ have a numerator that is greater than the denominator. An improper fraction can also be represented as a *mixed number*—the combination of a whole number and a fraction (e.g., $\frac{4}{3}$ = the mixed number $1\frac{1}{3}$).

☞ Try Probe 9.2 (pages 9-8 and 9-9).

9•1•2 LEARNING: UNDERSTANDING THE TASK CONFRONTING CHILDREN

Rational-number concepts are difficult for children to construct (Behr et al., 1992). *Why?* There are both psychological and instructional reasons for this difficulty.

Psychological Difficulties

Differences Between Common Fractions and Whole Numbers. Rational numbers are different from the whole numbers with which children are familiar. Common fractions are their first encounter with a set of numbers not based on counting (Behr & Post, 1988). Solving problems involving fractional parts entails instead equal partitioning. Moreover, rational numbers embody a multiplicative relationship, not an additive relationship with which young children are familiar (Vergnaud, 1983). For instance, equivalent fractions are determined by multiplying the numerator and the denominator by the same number (e.g., $\frac{2}{3} \times \frac{2}{2} = \frac{4}{6}$), not by adding the same amount to the numerator and denominator (e.g., $\frac{2}{3} \neq \frac{2+1}{3+1}$ or $\frac{3}{4}$). (See Figure 9.2

on page 9-9 for a summary of these and other differences.)

Developmental Implications. Even under ideal instructional circumstances, constructing an understanding of such a novel concept as rational numbers is a difficult and lengthy process. Expect children's whole-number knowledge to interfere (e.g., for them to view $\frac{2}{3}$ as two whole numbers, rather than as a relationship between two quantities, or to see $\frac{1}{3}$ as larger than $\frac{1}{2}$). Only gradually and by actively grappling with rational-number situations can children construct the understanding necessary to distinguish common fractions from whole numbers.

Instructional Deficiencies

Instruction on rational numbers often moves too quickly to working with abstract symbols and, thus, does not provide an adequate conceptual foundation (e.g., the ideas of equal partitioning and multiplicative relations) necessary to understand fractions (Behr et al., 1992). Furthermore, it often provides a narrow and disconnected view of common fractions (e.g., fraction symbols are not explicitly linked to quotient, ratio, and operator meanings) (Novillis, 1976; Novillis-Larson, 1980).

9•1•3 TEACHING

Given the difficulty of the topic, can common fractions be introduced in the early primary grades, or should instruction on this topic be delayed until children's thinking is more mature? Which rational-number meaning should serve as the basis for common fraction instruction? Because of the complexity of the ideas involved, is the investigative approach less appropriate than an approach involving direct instruction (Behr et al., 1992)? Although there is no consensus about when or how to teach rational numbers (Behr et al., 1992), we suspect that meaningful, inquiry-based fraction instruction can begin early in the primary grades. Below, we discuss four general guidelines for such instruction.

☞ Consider Probe 9.3 (page 9-10).

↬ **Introduce the concept of rational numbers concretely and informally with fair-sharing problems—a quotient meaning** (Streefland, 1993). Traditionally, instruction has introduced common fractions in terms of the (continued on page 9-11)

➤ Probe 9.2: Rational-Number Concepts and Representations

Part I: Rational-Number Meanings. A common fraction such as $\frac{3}{5}$ can represent four different rational-number meanings: (a) *part of a whole* (e.g., a three parts of a whole, which has been divided into five equal-size parts), (b) *quotient* (e.g., three items divided among five kids), (c) *ratio* (a comparison of two possibly different quantities such as $3 for 5 items), (d) *operator* (e.g., an in-out or function machine with a rule that converts an input of 20 into 12, 25 in 15, and 30 into 18). The aim of Part I of this probe is to help you construct an explicit understanding of these rational-number meanings. For each item below, identify which rational-number meaning is involved. Discuss your answers with your group or class.

1. Fair-sharing word problems such as those in Part II of Investigation 9.1 and the one below:

    ■ **An Unwelcomed Guest.** Trevor heated up five small pizzas for himself and four buddies. Unfortunately, Ruffus the dog ate one of the pizzas before everyone arrived. If four pizzas are shared fairly among the five friends, what portion of a pizza does each friend get?

2. A workbook question such as: *What fraction of the rectangle is shaded?*

3. A workbook question such as:
    Color in one-fourth of the circle.

4. A test question such as: Color in one-third of the set of circles.

5. A word problem such as:

    ■ **Deductions.** El Rob-o Robotics Inc. withheld $\frac{3}{7}$ of an employee's pay for federal, FICA, and state taxes; health insurance; retirement; parking; and the company sunshine fund. If Ganzalo's gross pay is $2,835 a month, how much does the company withhold from his pay each month?

6. A word problem such as:

    ■ Tristan saw 15 Chevys and 20 Fords pass his house one afternoon. Which of the following shows the number of Chevys spotted compared to the number of Fords?

    a. $\frac{3}{7}$ b. $\frac{3}{4}$ c. $\frac{7}{3}$ d. $\frac{4}{3}$ e. not given

✓ Part II: Concept Maps. The aim of Part II of this probe is to help you check and deepen your understanding of rational concepts and their representations (common fractions). Discuss your map with your group or class.

1. With the help of your group or class, draw a concept map involving the following: *the concept of division, fraction symbols (e.g., $\frac{3}{4}$), in-out machine with a halving rule, the concept of operator, part-of-a-whole fraction concept, rational-number meanings, the concept of ratios, the task of sharing 2 cookies among 3 people, and the task of representing a half-filled glass.*

2. Draw a concept map including the following: *common fractions, fractions that reduce to whole numbers, improper fractions, mixed numbers, nonunit fractions, proper fractions, and unit fractions.* Note that there may be more than one correct way of doing this.

Part III: Questions about Common Fractions. Common fractions represent complicated ideas (Bezuk & Cramer, 1989) and raise some interesting questions (see Figure 9.2 on the next page). To help you better understand this point, consider the following questions. Then discuss your answers with your group or class.

1. The quantity shown by the dark portion in the figure for Question 2 of Part I above can be represented by how many common fractions? (a) 1 (b) 2 (c) 12 (d) an infinite number (e) not a, b, c, or d.

2. Jasper ate one-half of the candies he collected Halloweening. Janine ate one-third of her candies. Which child ate more?

3. What common fraction or fractions are between $\frac{1}{2}$ and $\frac{1}{4}$?

Probe 9.2 continued

Figure 9.2: A Comparison of Common Fractions and Whole Numbers

Issue	Whole Numbers	Common Fractions
Type of quantity worked with:	Discrete quantities.	Discrete and continuous quantities.
Units worked with:	*Single* items (wholes) or groups of single items (e.g., tens).	Parts of items (wholes).
Key learning mechanism:	Counting.	Equal partitioning (e.g., fair sharing).
Form of symbol representation:	One numeral composed of one or more digits.	Composite numeral: *two* sets of one or more digits and a fraction bar.
Concept represented:	An integer.	A *relationship* between integers.
Type of relationship:	Additive.	Multiplicative.
Uniqueness of symbol representating a quantity:	Numeral represents a particular whole number.	Infinite number of equivalent fractions represent a rational number.
Value:	Absolute.	Relative.
Number of numbers within an interval:	A fixed number (e.g., between 4 and 7 are 5 and 6).	An infinite number (e.g., between $\frac{1}{4}$ and $\frac{1}{7}$ are $\frac{1}{5}$, $\frac{1}{6}$, $\frac{2}{9}$, $\frac{3}{13}$ . . .).
Next number:	Can be determined from the counting sequence.	No next fraction.
Ordering numbers:	Magnitude increases for each successive counting number.	With a constant denominator, magnitude increases with larger numerators (e.g., $\frac{1}{8}$, $\frac{2}{8}$, $\frac{3}{8}$ . . .). With a constant numerator, magnitude *decreases* with "larger" denominators (e.g., $\frac{1}{2}$, $\frac{1}{3}$, $\frac{1}{4}$, $\frac{1}{5}$, $\frac{1}{6}$ . . .).

4. On the number-line segment below, indicate $\frac{1}{2}$ with a mark. Then indicate all the other common fractions between 0 and 1 you can think of with a mark. What conclusion can you draw about common fractions?

5. On a number line, what common fraction comes just before and just after $\frac{1}{2}$?

Questions for Reflection

Traditional mathematics instruction has not adequately fostered the development of multiplicative concepts and reasoning necessary to understand intermediate-level topics (Behr et al., 1992). One particular deficiency is a lack of problem situations that involve composing subunits into units, decomposing units into subunits, and flexibly switching between levels of units and subunits. Consider, for example, two-thirds of a circular region.

1. The whole circular region is 1 unit.

2. The unit is partitioned into three parts.

3. Each part can be viewed as 1/3 of a unit.

4. Two of the three parts combined to make 2/3.

1. (a) Which of the four steps above involves composing subunits into a larger unit? (b) Which step involves decomposing a unit into subunits?

2. (a) How many different levels of units and subunits are represented above? (b) How is a multiplicative relationship involved?

➤ Probe 9.3: Solving Fair-Sharing Problems Informally

The aim of this probe is to help you appreciate the power of informal knowledge in solving fair-sharing problems before children have received formal fraction-division instruction.

1. (a) Consider how children might use a manipulative or a drawing to solve the fair-sharing problems below informally. (b) What questions arise from a task such as Problem 1?

    ■ **Problem 1.** Place four dolls, muppets, or stuffed animals and 10 paper cookies on a table. Explain that the four friends want to share the cookies fairly. Ask how they can share the cookies so that all the friends get a fair share.

    ■ **Problem 2.** The five members of the national Dashed Hopes Heavy Metal Band Fan Club decided to celebrate the two-stop national tour of the band by buying pizza. With the sum total of the club's assets, they bought eight 6-inch pizzas. Assuming the pizzas were shared fairly, how much pizza did each fan-club member get?

    ■ **Problem 3.** Marja had two cupcakes in her lunch. If she shared the cupcakes with her two friends and each of the three children got the same amount, what part of a cupcake did each child get?

2. Figure 9.3 illustrates three informal solutions that second graders devised for Problem 2.

    a. How do such informal solutions for solving fair-sharing (quotient) problems naturally lead to discussion of a part-of-the-whole meaning of fractions?

    b. How would each of the informal solution processes and solutions be represented symbolically?

    c. How might symbolically representing the different solutions, which represent a child's share size, help children understand equivalent fractions better?

    d. What arithmetic operation must a student (informally) perform to determine a child's share size using Solutions A and B?

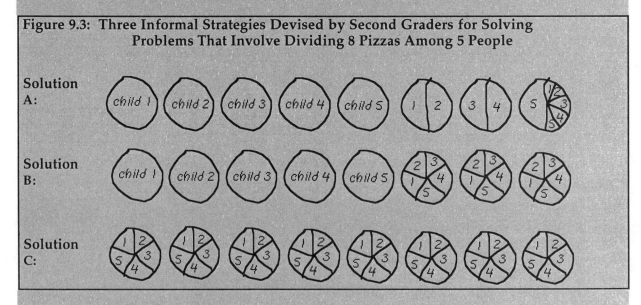

Figure 9.3: Three Informal Strategies Devised by Second Graders for Solving Problems That Involve Dividing 8 Pizzas Among 5 People

3. How could you exploit children's informal fair-sharing strategies to help them see that $14 \div 3$ is equal to both 4 r2 and $4\frac{2}{3}$ (that $4 r2 = 4\frac{2}{3}$)?

part-of-a-whole meaning. Yet, GIVEN CHILDREN'S FAMILIARITY WITH FAIR SHARING, IT MAKES SENSE TO INTRODUCE CHILDREN TO A QUOTIENT INTERPRETATION OF COMMON FRACTIONS *FIRST* (Freudenthal, 1983). Children can be informally introduced to rational numbers by exploiting or creating situations in which something (e.g., a candy bar or a box of crayons) must be shared among a number of them. Hypothetical problems like those in Probe 9.3 or those discussed on page 9-27 of the CHILDREN'S LITERATURE segment can also be used.

☞ **Initially, prompt children to estimate the outcome of fair-sharing situations** (Streefland, 1993). For example, ask children to estimate whether each person's share in a problem such as Problems 1, 2, or 3 in Probe 9.3 will be more or less than one and, if less than one, whether it will be more or less than one-half.

☞ **Later, encourage children to use objects, manipulatives, or drawings to solve fair-sharing problems informally.** As noted in chapter 5, dividing up an amount to share it among siblings or friends is a common, everyday experience. These and other informal experiences can provide a basis for understanding equal partitioning and solving fraction problems (see Mack, 1990). For example, given Problem 1 in Probe 9.3 (share 10 cookies among four friends), even some first graders will distribute the cookies so that each friend gets two and then cut the remaining two cookies in half and give each friend another half. When given Problem 2 in Probe 9.3 (How much would each of five children get if they shared eight pizzas?), even second-grade students can use a variety of informal strategies (see Figure 9.3 on page 9-10) (cf. Kieren, 1988).

Pose a task such as sharing a candy stick (see Part II on page 9-5 of Investigation 9.1) among three (or some other number of) children and encourage informal experimentation (e.g., estimating the size of a share, checking to see if that size share will give the number of shares needed, adjusting the estimate, and so forth) (Tzur, 1995).

Note that solving fair-sharing problems creates a *need* for a part-of-a-whole concept—fraction names such as "three-fourths" and "five-fourths" (see Figure 9.4 on page 9-12). Frames A to C in Figure 9.4 illustrate informal divvy-up solutions. The need to label the size of a person's share naturally raises the issue: *How can a part of a whole be described?* As Investigation 9.1 illustrated earlier, a useful solution is to subdivide the whole into equal-sized parts and compare each girl's share to a whole (see Frame D of Figure 9.4). Common fractions provide a convenient way of identifying the size of each girl's share (see Frame E in Figure 9.4).

To begin with, a teacher might ask a class how a candy bar could be shared fairly between two children. After divvying-up the candy bar, the teacher could ask: "What can we call this?" This naturally leads to a discussion of how many parts of interest there are relative to the total number of equal-sized shares in a whole (a part-of-a-whole interpretation).

☞ **Help students see that rational numbers have a wide variety of meanings (that fractions can represent meanings other than a part-of-a-whole meaning) and how the various meanings of rational numbers are related.** Provide them concrete and personally meaningful opportunities to discover the need for a part-of-the-whole meaning (see, e.g., Activity File 9.1), a quotient meaning (e.g., fair-sharing situations), a ratio meaning (e.g., a science unit on gears), and an operator meaning (e.g., a unit on deciphering and devising in-out machines involving a fractional rule). (Text continued on page 9-13.)

🖥️ 🍎 Activity File 9.1: A Unit on Estimating the Size of Dinosaurs

◆ Estimating measures of length + part-of-a-whole meaning + measuring + averages + proportional reasoning ◆ K-4 ◆ Any number

After reading a children's book on dinosaurs such as *Tyrannosaurus Was a Beast* by Jack Prelutsky (© 1988, Greenwillow Books), encourage students to look up information about the dinosaurs. The Prelutsky book, for example, includes the length and height of 14 dinosaurs (e.g., Tyrannosaurus was about 50 feet long and $18\frac{1}{2}$ feet tall, Brachiosaurus was 75 to 85 feet long and about 40 feet tall, and Triceratops was 25 to 30 feet long and about $9\frac{1}{2}$ feet tall). Note that this introduces the issue of fractional measures and what, for instance, one-half a foot means. (Activity file continued on page 9-12.)

Figure 9.4: How Fair-Sharing Problems Can Provide a Bridge Between Quotient and Part-of-a-Whole Interpretations of Fractions

A. Divide each pizza into four parts (pieces).

3 pizzas shared by 4

5 pizzas shared by 4

B. Divvy up the pieces among the four girls: Priscilla (P), Queen (Q), Ramella (R), & Shifra (S).

Each girl gets one of four equal shares of each pizza.

Each girl gets one of four equal shares of each pizza.

C. The results of divvying up the pieces.

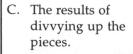

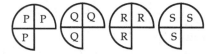

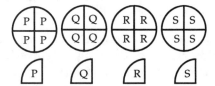

D. Naming the size of each girl's share relative to a whole pizza. (Note that this involves a part-of-the whole meaning.)

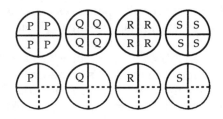

E. Symbolic representation of a share.

$$\frac{3}{4}$$

$$\frac{5}{4}$$

Activity File 9.1 continued

To foster a measurement sense, have the children relate the dinosaur measurements to a familiar reference or benchmark. Children may suggest, for instance, the typical (average) height of students in the class as a benchmark. (Note that this can create a need to measure heights and to introduce the concept and calculation of means.) Once this benchmark has been determined, encourage students to devise their own methods for translating dinosaur measurements into an equal number of typical student heights. For example, some children might reason that if the height of an average student is 4 feet 3 inches or $4\frac{1}{4}$ feet, then about $11\frac{3}{4}$ students would fit along the length of Tyrannosaurs (50 feet). (Note that solving these translation problems involves proportional reasoning. In effect 1 student is to $4\frac{1}{4}$ feet as x students are to 50 feet.

To make the proportion problem more manageable for younger children, a teacher may wish to begin with a round average height of, for instance, 4 feet and easily determined equivalents such as the height of Brachiosaurus, which was 40 feet or the equivalent of 10 students tall.)

9•2 COMMON FRACTIONS

Figure 9.5: A Child Driven to Desperation by Fractions

PEANUTS reprinted by permission of UFS, Inc.

As Figure 9.5 suggests, fractions are notoriously difficult for children. In Subunit 9•2•1, we discuss their learning of fraction concepts. In Subunit 9•2•2, we describe how instruction can help children *understand* these concepts.

9•2•1 LEARNING

In this subunit, we examine children's informal fair-sharing (equal-partitioning) strategies and their difficulties with common fractions.

Informal Fair-Sharing Strategies: Early Means of Equal Partitioning

The type of informal fair-sharing (equal-partitioning) strategy children use depends on the type of quantity involved.

Divvy-Up Strategy. To partition discrete quantities such as a collection of blocks into equal parts, children use the divvying-up (dealing-out) strategy discussed earlier in chapter 5.

Subdividing Strategies. With continuous quantities, children use a subdividing procedure (Hiebert & Tonnessen, 1978). To divide a string in half, for example, a relatively sophisticated child would examine the object to gauge its midpoint, subdivide the string at that point, and then check the resulting portions to ensure they are equal. Subdividing continuous quantities is harder for children than divvy-up discrete quantities for two reasons: (1) Unlike the divvy-up strategy, a subdividing strategy requires carefully planning ahead. (2) Whereas a divvy-up strategy can be used with any number of shares or any kind of discrete quantity, a subdividing

strategy varies from task to task (e.g., folding a sheet of paper into halves, thirds and fifths each requires a different procedure) and from shape to shape (e.g., folding a rectangle into thirds requires a different procedure than does folding a circle into thirds).

Common Difficulties with Common Fractions

Young children's understanding of fraction terms is usually narrow and incomplete. Some common difficulties with common fractions are outlined below.

1. Because instruction often uses circular-region (e.g., pie and pizza examples) almost exclusively, many children have difficulty relating fraction concepts to other continuous-quantity models (e.g., fractions of a rectangle), number-line representations, and discrete-quantity models.

2. Many children do not understand that gauging a part of a whole requires that partitioning the whole into parts of equal size and make errors like that illustrated in Figure 9.6.

Figure 9.6: Children Commonly Do Not Understand that Fractions Describe a Situation in Which All the Parts are Equal in Size

Write a fraction to show what part of the pie was eaten (the darker portion):

1/3

3. Some children do not recognize that common fractions involve a part of a whole and instead compare a part to the remaining parts of the whole (see Figure 9.7).

Figure 9.7: Part-to-Part Errors

Write a fraction to show what part of the pizza was eaten (the darker portion)? <u>2/3</u>

What fraction of the marbles are black? <u>2/3</u>

---

4. Many children do not have a good sense of fraction size. They do not understand that nonunit fractions can be built up from unit fractions. For example, they do not recognize that $\frac{3}{4}$ is literally three *one-fourths* ($\frac{1}{4} + \frac{1}{4} + \frac{1}{4}$ or $3 \times \frac{1}{4}$). Moreover, they have difficulty reasoning qualitatively about fractions. For instance, they do not have a good intuitive feel for what happens to the size of a fraction if its denominator is replaced with a larger digit.

5. Many children do not recognize equivalent common fractions. They may be able to label or create direct-correspondence models successfully but not indirect-correspondence models. For example, a child may have little difficulty labeling ●●○○○○ as "two-sixths" (because the model corresponds directly to the fraction) but not recognize that it can also be labeled "one-third" (because the model corresponds only indirectly to the fraction). Moreover, because many children do not realize that fractions involve a multiplicative relationship, they consider, for instance, $\frac{3}{4}$ equivalent to $\frac{6}{7}$ ($\frac{3+3=6}{4+3=7}$), rather than $\frac{6}{8}$ ($\frac{3 \times 2 = 6}{4 \times 2 = 8}$).

6. Research indicates that children typically have weak fraction-estimation skills.

7. Children frequently do not understand that a fraction represents a *relationship*, not a particular amount such as the size or the number of items. They believe, for example, that a half is always larger than one-third when, in fact, such fractions cannot be compared unless the size of each whole is known.

8. Many children have difficulty comparing common fractions (e.g., believe that $\frac{1}{3}$ is larger than $\frac{1}{2}$ because 3 is more than 2).

9. Many children do not recognize the importance of explicitly defining the whole or unit when solving fraction problems.

9•2•2 TEACHING

Even primary-level children can begin to learn about fractions in a meaningful manner, *if* instruction builds upon their informal strengths and they are given sufficient opportunities to work with fractions concretely before the topic is introduced formally.

A Meaningful Approach

As with any topic, it is usually helpful to move from relatively concrete and informal representations to relatively abstract and formal representations. A four-phase progression is outlined below.

Phase 1: Prefraction experiences with *equal partitioning*. PURPOSEFUL EQUAL-PARTITIONING EXPERIENCES THAT DO NOT EXPLICITLY INVOLVE FRACTION TERMS OR SYMBOLS CAN PROVIDE A CONCRETE BASIS FOR UNDERSTANDING FRACTION CONCEPTS AS EARLY AS KINDERGARTEN. Begin by having children share (divvy-up) collections of things (discrete quantities). Then move to the more complicated tasks of sharing or subdividing continuous quantities. Note that both types of experiences can be done in the context of everyday activities (e.g., sharing sheets of paper for a school assignment, dividing up markers to play a game, sharing a piece of poster paper for art, dividing a piece of paper in halves or thirds to prepare for a quiz, folding a letter into thirds to fit into an envelope). An additional example is described in Box 9.1 on the next page.

Phase 2A: Verbally label concrete models. *Link* spoken fraction terms to concrete representations of fractions. For example, after sharing eight pencils among four group members, have the children identify the size of each persons share: "one of four equal piles—one fourth of the piles—or two of eight pencils—two-eighths of the pencils."

Phase 2B: Concretely model verbal labels. Reverse Phase 2A by beginning with a verbal label like "one-fourth" and asking children to

Box 9.1: A Purposeful-Way of Introducing "Thirds"[2]

Vignette	Comments
Mr. Adams wanted his second-grade class to construct place-value mats so they could play a place-value game. He explained that the construction paper distributed to each child needed to be folded into three equal sections for a ones, a tens, and a hundreds portion. Mr. Adams asked the class how this could be done, and suggested using a regular piece of paper to experiment with. Several children tried folding the paper in the middle and found this did not work. Mr. Adams encouraged one of these students to explain what she had tried and why it didn't work. Barbara Ann noted, "The pieces aren't the same size if you do."	Note that Mr. Adams' "lesson" on fractions was introduced as a problem the class needed to solve so that they could play a game (which focused on another content area altogether). There are many opportunities during the school year to introduce basic mathematical skills and concepts in a purposeful manner as a means to achieving significant ends.
After some experimenting, Marcella found a way of doing it: "Fold one end halfway toward the other end and then fold the other end over it." The class listened and watched while Marcella explained and demonstrated.	Children are encouraged to speak and listen carefully about the genuine problem facing them.
Afterward, Mr. Adams pointed out that the construction paper was folded into thirds. Later, he had the class write about whether they would rather share a yummy cake that was cut into two equal pieces ("halves"), three equal pieces ("thirds"), four equal pieces ("fourths"), or five equal pieces ("fifths").	✐ To further consolidate the learning experience, the teacher has the class write about fractions using a personally meaningful context.

create a model of it. For example, a child can be given 12 cookies or a pizza (large paper circle) and asked to take one-fourth.

Phase 3A: Symbolically represent concrete and verbal representations. Introduce written symbols such as $\frac{1}{2}$, $\frac{3}{4}$, and $\frac{5}{3}$ after children are comfortable using verbal fraction terms in concrete situations. Relate fraction symbols such as $\frac{2}{3}$ to both divvy-up (quotient) and part-of-a-whole meanings:

Quotient meaning	Part-of-the-whole meaning
2 → Two things	2 → Two parts
— → shared fairly	— → of a whole divided into
3 → among three people	3 → three equal-sized parts

Phase 3B: Verbally label and concretely model fraction notation. Reverse Phase 3A by beginning with a fraction such as $\frac{1}{4}$ and asking children to identify it and create either a quotient or part-of-a-whole model of it.

Phase 4A: Use mental imagery of concrete model. Encourage children to mentally imagine a concrete model and use this mental image to reason out answers.

Phase 4B: Use fractions as abstract numbers. Prompt children to reason about fraction tasks without the physical models or even the mental image of such models so that they don't always rely on them.

☞ Consider Investigation 9.2 (pages 9-16 and 9-17). (Text continued on page 9-18.)

✿ Investigation 9.2: Using *Cuisenaire Rods* to Develop Common Fraction Concepts[*]

◆ Part-of-a-whole models and problem solving ◆ 2-6 ◆ Groups of four + class discussion

This investigation illustrates how *Cuisenaire rods* (white = 1 cm long, red= 2 cm long, light green = 3 cm long, purple = 4 cm long, yellow = 5 cm long, dark green = 6 cm long, black = 7 cm long, brown = 8 cm long, blue = 9 cm long, orange = 10 cm long) can be used to prompt reflection about common fractions and to help children construct a deeper understanding of them. (Note that the same activities could be done with other manipulatives such as *Fraction Circles*.) Try the following activities yourself either on your own or with your group. As you do, consider what children could learn from each activity. Answer the **Questions for Reflection** that follow and discuss your answers with your group or class.

Activity 1

a. If the brown rod is the whole, does a purple rod represent one-half? Why or why not?
b. If the orange rod is the whole, does a dark green rod represent one-half? Why or why not?

Activity 2

a. If the dark-green rod is the whole, what fraction does a red rod represent?
b. If the dark-green rod is the whole, then what does the brown rod represent?

Activity 3

a. If a blue rod represents the whole, what rod represents two-thirds?
b. If an orange and red rod were joined to make the whole, what rods could represent one-half?

Activity 4

a. If the light-green rod is $\frac{1}{3}$, what rod represents the whole?
b. If the red rod is $\frac{1}{4}$, what rod represents the whole?

Activity 5

a. If the red rod is $\frac{1}{4}$, what rod represents $\frac{3}{4}$?

b. If the red rod is $\frac{1}{5}$, what rod represents $\frac{1}{2}$?

c. If the light-green rod is $\frac{1}{4}$, what rod represents $\frac{1}{2}$?

d. If the purple rod is $\frac{2}{3}$, what rod represents $\frac{1}{2}$?

e. If the purple rod is $\frac{2}{3}$, what rod represents $\frac{7}{6}$?

f. If the light-green rod is $\frac{1}{2}$, what rod represents $\frac{9}{6}$?

Activity 6

a. Which rod or rods can you define as the whole and show one-third and one-sixth of it?
b. Which rod or rods can you define as the whole and show one-half and one-third of it?

---

[*] See, for example, *Everything's Coming Up Fractions* by J. Bradford (© 1981 by the Cuisenaire Company of America, New Rochelle, NY) for additional examples or ideas for using *Cuisenaire rods*. For a discussion of how to implement similar activities using easily made fraction strips, see "Let's Do It: Fractions with Fraction Strips" by J. A. Van de Walle and C. S. Thompson, *Arithmetic Teacher*, Vol. 32, No. 4 (December 1984), pp. 4-9.

Investigation 9.2 continued

Activity 7

a. If the dark-green rod is the whole, then what fraction does a white rod represent?
b. What fraction(s) do two white rods represent?
c. What fraction(s) do three white rods represent?
d. What fraction(s) do four white rods represent?
e. What fraction(s) do five white rods represent?
f. What fraction(s) do six white rods represent?
g. What fraction(s) do seven white rods represent?
h. What fraction(s) do nine white rods represent?

Activity 8

a. If the dark-green rod is the whole, two white rods would represent what fraction? What other number name can be given to two white rods? Hint: What rod is the same length as two whites and what fraction of a dark-green rod would this rod represent?
b. What other name can be given six white rods?
c. What other name can be given nine white rods?

Questions For Reflection

1. In Activity 1a, why is the brown rod referred to as a *whole* rather than *one*?

2. What is the purpose of Activity 1b?

3. a. If children responded verbally, which of the four phases in the meaningful approach to introducing common fractions, does Activity 2a represent: Phase 1 (Prefraction experiences with equal partitioning); Phase 2 (Verbally labeling concrete models and vice versa); Phase 3 (Symbolically representing concrete and verbal representations and vice versa); or Phase 4 (Mentally imagining concrete models)?

   b. If students responded with a written answer, this activity would be an example of which of the steps above?

4. For children just beginning fraction work, the intended answer to Activity 3b is a dark-green rod. Mathematically, though, is this the only possible answer?

5. Compare Activities 2, 3, and 4. (a) How do the tasks posed by each differ? (b) Which of these do you suppose is most often presented by textbooks, teachers, and tests? (c) Which of these do you think would be most challenging for children?

6. Activity 5 contains some fairly challenging tasks. What kind of reasoning is involved in determining the answer to these questions?

7. Activity 6 lays the groundwork for what arithmetic instruction later?

8. (a) What is the purpose of Activity 7f and the sequence of Activities 7a to 7e leading up to it? (b) What is the purpose of Activities 7g and 7h?

9. How could a teacher transform Activity 7 into an estimation tasks?

10. Activity 8 may help children construct what fraction concept?

Teaching Tips

Some teaching tips are outlined below.

↪ **Illustrate common fractions with a wide variety of examples, including discrete-quantity models** (see, e.g., Figure 9.8). It is important that children see more than the circular-region (pie or pizza) model of common fractions.

↪ **Help children *explicitly* recognize that fractions describe a particular type of partitioning situation: one in which all the shares or parts are equal.** Emphasize that $\frac{1}{2}$, for instance, represents one of two *equal shares* or *parts*. Nonexamples as well as examples should be used to underscore this point (see Activity 1 on page 9-16 of Investigation 9.2 and Box 9.2 below).

Figure 9.8: Different Models of the Fraction $\frac{1}{4}$

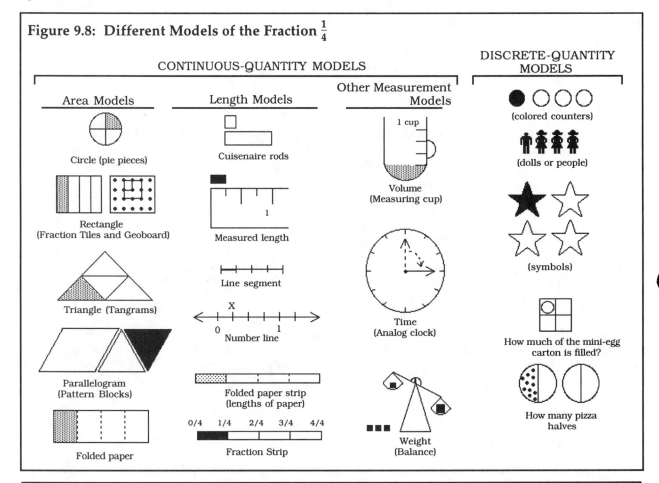

Box 9.2: Using a Real Nonexample to Underscore the Importance of Equal Parts[3]

Helene was referred to a diagnostic-teaching center partly because she was having difficulty with fractions. Her remedial instructor tried several explanations and demonstrations of fractions to no avail. To avoid more frustrating sessions for the child and herself, the instructor examined samples of Helene's school work for clues concerning the girl's misconceptions (see Figure 9.6 on page 9-13). She found that the girl did not understand that the parts had to be equal.

Because eating was one of Helene's passions,

the instructor began the next session by taking out a candy bar and saying, "I'll give you half of this candy bar." The instructor proceeded to cut the candy bar into unequal portions and offered Helene the smaller portion. This did not sit well with Helene. After the girl vociferously protested her unfair share, the instructor noted the importance of dividing a whole into equal-sized parts when determining a fraction of it. The demonstration reportedly had a significant impact on Helene. Indeed, most elementary children are quick to note when a collection or object has not been fairly shared with them.

✎ ✓ **Help children recognize that a common fraction can represent a relationship between a part and its whole.** Have them compare, contrast, and discuss examples and nonexamples of fractions. For instance, ask them to evaluate the part-to-part errors shown earlier in Figure 9.7 on page 9-14 and justify why these answers are incorrect. Children's understanding of part-whole relationships can be fostered (and evaluated) by posing questions requiring them to reverse their thinking (see Activity 4 on page 9-16 of Investigation 9.2 and the third type of problem illustrated in Figure 9.9 below).

✎ **To foster a sense of fraction size, encourage children to build up models of nonunit fractions from unit fractions** (as was done in Activity 7 on page 9-17 of Investigation 9.2). This can help them see, for instance, that *five-sixths* is literally made from five *one-sixths*. Note also that such building up activities can also help children construct an informal understanding of the multiplicative relationship represented by fractions (e.g., $\frac{1}{6}+\frac{1}{6}+\frac{1}{6}+\frac{1}{6}+\frac{1}{6}$ or $5 \times \frac{1}{6}=\frac{5}{6}$).

✎ ✓ **Use qualitative-reasoning tasks as teaching and evaluation tools** (see Activity I on page 9-20 of Investigation 9.3). Qualitative-reasoning tasks provide an opportunity for children to discuss and defend their informal ideas about fractions and to construct a more accurate understanding of fractions and fraction size. Such tasks underscore that what is important in mathematics is understanding and thinking, not memorizing facts or procedures. Such tasks are ideal for assessing an understanding of fractions and fraction size because they require understanding, rather than tap facts or procedures that can be memorized by rote.

☞ Try Investigation 9.3 (pages 9-20 to 9-23). (Text continued on page 9-24.)

Figure 9.9: Three Ways of Posing a Fraction Problem

Type	With a Discrete Quantity		With a Continuous Quantity	
Missing fraction (given a part and a whole, find the fraction)	Jerry got 3 of his sister's 12 candies. What fraction of the candies did Jerry get?	o o o o If o o o o is the whole, then o o is what fraction of this whole?	Rishi cut a pizza into 8 equal pieces and ate two of them. What fraction of the pizza did Rishi eat?	What fraction of the rectangle is dark? 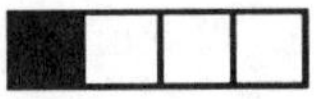
Missing part (given a whole and a fraction, find the part)	Jerry got 1/4 of his sister's 12 candies. How many candies did Jerry get?	o o o o If o o o o is the whole, then 1/4 is how many circles?	Rishi cut a pizza into 8 equal pieces. He ate one-fourth of the pizza. How many pieces did he eat?	Color in 1/4 of the rectangle 
Missing whole (given a part and a fraction, find the whole)*	Jerry got 3 of his sister's candies. This is 1/4 of what she had. How many candies did his sister have?	If o o is 1/4, then the whole is how many circles?	Rishi ate two pieces of pizza. This was one-fourth of a whole pizza. How many pieces did the whole pizza have?	1/4 of a rectangle is shown. Draw the whole rectangle.

✓ *This reverse-processing or "construct-the-whole" task (Behr & Post, 1988) indicates a relatively deep understanding of the part-whole concept (Steffe, Olive, Battista, & Clements, 1991) and, thus, provides a good evaluation tool as well as a good teaching device.

♻ Investigation 9.3: Informally Comparing Common Fractions

Many children have difficulty understanding that fractions such as $\frac{2}{3}$ and $\frac{4}{6}$ are equivalent or determining that $\frac{3}{4}$ is larger than $\frac{2}{3}$. Activity I portrays a qualitative-reasoning task that can help students reflect on such comparisons. Activity II suggests how a fair-sharing analogy can help students determine whether fractions are equivalent and, if not, which is larger. Activity III shows how a manipulative can concretely model equivalent fractions and ordering fractions. Activity IV illustrates how a pictorial model can do the same. To see what is involved, try the activities yourself either by yourself or, better yet, with your group. Discuss your answers with your group or class.

Activity I: **Qualitative Reasoning About Fraction Comparisons** (◆ Reasoning about the size of fractions ◆ 5-8 ◆ Any number)

For the questions below, w, x, and y are whole numbers and w > x > y.

1. Circle any of the following that is greater than 1: (a) $\frac{w}{x}$ (b) $\frac{y}{w}$ (c) $\frac{w+x}{y}$ (d) $\frac{w}{x+y}$

2. Which is larger? (a) $\frac{x}{y}$ or $\frac{x}{w}$ (b) $\frac{y}{w}$ or $\frac{y}{x}$ (c) $\frac{w}{w}$ or $\frac{x}{y}$

◌ **Teaching Tip.** Primary-level children can be given less difficult qualitative-reasoning tasks such as: If x in the fraction $\frac{x}{y}$ got smaller and y remained the same, would the fraction increase, decrease, or remain the same size?

Activity II: **A Fair-Sharing Analogy for Comparing Fractions Using** *Fraction Circles* (◆ Using a quotient interpretation to compare fractions ◆ 2-8 ◆ Any number)

A fair-sharing analogy can be used at the conceptual, the connecting, or the symbolic level to compare two fractions. *Fraction Circles* (shown below) are one manipulative that can be helpful in modeling the analogy.

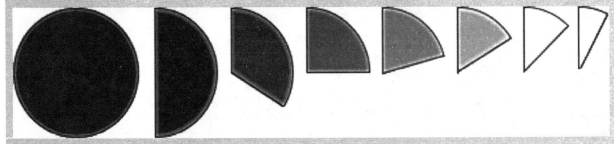

Black = 1, Orange = $\frac{1}{2}$, Green = $\frac{1}{3}$, Purple = $\frac{1}{4}$, Blue = $\frac{1}{5}$, Red = $\frac{1}{6}$, Brown = $\frac{1}{8}$, Yellow = $\frac{1}{10}$, and Beige = $\frac{1}{12}$.

1. For each of the following comparisons, consider how *Fraction Circles* could be used to model a fair-sharing analogy and to answer the following questions informally: *Are the fractions equal? If not, which is the larger?*

(a) $\frac{1}{2}$ versus $\frac{2}{4}$ (Note that $\frac{1}{2}$ could be interpreted as one pie shared fairly between two people. The fraction $\frac{2}{4}$ could be interpreted as two pies shared fairly among four people.) (b) $\frac{1}{3}$ versus $\frac{2}{6}$, (c) $\frac{1}{2}$ versus $\frac{1}{4}$, (d) $\frac{1}{2}$ versus $\frac{1}{3}$, (e) $\frac{1}{3}$ versus $\frac{2}{5}$, and (f) $\frac{1}{2}$ versus $\frac{2}{5}$

---

*Fraction Circles are available commercially from Creative Publications under the name *Fraction Circles PLUS*™.

Investigation 9.3 continued

2. For each of the following comparisons, illustrate how a drawing could be used to model a fair-sharing analogy and to answer the following questions informally: *Are the fractions equal? If not, which is the larger?*

   (a) $\frac{2}{3}$ versus $\frac{4}{6}$, (b) $\frac{3}{4}$ versus $\frac{6}{8}$, (c) $\frac{1}{2}$ versus $\frac{2}{3}$, (d) $\frac{3}{4}$ versus $\frac{5}{8}$, (e) $\frac{3}{4}$ versus $\frac{2}{3}$, (f) $\frac{3}{2}$ versus $\frac{5}{6}$, (g) $\frac{4}{3}$ versus $\frac{5}{4}$, (h) $\frac{2}{3}$ versus $\frac{3}{6}$

3. Why might a teacher wish to include items f and g above?

4. The three informal fair-sharing strategies illustrated in Figure 9.3 (page 9-10) are not equally useful in comparing fractions. Which strategy is the most useful in making each comparison in Question 2 above?

Activity III: Illustrating Equivalent (Part of the Whole) Fractions With *Fraction Tiles* (◆ Concretely modeling equivalent fractions ◆ 1-6 ◆ Groups of four)

Fraction Tiles* are transparent rectangles that come in the following sizes and colors:

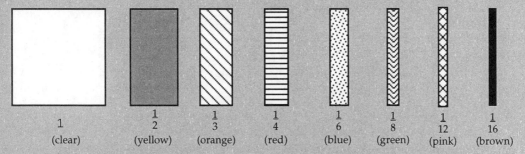

A teacher might wish to begin by helping students see that 2 halves (yellow tiles) covers (equals) a whole (clear tile), 3 thirds (orange tiles) equals a whole, 4 fourths (red tiles) covers a whole.

Questions 1, 2a, 2b, 3a, and 4 can be used to lead students to more challenging questions such as Questions 2c, 2d, 3b, and 5. Try these latter questions to get a sense of how to use the *Fraction Tiles* model.

1. a. How many fourths (red tiles) does it take to cover a half (yellow tile)?
   b. How many eighths (green tiles) does it take to cover a half (yellow tile)?
   c. How many sixteenths (brown tiles) does it take to cover a half (yellow tile)?

2. a. How many eighths (green tiles) does it take to cover a fourth (red tile)?
   b. How many sixteenths (brown tiles) does it take to cover a fourth (red tile)?
   c. How many eighths (green tiles) does it take to cover three-fourths (3 red tiles)?
   d. How many sixteenths (brown tiles) does it take to cover three-fourths (3 red tiles)?

3. a. How many sixteenths (brown tiles) does it take to cover an eighth (green tile)?
   b. How many sixteenths (brown tiles) does it take to cover five-eighths (5 green tiles)?

4. a. How many sixths (blue tiles) does it take to cover a third (orange tile)?
   b. How many twelfths (pink tiles) does it take to cover a third (orange tile)?
   c. How many twelfths (pink tiles) does it take to cover a sixth (blue tile)?

* Note that if commercially available *Fraction Tiles* are not available, fraction strips can be made from construction paper. Make sure that the strips are proportional in size (e.g., that two $\frac{1}{2}$ strips fit over 1, that two $\frac{1}{4}$ strips fit over a $\frac{1}{2}$ strip, and so forth. Laminating the strips will help their longevity and ease of use.

Investigation 9.3 continued

5. a. How many sixths (blue tiles) does it take to cover two-thirds (2 orange tiles)?
   b. How many twelfths (pink tiles) does it take to cover five-sixths (6 blue tiles)?

Activity IV: **The Rectangular Cake-Cutting Analogy for Comparing Fractions** (◆ Pictorial model for comparing fractions ◆ 2-8 ◆ Any number)

1. Ms. Socrates asked her class if $\frac{4}{8}$ of a rectangular-shaped cake is larger than, smaller than, or equal to $\frac{1}{2}$ of the cake. The class quickly recognized that the fractions were equal. "How could you use a graph-paper drawing to prove that four-eighths equals one half?" prompted the teacher. How would you answer Ms. Socrates's question?

2. Ms. Socrates then asked her class to use a graph-paper drawing to determine if $\frac{2}{3}$ of a rectangular-shaped cake is larger than, smaller than, or equal to $\frac{3}{4}$ of the cake. How would you answer?

3. In response to Question 2 above, several groups drew two same-sized rectangles one above the other. Using vertical lines, students divided the top rectangle into three equal parts and shaded the first two. Similarly, they divided the lower rectangle into four equal parts and shaded the first three. From the diagram (see Figure A below), it was clear that $\frac{3}{4}$ was larger. Ms. Socrates then asked "Is there another solution? What if the cakes were sitting side by side or what if the one cake was cut vertically and the other horizontally (as shown in Figure B below), and we could not line them up one beneath the other (as shown in Figure A below)?"

Figure A: Students' Easy-to-See Method for Comparing Fractions

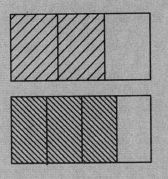

Figure B: Ms. Socrates's Hard-to-See Method for Comparing Fractions

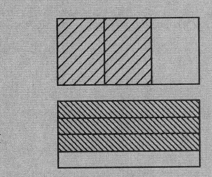

4. In response to Question 3, Priya suggested that both rectangles in Figure B be divided into equal size pieces. That would make comparing the two fractions easier. How could Priya's suggestion be implemented?

5. In response to Question 4, Skywalker suggested using three horizontal lines to further divide up the first rectangle and using two vertical lines to further divide up the second rectangle. This process divided each rectangle into 12 equal parts. The class dubbed this procedure, the "**rectangular-cake cutting method**" (Jencks & Peck, 1987). With graph paper, illustrate how this method can be used to complete the equations:

$$\frac{1}{3} = \frac{\square}{6} \quad \text{or} \quad \frac{2}{5} = \frac{\square}{10}$$

Investigation 9.3 continued

6. Illustrate how the rectangular-cake cutting analogy could be implemented with *Fraction Tiles* to compare $\frac{2}{3}$ and $\frac{3}{4}$.

7. Jencks and Peck (1987) gave children number sentences such as:

$$\frac{1}{3} = \frac{\Box}{2} \qquad \frac{2}{5} = \frac{\Box}{4}$$

   Impressively, children were able to use the rectangular-cake cutting analogy to complete such expressions. (a) How? (b) Briefly outline a plausible argument for each answer.

8. Illustrate how the rectangular-cake-cutting analogy could be used to determine the larger of the following fraction pairs: (a) $\frac{2}{5}$ or $\frac{1}{3}$ (b) $\frac{2}{3}$ or $\frac{3}{4}$ (c) $\frac{3}{5}$ or $\frac{4}{7}$ (d) $\frac{3}{4}$ or $\frac{5}{7}$ (e) $\frac{4}{5}$ or $\frac{5}{6}$

9. (a) Dividing a caking lengthwise and widthwise is an informal means for finding what? (b) By using the rectangular-cake-cutting analogy to answer questions such as Questions 2, 5, and 7 above, children might rediscover what formal procedure for finding an equivalent fraction? (c) By using the analogy to answer questions such as Question 8, children might rediscover for themselves what formal shortcut for comparing two fractions?

Activity V: *Fraction Trip* (♦ Practice comparing fractions ♦ 2-8 ♦ Individual or pairs of students)

The aim of this activity is to trace a path from the start to the finish. In the *Equivalent-Fraction Version*, a player may advance from one fraction to a connected fraction if they are equivalent. In the *Smaller-Fraction Version*, a player may advance from a fraction to a connected fraction if the latter is smaller. In the *Larger-Fraction Version*, which is illustrated below, a player may advance from a fraction to a connected fraction if the latter is larger. The solid line indicates one solution path for the grid below. Can you find others? Use any method of comparing fractions including intuitive reasoning strategies. Discuss and justify your solutions.

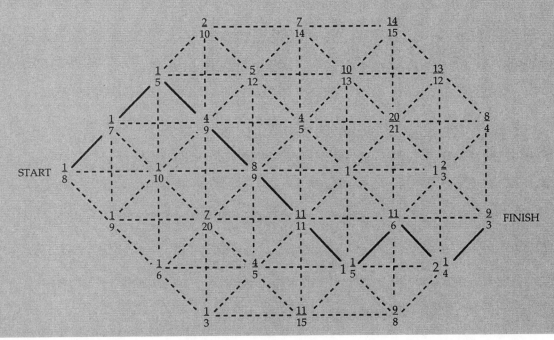

↪ **Use both a quotient and a part-of-a-whole interpretation to help children make sense of equivalent fractions.** In both cases, manipulatives can be invaluable in helping children to understand equivalent fractions.

• **Quotient meaning.** Exploring equivalent fair-sharing situations concretely can provide a sound informal basis for understanding equivalent fractions (see e.g., Activity II on page 9-20 of Investigation 9.3). Have children compare, for example, the size of a person's share when one pizza is shared fairly among four people ($\frac{1}{4}$) and when two pizzas are shared fairly among eight people ($\frac{2}{8}$) (see Figure 9.10). Children initially may be surprised to find that the size of a person's share in these two situations is the same.

• **Part-of-a-whole meaning.** Encourage children to build direct-correspondence and indirect-correspondence models side by side. For example, if a 6-cm dark green rod represents the whole, one-half can be represented directly by a 3-cm light-green rod or indirectly by three 1-cm white rods (see Activity 8 on page 9-17 of Investigation 9.2). *Fraction Circles* and *Fraction Tiles* (see Activity III on page 9-21 of Investigation 9.3) can also provide concrete models of equivalent fractions.

↪ **After children have a sound informal understanding of equivalent fractions, help them to recognize** *explicitly* **that determining equivalent fractions involves multiplication or division, not addition or subtraction.** Help students to redis-cover the *Fundamental Law of Fractions*: To find an equivalent fraction, multiply (or divide) both the numerator and denominator by the same natural number.

↪ **Estimating fractions should be an integral aspect of fraction instruction.** Skill in estimating fractions is a basic aspect of a fraction number sense and can provide a sound basis for ordering fractions and fraction arithmetic.

↪ **Help children explicitly understand that two common fractions cannot be compared unless their wholes are the same size (or at least identified).** Pose such questions as: "One-half of a cake is larger than one-third of a cake, but is one-half of a cupcake larger than one-third of a cake?" (See also Question 2 in Part III of Probe 9.2 on page 9-8). Concrete models, such as those shown in Figure 9.11 (on page 9-25), may also help. Moreover, encourage children to name the whole when comparing fractions (e.g., one-half of this cookie is larger than one-third of it).

↪ **A fair-sharing (the quotient meaning) can provide an easily understood and powerful analogy for interpreting fraction size and ordering fractions.** Consider the case of 8-year-old Arianne who had just been introduced to the analogy. Asked which was larger $\frac{1}{2}$ or $\frac{1}{3}$, she took a moment, indicated $\frac{1}{2}$, and explained that a person would get more if one pizza were shared between two people than if one pizza were shared among

---

Figure 9.10: Using a Fair-Sharing Analogy to Illustrate the Equivalent Fractions $\frac{1}{4}$ and $\frac{2}{8}$

■ **Pizza Lover** (◆ 2-4). On Saturday, Andre and three friends stopped at the local pizza parlor for a treat. The four friends shared a large-size pizza equally among them. On Sunday, Andre and seven friends stopped at the local pizza parlor again for a treat. The eight friends shared two large-size pizzas equally among them. Did Andre eat more pizza on Saturday or on Sunday, or did he eat the same amount on both days?

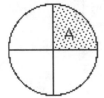 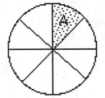 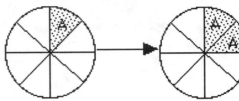

Andre's share if one pizza is shared fairly among four people: $\frac{1}{4}$

Andre's share if two pizzas are shared fairly among eight people: $\frac{2}{8}$ (the *same* amount as the situation represented by $\frac{1}{4}$).

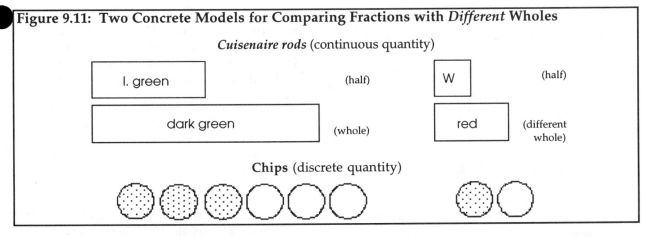

Figure 9.11: Two Concrete Models for Comparing Fractions with *Different* Wholes

three people. *Chooser* (Activity File 9.2 below) is an entertaining way to accustom children to the fair-sharing analogy and to practice ordering fractions.

☞ **Various manipulatives can provide a concrete model for ordering fractions of the same whole** (see Figure 9.12). Such models can help children to *see*, for example, that "one-half" (or

$\frac{1}{2}$) is larger than "one-third" (or $\frac{1}{3}$). By relating the comparison of spoken fraction terms such as *one-half* and *one-third* or formal symbols such as $\frac{1}{2}$ and $\frac{1}{3}$ to such concrete situations, children should be less prone to consider $\frac{1}{3}$ larger. The rectangular-cake analogy (described in Activity IV on page 9-22 of Investigation 9.3) can also provide a concrete means for ordering fractions.

Activity File 9.2: *Chooser*

◆ Practice comparing fractions ◆ 2-4 ◆ Two to six players or teams

Four digits from 1 to 9 are randomly drawn. A player or team must use two of the digits to make the largest (or smallest) fraction possible. The players or teams with the largest fraction are awarded a point. In the **Wide-Open** version, players can use improper fractions (e.g., $\frac{8}{2}$). In the **Restricted** version, players must make the largest fraction that is less than 1.

Figure 9.12: Two Concrete Models for Comparing Fractions of the *Same* Whole

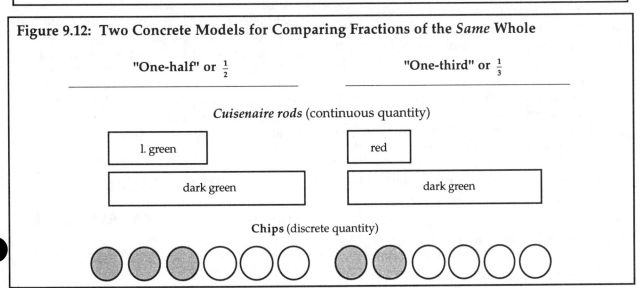

꩜ **Encourage children to devise, discuss, and use informal strategies such as utilizing $\frac{1}{2}$ as a reference point or benchmark** (see, e.g., Activity V on page 9-23 of Investigation 9.3). To compare $\frac{3}{5}$ and $\frac{4}{9}$, for example, some reason that because $\frac{3}{5}$ is somewhat more than half and $\frac{4}{9}$ is somewhat less than half, $\frac{3}{5}$ must be larger than $\frac{4}{9}$.

꩜ **Games can provide an entertaining and purposeful way to learn and practice fraction-ordering skills.** See, for instance, Activity V on page 9-23 of Investigation 9.3 and Activity File 9.2 on page 9-25.

꩜ **Encourage children to discover efficient ways of comparing fractions.** For example, pose the question: Which do you think is larger, $\frac{2}{9}$ or $\frac{4}{17}$? Children should recognize that comparing such fractions is difficult. Encourage them to devise a reliable way for judging the larger fraction. One solution they may suggest is finding a common denominator (e.g., $\frac{2}{9} = \frac{34}{153}$ and $\frac{4}{17} = \frac{36}{153}$). Then encourage students to find a shortcut for this common-denominator method: the cross-products method (e.g., $\frac{2}{9}$ vs. $\frac{4}{17} \rightarrow 2 \times 17 = 34$ and $4 \times 9 = 36$, so $\frac{4}{17}$ is larger).

A relatively concrete way of discovering the cross-products algorithm entails encouraging children to compare fractions by mentally imagining a rectangular-cake analogy (see Activity IV (on page 9-22 of Investigation 9.3). Asking children to rely on mental imagery may prompt some to invent a shortcut: the cross-products algorithm. Consider using the rectangular-cake analogy to compare $\frac{2}{5}$ and $\frac{3}{7}$ without the aid of paper and pencil: Lengthwise each cake will be divided into five pieces; widthwise, seven pieces. Two-fifths would be represented by two columns of seven squares each: 2 x 7 or 14 squares altogether. Three-sevenths would be represented by three rows of five squares each: 3 x 5 or 15 squares. This procedure, which is essentially an intuitive cross-products algorithm, shows that $\frac{3}{7}$ is more than $\frac{2}{5}$. Peck and Connell (1991) reports that a number of fifth-graders quickly discovered such a procedure after they were encouraged to compare fractions mentally using a rectangular-cake analogy.

꩜ **Encourage children to use the heuristic of "*explicitly* defining the whole" when solving fraction problems.** Pose problems such as those below and encourage students to consider and discuss what the whole of the solution should be.

■ **Problem 9.1 (◆ 4-8).** Argus had a box of 12 candies. If he shared his candies equally among himself and his two brothers, what fraction of the box did each brother get?

■ **Problem 9.2 (◆ 4-8).** Dante had two packs of gum with 5 sticks in each. While playing baseball, he chewed seven sticks of gum. How many packs of gum did he use while playing baseball?

PARTING THOUGHTS

"Fractions and rational numbers [can] take on numerous personalities" (Behr et al., 1992, p. 296). For children to construct a broad understanding of rational number, they need exposure to these various personalities (Kieren, 1976, cited in Behr et al., 1992). More specifically, it is important that elementary instruction introduce children to the quotient, ratio, and operator meanings of common fractions as well as to the part-of-a-whole meaning. A deep understanding of a rational-number concept comes from discerning what their meanings have in common—a multiplicative relationship, a relationship that is new to children.

Even so, "students bring to instruction a rich store of informal knowledge [about] fractions" (Mack, 1990, p. 132). They can use their informal knowledge about equal partitioning to solve quotient problems and in time part-of-a-whole, ratio, and operator problems in a meaningful way. Teachers, then, "should be like a consulting architect—knowing the ground of a pupil's knowledge and helping the pupil to build a knowledge structure on it" (Kieren & Behr, 1985, p. 178).

RESOURCES

SOME INSTRUCTIONAL RESOURCES

Described below are some valuable resources for fraction instruction.

☞ **Fractions with Pattern Blocks** by M. E. Zullie, © 1975, by Creative Publications. This workbook is appropriate for primary and intermediate grades. A wide variety of shapes (area models) illustrate fractions. The book incorporates worthwhile problem-solving lessons at the end of each section. It uses games and reverse processing for review and assessment. There is generally an attempt to relate concrete to symbolic representations.

☞ **Introduction to Fractions, Book I, A Peatmoss Math Book** by Donald M. Peck and Michael L. Connell, © 1989 by The Wild Goose Co. The book consists of 15 structured activities that introduce children to a quotient meaning of the fraction symbol and helps them to make fraction comparison decisions: whether a fraction is larger than, smaller than, or equal to another. The instructions for teachers underscores the point that a teacher should serve as a facilitator and encourage children to make their own decisions.

☞ **It's A Tangram World** by Lee Jenkins and Peggy McLean, © 1980 by Activity Resources Co., Inc. This resource illustrates various ways of using tangrams to foster fraction concepts and provide problem-solving experiences. The activities are intended to be used after children have been introduced to fractions with an area model and before they begin determining equivalent fractions at the symbolic level.

☞ **The Math Solution** by Marilyn Burns, © 1984 by Marilyn Burns Education Associates. The chapter on fractions contains an introduction and four sections of lessons. The introduction provides a conceptual framework for the topic and establishes a rationale for the lessons. It points out some common problems children have with fractions, emphasizes the importance of introducing concepts concretely, and suggests using a variety of discrete- and continuous-quantities models.

☞ **20 Thinking Questions for Fraction Circles: Grades 3-6** and **Grades 6-8** by Kathryn Walker and Kelly Stewart, © by Creative Publications. These two resources described inquiry-based lessons involving *Fraction Circles*.

A SAMPLE OF CHILDREN'S LITERATURE

☜ **Gator Pie** by Louise Mathews, © 1979 by Dodd, Mead & Company. This is a delightful story that would be suitable for primary-level children. Two alligators Alice and Alvin find a pie and decide to share it. But before they can, another gator joins the party, which necessitates cutting the pie into three parts (thirds). Next a fourth gator and then four more gators join the party. Finally, there are 100 gators at the party and the size of the pieces (one-one hundredth) has become slim pickings. Alvin raises the question whether each piece is exactly the same size. When a fight breaks out, Alvin and Alice abscond with the pie.

At a basic level, this story can serve to introduce children to the idea of fairly dividing up a whole and fraction names like *one-half*. The story can also serve as the basis for a class discussion, probing questions, and the development of a more explicit understanding of fractions by more advanced students. Note, for example, that story relates the number of people sharing a whole to the number of pieces and the fractional name for each share (e.g., 8 gators → 8 pieces → *eight* one-eighths). A teacher may wish to take this one step further and help students see that eight one-eighths is the same as eight-eighths or one whole or, symbolically, that $8 \times \frac{1}{8} = \frac{8}{8} = 1$.

By illustrating one-half, one-third, one-fourth, one-eighth, and one-hundredth, the story provides a basis for recognizing that a larger denominator means the whole is split up into smaller parts and that one-hundredth is much smaller than one-half or one-fourth: To underscore this point a teacher could follow-up with questions like, "Would you rather have one-fourth of a pie or one-third of a pie?"

The story ends by noting that Alice and Alvin each eat one-half of a pie. Because many children may not make the connection themselves, a good question to ask is, "What other fraction describes how much pie each got?" This may help students recognize that fifty-hundredths is equivalent to one-half.

🐚 **Fractions Are Parts of Things** by J. Richard Dennis, © 1971 by Thomas Y. Crowell. This book introduces one-half, one-third, and one-fourth by using a wide variety of shapes (area-model examples) and even a couple of discrete-quantity examples. It discusses and illustrates several ways children can use symmetry to gauge for themselves whether or not a shape has been split into halves: (1) Sometimes halves will match up when a shape is folded. (2) Sometimes halves will match up when the halves are cut apart.

🐚 **The Teacher from the Black Lagoon** by Mike Thaler, © 1989 by Scholastic. In this story, a boy, worried about who his new teacher might be, fantasizes about his first day of school. The boy imagines a green monster Mrs. Green slithering into his class. As mean as can be, she even assigns homework on the first day of school. "Your homework for today," grins Mrs. Green, smoke rising from her nostrils, "is pages 1 to 200 in your math book—*all* the fraction problems." When another boy protested that the class has never had fractions, Mrs. Green beckons the boy to the front of the room to help with a demonstration. She takes a big bite of the boy leaving only his trunk and intones, "This is half a boy. Now you've had fractions."

Evaluate Mrs. Green's fraction lesson. What were its strengths and weaknesses? Seriously, what principles of instruction did Mrs. Green observe and which did she violate? Aside from the unprofessional and distasteful aspects of her demonstration, was Mrs. Green's example of one-half adequate? Why or why not? Read the story to a group of children. Does the story accurately reflect their feelings about fractions? Do they think Mrs. Green's fraction example is good or bad? Oh, by the way, Mrs. Green did not really turn out to be a monster in the literal or the figurative sense.

TIPS ON USING TECHNOLOGY

Calculators

▦ **Math Explorer™ Calculator Job Cards®** by Shirley Hoogeboom and Judy Goodnow, © 1991 Creative Publications. This resource contains 20 jobcards ranging across such topics as operating on whole numbers, operating on fractions, changing fraction to decimals, changing percents to fractions, and powers. It also includes basic information on how to use the various keys of a *Math Explorer™* such as the clearing key and the memory keys. Particularly relevant to this chapter are Jobcards 6, 7, and 8. Card 6 introduces entering and simplifying fractions. To enter and simplify $\frac{12}{16}$, for example, use the following sequence of key strokes:

$\boxed{1}\ \boxed{2}\ \boxed{/}\ \boxed{1}\ \boxed{6}\ \boxed{\text{Simp}}\ \boxed{=}$. The calculator will display 6/8.

Card 7 details how a fraction can be reduced to lowest terms. One way is to use the simplification process just described and then keep entering $\boxed{\text{Simp}}\ \boxed{=}$ until a fraction will not reduce any further. (Note that by pressing $x \rightleftarrows y$ key, a student can discover what factor was used to reduce the fraction in each step of the simplification process.) Alternatively students can be encouraged to predict what factor they should divide by and then check their prediction with the calculator. For example, for $\frac{12}{16}$, a student might choose to divide the numerator and denominator by 2: $\boxed{1}\ \boxed{2}\ \boxed{/}\ \boxed{1}\ \boxed{6}\ \boxed{\text{Simp}}\ \boxed{2}\ \boxed{=}$. Pressing $\boxed{\text{Simp}}\ \boxed{=}$ would indicate that the fraction could, in fact, be simplified further and that a factor larger than 2 was needed to rename $\frac{12}{16}$ in simplest terms.

Card 8 describes how an improper fraction can be changed to a mixed number. For example, to change $\frac{10}{8}$ into a mixed number enter $\boxed{1}\ \boxed{0}\ \boxed{/}\ \boxed{8}\ \boxed{\text{Ab/c}}$. The calculator will indicate 1∪2/8 (1 unit and $\frac{2}{8}$ or $1\frac{2}{8}$). To simplify the expression, press $\boxed{\text{Simp}}\ \boxed{=}$.

Computers

🖥 **Fraction Attractions** published by Sunburst. Amusement park games can involve third- to eighth-graders in the following fraction concepts: ordering, equivalence, relative size, multiple representations, and location of fractions on a number line. Available in Mac or Windows formatted disk or CD.

10 UNDERSTANDING OPERATIONS ON COMMON FRACTIONS

THE MATH CORNER

Daily Challenge

A Fraction Problem.
Choosing from 1, 3, 4, 5, 6, and 7, fill in the boxes in the expression to the right to get the largest sum possible that is less than 1. A digit may be used only once.

$$\frac{\square}{\square} + \frac{\square}{\square}$$

Consumer Math

A Fraction Riddle. A salesman told me he could get me an item for a fraction of the regular retail price. After I bought the item, I discovered that I paid more for it than the regular retail price. The salesman claimed he did not lie. How could this be?

To foster interest in mathematics, dedicate part of your bulletin board space to a *Math Corner*. Part of this display can be a *Daily* (or *Weekly*) *Challenge*, which can consist of a problem, puzzle, or riddle. The fraction problem shown in the *Daily Challenge* above (from Behr, Wachsmuth, & Post, 1985) requires considerable thought and could serve as the basis for a discussion on fraction addition. Such a problem is ideal for fostering a fraction operation sense. (To make the problem illustrated above easier for third and fourth graders, eliminate the constraint that the sum of the fractions has to be less than 1.)

The second part of the bulletin board displayed above is titled *Consumer Math*. This can be a regular or semiregular feature of the *Math Corner* and can serve as a vehicle for discussing consumer-education issues as well as prompting discussions of mathematical ideas. The riddle above can be an entertaining way to deepen students' fraction operation sense.

☞ Try the bulletin-board tasks. Compare your answers with those of your group or class.

THIS CHAPTER

*O*perating on common fractions is needed in such everyday activities such as cooking or calculating the value of common stocks. In some cases, it is easier to use fractions to perform mental arithmetic than it is to use decimals. For exam-

ple, if a jacket is regularly priced at $96 and is on sale for 25% off, it is easier for most people to determine the amount of the savings by gauging $\frac{1}{4}$ of 96 than it is multiplying .25 times 96. Moreover, exploring operations on fractions can foster the multiplicative reasoning necessary to understand ratios and proportions (Streefland, 1993). For example, to add fractions such as $\frac{1}{2} + \frac{1}{3}$, children must discover that the denominator of the sum is derived from multiplying the denominators of the addends, not adding them.

In Unit 10•1, we illustrate how learning a variety of meanings for an arithmetic operation (see chapter 5) is crucial for comprehending operations on fractions, in general, and fraction multiplication and division, in particular. In Unit 10•2, we illustrate how to help children understand operations on common fractions. This understanding will make their task of understanding operations on decimals (addressed in chapter 11) considerably easier.

WHAT THE NCTM *STANDARDS* SAY

Grades K-4

"In grades K-4, the mathematics curriculum should include fractions so that students can:

◆ use models to explore operations on fractions . . . ;

◆ apply fractions . . . to problem situations" (NCTM, 1989, p. 57).

Grades 5-8

"In grades 5-8, [instruction] should develop the concepts underlying computation and estimation in various contexts so that students can:

◆ compute with . . . fractions . . . and rational numbers;

◆ develop, analyze, and explain procedures for computation and . . . estimation;

◆ use computation [and] estimation [procedures] to solve problems;

◆ use estimation to check the reasonableness of results" (NCTM, 1989, p. 94).

10•1 MATHEMATICS AND LEARNING

Figure 10.1: F-r-a-c-t-i-o-n A-r-i-t-h-m-e-t-i-c Spells "More Despair"

PEANUTS reprinted by permission of UFS, Inc.

In Subunit 10•1•1, we outline meaningful analogies for operations on fractions. In Subunit 10•1•2, we explore children's thinking for clues about where to begin instruction on fraction arithmetic and why it is often so onerous (see Figure 10.1).

10•1•1 MEANINGFUL ANALOGIES

What type of real-world situations or analogies can help children understand operations on fractions?

Addition and Subtraction. Change add-to unknown-outcome, part-part-whole unknown-whole, and change take-away unknown-outcome problems would make a good starting point for introducing addition and subtraction with fractions. Compare and equalize unknown-difference problems can be introduced later.

Multiplication. *Why does multiplying with a fraction less than one make something smaller when multiplying is suppose to make things bigger?* Although the common and familiar repeated-addition analogy is useful for making sense of, say, $4 \times \frac{1}{2}$ ($\frac{1}{2}$ added four times) or even $\frac{1}{2} \times 4$ (which can be thought of as $\frac{1}{2}$ *added four*

times), it makes little sense with an expression such as $\frac{1}{4} \times \frac{1}{2}$. Fortunately, there are interpretations that do make sense.

• *Groups-of* interpretation. All types of fraction multiplication expressions are readily interpretable in terms of a *groups-of* concept (Ott, 1990). For example, if children interpret 2×4 as "two groups of four," then $4 \times \frac{1}{2}$ can be interpreted as "four groups of one-half of a whole" and $\frac{1}{2} \times 4$ can be viewed as "one-half group of four." Even expressions such as $\frac{1}{2} \times \frac{1}{4}$ can make sense—"one-half group of one-fourth of a whole."

• *Area* interpretation. Multiplication with fractions also makes sense if we consider an area interpretation. The expression $\frac{1}{2} \times 4$ can be interpreted as, "What is the area of a rectangle $\frac{1}{2}$-units long and 4-units wide?" Similarly, the problem $\frac{1}{2} \times \frac{1}{4}$ can be interpreted as, "What is the area of a rectangle $\frac{1}{2}$-units long and $\frac{1}{4}$-units wide?"

• *Rate* interpretation. Rate situations can involve fractions. For example, a boy walks to school at the rate of $\frac{1}{2}$ miles per hour. In $\frac{1}{4}$ of an hour, he travels $\frac{1}{2} \times \frac{1}{4}$ or $\frac{1}{8}$ of a mile. A rate interpretation of fraction multiplication might be helpful with intermediate-level students.

☞ **Fraction-multiplication instruction should build on** *groups-of* **and** *area* **meanings of multiplication.** Children should be thoroughly familiar with these interpretations of multiplication before instruction on fraction multiplication begins.

Division. *Why does dividing by a fraction make something bigger when dividing is supposed to make things smaller? How can instruction build on existing knowledge (e.g., everyday analogies) to help children make sense of and solve expressions such as* $\frac{1}{2} \div \frac{1}{4}$? Although it is difficult to make sense of division expressions like $4 \div \frac{1}{2} = 8$, $\frac{1}{4} \div \frac{1}{8} = 2$, and $\frac{1}{8} \div \frac{1}{4} = \frac{1}{2}$ in terms of the familiar divvy-up analogy, two other analogies can be helpful: measure and area.*

• *Measure-out* interpretation. A measure-out meaning (an amount ÷ size of the group or share = number of groups or shares) provides a readily interpretable basis for introducing division by a fraction—whether a whole number is divided by a fraction (e.g., $8 \div \frac{1}{2}$) or a larger fraction is divided by a smaller one (e.g., $\frac{1}{4} \div \frac{1}{8}$). Using this interpretation, it makes sense that the answers for Problems 10.1 and 10.2 below are larger than the initial amount. If a child has 8 cookies and each share is $\frac{1}{2}$ of a cookie, then she has enough for 16 shares. If $\frac{1}{4}$ of a pie is left and each piece is $\frac{1}{8}$ of a pie, then there must be 2 pieces left because two one-eighths fit into one quarter.

■ **Problem 10.1: Cookies for Tea** (◆ 1-5). Topaz has 8 giant cookies. If she plans to give each person who comes to her tea half a cookie, how many friends can Topaz invite?

---

* In fact, a divvy-up analogy can make sense if you do not use examples involving fair-sharing among people (whole groups). In a "put-in" variation of the divvy-up analogy, an amount is used to form partial groups, and the quotient specifies the size of the whole group (Behr et al., 1992; Ott, Snook, & Gibson, 1991). For example, if four crayons fill half a box, how many fill a full box? Because of space limitations, we will not consider a put-in analogy further but focus on the more commonly used measure-out and area analogies.

■ **Problem 10.2: Leftover Pie** (◆ 2-5). One-quarter of a pie was left uneaten. If the original pie was divided into eighths, how many pieces of pie were left?

Measure-out problems are sometimes called "goes-into" problems. For example, $\frac{1}{4} \div \frac{1}{8}$ can be read: "How many eighths fit into a fourth?"

A measure-out meaning even makes sense in situations where a smaller fraction is divided by a larger one (e.g., $\frac{1}{8} \div \frac{1}{4}$). In Problem 10.3 below, for example, the amount available ($\frac{1}{8}$) is less than the size of one share ($\frac{1}{4}$). That is, $\frac{1}{8}$ of a whole is not enough to make one full share, which is $\frac{1}{4}$ of the whole. The quotient ($\frac{1}{2}$) represents the *fraction of a share* this amount makes— $\frac{1}{8}$ is $\frac{1}{2}$ of a $\frac{1}{4}$. The answer ($\frac{1}{2}$ of a share) can be larger than the available amount ($\frac{1}{8}$ of a pie) because $\frac{1}{2}$ and $\frac{1}{8}$ are fractions of different wholes.

■ **Problem 10.3: Less Than One Share of Pie** (◆ 3-6). Arianna found only one-eighth of a small-sized pizza left. If she wanted portions that were one-fourth of a pizza, how many portions did she have?

In Problem 10.3 above, note that Arianna has less than what she needs for one portion. More specifically, she has one-half of one portion.

• *Area* model. As with multiplication of fractions, division of fractions can be interpreted in terms of an area model. The expression $\frac{1}{4} \div \frac{1}{8}$, for instance, can represent the situation described in Problem 10.4 below:

■ **Problem 10.4: Missing Side** (◆ 3-6). A rectangle has an area of $\frac{1}{4}$-square units and a length of $\frac{1}{8}$-linear units. What is the width of the rectangle (in linear units)?

☞ **Instruction on fraction division should build on** *measure-out* **and** *area* **meanings of division.** Children should thoroughly understand these interpretations of division and how they differ from children's familiar divvy-up interpretation *before* symbolic fraction division is introduced. Such interpretations can help children understand why dividing by a fraction sometimes leads to an answer larger than the dividend.

10•1•2 CHILDREN'S THINKING

Informal Strengths. After Miss Brill found that her class was completely baffled by the fraction-division algorithm, she discussed her problem with Ms. Socrates. The experienced teacher counseled, "Consider building on your students' informal knowledge."

Mrs. MeChokemchild, who was hovering nearby, interjected, "Ms. Socrates, your head's goin' soft. What informal knowledge do kids have about dividing with fractions?"

For once, Miss Brill had to agree with Mrs. MeChokemchild. It seemed a little far-fetched that fifth graders would have any informal knowledge about fraction division.

☞ Try Probe 10.1 (page 10-5) before continuing.

"I'll show you," said Ms. Socrates, calmly ignoring Mrs. MeChokemchild's uncivility. "These [see Figure 10.2 on page 10-6] are some informal solutions to the *Lead-Heads* problem [Problem 4 in Probe 10.1] my students devised," she noted proudly. "My guess is that they are representative of children who have been encouraged to consider a variety of informal solutions. I should add that it is important to encourage children to share and to justify their strategies."

"But do they know the division algorithm?" demanded Mrs. MeChokemchild defensively.

"They will in time. Moreover, they'll *understand* what they're doing," added Ms. Socrates.

The moral of this tale is that even before they are taught formal algorithms, children can understand and solve real-world situations or word problems that involve operations on fractions. It is not necessary to know the standard algorithm to figure out the answer to, say, the *Lead-Heads* problem in Probe 10.1. The answer can be reasoned out. For example, if one pound contains 8 eighths, then three pounds contains 24 eighths. As each head requires 3-eighths and 3 fits in 24 *eight* times, eight heads can be made.

Common Difficulties. *Why is understanding operations on fractions so difficult?* One reason is how this topic is usually taught. The skills approach focuses on memorizing algorithms—learning the mechanics of fraction-arithmetic procedures—not understanding operations on fractions or why the algorithms work. It typically does not encourage or build on children's informal knowledge or help students construct the necessary supporting concepts (e.g., Post, Cramer, Behr, Lesh, & Harel, 1993). In particular, although "today's textbooks devote considerable attention to algorithms for multiplication and division with [fractions], they give little attention to" how whole-number meanings for these operations apply to situations involving fractions (Graeber & Tanenhaus, 1993). As one seventh-grader put it, "I know how to do [fraction arithmetic] but don't ask me to explain it." When operations on fractions is just more math magic, children do not develop a fraction operation sense or a positive disposition toward fractions, in particular, or mathematics, in general.

A second reason for difficulties is that many children narrowly view multiplication as repeated addition and division as divvying-up (Fischbein et al., 1985; Greer, 1989; Kouba, 1985).

10•2 TEACHING

Figure 10.3: Knowledge Is Power

I TOLD YOU TO BE HOME BY A QUARTER OF 12!

BUT I LEARNED IN MATH CLASS THAT ¼ OF TWELVE IS 3!

How can operations on fractions be taught so that they make sense to pupils and enhance their mathematical power (cf. Figure 10.3)? In Subunit 10•2•1, we describe general guidelines for helping children construct an understanding of operations on fractions. In Subunit 10•2•2, we focus on how instruction can be structured to help students reinvent the written algorithms for operating on fractions and understand why these formal procedures work. (Continued on page 10-7.)

➤Probe 10.1: Exploring Students' Informal Knowledge of Operations on Common Fractions

The aim of this probe is to help you reflect on the power of informal knowledge. Imagine yourself in the place of a fourth grader who has not yet learned the school-taught algorithms for operating on fractions. Try solving the problems below *without* using a formal procedure. Share your solution procedures with other members of your group or class. Ask at least three fourth- or fifth-graders who have not been introduced to formal procedures for operating on fractions to solve the problems below. Note whether each child is successful and what strategy was used. Share your results with your group or class.

■ **Problem 1: Crude and Rude** (◆ 4-6). On its first world tour, the Dashed Hopes Heavy Metal Band immediately alienated $\frac{1}{4}$ of the population of Goodsenseland by their utterly tasteless remarks when arriving at the Goodsenseland International Airport. Soon after, they alienated another $\frac{1}{3}$ of the population when the band tried to crash the wedding reception of the president's daughter. How much of Goodsenseland's population had the band alienated so far?

■ **Problem 2: Bad for Business** (◆ 4-6). After the international incident sparked by the Dashed Hopes Heavy Metal Band's visit to Goodsenseland, the stock of Very Bad Records, which sponsored the band's tour, dropped dramatically in value. If the stock had been selling at $9\frac{1}{4}$ per share and the value of a share fell $7\frac{3}{8}$ per share, what was the new value of the stock?

■ **Problem 3: Rebuilding Costs** (◆ 4-6). Very Bad Records was supposed to get $\frac{3}{4}$ of the money earned by Dashed Hopes' appearance in Goodsenseland. To make amends for the disruption and destruction caused by the band on their visit, Very Bad Records decided to donate $\frac{2}{3}$ of their earnings to the treasury of Goodsenseland. What fraction of the money earned by the Dashed Hopes' appearance in Goodsenseland was donated to the national treasury?

■ **Problem 4: The Lead Heads** (◆ 4-6). To help offset the costs of the Dashed Hopes Heavy Metal Band's visit to Goodsenseland, Very Bad Records decided to sell kits for making busts (head sculptures) of the band's leader, Deep Despair. Although grossly overpriced, Ariel, the president of a local Dashed Hopes Heavy Metal Band Fan Club, could not resist this sensational offer. She bought the mold and 3 pounds of lead. If each bust requires $\frac{3}{8}$ pounds of lead, how many busts of Mr. Despair could Ariel make with 3 pounds of lead?

Questions for Reflection

1. Did you have difficulty coming up with informal strategies for the problems above? If so, why?

2. (a) Try solving the *Lead-Heads* problem by using a school-taught algorithm. (b) Some students conclude that this problem can be solved by multiplying $\frac{3}{8} \times 3$. Does the answer $\frac{9}{8}$ or $1\frac{1}{8}$ make sense? Why or why not?

3. **Write-A-Word-Problem Problem.** Write a word problem for $\frac{1}{2} \div \frac{1}{4} = ?$

4. Illustrate with a diagram or with manipulatives, the expression $3\frac{1}{2} \times 2\frac{1}{4}$.

Figure 10.2: Some Informal Solutions for Problem 4 in Probe 10.1 (the _Lead-Heads_ Problem), Which Involved Finding How Many $\frac{3}{8}$ Fit Into 3)

Adrian's solution:

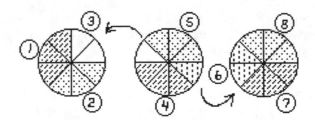

Each circle = 1 lb
Each head requires $\frac{3}{8}$ lbs.

Bryant's solution:

(drawn to solve 2 2/8 - 3/8)

Cyril's solution:

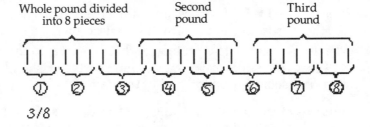

3/8

Darien's solution:

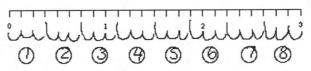

Erwin's solution:

3 pounds of lead divided into 8 pieces each

24 eighths
Each head gets 3 eighths of a pound.
So 24 eighths ÷ 3 eighths is 8 heads.

Fritz's solution: 3 = 24/8   24/8 ÷ 3/8 = 8

Greta's solution: $\frac{3}{8}$ is between $\frac{2}{8}$ or $\frac{1}{4}$ and $\frac{4}{8}$ or $\frac{1}{2}$. If each head took $\frac{1}{4}$-pound, then 3 pounds could make 12. If each head took $\frac{1}{2}$-pound, then 3 pounds could make 6. So $\frac{3}{8}$ makes halfway between 6 and 12 or 8 heads.

10•2•1 PREALGORITHMIC INSTRUC-TION: CONSTRUCTING A CONCEPTUAL FOUNDATION

Well before instruction focuses on written algorithms for operating on fractions, it should help children construct the conceptual foundation for inventing and understanding these procedures. In this subunit, we discuss how to foster an operation sense, promote inquiry, and understanding.

Fostering an Operation Sense

Because all phases of instruction should stress gauging whether an answer is reasonable and why, it is essential to promote children's operation sense. Two key ways of accomplishing this aim are regularly engaging children in tasks that involve qualitative reasoning and estimating. See Investigation 10.1 for sample tasks.

☞ Try Investigation 10.1 (pages 10-8 and 10-9).

Promoting Inquiry and Understanding

In this section, we describe how to promote inquiry and understanding during the conceptual and the connecting phases of instruction.

Conceptual Phase. Before symbolic expressions and written algorithms are introduced, children should be given ample opportunity to solve problems informally.

↬ **Ideally, begin by using an operation purposefully in real situations.** The focus of presymbolic instruction should be on *reasoning out* solutions to genuine and intriguing problems and helping children construct a conceptual basis for operating on fractions. Consider, for example:

• **Planning a class party.** Have the class consider how many pizzas need to be bought. This will require determining what is a *reasonable* number of pieces each student should get. If the consensus is that each of 24 people should get three pieces ($\frac{3}{8}$ of a pizza), the problem is: Twenty-four three-eighths makes how many pizzas?

• **Cooking projects.** Perhaps as a social studies lesson on different cultures, have the class prepare and cook dishes representative of different countries or parts of the United States. Students can also be involved in cooking projects as

part of a charity effort or preparations for a class party (see Box 10.1 on page 10-10). Cooking can involve, for example, halving, doubling, tripling recipes as well as other operations (e.g., $\frac{3}{4}$ cups of milk from one container and another $\frac{3}{4}$ cups from another makes how much altogether?).

• **Projects involving measuring.** In constructing a doll-house size replica of a Victorian-style house, for instance, students may need to determine how many $\frac{3}{4}$-inch rods can be cut from a 3-foot piece of doweling (in order to make a railing) or the wall area of a room that is $11\frac{1}{4}$ inches long, $6\frac{1}{2}$ inches wide, and $8\frac{1}{4}$ inches high (to ensure that remaining doll-house wallpaper is sufficient to cover the walls).

• **Unit on the stock market.** Creating a virtual stock market can involve students in, for instance, determining the total cost of 12 stocks bought at a cost of $27\frac{1}{8}$ each (multiplying) or figuring profits when the same stocks are sold at $34\frac{1}{4}$ each (multiplying and subtracting).

• **Consumer education unit.** Students could determine the relative values of an item that originally cost $68 on sale for 25% ($\frac{1}{4}$) off and the same item that originally cost $78 at another store for 33% ($\frac{1}{3}$) off.

• **Probability unit.** Determining the solutions to probability problems can involve students in adding and multiplying fractions, in particular (see Box 13.1 on page 13-3 for an example).

Word problems such as Problems A to O in Probe 10.2 are a good way to supplement real situations.

☞ Try Probe 10.2 (pages 10-11 and 10-12).

↬ **Encourage children to use what they know to invent their own procedures for operating on fractions.** THAT IS, INVITE THEM TO USE THEIR CONCEPTUAL UNDERSTANDING OF AN OPERATION AND MANIPULATIVES OR PICTURES TO DEVISE INFORMAL PROCEDURES (Bezuk & Bieck, 1993; Kieren, 1988) (see, e.g., Box 10.2 on page 10-13). IF CHILDREN INVENT INCORRECT PROCEDURES, POSE QUESTIONS OR USE OTHER INDIRECT MEANS TO PROMPT SELF-CORRECTION (see, e.g., Box 10.3 on page 10-13). (Text continued on page 10-14.)

✿ Investigation 10.1: Reasoning About Operations on Common Fractions

◆ Fraction operation sense (qualitative reasoning and estimating) ◆ 2-8 ◆ Any number

Children need to develop an operation sense for adding, subtracting, multiplying, and dividing fractions. Fostering qualitative reasoning and estimation skills are key components of such a sense. Qualitative-reasoning tasks can provide the foundation for understanding and monitoring operations on fractions (Behr et al., 1992). The conceptual phase of instruction should first focus on posing problem situations and helping children consider the direction of an answer (see Part I below). During the connecting phase, qualitative reasoning can be extended to doing the same with symbolic expressions such as $\frac{3}{4} \times \frac{2}{3}$ and $\frac{1}{8} \div \frac{3}{4}$ (see Part II below). Estimation activities put a premium on reasoning, particularly if children are encouraged to justify their answers. Estimation proficiency is important for evaluating the reasonableness of answers. In the conceptual phase, students can be encouraged to estimate the solutions to problems (see Part III). In the connecting and symbolic phases, they can be prompted to do the same with symbolic expressions (see Part IV). To understand what is involved and to perhaps deepen your own operation sense, try the four parts below. Discuss your answers with your group or class. Part V illustrates how qualitative reasoning and estimation can be useful in evaluating the reasonableness of an answer.

Part I: Qualitative Reasoning in the Conceptual Phase

For each of the following problems, indicate whether the answer will be larger than, smaller than, or equal to the starting amount. Briefly justify why.

■ **Problem A: Chow Hound** (◆ 2-4). Ruffus the dog chewed a hole in the bottom of a dry dog food bag and promptly ate half the contents of the bag. Later that day, he returned to eat another third of the bag's content. Altogether, did Ruffus eat less than a half, just one-half, or more than half of the bag's content?

■ **Problem B: Thirsty Dog** (◆ 2-4). After eating a whole bunch of dry dog food, Ruffus was very thirsty. His water bowl was half filled. If Ruffus drank one-third of a bowl of water, did he have less than, more than, or just half a bowl of water left?

■ **Problem C: The Pizza Pilfer** (◆ 3-5). Mary heated one-third of a pizza for her lunch. While the pizza was cooling on the table, Ruffus ate half of it. Did Ruffus eat less than a third, just a third, or more than a third of the whole pizza?

■ **Problem D: Rations for Ruffus** (◆ 3-5). Mary's mom said that Ruffus had to go on a diet and should be given only an eighth of a bag of dry food a day. Mary found that Ruffus' bag of dry dog food was half full. How many days should this last—less than, more than, or just half a day?

Part II: Qualitative Reasoning in the Connecting Phase

1. Without computing the answer, quickly indicate whether the quotient of $\frac{3}{4} \div \frac{3}{8}$ will be:

   (a) smaller than $\frac{3}{4}$ (b) larger than $\frac{3}{4}$ but less than 1, (c) larger than 1.

2. For the questions below, explain to students that the box, circle, triangle, and diamond each cover a digit.

   ➮ ✓ **Teaching or Assessment Tip.** Note that the following questions are useful either as the basis for prompting discussion and meaningful learning or for assessing conceptual understanding. Without a meaningful analogy to guide thinking, these questions would be difficult, if not impossible, to answer. Consider what meaning for the operation involved would be helpful.

Investigation 10.1 continued

a. In the expression to the right, indicate what would happen to the sum if the digit covered by (i) the box increased in value, (ii) the circle increased in value, (iii) the box and the digit covered by the circle increased in value, (iv) the triangle decreased in value, (v) the box increased in value and that covered by the circle decreased in value, and (vi) the circle decreased in value and that covered by triangle increased in value? For each case, indicate whether the sum would get larger, smaller, stay the same, or cannot be determined.

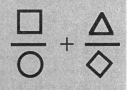

b. In the expression to the right, indicate what would happen to the product if the digit covered by (i) the box increased in value, (ii) the circle increased in value, (iii) the box and the digit covered by the circle increased in value, (iv) the triangle decreased in value, (v) the box increased in value and that covered by the circle decreased in value, and (vi) the circle decreased in value and that covered by triangle increased in value? For each case, indicate whether the product would get larger, smaller, stay the same, or cannot be determined.

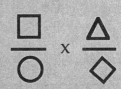

c. In the expression to the right, indicate what would happen to the quotient if the digit covered by (i) the box increased in value, (ii) the circle increased in value, (iii) the box and the digit under the circle increased in value, (iv) the triangle decreased in value, and (v) the box increased in value and that covered by the circle decreased in value? For each case, indicate whether the quotient would get larger, smaller, stay the same, or cannot be determined.

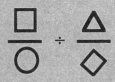

Part III: Estimation During the Conceptual Phases

1. Estimate the answers to Problems A, B, C, and D in Part I (on the previous page).

2. Make up a word problem involving an operation on a fraction. Share your word problem with your group or class. Have them estimate the answer to it.

Part IV: Estimation During the Connecting and Symbolic Phases

1. Without computing the answer, quickly indicate whether the sum of $\frac{12}{13} + \frac{7}{8}$ is closer to: (a) $\frac{1}{2}$, (b) 1, (c) 2, (d) 19, or (e) 21.

2. Take no more than 2 minutes to estimate the answers to the following items:

(a) $\frac{7}{8} + \frac{2}{5}$ (b) $4\frac{1}{7} + 5\frac{7}{16}$ (c) $2\frac{3}{5} + 3\frac{5}{8}$ (d) $1\frac{1}{9} + 2\frac{6}{13} + 5\frac{7}{16}$

(e) $3\frac{13}{15} - \frac{9}{10}$ (f) $5\frac{3}{5} - \frac{6}{7}$ (g) $7\frac{1}{10} - 5\frac{7}{10}$ (h) $9\frac{3}{4} + 6\frac{5}{7}$

(a) What estimation strategy or strategies did you use? (b) If you have not done so already, try rounding the addends off to the nearest whole and try again. Did this make the task easier? (c) Now try the more precise strategy of rounding the addends off to the nearest half.

Part V: Operation Sense

For the problem below, Rock computed an answer of $\frac{4}{5}$ and concluded that Raphaela had gone $\frac{4}{5}$ of a mile. Ann computed an answer of $\frac{4}{5}$ and concluded that the runner had gone $\frac{4}{5}$ of $\frac{3}{5}$ (or $\frac{12}{25}$) of a mile. Which, if either, is correct? Why?

■ **A Truncated-Run** (◆ 5-8). Every morning, Raphaela runs around her block a distance of $\frac{3}{5}$ of a mile. After caring for her rambunctious nephew the previous day, she was only able to run $\frac{3}{4}$ of this distance. How far did the exhausted aunt run?

Box 10.1: An Example of the Investigative Approach to Operations on Fractions

Vignette	Comments
Ms. Socrates proposed that the class bake their own cupcakes for an upcoming party. A recipe called for $\frac{3}{4}$ cups of sugar. Ms. Socrates noted that the recipe made 18 cupcakes but that they needed 27.	The teacher introduced fraction multiplication purposefully. Proposing a baking task naturally lead to the mathematical problem of multiplying $\frac{1}{2}$ and $\frac{3}{4}$.
After a discussion, the class agreed that they need to make $1\frac{1}{2}$ recipes. Sonia pointed out that would require $\frac{3}{4}$ cups of sugar and half of another $\frac{3}{4}$ cups.	
Ms. Socrates asked the class if a half of $\frac{3}{4}$ cups would be less than, equal to, or larger than $\frac{3}{4}$ cups. The class agreed that it should be less.	The teacher engaged the children in qualitative reasoning.
Each group of four children set about to determine the amount informally. Some groups drew a picture; others chose a manipulative such as *Fraction Circles*.	The class worked in small groups to devise their own informal solutions.
After the class agreed that the answer was $\frac{3}{8}$, Ms. Socrates asked how the problem and solution could be represented. Daktar suggested $\frac{3}{4} \div \frac{1}{2} = \frac{3}{8}$. Ms. Socrates prompted the students to analyze the suggestion in terms of what they knew about whole-number division. Lourdes commented that it didn't make sense to divvy up $\frac{3}{4}$ among half a person. Pia concluded that $\frac{3}{4}$ could be measured out in groups of a half but that would make [an answer of] more than 1, not $\frac{3}{8}$.	The teacher encouraged the students to connect the problem and their informal solution to a formal representation. When a student incorrectly proposed a division representation, the teacher created cognitive conflict by prompting students to interpret the symbolism in terms of their existing understanding of division.
James then conjectured that $\frac{1}{2} \times \frac{3}{4} = \frac{3}{8}$. Tabia argued that it couldn't be multiplication because multiplication always made the answer bigger, and $\frac{3}{8}$ was not bigger than $\frac{3}{4}$.	
Ms. Socrates asked the class if anyone could think of a counterexample to Tabia's conjecture. Bekka offered $3 \times 0 = 0$, and Lance proposed $5 \times 1 = 5$. The class then re-examined the equation $\frac{1}{2} \times \frac{3}{4} = \frac{3}{8}$ in terms of their familiar groups-of meaning ("one-half group of three-fourths is three-eighths") and concluded it made sense.	To counter a common misconception, the teacher asked the class to consider counterexamples (Fischbein, 1987). She then encouraged students to use a familiar analogy for multiplication to evaluate whether or not the multiplication representation made sense (Davis, 1984).

➤ Probe 10.2: Using Informal Knowledge to Invent Concrete Strategies for Operating on Fractions

In the investigative approach, a teacher might pose problems and encourage children to invent their own strategies for operating on fractions. This could serve as the conceptual basis for them later reinventing formal algorithms. To see how and to perhaps deepen your own understanding of operations on fractions, complete the three parts below either on your own or, preferably, with the help of your group. Discuss your solutions with your group or class.

Part I: Addition and Subtraction

1. Can you add apples and oranges? How is adding (or subtracting) unlike fractions comparable to adding apples and oranges?

2. Which of the following is assumed to be true when fractions are added or subtracted (e.g., $\frac{1}{4} + \frac{2}{3}$ or $\frac{3}{6} - \frac{1}{3}$)? Circle the letter of any correct statement.

    a. Each addend can represent a fraction of different-sized wholes.
    b. Each addend can represent a fraction of same-sized wholes.
    c. Each addend can represent a fraction of the same whole.
    d. None of the above.
    e. Statements a, b, and c are all true.
    f. Both statements b and c are true.

3. Put yourself in the place of an elementary-level child who does not know the algorithm for adding unlike fractions. Illustrate how you could use your knowledge of whole-number addition and manipulatives such as *Cuisenaire rods*, *Fraction Circles*, or *Fraction Tiles* to model and to solve Problem A below.

    ■ **Problem A: A Treat Tragedy (◆ 3-5).** Mary made a special treat for her birthday party—a tuna dip in the shape of a bunny. Ruffus her dog discovered the treat and ate one-half of it. Later he polished off another one-third of the (original) treat. What fraction of the bunny-shaped treat did Ruffus wolf down altogether?

4. A common solution children devise for Problem A is shown below. How could a teacher *create cognitive conflict* in order to prompt children to reconsider this incorrect solution and to discover a correct method for adding $\frac{1}{2}$ and $\frac{1}{3}$ with the rods?

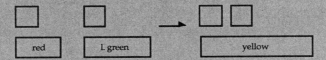

Part II: Groups-of and Area Meanings of Multiplication

Put yourself in the place of a child who does not know a fraction-multiplication algorithm. Illustrate how you could informally model and solve Problems B, C, D, and E using manipulatives such as *Cuisenaire rods*. Illustrate how you could informally solve Problems F and G using square tiles.

■ **Problem B: Mania for Order (◆ 3-6).** Mr. Carlton found six opened cartons of milk in the refrigerator. Each was three-quarters full. Because having so many opened and partially filled cartons of milk drove him crazy, Mr. C. decided to combine the contents of the milk cartons. How many cartons of milk would Mr. C. have after he finished his tidying-up project?

■ **Problem C: A Case of the Munchies (◆ 3-6).** Mr. Carlton found a third of a pie in his refrigerator and ate half of it. How much of the original pie did he eat?

Probe 10.2 continued

- **Problem D: Thirst Quencher** (◆ 4-6). If Mr. Carlton drank two-third of the milk in a carton that was three-fourths full, how much milk did Mr. C. drink?

- **Problem E: Still Snacking** (◆ 4-6). For a snack, Mr. Carlton ate a fourth of the pizza leftovers he found in his refrigerator. If the leftovers consisted of two-thirds of a pizza, how much of the original pizza did Mr. C. eat?

- **Problem F: Carpeted Cat Ramp** (◆ 4-6). Owen made a ramp for his cat window 3-yards long and $\frac{1}{2}$-yard wide. He wanted to carpet the top of the ramp. What is the area the carpet will cover?

- **Problem G: Carpeted Cat Platform** (◆ 4-6). Owen made a platform just below his cat window that was $\frac{1}{2}$-yard long by $\frac{1}{4}$-yard wide. He wanted to carpet the top of this platform. What is the area the carpet will cover?

Part III: Measure-Out and Area Meanings of Division

Put yourself in the place of a child who does not know a fraction-division algorithm. Illustrate how you could informally model and solve Problems H to M using *Cuisenaire rods* or some other manipulative. Illustrate how you could informally model and solve Problems N and O using square tiles.

- **Problem H: Burger Bribes** (◆ 3-6). To control Ruffus on his walk, Mary broke up two dog "burgers" into fourths. How many doggie bribes (pieces of dog burger) did Mary have?

- **Problem I: Pie Pieces Left** (◆ 3-6). Mrs. Smith brought home half a pie leftover from an office party. If the pie had originally had been cut into eighths, how many pieces of pie could she serve with supper?

- **Problem J: Tight Squeeze** (◆ 3-6). Mary was typing up a school report. She had only a $\frac{3}{4}$-inch space left on a page. If each line of type required $\frac{3}{8}$-inches, how many more lines can she fit on the page?

- **Problem K: Food Shortage** (◆ 4-6). Ruffus had $\frac{1}{2}$ bag of dog food left. If he ate $\frac{1}{3}$ bag a week, how many week's supply of dog food did Ruffus have left?

- **Problem L: Short on Sugar** (◆ 4-6). After Ruffus ate Mr. Smith's favorite cookies, the hungry dog owner decided to bake some more. Mr. Smith had $\frac{1}{8}$-cup of sugar, and a batch of cookies called for $\frac{1}{4}$-cup of sugar. What portion of a batch could he make?

- **Problem M: A Mowing Problem** (◆ 4-6). Ms. Alvez had $\frac{1}{3}$-gallon of gas for the lawn mower. If it takes $\frac{1}{2}$-gallon of gas to cut the lawn, how much of the lawn can she cut?

- **Problem N: Garden Length** (◆ 4-6). Mr. Weinstein wanted to plant a rectangular garden that covered a space of $\frac{3}{4}$-square yards. If one side of the garden had to be $\frac{1}{4}$-yards long, how long would the other side have to be?

- **Problem O: Plot Dimension** (◆ 5-8). Mr. Truillo had bought $\frac{1}{8}$-square mile of land from a neighbor. If the plot was rectangular in shape and the side bordering Mr. Truillo's property was $\frac{1}{2}$-mile long, how far did the other side of his land purchase extend?

Box 10.2: An Invented Procedure for Multiplying Fractions

Example 1. Before any formal instruction on fraction multiplication, a combined fourth-fifth grade class was asked to solve the following problem:

- ■ **Hungry Cat (◆ 4-8).** There was one-half a bag of dry cat food left. Tom the Cat ate one-third of it. What portion of the bag did Tom eat?

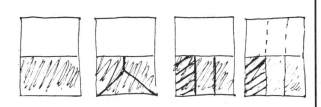

Figure A   Figure B   Figure C   Figure D

To represent half a bag of cat food, ten-year-old Arianne immediately drew Figure A to the right. She then experimented with dividing the half that was left into thirds (see, e.g., Figure B), finally drawing Figure C. Asked how much Tom ate, she used her existing knowledge of fractions to partition her drawing of the bag into six equal parts (see Figure D) and concluded he ate one-sixth of the bag.

Example 2.[1] Mr. Vanhille read a report of considerable personal interest to his fifth-grade students: a summary of the vote on the dress-code proposal for the junior high school. The report noted that almost 45% of the eligible voters voted and that 72% favored the proposal. This raised the question, "What percent of all the voters actually voted in favor of the proposal?" Mr. Vanhille asked for easy-to-use fractions close to the reported percentages. Students volunteered $\frac{2}{5}$ and $\frac{3}{4}$, respectively. The class then proceeded to use a method similar to that in Example 1: They pictorially represented two-fifths of a whole and then three-fourths of that—giving them an answer of $\frac{6}{20}$ or $\frac{3}{10}$.

Box 10.3: Creating Conflict About an Informal Solution

Using manipulatives does not guarantee that children will correctly model and solve problems involving operations on fractions. It is very likely that to solve a problem involving the addition of a half and a third, for example, some children will make the error illustrated below. (This concrete solution is equivalent to adding the numerator and adding the denominator separately for a symbolic expression—e.g., $\frac{1}{2} + \frac{1}{3} = \frac{2}{5}$).

When children arrive at such a solution, ask them if it is plausible. If they insist it is, create cognitive conflict in the following ways:

• **Encourage students to explicitly consider the size of the sum.** Ask, "If you had half a candy bar and got another third of the candy bar, would you have more or less than half the candy bar?" Have them compare their answer to their representation of the sum by asking, "Is your answer more or less than one-half? Children

should recognize that their answer of $\frac{2}{5}$ is less than $\frac{1}{2}$ (less than what they began with) and that there is something fundamentally wrong with their concrete procedure.

• **Encourage students to explicitly consider the underlying (and often unstated) assumption of fraction addition (or subtraction)—that each addend represents a fraction of the same whole or the same-sized wholes.** Students making the error above can be asked, for example, "Did you model one-half of a whole and one-third of the *same* whole?" or "How can a red rod and a light-green rod be used to show the same whole?"

• **Encourage children to explicitly consider the relative sizes of the addends represented.** Ask if one-half and one-third of the same whole can be the same size—can both be represented by a white cube.

With any luck, children will recognize that they have to find a rod (whole) that can be divided in both halves and thirds. In effect, this would entail discovering the concrete equivalent of finding a common denominator.

Connecting Phase. A key to teaching fraction operations meaningfully is to help children link the symbolism to their informal understandings and everyday experiences. Some general guidelines are outlined below.

☞ Consider Investigation 10.2 (pages 10-15 to 10-17).

🙶 **Introduce symbolism for fraction operations by having children represent problems and their informal solutions in a number sentence.** For example, after using manipulatives to solve the measure-out problem below, children could summarize their efforts with the number sentence $\frac{1}{2} \div \frac{1}{8} = 4$.

■ **Problem 10.5: How Many Signs?** (◆ 3-6). Delanna had a $\frac{1}{2}$ pint of paint. If it took $\frac{1}{8}$ of a pint of paint to cover each sign, how many signs could Delanna paint?

✔ 🙶 **Later, present symbolic expressions and have students make up an appropriate word problem.** This type of reverse-processing task provides a particularly good test of understanding. (Teachers should be able to respond to such tasks automatically. To promote meaningful learning, it is essential that a teacher be able to relate a symbolic expression to real situations.)

🙶 **Encourage children to *explicitly* connect the symbolism to familiar knowledge.** For example, use whole-number analogies such as adding different-denomination coins to help children see that you can add or subtract "apples and oranges" (different denominations), *if* you find a common name (denomination) (see, e.g., Box 10.4). Help students make the following symbol-to-model, symbol-to-real-life, and concept-to-concept links:

• **Encourage students to relate symbolic expressions to their conceptual understanding of an operation.** For example, an expression such as $\frac{1}{2} \div \frac{1}{6}$ can be related to a meaningful measure-out analogy. Help children see that in this interpretation, the dividend $\frac{1}{2}$ is the *amount*, the divisor $\frac{1}{6}$ is the *size of the groups (shares)*, and the quotient 3 is the *number of groups (shares)*. As Investigation 10.2 suggests, this is essential to inform and to guide their use of manipulatives. For example, in solving $\frac{1}{2} \div \frac{1}{3}$, pupils may see $\frac{1}{3}$ fits into $\frac{1}{2}$ one time but not under-

---

Box 10.4: *Can You Add Apples and Oranges?*

Because her review of adding unlike fractions was not going well, Miss Brill asked her experienced colleagues for advice. "With an expression like $\frac{1}{2} + \frac{1}{3}$," announced Mrs. MeChokemchild firmly, "I always tell them, You can't add apples and oranges." Miss Brill thought this sage advice; she could recall her own elementary teachers using these very same words.

Much to Mrs. MeChokemchild's disconsternation and Miss Brill's surprise, Ms. Socrates interjected, "But you can add apples and oranges. If I have five apples and three oranges, I can add them if I give them the *same name*: fruit. Adding fractions is not any different. I can add one-half and one-third if I give them the same name—if I find a common denominator."

"I like to use a coin analogy with my class," continued Ms. Socrates. "I ask them if I can add three dimes and two nickels." The answer, of course, is yes. You simply need to find a common denomination and the equivalent values in this common unit":

3 dimes	→	6 nickels		30 cents
+ 2 nickels		+ 2 nickels	or	+ 10 cents
?		8 nickels		40 cents

"By relating addition (and subtraction) to such whole-number analogies, the process of finding a common denominator is less mysterious to students," concluded Ms. Socrates.

---

stand what to do with the leftover part. Common errors include viewing it as a fraction of the whole (which results in an incorrect answer of $1\frac{1}{6}$) or as a fraction of the amount $\frac{1}{2}$ (which results in an incorrect answer of $1\frac{1}{3}$). In fact, the leftover part is a fraction of the $\frac{1}{3}$ (the size of the group or share). As $\frac{1}{6}$ is half of $\frac{1}{3}$, the correct answer is $1\frac{1}{2}$ shares. Figure 10.4 (on page 10-18) illustrates how the use of *Cuisenaire rods* can be explicitly connected to a measure-out meaning by having students define and label the *whole*, the amount available (*have*), the size of the groups (*size of each share*), and the answer, which specifies the number of groups (the *number of shares*). (Continued on page 10-18)

🍎 Investigation 10.2: Connecting Concrete and Symbolic Operations on Fractions Using *Fraction Tiles* as an Example

◆ Relating symbolic fraction arithmetic to concrete meanings and models
◆ 3-8 ◆ Groups of four + class discussion

During the connecting phase, instruction should help students relate symbolic expressions such as $\frac{1}{2} + \frac{2}{3}$, $\frac{1}{2} \times \frac{2}{3}$, and $\frac{1}{2} \div \frac{2}{3}$ to familiar analogies and encourage them to use these analogies to guide their use of manipulatives, drawings, or logical reasoning when determining the answer to these expressions. Part I involves considering how fraction addition and subtraction expressions can be modeled with *Fraction Tiles* (see page 9-21 of Investigation 9.3). Part II entails considering how *Fraction Tiles* and graph paper can be used to create meaningful models of fraction-multiplication expressions. Part III requires considering how *Fraction Tiles* can be used to create meaningful models of fraction-division expressions.

∞ **Teaching Tips.** Note that although this activity suggests using *Fraction Tiles* to model the meaning of many of the problems below, other manipulatives such as *Cuisenaire rods* (see page 9-16 of Investigation 9.2) and *Fraction Circles* (see page 9-20 of Investigation 9.3) could be used. Encourage children to use whatever manipulatives they feel comfortable with.

Tackle the investigations below yourself either on your own or, ideally, with your group. Then discuss your efforts with your group or class. Actually using your understanding of the operations to create models is important for three reasons. One is that it should help you better understand the need for and power of a conceptual understanding and concrete models. A second is to give you a better idea of where students may become confused when trying to use these models. A third, perhaps, is to help deepen your understanding of fraction operations. (Thinking through the creation of models can help students of any age construct a more complete understanding.)

Part I: Fraction Addition and Subtraction (◆ 3-5)

1. Consider how *Fraction Tiles* could be used to model (a) $\frac{1}{4} + \frac{1}{4}$, (b) $\frac{1}{4} + \frac{1}{2}$, (c) $\frac{1}{2} + \frac{1}{3}$, (d) $\frac{3}{8} + \frac{5}{16}$, and (e) $\frac{3}{4} + \frac{2}{3}$. Illustrate each model.

2. Consider how *Fraction Tiles* could be used to model (a) $\frac{3}{4} - \frac{1}{4}$, (b) $\frac{3}{4} - \frac{3}{8}$, and (c) $\frac{3}{4} - \frac{2}{3}$.

3. Children should be able to model fraction addition and subtraction with a variety of manipulatives. Consider how $\frac{1}{2} + \frac{1}{4}$, $\frac{1}{4} + \frac{1}{3}$, and $\frac{3}{4} + \frac{2}{3}$ could be modeled with discrete quantities. Illustrate your solution and share it with your group or class.

Part II: Multiplication (◆ 4-6)

1. (a) Which meanings of multiplication could guide an effort to concretely model fraction multiplication? (b) Illustrate how *Fraction Tiles* could be used to model these meanings for the following expressions: (i) $2 \times \frac{3}{8}$, (ii) $\frac{1}{2} \times \frac{1}{4}$, and (iii) $\frac{3}{4} \times \frac{2}{3}$.

2. How *Fraction Tiles* can be used to model a *groups-of* interpretation of $2 \times \frac{1}{6}$ is illustrated to the right.

   Consider how this manipulative could be used to model a groups-of interpretation of the following expressions: (a) $2 \times \frac{3}{8}$, (b) $3 \times \frac{5}{12}$, and (c) $\frac{3}{4} \times 1$.

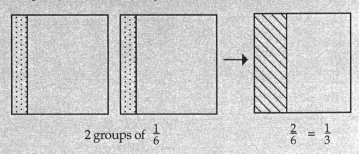

2 groups of $\frac{1}{6}$ $\frac{2}{6} = \frac{1}{3}$

Investigation 10.2 continued

3. Illustrate how you could use *Fraction Tiles* to model a *groups-of* interpretation of the following expressions: (a) $\frac{1}{2} \times \frac{1}{3}$, (b) $\frac{1}{8} \times \frac{1}{2}$, (c) $\frac{1}{4} \times \frac{1}{3}$, (d) $\frac{5}{6} \times \frac{1}{2}$, and (e) $\frac{3}{4} \times \frac{2}{3}$.

4. Ms. Socrates asked her class to show how *Fraction Tiles* could be used to model a *groups-of* meaning of $\frac{1}{2} \times \frac{1}{3}$. Several groups devised Method A depicted below. Several others invented Method B also shown below. Which model, if either, faithfully represents a *groups-of* meaning? Why or why not?

Step: 1. Represent 1/3 of a whole 2. Show 1/2 group of the 1/3 3. Determine the answer (1/6)

Method A (vertical method):

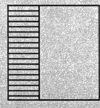 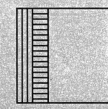 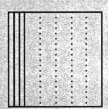

Orange tile is 1/3 of the whole. | Divide the 1/3 into halves. Because it takes 2 blue tiles to cover the orange tiles, 1/2 of 1/3 is 1 blue tile. | A blue tile is 1/6 of the whole.

Method B (cross-colored method):

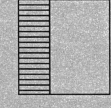 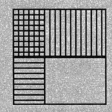 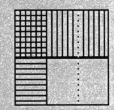

Orange tile is 1/3 of the whole. | Yellow tile (1/2) cuts the 1/3 in half widthwise. | The intersection of the two tiles is 1/6 of the whole.

5. How could *Fraction Tiles* be used to model an *area* meaning of the following expressions: (a) $1 \times \frac{3}{4}$, (b) $\frac{1}{8} \times \frac{1}{4}$, (c) $\frac{1}{2} \times \frac{1}{3}$, (d) $\frac{1}{4} \times \frac{1}{6}$, (e) $\frac{5}{6} \times \frac{1}{4}$, and (f) $\frac{3}{4} \times \frac{2}{3}$.

6. (a) Ms. Socrates informed Miss Brill that graph paper could be used to illustrate an area interpretation of fraction multiplication. *"For a problem like $\frac{1}{2} \times \frac{1}{3}$, how big should I make my unit box?"* asked Miss Brill. How many squares on the graph paper should Miss Brill enclose to make her unit? Why? (b) Rodney thought that $2\frac{2}{3} \times 1\frac{1}{2} = 2\frac{2}{6}$. On graph paper, illustrate an area interpretation of $2\frac{2}{3} \times 1\frac{1}{2}$. (c) In what way does Rodney's procedural knowledge appear to be incomplete or inaccurate? That is, what appears to have been wrong with his solution?

Part III: Division (♦ 4-8)

1. Illustrate how you could use *Fraction Tiles* to model a *measure-out* interpretation of the following expressions: (a) $1 \div \frac{1}{6}$, (b) $\frac{1}{2} \div \frac{1}{4}$, (c) $\frac{2}{3} \div \frac{1}{4}$, and (d) $\frac{1}{3} \div \frac{1}{6}$.

2. Now illustrate how you could use *Fraction Tiles* to model a *measure-out* interpretation of (a) $\frac{1}{4} \div 2$, (b) $\frac{1}{6} \div 2$, (c) $\frac{1}{4} \div \frac{1}{2}$, and (d) $\frac{1}{6} \div \frac{1}{3}$.

Investigation 10.2 continued

3. (a) Illustrate how you could use *Fraction Tiles* to model a *measure-out* meaning of $\frac{1}{2} \div \frac{1}{3}$. What answer did you get? Does it agree with those of others in your group? (b) How could you show $\frac{5}{8} \div \frac{1}{2} = 1\frac{1}{4}$? What does the 1 in the answer indicate? What does the $\frac{1}{4}$ in the answer mean?

4. How could you show (a) $\frac{1}{4} \div \frac{2}{3}$ and (b) $\frac{5}{8} \div \frac{3}{4}$? In each case, what is the answer a fraction of?

5. Hilarie used *Fraction Tiles* to model $\frac{3}{4} \div \frac{1}{3}$ and got an answer of $2\frac{1}{12}$. Christine claimed the answer was $2\frac{1}{9}$ and Shayla argued it should be $2\frac{1}{4}$. Who, if anyone, was correct? Briefly describe the likely basis for any errors?

Questions for Reflection

1. Miss Brill demonstrated to her class the following procedure she learned from Ms. Socrates: To model a measure-out meaning of $\frac{1}{4} \div \frac{1}{8}$, first represent and label the whole, then illustrate and label the amount (the dividend $\frac{1}{4}$), next represent and label the size of the share (the divisor $\frac{1}{8}$), and then determine how many shares the amount provides (the quotient). She pointed out that finding a common denominator can facilitate the last step of finding the number of shares. Because it takes two green tiles to cover the red tile—$\frac{1}{8}$ fits into $\frac{1}{4}$ two times (see figure below). (a) Was Miss Brill using the skills, the conceptual, the investigative, or the problem-solving approach? (b) What are the advantages and disadvantages of her approach?

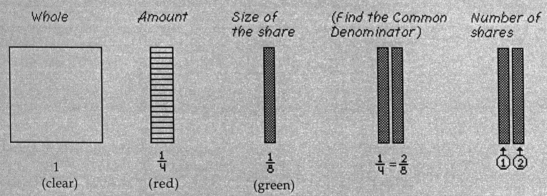

Whole	Amount	Size of the share	(Find the Common Denominator)	Number of shares
1 (clear)	$\frac{1}{4}$ (red)	$\frac{1}{8}$ (green)	$\frac{1}{4} = \frac{2}{8}$	①②

✓ 2. (a) Several days after Miss Brill showed her class how to model fraction division with *Fraction Tiles*, she gave them *Cuisenaire rods* and asked them to use this new manipulative to do fraction division. The class protested that they had not been shown how to use the rods to do fraction division. Miss Brill smiled and answered, "So?" What is the method behind her "madness." (b) What meaning of division should she encourage her students to use as they tried to construct a model with the rods?

3. Illustrate how (a) *Cuisenaire rods* and (b) *Fraction Circles* could be used to represent each of the expressions listed in Part III above.

4. Asking students to write word problems or to evaluate others' efforts can help connect symbolism to real situations. (a) Write a realistic measure-out problem for $\frac{3}{4} \div \frac{1}{8} = 6$. (b) Evaluate the following effort by Doreen: *Ducky has $\frac{3}{4}$ quarts of Super Juice. In each gulp, he drinks $\frac{1}{8}$ of the Super Juice. How many gulps will it take Ducky to finish the Super Juice?*

Figure 10.4: Using *Cuisenaire Rods* to Model a Measure-Out Interpretation of Fraction Division

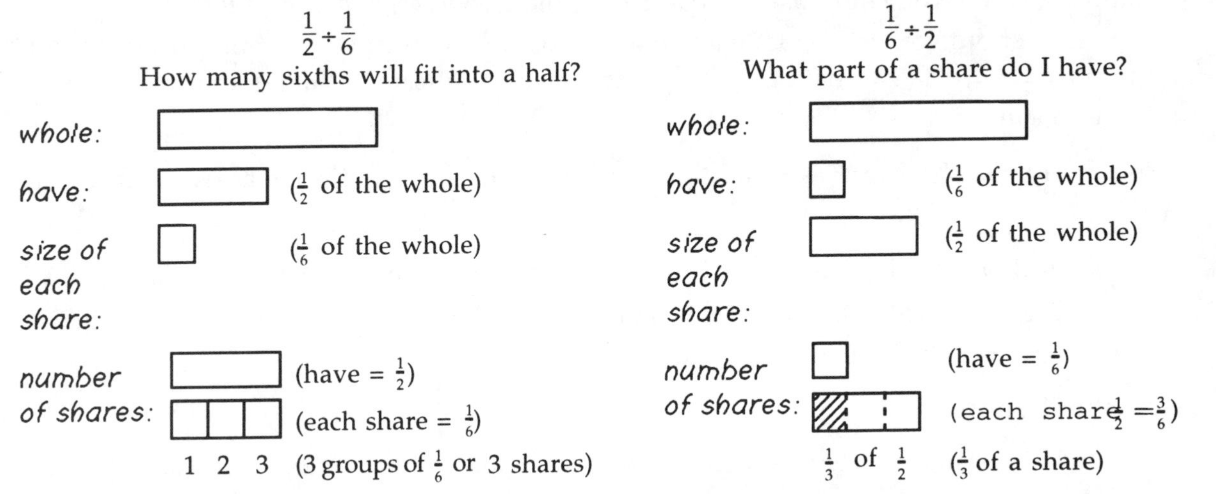

$\frac{1}{2} \div \frac{1}{6}$

How many sixths will fit into a half?

whole:

have: ($\frac{1}{2}$ of the whole)

size of each share: ($\frac{1}{6}$ of the whole)

number of shares: (have = $\frac{1}{2}$)

(each share = $\frac{1}{6}$)

1   2   3   (3 groups of $\frac{1}{6}$ or 3 shares)

$\frac{1}{6} \div \frac{1}{2}$

What part of a share do I have?

whole:

have: ($\frac{1}{6}$ of the whole)

size of each share: ($\frac{1}{2}$ of the whole)

number of shares: (have = $\frac{1}{6}$)

(each share $\frac{1}{2} = \frac{3}{6}$)

$\frac{1}{3}$ of $\frac{1}{2}$ ($\frac{1}{3}$ of a share)

• **Help children to see the connection between symbolic expressions and everyday applications of fraction arithmetic.** For instance, students should recognize that making $\frac{1}{2}$ of a recipe that requires $\frac{1}{3}$ pound of flour can be represented as $\frac{1}{2} \times \frac{1}{3}$, which can be interpreted as "one-half group of one-third."

• **Help students relate their understanding of one operation to another.** For example, to construct a deep understanding of fraction division, students should understand how a measure-out meaning is related to a groups-of meaning of multiplication (e.g., $\frac{1}{2} \div \frac{1}{8} = \Box \rightarrow \Box \times \frac{1}{8} = \frac{1}{2}$, where $\frac{1}{2}$ is the amount, $\frac{1}{8}$ is the size of the share, and $\Box$ = the number of shares).

☞ **Help children see how a formal representation can be represented by a variety of concrete and pictorial models.** Because some children may find one model more personally meaningful than others, initially they should be encouraged to use the manipulative of thier own choice. Take care to present problems that can be solved by the particular manipulative your class is using at the time. Note that children should already be familiar with how to use a particular manipulative so that their attention can be focused on how to solve the arithmetic problems. If children have not had previous experience with a manipulative such as *Cuisenaire rods*, help them first to learn how to represent fractions and determine equivalent fractions with the manipulative.

✔ **To check for understanding, have students determine the answer of symbolic expressions with a new manipulative.** Ultimately, students should be able to model fraction-arithmetic expression with any concrete model—including those that involve unfamiliar manipulatives. This indicates that a child has a deep understanding of the underlying concepts. If students think in terms of the measure-out meaning, they will be able to use the new manipulative. If they have memorized a manipulative procedure by rote, they will probably be unable to make the transfer.

☞ **In general, use fractions with denominations of 12 or less** (Bezuk & Bieck, 1993). That is, generally restrict computational examples to the most commonly used fractions. (When was the last time you used fractions such as $\frac{3}{17}$ or $\frac{4}{29}$?) By using the more familiar fractions students will be better able to visualize and conceptualize what is happening.

10•2•2 THE INVESTIGATIVE APPROACH TO ALGORITHMIC INSTRUCTION

Two general guidelines for the symbolic phase of instruction are listed below.

☞ **Prompt students to reinvent formal algorithms or their own algorithms for operating on** fractions. Ideally, instruction would encourage them "to look for patterns in the data they collect using manipulatives" or pictures and to find short cuts for their meaningful informal strategies (Bezuk & Bieck, 1993, p. 132).

☞ Instruction should focus on, and students be able to explain, *why* formal algorithms work. It is important for students to understand fraction-arithmetic procedures so that, if for no other reason, they see that mathematics makes sense. Understanding the underlying concepts of these procedures can also facilitate the learning and effective application of these procedures.

In this subunit, we illustrate how the two teaching tips just described apply to the teaching of fraction multiplication and division.

☞ Consider Probe 10.3 (pages 10-20).

Multiplication Algorithm

Because it is a relatively straightforward procedure, children should have little difficulty rediscovering the formal algorithm for multiplying fractions. This can be facilitated by encouraging children to find a shortcut to the cross-colored *groups-of* or area method. As a result of working with these concrete models, children may discover that the numerator of the answer is simply the product of the numerators of the factors and that the denominator of the answer is simply the product of the denominators of the factors (see Figure 10.5).

Division Algorithms

There are two formal fraction-division algorithms: (1) the *reciprocal procedure* and (2) the *common-denominator method.* "What?" you might well ask yourself. The reciprocal procedure is just a fancy name for the *invert-and-multiply procedure.* Although most adults are familiar with the reciprocal procedure, many are not familiar with the common-denominator method. In this subunit, we discuss how the two algorithms can be introduced meaningfully and which to introduce first. We also consider shortcuts to these procedures—shortcuts that students can reinvent themselves.

The Common-Denominator Method. By thinking in terms of a measure-out meaning of division, children can reinvent what is called the *common-denominator method* for determining the quotient of symbolic division expressions. Indeed, this algorithm is simply the symbolic equivalent of the concrete measure-out procedure illustrated on page 10-17 of Investigation 10.2 (see Box 10.5 on page 10-21).

Note that once the common denominator has been determined, the answer in each case can be determined simply by dividing the numerators. Consider the following example:

$$\frac{1}{2} \div \frac{1}{3} = \frac{3}{6} \div \frac{2}{6} = \frac{3}{\cancel{6}} \div \frac{2}{\cancel{6}} = 3 \div 2 = 1\frac{1}{2}$$

The answer is $1\frac{1}{2}$ whether you divide $\frac{3}{6}$ by $\frac{2}{6}$, $\frac{3}{7}$ by $\frac{2}{7}$, $\frac{3}{8}$ by $\frac{2}{8}$, and so forth.

Reciprocal Procedure. *Why do you invert and multiply when using the reciprocal procedure? For example, why does* $\frac{3}{4} \div \frac{1}{8} = \frac{3}{4} \times \frac{8}{1} = 6$? Although the invert-and-multiply procedure can be memorized by rote, it may be easier to learn and use if students understand its underlying rationale (see Box 10.6 on page 10-21.)

Figure 10.5:	Rediscovering the Fraction Multiplication Algorithm by Reflecting on the Cross-Colored *Groups-Of* or Area Model

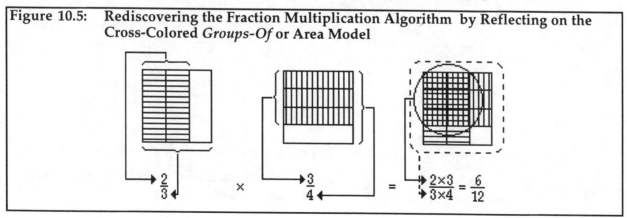

➤Probe 10.3: Rediscovering Fraction Multiplication and Division Algorithms

This probe illustrates how the investigative approach can be implemented for fraction multiplication and division by, for example, asking you to reinvent a formal algorithm.

Part I: Multiplying Fractions

1. What is the formal algorithm for multiplying fractions such as $\frac{1}{2} \times \frac{1}{3}$, $\frac{1}{6} \times \frac{3}{4}$, and $\frac{2}{3} \times \frac{5}{4}$?

2. Consider how the expressions listed in Question 1 could be solved using *Fraction Tiles* and (a) the vertical *groups-of* method (Method A illustrated on page 10-16 of Investigation 10.2), (b) the cross-colored *groups-of* method (Method B illustrated on page 10-16 of Investigation 10.2), and (c) the area-model method.

3. Which of the methods listed in Question 1 concretely model the formal algorithm and could, with reflection, lead to the discovery of the formal algorithm?

Part II: The Common-Denominator Algorithm for Dividing Fractions

1. Use a measure-out analogy and manipulatives to determine the quotient of the following symbolic expressions: (a) $\frac{1}{2} \div \frac{1}{4}$, (b) $\frac{2}{3} \div \frac{1}{6}$, (c) $\frac{1}{8} \div \frac{3}{4}$. Summarize symbolically each step of your concrete procedure. What written algorithm did you devise? Discuss your invention with your group or class.

2. Use the common-denominator method illustrated below to determine the quotient of the following expressions. You may wish to use manipulatives or drawings as an aid. Use the measure-out interpretation as a guide whether or not you use these aids.

   a. $\frac{1}{2} \div \frac{1}{8}$ b. $\frac{1}{2} \div \frac{1}{3}$ c. $\frac{3}{4} \div \frac{2}{3}$ d. $\frac{1}{8} \div \frac{1}{2}$ e. $\frac{1}{3} \div \frac{1}{2}$ f. $\frac{2}{3} \div \frac{3}{4}$

Step 1: *Find a common denominator and the equivalent fraction of each fraction.*
$$\frac{3}{4} \div \frac{1}{2} = \frac{6}{8} \div \frac{4}{8}$$

Step 2: *Use a measure-out interpretation to determine the quotient.*
There are $1\frac{1}{2}$ four-eighths in $\frac{6}{8}$.

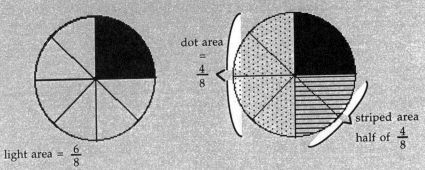

light area = $\frac{6}{8}$

dot area = $\frac{4}{8}$

striped area half of $\frac{4}{8}$

3. Examine your solutions to expressions 2a to 2f above. Can you find a shortcut for Step 2.

4. Should instruction first introduce symbolic fraction division with the common-denominator method or the reciprocal (invert-and-multiply) procedure?

Box 10.5: Reinventing the Common-Denominator Method

🍎 **A Fraction Division Game.** To practice computing quotients and comparing fractions informally and to create an opportunity for inventing algorithms, a teacher had his class play the *Largest Quotient of Fractions* game. This game entailed rolling a 10-sided die numbered 1 to 10. Players then recorded the digit in one of four boxes arranged as shown below. This process was repeated until all the boxes had a digit.

$$\frac{\square}{\square} \div \frac{\square}{\square}$$

The players were encouraged to use a measure-out meaning and manipulatives to determine their answers. Players then compared their answers to see whose answer was larger. A player with the largest answer was awarded a point.

Alexi's Procedure. While playing, Alexi formed the expression $\frac{1}{2} \div \frac{1}{3}$. Perhaps recalling his experience with manipulatives, he multiplied the two denominators to find a common denominator, determined the equivalent fraction

($\frac{1}{2} = \frac{3}{6}$ and $\frac{1}{3} = \frac{2}{6}$), wrote $\frac{3}{6} \div \frac{2}{6}$, and reasoned that the answer had to be $1\frac{1}{2}$ or $\frac{3}{2}$. This common-denominator method was dubbed *Alexi's Procedure* by the class.

The Need for a Lowest Common Denominator. *Alexi's Procedure* soon created a need for finding the lowest common denominator. For example, while playing the *Smallest Quotient of Fractions*, a student came up with the expression $\frac{1}{5} \div \frac{3}{10}$. Multiplying the denominators lead to a common denominator of 50! The teacher asked the class if there might be an easier way to figure out the quotient of the expression. This lead to discussion of what was the smallest whole that could be divided into both five and ten parts.

☞ **Teaching Tip.** The *Largest Quotient of Fractions* game can be done as a whole-class activity by dividing the class into teams of four. As the digits are read off by the teacher, each team must reach a consensus as to where to put it. In a follow-up discussion, the class can share the teams' strategies for placing digits, division solution strategies, and solutions.

Box 10.6: Rationale for the Invert-and-Multiply Algorithm

Consider the problem $\frac{1}{4} \div \frac{1}{8}$, which has been rewritten in a vertical format in Step a below. A useful heuristic in mathematics is to take a difficult problem and transform it into a simpler problem. How can we make division simpler? Certainly dividing by 1 is easy. Ideally, then, we would like to change the denominator $\frac{1}{8}$ into 1. This can be achieved by applying the identity principle—multiplying $\frac{1}{8}$ by its inverse $\frac{8}{1}$. Now if we multiply the denominator by $\frac{8}{1}$, we should do the same for the numerator to maintain an equivalent value. See Steps b and c below. Note that the traditional algorithm skips from step a to step d, leaving out the rationale for the procedure (steps b and c).

(a) $\dfrac{\frac{1}{4}}{\frac{1}{8}}$ = (b) $\dfrac{\frac{1}{4} \times \frac{8}{1}}{\frac{1}{8} \times \frac{8}{1}}$ = (c) $\dfrac{\frac{1}{4} \times \frac{8}{1}}{1}$ = (d) $\frac{1}{4} \times \frac{8}{1}$ = 2

Ideally, children can be encouraged to discover the reciprocal (invert-and-multiply) procedure for themselves. Two methods for doing so are noted below.

- **Method 1.** Encourage students to informally solve a series of problems or symbolic expressions such as those below, to record their answers, and to look for a shortcut. Note that it may be necessary to ask students for *another name* for an answer.

$\frac{1}{2} \div \frac{1}{3} = 1\frac{1}{2} = \frac{3}{2}$ $\qquad$ $\frac{1}{4} \div \frac{1}{3} = \frac{3}{4}$

$\frac{1}{3} \div \frac{1}{2} = \frac{2}{3}$ $\qquad$ $\frac{1}{3} \div \frac{1}{4} = 1\frac{1}{3} = \frac{4}{3}$

$\frac{1}{6} \div \frac{1}{2} = \frac{1}{3} = \frac{2}{6}$ $\qquad$ $3 \div \frac{1}{2} = \frac{3}{1} \div \frac{1}{2} = \frac{6}{1}$

$\frac{2}{3} \div \frac{4}{5} = \frac{10}{12}$ $\qquad$ $8 \div \frac{1}{4} = \frac{8}{1} \div \frac{1}{4} = \frac{32}{1}$

• **Method 2**. Point out that the format $6 \div 2$ is equivalent to $\frac{6}{2}$ and ask what the equivalent format of $\frac{3}{4} \div \frac{1}{8}$ would be? After $\frac{\frac{3}{4}}{\frac{1}{8}}$ is recorded on the chalkboard, the teacher could pose the problem, "How could this be solved?" After using the heuristic of transforming the expression into a simpler expression as discussed earlier, the students could be asked to solve a series of other expressions in the same way. With any luck, some students might recognize that all you have to do is invert the divisor and multiply. This discovery might be facilitated if a teacher explicitly encouraged students to look for a shortcut. Note that such an approach helps students understand the reciprocal method, while involving them in the *processes* of mathematics (problem solving, deductive reasoning, looking for a pattern). Thus, it underscores that mathematics is supposed to make sense and involves thinking, not memorizing by rote.

Box 10.7: Invention of an Informal Fraction-Division Procedure

While playing *Largest* (and *Smallest*) *Quotient of Fractions* (see Box 10.5 on page 10-21), fifth-grader Alison noticed the following pattern: To determine an answer, all you have to do is cross multiply. For example,

$$\frac{3}{4} \diamond \div \frac{1}{6} = \frac{18}{4}$$

There was some doubt that this was a correct procedure, as the answer was not consistent with a shortened common-denominator method that the class had adopted:

$$\frac{3}{4} \div \frac{1}{6} = \frac{9}{12} \div \frac{2}{12} = \frac{9}{2}$$

Arianne pointed out, "It [Alison's procedure] could work. It (her quotient) might be another answer [name for the quotient]."

The students checked out this conjecture and found that Alison's answer of $\frac{18}{4}$ was equivalent to $\frac{9}{2}$. They dubbed her discovery the *Envelope Method*, because the path of the first step looks like the back flap of an envelope.

Box 10.7 illustrates a self-invented algorithm for dividing fractions. Note that this informal method is actually more efficient than the formal reciprocal (invert-and-multiply) algorithm. In fact, the child had reinvented the cross-products procedure, which is sometimes taught as a shortcut for the reciprocal algorithm. Activity 10.1 illustrates how students can be guided to rediscover this shortcut.

🍎 Activity File 10.1: *Fraction Race*

◆ Guided discovery of the cross-products procedure for fraction division ◆ 5-8
◆ Any number

Ms. Socrates challenged her class to a "fraction race." She proposed that the class pit their fastest fraction divider against her in a race to determine the quotient of five expressions such as $\frac{3}{7} \div \frac{4}{5}$. The class quickly nominated Cammy.

Sensing a trick, Liam quipped: "You've already memorized the problems and the answers."

Ms. Socrates reassured the class, "No, we'll have three volunteers—other than my chosen opponent—choose the expressions." A committee was assembled and during recess chose the five expressions shown below:

$$\frac{4}{9} \div \frac{5}{8} \qquad \frac{8}{9} \div \frac{3}{5} \qquad \frac{6}{7} \div \frac{3}{4} \qquad \frac{7}{10} \div \frac{8}{9} \qquad \frac{11}{12} \div \frac{7}{9}$$

After recess, the challenge was about to begin when Ms. Socrates added a new twist. In addition to Cammy, the class can have a challenger who may use a calculator. A murmur went through the class. "Cammy is fast," Allen noted, "but Ms. Socrates doesn't stand a chance against a calculator." Vuk ("Mr. Electronics-Game Wizard") was quickly chosen to man the calculator.

While Ms. Socrates, Cammy, and Vuk armed with his calculator closed their eyes, the committee wrote the chosen expressions on the chalkboard. Tonja, the committee chair, then announced, "Go." Before Cammy and Vuk had recorded their answers to the fourth expression, Ms. Socrates handed her written answers to Tonja. The class was astounded and searched for an answer. Liam suggested that Ms. Socrates must have memorized all the basic fraction division facts. After this and several other conjectures were found to be implausible, Loretta advanced the cross-products procedure.

Should students be encouraged to first use the common-denominator method or the invert-and-multiply procedure? Initially, encourage children to use the common-denominator method. It can be used meaningfully by children who comprehend equivalent fractions and a measure-out meaning of division. The invert-and-multiply procedure can be used any time after children discover this shortcut for themselves or after they are ready to comprehend its rationale.

PARTING THOUGHTS

"The emphasis of instruction should . . . shift from the [memorization] of algorithms for performing operations on fractions to the development of a quantitative understanding of fractions" and operations on them (Bezuk & Cramer, 1989, p. 157). That is, operations on "fractions should be approached conceptually. An understanding of what happens when [for example] one divides by a fractional number (less than or greater than 1) is essential" (NCTM, 1989, p. 96). As with the introduction of common fractions, operations on common fractions should begin with children informally tackling real, realistic, and imaginary problems. Children should first be encouraged to use their whole-number conceptual knowledge and number sense to consider the direction of a solution (qualitative reasoning) and to estimate solutions. Next, they can be encouraged to use their conceptual understanding of operations to devise informal solutions using manipulatives and drawings. In time, they can be encouraged to look for shortcuts and reinvent the formal algorithms.

RESOURCES

SOME INSTRUCTIONAL RESOURCES

The two resources below provide helpful suggestions for building a sound basis for introducing operations on fractions meaningfully.

☛ **Fraction Circle Activities: A Sourcebook for Grades 4-8** by Barbara Berman and Fredda J. Friederwitzer, © 1988 by Dale Seymour Publications. This is a valuable aid for introducing fractions concepts and operations on fractions concretely with *Fraction Circles* (see page 9-20 of Investigation 9.3). The resource begins with different names for one (unit circle, one whole, one), discusses dividing the circle into equal parts (halves, thirds,

fourths, and so forth), introduces more different names for one (e.g., three-thirds), compares the size of unit fractions (e.g., one-half is the largest *Fraction Circle* and one-twelfth is the smallest), shows how *Fraction Circles* can be used to compare nonunit fractions, introduces equivalent fractions, illustrates how *Fraction Circles* can be used to add and subtract fractions with like or unlike denominators, and finally, discusses renaming fractions to lowest terms.

☛ **Mathematics: A Way of Thinking** written by R. Baratta-Lorton, © 1977 by Addison-Wesley. The book is highly organized, each lesson building on the prior lesson. Almost all lessons may be done with an entire class through guided instruction. Chapter 11 on fractions begins with three lessons that focus on defining common fractions and assigning them values. Lessons 4 through 8 involve finding the area of geometric shapes on the geoboard and set the stage for introducing multiplication with fractions with an area model (lessons 27 through 31). Lessons 9 through 12 use discrete quantities to move smoothly from defining fractions to adding and subtracting with fractions. These lessons use the students in the class as a set, with each student or row being a fraction of that set. Lessons 13 and 15 ask students to write word problems to describe a fraction or an operation with fractions, an excellent way to assess understanding. Lessons 16 and 17 use a continuous-quantity model (paper-folding activities) to introduce equivalent fractions (e.g., one piece of a sheet of paper folded in half equals two pieces of a sheet folded in quarters). Lessons 18 and 19 are designed to use paper folding and lists of equivalent fractions as aids in formulating the rules for adding and subtracting fractions with unlike denominators. Lessons 20 and 21 use unifix cubes, a discrete-quantity model, to find equivalent fractions (e.g., $\frac{1}{2} = \frac{2}{4} = \frac{4}{8}$). Lessons 22 to 25 suggest one way children find the lowest common denominators.

☛ **Seeing Fractions: A Unit for the Upper Elementary Grades**, © 1991, California Department of Education, Sacramento, CA. This fifth-grade replacement unit is widely available and nationally acclaimed (Parker, 1993). It involves a problem-solving and manipulative-based approach to fraction instruction and includes many worthwhile tasks.

A SAMPLE OF CHILDREN'S LITERATURE

The *Doorbell Rang*, discussed earlier as a way of introducing informal whole number division (see Box 3.1 on page 3-13, Activity File 5.5 on pages 5-21 and 5-22, and a description of the story on page 5-36), can also be used to introduce multiplication by a fraction (Whitin & Wilde, 1992). For instance, a situation where 12 cookies had to be shared fairly between two children ($12 \div 2 = 6$) could be thought of as each of two children getting one-half of the 12 cookies ($\frac{1}{2} \times 12 = 6$). Indeed, this story can create an opportunity for discussing the relationship between division by a number and multiplication by its inverse (e.g., $\frac{1}{2} \times 12 = 6$ and $12 \div 2 = 6$, $\frac{1}{4} \times 12 = 3$ and $12 \div 4 = 3$, $\frac{1}{6} \times 12 = 2$ and $12 \div 6 = 2$, and so forth).

TIPS ON USING TECHNOLOGY

Calculators

The Texas Instruments *Math Explorer* can perform operations on fractions and, thus, can serve to check children's informal or formal solutions or to look for patterns in an effort to devise shortcuts (rediscover formal algorithms). For example, $\frac{1}{2} + \frac{1}{3}$ would be keyed in the following manner:

$$1 \quad / \quad 2 \quad + \quad 1 \quad / \quad 3 \quad =$$

Consider the experience of one class that was accustomed to looking for shortcuts. After calculating and recording their answers to a number of such expressions ($\frac{1}{2} + \frac{1}{3} = \frac{5}{6}$; $\frac{1}{4} + \frac{1}{3} = \frac{7}{12}$; $\frac{1}{5} + \frac{1}{2} = \frac{7}{10}$ and $\frac{1}{3} + \frac{1}{7} = \frac{10}{21}$), one group of children proposed the following conjecture: "You just add the [denominators] to get the top [digit] of the answer and multiply the [denominators] to get the bottom [digit] of the answer." To help the class consider whether this conjecture was generally true, the teacher asked whether or not the short cut would work for nonunit fractions such as $\frac{3}{4} + \frac{2}{3}$.
Calculating several such examples quickly led the class to conclude that their shortcut always worked for finding the bottom digit of the sum (for finding a common denominator) but not for finding the top digit. This prompted the students to amend their short cut for adding nonunit fractions. With exploration, they discovered that once a common denominator had been found, the correct answer could be determined by changing the addends into equivalent fractions with the common denominator.

$$\frac{3}{4} + \frac{2}{3} \rightarrow \frac{?}{12} + \frac{?}{12} = \frac{9}{12} + \frac{8}{12} = \frac{17}{12}$$

Adding mixed fractions such as $1\frac{1}{2} + 4\frac{1}{8}$ is keyed in the following way:

$$1 \quad \text{unit} \quad 1 \quad / \quad 2 \quad + \quad 4 \quad \text{unit} \quad 1 \quad / \quad 8 \quad =$$

Subtracting, multiplying and dividing fractions would be done in the same way except that the appropriate operator key would be substituted for the + key.

Computers

In evaluating computer programs, consider the instructional guidelines for meaningful learning discussed in this chapter. A program should not jump too quickly into manipulating symbols, and it should help children see the connections among different representations (e.g., relate symbols to concrete models and spoken language) (Clements, 1989). The **IBM Elementary Mathematics Series** (by IBM/WICAT Systems, Inc.) does a relatively good job of presenting fraction and fraction-arithmetic models and encouraging students to act on them (Clements, 1989).

Children's Encyclopedia of Mathematics: Fraction Series (by AIMS and distributed by SoftWare House) includes six new CD ROM titles appropriate for 5-8[+]: *Caveman—Between the Whole Numbers, Gems—Subtracting with Fractions, Genie and the Clam—Comparing Rational Numbers, Knights Between Rational Numbers, Machine—Adding with Fractions,* and *Watermelon—Equivalent Fractions.*

Fraction-Oids I, II, and III (distributed by SoftWare House, available on CD ROM format, and appropriate for 3-8) address basic fraction concepts, addition and subtraction of fractions, and multiplication and division of fractions, respectively.

11 PLACE-VALUE REPRESENTATIONS OF FRACTIONAL PARTS: DECIMAL FRACTIONS, DECIMALS, AND OPERATIONS ON DECIMALS

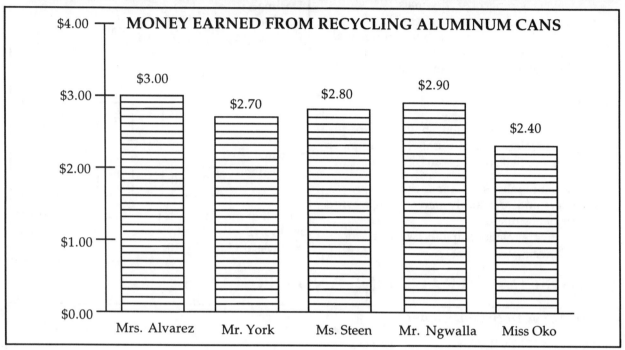

Constructing a bar graph to report school, grade-level, or classroom information can be an effective way of connecting decimal concepts to a concrete display and to children's lives. The bulletin board above stemmed from an extended unit on environmental sciences and was updated weekly. Note that the display also connects decimals to the relatively familiar and important everyday domain of money. Each subdivision of a bar represents an increment of 10¢, and 10 subdivisions, an increment of $1. A more elaborate graph could involve adding even smaller subdivisions to represent increments of 1¢.

A bar graph could also be constructed and regularly updated to represent, for example, an ongoing fund-raising effort to finance a field trip, new equipment, a charitable contribution, and so forth. Other bulletin board ideas include keeping a tally of books read, seasonal precipitation, kilowatts of energy consumed during a period of time, or the amount of water used by a class or school. One-time static displays could include summarizing the times (in seconds and tenths of seconds) of a class or grade-level athletic event such as the top

four runners in the 50-yard dash.

THIS CHAPTER

*I*n chapters 9 and 10, we introduced common fractions and operations on common fractions. In Unit 11•1 of this chapter, we discuss a particular kind of common fraction (decimal fractions) and decimals. Decimal fractions such as $\frac{1}{10}$, $\frac{3}{10}$, $\frac{27}{100}$, and $\frac{101}{1000}$ can provide a conceptual bridge between common fractions and decimals. As Figure 11.1 on page 11-2 illustrates, decimals permit us to represent common fractions in terms of our familiar base-ten, place-value numerals—and are often a more convenient way of representing portions of a whole than are common fractions. They are also a convenient way of representing irrational numbers such as $\sqrt{2}$. In Unit 11•2, we explore operations on decimals. Although this requires learning new procedures such as where to place the decimal point, students shouldn't panic. The underlying concepts or meanings are the same as those for operations on fractions.

WHAT THE NCTM *STANDARDS* SAY

Grades K-4

"In grades K-4, the mathematics curriculum should include . . . decimals so that students can:

◆ develop concepts of . . . decimals;
◆ develop number sense for decimals;
◆ use models to relate fractions to decimals [and] to explore operations on . . . decimals;
◆ apply decimals to problem situations" (p. 57).

Grades 5-8

"In grades 5-8, [instruction] should include the continued development of number and number relationships so that students can:

◆ develop number sense for decimals;
◆ understand and apply percents in a wide variety of situations;
◆ investigate relationships [between] fractions [and] decimals . . ." (p. 87).

Figure 11.1: Decimals as a Base-Ten, Place-Value Representation of Fractions
Common fraction: $924\frac{3}{8}$
Decimal fraction Equivalent: $924\frac{375}{1000} =$
$900 + 20 + 4 + \frac{300}{1000} + \frac{70}{1000} + \frac{5}{1000} =$
$900 + 20 + 4 + \frac{3}{10} + \frac{70}{100} + \frac{5}{1000}$

100	10	1	$\frac{1}{10}$	$\frac{1}{100}$	$\frac{1}{1000}$

| **Decimal equivalent:** | 9 | 2 | 4 . 3 | 7 | 5 |

100	10	1	$\frac{1}{10}$	$\frac{1}{100}$	$\frac{1}{1000}$

Note that moving each place to the left involves multiplying by 10; moving each place to the right involves dividing by 10.

11•1 DECIMAL FRACTIONS AND DECIMALS

Figure 11.2: A Decimal Disorder

YOUNG ONES' VIEW

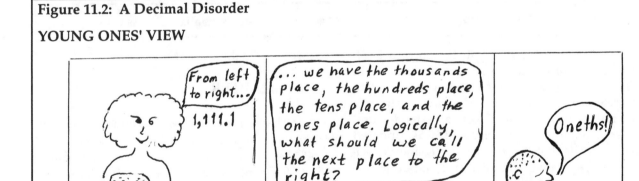

In this unit, we discuss what the traditional skills approach overlooks: the conceptual rationale underlying decimals (Subunit 11•1•1). We then discuss common difficulties children encounter in the skills approach (see, e.g., Figure 11.2) (Subunit 11•1•2) and how they can be helped to understand decimals (Subunit 11•1•3).

11•1•1 MATHEMATICS: DECIMAL NUMERATION

☞ Consider Probe 11.1 (page 11-3).

Fraction-Decimal Connections

If they represent the same thing as fractions, why were decimals ever invented? Basically, decimals are easier to work with in many situations. Consider the task of comparing two rational numbers. Is it easy to tell at glance which is larger, $\frac{7}{9}$ or $\frac{11}{15}$? What about the decimal equivalents of these fractions— $0.7\overline{7}$ or $0.73\overline{3}$? Moreover, operating on decimals is often easier than operating on fractions. For instance, decimals are (continued on page 11-4)

➤ Probe 11.1: Understanding Decimals

The aim of Part I of this probe is to prompt a discussion and an exploration of decimal numeration by raising questions or creating conflict. Answer the questions below. Share your answers with your group or class. The aim of Part II is to help you explicitly define and distinguish among the three types of decimals: terminating decimals (e.g., 0.5), infinitely repeating decimals (e.g., $0.3\bar{3}$), and infinitely nonrepeating decimals (e.g., $\sqrt{3} = 1.7320508...$). (➪ **Teaching Tip**. Note that this probe could also be used with intermediate-level students.)

Part I: Decimal Numeration

1. Circle the following fractions that can be expressed as a decimal.

    (a) $\frac{6}{100}$ (b) $4\frac{4}{10}$ (c) $\frac{5}{1}$ (d) $\frac{1}{7}$ (e) $\frac{3}{16}$ (f) $\frac{47}{159}$

2. Solve the following word problem:

    ■ **A Tale of Two Rain Totals (◆ 5-8).** In Urbana, weatherman Felix Fractions noted the week's precipitation as $\frac{5}{12}$", $\frac{1}{6}$", $1\frac{2}{7}$", $\frac{3}{8}$", $\frac{4}{9}$", 0", $\frac{6}{11}$". In Champaign, weatherman Dag Decimal noted the week's precipitation as 0.42", 0.17", 1.29", 0.38", 0.44", 0", and 0.55". What was the total precipitation in Urbana for the week? What was the total for Champaign? Which city got more rain for the week?

3. Which of the following is a decimal? Circle any correct choice.

    30   3   3.3   3.0   0.3   0.003

4. Which is the center of the decimal system, the decimal point or the ones place?

5. Write the numeral for *three hundred and forty-two thousandths*. Compare your answer with that of others in your group or class.

6. List the ways the decimal 2.86 can be read.

7. Is it correct to write three-tenths as .3 or 0.3?

Questions for Reflection

1. Can any common fraction (rational number) be expressed as a decimal?

2. In Question 2, was it easier to add fractions or decimals?

3. In regard to Question 3, what choices did your group or class conclude qualified as a decimal? What does the term *decimal* mean?

4. The places (. . . thousands, hundreds, tens, ones, tenths, hundredths, thousandths . . .) are symmetrical if which is considered the center of the decimal system—the decimal point or the ones place?

5. Did everyone in your group or class agree on how *three hundred and forty-two thousandths* should be written? What does the *and* in *three hundred and forty-two thousandths* represent?

Part II: Types of Decimals

1. Using the long-division algorithm, convert the following fractions into decimals by dividing the numerator by the denominator. Did the division leave a remainder and how is this related to what type of decimal resulted?

    $\frac{3}{4}$: $4\overline{)3.00}$ $\frac{3}{8}$: $8\overline{)3.000}$ $\frac{7}{16}$: $16\overline{)7.0000}$

2. Likewise, convert the following fractions into decimals. What do you notice about the remainders in these cases and how is this related to what type of decimal resulted?

    $\frac{7}{9}$: $9\overline{)7.00}$ $\frac{4}{15}$: $15\overline{)4.000}$ $\frac{5}{27}$: $27\overline{)5.000000}$

🖩 3. Use a calculator to determine the square roots of 2, 4, 5, 8, 9, 10, 16, and 17 and record your data. (a) The square root of perfect squares such as 4 can be represented by what type of decimal? (b) The square root of nonperfect squares such as 5 can be represented by what type of decimals?

4. On the Tree Diagram of the Real-Number Hierarchy on page 8-2 of chapter 8, label T those numbers represented by a terminating decimal, R those represented by an infinitely repeating decimal, N those represented by infinitely nonrepeating decimals.

easier to add and subtract than are fractions with unlike denominators. Consider Question 2 of Probe 11.1 (page 11-3). Although the amounts of precipitation recorded by Felix and Dag for the week were essentially identical ($\frac{5}{12}$ = 0.42; $\frac{1}{6}$ = 0.17, $1\frac{2}{7}$ = 1.29, and so forth), it is easier to determine the total precipitation expressed in decimals.

Types of Decimals

The division of two integers $\frac{a}{b}$ (where b ≠ 0) produces either a terminating decimal or an infinitely repeating decimal. Thus, all rational numbers are one of these two kinds of decimals. Unlike rational numbers, all irrational numbers can be expressed as infinitely nonrepeating decimals.

Terminating Decimals. If two integers can be divided until there is no remainder, then the number is called a *terminating decimal*. Consider the case of $\frac{1}{4}$: 1 ÷ 4 = 0.25 r0. Note that writing the decimal equivalent (0.25) does not introduce rounding error.

Nonterminating Decimals: Infinitely Repeating Decimals. If division of the two integers leaves a nonterminating pattern of remainders, then the number is called an *infinitely repeating decimal*. In the following cases, note that the remainders form an infinitely repeating cycle: $\frac{1}{3}$ = 1 ÷ 3 = 0.3 r1 = 0.33 r1 = 0.333 r1 and so forth and $\frac{3}{11}$ = .27 r3 = .272 r8 = .2727 r3 = .27272 r8 = .272727 r3 and so forth.

Nonterminating Decimals: Infinitely Nonrepeating Decimals. Such decimals never end or form a repeating pattern. For example, $\sqrt{2}$ can be represented by the nonterminating, nonrepeating decimal 1.414213562...; π, by 3.141592653....

11•1•2 LEARNING

Various studies and national surveys indicate that children typically do not develop a sound understanding of decimals and many test poorly on the topic, unable to solve even slightly unfamiliar tasks (Kouba et al., 1989; Wearne & Hiebert, 1988b). As with other domains, a key reason for such results is how decimals have traditionally been taught. Four common difficulties are: (a) not recognizing connections between fractions and decimals (e.g., that fraction can be converted into decimals by dividing); (b) not understanding

place-value notation of decimals (e.g., reading 4.2 minutes as *four and two oneths minutes* or as *four minutes and two seconds*); (c) comparing decimals in terms of whole-number knowledge (e.g., considering .23 larger than .4); and (d) not recognizing decimal equivalents (e.g., that two tenths plus three hundredths is equivalent to twenty three hundredths and that .3 is the same as .30).

11•1•3 TEACHING

In the *Curriculum Standards*, the NCTM (1989) recommends beginning decimal instruction in the primary grades. Although decimals have traditionally been introduced formally in fourth or fifth grade, there are good reasons for introducing this topic earlier. First, children need a sound conceptual basis for understanding decimal notation, and these ideas take a long time to construct. Second, decimal notation is used widely in everyday life. Even primary-level students encounter these symbols in many situations such as money notation (e.g., $2.35), data reported in newspapers and elsewhere (e.g., batting averages), and on digital stopwatches (e.g., 10.53 seconds). Primary-age children may also use calculators in school and at home, and most calculators display the quotient for division as a decimal[*] (e.g., 10 ÷ 3 = 3.3̄3). To comprehend these applications and facilitate their learning, children need to *understand* what decimal notation means.

Decimal Numeration

To foster an understanding of decimals, teachers can help children see (a) the connection between fractions and decimals and (b) the connection between decimals and base-ten, place-value concepts. Instruction should proceed from fractions to decimal fractions (e.g., $\frac{1}{10}$, $\frac{5}{10}$, $\frac{17}{100}$, $\frac{27}{1000}$) and then to decimals.

Conceptual Phase: Decimal Fractions. *Decimal fractions are common fractions with a denominator of 10 or a power of 10* and can serve as a conceptual bridge between fraction instruction and decimal instruction.

---

[*] The *Math Explorer* manufactured by Texas Instruments gives children the option of division ($\boxed{÷}$) or integer division ($\boxed{\text{INT} ÷}$). The latter displays a quotient and a remainder (e.g., 13 ÷ 3 → Q = 4, R = 1). If children use the division key of the *Math Explorer* or other calculators, they may well wonder what decimal answers mean.

Miss Brill's instruction on decimals was not going well. "What can I do?" she pleaded with Ms. Socrates.

The more experienced teacher counseled, "Build on their knowledge of common fractions. Although children may have informal knowledge of common fractions such as one-half, one-fourth, and one-third, they may have little or no exposure to decimal fractions outside of school. However, it is a short step from understanding common fractions such as one-half, one-fourth, and one-third to understanding decimal fractions such as one-tenth, four-tenths, one-hundredth, twenty-four hundredths, one-thousandth, and so on. Playing math games such as *If-Then—Decimal-Fraction Version* (see Part I of Investigation 11.1) is one way I use to introduce decimal-fraction concepts and terms. For example, I ask students, 'If a large cube represents one, then what do three large cubes, a flat, and a long represent?'"

☞ Consider Investigation 11.1 (page 11-6).

Miss Brill recognized that playing a game involving base-ten blocks could be an interesting and powerful way of introducing decimal fractions. Moreover, she saw that it also provided entertaining practice for adding unlike fractions, which entailed finding a common denominator and determining equivalent fractions. For example, translating three large cubes representing three wholes, a flat representing one-tenth, and a long representing one one-hundredth into a decimal fraction entailed adding $3 + \frac{1}{10} + \frac{1}{100}$, which involves recognizing that $\frac{1}{10} = \frac{10}{100}$. Nevertheless, Miss Brill was concerned about one aspect of the model: "*Won't using different blocks to represent one or a unit be confusing to children? Won't it be less confusing to define the large cube as one from the start?*"

Ms. Socrates responded, "Typically children easily adapt to redefining one as a large cube, a flat, or a long (e.g., Wearne, Hiebert, & Taber, 1991). Varying the block that represents a unit underscores the arbitrariness of units and encourages flexible thinking (Owens & Super, 1993)."

"To familiarize my students with decimal fractions," added Ms. Socrates, "I also have them use metric rulers to do projects, such as constructing a scene for a diorama to scale, or science experiments, such as measuring the amount of rainfall in different locales. Measuring with metric rulers can help children recognize decimal-fraction equivalents (e.g., that 10 tenths is one whole, 10 hundredths is a tenth, and 10 thousandths is a hundredth, and vice versa) and the division by 10 pattern (i.e., $1 \div 10 =$ tenths, tenths $\div 10 =$ hundredths, hundredths $\div 10 =$ thousandths . . .)."

Connecting Phase: Linking Decimals to Decimal Fractions. "Once children understand decimal fractions, it is just another small step to understanding decimals," continued Ms. Socrates. "I use the investigative approach and use base-ten blocks again to help children discover that decimal fractions can also be represented more easily with place-value notation—that is, as decimals. For example, I have my students play *Decimal-Fraction Derby* (see Part II of Investigation 11.1 on page 11-6). Note that keeping score for this game with base-ten blocks and a three-space place-value mat naturally creates the problem: How do you keep score of tenths of a point? What block represents tenths and where do you place these blocks on the score board? (see Step 1 of Box 11.1 on page 11-7) After my students have solved this problem, I challenge them to devise a less cumbersome written scoring procedure—one that involves base-ten, place-value notation rather than fractions and mixed numbers (see Step 2 of Box 11.1). This often leads students to reinvent decimal notation or to recognize that decimal notation is relevant to representing decimal fraction. If not, I introduce the standard decimal notation (the decimal point) as the conventional way of representing decimal fractions in the U.S."

"REAL CLASS ACTIVITIES OR GAMES THAT INVOLVE WORKING WITH MONEY, METRIC MEASURES, OR HUNDRED SQUARES CAN PROVIDE A PURPOSEFUL WAY OF INTRODUCING AND REINFORCING DECIMAL IDEAS," added Ms. Socrates. "For instance, my class has set up its own economic system (see Activity File 8.1 on page 8-28) and prints its own currency. To underscore grouping by ten, we use currency with values of $1000, $100, $10, $1, 10¢, and 1¢ only. This creates the opportunity to explicitly discuss that 10¢ is another name for $0.1 (one-tenth of a dollar) and 1¢ is another name for $0.01 (one one-hundredth of a dollar) and that grouping by ten applies to digits, to the right of the decimal as well as those to the left of it."

"In one activity, I give each student $1000 credit to invest in the stock market any way they please," elaborated Ms. (continued on page 11-7)

⚙ Investigation 11.1: Using Base-Ten Blocks to Introduce Decimals

◆ Decimal-fraction and decimal concepts ◆ 2-4 ◆ Any number

BASE-TEN BLOCKS ARE A PARTICULARLY USEFUL CONCRETE MODEL FOR INTRODUCING DECIMAL FRACTIONS AND LINKING THEM TO DECIMALS (Hiebert, 1987). To begin with, it may be less confusing to use only two denominations: ones and tenths (see Part IA). Then hundredths can be introduced by redefining a flat as one (see Part IB). Later, thousandths can be illustrated by redefining the large cube as one (see Part IC). Once students are familiar with decimal fractions, then decimals can be introduced as an alternative (place-value) representation (see Part II).

Part I. Conceptual Phase: Introducing Decimal Fractions

Play *If-Then—Decimal-Fraction Version*. Divide the class into teams of about four. Pose *if-then* questions such as these described below. Have each team record its answer on a minislate. Discuss the answers presented, why incorrect answers are incorrect, and why the correct answer was correct. Award teams with the correct answer a point.

A. Introducing Decimal Fractions Involving Tenths

1. If a long equals one, then what decimal fraction do the following represent: (a) a cube, (b) four cubes, and (c) two longs and six cubes?
2. If a long equals one, then what blocks would represent: (a) sixth tenths, (b) one and three tenths, and (c) three and nine tenths?

B. Introducing Decimal Fractions Involving Hundredths

1. If a flat equals one, then what decimal fraction do the following represent: (a) a long, (b) a cube, (c) a flat and nine cubes, (d) a long and a cube, (e) two longs and seven cubes, and (f) three flats, three longs, and three cubes?
2. If a flat equals one, then what blocks would represent: (a) three hundredths, (b) two and three tenths, (c) twenty-three hundredths, and (d) one and forty-two hundredths.

C. Introducing Decimal Fractions Involving Thousandths

1. If a large cube equals one, then what decimal fraction do the following represent: (a) a flat, (b) a long, (c) a cube, (d) a large cube and three cubes, (e) a long and a cube, (f) three longs and four cubes, and (g) two large cubes, a flat, a long, and a cube equal?
2. If a large cube equals one, then what blocks would represent (a) six tenths, (b) seven thousandths, (c) twenty-three hundredths, and (d) one and two hundred three thousandths?

Part II. Connecting Phase: Linking Decimal Numeration to Decimal Fractions

Play *Decimal-Fraction Derby*. Make up a deck of cards with whole numbers less than 6 (i.e., 1, 2, 3, 4, 5), decimal fractions involving tenths (e.g., $\frac{1}{10}, \frac{3}{10}, \frac{5}{10}, \frac{10}{10}, \frac{70}{10}, \frac{15}{10}, \frac{47}{10}$), and mixed numbers (e.g., $1\frac{1}{10}, 5\frac{1}{10}$). On their turn, players draw two cards, decide which has the larger number, and score the number points on their card of choice. Use base-ten blocks and a two-space place-value mat (tens and ones place) to keep score. The game ends at the conclusion of the round in which one or more players reach 50. The player with the largest total wins; the player with second largest total takes second place, and so forth. Play the game again. This time, keep a written score without using fractions.

Questions for Reflection

1. Playing *If-Then—Decimal-Fraction Version* involves practicing what fraction skills?

2. (a) Keeping score of *Decimal-Fraction Derby* with a two-space place-value mat should create what problem? (b) When asked to replay the game and keep a written score, what informal place-value notation system might children invent and use?

Box 11.1: Discovering How Decimal Fractions Can Be Represented as Decimals

Step 1: Discovering the Correct Position for Tenths. Create a situation where children need to model a number such as $132\frac{3}{10}$ using base-ten blocks. This may require some discussion about which block should be defined as 1. The discovery process may be facilitated by using place-value mats as shown below in Figure A. Note that using such a mat naturally raises the question, "Where should we put the tenths?" Some students may suggest adding a tenths place to the mat or making up a new mat with a tenths place. With any luck, students will conclude that a reasonable place for the tenths would be to the right of the ones place. Ask students to justify their placement. [Going from left to right the value of the digits gets smaller by a factor of 10. So, it does not make sense to place tenths to the left of the hundreds place.] Figure B below illustrates a model of $132\frac{3}{10}$ using the "expanded" place-value mat.

Step 2: Discovering a Shortcut for Decimal-Fraction Notation (Decimals). Ask students how they could write a number for the concrete model representing $132\frac{3}{10}$ without using a fraction. If necessary, a teacher might coax students by writing on the board:

hundreds	*tens*	*ones*
1	3	2

Prompts might include, "How can we show three-tenths without using a fraction and where should this symbol go? Some children—using the revised place-value mat for inspiration—might suggest indicating the three-tenths with a 3 placed to the right of the ones place.

hundreds	*tens*	*ones*	*tenths*
1	3	2	3

At this point, the teacher might conclude, so we can write one hundred thirty two and three-tenths as 1323. Such a suggestion should raise concern about distinguishing between $132\frac{3}{10}$ and 1,323. If the issue is not raised by the students themselves, a teacher might ask, "How can we note where the whole numbers end and the fractional parts of wholes begin?" With any luck, though, some children will suggest various ways of designating tenths (see Examples A to D below). An inspired child might suggest using a period to show the end of one "sentence" and the beginning of another (Example E).

132/3	132<u>3</u>	132 ③	132∧3	132.3
A	**B**	**C**	**D**	**E**

Figure A: Place-Value Mat

Hundreds	Tens	Ones	

Figure B: Expanded Place-Value Mat

Hundreds	Tens	Ones	Tenths

Socrates. Besides serving as a basis for an economics lesson (e.g., the role of the stock market in our economy), providing practice using the internet to obtain economic information, and creating a real need to collect and analyze data and statistics, this activity often helps students appreciate the value of decimals. Namely, it is usually easier to operate on the decimal equivalents of stock prices than it is to do the arithmetic on the reported prices, which involve fractions.

Decimal Number Sense

Comparing and Ordering Decimals. If decimals are introduced concretely and meaningfully, many students will not need direct instruction on comparing decimals. One study (Wearne & Hiebert, 1989), for instance, found that with conceptually-based instruction that used base-ten blocks, students were able to order decimals without explicit instruction on how to do this.

Fraction-Decimal Equivalents. To strengthen the connection between fraction and decimal knowledge and to foster a number sense for decimals, children should be able to recognize or determine the decimal equivalents of fractions and vice versa (see, e.g., Investigation 11.2). For example, initially encourage students to devise their own methods for converting fractions into decimals. If necessary, help them recognize that a fraction can be changed into a decimal by dividing its numerator by its denominator. In time, encourage children to rediscover the algorithms for converting decimals to fractions.

Approximating Decimals. Decimal number sense also entails approximating decimals. Rounding off decimals is particularly important with infinitely repeating and nonrepeating decimals but introduces "rounding error" (e.g., rounded to hundredths: $\frac{1}{8} = .125 \rightarrow .13$, $\frac{2}{3} = .66\overline{6}$ $\rightarrow .67$, $\sqrt{3} = 1.732... \rightarrow 1.73$). Problem 11.1 below illustrates a multistep rate problem that involves

approximation.

■ **Problem 11.1: Traveling Light (♦ 5-8).** How many hours does it take a ray of light to travel from the sun to the earth? Light travels approximately 186,000 miles per second. The earth is about 93 million miles from the sun. Give your answer to the nearest hundredth of an hour.

In some cases, fractions are required or are easier to use than decimals. This is a problem when the decimal is a nonrepeating decimal, because such decimals do not have a fractional equivalent. What is one to do? This dilemma can be resolved by converting a nonrepeating decimal into a terminating or repeating decimal of approximately the same size. For example, the nonrepeating decimal 0.1112131415 is reasonably close to $0.11\overline{1}$, which has the decimal equivalent of $\frac{1}{9}$.

☞ Try Investigations 11.2 (page 11-9 and 11-10) and 11.3 (page 11-11).

11•2 OPERATIONS ON DECIMALS

Decimal arithmetic has darkened many a student's day. As Figure 11.3 implies, because children do not understand the school-taught algorithms, many have trouble remembering, for instance, where to put that dang decimal point. This unit explores the most common difficulties children have with decimal arithmetic (Subunit 11•2•1) and how instruction can make decimal addition and subtraction, multiplication, and division understandable (Subunit 11•2•2).

11•2•1 LEARNING: COMMON DIFFICULTIES

Many children have little understanding of operations on decimals and perform poorly in this area. This subunit focuses on why children commonly have these difficulties.

☞ Try Investigation 11.4 (page 11-12).

Routine Expertise

Although many students in traditional programs do learn how to use the standard decimal-arithmetic algorithms correctly, they frequently have difficulty with questions that require conceptual understand- (continued on page 11-13)

Figure 11.3: That Dubious Decimal Point

Herman copyright 1991 Jim Unger. Reprinted with permission of Universal Press Syndicate. All rights reserved.

"Where do you want the decimal point?"

✎ Investigation 11.2: Exploring Decimal Patterns

◆ Fraction-decimal equivalents + calculator ◆ 2-8 ◆ Any number

This investigation illustrates how calculators can be used to explore decimal equivalents of fractions, to introduce the distinction between terminating decimals and infinitely repeating decimals, and to explore decimal patterns.

▦ Part I: Introducing Infinitely Repeating Decimals

While teaching decimal arithmetic, Miss Brill noticed that her students did not have a good decimal number sense. They did not recognize that fractions and decimals are equivalent forms of the same number. Indeed, when she asked what the decimal equivalent of $\frac{1}{2}$, $\frac{1}{3}$, or even $\frac{3}{10}$ was, her students had no idea. Moreover, they had no idea of how to use a calculator or long-division to convert fractions to decimals. Miss Brill decided to put off further instruction on decimal arithmetic until her students had a firmer idea of what decimals were.

After passing out *Math Explorer*™ calculators to the class, Miss Brill pointed out that the fraction bar can mean "divided by." She then proceeded to show the class how to convert $\frac{1}{2}$ by division with a calculator: Press clear $\boxed{c}$, key-in the numerator $\boxed{1}$, press the divide key $\boxed{\div}$, key in the denominator $\boxed{2}$, and press equals $\boxed{=}$. Miss Brill was surprised by the interest her students showed as they also converted other terminating decimals such as $\frac{1}{4}$, $\frac{3}{4}$, $\frac{1}{5}$, and $\frac{3}{10}$.

Next, Miss Brill gave them $\frac{1}{3}$ to convert and was delighted to hear gasps and several woowees. The calculator had done something unexpected by reeling out a repeating decimal. Miss Brill then had the class convert $\frac{2}{3}$, which was also greeted with glee. The stage was now set to explore the patterns of repeating decimals.

▦ Part II: Exploring Patterns of Infinitely Repeating Decimals

Ninths. Miss Brill had the class investigate fractions with denominators of 9. Using calculators, her students quickly discovered an interesting pattern. What is the pattern?

Elevenths. Miss Brill then introduced elevenths. Using calculators, the class quickly discovered that the decimal equivalents of elevenths formed a two-digit repeating cycle. If you have not already done so for *Dividing by Eleven Made Easy* (Activity V of Investigation 8.11 on page 8-34 of chapter 8), specify the rule underlying this pattern.

Sevenths. Miss Brill continued with the sevenths. The students created a table of equivalent values for $\frac{1}{7}$ to $\frac{6}{7}$. Use a calculator to complete the table below:

$\frac{1}{7} =$ $\frac{2}{7} =$ $\frac{3}{7} =$ $\frac{4}{7} =$ $\frac{5}{7} =$ $\frac{6}{7} =$

A repeating pattern was not readily evident. Andy pointed out that the last (seventh digit) of the decimal equivalent of $\frac{2}{7}$ ended with a 3 and a 3 did not even appear in the first seven digits of the decimal equivalent of $\frac{1}{7}$. He also noted that the last digit of the decimal equivalents for $\frac{4}{7}$ and $\frac{6}{7}$ ended in 6 and 9, respectively, and neither a 6 nor a 9 appeared anywhere else in their decimal-equivalent table. Andy concluded that the decimal equivalents of sevenths didn't form a repeating pattern.

Investigation 11.2 continued

1. (a) Could Andy be correct? (b) If sevenths could not be expressed as an infinitely repeating decimal, what is the alternative?

2. What has Andy overlooked about the data in the decimal-equivalent table?

3. Several students argued that the repeating pattern might involve many digits. By examining the table carefully and taking into account Andy's error, the class concluded that the repeating cycle involved six digits. They checked their conjecture by using the calculator function of their classroom computer, which could provide quotients (rounded off) to 11 decimal places. After the class discussed how the rounding could disguise a pattern, the students—without Miss Brill's help—used the computer to revise their decimal-equivalent list for sevenths.

Miss Brill, who had been spotted scheming with Ms. Socrates the previous day, boldly announced, "I bet Miss Magic could give you the decimal equivalent for any number of sevenths without writing numbers or using a calculator. But, I will need to wear my magic think-hat." (She put on a tall cone-shaped hat with a flowing silk streamer attached to the point.)

The class was skeptical, to say the least. "There isn't anyway," commented Rodney. "There's too many digits."

"Try me," challenged Miss Magic, alias Miss Brill. "Look at your table of fractions with denominators of seven. Tell me one of the fractions, and I will try to tell you the decimal equivalent. I think I can do it wearing this magic hat. Check my answer with your list."

"Okay, what is one-seventh?" replied Denise.

"Point one. . . (pause) four . . . two . . . eight . . . five . . . seven . . . ," noted Miss Magic and then quickly added, "one, four, two, eight, five, seven. Is that right?"

The class was in awe. Darlene next posed, "What is five-sevenths?"

"Point . . . ," said Miss Magic pausing for a moment, "seven . . . one, four, two, eight, five, seven, one, four, two, eight, five, seven. Is that right?"

"Yes. How do you do that?" rang out a chorus of voices.

"Maybe it's the magic hat," teased Miss Brill.

"She's just memorized them," hypothesized Judi.

"Not really," countered Miss Magic. "Try me on some unusual examples."

Janice was suddenly excited. She thought she had a fraction that would stump Miss Brill: "What is ten-sevenths?"

"One point . . . (pause) four, two, eight, five, seven, one, four, two, eight, five, seven, one," replied Miss Magic. "Check it with your calculator."

LeMar calculated ten divided by seven on the computer. Miss Brill was correct again. Some of the students followed Janice's lead and posed twenty-sevenths, fifty-sevenths, twenty-one sevenths (which is the whole number of three), and many others. As the computer confirmed, Miss Brill was always correct.

Although the class begged her to tell them the trick, Miss Magic resisted saying only: "I'll leave it up to you to tell me."

What is the basis of Miss Magic's "trick?" Use it to determine the decimal equivalents of fifteen-sevenths and one hundred-sevenths.

✂ Investigation 11.3: Some Challenging Decimal Tasks

◆ Decimal numeration + number sense ◆ 5-8 ◆ Groups of four + class discussion

This investigation includes a number of challenging tasks that can be used to foster discussion or to assess decimal connections, concepts, or skills. To check your understanding, try the questions yourself and then discuss your answers with your group or class.

☞ ✓ **Teaching and Assessment Tips.** Note that Questions 1 and 2, which are suitable for intermediate-level students, can be used as learning activities, assessment items, or both. Questions 3 and 4, which are suitable for both primary- and intermediate-level students, can be used to prompt discussion or diagnose systematic decimal-comparison errors. Question 5, suitable for students in fourth grade or above, can serve as the basis for a class discussion or gauging whether or not students understand the structure of the decimal system. Question 6, appropriate for middle-school students, can provide practice or check the approximation technique discussed on page 11-8.

1. Construct a concept map with the following concept terms: *Common Fractions (numerator and denominator are integers—e.g., $\frac{1}{2}$ or $\frac{2}{3}$), Decimals, Fractions, Infinitely Nonrepeating Decimals (e.g., 0.121221222... or 0.4714045...), Infinitely Repeating Decimals (e.g., $0.\overline{66}$ or $0.09\overline{09}$), Irrational Numbers, Other Fractions (numerator or denominator is not an integer—e.g., $\sqrt{2}/3$), Rational Numbers, Real Numbers, Symbols, and Terminating Decimals (e.g., 0.5 or 0.75).* Include the following linking words in your map: *are alternative forms* and *can be written as.*

2. Write a realistic word problem that would fit each of the following expressions:

   (a) $26 \div 3 = 8$ r 2 (d) $26 \div 3$ is about 10   (f) $26 \div 3 = 8.67$

   (b) $26 \div 3$ would be 8   (e) $26 \div 3 = 8\frac{2}{3}$ (g) $26 \div 3 = 8.\overline{66}$

   (c) $26 \div 3$ would be 9

3. Some of the digits of the two decimals below have been covered up. Can you tell which number is larger? Justify your answer.[†]

   (a) 0.■   (b) 0.■ ■ ■

4. (a) How would the value of the decimal 2.35 change if a zero was inserted (a) at A, (b) at B instead of A, (c) at C instead of A or B, (d) at D instead of A, B, or C, (e) at E instead of A, B, C, or D? Justify each answer.[†]

   $$\begin{array}{ccccc} A & B & C & D & E \\ \downarrow & \downarrow & \downarrow & \downarrow & \downarrow \end{array}$$

   $$2 \bullet 3 \; 5$$

5. (a) *Without using a calculator*, write a number ten times bigger than 437.56 . (b) For Question 5a, Chandra responded 437.560; and Sasi answered 4370.56. Which, if either, is correct? Why? For an incorrect answer, explain how the student may have arrived at the answer.

6. Listed below are the decimal equivalent of three irrational numbers. Name a common fraction that approximates each of these decimals.

   (a) $\sqrt{2}/2 = 0.707106...$ (b) $\sqrt{3} = 1.732050...$ (c) $\pi = 3.141592...$

[†]Based on tasks described in Resnick, Nesher, Leonard, Magone, Omanson, and Peled (1989).

✓ ☾ Investigation 11.4: Gauging Understanding of Decimal Multiplication and Division

◆ Operation sense + assessment tasks (decimal multiplication and division)
◆ 5-8 ◆ Individually or in small groups

Answer as many of the following questions as you can. You may wish to compare your answers with those of your group and class. By compiling the results of this investigation, your class can gauge which of the following assessment items are relatively easy and which are relatively difficult. If you have the opportunity, administer the items below to a sample of intermediate-level students to see how they respond.

1. Determine the product of (a) 0.25 x 0.8 and (b) 3.5 x 0.8

✐ 2. Write a realistic word problem that could be represented by the expressions (a) 0.25 x 0.8 and (b) 3.5 x 0.8.

3. Solve the following word problems:

   ■ **Problem A: A Run for the Border.** Caught red-handed pilfering fish from the neighborhood store, Ruffus the dog sprinted for home at a speed of 6 miles per hour. If he ran for 0.15 hours before collapsing in a pool of slobber, how far had Ruffus run?

   ■ **Problem B: Reduced Copy.** Celena wanted to include a picture in her report but it was too large. She reduced the picture to .75 its original size. If the picture was originally 12 inches tall, how tall was Celena's copy?

4. Illustrate how base-ten blocks could be used to determine the products of (a) 0.25 x 0.8 and (b) 3.5 x 0.8.

5. Without using a calculator, indicate where the decimal point for the following expression should go.

	A	B	C	D	E	F	G
	↓	↓	↓	↓	↓	↓	↓
4.55 x 6.108 =	2	7	7	9	1	4	

🖩 6. Use a calculator to determine the *remainder* of 31,859,642 ÷ 75,301. You may use any of the operations (+, -, x, and ÷). If you have TI *Math Explorer*, you may not use the INT ÷ function, which would automatically indicate the remainder.[†]

   ✓ **Assessment Tips. Assessment of students' knowledge of operations on decimals should tap conceptual understanding as well as mastery of procedures.** To gauge whether students understand operations on decimals, a teacher needs to assess more than correct use of the standard algorithm (e.g., Question 1 above). Assessment needs to include items like Questions 2 to 6:

   • writing realistic word problems for symbolic expressions;

   • choosing the correct operation for problems that involve various situations and settings;

   • constructing models to represent symbolic expressions; and

   • estimating answers (Owens & Super, 1993).

[†]Based on a task described by Simon (1993).

ing. More specifically, though many students have no difficulty determining the product of expressions such as 0.25 x 0.8 and 3.5 x 0.8 (Question 1 of Investigation 11.4 on page 11-12), they have considerable difficulty with Questions 2 to 6 in Investigation 11.4.

Common Sources of Confusion

Decimal Multiplication. Word problems or symbolic expressions involving a whole-number multiplier (e.g., 4 x 0.8) cause children relatively little difficulty because such items can be readily assimilated to their understanding of multiplication as repeated addition. Even multiplying a whole number by a decimal (e.g., 0.8 x 4) is understandable because multiplication is commutative and such expressions can be viewed as having a whole-number multiplier (e.g., 0.8 x 4 = 4 x 0.8).

As with fraction multiplication, children have difficulty understanding decimal word problems or symbolic expressions involving two nonunit decimals because such items do not fit their concept of multiplication as repeated addition. For 0.5 x 0.2, for instance, how can you count two-tenths *five-tenths* times? Moreover, from their whole-number experience, they incorrectly assume that multiplication always results in an answer bigger than the factors and quite the opposite happens when multiplying by a decimal less than one. When given word problems that involve a decimal multiplier less than one, such as Problems A and B in Investigation 11.4, children often have difficulty recognizing that multiplication is the appropriate operation (Greer, 1992).

Rate problems (e.g., Problem A in Investigation 11.4) are especially difficult for many children (Owens & Super, 1993), because they are unfamiliar with such problems.

Decimal Division. Word problems or symbolic expressions involving a whole-number divisor (e.g., 0.8 ÷ 4) cause children relatively little difficulty because such items can be readily assimilated to their understanding of division as divvying up. As with fraction division, children have difficulty understanding decimal word problems or symbolic expressions involving a divisor less than one (e.g., 4 ÷ 0.8) because such items do not fit their view of division as divvy up. Furthermore, it contradicts their whole-number experience that division always results in an answer

smaller than the dividend (the amount divvied up) (e.g., Graeber & Tirosh, 1990).

11•2•2 TEACHING

In this subunit, we describe how instruction can prepare children for challenging questions such as Questions 2 to 6 of Investigation 11.4. If you had difficulty with many of these questions—take heart that most adults do and that working through this subunit should greatly expand your own understanding.

Meaningful Instruction of Decimal Addition and Subtraction

In the investigative approach, children are encouraged to build on their existing conceptual knowledge to reason out decimal sums and differences and to construct decimal addition and subtraction algorithms.

Conceptual Phase. As with whole-number addition and subtraction, students probably should begin decimal addition and subtraction with problems that involve qualitative reasoning and estimation. Next, students should use manipulatives and their own informal strategies to solve problems requiring exact answers.

Connecting Phase. Three teaching tips for the connecting phase are listed below.

☞ **Encourage students to reinvent decimal addition and subtraction algorithms by reflecting on what they already know.**

☞ **Encourage students to reflect on how each step of a written algorithm corresponds to a step in their concrete models.**

☞ ✓ **Use uneven decimal expressions such as 3.25 + 1.5 to foster and to evaluate conceptual learning of addition and subtraction algorithms** (Wearne & Hiebert, 1988a).

Meaningful Instruction of Decimal Multiplication

Your efforts to understand fraction multiplication should help in understanding decimal multiplication. Many of the same teaching principles discussed in chapter 10 apply here. This subunit describes what analogies are useful, what role qualitative reasoning and estimation can play, and how concrete models can aid in the construction of an understanding of decimal multiplication during the conceptual and connecting phases. It then discusses how during the connecting phase, children can learn the procedure for placing a decimal point in a meaningful fashion.

☞ Consider Investigations 11.5 (page 11-15) and 11.6 (pages 11-16 and 11-17).

Meaningful Analogies. As with multiplying fractions, children must go beyond their informal conception of multiplication as repeated addition to understand decimal multiplication in all its forms. This section describes how a groups-of and an area analogy can help students make sense of multiplying by either a decimal less than one (e.g., 0.5 x 0.2 = 0.1) or a nonunit decimal larger than one (e.g., 3.5 x 0.2 = 0.7).

∞ **Introduce decimal multiplication with *groups-of* problems involving a whole-number multiplier.** Solving problems such as Problem A in Investigation 11.5 can make the transition from whole-number multiplication to decimal multiplication relatively easy. The conceptual phase can then build on children's understanding of the groups-of meaning by asking them to consider problems involving a multiplier of less than one, such as Problem B in Investigation 11.5, or a nonunit decimal greater than one, such as Problem C in Investigation 11.5.

∞ **During the connecting and symbolic phases, encourage children to relate symbolic expressions to a *groups-of* analogy.** As with fraction multiplication, a groups-of analogy makes sense whether the multiplier is a whole number, a decimal less than one, or a "mixed" decimal. For example, 3 x 0.2 can be viewed as *three groups of two-tenths of a whole*; 0.5 x 0.2, as *five-tenths groups of two-tenths of a whole*; and 3.5 x 0.2, as *three and five-tenths groups of two-tenths of a whole*. Note that this wording underscores that a multiplier less than one is a fraction of the second decimal and that the second decimal is a fraction of some whole.[1]

∞ **During the conceptual phase, introduce *area* problems in which one or both sides of a rectangle is a decimal. During the connecting phase, introduce the area analogy as an alternative interpretation of symbolic expressions such as 0.5 x 0.2.** Like a groups-of analogy, an area interpretation applies to any type of decimal multiplication situation. For instance, 0.5 x 0.2 can rep-

resent a situation in which the length of a rectangular section of land is 0.5 km and the width is 0.2 km and the task is to determine the area in square kilometers.

Qualitative Reasoning and Estimating. Even before children use manipulatives to determine exact answers, instruction on decimal multiplication, particularly that involving a nonunit multiplier, should involve qualitative-reasoning and estimation (e.g., Grossnickle & Perry, 1985).

∞ **Begin decimal-multiplication instruction by encouraging children to consider the general direction of a product.** During the conceptual phase, encourage students to analyze groups-of problems of all sorts (including a decimal multiplied by a nonunit decimal) and to note explicitly whether the answer will be larger or smaller than the size of the group (the multiplicand) and why (see, e.g., Question 2 in Investigation 11.5). Note that a groups-of interpretation can help children see why multiplication by a decimal less than one "makes the answer smaller." After all, five-tenths (or one-half) group of two-tenths has to be less than one (full) group of two-tenths. During the connecting phase, tasks such as Questions 3 and 4 in Investigation 11.5 can be posed.

∞ **During all phases of instruction, encourage children to estimate products.** During the conceptual phase, encourage children to estimate the products of groups-of problems (see Question 5 of Investigation 11.5). During the connecting phase, encourage children to relate symbolic expressions such as those in Question 6 of Investigation 11.5 to a groups-of meaning and estimate the answer. During the symbolic phase, estimating products can serve as a check for written work.

Concrete Models. Conceptually-guided use of concrete models can help students, even intermediate- and college-level students, make sense of decimal multiplication.

∞ **During the conceptual phase, encourage children to use base-ten blocks to devise informal strategies for solving decimal-multiplication problems involving *groups-of* or *area* situations.** Part I of Investigation 11.6 (page 11-16) illustrates one way of creating an opportunity for doing so.

• **Groups-of model.** Figure 11.4 (on page 11-18) illustrates a concrete solution for Problem B of Investigation 11.6. (Continued on page 11-18.)

☪ Investigation 11.5: Thinking About Decimal Multiplication

◆ Qualitative reasoning and estimating ◆ 3-6 ◆ Groups of four + class discussion

Decimal multiplication instruction should begin with sense-making activities such as qualitative-reasoning and estimation tasks, then move to computing exact products. Try the following tasks yourself. Discuss your answers with your group or class.

1. (a) Would a repeated-addition interpretation make sense for each of the following symbolic expressions: 6 x 0.3, 0.5 x 0.3, and 6.5 x 0.3? (b) In each case, would a groups-of analogy make sense? (c) In each case, would an area analogy make sense? (d) Where appropriate, devise a groups-of and/or an area word problem. Hint: Consider what you learned about fraction multiplication.

2. For each of the following word problems, gauge whether the answer (product) will be larger or smaller than the starting amount (multiplicand).

   ■ **Problem A: Yeasty Dough.** Mr. Canella added three 0.25 oz. packages of yeast to his bread dough. How much yeast did he add?

   ■ **Problem B: Less Yeasty Dough.** Because his last batch of dough baked up to the size of a small refrigerator, Mr. Canella decided to use less yeast. This time he added three-tenths of a 0.25 oz. package of yeast to his dough. How much yeast did he add?

   ■ **Problem C: Reasonably Yeasty Dough.** From his previous experiences with gigantic and miniature loafs of bread, Mr. Canella decided to add one and five-tenths 0.25 oz. package of yeast to his bread dough. How much yeast did he add?

3. In the equations below, a ■ covers a digit larger than 1 (i.e., a digit ranging from 2 to 9). (a) In each of the following cases, is the product smaller or larger than the starting amount (the multiplicand) or is it indeterminable? Briefly explain why. Hint: Consider an appropriate problem context or an analogous situation with fractions. (b) How would your answers change if ■ could equal any digit from 0 to 9?

Case	Multiplier		Multiplicand		Product
A.	■	x	■	=	?
B.	■	x	0.■	=	?
C.	■	x	■.■	=	?
D.	0.■	x	■	=	?
E.	0.■	x	0.■	=	?
F.	0.■	x	■.■	=	?
G.	■.■	x	■	=	?
H.	■.■	x	0.■	=	?
I.	■.■	x	■.■	=	?

4. Why does multiplying with a decimal less than one result in a product smaller than the multiplicand? For example, why is the product of 0.3 x 2 or 0.5 x 2 smaller than two?

5. For each problem in Question 2 above, *estimate* the answer.

6. Estimate the product for the following expressions: (a) 0.3̄3 x 10.75, (b) 0.75 x 19.45, and (c) 3.25 x 8.95.

✂ Investigation 11.6: Constructing the Conceptual Basis for Symbolic Decimal Multiplication

◆ Concretely modeling decimal multiplication + connecting symbolic decimal multiplication to a groups-of analogy and concrete models ◆ 4-6 ◆ Any number

After students have had opportunities to engage in qualitative reasoning about decimal multiplication and estimating products (see, e.g., Investigation 11.5 on page 11-15), they can then explore ways of determining exact answers of decimal multiplication. Part I asks students to consider how base-ten blocks could be used to devise an informal strategy for solving *groups-of* and *area* problems. The aim of Part II is to connect *groups-of* and *area* analogies and concrete models to symbolic expressions. Part III illustrates a discovery-learning activity that can help students induce the rules for placing the decimal point in a product. To really understand what is involved in this sequence and to perhaps deepen your own understanding of decimal multiplication, work through the parts below. It may be helpful to do so with your group or class. For the questions below, assume that large cubes, flats, longs, and cubes but not chips (tenths of a cube) are available.

Part I: Using Base-Ten Blocks to Devise Concrete Models of Decimal Multiplication Problems

1. Illustrate how you could use base-ten blocks to solve the *groups-of* problems below.

   ■ **Problem A: Ardent Exerciser.** For exercise, Zenobia liked to walk $2\frac{1}{2}$ miles a day. One day her kitten got loose and she chased it five times around the path surrounding her neighborhood. If the path was .8 miles around, how far did Zenobia chase her kitten and was this far enough to qualify for her daily walk?

   ■ **Problem B: Flea Powder.** Mary used five-tenths of the 0.2 liters of flea powder she had on hand to dust a very itchy Ruffus. How much of a liter did Mary use on her dog?

   ■ **Problem C: Anxious Father.** While waiting for his wife to give birth to their first child, Mr. Ngwalla paced the hallway surrounding the maternity ward 3.5 times. If this hallway was 0.2 miles around, how far did Mr. Ngwalla pace?

2. Illustrate how you could use base-ten blocks to solve the following *area* problems:

   ■ **Problem D: Crafted Desk**. Mrs. Echeverriarza built a desk 1.5 meters long by 1.2 meters wide. What was the area of the desk top?

   ■ **Problem E: Cover Up.** Ruffus scratched the dining room table while attempting to retrieve leftovers. To cover the scratched surface, Mary made a table mat 0.7 meters long by 0.2 meters wide. What area did Mary's table mat cover?

Part II: Connecting Symbolic Expression to Meaningful Analogies and Concrete Models

This part is particularly important for you to work through because it is not enough to know that base-ten blocks can be used to model decimal multiplication. A teacher must know how to use the blocks to make such models and why. With the aid of your group, try answering the following questions. Assume that you have available large cubes, flats, longs, and cubes but not chips (tenths of a cube).

1. (a) Illustrate how base-ten blocks could be used to model a *groups-of* interpretation of 3 x 0.2. (b) Do the same for an *area* interpretation.

2. Use base-ten blocks to model (a) a *groups-of* and (b) an *area* meaning of 0.3 x 2. This might necessitate redefining what block is called the unit. Illustrate your models.

3. Use base-ten blocks to model (a) a *groups-of* and (b) an *area* meaning of 0.3 x 0.2. Consider what block should be called the unit. Illustrate your model of 0.3 x 0.2.

4. (a) Would it be possible to use base-ten blocks to model a *groups-of* meaning of 0.3 x 0.02? Why or why not? (b) Would it be possible to use them to model an *area* interpretation of 0.3 x 0.02? Why or why not? (c) Illustrate any possible models of 0.3 x 0.02.

Investigation 11.6 continued

5. (a) Would it be possible to use base-ten blocks to model a *groups-of* interpretation of 0.3 x 0.002? Why or why not? (b) Would it be possible to use them to model an *area* interpretation of 0.3 x 0.002? Why or why not? (c) Illustrate any possible models of 0.3 x 0.002.

6. Miss Brill asked her class to make a *groups-of* model for the expression .01 x .3 with base-ten blocks. Evaluate each of the following models. Explain why the model is correct or not.

a. Jasper

   Long = .1,
   so .3 = 3 longs

   cube = .01

   Because 3 longs (.3) have 30 cubes (.01), the answer is 30

b. Jack

   Flat = .1, so .3 = 3 flats
   Long = .01, so .01 = 1 long
   Cube = .001

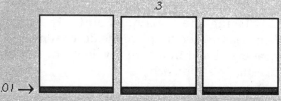

   Because there is 1 long for each of 3 flats, the answer = 3 longs or .03

c. Dianne

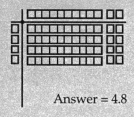

   If a long = .01, then three-tenths of a long = 3 cubes = .003

7. Adrienne created the area model of 1.2 x 0.4 shown to the right. Evaluate her model and answer. Do each make sense? Why or why not?

   Answer = 4.8

8. Miss Brill thought it would be a good idea to have her class concretely model multiplication expressions involving decimals. She asked her class to construct a *groups-of* model for the

following expressions with base-ten blocks: (a) .3 x .04 (.3 groups of .04) and (b) .05 x .3 (.05 groups of .3). Miss Brill realized that she had better try modeling these problems with blocks herself so that she would know how to guide her students' efforts. In working out the answers, she discovered her initial solution required regrouping. Illustrate a concrete model for each expression and its ungrouped and regrouped solution. What do these two answers illustrate about how we can think about decimals?

9. Miss Brill asked her class to use base-ten blocks to represent an *area* meaning of 1.2 x 3.4. (a) Illustrate how base-ten blocks could represent an *area* meaning of 1.2 x 3.4. (b) The written algorithm is shown to the right. What parallels exist between the expanded partial products of this algorithm and the area model?

   3.4
   x1.2
   .08 ⎫
   .6   ⎬ partial
   .4   ⎭ products
   3.
   4.08

10. Judi asked how 1.02 x 2.4 could be represented with base-ten blocks. Assuming that only large cubes, flats, longs, and cubes were available, would it be possible to model (a) a *groups-of* meaning of this expression and (b) an *area* meaning? Why or why not? If so, illustrate.

Part III: Discovering the Rule for Placing the Decimal Point in a Product

1. Put yourself in the place of a child who does not know the decimal multiplication algorithm or the rule for placing the decimal point in the product. Use a *groups-of* interpretation of multiplication to reason out the answers to the following expressions and to determine the position of the decimal point.

   (a) 0.1 x 4   (b) 0.5 x 4   (c) 0.01 x 4

   (d) 1 x 0.8   (e) 0.1 x 0.8   (f) 0.01 x 0.8

   (g) 1.5 x 4   (h) 1.5 x 0.4   (i) 1.5 x 0.04

2. How might answering Question 1 above help children discover the rule for noting where the decimal goes in the product of decimal multiplication such 0.3 x 0.02.

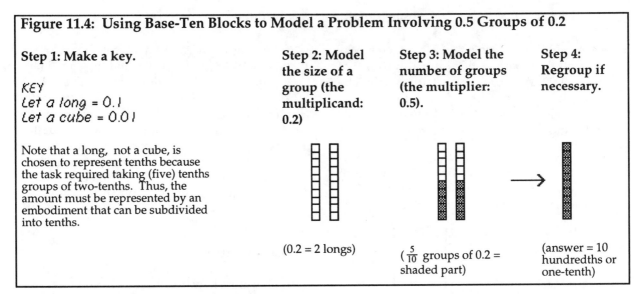

Figure 11.4: Using Base-Ten Blocks to Model a Problem Involving 0.5 Groups of 0.2

Step 1: Make a key.

KEY
Let a long = 0.1
Let a cube = 0.01

Note that a long, not a cube, is chosen to represent tenths because the task required taking (five) tenths groups of two-tenths. Thus, the amount must be represented by an embodiment that can be subdivided into tenths.

Step 2: Model the size of a group (the multiplicand: 0.2)

(0.2 = 2 longs)

Step 3: Model the number of groups (the multiplier: 0.5).

($\frac{5}{10}$ groups of 0.2 = shaded part)

Step 4: Regroup if necessary.

(answer = 10 hundredths or one-tenth)

• **Area model.** Figure 11.5 illustrates how base-ten blocks can be used to model Problem E (*Cover Up*) on page 11-16 of Investigation 11.6. An area model can help children see why multiplying two decimals less than one has a different effect than multiplying two whole numbers.

↪ **During the connecting and symbolic phases, encourage students to think explicitly in terms of a meaningful analogy when working with manipulatives** (see, e.g., Part II on pages 11-16 and 11-17 of Investigation 11.6) Using manipulatives alone may not be sufficient for children to comprehend the arithmetic they are doing or to get the correct answer. Questions 5 and 6 in Part II of Investigation 11.6 illustrate this problem. Jack, for example, apparently did not recognize that the .01 in the expression .01 x .3 is a fraction (one-hundredth group) of the .3, not the whole that .3 is a fraction of. Such an error is common among elementary students (and preservice teachers) who do not explicitly think in terms of the *groups-of* analogy and what each number in an expression represents. Students' use of manipulatives should be conceptually guided.

Placing the Decimal Point. To help students learn where to place the decimal point in a meaningful and thought-provoking way, use the investigative approach.

↪ **Encourage the use of** *groups-of* **interpretation to reason out and rediscover the rule for placing the decimal point when multiplying decimals** (see, e.g., Question 1 in Part III on page 11-17 of Investigation 11.6).

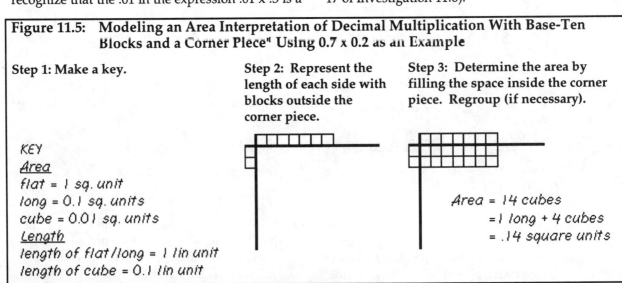

Figure 11.5: Modeling an Area Interpretation of Decimal Multiplication With Base-Ten Blocks and a Corner Piece" Using 0.7 x 0.2 as an Example

Step 1: Make a key.

KEY
Area
flat = 1 sq. unit
long = 0.1 sq. units
cube = 0.01 sq. units
Length
length of flat/long = 1 lin unit
length of cube = 0.1 lin unit

Step 2: Represent the length of each side with blocks outside the corner piece.

Step 3: Determine the area by filling the space inside the corner piece. Regroup (if necessary).

Area = 14 cubes
= 1 long + 4 cubes
= .14 square units

Meaningful Instruction of Decimal Division

This section addresses division of a decimal by a whole number and then division by a decimal.

☞ Consider Investigations 11.7 (page 11-20) and 11.8 (pages 11-21 to 11-24).

Division of a Decimal by a Whole Number. Similar to decimal multiplication, division of a decimal by a whole number can serve as the transition from whole-number division to division by a decimal.

• **Conceptual phase.** Division by a whole number can be readily interpreted in terms of a divvy-up (or a measure-out) meaning.

☞ Division of a decimal by a whole number can be introduced by encouraging children to estimate the quotient of divvy-up (or measure-out) situations or word problems (e.g., "Question 1 in Investigation 11.7). Problem situations involving money (e.g., Problem A and B in Investigation 11.7) are highly familiar to children and a good place to start. (If estimating division with money is too difficult for a child, try simpler situations involving tenths only.) Later, estimating the quotient of symbolic expressions can be introduced. If children have difficulty with this task, encourage them to think in terms of a divvy-up or measure-out model of division. For example, confronted with the task of $3\overline{)105.50}$, Arianne's teacher encouraged her to think of it as $105.50 shared fairly among three people. The fourth-grader then responded, "Well $25 would be [about what] four people [would get]. The girls' group then quickly concluded the answer had to be about $35.

☞ Next, encourage children to determine exact products by using an informal strategy and concrete manipulatives (e.g., Question 2 of Investigation 11.7). More specifically, they can use their informal divvying-up strategy to solve divvy-up problems or repeated subtraction strategy to solve measure-out problems.

• **Connecting phase.** After children can solve decimal-division-by-a-whole-number problems using informal strategies, they are ready to reinvent the distributive algorithm.

☞ Encourage children to reinvent the distributive algorithm for decimal division by challenging them to summarize their concrete divvying-up strategy as a written procedure (see, e.g., Question 3 of Investigation 11.7 on page 11-20). This essentially involves translating each step of a concrete (e.g., base-ten block) procedure into a parallel step with written numbers. Figure 11.6 (on page 11-25) illustrates this linking process using a money analogy.

☞ Encourage students to reflect on the links between the distributive algorithm for decimals and their familiar divvying-up strategy. This can be achieved by asking them to justify explicitly each step in the algorithm—indicate explicitly how it parallels a step in their concrete divvying-up strategy (see, e.g., Question 4 on page 11-20 of Investigation 11.7).

☞ Encourage children to consider explicitly what remainders in decimal division represent and how they can be represented. Pose problems or expressions that do not come out evenly, (e.g., Question 5 on page 11-20 of Investigation 11.7). By thinking in terms of a divvy-up meaning (see Figure 11.7), children should recognize that the remainder cannot be treated the same as it was in whole-number division (Susan's error in Question 6 of Investigation 11.7). Nor can the remainder simply be recorded in the next place to the right in the quotient (Michelle's error in Question 6 of Investigation 11.7). (Text continued on page 11-26.)

Figure 11.7: Decimal Division Remainders

```
      T O tth
        3 . 2
   4)1 3 . 1
   - 1 2
       1 1
      - 8
        3
```

T = tens place
O = ones place
tth = tenths place

Note that the remainder is *three tenths* (3.2 r .3), not *three* (3.2 r 3) or *three hundredths* (3.23).

Questions for Reflection

1. When decimal division does not come out evenly, such as with the expression above, what options does a student have?

2. Consider the situations in which each of these options would make the most sense.

⌣ Investigation 11.7: Dividing a Decimal by a Whole Number

◆ Constructing a conceptual basis for dividing a decimal by a whole number
◆ 3-8 ◆ Any number

Dividing a decimal by a whole number is relatively easy for students to understand and, thus, a logical place to start instruction on decimal division. The following questions and tasks are intended to help students to build on their existing knowledge. Complete them yourself and share your answers with your group or class.

1. Read the following word problems and estimate the answers of each. Indicate an upper and lower amount that would be reasonable.

   ■ **Problem A: Costly Rejection**. Fernández, Giorgio, and Homer were playing basketball. In a spectacular rejection, Giorgio, sent the ball crashing through a nearby house window. The window cost $46.17 to replace. Fernandez and Homer decided to help Giorgio with the cost. If the $46.17 was split evenly three ways, how much did each boy have to pay?

   ■ **Problem B: Antique Sale.** The Hansen quadruplets wanted money for their vacation trip. Their mother agreed that if they cleaned out all the old stuff stored in the basement, they could keep whatever they made in a garage sale. The old stuff sold for a total of $131.92. If this was shared fairly among the four Hansen children, how much would each quadruplet get?

2. (a) Problems A and B above are what type division problem? (b) Illustrate how base-ten blocks or play money could be used to solve each of these problems concretely and intuitively.

3. (a) Using the format $3\overline{)46.17}$, illustrate with numbers each step of the concrete solution procedure you devised in Question 2b to solve Problem A. (b) Using the format $4\overline{)131.92}$, illustrate with numbers each step of the concrete solution procedure you devised in Question 2b to solve Problem B.

4. With the help of your teacher, list the steps of the distributive long-division algorithm and describe how each step parallels a step in the concrete models you devised for Question 2.

5. Illustrate how base-ten blocks could be used to model the long division of the following expressions: (a) $3\overline{)46.18}$, (b) $5\overline{)243.17}$, and (c) $3\overline{)139.6}$

6. (a) For Expression 5c above, what problem did you encounter and what do you suspect the solution is? (b) For Expression 5c, Jodi, Leah, Michelle, and Susan disagreed about how to represent the remainder. Jodi claimed that the answer should be 46.5 r .1, Leah thought it should be 46.5 r .01, Michelle argued that 46.51 was correct, and Susan favored 46.5 r 1. Based on your model with base-ten blocks, who was correct and why? (c) If the remainder format or rounding is not used, what is the answer to Expression 5c?

✐ 7. Write your own divvy-up and measure-out word problems involving the division of a decimal by a whole number. Share your problems with your group and evaluate them. Indicate which share the same conceptual basis as the distributive algorithm. Illustrate how a child could solve those problems intuitively with base-ten blocks and how the steps of the concrete procedure parallel the distributive algorithm.

☙ Investigation 11.8: Dividing by a Nonunit Decimal

◆ Helping students construct an understanding of division by a decimal ◆ 5-8 ◆ Any number

This investigation outlines a sequence of explorations that can provide a basis for the meaningful instruction of dividing by a nonunit decimal. Part I illustrates qualitative-reasoning and estimating tasks that can serve to introduce dividing by a decimal. Part II asks students to consider how base-ten blocks could be used to devise an intuitive strategy for problems involving division by a decimal. The aim of Part III is to connect a meaningful analogy and concrete models to symbolic expressions. Part IV considers how students can be helped to reinvent the formal algorithm for dividing by a decimal. To really understand what is involved in the meaningful instruction of division by a nonunit decimal and to perhaps deepen your own understanding of it, try the following sequence of activities yourself. Working with others may be helpful.

Part I: Qualitative Reasoning and Estimation

1. (a) Ms. Socrates wanted to relate division with decimals to word problems to make the new topic more meaningful. What type of word problem(s) make(s) sense for division by a decimal less than one (e.g., $1.8 \div 0.3$)? (b) What type of word problem(s) make(s) sense for division by a decimal larger than one (e.g., $4.8 \div 2.5$)? Hint: Consider the analogous situations with fractions.

2. For each of the following word problems gauge whether the answer (quotient) will be larger or smaller than the starting amount (dividend).

   ■ **Problem A: Pile of Quarters.** Mrs. Osero had $52.50 worth of quarters. If she made piles worth $5 each, how many piles did she make?

   ■ **Problem B: Halloween Treats.** Mrs. Osero had $52.50 in quarters. If she made up Halloween treats with $.75 each, how many treats could she make up?

   ■ **Problem C: Halloween Treats Retreated.** Sure that only a few children would visit and feeling generous, Mr. Osero increased the treat. With $52.50, how many treats could Mr. Osero make if each treat was $1.75?

3. In the equations below, a ■ covers a digit larger than 1 (i.e., a digit ranging from 2 to 9). (a) In each of the following cases, is the quotient smaller or larger than dividend or undeterminable? Briefly explain why. Hint: Consider an appropriate problem context or an analogous situation with fractions. (b) How would your answers change if ■ could equal any digit from 0 to 9?

Case	Dividend		Divisor		Quotient
A.	■	÷	■	=	?
B.	0.■	÷	■	=	?
C.	■.■	÷	■	=	?
D.	■	÷	0.■	=	?
E.	0.■	÷	0.■	=	?
F.	■.■	÷	0.■	=	?
G.	■	÷	■.■	=	?
H.	0.■	÷	■.■	=	?
I.	■.■	÷	■.■	=	?

4. Within a minute, estimate the answer to the following expressions:

   (a) $3.8 \div 0.2$　　(b) $4.7 \div 0.09$　　(c) $19.6 \div 0.47$　　(d) $6.2 \div 1.89$　　(e) $2.1 \div 3.02$

   What strategy or strategies did you use? Share them with your group or class. Why might a student have difficulty making reasonable estimates?

Investigation 11.8 continued

Part II: Using Base-Ten Blocks to Devise Concrete Models of Division by a Decimal

For the questions below, assume that large cubes, flats, longs, and cubes but not chips (tenths of a cube) are available.

1. (a) What type of division word problem is Problem D below? (b) What informal strategy do children frequently use to solve this type of division problem? (c) Illustrate how you could use base-ten blocks to model this meaning of division and this informal strategy.

   ■ **Problem D: Water Rationing.** To help his scouts understand that national resources such as water are not unlimited and need to be conserved, Mr. Nagle rationed the water on their campout. If a water bottle had 0.8 gallons of water left and each scout was supposed to get 0.2 gallons, the water bottle would provide water for how many Scouts.

2. For each problem below, (a) identify the type of division problem represented and (b) show how you could use to solve it informally.

   ■ **Problem E: Water Rationing Revisited.** A water bottle containing 1.8 gallons would serve how many scouts if each got 0.3 gallons of water?

   ■ **Problem F: Pool Maintenance.** The alkalinity level in Mr. Leavitt's pool was extremely high. To lower the pH, he had to add muriatic acid. If Mr. Leavitt had to add 1.5 gallons of muriatic acid and was instructed to add 0.3 gallons of acid a day, how many days did he have to add acid to his pool?

   ■ **Problem G: Desk Width.** If a desk has an area of 1.2 square meters and a length of 0.6 meters, how wide is the desk? (✚ Hint: Consider how students could build on their knowledge of an area model of decimal multiplication.)

✎ 3. Write a measure-out, a rate, and an area problem involving decimal division. Share them with your group. Evaluate the problems and consider how you could use base-ten blocks to solve them.

4. (a) After solving Problem E above, Jenn asked, "What if this measure-out problem involved an amount of 1.2 gallons and each share was .15 gallons?" (b) Emily added, "What if it involved an amount of 1.9 gallons and each share was supposed to be 0.3 gallons?" In each of these cases, show how base-ten blocks could be used to determine the number of shares.

Part III: Modeling Symbolic Decimal Division with Base-Ten Blocks

This investigation asks students to interpret symbolic decimal-division expressions and to find their quotients by applying what they have learned in the conceptual phase. It also illustrates some of the pitfalls students of all ages and teachers can fall into when relating symbolic decimal division to concrete models. For the questions below, assume that large cubes, flats, longs, and cubes but not chips (one-tenths of a cube) are available.

1. Miss Brill wrote $0.9 \div 0.3 = ?$ on the chalkboard and recommended using base-ten blocks to determine the answer. Rodney spoke for many of the students when he asked, "How in the world can we do that?" (a) Miss Brill, as she was now apt to do, responded to Rodney's questions with a question, "What meaning of division might it be helpful to consider?" (b) Now use the base-ten blocks to model $0.9 \div 0.3$ in terms of that meaning.

2. LeMar suggested that as with fractions, it might be helpful to consider a measure-out interpretation. "So," continued Miss Brill, "how could you use the base-ten blocks to model a measure-out meaning of $0.9 \div 0.3$?"

Investigation 11.8 continued

(a) With a measure-out interpretation of 0.9 ÷ 0.3, what does the 0.9 represent? What does the 0.3 represent? What does the quotient 3 represent? (b) To represent 0.9, does it matter what blocks you let equal a tenth? (c) If you have not done so already, illustrate how you could use base-ten blocks to model a measure-out meaning of 0.9 ÷ 0.3 = 3. (d) How does the model and measure-out interpretation make clear why the answer is the whole number 3?

3. Miss Brill then asked the class to use the base-ten blocks to model a measure-out meaning of 2.1 ÷ 0.3. (a) Other than the fact that you need two types of blocks to represent the dividend 2.1, how is constructing this model different from that for 0.8 ÷ 0.2? Was Miss Brill wise in introducing expressions such as 2.1 ÷ 0.3 after expressions such as 0.8 ÷ 0.2 or would it have been easier to introduce expressions such as 2.1 ÷ 0.3 first? (b) Illustrate your model.

4. Judi, who always seemed to be stretching her knowledge, asked how using base-ten blocks could be used to solve expressions with hundredths. Miss Brill posed the expression 0.42 ÷ 0.06 = ? Illustrate how base-ten blocks could be used to construct a measure-out model of 0.42 ÷ 0.06.

5. a. Using a flat to represent 1, a long to represent 0.1, and a cube to represent 0.01, Judi constructed a measure-out model for the expression .28 ÷ .08. After working out the answer with manipulatives, she had four cubes leftover and recorded her answer as 3.4. Is her answer correct? Why or why not? Hint: Consider what the quotient represents in a measure-out interpretation. The four remaining cubes represent a fraction of what?

   b. Illustrate how base-ten blocks could be used to model a measure-out meaning of .30 ÷ .12.

   c. Without thinking, Miss Brill asked the class to use base-ten blocks to represent a measure-out meaning of 2.52 ÷ 1.4. The students seemed stymied by this task. Why? Can you think of how the blocks could be used to determine the quotient?

6. Judi's group asked for another problem. Miss Brill wrote 0.3 ÷ 0.6 and 1.2 ÷ 2.4 on the board and instructed the class to model a measure-out interpretation of these expressions. Judi gasped, "How can we, the divisor is bigger than the dividend?" Is it possible to model this problem as Miss Brill requested or not? Justify your answer.

7. Miss Brill asked the class to pose a problem. LeMar suggested 25.335 ÷ 2.4, and Darrin suggested 1.444 ÷ 2.5. The class discovered that they could not use base-ten blocks to determine an exact answer for either expression. How might Miss Brill have foreseen this?

8. Remembering their work with whole-number division, Judi asked if an area interpretation might also be useful for thinking about division with decimals. Illustrate how base-ten blocks could be used to model an area meaning for 2.1 ÷ 0.3.

9. a. In an area model of 2.1 ÷ 0.3, what does the dividend 2.1 represent? What does the divisor 0.3 represent? What does the quotient 7 represent?

   b. Paige recommended letting a flat equal 1. What does Paige need to clarify and why?

   c. If a flat equals 1 square unit, what equals 0.1 square units and 0.01 square units?

   d. If a flat equals 1 square unit, what equals 1 linear unit? What represents 0.1 linear units?

   e. To model an area meaning of 2.1 ÷ 0.3, what blocks do you need to represent the dividend 2.1?

   f. Illustrate how base-ten blocks can be used to determine the quotient of 2.1 ÷ 0.3.

   g. Stephen recommended letting the large cube equal one square unit. Would this be a good idea? Why or why not?

Investigation 11.8 continued

10. The class appeared to understand the area analogy until Michelle asked how would you make an area model of 0.8 ÷ 0.2. Judi confidently volunteered to solve the expression and wrote her solution on the chalkboard. Judi announced proudly, "The unknown side is four-tenths."

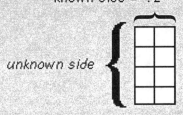

Violet punched .8 ÷ .2 into her calculator and found that the answer was 4, not 0.4. Confusion reigned. Miss Brill, perplexed by the conflicting answers, announced, "Let's see if we can reason this out. If a flat represents 0.1 square unit, what represents a length of 0.1 units?"

Judi answered, "The side of a flat."

(a) Is Judi correct or not; would the length of a flat be equal to 0.1 linear units? Why or why not? (b) To determine the answer of 0.8 ÷ 0.2, what should a flat represent? Why? (c) With an area model, can just any block (the large cube, flat, long, or small cube) represent 1 square unit?

11. (a) Illustrate an area model of 1.3 ÷ 0.4. (b) How could more advanced students use these leftover blocks to determine the quotient of 1.3 ÷ 0.4?

12. Without reflecting, Miss Brill asked the class to use base-ten blocks to model an area meaning for the following expressions: (A) 2.7 ÷ 5.4, (B) 2.42 ÷ 0.8, (C) 1.44 ÷ 2.5, (D) 4.5 ÷ 1.25, (E) 2.727 ÷ 0.9, and (F) 0.72 ÷ 0.012. Assuming that only large cubes, flats, longs, and cubes are available, (a) which can be modeled without interpolation? (Interpolation would involve comparing the leftover blocks with the total number of blocks needed to complete the row—in effect, determining what fraction of a complete side could be made with the leftover blocks.) Illustrate how. (b) Which of the expressions above require interpolation? Illustrate how. (c) Which of the expressions above *cannot* be represented with an area model using base-ten blocks? Why?

13. (a) Without interpolating, could base-ten blocks be used to create a measure-out model and determine the quotient for which expressions listed in Question 12? Illustrate how. (b) With interpolating, base-ten blocks could be used to create a measure-out model and determine the quotient for which expression in Question 12? Illustrate how.

Part IV: Reinventing a Formal Algorithm for Dividing by a Decimal

According to the syllabus, the next topic Miss Brill was supposed to teach was the division-by-a-decimal algorithm. Mrs. MeChokemchild recommended telling students the algorithm and then giving them plenty of practice to prevent forgetting. Ms. Socrates suggested, "Why not challenge students to invent the algorithm themselves? Miss Brill—still amazed by the differences in her colleagues approach to instruction—listened as Ms. Socrates guided her in how to use an investigative approach.

1. Assume you did not know the algorithm for dividing by a decimal. What problem-solving heuristic might be useful in figuring out an algorithm to solve an expression such as following expression:

   $0.3\overline{)20.1}$

2. Once Miss Brill's class figured out that they needed to move the decimal to the right to convert 0.3 into a whole number and then do the same for the dividend (see the figure to the right), Andy asked, "Why can you just move the decimal point in the division and the dividend?" How would you answer Andy's question?

   $0_\times3.\overline{)20_\times1.}$

3. (a) What are the advantages and disadvantages of Mrs. MeChokemchild's approach? (b) What are the advantages and disadvantages of Ms. Socrates' approach?

11-25

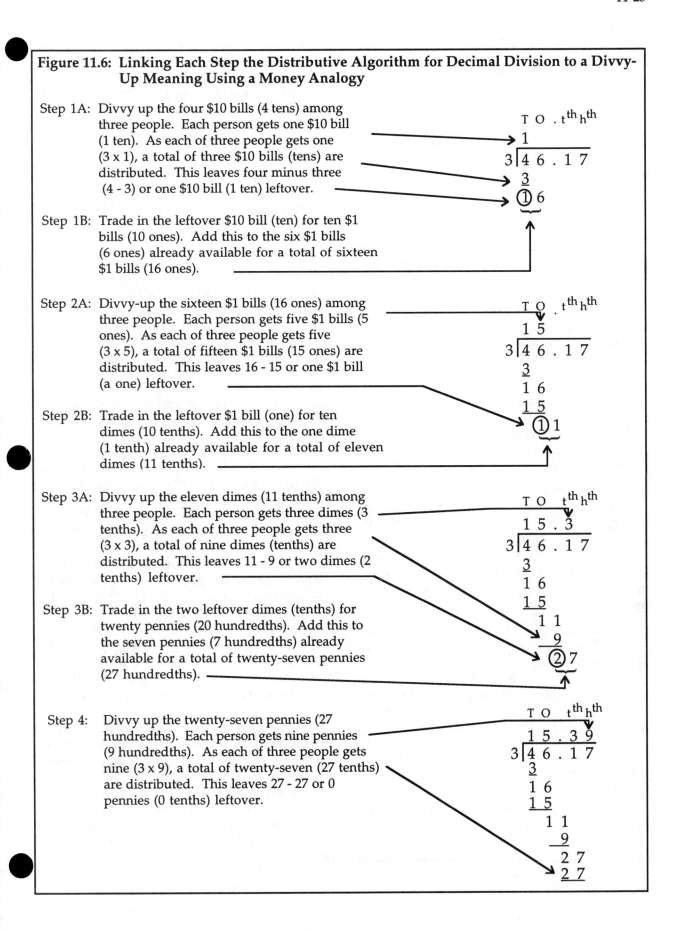

Figure 11.6: Linking Each Step the Distributive Algorithm for Decimal Division to a Divvy-Up Meaning Using a Money Analogy

Step 1A: Divvy up the four $10 bills (4 tens) among three people. Each person gets one $10 bill (1 ten). As each of three people gets one (3 x 1), a total of three $10 bills (tens) are distributed. This leaves four minus three (4 - 3) or one $10 bill (1 ten) leftover.

Step 1B: Trade in the leftover $10 bill (ten) for ten $1 bills (10 ones). Add this to the six $1 bills (6 ones) already available for a total of sixteen $1 bills (16 ones).

Step 2A: Divvy-up the sixteen $1 bills (16 ones) among three people. Each person gets five $1 bills (5 ones). As each of three people gets five (3 x 5), a total of fifteen $1 bills (15 ones) are distributed. This leaves 16 - 15 or one $1 bill (a one) leftover.

Step 2B: Trade in the leftover $1 bill (one) for ten dimes (10 tenths). Add this to the one dime (1 tenth) already available for a total of eleven dimes (11 tenths).

Step 3A: Divvy up the eleven dimes (11 tenths) among three people. Each person gets three dimes (3 tenths). As each of three people gets three (3 x 3), a total of nine dimes (tenths) are distributed. This leaves 11 - 9 or two dimes (2 tenths) leftover.

Step 3B: Trade in the two leftover dimes (tenths) for twenty pennies (20 hundredths). Add this to the seven pennies (7 hundredths) already available for a total of twenty-seven pennies (27 hundredths).

Step 4: Divvy up the twenty-seven pennies (27 hundredths). Each person gets nine pennies (9 hundredths). As each of three people gets nine (3 x 9), a total of twenty-seven (27 tenths) are distributed. This leaves 27 - 27 or 0 pennies (0 tenths) leftover.

Encourage children to consider what they can do if decimal division does not come out evenly. One option is to continue for a few more places to see if it might terminate. Another option is round off the answer. Yet another is to record the decimal remainder. Help children understand in what situations each of these options would make the greatest sense. One way to accomplish this would be to pose a question such as Question 2 of Investigation 11.3 (on page 11-11).

Division by a Decimal. Ms. Socrates had recommended introducing division by a decimal with estimation activities. So, Miss Brill devised a game where she presented expressions such as 0.8 ÷ 0.2, 0.27 ÷ 0.03, 3.8 ÷ 0.2, and 6.2 ÷ 0.89 and teams of students had to record their estimate on miniature slates within 15 seconds. Despite the class' initial enthusiasm, it soon became clear that most estimates were not even in the right direction (i.e., larger than the dividend). The class soon lost interest in the activity.

Miss Brill was disappointed that her lesson flopped. "I started with estimation as you suggested," she later complained to Ms. Socrates. "Moreover, I tried to make the lesson interesting by putting it in the context of a game. What went wrong?"

Why did Miss Brill's lesson bomb? "The estimation task required by the game," began Ms. Socrates as diplomatically as she could, "requires a conceptual foundation. They need to relate symbolism such as this (pointing to the 0.8 ÷ 0.2 card) to something meaningful in order to make an estimate of its quotient."

• **Conceptual basis for dividing by a decimal.** "I rushed too quickly into using symbolic math again," surmised Miss Brill. "I know, I know. I should have begun with problems and then related the symbolism to these problem situations. *But what kind of problem situations would lend themselves to division by a decimal?*" asked Miss Brill.

"What did you discover about the analogous situation of dividing by a fraction?" prompted Ms. Socrates.

"A divvy-up interpretation doesn't make much sense," recalled Miss Brill. "Perhaps that explains much of the confusion. Many of my students were trying to interpret the symbolism in terms of a divvy-up meaning, and it didn't make sense to them."

☞ **As with division by a fraction, the measure-out model provides one useful analogy for making sense of division by a decimal** (see, e.g., Figure 11.8 on the next page). Facilitating decimal division provides another reason for ensuring that children become familiar with this interpretation early in the context of whole-number division.

• **Qualitative reasoning and estimation.** As Ms. Socrates recommended to Miss Brill, instruction on division by a decimal should begin with qualitative reasoning and estimation.

☞ **Encourage children to consider the general direction of the quotient.** During the conceptual phase, encourage children to analyze measure-out problems of all sorts (i.e., a whole number divided by a whole number, a nonunit decimal divided by a whole number, a whole number divided by a nonunit decimal, and a nonunit decimal divided by a nonunit decimal), and to note explicitly whether the answer (quotient) will be larger or smaller than the starting amount (dividend) and why (see, e.g., Question 2 in Part I on page 11-21 of Investigation 11.8).

Note that measure-out situations can help children see why division by a decimal less than one results in an answer larger than the dividend. For example, if a silversmith has 0.8 pounds of silver and each silver decoration requires 0.2 pounds of silver, then clearly he has enough for 4 decorations. Even if the silversmith had only 0.1 pounds of silver, he would have enough for half of a decoration. During the connecting phase, tasks such as Question 3 in Part I of Investigation 11.8 can be posed. At both the conceptual and connecting levels, linking decimal division to measure-out situations involving money can be particularly helpful in predicting the direction of an answer (see Box 11.2 on the next page).

☞ **For all phases of instruction, encourage children to estimate the quotients of measure-out problems or expressions.** During the conceptual phase and even before children use concrete models to determine exact answers, encourage them to estimate the answers to measure-out problems such as Problem B in Investigation 11.8 (page 11-21). During the connecting phase, encourage pupils to relate symbolic expressions such as those in Question 4 in Part I on page 11-21 of Investigation 11.8 to a measure-out meaning and esti-

Figure 11.8: Using Base-Ten Blocks to Model Measure-Out Problems Involving Decimal Division

Situation: If each Scout is supposed to get 0.2 gallons of water and there is a total of 0.8 gallons available, how many scouts can receive a share of water?

Step 1: Make a key.

Let a long = 1 gallon
    cube = 0.1 gallon

Note that a key may need to be revised once a problem is started

Step 2: Represent the amount (0.8 gallons).

Amount = 0.8 gal.

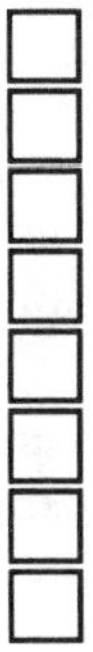

Step 3: Represent the size of each share.

Amount = 0.8 gal

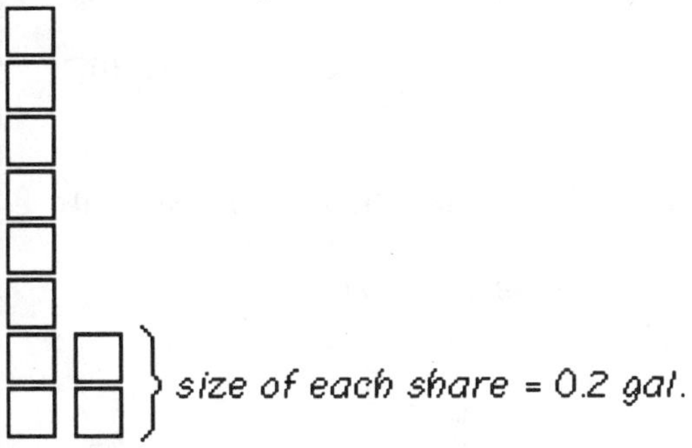

} size of each share = 0.2 gal.

Step 4: Determine the number of shares that fit into the amount.

Amount = 0.8 gal.

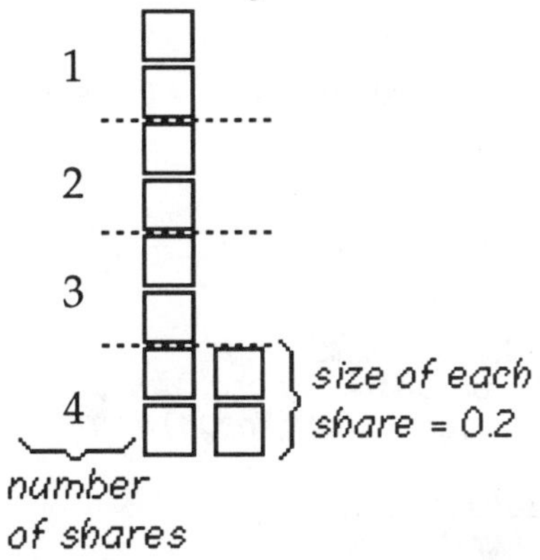

1

2

3

4

} size of each share = 0.2

number of shares

Box 11.2: Relating Division by a Decimal to Situations that Involve Measuring Out Money[†]

$1.00 \div 0.50 \rightarrow$ How many half dollars in a dollar?	$.50 \div 0.05 \rightarrow$ How many nickels in a half dollar?
$1.00 \div 0.25 \rightarrow$ How many quarters in a dollar?	$.50 \div 0.01 \rightarrow$ How many pennies in a half dollar?
$1.00 \div 0.10 \rightarrow$ How many dimes in a dollar?	$.25 \div 0.05 \rightarrow$ How many nickels in a quarter?
$1.00 \div 0.05 \rightarrow$ How many nickels in a dollar?	$.25 \div 0.01 \rightarrow$ How many pennies in a quarter?
$1.00 \div 0.01 \rightarrow$ How many pennies in a dollar?	$.10 \div 0.05 \rightarrow$ How many nickels in a dime?
$.50 \div 0.25 \rightarrow$ How many quarters in a half dollar?	$.10 \div 0.01 \rightarrow$ How many pennies in a dime?
$.50 \div 0.10 \rightarrow$ How many dimes in a half dollar?	$.05 \div 0.01 \rightarrow$ How many pennies in a nickel?

[†] Based on a suggestion by Graeber and Tanenhaus (1993).

---

mate answers. Note that estimation strategies used for fractions can also apply to decimals. For $19.6 \div 0.47$, for example, a child could round off 19.6 to 20 and 0.47 to 0.5 and think how many halves can 20 wholes make? During the symbolic phase, estimation can be used as a way of monitoring and checking written work.

• **Concrete models.** In addition to a measure-out model, rate and area analogies are other ways division by a decimal can be connected to real-world situations and, thus, made comprehensible. Below we discuss how children can use base-ten blocks to solve these three types of problems concretely. Note that these analogies and models apply equally well to situations or problems involving the division of a decimal by a whole number.

1. *Measure-out model.* Figure 11.8 (page 11-27) illustrates a four-step process that involves using an informal strategy to solve measure-out problems such as Problems D and E on page 11-22 of Investigation 11.8.

2. *Rate model.* For rate problems such as Problem F on page 11-22 of Investigation 11.8, the same concrete model as that illustrated in Figure 11.8 can be used.

3. *Area model.* Figure 11.9 illustrates how base-ten blocks can be used to solve area problems such as Problem G on page 11-22 of Investigation 11.8.

☞ **During the connecting phase, encourage children to interpret symbolic expressions such as 0.9 ÷ 0.3 in terms of a measure-out or an area meaning and to solve them by using base-ten blocks.** As Part III of Investigation 11.8 (pages 11-22 and 11-23) illustrates, modeling some expressions is challenging and requires the thoughtful application of a measure-out or an area analogy.

• **The division-by-a-decimal algorithm.** As Part IV of Investigation 11.8 (page 11-24) suggests, children can be challenged to reinvent the algorithms themselves. In reflecting on what heuristics might be useful, some students might recognize

---

Figure 11.9: Using Base-Ten Blocks to Model an Area Problem Involving Decimal Division

Situation: If the area of a rectangle is 1.8 square meters and the length is 0.6 meters, what is the width?

Step 1: Draw up a key.

Key
Use to Draw Sides:
length of a flat (or long = 1 (linear unit)
length of a small cube = 0.1 (linear) unit

Use to Show Area:
flat = 1 square unit
long = 0.1 square units
cube = 0.01 square units

Step 2. Draw out the length of the known side.

length = 0.6 m

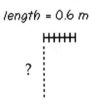

Step 3: Take blocks equal to the area (1.8 square units): 1 flat and 8 longs.

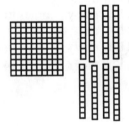

Step 4: Arrange the blocks so that they have a length of 0.6 (6 cubes long). Trade in blocks as necessary (i.e., trade in a flat for 10 longs).

length = 0.6 m

The unknown side is the length of 3 longs, which = 3 linear units

that they can translate an unfamiliar task into a familiar one by moving the decimal of the divisor to the right and making it a whole number. They may also recognize that to create an equivalent expression, the decimal point in the dividend needs to be moved to the right the same number of spaces. In effect, this converts division-by-a-decimal situation into a division-by-a-whole-number situation. The quotient can now be determined using the distributive algorithm (see Figure 11.6 on page 11-25).

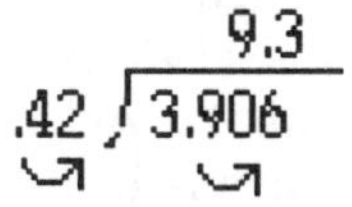

$$.42 \overline{)3.906} = 9.3$$

Why can you move the point in the decimal-division algorithm? Ideally, students would be encouraged to justify this procedure in their own way. An informal proof could involve modeling a measure-out interpretation of, say, 20.1 ÷ 0.3 and 210 ÷ 3 with base-ten blocks. In each case, the number of shares would be 67. More formally, students could build on their connection between division and fractions and their understanding of how to find equivalent fractions (see Figure 11.10 below).

Figure 11.10: A Rationale for the Division by a Decimal Algorithm

Step 1: Recognize that division can be expressed as a fraction.

$$0.3\overline{)20.1} = \frac{20.1}{0.3}$$

Step 2: Apply the algorithm for finding an equivalent fraction: Multiply the numerator and denominator by the same factor.

$$\frac{20.1 \times 10}{0.3 \times 10} = \frac{201}{3}$$

PARTING THOUGHTS

"Because evidence suggest that children construct [decimal] ideas slowly, it is crucial that teachers use physical materials, diagrams, and real-world situations in conjunction with ongoing efforts to relate their learning experiences to oral language [e.g., decimal-fraction terms] and symbols" (NCTM, 1989, p. 57). For example, "the opportunity to relate decimals to money is . . . con-

ceptually compelling" (Owens & Super, 1993, p. 143). Moreover, "decimal instruction should . . . relate fractions to decimals so that students . . . establish connections between the two systems" (NCTM, 1989, p. 59).

CHILDREN SHOULD BE ENCOURAGED TO USE THEIR UNDERSTANDING OF ARITHMETIC OPERATIONS TO INVENT PROCEDURES FOR OPERATING ON DECIMALS. For multiplying with a decimal, this will mean ensuring that children understand *groups-of* and *area* meanings of multiplication; for dividing by a decimal; *measure-out* and *area* meanings of division.

RESOURCES

SOME INSTRUCTIONAL RESOURCES

☞ **Base-Ten Mathematics: Interludes for Every Math Text** by Mary Laycock © 1977 by Activity Resources Company, Inc. This invaluable resource describes and illustrates how base-ten blocks can be used to model decimals to the thousandths place, to compare decimals, and to do decimal arithmetic. It also describes several decimal games. Furthermore, the resource illustrates how base-ten blocks can be used with a wide variety of mathematical topics including whole-number comparisons and arithmetic, primes, metric concepts, squares and square roots, and algebra.

A SAMPLE OF CHILDREN'S LITERATURE

The following references are useful for introducing primary-age children to *coin values* and other *money concepts*: **Dollars and Cents for Harriet** by Betsy and Giulio Maestro (© 1988 by Crown Publishers), **If You Made a Million** by David M. Schwartz (© 1989 Lothrop, Lee & Shepherd Books), and **Twenty-six Letters and Ninety-nine Cents** by Tana Hoban (© 1987 by Greenwillows Books).

✏ **Alexander, Who Used to be Rich Last Sunday** by Judith Viost, © 1978, Atheneum. After receiving a dollar from his grandparents, Alexander squanders his riches on a series of purchases. After reading about each purchase, a teacher could list the amount Alexander started with and how much he spent (e.g.,

$1.00 - $.15 for gum), and ask the class to determine how much is left. This can provide an opportunity to discuss the parallel between money notation and decimal notation and how to subtract with decimals. Follow-up activities could include asking children to imagine receiving a gift of $10 or more and detailing how they would spend the money or writing their own story about "losing a fortune."

Arthur's Funny Money by Lillian Hoban, © 1981, published by Harper Trophy, A Division of Collins Publishers. Arthur wants to buy a team T-shirt and cap, which together costs $5. After checking his savings, he finds he has only $3.78. His sister suggests setting up a bicycle-cleaning business to earn money. After buying soap for 53¢ and cleaning pads for 27¢, Arthur makes up a sign stating: *Bikes washed for 25¢.*

The story provides an entertaining context for discussing money notation and equivalents (e.g., 25¢ = one-quarter of a dollar or $.25). It can also provide realistic problems for discussing or practicing the addition and subtraction of decimals. For example, a teacher can ask: (a) If Arthur needs $5.00 and has $3.78, how much more money must he earn. (b) If soap costs $.53 and cleaning pads $.27, what were the start-up costs of his business? (c) How much must he earn now to get the $5 he needs?

Other problems that could be posed while reading the book include: (a) Arthur's first customers wanted a tricycle cleaned and argued that the charge should be half as much. What is one half of $.25? (b) The customer agreed to pay Arthur $.38 to clean a bike and a trike. In effect, how much was the customer paying for the trike cleaning?

The Greatest Guessing Game: A Book about Division by Robert Froman, © 1978, Thomas Y. Crowell. This book describes a variety of situations involving multidigit division and remainders, including some money-related situations. Children are encouraged to estimate and devise their own solution strategies for problems such as $6.00 shared among four friends or $8.27 shared among five.

TIPS ON USING TECHNOLOGY

Calculators

The Math Explorer, © 1988 by Texas Instruments. This calculator is ideally suited for intermediate-grade mathematics instruction. Among its functions is a key for changing a fraction to a decimal or vice versa.

A calculator can be an invaluable tool in exploring decimal-related concepts and patterns. Activity Files 11.1 and 11.2 can foster a basic number sense about decimals. Activity File 11.3 (page 11-31) illustrates a calculator-based game that involves applying a groups-of concept of multiplication to make an estimate and then making successive approximations. Activity File 11.4 (page 11-31) provides an entertaining way to practice (a) using a calculator or estimation to do decimal arithmetic and (b) ordering decimals.

Activity File 11.1: Halfway

◆ Decimal number sense and inductive reasoning
◆ 4-6 ◆ Class divided into small groups

After a class concludes that 0.5 is halfway between 0 and 1, challenge it to use calculators to come up with as many other pairs of numbers for which 0.5 is the halfway point. The pairs 0.2 and 0.8, 0.25 and 0.75, and 0.000001 and 0.999999, for example, are all acceptable answers. (A teacher may have to prompt students to consider pairs such as the latter two examples.) Encourage students to consider what they notice about the sum of each pair. Encourage students to find pairs of number in which other decimals such 1.6 and 2.75 are the midpoints.

Activity File 11.2: *Order Race*

◆ Ordering fractions and decimals ◆ 4-6
◆ Class divided into small groups

This activity can help illustrate that decimals are easier to use when ordering a number of rational numbers. On a handout, list fractions and their decimal equivalents as shown below:

List A:	$\frac{1}{6}$	$\frac{7}{12}$	$\frac{5}{8}$	$\frac{9}{16}$	$\frac{11}{20}$	$\frac{4}{15}$	$\frac{3}{32}$	$\frac{3}{25}$
List B:	$0.1\overline{6}$		$0.58\overline{3}$		0.625		0.5625	
	0.55		$0.2\overline{6}$		0.09375		0.12

Activity File 11.2 continued

Distribute the handouts face-down to each group. Challenge the participants to order each list. Discuss with the class the order of each list and which list was easier to order. Ask the class how fractions can be changed into decimals.

Note that this same activity could be done as an experiment. Randomly give half the groups just List A to order and the other half just List B. Determine which had the best performance overall—the groups working on List A or those working on List B.

As a follow-up to either approach above, give groups additional lists of fractions one at a time. Keep score of how much time each group takes to complete each list. If a group does not order the rational numbers correctly, they can be given a maximum score of, say, 5 minutes. The game of *Order Race* can provide an entertaining way to practice using a calculator to convert fractions to decimals and then ordering the decimals.

Activity File 11.3: Missing Multiplier

◆ Estimation of decimal multiplication ◆ 5-8
◆ Any number

On the chalkboard, write a missing-multiplier expression such as ＿＿ x 8 = 36 or ＿＿ x 8 = 7.2 (basic version), ＿＿ x 8 = 50.4 or ＿＿ x 8 = 1.28 (intermediate version), ＿＿ x 8 = 30.08 or ＿＿ x 8 = 6.216 (advanced version).

Encourage students to use a calculator to determine the missing multiplier. The activity can be played as a competitive game in which individual class members or small groups of students compete against each other to see who is the first to determine the missing factor. Encourage students to discuss their strategies.

Keystrokes—Calculator Activities for Young Students Exploring New Topics by Robert E. Reys et al., © 1980 by Creative Publications. This resource, intended for use in grades 5-8, devotes a unit to decimals (as well as integers, estimation, and square number and square roots). The decimal unit begins with uses of decimals. It introduces decimal ordering by asking children to locate decimals on a number line or to identify the decimal represented by a point on the number line. It introduces

Activity File 11.4: Decoding Decimals

◆ Practice calculating (or estimating) decimal-arithmetic answers and ordering decimals
◆ 5-8 ◆ Any number

Ms. Clark-Jones told her class she had an important message for them. When she passed out a copy of the message to each group of four, the class discovered that, unfortunately, the letters of the message were all scrambled. Ms. Clark-Jones noted that the message could be unscrambled by putting the decimal expression for each letter in order from largest to smallest. When a student asked if they could use their calculators, the teacher asked, "Do you think that would be a good idea?" Looking at the daunting calculations, the class readily agreed it would be a most excellent idea.

Note that without calculators this same activity could be used as an estimation exercise. This would require students to draw on their conceptual understanding of decimal arithmetic and would be far more challenging than using a calculator.

IMPORTANT MESSAGE

Unscramble the message below by putting the answer to the accompanying arithmetic expression for each letter in order from largest to smallest.

A → 1.683 ÷ 30.6	I → 3.2 - 2.205	S → 21.63 + 33.094
D → 0.25 x 0.832	N → 150.8 x 25.6	T → 0.5 ÷ 0.01
E → 562.48 - 75.99	O → 120 ÷ 0.05	T → 153.56 x 8.3
F → 0.8 x 16	R → 1.085 x 3.451	Y → 8 x 0.001

Questions for Reflection

1. What is the message that Ms. Clark-Jones was trying to pass onto her class? Try estimating and then calculating the answers.

2. In constructing such an activity as an estimation exercise, what things should a teacher keep in mind?

adding by tenths by relating formal expressions to counting by tenths (e.g., 4 + 0.1: "Counting by tenths, what number comes after 4?"). A similar approach is taken for adding hundredths, subtracting tenths, and subtracting hundredths. Consider, for example, how a teacher could relate 7.1 - 0.1 to children's intuitive counting knowledge. The unit goes on to compare decimals and fractions, and touch upon decimal addition, subtraction, multiplication, and division. Decimal-arithmetic activities involve graphing, finding patterns, and making connections with everyday applications of decimals.

Computers/Videotapes

Computer models such as the *IBM Elementary Mathematics Series*, mentioned in the previous chapters, enable students to work with base-ten block models of decimals and decimal operations without the logistical problems of using real blocks. Such models can illustrate each step of a decimal arithmetic algorithm.

⊟ **Blocks Microworld** by Patrick Thompson, and distributed by ABC Intellimation. This software is Macintosh compatible.

As with modeling whole numbers and operations on whole numbers, children can use base-ten blocks to model decimals and decimal arithmetic without reflection or understanding. Consider, for example, a child asked to model 0.324 with base-ten blocks. The child puts out three flats, two longs, and four cubes. The child appears to have modeled the decimal correctly, but does this mean she understands decimal place-value? In fact, it is not possible to tell whether this behavior reflects a true success or a false success. It is possible that the child had little or no understanding of decimals and so interpreted the decimal 0.324 in terms of her whole-number knowledge—as three hundred twenty-four (Thompson & Thompson, 1990). That is, the child created the correct model for the wrong reason. (This is another reason for varying which block is defined as the unit.)

Computers can be designed to minimize unreflective use of manipulatives (Thompson, 1992). For example, *Blocks Microworld* gives the user the option of selecting which block represents the unit. If the user does not make a choice, the default setting is a cube = 1 unit. If children mechanically use the *Blocks Microworld* in an effort to represent 0.324, the program will not recognize false successes. If a team select three flats to represent the three-hundredths in 0.324, the computer will identify the display as 300, not .3. Ideally, the chil-

dren would reflect on the display, discuss their situation, modify their solution strategy, or seek help. Put differently, because children bumped into a constraint posed by the computer, they must rethink what they are doing. Teachers can also create cognitive conflict by providing feedback about concrete block models if they recognize a false success and they happen to be available. The advantage of using a computer is that the constraint (feedback) is built into the program and is always there (Thompson, 1992).

The program also has the useful feature of giving the user the option of selecting different base systems. This can provide students the opportunity of exploring whole-number and "decimal" arithmetic in other bases.)

⊟ **Mathville Mindway** and **Mathville VIP** CDs, appropriate for grades 3 to 5 and 6 to 9, respectively, are distributed by SoftWare House. The first involves eight games that include fractions and decimals as well as other concepts. The second involves solving problems in everyday situations that entail using fractions and decimals as well as other content.

⊟ **Number Quest** and **Get to the Point** © Sunburst Communications. These programs are useful for developing a number sense by requiring students to think about number order. In the decimal version of *Number Quest* the child is shown a number line from 0 to 1 and must find a computer-chosen three-place decimal in as few guesses as possible. *Get to the Point* includes the game titled *Point of Order*. In this game, the computer displays two decimals that serve as end points. The aim of the game is to type in as many numbers that fall within the interval between the end points. The catch is that once an answer is entered, it becomes one of the end points by replacing the more distant end point. If the original end points were .425 and .800 and a player typed in .500, the end points for the next turn would be .425 and .500 (because .500 is farther away from .800 than it is from .425). Try playing the game with your group or class. Can you devise a winning strategy?

Videotapes

⊞ See the *Proportional Reasoning Unit* described on page 12-28.

12 COMPARING QUANTITIES FAIRLY: RATIOS, PROPORTIONS, AND PERCENTS

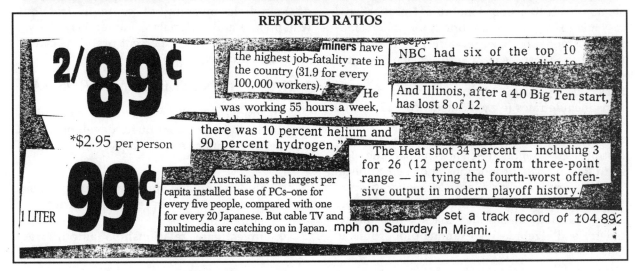

REPORTED RATIOS

2/89¢

*$2.95 per person

1 LITER 99¢

miners have the highest job-fatality rate in the country (31.9 for every 100,000 workers). He was working 55 hours a week,

there was 10 percent helium and 90 percent hydrogen,"

Australia has the largest per capita installed base of PCs–one for every five people, compared with one for every 20 Japanese. But cable TV and multimedia are catching on in Japan.

NBC had six of the top 10

And Illinois, after a 4-0 Big Ten start, has lost 8 of 12.

The Heat shot 34 percent — including 3 for 26 (12 percent) from three-point range — in tying the fourth-worst offensive output in modern playoff history.

set a track record of 104.892 mph on Saturday in Miami.

The bulletin board above titled *Reported Ratios*[†] can be one in a series named *Numbers in the News*. (Others in the series could be *Famous Fractions* and *Informative Integers*.) Each group of children can be asked to create a montage consisting of eight examples of ratios reported in newspapers, journals, or other periodicals. Have the groups cut out the advertisements, news reports, sports stories, and so forth and highlight the ratio. The class can discuss each group's montage before it is posted on the bulletin board (e.g., What are the different ways ratios are verbally expressed or symbolically represented in each montage?). More advanced students can discuss whether the ratio describes a part-whole relationship (the size of a part compared to its whole), a part-part relationship (one part of a whole compared to another), or a rate (a measure compared to a different measure).

Instead of the open-ended activity illustrated above, a teacher can ask students to collect examples of ratios about a single topic. This can serve to collect information and to stimulate discussion about the topic and, thus, provide a real reason for studying ratios as well as relating them to everyday life and other subjects such as social studies. For example, a group can assemble a montage about violence against women, titled **"What do the following statistics say about our society?"** *Three out of four women will be victims of at least one violent crime.* *A woman is beaten every 18 seconds.* *12.1 million U.S. women—1 in 8—have been raped.** *A woman is raped every 6 seconds.**

THIS CHAPTER

*T*he focus of primary-level instruction (chapters 4 to 7) is representing a single quantity (e.g., writing single and multidigit numerals) and operating on such quantities (e.g., adding or subtracting) to form a new single quantity. Intermediate-level instruction takes a monumental intellectual step by introducing how to represent *comparisons* of quantities (ratios) and the idea that two quantities can *covary*—get larger or smaller together—*in a fixed way* (proportions).

[†] Based partly on *Ratios in Advertising*, an activity described in *Hands-On Math* by F.M. Thompson and © 1994 by the Center for Applied Research in Education

* Data compiled by the Senate Judiciary Committee and reported by *Newsweek* 7/16/90.

**Data reported in an Associated Press news release 4/24/92.

Ratios are used everyday to compare and convey all sorts of information (see, e.g., the bulletin board on page 12-1). We examined one use of ratios in chapter 9: identifying the relative size of a portion by comparing the part to its whole. In Unit 12•1, we explore further the uses and meanings of ratios.

Because numerous "aspects of our world operate according to proportional rules," proportional reasoning is extremely important for understanding and modeling a wide variety of real-world phenomena (Post, Behr, & Lesh, 1988, p. 79). It is fundamental to sciences such as biology, chemistry, and physics. Other real-world applications include rates (e.g., If 3 items cost $2, then 9 items cost $6) and conversions (e.g., If $1 = 10 dimes, then $6 = 60 dimes). Investigation 12.1 illustrates an integrated science-mathematics lesson that involves proportions and their application to a real-world problem. Moreover, proportional reasoning underlies many aspects of more advanced mathematics and is a key tool for geometry and algebra. We examine proportions in Unit 12•2.

☞ Try Investigation 12.1 (page 12-3).

In Unit 12•3, we consider percent—a convenient and widely used notation for ratios. Percent is derived from the Latin *per centum* meaning *by the hundred* or *for every hundred*. For example, an 80 percent success rate means *80 of every 100* attempts were successful. Percent can also be thought of as another way to represent the part-of-the whole meaning of common fractions (Chapter 9) and decimals (Chapter 11). As we will see in this chapter, percent problems can be viewed as proportion problems.

WHAT THE NCTM *STANDARDS* SAY

"In grades 5-8, the mathematics curriculum should include the continued development of number and number relationships so that students can:

◆ understand and apply ratios, proportions, and percents in a wide variety of situations;
◆ investigate relationships among fractions, decimals, and percents" (p. 87).

12•1 RATIOS

Figure 12.1: A Misunderstood Ratio

FRANK AND ERNEST reprinted with the permission of Bob Thaves.

As Figure 12.1 implies, an accurate understanding of ratios is a key aspect of mathematical literacy. The aim of this unit is to foster an explicit understanding of ratios (Subunit 12•1•1) and how teachers can help students to do the same (Subunit 12•1•2). (Continued on page 12-4.)

✿ Investigation 12.1: Measuring Shadows and Other Things

◆ Proportional reasoning + data collecting + algebra ◆ 5-8 ◆ Any number

Many situations in everyday life involve proportional reasoning. The two activities below provide an informal and interesting way to introduce children to proportions. To see what is involved, try them yourself.

Activity I: The Length of Shadows

What factors affect the length of shadows? Experiment with a flashlight and an object such as a dark-green *Cuisenaire rod*. Holding the distance between the flashlight and the object constant, place the light source at different angles as shown below. What happens to the length of the object's shadow? Holding the flashlight at 45º above the object, move the light source away from the object. What happens to the length of the object's shadow?

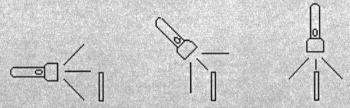

Activity II: Measuring an Inaccessible Height

■ **The Fearful Landscaper.** Mr. Krupa was a landscaper. Occasionally, customers asked him to uproot and relocate trees. The cost of such a job depends on the height of the tree, which indicates the extent of the root system and, hence, the amount of digging required. Mr. Krupa was asked to relocate a rather large pine. Unfortunately, Mr. Krupa was afraid of heights. Clearly the landscaper needed a way to measure the height of the tree without actually climbing and measuring it.

✚ **Hint:** On a sunny day, take a pencil or stick measuring 6-inches long, a 12-inch ruler, a yard stick, and another person or object 4 or 5 feet tall outside. Record the height of each item and the length of its shadow in the table below. Examine the table for a pattern. How could you determine the height of a very high tree or a flagpole without actually climbing the object and risking serious bodily injury?

Item	Height of item	Length of shadow

Alternatively, use *Cuisenaire rods* and a flashlight or an indirect light source such as ceiling lights. (To make the task of finding a relationship easier, find a place where the length of the shadow cast by an object is an easy multiple of the object's length such as half, twice, or three times as large.) Note that all objects should be measured from the same position. Why?

▦ Either with or without the aid of a graphing calculator, summarize your findings algebraically as a formula (an equation). Let h = the height of items or rods and l = the length of their shadow.

12•1•1 MATHEMATICS & LEARNING: UNDERSTANDING RATIOS

In this subunit, we touch on the uses of ratios, define ratios, and note how they differ from a part-of-the-whole meaning of common fractions.

☞ Try Probe 12.1 (page 12-5), Investigation 12.2 (page 12-6), and Probe 12.2 (page 12-7).

Uses of Ratios

Box 12.1 lists some of the many ways ratios are used in everyday life. This section focuses on one particularly important use of ratios (comparing quantities and strategies for doing so).

Comparing Quantities. Many everyday situations require comparing two uneven sets of data. *How can a fair comparison be made in such situations?* In the *Basketball Problem* in Probe 12.1, for example, how can one determine the best shooter when each boy had a different number of chances to shoot? Many children intuitively sense that the boy with the most baskets is not necessarily the best shot. After all, he had many more chances to shoot and make baskets. Likewise, with *A Best Buy* in Probe 12.1, the cheapest item—even if it is on sale—is not necessarily the best bargain.

Ratios can provide a *common basis* for comparing uneven sets of data. In the *Basketball Problem* in Probe 12.1, for instance, determining the rate of success (ratio of baskets to total shots) shows that Alfredo makes 2 baskets for every 4 shots or 10 of every 20 shots, which is better than Benito (4 for every 10 or 8 for every 20) or Curry (6 for every 20).

Comparison Strategies. *How can ratios be used to compare data?* Two methods are:

1. The *common-multiple method* entails (a) expressing the ratios involved as fractions, (b) finding a common denominator, (c) determining equivalent fractions, and (d) comparing the fractions. For the *Basketball Problem* in Probe 12.1, for example, this method would involve: (a) expressing the baskets-to-shots ratios as fractions ($\frac{2}{4}$, $\frac{4}{10}$, and $\frac{6}{20}$); (b) finding a common multiple of 4, 10, and 20 to serve as a common denominator (20); (c) determining that $\frac{2}{4} = \frac{10}{20}$, $\frac{4}{10} = \frac{8}{20}$; and (d) judging $\frac{10}{20}$ is the largest fraction.

2. The *common-unit method* entails changing ratios so that each has a common unit. Unit pricing is a good everyday example. In *A Best Buy* in Probe 12.1, it is difficult to determine the best value because each price is based on a different weight. Unit pricing allows a consumer to compare the prices of different brands of cat food based on the same weight. For example, if six 13 oz. cans of *Kitty Cuisine* is \$3.75, then the unit price is $\frac{\$3.75}{6 \times 13 \text{ oz}} = \frac{\$3.75}{78 \text{ oz}} = 4.8¢$ per oz.

Ratios Defined

What is a ratio?

A Fixed Relationship. As Investigation 2.2 illustrates, a ratio is a *fixed*, and thus a special type of, relationship. A fixed rate (e.g., \$5 per person) or a fixed scale (e.g., halving, doubling or tripling) both qualify as ratios. The length of a square's diagonal is always $\sqrt{2}$, or about 1.4, times the length of its side. Thus, when the side of a square is doubled, its diagonal also doubles. Relationships that are not fixed (e.g., doubling the length of square's side does not double its area) are not ratios. (Continued on page 12-8.)

Box 12.1: Some Everyday Uses of Ratios

• Shopping (e.g., 3 cans of cat food for \$1).

• Money (e.g., 5 nickels equal a quarter).

• Recipes (e.g., $1\frac{1}{2}$ cups of flour per serving).

• Home maintenance (e.g., 4 ounces of tint per gallon of paint; 1 gallon of paint for every 400 to 500 square feet of wall).

• Driving (e.g., 55 miles per hour, 24 miles per gallon).

• Music (e.g., in $\frac{4}{4}$ time, four beats per measure).

• Map reading (e.g., $1\frac{1}{2}$ inches = $\frac{1}{2}$ miles).

• Model railroading (e.g., with O-gauge model trains, $\frac{1}{4}$ inch represents 1 foot).

• Games of chance (e.g., the chances of drawing a heart from a poker deck is 13 in 52 or 1 in 4).

• Measurement (e.g., 10 miles = 16.1 km).

➤ Probe 12.1: Comparing Quantities

The aim of this probe is to help you explicitly understand why ratios are important in everyday life. With the help of your group, answer the questions below. Discuss your solutions with your class.

☞ **Teaching Tip**. Problems such as those below can be used with elementary-level students for the same purpose noted above. Primary-level students can begin with simpler problems—problems that involve comparing two quantities and rates that involve multiples (e.g., Which is the better value: 1 for $2 or 3 for $3, 1 for $2 or 3 for $6, 1 for $2 or 3 for $9, 2 for $4 or 3 for $9?).

Part I: Problem with a Basketball Problem

Miss Brill gave her fifth-grade class the following problem:

■ **A Basketball Problem**[†] (◆ 4-8). In their last basketball game, only three of the Bork School Blanks scored. The table below records the results of the game. Who is the best shooter?

player	shots	baskets
Alfredo	4	2
Benito	10	4
Curry	20	6

1. Andy's group constructed the table below. After examining it, they concluded that Alfredo was the most accurate shooter. What seems to be the rationale for the group's solution?

player	shots	successes
Alfredo	20	18
Benito	20	14
Curry	20	6

2. (a) Evaluate the strategy used by Andy's group. (b) Is their conclusion correct?

3. Would their strategy have worked if Alfredo had originally taken 6 shot instead of 4?

☞ **Teaching Tip**. A teacher may wish to pose just the *Basketball Problem* above and see what solutions his or her students devise. Questions 1 to 3 above could always be posed afterward to prompt further discussion.

Part II: A Consumer-Education Problem

■ **A Best Buy** (◆ 5-8). Sharleen was on a tight budget and always on the lookout for the most economical buy. While grocery shopping, her eye was caught by the following specials on cat food:

> four 5.5 oz. cans of *Gourmet Kitten* for $1.28;
> twelve 13 oz. cans of *Sea Catch for Cats* for $7.08;
> ten 5.5 oz. cans of *Feline Fuel* for $2.40; and
> six 13 oz. cans of *Kitty Cuisine for* $3.75.

Which was the best buy?

[†] Adapted from "A Study of Mathematics Education in Classroom Situations: A Methodological Research" by I. Hirabayashi. In L. Streefland (Ed.) *Proceedings of the Ninth International Conference for the Psychology of Mathematics Education* (1985, pp. 116-121). Utrecht, Netherlands: International Group for the Psychology of Mathematics Education.

☘ Investigation 12.2: Explicitly Understanding Ratios

◆ Identifying ratios ◆ 5-8 ◆ Groups of four + class discussion

The aim of this investigation is to help students explicitly define the concept of *ratio*. To see what is involved and to perhaps clarify your own concept of ratio, try the activity along with your group. Discuss your conclusions with your class.

Instructions: Which of the following involve a ratio? If the comparison involves a ratio, indicate with a R; otherwise, write NA.

_____ 1. **Double the Dough.** A father, anxious to teach his son Günter the virtue of thrift, promised to match dollar for dollar the amount the boy put in a savings account. To help his son appreciate the value of this deal, the father drew up the table below to illustrate *the relationship between the amount of the boy's contribution and the total deposit:*

Günter's contribution	$1	$2	$3	$4	$5	$6
Total deposited	$2	$4	$6	$8	$10	$12

_____ 2. **Mounting Admissions Costs.** A day's admission charge to *Walter Dizzy's Wonder-Why-You-Ever-Came World* was $50 for one person. For each additional family member the charge was reduced by $5. The sign above the ticket booth summarizes the *relationship between the number of family members and the admissions costs:*

Number in family	1	2	3	4	5	6	7	8	9	10
Admissions cost	50	95	140	185	230	275	320	365	410	455

_____ 3. **Relationship Between the Side and Area of a Square.** Use plastic square blocks or graph paper to explore what happens to the area of a square as its sides double. Complete the table below:

Length of side (cm)	1	2	4	8	16
Area (square cm)					

Is there a constant relationship between a square's length and its area?

_____ 4. **Relationship Between the Side and Diagonal of a Square.** Draw squares with sides of 3, 6, 9, 12, and 15 cm. Draw in a diagonal for each square. Measure the diagonals to the nearest mm. Better yet, use the Pythagorean theorem ($c^2 = a^2 + b^2$) to determine the length of each diagonal. Reduce irrational numbers to their simplest form (e.g., $\sqrt{72} = \sqrt{36 \cdot 2} = 6\sqrt{2}$). Summarize your data in the table below:

Length of side (cm)	3	6	9	12	15
Length of diagonal					

Is there a constant relationship between a square's length and its diagonal?

Questions for Reflection

1. Marci's group argued that all four situations above involved a constant relationship and, therefore, were ratios. In Situation 2, the admission cost (c) could be calculated in each case by multiplying the number of people (n) by 50 and subtracting the number of people minus one times five: $c = 50n - 5(n - 1)$. In Situation 3, the area could be determined by squaring the length of a side ($A = s^2$). Evaluate Marci's conclusion.

2. (a) How do Situations 2 and 3 above differ from Situations 1 and 4? (b) Do all four situations fit the definition of ratios agreed upon by the mathematical community?

➤ Probe 12.2: Distinguishing Between Ratios and Common Fractions Representing a Part-of-the-Whole Concept

As noted in chapter 9, common fractions can represent both a part-of-a-whole and a ratio meaning. However, there are some fundamental differences between these two meanings. The aim of this probe is to help you explicitly consider these difference. Answer the following questions, preferably with the aid of your group. Discuss your answers with group or class.

1. In Ms. Pines' class, two of every five football players got an A on the final math test. Both the fraction of all football players getting an A and the ratio of football players getting an A compared to the total number of football players could be represented by the common fraction $\frac{2}{5}$. (a) Could the part-of-a-whole situation be represented by the fraction $\frac{5}{2}$? (b) Could the ratio situation be represented by the fraction $\frac{5}{2}$?

2. In Ms. Pines' class, two football players got As for every three football players who didn't. Can this relationship be expressed as a common fraction representing (a) a part-of-a-whole meaning and (b) a ratio meaning?

3. Consider the following examples of ratios and common fractions that represent a part-of-a-whole meaning. What differences do you notice?

Ratios	Common Fractions (part-of-a-whole meaning)
a. 3 pies for $5 (3:5)	a. 3 of the five pies were eaten (3/5)
b. 80 miles in 2 hours (80:2)	b. 80 half-hour blocks of time (80/2)
c. 1 person, 1 vote (1:1)	c. The fraction of Grump Party members voting in the last election was 1/1

4. A road sign reads: *50 mph*. Is *50 mph* a ratio? Why or why not?

5. Other than a fraction, how can the ratio one to two be expressed?

6. (a) Are 3/0 and 100/0 acceptable as ratios? Why or why not? (b) Are they acceptable common fractions representing a part-of-a-whole meaning? Why or why not?

7. (a) Are ratios always rational? (b) Are common fractions representing a part-of-a whole meaning always rational? Why or why not? (c) For the right isoceles triangle shown to the right, what is the ratio of the hypotenuse to a side? Is this ratio rational?

 $$\frac{\text{hypotenuse}}{\text{side}} = \frac{?}{2}$$

8. Are all common fractions ratios? Are all ratios common fractions? Consider the definition of ratios on page 12-8. What, then, is the relationship between common fractions and ratios?

9. What is assumed when two common fractions such as $\frac{1}{2}$ and $\frac{1}{3}$ are compared to determine the larger? Does this same assumption hold when two ratios such as 1:2 and 1:3 are compared?

10. In the first half, Stephon made 2 of 6 free throws. In the second half, he made 7 of 8. (a) Overall, what was his success rate for free throws for the game? (b) For Question 10, Simone wrote $\frac{2}{6} + \frac{7}{8} = \frac{9}{14}$. Evaluate Simone's answer. (c) Is the addition of ratios and the addition of common factions comparable? (d) Do the ratios 1:3 and 7:8 add to yield a success equivalent to that of 2:6 plus 7:8? Why or why not?

A Multiplicative Relationship. A ratio such as $\frac{3}{5}$ indicates, not only the size of each quantity compared (three and five) but also, a particular relationship between the two (Behr & Post, 1988). More specifically, it represents a multiplicative, not an additive, relationship (Vergnaud, 1983). For example, $\frac{3}{5}$ specifies that 3 is three-fifths of 5 ($3 = \frac{3}{5} \times 5$) and 5 is five-thirds of 3 ($5 = \frac{5}{3} \times 3$), not that 3 and two more is 5 ($3 + 2 = 5$) or 5 is two more than 3 ($5 - 2 = 3$).

An Ordered Relationship. Furthermore, a ratio compares two quantities in *a particular order*. For example, 15,000 dollars per 1.25 acres is vastly different from 15,000 acres for 1.25 dollars. Yet, some students—unaware that order is important—will mechanically record the first (dollars to acres) comparison as 1.25/15,000—incorrectly implying a remarkable bargain. In brief, *a ratio compares two ordered quantities that share a fixed multiplicative relationship.*

A Comparison With Common Fractions Representing a Part-of-a-Whole Meaning

Ratios can differ from common fractions that represent a part-of-a-whole meaning in a number of important ways.

Different Types of Relationships. Like fractions representing a part-of-a-whole meaning, ratios can represent a relationship between a part and its whole (*part-to-whole ratios*). Unlike fractions representing a part-of-a-whole meaning, ratios can also represent a relationship between (a) a whole and its part (*whole-to-part ratios*), (b) one part of a whole and another part of the whole (*part-to-part ratios*), and (c) two different quantities (*rates*). For example, the ratio of all Ms. Pines' football players to those who got As in Question 1 of Probe 12.2 (page 12-7) could be represented by the whole-to-part ratio $\frac{5}{2}$ (as long as it is made clear that the fixed relationship is total number of football players to that part getting an A). The ratios of football players who got As to those who didn't (Question 2 of Probe 12.2) can be represented by the part-to-part ratio $\frac{2}{3}$. The ratio 3 pies for $5 (Question 3 of Probe 12.2) can be represented by the rate 3/$5. In each of these three examples, the fraction representing a ratio clearly imply something other than a part-to-whole relationship.

Single-Number Examples. By convention, some ratios are reported as single numbers, not as fractions. For example, 50 miles per hour is expressed as 50 mph, not $\frac{50 \text{ miles}}{1 \text{ hour}}$, and 24 miles to the gallon is represented as 24 mpg, not $\frac{24 \text{ miles}}{1 \text{ gallon}}$. (Note that in these examples, the 1 hour or 1 gallon is implied—much like the whole number 4 implies four wholes or $\frac{4}{1}$.)

Various Representations. The ratio of one to two can be expressed as 1:2, (1,2), 1→2, or 1 to 2 as well as in fraction form ($\frac{1}{2}$).

Ratios with Zero. Whereas the common fraction $\frac{9}{0}$ is not possible because a whole cannot be divided into *noneths*, a ratio such as 9:0 or 9/0 is possible. It could represent, for instance, the number of starters on a major league baseball team making a million dollars a year compared to those making less than a million. Such applications are relatively rare but do imply that ratios are not necessarily rational numbers.

Ratios with Nonrational Numbers. Ratios can involve nonrational numbers. For example, as you may have discovered in Investigation 12.2, the ratio of a square's side and its diagonal is $1:\sqrt{2}$. By definition, common fractions can only have elements that are integers. All common fractions, then, represent ratios, but not all ratios are represented by common fractions.

Comparing Ratios. Recall from chapter 9 that the comparison of two fractions such as $\frac{1}{2}$ and $\frac{1}{3}$ is not possible unless both fractions have the same whole. The same is not true of ratios. To compare two ratios, the whole need not be the same for each. For example, if 1 of every 2 seniors going to a football game buys a pennant from the Booster Club and 1 of every 3 juniors does so, the *ratio* of seniors buying a pennant ($\frac{1}{2}$) is more than the ratio of juniors buying a pennant ($\frac{1}{3}$). Moreover, this is true regardless of the number of seniors and juniors going to the game.

Combining Ratios. Ratios combine differently than do fractions. In Question 10 of Probe 12.2, it made sense to combine the success rates 2:6

and 7:8 to find an overall success rate of 9:14. An answer of $\frac{9}{14}$ for $\frac{2}{6} + \frac{7}{8}$ is not acceptable.

12•1•2 TEACHING

Although ratios are not introduced formally until the intermediate grades, informal exploration of ratios can begin at the primary level. In this subunit, we discuss how this can be done and how symbolic instruction can be linked to children's informal knowledge.

Conceptual Phase

☞ "INTRODUCE RATIOS "GRADUALLY THROUGH DISCUSSING THE MANY SITUATIONS IN WHICH THEY OCCUR NATURALLY" (NCTM, 1989, p. 89). Primary-level children can explore and discuss situations involving doubling and even tripling. Some of the everyday uses of ratios listed in Box 12.1 (page 12-4) appropriate for young children include money equivalents (e.g., 1 nickel makes 5 pennies, 2 nickels make 10 pennies, and so forth), music instruction (e.g., in $\frac{4}{4}$ time, 1 half note → 2 beats, 2 half notes → 4 beats), simple recipes (e.g., 1 cup of flour makes 4 servings; 2 cups, 8 servings; and so on), and measurement equivalents (e.g., 1 yard = 3 feet, 2 yards = 6 feet, etc.). Body parts (e.g., 1 mouth per person, 2 arms per person, 10 fingers per person) and packaging (e.g., 12 eggs per carton) also provide natural illustrations of ratios. Learning how to draw figures can involve examining the relative position and size of features (see, e.g., Activity File 12.1).

☞ Introduce ratios purposefully as a tool for solving comparison problems that require finding a common basis in order to compare two or more quantities. For example, present problems like those in Probe 12.1 (on page 12-5).

☞ Provide concrete activities such as counting and pairing the items of two collections as a first step in learning about ratios (Lamon, 1990). For example, in preparation for an art project, a teacher could give a group of four students eight straws, ask them to count how many children are at the table and the number of straws, and then instruct the students to share the straws fairly. Note that many kindergartners could solve such a task by using the divvying-up strategy described in chapters 5 and 9. In time, a teacher could pose more difficult problems such as, "Take two straws for each child at your table."

Activity File 12.1: Drawing Well-Proportioned Faces and Bodies

◆ Measuring + averages + ratios ◆ 3-8
◆ Any number

As part of an integrated art-mathematics unit on drawing people, draw an oval on the chalkboard to represent a human head. Draw a horizontal line at the chin line and head top, use three more equidistant horizontal lines to divide the oval into fourths, and label the line and spaces as shown in Figure A. Pose such questions as, Where should we draw the eyes, at the $\frac{1}{4}$ line, $\frac{2}{4}$ line, Space A, or Space B? Where should we put the nose, mouth, and hairline?

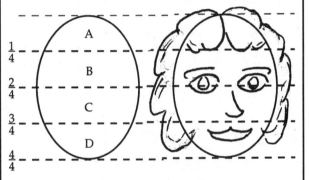

Figure A   **Figure B**

One way children can address the question above is by trial and error (e.g., drawing the eyes at the $\frac{1}{4}$ line). Another is to use tape measures to measure the spans of sample faces (top of the head to the chin) and to measure the distances from the top of the head to the hairline, to the eyes, to the top and to the bottom of the nose, and to the mouth. The students can then summarize each of these measurements as an average and compare the relative distance of each feature to the total span of a face. For example, if the average distance from the top of the head to the eyes was 3.8 inches and the average face span was 7.7 inches, then (rounded off) the ratio would be $\frac{4}{8}$ or $\frac{2}{4}$ (as shown in Figure B).

☞ Use the method outlined above to gauge the size of a head, arms, trunk, and legs relative to the total height of a person.

Connecting Phase

☞ Use examples *and* nonexamples to help students construct an explicit and accurate concept of ratios (NCTM, 1991). Investigation 12.2 (on page 12-6) can help them recognize that ratios involve a fixed multiplicative relationship. Examples and nonexamples can also help students recognize that the order of the terms in a ratio is important (see, e.g., Activity File 12.2). For instance, farmers and gardening buffs will recognize 25:3:8 lawn fertilizer as containing 25% nitrogen, 3% phosphorous, and 8% potash (a potassium compound), not some other chemical breakdown.

☞ **Help children explicitly distinguish between ratios and common fractions that represent rational numbers.** A task such as Probe 12.2 (page 12-7) can be used to promote a discussion of key differences. Computing cumulative averages such as batting averages (the ratio of *hits* to *times at bat*) can help, for instance, illustrate that ratios combine differently than fractions. If a batter gets 1 hit in 4 tries in game 1 and goes 2 for 3 in game 2, then her cumulative batting average is:

$$\frac{1+2}{4+3} = \frac{3}{7}, \text{not } \frac{1}{4} + \frac{2}{3} = \frac{11}{12}.$$

12•2 PROPORTIONS

☞ **Encourage students to consider explicitly what each element of a ratio represents.** They need to recognize that ratios can refer to *whole-to-part*, *part-to-part*, and *one quantity-to-a-different-quantity* (rate) situations, as well as to *part-to-whole* relationships.

Figure 12.2: Equivalent Distress

Proportions have numerous real-world applications including unit pricing, gas mileage, speed, acceleration, density, concentration, power, efficiency, chemical composition, and exchange rates (e.g., Heller, Ahlgren, Post, Behr, & Lesh, 1989). Gears, pulleys, and levers (see, e.g., Investigation 12.3) are all governed by proportional relationships. Moreover, along with fractions and rates, proportion is a "foundation for much of the mathematics students will subsequently study"

(Heller, Post, Behr, & Lesh, 1990). The aim of this unit is to foster an explicit understanding of proportions (Subunit 12•2•1), how children's proportional thinking develops (Subunit 12•2•2), and what elementary-level teachers can do to encourage this type of thinking (Subunit 12•2•3).

☞ Work through Investigations 12.3 (pages 12-11 and 12-12) and 12.4 (page 12-13) before reading on. (Text continued on page 12-14.)

✿ Investigation 12.3: Explicitly Understanding Proportions

◆ Identifying proportional situations + graphing + algebra ◆ 5-8
◆ Individuals or small groups of students + class discussion

The aim of this investigation is to help students to explicitly define directly proportional and inversely proportional situations. After trying the investigation yourself, discuss your answers with your group or class.

Part I. Solve the following problems. Record your solution strategy. Before continuing on to Part II, compare your solution strategy and answer with others in your group or class.

■ **Problem 1: Exhausted Examiners.** Elke and Faye corrected final exams at the same rate but Elke got a head start. When Elke had completed 12 exams Faye had finished only 4. When Elke had finished 60 exams, how many exams had Faye completed?

■ **Problem 2: A Metric Conversion.** If 6 inches is 15.24 cm, 9 inches is how many centimeters?

■ **Problem 3: An Exchange Rate.** If 5 Canadian dollars can be exchanged for 4 U.S. dollars, what is 35 Canadian dollars worth in U.S. dollars?

■ **Problem 4: Taken for a Ride.** A taxicab charged $1 plus 50¢ a mile. If it costs $3 to go four miles, how much would it cost to go 6 miles?

Part II. For Problem 1, Dayanara answered 52, and the others in her group (Kenya, Namarta, and Pavlina) answered 20. Kenya explained that *Exhausted Examiners* was a simple proportion problem: $\frac{4}{12} = \frac{X}{60}$; so $12X = 240$; thus, $X = 20$. Although she tried to explain that an answer of 20 was too low, Dayanara was out-voted. When they discussed the problem with the whole class, the group discovered that Dayanara had been correct all along. (1) Why is Kenya's solution not correct? (2) Describe how Dayanara may have arrived at the correct solution. (3) Of Problems 2, 3, and 4 above, which are proportion problems and which are not? Briefly justify your answers.

Part III. When the sides of a square double in length, what happens to the area? (2) When the sides of a cube doubles in length, what happens to the volume? (3) Which, if either, of these cases, involves a proportional relationship? Justify your answer.

Part IV. To distinguish between problems involving a direct proportion and nonproportion problems, it can be helpful to record the data in a table and to graph it. Draw a line connecting the dots of the graph. If necessary, extend the line so that it intersects the left or bottom side of the graph. (1) Graphs of directly proportional relationships have what characteristics? (2) Why do graphs of directly proportional relationships have the characteristic they do? (3) In what way are they different from graphs of nonproportional situations?

Problem 1:	Elke		12	16				36
	Faye	0	4						

Problem 2:	inches	0	3	6		9
	cm			15.24		

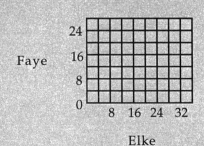

Elke / Faye

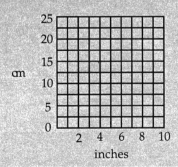

inches / cm

Investigation 12.3 continued

Problem 3

Canadian $	5		15				35
US $		4	8	12			

Problem 4

Miles	0	1	2	3	4	5	6
$		1	1.50		3		

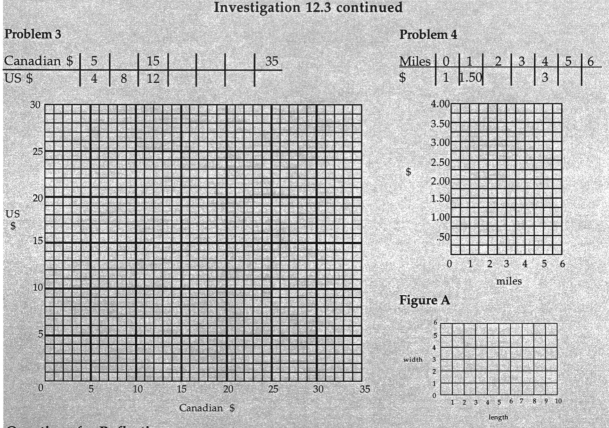

Figure A

Questions for Reflection

1. (a) How could students use the graph in Figure A to determine whether the relationship between the length and the width of similar rectangles measuring 2 units by 1 unit, 4 units by 2 units, and 6 units by 3 units was proportional or not? (b) How could they use a graph to determine if a 10-by-5 rectangle was similar to a 4-by-2 rectangle? (c) Many students think *all* rectangles are similar. Are all rectangles similar? Illustrate your answer using a graph.

2. (a) For each directly proportional situation in Part III, summarize the relationship between the quantities with an algebraic equation. Hint: Consider the relevant tables. Label the quantity in the top row x; label the quantity in the bottom row y. Next consider how y can be determined if x is known. (b) Using k to represent a constant factor, write a general algebraic equation that could represent any directly proportional situation.

3. (a) A graph of two inversely proportional quantities has what general characteristics? (b) Identify a real-world example of an inversely proportional relationship and graph some sample data. (c) One example of inversely proportional quantities is the relationship between the speed and time it takes to travel a set (constant) distance. If it takes 3 hours to drive a distance at 40 miles per hour, what speed would be required to drive this distance in 12, 6, or 4, 2, 1, or $\frac{1}{2}$ hours? On a piece of graph paper, graph these data and summarize this inverse relationship as an algebraic equation.

4. The data to the right illustrate a case where as x gets larger, y gets smaller. (a) Intuitively, are these data directly or inversely proportional? (b) Graph these data.

x	-3	-2	-1	0	+1	+2	+3
y	+6	+4	+2	0	-2	-4	-6

Does the shape of the graph correspond more closely to that you drew for directly or indirectly proportional situations? (c) Summarize the relationship of x and y as an algebraic equation. Does the equation more closely resemble that of a direct or an inverse relationship?

☽ Investigation 12.4: Teetering Teeter-Totter

Teeter-totters and balance beams are two examples of levers found in everyday life. Experimenting with them can serve as a basis for an integrated lesson on machines (science) and proportions (mathematics). In Part I, we describe how primary-level children can intuitively explore levers. In Part II, we illustrate how intermediate-level children can examine this type of machine more systematically. After reading Part I, try Part II with your group. Discuss your results with your class.

Part I (◆ Intuitive proportional reasoning ◆ K-4 ◆ Any number)

Begin by posing questions such as: *What happens when a heavy child and a light child get on opposite ends of a teeter-totter? If they want to balance the teeter-totter, what do they have to do? What factors determine whether or not a teeter-totter balances?* To explore these questions informally, volunteers can be weighed, don labels indicating their weights, and experiment on teeter-totters. Note that such an activity also involves reading and ordering multidigit numerals (e.g., identifying 54 pounds as more than 45 pounds). After children have observed that position (distance from the fulcrum or "balance point") is a key factor, encourage them to experiment further on teeter-totters to intuitively address the question: *How are weight and distance from the fulcrum or balance point related?* Further exploration of this issue can be done with a *Math Balance* or other balance beam.

Part II (◆ Explicit proportional reasoning + algebra ◆ 5-8 ◆ Groups of about four + class discussion)

To systematically explore the relationship between weight and distance from the fulcrum, older students can conduct the following experiment:

1. Using a *Math Balance*, systematically vary the weight and position of the weight on each arm. Record the results in the tables below. Enter = if the *Math Balance* balances—as when two 10-gram weights are placed on the left arm at position 1 and one 10-gram weight is placed on the right arm at position 2 (see Table A). Enter ∟ if the *Math Balance* tilts left—as when two 10-gram weights are placed on the left arm at position 3 and a 10-gram weight is placed on the right arm at position 4 (again see Table A). Enter ꓤ if the *Math Balance* tilts right—as when two 10-gram weights are placed on the left arm at position 4 and one 10-gram weight is placed on the right arm at position 9 (see Table A).

Table A

1 10-g. weight on right arm

2 10-g. weights on left arm	position →	1	2	3	4	5	6	7	8	9	10
	1		=								
	2										
	3				∟						
	4									ꓤ	

Table B

2 10-g. weights on right arm

3 10-g. weights on left arm	position →	1	2	3	4	5	6	7	8	9	10
	1										
	2										
	3										
	4										

Table C

2 10-g. weights on right arm

4 10-g. weights on left arm	position →	1	2	3	4	5	6	7	8	9	10
	1										
	2										
	3										
	4										

Table D

3 10-g. weights on right arm

6 10-g. weights on left arm	position →	1	2	3	4	5	6	7	8	9	10
	1										
	2										
	3										
	4										

2. (a) Examine the tables. When does the *Math Balance* balance? (b) Summarize your conclusion (the law of levers) algebraically as a formula (an equation).

12•2•1 MATHEMATICS: UNDER-STANDING PROPORTIONS

Definition

As Figure 12.2 (on page 12-10) illustrates, *proportions are equivalent ratios* (e.g., "1 is to 3 as 2 is to 6" or $\frac{1}{3} = \frac{2}{6}$). A proportion is essentially, then, a relationship between two relations (Yiu, 1992). This relationship is a special type of relationship—a *multiplicative* relationship.

Consider, for example, Problem 3 of Investigation 12.3 (page 12-11), which specified that 5 Canadian dollars is worth 4 U.S. dollars. There are two ways to determine what 35 Canadian dollars is worth in U.S. dollars, and both involve multiplication. One is to set up a table and extend the pattern. In Table A below, note that each new pair of entries is determined by multiplying the first pair of entries by the *same factor* (e.g., the third Canadian $ entry = 3 x 5 and the third U.S. $ entry = 3 x 4).

Table A: Canadian vs U.S. Dollars

Entry	1	2	3	4	5	
Canadian $	5	10	15	20	25	...
U.S. $	4	8	12	16	20	

The second method involves noting that each entry in the U.S. $ row in the proceeding table can be determined by multiplying the Canadian dollar amount by the exchange rate of $\frac{4}{5}$ (e.g., $35 Canadian x $4 U.S./$5 Canadian = $28 U.S.). This constant factor is called the *unit rate*.

Problems 1 and 4 of Investigation 12.3 (page 12-11) do not involve a multiplicative relationship and, hence, are not proportion problems. In Problem 1, for example, the relationship between the number of exams corrected by Elke and that corrected by Faye can be determined by subtraction and expressed algebraically as E - 8 = F

(e.g., if Elke has completed 20 exams, then Faye has completed 20 - 8 or 12 exams). Like Kenya in Part II of Investigation 12.3, though, many students incorrectly attempt to solve Problem 1 by setting up a proportion and using the standard cross-products algorithm (Cramer, Post, & Currier, 1993). The traditional skills approach promotes this kind of error by fostering the rote memorization and blind application of the cross-products algorithm.

Types of Proportion Problems

There are basically two types of proportions (Behr et al., 1992)—those involving direct proportions and those involving inverse proportions.

Direct Proportions. Examples of direct proportions include the relationship between the height of an object and the length of its shadow (Investigation 12.1 on page 12-3), metric conversions (Problem 2 on page 12-11 of Investigation 12.3), and exchange rates (Problem 3 of Investigation 12.3). In the sample shadow data shown below, note that shadow length (y) was always 1.25 times (a constant factor k) longer than rod height (x). The relationship between two directly proportional quantities can be summarized by the algebraic equations A and B in Figure 12.3 below. For example, the data in Table B below can be capsulized by the formula $y = 1.25 \bullet x$.

Table B: Sample Shadow Data (in cm)

height of rod (x)	2	3	4	5
length of shadow (y)	2.5	3.75	5	6.25

In *some* directly proportional situations, y is always a constant factor *smaller* than x. Consider, for instance, accounting or a "zero-sum" game, where someone's gain is another's loss. In Table C (on the next page), note that the more points a player scores, the more points the opponent loses and that the opponent's score (y) can be determined by multiplying the player's score (x)

Figure 12.3: Direct Versus Inverse Proportions

Direct Proportions		Inverse Proportions	
A. $\frac{y}{x} = k$	(the quotient of the variables is constant factor or unit rate)	C. $x \bullet y = k$	(the product of the variables is constant factor)
B. $y = x \bullet k$	(y varies directly with x)	D. $y = \frac{k}{x}$	(y varies directly with the *inverse* of x)

by the negative constant factor (-k) of -1. Such situations can be summarized in general terms by the algebraic equation $y = -k \cdot x$. For instance, the sample scores for a zero sum game below can be capsulized by the formula $y = -1 \cdot x$.

Table C: Sample Scores for a *Zero-Sum* Game

player's score (x)	-4	-1	0	+2	+5
opponent's score (y)	+4	+1	0	-2	-5

Inverse Proportions. Real-world examples of *inversely proportional quantities* include the law of levers (the relationship between distance from a fulcrum and weight illustrated by Investigation 12.4 on page 12-13), the relationship between the length and width of rectangles with same area, and the relationship between speed and time given a constant distance (see table below). In each case, two variables (x and y) have the same product (k) (summarized as formula C in Figure 12.3), and y can be predicted by dividing this constant product k by x (summarized as formula D in Figure 12.3). Thus, when k is positive, y gets smaller as x gets larger. When k is negative, y gets larger as x gets larger. For instance, the data for the constant distance of 60 miles below can be summarized by the formula $y = \frac{60}{x}$.

Table D: Data for the Constant Distance of 60 mi.

speed in mph (x)	1	10	15	30	45	60
time in hours (y)	60	6	4	2	$1\frac{1}{3}$	1

Identifying Proportional Situations

Setting up data in a table or depicting it in a graph can be helpful in distinguishing proportional relationships from other relationships. Setting up a table can make it easy to spot whether or not a relationship is multiplicative. For example, in Table E below, *all* entries of each row are clearly multiples of the first entry in the row. Moreover, each pair of entries was determined by a constant exchange rate (a unit rate of $\times \frac{5}{1}$). In Table F, however, only *some* of the entries of each row are multiples of the first entry, and there is not a constant exchange rate.

Table E: Directly Proportional Quantities

number of nickels	1	2	3	4	...
number of pennies	5	10	15	20	

Table F: Nonproportional Relationship

cows	1	2	3	4	...
fence sections	8	10	12	14	

Graphs of quantities that are directly proportional, then, have two characteristics—they (a) consist of a straight line and (b) pass through the origin (0,0). This is illustrated in Graph I, a plot of the data in Table E.[*] Note that Graph II, a plot of the data in Table F, involves a straight line but does not pass through the origin.

Graph I: Directly Proportional Quantities

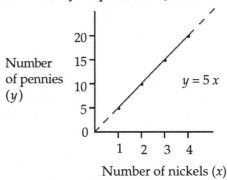

Graph II: Nonproportional Relationship

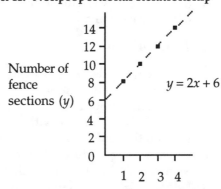

12•2•2 LEARNING: UNDERSTANDING CHILDREN'S PROPORTIONAL REASONING

In this subunit, we consider (a) whether or not elementary-level children are capable of proportional reasoning, (b) their informal strategies, and (c) some common difficulties.

---

[*] Directly proportional situations can be summarized by the formula $y = mx$, where m = slope. Note that if m is positive, y increases by the constant factor of m as x increases, and the line will go uphill. If m is negative, y decreases by the constant factor m as x increases, and the line will go downhill.

Developmental Views

Piaget and Inhelder (1958) argued that pre-adolescent children are not capable of proportional reasoning. Recent research suggests that given the right opportunities, elementary-level children can indeed develop this relatively abstract type of reasoning—albeit, not easily or quickly (see, e.g., Noelting, 1980a, 1980b).

Informal Strategies

Long before children are introduced to the formal methods for solving proportion problems (e.g., the cross-products methods), they can solve many such problems by using informal strategies. Even many young primary-age children can use their additive knowledge to devise a build-up or a "for-every" strategy. Consider the question: If 1 coloring book cost $2, how much will two coloring books cost? (This question could be represented symbolically as 1:2::2:?, which would be read one is two as two is to what?). If allowed to use objects, some primary children represent one book with, for example, a rod and dollars with, for instance, two blocks. By repeating this process until they have represented the prescribed number of book (two rods), they can determine the correct answer of four (see Figure 12.4).

Common Difficulties

In general, many students, and even many adults, do not perform well on proportional-reasoning tasks (Hoffer, 1988b; Lovell, 1961; Wollman & Karplus, 1974). Studies with seventh-graders have found that only about half were successful on such tasks (e.g., Behr et al., 1983). The success rate among adults is not much higher (Karplus & Peterson, 1970). This section discusses three common difficulties.

Additive Reasoning. When confronted with a proportional problem such as Problem 12.1 below, elementary-level children are prone to use additive reasoning rather than multiplicative reasoning (e.g., Hart, 1984a; Karplus, Karplus, & Wollman, 1974).

■ **Problem 12.1** (◆ 2-5). At the carnival, $2 buys 5 tickets. Shabana had $6. How many tickets could she buy?

Instead of considering how many times larger $6 is than $2 and multiplying 5 tickets by this rate of change, many children solve the problem by reasoning $6 is *$4 more* than $2, so Shabana can buy 5 + 4 or 9 tickets. Although additive reasoning is extremely prevalent, it is not an obstacle to instruction. It does not appear to be an invariant developmental phase that all children must pass through but rather "is strongly influenced by instruction" (Karplus, Karplus, Formisano, & Paulsen, 1979, p. 91).

Noninteger Multiplicative Relationships. Informally, direct proportion problems can be solved by either determining the factor of change or the unit rate. In Situation A of Box 12.2 on the next page, the factor of change is an integer and the unit rate is not, and so many children choose to informally determine the factor of change. In Situation B, the unit rate is an integer but the factor of change is not, and so many children choose to informally determine the unit rate. In Situation C, neither the factor of change nor the unit rate is an integer. Hence, children may have difficulty devising an informal strategy.

When students encounter a missing-value proportion problem that requires a noninteger solution (e.g., $\frac{35}{3}$ for Situation C), they often revert

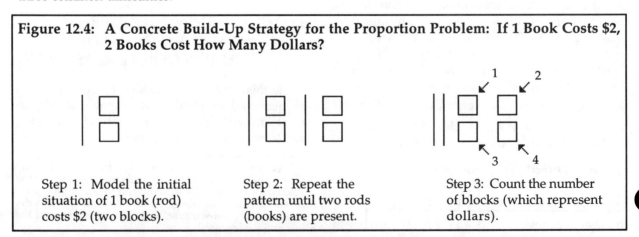

Figure 12.4: A Concrete Build-Up Strategy for the Proportion Problem: If 1 Book Costs $2, 2 Books Cost How Many Dollars?

Step 1: Model the initial situation of 1 book (rod) costs $2 (two blocks).

Step 2: Repeat the pattern until two rods (books) are present.

Step 3: Count the number of blocks (which represent dollars).

Box 12.2: Types of Situations Involving Noninteger Multiplicative Relationships

Situation A:	Situation B:	Situation C:
3 items for \$5,	3 items for \$6,	3 items for \$5,
12 items for ?	5 items for ?	7 items for?

factor of change = x 4   factor of change = $x\frac{5}{3}$ factor of change = $x\frac{7}{3}$

unit rate $= x\frac{5}{3}$ $\frac{3}{5} = \frac{12}{?}$

unit rate $= x\frac{6}{3}$ or $\times 2$ $\frac{3}{6} = \frac{5}{?}$

unit rate $= x\frac{5}{3}$ $\frac{3}{5} = \frac{Z}{?}$

? = 5 x 4 = 20   ? = 5 x 2 = 10

to using an additive strategy or claim that an answer cannot be determined (Karplus, Pulos, & Stage, 1983; Post et al., 1993). Students who can solve such proportion problems are operating at a relatively sophisticated level.

Problems With Formal Cross-Products Algorithm. With a skills approach, children are simply taught a procedure for solving problems involving a direct proportion—namely the cross-products algorithm. This algorithm specifies: (1) set up the proportion, (2) cross multiply, and (3) solve for the unknown. It is frequently used without thought or understanding to solve problems like Problem 12.2 below:

■ **Problem 12.2: An Unequal Party—Take 1** (◆ 6-8). The ratio of boys to girls at a party was 3 to 2. There were 21 boys. How many girls were at the party?

(1) $\frac{3}{2} = \frac{21}{x}$ (2) $3x = 21 \bullet 2$

(3) $x = \frac{21 \bullet 2}{3} = 14$

It is important to keep in mind that using the cross-products algorithm to solve stock proportion problems like Problem 12.2 does not necessarily involve an understanding of proportions (Hoffer, 1988a; Lesh, Post, & Behr, 1988). Indeed, the mechanical learning of the cross-products algorithm typically leads to errors when students encounter a problem like Problem 12.3 below.

■ **Problem 12.3: An Unequal Party—Take 2** (◆ 6-8). The ratio of boys to girls at a party was 3 to 2. There were 35 students at the party. How many were boys?

A common (incorrect) solution is:

$$\frac{3}{2} = \frac{x}{35} \qquad 2x = 3 \bullet 35 \qquad x = \frac{3 \bullet 35}{2} \qquad x = 52.5$$

The fact that the number of boys is greater than the total number of party goers or that the answer involves half a boy is often ignored! In brief, it makes little sense for children to learn and practice a formal proportion algorithm they do not understand.

Varying Format. Another thing that can add to students' confusion about proportions is that the format can vary. Problem 12.3 above can be set up either as shown in Figure A or Figure B below, but not, for example, as in Figure C.

Figure A: Within-Ratio Format

factor of change = x7

unit rate $= x\frac{5}{3}$ $\frac{3 \text{ (boys)}}{5 \text{ (students)}} = \frac{x \text{ (boys)}}{35 \text{ students}}$

Figure B: Between-Ratio Format

unit rate $= x\frac{5}{3}$

factor of change = x7 $\frac{3 \text{ boys}}{x \text{ boys}} = \frac{5 \text{ students}}{35 \text{ students}}$

Figure C: An Incorrect Format

no constant factor of change

no constant unit rate $\frac{3 \text{ boys}}{5 \text{ students}} = \frac{35 \text{ students}}{x \text{ boys}}$

12•2•3 TEACHING

To prepare children for formal proportion instruction that usually begins in the middle-school years, an informal exploration of the topic should begin much earlier. Basically, children should not use the cross-multiplication algorithm until they are ready to understand why it works or, better yet, reinvent it themselves. Instruction should focus on helping them make sense of proportion situations, estimating answers, and devising informal solutions.

Conceptual Phase

If teachers choose problems and activities carefully and encourage the use of informal strategies, intermediate-level, and even primary-level children, can successfully solve proportion problems. Indeed, it is important to provide children from an early age a wide variety of opportunities to engage in the kinds of comparative thinking that underlie proportional reasoning.

☞ **Foster qualitative reasoning about proportional situations with schoolchildren of all ages.** Research suggests that qualitative reasoning can help performance with quantitative proportional-reasoning problems and, perhaps, should even preceded such problems (Behr et al., 1992). Encourage children to intuitively make and informally test predictions about everyday situations involving direct proportions, such as the shadow lengths of various objects (see Activity I of Investigation 12.1 on page 12-3), and those involving indirect proportions, such as playing on a teeter-totter (see Investigation 12.4 on page 12-13).

☞ **Introduce and practice proportional reasoning in the context of real problems.** Some possibilities include mixing paint, adjusting recipes (see, e.g., Activity File 12.3), determining unit prices, building gears, using the length of shadows to de-termine inaccessible heights (see Activity II of Investigation 12.1 on page 12-3), and comparing free-throw success in a basketball game. Scaling activities, like those listed in Activity File 12.4 (on page 12-19), can also provide an interesting and purposeful vehicle for exploring proportions. Activity File 12.5 (on page 12-19) describes an imagination-fostering activity that can involve either imprecise scaling (appropriate for younger children) or more precise scaling (appropriate for more experienced students). Using proportions to make predictions can be engaging and illustrates

---

🍎 Activity File 12.3: Cooking

◆ Proportional reasoning ◆ K-8
◆ Whole class or small group

To prepare for a class, grade-level, or school party, picnic, lunch, bake sale, or whatever, have the students prepare cookies or other edibles. Choose a recipe and ask students to make the appropriate adjustments for the amount needed. The recipe below would be appropriate for intermediate-level children. It was chosen because it contained a good mix of numbers—several different whole numbers, four different fractions, and even a mixed number. (Recipes with just whole numbers or simple unit fractions like $\frac{1}{2}$ and $\frac{1}{4}$ could be chosen for primary-level children). Using a large cookie cutter, the recipe makes about two dozen cookies. If the class were making cookies for an entire grade level, the recipe might have to be tripled or quadrupled. Students would then have to figure out, for example, how many cups of shortening and how many teaspoons of vanilla they need.

Recipe for Easy Cut-Out Cookie[2]

<u>Cookies</u>	<u>Frosting</u>
$\frac{2}{3}$ cup shortening	1 cup powdered sugar
$\frac{1}{2}$ tsp vanilla	$\frac{1}{4}$ tsp vanilla
$1\frac{1}{2}$ tsp baking powder	1 to 4 tbsp milk
2 cups flour	food coloring
$\frac{3}{4}$ cups sugar	

Mix all of the cookie dough together, chill for 1 hour. Roll out the dough onto a floured surface. Roll to the desired thickness, then cut out desired shapes. Bake at 375° for 10 to 12 minutes. While cookies are cooling, mix the frosting ingredients together, add milk to achieve desired thickness. Use food coloring to color the frosting.

---

an important application. For example, if it took $1\frac{1}{2}$ hours to complete one-fourth of a job, how long will the whole job take? Or if Joe Slug is a .333 hitter (1 hit for every 3 at bats), how many hits can we expect Joe to get in a three-game series (about 12 at bats)?

☞ **Use a variety of problems to practice proportional reasoning.** For example, use problems that involve inverse relationships as well as those that involve direct proportions. With ad-

Activity File 12.4: Purposeful Scale-Drawing and Modeling Activities

◆ Proportional reasoning ◆ 3-8 ◆ Small group

• ⌨ As part of a social studies lesson, make scale drawings of, for example, historic buildings, rail cars, canal boats, or aircraft carriers.

• ⌨ To plan the arrangement of a display, decorations for a party, installment of equipment, or other real-life events, prepare a scale-drawn floor plan of the class, school wing, school, etc.

• ⌨ As part of a safety lesson, make scale-drawn floor plans of students' residences indicating, for example, the distance from a student's bedroom to the nearest outside door.

• As part of a social studies project, use balsa wood, clay, or other material to build a scale replica of a historical building, a famous ship, an Indian village, a Colonial town (e.g., Williamsburg), or other items of historical significance.

• Build train cars, houses, bridges, and so forth to a standard model-train scale.

• ⌨ As part of a social studies lesson, visit a battlefield and make a scale drawing of it. Then discuss the battle using the map.

• ⌨ To plan a class trip, make a scale drawing of the route.

Activity File 12.5: Shrink the Class†

◆ Qualitative or quantitative proportional reasoning ◆ 1-8 ◆ Whole class

Explain to the class that Tom Thumb was a legendary dwarf who was presumed to live in England at the time of King Arthur. Then have the class imagine that they were no larger than a thumb. Pass out an activity sheet with the outline of a child that is about the size of the children's thumb. Have the class pretend that a science demonstration has gone astray—as in the movie "Honey, I Shrunk the Kids"—and every thing in the classroom has been shrunk. Have the children draw in their shoes, desk, pencils, and other items. This should provoke discussions about how large to make each of these.

---

†Based on the Liz Thumb activity described in "Young Children (6-8) Ratio and Proportion" by J. van de Brink and L. Streefland, *Educational Studies in Mathematics*, (1979, *Vol. 10*, pp. 403-420.)

---

vanced children, use nonintegers as a unit rate and a factor of change.

☞ **Encourage children to devise their informal strategies to solve proportion problems** (e.g., the concrete build-up strategy illustrated earlier in Figure 12.4 on page 12-16). INSTRUCTION SHOULD FOCUS ON CREATING OPPORTUNITIES FOR CHILDREN TO INVENT AND SHARE THEIR OWN INFORMAL STRATEGIES rather than impose procedures on them (see, e.g., Box 12.3). In this way, instruction can encourage developmentally-appropriate strategies that should further the development of genuine proportional reasoning. Devising and using, for example, an informal build-up strategy can help children see—at least intuitively—that proportional situations involve a repeated-addition (multiplicative) relationship.

Connecting Phase

Setting Up Proportions. As with other mathematical topics, a first step in introducing

Box 12.3: Using a Table to Solve Proportion Problems Informally

The following problem would be appropriate for children already familiar with fractions and who have some experience with similar problems involving whole numbers.

■ **Building a Model-Train House.** With an O-gauge model train, $\frac{1}{4}$" equals 1' (e.g., one foot of real track would be $\frac{1}{4}$-inches long on the model). A 50 foot-long house would be how many inches long in such a model? (✚ Hint: Construct a table and look for a pattern.)

Real (feet)	1	2	3	4	5	. . .	50
Model (inches)	$\frac{1}{4}$	$\frac{2}{4}$	$\frac{3}{4}$	$\frac{4}{4}$	$\frac{5}{4}$		?

By constructing the table above, students should quickly recognize that the answer can be determined by multiplying $\frac{1}{4}$ by the factor of change: 50. (A factor-of-change strategy makes use of the within-the-Model-row pattern.) Some students may notice another (between-rows pattern)—that a real measurement can be converted into a model measurement by multiplying by $\frac{1}{4}$ (e.g., $1 \times \frac{1}{4} = \frac{1}{4}$, $2 \times \frac{1}{4} = \frac{2}{4}$, $3 \times \frac{1}{4} = \frac{3}{4}$) and use the unit-rate strategy to determine the answer ($50 \times \frac{1}{4}$).

proportions symbolically is to connect the symbolism to what they already understand.

☞ **Encourage students to summarize problem situations with symbols.** The proportion format can be introduced as a shorthand for describing problem situations.

☞ **Encourage students to draw a picture as an aid for setting up a proportion and solving it.** Consider Problem 12.4.

◼ **Problem 12.4: Home Improvements are Never as Simple as They Seem (◆ 3-8).** Ashanti bought 4 feet of PVC pipe at 75 cents a foot for a new vanity in his basement. After beginning his plumbing project, he realized that a direct route from the new sink to the main sewer line was not possible. How much would Ashanti have to pay if he needed another 28 feet of PVC to complete the project?

Making a drawing such as those shown in Figure 12.5 can help students set up the proportion correctly ($\frac{4}{75} = \frac{28}{x}$)—even though the information given in the problem was out of order. Note that drawing compares feet to feet and cents to (unknown) cents. (Some students may need guidance at first setting up their diagrams so that comparisons can be made.) The second advantage of making a drawing is that it should help students judge the relative size of the unknown. In the drawing above, students should quickly recognize that the answer should be considerably larger than 75¢.

Figure 12.5: Illustrating a Directly Proportional Situation

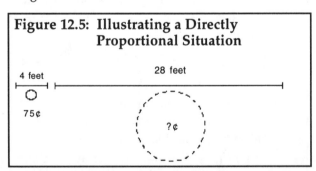

Developing an Explicit Understanding of Proportions. Teacher should build on children's informal knowledge of proportions to help them construct an explicit understanding of proportions.

☞ **Emphasize the mathematical characteristics of proportional situations**

(Cramer et al., 1993). In lessons developed by the Rational Number Project, this was done in the following ways: (a) Students conducted physical experiments with the proportional and nonproportional situations, collected data, summarized the data in tables, and determined the rule for relating pairs of numbers in the table. (b) Students also graphed the data from the experiments and were encouraged to consider the graphic characteristics of directly proportional situations—a straight line through the origin. They were then led to define directly proportional situations as those whose graph could be expressed by the rule $y = mx$. (Note that m or the slope, is the unit rate and that equation always results in a straight-line graph. Moreover, note that when $x = 0$, $y = 0$, and so the graph passes through the point 0,0 on the origin.)

Symbolic Phase

☞ **Foster discussion about alternative formats.** Students should recognize that the within-ratio format ($\frac{a_1}{b_1} = \frac{a_2}{b_2}$) and the between-ratio format ($\frac{a_1}{a_2} = \frac{b_1}{b_2}$) are equivalent and that they can choose freely between them. There is a good chance that some students will spontaneously use the format $\frac{a_1}{a_2} = \frac{b_1}{b_2}$. Encourage the class to discuss this solution procedure and whether it is correct (e.g., Does it consistently yield the correct answer—the same answer as $\frac{a_1}{b_1} = \frac{a_2}{b_2}$ format?). Otherwise, a teacher can illustrate this solution ("One student I knew solved the problem this way...") and ask the class to evaluate it.

☞ **Encourage students to label their symbolic solutions to ensure that proportions are set up correctly.** Labeling each term in a proportion can help students identify the correct part-part or part-whole relationship. For Problem 12.3 (If there are 3 boys for every 2 girls and 35 students total, how many boys are there?), for example, mismatched labels indicate a problem.

$$\frac{boys}{girls} \quad \frac{3}{2} = \frac{Y}{35} \quad \frac{boys}{students}$$
incorrect set-up (part:part::part:whole)

$$\frac{boys}{students} \quad \frac{3}{5} = \frac{Y}{35} \quad \frac{boys}{students}$$
correct set-up (part:whole::part:whole)

This labeling technique can be modified as shown below to help students distinguish the two correct formats from incorrect formats:

boys →   <u>3</u> = <u>Y</u> ← boys (total)
students → 5   35 ← students (total)
     correct set-up (within-ratio format)

boys →   <u>3</u> = <u>5</u> ← students
boys (total) → Y   35 ← students (total)
    correct set-up (between-ratio format)

boys →   <u>3</u> = <u>35</u> ← students (total)
students → 5   Y ← students (total)
     incorrect set-up

boys →   <u>3</u> = <u>35</u> ← students (total)
boys (total) → Y   5 ← students
     incorrect set-up

12•3 PERCENT

Figure 12.6: Truth in Advertising

SHOE reprinted by permission of the Tribune Media Service.

As an *application* of mathematical concepts, percent does not involve developing new concepts. It is included in the elementary mathematics curriculum because it is so widely used (e.g., see Figure 12.6). In Subunit 12•3•1, we discuss the connections between percent and its underlying concepts and the role of percent; in Subunit 12•3•2, common difficulties; and in Subunit 12•3•3, the investigative approach to percent instruction.

12•3•1 MATHEMATICS: UNDERSTANDING PERCENT

Connections with Mathematical Concepts

Percents are simply another symbol for—another way of representing—fractions, decimals, and ratios. More specifically, they are another name for *hundredths*. For instance, $\frac{12}{100}$ or 0.12 can be thought of as 12 percent or 12%. Percents can also be viewed as a symbol for a special kind of part-to-whole ratio—one in which the whole is

100. Thus, 12%, for example, is a way of representing *12 for every 100* (12 per centum).

☞ Try Probe 12.3 (page 12-22).

The Role of Percent

Percent is probably the most widely used ratio notation in everyday life. It is also widely misused and abused.

Uses. Percents are a convenient way to compare data because they have the common base of 100. As Question 1 in Probe 12.3 illustrates, for example, comparing the ratios (scores) $\frac{17}{19}$ and $\frac{27}{30}$ cannot be done easily because they do not have a common basis of comparison. By reporting each ratio as a percent (89% and 90%, respectively), the better score becomes readily apparent.

As Question 2 of Probe 12.3 underscores, percents are a convenient way to represent and remember ratios, particularly when they involve large numbers. One has (continued on page 12-23)

Probe 12.3: Exploring Percent

The aim of this probe is to help you construct a deeper understanding of percent. With the help of your group, answer the questions below. Discuss your answers with your class.

1. Consider the following word problem:

   ■ **Competitive Sisters.** Ming-Ling and Ming-Yeh were sisters assigned to different fifth-grade classes. Nevertheless, they still competed with each other. After school, they compared scores on their weekly math test. Ming-Ling got 17 of a possible 19 points on her test. Ming-Yeh got 27 of 30 points. (a) Can you tell from looking at the ratios $\frac{17}{19}$ and $\frac{27}{30}$ which sister did better? (b) If not, express the ratios in a way that will allow you to compare their homework scores.

2. Try the following experiment. Your task is to remember the following information about Zorkian television programming. Take 20 seconds and read through the data. You may not write anything down. Then answer the questions that follow the data.

   Data about Zorkian T.V. Programming. Of the 6,783,925,104 who watched television at 2AD (2 Zork time units after dark), 2,261,308,368 (33%) tuned in *My Favorite Human*, a zany comedy about a bumbling space alien, and 1,695, 981, 276 (25%) viewed *My Mother the Garbage Vehicle* about an orphan who adopts a crashed spaceship full of nuclear waste.

   Questions. Answer the following questions without looking back at the data.

   a. How many Zorkians watched television at 2 AD?

   b. How many of these watched *My Favorite Human*?

   c. How many watched *My Mother the Garbage Vehicle*?

   d. What percent of the Zorkians watching TV, watched *My Favorite Human*?

   e. What percent watched *My Mother the Garbage Vehicle*?

   Moral. Now check your answers by rechecking the data about Zorkian programming. Which question above did you answer correctly? Compare your results with those of others in your group or class. What point about percent should emerge from this experiment?

3. (a) What is the answer to the following word problem? (b) What point about percent could a discussion of this problem raise?

   ■ **Diet Burgers.** A fast-food chain boasted that its diet burgers were 94% fat free. How many grams of fat are there in a quarter-pound diet burger? (Two pounds is approximately 1,000 grams.)

4. Percents can be deceptive. Critically analyze the following examples. How might they be misleading?

   Example A: Newspaper Advertisement by Dark's Discounts. Gigantic spring sale. Everything in the store must go. Everything 75% off.

   Example B: Mr. Big's Big Claim. In an effort to justify an utterly indecent salary hike for himself, Mr. Big, CEO of Mega Industries, explained to the company's board of directors, "Our profits for this past year were up 200%."

   Example C: Magazine Advertisement by the Crafty Collectibles Company. SAVE SAVE SAVE on this once-in-a-lifetime offer. A sheet of 50 Elvis stamps for 50% OFF a nationally advertised price.

only to leaf through a newspaper to see how much we depend on this notation system. It is used extensively, for example, to report news, to advertise goods, and to indicate sales tax or interest rates.

Misuses. Although percents can make comparisons easier, they can be deceptive when the whole is not identified. Does the 75% off in the newspaper advertisement by Dark's Discounts (Example A of Question 4 in Probe 12.3 on page 12-22) mean 75% off the store's normal low discount prices, 75% off the bloated manufacturer's suggested retail prices, or 75% of the current national debt? Without knowing 75% of what, the consumer is in the dark.

When the whole is not reported, percents can disguise the size of the numbers involved in a ratio. They are sometimes used to make the actual number involved seem larger than it really is. Consider the following examples:

> **Example 12.1:** "Increasing the dues by 33% would be an undue financial hardship on many members." (Versus: "Increasing our dues of $3 by $1 would be . . . .")

> **Example 12.2:** Of the dentists surveyed, 75% recommended Scum Away brand toothpaste over all other brands." (Versus: "Three of the four dentists we surveyed recommended . . . .")

Percents are also sometimes used to make the actual number involved seem smaller than it is. Consider the following two applications from a drug company to the FDA for approval of a new drug:

> **Example 12.3: Draft of FDA Application.** Clinical trials indicate that the harmful side effects of N-RICH-US—including blindness, psychosis, bleeding from every pore in the body, and death—should affect only 10 in every 1,000 users.

> **Example 12.4: Revised Application Actually Sent to the FDA.** Clinical trials indicate that the harmful side effects of N-RICH-US—including blindness, psychosis, bleeding from every pore in the body, and death—should affect only 1% of the users.

Psychologically, 10 is not an unsubstantial number of people. However, because 1 is psychologically a small number, an unwary FDA administrator

might conclude that the side effects of N-RICH-US are negligible.

Indeed, sometimes efforts at persuasion involve cynically choosing a misleading whole. Consider Mr. Big's claim (Example B in Question 4 of Probe 12.3 on page 12-22) that his company's profits were up 200% in the last year. Unfortunately, he did not report that this was in comparison to the previous year's earning that totaled a meager $100. Had Mr. Big chose as the whole the company's average profits from the 10 years just before he took over as CEO—a figure of 100 million dollars—the percent reported would have been dramatically different. It would have been even more different if he chose as the basis of comparison, the company's record high annual profit.

Sometimes, efforts at persuasion involve unscrupulously misleading others about the whole. The magazine advertisement by Crafty Collectibles, Example C in Question 4 of Probe 12.3 on page 12-22, is a ploy consumers should be alert to. Unwary consumers might incorrectly assume that 50% of the nationally advertised price implies 50% off the standard catalogue price (the typical price)—not realizing that it actually means 50% off Crafty Collectibles' usual exorbitant price.

Types of Percent Problems

There are basically three types of percent problems (see Box 12.4)—unknown part (e.g., Problem 12.5 below), unknown percent (e.g., Problem 12.6), and unknown whole (e.g., Problem 12.7).

Box 12.4: Three Types of Percent Problems		
Unknown Part:	7% of 3 is what?	7% x 3 = ☐
Unknown Percent:	0.21 is what percent of 3?	☐% x 3 = 0.21
Unknown Whole:	0.21 is 7% of what number?	7% x ☐ = 0.21

■ **Problem 12.5: Unknown Part.** If the sales tax was 7%, how much sales tax would be added for an item costing $3?

■ **Problem 12.6: Unknown Percent.** If an item cost $3 and sales tax came to 21 cents. What percent sales tax was charged?

■ **Problem 12.7: Unknown Whole.** Mary wanted to return a defective binder, but Ruffus her dog had chewed up the receipt. Mary could still see that the sales tax came to $0.21. If the sales tax was 7%, what was the cost of the binder?

12•3•2 LEARNING: UNDERSTANDING CHILDREN'S DIFFICULTIES

Five common difficulties are: (a) incorrectly translating decimals into percents and vice versa; (b) not recognizing that percent is based on 100; (c) unfamiliarity with unknown-percent and unknown-whole problems; (d) unfamiliarity with problems involving more than 100%; and (e) unfamiliarity with problems involving a percent of a percent.

12•3•3 TEACHING

As with ratios and proportions, the conceptual groundwork for percent should be laid in the primary grades. This will provide a sound basis for the connecting phase—for introducing percent symbols in the fifth grade (if not sooner).

Fostering Connections

Connections with Real-World Applications. During all phases of instruction, children should be helped to understand the uses and misuses of percent.

↬ **The introduction and practice with percent should be done purposefully by exploring real or realistic applications.** To help children understand the utility of percent, have a class read or make reports with percents. For example, as part of a science unit on genetic variation, have the class check the eye color, hair color, or height of 100 same-aged students and report their results as percents. Note that using a sample of 100 makes it easy to translate the data into percents. A more challenging task—and one which underscores the real value of percent—is comparing different-sized samples, say, fifth-grade boys and girls at various height ranges (e.g., 4 feet 6 inches to 4 feet 8 inches). Moreover, real or realistic problems can provide an interesting way to practice using percent and can serve as the basis for instruction in other content areas (see, e.g., Activity File 12.6). For example, problems involving advertising, such as Questions 3 and 4 of Probe 12.3 on page 12-22, can serve as the basis for a consumer-education lesson.

↬ ✐ **Encourage children to find examples or create stories that involve misusing percents to disguise the actual numbers involved in a comparison.** Analyzing the deceptive use of percent is a good way to introduce children to the issue of clearly defining the whole and how percent can be misused (see, e.g., Questions 3 and 4 of Probe 12.3 on page 12-22). Finding examples of misuse and explaining how percents are used in a deceptive manner or creating a story about such misuse requires understanding.

Connections with Prior Knowledge and Models Conceptual-level instruction should build on children's existing knowledge of fractions and decimals and use concrete or pictorial models to develop their vocabulary and understanding of percent. At the connecting level, instruction should help children explicitly link percent symbolism to their conceptual knowledge of decimal fractions, decimals, and percent.

↬ **Introduce percent by building on children's understanding of decimal fractions and decimals.** Ensure that students have a sound basis for understanding percent. In particular, they should have

---

 Activity File 12.6: Estimating the Percent of Oxygen in the Air

◆ Measurement + percent ◆ 5-8 ◆ Any number

As part of a science unit on the atmosphere, Mr. Burger had his class do the following study to estimate what percent of the atmosphere is oxygen. Steel wool was soaked in aged vinegar. The vinegar acted as a catalyst to promote rusting (oxidation). The steel wool was then stuffed into the bottom of a glass jar. The jar was turned upside down and carefully lowered into a pan half filled with water. Mr. Burger noted that there was no water in the jar and asked why. The class agreed that the air in the jar kept the water pushed back. After several days, the class found that the steel wool was quite rusty and that the water level in the jar had risen. After discussing why these things had occurred (the oxygen in the jar was used up in the oxidation process), the class measured the distance the water had risen ($1\frac{1}{2}$ inches) and the height of the jar (7 inches)—after some discussion, the students agreed that $1\frac{1}{2}/7$ = 3/14 = .21 and concluded that the atmosphere was about 21% oxygen.

a solid *understanding* of decimal fractions and decimals *before* the concept of percent is introduced. Help students connect this new concept to their existing concepts. Specifically, help them see that percent is nothing more than another name for hundredths. For example, *twenty-five hundredths* ($\frac{25}{100}$ or .25) can also be named *twenty-five percent* (25%). Then, help children to recognize that decimal fractions such as *nine-tenths* ($\frac{9}{10}$) or decimals such as .9 can be expressed as percents by considering their equivalents in hundredths (e.g., $\frac{9}{10} = \frac{9}{100}$ = 9%). In brief, underscore that percent is simply a new term and notation for a concept they already understand.

☞ ✔ **Use a variety of models and examples to illustrate and check the concept of percent.** Both concrete models such as base-ten blocks and pictorial models such as 10 x 10 grids can help children make the connection between percent and decimal fractions and decimals.

Number Sense for Percent

In this section, we discuss how to foster a number sense, in general, and a sense for percent equivalents, in particular.

General Percent Sense. At all phases of instruction, instruction should help students cultivate a number sense for percent.

☞ **Emphasize that percents involve using 100 as the common basis of comparison and other key characteristics of percents.** CHILDREN SHOULD UNDERSTAND THAT PERCENTS ARE A CONVENIENT WAY FOR MAKING COMPARISONS BECAUSE THEY HAVE THE COMMON BASE OF 100. Help children to recognize that, for example, *twenty-five percent* or 25% literally means 25 per hundred—25 in every 100.

☞ ✔ **As a way of fostering and evaluating an understanding of percent, challenge students with qualitative-reasoning tasks.** For example, ask them what it means "to give a 110% effort" or "to take 125% off the original price."

☞ **Encourage estimating the solutions to percent problems before expecting exact answers and afterward as a way of checking.** Initially, create opportunities to estimate with relatively easy percents such as 50%, 25%, $33\frac{1}{3}$%, 1%, and 10%. Later, encourage students to *simplify* a problem (e.g., 68% of $19.99 is about 70% of $20).

Percent-Fraction or -Decimal Equivalents. A key aspect of a percent number sense is the ability to convert a percent into a fraction or a decimal.

☞ **Begin with direct translations involving 100.** At the connecting level, help children link percents to decimal fractions, decimals, and apparent models (models with 100 subdivisions). For example, 37% can be viewed as *37 hundredths* or $\frac{37}{100}$.

☞ **For familiar fractions, encourage the automatic recognition of nondirect equivalents.** A key aspect of a number sense is the ability to recognize 50% as $\frac{1}{2}$, 25% as $\frac{1}{4}$, 10% as $\frac{1}{10}$, 20% as $\frac{1}{5}$, as well as the percents equal to other fourths, tenths, and fifths. This knowledge can build on children's understanding of fraction equivalents. If 50% = $\frac{50}{100}$ and $\frac{50}{100} = \frac{1}{2}$, then 50% = $\frac{1}{2}$. In time, children should also be able to immediately recognize 33% or $33\frac{1}{3}$% as $\frac{1}{3}$, 67 or $66\frac{2}{3}$% as $\frac{2}{3}$, 12.5% as $\frac{1}{8}$, 37.5% as $\frac{3}{8}$, 62.5% as $\frac{5}{8}$, and 87.5% as $\frac{7}{8}$.

☞ **Foster an informal understanding of small percents.** Instruction should help students understand percents between 0 and 1%. Challenge students to represent $\frac{1}{2}$% or 0.5% on a 10 x 10 grid. If they are stymied, have them first consider how 1% would be represented. By recognizing that each small square is 1%, students should recognize that $\frac{1}{2}$% or 0.5% is one-half of a small square (see Figure 12.7 on the next page). Then challenge them to consider what fraction and what decimal this would represent. Because a fraction must involve equal-sized parts, $\frac{1}{2}$% must equal $\frac{1}{200}$. Children can also be encouraged to reason out the decimal equivalent of $\frac{1}{2}$%. If 1% is equal to .01, then $\frac{1}{2}$% must be less than .01—one half of .01 to be precise. If children have studied decimal multiplication, this translates to 0.5 x .01, the product of which can be determined with base-ten blocks. Otherwise, they can use base-ten blocks to represent 1% or .01 and then $\frac{1}{2}$% or .005.

☞ **Foster a conceptual understanding of percents greater than 100%.** Help students make sense of percents greater than 100%. Challenge them to represent, say, 200% or 125% concretely with base-ten blocks or pictorially with 10 x 10

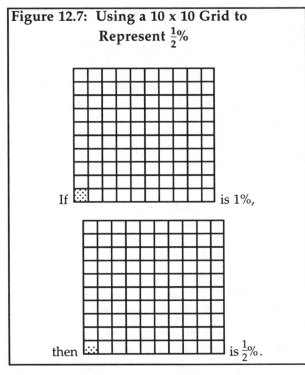

Figure 12.7: Using a 10 x 10 Grid to Represent $\frac{1}{2}$%

If [grid] is 1%,

then [grid] is $\frac{1}{2}$%.

grids. If they have difficulty, encourage them to first consider how 100% would be represented.

Percent Problems

☞ **Students should work with a variety of percent problems so that they become accustomed to explicitly defining the whole and the unknown element.** More specifically, students should work with (a) unknown-whole problems as well as unknown-part and unknown-percent problems; (b) problems that involve more than 100%; and (c) problems that involve a percent of a percent.

☞ **Initially, encourage students to use concrete models or drawings and informal solution strategies.** Do not impose a procedure on students. Instead, help them work out a strategy that makes sense to them.

☞ **Help children see that percent problems are essentially fraction and decimal problems using new terms.** Investigation 12.5 illustrates how percent problems can be related to proportions.

☞ Try Investigation 12.5 (page 12-27).

PARTING THOUGHTS

"The fact that many aspects of our world operate according to proportional rules makes proportional reasoning abilities extremely useful in the interpretation of real world phenomena" (Post et al., 1988, p. 79). "Proportional reasoning involves an understanding of the [multiplicative] relationships embedded in proportional situations" (Cramer et al., 1993, p. 168). To help children understand such relationships, "traditional methods . . . have focused heavily on memorization of the multiplication [table]. However, indirect approaches may turn out to be more effective" (Resnick & Singer, 1993, p. 127). Students need to see many problem situations that can be modeled and solved through proportional reasoning" (NCTM, 1989, p. 82). "It is important not to promote specific strategies" (Lamon, 1993, p. 153). In solving ratio and proportion problems even before they had instruction in the domain, many children showed they had a repertoire of powerful [informal] strategies at their command" (Lamon, 1993, p. 150). "Ideally, instruction should be designed to take advantage of students' . . . invented strategies" (Lamon, 1993, p. 151). That is, they should be encouraged to choose among, discuss, evaluate, and extend these strategies.

RESOURCES

SOME INSTRUCTIONAL RESOURCES

☎ **Fractions, Decimals, Ratios, & Percents: Hard to Teach and Hard to Learn?** edited by Carne Barnett, Donna Goldstein, and Babette Jackson, © 1994, Heinemann. Elementary teachers describe their experience with teaching fractions, decimals, ratios, and percents.

☎ **My Travels with Gulliver** © by Wings on Learning. This resource focused on situations in *Gulliver's Travels* that involve using ratios and proportions.

☎ **Understanding Rational Numbers and Proportional Reasoning** by Frank Curcio and Nadine Bezuk, © 1994 by the NCTM. This component of the NCTM Middle Grades Addenda series is an excellent source of classroom-ready activities involving data collection, fractions, ratios, proportions, and percents. The reference illustrates how rational numbers and proportions are an integral aspect of many real-world situations and includes suggestions for integrating technology into instruction and implementing alternative assessment. (Continued on page 12-28.)

⌣ Investigation 12.5: Introducing the Ratio Method for Solving Percent Problems

◆ Connecting percents to proportions + problem solving ◆ 5-8 ◆ Groups of four + class discussion

Percent problems often give students considerable difficulty. This activity illustrates a technique for translating a percent problem into a proportion, which can then be solved by using the cross-products procedure. To see how this can be a useful technique for solving percent problems, try the activity yourself, preferably with the aid of your group. Discuss your solutions with your group or class.

Part I: Review—Using Line Segments to Solve Proportion Problems.
Problem A below can be represented by line segments 5, 4, 30, and x units long (where the line for x is shorter than that for 30). This drawing implies the proportion $5/4 = 30/x$. Using the cross-products procedure, we find that $x = 24$.

■ **Problem A: A Speedy Delivery.** Mr. Buya's wife was about to have a baby. He drove the first 5 miles to the nearest hospital in 4 minutes. The hospital was another 30 miles away. Assuming he could maintain the same rate of speed for the rest of his trip, how long would the rest of the trip take Mr. Buya to drive?

Part II: A Transition—Extending the Technique to Equivalent Fractions.
Equivalent fractions can be viewed as proportions. Because two equivalent fractions have the same whole, we know that the line segments for each fraction must be the same length. To help visualize the equivalent fractions $\frac{2}{3}$ and $\frac{6}{9}$, the two line segments in Figure A are placed one above the other rather than side by side. Use a line segment to represent the equivalent-fraction problems below. Use a ☐ to indicate the unknown. Then use the cross-products algorithm to determine the unknown.

■ **Problem B:** Hart's recipe called for $\frac{3}{4}$ cup of milk. He wanted to make only half the recipe. In order to work with an easier number, Hart decided to convert $\frac{3}{4}$ into eighths. Three-fourths cups of milk is how many eighths cups of milk?

■ **Problem C:** Hermila and Jillandra wanted to buy a cake at the school fair. Because Hermila contributed more money, the girls decided she should get $\frac{2}{3}$ of the cake. If the cake was divided into 9 equal shares, how many ninths should Hermila get?

Part III: Extending the Technique to Percent Problems.
How could the following percent problems be represented by the line-segment technique? Hint: Recall that 15%, for example, can be represented by the fraction $\frac{15}{100}$ (part = 15; whole = 100). For each of the three problems below, illustrate how your drawing can help in setting up as a proportion that can then be solved using the cross-products method.

■ **Problem D: Part Unknown.** The list price of car is $21,000. The dealer's cost of the car is 15% below the list price. (The dealer's margin of profit is 15% of $21,000.) What is the margin of profit for the dealer?

■ **Problem E: Percent Unknown.** The list price of a car $21,000. A dealer agrees to sell you the car for $19,500. What percent of the total cost is this price?

■ **Problem F: Whole Unknown.** In a financial disclosure statement, you discover that $21,000 is only 80% of the true cost of the car when financing and an extended warranty are included in the cost of the car. What is the true cost of the car?

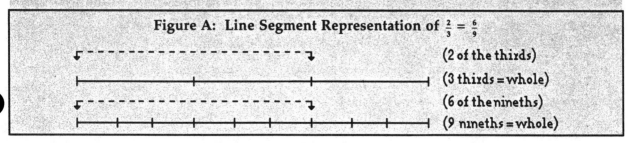

Figure A: Line Segment Representation of $\frac{2}{3} = \frac{6}{9}$

(2 of the thirds)
(3 thirds = whole)
(6 of the nineths)
(9 nineths = whole)

A SAMPLE OF CHILDREN'S LITERATURE

🔖 Stories that involve *changing scale* include **Alice's Adventures in Wonderland** by Lewis Carroll (© 1985, Scholastic), **The Borrowers** by Mary Norton (© 1953, Harcourt, Brace, Jovanovich), **Gulliver's Travels** by Jonathan Swift (© 1947, Putnam), and **Stuart Little** by E. B. White (© 1945, Harper). With *Gulliver's Travels*, for example, students could use pictures in the text to gauge the relative size (size ratio) of Gulliver and the (6-inch tall) Lilliputians.

Stories that discuss *rates of growth* include **Germs Make Me Sick!** by Melvin Berger, **The Habits of Rabbits** by Virginia Kahl, and **Melisande** by E. Nesbit. In the latter story, a bald Melisande wishes her hair would grow. When she gets her wish, her hair grows 1 inch each night. After being cut, it grows 2 inches each night; a second cut results in growth of 4 inches per night, and so forth. After each haircut a teacher can ask students how many nights it would take for Melisande's hair to grow 2 yards if her head was shaved (Whitin & Wilde, 1992). Note that solving the problem can involve proportional reasoning (e.g., if 1 yard = 36 inches, then 2 yards = 72 inches) and rates (e.g., ☐ days x 2 inches/day = 72 inches, so ☐ = 36 days).

🔖 **The Magic School Bus: Lost in the Solar System** by Joanna Cole, © 1990 Scholastic. This book can serve to introduce an integrated science-mathematics unit on the solar system, measures of weight, and proportions.[3] In this volume of the *Magic School Bus* series, a child travels to the planets of our solar system and discovers that his weight is different on each. For example, his weight on earth was 85 pounds, but on Venus, Mars, Jupiter, and Saturn it's 77, 32, 247, and 90 pounds, respectively. After reading the story, a teacher can pose proportion problems such as: About how much do you think 170 pound man (twice the weight of the boy) would weigh on each of the other planets in our solar system? About how much would a 42.5 pound box of supplies (half the boy's weight) weigh? About how much would 255 pounds (three times the boy's weight) weigh? Children in third to fifth grade could first be encouraged to use qualitative reasoning to es-

timate the answers. Later they could be encouraged to use informal strategies to solve such problems. Children in the latter intermediate grades can be given more difficult problems (i.e., those with a factor of change other than 2, $\frac{1}{2}$, and 3) and encouraged to invent informal procedures for solving them or to even reinvent the cross-products algorithm.

TIPS ON USING TECHNOLOGY

Computers/Videotapes

Computers could be used to "represent dynamically situations in which quantities vary with a constant ratio, such as the number of turns of the winch and the change in height of a well bucket" (Greer, 1992, p. 292). "Applying the Computer's Representational Plasticity to Create Bridging Notations to Ramp from the Concrete to the Abstract" (by J. Kaput, pp. 63-70 in *Designing for Learning*, edited by B. Bowen and © 1990 by Apple Computers, Cupertino, CA) includes a description of software designed to represent rates (e.g., three umbrellas for every two animals). "A LOGO-Based Microworld for Ratio and Proportion" (by C. Hoyles, R. Noss, & R. Sutherland, pp. 115-122 in the *Proceedings of the Thirteenth Annual Conference of the International Group for the psychology of Mathematics Education, Vol. 2*, edited by G. Vergnaud, J. Rogalski, & M. Artigue and © 1989 by G. R. Didactique, Paris) suggests, for example, using computer-generated, geometrically similar figures to counter common errors in proportional reasoning.

💾 **Gears** designed by Robert Kimbal and available from Sunburst. By experimenting with gears, students can discover gear ratios and relationships that will permit them to predict the rate and direction the last gear in a series of gears will turn. Available in disks formatted for Apple, IBM, Macintosh. Network versions are also available.

📼 **Proportional Reasoning Unit**, distributed by Sunburst, includes four videotapes that illustrate real-world applications of proportional reasoning such as horse training, architecture, and biochemistry: (1) *Percents: Say It with Hundredths*, (2) *Rates and Ratios: Comparisons*, (3) *Proportions: Expressing Relationships*, and (4) *Proportions: The Shrinking and Stretching Machine*.

13 MAKING SENSE OF INFORMATION AND USING IT TO MAKE EVERYDAY DECISIONS: STATISTICS AND PROBABILITY

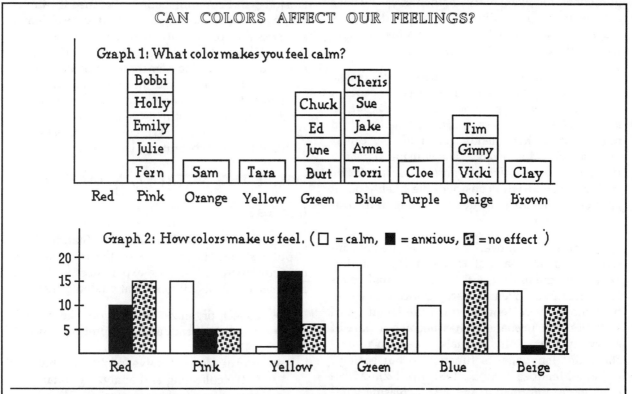

CAN COLORS AFFECT OUR FEELINGS?

Graph 1: What color makes you feel calm?

Red	Pink	Orange	Yellow	Green	Blue	Purple	Beige	Brown
Bobbi					Cheris			
Holly				Chuck	Sue			
Emily				Ed	Jake		Tim	
Julie				June	Anna		Ginny	
Fern	Sam	Tara		Burt	Torri	Cloe	Vicki	Clay

Graph 2: How colors make us feel. (□ = calm, ■ = anxious, ▦ = no effect)

We did an opinion poll and an experiment to see how colors might affect how we feel. We used a computer to graph our data and write this report. Graph 1 shows the result of the opinion poll of our class. Blue and green got the most votes for making people feel calm. Graph 2 shows the results of our experiment. We showed 25 students chosen randomly from the sixth-grade classes a color for a minute and asked them if they felt calmer, more anxious, or the same. Most said that Pink, Green, Blue, and Beige made them feel calmer. Most students said red and yellow made them feel more anxious.

Bulletin boards can serve to display the results of students' investigations of an issue, a question, or a problem. A display can include the aim of the investigation, a summary of the data collected, and the conclusions drawn (an interpretation of the data). The bulletin board above, for example, summarizes a class' exploration into the effects of color on people's feelings. This exploration served as a basis for an integrated unit on expressive arts (using colors in songs, literature, and music to portray feelings), science (reflection, absorbtion, and perception of color), and mathematics. Note that collecting, organizing, and analyzing the data for such an investigation provide children a real purpose for learning about statistics and creating graphs. Note also that the bulletin board underscores the importance of graphs as a valuable way of summarizing and communicating data. 💻 Computers can be used to collect, analyze, and graph data (spreadsheet function) and to write up reports (word processing).

☞ Can the colors we wear or the color of a room affect our mood? Can the color of soap box or a political poster influence how we feel? With your group or class design a study to address one or more of these questions.

THIS CHAPTER

"*S*tatistics and probability," choked Miss Brill as she read through the district's new guidelines for elementary mathematics. "That's college material studied by math and science majors. What normal person, let alone a child, uses statistics and probability?"

"In fact," noted the ever patient Ms. Socrates, "even young children encounter these concepts in their everyday lives. *Statistics, simply put, is using and making sense of data.* When a child notes that all her friends get at least a dollar more a week in allowance, she is using statistics. *Probability is basically an effort to predict future events.* A child who considers the likelihood of getting caught for a misdeed is engaging probabilistic thinking."

Although often overlooked by elementary instruction in the past, statistics and probability are among the most useful topics in a mathematics curriculum. "Even a cursory glance at newspapers shows the extent to which the language of statistics and probability has become a part of everyday life . . . . Individuals need [to understand this language] to function in our society" (Pereira-Mendoza & Swift, 1981, pp. 1-2). Moreover, in our information age, it is increasingly important that students know how to collect, organize, describe, display, and interpret data (NCTM, 1989). They also need to know how to use information as a basis for making predictions and choices. In brief, knowledge of statistics and probability is crucial today for mathematical literacy and for numerous everyday decisions.

Knowledge of statistics and probability are fundamental to solving many significant practical problems that are inherently interesting to children (NCTM, 1989). Thus, the study of statistics and probability can promote children's mathematical power in at least three interrelated ways. (1) It can promote a positive disposition by (a) providing rich opportunities for intuitive exploration and exciting discoveries, (b) expanding children's view of mathematics, (c) creating a purpose for learning other content areas,

and (d) underscoring the usefulness of mathematics. As illustrated in Box 13.1 (on the next page), children can see that mathematics is a useful tool for exploring the questions raised in other subject areas such as science, social studies, and consumer education. (2) As Box 13.1 also illustrates, explorations involving statistics and probability can actively involve children in the processes of mathematical inquiry—problem solving, searching for patterns, conjecturing, drawing logical conclusions, and communicating. Because it can involve devising strategies to solve problems, statistics and probability instruction can serve as a basis for problem-solving instruction. (3) Moreover, solving problems in these domains can involve the application and meaningful learning of other mathematical knowledge such as number, written arithmetic, estimation, and measurement (again, see Box 13.1). We consider statistics in Unit 13•1 and probability in Unit 13•2.

WHAT THE NCTM *STANDARDS* SAY

Grades K-4

Statistics and Probability. Standard 11 stipulates that "in grades K-4, the mathematics curriculum should include experiences with data analysis and probability so that students can:

- ◆ collect, organize, and describe data;
- ◆ construct, read, and interpret displays of data;
- ◆ formulate and solve problems that involve collecting and analyzing data;
- ◆ explore concepts of chance" (p. 54).

Grades 5-8

Statistics. According to Standard 10, "in grades 5-8, the mathematics curriculum should include exploration of statistics in real-world situations so that students can:

- ◆ systematically collect, organize, and describe data;
- ◆ construct, read, and interpret tables, charts, and graphs;
- ◆ make inferences and convincing arguments that are based on data analysis;
- ◆ evaluate arguments that are based on data analysis;
- ◆ develop an appreciation for statistical methods as powerful means for decision making" (p. 105).

Box 13.1: A Chance Opportunity to Learn

During a team meeting, Mrs. Fermanian the science-health teacher quietly addressed Mr. Yant, "My health classes are studying about venereal disease, and I'd appreciate your help in making an important point." Mr. Yant cautiously agreed to do what he could. "Our health literature indicates that 1 in 5 teens has VD," continued Mrs. Fermanian, "I want to impress on my students the dangers of casual sex with multiple partners. What is the probability of encountering someone with VD if a person has sex with two partners?"

Mr. Yant recognized this situation created a marvelous opportunity to work on probability. He further saw that solving this probability problem would naturally create a chance to review and practice operations on fractions. He arranged to co-teach Mrs. Fermanian's class.

Jackson argued that the probability of each of two partners having VD was one in five, so the probability overall should still be one in five. Germaine argued that Jackson's conclusion didn't make sense, "Contact with the infection should be more likely, because there are more opportunities for contact." Building on Germaine's argument, Alysen suggested adding the probabilities $\frac{1}{5} + \frac{1}{5}$ and proposed an answer of $\frac{2}{10}$ —an answer that met with the approval of many classmates. Mr. Yant decided to use Alysen's error as a springboard for what appeared to be a much needed review of fraction addition and equivalent fractions. To prompt reflection, he asked, "What is another name for $\frac{2}{10}$? This led to a discussion of how to reduce fractions. The class soon recognized that $\frac{2}{10}$ was equivalent to $\frac{1}{5}$. Having intuitively concluded that the probability of encountering VD with three partners should be greater, Alysen and her classmates now saw that $\frac{2}{10}$ did not make sense as the solution to the problem. Kimo, whose dissent had been ignored earlier, noted that the trouble was that Alysen added the fractions incorrectly. After discovering that correctly adding fractions produced what seemed like a sensible answer ($\frac{1}{5} + \frac{1}{5} = \frac{2}{5}$), Mr. Yant created cognitive conflict by challenging the class to consider the probability of contacting VD with six partners. After the class recognized that simply adding the probabilities ($\frac{1}{5} + \frac{1}{5} + \frac{1}{5} + \frac{1}{5} + \frac{1}{5} = \frac{6}{5}$) didn't make sense, Mr. Yant suggested that the class informally explored other methods for determining the answer.

☞ With the help of your group or class, informally solve the problems posed above.

Probability. According to Standard 11, "in grades 5-8, the mathematics curriculum should include explorations of probability in real-world situations so that students can:

- model situations by devising . . . experiments or simulations to determine probabilities;
- appreciate the power of using a probability model by comparing experimental results with mathematical expectations;
- make predictions that are based on experimental or theoretical probabilities;
- [appreciate] the pervasive use of probability in the real world" (p. 109).

13•1 STATISTICS

Statistics are used in many aspects of everyday life including business, sports, science, government, journalism, and so forth. Making decisions in today's world—evaluating, for example, advertising claims, the relative value of football players, weather reports, government reports, and DNA evidence—requires an ability to interpret and analyze statistical information (Bright & Hoeffner, 1993). Moreover, as Figure 13.1 (on the next page) suggests, statistics can be manipulated to make a case. As a famous quote goes, "There are three kinds of lies: lies, damned lies, and statistics."[*] An understanding of statistics, then, is imperative for students to become informed consumers and citizens.

In Subunit 13•1•1, we explain a rationale for collecting real data in teaching statistics. In Subunit 13•1•2, we address graphing—an invaluable

---

[*] According to *Respectfully Quoted* edited by Suzy Platt (Congressional Reference Division, Library of Congress, Washington, 1989), in his autobiography, Mark Twain attributes this remark to Disraeli, a famous British politician. It has also been attributed to others.

Figure 13.1: A Tool of Persuasion

tool in organizing, describing, and analyzing information. In Subunit 13•1•3, we discuss *descriptive statistics*—statistics that *measure or describe a set of data and that can be used in their analysis.* In Subunit 13•1•4, we touch on how statistics can be used to make predictions—more specifically, how *a conclusion or inference about a larger group can be drawn from data collected with a sample of the group.*

13•1•1 A NEW DIRECTION IN STATISTICS INSTRUCTION: COLLECTING REAL DATA

Addressing everyday problems and questions frequently begins by collecting needed data. As Activity File 3.1 illustrates, CHILDREN SHOULD GAIN EXPERIENCE IN HOW TO COLLECT DATA PURPOSEFULLY—AS A WAY FOR INVESTIGATING INTERESTING ISSUES. Teaching tips on implementing the investigative approach are outlined below.

↪ **In general, children should collect their *own* data rather than used contrived data.** Textbook or worksheet exercises with "canned" data are often uninteresting to children. Investigation 13.1 illustrates how a genuine investigation can involve students in collecting real data and then organizing, analyzing, and describing it.

☞ Try Investigation 13.1 (pages 13-5 and 13-6).

↪ **Encourage children to propose and explore their own questions.** "Children's questions about the physical world can often be answered by collecting and analyzing data. After generating questions, they decide what information is appropriate and how it can be collected, displayed, and interpreted to an- (continued on page 13-7)

🍎 Activity File 13.1: Toothpick-Bug Hunt

◆ Collect, organize, and analyze data ◆ K-5
◆ Whole class

This science lesson on protective coloring creates a real need to collect, organize, and analyze data. Before class, use food coloring or tempera to dye an equal number of toothpicks red, yellow, orange, dark green, and brown. Dye at least 50 of each color. (Multicolored macaroni can be used instead of toothpicks.[1]) Place the toothpicks outside in the grass, in dirt, on tree trunks, and on tree or plant leaves. The search area should be well defined so that students do not get lost, cross roads, or otherwise encounter danger.

Tell the class that they are going to pretend to be toothpick birds. Further explain that a toothpick bird's favorite food is toothpick bugs and that they are going outside to find their favorite food. Show the class some sample toothpick bugs so that they know what to look for.

Give the class a specific amount of time to search for the toothpick bugs (e.g., 10 minutes). Have the children reassemble in the classroom with their catches. Ask what color toothpick bug they caught most often and what they caught least often. Encourage the class to count the number of toothpick bugs of each color and organize the data so that the most likely and least likely victim can be identified. This creates a real need for discussing and learning about graphs or charts. After compiling the data in a graph or chart, ask the students why the results turned out as they did. This should lead to a discussion of protective coloring.

🍎 Investigation 13.1: How Far and Why?[†]

◆ Collecting, analyzing, and graphing data + measuring + determining averages
◆ 4-8 ◆ Small groups of four

This integrated science-mathematics lesson can begin with the question, *What affects how far a marble rolled down an incline will travel from the incline?* Reasonable conjectures include (a) the height of the incline, (b) the weight of the marble, and (c) the length of the incline. The following experiment focuses on answering the question, *Does the height of the incline affect the roll distance and, if so, what height will maximize the roll?* Try it yourself to see what is involved.

The experiment involves dropping a marble down a paper-towel tube held at various heights and measuring how far the marble rolls each time (see the figure below). Start with a height of 5 cm and increased it by 5 cm increments up to 25 cm.

Step 1: Predict the height at which the marble will roll the farthest, the second farthest, and so forth. Record your predictions in the table and Graph A on the next page.

Step 2: At each height, run three trials and determine an average. (*Why run three trials and take the average for each height?* Note that if a mean is used, the students will practice decimal addition and division.) Record the data in the table on the next page.

Step 3: Plot the average distance rolled for each height in Graph B on the next page and analyze the data. Did the results turn out as expected? What is the relationship between height and distance? Consider why the results turned out as they did.

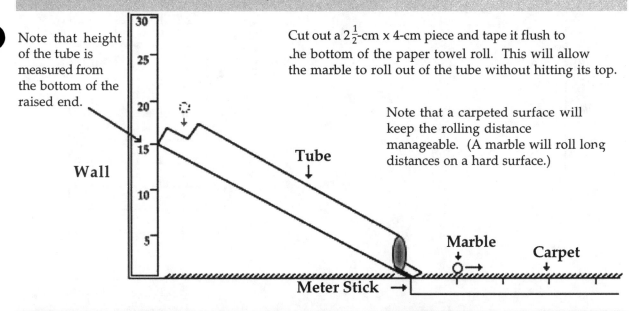

Note that height of the tube is measured from the bottom of the raised end.

Cut out a $2\frac{1}{2}$-cm x 4-cm piece and tape it flush to .he bottom of the paper towel roll. This will allow the marble to roll out of the tube without hitting its top.

Note that a carpeted surface will keep the rolling distance manageable. (A marble will roll long distances on a hard surface.)

Wall **Tube** **Marble** **Carpet**

Meter Stick →

Questions for Reflection

1. (a) From the data collected, *Can you be certain you have identified the height that produces the maximum distance?* (b) *How could you check for the height that produces the maximum distance?*

2. (a) Would it make sense to connect the dots in Graph B with lines? Why or why not? (b) The variables *height* and *distance* are what kind of data, categorical or numerical data? (c) If the latter, do they represent discrete or continuous quantities? (d) Would it make sense to connect the dots of a graph that plotted *favorite TV show* and *number of people who chose the show*? Why or why not? (e) Would it make sense to connect the dots of a graph that plotted *favorite (whole) number* and the *number of people who chose the number*? Why or why not?

Investigation 13.1 continued

Table

Height of Tube (cm)	Predicted Distance*	Trial 1	Trial 2	Trial 3	Average	Actual Order
5						
10						
15						
20						
25						

* Rank the predicted distances from 1 (for longest) to 5 (for the shortest).

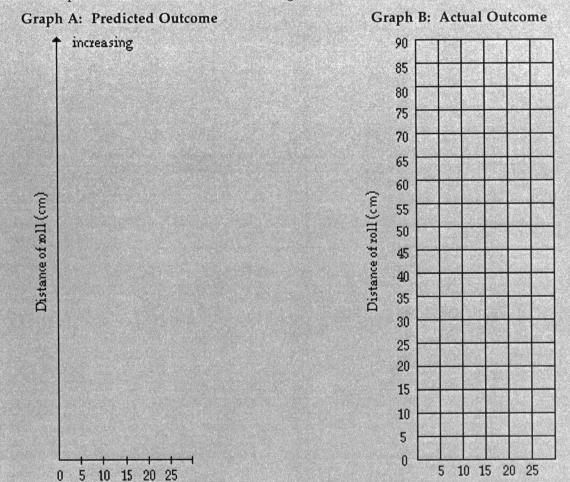

Graph A: Predicted Outcome   Graph B: Actual Outcome

✦ **Extensions**. To test whether or not weight is a factor, repeat the experiment with a steel marble (a ball bearing). Graph these results in a different color on Graph B. Is there a constant difference or not? To test whether or not the length of the incline is a factor, repeat the experiment with inclines of different length. (Suggestion: Cut a 2-inch diameter PVC pipe in half and cut the halves to various lengths). Over the various incline lengths, is there a constant angle that maximizes distance? What other questions do the data raise? Other variations of the investigation can include using carpets of different naps or different floor surfaces. These changes have what effects on the distance traveled?

† Based on an activity described in *Making Sense of Data* (Addenda Series, Grades K-6) by M. M. Lindquist with J. Luguire, A. Gardner, and S. Shekaramiz, © 1992 by the National Council of Teachers of Mathematics.

swer their questions" (NCTM, 1989, p. 54). Note that such investigations often lead to new questions and conjectures to explore. The process of answering interesting questions underscores the usefulness of mathematics and fosters a positive disposition toward it.

13•1•2 GRAPHING—ORGANIZING, DESCRIBING, AND ANALYZING DATA

Once needed data are collected, this raw information must be transformed into usable, sensible information by organizing, describing and analyzing it. These processes can be aided by creating visual displays of the information—that is, by summarizing the information in graphs. This subunit expands on why graphing instruction is important and outlines general guidelines for effective instruction.

Mathematics: Reasons for Graphing Instruction

Graphs are invaluable in mathematics and everyday life. By organizing data so that it is easier to see relationships, graphs can facilitate problem solving or making predictions. Moreover, by summarizing large amounts of information in a concise and visual format, they can facilitate the communication of ideas. Parenthetically, graphing instruction can provide purposeful computational practice and, because graphs are useful in a wide variety of fields, it can help connect mathematics with other subject areas.

Learning: Understanding Children's Difficulties

Many students have difficulty interpreting graphs because of insufficient opportunities to make sense of them. They have trouble determining relationships among depicted quantities (e.g., answering the following question about Graph 1 on page 13-1: Which colors made students feel calmer than either pink or beige?), interpolating (determining the value between two points on a scale), or extrapolating (extending a graph to determine unillustrated values). Many children expect all graphs to reflect their visual image of a situation (Bright & Hoeffner, 1993). For instance, whereas the graph of a roller coaster's height

over time resembles the silhouette of the roller coaster, the graph of its speed over time does not.

Teaching: Guidelines for Effective Graphing Instruction

Two tips on teaching graphing follow.

☞ **To underscore the reasons for graphing, begin with a problem and an effort to collect relevant data** (Russell & Friel, 1989) **or create a genuine need to make predictions or communicate information.** Graphing activities should be purposeful (e.g., needed to make relationships transparent or to summarize results).

☞ **Focus on interpreting graphs rather than the mechanics of constructing graphs.** Investigation 13.2 illustrates sample interpretation activities that put a premium on sense-making.

☞ Try Investigation 13.2 (page 13-8).

13•1•3 DESCRIPTIVE STATISTICS— DESCRIBING AND ANALYZING DATA

After data have been collected and organized, descriptive statistics can serve to summarize (describe) and to examine (analyze) the information numerically. In this subunit, we focus on the definitions of, common difficulties with, and the meaningful instruction of the most common descriptive statistics.

Mathematics: Understanding Elementary Statistics

The most commonly used descriptive statistics are averages (an indication of the typical score), spread (an indication of how dispersed the scores are), correlations (measures of how closely related two sets of data are), and ratios (an indication of frequency or rate; see chapter 12).

☞ Try Probe 13.1 (pages 13-9 and 13-10), and Investigation 13.3 (pages 13-11 and 13-12).

Learning: Understanding Children's Difficulties

Because of inadequate instruction, most students have little under- (continued on page 13-13)

⌘ Investigation 13.2: Picturing Relationships

◆ Graph sense ◆ 7-8 ◆ Small groups of four + class discussion

Interpreting graphs is fundamentally important to many aspects of everyday life. Children need to be able to picture in real terms what a graph means. Activity I relates graphing to everyday situations. Activity II requires students to translate a graph on rates into physical actions. Note that both interpretation activities put a premium on thinking.

Activity I: Relating Graphs to Everyday Situations. Match each of the following situations with an appropriate graph below. (For all graphs, time is represented by the horizontal axis.) Explain why each situation fits the graph.

a. The height of a baseball as it is thrown from deep center field to home plate.
b. The (vertical) speed of the baseball described above.
c. The water level in a bathtub including the time the tub was filled, the bather got in, the bather got out to answer the phone, the bather got back in, the bather added hot water, the bather got out, and the water was let out.
d. The temperature of a can of frozen orange juice concentrate set out to defrost, later mixed with tap water to make juice, and set out on a table for brunch.
e. The temperature of a microwave dinner including the time it was in the freezer, in the microwave overcooking, on the kitchen counter cooling, and in the trash.
f. The commercial value of a diamond ring purchased retail and kept for a lifetime.

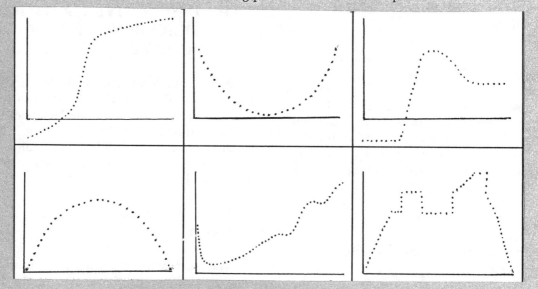

Activity II: Acting Out Graphic Representations. Study the graph to the right and then either physically act out the represented situation or instruct another student to do so.

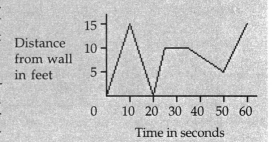

🖥 🖻 Motion sensors can be hooked up to graphing calculators (e.g., a TI 82) through a CBL (Calculator-Based Laboratory) interface, made by Vernier Software. Other probes can be used with the CBL to collect data on temperature, voltage, and light intensity. With calculators and computers, programs are needed to use the probes (date-collection devices). The programs can be downloaded from a TI with Graphlink. For Macintoshes, the motion detector program is MacMotion. Information about sensors can be obtained by calling 1-800-TI CARES or visiting TI web site (www.ti.com). The number for the equipment loan center is 972-917-6411.

➔ Probe 13.1: Using an Everyday Classroom Situation as a Basis for Investigating Averages and Spread

Averages describe a typical score and include the *mean (the number that would result if the total were evenly divided)*, the *median (the middle score)*, and the *mode (the most frequent score)*. For example, a mean of 80% on 10 quizzes describes succinctly a student's overall level of performance. However, an average by itself often does not provide a clear summary of a set of data. Measures of spread, such as the range (the difference between the largest and smallest value), are often essential for making sense of data. Ideally, the exploration of averages and spread would stem from real classroom situations. To see how this might occur and to deepen your own understanding of averages, complete Parts I, II, and III with your group and discuss your answers with your class.

Part I: A Fair Scoring Procedure

1. Miss Brill decided to play the *Names-for-a-Number Game*, which had recently been described to her by Ms. Socrates. She told the class that the aim of the game was to write down as many names for a as they could in one minute. Using 9 as an example, Miss Brill asked for other ways nine could be expressed. Suggestions included $8 + 1, 9 + 0, 3 \times 3, 3^2, \frac{9}{1}$, *nine, nueve,* nine base-ten cubes, IX, and |||||||||| (Egyptian hieroglyphics). She had her students take out their minislates for recording their answers and break into their math groups (five groups of three to five students each). She explained that the group that recorded the largest number of unique names would win (unique was defined as a name no other group recorded). Ask your instructor to play the game above with your class and, afterward, answer the following questions:

   a. Playing *Names-for-a-Number* might foster the learning of what mathematical content?

   b. Miss Brill's scoring procedure might raise what questions or issues?

2. Miss Brill wrote the number 36 on the chalkboard and gave the groups 1 minute to record other names for it. She then asked Group A for their answers. As each answer was read off, Miss Brill checked with the other groups to see if anyone else had recorded the answer. If the answer was unique, Miss Brill listed it on the chalkboard below the group's name. If the answer was not unique, she noted, "Everyone strike that answer from your list." (This saved time recording the answers of the other groups on the board.) After Miss Brill had, in turn, checked each group's answers, she tallied the answers for each group and recorded it on the chalkboard.

A	B	C	D	E
7	8	6	5	7

   "It looks like Group B came in first and Groups A and E are tied for second," announced Miss Brill.

   "It wasn't fair Miss Brill," interjected Michelle, "our group and Group D had only three people today. Groups A and B both had five people, and Group E had four."

   Miss Brill, who was becoming more accustomed to being challenged by students and to seizing spontaneous learning opportunities, commented, "So you think our scoring procedure is unfair because having more heads in a group makes it easier to come up with more possibilities." When other students agreed with Michelle's objection, Miss Brill posed the question, "How can we score the groups fairly—take into account that the groups had different numbers of people?

   a. How do you think Miss Brill's class could resolve this problem?

   b. What mathematics does your solution entail?

3. LeMar suggested using the average number of answers for each group. How would students informally compute each group's mean number of answers?

Probe 13.1 continued

4. Judi looked up averages in her math textbook and reported, "You have to add up the answers each person in a group contributed and divide by the number of people in the group." Why do you add the scores and divide by the number of scores to determine a mean? How might this formal procedure be derived from an informal method or explain in terms of meaningful analogy?

Part II: A Case of Peculiar Experimental Results

Ms. Socrates had her class do a science experiment described in Investigation 13.1 on pages 13-5 and 13-6. To prepare for the experiment, the class discussed the importance of doing multiple trials and taking an average (e.g., to minimize the impact of a freak occurrence), informally defined the mean as a "fair share," and agreed that a mean could be informally calculated by pooling (adding) everyone's scores and then divvy-up the scores among everyone (dividing by the number of scores).

After collecting, averaging, and graphing their data in their groups of four, the students met as a class to discuss their findings and conclusions. Everyone was surprised that roll distance did not simply increase as the height of the incline increased. But after thinking about the results, Franklin offered they made sense because when the incline was too steep, the marble bounced harder against the floor.

Excitedly, Julia interjected, "I can understand that. But our roll distance went up and down, up and down again."

After examining the graph constructed by Julia's group, Ms. Socrates summarized, "You have two peaks. What would cause that?" This prompted calls to see the group's data. Julia summarized her group's data on the chalkboard.

Tube ht	Trial 1	Trial 2	Trial 3	Trial 4	Trial 5	Mean
5	12	10	12	11	13	11.6
10	35	37	34	36	38	36.0
15	40	38	41	13	39	34.2
20	44	44	47	45	43	44.6
25	8	7	10	8	6	7.8

1. What accounts for the anomalous results of Julia's group?

2. Jana suggested redoing Trial 4 for a tube height of 15 cm because 13 cm was so different from the other four results. (a) What effect did this "outlier" have on the mean? (b) Is a mean of 34.2 cm really representative (a typical score) of the roll distances Julia's group obtained for a height of 15 cm? (c) Does an outlier usually have such a strong effect on a mean?

3. Courtney commented that her father was a scientist and that he said you shouldn't tamper with your data even if it doesn't come out the way you wanted. If Julia's group agreed and didn't redo Trial 4 for a height of 15 cm, what could they do to obtain overall scores that were more typical of roll distance at each height?

Part III: A Case of Uneven Distribution

To raise money for a field trip, Mr. Rosed's class decided to sell lightbulbs. To recognize the group that made the best effort at obtaining support for their trip, Mr. Rosed promised that the group with best overall sales could have first choice of bus seats. The class summarized the sales for each group on a bar graph and quickly concluded that the Unicorns should get the sales award because their bar was the highest. The Cherubs protested, pointing out that they finished second simply because their group had only four people whereas the Unicorns had five. The class agreed that a fair way to compare the two groups' sales was to compute averages. The class calculated the Unicorn's and Cherub's average to be $52 and $55, respectively. Ivana and the other Cherubs were jubilant. The Unicorns complained that the only reason the Cherubs had such a good showing was that Ivanna's father sold $185 worth of lightbulbs at his factory. Explain why the Unicorns might have a legitimate case. What additional information about the Unicorns' sales could helpful in supporting their case?

℃ Investigation 13.3: Investigating Relationships

◆ Measurement with standard units + correlations + graphing (scatterplots)
◆ 5-8 ◆ Whole class working in groups of four

A fundamental aspect of economics, meteorology, physics, psychology, or any science is making predictions. This requires knowing or discovering relationships among variables. Indeed, solving many everyday problems often requires understanding if, how much, and in what way two (or more) factors are related. For example, is studying (effort) associated with mathematical achievement? Was the gender of a candidate related to who won or lost in the last election? How much effort does the level of school spending have on pupil achievement? Does education or gender have a bigger impact on a corporation's salaries? How does increasing the number of students in cooperative learning group affect its problem-solving performance? Will doubling a company's TV advertising budget in a market area reduce sales, have a minimal effect, double sales, or quadruple sales?

The following activity illustrates one way the investigative approach could be used to introduce or to practice measurement with standard units, graphing scatterplots, and using such graphs to detect relationships. To see what is involved and to perhaps deepen your own graphing and statistical sense, try the activity yourself. You will need at least 12 people to measure.

As readers of detective novels such as *Sherlock Holmes* know, good criminologists use relationships they have noticed to make useful predictions. Consider the following case.

■ **Predicting Height: The Case of Commodegate.** Rhett Burns was furious. Someone had broken into his campaign office during the night and placed a toilet in the front window with a sign that read, A WIN FOR RHETT, AND WE'RE IN THE TOI-LĒT'.

When Detective Lu arrived, Rhett was futilely trying to dissuade the press from printing the pictures of the spectacle. "We need to get politics out of the sewer," he pronounced with calm dignity. Turning to Detective Lu, he hissed hysterically, "I want the perpetrator of this contemptible dirty trick prosecuted to the full extent of the law!"

Ever the professional, Detective Lu dryly observed, "The trickster used phonetic symbols to suggest a nonstandard pronunciation of toilet," and began looking for evidence. In the back of the building, the detective found hand prints and footprints in the mud below a window from which the trickster had apparently jumped to flee the scene. Checking the window area, the detective found a jacket and hat that the trickster had apparently removed once inside and had left behind in his panicky escape. "From this evidence," noted Detective Lu, "we can determine the trickster's hand size, foot size, arm size, arm span (distance finger tip to finger tip of arms extended), and head size. But it sure would help if we knew the trickster's height."

1. How could Detective Lu determine the trickster's arm span from the evidence collected?

2. Can the height of people be predicted from their hand size, foot size, arm size, arm span, or head size?

Investigation 13.3 continued

To answer Question 2 above, a class can undertake an investigation in which students measure their own heights, hand size, foot size, and so forth, compile the data, and then analyze it. Encourage students to consider questions such as, *How should hand size be measured*? Suggestions might include hand span (the distance from thumb to little finger with the fingers stretched out), the length of the hand (the distance from the tip of the middle finger to the wrist), the width of the hand (the distance across the hand with the fingers closed, and the length of the first finger. (Note that more than one measure of hand size can be used.) Prompt them to consider whether a ruler or a tape measure and whether inches or centimeters would be easier to work with. Encourage students to consider how they will determine if a body-part measurement can predict height or decide which is the best predictor. With your group or class, try this activity yourself. What conclusions can you draw?

Ideally, students will suggest that graphing the data may help to see if a relationship exists between the various body parts listed above and height. Using graph paper, summarize your data in scatterplots.

☞ Teaching Tips

• One way to manage this activity is to have each group make up separate data sheets for each body part. Each data sheet should also include the height for each person. One group can collect the data sheets for hand size from the class and graph the data for hand size vs. height. Another group can collect the data sheets for foot size and graph these data against height. And so forth. After the groups have constructed their graphs, they can present their results and analysis to the class. The class can then compare the graphs to see which body part has the closest relationship to height.

• Note that this activity may raise the issue of scale. For example, if the data are all bunched into one corner, a graph may be hard to read. Changing the scales can stretch out the data and make the graph more readable.

✦ **Extension.** Is the best predictor of height the same for children as it is for adults? Is the relationship the same, stronger, or weaker for children?

Questions for Reflection

1. If there was a perfect relationship between hand size and height (e.g., if the person with the largest hand was also the tallest, the person with second largest hand was also the second tallest, and so forth), what would the scatterplot look like? Illustrate your answer on graph paper.

2. If there was a strong relationship between hand size and height (e.g., people with large hands generally were taller than average), what would the scatterplot look like? Illustrate your answer on graph paper.

3. If there was a mild relationship between hand size and height, what would the scatterplot look like? Illustrate your answer on graph paper.

4. If there was no relationship between hand size and height (e.g., if people with the largest hands had above average, average, and below average height), what would the scatterplot look like? Illustrate your answer on graph paper.

5. If there was a perfect but negative relationship between hand size and height (e.g., the person with the largest hand was the shortest, the person with the next largest hands was the second shortest, and so forth), what would the scatterplot look like? Illustrate your answer on graph paper.

standing of averages, spread, or correlations. For example, although seventh-graders know how to calculate a mean, many do not understand conceptually what it means (Brown & Silver, 1989) and assume that any difference in mean scores is significant (Shaughnessy, 1992). Many people believe that a correlation implies a cause-and-effect relationship. An example of a *correlation fallacy* is noting that, as schools' per-student costs increase, their average achievement tends to drop and concluding that spending more money won't improve education. This conclusion does not take into account a real reason for high per-student costs: Schools with large populations of low achieving special needs children receive more special education funding.

Teaching

To prepare children for a world that relies on statistics, it is important to help them understand their purposes and informally construct an understanding of statistical procedures.

↪ **To highlight the purposes of statistics and to promote an informal understanding of them, exploit or create a real need for statistics.** For example, Part I of Probe 13.1 (page 13-9) illustrate how determining fair scores with uneven teams can create a need to discuss averages in general and means in particular. By relating means to their informal understanding of fair sharing, children can construct for themselves a procedure for computing averages: Pool the individual contributions and then partition the pool among the individuals (e.g., in Part I of Probe 13.1, after tallying its members scores, Group C had a total of six points, which could then be divided up among three people for a mean score of two points each). Note that this parallels and can be summarized as the formal procedure: Add the scores and divide by the number of scores.

As illustrated in Part II of Probe 13.1 (page 13-10), there are many everyday situations in which a mean can give a misleading picture of central tendency (the typical score) and, thus, is not appropriate to report as the average. In the example illustrated, a more appropriate average would have been the *medians* (the *middle value* of each condition).

As illustrated in Part III of Probe 13.1, the mean sales of the Cherubs ($55) was greater than that of the Unicorns ($52), but this does not guarantee that all of the Cherubs contributed more than any of the Unicorns. Indeed, if the lower limit of the Unicorn's range was $36 or more, only the top salesperson of the Cherubs would have had more sales. (If the four Cherubs averaged $55 in sales, then their total sales was 4 x $55 or $220. If Ivana—the top salesperson of the Cherubs—had $185 in sales, then the other three Cherubs must have had a total of $220 - $185 or $35 in sales. If the five Unicorns had sales of, for example, $36, $48, $54, $59, and $63, then their member with the smallest sales still outperformed all but one of the Cherubs. Moreover, if the groups other than the Cherubs and Unicorns had an upper limit of $35 or less, then the Unicorns could legitimately claim that they had five of six top sales people and that they deserved recognition as the most productive group.)

As illustrated in Investigation 13.3 (pages 13-11 and 13-12), an informal idea of correlations can grow naturally out of investigations that explore everyday relationships. Scatterplots provide a visual way of depicting the size and the nature of the relationships. Our experience suggests that even fifth- and sixth-graders can deduce for themselves that a perfect (positive or negative) correlation is represented by a straight line, no correlation is represented by a "blob of dots," and that intermediate correlations are shown by elliptical distributions of dots.

13•1•4 USING STATISTICS TO MAKE PREDICTIONS—ANALYZING DATA

Inferential statistics involves using probability to determine whether or not a conclusion can be drawn about a population from data collected on a sample. It is a powerful and widely used analytic technique (e.g., a basis for science and polling). However, elementary instruction typically focuses on descriptive statistics and overlooks inferential statistics altogether. The ideas of sampling and chance provide the conceptual foundation for inferential statistics and should be introduced to elementary students (Jacobs & Lejoie, 1994). In this subunit, we focus on sampling; in Unit 13•2, we discuss chance.

Mathematics: Understanding Sampling

☞ Try Investigation 13.4 (page 13-14). (Text continued on page 13-15.)

✣ Investigation 13.4: Sampling

◆ Statistics ◆ 3-8 ◆ Class working in small groups of about four

The activities below (a) illustrate how a sample can be useful in predicting a population characteristic and (b) raise key issues about sampling. To see how and to perhaps deepen your own understanding of sampling, try the activities below along with your class.

Activity I: Fish Counts[†1]

The following activity can be done with primary- or intermediate-level children. Try the activity yourself. Have *one* person in your group or class serve as the teacher. The teacher should read the following instructions to him- or herself and demonstrate the activity for everyone in your group or class.

Instructions for the Teacher: Put a large number of counters, preferably at least several hundred, in a bag. Then pose the following problem:

■ **Total Fish Population.** A game warden wanted to gauge the total number of fish in a pond (the number of counters in the bag). How could she do this?

1. Without catching and counting every fish (which would be impractical), how could the problem above be solved? Justify your solution procedure.

2. One way to solve the *Total Fish Population* problem is to use the following sampling technique: Randomly net and tag an initial sample of fish. Replace the initial sample and let it mix with the population. Then take a second sample and use this information to determine the total population. Consider the following example using counters: An initial sample of 10 counters was removed from a bag and marked. The marked counters were replaced in the bag and thoroughly stirred among the unmarked counters. If 10 fish (counters) were initially marked, and if 2 of a second sample of 60 were marked, what is the total population of fish?

3. Try the following experiment. Randomly select and mark an initial sample of 20. After mixing the initial sample back into the population of counters, take a second sample of 15 and estimate the total population. After replacing the previous second sample and remixing it, redo the experiment with second samples of 30, 60, and 120. Determine the actual number of counters in the population. Did the size of the second sample have an effect on the accuracy of your predicted population size? Justify your conclusion.

◆ 4. Redo the experiment with larger initial samples of 40, 80, and/or 120 and second samples of 15, 30, 60, and 120. (a) Did the size of the initial sample have an effect on the accuracy of your predicted population size? Briefly justify your conclusion. If so how and why? (b) Which, if either, had a bigger impact on the accuracy of your prediction—the size of the initial sample or the size of the second sample?

Activity II: Evaluating Advertisements

Analyze and evaluate the following advertisements:

Example A. Nine out of 10 doctors surveyed recommended *MaimPain* brand aspirin for their patients who suffered from headaches.

Example B. We gave Miss Sneeze our taste test, and she couldn't tell the difference between *Mal de Mer* Margarine and real butter. *Mal de Mer* tasted just like real butter.

[†] Inspired by a lesson on the art of tag and recapture (pages 205-213) in *The Challenge of the Unknown*, ©1986 by J. C. Crimmins & Co.

The Need for Sampling. A union representative needs to know quickly how the teachers in a large school district feel about a new administration proposal. A presidential candidate wants to know how popular she is with the voters. A company wants to know how consumers perceive a new product. In these, and many other situations, there is a need to collect information about a population of people, but it is not practical to check with everyone in the population. Sampling provides a practical way of gauging the opinion of the population by checking with just some members of the population. *But will any sample do?*

Importance of a Representative Sample. To make a good guess about the opinion of the whole population, it is important to have a *representative sample*—one that accurately reflects the whole population. As Activity I of Investigation 13.4 (on page 13-14) illustrates, one aspect of such a sample is obtaining a sufficiently large sample. The larger the sample, the more likely it is to be representative of the whole population and, thus, fair. What are some other considerations about obtaining a representative sample?

Learning: Children's Thinking

Children typically have informal but incomplete knowledge about sampling. One example is the base-rate fallacy (Shaughnessy, 1992)—the tendency to use subjective factors such as fairness rather than a factual basis for choosing a sample (e.g., insisting that a sample consist of 50% boys and 50% girls even though a school population consists of 40% boys and 60% girls).

Teaching: Two Tips

☞ **To help students reflect on, discuss, and construct an explicit understanding about the need for sampling and the importance of representative samples, create opportunities where they *need* to use samples to make a prediction.** Key issues about sampling can be raised by having students take their own poll or survey. Conducting sampling activities (see, e.g., Activity I of Investigation 13.4 and Investigation 13.5) and evaluating advertising claims (see, e.g., Activity II of Investigation 13.4) can also serve this purpose.

☞ Try Investigation 13.5 (pages 13-16 to 13-18).

☞ **To help students recognize the base-rate fallacy (using subjective factors rather than a factual basis for making sampling decisions), encourage them to discuss differences in opinions about samples and the rationale for their samples.** For example, encourage students who believe that a sample should consist of 50% boys and 50% girls because it is fair to debate those who believe that the sample should be 40% boys and 60% girls because it would be representative of the population under study.

13•2 PROBABILITY

Figure 13.2: Probability in Everyday Life

GARFIELD reprinted by permission of UFS.

Probability is concerned with the likelihood of a particular event occurring. Everyday experience suggests that some things are impossible (e.g., an eggplant becoming a rocket scientist), other things are improbable (e.g., winning the lottery or, as shown in Figure 13.2, a flipped coin coming to rest on its side), other things are probable (e.g., studying [continued on page 13-19]

🍎 Investigation 13.5: The Secret Code†

◆ Collecting, analyzing, and graphing data (descriptive statistics) + making inferences based on a sample (inferential statistics) + concepts of spread and averages (means) + inductive and deductive reasoning ◆ 4-8 ◆ Small groups + whole-class collaboration

Like Investigation 13.1 (pages 13-5 and 13-6), Probe 13.1 (page 13-9), and Investigations 13.3 (pages 13-11 and 13-12) and 13.4 (page 13-14), this entertaining activity illustrates the investigative approach to statistics instruction. To see for yourself what is involved, try solving the following problem with the help of your group. Go on to the next page after you have solved the problem or have become hopelessly blocked.

■ Activity I: A *Secret Code* Problem

Mr. Del-Ryan's class entered their classroom to find a sheet of paper at each group's table. The sheet had some funny writing on it. "What is this?" students' asked.

"It appears to be a message in a secret code," commented the teacher.

"Did you put this on our desks?" asked students suspiciously.

"No," Mr. Del-Ryan responded, "the message is not from me."

"Then who?" inquired a student.

"I guess you'll have to decode the message," answered the teacher adding to the mystery.

The mysterious letter said:

5...10...95

* { ...) $ # + # / % # = ...@ * % } * / ...% } # ... / # , % ...% @ (...@ # # : +

...... % } # ...? # - $ # $ ...({ ...% } * + ... / (% # ...} - + ... % } # ...

$ * [} % ...% (...+) $ - ^... @ - % # $ ...(/ ...% } # * $...% # - > } # $ ...

(/ ...{ * # ; = ...= - ^......- + :...% } # * $...% # - > } # $...% (...

+ * / [...- ...+ (/ [...({ ...% } # * $ ...> } ((+ * / [...@ * % } * / ...% } # ...

; * \ * % + ...({ ...+ (> * - ; ...- > > #) % - ? * ; * % ^ ...... $ # ! & * $ # ...

% } # * $ ...% # - > } # $ ...% (...@ - ; :...? - > : @ - $ = + ...{ ($ ...

} - ; { ...- / ... } (& $ ...... ($ ...% (.../ # [(% * - % # ...@ * % } ...\ # ...

{ ($ ...- / ^ ...(% } # $ ...) $ * / > *) - ;

= & > - % * (/ - ; ; ^

^ (& $ ...) $ * / > *) - ;

___

†Inspired by an activity described in *Probability and Statistics*, the Nuffield Mathematics Project, © 1969 by the Nuffield Foundation and published in the U.S. by John Wiley & Sons, Inc., New York.

Investigation 13.5 continued

Note that additional coded messages can be constructed by using icon fonts. For example, with a Macintosh, a Cairo, Mobile, or Zaph Dingbats font could be used. If you typed *the children are home* (lower case), the Cairo font would automatically translate this sentence into the following:

Activity II: A Solution Clue

There are various ways of solving the *Secret Code*. One method is discussed below. Ideally, students would suggest such an approach themselves. Otherwise, a teacher can provide a hint to the approach by having the students play *Scrabble* ® (Milton Bradley) and asking why the letters have different values.

Gauging Letter Frequency. One way to approach the problem is to compare the frequency of the symbols in the message with the relative frequency of the letters. If the coded message uses a typical sample of words, then the symbols for common letters should appear frequently and the symbols for uncommon letters should appear infrequently. This raises the question, *what is the average frequency of each letter?*

Students could each pick a sample paragraph from sample books and count the number of times each letter appears in their samples. The class could then compile the data either in a table or a graph. Before doing so, read on.

Predicting Frequency. This activity can be elaborated on by asking students to predict the relative frequency of letter use. The class can decide on how many categories to use. For example, they may wish to categorize letters as high in frequency (H), moderate in frequency (M), or low in frequency (L). An even more challenging task is to predict the top fourth, the second fourth, the third fourth, and the lowest fourth. In either case, students will need to decide how to divide 26 items. (For example, 26 items divided among four categories would mean six letters per category and two letters left over. Students would need to decide which category or categories would get an extra letter. What are the different possibilities? Which makes the most sense?) Have students record their individual predictions (see data sheet on the next page).

After students make their individual predictions, overall class predictions can be compiled. The class will have to decide how to accomplish this. For instance, they could agree that the overall prediction for a letter would be determined by majority vote. That is, a letter would be assigned to the category with largest number of votes. This may raise of questions of spread and fairness. Consider the results in the table below:

letter	bottom 6	lower mid 7	upper mid 7	top 6
F	8	8	9	0
P	1	10	11	2

According to a majority vote, both F and P would be placed in the same upper-mid category. What might be a fairer way to summarize the overall class prediction for each letter?

Individual students could then determine the frequency of each letter in their sample, and the class could compile a total frequency for each letter and rate the actual frequency of each letter. These data could also be recorded in the chart on the next page. Students could circle their individual predictions that matched and then do the same for the overall class prediction (see sample below). Generally, there will be more matches for the latter than the former—underscoring the value of diverse input and a collective intelligence.

Investigation 13.5 continued

	My Prediction	Overall Prediction for the Class	Frequency in my Sample	Total (class) Frequency	Actual Rating
A	(H)	(H)	18	448	H
B	M	(L)	1	30	L
C	H	(M)	4	180	M

Note that matches between My Prediction and the Actual Rating are circled. The same has been done for matches between the Overall Predictions for the Class and the Actual Ratings.

Data Sheet

	My Prediction	Overall Prediction for the Class	Frequency in my Sample	Total (class) Frequency	Actual Rating
A					
B					
C					
D					
E					
F					
G					
H					
I					
J					
K					
L					
M					
N					
O					
P					
Q					
R					
S					
T					
U					
V					
W					
X					
Y					
Z					

hard typically leads to a passing grade), and some things are certain (death and taxes).

Probability touches our everyday lives in countless ways. For example, weather forecasts, medical advice, election predictions, team tendencies, forecast of sporting events, lottery tickets, marketing analyses and projections, and military plans all typically involve gauging or reporting the likelihood of future events.

In the past, insufficient attention was paid to this important topic, and many students did not develop a probability sense. A consequence of this mathematical illiteracy is a tendency to make much of coincidences. Consider, for example, two strangers who discover that the brother of one dated the friend of the other. Although this may seem remarkable—evidence of fate or a uniting harmony—such coincidences are surprisingly common (Paulos, 1988).*

We explore probability in Subunit 13•2•1, children's probabilistic thinking in Subunit 13•2•2, and how probability can be taught meaningfully in Subunit 13•2•3.

13•2•1 MATHEMATICS: UNDERSTANDING PROBABILITY

In this subunit, we define key probability terms. *Empirical probability involves using the results of an experiment to determine the chances of something happening.* In contrast, *theoretical probability involves a logical analysis of a situation to determine the chances of something happening.* This requires defining the *sample space: specifying all possible outcomes of a situation.* (An outcome is one of the possible things that can happen.) *An event is any portion of the sample space—one outcome or a combination of outcomes.*

Because empirical and theoretical probability each indicate the *relative* frequency we can expect an event to occur, both can be expressed as a fraction, decimal, percent, or ratio. For example, the sample space for correctly (+) or incorrectly (-) guessing the answers to two true-false ques-

tions is: ++ (correct on both questions), +- (correct on the first but not the second question), -+ (correct on the second question only), -- (incorrect on both). One possible event is guessing incorrectly on at least one question (+-, -+, or --). The theoretical probability of this event is $\frac{3}{4}$, .75, 75%, or 3:4.

☞ Consider Investigations 13.6 (page 13-20) and 13.7 (page 13-21).

13•2•2 LEARNING: UNDERSTANDING CHILDREN'S PROBABILISTIC THINKING

In this subunit, we provide an overview of how children's probabilistic thinking develops and some of their common difficulties.

Developmental Trends

Children's probability sense grows gradually *with experience* (Jones, Thornton, & Langrall, 1997).

Level 1: Subjective (No Sense of the Possible). Children just beginning school seem to have little, if any, informal understanding of chance and probability (Piaget & Inhelder, 1975). Their thinking is highly deterministic (there is a reason for everything) and idiosyncratic (based on personal opinion). Consider, for example, a situation where one red marble and four white marbles are put in a container in full view of a group of young children. Asked to predict which color is more likely to be drawn, they typically overlook the facts of the situation—that chance favors picking a white marble—and adduce such conjectures as "Red because it is my favorite color," "Red because it is the *special* one," "Red because red was drawn before," or "Red because white was drawn before, and it wouldn't be fair to draw another white one."

Level 2: Transitional (Nonsystematic Sense of the Possible). In time, children recognize that uncertainty or chance can play a role in many aspects of life, but their understanding of probability is highly intuitive. Although they may be able to list all the possible outcomes for simple situations (e.g., flipping a coin), Level 2 children may not be able to do so for more complicated two-stage problems (e.g., flipping two coins). Moreover, they do not understand that probabilities are ratios. (Continued on page 3-22.)

---

* Paulos (1988, p. 29) explains that if each of about 200 million adults knows roughly 1,500 people, then the probability of having a common acquaintance is approximately $\frac{1}{100}$. If both people are from the same community, the probability of a common acquaintance is even higher.

♧ Investigation 13.6: Fair Game?

◆ Probability sense + problem solving

Analyzing the fairness of games can help children explore probability, including ideas that are counterintuitive. To see how and to perhaps deepen your own probability sense, try analyzing the games below with your group. Discuss your conclusions with your class.

■ **Game 1:** *Two Flips* (◆ 2-8 ◆ Groups of three + class discussion). Each of the three players roll a die. The player with highest roll is designated the *one-head player*; the second highest, the *two-heads player*; and the lowest, the *no-heads player*. Two coins are flipped. If two heads come up, the *two-heads player* wins. If one head comes up, the *one-head player* wins. If no heads come up the *no-heads player* wins.

1. (a) Do you think *Two Flips* is fair? That is, does each player have an equal chance of winning? (b) If three players played *Two Flips* 12 times, how many games would you predict the one-head player, two-heads player, and the no-heads would each win? (c) Compare your predictions with your group or class. Does everyone agree the game is fair or not? (d) Regis' group conjectured that each player should win one-third of the time or 4 of 12 games. Duc's group argued that there were two ways to get one head (heads-tails and tails-heads) and so the one-heads player should win twice as often as the others. Regis countered that you couldn't distinguish between heads-tails and tails-heads and, even if you could, the result was still the same. Who, if anyone, is correct?

2. How could you determine whether or not *Two Flips* is fair?

3. One way to determine the fairness of *Two Flips* is actually play the game (determine the empirical probability of each of the three events: two heads, one-head, no heads). (a) Play 12 games and keep a record of how many times the two-heads, one-head, and no-heads player each win. (b) Compile the data across groups. What do your results suggest about the fairness of the game?

♦ 4. The conjecture made by Regis' group that two heads, one head, and no heads are equally likely is based on what incorrect assumption (common misconception)?

5. (a) What is the theoretical probability of each player winning? (b) What problem-solving heuristic could you use to informally determine the theoretical probability or prove your answers to skeptics?

■ **Game 2:** *Take Your Chances* (◆ 3-8 ◆ Pairs of students + class discussion). Each player picks numbers from 2 to 12. Two 6-sided dice (each numbered 1 to 6) are rolled and, if the sum equals a player's number, that player gets a point.

1. Allan challenged Bert to a game of *Take Your Chances* and offered, "I'll give you a break Bert. I will pick only four numbers—*five, six, seven,* and *eight*. You can have all the rest." Is Allan a swell guy who doesn't mind losing, is he outsmarting Bert, or is his offer fair?

2. One way to determine if Allan's version of *Take Your Chances* is fair is to play the game and determine the empirical probability: (a) With a partner, play *Take Your Chances* 36 times to determine if the game is fair. (b) Compile the data across pairs and analyze the class results. What do these data suggest about the fairness of the game?

3. (a) What are all the possible sums of two 6-sided dice each numbered 1 to 6? (b) Are they equally likely? Why or why not?

4. What is the theoretical probability of Allan winning? Of Bert winning?

5. If Allan took the even sums and Bert took the odd sums, would this game be fair? Why or why not?

6. If Allan and Bert used a 0 to 5 die, would the game be fair if Allan took the even sums and Bert took the odd sums? Why or why not?

✿ Investigation 13.7: Some Problems Involving Probability

◆ Application of problem-solving skills to probability problems
◆ Small groups of about four + whole-class discussion

Students should be given ample experience solving probability problems, including those with counterintuitive solution. Try solving the following probability problems yourself. Discuss your strategy and solution with your group or class.

■ **Problem 1: A Love Story** (◆ 7-8). Dick and Jane met at a dance. Not particularly clever at making conversation, Dick resorted to the old standby: "What's your sign?" When Jane answered Leo, a stunned Dick exclaimed, "Leo! Far out. That's really weird. We must have been meant for each other." On the basis of what seemed like a remarkable coincidence, Dick and Jane married the following week. (a) Just what are the chances that two people meeting at random would have the same Zodiac sign? (There are 12 Zodiac signs. Assume that an equal number of people are born under each sign.) (b) Can Dick and Jane's meeting be considered a remarkable coincidence or not?

■ **Problem 2: The Marble Argument** (◆ 5-8). Monique and Unique were arguing over who owned two special marbles. To end the rife, their father put the two special marbles in a bag along with two regular marbles. The girls flipped a coin to see who would blindly choose two of the four marbles. (a) What is the probability of Monique winning the coin flip *and* picking a special marble on her first try? (b) If Monique won the coin flip, what is the probability of her picking a special marble on her first try *and* on her second try?

■ **Problem 3: Cube Confusion** (◆ 5-8). A red cube, two yellow cubes, and a blue cube are placed in a box. A cube is picked at random, put back in the box, and a cube is again picked at random. (a) What is the probability of picking a red *and* a yellow cube? (b) What is the probability of picking a red cube *and* then a yellow cube? (c) What is the probability of picking a red cube *or* a yellow cube on the first try? (d) What is the probability of picking a red cube *or* a yellow cube on each of two tries? (e) What is the probability of picking two red cubes *or* two yellow cubes?

■ **Problem 4: Foul Forecast** (◆ 4-8). (a) The weather report predicted a 50% chance of rain on Saturday *and* a 50% chance of rain on Sunday. What is the probability of it raining on at least one of these weekend days? (b) If there was a $33\frac{1}{3}$% chance of rain on Saturday *and* on Sunday, what is the probability of it raining on at least one day of the weekend?

Questions for Reflection

1. Luis' group concluded that the solution to Problem 1 above was just $\frac{1}{12}$. Carla's group disagreed, arguing for an answer of $\frac{1}{144}$ because $\frac{1}{12} \times \frac{1}{12}$ is 144. With which, if either, do you agree? In the investigative approach, how might a teacher handle such a disagreement?

2. For Problem 4 above, Mara concluded that it was sure to rain some time over the weekend. Do you agree or disagree? How could you prove or disprove your answer?

3. How could encouraging children to use qualitative reasoning help them to solve the problems above—particularly those involving *and* or *or* (Problems 2, 3, and 4)?

4. (a) Does the term *and* in a problem always imply multiplying? (b) Does the term *or* in a problem always imply adding? (c) How does this investigation illustrate the need for fostering adaptive rather than routine, expertise? (d) How does it illustrate that language arts are an integral aspect of mathematics?

5. How could using making a list, constructing a table, drawing a picture (tree diagram), or some other problem-solving heuristic help children solve the problems above informally?

Children in Phase 2 believe that there is a better chance of picking a black marble from Box B below—even though the probability is, in fact, the same for doing so from Box A.

 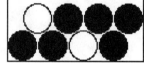

Box A (probability of choosing black = $\frac{3}{4}$)   Box B (probability of choosing black = $\frac{6}{8} = \frac{3}{4}$)

Level 3: Informal Quantitative (Semi-Systematic Sense of the Possible). In time, children can informally consider all possible outcomes for two-stage problems and devise own informal terminology (e.g., "Three out of four").

Level 4: Numerical (Formal Knowledge). With *sufficient* experience, children develop the facility to analyze probability situations theoretically (e.g., can consider all possible outcomes for any-stage problems and recognize probabilities as ratios).

Common Difficulties

More so than most other mathematical topics, children frequently have many misconceptions and misleading intuitions about probabilistic situations (NCTM, 1989). In Game 1 of Investigation 13.6 (*Two Flips* described on page 13-20), for instance, many students (like Regis' group) assume that the three events (heads on both a first and second coin flip, heads on one of the flips, no heads on either flip) are equally likely. Unfortunately, traditional instruction does little to foster probabilistic understanding or thinking (Shaughnessy, 1992). Its focus on memorizing procedures for computing theoretical probabilities often leaves students confused, for example, about whether to multiply or add the probability of outcomes when solving probability problems.

13•2•3 TEACHING

Despite the difficulty of the topic and the fact that solutions often seem counterintuitive, even primary-level children's understanding of probability can improve with instruction (Bright & Hoeffner, 1993; see, e.g., Fischbein & Gazit, 1984). ELEMENTARY INSTRUCTION SHOULD FOCUS ON DEVELOPING A *PROBABILITY SENSE*—AN INFORMAL CONCEPT OF CHANCE. IN TIME, IT SHOULD ENABLE STUDENTS TO ANALYZE AND TO SOLVE PROBLEMS INFORMALLY. Middle-school instruction can help students reinvent formal procedures by building on their probability sense and informal knowledge of probability.

Phase 1: Probability Sense (Conceptual Phase and Beyond)

Guidelines for laying the conceptual groundwork for probability instruction are described below. Note that development of a probability sense can begin even before fractions are introduced to represent probabilities and can continue throughout instruction.

☞ **To help lay a conceptual foundation for probability, have children solve problems and explore activities involving the Fundamental Counting Principle and advanced counting techniques (combinations and permutations).** Solving problems such as *Rosa's Outfits* in Box 2.6 (page 2-18) and *Combination Problems A and B* on page 3-9 of Investigation 3.1 can help lay the groundwork for understanding combinations and the multiplicative reasoning necessary to understand probability—particularly the probability of compound events.

☞ **Encourage children to make intuitive predictions and to use probabilistic language.** Everyday events, science experiments, and games can all provide genuine opportunities for informally estimating the likelihood of an event. Primary-level children should be familiar with the terms *certain* or *sure* and *uncertain* or *unsure, likely* or *probable* and *unlikely* or *improbable,* and *maybe* or *possible* and *impossible.*

☞ **Games of chance are an excellent vehicle for fostering a probability sense, raising instructional issues, challenging naive concepts, and devising or practicing informal solution strategies.** Initially, playing games can provide entertaining opportunities to discuss the role of uncertainty and chance in everyday life, to introduce probabilistic language, and to make predictions. In time, analyzing the fairness of games can be an interesting way of introducing and discussing probability concepts or procedures (see, e.g., Investigation 13.6 on page 13-20).

☞ **To develop a probability sense, children need regular exposure to probabilistic situations and probability problems—particularly those** with counterintuitive solutions—throughout the elementary grades (see, e.g., Investigations 13.6 and 13.7 on pages 13-20 and 13-21, respectively). Tasks that can challenge children's strongly held but faulty intuitions are particularly important. The cognitive conflict caused by unexpected results can prompt students to rethink their assumptions and motivate a logical analysis of probabilistic situations.

∞ **Initial efforts to solve probability problems should focus on using *qualitative reasoning* and sharing informal explanations.** Before asking children to determine exact probabilities, encourage them to consider, for example, the *relative size* of probabilities or the *direction* of a solution (i.e., whether or not an answer should be larger, smaller, or equal to a probability given in a problem). Moreover, encourage children to justify their answers to problems in their own terms (using natural language). Consider, for instance, Problem 13.1 below:

■ **Problem 13.1: Two Buckets of Marbles** (◆ 3-8). A red and green bucket each have a mixture of 100 black and 100 white marbles. You randomly choose a bucket by flipping a coin and then randomly choose a marble from that bucket. What do you think is more likely to happen—(a) you will get a black marble, or (b) you will choose the green bucket and get a white marble?

Alison noted, "This [choice b] is more exact." Arianne explained, "It's more harder to flip a coin and get the green bucket *and* get a white marble." Alexi commented, "There are more chances to mess up [with choice b]. With [choice] a, you can mess up once. With [choice] b, you have a chance to mess up twice."

Phase 2: Analyzing and Informally Solving Probability Problems (Initial Connecting Phase)

Once children have had the opportunity to construct an intuitive probability sense, introduce common fractions as a way of representing probability and help them devise more precise means of analyzing probability situations (e.g., defining the sample space) and informally solving problems (e.g., intuitively deciding what to do with the probabilities).

∞ **To help students specify the probability of an event, link formal terminology and symbols to informal terminology.** Initially, the probability of choosing, for example, 3 white marbles from a bag of 8 marbles can be described informally as *three out of eight marbles*. Later, it can be described more formally as *three chances out of eight* or simply *three out of eight*. The fraction symbolism ($\frac{3}{8}$) can then be linked to these terminologies.

∞ **To help children analyze probability problems informally, encourage them to list the possible outcomes and to specify the probability of each event (i.e., decide whether or not each is equally likely).** See, for instance, Question 3 in Game 2 of Investigation 13.6 on page 13-20. Solving problems such as Problem 13.2 and 13.3 below can also help set the stage for more formal analyses of probability in the intermediate grades.

■ **Problem 13.2: Two Coins** (◆ 2-3). If a penny is flipped, it can come up heads or tails. A nickel can also come up heads or tails. If both a penny and a nickel are flipped, what are the ways they can come up? How many of these ways involve one head and one tail?

■ **Problem 13.3: Three Coins** (◆ 3-4). If a penny, a nickel, and a dime are flipped, they can each come up heads. How many other ways can three coins come up? How many of these involve two heads and a tail? How many involve one head and two tails? How many involve three tails?

∞ **Encourage children to use their probability sense (e.g., qualitative reasoning) and informal methods for solving probability problems instead of imposing formal procedures.** In general, instruction should begin with gauging empirical probabilities, move to determining theoretical probabilities informally, and then introduce computing theoretical probabilities. After experience considering the likelihood of personally familiar events (informally estimating empirical probabilities), children can determine empirical probabilities either by collecting data on the actual event or by using models (i.e., creating a simple simulation using coins, dice, or spinners). For Problem 13.1 above, for example, primary-level children could gauge the empirical probability by repeatedly carrying out an experiment with a red and a green bucket each filled with a mix of 100 black and 100 white marbles. Developmentally more advanced students could create a simulation of the event. That is, they could model choosing a bucket by flipping a coin and randomly selecting a marble by flipping a second coin. (Note that students would need to recognize that the probability of choosing a black marble and a white marble is even.) Even more advanced children could solve the problem informally be drawing a tree diagram such as the one below:

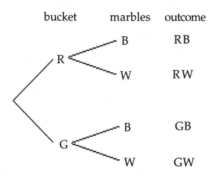

☞ To better appreciate the teaching tip above, try Investigation 13.8 (pages 13-25).

Phase 3: Toward More Formal Instruction (Advanced Connecting Phase)

After children have a solid probability sense and are comfortable solving probability problems informally, they can be encouraged to adopt more formal procedures.

☞ Try Investigation 13.9 (pages 13-26).

∽ **Intermediate-level students can be encouraged to devise systematic simulations of relatively simple everyday events.** Investigation 13.9 outlines guidelines for creating a systematic simulation and poses a number of everyday situations that intermediate-level students should find manageable to simulate. Box 13.2 (on pages 13-27 and 13-28) illustrates an inquiry-based and extended unit on statistics and probability that incorporates designing a simulation of a popular sport.

∽ **Encourage children to devise formal calculational procedures as a shortcut for their informal procedures.** By the end of the elementary years, for example, students should recognize that they have to multiply to determine the probability of two or more independent events oc-

curring together (see, e.g., Investigation 3.1 on page 3-9). Consider Problem 13.1 on page 13-23. As the probability of choosing the green bucket is $\frac{1}{2}$ and the probability of choosing a white marble from it is $\frac{100}{200}$ or $\frac{1}{2}$, the probability of choosing the green bucket *and* a white marble is $\frac{1}{2} \times \frac{1}{2}$ or $\frac{1}{4}$.

∽ **To help children choose the correct operation, encourage them to use their probability sense (e.g., qualitative reasoning).** For example, asked to determine the probability of rolling two 1s with a pair of dice, a student suggested adding one-sixth and one-sixth and offered an answer of two-sixths. The teacher asked the class if rolling two 1s was harder, easier, or as likely as rolling a single 1. The class agreed that rolling two 1s should be harder than rolling a single 1. This led them to recognize that $\frac{2}{6}$ (adding the individual probabilities) did not make sense, because it is greater than $\frac{1}{6}$ (the probability of rolling a single one).

PARTING THOUGHTS

"I soon found that . . . getting people to use [statistics and probability] in their judgments and decisions . . . is not easily remedied just by 'teaching them the right way'" (Shaughnessy, 1992, p. 465). Instead of simply teaching students a series of techniques, instruction should help them understand why statistics and probability are useful and develop a statistics and probability sense. Toward these ends, "a spirit of investigation and exploration should permeate statistics [and probability] instruction" (NCTM, 1989, p. 54). Indeed, the study of these domains should flow naturally from children's explorations of interesting tasks, questions, and problems—from a real need to collect, organize, and interpret information and to use it to make predictions about future events.

RESOURCES

SOME INSTRUCTIONAL RESOURCES

Statistics

☞ **Making Sense of Data—(Addenda Series, Grades K-6)** by Mary M. Lindquist with Jan Luquire, Angela (text continued on page 13-29)

🍎 Investigation 13.8: More "At Least" Problems

◆ Probability sense + problem solving ◆ Small groups + class discussion

Like the problem in Box 13.1 (page 13-3) and Problem 4 of Investigation 13.7 (page 13-21), the problems below involve probability situations not normally addressed in elementary instruction. By using informal strategies, though, students can solve them. To deepen your own probability sense, tackle the problems with your group. Discuss your findings with your class.

■ Problem 1: A Winning Strategy for *Piggy* (◆ 3-8 ◆ Groups of four)

The aim of *Piggy* is to be the first player to score 100 points. There are three simple rules:

1. On their turn, players roll a die with faces numbered 0 to 5 and score the number of points that come up.
2. Players may roll the die as many times as they wish (i.e., one or more times). However, the number of rolls must be specified at the beginning of a turn.
3. The score is accumulative—with one exception. If a player rolls a *zero*, his or her score automatically becomes and REMAINS 0! (Note if all opponents have been eliminated from the game, the remaining player wins by default.)

The Problem. Try playing the game with your group. Intuitively, what is the winning strategy for *Piggy*?

✦ **Suggestions for Following Up.** With more advanced students, a teacher may wish to encourage a more systematic investigation of the problem. Try the following suggestions yourself:

• **Investigating the Empirical Probability of *Piggy*** (◆ 3-8). Devise an experiment to determine if it is better to roll the die just once, twice, three times, six times, or even more per turn.

• **Investigating the Theoretical Probability of *Piggy*** (◆ 5-8). What is the theoretical probability of getting a 0 on one roll? What is the theoretical probability of rolling a 0 at least once in (a) two rolls and (b) three rolls?

■ Problem 2: A Problem Created by Playing a Largest-Sum Game (◆ 5-8 ◆ Class divided into teams of four)

To practice decimal addition, Miss Brill had her class play *Largest Decimal Sum*, an adaptation of the *Largest-Sum* game (Investigation 6.4 on page 6-21). The first two rolls of a 0 to 9 die came up a 1 and a 0. LeMar's group placed these digits as shown to the right. On the next roll, a 6 came up. "Should we place the 6 in the box on the far left or in one of the middle boxes?" Andy asked.

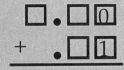

"If we put the 6 in the box on the far left," LeMar thought out loud, "and a 7, 8, or 9 comes up on either the last two rolls, we lose." What is the probability of rolling at least one 7, 8, or 9 if a 10-sided die (with faces 0 to 9) is rolled twice?

↪ **Teaching Tips.** Instead of presenting the class with the stock problem above, a teacher could wait for a similar situation to arise while actually playing a game. This should make solving the problem more purposeful. Note that problems similar to that above would be a natural outcome of playing *Largest Sum* (or its variations) with whole numbers also.

■ Problem 3: Two-Coin Flip Experiment Revisited (◆ 5-8 ◆ Groups of four)

Fyvush flipped a fair coin three times; Gillian flipped a fair coin six times. Is the probability of Fyvush getting at least two of three heads the same, smaller, or greater than that of Gillian getting at least four of six heads? Why?

✿ Investigation 13.9: Systematic Simulations of Everyday Situations

◆ Devising simulations of real or realistic events ◆ 5-8 ◆ Whole class, small group, or individual

A simulation is a model that faithfully represents the critical features of a real situation. It is a valuable way of determining the empirical probability of a situation and solving probability problems. Consider the following problem:

■ **Problem 1: Taking Her Chances.** Hedda had a true-false Social Studies exam the next day and knew she had to get 7 of 10 items correct to pass the test. If she did not study and simply guessed on each item, how likely is it Hedda would pass?

The Quantitative Literacy Project[†] suggests the following guidelines for creating a simulation:

Step 1: Identify the key elements and assumptions of the problem situation. The key element in Problem 1 is that Hedda needed to correctly answer at least seven of 10 true-false items. The assumption is that she has no means for responding correctly other than guessing.

Step 2: Select a random device to simulate the situation. Flipping a coin could model the key elements and assumptions of Problem 1. If a guessing strategy is used, each exam item involves two possible outcomes (correct or incorrect) that are equally likely. This can be simulated by flipping a coin (e.g., let heads = correct and tails = incorrect).

Step 3: Define a trial. To complete the simulation of Problem 1 would require 10 coin flips—one each to simulate a guess for each of the 10 test items. Simulating each key component (the 10 flips) once constitutes a trial.

Step 4: Collect the data. Carry out a large number of trials and record the results. The more trials completed, the better you will be able to predict the results of a problem.

Step 5: Draw conclusions from the data. Based on your results, how likely is it that Hedda in Problem 1 will pass by using a guessing strategy?

Use the guidelines above, solve Problems 2 to 4 below by creating a simulation.

■ **Problem 2: Taking More Chances.** Hedda's Social Studies teacher made a surprise announcement: "Would you rather have a 10-item test or a 100-item test?" Keeping in mind that 70% is passing and Hedda's utter lack of knowledge, would she be better off voting for the 10-item test, would she be more likely to pass the 100-item test, or is she equally likely to pass (by sheer luck) either the 10-item or the 100-item test?

■ **Problem 3: Taking Her Chances Revisited.** Hedda decided to take her chances and did not study for her Social Studies exam. And boy, was she in for a surprise. Instead of a true-false test, her teacher handed out a 10-item, multiple-choice test with four choices per test item. Now how likely is it that Hedda will get 7 items correct by guessing alone?[1]

■ **Problem 4: Productive Hitter.** Joe Megabucks had a batting average of .333. Mr. Wilson drove 3 hours to Wrigley Field because he wanted to see Joe make his 2500th hit. What are the chances that Joe will go hitless in the game, gravely disappointing Mr. Wilson? Assume that Joe typically hits four times in a game.

■ **Problem 5: Coinciding Birthdays.** In a classroom of 25 students, what is the probability that two students will have the same birthday?

✦ **Extension for Problems 3 to 5 (◆ 7-8).** Determine the theoretical probability in each case.

[†] See *The Art and Techniques of Simulation: Quantitative Literacy Series* by M. Gnandesikan, R. Schaeffer, & J. Swift, © 1987 by Dale Seymour.

🍎 Box 13.2: A League of Their Own[2]

To involve her students with statistics, probability, and other topics in a purposeful way, Ms. Socrates posed the following problem:

■ **Problem A: Building a Baseball Franchise** (◆ 3-8). Pretend that each group owns a baseball team. Because of a catastrophic players' strike, your team was disbanded, and you must draft a new team. The draft will be held in two weeks. Try to assemble the best team you can. For the purposes of our project you will need to draft four pitchers, a player for each of the other eight positions, and a designated hitter. Each team will have a salary cap of $35,000,000 to spend on its players.

The problem raised a number of questions: What number does 35,000,000 represent? How many large base-ten cubes (a familiar benchmark for 1,000) is this? On what basis should a group make its decisions and where could they get the information needed to make them?

After exploring the first two questions, the class tackled the task of collecting needed data. Several students suggested that baseball books, the web, or baseball cards could provide helpful information. The next day, Myron brought in his collection of baseball cards. Ms. Socrates had him pass out a set of cards to each group. The students examined the cards to see for themselves what information might be helpful in making their decisions. This raised a number of questions. What did abbreviations such as AB (at bats), H (hits), 2B (doubles), HR (home runs), RBI (runs batted in), and SLG (slugging average), and AVG (batting average) mean?

🖩 These questions raised a number of interesting mathematical questions, such as What is an average? and What does a batting average of .284 mean? To address the first question, Ms. Socrates began with problems involving a whole-number average and a fair-sharing analogy (see Part I of Probe 13.1 on page 13-9). She then had the class consider several problems involving a decimal average greater than one (e.g., the average of 1, 3, 4, 5 is 3.25). To address the second question and review decimals, Ms. Socrates next asked the class to read the decimal .284. This raised the question, "Why were batting averages expressed as decimals to thousandths?" The class finally agreed that it indicated the number of hits in 1000 at bats, which is a more precise measure than using 100 at bats. Ms. Socrates asked what a player's batting average would be if he was at bat 1000 times and got a hit every time, 250 times, or 72 times. She then asked what a player's batting average would if he was at bat 500 times and got a hit every time, 250 times, or 72 times. Next, she asked what a player's batting average would be if he was at bat 300 times and got a hit every time, 250 times, or 72 times. This provided an opportunity to learn how to use a calculator to convert fractions to decimals (e.g., 72/300 = 0.240).

Over the next two weeks, the groups used some class time and free time to consider their draft choices. To make effective comparisons, students quickly found that they had to organize the mass of information. Someone suggested sorting the baseball cards by position and making a chart to summarize key information.

Before the player draft, Ms. Socrates posed Problem B below. This served to explore theoretical probability informally.

■ **Problem B: Devising a Baseball Simulation** (◆ 5-8). Using two 10-sided dice (each numbered 0 to 9) and the operation of multiplication, create a baseball simulation.

One group proposed a simulation involving six categories of pitchers (lifetime percent of wins ≥ 75%, 65-74%, 55-64%, 45-54%, 35-44%, and 25-34%), each broken down by 15 hitter categories (lifetime batting average ≥ .300, .290-.299, .280-.289, and so forth). The class concluded that creating the simulation would require an enormous effort. Six pitching levels by 15 batting levels meant 6 x 15 or 90 charts each consisting of 81 entries for a total of 7,290 entries!

Another group proposed a simpler simulation involving only three pitching levels and three batting levels (3 x 3 or 9 charts). To define high, average, and low pitchers, the students used a sampling method: randomly selected the cards of 30 pitchers, checked the lifetime percent of wins for each, listed the players in order, and divided them into three equal groups. The

Box 13.2 continued

top third (*high pitchers*) won 55% or more of their games; the middle third (*average pitchers*), 46% to 54%; and the lower third (*low pitchers*), 45% or less. Based on their sample of 30 other players, the students designated a player with a batting average of .280 or higher as a *high hitter*; one with an average of .250 to .279, as an *average hitter*; and one with an average of below .250, as a *low hitter*. The pitching charts for the high pitchers were given the lowest probability of getting a hit. Against a high pitcher, a high hitter was given a $\frac{28}{100}$ chance of getting a hit; an average hitter, a $\frac{26}{100}$ chance; and a low hitter, a $\frac{24}{100}$ chance.

Instead of 9 charts, Alexi proposed using 7: Chart 1 (high hitter vs. low pitcher) listed 30 of the 100 possibilities as hits; Chart 2 (high hitter vs. average pitcher), 29; Chart 3 (high hitter vs. high pitcher or average hitter vs. low pitcher), 28; Chart 4 (average hitter vs. average pitcher), 27; Chart 5 (average hitter vs. high pitcher or low hitter vs. low pitcher), 26; Chart 6 (low hitter vs. average pitcher), 25; and Chart 7 (low hitter vs. high pitcher), 24.

Making up the charts involved identifying all the possible outcomes of multiplying two numbers 0 to 9 (10 x 10 or 100) and noting the likelihood of each product (e.g., 0 occurs 19 of 100 times; 1s 1/100; 2s or 3s, 2/100; 4s, 3/100, and so forth). To construct Pitching Chart 7 (a portion of which is shown below), for example, students decided on assigning the products 1 (1/100); 4 (3/100); and 6, 8, 12, 18, and 24 (each 4/100) as hits (H) and all other outcomes as outs (O) (total probability of a hit = 24/100).

Pitching Chart 7: Low Hitter vs. High Pitcher

```
0   1   2   3   4   5   6   7   8   9       81
O   H   O   O   H   O   H   O   H   O  ...  O
```

To distinguish between power hitters (those who frequently get extra-base hits) and contact hitters (those who typically get singles) and thus make the simulation even more realistic, the class also used the SLG data. Unlike a regular batting average in which all types of hits are treated the same, a slugging average is a *weighted average*. It weighs the importance of a hit according to the number of bases a hitter

advances: a single is worth 1; a double, 2; a triple, 3; and a home run, 4. Thus, a hitter who had a double and a triple in eight at bats would have an SLG of $\frac{2+3}{8} = \frac{5}{8}$ or .624. From a sample of players, the students gauged the average number of times players with a high SLG get a double (17%), a triple (3%), and a homerun (15%). They did the same for players with a medium SLG and for those with a low SLG. These averages were then built into an extra-hit chart. That is, when a high SLG player got a hit, they rolled two dice and consulted a *high SLG extra-base chart* that provided a $\frac{15}{100}$ chance of getting a homerun, a $\frac{3}{100}$ chance for a triple, and a $\frac{17}{100}$ chance for a double. Different charts gave medium SLG and low SLG players fewer chances for extra base hits.

The class randomly chose the cards of 20 pitchers (4 for each of five teams), 5 players for each of the other positions, and 5 designated hitters. To facilitate the selection process during the draft, the students summarized key information for each player on 3 x 5 cards. For each pitcher, they recorded the player's name, P (for pitcher), and H (high), A (average), or L (low) depending on the pitcher's lifetime winning percent. For each of the other players, they recorded the player's name, his position, hitting level, and his SLG level. The cards were then organized by position and relative performance.

Before the day of the draft, Mrs. Socrates posed the problem of how to devise a team picking order that was fair. On draft day, the team with the first pick, deducted the player's salary from their total, and took possession of the player's card. Note that this involved practicing subtraction with large numbers. The next group chose from the remaining cards and so forth. Playing the game served to practice basic multiplication facts and provided an opportunity to collect, organize, and analyze data.

⌨ A computer could be used to create charts summarizing the player data for the draft, make the pitching and SLG charts, devise a simulation and provide real programming experience, facilitate setting up and printing a schedule, collecting team and individual data, and generating appropriate statistics.

Gardner, and Sandra Shekaramiz, ©1992 by the NCTM. The introduction of this outstanding reference notes: "We live in a world of information. Stop and think a moment about the number of facts, figures, and other data that confront us each day. What do we do with all this information? We ignore some of it, we organize some of it to fit what we already know, or we summarize it . . . . [T]his information . . . is presented in written descriptions, in graphs or tables, or in summary numbers such as averages. . . . [W]e need to help our students—from the time they first enter school—to make sense of data" (p. 1). It goes on to describe for each grade K through 6 activities that involve age-appropriate ways of collecting, representing, and analyzing data. Each activity is based on answering questions—many of them directly related to children's personal lives. The intent is that the activities be purposeful and interesting. The activities also involve using mathematical content other than statistics. For example, in addition to *How Far and Why?* (the basis for Investigation 13.1 on pages 13-5 and 13-6), the Fourth-Grade chapter describes the activity summarized in Activity File 13.2 below.

Activity File 13.2: Which Paper Towel Gets the Wettest

◆ Area (measurement) + statistics ◆ 3-8
◆ Small groups about four

This activity begins with a question like, Are advertising claims that Brand X is more absorbent than other paper towels valid? Have students consider how to measure absorbency. Note that the same amount of water (e.g., 4 drops) should be used with each towel sample. Use a transparent square-centimeter grid to measure the area of the towel wetted. Note that adding tempera paint will leave a stain on the towel, making it easier to measure the area. This activity can further be extended by asking: Does twice as much water wet twice the towel area? What is the relative absorbency of napkins, butcher paper, newspaper, notebook paper?

☞ **Pictorial Representation** developed by the Nuffield Mathematics Project, © 1969 by the Nuffield Foundation, and published in the U.S. by John Wiley & Sons, Inc. This refer-

ence includes project ideas appropriate for K-6 classes. It pictures various types of graphs including a line graph, which is not discussed in this chapter. (A line graph is similar to a bar graph but uses a line instead of a rectangle.) It is richly illustrated with many examples of child-made graphs.

☞ **Used Numbers: Real Data in the Classroom,** developed by TERC and Lesley College (Used Number Project), © 1996-1997, and published by Dale Seymour. This activity-based program for grades K-6 involves students in collecting, displaying, and interpreting data. It includes the following units: **Counting: Ourselves and Our Families** by Antonio Stone and Susan Jo Russell, © 1990, for grades K-1; **Measuring: From Paces to Feet** by Rebecca B. Corwin & Susan Jo Russell, © 1990, for grades 3-5; **Sorting: Groups and Graphs** by Susan Jo Russell & Rebecca B. Corwin, © 1990, for grades 2-3; **Statistics: Middles, Means, and In-Between** by Susan N. Friel, J. Rebecca Mokros, & Susan Jo Russell, © 1992, for grades 5-6; **Statistics: Prediction and Sampling** by Rebecca B. Corwin & Susan Jo Russell, © 1990, for grades 5-6; and **Statistics: The Shape of the Data** by Susan Jo Russell & Rebecca B. Corwin, © 1989, for grades 4-6.

Statistics and Probability

☞ **Dealing with Data and Chance** (Addenda Series, Grades 5-8) by Judith S. Zawojewski with Gary Brooks, Lynn Dinkelkamp, Eunice D. Goldberg, Howard Goldberg, Arthur Hyde, Tess Jackson, Marsha Landau, Hope Martin, Jeri Nowakowski, Sandy Paull, Albert P. Shulte, Philip Wagreich, and Barbara Wilmot, © 1991 by NCTM. This reference considers intuitive understandings and everyday uses of data and chance and how to build on intuitive knowledge.

☞ **Fantasy Baseball** written by Tim Scheidt and distributed by Dale Seymour. This resource provides for a 5- to 8-week unit that involves ratios, fractions, percentages, graphing, and probability. Suitable for grades 6 to 8.

☞ **Probability and Statistics** developed by the Nuffield Mathematics Project, © 1969 by the Nuffield Foundation and published in the U.S. by John Wiley & Sons, Inc. This valuable resource describes activities and games for involving 5- to 13-year-olds in the intuitive exploration of statistics and probability.

☞ **Teaching Statistics and Probability** (1981 Yearbook) edited by A. P. Shulte, © 1981 by NCTM. Elementary school teachers will be particularly interested in Part I (*The Case for Teaching Statistics and Probability*) and Part III (*Classroom Activities*) of this NCTM yearbook. Part III includes chapters on graphs, activities that involve using statistics and probability, a sampling activity using popsicle sticks, analyzing the fairness of games (see, e.g., Activity File 13.3 in the next column), using graphs and pictures to determine averages, using games to practice computation and to introduce probability, and a simulation activity.

☞ **Quantitative Literacy Series** evolved out of the *Qualitative Literacy Project* run by the American Statistical Association and the NCTM and is published by Dale Seymour. **From Home Runs to Housing Costs** by Center for Statistical Education (ASA) and also published by Dale Seymour includes more than 30 sets of data to supplement the QLS series. The QLS series includes the following references on teaching statistics and probability in the intermediate grades: **The Art and Techniques of Simulation** by Mrudulla Gnanadesikan, Richard L. Scheaffer, & Jim Swift, © 1987; **Exploring Data** by James Landewehr & Ann E. Watkins, © 1986; **Exploring Measurements** by Peter Barbella, James Kepner, & Richard L. Scheaffer; **Exploring Probability** by Claire M. Newman, Thomas E. Obremski, & Richard L. Schaeffer, © 1987; and **Exploring Surveys and Information From Samples** by James Landewehr, Jim Swift, & Ann E. Watkins, © 1987.

Probability

☞ **Probability** by E. Phillips, G. Lappan, M. J. Winter, & W. Fitzgerald, © 1986 by Addison-Wesley. This reference was the product of the *Middle Grades Mathematics Project*.

☞ **What Are My Chances?** by Albert P. Shulte and Stuart A. Choate and distributed by Dale Seymour. This resource includes more than 70 hands-on activities. Book A includes expressing probability as fractions, decimals, and percents. Book B includes the multiplication

---

 Activity File 13.3: Which is Fairer?[†]

◆ Empirical or theoretical probability ◆ 3-8 ◆
Pairs of students + whole-class discussion

The aim of this activity is to have students determine which of the two games described below is fairer and why. Less developmentally advanced students can play the games and record their results. The empirical probability can be determined by compiling the results of all the pairs. Developmentally more advanced students can be encouraged to determine the theoretical probability by using, for example, a table.

Game 1: Odd or Even Difference. One player is designated the *odd* player; the other, the *even* player. Two dice numbered 0 to 5 are rolled, and the difference between them is determined. If the difference is odd (e.g., 5 - 2 = 3 or 2 - 1 = 1), the *odd* player scores a point. If the difference is even (e.g., 5 - 3 = 2 or 4 - 0 = 4), the *even* player scores the point. After two minutes, the player with the most points wins.

Game 2: Odd or Even Product. The game is played like Game 1, except that the players use the product of the two dice rather than their difference.

◆ **Extensions.** Encourage students to play or to analyze *Odd or Even Sum* to see if this game is fair. (The game is played like Game 1, except that the players use the sum of the two dice rather than the difference. Have them consider *Odd or Even Quotient*. Students should quickly recognize that order matters (e.g., $4 \div 2 = 2$ and $2 \div 4 = \frac{1}{2}$) and that a rule must be made up to specify which digit serves as the dividend and which as the divisor. They should also quickly realize that many quotients are neither odd nor even. This could lead to a spin-off game *Whole Number or Fraction* where one player is designated *whole number* and the other, *fraction*. Is the game fair? Why or Why not?

[†] Games 1 and 2 are based on *Developing Mathematical Processes*, Level 6, Topic 85, developed at the University of Wisconsin Research and Development Center for Cognitive Learning and reported in Chapter 8 "Fair Games, Unfair Games" by G. W. Bright, J. G. Harvey, and M. M. Wheeler of *Teaching Statistical and Probability* (1981 *Yearbook*), edited by A. P. Shulte and J. R. Smart, © 1981 by NCTM, Reston, VA.

principle, combinations and permutations, and conditional probability.

A SAMPLE OF CHILDREN'S LITERATURE

Statistics

Box 13.3 illustrates an extended, literature-based unit on fear (affective education), a unit that entails purposefully collecting, graphing, and analyzing data. The reference below could serve as an aid for introducing averages.

📖 **Averages** by Jane Jonas Srivastana, © 1975 by Thomas Y. Crowell. This useful reference describes various activities involving means, medians, and modes appropriate for primary-age children. The types of averages are humorously illustrated with pictures. The mode is clearly defined as the *most-of* average.

Probability

Children's literature could serve as a basis for an extended and integrated unit on weather and probability. The first book below could be used to provide a general introduction to probability. The second could be used to introduce an important everyday application of probability: meteorology (the examination of weather patterns in order to predict future weather).

📖 **Probability: The Science of Chance** by Arthur G. Razzell and K. G. O. Watts, © 1964 by Doubleday. This book from the *Exploring Mathematics* series is well suited for fifth and sixth graders. It begins with a discussion of people's desire to foretell the future and various methods used to fulfill this desire (e.g., palmreading and astrology). The book discusses how the science of probability grew out of gamblers' desires to predict the outcome of dice, tossed coins, and cards and how probability serves as a basis for the insurance industry. It makes the key point that probability is concerned with what happens in the long run. The book also discusses sampling.

📖 **Cloudy with a Chance of Meatballs** by Judi Barrett, © 1978, Atheneum. The town of Chewandswallow had unusual weather: Three times a day it rained foods such as soup or hamburgers. This made obtaining food for the town folk easy until a terrible turn in the weather. In a follow-up discussion, encourage students to consider why it is important to predict the weather and to explore how they could do so. For example, have them collect data on the color of the sky at dawn and sunset and the weather that follows. By collecting, organizing, and analyzing these data,

---

📖🍎 Box 13.3: What's Scary to You?

Ms. Born-Free knew that children had many fears and that it could help to talk them out. Over the course of two weeks, she read and discussed books from the *Berenstain Bears* series by Stan and Jan Berenstain, including *Go to the Doctor, Visit the Dentist, Moving Day, Go to Camp, Learn about Strangers, Bad Dream, Double Dare, The Truth, Get Stage Fright,* and *In the Dark.* The following week, Ms. Born-Free instructed, "I want you each to list the three scariest things to you." She circulated around the room, helping

children formulate their ideas in words. Afterward, she discussed with the class how they could determine what things were the scariest and otherwise make sense of all their data. One question that came up, for example, was: Are boys and girls fearful of the same or different things? Each group set about summarizing and portraying the data. Two samples (a bar graph and stem-and-leaf plot) are shown below (*Key for both:* ▦ = *boys,* ☐ = *girls*).

children may rediscover the ancient rule of thumb: Red skies at night, sailors delight; red skies at morning, sailors take warning. A series of additional activities are described in *Storytime Mathtime: Math Explorations in Children's Literature* by Patricia Satariano.

TIPS ON USING TECHNOLOGY

Calculators

With intermediate-level students, graphing calculators can eliminate the tedium of plotting data and can help focus efforts on analyzing and interpreting graphs.

Computers

Statistics. The Internet provides a wealth of data that students can collect, graph, and analyze to address real issues. For example, "The Globe Program" (www.globe.gov) involves thousands of classes around the world in collecting and posting environmental data, which could serve as the basis for an integrated science and statistics lesson. As part of an extended and integrated math-social studies-science project on world population, have students visit the "World Population" Web page at http://sunsite.unc.edu/lunarbin/worldpop and record the current world population each month over the course of six months. Have students calculate (a) the population increase for each month and (b) the average monthly increase over the six-month period. Determine the percentage of increase for each month and the six-month period.

Reasons for using computers to teach statistics include: (1) Increasingly powerful computer tools for doing statistical analyses are becoming readily available and important in the workplace. Students should have a basic familiarity with the capabilities of this technology. (2) Using computers to do the number crunching leaves students free to analyze statistics and discover relationships (e.g., the effects of changing scores on averages or graphic representations). In brief, it can help students understand statistics better. After students have collected data, the spreadsheet function of such programs as *AppleWorks* provides a ready means for listing scores in order and calculating their mean. Several examples of educational programs developed to teach statistics are described below.

Data Insights by Edwards and Keogh, © 1990. After students have collected their own data, they can use *Data Insights* to create box-and-whiskers plots as well as spreadsheets.

Statistics Workshop was developed by the *Reasoning Under Uncertainty Project* run by BBN, (Bolt, Beranek, and Newman) Laboratories and © 1991 by Sunburst Communications, Inc.) This computer tool, for Macintosh Plus or later with 800K disk drives, provides an opportunity to explore fundamental statistic concepts and pictorial representations of data. Students can use data provided or enter their own. By opening the *Datasheet* menu and selecting *Column Statistics*, the program will list statistics such as the mean, the minimum and maximum score, the range, and the lower and upper quartile for the data set chosen. By opening the *View* window, students can have the computer generate a histogram, bar chart, box-and-whiskers plot, or a scatterplot. By experimenting with sets of data students can discover the effects of extreme scores on means. By examining and discussing the scatterplots of various sets of data, intermediate-level students should be able to reason out what the scatterplots of various correlations should look like.

Table Top developed by C. Hancock and J. Kaput (see, e.g., C. Hancock, *Data Modeling with the Table Top* [Technical Report, 1990], Cambridge, MA: Technological Educational Resource Centers (TERC). Available on disks formatted for Macintosh or Windows, *Tabletop Jr.* is suitable for grades K-6; Tabletop Sr., grades 6-8. This easy-to-use database system allows students to create Venn diagrams, one dimensional graphs (e.g., list cereals by sugar content), or two-dimensional graphs (e.g., a scatterplot illustrating cereals by sugar content and price per serving). Students can use either canned data or enter their own.

Probability. Two examples of software that can be used to devise simulations and explore empirical probabilities are **Chance Plus** developed by C. Konold (© 1991 by Scientific Reasoning Institute, Hasbrouk Hall, University of Massachusetts) and **Probability Constructor** (published by LOGAL, Kiyat Shmona, Israel, and distributed by Sunburst).

14 THE MATHEMATICS OF OUR ENVIRONMENT: GEOMETRY AND SPATIAL SENSE

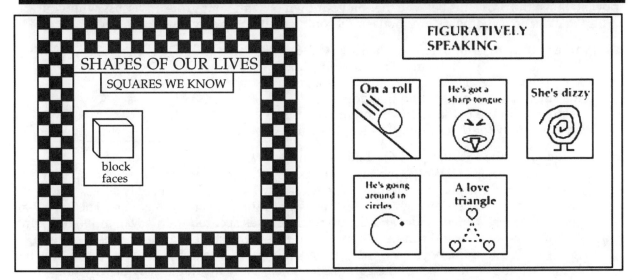

A bulletin board can highlight mathematical connections. The one above illustrates three ways geometry touches our everyday lives.

 We live in a world of objects with various geometric forms. *Shapes of Our Lives* can prompt children to reflect on the occurrence of a shape in their everyday lives. For the bulletin board above, for example, a teacher could take students on a "shape safari" or simply ask them, "Where do you see squares in school, outdoors, in your home, or downtown?" Children could then take photographs or draw, paint, or construct pictures of their examples. One option for a bulletin board is to have a series of displays—periodically introducing a new shape (e.g., *The Shape of the Week* or *The Shape of the Month*). Another option is to have a single display of various shapes (e.g., *Squares We Know, Typical Triangles, Common Circles,* and *Routine Rectangles*).

 Designing layouts, borders, and backgrounds for bulletin boards, cards, calendars, announcements, and so forth by hand or by computer can provide purposeful experiences with geometric patterns. The border for the *Shapes of Our Lives* is appropriately constructed of squares. This pattern is an example of a tessellation (see page 14-18) and was created using *Superpaint*.

 Geometric analogies or allusions are commonly used in everyday conversations. *Figuratively Speaking* can prompt children to consider the connection between these language tools and mathematics. After giving a class several examples, a teacher can encourage students to come up with their own examples or to look for examples in their reading. Students can then draw, paint, or construct a picture illustrating their examples (e.g., use the *Color It* program).

Students can also construct their own books, titled *Shapes of My Life, Patterns I've Designed,* and *Figuratively Speaking,* and regularly add to them, making the exploring of geometric connections an ongoing process. Sharing their examples with the class can prompt further reflection.

THIS CHAPTER

☞ Try Investigation 14.1 (page 14-2).

Geometry is the science of shapes and space. "*Spatial sense is an intuitive feel for one's surroundings and the objects in them*" (NCTM, 1989, p. 49). As "shapes are patterns" (Senechal, 1990, p. 139), the study of geometry extends the exploration of patterns begun in chapter 2. It also involves learning about the space we live in. (Continued on page 14-3.)

☾ Investigation 14.1: Exercising Geometric Thinking

◆ Problem solving involving geometric thinking ◆ Small groups of four

What is geometry? In essence, it is the study of shapes and space. All of us have informal knowledge about the shapes around us and the space we live in. This knowledge can be a powerful aid in understanding a wide variety of mathematical ideas and in solving all sorts of problems. Increasing our understanding of geometry can greatly expand our mathematical power. Solve the problems below either on your own or with your group. Discuss with your group or class how geometric intuitions or reasoning could help solve these problems.

■ **Problem 1: Length of a Triangle's Side** (◆ 3-6).
Side A of the triangle to the right is 3 cm long, and
side B is 4 cm long. How long is side C? Assume
that a ruler is not available and that you are
unfamiliar with the Pythagorean theorem. Devise an
informal strategy for determining the length of side C.

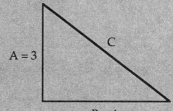

■ **Problem 2: Roped Rover** (◆ 4-6). LaFranz and
Pices wanted to see Mr. Wolverine's new attack dog Rover, which was kept tied up in the backyard behind the garage. Because the backyard was fenced in, the only access to the back of the garage and the dog was a walkway that ran along side the garage. The back wall of the garage was 10-feet wide, and the dog's chain was secured to this wall at its midpoint. Mr. Wolverine's dog could run straight out from where the chain was secured a maximum distance of 7 feet. If the boys used the sidewalk along the side of the garage, would they be able to reach the back corner of the garage and safely view the dog? Why or why not?

■ **Problem 3: A Garden Plot** (◆ 4-8). Francesca has a garden plot that measures 8 feet by 10 feet. If she plants strawberry plants at least 1 foot apart, what is the *maximum* number of strawberry plants she can plant in her garden?

Questions for Reflection

1. Many students jump to the conclusion that the solution to Problem 3 is 8 x 10 or 80. What problem-solving heuristic would be invaluable in solving the *Garden Plot*?

2. For *The Garden Plot*, Alexi (age 11), Alison (age 11), and Arianne (age $9\frac{1}{2}$) each thought to draw a picture but came up with a different answer—80, 90, and 99, respectively. Alexi drew a picture with 10 rows of 8 plants each, numbering the *rows* 1 to 10 and the *plants* 1 to 8. He justified his drawing and answer by noting that the problem specified that the plot was *8 feet* by *10 feet*. Alison and Arianne drew a picture with *11 rows* of *9 plants each*. (a) In the investigative approach, how would a teacher deal with such discrepant solutions? (b) Who was correct and why?

3. After completing her drawing, Alison started to determine her answer by counting each pictured plant. Her teacher noted that counting each item was one way to determine the total number of plants but encouraged her to consider a shortcut. (a) What short cut would be appropriate? (b) Alison counted the number of plants in the first row and noted there were 9. She then counted the number of rows by pointing to the first item in each row. However, she skipped the first item of the first row because, she explained, "You can't count a plant twice." As a result, she counted only 10 rows and came up with answer of 90 plants (10 rows of 9 plants per row). How could a teacher help Alison recognize that she needed to count all the rows?

4. Is Arianne's answer of 99 really the maximum number of plants possible?

Geometry is unlike other aspects of elementary school mathematics and yet can be a key to understanding them. As the subject of shapes and space, geometry is quite different from arithmetic with its focus on collections and numbers. It provides children a different view of mathematics (NCTM, 1989)—and thus a more complete understanding of it.

Partly "because their spatial capabilities frequently exceed their numerical skills," "children are naturally interested in geometry and find it intriguing" (NCTM, 1989, p. 48). Indeed, it often provides a refreshing break for children less skilled in arithmetic and gives them an opportunity to shine. Consider the case of $9\frac{1}{2}$-year old Arianne—19 months younger and with a full year less formal arithmetic learning than the other members of her group. Shown a right triangle with shorter sides of 3 and 4 and asked the length of the third side (Problem 1 of Investigation 14.1 on page 14-2), her group mates were unsure how to proceed. Using her first finger and thumb, Arianne promptly measured the side labeled *4* and, then using the span between these two fingers, compared the known side to unknown and estimated its length to be *five*. Although this procedure could have been performed more precisely, she understood its essence. Although less sophisticated in arithmetic thinking, Arianne was able to excel on a task requiring geometric thinking.

Because of its intuitive appeal, geometry can be a great aid in solving problems and communicating ideas. After all, the heuristic of drawing a picture is simply a device for translating and summarizing verbal information as geometric information—a process that can facilitate understanding. (Drawing a picture can, for example, be helpful in solving a problem such as Problems 2 and 3 of Investigation 14.1.)

As illustrated throughout this guide, geometric models can also serve to help students understand a wide variety of mathematical concepts and procedures (e.g., in chapter 5, using a number line to represent multiplication of whole numbers; in chapter 7, using a number grid to model multidigit addition; in chapter 8, using a volume model to explain and determine cube roots; in chapter 9, using pattern blocks or Cuisenaire rods to model fractions; in chapter 10 and 11, using an area model to represent fraction and decimal multiplication; in chapter 12, using graphs to identify proportional and nonproportional situations; in chapter 13, using a block-leveling model to illustrate the concept of *mean*). The special connection between geometry and measurement will be explored in the next chapter. (The term *geometry* is derived from the Greek *geometria—geo* meaning the earth or land and *metria* meaning to measure—to measure the earth or land.) Geometric models useful in algebra will be examined in chapter 16. In brief, "children who develop a strong sense of spatial relationships and who master the concepts and language of geometry are better prepared to learn number and measurement ideas as well as other advanced topics " (NCTM, 1989, p. 48).

In this chapter, we examine the value of geometry and the nature of geometric learning (Unit 14•1) and then focus on how geometry can be taught in a stimulating manner (Unit 14•2).

WHAT THE NCTM *STANDARDS* SAY

Grades K-4

"In grades K-4, the mathematics curriculum should include two- and three-dimensional geometry so that students can:

◆ describe, model, draw, and classify shapes;
◆ investigate and predict the results of combining, subdividing, and changing shapes;
◆ develop spatial sense;
◆ relate geometric ideas to number and measurement ideas;
◆ recognize and appreciate geometry in their world" (p. 48).

Grades 5-8

"In grades 5-8, the mathematics curriculum should include the study of the geometry of one, two, and three dimensions in a variety of situations so that students can:

◆ identify, describe, compare, and classify geometric figures;
◆ visualize and represent geometric figures with special attention to developing spatial sense;
◆ explore transformation of geometric figures;
◆ represent and solve problems using geometric models;
◆ understand and apply geometric proper-

ties and relationships;
- ◆ develop an appreciation of geometry as a

means of describing the physical world" (p. 112).

14•1 GEOMETRY AND CHILDREN'S GEOMETRIC THINKING

Figure 14.1: A Parallel Young Ones' View

Both literally and figuratively, we live in a geometric world. We encounter parallel lines on ruled paper, printed pages, railroad tracks, and so forth; and we think about our world—including our personal relationships—in terms of geometric analogies (see Figure 14.1). In Subunit 4•1•1, we consider the reasons for studying geometry; in Subunit 4•1•2, the nature of children's learning.

4•1•1 MATHEMATICS: THE NEED FOR GEOMETRY

According to the NCTM (1989) *Curriculum Standards*, geometry should be an important and integral component of the K-8 curriculum. *But why is it so important to study geometry?*

☞ Consider Investigation 14.2 (page 14-5).

There are two key reasons for studying geometry in the elementary school.

1. As the bulletin board on page 14-1 and Investigation 14.2 illustrate, geometry is an integral aspect of everyday life. A spatial sense is necessary for understanding and functioning effectively in our environment. Geometry can help us represent, describe, and understand our natural and human-made world (NCTM, 1989). Moreover, it is a key part of such jobs as fashion design, engineering, architecture, and art and plays a central role in other aspects of everyday life such as planning the layout of a garden, choosing picture frames and arranging pictures, and decorating a cake.

2. Geometry can enhance mathematical power in three ways: (a) As Investigation 14.2 illustrates, geometry can be a great deal of fun and can help foster a positive disposition toward mathematics. (b) As Investigations 2.5 (on page 2-38) and 14.1 (page 14-2) illustrated earlier, geometry provides numerous opportunities to involve children in the processes of mathematical inquiry—problem solving, conjecturing, reasoning, and communicating. (c) As we have seen throughout this text, geometric models can help make other mathematical content topics more concrete and comprehensible.

14•1•2 LEARNING

In this subunit, we describe a model that can be helpful in understanding the development of children's geometric thinking and why many encounter difficulty learning geometry.

Understanding the Development of Children's Geometric Thinking

As with other domains of mathematics, children's geometric thinking develops gradually. Initially, children's geometric knowledge is incomplete and their reasoning is based on general appearances. As children construct a more complete understanding of geometric concepts, they rely less on appearances but may still have important gaps in their knowledge and reasoning. In time, they may construct (continued on page 14-6)

⌨ Investigation 14.2: Informal Geometry

◆ Informally and creatively exploring geometry and its everyday applications
+ spatial sense ◆ K-8 ◆ Any number

At the primary-level particularly, instruction should focus on informal geometry. This can be done in various creative and interesting ways that also help children see the connection between geometry and everyday life. Try the sample of activities below to see how.

Activity I: Tiling a Hallway. Mr. Argo decided to tile a hallway, which was 100 square feet in area. Unable to decide between a blue tile and a yellow tile, he decided to buy 50 1-foot x 1-foot tiles of each color. When he got back home, Mrs. Argo asked, "Now what are going to do with two colors? " Illustrate some patterns Mr. Argo could create with the tiles he bought.

Activity II: Evocative Ads. Design an advertisement so that the lettering evokes a mental image of your message. For example, note that the lettering of *Splash Pools* evokes the image of waves.

designed
by AAB

Activity III: Stamp Designs. Each year the U.S. Postal Service issues stamps commemorating a person or event. The designers of stamps often use geometric designs to make stamps attractive. For example, a stamp commemorating the poultry industry inscribed the value of the stamp inside an egg. Choose a person or event you think should be honored on a postage stamp. Design a stamp that would vividly portray the person or event. Incorporate appropriate geometric shapes or patterns.

Activity IV: Flag Designs. National, state and other flags involve geometric considerations. One is the shape of the flag itself (e.g., rectangular, square, triangular, and so forth). Another is the use of geometric shapes such as five-pointed stars, (horizontal, vertical, and/or diagonal) bars, and (rectangular, square, or circular) fields or insets. Yet another is the overall design or arrangement of the elements. Design an individual, a group, or a class flag to represent what is important to you.

Activity V: Geowords. *Geowords* are geometry terms designed to highlight their meaning (see Examples A and B to the right). (a) Fashion ARC, BISECT, PERPENDICULAR, RIGHT ANGLE, ROTATION, and TESSELATION into geowords. Experiment with different ways these words can be fashioned. (b) What other geometric terms can you fashion into geowords?

Ⱥcute Ⱥngle   PARA‖E‖INES

Example A   **Example B**

✑ Teaching Tips

Note that Activity I could be posed as a real problem (e.g., covering over a bulletin board or wall). Activity II could be done as part of a creative writing lesson, and Activities III and IV could be done as part of an integrated social studies-art-mathematics lesson. One way of introducing Activity IV would be to have students examine the flags of the states or world's nations and try to classify them. This open-ended task should prompt a discussion of geometric considerations involved in flag designs. It might also raise the issue of how color is used to represent ideas. Note that in addition to encouraging students to think about the meaning of the geometric terms, devising geowords fosters imagination and creativity. Activity V can be used to underscore that the mathematical meaning of a term is not necessarily identical to its everyday meaning. For example, the geoword BI SECT is consistent with everyday language meaning of bisect, divide into two parts—usually equal parts. Mathematically, the term unambiguously means *divide into equal parts*.

⌨ Students could be encouraged to use drawing applications such as *Claris Draw*, *Color It*, and *Super-Paint* to experiment with and complete the design activities above, particularly Activities II and IV.

a more complete understanding of concepts, which better enable them to reason logically about geometric problems. Levels of geometric thinking have been described by two Dutch educators, Pierre van Hiele and Dina van Hiele-Geldof (see Hoffer, 1981, 1983; van Hiele, 1986).

Van Hiele Levels of Geometric Thinking. The first three of the five van Hiele levels summarized below are relevant to elementary-age children.

• **Level 0: visualization.** At this level, children use general appearances to *recognize* and to *name* geometric shapes. They do not focus on the properties of a geometric shape. "There is no why"; a rectangle is a rectangle because it "looks like one" (van Hiele, 1986, p. 83). If an example of a shape does not conform to their particular mental image of the shape, children assume it is a different shape. For example, if a child associates rectangles with an oblong shape, she will identify a ▭ , but not a ◻ , as a *rectangle*. Indeed, if a square is turned up onto a vertex (◻ → ◇), it is no longer a square but a diamond in a child's eyes.

• **Level 1: analysis.** At this level, children begin to *analyze* and to *describe* the properties or attributes of geometric shapes. An attribute is a characteristic of a particular example but not necessarily one that is shared by all examples of a concept. For example, children may describe rectangles as having four sides—two long sides and two short sides. Although *four sides* is characteristic of all rectangles, *two long sides and two short sides* is not (e.g., it incorrectly excludes squares from the family of rectangles). Put differently, their preliminary analysis does not allow children to see how different shapes are related. Moreover, it does not include seeing how the attributes of a shape are interrelated. For example, children may note that a rectangle has parallel opposite sides, equal opposite sides, and four right angles, not recognizing that if the opposite sides of a four-sided figure are parallel and if one interior angle is 90°, then all four angles must be right angles and that the opposite sides must be equal.

• **Level 2: informal deduction.** At this level, children consider *relationships*. They discover the *critical attributes of shapes (the characteristics shared by all examples of a concept)*, and this allows them to deduce whether or not two concepts or examples are related. For instance, once children recognize that the critical attributes of a rectangle are four sides, parallel and equal opposite sides, and four right angles, they may notice that a square has all of these attributes and, thus, must be a rectangle—albeit a special kind of rectangle. Or, they may compare the example of a ◇ to the critical attributes of a square (four equal and parallel sides and four right angles), recognize that it shares all of these critical attributes, and deduce that it must be an example of a square. At this level, children also begin to recognize how the critical attributes of a shape are interrelated. As they see how attributes are interrelated, children can begin to define a shape in terms of a minimal set of *critical attributes (the fewest characteristics needed to define it)*. For example, instead of defining a rectangle as a parallelogram with *four* right angles, it can be defined as a parallelogram with *a* right angle (because it logically follows that all the interior angles of such a figure would be right angles).

• **Level 3: formal deduction.** At this level, children can develop proofs using axioms and definitions.

• **Level 4: rigor.** At this level, children can use different premises to develop different geometries.

Key Points About the Van Hiele Model. This model suggests the following three points about the development of geometric thinking:

1. It is gradual and sequential, and instruction that is too far above a child's level of thinking will probably not make sense.

2. Each successive level involves developing an explicit understanding of what was explored implicitly and intuitively the level before (e.g., Level 1 thinkers focus explicitly on the properties of objects, which as Level 0 thinkers they may have considered nonconsciously).

3. The level of a child's geometric thinking depends on *experience* rather than age and can vary from concept to concept.

Common Difficulties

Traditionally, elementary instruction has included little geometry and almost no geometry of substance (e.g., Bruni & Seidenstein, 1990; Fuys &

Liebov, 1993). Because the skills approach focuses on memorizing the names of shapes and provides limited examples of concepts, it only reinforces Level 0 (appearance-based) thinking and impedes children's progress to higher Van Hiele levels.

14•2 TEACHING

Figure 14.2: Why Informal Geometry Is Important

Figure 14.2 underscores the point made earlier that highly abstract geometry instruction can leave children bewildered. This unit outlines general guidelines for meaningful instruction (Subunit 14•2•1). It also describes specific teaching suggestions regarding topology (Subunit 14•2•2), other aspects of spatial sense (Subunit 14•2•3), transformation geometry (Subunit 14•2•4), and two- and three-dimensional geometry (Subunit 14•2•5).

14•2•1 GENERAL GUIDELINES

Three general guidelines are outlined below.

↪ **Integrate geometry instruction with that of other mathematical domains and other subject areas.** This provides for purposeful and meaningful (well-connected) learning. See, for example, Investigation 14.1 (on page 14-2), which involves problem solving, and Investigation 14.2 (on page 14-5), which involves art and social studies. Activity File 14.1 on pages 14-8 and 14-9 illustrates an example of the investigative approach to geometry instruction. Note that this activity involves both other mathematical domains and other subject areas.

↪ **ELEMENTARY INSTRUCTION, PARTICULARLY PRIMARY-LEVEL INSTRUCTION, SHOULD FOCUS ON INFORMAL GEOMETRY.** The basic aim is to develop an intuitive spatial sense and informal geometric concepts. As Investigations 14.1 and 14.2 and Ac-

tivity File 14.1 illustrate, informal geometry can involve: (a) an engaging problem, puzzle, *or* challenge; (b) a *hands-on activity* that provides opportunities to experiment with objects or to explore space; (c) artistry and creativity; and (d) having fun (Van de Walle, 1994).

↪ **FOCUS ON THE DEVELOPMENT OF *GEO-METRIC THINKING* AS WELL AS CONTENT KNOWLEDGE.** A key aim of instruction should be helping children achieve the next van Hiele level of geometric thinking.

• **To prompt Level 1 thinking, encourage students to analyze a *variety* of examples *and* nonexamples of a shape and to induce its attributes.** Part I of Investigation 14.3 (page 14-10) illustrates how carefully chosen examples and nonexamples can help clarify a geometric concept that most adults do not fully understand. Part II (page 14-11) illustrates how an incomplete concept can arise if a full range of examples or nonexamples are not included.

• **To promote Level 2 thinking, help children focus on the *critical* attributes of concepts and informally deduce the minimal set necessary to define concepts.** Present a variety of examples of a concept and encourage them to explicitly consider whether an attribute can be found in all or only some of the examples. Prompt pupils to evaluate definitions—to consider if a minimal set of critical attributes is used. (Continued on page 14-9.)

🍎 Activity File 14.1: An Extended and Integrated Unit on Quilting[1]

◆ Geometric problem solving + tessellations + other mathematical content (e.g., inductive reasoning, combinations, and probability) + other subject areas (e.g., reading and social studies) ◆ 3-8 ◆ Whole class working in groups of four

✎ A unit on quilting can be a rich source of mathematical problems. This unit was designed to accompany the reading of *The Patchwork Quilt* by Valerie Flournoy (© 1985, Dial Books for Young Readers) and *The Keeping Quilt* by Patricia Polacco (© 1988, Simon & Schuster Books for Young Readers). For a discussion of how early American patchwork patterns may have gotten their names, see *Eight Hands Round: A Patchwork Alphabet* by Ann Whitford Paul (© 1991, Harper Collins).

Combinations. After solving some simpler combination problems, Mrs. Ryherd posed the following problem:

■ **Color Combinations.** Some time after making her first patchwork quilt with Grandma, Tanya decided to make a two-color quilt. She had red, blue, black, white, and pink fabric. How many two-color combinations could she make from the five colors available?

The children were encouraged to solve the problem intuitively. One group made the list below and counted the listed items to determine the solution.

red-blue   blue-black   black-white   white-pink
red-black   blue-white   black-pink
red-white   blue-pink
red-pink

While the group was sharing their solution, Mrs. Ryherd recognized that it could be viewed as the sum of an arithmetic series. Although she had not planned to discuss this topic, she seized on the opportunity. Mrs. Ryherd asked the class how the solution could be summarized as a number sentence. The class agreed on the following representation, which was recorded on the chalkboard:

$$4 + 3 + 2 + 1 = 10$$

Mrs. Ryherd then asked how many two-color combinations Tanya could make if she found a sixth color (yellow). After determining the answer intuitively by making a list, the class summarized the solution as a number sentence.

$$5 + 4 + 3 + 2 + 1 = 15$$

Mrs. Ryherd then asked how many two-color combinations could Tanya make if she had 50 different colors. After some eye rolling and discussion, the class agreed that this task could be solved by adding $49 + 48 + 47 + 46 \ldots + 3 + 2 + 1$. They also concluded that adding up all those numbers would be a lot of work. At this point, Mrs. Ryherd encouraged the class to look at the simpler examples to see if they could find any shortcuts for adding series of numbers.

Probability. The next day, Mrs. Ryherd posed the following problem:

■ **Difficult Choices.** Tanya could not decide what two colors to use for her quilt. She put one piece of each of the five fabrics in a bag. Then, without looking, she chose two pieces. What are the chances of her choosing a red-blue combination?

The class discussed how such a problem could be solved. One child suggested trying it. This led to a discussion of repeating the experiment many times. After gauging the empirical probability, Mrs. Ryherd encouraged the class to use the list of combinations made up the previous day to determine the theoretical probability. After defining theoretical probability as the number of desired outcomes over the total number of outcomes, the class could see from their chart that the probability of a red-blue combination was $\frac{1}{10}$.

Geometric Problem Solving. On the third day of the unit, Mrs. Ryherd posed the following problem:

■ **Patch Tetrominoes.** Tanya decided to make her quilt by repeating the same pattern of four square pieces. How many different patterns could Tanya make from four square pieces? Note that unlike Figure A (below), two pieces must be joined by sewing along a complete side of each (see Figure B).

Activity File 14.1 continued

Figure A ▢▢▢▢   Figure B ▢▢▢▢

Mrs. Ryherd had available colored tiles and graph paper to facilitate the children's explorations for this problem and the next.

Tessellation and Symmetry. The day after students shared and discussed their solutions to the *Patch Tetrominoes* problem above, Mrs. Ryherd had the class explore the following problem:

■ **Tessellating Tetrominoes.** Could Tanya use each tetromino pattern to make a quilt? For example, could she sew together many examples of the pattern below without leaving any space between them?

Note that to make this problem even more pur-

poseful, a teacher could have students make their own quilt or miniquilt. The ideas of tessellation (see page 14-18) and slide (translation) symmetry could be highlighted by sewing together four cloth pieces of the same color to make a pattern and then alternate colors when the patterns are sewn together as shown below:

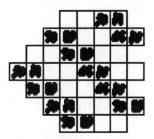

⌨ Note that a computer drawing application such as *Claris Draw*, *Color It*, or *SuperPaint* can facilitate experimenting with and designing quilt patterns.

• To foster Level 2 thinking, prompt students to discover relationships among geometric shapes (e.g., that a square is a special kind of rectangle). Investigation 14.4 (page 14-12) illustrates four different ways to help students explore the relationships among polygons, namely Venn diagrams, concept mapping, error analyses, and tree diagrams.

• To prompt Level 2 thinking, encourage conjecture-making and -testing, informal deductive reasoning, and informal proofs. For instance, in constructing a concept map or Venn diagram, encourage students to consider where a new concept such as *trapezoid* fits. Encourage groups to evaluate a new shape or their conjectures about it in light of the critical attributes of known concepts (see Box 14.1). In addition to informal deductive logic, informal proofs can consist of collecting examples consistent with a conjecture and informal disproofs can involve finding a counterexample (Geddes & Fortunato, 1993).

☞ Try Investigations 14.3 (pages 14-10 and 14-11) and 14.4 (page 14-12).

14•2•2 INFORMAL TOPOLOGY

In this subunit, we define *topology* and make a case for including the topic in the elementary curriculum. (Continued on page 14-13.)

Box 14.1: Does It Walk and Quack Like a Duck?

After presenting a number of examples and nonexamples of *trapezoids*, Ms. Socrates asked her students to define the new concept by indicating where it would go in their concept map. Arguing for her group, Roma suggested placing *trapezoid* under *parallelogram* because it had two parallel sides.

"Does it walk and quack like a duck?" asked Ms. Socrates. "How did we agree to define a parallelogram?"

"It's a four-sided figure with opposite sides parallel and equal," commented Lili.

"Does a trapezoid have these characteristics?" followed up Ms. Socrates.

"Only kind of," allowed Roma. "It's four-sided but both [sets of] sides are not parallel and equal."

"So it walks but doesn't quack like a duck," added Lili, now familiar with Ms. Socrates' standard refrain. "Our group put traps under quads." Asked why, Lili replied, "Like quadrilaterals, a trapezoid is a four-sided enclosed figure. If it walks and quacks like a duck, then it's a duck."

☼ Investigation 14.3: Using Examples and Nonexamples to Induce the Critical Attributes of Geometric Concepts

◆ Discovering definitions ◆ 5-8 ◆ Any number

Many students do not have an explicit understanding of *diagonals*. Part I illustrates how examples and nonexamples can help students construct an explicit definition of this concept. Part II illustrates a key point about using examples and nonexamples. After completing each part, discuss your conclusions with your group or class.

Part I: Diagonals

Consider the examples and nonexamples below and then answer the following questions.

A. $\overline{BD}$ is a diagonal.	B. $\overline{AC}$ is a diagonal.	C. $\overline{AD}$ is not a diagonal.
D. In the rectangle ABCD below, $\overline{AC}$ and $\overline{BD}$ are diagonals, but $\overline{AB}$, $\overline{BC}$, $\overline{CD}$, and $\overline{DA}$ are not.	E. In the pentagon ABCDE below, $\overline{BE}$ is a diagonal; $\overline{BC}$ and the zig-zag line from B to D are not.	F. In the hexagon ABCDEF below, $\overline{DB}$ and $\overline{DF}$ are diagonals; $\overline{DC}$ and $\overline{DE}$ are not.

1. Define a diagonal. _____
   _____

2. How many diagonals does triangle ABC in Figure A below have? Why?

3. Which of the following are diagonals for polygon ABCDEFGH (shown in Figure B below): $\overline{BD}$, $\overline{CG}$, $\overline{DE}$, $\overline{DF}$, $\overline{EG}$?

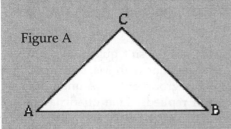

Figure A

Figure B

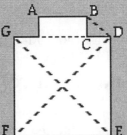

Investigation 14.3 continued

Part II: Trianquads†

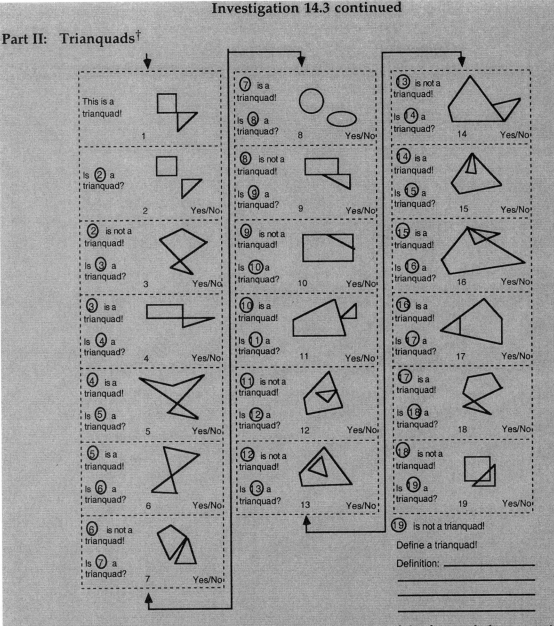

1. From the examples and nonexamples above, can you tell if the figures below are trianquads? Why or why not?

    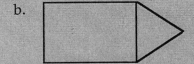   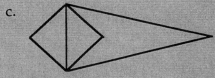

a.   b.   c.

2. What definition of trianquads would include the figures above? What would not?

3. How could a teacher amend the illustration above to clarify which definition of trianquads is accurate?

✿ Investigation 14.4: Explicitly Examining Relationships Among Figures

◆ Fostering Level 2 geometric thinking ◆ 5-8 ◆ Any number

To check and help clarify your understanding of the relationships among various polygons, try the following activities. Discuss your answers with your group or class.

Activity I: Using Venn Diagrams to Explore Relationships

Draw a Venn diagram that represents the relationships among polygons, quadrilaterals, parallelograms, rectangles, and squares.

Activity II: Using Concept Mapping to Explore Relationships

If you did not do Part III of Probe 3.4 (on pages 3-33 and 3-34 in chapter 3), draw a concept map that includes the following concepts: *parallelograms, polygons, quadrilaterals, rectangles, rhombuses, squares,* and *trapezoids*. Be sure to use clear and specific linking phrases.

Activity III: Using Error Analysis to Explore Relationships

1. Miss Brill asked her class to draw a Venn diagram illustrating the relationships among parallelograms (P), rectangles (Rec), rhombi (Rh), and squares (S). Evaluate the following efforts. If a child's drawing is incorrect, specify how it misrepresents a relationship.

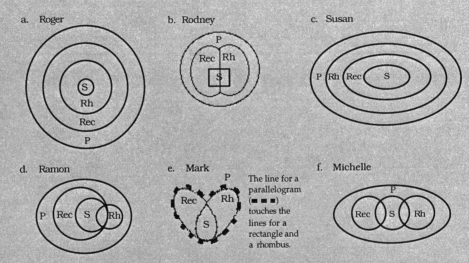

2. Miss Brill asked her class to draw a tree diagram to represent the relationships among quadrilaterals, trapezoids, parallelograms, rhombi (or rhombuses), rectangles, and squares. Evaluate the following efforts. If a child's diagram is incorrect, specify how it misrepresents a relationship.

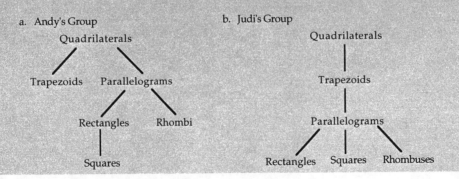

☞ Try Investigation 14.5 (pages 14-14 to 14-16).

Mathematics: Understanding Topology

Topology can be thought of as the geometry of *elastic motions*—as a *geometry without concern for straightness or length*. Topological transformations can change shape or size. Distortions (e.g., the image in a curved mirror) change the shape of a figure, and dilations (stretching and shrinking) change the size of a figure.

Definition. More specifically, *topology is the branch of geometry that studies what properties of a figure or surface remain the same when it is changed by bending, twisting, enlarging, or shrinking into another shape.* It can rightly be called the "mathematics of distortion."

Examples of Topological Aspects. Topology is concerned with spatial relationships—how objects and positions in space are related and what relationships remain the same as objects or space change. As Activities 1 and 2 of Investigation 14.5 (on page 14-14) illustrate, certain characteristics—betweenness (order along a path), closed or not closed, connectedness (all one piece or not), inside or outside relationships, and intersecting or not intersecting—do not change when a figure or surface is distorted. (Because length and straightness can be changed by distortions, topology can be thought of as the geometry without length or straightness.) As Activities 2 to 4 of Investigation 14.5 (on pages 14-14 and 14-15) illustrate, another characteristic that does not change with distortion is the number of holes through a figure.

Teaching

Some research indicates that topology is a good place to begin geometry instruction (Fuys & Liebov, 1993). There are two good reasons for introducing qualitative activities, such as those illustrated in Activities 1 to 4 of Investigation 14.5, before activities that involve quantifying size (measurement):

1. *Spatial sense.* An intuitive feel for spatial relationships is necessary for successfully engaging in many everyday activities and solving many mathematical problems. Throwing a ball accurately; drawing or painting a picture; reading a circuit diagram or a road map; and designing a dress, a landscape, an automobile, or a building layout all entail a sense of how objects and space are related even as they change because of motion (e.g., change in position or viewpoint). Many mathematical problems, such as the *Garden Plot Reconsidered* (Problem 3 in Investigation 14.1 on page 14-2), require visualizing spatial relationships.

2. *Recognition of different geometries.* Teaching topology as well as traditional Euclidean geometry can help children understand that figures can be analyzed from different perspectives and that each perspective has its own set of rules. Consider, for example, Activity 3 of Investigation 14.5. Working from the rules (premises) that a figure can be transformed but not cut or folded onto itself, children can discover that a doughnut and a coffee cup actually belong to the same group of things (things with a single hole through them). In time, they can recognize that by beginning with a different set of premises, they can build different geometries that provide other perspectives on objects and space.

14•2•3 OTHER ASPECTS OF SPATIAL SENSE

Activities that involve analyzing, constructing, and drawing activities (Subunit 14•2•1) and topology activities (Subunit 14•2•2) are all useful for fostering a spatial sense—an intuitive and largely qualitative understanding of space. In this subunit, we focus on how a spatial sense can be promoted by activities involving sighting and projecting, orienting and locating, and spatial reasoning. Transforming and measuring activities—also useful for this purpose—are discussed in the next subunit (Subunit 14•2•4) and next chapter (chapter 15), respectively.

☞ Try Investigation 14.6 (pages 14-17 & 14-18).

• **Projecting and sighting.** Shadow geometry (see Part I on page 14-17 of Investigation 14.6) is an example of *projecting (using rays of light to create an image)*. Whereas topology can be thought of as geometry without regard to straightness or length, shadow geometry is an example of geometry concerned with straightness but not length. For example, over the course of a day, the shadow of a flagpole will change length but not straightness. As Investigation 14.6 illustrates, students can compare shadow geometry with topology by systematically examining what properties do and do not change. The concept of straight lines is also (continued on page 14-19)

⚘ Investigation 14.5: Informal Topology

◆ Informal geometry ◆ K-8 ◆ Any number

Topology can be thought of as the geometry of elastic motions and explored informally and concretely with balloons, rubber sheets, and clay. This activity describes a sample of topological activities, activities that children and adults alike find engaging. Parts I and II explore the effects of distortion with balloons and clay, respectively. Part III—Investigations into one-sided strips called Mobius strips—can tease children's imaginations. Part IV provides hands-on experience with key principles of map making (cartography) and can be combined with social studies lessons. To see what is involved and to perhaps expand your own knowledge of geometry, try them yourself.

Part I: Balloon or Rubber Sheet Activities (◆ K-8)

What happens when we change the shape of a figure or surface by bending, twisting, enlarging, or shrinking it? Do all of its characteristics change or do some stay the same?

Activity 1. With a marker, draw a square and a triangle on a partially inflated balloon or a rubber sheet: Inflate the balloon or stretch the rubber sheet. Is the length of each line in the shapes preserved or not? Is straightness of the lines making up the shapes preserved or That is, can a straight line be made curved or crooked?

Activity 2. This investigation extends Activity 1 by examining additional properties. With a marker, draw a picture such as the one shown to the right on a partially inflated balloon or a rubber sheet. Inflate the balloon or stretch the rubber sheet and answer the questions a to g below. This may require deflating and inflating the balloon several times.

☞ **Teaching Tip.** Classroom teachers may choose to do this activity as a whole class or as a small group activity. Particularly for the latter, it may be less confusing to begin with simpler designs and analyze one or two aspects at a time. For example, to examine *betweenness* a group could draw A B C on a partially inflated balloon and then inflate it.

Which of the following characteristics change, and which do not?

a. area of a figure (e.g., the size of O or △)

b. betweenness (e.g., on line A B C, Point B is between A and C)

c. closed-open (e.g., ⬭ is a closed figure; ∠ is an open figure)

d. connectedness (e.g., ∠ is connected; is not connected)

e. inside-outside (e.g., the dot in ⦿ is inside the circle, the dot next to the ellipse •⬭ is outside it)

f. intersection (e.g., 0 has no common points, † or x has one common point, # has four common points)

g. shape

Part II: Clay Forms and Holes (◆ K-8)

Direct experimentation with clay can help students uncover yet another characteristic that does not change with distortions.

Activity 3. *Without tearing or folding a shape onto itself,* can a clay cube be molded into a ball? Into a doughnut? Can a clay ball be molded into a doughnut? Can a doughnut be molded into a coffee cup? Into a sugar bowl? Likewise, can a 0 can be molded into any other numbers? What about 1?

Investigation 14.5 continued

Activity 4. Consider the following series of transformations:

A.

cube	sphere	blob

B.

doughnut	craft project gone awry	coffee mug

C.

sugar bowl	melting sugar bowl	lump left by melted sugar bowl

1. For Transformation A above, what do the cube, sphere, and blob have in common?
2. For Transformation B above, what do the doughnut, craft project, and coffee mug have in common?
3. For Transformation C above, what do the sugar bowl, melting bowl, and lump have in common?

Activity 5. The items in Example A above have no holes that go through the shape. (In formal terms, a cube, sphere, or blob has a genus of 0.) The items in Example B above each have a single hole that goes through the shape. (In formal terms, a doughnut has a genus of 1.) The items in Example C above each have two holes that go through the shape. (In formal terms, a sugar bowl has a genus of 2.) Items with three or more holes have a genus of 3 or more. For each of the following items below, identify what examples have a genus of 0, what examples have a genus of 1, what examples have a genus of 2, and what items have a genus of 3 or more.

1. Clay numerals 0, 1, 2, 3, 4, 5, 6, 7, 8, 9.
2. Clay capital letters of the alphabet (A, B, C, D, E, F...).
3. The following everyday objects.

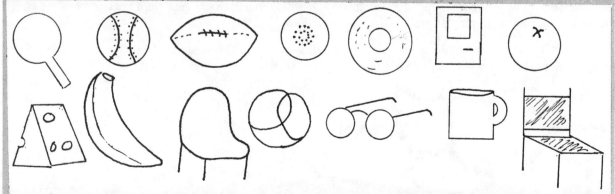

☞ **Teaching Tip.** Encourage students to find various other everyday examples of genus 0, 1, 2, and 3 or more. Encourage students to defend their classification.

Investigation 14.5 continued

Part III: Mobius Strip (◆ 2-8)

A ninth-century German mathematician named Augustus Ferdinand Möbius created a fascinating object now called a Mobius strip.

Activity 6. Making a Mobius strip is easy. (1) Cut a strip of (white) construction paper. (2) Give the strip a half twist, and (3) tape the two ends together to form a closed ring.

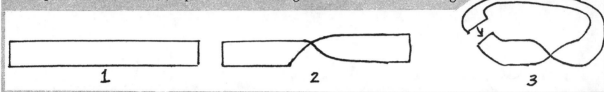

Activity 7. A Mobius strip has some strange and unexpected properties. Color each side of a regular strip with a different-color crayon. Now try to do the same with your Mobius strip. What happens? What does this imply about a Mobius strip?

Activity 8. Consider another property of a Mobius strip. Draw a line down the middle of such a strip and cut along the line. What would you predict would happen? What happens when you actually make the cut? Repeat the experiment by cutting a strip into thirds.

Halving   Cutting into thirds

Part IV: Map Coloring (◆ 4-8)

One practical application of topology is map making.

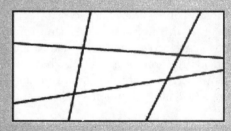

Activity 9. The map to the right is made entirely of straight lines that begin and end at an edge. What is the fewest colors needed to color the regions of the map such that no two adjacent areas (areas sharing a common line) have the same color? Try this experiment with other similar maps. What conclusion can you draw? Does it matter how many straight lines are used? To check, add a straight line that begins and ends with an edge to map above. Would this require additional colors?

Activity 10. In the map depicted in Figure A below, what is the fewest colors needed to shade in the states so that adjoining states have a different color?

Activity 11. Why is the answer to Activity 10 what it is? Consider a relatively simple case. How many colors are needed to shade in Figure B below so that adjoining regions have different colors?

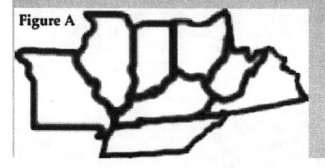

Figure A

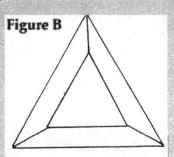

Figure B

☪ Investigation 14.6: Expanding Spatial Sense

Part I: Shadow Geometry[†] (◆ Informal projective geometry ◆ K-8 ◆ Any number)

Balloon or rubber-sheet geometry (see Part I of Investigation 14.5 on page 14-14) investigated situations where straightness and length did not remain constant when a figure or surface was changed. Shadow geometry encourages students to consider which properties remain the same and which change in a different situation. Use pipe cleaners, wire, or other flexible material that can hold a shape. (A telephone wire can be cut open to obtain the color-coded insulated strands inside. Waste wire can be obtained for free from telephone workers or companies. Be sure to leave the rubber insulation on the strands.)

Activity 1. (a) Take a straight object, such as an unbent pipe cleaner, a Cuisenaire rod, a long, or a ruler, and examine the shadows it makes. Can the length of the shadow be made larger or smaller? Can the straight object be positioned to cast a curved or crooked shadow on a surface that is flat? Which characteristic, if either, is preserved? (b) Take a curved object, such as a bent pipe cleaner or a roll of tape, and examine the shadows it makes. Can such an object be positioned to cast a straight shadow? Is the characteristic of curvedness preserved?

Activity 2. This investigation extends the analysis of Activity 1. Which of the following characteristics are shared by all shadows of an item and which are not? Compare your results with those you obtained with balloon geometry (Activity 2 on page 14-14 of Investigation 14.5).

a. area of a figure (e.g., the size of ○ or △)

b. betweenness (e.g., on line _A_•_ _B_•_ _C_•_, Point B is between A and C)

c. closed-open (e.g., ⬭ is a closed figure; ◺ is an open figure)

d. connectedness (e.g., ◺ is connected; ◿ is not connected)

e. inside-outside (e.g., the dot in ⊙ is inside the circle, the dot next to the ellipse •⬭ is outside it)

f. intersection (e.g., 0 has no common points, † or x has one common point, # has four common points)

g. shape

Activity 3. This investigation explores the property of intersection. (a) Make a circular wire and examine its various shadows. Summarize your results in table below and compare them to those of balloon geometry. (b) Bend the wire circle along a diameter so that the two halves of the circle are in perpendicular planes. Does this change any of the results above? What conclusions can you draw about intersections in shadow geometry?

Could an O look like the following:	Shadow geometry	Balloon geometry
⬭		
—		
∞		

[†]Based on material in chapter 9 (*Geometry* written by Edith Robinson) appearing in *Mathematics Learning in Early Childhood* (the 37th Yearbook edited by J. N. Payne and © 1975 by the NCTM).

Investigation 14.6 continued

Part II: Geometric Puzzles (◆ Fostering spatial sense and spatial reasoning ◆ Any number)

Geometric puzzles can be an entertaining way to foster a spatial sense and spatial reasoning.

Activity 1: Tangrams (◆ K-5). Using two or more pieces of a tangram, is it possible to make a triangle? A parallelogram? A rectangle? A trapezoid? A pentagon? A hexagon? How many different ways can you make a particular shape?

Activity 2: Joined Polygons. Problem 4 of Investigation 2.2 on page 2-13 of chapter 2 introduced tetrominoes. The problems below are extensions of *Tetrominoes*. Hexominals is quite challenging.

- ■ **Pentominoes** (◆ 1-5). How many possible shapes can be made by joining five squares so that each square has at least one whole side in common with another square?

- ◆ **Hexominals** (◆ 6-8). How many possible shapes can be made by joining six squares so that each square has at least one whole side in common with another square?

Activity 3: Tessellation. *Tessellation involves covering a surface with one or more shapes in a repeating pattern with no gaps* (see, e.g., Activity I of Investigation 14.2 on page 14-5).

- 🍎 **Tessellating Pattern Blocks** (◆ 1-4). What pattern block shapes can tessellate by themselves? Why? What shapes must be used in combination with other shapes? Why?

- ■ **Tessellating Pentominoes** (◆ 4-8). How many of the pentominoes can tessellate? Use graph or grid paper to illustrate your answer.

Part III: Geometric Problems[†] (◆ Spatial sense and spatial reasoning ◆ 1-8 ◆ Individually, small group, or whole class)

Reasoning about spatial relationships is crucial for many everyday situations. Try the following sample of spatial-reasoning tasks. For each, consider whether intuitive, inductive, and/or deductive reasoning is involved. Consider how the more difficult tasks could be simplified so that they are appropriate for primary-level students.

Task 1: Constructing a Block Building From Three Views (◆ 4-8). The top, front, and side view of a block building are shown below. Use blocks to construct this building. Compare and discuss your results with others in your group or class.

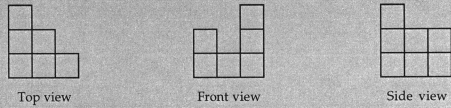

Top view   Front view   Side view

Task 2: Cube Houses (◆ K-4). How many different houses can you build with four blocks?

Task 3: Equal Areas? (◆ 7-8). In the figure to the right, is the area of A equal to the area of B? Why or why not?

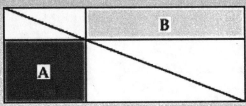

[†] Tasks 1, 2, and 3 are based on suggestions in "Geometry Instruction (Age 4-14) in the Netherlands—The Realistic Approach" by E. de Moor. In L. Streefland (Ed.), *Realistic Mathematics Education in Primary School* (pp. 119-138), © 1991 by the Freudenthal Institute, The Netherlands.

central to the everyday phenomenon of *sighting* (*lining up objects in a straight line*).

• **Orienting and locating.** *Orienting (defining your position relative to the surrounding space and finding your way from one point to another)* and *locating (defining the relative position of some other object in space)* are both key everyday competencies.

• **Spatial Reasoning.** Spatial reasoning can be cultivated by prediction tasks (e.g., predicting what shape will result from joining two squares), geometric puzzles (see, e.g., Part II of Investigation 14.6 on page 14-18), and geometric problems (see, e.g., Part III of Investigation 14.6).

14•2•4 TRANSFORMATION GEOMETRY

☞ Try Investigation 14.7 (pages 14-20 & 14-21).

Mathematics. Whereas topology can be considered the geometry of elastic motions, *transformation geometry can be viewed as the study of nonelastic or rigid motions.* Activity I of Investigation 14.7 (on page 14-20) should make clear that in this geometry, unlike balloon geometry (topology) or shadow geometry, both straightness and length are preserved as a (rigid) figure moves. The study of transformation geometry is also important because it can promote spatial visualization.

Teaching. Primary-level students can be introduced to the basic motions of slides, turns, and flips and combinations of these motions with activities involving body or object motions (e.g., see Activity II on page 14-20 of Investigation 14.7). These physical motions serve as concrete analogies for the mathematical concepts of translations, rotations, and reflections, respectively. Intermediate-level students can begin more formal explorations of these motions, including the properties of each (see, e.g., Activity III on pages 14-21 of Investigation 14.7). All three of these motions have the property of preserving size and shape. Other activities that can prompt intuitive or explicit exploration of the basic motions include tiling or tessellating activities such as Activity 3 on page 14-18 (slides); using metal mirrors, *Miras*, or *Reflectas* to make mirror images (flips); and detecting patterns in clothes, book covers, or wallpaper (slides, turns, and/or flips). With tessellations or other patterns, challenge older students to consider whether a repeating design or successive impressions are produced by slides, turns, or flips.

14•2•5 TWO- AND THREE-DIMENSIONAL GEOMETRY

Euclidean geometry can be thought of as the study of stationary figures with a rigid or fixed shape. It includes plane (two-dimensional) geometry and solid (three-dimensional) geometry. Plane geometry is important partly because most of our current media (e.g., books, chalkboards, computer displays, maps, movies, and television) are two dimensional; solid geometry, because we live in a three-dimensional world (Banchoff, 1990). Part III of Investigation 14.6 (page 14-18) illustrates several interesting problems that involves two- and three-dimensional objects. Part I of Investigation 14.8 (on pages 14-22 and 14-23) illustrates activities for informally exploring some special relationships of polygons. Part II (on page 14-24) illustrates activities for informally exploring the connection between plane and solid geometry; Part III (also on page 14-24), activities for informally exploring solids.

☞ Try Investigation 14.8 (pages 14-22 to 14-24).

PARTING THOUGHTS

"Geometry . . . provides a rich context for . . . the development of mathematical thinking" (Fuys & Liebov, 1993, p. 190). "Spatial understandings are necessary for interpreting, understanding, and appreciating our inherently geometric world" (NCTM, 1989, p. 48). To prepare children to live in this world, instruction "should initiate geometric *actions, drawing,* and *thinking*" (Schipper, 1983, p. 296, italics added). "Too often, the first time a student is encouraged to think about what [a geometric concept such as] volume means is the same day that he or she is given a formula . . . . To encourage fluency in the language of geometry, we need a good deal more 'pre-geometry' throughout the school experience, and that should include 'pre-solid' as well as 'pre-plane' geometry" (Banchoff, 1990, p. 14). Indeed, geometry instruction needs to encompass a variety of geometries and topics. "Just as Shakespeare is not sufficient for literature . . . so Euclid is not sufficient for geometry. [His geometry does] *not* include the geometry of maps, networks, or flexible forms, all of which are of central importance today" (Senechal, 1990, p. 140). (Continued on page 14-25.)

☙ Investigation 14.7: Exploring Transformation Geometry

◆ Spatial sense ◆ K-8 ◆ Individually, small groups, or whole class

Transformation geometry examines the motion of rigid figures. This investigation describes a sample of informal activities that explore this geometry—activities that students of all ages find intriguing. To see what is involved or perhaps extend your own knowledge of geometry, try the following activities yourself.

Activity I: Informal Explorations of Transformation Geometry

1. Cut out an 𝔽. What characteristics are preserved as you moved the cut-out F around? Fill in Chart A below and compare your results with those of balloon and shadow geometry.

2. Can the cut-out be moved to look like the examples listed in Chart B below? Fill in the chart and compare your results with those of balloon and shadow geometry.

Chart A	on a balloon	with a shadow	with a cutout		Chart B	on a balloon	with a shadow	with a cutout
a. area								
b. betweenness (e.g., A B C)								
c. openness								
d. connectedness								
e. intersections (two)								
f. length of each line segment								
g. shape								
h. straightness of line segments								

Activity II: Informal Explorations of Basic Motions

The following questions examine three basic types of motions.

1. How could you get the F from position A to position B with the least amount of movement?

2. How could you get the F from position A to position C with the least amount of movement?

3. (a) How could you get the F from position A to position D with the least amount of movement? (b) Could you move the F from position A to position D with the move you used in Question 1 or 2 or with a combination of those moves?

Investigation 14.7 continued

4. A (metal) mirror, Mira (a see-through plastic mirror), Reflecta, or other reflecting surface can be used to "transport" the letter **F** in Position A to what other position, Position B, C, or D?

🍎 With a Mira, a student can use a pencil to trace an image on a piece of paper. The paper should be placed behind the reflecting surface—on the side opposite the object.

Activity III: More Formal Explorations of Basic Motions

• **Slides** involve changing the position of a figure by sliding it along a straight line (e.g., in Question 1 of Activity II, the letter 𝔽 could be slid straight from Position A to Position B).

• **Turns** involve changing the position of a figure by rotating it (e.g., in Question 2 of Activity II, the letter 𝔽 could be turned from Position A to Position C).

• **Flips** involve changing the position of a figure by flipping it over (e.g., to get the letter 𝔽 from Position A to Position D in Activity II, it could be flipped over).

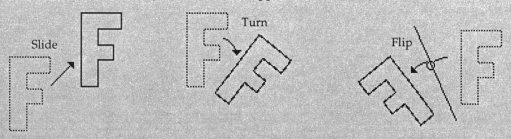

Slides, turns, and flips provide concrete analogies for the transformations of translations, rotations, and reflections, respectively.

1. From Point A in the letter **L** to the right, draw a straight line a given distance. Label the new end point A'. From Point B, draw a straight line that is parallel to the line you just drew from A to A' ($\overline{AA}'$) and the same length as $\overline{AA}'$. Label the new end point of this line B'. Do the same for Point C. Connect Points A, B', and C' with a straight line. (a) This process involves what kind of transformation—a translation (slide), rotation (turn), or reflection (flip)? (b) What are the properties of this transformation? That is, what characteristics (e.g., size [such as the length of line segments], shape [including the size of angles and parallelism], heading [direction in which the figure is pointing], orientation) did the move preserve, and what characteristics did it change?

2. From Point A in the Letter L below draw a straight line perpendicular to the line *l* (line of symmetry). Measure the length of this line. Now extend this line the same distance on other side of *l*. Label the end point of this line A'. Do the same for Points B and C labeling the new ends B', and C', respectively. Connect Points A', B' and C'. (a) This process involves what kind of transformation—a translation, a rotation, or a reflection? (b) What are the properties of this transformation? That is, what characteristics (e.g., size, shape, up-down orientation, left-right orientation) did the move preserve, and what characteristics did it change?

Questions for Reflection

1. Are a flip and a reflection really identical processes? Why or why not?

2. (a) How could reflection, rotation, and translation be used to define congruence? (b) How could these motions serve as analogies for line (flip), rotation (turn), and translation (slide) symmetry.

🍎 Investigation 14.8: Exploring Two- and Three-Dimensional Geometry

Part I: Exploring the Properties of Polygons
(◆ Informal 2-D geometry + measurement ◆ Whole class or small groups)

Triangles and other polygons have a number of interesting properties that students can discover. To see for yourself, try Activities 1 to 4, preferably with the help of your group. Discuss your findings with your group or class.

Activity 1: Experimenting with the Size of a Triangle's Sides (◆ 3-8). Using *Cuisenaire* rods, solve the problem below.

■ **A Triangular Fence.** After building a fence around his side yard Mr. Garett had three pieces of fence section left—one 3 feet long, one 4 feet long, and one 5 feet long. He decided to use the scrap fence section to build a triangular wall around an abandoned well in his backyard. (Figure A illustrates how this can be done using rods of 3, 4, and 5 units.) When Mr. Garett went to retrieve the fence sections, he discovered that his son Roger had sawed the 4-foot section in half to make a trap door for his tree house. (a) Could Mr. Garett make a triangular wall of fence sections 2, 3, and 5 feet long? What about sections 2, 3, and 4 feet long or 2, 3, and 3 feet long? (Use rods to model these situations. Note that after joining two rods at a corner, use the inside length of the rods to represent the length of the fence section, not the outside length of the rods.) (b) *Can the lengths of the sides of a triangle be any three numbers?* Try putting together rods of various lengths up to 14 or so. (Fourteen can be represented with two orange 10 cm rods and a purple 4 cm rod.) Fill in the table in the next column. What can you conclude about the sum of any two sides of a triangle?

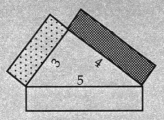

Figure A

Length of the Sides

Side 1	Side 2	Side 3	Triangle possible?

Activity 2: Sum of the Angles of a Triangle (◆ 3-8).
Cut out a paper triangle (e.g., cut a $8\frac{1}{2}$- x 11-inch piece of paper along a diagonal). Use a different-colored crayon to color in each angle. Cut the triangle into three parts so that each part contains one of the angles (i.e. don't cut through a vertice), and try fitting the three angles together. (Alternatively, fold the top angle down to meet the base and then fold the remaining angles inward so that the vertices of all three angles meet.)

1. (a) What do the three angles form? (b) The answer to the previous question involves an angle of how many degrees? (c) What does this activity imply about the three angles of your triangle? (d) Is your conclusion true for *all* types of triangles? Try this activity with triangles of different shapes to find out.

2. (a) Repeat the experiment above with quadrilaterals, pentagons, and hexagons. In each case, the angles sum to what? (b) Record your data for Question 1 and 2a in a table. Given the number of sides of a polygon, what rule predicts the sum of its angles? (c) Summarize the rule as an algebraic equation.

Activity 3: An Interesting Property of Right Triangles[2] (◆ 7-8).
Mr. Yant gave his class the following problem:

Investigation 14.8 continued

■ **A Tiling Problem.** An apprentice contractor was assigned the task of laying the floor tiles for three square-shaped rooms adjacent to a triangular foyer. The triangular foyer met a right and had two sides that were each 15 feet long (see Figure B below). (a) What was the area of each room? (b) If the contractor used white and black triangular tiles like those shown in Figure C below, how many triangular tile pieces of each color would he have to order for the job?

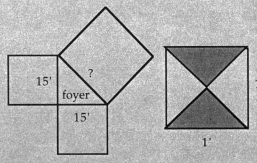

Figure B	**Figure C**

1. From the information given, Alf had no difficulty determining the area of the two smaller square rooms. However, not knowing the side of the larger square room, he could not compute its area. Without actually measuring the length of the room, how could he *informally* solve this problem?

2. Jackie suggested examining some simpler examples. Use the 1 cm square-diagonal grid below to determine the area of the largest square adjacent to each side of a right trian-

gle with shorter equal sides of (a) 1 cm, (b) 2 cm, (c) 3 cm, and (d) 4 cm. Summarize your results in the table at the bottom of the page.

3. Mr. Yant then asked his class to draw the following right triangles on graph paper: (a) shorter sides of 3- and 4-units and (b) shorter sides of 6- and 8-units. In each case, use cubes or a graph-paper drawing to determine the length of the larger side and the area of the squares adjacent to the sides of the triangle. Enter your results in the table below.

4. (a) Summarize verbally how the area of the largest square adjacent to a right triangle could be determined from knowing the two shorter sides of the right triangle. (b) Summarize this relationship as an algebraic equation (formula).

Activity 4: A Shortcut for Determining the Number of Diagonals (◆ 7-8).
(a) To devise a shortcut for determining the number of diagonals for a figure, compare the number of sides of a figure to the number of diagonals that can be drawn from the first vertex (angle A). What pattern do you detect? Now consider the total number of diagonals for the other vertices. What pattern do they form and what shortcut could be applied to summarize the number of diagonals? (b) Another way to approach the problem is to construct a table and look for a pattern.

number of sides	4	5	6	7				12
total number of diagonals		5						

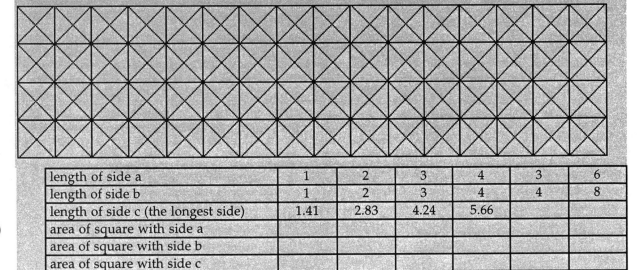

length of side a	1	2	3	4	3	6
length of side b	1	2	3	4	4	8
length of side c (the longest side)	1.41	2.83	4.24	5.66		
area of square with side a						
area of square with side b						
area of square with side c						

Investigation 14.8 continued

Part II: Exploring Connections Between Two- and Three-Dimensional Shapes (◆ Euclidean geometry + spatial reasoning ◆ 5-8 ◆ Any number)

To stretch your spatial reasoning, try the following activities. Discuss your conclusions with your group or class.

Activity 5: Flatland. Pretend you are an inhabitant of a two-dimensional space called *Flatland*. One day a fleet of alien space ships lands on Flatland. One spaceship is in the form of a right cylinder; another, a cube; and the last, a right triangular prism. What would these space ships look like on the two-dimensional Flatland? What would a Flatlander see as the cube-shaped space ship landed?

Activity 6: Cutting Clay. *What two-dimensional shape results when a plane cuts through a solid?* Using an oil-based modeling clay (which will not dry out), make various solid shapes such as those below. Predict the shape of the slice face before you cut the solid with a "piano wire" (see Figure D below).

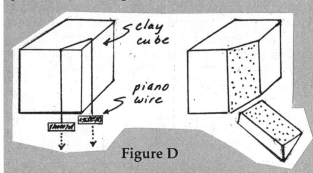

Figure D

Activity 7: Imaginary Solids. An excellent visualization activity is considering what three-dimensional shape results from sliding or turning a two-dimensional shape.

1. Consider a triangle such as Figure E below. (a) What solid is formed by sliding it across a flat surface along side $\overline{BC}$? (b) What is formed by turning it 360° about line segment $\overline{AB}$. (c) To reverse the process, consider what instructions would have to be followed to create Figure E from a cone.

2. (a) What solid is formed by sliding the rectangle illustrated in Figure F? (b) What solid is formed by rotating it around side $\overline{AB}$? (c) What is formed by rotating it around side $\overline{BC}$? (d) What is formed by rotating it around a vertical line of symmetry?

3. (a) What solid is formed by sliding the circle illustrating in Figure G straight up? (b) What is formed by sliding it up at an angle? (c) What solid is formed by turning the circle about point q? (d) What is formed by rotating it about the line of symmetry xy?

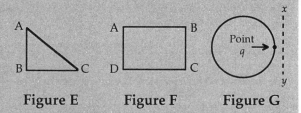

Figure E   **Figure F**   **Figure G**

Part III: Regular Polyhedra (◆ Informally exploring regular solids ◆ 5-8 ◆ Class working in small groups of four)

Regular polyhedra are three-dimensional shapes whose sides (faces) are constructed entirely from congruent regular polygons.

Activity 8: Using Equilateral Triangles, Using Squares, and Regular Pentagon. (a) Cut out congruent equilateral triangles from oaktag or other stiff paper. Can you tape them together to form a regular polyhedron? If so, how many different regular polyhedra can you construct from congruent equilateral triangles? If not, why not? (b) Cut out congruent squares from oaktag or other stiff paper. Can you tape them together to form a regular polyhedron? If so, how many different regular polyhedra can you construct from squares? If not, why not? (c) Cut out congruent regular pentagons from oaktag or other stiff paper. Can you tape them together to form a regular polyhedron? If so, how many different regular polyhedra can you construct from pentagons? If not, why not?

Activity 9: Using Larger Regular Polygons. Cut out congruent regular hexagons, heptagons, and octagons from oaktag or other stiff paper. Can you tape each type together to form a regular polyhedron? If so, how many different regular polyhedra can you construct from each? If not, why not?

RESOURCES

SOME INSTRUCTIONAL RESOURCES

Informal Geometry

☞ The following five resources describe a variety of informal geometry activities: **Cooperative Informal Geometry** written by Wade H. Sherard III and published by Dale Seymour; **Geometry and Visualization** developed by the Mathematics Resource Project, © 1978 by Creative Publications; **Geometry for grades K-6, Readings from the Arithmetic Teacher** edited by J. M. Hill, © 1987 by NCTM; **Ideas from Arithmetic Teacher, grades 4-6, intermediate school** compiled by F. Fennell & D. Williams, © 1986 by NCTM; and **Informal Geometry Explorations** by Margaret J. Kenney, Stanley J. Bezuszka, and Joan D. Martin and published by Dale Seymour.

☞ **It's a Tangram World** (2nd ed.) by Lee Jenkins and Peggy McLean, © 1980 by Activity Resources Co. and **Tangram Treasury (Books A, B, and C)** by J. Fair, © 1987 by Cuisenaire Company of America. In addition to illustrating some animal designs that can be created from tangrams, *It's a Tangram World* shows how tangrams can be used to model fractions, make fraction comparisons concretely, and model fraction arithmetic. It also illustrates how they can be used to model continents and compare their relative size.

☞ **Introduction to Tessellations** by Dale Seymour and Jill Britton and **Teaching Tessellating Art** by Jill and Walter Britton; both published by Dale Seymour. *Introduction to Tessellations* (for grades 6 to 8), explores, for instance, Escher-type tessellations, Islamic art designs, and tessellating letters. *Teaching Tessellating Art* (for grades K-8), includes an explanation of how computers can be used to create tessellations.

Geometry and Spatial Sense

☞ In addition to the **Marilyn Burns geometry replacement units for grades 2 and 3** and the **February 1990 issue** of the **Arithmetic Teacher**, which is devoted to instructional ideas for developing a spatial sense, teachers should find the following references valuable:

☞ **Geometry and Spatial Sense** (Curriculum and Evaluation Standards for School Mathematics: Addenda Series, Grades K-6) by John Del Grande and Lorna Morrow, © 1993 by NCTM. This rich resource describes geometry activities for each grade K-6.

☞ **Geometry in the Middle Grades** (Curriculum Standards Addenda Series, Grades 5-8) by Dorothy Geddes and others, © 1992 by NCTM. The introduction of this valuable resource includes a rationale for teaching geometry, several examples of how the NCTM (1989) *Curriculum Standards* can be implemented, a summary the van Hiele model, and sample activities.

☞ **Learning and Teaching Geometry, K-12 (1987 Yearbook)** edited by M. M. Lindquist and A. Shulte, © 1987 by NCTM. This resource includes numerous ideas for teaching geometry and spatial sense. For example, in *Geometry: An Avenue for Teaching Problem-Solving in Grades K-9* (pp. 59-68), L. J. DeGuire suggests that one way to introduce geometry and problem solving is to encourage children to copy, find, and create patterns.

☞ **Visual Mathematics** © 1991 by the Mathematics Learning Center. *Visual Mathematics* is a course guide for teaching mathematics in an integrated, problem-oriented fashion. It is based on the philosophy that a teacher should serve as a facilitator of learning and that students should be actively involved in constructing knowledge. Together with the *Mind and the Mind's Eye* teaching materials, the two-volume course guide provides a complete one- or two-year curriculum.

A SAMPLE OF CHILDREN'S LITERATURE

☞ The following article describes a number of children's books on geometry: **Selected Books for Geometry** by D. Thiessen and M. Mathias, *Arithmetic Teacher*, 1989, volume 36, number 6. As a basis for *informal geometry*, consider such children's books as **Sam Loyd's Book of Tangram Puzzles** by Peter Van Note (© 1968, Dover), **The Shape of Me and Other Stuff** by Dr. Seuss (© 1973, Random House), **The Shapes Game** by Paul Rogers (© 1989, Holt), **Tangrams, 330 Puzzles** by Ronald C. Read (© 1965, Dover), **Topsy-Turvies:**

Pictures to Stretch the Imagination by Anno Mitsumasa (© 1970, Walker), and **The Upside Down Riddle Book** by Louis Phillips (© 1982, Lethrop, Lee, and Shepard). Some books on *paperfolding* include **The ABC's of Origami: Paper-folding for Children** by Claude Sarasas (© 1964, Charles E. Tuttle), **Exploring Triangles: Paper-folding Geometry** by Jo Phillips (© 1972, Thomas Y. Crowell), and **Sadako and the Thousand Paper Cranes** by Eleanor Coerr (© 1977, Putnam). Books that relate geometry to *real-world applications* include: **Architecture: A Book of Projects for Young Adults** by Forrest Wilson (© 1968, Reinhold), **Environmental Geometry** by The Nuffield Mathematics Project (© 1969, The Nuffield Foundation), **Round Buildings, Square Buildings, and Buildings that Wiggle like a Fish** by Philip M. Isaacson (© 1988, Knopf), **Shadowland** by Anno Mitsumasa (© 1988, Orchard), and **The Village of Round and Square Houses** by Ann Grifalconi (© 1986, Little Brown). Children's books on *topology* include **Maps, Tracks and the Bridges of Königsberg: A Book about Networks** by Michael Holt (© 1975, Thomas Y. Crowell), **Over, Under and Through, and Other Spatial Concepts** by Tana Hoban (© 1972, Macmillan), and **Rubberbands, Baseballs and Doughnuts: A Book about Topology** by Robert Froman (© 1972 by Thomas Y. Crowell). Books pertaining to *shadow geometry* include **Shadows and Reflections** by Tana Hoban (© 1990, Greenwillow) and **Shadows, Here, There and Everywhere** by Ron and Nancy Goor (© 1981, Thomas Y. Crowell). Children's books on *transformation geometry* include **'M' is for Mirror** by Duncan Birmingham (© 1988, Tarquin Publications) and **Reflections** by Ann Jonas (© 1983, Greenwillow). There are numerous children's books on *two- and three-dimensional geometry*, including: **Animal Shapes** by Brian Wildsmith (© 1980, Oxford), **The Boy with Square Eyes** by Juliet and Charles Snape (© 1987, Simon and Schuster), and **Shapes, Shapes, Shapes** by Tana Hoban (© 1970, Greenwillow). Two additional books on shapes are:

🕮 **The Greedy Triangle** by Marilyn Burns, © 1994 by Marilyn Burns Education Associates, and published by Scholastic. This *Marilyn Burns Brainy Day Book* illustrates everyday examples of triangles. When a triangle becomes bored, it repeatedly asks for one more side and angle and becomes, in turn, a quadrilateral, a pentagon, and so on. After a getting a good many sides and angles the "greedy triangle" rolled down a hill. (Children may notice that the more sides and angles a polygon has, the more it resembles a circle.)

🕮 **Shape** and **Size,** by the Nuffield Mathematics Project, © 1967 by the Nuffield Foundation and published in the U.S. by John Wiley & Sons, Inc. These books are a rich source of instructional ideas and are lavishly illustrated with examples of children's work.

🕮 The following fantasies introduce the idea of other dimensions: **...and He Built a Crooked House** by Robert Heinlein in *Fantasia Mathematica* edited by Clifton Fadiman (editor) (© 1958, Simon & Schuster), **A Wrinkle in Time** by Madeleine L'Engle, (© 1962, Farrer, Straus, and Giroux), and **Flatland** by Edwin Abbott (© 1884, Seeley & Co., London, England, and reprinted in 1952 by Dover).

TIPS ON USING TECHNOLOGY

Computers

The world wide web has the following geometry-related websites that may be of interest to students: "The Geometry Center" (www.geom.umn.edu), "The Geometry Forum" (forum.swarthmorme.edu), "Fractal Lesson for Elementary and Middle School Students" (http://cml.rice.edu/~lanius/ frac/), and "Origami" (http://www.fascinating-folds.com/). A sample of geometry-related software is described below.

💾 **Factory** and **Super Factory** © 1986 by Wings for Learning/Sunburst Communications. This program displays square objects that are transformed in several ways (e.g., punched and rotated). Students must try to make a duplicate by visualizing the sequence of transformations. *Factory* is available on disks formatted for Apple, IBM, or Macintosh computers. A Windows version is also available. *Super Factory* is available on disk formatted for Apple and IBM computers.

💾 **Geometric Supposer Series** designed by Education Development Center, Judah Schwartz, and Michal Yerushalmy, © 1985, distributed by Sunburst. This computer tool allows students to create, explore, or measure two-dimensional shapes. The *Triangles* and *Quadrilaterals* versions are available on disks formatted for Apple, IBM, or Macintosh computers; the *Circles*, and *preSupposer*, on disk formatted for Apple and IBM computers. Students can choose to draw shapes free hand or ask the computer to generate a shape such as an isosceles triangle. They can then choose from a menu additional constructions (e.g., bisect an angle, circumscribe or inscribe a circle, draw parallel or perpendicular lines, extend or partition a line segment, or join points) or measurements (angles, areas, or lengths). This *Geometric Supposers* can be very useful in prompting students to make and to test conjectures and to discover and to explore relationships. With the *Quadrilaterials* version, for example, students can readily test the conjecture that increasing the perimeter of a rectangle always increases its area.

Geometer's Sketchpad © 1992 by Key Curriculum Press. This program accomplishes the same thing as the *Supposers* program but is even more powerful. It can save drawings and examine slide (translation), turn (rotation), flip (reflection), and dilation transformations or combinations of these transformations. The program (or a TI92) can be used to discover generalizations such as the sum of the interior angles of a polygon. Working in groups of two or three, each group can construct a triangle. The program will display the number of degrees for each angle and the sum of the angles. By comparing their results with those others who drew different triangles, students should readily recognize that sum of the angles for any triangle is 180°. Analogous discoveries can be made for four-, five-, and six-sided polygons.

The Geometric Golfer developed by MECC and distributed by Dale Seymour. This Macintosh Plus program enables students to explore the basic motions of transformation geometry plus dilation. Suitable for grades 7 and 8.

Logo-Based Geometry Curriculums: K-6 by D. H. Clements and M. T. Battista, ©1991 by Silver Burdett & Ginn. This Logo-enhanced curriculum has as its aims the development of: (a) geometric concepts and skills; (b) geometric problem-solving abilities including problem-solving heuristics (e.g., looking for patterns); and (c) related processes such as spatial visualization, estimation, and conjecturing.

The *Geometric Shapes: Special Paths* strand introduces angles and polygons such as triangles and rectangles as special paths. *Motions* introduces geometric transformations (translations, rotations, and reflections) and provides practice for such spatial skills as mentally rotating shapes.

The *Geotools* strand enables users to label points with letters and to measure angles or line segments indicated by these letters. This can help students make the transition to more formal (Euclidean) geometry (Clements, 1990). In Logo, children must give *relative directions*—directions from the perspective of the turtle, on the screen (in the plane). For example, if the turtle is facing down (∇) and they want it to head to the right side of the screen, children would have to enter the command LEFT 90 (turn left 90°), not RIGHT 90. Such activities help children see that there are times when you must take the perspective of others rather than always view things from one's vantage (e.g., when giving map directions). Although psychologically an important lesson, school-taught plane geometry typically assumes a standard perspective—the perspective of someone standing outside the plane. By labeling points, Geotools can help children discuss their Logo constructed shapes, which were designed from a relative perspective, in terms of the standard geometry perspective (Battista & Clements, 1988).

A basic difference between traditional and Logo geometry instruction is that with the former, children learn "about mathematics"; with the latter, they learn "to be mathematicians" (Taylor, 1980). Put differently, Logo can promote children's geometric thinking as well as factual learning (Battista & Clements, 1988). For instance, in contrast to traditional instruction that focuses on identifying rectangles (a Level 0 or visualization-level activity in the van Hiele hierarchy), Logo students must construct a program (sequence of commands) to draw the rectangle. "They must analyze the visual characteristics of the rectangle and establish relationships among its component parts. For example, students who think of a rectangle as 'a figure with two long sides and two short

Box 14.2: Analytic Thinking Promoted by Logo[†]

A. Discovery of common features among different examples of a rectangle: What do these programs have in common? How do they differ?

```
TO RECTANGLE.1
FORWARD 30
RIGHT 90
FORWARD 50
RIGHT 90
FORWARD 30
RIGHT 90
FORWARD 50
RIGHT 90
END
```

```
TO RECTANGLE.2
FORWARD 40
RIGHT 90
FORWARD 20
RIGHT 90
FORWARD 40
RIGHT 90
FORWARD 20
RIGHT 90
END
```

B. Construction of a general program for rectangles: Summarize the common features of rectangles by devising a general program. (The example below was drawn using: GENERAL.RECTANGLE 20 45)

```
TO GENERAL.RECTANGLE
:SIDE 1 :SIDE 2
FORWARD :SIDE 1
RIGHT 90
FORWARD :SIDE 2
RIGHT 90
FORWARD :SIDE 1
RIGHT 90
FORWARD :SIDE 2
RIGHT 90
END
```

C. Discovery that a square is a special kind of rectangle: What does the program below have in common with that for a rectangle. How is it different?

```
TO SQUARE
FORWARD 20
RIGHT 90
FORWARD 20
RIGHT 90
FORWARD 20
RIGHT 90
FORWARD 20
RIGHT 90
END
```

_____

[†] Based, in part, on "A Case For Logo-Based Elementary School Geometry Curriculum" by B. T. Battista and D. H. Clements. *Arithmetic Teacher, Vol. 38*, No. 3 (November 1988), pp. 11-17.

sides' must be more precise and complete to write a Logo procedure for a rectangle; they must explicitly address the properties of rectangles, such as opposite sides being equal in length and adjacent sides being perpendicular" (Battista & Clements, 1988, p. 14). See Frames A and B in Box 14.2 on the next page. Devising a procedure for controlling the turtle requires children to consider explicitly their intuitive expectations and, thus make them more accessible to reflection and revision (Papert, 1980a). In brief, it can help propel children toward Level 1 (the analysis level) and Level 2 (the informal-deduction level) in the van Hiele hierarchy.

Moreover, comparing the programs of different shapes can further reinforce the idea that definitions, not appearance, are the basis for categorizing shapes. Moreover, this can lead children to discover relationships among shapes and the hierarchial classification of polygons—that is, promote Level 2 (informal inductive) thinking. For example, in comparing the program for a square (see Frame C in Box 14.2) with that of a rectangle (Frame B in Box 14.2), children may discover that a

square is simply a rectangle in which all the sides are the same.

Like using concrete manipulatives, however, using Logo does not guarantee learning. Simply exposing children to a Logo environment may distract children from mathematical ideas and may not increase mathematical achievement (Clements & Battista, 1989). But with reflection prompted by teacher guidance and peer interaction, Logo can help children construct geometric concepts, while providing them experience with independent problem solving (Clements & Battista, 1989).

Additional Logo references include **Discovering Apple Logo: An Invitation to the Arts and Pattern of Nature** (by David D. Thornburg) and **Teaching with Logo: Building Blocks for Learning** (by Molly and Daniel Watt) both published by Addison-Wesley.

TesselMania! developed by MECC and distributed by Dale Seymour. Available on CD (Macintosh and Windows compatible) and suitable for grades 3-8[+].

15 SIZING UP THINGS: MEASUREMENT AND MEASUREMENT FORMULAS

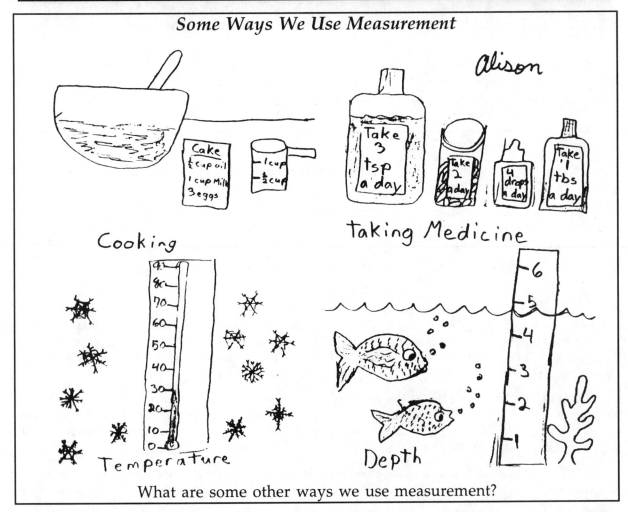

Some Ways We Use Measurement

What are some other ways we use measurement?

A bulletin board like the one above can help children see how measurement is relevant to their everyday lives. They can be encouraged to add their own examples. Moreover, children can be prompted to analyze the examples and indicate what attribute (e.g., length, area, volume, speed, time, pressure) is being measured for each. Intermediate-level children might be urged to identify *derived measures*—measures that express a relationship between two quantities (e.g., speed expresses a relationship between distance and time).

This activity can easily be integrated with a social studies lesson on occupations. Have different teams of children choose an occupation and construct a display of how it uses measurement (e.g., doctors measure a patient's height, weight, temperature, blood pressure, levels of cholesterol, white-cell counts, heart rate, level of depression, and so forth). Alternatively, the examples could be assembled into a book as part of a "Measurement on the Job" series and shared with other pupils in the class or school, with parents, or others.

THIS CHAPTER

☞ Consider Probe 15.1 (pages 15-2 and 15-3).

Measurement involves gauging the size of a quantity. As Part I of (continued on page 15-4)

➤ Probe 15.1: Measurement Connections

Measurement is integral to numerous aspects of everyday life, mathematics, and other curriculum areas. The aim of this probe is to prompt reflection on its many practical applications and its value in fostering mathematical processes such as problem solving and learning mathematical content such as fractions. Answer the following questions with your group. Then discuss your conclusions with your class.

Part I: Connections with Everyday Life. Take a moment to list ways you have used measurement in the last 24 hours.

Part II: Connections with Other Curriculum Areas. Science projects, such as those described in Activity File 15.1 below, can serve as a basis for the investigative approach to measurement instruction. To get a better sense of what is involved with these projects, carry them out yourself. Then answer the questions that follow. Re-examine these questions after reading the chapter.

🍎 Activity File 15.1: Plant-Growth Experiments[1]

◆ Measurement of length with either nonstandard or standard units +
data collection + graphing ◆ 1-8 ◆ Class working in small groups

To introduce a unit on Life Sciences, Mrs. Sayre asked her class what things were necessary for a plant to grow. Sascha suggested sunlight, Melanie proposed water; Jennifer offered warmth; Laura, posed soil; and Stacy added air. Mrs. Sayre recorded the hypotheses on the chalkboard:

sunlight–no sunlight   water–no water   warmth–cool   soil–no soil   air–no air

The teacher then proposed doing a controlled experiment with lima bean seeds. The class discussed the reason for a controlled experiment and how to set one up to test their hypotheses. Mrs. Sayre proposed that each of the six groups conduct their own experiment and then combine their data. She further proposed that each group use a number of seeds for each condition. After Lisa suggested four per condition, Mrs. Sayre asked the class to determine how many seeds each group would need. The following week the groups noted how many of their plants grew and by how much.

☞ **Teaching Tips.** Note that the complexity of this science experiment can be tailored to the developmental level of students. Young children could, for example, examine a few factors and do so one at a time. Young children could use nonstandard units of length. Ask the class to brainstorm about what might serve as an appropriate unit.

🖳 Children can be encouraged to use a computer to record and graph their data and to write up and print out their report.

✦ **Extensions.** Some of the numerous ways this activity could be extended are listed below.

• Replicate the experiment above with different kinds of seeds (e.g., radish, corn, pumpkin, and bean seeds). Do different plants have different growing requirements?

• Try germinating and growing plants with different amounts of water. Is there an optimal amount of water for a particular type of plant? Do different plants require different amounts of water? Is it possible to overwater a plant?

• Try watering seeds and plants with different liquids (e.g., rain water, tap water, distilled water, sugar water, orange juice). Does it make a difference for a particular type of plant? Does the effect vary for different types of plants?

• Try germinating seeds and growing plants under different air and soil temperatures. Which is more critical for germination and growth, soil temperature or air temperature? Is there an optimal soil or air temperature for a particular kind of seed?

• Try germinating seeds and growing plants under different soil conditions (e.g., potting soil, regular soil, sand, clay). Which type of soil is optimal for germination and growth?

Probe 15.1 continued

Activity File 15.1 continued

• Try germinating seeds and growing plants with soils differing in pH (e.g., *Miracid*, which can be obtained at gardening stores, and baking soda can be added to soil to lower and raise its pH, respectively). Is there an optimal pH range for a particular type of plant?

• Try germinating seeds at different soil depths. Is there an optimal range for a particular plant? Does this range vary from plant to plant?

1. (a) How could you set up a controlled experiment to test all of the factors Mrs. Sayre listed above? (b) Why is a controlled experiment necessary in determining which factors are critical to germination or to growth?

2. (a) For what pedagogical reasons did Mrs. Sayre have each group conduct their own experiment? (b) What is the statistical advantage of doing so? (c) Consider what statistical concepts and arithmetic skills might be involved in combining the groups' data.

3. (a) To combine and average data, would it be easier to use inches or centimeters as the unit of length? (b) Why?

4. (a) For Mrs. Sayre's class to test all five factors mentioned above in a controlled experiment would require a total of how many different conditions (e.g., sunlight with water, warmth, soil, and air; no sunlight with water, warmth, soil and air; . . .)? (b) If a group used four seeds per condition, how many seeds would each group need? If there are six groups, how many seeds would Mrs. Sayre need?

Part III: Connections with Other Mathematical Areas. Read the following example of the investigative approach (Activity File 15.2) and answer the questions that follow.

Activity File 15.2: Follow the Yellow-Brick Road[2]

◆ Various measurement concept and skills + problem solving + arithmetic skills ◆ 1-5
◆ Whole class working in small groups

Mrs. Plant announced to her class, "The theme for this year's reading-incentive program is 'Follow the Yellow-Brick Road.' If the students in each of the 13 classes reach their 6-month reading goal, they may choose which Wizard of Oz character Mr. Chow, the school principal, will appear as at the year-end assembly. After each class completes its reading requirement for the month, it will earn one paper brick to complete the Yellow-Brick Road. The path of the Road should lead from the entrance of the school to the principal's office. The paper bricks will be taped along the ceiling edge of the path so that everyone can keep track of the school's progress."

■ **The Yellow-Brick Road Problem.** If there are 13 classes and each class can earn one paper brick a month over a 6-month period, what is the maximum number of paper bricks we need? How big must we make each paper brick so that this number of bricks will reach from the front door to the principal's office?

1. (a) What heuristics might be helpful in solving the problem above? (b) Solving this problem might entail what other mathematical processes?

2. (a) Solving the problem above would involve using and practicing what arithmetic skills? (b) How does the activity above purposefully involve statistics? (c) What other areas of mathematics does the activity touch on?

3. (a) What measurement issues are raised by the need to measure the distance from the front entrance to the principal's office? (b) Mrs. Plant noted that they would have to measure around corners and asked how they could do that. How could this be done? (c) After the class suggested various measurement instruments, Mrs. Plant asked whether using a yard stick or a meter stick would be more accurate and which would be easier to use. How would you answer these questions?

Probe 15.1 (page 15-2) should demonstrate, instruction on this topic is important because of its innumerable practical applications. From the moment we get up in the morning until we go to sleep at night, we use numerous measurements. The alarm clock at our bedside keeps time. We chose clothing according to size. Some may take medicine or diet supplements (e.g., vitamins) in prescribed amounts. Weight-conscious people may eat a prescribed amount of food so as not to exceed a particular calorie level (a measure of energy). Health-conscious people may check food for fat or cholesterol contents. Drivers periodically check their gas gauge, speedometer, odometer, and various other instruments. Some students evaluate assignments in terms of size (e.g., "Well my assignment is a real killer, I have 100 pages to read") and their educational progress (perhaps too narrowly) in terms of grades. The list could go on and on. In brief, measurement instruction can help students see that mathematics is useful in everyday life (NCTM, 1989). Moreover, as Part II of Probe 15.1 (pages 15-2 and 15-3) illustrates, it is intimately connected to other subject areas such as science, health, and consumer education.

Measurement instruction can also be a powerful tool for helping children learn a wide variety of mathematical skills and concepts (NCTM, 1989). As both Parts II and III of Probe 15.1 (pages 15-2 and 15-3) show, measurement problems provide invaluable opportunities to learn or practice processes of mathematical inquiry and mathematical content in a purposeful manner. Many of the problems in chapter 2 used to hone problem solving skills involved measurement. In chapter 4, we examined counting. Enumerating collections is actually a form of measurement because it involves determining the size of a quantity. In the case of counting, we are measuring a discrete quantity. In this chapter, we focus on the measurement of continuous quantities. Although we have waited until now to discuss measurement, it is a natural context to create a need for fractions (chapters 9 and 10) and decimals (chapter 11) and, thus, introduce these topics (NCTM, 1989). As we will see in this chapter, geometry (introduced in chapter 14) involves such measurement concepts as length and width, perimeter, area, volume, and angles.

In the traditional skills approach, instruction focuses on memorizing measurement procedures and formulas. Unfortunately, "premature use of instruments or formulas leaves children without the understanding necessary for solving measurement problems" (NCTM, 1989, p. 51). Moreover, a focus on memorizing facts (e.g., metric equivalents such as 1 meter = 39.37 inches), procedures (e.g., metric conversion methods), and formulas (e.g., area formulas) turns off many students. In this chapter, we first discuss how to help children construct a basic understanding of measurement (Unit 15•1). We then address the issue of how to help children learn measurement formulas in a way that can make sense to them (Unit 15•2).

WHAT THE NCTM *STANDARDS* SAY

Grades K-4

Standard 10 for grades K-4 specifies that the "mathematics curriculum should include measurement so that students can:

- ◆ understand the attributes of length, capacity, weight, area, volume, time, temperature, and angle;
- ◆ develop the process of measuring and concepts related to units of measurement;
- ◆ make and use estimates of measurement;
- ◆ make and use measurements in problem and everyday situations" (p. 51).

Grades 5-8

Standard 13 for grades 5-8 notes that "the mathematics curriculum should include extensive concrete experiences using measurement so that students can:

- ◆ extend their understanding of the process of measurement;
- ◆ estimate, make, and use measurements to describe and compare phenomena;
- ◆ select appropriate units and tools to measure to the degree of accuracy required in a particular situation;
- ◆ understand the structure and use of systems of measurement;
- ◆ extend their understanding of the concepts of perimeter, area, volume, angle measurement, capacity, and weight and mass;
- ◆ develop the concepts of rates and other derived and indirect measurements;
- ◆ develop formulas and procedures for determining measures to solve problems" (p. 116).

15•1 FOSTERING AN UNDERSTANDING OF MEASUREMENT

Figure 15.1: A Nonstandard Measure[3]

YOUNG ONES' VIEW

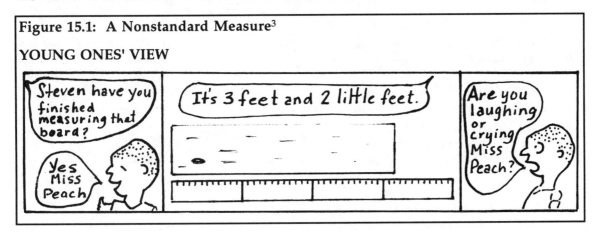

The skills approach focuses on *how to measure*, not on *what it means to measure* (Van de Walle, 1994). As Figure 15.1 illustrates, this can results in curious answers. In this unit, we consider what it means to measure (Subunit 15•1•1), how children's thinking about measurement develops (Subunit 15•1•2), and how to help them learn what it means to measure (Subunit 15•1•3).

15•1•1 MATHEMATICS: UNDER- STANDING MEASUREMENT

"How big is it?" is a fundamental question in almost all everyday activities. "This question is at once simple yet subtle, elementary yet difficult. Students who grow up recognizing the complexity of measurement may be less likely to accept unquestioningly many of the common misuses of numbers and statistics. Learning [what it means] to measure is the beginning of numeracy" (Steen, 1990b, p. 6). In this subunit, we outline the basic concepts underlying what it means to measure and explain the relationship between measurement and estimation.

☞ Consider Probe 15.2 (pages 15-6 and 15-7).

What It Means To Measure

Comparing the size of two discrete quantities, such as the number of windows on the front side of two houses, simply involves counting each collection and comparing the resulting numbers. Comparing two continuous quantities, such as the size of two house lots (Question 1 of Probe 15.2 on page 15-6), requires measuring each and comparing the measurements. Although measuring is a more complicated process than counting, at heart it involves a fundamentally simple idea—partition the continuous quantities into equal-size units so that the number of units in each can be counted. Understanding how to measure entails comprehending the following four-step process:

Step 1: Determine the Attribute To Be Measured. Objects have many characteristics (attributes) that can be measured. When presented a task that involves measurement, it is essential then to decide what attribute needs to be measured. In Question 3 of Probe 5.2, for instance, Rodah should ask Mr. Picky to clarify what he wants measured. Is it the height, length, or width of the cereal box (linear units)? Is it the size of the box front (area), the amount of Crunchy cereal the box holds (capacity), the amount of space occupied by the box (volume), its heaviness (weight), its ability to withstand crushing (tensile strength), or what? Regardless of the attribute chosen, the remaining steps in the measurement process are identical.

Step 2: Choose an Appropriate Unit of Measurement. The selection of a unit involves understanding the following ideas:

•**A unit of measurement must be appropriate for the attribute chosen** (e.g., length can be measured by a ruler in inches but not by a scale in pounds).

•**Within this restriction, the choice of unit is arbitrary**. An attribute can be measured by different units of measurement (e.g., a length can be measured in paperclips, inches, or centimeters).

•**However, a unit must be appropriate for the size of an object** (e.g., whereas an inch is appropriate for gauging the size of a pencil, a mile or a light-year is not). (Continued on page 15-8.)

→ **Probe 15.2: Basic Measurement Concepts**

The aim of this probe is to foster reflection on, and an explicit understanding of, key ideas underlying measurement. Answer the following questions, preferably with your group. Discuss your answers with your class.

1. Solve the following problem:

   ■ **Confused Lot Buyer.** Mr. O'Reilly wanted to buy the largest lot possible to build his new house. He examined a survey map of a housing subdivision—a part of which is illustrated below. Which of the two lots shown is larger?

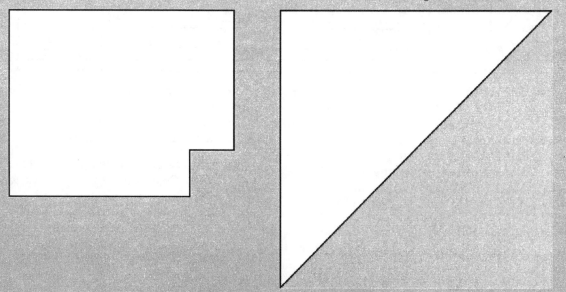

2. A primary-level teacher asked her class to measure a distance on a wall map. Although such a process would be automatic for most adults, it may not be for young children. Consider what is involved in measuring the map distance illustrated below. Hint: Assume you know nothing about measuring, what questions would you need to ask?

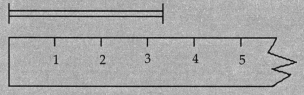

3. The Peppy Box Company had just developed a new box for Crunchy Cereal. Mr. Picky, the president of Peppy Boxes was preparing a talk for Crunchy Cereal executives and left Rodah, his Executive Secretary, a sample box and the message, "Get me the measurements on this box immediately." Aside from some pointers on manners, what does Rodah need to talk to Mr. Picky about?

Crunchy Cereal

4. Your student teacher announces to the class, "I don't want you to estimate the lengths of the objects listed. You need to measure each item carefully to get an *exact* measurement." Is there anything you should tell your student teacher about measurement?

5. Consider the task of measuring a distance on a wall map (e.g., see the diagram for Question 2 above). How is the process of measuring similar to the process of rounding?

Probe 15.2 continued

6. The activity file below illustrates how instruction in other content areas can serve as a basis for the investigative approach to measurement instruction. After reading it, answer the following questions: (a) Even if Paulie's measurement of 25,333 miles is used, what does the activity illustrate about the nature of measurement? (b) Why did Miss Brill run her finger from 0 to 1 to show 1 inch rather than simply point to the 1 on the tape measure? (c) What mathematical content areas other than measurement were involved in this measurement activity?

 Activity File 15.3: Measuring the Circumference of a Globe[4]

◆ Integrated measurement activity ◆ 4-8 ◆ Small groups of four to six

After estimating the circumference of the earth (Task 2 of Investigation 7.7 on page 7-19 of Chapter 7), Miss Brill's class was curious about what this distance actually was. LeMar suggested using the globe sitting on Miss Brill's desk. With the help of Andy, LeMar wrapped a tape measure around the equator of the globe and found it was *about* 38 inches long. Using the scale on the globe, the boys then found 1000 miles was approximately $1\frac{1}{2}$-inches. Each group then set about trying to determine the circumference of the earth from these data.

LeMar suggested to his group that they divide 38-inches by $1\frac{1}{2}$-inches to see how many $1\frac{1}{2}$-inches there were in 38-inches.

Several groups had difficulty getting starting. So, Miss Brill tried to make the problem more concrete for them. After taping a strip of butcher paper to a table, she had the students lay out a tape measure on the paper and tape it down on one end and again just past the 38-inches mark. She then had the students summarize what they knew about the problem.

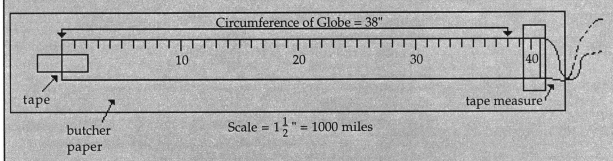

Scale = $1\frac{1}{2}$ " = 1000 miles

Kevin suggested marking off $1\frac{1}{2}$-inch segments. Because she suspected that Jimmy had little measurement experience, Miss Brill took this opportunity to help him follow Kevin's suggestion. Asked to mark off $1\frac{1}{2}$", Jimmy was unsure what to do. Miss Brill ran her finger from 0 to 1 and noted, "This is one inch. What would be an inch and a half?" Jimmy then indicated this distance and marked it on the butcher paper. Asked what would be another inch and a half, Jimmy ran his finger up to 3 and marked it. After completing this process, the students noted they had 25 marks and $\frac{1}{2}$-inch left. They quickly surmised that the circumference of the earth must be 25,000 miles and then some.

Miss Brill posed the question, "If $1\frac{1}{2}$-inches represents 1000 miles, then $\frac{1}{2}$-inch would represent how many miles?" Judi quickly recognized that there were three half inches in $1\frac{1}{2}$-inches and suggested dividing the 1000 miles into three equal groups. She estimated 100, but quickly recognized that was not nearly enough. She then tried 200, but again three 200s was short of 1000. Next Judi tried 300, but three 300s was again short of 1000. She tried 400, but three 400s (1200) was over 1000. The girl settled on 300 because 900 was closer to 1000 than 1200. Adding 300 to 25,000, she arrived at answer of 25,300. Paulie divided 1000 by 3 and got an answer of 333 r1. He recorded the circumference of the earth as 25,333.

•**The number of units varies inversely with the size of the units.** Measuring an attribute of an object with a larger unit such as feet will result in fewer units than measuring it with a smaller unit such as inches.

•**Even though different units of measure can be chosen, one cannot change units during the measuring process.** For instance, once inches are chosen to measure the length of a desk, only these units can be applied; switching to centimeters in midstream is unacceptable.

Step 3: Compare the Unit to the Object to Determine the Number of Units. Comparing the selected unit to an object essentially enables us to divide a continuous quantity into units of measurement—into something countable. (In effect, it transforms a continuous quantity into a discrete quantity.) Learning how to make such comparisons is not obvious. A child needs to learn, for instance, where to start comparing a unit to an object and how to interpret partial units (e.g., see Figure 15.1 on page 15-5). It is further complicated by the fact that each attribute requires a different comparison process (e.g., measuring length, area, and volume each entail different measurement skills).

Step 4: Report the Number of Units *and* the Name of the Unit. Because different units can be chosen and the number of units depends on the size of the unit, it is essential to report the name of the unit as well as the number of units.

The Relationship Between Measurement and Estimation

Estimating plays a central role in measuring. Indeed, all measurements are basically estimates.

Everyday Measurement. Although many everyday uses of measurement involve specifying an exact value (e.g., speed limit 30 miles per hour, use $\frac{3}{4}$ cups of milk, the ideal weight for your height is 120 pounds), we more often use less specific measures (e.g., I am only going about 30 miles per hour, I use about $\frac{3}{4}$ cups of milk, I weigh about 120 pounds).

The Inexact Nature of Measurement. Question 4 of Probe 15.2 (on page 15-6) highlights the common misconception that measurements can be exact. In fact, measurements are never entirely

precise. Some students wonder, *How can this be true when you can request a specific amount such as 4 pounds of meat or 6 gallons of gasoline?* The truth is that there is no way of measuring out 4 pounds of meat or 6 gallons of gasoline with absolute precision. Because it is not humanly or mechanically possible to measure length exactly, for example, a lumber order for boards 6-feet long actually come in various sizes (e.g., $6'\frac{1}{16}"$, $5'\frac{31}{32}"$, $6'\frac{2}{45}"$). For one thing, our vision is only so precise. For another, the units of a ruler could not exactly replicate the standard units. Because no measurement or measurement device can be entirely exact, even "specific" measurements are really just estimates.

Parallels with Rounding. Because measurements are never exact, the process of measuring—as Question 5 of Probe 15.2 (on page 15-6) implies—is similar to the process of rounding. With rounding whole numbers or decimals, the level of accuracy needed dictates to what place you round. Similarly, measurement requires deciding how precise a measure needs to be. Does a task require accuracy to inches, eighths of an inch, millionths of an inch, or what? Given the equipment available, what level of precision is even practical? After a level of precision is chosen, rounding requires deciding whether a number is closer to the next smaller or the next larger unit. Likewise, after a unit of measurement is chosen, measuring requires deciding what to do with partial units. For example, assume that you need to determine a map distance to the nearest centimeter. If this distance is less than halfway between 3 cm and 4 cm, then the measurement would be rounded to 3 cm.

15•1•2 LEARNING: UNDERSTANDING CHILDREN'S THINKING

In this subunit, we briefly outline how children's understanding of measurement develops and why many have difficulty learning measurement concepts and skills.

The Development of Measurement Concepts

Surprising Informal Knowledge. From everyday experiences, children construct informal concepts about measurement. They intuitively compare things in terms of height, weight, and so forth. For example, children intuitively brace their arm when given a large, heavy-looking object (Bower, 1974).

One study found that children from 3- to 9-years old spontaneously used informal measurement procedures to share various types of continuous quantities (Miller, 1984). For example, children were asked how colored water ("Kool-Aid") could be shared among three turtles. Although one-fourth of the three-year-olds apparently poured an arbitrary amount of colored water into each turtle's glass, the dominant strategy was to pour some water into each glass, compare the levels, and then pour additional water to even up the glasses (Campbell, 1990).

From Appearances to Concept. As with other mathematical concepts, measurement concepts begin with intuitions based on appearances and—with experience and reflection—gradually become more complete, coherent, and logical (e.g., Piaget & Inhelder, 1967; Piaget, Inhelder, & Szeminska, 1960). Consider children's reactions to the conservation-of-volume task. If shown two identical glasses with the same level of water, young children will readily agree that the glasses have the *same* amount (volume) of water. If one glass is poured into a tall thin glass and the other is poured into a short, squat glass, they then conclude that the taller glass has *more*. At both times, young children focus on appearances—the height of the water level. In effect, they consider only this one dimension, not the compensating change (the taller glass is also thinner).

Through real experiences and reflection, children gradually construct a concept of measurement unit, which enables them to disregard the misleading perceptual cues such as those created by conservation tasks (Bearison, 1969). That is, they recognize that comparing quantities involves considering the number of units of measurement that "fit" each quantity, not their appearances. For example, on the conservation-of-volume task, children recognize that if the same number of cups of water are put into each glass, the glasses have the same amount of water unless water is added or taken from one of the glasses. Moreover, they recognize that this is true despite superficial changes in appearances—as when the water is poured into a taller but thinner container. (Because they can think in terms of units, children now understand that *both* height and width must be taken into account—that tallness

by itself does not necessarily reflect volume.) Children often construct a concept of unit for length first, then for area next, and for volume last (Hart, 1984b; Piaget et al., 1960).

Difficulties

Instruction that does not actively involve children in measuring and reflection can impede conceptual development. Unfortunately, the traditional textbook-based skills approach focuses on memorizing by rote measurement facts (e.g., equivalent measures such as 12 inches = 1 foot) and measurement procedures (e.g., how to use a ruler). This does not provide children the opportunity to construct an understanding of the process of measurement or a concept of measurement unit. This often leads to mechanical and incorrect use of measurement knowledge and tools. For example, many elementary-level children confuse area with perimeter and vice versa (e.g., Lindquist & Kouba, 1989). Common errors when using a ruler include counting the number of hash marks starting with 0 rather than the units between the marks (Bright & Hoeffner, 1993), treating the 1 hashmark as the starting point instead of the 0 hashmark and counting the 2 hashmark as *one*,[5] and placing the edge of an object at the 1-inch hashmark rather than the 0 hashmark.*

15•1•3 TEACHING WHAT IT MEANS TO MEASURE

Three general teaching tips follow.

☞ **Measurement instruction should actively involve students in making real measurements** (e.g., Bright & Hoeffner, 1993). They must actively construct measurement concepts for themselves (Wilson & Rowland, 1993). This is best accomplished by INVOLVING CHILDREN IN PERSONALLY MEANINGFUL TASKS THAT REQUIRE MEASUREMENT. As noted elsewhere, active involvement entails more than physical manipulation of objects. It entails actively reflecting on experiences, writing about these reflections, sharing them with others, and revising conjectures.

In particular, "students must have opportunities to use measurement skills to solve real problems if they are going to develop understanding"

---

*Constance Kamii's (e.g., Kamii & Clark, 1997) recent research on the use of rulers as a measuring tool suggests marking 0 on rulers.

of the measurement process (Bright & Hoeffner, 1993, p. 79). Analyzing measurement problems may help them understand such fundamental measurement concepts as: units translate a continuous quantity into something countable, the same units must be used to complete a measurement, and the number of units varies inversely with the size of the units.

Science experiments (Activity File 15.1 on pages 15-2 and 15-3 and Activity File 15.3 on page 15-7), long-term projects (Activity File 15.2 on page 15-3), and everyday classroom situations (Activity File 15.4 to the right) can create a real need to measure things. Box 15.1 illustrate an example of the investigative approach to measurement instruction. (Text continued on page 15-13.)

♎ Activity File 15.4: Class Olympics

◆ Measuring length, height, and speed ◆ 1-8
◆ Any number

Challenge students to consider how to gauge and compare their efforts in such events as a broad jump, shot put (softball throw), high jump, or foot race. This raises the issue of what attribute is being measured and how to measure the attribute. They can also be encouraged to consider what nonstandard unit of measure can be used in each event and how to devise informal measurement instruments (e.g., using interlocking blocks to measure distance). Older students can be encouraged to use standard units and conventional measurement tools. Such an activity could be one way of introducing metric units of length.

Box 15.1: Examples of the Investigative Approach to Measurement Instruction

Vignette	Comments
Example 1. Mr. Burley suggested that as a service project, his class could seed the patch of lawn that had recently been dug up to repair water pipes. He pointed out that covering the seeded area with plastic would facilitate the growth of grass. To determine how much plastic would be needed, a team was assigned to measure the length and width of the rectangular plot of ground. Mr. Burley included Ariel and Chad on the team because testing had indicated they were unsure of measurement concepts and skills.	The lesson was based on a real project. In addition to providing a service to the school community and learning gardening skills, the task was mathematically rich. This complex task provided an opportunity to inquire into new topics and review old topics in a purposeful manner. Note that this lesson reviewed measurement concepts and skills by *actually* involving children—particularly those who need the review most—in measuring things.
The measurement team reported back that the plot was 21 feet, 7 inches long by 7 feet, 4 inches wide (rounded off to the nearest inch).	The teacher used this opportunity to review rounding procedures.
The groups set about trying to determine the area. Based on their knowledge of area, Alex's group devised the procedure to the right. $$\begin{array}{r} 21' \ 7'' \\ \times \ 7' \ 4'' \\ \hline 147' \ 28'' \end{array}$$	The teacher did not tell the class how to solve the problem. Instead, he allowed them to use what they already know to devise their own solution. (Note that Alex's answer should actually read 149 *square* feet and 28 *square* inches).
Mr. Burley then asked the groups to share their solutions. After Alex presented his group's solution, children in several other groups noted their disagreement. "We're not sure exactly what the answer is," noted Alysen, "but we think it has to be more than Alex's answer."	The teacher withheld judgment and encouraged the children to share ideas and judge for themselves what was reasonable.
"Class, Alysen's group disagrees," commented Mr. Burley enthusiastically. "Let's explore this. Alysen, why do you think the answer has to be more than 147 square feet and 28 square inches?"	The teacher welcomed the conflict because this can motivate students to explore ideas. He asked Alysen to justify her conjecture.

Box 15.1 (continued)

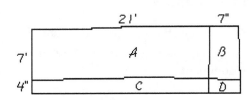

Alysen drew the diagram to the right on the board. "This area," she noted [pointing to part A], "is 147 square feet, and this part [pointing to part D] is 28 square inches. We haven't even figured out what the other two parts are yet."

"Yah, I can see that," conceded Alex graciously.

The peer-peer dialogue helped Alex see why his group's procedure was incorrect

"But," continued Alysen, "we don't know how to multiply feet and inches" (e.g., 21' x 4").

Shari suggested, "Why not change the inches to decimals?" She proceeded to write on the chalkboard: $21' 7" = 21.7'$ and $7' 4" = 7.4'$. The class enthusiastically embraced Shari's suggestions.

Note that using decimals can make doing arithmetic easier.

"How would you change 7' 11" into a decimal?" asked Mr. Burley. Shari responded by quickly writing 7.11 on the board and then paused to consider what she had written.

Seeing that the class was heading down a wrong path without any dissent, the teacher asked a question aimed at prompting reflection. Note that he did not simply tell Shari she was wrong but instead attempted to prompt doubt and conflict.

Drawing on his knowledge of decimals, Chico offered, "I don't think that's right?"

"No, it can't be," confirmed Shari, 7' 11" is more than 7'4" and 7.11 is not more than 7.4."

Note that the lesson spontaneously lurched into a review of decimal ordering and place value.

"Asked why, Shari added, "Because 7.11 is seven wholes, one tenth and one hundredth and 7.4 is seven wholes and four tenths, which is more."

"How can we change 7' 4" into a decimal then?" asked Mr. Burley. When there were no responses after several minutes, he prompted: "What's our whole?"

The teacher used a series of question to help the students redefine 4" as a fraction of a foot.

"Feet," responded Ariel.

"And what part of our whole is four inches?" prodded Mr. Burley.

Looking at her ruler, Ariel offered, "Oh, $\frac{4}{12}$?"

Chico quickly agreed, "That's right, because there's 12 inches in a foot."

"How can we change $\frac{4}{12}$ into a decimal?" asked Mr. Burley. Marsha noted that $\frac{4}{12}$ was equal to $\frac{1}{3}$ and $\frac{1}{3}$ was equal to the decimal $.33\overline{3}$. After the class agreed that 7" was $\frac{7}{12}'$, Mr. Burley asked

The problem led to a review of fraction-decimal equivalents. Although the teacher had hoped that the class would recall that fractions can be changed into decimals by dividing the numerator by the denominator, he did not insist they use this procedure.

Box 15.1 continued

how $\frac{7}{12}$ could be changed into a decimal. He then allowed the students to work on this task without further comment.

One boy used his existing knowledge and logical reasoning to devise an elegant informal solution.

Exploiting the fraction-decimal equivalents he knew, Alexi offered the following line of reasoning:[6]

$$3" \quad = \quad \tfrac{1}{4} \text{ of } 12 = \quad .25$$
$$\underline{+\ 4"} \quad = \quad \underline{+\ \tfrac{1}{3}} \text{ of } 12 = \quad \underline{+\ .33\overline{3}}$$
$$7" \qquad\qquad\qquad = \quad .58\overline{3}$$

So $21'\ 7" \quad = \quad 21.58\overline{3}\ '$

In effect, $\frac{3}{12} + \frac{4}{12} = \frac{7}{12}$

As $\frac{3}{12} = \frac{1}{4}$ and $\frac{4}{12} = \frac{1}{3}$, $\quad \frac{3}{12} + \frac{4}{12} = \frac{1}{4} + \frac{1}{3}$

As $\frac{1}{4} = .25$ and $\frac{1}{3} = .33\overline{3}$, then $\frac{1}{4} + \frac{1}{3} =$

$.25 + .33\overline{3}$ or $.58\overline{3}$

After congratulating Alexi, Mr. Burley asked if there were other ways to change a fraction into a decimal. One student recalled that a calculator could be used by couldn't remember the procedure. Mr. Burley encouraged the class to check their textbook for the procedure. After the class had rediscovered that a fraction can be converted into a decimal by dividing the top digit by the bottom one, Mr. Burley asked them why dividing made sense. He further prompted them to consider what meanings fractions could have.

The textbook was used as a resource.

The teacher wanted his students to understand the rationale for the procedure. He reasoned that by connecting the *how* to the *why*, his students might remember the procedure better.

Alicia recalled that fractions could have a division, as well as a part-of-a-whole, meaning—and that's why you divide.

A common fraction such as $\frac{2}{3}$ can represent two things divided among three groups, as well as two parts of a whole divided into three parts.

Example 2. McClain, Cobb, and Gravemeijer (1997) reported on a primary-level class that adopted *Unifix* cubes as a unit of length. After carrying around bags of the cubes to complete various measurement activities, students suggested using a ten-bar (10 cubes pushed together) instead.

The class used an informal measure ("Smurf cans," which were represented by *Unifix* cubes). In the natural course of using this informal measure, children invented their own, more convenient, measuring tool (the ten-bar ruler). Use of this tool provided practice skip counting by ten.

During the course of one activity, children had to determine a length 23 units long. Jordana noted that it would be less than two ten-bars long (see Figure A). Sarah suggested that it would be more than two ten-bars long (see Figure B). Jordana argued that Figure B represented 33, not 23, because the three was in the "thirties bar." Sarah countered that the last cube in the first ten-bar was ten, the last cube in the second ten-bar was twenty and the third cube of the third ten-bar was 23.

A.

B.

During the course of a real measurement activity, the issue of how to use a ruler to measure is raised. The teacher allowed the children to debate their conflicting views. The children successfully resolve the debate themselves.

This explanation satisfied Jordana and the rest of the class.

In the course of measuring and comparing heights, a group had to determine the difference of 67 and 72 cubes. Lynn offered "six" as an answer. Anticipating Lynn's error, Shana offered "Did you count *from* 67 and not the 67?"

During the course of a measurement activity, one child again helps another understand how to use a ruler as a measuring tool and that measuring length involves counting units of length from one end to another.

☞ **Use the five-phase teaching sequence outlined below with each attribute** (Wilson & Rowland, 1993). For each new attribute, it is important to lay the conceptual groundwork and help children link the formal terms, symbols, procedures, and formulas to this conceptual groundwork. Phases 1 to 3 can be thought of as aspects of the conceptual phase. Phases 4 and 5 are analogous to the connecting phase. As children learn more about measurement, the time needed to proceed through these phases will probably decrease. Primary-level instruction should focus on Phases 1 to 4, intermediate-level, on Phase 5. In this unit, we discuss Phases 1 to 4; in Unit 15•2, we consider Phase 5.

Phase 1: Identifying attributes. Initially, measurement instruction should help students distinguish among attributes and explicitly define them. Help them see that things have many different measurable attributes and that it is important to specify clearly which attribute is to be measured. Ideally this would be done in the context of solving a problem (see, e.g., Question 2 on page 15-6 of Probe 15.2). This would provide a real purpose for distinguishing a particular attribute from others and measuring it.

Phase 2: Making direct comparisons. Direct comparisons involve comparing two items directly without measurement tools or units. For example, to determine the taller of two children (see Part 1 of Activity File 15.5 on the next page), one can simply stand them back to back and see who is taller. Note that such a comparison simply involves intuitively using appearances. Although children typically do not need instruction to make direct comparisons, such activities provide an opportunity to foster vocabulary associated with measurement (NCTM, 1989).

Phase 3: Using the four-step measurement process to make indirect comparisons. Phase 3 of instruction should focus on helping children over-

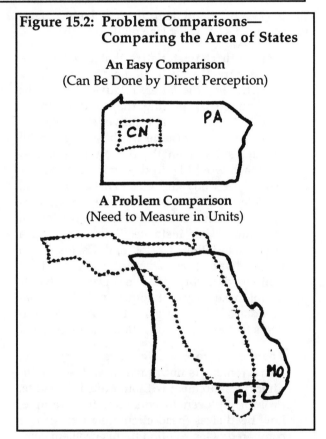

Figure 15.2: Problem Comparisons—Comparing the Area of States

An Easy Comparison (Can Be Done by Direct Perception)

A Problem Comparison (Need to Measure in Units)

come their reliance on using appearances by guiding them to construct an understanding of measurement units. This can be done by posing *problem comparisons*—comparisons where it is not intuitively clear which item is larger (Wilson & Rowland, 1993) (see Figure 15.2 above). Problem comparisons (e.g., see Parts 2 and 3 of Activity File 15.5 on page 15-14) can help students understand the need for measurement units and that measurement is a process of comparing a unit (a known quantity) to an unknown quantity. During Phase 3, they should also begin to construct an explicit understanding of the four-step measurement process: (a) determine the attribute to be measured, (b) choose an appropriate unit, (c) compare the units to the object, and (d) report both the number of units and the name of the units.

🍎 Activity File 15.5: Comparing the *Size* of Body Parts

◆ Creating a need for indirect measurement ◆ 1-8 ◆ Any number

As part of an ongoing science unit on human growth, have a class determined the relative sizes of its members. (To make the data analyses richer, boy-boy, girl-girl, and boy-girl comparisons could be made.) Encourage the students to consider the various ways body size could be defined (height, hand length, arm length, feet length, head size, waist size, and so forth).

1. **Start with characteristics that can be measured directly such as height and hand length.** For the latter, relative size can be determined by putting the hands palm to palm. Note that a relatively simple approach is to determine the boy or girl with the largest hand length. A more complicated approach would be to determine the relative size of each boy and girl. This could entail considering how to organize the comparisons systematically. It might also involve logical reasoning. For instance, if Brendan has a larger hand than Carlos and Carlos has a larger hand than Damon, then a direct comparison of Brendan's and Damon's hands is not necessary. It logically follows that Brendan's hand is larger. (Encourage the students to make such deductions themselves.)

2. **Then move to characteristics where direct measurement is not practical and where indirect measurement without units is possible.** Prompt children to consider, for example, how head sizes (head circumferences) can be compared. One solution to this problem comparison is to use a string or other flexible material that can wrap around a head. Then this string can be stretched out and its length compared to that of other lengths of string. Such an approach can serve as a *transition* from direct measurement to indirect measurement *with units*.

3. **Finally, use problem comparisons to create a need for indirect measurement with units.** For example, have students measure and compare the size (area) of their feet. Because one child's foot might be longer but thinner than another child's foot, direct comparisons or indirect comparisons without units is not practical. Children can trace an outline of their feet on grid paper and tally the number of grids (Burns, 1987).

One way to create a need for units is to request the comparison of many measurements. Measuring in units greatly simplifies the comparison process. Basically, the *number* of units can be ordered without comparing actual lengths. For example, if Brendan is 40 blocks (units) tall, Carlos is 36 blocks tall, and Damon is 34 blocks tall, then children can simply use their knowledge of the counting sequence to order and to compare measurements. A second way is to encourage a class to consider how they can record their personal measurements so that their amount of growth can be determined and compared later (e.g., at the end of the year). Note that recording long lines to represent a measurement, for example, is not convenient. If a length is marked off in units, on the other hand, the *number* of units can be recorded in a compact manner. Note also that recording measurements should underscore the importance of reporting the name of the unit as well as the number. A third way of creating a need for measurement units is to ask, for instance, "How much taller is Brendan than Carlos?" or "How could we determine how much you will grow this year?"

Phase 4: Moving from nonstandard to standard units of measurement. Measurement instruction should begin with nonstandard units (see, e.g., Activity 1 of Investigation 15.1 on page 15-15) and then introduce standard units (see, e.g., Activity 2 of Investigation 15.1 on page 15-16). Working with nonstandard units during Phases 1 to 3 can, for example, help children realize that measurement units are arbitrary.

☜ **Make estimation an *integral* aspect of Phases 2 to 4** (see, e.g., Activity I of Investigation 15.2 on page 15-17). Help students construct mental benchmarks of common units of measurement (see, e.g., Activity II of Investigation 15.2).

☞ Try Investigations 15.1 (pages 15-15 and 15-16) and 15.2 (page 15-17). (Text continued on page 15-18.)

☕ Investigation 15.1: Measuring Angles

In this investigation, students explore two interesting ways an angle (*the amount of turn*) can be measured informally. To see what is involved, try the two activities below with your group.

Activity 1: Using Pattern Blocks (◆ Nonstandard unit of angular measure ◆ 3-5 ◆ Small groups of about four)

This conceptual-level activity illustrates a concrete method for measuring the amount of turn. Ask students how many green triangles it takes to swing back to a vertical starting line. Do the same using the orange square, blue rhombus, clear-wood rhombus, yellow hexagon, and red trapezoid.

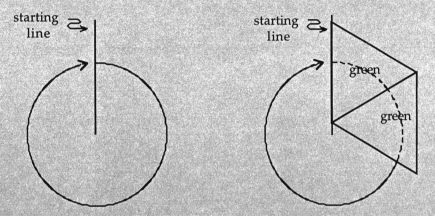

Answer the following questions and discuss your answers with your group or class.

1. How many of each type of pattern block mentioned above was needed to swing around back to the vertical line?

2. Miss Brill's class agreed unanimously about the green triangle, orange square, and yellow hexagon but had sharp disagreements about the blue rhombus, the clear-wood rhombus, and the red trapezoid. With the blue rhombus, for example, Andy found it took three to turn completely around, LeMar found it took four, and Rodney found it took six. (a) Why did this disagreement arise? (b) Which boy, if any, is correct? (c) What does Miss Brill need to clarify to her students?

3. Which blocks would be useful for illustrating half a turn?

4. Miss Brill's class labeled the angles of a green triangle *one-sixth of a (complete) turn*. What could the angles of the other pattern blocks be called?

5. Miss Brill had her class measure various angles with the pattern blocks. What fraction of a (complete clockwise) turn would the following angles be? (Note that answering this question involves fraction addition.)

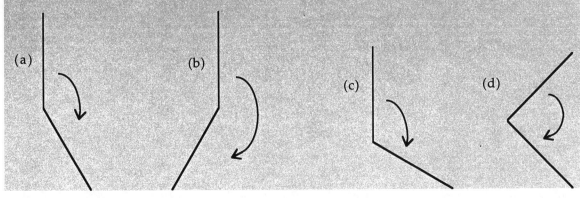

Investigation 15.1 continued

Activity 2: Using Hinged Mirrors[†] (◆ Standard unit of angular measure ◆ 6-8 ◆ Groups of four)

This connecting-level activity illustrates how *degrees* can be introduced as a measure of angles.

Part I. Have students close two hinged mirrors until the sides of the mirror touch two adjacent sides of a pattern block. Have them consider the questions below. Experiment with the hinged mirrors and pattern blocks and answers the questions below yourself.

1. (a) Counting the block and all its reflections, how many green triangles did you see? (b) How many orange squares? (c) How many yellow hexagons?

2. (a) How many blue rhombi did you see? (b) What happens to the number of blue rhombi visible when the shape is turned so that the hinged mirrors enclose an adjacent angle and why?

3. (a) In what ways do the results of this activity parallel the results of Activity 1? (b) In effect, enclosing a block in the mirror shows what?

Part II. The hinged mirrors effectively provide a panoramic view of the blocks—a view from all directions. Ask students what turning completely around on a skateboard, ice skates, or skis is called (*a 360*). Relate this to the standard convention of labeling a complete turn 360°. Then have the class analyze the angles of the pattern blocks in terms of degrees. Consider the following questions you could pose students.

1. (a) Each green triangle is what fractional part of the actual block and its reflections in the hinged mirrors? (b) If a complete view (complete turn) is 360°, then the angle of a green triangle is how many degrees? (c) An angle of each other pattern block is how many degrees?

2. Translate the angles measured in Question 5 of Activity 1 into degrees.

Part III. Have students draw a straight line and, about $1\frac{1}{4}$-inch below the line, a dot as shown in Figure A below. Have them place the top of the green triangle on the line just above the dot as shown in Figure B. Then enclose the top two sides with the hinged mirrors. How many dots (including the drawn and reflected dots) can be seen?

| Figure A | Figure B |

Predict the number of dots that would be visible if an orange square was enclosed in the hinged mirrors instead of a green triangle. Check your prediction. Now, without pattern blocks, have students experiment with opening the hinged mirrors different amounts. Encourage them to consider the following questions: *(1) When 10 dots are visible, the hinged mirrors are opened at what angle? (2) When 20 dots are visible, the hinged mirror is open at what angle? (3) How many dots would be visible if the mirrors were open 10°? (4) In theory, how many dots would be visible if the mirrors were open only 1°?* Answer these questions yourself and discuss your answers with your group or class.

[†] Based, in part, on chapter 6 in *A Collection of Math Lessons From Grades 6 through 8* by Marilyn Burns and Cathy McLaughlin and © 1990 by The Math Solutions Publication.

☪ Investigation 15.2: Measurement Estimation

◆ Measurement sense ◆ Groups of four + class discussion

Estimation should be an integral part of measurement instruction from the start of school. Initially, children can use direct perception to judge the relative size of easy and then problem comparisons. In time, they can estimate size in terms of nonstandard units and, later yet, in standard units. This activity involves estimating area with either nonstandard or standard units. To see what is involved and to perhaps deepen your own measurement sense, try the following activities yourself, preferably with the help of your group. Discuss your conclusions with your class.

Activity I: Estimating Area (◆ 4-8)

After students have been introduced to measuring the area of rectangles and squares, pose a problem such as that below.

- ■ **The Approximate Area of a Circle.** Distribute pie tins or other circular objects to students and ask them to estimate the area of the tin. If students have already learned the formula for the area of a circle, instruct them to devise their own (nonalgorithmic) method. (✚ Hint: Consider how students can use their knowledge about finding the area of the rectangles and squares to estimate the area of a pie tin.)

Questions for Reflection

1. (a) How might your strategy be refined to give a more accurate estimate? (b) Discuss the relative accuracy of the strategies used by different people in your group or class.

2. (a) How might beans be used to estimate the area of a circle? (b) How might weight be used?

3. When presented Problem B above, Erza proposed, "Wrap a string around the pie tin and then [fashion] the string into a square. Compute the area of the square, and this will tell you the area of the pie tin. (a) Is Erza's conjecture correct or not? *Do polygons with the same perimeter have the same area?* (b) How could this conjecture be tested?

Activity II: Devising Estimation Benchmarks (◆ 1-8)

As with estimating the sizes of collections, benchmarks can be helpful in estimating the sizes of continuous quantities. This activity asks students to devise handy references for several measures. To see what is involved and to perhaps expand your own measurement sense, try the activity with your group. Discuss your ideas with your class.

1. Consider what could serve as a handy benchmark for (a) linear measures such as an inch, a foot, a yard, a centimeter, a meter, (b) area measures such as a square inch, a square foot, a square yard, a square centimeter, a square meter; and (c) volume measures such as 1 cup, 1 quart, 1 liter? Include in your list manipulatives and other familiar objects that would be available in a classroom.

2. (a) Measure the length of various common objects such as different-sized paper clips and the distance between the knuckles of the first finger. Record your results in a chart. Try to find an item that could serve as benchmarks for an inch, a foot, a yard, a centimeter, and a meter. (b) Collect various common items and measure their area. Record your results in a table. Try to find an item that could serve as benchmarks for a square inch, a square foot, a square yard, a square centimeter, and a square meter. (c) Collect various common containers and measure their volume. Record your results in a table. Try to find containers that could serve as a benchmark for 1 cup, 1 quart, 1 milliliter, and 1 liter.

15•2 DEVISING MEASUREMENT FORMULAS

Figure 15.3: Mechanical Learning of Formulas Can Lead to Miserable Results

CALVIN AND HOBBES copyright 1995 Watterson. Dist. by UNIVERSAL PRESS SYNDICATE. Reprinted with permission. All rights reserved.

Children often have difficulty learning or remembering measurement formulas because instruction focuses on memorizing them by rote (Hirstein, Lamb, & Osborne, 1978). In this unit, we describe how the investigative approach can promote the meaningful learning of measurement formulas. More specifically, we consider how instruction can help students devise the formulas for area and perimeter in Subunit 15•2•1 and the formulas for volume in Subunit 15•2•2.

15•2•1 AREA AND PERIMETER

Perimeter and Area of Polygons

Children can be encouraged to look for patterns and to use what they know to reinvent area and perimeter formulas. Deriving these formulas themselves can promote mathematical power in three ways: increase their confidence that they can make sense of mathematics, engage them in genuine mathematical thinking, and foster understanding. Promoting adaptive expertise makes it less likely children will forget the formulas, more likely they can reconstruct them if they do, and far more likely they will be able to devise new formulas on their own.

Rectangles. By working with a geoboard or dot-matrix paper, for example, third-graders can quickly discover that the number of squares in (the area of) a rectangle can easily be determined by the shortcut: multiply the length of the rectangle by its width (see Activity File 15.6 on page 15-19).

☞ Try Investigations 15.3 (page 15-20) and 15.4 (pages 15-21 and 15-22).

Squares, Parallelograms, and Triangles. Once children rediscover the formula for the area of a rectangle and recognize squares as a special type of rectangle, they should have little trouble deducing that the formula for the area of a square is $A = s^2$ (where s = the length of a side).

Children can derive the formulas for the area of a parallelogram and a triangle by using the heuristic: TRANSFORM A FIGURE INTO ONE FOR WHICH YOU ALREADY KNOW THE AREA FORMULA. For example, a parallelogram can be transformed into a rectangle by drawing a height, cutting along this height, and placing the resulting triangle on the other side of the parallelogram. Given that the area of this rectangle equals length and width ($A_r = l \times w$), the base of the parallelogram equals the length of the rectangle (b = l), and the height of the parallelogram equals the width of the rectangle (h = w), it follows that the area of a parallelogram equals base times height ($A_p = b \times h$).

Circumference and Area of a Circle— Examples of the Investigative Approach

Posing a problem such as *A Bicycle Problem* (see Box 15.2 on pages 15-23 and 15-24) can lead children to explore the relationship between the diameter and circumference of a circle and to rein-

♣ Activity File 15.6: Rediscovering the Formula for the Area of a Rectangle

◆ Inductive reasoning + measurement (area) ◆ 3-5 ◆ Class working individually or in small groups

This lesson has multiple aims. In addition to giving children an opportunity to look for patterns (inductive reasoning) and reinventing the formula for a rectangle, it can serve as an introduction to square numbers and as practice of multiplication combinations.

After introducing the concept of area with square tiles and geoboards, Mr. Mihelich distributed to each child four sheets of dot-matrix paper similar to Figure A below and a sheet for a table (see Figure B below) all stapled together. The following instructions were on the first page of the handout: On each dot matrix below, draw four different rectangles that each have a width of 1 unit. After discussing what width meant and encouraging a student to illustrate an example on a matrix drawn on the chalkboard, the students tackled the task. After sharing their results, Mr. Mihelich asked the children what the area of a one-by-one, two-by-one, three-by-one, and a four-by-one rectangle were. The class agreed to measure area as the number of one-by-one boxes contained in a rectangle. He summarized the findings in a table. On the second dot-matrix page, he then asked them to draw four differently-shaped rectangles with a width of 2 units. He again had the class discuss their results and determine the area of the four possibilities (1 by 2, 2 by 2, 3 by 2, and 4 by 2). These results were also summarized in the table. This same process was repeated for widths of three and widths of four. During the course of summarizing these data, a number of children recognized that the area was the product of the length and the width. Mr. Mihelich followed up this discovery by noting that, for example, a three-unit long by four-unit wide (a three-by-four) rectangle can be represented by the expression 3 x 4 and its area by the product 12. To introduce square numbers, he asked his class what they noticed about the special rectangles—the squares. A number of students quickly recognized that each square had a length equal to its width.

Figure A: Example of Dot-Matrix Page

Draw four different rectangles that each have a width of 1 unit.

Figure B: Table Page

Table

Length	Width	Area
1	1	1
2	1	2
3	1	3
4	1	4
1	2	2
2	2	4
3	2	6
4	2	8
1	3	3
2	3	6
3	3	9
4	3	12
1	4	4
2	4	8
3	4	12
4	4	16

invent the formula for the circumference of a circle. Note that the investigation illustrated in Box 15.2 also created a need for measuring, discussing measurement equivalents, operating on decimals, and introducing geometry vocabulary (e.g., the terms *radius*, *diameter*, and *circumference*). Moreover, this investigation also involved students in the processes of mathematical inquiry (e.g., making and testing conjectures, using problem-solving heuristics such as *use a model* and *looking back*, and inductive and deductive reasoning), collecting and organizing data (including graphing), using a calculator, and purposeful computational practice.

Like the *Bicycle Problem*, the *Strung-Out* problem (Activity I on page 15-21 of Investigation 15.4) can prompt an exploration of circles. Intuitively, it would seem that a huge amount of additional string would be needed if a string around the equator of the earth were pulled outward 1-inch from the surface. But how could we find out if this intuition is correct or not? (Continued on page 15-24.)

♻ Investigation 15.3: Devising Formulas for the Area of Polygons

◆ Reinventing the area formulas for squares, parallelograms, and triangles
+ deductive reasoning ◆ 5-8 ◆ Any number

Do you recall the formulas for the area of a square, parallelogram, and a triangle? Instruction should help students use their existing knowledge to devise for themselves the area formulas for polygons. This can facilitate meaningful memorization of these formulas or, at very least, empower students to reconstruct them when needed. To see how, do the following investigations with your group or class.

Part I: Squares

After rediscovering the formula for the area of a rectangle, students should be able to deduce the formula for the area of a square. Begin with the formula for the area of a rectangle (A = l x w), consider what you know about the relationship between a rectangle and a square, and informally devise a formula yourself. It may help to consider a concrete example such as the 4-cm by 4-cm square below.

Part II: Parallelograms

A key heuristic for devising the formula for the area of figures such as a parallelogram is to consider how the figure can be *cut up and rearranged to look like a figure for which the area formula is already known*. Consider how this could be done for the parallelogram to the right.

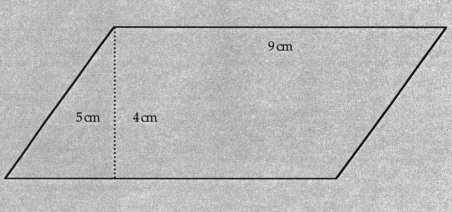

Part III: Triangles

Consider how students could build on what they already know to devise the formula for the area of a triangle. Briefly explain using the triangle to the right as an example.

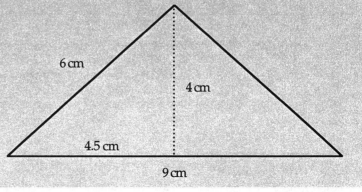

⏚ Investigation 15.4: Circular Explorations

◆ Conceptual basis for the formulas for the perimeter and area of circles ◆ 4-8 ◆ Groups of four to six

Do you recall the formulas for the perimeter and the area of a circle? Do you get the two formulas confused? *Why does π appear in these formulas, and what does π mean anyway?* The aim of this investigation is to help students answer these questions.

To get students thinking about the relationship between the diameter and perimeter, pose the *Strung-Out* problem (Activity I) below. Activity II (An Experiment in Measuring the Diameter and Circumference of Circles) can help them consider this relationship in a more structured and explicit manner. Activity III (Devising the Formula for the Area of a Circle) then builds on what students learned in Activity II. Activity IV explores the relationship between the area of polygons inscribed in circles and the number of sides of a polygon. To better understand the formulas for the perimeter and area of a circle, try these four activities yourself.

Activity I: A Problem Involving Circumferences. Consider the following problem:

■ **Strung-Out.** A string is wrapped around the earth at the equator. Assume the earth is a sphere with a smooth surface. Then, the string is pulled outward from the earth's surface so that the string is always one-inch away from the earth's surface all the way around the equator. How much more string will be needed to complete this new circle?

1. Intuitively estimate how much additional string will be needed.

    a. Several inches of additional string
    b. Several feet of additional string
    c. Several yards of additional string
    d. Several miles of additional string
    e. Many miles of additional string

2. Share your intuitive guess to Question 1 with your group or class. Summarize your choices in a table or a graph.

3. The *Strung-Out* problem is very difficult for most students to solve. What problem-solving heuristic might be helpful? Activity II below suggests one way to tackle this challenging problem.

Activity II: An Experiment in Measuring the Diameter and Circumference of Circles. To help students examine the relationship between the diameter and circumference of a circle, have them conduct the following experiment.

1. Find a number of circles of different diameters (e.g., caps to jars, wooden discs, cans). It is best to use circles that are all at least 2 inches

in diameter and fairly thick, this makes measuring the diameter and circumference easier and more accurate. Circles can be cut from sturdy material such as cardboard or plywood. For younger students, use convenient diameters for these circles (e.g., 2 in., 7 in., 10 in., 14 in., 10 cm, 20 cm, 30 cm, 40 cm, 50 cm).

2. Use a tape measure to measure the diameter and circumference of each circle. (Measuring in centimeters rather than inches will give you a more precise measurement and will be easier to convert to decimals.) If a tape measure is not available, wrap a string or another flexible material around the circles and measure the length of string needed for each circle. (To maximize the precision of your measurements, secure the end of the tape measure or string with transparent tape.) Enter the data in the chart below.

diameter d	circumference c

3. (a) Overlooking measurement error, is there a constant a relationship between the diameter of a circle and the circumference of the circle? (b) How could drawing a graph prove whether or not a relationship exists? Plot your data in a graph and see.

Investigation 15.4 continued

4. Summarize the relationship between the circumference of a circle and the diameter of the circle with an algebraic equation (formula).

5. (a) What is the circumference of a circle if its diameter is 8 cm? (b) What is the circumference of a circle 10 cm in diameter? (c) What is the circumference of a circle 12 cm in diameter?

6. What you have learned about the relationship between the diameter and perimeter of a circle is sufficient to solve the *Strung Out* problem. (a) Now, what is the solution to this problem? (b) Is the solution surprising?

Activity III: Devising the Formula for the Area of a Circle. Once children know the formula for the area of a rectangle and the perimeter of a circle, they have the basis for reinventing

the formula for the area of a circle. Try devising the formula. Working with a group might be particularly helpful in solving this problem. Also, what problem-solving heuristic would be helpful in solving this problem? Recall how you derived the area of a parallelogram in Part II on page 15-20 of Investigation 15.3.

Activity IV: Further Exploration. Using the formula derived in Activity III, compute the area of the circle in Figure A below. Let the vertical or horizontal distance between two dots equal 1 linear unit. In Figure B, inscribe the largest triangle possible in the circle and estimate its area. In Figure C, inscribe the largest square possible in the circle and calculate its area. In Figures D, E, and F, inscribe the largest possible pentagon, hexagon, and octagon, respectively, and estimate the area of each. What relationship do you notice about the area of a polygon inscribed in a circle and the number of its sides?

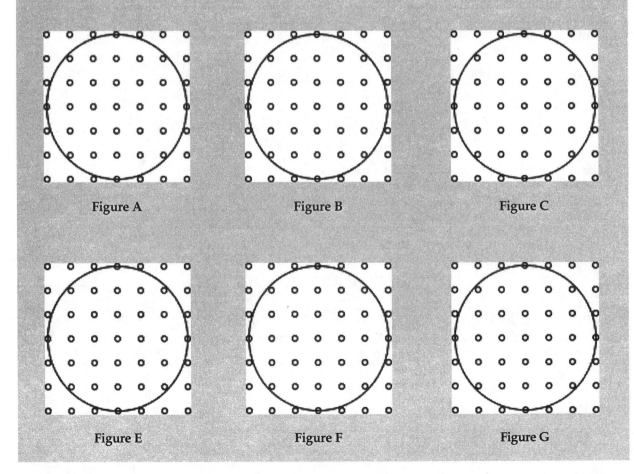

Figure A   Figure B   Figure C

Figure E   Figure F   Figure G

▦ 🍎 Box 15.2: Investigating a Bicycle Problem[7]

In selecting a problem to initiate a study of circles, Mrs. Stoffel considered how her fourth-grade students might use circles in their own lives (circular swimming pools; frisbees; a dog's path if chained to a stake in the yard; a path of a battery-operated airplane tethered to a swivel; wheels on rollerblades, bicycles, or cars; round foods such as cakes, pies, pizzas; and so forth). She settled on bicycles because this topic involved a simple machine (the wheel), which was one of her science goals.

Mrs. Stoffel began by posing the following problem:

■ **A Bicycle Problem (◆ 4-8).** A straight line from the center of a bicycle wheel to its edge (the radius) is 13 inches. How many revolutions must the wheel make to go 1 mile?

"What might help solve this problem?" prompted Mrs. Stoffel.

"It would help if we had the bicycle wheel," suggested Kathie.

"Maybe we could model a wheel," offered David.

Asked how a model might help, Nicole offered, "If we can figure out how far a little wheel can go, maybe we can figure out how far a big one can go."

Claudia retrieved a box of wooden and plastic discs and distributed them to the class. After lining up a row of discs, Rebecca offered an interesting conjecture, "If we know how far across a circle is in inches and we know how many inches are in a mile, then all we have to do is see how many circles fit in a mile." She drew the figure below on the chalkboard:

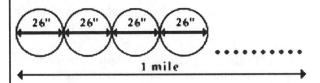

Claudia asked why 26 inches was used. Rebecca explained that the distance across a circle

was two radiuses. Mrs. Stoffel pointed out that Rebecca was referring to the *diameter* of a circle.

So Eva summarized, "All we have to do is divide the diameter into the number of inches in a mile."

In groups of four the class set about trying to determine how many inches are in a mile. After the class agreed that there were 63,360 inches in a mile, Mrs. Stoffel asked them about how many 26-inch wheels would fit into 63,360. After this estimation exercise, Lauren used a calculator to determine the exact answer (2436.9231).

Mrs. Stoffel then encouraged the class to look back, "How can we be sure this is the correct solution to our problem?"

Jeannie proposed checking their solution with a model, "How many times does a circle with a diameter of $3\frac{1}{2}$-inch have to go around to go 1 foot?"

Based on Rebecca's conjecture, Marcy punched $\boxed{1}$ $\boxed{2}$ $\boxed{\div}$ $\boxed{3}$ $\boxed{.}$ $\boxed{5}$ $\boxed{=}$ into her calculator, rounded off the quotient 3.4285714, and offered, "about three and a half times."

"How can we test whether or not this solution is accurate?" prompted Mrs. Stoffel.

Wendy suggested, "Roll the circle a foot and see how many times it goes around."

Kim tried rolling one of circles but lost track of when it went around. Kristin suggested using a pencil to mark the starting point of the circle. Taking great care to roll the circle, Kim found that, in spanning 1 foot, it went around just a little over one time.

"Maybe she did it wrong," Kristin suggested. This moved others to check Kim's effort. After multiple efforts to check Kim's results, the class concluded that Rebecca's conjecture was wrong and that they had not solved *A Bicycle Problem* correctly.

After her class examined and discussed the rolling motion of the model wheel, Mrs. Stoffel

Box 15.2 continued

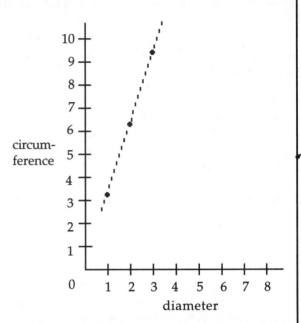

summarized its discovery, "When a circle makes a complete revolution, it travels the distance around its outside, which we call the *circumference*. Unfortunately, our problem doesn't specify what the circumference of the bicycle wheel is. Might there be a way of determining the circumference from what we know?"

David observed that the circumference of the model was about three times larger than the diameter. Nicole cautioned, "But can we be sure that this is always true?" In groups of four, the class set out to see. The students measured the diameters and circumferences of circles of various size. One group graphed the data (see the graph to the right) and found that it basically formed a straight line—suggesting a relationship.

Another group made up a table and came to the conclusion that the circumference was always about three times larger than the diameter.

diameter	1	2	3	4	5
circum.	3.1	6.5	9.3	12.5	16

After the class averaged all the available data together, it determined that the circumference of a circle was always about 3.1 times larger than its diameter. Using this information, they were then able to solve *A Bicycle Problem*.

Some students may suggest considering a simpler case:[8] Find a circle with a diameter of several inches. Measure its diameter and circumference. Then find another circle with a diameter 2 inches larger than the first. (This simulates pulling a string outward so that it is 1-inch from the first circle. In effect, pulling the string out 1-inch increases the diameter 1-inch on each side of the original circle, thus, increasing the diameter by 2-inches.) Measure the circumference of the new circle and determine how much it increased. Other students may counter that considering a smaller case will not help solve the *Strung-Out* problem because of the huge difference in dimensions. Prompt the class to consider how this counterclaim could be evaluated. (To see if there is a pattern, the class could, for example, repeat the simulation with two different circles, again one 2-inches larger in diameter than the other.)

☞ Try the experiment suggested above yourself. By how much did the circumference increase in each case? Can your results be applied to the *Strung-Out* problem?

One way to solve the *Strung-Out* problem is to have students consider the relationship between the circumference and the diameter of a circle. Activity II on pages 15-21 and 15-22 of Investigation 15.4 illustrates an experiment that can lead students to discover this relationship.

Measuring Circumferences. Note that efforts to solve the *Strung-Out* problem can lead students to consider how to measure the circumference of a circle. This issue can also be raised by posing a problem such as Problem 5.1:

■ **Problem 5.1: Big Wheel (◆ 4-8).** Have you ever seen a monster construction truck? These huge trucks are used to move enormous amounts of dirt and sand to build highways and airports. They have giant wheels bigger than a full-grown person—tires as tall as this room. (Note that a picture of one of these vehicles could help emphasize the enormity of the tires.) Suppose our class has been given the job of finding the distance around one of these monster tires. How can we do this?

Because a circle is a curve, it should be apparent that directly measuring its circumference with straightedge instruments such as a ruler, meter stick, or yard stick is not possible and that a more creative solution is needed. Encourage students to contemplate the problem in groups, discuss possibilities, devise solutions, and make a report of their findings. (With the *Big Wheel* problem above, the presence of a tire, even a bicycle tire, or some large circular item, might facilitate discussion.) Suggestions from students might include:

1. Wrap a string around the tire. Then, straighten the string and measure it.

2. Use a tape measure, one that bends. Wrap it around the tire.

3. Place a mark on the tire and mark where the tire touches the ground. Drive the truck forward and stop when the mark on the tire has gone all the way around. Measure how far the tire moved.

4. Cut the tire so that it can be straightened out into a line and measure it.

An Important Relationship. By carefully measuring the circumference and diameter of various circles and recording the data in a table such as the one below, students can discover an important relationship between the circumference and diameter of a circle.

diameter	circumference
3 cm	9.5 cm
6 cm	19 cm
10 cm	31 cm
15 cm	47 cm
20 cm	63 cm
7,926.41 mi	24,901.55 mi

An examination of such results should lead students to conclude that the circumference of a circle is always just over three times the diameter. By prompting students to consider how they could determine an even more accurate estimate of the relationship between circumference and diameter, a teacher can set the stage for a using functions and averages. Note that a more accurate estimate of this constant relationship can be computed by dividing the circumference of each circled measured by the diameter and averaging the quotients. The quotients for the data in the table above are 3.17, 3.17, 3.1, 3.13, 3.15, and 3.14 and the mean is 3.14—the approximate value of pi (π).[*] The approximate value will vary from group to group because, for instance, differences in the tautness of the string and the precision of measurements. Some teachers may wish to take this opportunity

to discuss and to contrast mathematical error and human error. It also provides an opportunity to discuss the value of averaging data.

The circumference of a circle, then, is *directly proportional* to its diameter. As diameters increase and decrease in measure, the circumference increases or decreases at the same rate, π. The constancy of the ratio c:d is one example of the order around us mathematics can help reveal.

The Circumference Formula. Summarizing the results of Activity II of Investigation 15.4 (pages 15-21 and 15-22) algebraically (in general form) yields the equation $c = \pi \cdot d$. Because the length of a diameter is equivalent to the sum of the lengths of two radii ($d = 2r$), the formula $c = \pi d$ is equivalent to the formula $c = 2\pi r$. Note that the equation $c = \pi \cdot d$ can be rewritten as $\pi = \frac{c}{d}$. *Pi* (π), then, is the ratio of a circle's circumference to its diameter.)

Application to the *Strung-Out* Problem. Once students understand the relationship between the circumference and diameter of a circle, they have a basis for solving the *Strung-Out* problem (see Activity I on page 15-21 of Investigation 15.4). If the ratio of the circumference to the diameter of a circle is about 3.14, then increasing the diameter of a circle 1 unit would increase the circumference 1 unit x 3.14. For example, if a circle has a diameter of 2 cm, then its circumference is approximately 2 cm x 3.14 or 6.28 cm. If the circle's diameter is increased to 3 cm, then its new circumference is 3 cm x 3.14 or 9.42 cm. Thus increasing the diameter of a circle by 1 cm increases its circumference by 9.42 cm - 6.28 cm or 3.14 cm.

If the string around the equator was pulled out 1 inch from the earth, the diameter of the new circle would increase by 2 inches. Thus, the circumference would increase by about 2 inches x

---

[*] The ratio c:d is not exactly 3.14 or $\frac{22}{7}$. These numbers are close approximations for c:d ratio that permit calculations accurate enough for most purposes. The exact value of π cannot be written as a fraction. As a decimal, π, does not terminate. There is no ending digit and these non-terminating digits do not repeat in a predictable cycle. The value of π is, therefore, an irrational number, usually the first irrational number that students encounter. Exploration of the chronological development of π may be of interest to curious students and can be found in books devoted to the history of mathematics.

3.14 or *6.28 inches*. The size of the diameter of the original circle does not matter in this problem. If the original circle had a diameter of 1 inch, 10 inches, 100 inches, 100 miles, or 24,000 miles, increasing the radius 1 inch would increase the circumference by 6.28 inches. An algebraic solution is illustrated in Box 15.3.

Box 15.3: An Algebraic Solution to the *Strung-Out* Problem

Original circle:	With radius increased by one unit:
radius = r	radius = r+1
circumference = 2πr	circumference = 2π(r+1)
	= 2πr + 2π

How much the circumference changed can be determined by taking the difference of the two circles (circumference of the larger circle minus the circumference of original circle): (2πr + 2π) - 2πr = 2π. Thus, increasing radius of a circle by 1 unit increases its circumference by 2π units (2 • 3.14...) or about 6.28 units.

The Area Formula. Once children understand the formula for the circumference of a circle they are ready for Activity III of Investigation 15.4 (page 15-22)—ready to reinvent the formula for the area of circle (see Box 15.4).

15•2•2 VOLUME

As with area formulas, instruction should be designed to encourage children to discover the formulas for volume themselves. See Investigation 15-5.

☞ Try Investigation 15-5 (page 15-28).

PARTING THOUGHTS

Elementary instruction should establish "a firm foundation in the basic underlying concepts and skills of measurement. Children need to understand the attribute to be measured as well as what it means to measure. Before they are capable of such understanding, they must first experience a variety of activities that focus on comparing objects directly, covering them with various units, and counting the units" (NCTM, 1989, p. 51). The investigative approach is an ideal way of teaching measurement skills and concepts. In this

---

🍎 Box 15.4: Devising the Formula for the Area of a Circle

Mr. Brandon's sixth-grade class was doing a science unit on dinosaurs. The class read that climatic changes brought about by the impact of a giant meteor may have helped cause their extinction. According to their science reference, the meteorite was thought to be 6 miles or 9.6 km across. The class read that the resulting crater was estimated to be about 30 miles across. To help the class understand the size of the crater, Mr. Brandon asked them to compare its area to the area of the city they lived in, a figure which they had previously looked up for a social studies lesson. Soin protested, "But we don't know how to calculate the area of circle."

Mr. Brandon responded, "Why not make up your own formula?" After a moment of stunned silence, he continued, "How did we derive the formula for the area of a parallelogram?"

"By changing it into a rectangle," offered Maryam.

"How can we change a circle into a rectangle?" asked Mr. Brandon.

"We could squash it," offered Romero.

"I suppose if you squashed it just right," commented Mr. Brandon. "Let's think about this more."

Dee Dee offered, "What if we cut up the circle? Would that help?"

The children experimented with cutting up circles in various ways. Suddenly, Jodi exclaimed, "I've got it. Cut the circle into eights and line them up head to toe. It kinda looks like a rectangle (see Figure A below)."

Figure A

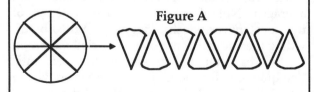

"It would look even more like a rectangle," added Fernando, "if you cut the circle up even more into sixteenths, thirty-secondths, and so on (see Figure B on the next page)."

Box 15.4 continued

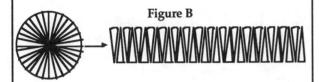

Figure B

"If we made enough cuts and lined up the wedges, they would—for all practical purposes—form a rectangle," noted Mr. Brandon. "So what's the area of our rectangle?

"Length times width," answered Alfonse.

"What's the length?" asked Mr. Brandon.

"The circumference of the circle," answered Anthony.

Asked why, Anthony accounced, "Because the circumference of the circle forms the top and bottom of the rectangles."

"So length would be *half* the circumference, because half is the top length and half is on the bottom length," corrected Alfonse.

"What's the width?" queried Mr. Brandon.

"That's the radius," answered several students in chorus.

"So," summarized Mr. Brandon writing $A = \frac{c}{2} \bullet r$ on the chalkboard, "the area is half the circumference times the radius. Earlier we find c is equal to what?"

Checking their notebooks, the students answered, "C equals the diameter times pi or twice the radius times *pi*."

Mr. Brandon wrote on the board: $c = 2r\pi$. "Putting $2r\pi$ in place of c in our formula we get: $A = \frac{c}{2} \bullet r = \frac{2r\pi}{2} \bullet r$

"Oh, the twos reduce and you get pi times the radius squared," noted several students. Mr. Brandon summarized the finding on the board:

$$\frac{2r\pi}{2} \bullet r = \pi r^2$$

way, measurement instruction can be integrated with other mathematical domains and other curriculum areas. "Children can see the usefulness of measurement if classroom experiences focus on measuring real objects, making objects of given sizes, and estimating measurements. Textbook experiences cannot substitute for activities that use measurement to answer questions about real problems" (NCTM, 1989, p. 53). "From their explorations, students should develop multiplicative procedures and formulas for determining measures" (NCTM, 1989), p. 116).

RESOURCES

SOME INSTRUCTIONAL RESOURCES

☎ **Children Learn to Measure,** edited by J. Glenn, ©1980 by Harper and Row of London. This resource includes 64 activities.

☎ **Clear Plastic Volume Set** manufactured by Learning Resources and **Power Solids** manufactured by Cuisenaire; both distributed by, for example, Dale Seymour. Both sets of manipulatives can be used to investigate volume intuitively (primary grades) or more formally (intermediate grades). The first includes 6 solids; the latter, 12.

☎ **Discover It!** by Manual Dominquez, and Mary Laycock. By using transparent figures and the 32-page guide, students can rediscover area and permiter formulas as well as the Pythagorean theorem and the Golden Ratio.

☎ **How to Teach Perimeter, Area, and Volume** by Verne Beaumont, Roberta Curtis, and James Smart, © 1986 by NCTM. This resource provides numerous teaching tips and activities for teaching perimeter, area, and volume. It includes a pattern for making a trundle wheel, a device for measuring linear distance, including the perimeter of circles.

☎ **Measurement in School Mathematics (1976 Yearbook),** edited by D. Nelson & R. Reys, © 1976 by NCTM.

A SAMPLE OF CHILDREN'S LITERATURE

Children's books involving *comparisons* include **Animal Superstars: Biggest, Strongest,**

⚠ Investigation 15.5: Exploring Volume

◆ Informal and formal investigations of volume ◆ K-8 ◆ Small groups of about four

The following discovery-learning activities encourage you to use concrete explorations and your existing knowledge to devise volume formulas. Discuss your findings with your group or class. (The *Clear Plastic Geo Volume Set* made by Learning Resources contains the forms shown below.

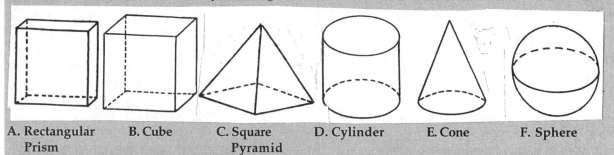

A. Rectangular   B. Cube   C. Square   D. Cylinder   E. Cone   F. Sphere
Prism   Pyramid

Activity I: Right Rectangular Prism. To help students discover the volume formula for rectangular solids, encourage them to fill the solid illustrated in Figure A with 1-inch cubes and to construct additional examples of rectangular solids with 1-inch cubes. (1) The solid illustrated by Figure A was how many cubes long, wide, high? What was its volume (the total number of cubes filling the solid)? (2) Build additional examples of rectangular solid consisting of a single layer of cubes (e.g., two rows of five cubes and three rows of four cubes). In each case what area was covered by the blocks? In each case what is the volume of the rectangular solid? (3) Now build multilayer examples. Construct a two layer and a five layer rectangular solid involving three rows of four blocks. In each case, what is the area covered by the blocks? What is the volume of the rectangular solid? Write two formulas that summarize how the volume of a rectangular solid can be determined.

Activity II: Cube. Fill the solid illustrated in Figure B with 1-inch cubes, and build a three layer rectangular solid involving three rows of three blocks each. (1) What is the volume of the cube? (2) How could the formula for right rectangular prism be simplified for cubes?

Activity III: Prisms. Consider the prism illustrated in Figure G to the right. Compare this prism to the right rectangular prism illustrated in Figure A. What do you suppose the formula for the volume of

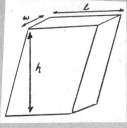

Figure G

Figure G is? Construct an informal proof to support your conjecture.

Activity IV: Square Pyramids (Cones with a Square Base). (1) Compare the square pyramid (the solid illustrated in Figure C) with the cube (Figure B). Note that the base and height of each is equal. What would you estimate the volume of the square pyramid to be? (2) Fill the square pyramid with plastic rice and empty it into the cube. About how much of the cube is filled? (3) Write a formula for the volume of the square pyramid. (4) Write a formula for the volume of a square pyramid in which the height is not equal to the base.

Activity VI: Volume of Cylinders. (1) Compare the cylinder (illustrated in Figure D) with the cube. Note that both have the same height. Is the volume of the cylinder grater than, less than, or equal to the cube? (2) If the volume of the cube can be thought of as area of the base times the height, what do you suppose the formula for the volume of a cylinder is?

Activity VII: Volume of Cones. (1) Fill the cone (Figure E) with plastic rice and put it into the cylinder. About how far did the rice fill the cylinder? (2) Devise a formula for the volume of a cone.

Activity V: Volume of Spheres. (1) Compare the sphere (illustrated by Figure F) with the cylinder. The volume of the sphere is about what? (2) Fill the sphere with plastic rice and empty it into the cylinder. About how much of the cylinder did it fill? (3) Write a formula for determining the volume of a sphere.

Fastest, Smartest by Russell Freedman (© 1981, Prentice-Hall), Book Cooks: Literature-Based Classroom Cooking by Marlene Beierle and Pat Ferraro (© 1992 by Creative Teaching Press), The Dinosaur is the Biggest Animal that Ever Lived, and Other Wrong Ideas You Thought Were True by Seymour Simon (© 1984, Lippincott), The Dinosaur Who Lived in My Backyard by B. G. Hennessy (© 1988, Viking Kestrel), I'm Too Small. You're Too Big by Judy Barrett (© 1981, Atheneum), Is It Larger? Is It Smaller by Tana Hoban (© 1985 by Greenwillow Books), and Much Bigger than Martin by Steven Kellogg (© 1976, Dial). Books on *linear measurement* include How Big is a Foot? by Rolf Myllar (© 1991, Dell), Length by Henry Pluckrose (© 1988, Franklin Wats), and Paul Bunyon: A Tall Tale by Steven Kellogg (© 1984, William Morrow). Children's books on *weight* include Weighing and Balancing by Jane Jonas Srivastava (© 1974, Thomas Y. Crowell) and Who Sank the Boat? by Pamela Allen (© 1983, Coward, McCann, and Geoghegan). Two of the many children's books on *time* are Time for Horatio by Penelope Paine and Waiting for Sunday by Carol Blackburn (© 1991, Scholastic). Several more books are described below:

How Little and How Much: A Book About Scales by Franklyn M. Branley, © 1976 by Thomas Y. Crowell, Co. This book is geared to second- and third-graders. It introduces the idea of scales and how they help us measure. It begins by discussing where a reader would put ice cream on a 1 to 10 scale and then asks, "Does a rating of 5 mean the same thing to everyone?" This leads to a discussion about imprecise scales and the need for making comparisons and using standard units. For example, preference for ice cream can be compared to a preference for cake. Besides desserts, the book suggests students construct "Like Scales" for months, pets, and school subjects.

Standard units are introduced by discussing tallness. Although the height of a child could be compared to other items (e.g., taller than a cat, but not as tall as the ceiling), a more precise way to gauge height is to use a unit. Using a (nonstandard) unit of height, we can now specify that a child about 5 feet tall about is eight pencils tall. This book goes on to discuss standard units—both in English and metric systems.

Long, Short, High, Low, Thin, Wide by James T. Fey, © 1971 by Thomas Y. Crowell, Co. This book is geared to primary-level students. It begins with nonstandard units and touches on the issue of choosing an appropriately-sized unit. It uses a realistic example to explain the need for standard units. A man wants a house built that is 10 paces long by 20 paces wide. Unfortunately, the carpenter has shorter legs than the man. The book introduces both the English and metric systems. It provides a brief but interesting historical account of the development of some standard units of measurement.

Importantly, this book begins with questions that children may have asked themselves or that may be important to them (e.g., from page 1, "Have you ever wondered how tall am I? How high is the ceiling in my house?"). It goes on to note that we can answer questions about how tall, short, long, high, or wide by measuring and suggests comparing an item to other items (e.g., a pencil is longer than a thumb but not as long as a belt). The book goes on to introduce more exact measurement with nonstandard units (e.g., compare length to a familiar object such as a toothpick).

The book pictures how to position a unit at the end of an item and implies that it is important to measure from end to end. However, a teacher may wish to help students understand explicitly why this is done.

The book suggests an interesting activity. Have children spread their fingers out on a piece of paper and trace around them with a crayon. Then encourage them to measure the span of their hand from thumb to little finger with various nonstandard units such as toothpicks and paper clips. More advanced students can measure their handspan using standard units.

Measure with Metric by Franklyn M. Branley, © 1975, Thomas Y. Crowell and Metric Measurement by June Behrens, © 1975 by Children's Press. The latter introduces metric measures for length, weight, volume, and temperature. It uses familiar, everyday examples to help readers create a mental image of metric units. For example, a meter is compared to the length of a softball bat, a gram to the weight of a paperclip, and a liter to the volume of four tall glasses of milk. In addition to considering different attributes, the book also raises the issues of choosing an appropriate unit. For example, it introduces kilometers as a way of measuring long distances (e.g., the distance from home to school) and centimeters as a way of measuring things that are not as long as a meter.

🖙 **Science Experiences Measuring** by Jeanne Bendick © 1971 by Franklin Watts, Inc.) addresses basic measuring concepts, includes experiments, compares the English and metric systems, and touches on estimating measurements.

TIPS ON USING TECHNOLOGY

Computers

Some Internet web pages that can serve as references on measurement include "Common Equivalent Weights and Measures" (http://www.cchem.berkeley.edu/ChemResources/Weights-n-Measures/weights-n-measures.html) and "Numbers and Units" (http://www.math-science.sfasu.edu/physics101/NUMBERS&UNITS.html). The following web site might be helpful for an activity that involve the estimation of distances or a project that entails planning a trip around the world: "How Far Is It?" (http://www.indo.com/distance).

🖥 **Geo-Logo** by Douglas H. Clements and Julie S. Meredith, © 1994 by Logo Computer Systems. This modified Logo program can serve as a transition between physical experiences, such as moving and turning, and abstract mathematics including the measurement of lengths and angles with standard units (Battista & Clements, 1990). For example, after walking out paths themselves, children can be encouraged to view the Logo "turtle's actions as ones they . . . could perform . . . . In so doing, they are performing a mental action—an internalized version of their own physical movements" (Battista & Clements, 1988). Moreover, because Logo requires children explicitly and precisely formulate their intuitive concepts, it can help them internalize geometric ideas in a more abstract form. For example, children's intuitive idea of a straight line may be redefined more explicitly as a

path with no turns (Battista & Clements, 1988) and their intuitive idea of a "square angle" may be redefined more precisely as a turn of 90°. In fact, after Logo training, children were more likely to define angle dynamically as a turn rather intuitively (e.g., "Like a line that goes on a slant or corner") (Clements & Battista, 1989).

Logo can help children construct more precise, abstract, and coherent geometric concepts because it actively involves them in manipulating and exploring geometric ideas such as moving a distance or turning. It can help even young children construct measurement concepts, such as the length of a path is the sum of the lengths of its individual segments or the number of units varies inversely with the size of units (Campbell, Fein, & Schwartz, 1991). At the same time, Logo provides an opportunity to *do* mathematics—make, test, evaluate, and redefine conjectures.

Consider the task of constructing a rectangle before children have devised a routine for this shape (a set procedure for drawing rectangles). For example, after drawing a base of 50 units and a side of 30 units, children must figure out how long to draw the third side. Although it is obvious to adults that the third side should be 50 units, for primary-age children the solution to this missing-length problem may not be apparent. Young children may have to experiment, perhaps, trying the command *forward 40* first. Because of the immediate feedback of the display, they can see *for themselves* that the line is shorter than the base. They may then explicitly recognize that that third side must have the same length measurement (50 units) as the base and change their command to *forward 50* (Clements, Battista, Sarama, Swaminathan, & McMillen, 1997).

By constructing geometric forms such as rectangles, children will also have to estimate the amount of turn and experiment with different degrees of turn. Playing Logo games such as **Hit the Spot** can further involve children in predicting distances and angles and revising their commands (Battista & Clements, 1990). (The game involves placing a sticker on the screen and challenging players to reach this point using the fewest number of commands possible.)

16 THE TRANSITION FROM ARITHMETIC TO ALGEBRA: PREALGEBRA AND FUNCTIONS

xxxxxxxxxxxxxxxxxxxxxxxxxxxxxxx **MATH CORNER** xxxxxxxxxxxxxxxxxxxxxxxxxxxxxxx

■ **Botched Travel Arrangements** (◆ 7-8[+]). You are going on a ship cruise. Unfortunately, your plane was delayed and, by the time you arrived dockside, the ship had left. You charter a helicopter to catch up with your ship. If the ship left five hours ago and sailed at a speed of 22 mph and your helicopter can fly at 90 mph, how many hours will it take you to catch up with the ship? Illustrate how the problem can be solved using (a) arithmetic, (b) a graph, and (c) algebra. (Source: Chiu, 1996.)

nnnnnnnnnnnnnnnnnnnnnnnnnnnnnnnnnnnnnnnnnnnnnnnnnnnnnnnnnnnnnnnnnnnnnnnnnnnnnnnnnnnnnnnnnnnnnnnnnnnnnnnnnn

A teacher can use the bulletin-board above to underscore the connections between algebra and students' familiar knowledge of arithmetic and between algebraic and graphic representations. It may also help them see that mathematics in general and algebra in particular are useful in solving a variety of everyday problems.

☞ Try solving *Botched Travel Arrangements*.

THIS CHAPTER

*A*fter school, Miss Brill went over to Ms. Socrates' class to plan the spring field-day activities. She noticed the student work scrawled on the chalkboard earlier. There were letters among those numbers. A long-hidden memory stirred deep inside Miss Brill's brain. "That looks like algebra," she blurted. "You can't possibly be doing algebra in the elementary school. I took algebra in high school and didn't understand a thing about it. It was even more incomprehensible than arithmetic."

"Traditionally," Ms. Socrates commented, "algebra has been introduced in the first year of high school as a new topic with its own set of rules—utterly unrelated to the arithmetic taught the first nine years of school. Instruction immediately jumped into using letters and focused on how to manipulate algebraic symbols. Students memorized how to solve various types of equations and word problems by rote. To make a bad situation worse, instruction frequently did not point out the purposes of algebra or the algebraic manipulations."

"Although some students find algebra exhilarating," continued Ms. Socrates, "too many others find it to be the educational equivalent of an avalanche. They see little or no connection between algebra and what they already know. Many react to the flurry of new incomprehensible rules for manipulating expressions with letters by mentally shutting down. Numerous overwhelmed victims tell tales in their adulthood of how they had done all right in mathematics until they met the horrid algebra. For many students, the leap of conceptual thinking is too sudden and too great. However, algebra need not be foreign, mysterious, and senseless—so much gibberish."

Prealgebra can provide a bridge between arithmetic and algebra. It can *give students the opportunity to informally construct an understanding of algebraic concepts and procedures by building on their existing knowledge of arithmetic and geometry* (Kieran & Chalouh, 1993). In Unit 16•1, we focus on prealgebra and initial algebra instruction.

Many mathematics educators believe that functions should serve as "the primary concept around which algebra should be developed" (NCTM, 1992, p. 6). A function is merely a special kind of relationship. In chapter 2, we encountered functions in the form of *In-Out Machines*. Proportional situations studied in chapter 12 are one type of function. A child who knows that one quarter is needed to buy a pack of gum, two quarters (50¢) are needed to buy two packs, and so forth is informally thinking in terms of a function. In Unit 16•2, we examine functions.

WHAT THE NCTM *STANDARDS* SAY

Grades K-8

The standards below were written for grades 5-8 (NCTM, 1989). However, except for the use of formal methods, all the aims below also apply to the K-4 level, albeit at a basic and an intuitive level (see NCTM, 1992).

Prealgebra and Algebra. "The mathematics curriculum should include exploration of algebraic concepts and processes so that students can:

◆ understand the concepts of variable, expression, and equation;

◆ represent situations and number patterns with tables, graphs, verbal rules, and equations and explore the interrelationships of these representations;

◆ analyze tables and graphs to identify properties and relationships;

◆ develop confidence in solving linear equations using concrete, informal, and formal methods;

◆ apply algebraic methods to solve a variety of real-world and mathematical problems" (p. 102)

Patterns and Functions. The mathematics curriculum should include explorations of patterns and functions so that students can, in part:

◆ "describe and represent relationships with tables, graphs, and rules;

◆ analyze functional relationships to explain how a change in one quantity results in a change in another;

◆ use . . . functions to represent and solve problems" (p. 98).

16•1 PREALGEBRA AND ALGEBRA

Figure 16.1: Algebra Confuses Many Students

Other than to fill some course requirement, many students have no idea why they study algebra. Moreover, because their instruction focus on memorizing mechanics (fostering routine expertise), many—such as Paige in Figure 16.1—do not have a good algebraic sense (an intuitive feel for what algebraic symbols and manipulations represent). To foster a positive disposition toward algebra and adaptive expertise, it is essential that students understand why algebra is important and what algebraic symbols and manipulations really mean. In Subunit 16•1•1, we discuss the role of algebra in mathematics and the role of prealgebra as a way of connecting algebra to what children already know. In Subunits 16•1•2 and 16•1•3, we focus on two crucial aspects of the conceptual foundation for understanding algebraic symbols and manipulations: (a) using letters to represent numbers (the concept of variables) and (b) reflecting on and representing solution processes (the symbolization of method). In Subunit 16•1•4, we consider how children can learn to solve algebraic equations meaningfully.

16•1•1 THE ROLE OF ALGEBRA

Mathematics: An Invaluable Tool

Algebra is a valuable tool because it can make communicating mathematical ideas and solving mathematical problems easier.

☞ Try Investigation 16.1 (pages 16-4 to 16-6) and then continue.

Communicating Ideas. If mathematics can be viewed as a language, then algebra can be viewed as the *shorthand* of mathematics (Sawyer, 1971). Many mathematical ideas would be long and complicated when expressed in everyday language. Algebraic expressions (e.g., 2 x □ + 1 or $2x + 1$) and algebraic equations (e.g., 2 x □ + 1 = 8 or $2x + 1 = 8$) allow us to express these ideas efficiently in a compact form. (Note that an *algebraic expression does not involve an equal sign, whereas as algebraic equation does*. In effect, an algebraic equation consists of equivalent algebraic expressions.) Algebra, then, can serve as a tool for *concisely* making general statements and offering explanations.

• **A shorthand for making general statements.** As Problems 1 and 2 on page 16-4 of Investigation 16.1 illustrate, algebra allows us to summarize concisely arithmetic and other mathematical relationships we discover in an open-ended way. This makes giving mathematical directions easier than writing out instructions in words. For example, the fact that the circumference of a circle is about 3.14 times as large as its diameter can be capsulized as the algebraic equation C = 3.14 x d or C = πd—a formula that can be used to determine the circumference for *any* circle given its diameter or the diameter of any circle given its circumference.

• **A shorthand for making explanations.** As Problems 3 and 4 on page 16-5 of Investigation 16.1 illustrate, algebra also provides a convenient way of explaining mathematical processes and, thus, proving why things work out as they do. Although it may seem mysterious that the an-

swer to Problem 4, for instance, always comes out five, the reason is quite simple. Drawing a picture can help (see Frame A of Figure 16.2 on page 16-7). The symbolic representation (Frame B of Figure 16.2) is an intermediate step to using an algebraic representation (Frame C of Figure 16.2). Although the pictorial representation in Frame A of Figure 16.2 illustrates how the magic trick works with the *specific* initial choice of three, the symbolic and algebraic representations illustrate concisely why it works for *any* initial choice. Note that, for any number chosen, Step 5 undoes what happens to the number in Step 3 and Step 6 undoes Step 1. What is left is the result of Steps 2 to 5: adding 8, doubling it (which produces 16), subtracting 6 (which leaves 10) and dividing by 2 (which reduces 10 to 5).

Solving Problems. The value of algebra goes beyond recording and communicating mathematical ideas in a general and abbreviated form. Algebra can also be a useful tool in solving problems.

• **A relatively efficient means of solving many problems.** Algebra makes solving many problems easier. Indeed, without it, some problems would be difficult or impractical to solve. For example, although Problem 5 on page 16-6 of Investigation 16.1 can be solved informally in a number of ways (see Frames A, B, and C in Figure 16.3 on page 16-8), it can be solved very quickly by using algebra (see Frame D in Figure 16.3). Moreover, imagine trying to solve Problems 6 and 7 on page 16-6 of Investigation 16.1 without algebra.

• **A means for modeling situations, particularly dynamic situations.** Algebra is an invaluable tool for representing and solving many complex real-world problems (see, e.g., Problem 8 on page 16-6 of Investigation 6.1). Indeed, it has been characterized as "the study relationships among . . . changing quantities" (Heid and others, 1995, p. 1). For example, a publisher can create an algebraic equation to predict the total cost of producing a book of a given length, type of binding, number of figures, and so forth. The rules of algebra can then be applied to manipulate the information, and the results can provide a better understanding of the situation (NCTM, 1992). For example, the publisher may recognize that there is leeway to increase the number of figures included in a book. (Continued on page 16-7.)

ᴳ Investigation 16.1: Some Problems to Consider

◆ Problem solving + algebra ◆ 2-8 ◆ Small groups of four + class discussion

Why is algebra important? With your group, consider the following problems. Discuss your solutions with your class.

■ **Problem 1: Painted Cubes**[†] (◆ 7-8). To investigate cubic numbers and surface area, Mr. Wantell showed his class 1-inch cube blocks and asked them to imagine a 30-inch x 30-inch x 30-inch cube built from such blocks. (a) How many 1-inch cube blocks would it take to build this large cube? (b) If the surface of the large cube was painted, how many blocks would be painted on three faces, two faces, one face, no faces? (✦ Simplify the problem and look for a pattern.)

■ **Problem 2: Temperature Conversions** (◆ 5-8). As part of a global KIDLINK project (http://www.kidlink.org), an eighth-grade class decided to examine soil temperature at various depths over the course of a year. Miss Carson saw this as an opportunity to do some real mathematics, as well as explore the topics of soil science and temperature. She pointed out that, as most people in the world use the Celsius scale, the class needed to change their Fahrenheit readings to Celsius readings. Reporting the results on the World Wide Web, then, created a real need to use the formula for converting Fahrenheit readings to Celsius readings. Do you recall this conversion formula?

Miss Carson wanted her students to construct the formulas for themselves. She had her class collect their data in °F and then proposed to record their results in both °F and °C. The class wondered how this could be done. Alexi proposed examining a thermometer with both °F and °C, but students found the two scales did not match up. Although they could estimate the Celsius reading for a Fahrenheit reading, Miss Carson insisted on a more accurate conversion. She suggested starting with what they knew about the two scales. After some discussion, the teacher listed on the chalkboard the following known facts about the Fahrenheit and Celsius scales:

	°F	°C
freezing point of water	32°	0°
boiling point of water	212°	100°

1. "Use these facts and your knowledge of arithmetic to convert your Fahrenheit readings to Celsius readings," prompted Miss Carson. With your group, try to find the Celsius equivalent for the following temperatures: (a) 50°F, (b) 77°F, (c) 95°F. (↬ **Teaching Tips.** Questions 2 to 11 that follow stem from one combined seventh-eighth-grade class's efforts to answer Question 1 and illustrate how inquiry into this question might proceed. In an open-ended exploration of Question 1, the following questions could serve as probes as needed. If a more structured environment is desired, a teacher could pose Question 2 to 11 in turn.)

2. Alison suggested subtracting 32° from a Fahrenheit reading and using the difference as the Celsius reading (e.g., 50°F - 32°C = 18°C). Miss Carson asked her class if Alison's method and answer of 18°C made sense. (a) What is the rationale for Alison's method? (b) Does her answer make sense?

3. When her class intuitively concluded that Alison's answer seemed right, Miss Carson asked for informal proof. How could you informally prove that Alison's answer made sense or not?

4. To evaluate Alison's answer, the class tried several additional examples including 200°F. (a) Should the equivalent Celsius reading for 200°F be above, below, or equal to 100°C? (b) Why? (c) What answer do you get when you apply Alison's method? (d) Does the answer you obtained using qualitative and deductive reasoning agree with the answer obtained with Alison's method?

[†] Source: Page 99 of *Curriculum and Evaluation Standards for School Mathematics*, © 1989 by the National Council of Teachers of Mathematics.

Investigation 16.1 continued

5. Miss Carson hinted that it might be helpful to use what they studied earlier. Alexi intuitively suggested proportions. Arianne set up the proportion $\frac{32°F}{50°F} = \frac{0°C}{x}$. What answer does this method produce and does it make sense?

6. After trying to convert Fahrenheit readings to Celsius using a proportion with 0°C with one term, the class realized this method would always result in the nonsensical answer of 0°C. They tried setting up the proportion differently. How would you set it up?

7. Virginia tried to solve the problem by using the boiling points of water instead of its freezing points. She suggested setting up the proportion as $\frac{50}{212} = \frac{x}{100}$. Does this method work? That is, is the answer sensible or not?

8. Using Virginia's equation, the class agreed that 50°F equals 23°C. Asked if an answer of 23°C made sense, Arianne responded, "Kinda; yeah." How could you informally prove or disprove that the answer made sense?

9. Miss Carson asked her class where 50°F stood relative to the reference points 32°F and 212°F. This led to a discussion of what was halfway. One student proposed 212 ÷ 2 = 106°F; another, 180 ÷ 2 = 90°F; a third, (180 ÷ 2) + 32 = 122°F. Which, if any, is correct and why?

10. After determining that 50°F was less than a half of half the way between the two Fahrenheit reference points, the class turned it's attention to where 23°C stood in relationship to the Celsius reference points 0°C and 100°C. (a) About where does 23°C stand? (b) Your answer to Question 10a leads to what conclusion about Virginia's method and answer?

11. After using arithmetic to convert several Fahrenheit readings to Celsius readings, summarize your method as a formula—that is, write an equation for changing *any* Fahrenheit reading into a Celsius reading.

12. ✦ **Extension:** (a) Using arithmetic and the Fahrenheit-Celsius equivalents you know, convert 20°C and 35°C to Fahrenheit readings. (b) Summarize your procedure as an algebraic equation (formula for converting any Celsius reading into a Fahrenheit reading).

■ **Problem 3: A Curious Pattern**[†] (✦ 6-8). Write down three consecutive integers, square the middle number, and then subtract the product of the other two numbers from this square. Compare your results with those of your group or class. Use algebra to illustrate why your results hold true for *any* three consecutive numbers.

■ **Problem 4: A "Magic Trick"** (✦ 6-8). Miss Brill had on a black rain coat again. The class knew it was time once again for Miss Magic. Sure enough, Miss Brill announced that she was going to perform a new, truly mind-boggling trick. The teacher gave the following set of instructions:

Step 1:   Write a number—any number—on a piece of paper.
Step 2:   Add eight to the number.
Step 3:   Double the sum.
Step 4:   Subtract 6.
Step 5:   Divide by two.
Step 6:   Subtract the number chosen in Step 1.

[†] Based on a problem on page 184 in "Prealgebra: The Transition from Arithmetic to Algebra" by C. Kieran & L. Chalouh. In *Research Ideas for the Classroom: Middle Grades Mathematics*, edited by D. T. Owens and © 1993 by the National Council of Teachers of Mathematics.

Investigation 16.1 continued

Miss Brill then instructed each group to record its result, turn the paper over, and write the chosen number on the back. "From the number you chose, Miss Magic will be able to predict your group's result," boasted Miss Brill. When the first group finished, Miss Brill asked what number they chose. After the group indicated "Three," Miss Brill acted as if she was really straining her brain. She then quietly whispered to them that their result was *five*. The group was amazed that she was correct. Several more groups finished. One group had chosen 1000; another, 0; and yet another, -12. For each, Miss Brill correctly predicted the results. What is the outcome in each case and how did Miss Brill know it?

■ **Problem 5: Chickens and Pigs** (◆ 2-8). Farmer Hannibal loaded 18 animals into a covered van. Some were chickens, and some were pigs. If 50 legs were visible under the cover, how many chickens and how many pigs did Hannibal have in the van?

■ **Problem 6: Plain and Sugar-Coated Donuts** (◆ 7-8). On Monday, Pia ordered three plain doughnuts and two sugar-coated doughnuts. Her bill came to $2.95. On Tuesday, she bought seven plain doughnuts and five sugar-coated doughnuts. Her bill was $7.10. How much did Pia pay for each type doughnut?

■ **Problem 7: If Dimes Were Quarters** (◆ 7-8). Gary had 20 coins consisting of dimes and quarters. If his dimes were quarters and his quarters were dimes, he'd have 90¢ more. How many dimes and quarters did Gary have?

■ **Problem 8: Car-Resale Value** (◆ 8). Mrs. Flickinger knew that many of her eighth graders were already looking forward to learning how to drive and to buying their own cars. So she posed the following problem[1]:

A Fantasy Come True: Shopping for a New Car. Your grandparents are so proud of your achievements in school, they have offered to buy you a new car. Because they are very careful with their money, they ask you justify your selection of a car. What factors should you consider in buying a new car?

Working in groups of four, Mrs. Flickinger's students come up with various factors. In a class discussion, each group justified and defended its choices. The class finally agreed on 10 key factors including the resale value of the car. Mrs. Flickinger then had the groups use the internet to collect information on the 10 key factors for each of the cars the group was considering. The following table indicates the retail and resale prices of one of the cars considered:

Model year	1996	1995	1994	1993	1992	1991	1990	1989	1988	1987
Age of car (in years)	0	1	2	3	4	5	6	7	8	10
Retail/resale value	20,795	17,825	16,050	13,950	12,500	11,000	9,200	7,900	6,800	5,100

Mrs. Flickinger used these data to pose the question, "What if your grandparents expected you to keep your car for 12 years? What would be the resale value of your car then?

1. (a) How would you try to answer Mrs. Flickinger's question above? (b) What is your answer to the question? (c) Does it agree with that of other students or groups?

2. Is the relationship between age and value linear, curvilinear, or something else?

3. ◆ **Extension:** (a) What other factors should you consider in buying a new car? (b) Use the Internet to collect data on a factor and use it to compare several car models.

↬ **Teaching Tip.** Mrs. Flickinger had her class key the age and value data above into a graphing calculator and used it to generate a graph and an algebraic equation, both of which could be used to predict the resale value for any given age.

Figure 16.2: Demystifying a Magic Trick (Problem 5 on Page 16-6 of Investigation 16.1)

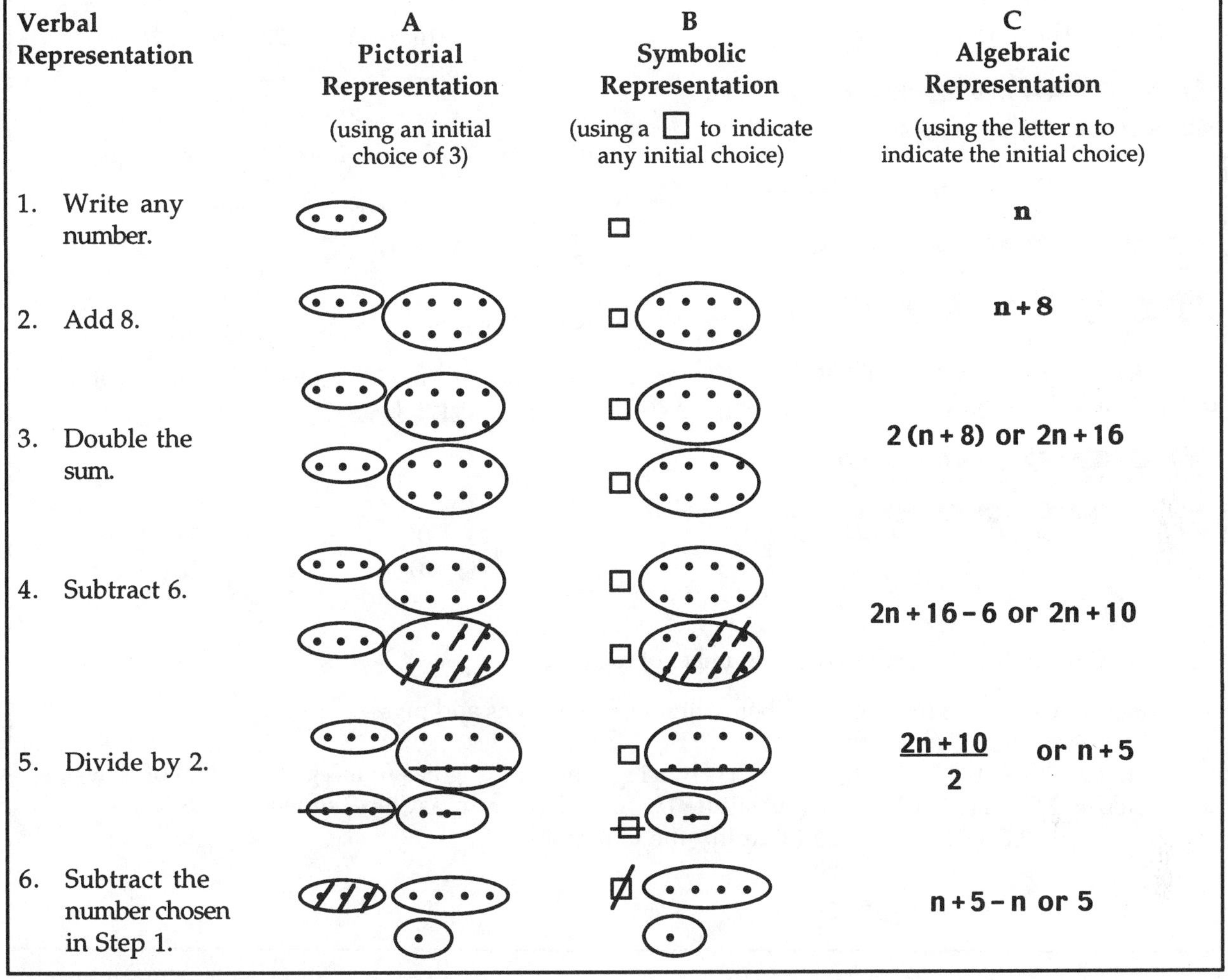

Verbal Representation	A Pictorial Representation (using an initial choice of 3)	B Symbolic Representation (using a ☐ to indicate any initial choice)	C Algebraic Representation (using the letter n to indicate the initial choice)
1. Write any number.			n
2. Add 8.			$n + 8$
3. Double the sum.			$2(n + 8)$ or $2n + 16$
4. Subtract 6.			$2n + 16 - 6$ or $2n + 10$
5. Divide by 2.			$\dfrac{2n + 10}{2}$ or $n + 5$
6. Subtract the number chosen in Step 1.			$n + 5 - n$ or 5

Teaching: Prealgebra and Algebra Instruction

To foster meaningful learning, when and how algebra is taught needs to be changed.

Algebra's Place in the Elementary Curriculum. *When should children begin to prepare for algebra?*

• **Conceptual bases.** To prepare students to understand algebra, its conceptual basis needs to be laid throughout the elementary grades (NCTM, 1992). This can include the following topics discussed earlier in this guide:

- identifying, continuing, describing, generalizing, and generating patterns (chapter 2);
- recognizing the connections among multiple representations such as natural language, concrete models, and written symbols and translating between them (e.g., chapters 3 to 6 and 9 to 15);
- solving missing-addend or factor problems (chapter 5);
- understanding arithmetic properties such as commutativity (chapter 5);
- understanding the relational meaning of the equals sign (chapter 5);
- creating algorithms to perform a particular task (chapters 5, 6, 10, and 11);
- number theory topics such as primes and factors, divisibility, exponents and roots, and integers (chapter 8);
- understanding ratios such as scales and rates (chapter 12); and
- interpreting and plotting graphs and using graphs to make predictions (chapter 13);
- devising formulas to short-cut the measurement of area and volume (chapter 15).

Figure 16.3: Solutions to *Pigs and Chickens* (Problem 5 on Page 16-6 of Investigation 16.1)

A. Draw a Picture

Step 1: There are 18 animals.

Step 2: All have at least two legs.

Step 3: That's 36 legs. I'll add pairs of legs until I have 50.

D. Algebra

Let C = number of chickens and P = number of pigs

Step 1: C + P = 18 (the total number of animals—chickens and pigs—is 18.)
Step 2: P = 18 - C (Solve for P.)
Step 3: 2C + 4P = 50 (Each chicken has two legs and each pig has four legs for a total of 50 legs.)
Step 4: 2C + 4 (18 - C) = 50 (Substitute 18 - C for P because, as Step 2 shows, P = 18 - C.)

$$2C + 72 - 4C = 50 \text{ (Simplify the expression.)}$$
$$72 - 2C = 50$$
$$-2C = -22$$
$$C = 11$$

B. Try and Adjust

10 chickens → 20 legs
8 pigs → 32 legs
52 legs

Fifty-two is too many; I need two fewer legs.

11 chickens → 22 legs
7 pigs → 28 legs
50 legs

C. Use a Table

# of Chickens	# of Chicken Legs	# of Pigs	# of Pig Legs	Total # of Legs
1	2	17	68	70
.	.	.	.	.
.	.	.	.	.
9	18	9	36	54
10	20	8	32	52
11	22	7	28	50

• **Algebra content.** Moreover, some algebra content that has traditionally been taught in the upper grades, such as using letters, should be explored in the elementary grades (NCTM, 1992). By reinforcing and building on these algebraic concepts throughout their education, children will have a solid basis for understanding and applying algebra later. This is discussed further in Subunits 16•1•2 to 16•1•4.

The Nature of Instruction. How algebra is taught also needs to change.

↪ **Ideally, algebra should arise as a natural by-product of children's exploration of arithmetic and geometry** (Peck & Jencks, 1988). Even at the primary-level, ALGEBRA CAN BE INTRODUCED AS A SHORTHAND FOR SUMMARIZING A PROBLEM SITUATION (see, e.g., Investigation 16.2 on the next page) OR A DISCOVERED RELATIONSHIP. For example, create a need for students to convert Fahrenheit temperatures (°F) to Celsius tempera-

tures (°C) and encourage them to use what they know (e.g., 32° F = 0° C, 212° F = 100° C, and arithmetic) to make the conversions (see Problem 2 on pages 16-4 and 16-5 of Investigation 16.1). After using arithmetic to make a number of conversions, ask students to use letters to summarize their arithmetic solution procedure for any given Fahrenheit reading. By deriving the algebraic equation, $C = \frac{5}{9}(F - 32)$ themselves, students should recognize that formulas have a common sense basis and that algebra makes such shorthand statements possible.

☞ Consider Investigation 16.2 (page 16-9).

↪ **Prealgebra and algebra instruction should be holistic** (NCTM, 1992). For example, Problem 2 (*Temperature Conversions*) of Investigation 16.1 encountered earlier involves proportions, whole-number and fraction arithmetic, and decimals as well as algebra. (Continued on page 16-10.)

☞ Investigation 16.2: A Science Problem

◆ Problem solving + algebra + integer addition + fractions
◆ 5-8 ◆ Whole class or small groups

Ideally, algebra instruction would evolve from real problems confronting a class. The problem below grew out of a science lesson and involved several mathematical ideas, including the use of letters to represent unknowns. To get a sense of how a purposeful prealgebra lesson might evolve, try the following investigation yourself, preferably with the aid of your group. Discuss your findings with your group or class.

Before posing the following problem, the class should understand that an atom is composed of protons, neutrons, and electrons. While all electrons appear to be similar and, thus, are probably elementary particles (not themselves composed of smaller components), the same does not appear to be true for protons and neutrons. These latter atomic components appear to have their own components called *up quarks* and *down quarks*.

■ **Quark Charges.** A proton has a net charge of +1 and consists of two up quarks and a down quark; a neutron has a net charge of 0 and consists of one up quark and two down quarks. What charge must up quarks have? What charge must down quarks have?

1. If this problem was read to a class, how could students use algebra as a shorthand to summarize the information?

2. Try solving the problem above by yourself or with your group. Share your strategy and solution with your group or class.

3. (a) In each of the following cases, describe how the student may have arrived at the answer he or she did. (b) Explain how a teacher could help these students to evaluate the correctness of their answers for themselves.

   Case I. One fifth-grade student quickly concluded that each up quark had a single positive charge (+1) and each down quark had a single negative charge (-1).

   Case II. Alison was the first to recognize that a fractional charge might be needed. She asked, "Would it work this way? If 2D [canceled] 1U, then D would have to be $-\frac{1}{2}$?"

   Case III. After recognizing that D could not be $-\frac{1}{2}$, Alison suggested, "What if 3D [canceled] 1U, D would equal $-\frac{1}{3}$ and U would equal +1?"

4. After recognizing that her answer of $D = -\frac{1}{2}$ and $U = +1$ would fit the equation $1U + 2D = 0$ but not the equation $2U + D = +1$, Alison asked, "Well one must be a whole, no?" To solve the equation $1U + 2D = 0$, is it possible for the up quark to have a whole charge (a charge of +1)? Why or why not? What knowledge of fractions is relevant here?

5. Fifth graders finally solved the problem using an informal try-and-adjust substitution strategy. How could algebra be used to solve the problem *Quark Charges* efficiently?

☞ **Select problems to illustrate the power of algebra.** To help students see the connection between their existing knowledge and algebra and to help them appreciate the value of algebra, begin with problems that they can solve using their arithmetic knowledge but that could be solved more easily by algebra (e.g., Problem 5 on page 16-6 of Investigation 16.1). Later, introduce problems that would be difficult to solve with arithmetic (e.g., Problems 6 and 7 on page 16-6 of Investigation 16.1) (NCTM, 1992). To underscore the power of algebra, a teacher should discuss with children how using algebra makes solving problems easier or feasible.

16•1•2 THE CONCEPT OF VARIABLES

Mathematics: Uses of Letters

Many students think of letters as representing a *specific unknown*. In fact, letters are used in mathematics in various ways, including representing quantities that change (Heid et al., 1995). To construct an explicit understanding of variables, see Probe 16.1.

☞ Consider Probe 16.1 (page 16-11).

Learning: Children's Understanding of Variables

Uses of Variables. Children typically have an incomplete understanding of how letters can be used in mathematics (e.g., Booth, 1988; Chalouh & Herscovics, 1988). Children commonly interpret a letter as representing a specific number (as a name for a particular number). For example, some middle-school students conclude that $7w + 22 = 109$ and $7n + 22 = 109$ have different solutions—that w and n represent different numbers (Wagner, 1981).

Children's incomplete understanding of variables is at least partly due to the limited examples of variables used in the elementary grades. In the primary grades, they see expressions such as $52 = 5$ tens __ ones in which the unknown (blank or box) has a specific value. Elementary-level students also see boxes and letters used to represent a specific unknown (e.g., $7 + \square = 10$ or $7 + A = 10$). They rarely see cases where letters are used as general unknowns or pattern generalizers—used to represent a given. Probably the most difficult aspect of a concept of variables for chil-

dren to understand is using letters to represent varying values.

Unconnected Knowledge. For many students, algebraic equations such as $5 + a = 12$ are merely abstract symbols with little or no connection to reality. Asked what the letter in $5 + a = 12$ meant, only some seventh graders responded with an interpretation faithful to the equation—*something added to five to make twelve* (Kieran, 1981). A more typical response described the process of solving for a—twelve minus five is seven.

Teaching: Fostering an Understanding of Variables

According to the NCTM (1989, p. 103) *Curriculum Standards*, "students need to be able to use variables in many different ways." Some examples of how to purposefully introduce students to various types of variables are discussed below.

Name for a Particular Number. After her class had concluded that the a circle's circumference is always about 3.1 times larger than its diameter (see Box 15.2 on pages 15-23 and 15-24 or Activity II of Investigation 15.4 on page 15-21), Mrs. Stoffel pointed out that this constant relationship between a circle's diameter and circumference was called *pi* and symbolically represented by the variable π. She had her students find and press the π key on their *TI Math Explorer* calculators, a process that indicated that π was equal to 3.1415927....

Representing a Specific Unknown. To prompt his second graders to use letters as place holders, Mr. Sorrentino read them missing-addend problems such as Problem 16.1 below.

■ **Problem 16.1: Missing Doggie Bones (♦ 1-4).** For a picnic, Mary packed 10 doggie bones—half were for Ruffus; half, for Bruno the Beagle. Unfortunately, Ruffus found the picnic basket early and ate some of the bones. How many bones did Ruffus eat if there were 6 bones left? (♦ How much of Ruffus' share was left for the picnic?).

This created a need to record the key information in the problems. A class discussion revealed that many children summarized Problem 16.1 as $10 - \_ = 6$ (used a space to indicate the unknown). Jillian proposed using a question mark; Breva suggested a blank (_). (Continued on page 16-12.)

➤ Probe 16.1: Uses of Letters

The aim of this probe is to help you construct an explicit understanding of the four ways letters (variables) are used in mathematics. With the help of your group, answer the following questions. Discuss your answers with your class.

1. Each of the five cases below illustrate a way letters can be used. (a) Consider the examples in each case below and determine how a letter is used. (b) How does the use of letters differ among the cases?

Case I

  Example 1: π

  Example 2: e

Case II

  Example 3: $2 + x = 7$

  Example 4: $5y = 35$

Case III

  Example 5: $2n + 4n = 6n$

  Example 6: $3n - 2n = n$

Case IV

  Example 7: $n \times 0 = 0$

  Example 8: $a + b = b + a$

Case V

  Example 9: $y = 2 + x$

  Example 10: $y = 2x$

2. Letters have four mathematical uses.

   i. **Name for a particular number**. In Case I above, a letter is used as the *name for a particular number*. For example, the sixteenth letter in the Greek alphabet π (*pi*) represents the ratio between a circle's circumference and its diameter (3.14...).

   ii. **Specific unknown.** In Case II, a letter represents *a specific unknown*. For example, in the equation $2 + x = 7$, the letter x represents one and only one possible solution—the number 5. Before about 250 A.D., people used ordinary language to describe unknowns rather than symbols or special signs (Kieran & Chalouh, 1993). Until the end of the sixteenth century, letters were used exclusively to represent a specific unknown.

   iii. **General unknown or pattern generalizer.** In Cases III and IV, a letter represents a *general unknown*—a range of values. For example, with $2n + 4n = 6n$, n can represent any and all numbers you can think of. Once it was recognized that letters could represent general numbers, they became a tool for summarizing patterns—including mathematical rules or principles (e.g., a + b = b + a represents the commutativity principle). That is, an algebraic expression or equation could now serve as a "*pattern generalizer*" (Usiskin, 1988). With the use of letters to represent a range of numbers (or a *given*), mathematicians were finally able to express general solutions with symbols and use algebra as a tool for proving rules (Kieran & Chalouh, 1993).

   iv. **Varying values.** The letters in Case V illustrate *varying values*—an unknown number that varies with respect to another. For example, in the equation $y = 2 + x$, the value of y *depends on* the value x. For example if $x = 1$, then $y = 3$; if $x = 5$, then $y = 7$. The value of y has a specific value for a given value of x but can vary as the values of x change.

Consider the formula for the area of a rectangle ($A = 1 \bullet w$). (a) Is there any situation where the letter A could represent a particular number? (b) Is there any situation where it could represent a specific unknown? (c) Is there any situation where the A could represent a generalized pattern (any unknown)? (d) Is there any situation where it could represent varying values (a value that varies according to other values)?

Arlette said she had seen boxes used in her math text and thought that would be a good place holder. Mr. Sorrentino asked if other shapes such as circles or triangles could be used to represent an unknown. The class concluded, "Why not!" Fannie proposed using the letter b to represent the unknown number of bones, an idea that met with wide approval. (Note that Problems 2, 5, 6, and 7 in Investigation 16.1 on pages 16-4 to 16-6 and Investigation 16.2 on page 16-9 also create a need for representing specific unknowns.)

Representing Generalized Numbers. After Mr. Mihelich helped his class discover that the area of rectangle could be determined by multiplying the length and width (see Activity File 15.6 on page 15-19), he prompted them to summarize their discovery with letters: $A_{rec} = l \times w$. In addition to summarizing their discoveries about determining the area, perimeter, or volume of geometric forms, students can be involved in representing generalized numbers by developing other formulas (e.g., Problem 2 on page 16-4 of Investigation 16.1) or devising proofs about generalizations (see, e.g., Problems 3 and 4 on pages 16-5 and 16-6 of Investigation 16.1).

Varying Values. After his students discovered the law of levers (see Investigation 12.4 on page 12-13) and summarized it algebraically ($d_1 \bullet w_1 = d_2 \bullet w_2$, where d = distance from the fulcrum and w = weight), Mr. Yant had them place two 10-gram weights at position 6 on the right arm of their *Math Balances* ($d_1 \bullet w_1 = 6 \bullet 20 = 120$). He then asked them what weights at what location on the left arm would make the *Math Balances* balance? He had the students record, graph, and analyze their date. The students found that it took 12 10-gram weights at Position 1; 6, at Position 2; 4, at Position 3; and 3, at Position 4—that w_2 varied inversely with d_2: that as d_2 increased, the amount of weight needed to balance the *Math Balance* (w_2) decreased.

16•1•3 THE SYMBOLIZATION OF METHOD

In this subunit, we first discuss key psychological barriers to understanding the use of letters as a shorthand for representing mathematics processes (the symbolization of method) and then consider how instruction can help children overcome these barriers.

☞ Try Probe 16.2 (on pages 16-13 and 16-14).

Learning: Understanding Children's Thinking

Algebra can cause "culture" shock, because unlike traditional arithmetic instruction, it focuses on the solution process or method, not the numerical answer. Moreover, reading and writing algebraic expressions or equations require adaptive expertise, not routine expertise (see, e.g., Question 1 in Part I of Probe 16.2 on page 16-13).

Teaching

Next, we discuss prealgebra and initial algebra instruction on the symbolization of method.

Prealgebra. The groundwork for the symbolization of method can and should be laid throughout the K-8 grades. Virtually all meaningful instruction—particularly that which encourages children to invent strategies and to examine why and how solution strategies work—helps lay a foundation of algebra. *Strategy problems* are particularly valuable in setting the stage for algebra because they ask students to focus on and justify solution strategies, not solutions.

Initial Algebra Instruction. The symbolization of method can be broached in the primary grades and revisited with increasing frequency in the intermediate grades. With the advent of computing technologies such as the graphing calculator, instruction no longer needs to focus on inculcating and fine tuning paper-and-pencil techniques for manipulating symbols and fixed procedures for solving classes of problems such as mixture or distance-rate-time problems (Heid et al., 1995). TODAY THE MAIN AIM OF INSTRUCTION SHOULD BE TO HELP STUDENTS APPRECIATE THE USES OF ALGEBRA AND DEVELOP AN ALGEBRAIC SYMBOL SENSE (CONCEPTUAL UNDERSTANDING).

☞ To help students appreciate the value of algebra and to create a need to learn algebraic representations and procedures, use a top-down (investigative) approach. As with any aspect of mathematics, algebra is most effectively taught in the context of tackling genuinely challenging task that is personally significant (NCTM, 1992). As Investigations 16.1 (pages 16-4 to 16-6) and 16.2 (page 16-9) and Probe 16.2 (pages 16-13 and 16-14) illustrate, (continued on page 16-15)

➤ Probe 16.2: Algebraic Symbol Sense

An algebraic symbol sense entails understanding how to represent situations and understanding the meaning of algebraic notation and manipulations.

☞ **Teaching Tip.** Note that both Parts I and Part II of this probe could be used as the basis of an error-analysis activity with sixth- to eighth-graders.

Part I: Representing Mathematical Processes

1. a. Without help from others, write an algebraic equation for each of the following situations:

    ■ **Problem A.** At Ideal University, there are six times as many students as professors. Let S indicate the number of students and P indicate the number of professors (Clement, Lochhead, & Monk, 1981).

    ■ **Problem B.** Cecil made $50 more than Ross. Let C = Cecil's amount and R = Ross'.

    b. Compare your equations with those of your group or class. If the results were not unanimous, what equation did the majority record?

    c. Many students have difficulty writing expressions or equations to represent situations described in word problems (Kieran, 1992). Instead of thoughtfully interpreting the mathematical meaning of word problems, they use a direct-translation approach analogous to a key-word approach for solving arithmetic word problems. In effect, they mechanically translate word problems phrase-by-phrase into algebraic equations—often with disastrous results. For example, a common response to Problem A is $6S = P$, an equation that implies a truly remarkable student-professor ratio of 1 to 6. For example, if Ideal University had 1000 students, the equation implies that the University employed 6,000 professors! How could using a *Math Balance* and a balance-beam analogy (the equal sign can be thought of as the fulcrum of a balanced balance beam) help students understand that $6S = P$ is incorrect and devise the correct equation?

    d. How could the balance-beam analogy be used to check or correct your answer to Problem B?

2. To solve *If Dimes Were Quarters* (Problem 7 on page 16-6 of Investigation 16.1), a class agreed that the total number of coins could be represented by $d + q = 20$ (where d = number of dimes and q = the number of quarters). To represent that switching the value of quarters and dimes would result in 90¢ more, Alexi wrote $(25d + 10q) - (10d + 25q) = 90$; Alison, $25d + 10q = (10d + 25q) + 90$. (a) Which, if either, is correct? Why or why not? (b) How could you prove the two equations were equivalent or not? (c) In simplifying Alexi's equation, Miriam wrote $15d + 35q = 90$. Is she correct or not? Why?

Part II: Making Sense of Algebraic Notation and Manipulations

For each of the following cases, consider how you could build on what children already know to help them interpret the symbolism meaningfully and, if necessary, correct themselves.

1. Miss Brill asked her students to use their knowledge about the area of a rectangle ($A = l \bullet w$) to deduce the formula for the area of square. LeMar reasoned that if $l = w$, then the area of square was $l \bullet l$ or $2l$). Andy countered that the formula was $A = l^2$. Marcus suggested that there was no conflict because $2l = l^2$.

2. (a) While trying to devise an algebraic proof for the *Magic Trick* (Problem 4 on pages 16-5 and 16-6 of Investigation 16.1), Alesia wrote $2(n + 8)$ to represent Step 3. To represent Step 4 (subtract 6), she wrote $2(n + 8) - 6 = 2n + 8 - 6 = 2n - 2$. (b) While devising her own magic trick, ("1. Pick any number, 2. add four, 3. double the sum, 4. subtract two, 5. divide by two . . ."), Joletta used algebra to determine her final ("magical") outcome. For Step 5, she recorded $\frac{2n+6}{2}$, but was confused about how to divide by 2. "Is the answer $n + 6$, $n + 3$, or $2n + 3$?" she asked.

Probe 16.2 continued

3. To create a need to discuss the meaning of algebraic notation and manipulations, Mr. Yant created decks of 20 equations (e.g., $3x + \frac{x}{x} = 13$, $\frac{x^2}{x} - 5 = 0$, $x^2 = 100$, $\frac{x}{2} - 2 = 48$, $\frac{x^2}{2} = 8$, $\frac{x}{2} + 3 = 4$, $\frac{x-5}{2} = 1$, $3x + x = 28$, $4(x - \frac{0}{2}) = 1$, $\frac{1}{x} = \frac{1}{10}$, $\frac{1}{x} = 4$, $x^2 - 1 = 63$, $x = 16 - x$, $2x + 2 = 12$, $x + x + x = 18$, $\frac{x^2}{20^2} = 25$, $\frac{2x-2}{2} = 5$, $2(x + 4) = 14$, $3x - 2 = 7$, and $4x + 2x = 12$). In groups of four, he had his class play *Algebra Match* by placing the cards face down in four rows of five. The order of play was determined by rolling a die. On their turns, if players flipped over two cards that matched, they kept the cards and took another turn. The object of the game was to be the player that collected the most cards. (a) Create Mr. Yant's deck and play *Algebra Match* with your group. (Otherwise, simply evaluate the equations listed above.) What questions did this raise? (b) How could you help students make sense of: $\frac{x}{x}$, $\frac{x^2}{x}$, and $x^2 = 100$? (c) For $\frac{x}{2} - 2 = 48$, Arianne wasn't sure whether to multiply each side by 2 or add 2 to them first. For $2(x + 4) = 14$, she wasn't sure whether to divide each side by 2 or subtract 4 from them first. In each case, does it matter what she did first? Why or why not?

4. Many students are not sure whether $4x - 3x$ is 1 or x. (a) What do you think the difference is? (b) How might you help students resolve their confusion?

Questions for Reflection

Algebra Tiles[†] can be helpful in constructing an algebraic symbol sense. This manipulative include the following pieces:

☐   (yellow cube) = length of 1 unit

▭▭▭▭   (yellow rod) = length of 5 units

(yellow square) = area of 25 square units

short blue rod = unknown length x

small blue square = x^2 (area of a square with an unknown length x

long blue rod = unknown length y

1. What do each of the following *Algebra Tiles* represent?

a. Large blue square   b. Small blue rectangle (subdivided)   c. Large blue rectangle (subdivided)   d. Medium-size blue rectangle

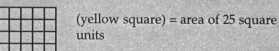

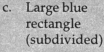

2. Show how *Algebra Tiles* and a take-away analogy could be used to make sense of $4x - 3x$.

3. Show how *Algebra Tiles* and an area analogy could be used to model and find the product of $2(x + 4)$.

4. Show how *Algebra Tiles* and divvy-up analogy could help students simplify the expression $\frac{2x+6}{2}$.

algebra instruction can evolve from solving real, realistic, or mathematical problems (NCTM, 1992).

↬ **To foster flexibility, encourage and discuss alternative algebraic representations and solutions.** Helping students recognize that different representations are possible can foster mathematical power and adaptive expertise (see, e.g., Question 2 in Part I of Probe 16.2 on page 16-13). Asking for alternative representations and solutions can, for instance, prompt discussion of equivalent operations (e.g., $n \bullet \frac{1}{3} = \frac{n}{3}$ or $n \div 3$).

↬ **Focus on helping students make sense of algebraic expressions and equations** (see, e.g., Probe 16.2). Encourage children to apply what they already know about numbers and arithmetic to interpret expressions such as $4x - 3x$ (four groups of a number take away three groups of that number leaves one group of the number, not one), $\frac{x}{x}$ (a number divided by itself is one), and $\frac{6x+8}{2}$ (six groups of a number and another 8 items shared fairly between two people would mean each person gets three groups of a number and another four items: $3x + 4$, not $3x + 8$ or $6x + 4$). Using manipulatives such as *Algebra Tiles* can help students visualize these processes. For example, $\frac{6x+8}{2}$ could be represented by six short blue rods and eight yellow cubes, all of which are evenly distributed into two piles. A *Math Balance* and balance-beam analogy can be particularly helpful in writing algebraic equations (see Box 16.1).

16•1•4 SOLVING ALGEBRAIC EQUATIONS MEANINGFULLY

In this subunit, we discuss strategies for, common difficulties with, and meaningful instruction on solving algebraic equations.

Mathematics: Solution Strategies

Algebraic equations can be solved by both informal and formal strategies.

Informal Strategies. Research has found that algebra students use various informal strategies (Kieran, 1992). For instance, with an equation such as $3n + 5 = 23$, many students use a *try-*

Box 16.1: Using a Math Balance to Write Equations

After reminding his students that an equation could be thought of as a balanced balance beam, Mr. Yant asked them to write an equation for the following situation: *Osmany had twice as many absences as Blake.*

Alexander's group proposed 2O = B; Alecia's group, O = 2B. After some fruitless debate, Mr. Yant suggested using a *Math Balance* to resolve the conflict. To disprove 2O = B, Alecia place a weight at Position 10 on the left arm of a *Math Balance* to represent Osmany's (10) absences and a weight of Position 5 on the right arm to represent Blake's (5) absences. "See," Alecia argued, "Osmany has twice as much as Blake but the scale doesn't balance."

Alexander objected, "My model is clearer. See, I put two weights at Position 1 on the left side to show Osmany's absences and one weight at Position 1 on the other side to show Blake's absences."

"Yeah, but like you still prove our point," countered Shoreen. "The *Math Balance* isn't balanced. So your model won't represent an equation."

"Oh yeah," exclaimed Alexander with the force of sudden insight, "O = 2B is right. If Osmany had twice as many as Blake, then Blake would have to double his amount to have the same number as Osmany."

---

and-adjust substitution strategy: Try substituting a number for the unknown (e.g., 5 for n), perform the arithmetic ($3 \bullet 5 + 5 = 20$), compare the outcomes ($20 \neq 23$), and try substituting a new number (e.g., let $n = 6$). Others use an *undoing* or *working backwards* strategy: start with 23, next subtract 5, and then divide by 3.

Formal Strategies. Two formal strategies commonly taught in the U.S. are described below.

• **Performing the same operation on both sides.** This procedure is similar to an informal undoing (working backwards) strategy but, unlike its informal counterpart, it underscores the relational meaning of equals. This procedure involves isolating the variable by performing the same operation on each side of the equation. Consider, for example, $3n + 5 = 23$. To get n alone, a student would subtract 5 from the left-hand side of the equation. To keep the equation balanced, 5 would also be subtracted from its right-hand side of the equation:

$$3n + 5 - 5 = 23 - 5$$
$$3n = 18$$

To further isolate n, each side of the equation is then divided by 3: $\frac{3n}{3} = \frac{18}{3}$ and so $n = 6$.

• **Transposing (change-sides, change-sign rule).** This procedure is simply a shortcut for *performing the same operation on both sides.* For $3n + 5 = 23$, this procedure would involve:

(1) 5 changes sides and sign $(+ \rightarrow -)$: $3n = 23 - 5 = 18$

(2) 3 changes sides and sign $(\times \rightarrow \div)$: $n = \frac{18}{3} = 6$

Learning: Traditional Instruction and Student Difficulties

Overlooking Informal Strategies. In the traditional skills approach, little—if any—effort is made to encourage informal strategies. After a brief introduction to informal strategies such as try-and-adjust substitution and working backwards, instruction quickly jumps to formal procedures. In some cases, instruction begins immediately with formal procedures.

Focusing on the school-taught algorithm promotes blind and nonadaptive use of a formal algorithm. Students fail to use informal strategies even when they might be easier and quicker to use. For example, using a known number combination would probably be easier to evaluate $x + 5 = 12$ than performing the same operation on both sides. Moreover, many students stop using a try-and-adjust substitution strategy after they learn a formal algorithm, even though this strategy would be a good way to check their work (Kieran, 1992).

Learning of Formal Algorithms by Rote. To compound students' difficulties, traditional instruction often makes little or no effort to explain formal procedures. For example, sometimes students are simply told to perform the same opera-

tion on both sides of the equation without helping them understand the need for doing so. Other times students are simply taught the change-side, change-sign rule without helping them recognize that it is a shortcut for the *perform-the-same-operation-on-both-sides* procedure. Not surprisingly, many children have little understanding of algebraic manipulations and experience difficulty solving algebraic equations.

Teaching

To help students develop adaptive, rather than routine, expertise at solving algebra equations, instruction should promote informal strategies and help students reinvent or at least comprehend the rationale for formal algorithms.

Informal Strategies. Students should be encouraged to devise, share, and use informal strategies long before and even after the introduction of formal procedures. In the long term, the aim should be the development of flexible and thoughtful use of strategies—choosing the strategy that makes sense and that minimizes labor. Substituting a numerical value should be encouraged both as an informal strategy and as a vehicle for checking formal solutions.

Formal Procedures. Formal procedures for solving algebraic equations can be introduced after children have had ample experience with informal strategies and after the conceptual ground for the procedures is laid.

☞ Try Investigations 16.3 (page 16-17) and 16.4 (page 16-18).

☞ Try Investigations 16.3 (page 16-17) and 16.4 (page 16-18).

↪ **The rationale for the *performing-the-same-operation-on-both-sides* procedure needs to be explicitly understood by students.** To lay the ground work for this understanding, elementary-level children can use a *Math Balance* (see, e.g., Investigation 16.3) or other scale (see Box 16.2 on page 16-19). The formal algorithm can then be related explicitly to this concrete balance model.

↪ **Encourage students to solve algebraic equations concretely and to rediscover procedural shortcuts themselves.** For instance, Investigation 16.4 illustrates how *Algebra Tiles* and an area model can help students make sense of polynomial multiplication and rediscover FOIL. (Continued on page 16-19.)

✿ Investigation 16.3: Using a *Math Balance* to Solve Algebraic Equations Informally

◆ Equality and inequality + algebraic equations ◆ Groups of four + class discussion

A balance-beam analogy provides a concrete model and rationale for the *performing-the-same-operation-on-both-sides-of-an-equation* rule. Indeed by representing equations on a balance beam and experimenting with such representations, students can induce this rule for themselves. For each problem below, consider how a *Math Balance* could be used to represent the data given and to determine the solution. Discuss your conclusions with your group or class.

Part I: Evaluating the Equality or Inequality of Two Number Expressions (◆ 3-8)

To familiarize yourself with the *Math Balance* and set the stage for solving algebraic equations, use this manipulative to solve the arithmetic problem below:

■ **Problem 1: Salesmen.** Ashad and B.J.'s scout council were selling popcorn as a fundraiser. The scout who sold the most popcorn would win two free weeks at scout summer camp. Best friends, Ashad and B.J. each wanted to sell the most so that they could share the prize between them. (a) On Saturday morning, Ashad sold 3 six-box packages (six-packs) of popcorn to Mrs. Golden and 5 single boxes to Mrs. Rhiner. B.J. sold 4 six-packs to his Aunt Grunda. Did the boys sell an equal amount or did one sell more? (b) On Saturday afternoon, Ashad sold 5 six-packs to his grandmother and single box to his neighbor. B.J. sold 4 six-packs to his soccer coach, half a six-pack to his piano teacher, and 4 single boxes to various individuals. On Saturday afternoon, did the boys sell an equal amount or did one sell more? (c) Write a number sentence that summarizes each question (Questions a and b) above.

Part II: A Single Unknown (◆ 4-8)

Now try using the *Math Balance* to solve for a single unknown:

■ **Problem 2: Salesmen II.** After a week, Ashad and B.J. had sold exactly the same number of boxes of popcorn. If Ashad sold 3 more six-packs of popcorn, B.J. sold 2 more six-packs and some single boxes, and the boys sold 35 boxes altogether, how many single boxes did B.J. sell? (a) Using a box, letter or other symbol to show the unknown, summarize the information above in a number (algebraic) sentence. (b) Then determine the value of the unknown using a *Math Balance*.

Part III: More Complicated Problems (◆ 5-8)

■ **Problem 3: What Number?** What number added to 8 is equal to three times the number? (a) Using a □, a letter, or some other symbol to show the unknown, write a number sentence that summarizes the information in the problem. (b) Using a *Math Balance*, determine the value of the unknown.

■ **Problem 4: What Number?—Two Different Unknowns.** Three times what number plus a second number is twice the second number minus 4? What is the second number? (a) Using a □ and a △, letters, or some other symbols to show the unknowns, write a number sentence that summarizes the information in the problem. (b) Using a *Math Balance*, determine the values of the unknowns.

■ **Problem 5: Tug of War.**[†] Illustrate how each of the following tug-of-war events could be represented with a *Math Balance* and answer the questions posed. (a) **First Event**. On one team are six Musclebound Mudpuppies who have trained for this event by swimming against the current of Raging River. All six are of equal strength. The other team consists of five Octogenarians, a tugging team that has well-developed muscles from playing croquet with sledgehammers and cannon balls. They are also all of equal strength. In a strenuous contest between these two teams the result is a draw. Neither team can pull the other into the middle, a pit filled with chocolate pudding. (Hint: At what position on a *Math Balance* would the weight(s) representing the six Mudpuppies have to be placed to balance those representing the five Octogenarians? What relative value, then, does each Mudpuppy have? What relative value does each Octogenarian have?) (b) **Second Event**. On one team is the miniature elephant, Tuska-loosa, who has perfected rope pulling by lifting elevators in some of the world's tallest buildings. Tuska-loosa will be matched against a team consisting of three Mudpuppies and two Octagenarians. This event also results in a draw. Tuska-loosa's strength has what relative value? (Hint: It will not be possible to represent Tuska-loosa's relative strength by placing a single weight on the balance beam.) (c) **Third Event**. One team has Tuska-loosa and two Octogenarians. To have a draw, the opponents would have to consist of four Octogenarians and how many Mudpuppies? Why? (d) **Fourth Event**. If Tuska-loosa and one Mudpuppy were on one team, how many Mudpuppies and Octogenarians would have to be on the second team to have a draw? (e) **Fifth Event**. Make up two teams that will not end in a draw. Show which team will win and provide proof for your result.

[†] Based on an idea presented by Toni Meyer, New York State Education Department at the 32nd annual AMTNYS summer workshop (August, 1994) at Siena College, Londonville, NY.

⌘Investigation 16.4: Using *Algebra Tiles* to Solve Algebra Problems & Equations Concretely

◆ Multiplying polynomials + rediscovering FOIL + polynomial factoring ◆ 5-8
◆ Small groups + whole class discussion

Using manipulatives such as *Algebra Tiles* and an area model can help students relate abstract expressions such as $4x^2 + 2xy + 6x + y + 2$ to something concrete and help them understand algebraic manipulations and solutions. To see how, use *Algebra Tiles* to solve the problems below. Discuss your answers with your group or class.

▪ **Problem 1: Ruffus in the Dog House.** To minimize the damage caused by Ruffus, Mr. Smith decided to fence in his frenetic pet. Unsure how big he wanted to make the dog pen, he drew the sketch to the right. (a) What is the area of the dog pen (the area inside the fence, including the dog house)? (b) Camille wrote A = (x + 5) (x + 4); Ramzi, A = x^2 + 9x + 20; Cornelius, A = $20x^2$; and Vicki, A = x^2 + 9x. How might *Algebra Tiles* be used to determine which answers above are equivalent? (c) How might those who answered incorrectly have arrived at the answers they did? (d) Use an informal strategy and a calculator to determine the length of the south- or lower-side and east- or right-side extensions from the dog house (both labeled x) rounded to the nearest whole number, if the dog pen was to have an area of 1000 square feet.

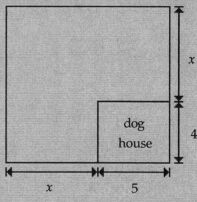

▪ **Problem 2: A Doll House.** Reggie wanted to surprise his sister by building her a doll house of balsa wood. He was not sure what length and width to make the doll house and so decided to experiment with bars of wood. He decided to make the length two bars and the width one bar. (The bars were all the same size.) However, he realized that the width would have to be another 2 inches long to accommodate his sister's doll and doll furniture. (a) What is the area of Reggie's dollhouse? (b) Ichiro wrote an equation A = 2x(x + 2); Annetta, A = (x + x) (x + 2); Adrian; A = $2x^2$ + 2, and Lenore, A = $2x^2$ + 4x. Illustrate how these students could use *Algebra Tiles* to determine which answers are equivalent. (c) Whose formula best addresses the problem? Why? (d) Use an informal strategy and a calculator to determine what the value of x would have to be (rounded to the nearest whole centimeter) to have a doll house with an area of at least 2000 square cm.

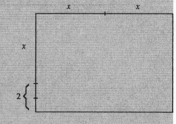

✦ **Extension for Problem 2.** The dollhouse still did not have enough room. Reggie decided to add a longer wooden bar (y) to the length (2x) and keep the width (x + 2) the same. Write a formula for the area of the new dollhouse.

Questions for Reflection

1. Use *Algebra Tiles* to determine the product of the following binomials: (a) (y + 2) (y + 1), (b) (3x + 1) (x + 4), (c) (x + 3) (y + 2), (d) (2x + 4) (3y + 5).

2. Consider the expressions in Question 1 and their products. Consider also the following equations: (x + 5) (x + 4) = x^2 + 9x + 20 and (2x + y) (x + 2) = $2x^2$ + 4x + xy + 2y. Devise a shortcut for multiplying binomials.

3. In the FOIL algorithm, what do F, O, I, and L represent?

4. Consider how the area model could be used to interpret factoring polynomials and illustrate how *Algebra Tiles* could be used to determine the factors of (a) $6x^2$, (b) 4x + 2, (c) $2x^2$ + 8x + 6, (d) 2xy + 8x + y + 4, (e) $4x^2$ + 2xy + 6x + y + 2.

Box 16.2: A Balance-Beam Model for Solving Algebraic Equations Using $n + 3 = 5$ as an Example

A. Represent the equation. For example, represent the left-hand side of the equation ($n + 3$) with an unknown weight and three 1-unit weights. Represent the right-hand side of the equation (5) with five 1-unit weights.

B. Isolate the variable. Ask students how they can get the unknown weight alone. Students should recognize that this can be done by removing the three 1-unit weights from the left pan.

C. Re-establish the balance (equality). Ask the students how the balance-beam can be balanced again. Students should recognize that removing three 1-unit weights from the right pan will rebalance the balance beam.

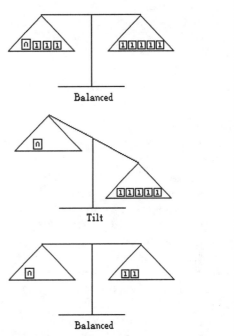

16•2 FUNCTIONS

Figure 16.4: Functions Can Be Useful in Analyzing Many Aspects of Everyday Life

Functions tie together many aspects of mathematics and can be used to describe and analyze many real-world situations. For example, as Figure 16.4 implies, speed is a function of two measurements—distance and time. More specifically, speed is the ratio of distance (d) to time (t), which can be expressed as the formula $s = \frac{d}{t}$. Such formulas, shorthand expressions for functions, play an important role in mathematics—particularly geometry (see chapter 15)—as well as other fields such as science. In Subunit 16•2•1,

we explore functions; in Subunit 16•2•2, we examine how this topic can be taught in a meaningful and stimulating way to elementary-level children.

16•2•1 MATHEMATICS: UNDERSTANDING FUNCTIONS

☞ Try Investigations 16.5 (pages 16-20 to 16-22) and 16.6 (pages 16-23) before reading on. (Text continued on page 16-24.)

✿ Investigation 16.5: In-Out (Function) Machines

In-out machines can be an invaluable model for introducing and exploring functions. To see how and to perhaps deepen your own understanding of this topic, try the investigations below yourself. Discuss your findings with your group or class.

Part I: An Informal Model of Functions (◆ Introducing functions informally + inductive and deductive reasoning + arithmetic practice ◆ K-8 ◆ Individually, small group, or whole class)

In-Out Machines, introduced in Probe 2.3 (page 2-25 of chapter 2), provide a dynamic and relatively concrete analogy for the concept of functions. Such a machine takes what you put into it (an input) and *consistently* produces a result (an output)—through some invisible internal process (a rule or function). For example, when 7 is put in Machine A to the right, 14 comes out the other end. When 4 is put in, 11 comes out. When 0 is put in, 7 comes out. When 13 is put in, 20 comes out. Note that summarizing such information in a table can help students figure out what the In-Out Machine is doing—what the rule or function is.

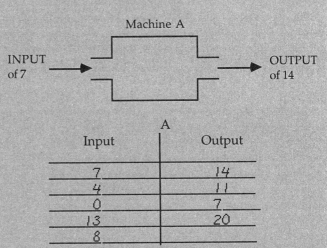

Input	Output
7	14
4	11
0	7
13	20
8	

1. (a) What is the rule (function) used by Machine A? (b) What type of reasoning was used to determine the function?

2. (a) What would you predict the output would be if the input were 8? (b) What type of reasoning was involved in making this prediction?

3. Machine A would be appropriate for what grade level?

4. Find the missing inputs or outputs for In-Out Machines B to H. Use only whole numbers 0 or larger. Be sure to give all possible answers. Indicate answers that are *not possible* with NP.

B Input	B Output		C Input	C Output		D Input	D Output
4	0		5	12		3	12
9	5		3	8		5	20
11	7		2	6		7	28
12			10	22		1	
19	15		15	32		10	
	10		7				16
	8		4				18
0			0				36
2				18			0
				50			
				27			

Investigation 16.5 continued

E Input	E Output		F Input	F Output		G Input	G Output		H Input	H Output
3	7		47	40		1	1		7	1
2	5		32	30		6	216		5	2
5	11		16	10		3	27		9	0
10	21		39	30		8	512		14	2
20	41		312	310		2			6	0
6			80	80			64		4	1
4			7			0				0
	9		52						8	
	10		108							
	27			10						
0				120						

5. As Table I to the right suggests, more than one input can be fed into a machine at a time. In the case illustrated by Table I, the machine works on both inputs and a single output comes out. For Tables I and J, fill in the missing inputs and outputs. Use only whole numbers larger than 0. Be sure to give all possible answers. Indicate answers that are not possible with NP.

I Input	I Output		J Input	J Output
(2,5)	7		(17,3)	NP
(6,3)	9		(13,2)	NP
(1,5)	6		(14,1)	14
(4,7)			(20,5)	4
(6,6)			(28,4)	7
	8			1
	7		(0,7)	
	10		(6,0)	

6. How can In-Out Machine exercises counteract the belief that there is always *a* correct answer?

Part II: Defining Rules Explicitly and Algebraically (◆ Inductive reasoning + variables + symbolization of method ◆ 3-8 ◆ Any number)

In-Out Machines provide an opportunity for summarizing arithmetic processes as algebra expressions. Initially, students can be encouraged to summarize the rule for an In-Out Machine in writing (using a natural language). They can then be encouraged to do the same thing algebraically. Children should quickly recognize that describing a rule with an algebraic expression is much easier than doing so with natural language.

1. To see for yourself: (a) determine the rule for the following machines, (b) summarize the rule in words, and then (c) summarize the rule with an algebraic expression.

K Input	K Output		L Input	L Output		M Input	M Output
2	7		0	1		1	4
6	15		1	$\frac{1}{2}$		2	8
9	21		2	$\frac{1}{4}$		3	16
11	25		4	$\frac{1}{16}$		4	32

2. For Machine L, Previa proposed the rule $\left(\frac{1}{n}\right)^2$. Evaluate her conjecture.

Investigation 16.5 continued

Part III: **Discovering the Key Characteristics of Functions** (◆ Explicitly defining functions ◆ 7-8 ◆ Any number)

1. Can you predict the last output for Tables N, O, and P below? Can you predict the last output for Tables Q, R, and S below?

N			O			P	
Input	Output		Input	Output		Input	Output
4	8		4	0		(1,12)	12
7	14		0	0		(2,6)	12
5	10		5	0		(3,4)	12
3	6		9	0		(10,1)	10
2	4		2	0		(5,2)	10
2			2			(5,2)	

Q			R			S	
Input	Output		Input	Output		Input	Output
4	4		0.5	$\frac{5}{10}$		(1,12)	7
4	1		0.5	$\frac{12}{24}$		(1,12)	2
4	5		0.5	$\frac{1}{2}$		(1,12)	10
4			0.5			(1,12)	
2	7		0.25	$\frac{250}{1000}$		(2,7)	5
2			0.25			(2,7)	

2. Tables N, O, and P summarize the inputs of and outputs of working In-Out Machines—examples of functions. Tables Q, R, and S illustrate broken machines—nonexamples of functions. By examining these examples and nonexamples of a function above, what is *the crucial requirement for a function*?

3. Circle the letter of any correct statement about an In-Out Machine.

   a. An input of an In-Out Machine must produce an unique output—an output unlike that of any other input.

   b. Each input must be different from all other inputs (once entered an input cannot be entered again).

   c. An In-Out Machine must be reliable—produce the same output every time a particular input is entered.

4. More formally, a function is a special type of relationship in which *each input has one and only one output*. Sixth-grader Alison asked if the following rule was a function: *If the number is even add four; if it is odd, add three.* Examples are listed in Table T below:

	Input	2	3	4	5	8	9
T							
	Output	6	6	8	8	12	12

(a) In the words of Ms. Socrates, does Example T "walk and quack like a duck"—that is, fit the criterion of a function? (b) Steffi argued that it did not "because you can't reverse" (determine the input from the output). Evaluate Steffi's argument.

☾ Investigation 16.6: Arrow Diagrams

Arrow diagrams are a way of representing a relationship. Part I illustrates a task that can be used to introduce such diagrams. As a special type of relationship, functions can also be represented by arrow diagrams. Part II illustrates how. To familiarize yourself with this technique, try Parts I and II.

Part I: The Connect-Four Tournament[†] (◆ Interpreting an arrow-diagram + deductive reasoning ◆ 4-6 ◆ Any number).

Mrs. B'Good's class held a *Connect-Four*[††] Tournament. A *Connect-Four* stand is illustrated below. The object of this two-player game is to get four checkers in a row either vertically, horizontally, or diagonally— and to keep your opponent from doing the same. On their turn, players put a single checker of their chosen color in the stand.

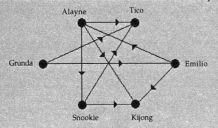

Six children made the finals, and each played each of the other finalists. To help them keep track of who played whom and who won, Mrs. B'Good's class used an arrow diagram. In the picture below, a line drawn between two players indicates they have played a game. The arrow points from the winner to the loser.

Connect-Four Tournament As of May 5

1. Summarize the current standings in the table below. Before doing so, consider the following questions: (a) Should a player's place in the standings be determined by his or her wins or percentage of wins? Why? (b) Snookie and Emilio have not played yet. Based on what has happened so far in the

tournament, who would you predict would win when they play? Justify your answer. (c) What must be true about the total number of wins and losses: (i) They should be equal; (ii) The total wins should be greater than the total number of losses. (iii) The total losses should be greater than the total number of wins; or (iv) The relationship between the total number of wins and the total number of losses can't be determined? Justify your answer.

Place	Name	Wins	Loses	Win %
1.				
2.				
3.				
4.				
5.				
6.				

2. How many more games must be played before each player plays all others in the tournament? Justify your answer.

Part II: Identifying Which Arrow Diagrams Represent Functions (◆ Relating an explicit definition of functions to a graphic representation ◆ 7-8 ◆ Any number).

Diagram A below represents a 1-to-1 correspondence: For each unique *x* value there is a single, unique *y* value. Diagram B represents a many-to-1 relationship: Multiple values of *x* are associated with a value of *y*. Diagram C represents a 1-to-many relationship: For each value of *x*, there are many values of *y*. Diagram D represents a combination of A and B: Some value(s) of *x* has (have) a distinct *y* value, while other values of *x* share the same *y* value. Diagram E represents a combination of A and C: Some value(s) of *x* has (have) a distinct *y* value; others have multiple *y* values. Based on the definition of a function, which of the diagrams below illustrate a function?

[†] Based on an activity titled the "Checkers Tournament" in *Measuring Up: Prototypes for Mathematics Assessment* (Mathematical Sciences Education Board and the National Research Council, 1993).
[††] *Connect Four* is the trademark game of the Milton-Bradley Company.

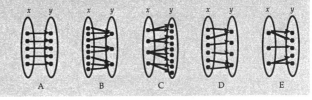

Functions involve a relationship, but not just any type of relationship. In terms of an In-Out machine, a function is a relationship in which an input has one and only one output. Thus, the key characteristic of function is *reliability*. If a particular input is entered into an In-Out machine, you can expect the same output every time. Machine O on page 16-22 of Investigation 16.5, for example, is an example of a working function machine because with a rule of *multiply by zero* (or subtracting the input from itself), you can always predict that an input of 2 will yield an output of 0. Table S on page 16-22 of in Investigation 16.5 illustrates a relationship (namely a *number between*) but not a function. For (2,7) then, the answer might be one of the following *four* numbers: 3, 4, 5, 6. In more general terms, *a function can be defined as a relation between two sets A and B, where each element in Set A has one and only one corresponding partner in Set B.**

16•2•2 TEACHING

THE STUDY OF PATTERNS AND FUNCTIONS IS A CENTRAL THEME OF MATHEMATICS AND SHOULD BE WOVEN THROUGHOUT THE ELEMENTARY CURRICULUM (NCTM, 1991). It should begin in the primary grades with informal investigations. At the immediate level, instruction should put even more emphasis on exploring functions (NCTM, 1991). Although the emphasis at this level should still be on informal explorations, instruction can begin a more formal exploration of the topic (e.g., explicitly defining functions as having one and only one output for an input, explaining why one graph represents a function but another does not). Two teaching tips are discussed below.

☞ Try Investigation 16.7 (page 16-25 and 16-26) and Probe 16.3 (pages 16-27 and 16-28).

↩ **Encourage elementary children to find, explain, and generalize functions informally.** In-Out Machines provide an informal analogy for introducing or exploring functions by children K-8 (see Part I of Investigation 16.5 encountered earlier on pages 16-20 and 16-21). As Investigation 16.7 illustrates, informally examining situations involving functions can provide a purposeful way of introducing the use of two or more letters in an equation, letters as pattern generalizers, and letters as varying values.

---

* Later in high school, Set A will be defined as the *domain*, Set B, as the *range*.

↩ **Relate arithmetic representations of functions (tables of data or sets of ordered pairs) to geometric representations (graphs or arrow diagrams) and algebraic representations (formulas).** Arithmetic representations of functions such as tables of data can be first related to graphs (see, e.g., Part I of Investigation 16.5 on pages 16-20 and 16-21 and Investigation 16.6 on page 16-23). Ideally, this process would begin by collecting and graphing real data to investigate real problems and relating graphs to everyday situations. Representing functional relationships graphically can begin in the primary grades. Then, in the intermediate grades, arithmetic representations of data can then be related to both graphs and equations (see, e.g., Part II of Investigation 16.5 on page 16-21 and Probe 16.3).

PARTING THOUGHTS

"Algebra serves as a stepping stone to academic success . . . . It is important that . . . all students are encouraged to [take this step]" (NCTM, 1992, p. 4). "It is essential that [elementary-level] students explore algebraic concepts in an informal way to build a foundation for subsequent formal study of algebra" (NCTM, 1989, p. 102), "First [encounters] with algebra should be through rich mathematical settings and applications followed by abstraction that comes from the need to describe or represent the patterns in these settings" (NCTM, 1992, p. 11). "Algebra . . . should be organized around the concept of function" (NCTM, 1992, p. 32). As an expression of regularities and patterns, this concept "is one of the big ideas or common threads that pervade a large portion of mathematics" (Van de Walle, 1994, p. 423).

RESOURCES

SOME INSTRUCTIONAL RESOURCES

Algebra

Algebra for Everyone (edited by Edgar L. Edwards, © 1990, NCTM) makes the case for teaching algebra to all students. It also includes teaching suggestions.

Numerous commercially available resources are available to make initial algebra instruction more concrete and meaningful. A sample is described below. (Continued on page 16-29.)

☝ Investigation 16.7: Bridges[†]

◆ Informally exploring functions + summarizing functions symbolically ◆ 3-8
◆ Individually or small groups of two to four

Many everyday phenomena involve a functional relationship. This investigation illustrates an engineering-related example that creates an opportunity for elementary-age children to explore functions informally using concrete models and logical reasoning. Note that solving the problems involved in the following investigations also provides purposeful practice of computational skills. More advanced students can also translate rules they have described in informal terms into algebraic formulas. To see what is involved, try the investigation yourself or with your group. Discuss your findings with your group or class.

Part I: The Two-Support Bridge

Aida used rods to build a bridge. She used yellow rods 5-cm long for the spans and red rods 2-cm long for the supports. Figure A below shows her bridge after completing two spans.

Figure A

1. (a) Build a 3-span bridge and answer the questions listesd in the table below. Do the same for a 4-span and 5-span bridge. (c) Without actually building a 15-span and 21-span bridge, complete the table below.

	3-spans	4-spans	5-spans	15-spans	21-spans
How many yellow rods did you need?					
How long was your bridge?					
How many red rods did you need?					
How many rods of both colors did you need?					

2. If the number of spans are known, what rule could translate this information into (a) the total number of rods, and (b) the length of the bridge?

3. (a) What is the total number of rods needed to build a 100-span bridge? Why? (b) What is the length of such a bridge? Explain your answer.

4. (a) Write a formula for determining the total number of rods (t) given the number of spans (s). (b) Write a formula for determining the length of the bridge (l) given s.

5. (a) What is the total number of rods needed to build a 187-span bridge? (b) What is the length of such a bridge?

[†] Based on a unit titled *"Bridges"* in *Measuring Up: Prototypes for Mathematical Assessment*. (Mathematical Sciences Education Board and the National Research Council). Reprinted with permission from MEASURING UP: PROTOTYPES FOR MATHEMATICAL ASSESSMENT. Copyright 1993 by the National Academy of Sciences. Courtesy of the National Academy Press, Washington, D.C.

Investigation 16.7 continued

Part II: The One-and-a-Half Support Bridge

Placido built a bridge using brown rods 8 cm-long for the spans and light-green rods 3 cm-long for the supports. Figure B below illustrates his bridge after completing two spans.

Figure B

1. (a) Build a 3-span bridge and answer the questions listed in the table below. Do the same for a 4-span and 5-span bridge (c) Without actually building a 15-span and a 21-span bridge, complete the table below.

	3-spans	4-spans	5-spans	15-spans	21-spans
How many brown rods did you need?					
How long was your bridge?					
How many light-green rods did you need?					
How many rods of both colors did you need?					

2. Describe the rule for figuring out (a) the total number of rods and (b) the length of the bridge—if you know the number of spans.

3. Write a formula for determining (a) the total number of rods and (b) the length of the bridge—if you know the number of spans. Let s = the number of spans, r = the total number of rods, and l = length of the bridge.

4. (a) What is the total number of rods needed to build a 187-span bridge? (b) What is the length of such a bridge?

5. How many brown rods and light-green rods would you need to build a bridge across a make-believe river 217 cm wide?

Questions for Reflection

1. How is the letter l in the formula written for Question 3 of Part II used—(a) as a name for a particular number, (b) to represent a specific unknown, (c) to serve as a pattern generalizer, or (d) to represent varying values?

2. In Question 4 of Part II, if 187 is substituted in the formula derived in Question 3, does this change how the variable l is used? Why or why not?

3. Note that the bridge problems above involve multiplicative thinking. For example, in Part I, determining the total number of rods for a 15-span bridge involves multiplying 15 x 3. (a) What are some other ways the problems above involve multiplicative reasoning? (b) How might these problems involve proportional reasoning?

4. For Question 5 of Part II, many students respond with an answer of 27. How might they have arrived at this answer and what does it overlook?

➤ Probe 16.3: Linking Different Representations of Functions

Functions can be represented in various ways. As Investigations 16.5 and 16.6 (pages 16-20 to 16-23) illustrated, they can be represented by *In-Out Machines*, *data tables*, and *arrow diagrams*. Functions can also be represented by *sets of ordered pairs* (e.g., {(3,5), (4,7), (5,9), (6,11)} represents "a doubling minus one" rule), *graphs* (e.g., the graph of the "doubling minus one" function is a straight line that has an x-intercept of $\frac{1}{2}$ and a y-intercept of -1), and *formulas* (e.g., the "doubling minus one" function can be summarized as the formula $y = 2x - 1$. The aim of this probe is to help you reflect on the connections among these representations of functions and how they relate to real situations.

Part I: Connecting Data Tables, Sets of Ordered Pairs, or Equations with Graphs

1. Each of the following tables and sets of ordered pairs is a sample of points in a graph below. For each, write the Roman numeral of the graph in which all the values would be found. A Roman numeral may be used more than once.

_____ a.

x	y
2	-4
1	-2
0	0
-1	2

_____ b.

x	y
2	1
3	1.5
4	2
5	2.5

_____ c.

x	y
2	0
3	1
4	2
4	3

_____ d.

x	y
2	4
1	1
0	0
-1	1

_____ e. {(1,3) (2,4) (-2,0)}

_____ f. {(1,-2) (2,-4) (-3,6)}

_____ g. {(1,1) (2,2) (-3,-3)}

_____ h. {(1,1) (2,4) (-3,9)}

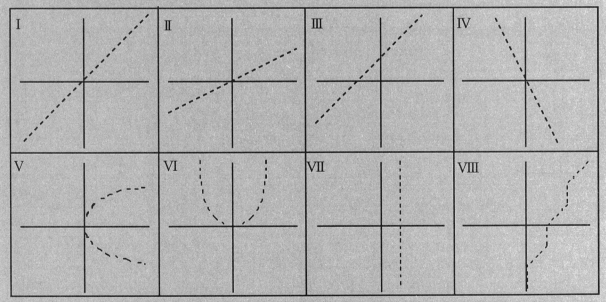

2. For each equation below, write the Roman numeral of the graph that portrays the relationship in the algebraic sentence. A Roman numeral may be used more than once.

_____ a. $y = x$ _____ b. $y = \frac{1}{2}x$ _____ c. $y = \pm\sqrt{x}$ _____ d. $y = x^2$

_____ e. $y = -2x$ _____ f. $x = 2$ _____ g. $y = x + 2$ _____ h. $y = \frac{x}{2}$

3. Indicate with a * each graph that represents a function. (What is the definition of a function?) Do some or all graphs represent a function? Justify your answer.

Probe 16.3 continued

4. Is $y = \pm\sqrt{x}$ a function? Why or why not?

5. (a) Which of the graphs on page 16-27 illustrate relationships that are directly proportional?
   (b) What can you conclude about the relationship between proportions and functions?

Part II: Interpreting Graphs and Algebraic Equations in Real Terms

Many students have routine expertise about graphs and related algebraic equations. They have no difficulty memorizing, for instance, that a linear plot can be represented by the general algebraic equation $y = mx + b$. They may even be able to specify what each term of the equation represents graphically (e.g., that m represents the slope). However, when presented with graphs of real-world relationships, they cannot explain, for instance, what the slope means in real terms. The task below asks students to consider a graphic and an algebraic representation in concrete terms.

On December 1, Jon borrowed money from his parents to buy a new car. He promised that beginning with the new year, he would make regular monthly payments on his debt. The graph to the right illustrates the amount of his debt after each payment for the first 6 months of the year.

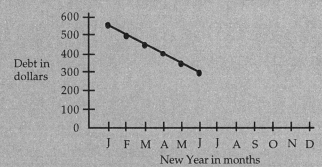

1. Summarize the graph to the right as an algebraic equation.

2. The plot illustrated can be represented by the algebraic equation $y = -50x + 600$. What do each of the following terms represent graphically? (a) y, (b) -50, (c) x, and (d) + 600

3. What does each term listed in Question 1 represent in terms of the story about Jon above?

4. Can you determine how much money did Jon borrow from his parents? If so, how and how much did he borrow? If not, why not and what additional information might help?

5. In what month would you predict he will pay off his debt?

Questions for Reflection

1. Examine the data and graphs for Problems 1 to 4 on pages 12-11 and 12-12 of Investigation 12.3 in Chapter 12. (a) Summarize each situation as an algebraic equation.

2. Reexamine your graph for Problem 4 of Investigation 12.3. (a) In $y = \frac{1}{2}x + 1$ (the equation for this graph and problem), what does the $\frac{1}{2}$ represent in the problem? (b) What does it represent in the graph? (c) What does the +1 represent in the problem? (d) What does it represent in the graph?

3. One of Mr. Brady's students noted that the $\frac{1}{2}$ in $y = \frac{1}{2}x + 1$ represents the slope. What does the slope show? (Hint: Reexamine the graphs for Problems 1 to 4 in Investigation 12.3 and the graph in Part II above.)

4. After concluding that, for instance, the $\frac{1}{2}$ in $y = \frac{1}{2}x + 1$ represent how steep a line is and, more specifically, how far up and over you go each time (rise over run), Mr. Brady asked what the 2 in $y = 2x + 1$ meant. Alfonso argued, "It means the rise is two and the run is 0. (a) Is Alfonso correct? Why or why not? (b) How could you prove he was correct or not?

5. What does a negative slope such as the -4 in $y = -4x$ indicate?

☞ **Algebra Thinking: First Experience** by Linda Holden Charles © 1990 by Creative Publications. This is a useful resource for intermediate-level teachers. Eight sections cover ratios and proportions, number patterns leading to rules, operations with integers, permutations and combinations, solving equations, solving problems using tables, simultaneous equations, and balance logic (substitution).

☞ **Hands-On Equations** by Henry Borenson, © 1991 by Borenson and Associates. The balance-beam model allows children to solve linear equations such $2x + x = x + 8$ successfully as early as the third or fourth grade. Although the model uses a pictured balanced beam rather than a real one, children do use pawns (▲) to represent a variable and cubes (■) numbered 0 to 10.

Level I of three levels consists of seven lessons—all suitable for elementary students. The first lesson underscores that the two sides of a scale must have the same value to balance. In Figure A below, for example, children should discern that each pawn is worth 4. What is the value of the pawn in Figure B?

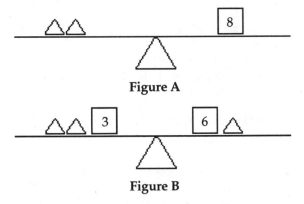

Figure A

Figure B

Children are encouraged to use a try-and-adjust strategy to determine the value of the pawn. For instance, for Figure B, a child might substitute 1 for a pawn ("x"). However, $1 + 1 + 3 \neq 12 + 1$, and so the child must try another value for x.

In the second lesson, students are asked to model equations such as $3x + x = x + 6$ and then solve them using a try-and-adjust strategy.

The third lesson introduces equations that may be difficult for many students to solve by

a try-and-adjust strategy (e.g. $5x + 1 = 4x + 9$). This creates an opportunity to introduce the undoing strategy. For the example illustrated in Figure C below, a teacher can ask if the scale will remain balanced or tilt if (a) a pawn is removed from one side (tilt), (b) if a pawn is removed from each side (balance), (c) if two pawns are removed from one side and one from the other (tilt), or (d) if three pawns are removed from each side (balance). By removing four pawns from each side (see Figure D below), students can see that $x + 1$ is the same number as 9 and conclude that x must be 8.

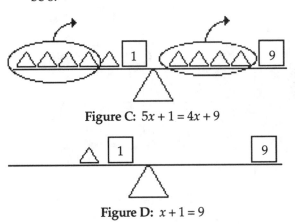

Figure C: $5x + 1 = 4x + 9$

Figure D: $x + 1 = 9$

Subsequent lessons introduce more complex equations and the use of parentheses.

☞ **The Ideas of Algebra, K-12** (1988 Yearbook), edited by Arthur F. Coxford, © 1988 by NCTM). One chapter (*Using Polynomials to Amaze* by C. H. Mulligan) includes a collection of amazing facts can prompt students to look for patterns and use algebra as a way of summarizing generalities and even justifying rules. For example, once students discover the pattern underlying the Fibonacii sequence (1, 1, 2, 3, 5, 8, 13, 21 ...), they can be encouraged to summarize the pattern as an algebraic expression.

Functions

☞ **Graphs Leading to Algebra** developed by the Nuffield Mathematics Project, © 1969 by the Nuffield Foundation, and published in the U.S. by John Wiley & Sons, Inc. This reference is appropriate mainly for intermediate-level teachers. It discusses introducing coordinate graphs, using graphs to represent algebraic equations such as $\square + 2 \triangle = 8$, and using more than one quadrant.

☞ **The Language of Functions and Graphs**, © 1985 by the Shell Centre for Mathematical Education, University of Nottingham, England. This excellent reference focuses on making sense of graphed data. Two graph-interpretation activities are illustrated below.

Example 1:   The Bus Stop Queue. Who is represented by each point on the scattergraph below?

Alice   Brenda   Cathy   Dennis   Errol   Freda   Gavin

Example 2:   Two Aircraft.

A   B

The following quick sketch graphs describe two light aircraft (Note: the graphs have not been drawn precisely).

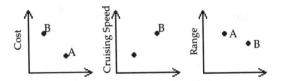

The first graph shows that aircraft B is more expensive than aircraft A. What else does it say?

• Are the following statements true or false?

"The older aircraft is cheaper."
"The faster aircraft is smaller."
"The larger aircraft is older."
"The cheaper aircraft carries fewer
    passengers."

• Copy the graphs below. On each graph, mark and label two points to represent A and B.

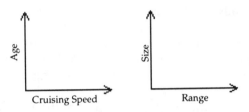

☞ **Patterns and Functions** by Elizabeth Phillips with Theodore Gardella, Constance Kelly, and Jacqueline Stewart, © 1991 by the NCTM. This outstanding resource is part of the *Curriculum and Evaluation Standards for School Mathematics Addenda Series for Grades 5-8.* It illustrates how pattern exploration can serve to foster an understanding of functions as well as other concepts such as exponents, primes, probability, rational numbers, and geometry.

☞ **Through Mathematical Eyes: Exploring Functional Relationships in Math and Science** edited by Ron Ritchhart, Dennie Palmer Wolf, and Julie Craven, ©1997, Heinemann.

A SAMPLE OF CHILDREN'S LITERATURE

📖 **A Game of Functions** by Robert Froman, © 1974 by Thomas Y. Crowell Company. This book begins by asking a question that gets at the heart of functions: "Have you noticed how some things depend on other things?" It then illustrate everyday functional relationships. The book goes on to describe a simple game for concretely introducing a coordinate grid and slope. A child is instructed, for instance to take one step out from a corner, and then one step up. After marking this child's position, another child can be instructed to take two steps out and two steps up, and a third child, three steps out and so forth. Later, more difficult relationships such as three steps out and one step up can be introduced.

📖 **666 Jellybeans! All That? An Introduction to Algebra** by Malcolm E. Weiss, © 1976, Thomas Y. Crowell. Readers are asked to determine if several number tricks will always work. Pictorial and algebraic proofs (like those shown in Frames A and C of Figure 16.2 on page 16-7) are included.

TIPS ON USING TECHNOLOGY

Calculators

Several recent advances in calculator technology can facilitate students exploration of algebra and functions. Some calculators are now designed to use (a) parentheses for grouping and (b) algebraic logic. The Texas Instruments *Mathmate*™ and *Math Explorer*™, for instance, can be used to correctly evaluate numerical expressions such as 5 + 2 x 3. A regular calculator would performed the arithmetic operations in the order they are key in.

Key: [5] [+] [2] [x] [3] [=]

Display: 5   2   7   3   21

Note that 5 and 2 are summed when the next operation (x) is keyed in. The *TI Mathmate*™ and *Math Explorer*™, take into account the rules of order (e.g., that multiplication is done before addition).

Key: [5] [+] [2] [x] [3] [=]

Display: 5   2   3   11

Note that the 5 and 2 are not summed when the next operation (x) is keyed in. To override the rules of order, parentheses can be keyed in. For example if a situation involved adding 5 and 2 and multiplying the sum by 3, a student would do the following:

Key: [(] [5] [+] [2] [)] [x] [3] [=]

Display: [5   2   7   3   21

Graphing calculators allow one to store values "in" a variable. For example, if you enter [3] [→] [x] (store 3 in *x*) and [4] [→] [y] (store 4 in *y*) and then enter [5] [(] [x] [+] [y] [)], 35 will be displayed. If, later, 2 is entered for *x* and the expression 5 (*x* + *y*) is key in, 30 will be displayed.

A major advantage of *graphing calculators* is that they can quickly translate an algebraic equation into a graph and vice versa. This can help students explore the connections between these two representations without the tedious effort of plotting points.

Suggestions for using calculators (and computers) for teaching graphing and functions to elementary students can be found in the following references: (a) **Functions, Graphing, and Technology** by C. Kieran. In *Integrating Research on the Graphical Representation of Function* edited by T. A. Romberg, E. Fennema, and T. P. Carpenter (© 1993 by Erlbaum). (b) **The Impact of Graphing Calculators on the Teaching and Learning of Mathematics**. In *Teaching and Learning Mathematics in the 1990s* (1990 Yearbook, pp. 205-211), edited by T. J. Cooney (NCTM). (c) **Uses of Technology in Prealgebra and Beginning Algebra** by M. K. Heid. *Mathematics Teacher, 83* (3), 194-198.

Computers

The following web site might be of interest to teachers or students of algebra: "The Algebra Word Problem Tutor" (http://sands.psy.cmu.edu/ACT/awpt/awpt-home.html).

The *SCANS* (Secretary Commission on Achieving Necessary Skills) Report (U.S. Department of Labor, Washington, D.C., 1990) recommended that in addition to competence with graphing calculators, students be able to use computers for generating spreadsheets and word processing and be familiar with dynamic software such as *Green Globs, Guess My Rules, Function Analyzer* and *Function Supposer* and such active application programs as *Geometer's Sketchpad* and *MathCad*.

Microcomputers such as the Power Macintosh 6400/200 now come with graphing software. The graphing function is easy to use and quickly translates algebraic expressions or sets of data into two- and three-dimensional graphs.

Box 16.3 on the next page illustrates how translating a problem situation into an algebraic equation and using technology can be invaluable labor-saving tools.

🖥 Box 16.3: Using an Everyday Problem as a Basis for Exploring Algebra

Some of Mr. Yant's students were having an animated discussion about their phone bills. Kimo commented that his parents made him pay for the line charges he ran up using the Internet. Anisha, who had her own phone line, was bemoaning her long-distance bills to her boyfriend. Mr. Yant saw these personal problems as an opportunity to introduce generalized number in an inquiry-based manner that also illustrated the usefulness of computers.

The class decided to tackle Anisha's problem first. After a review of her finances, everyone agreed that she had to budget her long-distance costs; a limit of four calls per week totaling $3.00 each was set. Anisha immediately wanted to know how many minutes each call could last. Taking into account her rate of 32¢ for the first minute and 22¢ for additional minutes, the class created the chart below. This showed she could talk for 13 minutes or less each time.

minutes	1	2	3	4	5	6	. . .	13	14
cost (¢)	32	54	76	98	120	142		296	318

Anisha then added, "Sometimes my grandparents send me money, sometimes I get extra money for babysitting, and sometimes I get money for gifts. So sometimes I have $50 or more dollars I could spend."

The students recognized that simply expanding table was not a practical solution. Marissa suggested using the computer. The class concluded that by letting the letter a represent the unknown (the number of *additional minutes* in a phone call), the cost of the call could be represented by the expression: **$32 + 22a$**. This expression was programmed into a microcomputer to create a spread sheet[*] shown below.

```
File: TELEPHOCOST                      REVIEW/ADD/CHANGE                    Escape:  Main Menu
=========A=========B=========C=========D=========E=========F=========G=========H=========
 1
 2              NUMBER OF          COST OF
 3              MINUTES            THE CALL
 4-----------------------------------------------------------
 5              +B4+1              +32+(22*B4)
 6              +B5+1              +32+(22*B5)
 7              +B6+1              +32+(22*B6)
 8              +B7+1              +32+(22*B7)
 9              +B8+1              +32+(22*B8)
10              +B9+1              +32+(22*B9)
11              +B10+1             +32+(22*B10)
12              +B11+1             +32+(22*B11)
13              +B12+1             +32+(22*B12)
14              +B13+1             +32+(22*B13)
15              +B14+1             +32+(22*B14)
16              +B15+1             +32+(22*B15)
17              +B16+1             +32+(22*B16)
18              +B17+1             +32+(22*B17)
-----------------------------------------------------------------------------------------
```

D3: (Label, Layout-C) THE CALL

Type entry or use @ commands   @-? for Help

---

[*]This spreadsheet was created through a series of formulas reflecting the algebraic expression 32 + 22a. Though there are many formulas in the spreadsheet, it is necessary to enter only the two formulas on line 5 shown below. In cell B5 (identified by column B and line 5), a formula +B4+1 is entered to create the value 1. (B4 has no numerical entry and thus is zero.) Through some simple commands the computer will copy the formula +B4+1 (the first + is an indicator to the computer that the characters following it represent a formula) into the cells below it in the column and will then make the expression relative to the row it is in. So, B4 becomes B5 in line 6, B6 in row 7, etc. The number of minutes will thus increase by one for each row. In cell D5, the cost of the call is determined by the formula +32+(22*B4). B4 represents the number of additional minutes beyond the first minute. In this line, the number of additional minutes is zero. In succeeding lines the number of additional minutes will always be one less than the total time of the call. This expression is then copied to the other cells in this column and made relative to the line it is in. Again, B4 becomes B5 in line 6, B6 in line 7, and so forth. These formulas are produced in a matter of seconds. These formulas then do the calculations instantaneously and produce the actual numerical values. Most software function similarly. In this example, Appleworks was used.

17 REFLECTIONS ON TEACHING: ORGANIZING INSTRUCTION TO ENHANCE MATHEMATICAL POWER, PROFESSIONAL DEVELOPMENT, AND EPILOGUE

What We Have Learned About Mathematics

Math is about solving problems. When I come to a hard problem is to drawn a picture or make a graft. Then I look for patterns. The patterns help me solve problems easier.

Arianne

Math is about finding patterns. Patterns are helpful in solving problem. Math can help solve problems. Using math you can solve a problem in a shorter time. Math makes problem solving easier and makes math fun to learn.

Alison
May 19, 1995

Mathematics is about solving problems, finding patterns and making shortcuts.
Making pictures and graphs can be helpful. For example, I used the graph below to solve the problem:
One of the Tempia triplets has a candy hidden in her hand. What are the chances Tim will pick the triplet with the candy and then pick the hand with the candy.
Alexis 5-19-95

Each 1/3 is a triplet, each 1/6 is their 6 hands. Only one hand has the candy so the answer is 1/6.

⌨ ✐ *What I have learned about mathematics?* can be a year-end journal assignment, which can also serve as a bulletin board display. Such a writing or computer assignment asks children to reflect on their mathematical experience and consider what it has taught them about the role of mathematics in their lives. At the end of each school year, teachers might benefit from reflecting on the question, *What I have learned about teaching mathematics?*

THIS CHAPTER

This is it—the final chapter. Although your long journey through this guidebook is nearly at an end, it is really only a beginning of a longer journey. We hope that this guide has helped foster a career-long interest in learning about math-

ematics education and improving mathematics instruction. We also hope that this guide has helped give you a better idea of how to create a learning environment that will spark a life-long love of mathematics and inquiry among your students.

In chapters 1, 2, and 3, we described a new way of teaching mathematics—a way that enhance children's mathematical power. In chapters 4 to 16, we discussed how this general approach can be used to teach specific content areas. This chapter closes out our exploration with some general reflections on teaching mathematics. In Unit 17•1, we consider how to organize instruction to enhance mathematical power. In Unit 17•2, we comment on how to further your professional development. The Epilogue brings our tale of Miss Brill to a fitting end.

17•1 ORGANIZING INSTRUCTION TO ENHANCE MATHEMATICAL POWER

Figure 17.1: No Plan, No Production

Teaching, like most endeavors in life such as taking a test (see Figure 17.1), requires planning. In Subunit 17•1•1, we discuss the role of planning and instructional management in maximizing students' mathematical power. In Subunit 17•1•2, we extend the discussion begun in chapters 1 and 2 about building a mathematical community. In Subunits 17•1•3 and 17•1•4, we discuss meeting individual needs and the needs of various types of children so that instruction can foster the mathematical power of *all* children. In Subunit 17•1•5, we consider what role technology should play in enhancing children's mathematical power.

17•1•1 PLANNING AND CONDUCTING MATHEMATICS INSTRUCTION

"The way in which instruction is planned and supported by the classroom environment" sends an unspoken message about what counts in learning and doing mathematics and, thus, "is crucial to what students learn" (Thornton & Wilson, 1993, p. 269). During her first year of teaching, Miss Brill learned a great deal about planning and conducting mathematics instruction.

Planning Instruction

The first-year teacher now understood what Ms. Socrates meant at the beginning of the year by, "PLAN AHEAD CAREFULLY, BUT DO NOT IMPLEMENT YOUR PLAN RIGIDLY. KEEP IN MIND THAT MATHEMATICAL THINKING AND UNDERSTANDING ARE LONG-RANGE GOALS."

Planning Ahead. Miss Brill now had a real appreciation for one of her education professor's favorite dictum, "The Seven Teaching Ps: *Poor Prior Planning Produces Pretty Poor Pedagogy.*" No doubt about it, reflected Miss Brill, when I did not plan ahead carefully, there was usually big trouble. Students were confused by inadequate instructions or groundwork; they become distracted while I searched for needed materials; they were perplexed or bored by instruction not suited to their developmental level or interests. She now recognized that poorly planned and uninspiring lessons were the key cause of nearly all of her discipline problems.

☞ **Planning ahead is essential for coherent mathematics instruction and for creating lessons that engage students' interests and thinking.** Miss Brill now recognized that even before school began, she needed an overview, which included a preliminary outline of when and how all the mathematical strands would be covered during the school year (Parker, 1993). This would better ensure that children had the prerequisite knowledge to build on and to tackle worthwhile tasks autonomously. Planning ahead is particularly important for lessons that entail active student involvement. It can lead students to greater levels of thinking and learning (Romberg & Carpenter, 1986; Thornton & Wilson, 1993) and can minimize discipline problems.

Flexibility. On the other hand, Miss Brill now recognized that a plan was merely a guide, not directions set in concrete. On many occasions, her lessons had taken an unexpected but useful turn. Often prepared problems, activities, or material prompted questions that led to interesting conjectures, debates, or explorations that served to actively involve students in mathematical inquiry and to deepen their understanding of mathematics (see, e.g., Box 17.1).

▨ Box 17.1: An Unexpected But Valuable Twist

To introduce the distinction between terminating decimals and infinitely repeating decimals, Miss Brill had her students use calculators to convert common fractions such as $\frac{3}{4}$ and $\frac{2}{3}$ to decimals. This prompted Aliya to ask an interesting question, "Our calculator only goes to seven decimal places. For example, when I changed one-seventh into a decimal, I got 0.1428571. How can I tell if it will stop at some point or if it will start repeating a pattern?"

Rodney offered, "Based on the example you've given us ($\frac{1}{2} = 0.5$, $\frac{3}{4} = 0.75$, $\frac{4}{10} = 0.4$, $\frac{3}{20} = 0.15$, $\frac{1}{3} = .33\overline{3}$, $\frac{2}{9} = 0.22\overline{2}$, and $\frac{4}{11} = .36\overline{36}$), I'd say if the bottom part of a fraction is even, then its decimal is terminating and, if the bottom part is odd, then its decimal is repeating."

"What do the rest of you think of Rodney's conjecture?" queried Miss Brill.

"I don't think so," intoned Michelle. "Look one-fifth is equal to point two." Others quickly came up with additional counterexamples to Rodney's conjecture.

Aliya offered, "Maybe the bottom has to be prime to be equal to a terminating decimal."

"No way," Andy interjected. "Three is prime, and one-third converts to a repeating decimal."

Impressed by how involved her student were in the process of mathematical inquiry, Miss Brill abandoned the rest of her planned lesson and encouraged the class to classify and to analyze more examples and to propose and to test additional conjectures. Andy suggested, "All our examples of fractions that convert to terminating decimals have a bottom part like two or ten that are factors of 100—that divide into 100 evenly; those that convert to repeating decimals have a bottom part like 3 or 15 that are not factors of 100."

"Interesting conjecture," remarked Miss Brill, "Can anyone find a counterexample?"

Soon after, Judi offered, "One one-thousandth equals the terminating decimal .001, and 1000 is not a factor of 100."

"Maybe the bottom part has to be a factor of 1000," offered Andy, trying to salvage his conjecture.

"But what about one ten-thousandth?" countered Judi. The class saw that this line of argument could go on indefinitely, but at least it got them thinking in the right direction.

"I know," pronounced LeMar, "If the denominator has two or five as a factor, then the fraction equals a terminating decimal."

Despite a murmur of satisfaction from the class, Miss Brill persisted, "Can anyone find a counterexample?"

Diego offered, "What about one-fifteenth? Five is a factor of fifteen but one-fifteenth equals a repeating decimal. The class ended without resolving Aliya's question.

The next day, Aliya proposed a refinement of LeMar's conjecture—fractions whose bottom part had (prime) factors of *only* 2 and 5 (e.g., $\frac{1}{4} = \frac{1}{2 \cdot 2}$, $\frac{1}{10} = \frac{1}{2 \cdot 5}$, $\frac{1}{25} = \frac{1}{5 \cdot 5}$) could be changed into terminating decimals and those with some other factor (e.g., $\frac{2}{15} = \frac{2}{5 \cdot 3}$, $\frac{1}{12} = \frac{1}{2 \cdot 2 \cdot 3}$, or $\frac{1}{35} = \frac{1}{7 \cdot 5}$) could be changed into repeating decimals. This pronouncement was dubbed and thereafter referred to as *Aliya's rule*.

Miss Brill was glad the class had taken the detour. Not only had it created an opportunity for students to propose and test conjectures, they made a connection between previously studied material (prime factoring) and types of decimal, thus, deepening their understanding.

☞ **Seize on unplanned opportunities to engage students in mathematical inquiry and the exploration of concepts.** Taking the time to evaluate students' spontaneous conjectures and questions *on the spot* can, perhaps, do more than anything to create a spirit of inquiry and help children understand and value the processes of mathematical inquiry. It can be more motivating than waiting to cover the material later when you had planned. Learning is like eating an apple, which is more delicious when ripe.

Long-Range Planning and the Spiral Curriculum. After watching students struggle to construct mathematical concepts, Miss Brill better understand that meaningful learning takes time. Moreover, she recognized that while a teacher should strive to make each lesson understandable to students, a deep understanding requires making many connections, and this typically requires revisiting an idea many times. For these reasons, she concluded, planning to teach a mathematical idea in a single discrete lesson usually did not make sense. She recognized that lessons needed to be planned carefully in the context of a unit and that ideas had to be revisited again and again in later units.

Curriculum Issues

Miss Brill now recognized that, as a professional, she (not a textbook) should dictate the curriculum.

Using Textbooks. At the beginning of the year, the new teacher could not fathom Ms. Socrates' comment that "an obstacle to achieving the vision presented by the NCTM *Standards* is reliance on the textbook as a means of delivering appropriate curriculum. Teachers must make decisions about the content of a text and reorganize it in ways that will help them teach the key ideas" (NCTM, 1992, p. 62). As Miss Brill compared Mrs. MeChokemchild's and her own textbook-based approach with Ms. Socrates's approach that built on worthwhile tasks, she recognized that relying heavily on a textbook, even their new and improved one, did not adequately foster mathematical power. The instructors' manual to their textbook laid out clearly what the teachers should say and do but was less informative about how to involve students in the processes of mathematical inquiry. In contrast, while Ms. Socrates actively created, monitored,

and guided learning situations, it was her students who spent most of the class time talking (e.g., conjecturing, justifying and debating ideas) and doing mathematics (e.g., solving problems, finding patterns, logically proving conjectures). Their textbook still treated mathematics largely as information that had to be transmitted to students. For example, procedures for operating on fractions and decimals were simply laid out for children, whereas Ms. Socrates created opportunities for her students to invent their own procedures and to rediscover formal ones. Their textbook provided pages of sterile drill exercises, whereas Ms. Socrates provided purposeful and often entertaining practice. Moreover, content was still basically introduced discretely by topics, rather than in Ms. Socrates's integrated fashion. "A typical text [also] often precludes the use of technology, which should play an integral part in any discussion of mathematics reform" (NCTM, 1992, p. 62) (see Subunit 17•1•5). In brief, proceeding through a typical textbook chapter by chapter can serve as the foundation for the skills or the conceptual approach, but it is not an adequate basis for the investigative approach.

In a purposeful, inquiry-based, and meaningful approach, textbooks are *one* resource from which teachers can pick and choose material to meet their instructional goals (Madsen & Baker, 1993). Newer textbooks generally contain many interesting problems, activities, investigations, and other teaching ideas that can serve as worthwhile tasks. Moreover, textbooks can serve as an invaluable reference to students as they try, for instance, to clarify the meaning of a term, to find an example of a concept, or to convert units of measure, and so forth.

Teacher-Designed Instruction. To avoid the textbook-induced tendency to teach an entire strand before beginning another, Mr. Yant's team decided to construct its own integrated mathematics curriculum so that students could better see the interconnectedness of mathematical topics. To do this, they compiled a list of concepts that they felt eighth graders should understand. They noted each on a notecard and sorted them by strands (e.g., rational numbers, geometry, algebra). Under each strand, they sequenced the cards vertically by relative difficulty—taking into account prerequisite knowledge. They then looked horizontally across different strands to see which concepts could be taught together and which were prerequisites for other concepts. They kept raising and lowering the cards to create a developmentally appropriate order. During this process, the team chose or devised problems that involved the concepts of approximately the same developmental level.

Replacement Units: An Intermediate Measure. In between relying on a textbook and devising your own curriculum is the intermediate step of using curriculum replacement units such as the Marilyn Burns Replacement Units (e.g., see pages 5-34 and 6-29), *Seeing Fractions: A Unit for the Upper Elementary Grades* (see page 10-23), and *Used Numbers: Real Data in the Classroom* (see page 13-29). These can serve as a stopgap measure while teachers built heir own program.

Models of Classroom Instruction

Miss Brill quickly recognized that the way she had always been taught mathematics (the traditional skills approach) was not an interesting or effective way to teach. This conclusion was hastened by her students' reactions to math class—groans and comments such as, "Time to hit the snooze button," "Time out *from* thinking," "Not fractions again—we study this stuff every year, and I still don't get it," and "Say what???"

From observing experienced and effective teachers and from her own experience, Miss Brill also recognized that no single alternative teaching method was sufficient to sustain student involvement and to foster their mathematical power (Mathematical Sciences Education Board, National Research Council, 1987; Rowen & Cetorelli, 1990; Thornton & Wilson, 1993). That is, some situations call for the conceptual approach; others, for the investigative approach; and yet others, for the problem-solving approach. Tips on organizing the investigative approach are discussed below.

↪ **Be on the lookout for worthwhile tasks that can serve as the basis for purposeful and meaningful inquiry.** Because Miss Brill wanted to incorporate problem-solving into her instruction but also felt compelled to cover the content outlined in her district's curriculum, she often tried the investigative approach—a blend of the teacher-directed conceptual approach and the student-centered problem-solving approach. The

real trick to this inquiry-based approach was finding a problem or project that would raise the questions or issues that would naturally lead to an exploration of the content she wanted to introduce. Her experienced colleague, Ms. Socrates, shared with her a number of good ideas. And as her teaching, reading, graduate course work, inservice workshops, and everyday experiences helped her construct more and more mathematical connections, Miss Brill saw more and more opportunities for inquiry-based content instruction.

↪ **Integrating whole-class instruction and discussion and small-group work can be a highly effective approach.** Such an approach has been shown to be more effective in promoting higher-level thinking than direct instruction alone (Peterson, 1988; Thornton & Wilson, 1993). A general plan that Miss Brill found useful was to cycle between teacher-directed whole-class interaction and student-centered individual or group activities (see Figure 17.2). This allowed her to frame a problem or project for the class, answer questions and clarify the task demands, and specify directions or expectations. This phase was typically brief. Students then worked semi-independently while Miss Brill circulated among them. She seldom answered questions directly but provided guidance by asking questions, such as *Does your answer make sense? Does everyone agree? Is there anything you have overlooked?* This phase usually took the bulk of the time. For those students or groups that finished early, she tried to have a problem extension or enrichment activity ready. Afterward, the students shared, justified, and debated their strategies, solutions, ideas, or creations. This provided an opportunity for Miss Brill or a student to summarize explicitly what had been learned. It also often led to new questions for exploration. The time for this phase varied considerably.

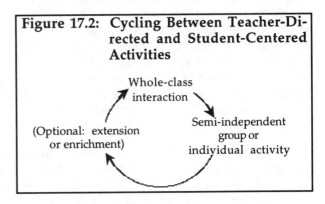

Figure 17.2: Cycling Between Teacher-Directed and Student-Centered Activities

Whole-class interaction

Semi-independent group or individual activity

(Optional: extension or enrichment)

☞ **Begin with guided inquiry and use menus as a way of preparing children for self-directed exploration.** This may be particularly important for young children, students who are accustomed to the skills approach, or children with learning difficulties. Providing menus can be a useful compromise or an intermediate step between guided and autonomous inquiry. *Menus can consist of several required tasks and a choice of additional required tasks or optional tasks.* Typically, a time limit is specified for completing the required tasks. Students can be given the choice to work on tasks individually, with their group, or other children. To assess individual or group progress, students can keep a menu book or record of their efforts and findings. In brief, menus give children the opportunity to make decisions themselves—choices about what tasks to work on, when and how to complete the work, with whom to work with, and with how to document their efforts.

Mathematics Learning Centers and Stations

Permanent mathematics learning centers or temporary mathematics learning stations can support the independent explorations of individual students or groups of students.

Mathematics Learning Center. A math center is a permanent place in the classroom for housing books (including children's literature, activity books, textbooks, and references), equipment (including computers and calculators), and materials (including manipulatives, graph paper, dot-matrix paper, and hundreds chart). It is a place where students know they can turn to look up information or to find materials for solving a problem, checking a conjecture, demonstrating a point or strategy, and so forth. A math center can be a place where students feel free to explore their own mathematical questions or teacher-designed, inquiry-based activities. Ideally the latter should involve a variety of mathematical rich tasks to accommodate children with a range of developmental levels and interests. A math center can include a table, bookcase and a bulletin board. It might also include a carpeted area where children can read, experiment with manipulatives, draw, and so forth.

Mathematics Learning Stations. A math station is a temporary set up that invites student-initiated exploration of a specific idea. It can either be set up as a part of, or apart from, a math

center using a desk, a table, a bulletin board, a computer station, or carpeted room corner. A math station can involve playing a familiar math game; open-ended or prescribed building or drawing activities; designing patterns (e.g., tessellations); using a computer to play a computer game, to work through an instructional lesson, or to engage in a programming activity (e.g., LOGO); listening to a reading of a children's literature book involving mathematics and following along in the book; engaging in a discovery-learning activity; solving one or more mathematical word problems or puzzles; writing about a mathematics-related topic; and so forth. Some activities may be appropriate for children of all ability levels; others may not be. For the latter, a station can offer alternative activities appropriate for children of different ability levels. Note that all the station activities should have instructions that are clear and self-explanatory. Instruction can be written on, for example, laminated 5 x 8 cards or sheets of paper secured in a notebook or presented orally using a tape recorder and earphones.

Homework

Miss Brill had been confused about homework. As a student, she had hated it. While at college, she had read that a school board had actually banned homework. She really wondered if it was necessary to inflict this time honored punishment on her students.

However, some of her colleagues treated her doubts as sacrilege. "No homework," roared Mrs. MeChokemchild charging at Miss Brill with her mouth open so wide the new teacher feared her head would be bit off. "Are you mad? Homework—and lots of it—are absolutely necessary for school achievement!"

"I agree that homework is important," added Ms. Socrates—to the complete surprise of Miss Brill, "But homework—like teacher talk, group work, or manipulatives—is a teaching tool that should be used thoughtfully and carefully."

Meaningful Homework. "The quality of homework is more important than its quantity," continued Ms. Socrates. "Several interesting and challenging tasks can accomplish as much as, if not more than, tons of tedious exercises. Students can get all the practice of basic skills they need by regularly solving problems, playing math games, or doing personally meaningful projects. I never use worksheets with rows and rows of computations."

"Home Connections." One way homework can be very useful is in helping children see the connection between school mathematics and everyday life at home. Encouraging children to apply what they learned in school to their personal life can help them construct a deeper understanding of school mathematics in a personally meaningful way.

Home Connections can also actively involve children's parents or guardians with their learning and practice of school mathematics (see, e.g., Box 17.2). For example, a parent can play games, provide opportunities to cook, undertake craft projects, share hobby interest, or otherwise extend the mathematical instruction and practice provided by school. Moreover, such parental involvement can help bring families closer together and foster the belief that mathematics is valued by all family members.

17•1•2 PROMOTING A MATHEMAT-ICAL COMMUNITY

In chapters 1 and 2, we discussed various methods for promoting a mathematical community. In this subunit, we discuss three additional factors—classroom arrangement, the role of questions, and parental support.

Classroom Arrangement

At the beginning of the school year, Miss

Box 17.2: Example of a *Home Connections* Message

Home Connections

Dear Parent or Guardian:

Our class has been studying different types of symmetries. Would you ask your child to explain slide symmetry, turn symmetry, and flip (or mirror) symmetry to you? Would you then help your child to find two examples of each in your house. Please have your child draw a picture, describe, or otherwise record each example.

Thank you for your help.

Brill found her classroom organized as she had remembered her elementary classrooms. The desks were neatly lined up in rows (see Frame A of Figure 17.3). She soon discovered that this arrangement made small-group problem solving and discussions difficult. It was hard for her to circulate and to keep tabs on each group's or each individual's progress. Moreover, it impeded discussion (e.g., children in the back often got "lost"). Miss Brill found that arranging the desk in groups of four to six (use Frame B of Figure 17.3) facilitated small-group work and allowed her to circulate freely, better ensuring that no one was left out.

Using Questions to Prompt Classroom Interaction

Classroom interaction is "the heartbeat of the teaching-learning process" (Koehler & Prior, 1993, p. 282). Teacher-student and student-stu-

---

Figure 17.3: Two Classroom Arrangements

A. **Traditional rows of desks**

B. **Groups of 4 to 6 desks**

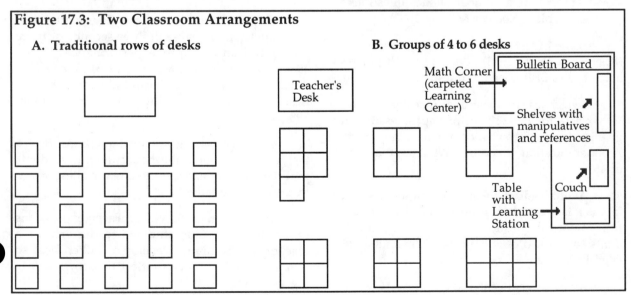

dent interactions are key to exchanging ideas, creating cognitive conflict or doubt, and otherwise prompting reflection and adjustments in thinking. In chapter 2, we examined several tools for promoting classroom interaction such as inviting justifications and class consensus and promoting group work (see Subunit 2•3•2). In this section, we focus on how teachers' and students' questions can promote the development of a mathematical community.

Asking Effective Questions. Miss Brill discovered that asking students good questions required considerable thought and skill.

↪ **Rely on questions that require understanding and prompt thought rather than factual recall** On her first observation of Miss Brill's class, the school principal noted that like many teachers, the new teacher asked a good number of questions, but nearly all simply required students to recall a fact (see, e.g., Fennema & Peterson, 1986; Hart, 1989; Suydam, 1985, all cited in Koehler & Prior, 1993). "Students can answer such questions by merely using knowledge they have memorized by rote," advised Mrs. Dew-Wright. "Try to work toward including more questions that involve higher levels of cognitive functioning. Ask questions that require students to *explain* an answer, to *analyze* a situation, to *apply* learned material, to *integrate* ideas, and to *evaluate* whether or not a position makes sense. Such questions will promote reasoning and communicating skills as well as deeper understanding. Because thought-provoking questions can be difficult to construct on the spot, it may help to plan some ahead—to include a number of such questions in your lesson plan (Koehler & Prior, 1993).

↪ **Use effective questioning techniques** (Koehler & Prior, 1993). Mrs. Dew-Wright also helped Miss Brill hone her questioning technique.

• **Avoid *yes-no* questions.** Questions such as "Is six a factor of 48?" can prompt guessing and give students a 50% chance of guessing correctly. A better question would be, "What are the factors of 48?"

• **Avoid leading questions.** Questions such as "Six is a factor of 48 is it not?" can be tantamount to a rhetorical question that do not require students to think (Posamentier & Stepelman, 1986, cited in Koehler & Prior, 1993).

• **Avoid teacher-centered questions.** Use

questions such as "Tell the *class* a factor of 48" rather than questions such as "Tell *me* a factor of 48." The former suggests that the whole class should listen to the answer and evaluate it. The latter question suggests that only the teacher should do so.

• **Avoid labeling questions as *easy* or *hard*.** Students who answer questions labeled *easy* won't get much satisfaction and those who can't will feel incompetent (Johnson, 1982). Labeling questions as *hard* may discourage some students.

• **Avoid verbal and nonverbal clues.** Questions with an uneven tone of voice (e.g., "Does the problem involve addition or SUBTRACTION?") or accompanied by facial gestures (e.g., "Does the problem involve addition [eyes downcast] or subtraction [eyes bright and straightward]?") can readily give away an answer.

Responding to Student Replies. From hard experience, Miss Brill also learned that *how* a teacher responded to students' replies was crucial to promoting a mathematical community.

↪ **Give students the opportunity to air *their* views.** When Miss Brill began teaching, she focused on getting through the material. Her concern about completing lessons led to impatience and response techniques that blocked open communication. If students did not respond immediately to a question, she would simply answer it herself. If students did try to answer, her smiles, nodding, grimaces, hand clenching, and so forth lead them to a predetermined answer she had in mind.

• **Regularly use wait time.** Pause after asking a question. A pause of three seconds or more can significantly improve performance (Rowe, 1986, cited in Koehler & Prior, 1993). It can give students the time to think carefully and gain confidence before responding (Clark & Peterson, 1986, p. 9).

• **Avoid answering your own questions.** Such a technique promotes the belief among students that they are not expected to answer questions or that they are unable to.

• **Avoid nonverbal clues.** Facial expressions or gestures can clue students to the answer a teacher has in mind. Develop a "poker face" so that students' responses reflect their own thinking, not yours.

Encouraging Student Questions. As a preservice teacher, Miss Brill learned that student questions could provide a springboard to inquiry and genuine learning. This remained an unused intellectual abstraction until she saw the excitement a student's spontaneous question could produce. With experience, Miss Brill felt more and more comfortable about taking time to address these "interruptions" to her planned lesson. She recognized that student questions typically stemmed from curiosity, puzzlement, and a real need to know. And, as a teacher, it was crucial to take advantage of these learning moments. From her own experience as a student, Miss Brill knew that encouraging student questions required more than saying, "If you have any question, just ask" (see Box 17.3).

Box 17.3: How a Teacher Responds to Student Questions Can Greatly Affect Their Willingness to Participate

I was always anxious and fearful of math. My instructors would always tell us to ask questions if we did not understand, so I would . . . . When I did, they often addressed me in a condescending tone, and in the classes that followed they would ask that all questions be held until the end of the class (on account of time). Eventually I stopped asking questions all together. This led to me falling further and further behind. I was never talked to by instructors (because my grades were never lower than a C). I . . . had the impression that they did not care—the ones who got it got it and those who didn't so what.—Bonnie McArthur

---

↪ **By word *and* deed encourage students to ask questions.** Miss Brill had a most impersonal and stern eighth-grade math teacher. Even so, this teacher had said one thing that impressed her, "If you have a question, ask it. Your question will probably benefit others, because it may be one they have or should have had." Miss Brill made sure to tell her class this and that questions were a sign of thinking. Perhaps more importantly, she learned how to respond to spontaneous questions so that her students saw they were valued. She took class time to explore questions of general interest and promptly and consistently got together privately with an individual or group who raised a questions of local concern.

Parental Support

Miss Brill was upset by the reaction of some of the parents at her last open house. "I noted that we were moving toward an investigative approach," she explained to Mrs. Socrates, "using projects and other worthwhile tasks to make mathematics instruction interesting and purposeful, to involve children in problem solving, reasoning, and communicating, and to make learning meaningful. I thought parents would be pleased. Instead some of them seemed upset. One father angrily said, 'I don't want my kid having fun or solving problems. I want him to memorize basic facts and computational procedures. I want him to bring home worksheets!' I was so caught off guard, I couldn't summon a good counterargument."

"The vast majority of parents and guardians are products of the traditional skills approach," replied Ms. Socrates, "and their beliefs about teaching mathematics are similar to those of Mrs. McChokemchild. To successfully implement the investigative approach you will need to convince them that mathematics can be interesting and fun and that it involves more than memorizing facts and procedures by rote. Changing parents' beliefs is important because they can profoundly affect their children's beliefs and willingness to join your mathematical community. Moreover, hostile parents can not only make teaching less pleasant, they may involve administrators and school board members, who in turn may interfere with the way you want to teach. Thus, it is important to develop a plan for bringing parents 'on board.' Here are some tips:

1. First thing in the fall, I hold a *Family Entertainment Night*. We play a math game such as *Equal Nim* (see Box 0.1 on page 0-16) or tackle some other interesting math task such as the *Horse* problem: If I bought a horse for $50, sold it for $60, bought it back for $70, and resold it for $80, what profit would I make if any? (from the *Mathematics: What Are You Teaching My Child* videotape featuring Marilyn Burns and distributed by Scholastic). The point of the event is that doing mathematics can be fun. Family Entertainment Night was so popular, I hold one every quarter now.

2. At my first open house, I explain the rationale for using the investigative approach. I briefly outline how this approach enhances

mathematical power better than the traditional skills approach (see chapter 1 and Box 2.2 on page 2-12). I note that I'm not 'throwing the baby out with the bath water' (Ohanian, 1992)—overlooking the mastery of basic skills while forsaking traditional teaching methods. I emphasize that, in fact, the investigative approach is more effective than the traditional skills approach in fostering skill mastery (see, e.g., Probe 1.3 on page 1-26 and Probe 3.1 on pages 3-4 and 3-5).

✐ 3. I regularly sent home *Home Connections* messages (see Box 17.2 on page 17-7) and *Student-Parent Letters*. The latter entails a writing assignment such as "What Math Did I Learn in the Plant-Growing Project?" This requires students to explicitly reflect on what they have learned. Sending the letter home provides parents with a sample of their children's writing performance and informs them about what their children are learning in mathematics.

✐ ⌨ 4. Monthly, I sent home a *class newspaper*. Regular pieces include a feature article about what we have done the previous month that involved mathematics (e.g., "various ways to solve a problem mentally" or "how geometry and multiplication are related"); a math riddle, puzzle, or problem; math games that reinforce concepts and skills learned in school; suggested children's literature, useful references (e.g., *Beyond Facts & Flashcards: Exploring Math With Your Kids* by Jan Mokros, © 1996, Heinemann), and web sites of particular interest to parents (e.g., "Helping Your Child Learn Math" made available by the U.S. Department of Education at www.ed.gov/pubs/parents/math/). Most of the material is collected and written by the math editors and other children. The class newspaper involves students in researching and writing about mathematics and using word processing and computer graphic skills. Laying out the paper engages geometric (spatial reasoning) skills. The parents are kept informed and many actually find the newspaper entertaining."

17•1•3 MEETING INDIVIDUAL NEEDS

A teacher—even at the kindergarten level—can expect significant individual differences and readiness to solve problems and to learn new concepts. In this section, we address the issue of heterogeneous versus homogeneous grouping and how a classroom teacher can organize instruction to meet the diverse needs of their students.

Heterogeneous versus Homogeneous Grouping

"Should math instruction always involve children of mixed abilities or developmental levels?" wondered Miss Brill.

A Case for Mixed-Ability Grouping. Several colleagues argued passionately that groups should always involve children of mixed abilities. As Miss Pickney explained, "By working with developmentally more advanced students, developmentally less advanced have many helpers instead of just one (the teacher). They are much more likely to be stimulated and to learn by watching and listening to high-ability kids than they would if they were stuck with other low-ability kids. Tracking tends to perpetuate or even accentuate achievement differences. And finally, grouping by ability exposes and stigmatizes slow learners."

A Case for Some Ability Grouping. "Oh fiddle-faddle," barked Mrs. MeChokemchild. "You think the kids don't know who is sharp in math and who isn't? Do you think by pretending that there are no differences, the differences disappear? Get a grip on it."

Ms. Socrates entered the fray, "Generally speaking, I work with my whole class or have students work in small heterogeneous groups. But sometimes whole-class discussions or heterogeneous grouping cannot provide developmentally less advanced children what they need. Moreover, it is important to provide my developmentally more advanced children opportunities to explore material in more depth than their peers are ready or care to explore."

"It seems to me," continued Ms. Socrates, "one of our fundamental tasks as educators to prepare our students to respect individual differences in talent and interest. Thank goodness we are not all good at or fascinated by the same things. I try to help my students see that each of us has strengths. One child might be good at arithmetic computations but not visualizing situations. Another might be weak at arithmetic computations but terrific at visualizing situations. The flip side is that all of us need help with something, and there's no shame in getting that help. All of us—including me—are on a journey toward more complete knowledge."

☞ **Flexible grouping can provide a balance between mixed-ability and same-ability grouping.** How a child is grouped can be varied according to topic—specifically, the child's developmental level and interest in the topic and his or her need for practicing it or readiness for extension in it (Thornton & Wilson, 1993). Grouping can also vary with instructional aim. For example, problem solving might involve mixed grouping whereas reviewing a concept might be done in homogeneous groups. (This would free children who already understand the concept to work on enrichment activities and free the teacher to focus on those struggling to construct the concept.)

Organizing Instruction to Provide More Individualized Attention

Concerned that not all of her children were receiving the individualized help they needed, Miss Brill pleaded, "I know that it is important to individualize instruction, particularly for those students who are struggling. But I'm already overwhelmed. *How can I possibly provide 25 or so students individual attention?*"

"It's hard at best," responded Ms. Socrates knowingly. "To provide more individual contact, teachers can free up time by using round-robin learning stations and additional helpers such as parent volunteers and cross-age or peer tutors."

Round-Robin Learning Stations. Round-robin learning stations are a series of mathematics learning stations that groups of children rotate through. While one group is meeting with the teacher, the other groups are productively engaged in one of the learning stations. (There should be one station for each group not meeting with the teacher.) The teacher then is free to focus on about four to six children. The teacher-led group can work on solving a problem that involves the particular concepts or skills the group needs to learn or practice, experimenting with manipulatives to better understand a concept or procedure, analyzing examples and nonexamples of a concept, playing an error-detection game, analyzing and discussing common errors, or other instructional or remedial activity helpful for the individuals in the group.

Additional Helpers. "I tried using my more

developmentally advanced students as tutors," noted Miss Brill, "but it didn't work out well."

"With all helpers, be they parent, student teacher, older child, or class member," responded Ms. Socrates, "you will need to take some time to help them become good teachers. Helpers need to realize, for example, that teaching is not simply giving a student the answer. Good teaching involves helping others formulate or discover answers, and this requires, for instance, patience and careful thought-provoking questions." Moreover, helpers are typically most effective when implementing a specific idea planned by a teacher.

17•1•4 EMPOWERING ALL CHILDREN

"I read the *Mathematical Power* book you lent me," Miss Brill commented to Ms. Socrates. "Parker (1993) made a good point, 'There are well-ingrained myths in this country about who can and who can't learn math' (p. 4). For most of my life I believed that girls were among those who couldn't."

"This myth has also hampered minority children and children with learning difficulties," added Ms. Wise. "Often, these children were considered particularly incapable of mathematical thinking and understanding and, as a result, weren't given the encouragement or even a chance to learn worthwhile mathematics."

"It was a real eye opener to read that 'the heart of mathematics reform efforts is a belief that mathematics is for *all* children. All children have the right to a mathematics education that engages them with important mathematical ideas, requires thinking, and develops understanding' (Parker, 1993, p. 4)," added Miss Brill enthusiastically.

"Speaking of all children," commented Ms. Socrates, "Our student population is more diverse than when I was in elementary school. My fifth-grade class was nearly all middle-class and did not have a single minority, physically handicapped, or mentally handicapped child in it. And the trend is toward even more diverse classes in the future."

"My background didn't prepare me well to handle the assortment of children in my class," confided Miss Brill.

To help you prepare for teaching a diverse population, we examine the impact of teacher expectations and provide a perspective and tips on working with various populations of children.

The Role of Teacher Expectations

In chapter 1, we explored three factors that heavily influenced the decisions teachers make—their beliefs and knowledge about mathematics, children, and teaching techniques. Another key factor is the expectations teachers have for individual students. Accurate expectations are essential for adjusting instruction so that it matches the interest, needs, and developmental level of individual pupils. High (but reasonable) expectations can create a self-fulfilling prophecy that maximize students' mathematical power. Inaccurately low expectations can create a self-fulfilling prophesy also, but one that cheats a student. Figure 17.4 (below) illustrates how this self-fulfilling prophesy (the Pygmalion Effect). *How can a teacher use expectations effectively—to maximize the benefits of the Pygmalion Effect and to minimize its harm?* Three suggestions are noted below.

☞ **Consciously recognize, monitor, and control your expectations.** The first key in dealing with the Pygmalion Effect effectively is understanding the power of expectations and how they are communicated both verbally and nonverbally. Second, it is important to develop a healthy skepticism for all sources of information on which expectations can be based—including the scores of achievement or IQ tests and other apparently authoritative sources. Third, teachers should confront their stereotypes and not use them to prejudge children. Fourth, teachers should consider what expectations they communicate explicitly or implicitly.

☞ **Use expectations constructively—have high expectations for all students.** Frequently, this will cause students to blossom or at least achieve far more than otherwise.

☞ **Treat children as individuals, regardless of IQ, achievement level, gender, race, or other label** (see Box 17.4 on the next page). Research regularly finds immense differences in the mathematical performance of what are often assumed to be a homogeneous group of children. For example, Baroody (1996) found that, although often characterized as passive learners incapable of adaptive expertise, some mentally handicapped children spontaneously invented more efficient strategies for determining sums. Moreover, he found that IQ level ("mildly retarded" or having an IQ 51-75 versus "moderate retarded" or having an IQ 26-50)—which should distinguish adap-

---

Figure 17.4: Mechanisms for Self-Fulfilling Prophecies[†]

TEACHER EXPECTATIONS	→ TEACHER BEHAVIOR	→ STUDENT ATTITUDES AND BEHAVIOR
Sources of expectations: 1. Social class 2. Race 3. Gender 4. IQ score 5. Grade records 6. Other teachers' comments 7. Track or grouping 8. Initial interaction 9. Previous siblings 10. Appearance 11. Labels such as *gifted, learning disabled,* or *mentally handicapped*	Means by which teacher's attitudes are transmitted 1. *Climate:* Teacher treats favored students more warmly. 2. *Feedback:* Teacher praises and discusses the efforts of favored students more. 3. *Input:* Teacher presents favored students more material and more difficult material. 4. *Output:* Teacher gives favored students more opportunity to respond and ask questions.	The teacher's behavior may have the effect of encouraging (rewarding) or discouraging (punishing) the child's academic, athletic, or social behavior. Also, from the teacher's behavior, the child may sense the teacher's opinion of him/her. The child may come to believe the teacher is correct and incorporate this opinion into his/her self-concept.

[†] Adapted from The Pygmalion Effect Lives by R. Rosenthal, *Psychology Today,* 9/73.

Box 17.4: A Change of Heart or The Case of a Misleading Label

"At the beginning of the year," reminisced Miss Brill, "I really misjudged . . . prejudged LeMar. Ms. Finkel, his fourth-grade teacher, had warned me to watch out for him because he was a trouble maker. His school records indicated he was *learning disabled* in mathematics, and . . . he is black. Putting all this information together, I concluded—I'm ashamed to say—that LeMar was beyond my help. Worse, I assumed he was going to be nothing but a problem, and I feared him."

"We didn't get off to a good start," continued Miss Brill. "I did not expect that LeMar would do well in school math and he responded accordingly. He was disruptive, and I responded defensively. I took his misbehavior personally—as a rebuke of me."

"But I discovered," added Miss Brill, "that, in fact, he was bright, curious, and imaginative—that he is probably mathematically gifted. I also found that he could be amiable, charming, and funny. He seemed learning disabled because he refused to play the game of school—make an effort to learn even if the material didn't make sense or wasn't important to him. LeMar just wasn't interested in getting grades or learning something because maybe it would be important years later. He acted out because of frustration. He was intensely curious and school math was just plain boring. School was driving him crazy. When I changed the way I taught—when I introduced problem solving and we began to grapple with some real projects—LeMar was transformed from Mr. Hyde into Dr. Jeckle. We became kindred spirits; I really came to treasure him. I can't believe I could so completely misjudge a person."

"I can understand why you were misled by LeMar's classification as learning disabled," commented Ms. Socrates. "It is a confusing term that is frequently not used precisely or carefully. Historically, it has been used to describe children of average intelligence who had difficulty learning specific content because something wasn't right in their brain. Our education system typically uses it to describe children of average intelligence whose achievement is two years behind their grade level. Although neurological evidence is seldom used to label children *LD*, many parents and educators assume such children have brain damage. That is, they confuse the histori-

cal definition and its criterion with the educational definition and its criterion. In recent years, I've had five children labeled *LD* in my classes, and in only one of these cases was there medical evidence of brain dysfunction."

"All too often," continued Ms. Socrates bitterly, "the *LD* label is used to blame the children for their difficulties and as an excuse to water down their instruction. I remember when my own daughter was doing poorly in math. The reading specialist suggested she was learning disabled and probably had a figure-ground difficulty, meaning she could not distinguish an object from its background. I asked her if she had ever watched my daughter navigate a playground or read a book she was interested in? Then the reading specialist said that may be she had a memory deficit instead. I felt like saying, 'Are you crazy? Have you ever played a game with my daughter like *Concentration*, where you had to remember the location of items over long periods of time? She has an incredible memory when she wants to use it! Beware of jargon that pass as easy explanations."

"What was wrong with your daughter?" asked a curious Miss Brill.

"Nothing was wrong with my daughter," responded Ms. Socrates. "She was *learning disinterested*, not learning disabled. She didn't find school learning interesting because of meaningless and purposeless instruction and practice. Indeed, I suspect that most children labeled *LD* are *instructionally disabled*, not learning disabled. That is, they are the victims of poor instruction, not miswired brains or laziness. These children have difficulty because their instruction is incomprehensible and boring. I found that when taught in a meaningful and stimulating manner, my daughter and my four non-neurological impaired *LD* students learned quickly and eagerly. Indeed, I found several of my so-called *LD* kids to be exceptionally bright."

"Like my LeMar," added Miss Brill.

"Moreover, meaningful and stimulating instruction is more likely to be effective with children with a genuine learning disability than is a traditional tell-and-drill approach," added Ms. Socrates.

tiveness—was not predictive of which children progressed and which did not. Indeed, the only two children who invented the relatively advanced strategy of counting-on in Baroody's (1997) study were both moderately retarded.

Teaching a Diverse Student Population

Although not all children have the same interest and capability in mathematics, it is important to foster each child's mathematical curiosity and thinking, regardless of age, gender, race, social background, or label (e.g., learning disabled or mentally handicapped).

Gender. Research indicates that beyond the elementary level, boys generally out achieve girls in mathematics (e.g., Fennema, 1984, 1990; Fennema & Meyer, 1989), and girls tend to lose interest in mathematics, to avoid mathematics courses, and to choose careers not requiring mathematics (Bush & Kincer, 1993). Research further suggests that this state of affairs is largely due to cultural expectations. Even when interactions for disciplinary reasons are excluded, teachers tend to interact more with boys than girls during mathematics instruction (Brophy, 1985). Moreover, teachers tend to ask boys more challenging and thought-provoking questions than they do girls.

☞ **Teachers need to communicate verbally and nonverbally that it is important for both girls and boys to learn mathematics.** Additionally, women teachers have a special responsibility to model interest in mathematics. Other guidelines for encouraging the mathematical power of girls are outlined in Box 17.5.

Minority Children. The mathematical achievement of elementary-level African American and Hispanic children is significantly lower than that of white children, and this achievement gap widens further in high school (see, e.g., Dossey, Mullis, & Jones, 1993; Secada, 1992; Stiff & Harvey, 1988). Such children fall behind at an early age, are denied the mathematics instruction provided their peers, and then fall further and further behind (Campbell & White, 1997). With traditional practices, the end result is that a large number of minority children, particularly African American children, are left innumerate and, thus, find their economic opportunities severely limited.

In addition to the guidelines described in Box 17.5, *what can be done to ensure that minority*

Box 17.5: Characteristics of Exemplary Mathematics Programs for Women and Minorities

Research indicates successful mathematics programs for women and minorities, such as Project IMPACT (Increasing the Mathematical Power of All Children and Teachers), have the following features:

• "A strong academic component focused on problem solving, understanding, and applications;
• early sustained instruction rather remediation;
• high expectations with positive, substantive teacher-student interactions;
• [substantive interaction] among students;
• multiyear involvement with students;
• teacher enhancement to ensure that teachers were competent in the subject matter and approach;
• use of a variety of instructional strategies including hands-on manipulative teaching;
• teachers convinced of students' ability to learn; . . .
• parental involvement" (Campbell & White, 1997, p. 312); and
• fostering understanding by building on prior knowledge, particularly intuitive knowledge or unique experiences the children had outside of school" (Campbell & White, 1997, p. 313).

In brief, the guidelines for effectively teaching girls and minorities are essentially the same for the investigative approach recommended for all children.

---

children achieve the mathematical power to participate fully in our economy and society?

☞ **Invite and encourage the mathematical learning and thinking of all students.** Many African American students, in particular, feel that their teachers don't care whether or not they achieve. Teachers can have a profound effect on minority students by simply demonstrating that they care (Walker & McCoy, 1997). Making a point to ask minority students questions or to share their strategies or solutions can also help them feel "welcomed."

☞ **Encourage parental involvement.** Many African American children are apathetic toward mathematics because, in part, their peers don't value it. Parent support, however, is the most important influence on student mathematical achievement (Walker & McCoy, 1997).

☙ **Help all children see how mathematics is important for their future.** Many African American children, particularly, do not appreciate the importance of studying mathematics (Walker & McCoy, 1997). Relate mathematics to students' everyday life, interests, and ambitions.

☙ **Culturally responsive educational practices can improve minority children's mathematical disposition and learning** (Mallory, 1997). Some research suggests, for example, that African American children—like many other children—learn better from interactive instruction involving a relational and intuitive approach, rather than expository instruction involving a linear and analytic approach (Mallory, 1997). Teachers should endeavor to recognize minority children's culture by integrating it into instruction. For example, children can be encouraged to use *Logo* to reproduce designs from American Indian artwork or to use the Building Taos Pueblo kit (*The Complete Guide to Building Taos Pueblo* by Louann C. Jordan, © 1989, Museum of New Mexico Press, Santa Fe, NM) to create a scale model of a pueblo (Taylor, 1997). Respect for cultural background can be shown by considering whether all students in a class would feel comfortable calculating the price of a meal involving pork or analyzing the probability of a gambling game (Thomas, 1997).

Non-English Speaking Children. Children who don't speak English often fall behind in mathematics because they have difficulty understanding the instruction. Thomas (1997) suggests the following guidelines for such children:

1. **Develop the mathematical concepts while children are learning English** (see also Flores, 1997). Using concrete models and allowing children to discuss mathematical ideas first in their own language can be helpful.

2. **Allow sufficient time to learn concepts.** Non-English speaking children will probably require even more time than English-speaking children to construct mathematical concepts and the English to explain them.

3. **Recognize that mathematical symbols, units of measurement, and so forth are not universal.** Not all children will necessarily be familiar with Hindu-Arabic numerals or the English measurement system. Help children see the connections between what is familiar to them and new symbols or systems.

4. **Encourage non-English speaking children to communicate in English in various modes.** Such children need practice speaking, listening to, reading, and writing English. Because some children may not come from backgrounds where they were expected to discuss their ideas, teachers may need to explain the importance of discussing mathematical ideas. Reading practice should involve familiar contexts, avoid difficult linguistic constructions, and help students develop reading strategies. Writing mathematics should be purposeful and involve learning, not simply recording the obvious for the sake of practice.

Low-Achieving Children. It is particularly easy to have low expectations for children labeled low-ability, learning disabled, or mentally handicapped. Research indicates that teachers treat such children differently—giving them less instruction, assistance, encouragement, or opportunity to discuss ideas (Lanier, 1981, cited in Koehler & Prior, 1993). Indeed, in some cases, teachers conclude that helping such children is futile and abandon serious efforts to teach them (Good & Brophy, 1978). Sometimes, parents and teachers feel sorry for a child with learning difficulties and, in a misguided effort to keep the child from frustration and failure, compound learning difficulties by avoiding more challenging concepts or instruction altogether.

☙ **Particularly with a child having difficulty learning mathematics, a teacher needs to work on making instruction meaningful and interesting, getting the child involved actively, and providing support and encouragement.** This may well include going back and helping the child construct a solid understanding of concepts introduced in earlier grades. Recent research (Ezawa, 1996; personal communication, August 27, 1997) indicates that even mentally handicapped children can profit from an investigative approach that focuses on patiently helping them construct basic counting, number, and arithmetic skills and concepts.

Gifted (Top 4%) and Upper-Ability Children. "In many ways," Miss Brill confessed to Ms. Socrates, "I am least effective with children who are mathematically advanced. They got so little of my time because I focused so much of my effort on children who were having difficulty. I figure the bright ones could take care of themselves and that the others need my help more. But still, I feel that I cheated the bright ones."

"It's a common problem," added Ms. Socrates. "We frequently don't do nearly enough for our more advanced children."

"It's not just that my time is limited," continued Miss Brill, revealing deeper truths. "I feel more comfortable teaching the other kids. I mean kids like LeMar and Judi really threw me. They continually asked questions such as 'Why is this important to learn, Miss Brill?' and 'Why is it necessary to do it this way?' At first I was horrified and threatened by such questions. But now I'm handling it better. Now I appreciate their inquisitiveness; so I'm not horrified, just threatened," continued Miss Brill only somewhat facetiously. "I just don't have the mathematical knowledge to challenge or keep up with these kids."

"You've taken the first steps to handling mathematically advanced students better," responded Ms. Socrates with a smile. "You recognize your feelings about them and appreciate their curiosity—their drive to understand. You will feel more comfortable with such kids as your own knowledge grows. I also find that it really helps to prepare ahead. When doing problem solving, it is particularly important with bright students to have extensions of problems ready. When doing content instruction, it is useful to have ready projects that require application and extension of the content. Over the years, I have slowly been collecting such project ideas."

Miss Brill wondered, *"When bright kids finish learning the regular content earlier, should I have them go on and do more advanced stuff?"*

☞ **"Enrichment is generally preferable to acceleration through the curriculum,"** noted Ms. Socrates. There are so many connections children can make. In general, it is better to deepen understanding rather than speed up the pace of study and simply add superficially understood concepts.

Hearing-Impaired Children. Research has regularly indicated that deaf children demon-

strate substantially lower achievement than their hearing peers (e.g., Pau, 1995). A common assumption is that a hearing impairment hinders or even prevents hearing the counting sequence and thus, interferes with learning it and numerical concepts. Recent research by Nunes and Moreno (in press) suggests that even a severe hearing loss does not preclude the construction of number and arithmetic concepts or that the degree of hearing loss predicts the extent of learning difficulties. These researchers concluded that a haring impairment should be considered a *risk factor*, not a direct cause, for learning difficulties with numerical concepts (see also Secada, 1984).

Although a hearing impairment creates an extra hurdle in learning the counting sequence and using it to solve arithmetic problems, hearing-impaired children can, with the proper support, construct numerical concepts, albeit more slowly. Research suggests the following three guidelines:

1. **Encourage the development of informal mathematical knowledge both at home and in school.** As with hearing children, the level of informal knowledge appears to be a significant predictor of school achievement (Nunes & Moreno, in press).

2. **Stress learning the counting sequence.** This is likely to have a positive impact on the numerical knowledge of hearing-impaired children (Nunes & Moreno, in press).

3. **Encourage hearing-impaired children to invent their own informal arithmetic procedures.** Nunes and Moreno (1997) found that although such children had difficulty using sign language to compute sums and differences in using the informal counting strategies discussed in chapter 5, some apparently invented their own signed counting-on algorithm. To add 8 and 7, for example, the children signed eight on their left hand and seven on their right. They then simultaneously represented an increment of one (nine) on their left hand and a decrement of one (six) on their right. They continued this process until 15 was represented on their left hand and 0 was represented on their right hand, which indicated there was nothing more to count-on.

17•1•5 THE USE OF INSTRUCTIONAL TECHNOLOGY

"Appropriate use of technology will make the changed curriculum more accessible to all students" (NCTM, 1992, p. 62).

Calculators

Won't the use of calculators interfere with the mastery of basic skills? Why would a teacher let children use them anyway? At what age should children begin to use calculators?

The development of readily available, inexpensive hand-held calculators in the early 1970's prompted heated discussion about their use in school. Various governmental and educational organizations, including the National Advisory Committee on Mathematics Education and the National Council of Teachers of Mathematics, recommended their use. However, many educators resisted—and still resist—their use because of unwarranted fears. Many others overlook the use of calculators, because they do not understand the potential benefits of this technology.

When Miss Brill asked her colleagues about calculators, she got an icy I-can't-believe-this-stupid-question stare from Mrs. MeChokemchild, who then launched into a diatribe about the evils of technology. "If you let kids use calculators, they'll get lazy and won't ever master the basic facts or the standard computational algorithms. This is why so many parent wisely oppose their use and will go absolutely bonkers if you introduce them. Drooling-stupid kids and frothing angry parents is a very bad combination Missy."

"Now, Esmeralda," countered Ms. Socrates, "The facts, madam, just the facts. Numerous studies have consistently found that calculators increase or at least don't hurt computational skills or mathematical achievement (see, e.g., Hembree & Dessart, 1986; Suydam, 1983).

"But how can I justify to parents letting students use calculators?" asked Miss Brill.

Ms. Socrates launched into a well-prepared defense (see, e.g., Campbell & Stewart, 1993; Coburn, 1987; Shumway, 1988; Suydam, 1983).

• **Calculator literacy is now a basic survival skill.** Because they are widely used in everyday life, children should be familiar with when, why, and how to use this basic tool. How better to accomplish this than by actually using calculators when needed in the classroom?

• **Calculators can be invaluable in discovering patterns or relationships, which, in turn, can facilitate calculational skills.** Calculators free children from the tedium of calculation, so that they can focus their attention on looking for patterns and relationships, increasing the chances that these key elements of concept development are discovered. For example, using a calculator makes it more likely that a child will see a connection between basic addition and subtraction combinations such as 5 + 3 = 8 and 8 - 5 = 3, and, thus, master the basic subtraction combinations. Likewise, multiplying various numbers by 10 on a calculator can lead to the discovery that the answer to such expressions is simply the number with a 0 added on the right (e.g., 32 x 10 = 320, 421 x 10 = 4210).

• **Calculators can serve to practice basic skills.** Calculator-based games can provide an entertaining way of practicing various elementary-level skills including the basic arithmetic combinations, place value, and estimation.

• **Calculators can serve to check paper-and-pencil or mental calculations.** Children should get into the habit of checking their work; the calculator provides a relatively painless way for them to do so.

• **Calculators can also serve as an aid when solving problems.** For example, they can be used to fill in a table so that a pattern is more evident.

• **The use of calculators results in a better disposition toward mathematics.** For example, calculator users seem to exhibit greater confidence and persistence in problem solving.

☞ **"Appropriate calculators should be available to all students at [almost] all times"** (NCTM, 1989, p. 8). Although there may be times when a teacher may wish to limit their use in order to achieve a particular goal (e.g., practice mental calculations), calculators should generally be an integral part of mathematics instruction from the start. Even young children can quickly learn how to use them.

Computers

The advent of relatively inexpensive microcomputers in the 1980's led to a heated debate about whether or not their use was developmentally appropriate for elementary-level and, particularly primary-level, children (see, e.g., Sloan, 1985). It is now generally conceded that microcomputers should be included at all levels of instruction (Campbell & Stewart, 1993; National Research Council, 1989). Clearly, though, microcomputers are not a cure-all, and simply using them should not be the goal. "They are resources .... Research is clear . . . when a teacher used technology without first making conscious decisions about the curriculum objectives served, children's understanding of mathematics is not improved" (Jensen & Williams, 1993, p. 227). In brief, the key issue is not whether computers should be used but how (Campbell & Stewart, 1993). This section outlines the educational uses of microcomputers and addresses the questions: *Why is integrating technology into mathematics instruction important? What role microcomputers should play in a classroom?* It also considers some of the advantages of using computers and a teacher's role in a technological environment.

Rationale. The Panel on Educational Technology or PET (1997) noted that computer technology "has fundamentally transformed America's offices, factories, and retail establishments" (p. 6) and that American education is not adequately preparing students for this radically different work environment. "It is widely believed that a continuing acceleration in the pace of technological innovation . . . will result in more frequent changes in the knowledge and skills that workers will need if they are to play high-level roles within the global economy of the twenty-first century. Our children will thus need to be prepared not just with a larger set of facts or a larger repertoire of specific skills, but with the capacity to readily *acquire* new knowledge, to solve new problems, and to employ creativity and critical thinking in the design of new approaches to existing problems" (PET, 1997, p. 15). In order to achieve these objectives, students not only need to learn about technology but they need to *use* technology to facilitate their learning and thinking (PET, 1997).

Instructional Uses. Educationally computers can be used in four qualitatively different ways (cf. Taylor, 1980).

1. **Trainer.** The computer can serve as an "electronic workbook"—as a perhaps more entertaining way to practice basic skills (Jensen & Williams, 1993).

2. **Tutor.** It can serve as a teaching machine—as a way of presenting information at a speed and, perhaps, a manner tailored to individual needs. Well-designed tutorial programs can provide different levels of instructional difficulty, needed prompts, immediate feedback, remedial instruction, and different modes of presentation.

3. **Tutee.** The computer can be programmed and, thus, serve as a learning machine. In this use, students are in charge and program the computer to perform a desired action—in effect, using a logical sequence of instructions in a computer language to teach the computer what to do.

4. **Tool.** It can serve as a tool kit for writing texts (word processor); drawing or reproducing pictures (graphic tools); filing, organizing, and reporting information (database); analyzing, graphing, or performing calculations on data (spreadsheet); communicating information (e.g., computer networks), or combining two or more of the functions listed above (e.g., hypermedia).

Using Computers in the Classroom. "There is no substitute for hands-on experience with a computer" (Bright, 1987, p. x). However, not all computer experiences are equally valuable. In the past, computer-assisted instruction (CAI) was used primarily as a trainer and a tutor—focused on drilling and teaching basic skills. Research (e.g., Goldman, Pellegrino, & Mertz, 1987; Suppes & Morningstar, 1972) indicates that computer technology provides a practical means of tailoring practice and instruction to individual needs (Resnick & Ford, 1981). It also indicates that: (a) computerized practice is at least as effective as noncomputerized drill (e.g., Wilson, 1987); (b) when used to supplement traditional instruction, CAI is more effective than traditional instruction alone—particularly for low- and high-achieving students; and (c) CAI improves students' disposition (Jensen & Williams, 1993).

However, there is widespread recognition that computer-based education should go beyond drilling and teaching factual knowledge (e.g., Campbell, 1988; Hatfield, 1984; Papert, 1972, 1980a, 1980b). The computer's role of tutor needs to be widened to include conceptual learning and problem solving. Computers, for example, can be an effective means for guided-discovery lessons that highlight patterns or relationships (such as those among number combinations discussed in chapters 5 and 7) or use examples and nonexamples to define a concept (such as the geometry terms discussed in chapter 14).

But can a computer provide the concrete experience and active involvement necessary for meaningful learning? In fact, the medium (objects, pictures of objects, or video displays of pictured objects) on which children mentally act may be unimportant. Actively manipulating icons and reflecting on such actions may be as effective as actively manipulating objects and reflecting on these actions. Moreover, computer technology and design are now sufficiently sophisticated that it may be able to provide meaningful instruction in a "user-friendly" manner (see, e.g., Collins & Brown, 1988; Connell, 1988). The recent developments of touchscreen, clear computer speech, flexible graphics, and so forth finally may make feasible active and interactive instruction for children even at the primary level.

Moreover, educational uses of computers should be expanded to involve them as tutees and tools. In these roles, computers can promote mathematical thinking as well as foster conceptual understanding and problem-solving ability (e.g., Bright, 1987; Papart, 1972, 1980a). For example, constructing a program can encourage students to analyze a procedure carefully (see, e.g., Box 17.6) and result in a deeper understanding of the underlying mathematics (Jensen & Williams, 1993). Some experts recommend working on short programs because this is generally more practical at the elementary level (e.g., Hatfield, 1983). In the investigative approach, a teacher would create a real need to use computers as tutees and tools (e.g., see Box 17.7 on the next page). For instance, **planning a class or band trip** can create a real need to surf the Internet to collect travel and sightseeing information and to make travel arrangements such as booking hotel rooms (see, e.g., Microsoft Expedia at http://expedia.com). Box 17.8 (on pages 17-20 and 17-21) lists how computers might be used in the investigative approach and where examples of these uses can be found in this guide.

Several new curricula, such as the technology-enhanced *Six Through Eight Mathematics* (*STEM*) Project and the technology-based Systematic Initiative for Montana Mathematics and Science Integrated Mathematics: A Modeling Approach Using Technology (SIMMS) Project, illustrate how available technology can be used as tools rather than tutors. See page 17-28 for a description of these innovative curricula.

Advantages of Computer Use. Computers have the potential of making the conceptual, the

Box 17.6: A Game Program

After they have had some programming instruction, intermediate-level children can be challenged to devise a program for the *Number-Guess Game*. A program written in BASIC is delineated below. Note that students may need to be given line 20—the instructions for randomly selecting a number.*

```
10   PRINT "THE NUMBER-GUESS GAME"
20   LET R = RND (100)
30   PRINT "A SECRET NUMBER FROM 1 TO
     100 HAS BEEN SELECTED."
40   PRINT "WHAT IS YOUR GUESS?"
50   INPUT G
60   IF G > R THEN GOTO 130
70   IF G < R THEN GOTO 150
80   IF G = R THEN GOTO 90
90   PRINT "YOU GUESSED IT.  CON-
     GRATULATIONS!  DO YOU WANT TO
     PLAY AGAIN? (Y or N)"
100  INPUT P
110  IF P = "N" OR "n" THEN GOTO 170
120  IF P = "Y" OR "y" THEN GOTO 20
130  PRINT "LOWER"
140  GOTO 40
150  PRINT "HIGHER"
160  GOTO 40
170  END
```

Primary-level teachers can use the program above to create a computerized version of *Number Guess* for their students. Playing this game can foster number sense and logical (deductive) reasoning.

_____
*Line 20 is for IBM PCs and IBM compatibles. The instruction for randomly selecting a number may be different for other computers. For example, for an Apple Macintosh, line 20 would be replaced by:

   20 RANDOMIZE 1
   25 PRINT INT (RND*100).

NOTE. Line 80 is not really necessary. If INPUT G does not fit the conditions specified in Lines 60 and 70 (i.e., if G is not greater or lesser than R, the secret the number), the computer will automatically go to Line 90 (in effect, assume that G = R). Line 80 is included because it might be easier for many children to follow the logic of the program.

Box 17.7: A Real Need to Use the Internet and Computer Programming

Mr. Brady's eighth-grade class was trying to determine whether a student who relied on guessing stood a better chance of getting 70% or above on a 10-item or a 100-item true/false test (Problem 2 of Investigation 13.9 on page 13-26 of Chapter 13). The class devised a simulation for each situation and decided that 100 trials for each simulation would be a fair test. For the 100-item simulation, this meant flipping a coin 100 x 100 or 1,000 times, which for a class of 25 meant each student had to make 40 coin flips. Several students commented that this was a lot of flipping.

Mr. Brady seized the opportunity to discuss the value of computer simulations. "How could we make our empirical test even more reliable?" he asked. After some discussion, the class agreed that increasing the number of trials of the simulations should make the empirical probabilities more accurate. "Let's run our simulations for 1000 trials then," Mr. Brady added. There was an au-

dible gasp followed by protests such as "Are you kidding? That will take all day." Mr. Brady then explained that computers were often used to do the brute labor of simulations.

This led to a discussion of how to program a simulation. As the Macintoshes available to the class did not have a programming language, Alexi suggested checking the web searcher *Yahoo!* (http://www.yahoo.com). Among the list of topics that could be searched was *computers and Internet*. This led to a list of programming languages, among which was Chipmunk BASIC v3.5.0 (© 1996 by Ronald H. Nicholson, Jr.; web address: www.nicholson.com/rhn/basic). This option was attractive because it ran on all Macs, and could be downloaded for free.

Groups of students then worked on devising the following BASIC program that could simulate any number of flips and provide the total:[1]

```
10   cls                         80   if b = 1 then t = t + 1       150  print "It would take over 5
20   print "How many trials?"    90   next i                             minutes to do that amount"
30   input a                     100  c = h + t                     160  print "Wish to continue?"
40   if a >= 15600 then 150      110  print c; "--trials done"      170  input d$
50   for i = 1 to a              120  pring h; "--heads"            180  if d$ = "Y" then goto 50
60   b = rnd(2)                  130  print t; "--tails"            190  print "Bye"
70   if b = 0 then h = h + 1     140  end                           200  end
```

Box 17.8: Constructivist Applications of Technology

According to the President's Panel on Educational Technology (1997, pp. 36-37), computers can be used to facilitate student-initiated and mixed-initiative projects, inquiries, explorations, and problem-solving activities in the following ways:

Computer as (Advanced) Tutor

- Afford "an environment for domain-specific problem-solving" and discovery learning (see, e.g., **Box 0.3**, page 0-24; Technology Tips on page 2-40, particularly *The Adventures of Jasper Woodbury; Hot Dog Stand: The Works*, page 3-40; **Box 7.3**, page 7-31; *The Whatsit Corporation: Survival Math Skills*, page 7-34; *Gears*, page 12-28; **Investigation 13.2**, page 13-8; *The Globe Program*, page 13-32; *Statistic Workshop*, page 13-32; *Geometric Supposer Series, Geometer's Sketchpad, Logo-Based Geometry Curriculum*, and **Box 14.2**, pages 14-26 to 14-28; *Geo-Logo*, 15-30;

Problem 2: Temperature Conversions stemming from a KIDLINK project, pages 16-4 and 16-5 of Investigation 16.1; **class newspaper**, page 17-10; project ideas in *Integrating Computers in Your Classroom: Middle and Secondary Math*, page 17-27; *Hypercard Projects* **14.2**, pages 14-26 to 14-28; *Geo-Logo*, 15-30; *for Mathematics*, page 17-27; and *SIMMS*, page 17-28);

Computer as Tutee

- Furnish "a user-friendly environment for the acquisition of basic programming and system design skills" (see, e.g., **Box 0.3**, page 0-24; **Activity File 7.10**, page 7-34; *Mathematics* by Irving Adler, page 8-32; **Box 13.2**, pages 13-27 and 13-28; *Logo-Based Geometry Curriculum: K-6*, and **Box 14.2**, pages 14-27 and 14-28; *Geo-Logo*, 15-30; **Box 17.6**, page 17-19; **Box 17.7**, page 17-20);

Box 17.8 continued

Computer as Tool

- Supply "a word processing, document preparation, or outlining system" (see, e.g., the discussion of **problem posing** on page 2-16; *SemNet*, page 3-40; **bulletin board on page 13-1**; **Box 13.2**, pages 13-27 and 13-28; **Activity File 15.1**, pages 15-2 and 15-3, **bulletin board on page 17-1**; **class newspaper**, page 17-10);

- Act as "a 'digital workbench' for the creation of musical, artistic, and other creative works" (see, e.g., **Activity File 12.4**, page 12-19; **bulletin board on page 14-1**; **Investigation 14.2**, page 14-5; **Activity File 14.1**, pages 14-8 and 14-9; *Discovering Apple Logo: An Invitation to the Arts and Pattern of Nature* and *TesselMania!* on page 14-28; **reproducing Indian artwork with Logo**, page 17-15; **class newspaper**, page 17-10);

- Serve as an "engineering workstation supporting the design of mechanical or electrical devices, architectural projects, or even organic molecules" (see, e.g., **Activity File 12.4**, page 12-19);

- Provide "a facility for the collection, examination, and analysis of statistical data, which might be used in connection with any of a wide range of experimental or survey applications" (see, e.g., **Box 2.10**, page 2-32; **Box 7.3**, page 7-31; **scientific-notation project idea**, page 8-32; **bulletin board on page 13-1**; **Box 13.2**, pages 13-27 and 13-28; *The Globe Program, Statistics Workshop*, and *Table Top* on page 13-32; **Activity File 15.1** on pages 15-2 and 15-3);

- Serve as "an information retrieval or database search engine capable of extracting information from a single site system or from sites distributed across the global Internet" (e.g., **Box 2.11**, page 2-36; **Box 7.3**, page 7-31; **scientific-notation project idea**, page 8-32; *The Globe Program*, page 13-32; **Problem 8: Car-Resale Value**, page 16-6 of Investigation 16.1; **class-trip example**, page 17-19; **Box 17.7**, page 17-20);

- Provide "a flexible laboratory instrument supporting the collection of scientific data from various physical sensors and the flexible manipulation of [these] data under student control" (e.g., **Investigation 13.2**, page 13-8);

- Furnish "a general or application-specific spreadsheet" (see, e.g., **Box 13.2**, pages 13-27 and 13-28; **Box 16.3**, page 16-32; *Spreadsheet Activities in Middle School Mathematics*, page 17-27; *STEM*, page 17-28);

- Provide "a tool for the symbolic manipulation or graphical display of mathematical functions, equations, and proofs" (see, e.g., *The Hot Dog Stand: The Works* on page 3-40; Box 16.3, page 16-32; *STEM*, page 17-28);

- Provide "a medium for communication with teachers, parents, community members, experts, and other students, both locally and over great distances, and for the organization and coordination of group projects" (see, e.g., **Box 1.6**, page 1-20; **Box 2.10**, page 2-32; **Problem 2: Temperature Conversions** (stemming from a KIDLINK project), pages 16-4 and 16-5 of Investigation 16.1; see **bulletin board on page 17-1**; **class newspaper**, page 17-10; **class-trip example**, page 17-19; *The Web Page Creator for School*, page 17-27);

- Furnish "an environment for the facilitation of group collaboration" (see, e.g., **Box 1.6**, page 1-20; *Hot Dog Stand: The Works*, page 3-40; *The Whatsit Corporation: Survival Math Skills*, page 7-34; **Box 13.2**, page 13-28; *The Globe Program, Statistics Workshop*, and *Table Top* on page 13-32; *STEM*, page 17-28);

- Serve "as an interactive hypertext encyclopedia incorporating various forms of multimedia illustrations, and supporting the rapid traversal of cross-reference links";

- Serve as "a vehicle for various forms of interactive exhibits and demonstrations"; and

- Furnish "an environment for the simulation of any of a wide range of devices and machines, physical systems, work environments, human and animal populations, industrial processes, or other natural or artificial systems (see, e.g., *Hot Dog Stand: The Works*, page 3-40; *The Whatsit Corporation: Survival Math Skills*, page 7-34; **Box 13.2**, page 13-27 and 13-28; *Chance Plus* and *Probability Constructor*, page 13-32; **Box 17.7**, page 17-20; *STEM*, page 17-28).

investigative, or the problem-solving approach to mathematics instruction more practical in at least four ways (e.g., Glass, 1984).

1. Computers can provide a way to actively involve many students at one time. In effect, they can free a classroom teacher—responsible for a large number of students and a variety of subjects—from an overreliance on whole-class lectures, drill, and written seatwork (Dwyer, 1980).

2. Computer technology makes individualized instruction more manageable. Students or small groups of students can tackle a concept or a problem at their own pace.

3. Interactive computers have several advantages over using manipulatives (Champagne & Rogalska-Saz, 1984). One is that it can be designed to highlight the correspondence between the pictorial model and the symbolic mathematics. This can help a child to see the links between these representation without requiring a teacher's intervention. Well designed computer-based instruction can also minimize the management problems created by using manipulatives.

4. Computer displays can readily supplement other models so that children see multiple representations of mathematical concepts and processes (Champagne & Rogalska-Saz, 1984).

A Teacher's Role in a Technological Environment. *Won't computers replace teachers and dehumanize elementary instruction?* In fact, used flexibly in conjunction with other effective instructional techniques such as teacher questioning, whole-class or small-group discussions, or cooperative-learning groups, the microcomputer can provide a means of *increasing* teacher-student and student-student interactions. For instance, even with a well designed program, a teacher can play a key role by asking questions that can prompt conflict, doubt, reflection, and/or discussion. Indeed, adequate computer facilities can free a teacher to be more responsive to an individual's or a group's questions, difficulties, or needs. In brief, computers can make instruction more effective by supporting person-to-person communication, not replacing it (Bright, 1987; Dwyer, 1980).

17•2 PROFESSIONAL DEVELOPMENT

Figure 17.5: Learning about Mathematics (and Mathematics Teaching) Should Be a Life-Long Pursuit

FOX TROT copyright 1984 Bill Amends. Dist. by UNIVERSAL PRESS SYNDICATE. Reprinted with the permission. All rights reserved.

On the last day of school, Miss Brill felt a mix of emotions. There was a sense of relief. She had completed her first hectic year of teaching and was looking forward to taking a well-deserved vacation. She welcomed reading up on several content areas and exploring a number of teacher resources. She savored the thought of planning and preparing lessons in advance—with time for reflection.

Yet her predominant feeling was sadness. She had started the school year with 24 strangers; now she had 24 comrades. And she was losing them. The loss seemed all the worse because Miss Brill felt she had failed them. As she explained to Ms. Socrates, "I made so many mistakes—especially in math. There are so many things I do would differently now *if only* I could do them over."

"Certainly we should strive to do our best, but none of us are perfect," comforted Ms. Socrates. Focusing on *if only* won't change what is past and only make us feel badly. Why not think about your first year of teaching in terms of all you have learned."

"I have learned much," Miss Brill said brightening momentarily. "But I have so much to learn and so much to do to become a good teacher," she continued sinking back into despair (cf. Figure 17.5).

Key Characteristics of Good Teachers

Ms. Socrates tried to reassure her colleague Miss Brill by describing the signs of a good teacher the new teacher already exhibited.

Student Focused. "You really care about the children, and your teaching focuses on them," elaborated Ms. Socrates. "You've come a long ways in a year. Remember your first weeks? Like many new teachers, your focus was on yourself. Remember asking if you would survive, worrying about whether the students would listen to you and obey you? Recall sending LeMar to the office because you felt challenged and threatened by him? What impressed me about you was how quickly you got past worrying about yourself and began focusing on your job performance. Remember all your questions about the mechanics of teaching such as, 'How do I set up group learning?' or 'How will I get through the whole math curriculum?' What was even more impressive was that in your first year, your focus began to shift again. Like the best teachers, the welfare of your students became your primary concern. In recent months, your questions more and more were about what your students were thinking and how you could help them."

Self-Fulfillment. You also enjoy teaching; helping others brings you personal satisfaction," Ms. Socrates noted further. "It's not simply a job—a means to some ends such as money, vacation time, or retirement."

Reflective Teaching. "Both your short- and long-term planning is guided by constant reflection," concluded Ms. Socrates. "You—unlike some of our colleagues who will go unnamed—are open to change. You monitor your students carefully to see how they are responding. You listen carefully and consider thoughtfully their comments, suggestions, and complaints because you recognize it as an invaluable source of input. You seek out the advice of others and welcome suggestions of your colleagues and supervisors accept constructive criticism nondefensively. You are constantly pondering how to adjust your instruction tomorrow or how you revise it for next year. This is good, because what worked wonderfully with one class can flop with another. Because of the complexity of teaching, a good teacher must be open minded and reflective."

Thirst for Knowledge. "Your hunger to learn is another key ingredient of a good teachers," Ms. Socrates continued. "I don't know how teachers can get children excited about exploring ideas unless they themselves are curious. Besides, one of the wonderful things about our profession is that it doesn't get boring. There is always more you can learn about the subjects and children we teach and about how to teach them." Even after all my years of teaching, I'm still learning. Just when I think I've figured out the ideal way to teach a topic, I learn something new and find an even better way to teach it.

Striving to Meet the Goals of the NCTM *Curriculum and Professional Standards*: A Long But Richly Rewarding Journey

"For the sake of my students, I wish I could do all the things you do so well," commented Miss Brill sincerely.

"Have patience," replied Ms. Socrates. "Becoming a better teacher is a slow building process. It took me many years to get where I am now, and—as I said before—I am still learning and making improvements."

Miss Brill was beginning to put things in perspective and to feel better about herself. The bell rang, and the class quickly filled with children. LeMar came up to her desk and handed her a card made of construction paper. The cover read, TO THE *BEAST* TEACHER OF ALL.

For a moment, Miss Brill was in shock. Then she looked into LeMar's tearing eyes and realized that the card was not a cruel joke. She considered correcting the lad's misspelling of *best*, but instead let him speak.

"Open it up Miss Brill; the whole class signed it," LeMar instructed.

"Thank you, class," choked Miss Brill barely able to control her emotions, "I can't think of anything I needed more right now. I'll keep this card always to remember my first class."

To improve mathematics instruction in future years, Miss Brill now recognized that she would have to work at educating herself further, at reformulating her aims and methods of instruction, and at educating her colleagues.

Teacher as Learner. Recognizing that she needed to expand her professional knowledge of teaching, Miss Brill took the following steps over the course of the next several years: (a) She joined the NCTM and began to read *Teaching Children Mathematics* and *Mathematics Teaching in the Middle School*, both of which contained numerous teaching ideas. (b) She participated in local, state, and national workshops and conferences, such as Cognitively Guided Instruction, Math Their Way, and Mt. Holyoke College's summermath for teachers (413-538-2063; e-mail: jpaquett@mtholyoke.edu) workshops and NCTM regional and national conferences). (c) She read books on teaching mathematics. (d) She went back to graduate school, took additional courses in mathematics education, including educational applications of computers. (e) She surfed the Internet, collecting suggestions from web sites, teacher bulletin boards, and teacher chat rooms.

Stages of Change. Miss Brill could see that she had come quite a ways in her first year. She had begun with the skills approach and shifted to the conceptual approach. She had even begun to break away from the textbook and to use replacement units and problems. Now she was looking forward to the challenge of going even further—building her own fifth-grade program. But why stop there? she thought. What we really need is a whole new K-8 curriculum.

Working as a School Team. Miss Brill recognized that her job teaching mathematics was made much harder because nearly all the primary-grade teachers used the traditional skills approach. Moreover, she worried about how her students would react when thrown back into a traditional program the following year, *"Won't*

they be confused and just hate going back to the traditional skills approach? I sometimes wonder if we are really doing our children a service by teaching them differently."

"Will they like going back to a traditional approach?" replied Ms. Socrates. "Probably not. Will my instruction hurt them. I don't think so. How can understanding and problem solving skills hurt them? Besides, what is the alternative—teach them in the traditional manner? No, I try to give my students the best experience I can. If nothing else, I hope they get a sense of what mathematics can be."

"I also see it as my responsibility to help educate my colleagues," continued Ms. Socrates. "That's why I joined the math curriculum committee and give in-house workshops. If I can help my primary-level colleagues teach math better, then my students will be better prepared and I'll be able to do even more interesting things with them. Moreover, to best prepare our students, I believe that teachers at all grade levels in our school and school district work together (Madsen & Baker, 1993). Our students would greatly benefit from a coordinated K-12 curriculum based on the NCTM (1989) *Curriculum Standards*. That's why I work on the district curriculum committee and keep bugging central administration about improving our math curriculum."

↬ **Implementing the investigative approach takes a team effort.** Because the problems teachers face when attempting to implement the investigative approach are far different than those faced by using the traditional skills approach (Simon, 1995; Stein et al., in press), support from others can be invaluable. Indeed, "a collegial relationship [among] teachers has been identified as a critical aspect . . . of schools that evidenced change" (Campbell & White, 1997, p. 324).

EPILOGUE

Miss Brill continued to grow as a teacher. Each year her understanding of mathematics, children's thinking, and how to teach mathematics grew. Mathematics was making more and more sense to her. She saw better its connections and power. Moreover, just when Miss Brill thought she really understood a topic, a student would ask her a question that forced her to delve into the topic deeper and rethink it. She now eagerly awaited those tough student questions she could not readily answer because they meant opening new doors—an exciting experience.

As time went on, Miss Brill became increasingly impressed by the power of children's informal knowledge and became willing to release more and more control to her students. She gradually understood better how children's thinking develops and their difficulties.

As her understanding of mathematics grew, she saw better how to help children see connections and appreciate the power of mathematics. As her understanding of children grew, she saw better how to build on their informal knowledge, how to create cognitive conflict, and how to choose problems that would be challenging and raise key content questions, and how to help students avoid common learning pitfalls. She increasingly became more comfortable with experimenting with techniques and the idea of constantly rethinking how she would teach.

A number of years after she began teaching, Miss Brill married Mr. Yant and took the name Mrs. Brill-Yant. Her students, though, addressed her as *Mrs. Brilliant*, even after repeated corrections. "Why do my students mispronounce my name?" she mused.

Brilliant is familiar to them," replied her friend Ms. Socrates. "Besides," she said with a smile, "the name fits."

RESOURCES

SOME INSTRUCTIONAL RESOURCES

Planning and Conducting Mathematics Instruction

☛ **The Annenberg/CPB Math and Science Collection**, Corporation for Public Broadcasting, 901 E. Street, NW, Washington, DC 20004-2037 (800-965-7373). The collection contains videos, software, and printed guides that document strategies for improving elementary (and secondary) mathematics and science instruction in various environments (urban setting, rural areas, public school, private academies). One set of materials is designed for the professional development of preservice and in-service teachers; another, for

parents. A third set of materials, titled "Taking the Lead" provides a guide to reforming mathematics and science instruction.

☛ **Classroom Organization and Models of Instruction** by C. A. Thornton & S. J. Wilson. In *Research Ideas for the Classroom: Early Childhood Mathematics* (pp. 269-293) edited R. J. Jensen, © 1993 by NCTM.

☛ **The Directory of Innovations in Elementary Schools** by Jane McCarthy and Suzanne Still, © 1997, Eye on Education. Provides information about successful use of indisciplinary curriculum, alternative assessment, family and community support, technology, and staff development.

☛ **Empowering Students by Promoting Active Learning in Mathematics: Teachers Speak to Teachers** edited by Dorothy Buerk, © 1994 by NCTM. This reference describes the efforts of five teachers in grades 5 and beyond to implement the NCTM *Standards*.

☛ **Implementing the K-8 Curriculum and Evaluation Standards: Readings from the *Arithmetic Teacher*** edited by Thomas E. Rowan and Lorna J. Morrow, © 1993 by NCTM. This compilation of articles from the *Arithmetic Teacher* offers practical suggestions for implementing the NCTM *Curriculum Standards* in a variety of content areas.

☛ **Prospects for School Mathematics** edited by Iris M. Carl, © 1995 by NCTM. Twenty-one essays consider reform issues including why mathematics instruction must accommodate individual differences.

☛ The following articles in the *Arithmetic Teacher* discuss effective questioning techniques: (a) **The Role of Questioning** by M. Burns, 1985, *Volume 32*, Number 6 (February, 1985), pages 14-16; (b) **Catering to All Abilities Through "Good" Questions** by P. Sullivan & D. Clarke, *Volume 39*, Number 2 (October, 1991), pages 14-18; and (c) **Questions** by M. Suydam, *Volume 32*, Number 6 (February, 1985), page 18. The book **Open-Ended Questioning** (by Robin Lee Harris Freedman, © 1994 by Addison-Wesley) discusses posing questions to encourage higher-level thinking and a variety of responses.

Empowering All Children

☞ See the following references: **How to Encourage Girls in Math & Science** (by Joan Skolnick, Carol Langbort, and Lucille Day, © 1982 by Prentice-Hall; **Math Equals: Biographies of Women Mathematicians + Related Activities** (by Teri Perl, © 1978 by Addison-Wesley); **Multicultural and Gender Equity in the Mathematics Classroom: The Gift of Diversity** (1997 Yearbook) edited by Janet Trentacosta and Margaret J. Kenney, © 1997 by NCTM); **New Directions for Equity in Mathematics Education** (edited by Walter G. Secada, Elizabeth Fennema, and Lisa Byrd Adajian, © 1994, NCTM); **Providing Opportunities for the Mathematically Gifted, K-12** (edited by Peggy A. House, © 1987, NCTM); and **Windows of Opportunity: Mathematics for Students with Special Needs** (by Carol A. Thornton and Nancy Bley, © 1994, NCTM).

Professional Development

☞ **Professional Development for Teachers of Mathematics** (1994 Yearbook) edited by D. B. Aichele, © 1994, NCTM. Part I discusses professional-development issues, including the issue of teacher autonomy and adaptiveness. Part II addresses how preservice teachers should be educated. Part III considers the professional development of in-service teachers, including a district-wide strategy for change, teachers empowering teachers, and building reflection into continuing professional development.

☞ **What's Happening in Math Class? Envisioning New Practices Through Teacher Narratives (Volume 1)** and **Restructuring Professional Identities (Volume 2)** edited by Deborah Schifter, © 1996, Teachers College Press. These books consist of essays written by teachers as they struggled to understand constructivism and implement the NCTM *Standards* in their classrooms.

A SAMPLE OF CHILDREN'S LITERATURE

✎ The following focus on *calculators*: **Calculator Fun** by David A. Adler (© 1981 Franklin Watts), **Calculators** by Jan P. Haney (© 1985, Raintree Publications), and **A Calculator Tutorial: Acquiring Skill with Classroom Cal-**

culators by William L. Merrill (distributed by Dale Seymour).

✎ The following discuss *computers* or *computer programming*: **BASIC Fun: Computer Games, Puzzles, and Problems Children Can Write** by Susan Drake Lipscomb and Margaret Ann Zuanich (© 1982, Avon Books) and **Using Computers: Programming and Problem Solving** by Gerald H. Elgarten and Alfred S. Posamentier (distributed by Dale Seymour). The latter resource helps students to use the computer as a tool for solving mathematical and business problems.

TIPS ON USING TECHNOLOGY

Calculators

▦ The following references describe how calculators can be used as a basis for mathematics instruction: **Calculators for Classrooms: Videotape and Discussion Guide** compiled by the Calculator-enhanced Mathematics Instruction Steering Committee of the NCTM; **Calculators in Mathematics Education (1992 Yearbook)**, edited by James T. Fey and © 1992 by NCTM; **Creative Mathematics Teaching with Calculators** written by David E. Williams and distributed by Dale Seymour; **How to Teach Mathematics Using a Calculator** by Terrence Coburn, © 1987 by NCTM; and **Using the Math Explorer™ Calculator** by Gary G. Bitter and Jerald L. Mikesill, © 1990 by Addison-Wesley.

Computers

References on Using Computers in the Classroom. The following resources discuss a rationale and teaching tips for using computers.

▢ **Computers in Elementary Mathematics Education** by D. H. Clements, © 1989 by Prentice-Hall. Part I (*Foundations of a New Vision*) provides an overview of (a) the problems in elementary mathematics education, (b) current theories of learning, and (c) how computers can be used effectively. Part II discusses computer-assisted instruction (the computer as trainer or tutor), computer uses such as spread sheets and graphing (the computer as tool), and computer programming with a focus on Logo (the computer as tutee). Part III discusses how the computer can help achieve the new curriculum goals as outlined in, for example, the *Curriculum Standards* (NCTM, 1989). Chapters in this part include Problem Solving, Logical Foundations and numbers; Computation; Fractions, Decimals, Percents, Ratio, and Proportions; Geometry and Measurement; Statistics, Graphs, Probability, and Estimation. Each chapter of Part III includes an annotated list of computer software as well as a discussion of key features education programs should have. Part IV provides general teaching tips about using computers.

Computers in Mathematics Education (1984 Yearbook), edited by V. P. Hansen & M. J. Zweng, © 1984 by NCTM. The chapters by Champagne & Rogalska-Saz, Damarin, Kraus, and Shumway, in particular, provide helpful instructional suggestions.

The Integrated Technology Classroom: Building Self-Reliant Learners by Joan Riedl and © 1995 by Allyn & Bacon. This reference is appropriate for K-8 teachers and describes how computers can serve as learning stations to promote individual and small-group learning.

Integrating Computers in Your Classroom: Middle and Secondary Math written by Peter Dudlin and others, © 1994 by Harper Collins. distributed by Carolina Biological Supply Company. This resource describes 28 projects covering prealgebra, algebra, and geometry.

Microcomputer Applications in the Elementary Classroom: A Guide for Teachers by G. W. Bright, © 1987 by Allyn & Bacon. This well-written reference discusses how microcomputers can be integrated into existing programs to improve classroom instruction. It discusses why computers are instructionally important, good and bad features of drill and tutorial programs, what computer games can teach, the role of computer simulations, the use of computers to diagnose errors, how to evaluate software, the instructional value of programming, and other uses of microcomputers (e.g., keeping grades and networking).

Report to the President on the Use of Technology to Strengthen K-12 Education in the United States by the Panel on Educational Technology of the President's

Committee of Advisors on Science and Technology, March 1997. This wide ranging report discusses such issues as the potential significance and role of technology in education, constructivist applications of technology, economic considerations, and equitable access. Copies of the report can be obtained by calling 212-478-0608 or e-mailing garrett-deckel@deshaw.com. The report is also accessible at the following web site: http://www.whitehouse.gov/WH/EOP/OSTP/NSTC/PCAST/K-12ed.html.

Teaching Children to Use Computers: A Friendly Guide by S. D. Savas & E. S. Savas, © 1985 by Teachers College Press. This introduction to instructional uses of computers discusses how to tell a computer what to print on the screen, do math on a computer, make pictures on the screen, and create loops.

Teaching with Technology edited by Judith Haymore Sandholtz, Cathy Ringstaff, and David C. Dwyer, © 1997, Teachers College Press. Case studies address such common concerns as managing computer-based learning and the role of the teacher in a technological environment.

Computer Tools for the Classroom. The following resources are computer tools for teachers, students, or both: **Curriculum Graphics CD Library** (published by Ventura Educational Systems and distributed by Dale Seymour) includes **Elementary Math Graphics CD Library** (grid and chart graphics), **School Productivity Graphics** (graphics for, e.g., school events), and **Creative Character Graphics** (e.g., animal cartoons). **HyperCard Projects for Mathematics** (produced by Ventura Educational Systems) and **HyperCard Projects for Teachers** (written by Fred Ventura and Marilyn Grovers) are both distributed by Dale Seymour. The first resource shows how to use HyperCard to enhance reasoning and problem-solving skills. The second resource includes a Macintosh disk and instructions on how to design tutorials, puzzle, game, and multiple choice quizzes with scorekeeping. **Spreadsheet Activities in Middle School Mathematics** (by John C. Russell © 1992, NCTM) includes an Apple IIe diskette. **The Web Page Creator for School** (designed by Vividus Corporation and published by Sunburst) is available in Macintosh, Power Macintosh, or Windows diskette or CD.

▣ STEM (published by McDougal Littell/Houghton Mifflin, © 1997) and SIMMS (published by Simon & Shuster Custom Publishing Company) were both developed by a cooperative adventure of the Montana Council of Teachers of Mathematics, the state of Montana, and the National Science Foundation. Both are based on the constructivist view that learning occurs best by children actively constructing knowledge in real-world investigations, not passively absorbing facts and procedures out of context. Both embody integrated content instruction, utilize open-ended problems, emphasize the processes of mathematical inquiry, and integrate assessment and instruction. The STEM curricula, designed for grades 6 to 8, can be done without technology, but provides guidelines as to how technology can enhance instruction. Information about this curriculum can be obtained by calling the publisher (800-289-2558, extension 3857) or Dr. Rick Billstein (406-243-2603) or visiting the following website: www.math.umt.edu/~stem. The SIMMS curriculum is designed for grades 9 to 12, but Level 1 could also be used for grade 8. Each module in Level 1 presents such mathematics as direct and inverse proportions, data collection and analysis, probability, linear and exponential functions, and graph theory in such applied contexts as the properties of reflected light, population growth, the spread of disease, and the manufacture of cardboard containers. Information about SIMMS can be obtained by calling the SIMMS Project (800-693-4060) or the publisher (888-339-0529) or by visiting the following web site: http://www.montana.edu/wwwsimms/.

World Wide Web (WWW) Resources. The WWW is a hypertext tool for publishing or obtaining information on the Internet. Web documents (web pages) can combine text, graphics, sounds, and video. Use of the web can promote learning and flexibility (Owston, 1997). The information available on the WWW, including instructional activities and games, is expanding daily. Teachers can obtain more information about the WWW by reading, for example, **The Educator's Guide to the Internet: Resources and Classroom Activities** (developed by Virginia Space Grant Consortium and © 1997 by Addison-Wesley) and **Internet Adventure: A Guide to Educational Resources on the Internet** (published by Allyn & Bacon). The first reference is appropriate for all teachers; discusses e-mail, Gopher, and the World Wide Web; and includes 40 inter

disciplinary lesson plans.

A sample of web sites that might be of interest to teachers follows: (1) **Ask Eric** (http://ericir.syr. edu/) includes ERIC (Educational Research and Information Clearinghouse) lesson plans and summaries of educational research; (2) **Bookmarks Online** (http://www.connect-time.com) includes tutorials on how to use such WWW resources as e-mail and search engines; (3) **California State University-Northridge Web Sites and Resources for Teachers** (http://www. csun.edu/~vceed009/math.html) includes lesson plans, search engines for finding particular topics, teaching ideas, mathematical puzzles and challenges, and links to the "EQUALS Project" and "Family Math." (4) **CyberSchool Magazine** (www.cyberschool mag.com) features articles for both teachers and students on a variety of topics from classroom ethics to space exploration; (5) **Guided Educational Tours** (http: //www.newnorth.net/get) features quality internet-based thematic units; (6) **Index of WWW Servers on Mathematics** (http:// www.math. psu.medu/ Math-Lists/Contents. html); (7) **The Maryland Collaborative for Teacher Preparation** site (http://www.inform.umd.edu:8080/UMS+ State/ UMDProjects/MCTP/ WWW/MCTPHone Page. html) includes essays on constructivism, information on other resources, and information on using technology. (8) **NASA Online Educational Resources** (http://www.gsfc.nasa.gov/nasa_on-line_education.html) includes in its net directory the *Eisenhower National Clearinghouse for Mathematics and Science Education*, which includes among its online documents the NCTM *Standards*; (9) **Teacher's Edition OnLine** (http://www.teachnet.com/); (10) **Teachers Network** (www.teachernet.org) offers a data base 500 classroom tested projects and a "Let's Talk" bulletin board where teachers can exchange ideas; and (11) **Wed Ed K-12 Curriculum Links** (http:// badger. state.wi.us/ agencies/dpi/www/ webed. html).

K-8 students may find **Internet for Kids** by Craig N. Bach (published by Future Kids and distributed by Sunburst) and the following websites of interest: "The Kids Identifying and Discovery Sites" or K.I.D.S." (www.scout.cs.wisc. edu/scout/KIDS/index.html), which includes evaluations of educational web sites by students, and KIDLINK (http://www.kidlink. org), which can involve global dialogs and projects.

APPENDIX A: FOOTNOTES

Chapter 1

[1]This project idea is based, in part, on a lesson plan developed by Willie Crittendon, a teacher in the Chicago area.

Chapter 2

[1]Our thanks to Dr. Steve Tozer, now at the University of Illinois at Chicago, for contributing this case.

[2]The children's solutions depicted in this box are based on those proposed by Jo Lynn Baldwin's third graders at the Lincoln Trails Elementary School (Mahomet, IL).

[3]Based on a lesson with Jo Lynn Baldwin's third-grade class at the Lincoln Trails Elementary School (Mahomet, IL).

[4]Tara was a student in Dianne Dutton's fourth-grade class at the Lincoln Trails Elementary School (Mahomet, IL). ,

Chapter 3

[1]Cassie was a student in Mrs. Sweeney's fourth-grade class, Lincoln Trails Elementary School, Mahomet, IL. The data on Deborah were collected with the help of Dr. Barbara S. Allardice, the mathematics coordinator of the Learning Development Center at the Rochester Institute of Technology. The case of Pam was reported to us by Dr. Allardice.

[2]Doug Clements described a similar example in a 1994 AERA presentation ("Students' Development of Length and Turn Measurement Concepts in a Computer-Based Unit on Geometric Paths").

[3]Thanks to Sharon C. Baroody for sharing this case study with us. This vignette was first reported in *Children's Mathematical Thinking* (Baroody, 1987).

Chapter 4

[1]Provided by Carole Sweeney, Sangamon Elementary School, Mahomet, IL; original source unknown.

[2]Compiled with the assistance of Kendra L. Kett of Lombard, IL, formerly a graduate student at the University of Illinois at Urbana-Champaign (UIUC), and Suzanne Costner, formerly a preservice teacher at the University of Tennessee at Knoxville.

Chapter 5

[1]This approach was suggested by Kyoung-Hye Seo, formerly a graduate student of Dr. Herbert Ginsburg at Teachers College, Columbia University.

[2]This problem was written by Liz Anderson, Kristen Dagley, Cindy False, Jenny Kuta, and Tracy Pinks, who were preservice teachers at UIUC.

Chapter 6

[1]The questions described in Question 4 of Investigation 6.1 were raised by students in Mrs. Dianne Dutton's third-grade class, Lincoln Trails Elementary School, Mahomet, IL. Julius was a member of Linda Moore's second-grade class in the Sangamon Elementary School (Mahomet, IL).

[2]Jacqueline Smith, formerly a preservice teacher at UIUC, reported this incident while doing her student teaching.

[3]Thanks to Dick Dennis, now retired from the College of Education at UIUC, for bringing this pig-identification system to our attention and providing us a Spotted Swine Mandatory Earnotching Chart.

[4]This question arose in Linda Moore's second-grade teacher at the Sangamon Elementary School (Mahomet, IL).

[5]Our thanks to Karen Jurgovan, formerly a graduate student at UIUC for sharing this observation with us.

[6]This activity file is based, in part, on lesson taught by Susan Quarles of the Lincoln Trails Elementary School (Mahomet, IL).

Chapter 7

[1]This exchange was overhead by Patti Stoffel and Christy Cornell, formerly at the Prairie Elementary School (Urbana, IL).

[2]This case was reported by Carol Hatfield, a third-grade teacher at the St. Matthews school in Champaign, IL.

[3]Thanks to Chip Bruce, a science educator at UIUC, for suggesting this activity.

Chapter 8

[1]Our thanks to Dr. Peter Glidden, now at West Chester University, for pointing out this historical fact.

[2]Our thanks to Joel Paque, formerly a preservice at UIUC, for sharing his analogy with us.

[3]Thanks to Carol Castellon, formerly a teacher and now the principal at the University High School (Urbana, IL) for pointing out this common difficulty.

[4]Based on a lesson plan submitted by Rachael Abarbanel, Alison Bullerman, Heather Gould, Todd

Medintz, and Kristin Zage, formerly preservice teachers at UIUC.

[5]Thanks to Kerri Smith, formerly a preservice teacher at UIUC, for suggesting this scoring system.

Chapter 9

[1]Based on a colloquium presentation (Teaching-Learning Interaction in a Computer Microworld: Children's Construction of Fraction Schemes) given by Ron Tzur on 4-28-95.

[2]Based on a lesson with Linda Moore's second-grade class at the Sangamon Elementary School (Mahomet, IL).

[3]This case study was reported to us by Karen Combs, then a diagnostic-teaching instructor at the Learning Development Center, Rochester Institute of Technology, Rochester, NY. A more detailed account of this case is reported in Baroody (1987).

Chapter 10

[1]Thanks to Lee Vanhille, formerly a fifth-grade teacher in Utah and graduate student at UIUC.

Chapter 11

[1]Our thanks to Todd Medintz, formerly a preservice teacher at UIUC, for pointing this out.

Chapter 12

[1]Thanks to Jerry Dewhirst, an engineer living in Mahomet, IL, for pointing out this example.

[2]Kathryn Rose's recipe was taken from *Our Town Our Taste*, compiled by the Mahomet (IL) Town and Country Women's Club and printed in 1992 by Jumbo Jack's Cookbooks P.O. Box 247, Audubon, Iowa 50025.

[3]Based, in part, on a lesson plan developed by Rebekah Calhoun, Lori Caravia, Julie Luebbers, Michelle Luneckas, Beth Mikucki, and Kathy Pagakis, formerly preservice teachers at UIUC.

Chapter 13

[1]Thanks to Jay Wilkins, formerly a doctoral student at UIUC, for this suggestion.

[2]Based, in part, on a lesson plan (*Take Me Out to the Ballgame*) submitted by Meg Dawczak, Maureen McDevitt, Carol Finnen, and Akemi Sessler, teachers in the Chicago area.

[3]Sixth graders Alison and Alexi Baroody and fifth-grader Arianne Baroody devised the simulation described. Alexi proposed the solution of using seven different charts.

Chapter 14

[1]Based, in part, on a unit designed by Becky Ryherd, a fourth-grade teacher at the Lincoln Trails Elementary School, Mahomet, IL

[2]Based on a lesson plan developed by Malvina Papadaki, formerly a graduate student at UIUC and now teaching in Greece.

Chapter 15

[1]Based, in part, on a lesson plan developed by Judith Sayre, a teacher from Hinsdale, IL.

[2]Based on a lesson plan developed by the following former UIUC preservice teachers: Patricia Plant, Stacey Barrett, Valerie Prescott, and Latacia Morgan.

[3]Based on case reported by Betsy Ginzburg, formerly a preservice teacher at UIUC.

[4]LeMar's solution was suggested by Alexi A. Baroody. Judi's solution was suggested by Alison E. Baroody. Both were 11-years-old at the time.

[5]Kathryn Endsley, formerly a preservice teacher at UIUC, observed that when her kindergarten class began working with centimeters, the most common error was counting from one.

[6]Sixth-grader Alexi A. Baroody devised this informal strategy.

[7]Based on a lesson plan prepared by Patricia Stoffel, formerly a teacher at the Prairie Elementary School (Urbana, IL), and now teaching at UIUC.

Chapter 16

[1]This lesson was developed by Beth Flickinger, formerly a graduate student at UIUC, and currently a teacher in Bement, IL.

Chapter 17

[1]Alexi A. Baroody developed this program.

APPENDIX B: BIBLIOGRAPHY

Ashlock, R. B. (1998). *Error patterns in computation* (7th ed.). Upper Saddle River, NJ: Prentice-Hall.

Ausubel, D. P. (1968). *Educational psychology: A cognitive view.* New York: Holt, Rinehart, & Winston.

Balacheff, N. (1988, April). *A study of students' proving processes at the junior high school level.* Paper presented at the annual meeting of the National Council of Teachers of Mathematics. Chicago, IL.

Baker, D., Semple, C., & Stead, T. (1990). *How big is the moon? Whole maths in action.* Portsmouth, NH: Heinemann.

Ball, D. L. (1990). The mathematical understandings that prospective teachers bring to teacher education. *The Elementary School Journal, 90,* 449-466.

Ball, D. L. (1991). Research on teaching mathematics: Making subject-matter knowledge part of the equation. In J. Brophy (Ed.), *Advances in research on teaching: Vol. 2. Teachers' knowledge of subject matter as it relates to their teaching practice* (pp. 1-48). Greenwich, CT: JAI Press.

Banchoff, T. F. (1990). Dimensions. In L. A. Steen (Ed.), *On the shoulders of giants* (pp. 11-59). Washington, DC: National Academy Press.

Baratta-Lorton, M. (1976). *Mathematics their way.* Menlo Park, CA: Addison-Wesley.

Baroody, A. J. (1987). *Children's mathematical thinking: A developmental framework for preschool, primary, and special education teachers.* New York: Teachers College Press.

Baroody, A. J. (1989). *A guide to teaching mathematics in the primary grades.* Boston: Allyn and Bacon.

Baroody, A. J. (1994). An evaluation of evidence supporting fact-retrieval models. *Learning and Individual Differences, 6,* 1-36.

Baroody, A. J. (1995). The role of the number-after rule in the invention of computational short cuts. *Cognition and Instruction, 13,* 189-219.

Baroody, A. J. (1996). Self-invented addition strategies by children classified as mentally handicapped. *American Journal on Mental Retardation, 101* (1), 72-89.

Bartels, B. H. (1995). Promoting mathematical connections with concept mapping. *Mathematics Teaching in the Middle School, 1,* 542-549.

Battista, M. T. (1983). A complete model for operations on integers. *Arithmetic Teacher, 30*(9), 26-31.

Battista, M. T., & Clements, D. H. (1988). A case for a Logo-based elementary school geometry curriculum. *Arithmetic Teacher, 36*(3), 11-17.

Battista, M. T., & Clements, D. H. (1990). Constructing geometric concepts in Logo. *Arithmetic Teacher, 38*(3), 15-17.

Bearison. (1969). Role of measurement operations in the acquisition of conservation. *Developmental Psychology, 1,* 653-660.

Bebout, H. C., & Carpenter, T. P. (1989). Assessing and building thinking strategies: Necessary bases for instruction. In P. R. Trafton & A. P. Shulte (Eds.), *New directions for elementary school mathematics* (1989 Yearbook, pp. 59-69). Reston, VA: National Council of Teachers of Mathematics.

Behr, M. J., Erlwanger, S., & Nichols, E. (1980). How children view the equals sign. *Mathematics Teaching, 22,* 13-15.

Behr, M. J., Harel, G., Post, T., & Lesh, R. (1992). Rational number, ratio, and proportion. In D. Grouws (Ed.), *Handbook of research on mathematics teaching and learning* (pp. 296-333). New York: Macmillan.

Behr, M. J., Lesh, R., Post, T., & Silver, E. A. (1983). Rational-number concepts. In R. Lesh and M. Landau (Eds.), *Acquisition of mathematics concepts and processes* (pp. 92-126). Orlando, FL: Academic Press.

Behr, M. J., & Post, T. R. (1988). Teaching rational number and decimal concepts. In T. R. Post (Ed.), *Teaching mathematics in grades K-8.* Boston: Allyn and Bacon.

Behr, M. J., Wachsmuth, I., & Post, T. R. (1985). Construct a sum: A measure of children's understanding of fraction size. *Journal for Research in Mathematics Education, 16,* 120-131.

Bell, A. W. (1976). A study of pupils' proof-explanations in mathematical situations. *Educational Studies in Mathematics, 7,* 23-40.

Bell, M. S. (1974). What does "everyman" really need from school mathematics? *Mathematics Teacher, 67,* 196-202.

Bezuk, N. S., & Bieck, M. (1993). Current research on rational numbers and common fractions: Summary and implications for teachers. In D. T. Owens (Ed.), *Research ideas for the classroom: Middle grades mathematics* (pp. 118-136). Reston, VA: National Council of Teachers of Mathematics.

Bezuk, N. S., & Cramer, K. (1989). Teaching about fractions: What, when, and how? In P. R. Trafton & A. P. Shulte (Eds.), *New directions for elementary school mathematics* (1989 Yearbook, pp. 156-167). Reston, VA: National Council of Teachers of Mathematics.

Bisanz, J., Lefevre, J., Scott, C., & Champion, M. A. (1984, April). *Developmental changes in the use of heuristics in simple arithmetic problems.* Paper presented at the annual meeting of the American Educational Research Association, New Orleans.

Booth, L. R. (1988). Children's difficulties in beginning algebra. In A. F. Coxford (Ed.), *The ideas of algebra,*

K-12 (1988 Yearbook, pp. 20-32). Reston, VA: National Council of Teachers of Mathematics.

Borasi, R. (1992). *Learning mathematics through inquiry.* Portsmouth, NH: Heinemann.

Borasi, R. (1994). Capitalizing on errors as "springboards for inquiry": A teaching experiment. *Journal for Research in Mathematics Education, 25,* 166-208.

Bower, T. (1974). *Development in infancy.* San Francisco: Freeman.

Brainerd, C. J. (1973). The origins of number concepts. *Scientific American,* March, 101-109.

Bright, G. W. (1987). *Microcomputer applications in the elementary classroom: A guide for teachers.* Boston: Allyn & Bacon.

Bright, G. W., & Hoeffner, K. (1993). Measurement, probability, statistics, and graphing. In D. T. Owens (Ed.), *Research ideas for the classroom: Middle grades mathematics* (pp. 78-98). Reston, VA: National Council of Teachers of Mathematics.

Brophy, J. (1985). Interactions of male and female students with male and female teachers. In L. C. Wilkinson & C. B. Marrett (Eds.), *Gender influences in classroom interaction* (pp. 115-142). New York: Academic Press.

Brown, C. A., & Silver, E. A. (1989). Discrete mathematics. In M. M. Lindquist (Ed.), *Results from the Fourth Mathematics Assessment of the National Assessment of Educational Progress* (pp. 19-27). Reston, VA: National Council of Teachers of Mathematics.

Brownell, W. A. (1935). Psychological considerations in the learning and the teaching of arithmetic. In D. W. Reeve (Ed.), *The teaching of arithmetic* (10th Yearbook of the National Council of Teachers of Mathematics, pp. 1-31). New York: Bureau of Publications, Teachers College, Columbia University.

Bruni, J. V., & Seidenstein, R. B. (1990). Geometric concepts and spatial sense. In J. Payne (Ed.), *Mathematics for the young child* (pp. 203-227). Reston, VA: National Council of Teachers of Mathematics.

Bunt, L. N. H., Jones, P. S., & Bedient, J. D. (1976). *The historical roots of elementary mathematics.* Englewood Cliffs, NJ: Prentice-Hall.

Burns, M. (1987). *A collection of math lessons from grades 3 through 6.* The Math Solution Publication. Distributed by Cuisenaire Company of America, New Rochelle, NY.

Bush, W. S., & Kincer, L. A. (1993). The teachers' influence on the classroom learning environment. In R. J. Jenson (Ed.), *Research ideas for the classroom: Early childhood mathematics* (pp. 311-328). Reston, VA: National Council of Teachers of Mathematics.

Buswell, G. T., & Judd, C. H. (1925). Summary of educational investigations relating to arithmetic. *Supplementary Educational Monographs,* No. 27. Chicago: University of Chicago Press.

Byrkit, D. R., & Sanchez, G. I. (1989). Mayan numeration systems. In *Historical topics for the mathematics classroom* (pp. 45-46). Reston, VA: National Council of Teachers of Mathematics.

Caldwell, O. W., & Courtis, S. A. (1925). *Then and now in education, 1845-1923: A message of encouragement from the past to the present.* Yonkers-on-Hudson, NY: World Books.

Campbell, P. F. (1988). Microcomputers in the primary mathematics classroom. *Arithmetic Teacher, 35*(6), 22-30.

Campbell, P. F. (1990). Young children's concept of measure. In L. P. Steffe & T. Wood (Eds.), *Transforming children's mathematics education* (pp. 92-99). Hillsdale, NJ: Erlbaum.

Campbell, P. F. (1997). Connecting instructional practice to student thinking. *Teaching Children Mathematics, 4*(2), 106-110.

Campbell, P. F., Fein, G. G., & Schwartz, S. S. (1991). The effects of Logo experience on first-grade children's ability to estimate distance. *Journal of Educational Computing Research, 7,* 331-349.

Campbell, P. F., & Stewart, E. L. (1993). Calculators and computers. In R. J. Jenson (Ed.), *Research ideas for the classroom: Early childhood mathematics* (pp. 251-268). Reston, VA: National Council of Teachers of Mathematics.

Campbell, P. F., & White, D. Y. (1997). Project IMPACT: Influencing and supporting teacher change in predominantly minority schools. In E. Fennema & B. S. Nelson (Eds.), *Mathematics Teachers in Transition* (pp. 309-355). Mahwah, NJ: Erlbaum.

Carey, D. A., Fennema, E., Carpenter, T. P., & Franke, M. L. (1995). Equity and mathematics education. In W. G. Secada, E. Fennema, & L. B. Adajian (Eds.), *New directions for equity in mathematics education* (pp. 93-125). New York: Cambridge University Press.

Carlow, C. D. (1986). Critical balances and payoffs of an estimation program. In H. L. Schoen & M. J. Zweng (Eds.), *Estimation and mental computation* (1986 Yearbook, pp. 93-102). Reston, VA: The National Council of Teachers of Mathematics.

Carnegie Forum on Education and the Economy. (1986). *A nation prepared: Teachers for the 21st century.* New York: Carnegie Corporation.

Carpenter, T. P. (1986). Conceptual knowledge as a foundation for procedural knowledge: Implications from research on the initial learning of arithmetic. In J. Hiebert (Ed.), *Conceptual procedural knowledge: The case of mathematics* (pp. 113-132). Hillsdale, NJ: Erlbaum.

Carpenter, T. P., Coburn, T. G., Reys, R. E., & Wilson, J. W. (1976). Notes from national assessment: Estimation. *Arithmetic Teacher, 23*(4), 297-302.

Carpenter, T. P., Fennema, E., Peterson, P. L., & Carey, D. A. (1988). Teachers' pedagogical content knowledge of students' problem solving in elementary arithmetic. *Journal for Research in Mathematics Education, 19,* 385-401.

Carpenter, T. P., Fennema, E., Peterson, P. L., Chiang, C. P., & Loef, M. (1989). Using knowledge of children's mathematics thinking in classroom teaching: An experimental study. *American Educational Research Journal, 26*, 499-532.

Carpenter, T. P., Matthews, W., Lindquist, M. M., & Silver, E. A. (1984). Achievement in mathematics: Results from the National Assessment. *Elementary School Journal, 84*, 485-495.

Carpenter, T. P., & Moser, J. M. (1982). The development of addition and subtraction problem-solving skills. In T. R. Carpenter, J. M. Moser, & T. A. Romberg (Eds.), *Addition and subtraction: A cognitive perspective* (pp. 9-24). Hillsdale, NJ: Erlbaum.

Carpenter, T. P., & Moser, J. M. (1984). The acquisition of addition and subtraction concepts in grades one through three. *Journal for Research in Mathematics Education, 15*, 179-202.

Carpenter, T. P., Moser, J. M., & Bebout, H. C. (1988). Representation of addition and subtraction word problems. *Journal for Research in Mathematics Education, 19*, 345-357.

Carraher, T. N., Carraher, D. W., & Schliemann, A. D. (1987). Written and oral mathematics. *Journal for Research in Mathematics Education, 18*, 83-97.

Cazden, C. B. (1986). Classroom discourse. In M. C. Whittrock (Ed.), *Handbook of research in teaching* (3rd ed., pp. 432-463). New York: Macmillan.

Chalouh, L., & Herscovics, N. (1988). Teaching algebraic expressions in a meaningful way. In A. F. Coxford (Ed.), *The ideas of algebra, K-12* (1988 Yearbook, pp. 33-42), Reston, VA: National Council of Teachers of Mathematics.

Champagne, A. B., & Rogalska-Saz, J. (1984). Computer-based instruction. In V. P. Hansen & M. J. Zweng (Eds.), *Computers in mathematics education* (1984 Yearbook, pp. 43-53). Reston, VA: National Council of Teachers of Mathematics.

Charles, R. I., & Lester, F. K. (1982). *Teaching problem solving: What, why and how.* Palo Alto, CA: Dale Seymour Publications.

Chiu, Ming Ming (1996). *Building Mathematical Understanding During Collaboration: Students Learning Functions and Graphs in an Urban, Public High School.* Doctoral dissertation. University of California, Berkeley.

Civil, M. (1990). *Doing and talking about mathematics: A study of preservice elementary teachers.* Doctoral dissertation, University of Illinois, Urbana.

Clark, C. M., & Peterson, P. L. (1986). Teachers' thought processes. In M. C. Wittrock (Ed.), *Handbook of research on teaching* (3rd ed., pp. 255-296). New York: Macmillan.

Clement, J., Lochhead, J., & Monk, G. (1981). Translation difficulties in learning mathematics. *American Mathematical Monthly, 88*, 286-290.

Clements, D. H. (1989). *Computers in the elementary mathematics instruction.* Englewood Cliffs, NJ: Prentice-Hall.

Clements, D. H., & Battista, M. T. (1989). Learning of geometric concepts in a Logo environment. *Journal for Research in Mathematics Education, 20*, 450-467.

Clements, D. H., & Battista, M. T. (1992). Geometry and spatial reasoning. In D. A. Grouws (Ed.), *Handbook of research on mathematics teaching and learning* (pp. 420-464). New York: Macmillan

Clements, D. H., Battista, M. T., Sarama, M. T., Swaminathan, S., & McMillen, S. (1997). Students' development of length measurement concepts in a Logo-based unit on geometric paths. *Journal for Research in Mathematics Education, 28*, 70-95.

Clements, D. H., & Callahan, L. G. (1983). Number or prenumber foundational experiences for young children: Must we choose? *Arithmetic Teacher, 31*(3), 34-37.

Clements, D. H., & McMillen, S. (1996). Rethinking "concrete" manipulatives. *Teaching Children Mathematics, 2*(5), 270-279.

Cobb, P. (1985). A reaction to three early number papers. *Journal for Research in Mathematics Education, 16*, 141-145.

Cobb, P. (1988). The tension between theories of learning and instruction in mathematics education. *Educational Psychologist, 23*, 87-103.

Cobb, P., & Merkel, G. (1989). Thinking strategies: Teaching arithmetic through problem solving. In P. R. Trafton & A. P. Shulte (Eds.), *New directions for elementary school mathematics* (1989 Yearbook, pp. 70-81). Reston, VA: National Council of Teachers of Mathematics.

Cobb, P., & Wheatley, G. (1988). Children's initial understanding of ten. *Focus on Learning Problems in Mathematics, 10*(3), 1-28.

Cobb, P., Wood, T., & Yackel, E. (1991). A constructivist approach to second grade mathematics. In E. von Glasersfeld (Ed.), *Constructivism in mathematics education* (pp. 157-176). Boston: Kluwer.

Cobb, P., Yackel, E., & Wood, T. (1989). Young children's emotional acts while engaged in mathematical problem solving. In D. B. McLeod & V. M. Adams (Eds.), *Affect and mathematical problem solving* (pp. 117-148). New York: Springer-Verlag.

Coburn, T. G. (1987). *How to teach mathematics using a calculator.* Reston, VA: National Council of Teachers of Mathematics.

Coburn, T. G. (1989). The role of computation in the changing mathematics curriculum. In P. R. Trafton & A. P. Shulte (Eds.), *New directions for elementary school mathematics* (1989 Yearbook, pp. 43-58). Reston, VA: National Council of Teachers of Mathematics.

Collins, A., & Brown, J. S. (1988). The computer as a tool for learning through reflection. In H. Mandl &

A. Lesgold (Eds.), *Learning issues for intelligent tutoring systems*. New York: Springer-Verlag.

Conant, L. L. (1956). Counting. In J. R. Newman (Ed.), *The World of Mathematics* (pp. 432-441). New York: Simon and Schuster.

Connell, M. L. (1988, March). *Using microcomputers in providing referents for elementary mathematics*. Paper presented at annual conference for Microcomputers in Education, Tempe, AZ.

Connolly, P. (1989). Writing and the ecology of learning. In P. Connolly & T. Vilardi (Ed.), *Writing to learn mathematics and science* (pp. 1-14). New York: Teachers College Press.

Court, S. R. A. (1920). Numbers, time, and space in the first five years of a child's life. *Pedagogical Seminary, 27*, 71-89.

Cramer, K., Post, T., & Currier, S. (1993). Learning and teaching ratio and proportion: Research implications. In D. T. Owens (Ed.), *Research ideas for the classroom: Middle grades mathematics* (pp. 159-178). New York: Macmillan.

Curcio, F. R. (1990). Mathematics as communication: Using a language-experience approach in the elementary grades. In T. J. Cooney & C. R. Hirsch (Eds.), *Teaching and learning mathematics in the 1990s:* (1990 Yearbook, pp. 69-75). Reston, VA: National Council of Teachers of Mathematics.

Dantzig, T. (1954). *Number: The language of science.* New York: The Free Press.

Davidson, N. (1990). Small-group cooperative learning in mathematics. In T. J. Cooney & C. R. Hirsch (Eds.), *Teaching and learning mathematics in the 1990s:* (1990 Yearbook, pp. 52-61). Reston, VA: National Council of Teachers of Mathematics.

Davis, H. T. (1989). History of computation. In *Historical topics for the mathematics classroom* (pp. 87-117). Reston, VA: National Council of Teachers of Mathematics.

Davis, R. B. (1983). Complex mathematical cognition. In H. P. Ginsburg (Ed.), *The development of mathematical thinking* (pp. 254-290). New York: Academic Press.

Davis, R. B. (1984). *Learning mathematics: The cognitive science approach to mathematics education.* Norwood, NJ: Ablex.

Davis, R. B. (1992). Reflections on where mathematics education now stands and on where it may be going. In D. A. Grouws (Ed.), *Handbook of research on mathematics teaching and learning* (pp. 724-734). New York: Macmillan.

DeCorte, E., & Verschaffel, L. (1987). The effects of semantic structure on first graders' strategies for solving addition and subtraction word problems. *Journal for Research in Mathematics Education, 18*, 363-381.

de Lange, J., Burrill, G., Romberg, T., & Van Reeuwijk, M. (1993). *Learning and testing mathematics in context:*

The case: Data visualization. Scotts Valley, CA: Wings for Learning.

DeRuiter, J. A., & Wansart, W. L. (1982). *Psychology of learning disabilities.* Rockville, MD: Aspen.

Dewey, J. (1933). *How we think.* Boston: D. C. Heath.

Dewey, J. (1958). *Art as experience.* New York: Capricorn Books.

Dewey, J. (1963). *Experience and education.* New York: Collier.

Dienes, Z. P. (1960). *Building up mathematics.* New York: Hutchinson.

Donaldson, M. (1978). *Children's minds.* New York: W. W. Norton & Co.

Dossey, J. A. (1992). The nature of mathematics: Its role and its influence. In D. A. Grouws (Ed.), *Handbook of research on mathematics teaching and learning* (pp. 39-48). New York: Macmillan.

Dossey, J. A., Mullis, V. S., & Jones, C. O. (1993). *Can Students Do Mathematical Problem Solving?* Washington, D.C.: U.S. Department of Education and National Center for Education Statistics.

Dossey, J. A., Mullis, I. V. S., Lindquist, M. M., & Chambers, D. L. (1988). *The mathematics report card: Are we measuring up? Trends in achievement based on the 1986 national assessment.* Princeton, NJ: Educational Testing Service.

Driscoll, M. J. (1981). *Research within reach: Elementary school mathematics.* Reston, VA: National Council of Teachers of Mathematics.

Duckworth, E. (1982) A case study about some depths and perplexities of elementary arithmetic. In J. Bamberger & E. Duckworth (Eds.), *An analysis of data from an experiment in teacher education* (Grant No. G81-0042, pp. 44-170). Washington, DC: National Institute of Education.

Dwyer, T. (1980). Some thoughts on computers and greatness in teaching. In R. P. Taylor (Ed.), *The computer in the school: Tutor, tool, tutee* (pp. 113-118). New York: Teachers College Press.

Ellis, A., & Harper, R. A. (1975). *A new guide to rational living.* North Hollywood, CA: Wilshire.

Engelhardt, J. M., Ashlock, R. B., & Wiebe, J. H. (1984). *Helping children understand and use numerals.* Boston: Allyn & Bacon.

English, L. D. (1997). Promoting a problem posing classroom, *Teaching Children Mathematics, 4*, 172-179.

English, L. D., Cudmore, D., & Tilley, D. (in press). Problem posing and critiquing: How it can happen in your classroom. *Mathematics Teaching in the Middle School.*

Erlwanger, M. (1975). Benny's concept of rules and answers in IPI mathematics. *Journal of Children's Mathematical Behavior, 1*, 7-25.

Ernest, P. (1988, July). *The impact of beliefs on the teaching of mathematics*. Paper presented at 6th meetings of the International Group for the Study of the Psychology of Mathematics Education, Budapest, Hungary.

Even, R., & Lappan, G. (1994). Constructing meaningful understanding of mathematics content. In D. B. Aichele & A. F. Coxford (Eds.), *Professional development for teachers of mathematics* (1994 Yearbook, pp. 128-143). Reston, VA: National Council of Teachers of Mathematics.

Ezawa, B. (1996). *Zählen und rechnen bei geistig behinderten schülern: Leistungen, konzepte und strategien junger erwachsener mit hirnfunktionsstörungen* (Counting and calculating of students with mental retardation: Capabilities, concepts and strategies of young adults with brain dysfunction). Frankfurt, Germany: Peter Lang.

Feinberg, M. M. (1988). *Solving word problems in the primary grades: Addition and subtraction*. Reston, VA: National Council of Teachers of Mathematics.

Fennema, E. (1984). Girls, women, and mathematics. In E. Fennema & M. J. Ayer (Eds.), *Women and education: Equity or equality?* (pp. 137-164). Berkeley, CA: McCutchan.

Fennema, E. (1990). Justice, equity, and mathematics education. In E. Fennema & G. C. Leder (Eds.), *Mathematics and gender* (pp. 1-9). New York: Teachers College Press.

Fennema, E., Carpenter, T. P., Franke, M. L., Levi, L., Jacobs, V. R., & Empson, S. B. (1996). A longitudinal study of learning to use children's thinking in mathematics instruction. *Journal for Research in Mathematics Education, 27*, 403-434.

Fennema, E., & Franke, M. L. (1992). Teachers' knowledge and its impact. In D. A. Grouws (Ed.), *Handbook of research on mathematics teaching and learning* (pp. 147-164). New York: Macmillan.

Fennema, E., & Meyer, M. R. (1989). Gender, equity and mathematics. In W. G. Secada (Ed.), *Equity in education* (pp. 146-157). Bristol, PA: Falmer.

Fey, J. T. (1990). Quantity. In L. A. Steen (Ed.), *On the shoulders of giants* (pp. 61-94). Washington, DC: National Research Council.

Fischbein, E. (1987). *Intuition in science and mathematics*. Dordrecht, The Netherlands: Reidel.

Fischbein, E., Deri, M., Nello, M. S., & Marino, M. S. (1985). The role of implicit models in solving verbal problems in multiplication and division. *Journal for Research in Mathematics Education, 16*, 3-17.

Fischbein, E., & Gazit, A. (1984). Does the teaching of probability improve probabilistic intuitions? *Educational Studies in Mathematics, 15*(1), 1-24.

Flexer, R. J. (1986). The power of five: The step before the power of ten. *Arithmetic Teacher, 34*(3), 5-9.

Flores, A. (1997). Sí se puede, "It can be done": Quality mathematics in more than one language. In J. Trentacosta & M. J. Kenney (Eds.), *Multicultural and gender equity in the mathematics classroom: The gift of diversity* (1997 Yearbook, pp. 81-91). Reston, VA: National Council of Teachers of Mathematics.

Folsom, M. (1975). Operations on whole numbers. In J. N. Payne (Ed.), *Mathematics learning in early education* (37th Yearbook, pp. 161-190). Reston, VA: National Council of Teachers of Mathematics.

Freudenthal, H. (1983). *Didactical phenomenology of mathematical structures*. Boston: Reidel.

Fuson, K. C. (1988). *Children's counting and concepts of number*. New York: Springer-Verlag.

Fuson, K. C. (1992a). Research on learning and teaching addition and subtraction of whole numbers. In G. Leinhardt. R. T. Putnam, & R. A. Hattrup (Eds.), *The analysis of arithmetic for mathematics teaching* (pp. 53-187). Hillsdale, NJ: Erlbaum.

Fuson, K. C. (1992b). Research on whole number addition and subtraction. In D. Grouws (Ed.), *Handbook of research on mathematics teaching and learning* (pp. 243-275). New York: Macmillan.

Fuson, K. C., & Burghardt, B. H. (1993). Group case studies of second graders inventing multidigit addition procedures for base-ten blocks and written marks. In J. R. Becker & B. J. Pence (Eds.), *Proceedings of the Fifteenth Annual Meeting of the North American Chapter of the International Group for the Psychology of Mathematics Education* (pp. 240-246). San José, CA: The Center for Mathematics and Computer Science Education.

Fuson, K. C., & Hall, J. W. (1983). The acquisition of early number word meanings: A conceptual analysis and review. In H. P. Ginsburg (Ed.), *The development of mathematical thinking* (pp. 49-107). New York: Academic Press.

Fuys, D. J., & Liebov, A. K. (1993). Geometry and spatial sense. In R. J. Jensen (Ed.), *Research ideas for the classroom: Early childhood mathematics* (pp. 195-222). Reston, VA: National Council of Teachers of Mathematics.

Garofalo, J. (1987). Metacognition and school mathematics. *Arithmetic Teacher, 34* (9), 22-23.

Geddes, D., & Fortunato, I. (1993). Geometry: Research and classroom activities. In D. T. Owens (Ed.), *Research ideas for the classroom: Middle grades mathematics* (pp. 199-222). Reston, VA: National Council of Teachers of Mathematics.

Gelman, R., & Gallistel, C. (1978). *Young children's understanding of number*. Cambridge: Harvard University Press.

Gibb, E. G., & Castaneda, A. M. (1975). Experience for young children. In J. N. Payne (Ed.), *Mathematics learning in early childhood* (37th Yearbook, pp. 96-124). Reston, VA: National Council of Teachers of Mathematics.

Ginsburg, H. P. (1989). *Children's arithmetic* (2nd ed.). Austin, TX: Pro-Ed.

Ginsburg, H. P., Klein, A., & Starkey, P. (1998). The development of children's mathematical thinking: Connecting research with practice. In I. E. Sigel & K. A. Renninger (Eds.), *Handbook of Child Psychology: Vol. 4. Child Psychology in Practice* (5th Ed., pp. 401-476). New York: Wiley.

Ginsburg, H. P., Posner, J. K., & Russell, R. L. (1981). The development of mental addition as a function of schooling. *Journal of Cross-Cultural Psychology, 12,* 163-178.

Glass, E. M. (1984). Computers: Challenge and opportunity. In V. P. Hansen & M. J. Zweng (Eds.), *Computers in mathematics education* (1984 Yearbook, pp. 10-14). Reston, VA: National Council of Teachers of Mathematics.

Goldman, S. R., Pellegrino, J. W., & Mertz, D. L. (1987, April). *Microcomputer use in skill development for basic math facts.* Paper presented at the annual meeting of the American Educational Research Association, Washington, DC.

Good, T. L., & Brophy, J. E. (1978). *Looking in classrooms.* New York: Harper & Row.

Goodnow, J., & Levine, R. A. (1973). "The grammar of action": Sequence and syntax in children's copying. *Cognitive Psychology, 4,* 82-98.

Graeber, A. O., & Tanenhaus, E. (1993). Multiplication and division: From whole numbers to rational numbers. In D. T. Owens (Ed.), *Research ideas for the classroom* (pp. 99-117). Reston, VA: National Council of Teachers of Mathematics.

Graeber, A. O., & Tirosh, D. (1990). Insights fourth and fifth graders bring to multiplication and division with decimals. *Educational Studies in Mathematics, 21,* 565-588.

Greer, B. (1989). Conceptual obstacles to the development of the concepts of multiplication and division. In H. Mandl, E. de Corte, S. N. Bennett, & H. F. Friedrich (Eds.), *Learning and instruction: European research in an international context* (Vol. 2.2, pp. 461-476). Oxford: Pergamon.

Greer, B. (1992). Multiplication and division. In D. Grouws (Ed.), *Handbook of research on mathematics teaching and learning* (pp. 276-295). New York: Macmillan.

Grossnickle, F. E., & Perry, L. M. (1985). Division with common fractions and decimal divisors. *School Science and Mathematics, 85*(7), 556-566.

Gundlach, B. H. (1989). The history of numbers and numerals. In *Historical topics for the mathematics classroom* (pp. 18-36). Reston, VA: National Council of Teachers of Mathematics.

Hart, K. (1984a). *Ratio: Children's strategies and errors.* Windsor, England: NFER-Nelson.

Hart, K. (1984b). Which comes first—Length, area, or volume? *Arithmetic Teacher, 31*(9), 16-18, 26-27.

Hart, L. E., & Walker, J. (1993). The role of affect in teaching and learning mathematics. In D. T. Owens (Ed.), *Research ideas for the classroom: Middle grades mathematics* (pp. 22-38). Reston, VA: National Council of Teachers of Mathematics.

Hatano, G. (1988). Social and motivational bases for mathematical understanding. In G. B. Saxe & M. Gearhart (Eds.), *Children's mathematics* (pp. 55-70). San Francisco: Jossey-Bass.

Hatfield, L. L. (1983). Teaching mathematics with microcomputers: Junior high school. *Arithmetic Teacher, 30*(6), 44-45, 68-69.

Hatfield, L. L. (1984). Toward comprehensive instructional computing in mathematics. In V. P. Hensen & M. J. Zweng (Eds.), *Computers in mathematics education* (1984 Yearbook, pp. 1-9). Reston, VA: National Council of Teachers of Mathematics.

Heid, K., Choate, J., Sheets, C., & Zbiek, R. M. (1995). *Algebra in a Technological World: Addenda Series, Grades 9-12.* Reston, VA: National Council of Teachers of Mathematics.

Heller, P., Ahlgren, A., Post, T., Behr, M., & Lesh, R. (1989). Proportional reasoning: The effect of two context variables, rate type and problem solving. *Journal for Research in Science Teaching, 26*(3), 205-220.

Heller, P., Post, T., Behr, M., & Lesh, R. (1990). Qualitative and numerical reasoning about fractions and ratios by seventh and eighth grade students. *Journal for Research in Mathematics Education, 21*(5), 388-402.

Hembree, R., & Dessart, D. J. (1986). Effects of hand-held calculators in precollege mathematics: A meta-analysis. *Journal for Research in Mathematics Education, 17*(2), 83-99.

Hersh, R. (1986). Some proposals for reviving the philosophy of mathematics. In T. Tymoczko (Ed.), *New directions in the philosophy of mathematics* (pp. 9-28). Boston: Birkhäuser.

Hiebert, J. (1984). Children's mathematics learning: The struggle to link form and understanding. *Elementary School Journal, 84,* 497-513.

Hiebert, J. (1987). Research report: Decimal fractions. *Arithmetic Teacher, 34*(7), 22-23.

Hiebert, J., & Carpenter, T. P. (1992). Learning, teaching with understanding. In D. Grouws (Ed.), *Handbook of research on mathematics teaching and learning* (pp. 65-97). New York: Macmillan.

Hiebert, J., & Tonnessen, L. H. (1978). Development of the fraction concept in two physical contexts: An exploratory investigation. *Journal for Research in Mathematics Education, 9,* 374-378.

Hiebert, J., & Wearne, D. (1992). Links between teaching and learning place value with understanding in first grade. *Journal for Research in Mathematics Education, 23,* 98-122.

Hirstein, J., Lamb, C., & Osborne, A. (1978). Student misconceptions about area measure. *Arithmetic Teacher, 25*(10), 10-16.

Hoffer, A. R. (1981). Geometry is more than proof. *Mathematics Teacher, 74,* 11-18.

Hoffer, A. R. (1983). Van Hiele-based research. In R. Lesh & M. Landau (Eds.), *Acquisition of mathematics concepts and processes* (pp. 205-227). New York: Academic Press.

Hoffer, A. R. (1988a). Geometry and visual thinking. In T. R. Post (Ed.), *Teaching mathematics in grades K-8: Research-based methods* (pp. 232-261). Boston: Allyn & Bacon.

Hoffer, A. R. (1988b). Ratios and proportional thinking. In T. R. Post (Ed.), *Teaching mathematics in grades K-8: Research-based methods* (pp. 285-313). Boston: Allyn & Bacon.

Holt, J. (1964). *How children fail.* New York: Delta.

Holt, J. (1970). *What do I do on Monday?* New York: E. P. Dutton & Co.

Hope, J. A. (1986). Mental calculation: Anachronism or basic skill: In H. L. Schoen, & M. J. Zweng (Eds.), *Estimation and mental computation* (1986 Yearbook, pp. 45-54). Reston, VA: National Council of Teachers of Mathematics.

Hope, J. A., & Sherrill, J. M. (1987). Characteristics of unskilled and skilled mental calculators. *Journal for Research in Mathematics Education 18*, 98-111.

Howden, H. (1989). Teaching number sense. *Arithmetic Teacher, 36*(6), 6-11.

Hughes, M. (1986). *Children and number: Difficulties in learning mathematics.* New York: Basil Blackwell.

Irons, R. R., & Irons, C. J. (1989). Language experiences: A base for problem solving. In P. R. Trafton & A. P. Shulte (Eds.), *New directions for elementary school mathematics.* (1989 Yearbook, pp. 85-98). Reston, VA: National Council of Teachers of Mathematics.

Jacobs, H. R. (1982). *Mathematics: A human endeavor* (2nd ed.). San Francisco: W. H. Freeman.

Jacobs, V. R., & Lajoie, S. P. (1994, April). *Statistics in middle school: An exploration of students' informal knowledge.* Paper presented at the annual meeting of the American Educational Research Association, New Orleans, LA.

Jacobson, M., Lester, F., & Stengel, A. (1980). Making problem solving come alive in the intermediate grades. In S. Krulik & R. E. Reys (Eds.), *Problem solving in school mathematics* (1980 Yearbook, pp. 127-135). Reston, VA: National Council of Teachers of Mathematics.

Jamski, W. D. (1989). Dürer's magic squares. *Arithmetic Teacher, 37*(4), 2.

Jencks, S. M., & Peck, D. F. (1987). *Beneath rules.* Menlo Park, CA: Benjamin Cummings.

Jensen, R. J., & Williams, B. S. (1993). Technology: Implications for middle grades mathematics. In D. T. Owens (Ed.), *Research ideas for the classroom: Middle grades mathematics* (pp. 225-243). Reston, VA: National Council of Teachers of Mathematics.

Johnson, D. R. (1982). *Every minute counts: Making your math class work.* Palo Alto, CA: Dale Seymour.

Johnson, D. W., & Johnson, R. T. (1989). Cooperative learning in mathematics. In P. R. Trafton & A. P. Schulte (Eds.), *New directions for elementary school mathematics* (1989 Yearbook, pp. 234-245). Reston, VA: National Council of Teachers of Mathematics.

Jones, G. A., Thornton, C. A., & Langrall, C. W. (1997, October). *Probability instruction informed by children's thinking.* Paper presented at the annual meeting of the North American Chapter of the International Group for the Psychology of Mathematics Education, Bloomington, IL.

Kamii, C. (1985). *Young children reinvent arithmetic: Implication of Piaget's theory.* New York: Teachers College Press.

Kamii, C. (1989). *Young children continue to reinvent arithmetic—2nd grade.* New York: Teachers College Press.

Kamii, C. (1990a). *Achievement testing in the early grades: The games grown-ups play.* Washington, DC: National Association for the Education of Young Children.

Kamii, C. (1990b, June). *Multidigit addition and subtraction: Learning to follow conventional rules or to do one's own thinking.* Paper presented at the Conference on Supporting Invention of Multidigit Addition and Subtraction in the Classroom, Evanston, IL.

Kamii, C., & Clark, F. B. (1997). Measurement of length: The need for a better approach to teaching. *School Science and Mathematics, 97*, 116-121.

Kaput, J. J. (1992). Technology and mathematics education. In D. A. Grouws (Ed.), *Handbook of research on mathematics teaching and learning* (pp. 515-556). New York: Macmillan

Karplus, R., & Peterson, R. W. (1970). *Intellectual development beyond elementary school IV: Ratio, a survey.* Berkeley: University of California, Lawrence Hall of Science.

Karplus, R., Karplus, E., & Wollman, W. (1974). Intellectual development beyond elementary school. IV: Ratio, the influence of cognitive style. *School Science and Mathematics, 74,*(6), 476-482.

Karplus, R., Karplus, E., Formisano, M., & Paulsen, A. (1979). Proportional reasoning and control of variables in seven countries. In J. Lochhead, & J. Clement (Eds.), *Cognitive process instruction* (pp. 47-103). Philadelphia: Franklin Institute.

Karplus, R., Pulos, S., & Stage, E. K. (1983). Proportional reasoning in early adolescents. In R. Lesh & M. Landau (Eds.), *Acquisition of mathematical concepts and procedures* (pp. 45-89) New York: Academic Press.

Kennedy, L. M., & Tipps, S. (1994). *Guiding children's learning of mathematics* (7th ed.). Belmont, CA: Wadsworth.

Kennedy, M. M., Ball, D. L., McDiarmid, G. W., & Schmidt, W. (1991). *A study package for examining and tracking changes in teachers' knowledge* (Technical Series 91-1). East Lansing, MI: The National Center for Research on Teacher Education at Michigan State University.

Kieran, C. (1981). Concepts associated with the equality symbol. *Educational Studies in Mathematics, 12*(3), 317-326.

Kieran, C. (1992). The learning and teaching of school algebra. In D. A. Grouws (Ed.), *Handbook of research on mathematics teaching and learning* (pp. 390-419). New York: Macmillan.

Kieran, C., & Chalouh, L. (1993). Prealgebra: The transition from arithmetic to algebra. In D. T. Owens (Ed.), *Research ideas for the classroom: Middle grades mathematics* (pp. 179-198). Reston, VA: National Council of Teachers of Mathematics.

Kieren, T. E. (1988). Personal knowledge of rational numbers: Its intuitive and formal development. In J. Hiebert & M. Behr (Eds.), *Number concepts and operations in the middle grades* (pp. 162-181). Reston, VA: National Council of Teachers of Mathematics.

Kieren, T., Behr, M. (1985). Fractions: Summary. In A. Bell, B. Low, & J. Kilpatrick (Ed.), *Theory, research, and practice in mathematical education* (pp. 176-185). Nottingham, England: Shell Centre for Mathematical Education, University of Nottingham.

Kilpatrick, J. (1985a). Doing mathematics without understanding it: A commentary on Higbee and Kunihira. *Educational Psychologist, 20*, 65-68.

Kilpatrick, J. (1985b). A retrospective account of the past twenty-five years of research on teaching mathematical problem solving. In E. A. Silver (Ed.), *Teaching and learning mathematical problem solving* (pp. 1-15). Hillsdale, NJ: Erlbaum.

Kline, M. (1974). *Why Johnny can't add*. New York: Vintage.

Koehler, M. S., & Grouws, D. (1992). Mathematics teaching practices and their effects. In D. A. Grouws (Ed.), *Handbook of research on mathematics teaching and learning* (pp. 115-126). New York: Macmillan.

Koehler, M. S., & Prior, M. (1993). Classroom interactions: The heartbeat of the teaching/learning process. In D. T. Owens (Ed.), *Research ideas for the classroom: Middle grades mathematics* (pp. 280-298). Reston, VA: National Council of Teachers of Mathematics.

Kouba, V. L. (1989). Children's solution strategies for equivalent set multiplication and division word problems. *Journal for Research in Mathematics Education, 20*, 147-158.

Kouba, V. L., & Franklin, K. (1993). Multiplication and division: Sense making and meaning. In R. J. Jensen (Ed.), *Research ideas for the classroom: Early childhood mathematics* (pp. 103-126). New York: Macmillan.

Kouba, V. L., Carpenter, T. P., & Swafford, J. O. (1989). Numbers and operations. In M. M. Lindquist (Ed.), *Results from the Fourth Mathematics Assessment of the National Assessment of Educational Progress* (pp. 64-93). Reston, VA: National Council of Teachers of Mathematics.

Labinowicz, E. (1985). *Learning from children: New beginnings for teaching numerical thinking*. Menlo Park, CA: Addison-Wesley.

Lamon, S. J. (1990, April). Ratio and proportion: Cognitive foundations in unitizing and norming. Paper presented at the Annual Meeting of the American Educational Research Association, Boston, MA. (ERIC Document Reproduction Service No. 325 335).

Lamon, S. J. (1993). Ratio and proportion: Children's cognitive and metacognitive processes. In T. P. Carpenter, E. Fennema, & T. A. Romberg (Eds.), *Rational numbers: An integration of research* (pp. 131-156). Hillsdale, NJ: Erlbaum.

Lampert, M. (1986). Knowing, doing, and teaching multiplication. Occasional Paper No. 97. East Lansing, MI: Michigan State University, Institute for Research on Teaching. (ERIC Document Reproduction Service No. ED 273 438).

Lappan, G., & Briars, D. (1995). How should mathematics be taught? In I. Carl (Ed.), *Seventy-five years of progress: Prospects for school mathematics* (pp. 131-156). Reston, VA: National Council of Teachers of Mathematics.

Lappan, G., & Schram, P. W. (1989). Communication and reasoning: Critical dimensions of sense making in mathematics. In P. R. Trafton & A. P. Shulte (Eds.), *New directions for elementary school mathematics* (1989 Yearbook, pp. 14-30). Reston, VA National Council of Teachers of Mathematics.

Laycock, M. (1977). *Base ten mathematics: Interludes for every math text*. Hayward, CA: Activity Resources Company.

Layzer, D. (1989). The synergy between writing and mathematics. In P. Connolly & T. Vilardi (Eds.), *Writing to learn mathematics and science* (pp. 121-133). New York: Teachers College Press.

LeFevre, J., Sadesky, G. S., & Bisanz, J. (1996). Selection of procedures in mental addition: Reassessing the problem size effect in adults. *Journal of Experimental Psychology: Learning, Memory, and Cognition, 22*, 216-230.

Leinhardt, G., & Smith, D. (1985). Expertise in mathematics instruction: Subject matter knowledge. *Journal of Educational Psychology, 77*, 247-271.

Lesh, R., & Lamon, S. J. (Eds.). (1992). *Assessment of authentic performance in school mathematics*. Washington, DC: American Association for the Advancement of Science.

Lesh, R., Post, T., & Behr, M. (1988). Proportional reasoning. In J. Hiebert & M. Behr (Eds.), *Number concepts and operations in the middle grades* (pp. 93-118). Reston, VA: The National Council of Teachers of Mathematics.

Lester, Jr., F. K. (1980). Research on mathematical problem solving. In R. J. Shumway (Ed.), *Research in mathematics education* (pp. 286-323). Reston, VA: National Council of Teachers of Mathematics.

Lester, Jr., F. K. (1989). Reflections about mathematical problem-solving research. In R. I. Charles & E. A.

Silver (Eds.), *The teaching and assessing of mathematical problem solving* (pp. 115-124). Reston, VA: The National Council of Teachers of Mathematics.

Lester, Jr., F. K., Garofalo, J., & Kroll, D. L. (1989). Self-confidence, interest, beliefs, and metacognition: Key influences on problem-solving behavior. In D. B. McLeod & V. M. Adams (Eds.), *Affect and mathematical problem-solving* (pp. 75-88). New York: Springer-Verlag.

Leutzinger, L. P., Rathmell, E. C., & Urbatsch, T. D. (1986). Developing estimation skills in the primary grades. In H. L. Schoen & M. J. Zweng (Eds.), *Estimation and mental computation* (1986 Yearbook, pp. 82-92). Reston, VA: National Council of Teachers of Mathematics.

Lindquist, M. M. (1989). It's time for change. In P. R. Trafton & A. P. Shulte (Eds.), *New directions for elementary school mathematics* (1989 Yearbook, pp. 1-13). Reston, VA: National Council of Teachers of Mathematics.

Lindquist, M. M., & Kouba, V. L. (1989). Measurement. In M. M. Lindquist (Ed.), *Results from the fourth mathematics assessment of the National Assessment of Educational Progress* (1989 Yearbook, pp. 35-43). Reston, VA: National Council of Teachers of Mathematics.

Lovell, K. (1961). A follow-up study of Inhelder and Piaget's the growth of logical thinking. *British Journal of Psychology, 52*(2), 143-153.

Mack, N. K. (1990). Learning fractions with understanding: Building on informal knowledge. *Journal for Research in Mathematics Education, 21*, 16-32.

Madell, R. (1985). Children's natural processes. *Arithmetic Teacher, 32*(7), 20-22.

Madsen, A. L., & Baker, K. (1993). Planning and organizing the middle grades mathematics curriculum. In D. T. Owens (Ed.), *Research ideas for the classroom: Middle grades* (pp. 259-279). Reston, VA: National Council of Teachers of Mathematics.

Mainville, Jr., W. E. (1989). Capsule 35: Fractions. In *Historical topics for the mathematics classroom* (pp. 135-137). Reston, VA: National Council of Teachers of Mathematics.

Mallory, C. E. (1997). Including African American students in the mathematics community. In J. Trentacosta & M. J. Kenney (Eds.), *Multicultural and gender equity in the mathematics classroom: The gift of diversity* (1997 Yearbook, pp. 23-33). Reston, VA: National Council of Teachers of Mathematics.

Markovits, Z., & Sowder, J. (1994). Developing number sense: An intervention study in Grade 7. *Journal for Research in Mathematics Education, 25*, 4-29.

Mathematical Sciences Education Board, National Research Council. (1987). *The teacher of mathematics: Issues for today and tomorrow.* Washington, DC: National Academy Press.

Mathematical Sciences Education Board, National Research Council. (1993). *Measuring up: Prototypes for mathematics assessment.* Washington, DC: National Academy Press.

McClain, K., Cobb, P., & Gravemeijer, K. (1997, October). *An analysis of students' development of reasoning strategies within the context of measure.* Paper presented at the annual meeting of the North American Chapter of the International Group for the Psychology of Mathematics Education. Normal, IL.

McLeod, D. B. (1992). Research on affect in mathematics education: A reconceptualization. In D. A. Grouws (Ed.), *Handbook of research on mathematics teaching and learning* (pp. 575-596). New York: Macmillan.

McKnight, C. C., Crosswhite, F. J., Dossey, J. A., Kifer, E., Swafford, J. O., Travers, K. J., & Cooney, T. J. (1987). *The underachieving curriculum: Assessing U. S. school mathematics from an international perspective.* Champaign, IL: Stipes.

Meyers, M. J., & Burton, G. M. (1989). Yes you can . . . plan appropriate instruction for learning disabled students. *Arithmetic Teacher, 36*(7), 46-50.

Miller, K. (1984). Child as the measurer of all things: Measurement procedures and the development of quantitative concepts. In C. Sophian (Ed.), *Origins of cognitive skills* (pp. 193-228). Hillsdale, NJ: Erlbaum.

Miura, I. (1987). Mathematics achievement as a function of language. *Journal of Educational Psychology, 79*, 79-82.

National Commission on Excellence in Education. (1983). *A nation at risk.* Washington, DC: U.S. Government Printing Office.

National Council of Teachers of Mathematics. (1989). *Curriculum and evaluation standards for school mathematics.* Reston, VA: Author.

National Council of Teachers of Mathematics. (1991). *Professional standards for teaching mathematics.* Reston, VA: Author.

National Council of Teachers of Mathematics. (1992). *Algebra for the twenty-first century: Proceedings of the August 1992 conference.* Reston, VA: Author.

National Council of Teachers of Mathematics (1995). *Assessment standards for school mathematics.* Reston, VA: Author.

National Research Council. (1989). *Everybody counts: A report to the nation on the future of mathematics education.* Washington, DC: National Academy Press.

Noddings, N. (1985). Small groups as a setting for research on mathematical problem solving. In E. A. Silver (Ed.), *Teaching and learning mathematical problem solving: Multiple research perspectives* (pp. 345-359). Hillsdale, NJ; Erlbaum.

Noelting, G. (1980a). The development of proportional reasoning and the ratio concept: Part I—Differentiation of stages. *Educational Studies in Mathematics, 11*, 217-253.

Noelting, G. (1980b). The development of proportional reasoning and the ratio concept: Part II—Problem structure at successive stages; problem solving strategies and the mechanism of adaptive restructuring. *Educational Studies in Mathematics, 11,* 331-363.

Novillis, C. G. (1976). An analysis of the fraction concept into a hierarchy of selected subconcepts and the testing of the hierarchical dependencies. *Journal for Research in Mathematics Education, 7,* 131-144.

Novillis-Larson, C. G. (1980). Locating proper fractions. *School Science and Mathematics, 53,* 423-428.

Nunes, T. (1992). Ethnomathematics and everyday cognition. In D. A. Grouws (Ed.), *Handbook of research on mathematics teaching and learning* (pp. 557-574). New York: Macmillan.

Nunes, T., & Moreno, C. (1997). Solving problems with different mediators: How do deaf children perform? *Educational Studies in Mathematics.*

Nunes, T., & Moreno, C. (in press). Is hearing impairment a cause of difficulties in learning mathematics? In C. Donlan (Ed.), *The development of mathematical skills.* Hove, East Sussez: Psychology Press.

Ohanian, S. (1992). *Garbage pizza, patchwork quilts, and math magic: Stories about teachers who love to teach and children who love to learn.* New York: W. H. Freeman and Co.

Ohlsson, S. (1988). Mathematics meaning and applicational meaning in the semantics of fractions and related concepts. In J. Hiebert & M. Behr (Eds.), *Number concepts and operations in the middle grades* (pp. 53-92). Reston, VA: The National Council of Teachers of Mathematics.

Ott, J. M. (1990). A united approach to multiplying fractions. *Arithmetic Teacher, 37*(7), 47-49.

Ott, J., Snook, S. L., & Gibson, D. L. (1991). Understanding partitive division of fractions. *Arithmetic Teacher, 39*(2), 7-11.

Owens, D. T., & Super, D. B. (1993). Teaching and learning decimal fractions. In D. T. Owens (Ed.), *Research issues for the classroom: Middle grades mathematics* (pp. 137-158). Reston, VA: National Council of Teachers of Mathematics.

Owston, R. D. (1997). The World Wide Web: A Technology to Enhance Teaching and Learning? *Educational Researcher, 26*(2), 27-33.

Panel on Educational Technology, President's Committee of Advisors on Science and Technology. (1997). *Report to the President on the use of technology to strengthen K-12 education in the United States.* Washington, D.C.

Papert, S. (1972). Teaching children to be mathematicians versus teaching about mathematics. *International Journal of Mathematical Education in Science and Technology, 3,* 249-262.

Papert, S. (1980a). *Mindstorms: Children, computers, and powerful ideas.* New York: Basic Books.

Papert, S. (1980b). Teaching children thinking. In R P. Taylor (Ed.), *The computer in the school: Tutor, tool, tutee* (pp. 161-176). New York: Teachers College Press.

Parker, R. E. (1993). *Mathematical power: Lessons from a classroom.* Portsmouth, NH: Heinemann.

Pau, C. S. (1995). The deaf child and solving problems of arithmetic: The importance of comprehensive reading. *American Annals of the Deaf, 140,* 279-286.

Paulos, J. A. (1988). *Innumeracy: Mathematical illiteracy and its consequences.* New York: Hill and Wang.

Payne, J. N., & Huinker, D. M. (1993). Early number and numeration. In R. J. Jensen (Ed.), *Research ideas for the classroom: Early childhood mathematics* (pp. 43-71). Reston, VA: National Council of Teachers of Mathematics.

Payne, J. N., & Rathmell, E. C. (1975). Number and numeration. In J. N. Payne (Ed.), *Mathematics learning in early childhood* (37th Yearbook, pp. 125-160). Reston, VA: National Council of Teachers of Mathematics.

Peck, D. M., & Connell, M. L. (1991). Using physical materials to develop mathematical intuition in fraction part-whole situations. *Focus on Learning Issues in Mathematics.* Albany, NY: SUNY.

Peck, D. M., & Jencks, S. M. (1988). Reality, arithmetic, algebra. *Journal of Mathematical Behavior, 7*(1), 85-91.

Peck, D. M., Jencks, S. M., & Connell, M. L. (1989). Improving instruction through brief interviews. *Arithmetic Teacher, 37*(3), 15-17.

Pellegrino, J. W., Hickey, D., Heath, A., Rewey, K., Vye, N. J., & the Cognition and Technology Group at Vanderbilt. (1991). *Assessing the outcomes of an innovative instructional program: The 1990-1991 implementation of the "Adventures of Jasper Woodbury* (Tech. Rep. No. 91-1). Nashville, TN: Vanderbilt University Learning and Technology Center.

Pengelly, H. (1988, July-August). *Mathematical learning beyond the activity.* Paper presented at the International Conference on Mathematics Education (ICM 6), Budapest.

Pereira-Mendoza, L., & Swift, J. (1981). Why we teach statistics and probability: A rationale. In A. P. Shulte (Ed.), *Teaching statistics and probability* (1981 Yearbook, pp. 1-7). Reston, VA: National Council of Teachers of Mathematics.

Perry, W. G. (1970). *Forms of intellectual and ethical development in the college years.* New York: Holt, Rinehart, and Winston.

Peterson, P. L. (1988). Teaching for higher order thinking in mathematics: The challenge for the next decade. In D. A. Grouws, T. Cooney, & D. Jones (Eds.), *Perspectives on research on effective mathematics teaching* (pp. 2-26). Reston, VA: National Council of Teachers of Mathematics.

Peterson, P. L., Fennema, E., & Carpenter, T. P. (1991). Teachers' knowledge of students' mathematics problem-solving knowledge. In J. Brophy (Ed.), *Advances in research on teaching: Vol. 2. Teachers' knowledge of subject matter as it relates to their teaching practice* (pp. 49-86). Greenwich, CT: JAI Press.

Peterson, P. L., Fennema, E., Carpenter, T. P., & Loef, M. (1989). Teachers' pedagogical content beliefs in mathematics. *Cognition and Instruction, 6*, 1-40.

Piaget, J. (1928). *Judgment and reasoning in the child.* New York: Harcourt, Brace, and Co.

Piaget, J. (1964). Development and learning. In R. E. Ripple & V. N. Rockcastle (Eds.), *Piaget rediscovered* (pp. 7-20). Ithaca, NY: Cornell University.

Piaget, J. (1965). *The child's conception of number.* New York: Norton.

Piaget, J., & Inhelder, B. (1958). *The growth of logical thinking from childhood to adolescence.* London: Routledge & Kegan Paul.

Piaget, J., & Inhelder, B. (1967). *The child's conception of space* (F. J. Langdon & J. L. Lunzer, Trans.). New York: Norton.

Piaget, J., & Inhelder, B. (1975). *The origin of the idea of chance in children.* New York: Norton.

Piaget, J., Inhelder, B., & Szeminska, A. (1960). *The child's conception of geometry.* (E. A. Lurnzer, Trans.). New York: Basic Books.

Plunkett, S. (1979). Decomposition and all that rot. *Mathematics in Schools, 8*(3), 2-5.

Pólya, G. (1949). On solving mathematical problems in high school. Reprinted in S. Kulik & R. E. Reys (Eds.), *Problem solving in school mathematics* (1980 Yearbook, pp. 1-2). Reston, VA: National Council of Teachers of Mathematics.

Pólya, G. (1957). *How to solve it* (2nd ed.). Garden City, New York: Doubleday Anchor Books.

Pólya, G. (1973). *How to solve it* (39th ed.). Princeton, NJ: Princeton University Press.

Pólya, G. (1981). *Mathematical discovery: On understanding, learning, and teaching problem solving.* New York: Wiley.

Post, T. R., Behr, M. J., & Lesh, R. (1988). Proportionality and the development of prealgebra understanding. In A. Coxford (Ed.), *Algebraic concepts in the curriculum K-12* (1988 Yearbook, pp. 78-90). Reston, VA: National Council of Teachers of Mathematics.

Post, T. R., Cramer, K. A., Behr, M., Lesh, R., & Harel, G. (1993). Curriculum implications of research on the learning, teaching and assessing of rational number concepts. In T. P. Carpenter, E. Fennema, & T. A. Romberg (Eds.), *Rational numbers: An integration of research* (pp. 327-362). Hillsdale, NJ: Lawrence Erlbaum.

Putnam, R. T., Lampert, M., & Peterson, P. L. (1990). Alternative perspectives on knowing mathematics in elementary schools. In C. B. Cazden (Ed.), *Review of research in education* (Vol. 16, pp. 57-150). Washington, DC: American Educational Research Association.

Rathmell, E. C. (1978). Using thinking strategies to teach basic facts. In M. N. Suydam & R. E. Reys (Eds.), *Developing computational skills* (1978 Yearbook, pp. 13-50). Reston, VA: National Council of Teachers of Mathematics.

Renga, S., & Dalla, L. (1993). Affect: Critical component of mathematical learning in early childhood. In R. J. Jensen (Ed.), *Research ideas for the classroom: Early childhood mathematics* (pp. 22-89). New York: Macmillan.

Resnick, L. B. (1983). A developmental theory of number understanding. In H. P. Ginsburg (Ed.), *The development of mathematical thinking* (pp. 109-151). New York: Academic Press.

Resnick, L. B. (1989). Treating mathematics as an ill-structured discipline. In R. I. Charles & E. A. Silver (Eds.), *The teaching and assessing of mathematical problem solving* (pp. 32-60). Reston, VA: National Council of Teachers of Mathematics.

Resnick, L. B., & Ford, W. W. (1981). *The psychology of mathematics for instruction.* Hillsdale, NJ: Erlbaum.

Resnick, L. D., Nesher, P., Leonard, F., Magone, M., Omanson, S., & Peled, I. (1989). Conceptual bases of arithmetic errors: The case of decimal fractions. *Journal for Research in Mathematics Education, 20*, 8-27.

Resnick, L. B., & Singer, J. A. (1993). Protoquantitative origins of ratio reasoning. In T. P. Carpenter, E. Fennema, & T. A. Romberg (Eds.), *Rational numbers: An integration of research* (pp. 107-130). Hillsdale, NJ: Erlbaum.

Reyes, L. H. (1984). Affective variables and mathematics education. *Elementary School Journal, 84*, 558-581.

Reys, B. J. (1986). Teaching computational estimation: Concepts and strategies. In H. L. Schoen, & M. J. Zweng (Eds.), *Estimation and mental computation* (1986 Yearbook, pp. 16-30). Reston, VA: National Council of Teachers of Mathematics.

Reys, B. J., Barger, R., Dougherty, B., Lemdke, L., Parnas, A., Sturdevant, R., Bruckheimer, M., Hope, J., Markovits, Z., Reehm, S., & Weber, M. (1991). *Developing number sense in the middle grades.* Reston, VA: National Council of Teachers of Mathematics.

Reys, R. E. (1984). Mental computation and estimation: Past, present, and future. *Elementary School Journal, 84*, 544-557.

Romberg, T. A., & Carpenter, T. P. (1986). Research on teaching and learning mathematics: Two disciplines of scientific inquiry. In M. C. Wittrock (Ed.), *Handbook of research on teaching* (3rd ed., pp. 850-873). New York: Macmillan.

Rose, B. (1989). Writing and mathematics: Theory and practice. In P. Connolly & T. Vilardi (Eds.), *Writing to learn mathematics and science* (pp. 15-30). New York: Teachers College Press.

Ross, S. H. (1989). Parts, wholes, and place value: A developmental review. *Arithmetic Teacher, 36*(6), 47-51.

Rowen, T. E., & Cetorelli, N. D. (1990). A model for teaching elementary school mathematics. In T. J. Cooney & C. R. Hirsch (Eds.), *Teaching and learning mathematics in the 1990s* (1990 Yearbook, pp. 62-68). Reston, VA: National Council of Teachers of Mathematics.

Russell, S. J., & Friel, S. N. (1989). Collecting and analyzing real data in the elementary school classroom. In P. R. Trafton (Ed.), *New directions for elementary school mathematics* (1989 Yearbook, pp. 134-148). Reston, VA: National Council of Teachers of Mathematics.

Sawyer, W. W. (1971). *Mathematician's delight*. Middlesex, England: Penguin.

Saxe, G. B. (1988). Candy selling and mathematics learning. *Educational Researcher, 17*(6), 14-21.

Schipper, W. (1983). The topological primacy thesis: Geometric and didactic aspects. *Educational Studies in Mathematics, 14*, 285-296.

Schoenfeld, A. H. (1982). Some thoughts on problem-solving research and mathematics education. In F. K. Lester, Jr., & J. Garofalo (Eds.), *Mathematical problem solving: Issues in research* (pp. 27-37). Philadelphia: Franklin Institute Press.

Schoenfeld, A. H. (1985). *Mathematical problem solving*. New York: Academic Press.

Schoenfeld, A. H. (1992). Learning to think mathematically: Problem solving, metacognition, and sense making in mathematics. In D. A. Grouws (Ed.), *Handbook of research on mathematics teaching and learning* (pp. 334-370). New York: Macmillan.

Schroeder, T. L., & Lester, Jr., F. K. (1989). Developing understanding in mathematics via problem solving. In P. R. Trafton & A. P. Shulte (Eds.), *New directions for elementary school mathematics* (1989 Yearbook, pp. 31-42). Reston, VA: National Council of Teachers of Mathematics.

Secada, W. G. (1984). *Counting in Sign: The number string, accuracy and used*. Unpublished doctoral dissertation, Department of Education, Northwestern University, Evanston, IL.

Secada, W. G. (1992). Race, ethnicity, social class, language, and achievement in mathematics. In D. A. Grouws (Ed.), *Handbook of Research on Mathematics Teaching and Learning* (pp. 623-660). New York: Macmillan.

Senechal, M. (1990). Shape. In L. A. Steen (Ed.), *On the shoulders of giants* (pp. 139-181). Washington, DC: National Academy Press.

Shaugnhessy, J. M. (1992). Research in probability and statistics: Reflections and directions. In D. A. Grouws (Ed.), *Handbook of research on mathematics teaching and learning* (pp. 456-494). New York: Macmillan.

Shaughnessy, J., Haladyna, T., & Shaughnessy, J. M. (1983). Relations of student, teacher, and learning environment variables to attitude toward mathematics. *School Science and Mathematics, 83*(1), 21-37.

Shumway, R. J. (1988). Calculator and computers (Chapter 12). In T. R. Post *Teaching mathematics in grades K-8* (pp. 334-383). Boston: Allyn & Bacon.

Silver, E. A. (1994). On mathematical problem posing. *For the Learning of Mathematics, 14*(1), 19-28.

Silver, E. A., Kilpatrick, J., & Schlesinger, B. (1990). *Thinking through mathematics: Fostering inquiry and communication in mathematics classrooms*. New York: College Entrance Examination Board.

Simon, M. A. (1993). Prospective elementary teachers' knowledge of division. *Journal for Research in Mathematics Education, 24*, 233-254.

Simon, M. (1995). Reconstructing mathematics pedagogy. *Journal for Research in Mathematics Education, 26*, 114-145.

Skemp, R. R. (1978). Relational understanding and instrumental understanding. *Arithmetic Teacher, 26*(3), 9-15.

Slavin, R. (1983). *Cooperative learning*. New York: Longman.

Sloan, D. (1985). Introduction: On raising critical questions about the computer in education. In D. Sloan (Ed.), *The computer in education: A critical perspective* (pp. 1-9). New York: Teachers College Press.

Sophian, C., & McCorgray, P. (1994). Part-whole knowledge and early arithmetic problem-solving. *Cognition and Instruction, 12*, 3-33.

Sowder, J. T. (1992). Estimation and number sense. In D. A. Grouws (Ed), *Handbook of research on mathematics teaching and learning* (pp. 371-389). New York: Macmillan.

Sowder, J. T., & Kelin, J. (1993). Number sense and related topics. In D. T. Owens (Ed.), *Research ideas for the classroom: Middle grades* (pp. 41-57). New York: Macmillan.

Sowell, E. J. (1989). Effects of manipulative materials in mathematics instruction. *Journal for Research in Mathematics Education, 20*, 498-505.

Stanic, G. M. A., & Kilpatrick, J. (1989). Historical perspectives on problem solving in mathematics curriculum. In R. I. Charles & E. A. Silver (Eds.), *The teaching and assessing of mathematical problem solving* (pp. 1-22). Reston, VA: The National Council of Teachers of Mathematics.

Steen, L. A. (Ed.). (1990a). *On the shoulders of giants: New approaches to numeracy*. Washington, D.C.: National Academy Press.

Steen, L. A. (1990b). Pattern. In L. A. Steen (Ed.), *On the shoulders of giants: New approaches to numeracy* (pp. 1-10). Washington, D.C.: National Academy Press.

Steffe, L. P., Olive, J., Battista, M. T., & Clements, D. H. (1991). The problem of fractions in the elementary school. *Arithmetic Teacher, 38*(9), 22-24.

Steffe, L. P., von Glasersfeld, E., Richards, J., & Cobb, P. (1983). *Children's counting types: Philosophy, theory, and application.* New York: Praeger Scientific.

Steffe, L. P., & Wood, T. (Eds.). (1990). *Transforming children's mathematics education.* Hillsdale, NJ: Erlbaum.

Stein, M. K., Silver, E. A., & Smith, M. S. (in press). Mathematics reform and teacher development: A community of practice perspective. In J. Greeno & S. Goldman (Eds.), *Thinking practices: A symposium on mathematics and science learning.* Hillsdale, NJ: Erlbaum.

Steinberg, R. M. (1985). Instruction on derived fact strategies in addition and subtraction. *Journal for Research in Mathematics Education, 16,* 337-355.

Stevenson, H. W., Lee, S. Y., & Stigler, J. W. (1986). Mathematics achievement of Chinese, Japanese, and American children. *Science, 231,* 693-699.

Stiff, L. V., & Harvey, W. B. (1988). On the education of black children in mathematics, *Journal of Black Studies, December,* 190-203.

Stiggins, R. J., & Bridgeford, N. J. (1985). The ecology of classroom assessment. *Journal of Educational Measurement, 22*(4), 271-286.

Stigler, J. W., Fuson, K. C., Ham, M., & Kim, M. S. (1986). An analysis of addition and subtraction word problems in American and Soviet elementary mathematics textbooks. *Cognition and Instruction, 3,* 153-171.

Streefland, L. (1993). Fractions: A realistic approach. In T. P. Carpenter, E. Fennema, & T. A. Romberg (Eds.), *Rational numbers: An integration of research* (pp. 289-325). Hillsdale, NJ: Erlbaum.

Suppes, P., & Morningstar, M. (1972). *Computer-assisted instruction at Stanford, 1966-68: Data, models, and evaluation of the arithmetic programs.* New York: Academic Press.

Suydam, M. N. (1983). Achieving with calculators. *Arithmetic Teacher, 31*(3), 20.

Suydam, M. (1984). Research report: Manipulative materials. *Arithmetic Teacher, 31*(5), 27.

Suydam, M., & Weaver, J. F. (1975). Research on mathematics learning. In J. N. Payne (Ed.), *Mathematics learning in early childhood* (37th Yearbook, pp. 43-67). Reston, VA: National Council of Teachers of Mathematics.

Taylor, L. (1997). Integrating mathematics and American Indian cultures. In J. Trentacosta & M. J. Kenney (Eds.), *Multicultural and gender equity in the mathematics classroom: The gift of diversity* (1997 Yearbook, pp. 169-176). Reston, VA: National Council of Teachers of Mathematics.

Taylor, R. P. (Ed.) (1980). *The computer in the school: Tutor, tool, tutee* (pp. 177-196). New York: Teachers College Press.

Tennyson, R. D., Youngers, J., & Suebsonthi, P. (1983). Concept learning of children using instructional presenting forms for prototype formation and classification-skill development. *Journal of Educational Psychology, 75,* 280-291.

Thomas, J. (1997). Teaching mathematics in a multicultural classroom. Lessons from Australia. In J. Trentacosta & M. J. Kenney (Eds.), *Multicultural and gender equity in the mathematics classroom: The gift of diversity* (1997 Yearbook, pp. 34-45). Reston, VA: National Council of Teachers of Mathematics.

Thompson, A. (1992). Teachers' beliefs and conceptions: A synthesis of the research. In D. Grouws Ed), *Handbook of research on mathematics teaching and learning* (pp. 127-146). New York: Macmillan.

Thompson, C., & Van de Walle, J. (1984). Let's do it: The power of 10. *Arithmetic Teacher, 32*(7), 6-11.

Thompson, P. W. (1992). Notations, conventions, and constraints: Contributions to effective uses of concrete materials in elementary mathematics. *Journal for Research in Mathematics Education, 23,* 123-127.

Thompson, P. W., & Thompson, A. (1990). Salient aspects of experience with concrete manipulatives. In G. Booker, P. Cobb, & T. Menendicuti (Eds.), *Proceedings of the 14th International Conference for the Psychology of Mathematics Education* (pp. 337-343). Oaxtepec, Mexico.

Thornton, C. A., & Smith, P. J. (1988). Action research: Strategies for learning subtraction facts. *Arithmetic Teacher, 35*(8), 8-12.

Thornton, C. A., & Toohey, M. A. (1985). Basic math facts: Guidelines for teaching and learning. *Learning Disabilities Focus, 1*(1), 44-57.

Thornton, C. A., & Wilson, S. J. (1993). Classroom organization and models of instruction. In R. J. Jensen (Ed.), *Research ideas for the classroom: Early childhood mathematics* (pp. 269-293). New York: Macmillan.

Tobias, S. (1989). Writing to learn science and mathematics. In P. Connolly & T. Vilardi (Eds.), *Writing to learn mathematics and science* (pp. 48-55). New York: Teachers College Press.

Trafton, P. R. (1978). Estimation and mental arithmetic: Important components of computation. In M. N. Suydam & R. E. Reys (Eds.), *Developing computational skills* (pp. 196-213). Reston, VA: National Council of Teachers of Mathematics.

Trafton, P. R. (1986). Teaching computational estimation: Establishing an estimation mindset. In H. L. Schoen & M. J. Zweng (Eds.), *Estimation and mental computation* (pp. 16-30). Reston, VA: The National Council of Teachers of Mathematics.

Trafton, P. R. (1989). Reflections on the number sense conference. In J. T. Sowder & B. P. Schappelle (Eds.), *Establishing foundations for research on number sense and related topics: Report on a conference* (pp. 74-77). San Diego: San Diego State University Center for Research in Mathematics and Science Education.

Trafton, P. R., & Shulte, A. P. (Eds.), (1989). *New directions for elementary school mathematics* (1989 Yearbook). Reston, VA: National Council of Teachers of Mathematics.

Tzur, R. (1995, April). *Teaching-learning interaction and children's construction of the equi-partitioning scheme.* Paper presented at the annual meeting of the American Education Research Association. San Francisco, CA.

Underhill, R. (1988). Mathematics learners' beliefs: A review. *Focus on Learning Problems in Mathematics, 10,* 55-69.

Usiskin, Z. (1988). Conceptions of school algebra and uses of variables. In A. F. Coxford (Ed.), *The ideas of algebra, K-12* (1988 Yearbook, pp. 8-19). Reston, VA: National Council of Teachers of Mathematics.

van Hiele, P. M. (1986). *Structure and insight.* Orlando, FL: Academic Press.

Van de Walle, J. A. (1994). *Elementary school mathematics: Teaching developmentally* (2nd ed.). New York: Longman.

Van de Walle, J. A., & Watkins, K. B. (1993). Early development of number sense. In R. J. Jensen (Ed.), *Research for the classroom: Early childhood mathematics* (pp. 127-150). Reston, VA: National Council of Teachers of Mathematics.

Vergnaud, G. (1983). Multiplicative structures. In R. Lesh & M. Landau (Eds.), *Acquisition of mathematics concepts and processes* (pp. 127-174). New York: Academic Press.

Wagner, S. (1981). Conservation of equation function under transformations of variable. *Journal for Research in Mathematics Education 12,* 107-118.

Walker, E. N., & McCoy, L. P. (1997). Students' voices: African Americans and mathematics. In J. Trentacosta & M. J. Kenney (Eds.), *Multicultural and gender equity in the mathematics classroom: The gift of diversity* (1997 Yearbook, pp. 71-80). Reston, VA: National Council of Teachers of Mathematics.

Wearne, D., & Hiebert, J. (1988a). A cognitive approach to meaningful mathematics instruction: Testing a local theory using decimal numbers. *Journal for Research in Mathematics Education, 19,* 371-384.

Wearne, D., & Hiebert, J. (1988b). Constructing and using meaning for mathematical symbols: The case of decimal fractions. In J. Hiebert & M. Behr (Eds.), *Number concepts and operations in the middle grades* (pp. 220-235). Hillsdale, NJ: Erlbaum; Reston, VA: National Council of Teachers of Mathematics.

Wearne, D., & Hiebert, J. (1989). Cognitive changes during conceptually based instruction on decimal fractions. *Journal of Educational Psychology, 81,* 507-513.

Wearne, D., Hiebert, J., & Taber, S. (1991). Fourth graders' gradual construction of decimal fractions during instruction using different physical representations. *Elementary School Journal, 91*(4), 321-341.

Wertheimer, M. (1959). *Productive thinking.* New York: Harper & Row.

Whitin, D. J. (1989). Number sense and the importance of asking "Why?" *Arithmetic Teacher, 36*(6), 26-29.

Whitin, D. J., & Wilde, S. (1992). *Read any good math lately: Children's books for mathematical learning.* K-6. Portsmouth, NH: Heinemann.

Wilde, S. (1991). Learning to write about mathematics. *Arithmetic Teacher, 39*(6), 38-43.

Wilson, P. S. (1987). Microcomputer use in the elementary school. *Arithmetic Teacher, 35*(4), 33-34.

Wilson, P. S., & Rowland, R. E. (1993). Teaching measurement. In R. J. Jensen (Ed.), *Research ideas for the classroom: Early childhood mathematics* (pp. 171-194). Reston, VA: National Council of Teachers of Mathematics.

Wollman, W., & Karplus, R. (1974). Intellectual development beyond elementary school V: Using ratio in differing tasks. *School Science and Mathematics, 74,* 593-613.

Wynroth, L. (1986). *Wynroth math program—The natural numbers sequence.* Ithaca, NY: Wynroth Math Program.

Yackel, E., Cobb, P., Wood, T., Wheatley, G., & Merkel, G. (1990). The importance of social interaction in children's construction. In T. J. Cooney (Ed.), *Teaching and learning mathematics in the 1990s* (1990 Yearbook, pp. 12-21). Reston, VA: National Council of Teachers of Mathematics.

Yiu, T. (1992). *A study of children's understanding of fraction size and its relationship to proportional reasoning.* Unpublished doctoral dissertation, University of Illinois, Urbana-Champaign.

APPENDIX C: PUBLISHERS OR DISTRIBUTORS OF
EDUCATIONAL MATERIALS

ABC Intellimation
P.O. Box 1922
Santa Barbara, CA 93116-1922
800-346-8355
FAX: 805-968-8899

Activity Resources Company, Inc.
P.O. Box 4875
Hayward, CA 94540
510-782-1300
FAX: 510-782-8172

Addison-Wesley Publishing Co.
Route 128
Reading, MA 01867
800-552-2759
FAX: 800-333-3328

AIMS Education Foundation
P.O. Box 8120
Fresno, CA 93747-8120
209-255-4094
FAX: 209-255-6396

Carolina Biological Supply Company
2700 York Road
Burlington, NC 27215-3398
800-334-5551
FAX: 800-222-7112

Center for Applied Research in Education
West Nyack, NY 10995-9901
800-288-4745
http://www.phdirect.com

COMAP
60 Lowell Street
Arlington, MA 02174-4131
617-641-2600
FAX: 617-643-1295

Creative Publications
Order Department
5623 W. 115th Street
Alsip, IL 60803
800-624-0822
FAX: 800-624-0821

Cuisenaire Company of America, Inc.
10 Bank Street
White Plains, NY 10606-1951
800-237-3142
FAX: 914-576-3480

CCV Software
P.O. Box 6724
Charleston, VA 25362-0724
800-843-5576
FAX: 800-321-4297
ccv@ccvsoftware.com

Dale Seymour Publications
P.O. Box 5026
White Plains, NY 10602-5026
800-872-1100
FAX: 800-551-7637
http://www.aw.com/dsp/

Delta Education
P.O. Box 3000
Nashua, NH 03061-3000
800-442-5444
FAX: 800-282-9560

Dial Books for Young Readers
A Division of E. P. Dutton, Inc.
2 Park Avenue
New York, NY 10016

Didax
395 Main Street
Rowley, MA 01969-0907
800-458-0024
FAX: 800-350-2345
http://www.Didaxinc.com

ETA
620 Lakeview Parkway
Vernon Hills, IL 60061-9923
800-445-5985
FAX: 800-ETA-9326
info@etauniverse.com

Everyday Learning Corporation
P.O. Box 812960
Chicago, IL 60681
312-540-0210
800-382-7670

Eye on Education
6 Depot Way, Suite 106
Larchmont, NY 10538
914-833-0551
FAX: 914-833-0761

Gameco Educational Materials
P.O. Box 1911G2
Big Springs, TX 79721
800-351-1404
FAX: 915-267-7480

Good Apple
1204 Buchanan, Box 299
Carthage, IL 62321-0299
800-435-7234
FAX: 217-357-3987

Heinemann
361 Hanover Street
Portsmouth, NH 03801-3912
800-541-2086
FAX: 800-847-0938
http://www.heinemann.com

Innovative Learning Publications
(see Addison Wesley)

Key Curriculum Press
P.O. Box 2304
Berkeley, CA 94702-0304
800-995-MATH
FAX: 800-541-2442
http://www.keypress.com

LEArning, Inc.
10 Industrial Avenue
Mahwah, NJ 07430
800-926-6579
FAX: 201-236-0072
E-mail: orders@erlbaum.com

The Learning Team (MathFinder CD)
84 Business Park Drive
Suite 307
Armonk, NY 10504
800-793-TEAM
FAX: 914-273-2227

Mathematics Learning Center
P.O. Box 3226
Salem, OR 97302
503-370-8130
FAX: 503-370-7961
To arrange workshops, contact
    MLC Workshops
    P.O. Box 1491
    Portland, OR 97207
    503-725-3041

McGraw-Hill
1221 Avenue of the Americas
New York, NY 10020
800-262-4729
FAX: 212-512-6285

MindWare
6142 Olson Memorial Hwy.
Golden Valley, MN 55422
800-999-0398
FAX: 612-595-8852

Nasco Math
901 Janesville Ave.
P.O. Box 901
Fort Atkinson, WI 53538-0901
800-558-9595
FAX: 209-545-1669

National Council of Teachers
    of Mathematics
1906 Association Drive
Reston, VA 20191-1593
703-620-9840
FAX: 703-476-2970
http://www.nctm.org
e-mail: infocentral@nctm.org

Optical Data Corporation
30 Technology Drive
Warren, NJ 07059
800-524-2481
FAX: 908-668-1322

Pro-Ed
8700 Shoal Creek Boulevard
Austin, TX 78758
800-897-3202
FAX: 800-397-7633
http://www.proedinc.com

Scholastic Software Club
2931 East McCarty Street
P.O. Box 7500
Jefferson City, MO 65102
800-724-4811
http://scholastic.com

Shell Centre for Mathematical Education
University of Nottingham
Nottingham, ENGLAND NG72RD
Telephone: (0115) 951-4412
FAX: (0115) 979-1813
e-mail: rszms@unicorn.nott.ac.uk

SoftWare House
P.O. Box 9204
Fargo, ND 58106-9204
800-541-6078
FAX: 800-457-6953
http://www.ccvsoftware.com
e-mail: swh@ccvsoftware.com

Sunburst Communications, Inc.
101 Castleton Street
Pleasantville, NY 10570
800-321-7511
FAX: 914-747-4109
http://www.SUNBURSTonline.com

Teachers College Press
1234 Amsterdam Avenue
New York, NY 10027-6694
800-575-6566
FAX: 802-864-7626
http://www.tc.columbia.edu/~tcpress

Teaching Resource Center
P.O. Box 1509
San Leandro, CA 94577
800-833-3389
FAX: 800-972-7722

Tricon Publishing
Box 146
Mt. Pleasant, MI 48804
517-772-2811
FAX: 517-773-5894

The Wild Goose Co.
375 Whitney Avenue
Salt Lake City, UT 84115
801-466-1172
FAX: 801-466-1186

WINGS *for learning* Sunburst
1600 Green Hills Road
P.O. Box 660002
Scotts Valley, CA 95067-0002
800-321-7511
FAX: 408-438-4214

APPENDIX D: SUBJECT INDEX
(Abbreviations: AF = Activity File, Fig = Figure, Inv = Investigation, Pr = Probe)

teacher expectations, role of, 17-12 (text & Fig 17.4), 17-13 (Box 17.4), 17-14 (text & Box 17.5)
teaching tips, 17-12, 17-14

Enumeration
activities, 4-11 (AF 4.3 & 4.4), 4-14 (AF 4.5)
cardinality principle, 4-8, 4-12
definition, 4-4 & 4-5 (Pr 4.1)
learning, 4-8
teaching tips, 4-11, 4-12

Error analysis
as a diagnostic tool
as a teaching-learning tool, 3-36, 6-20 (Box 6.2), 14-9, 14-12, 16-13, 16-14
reader inquiries, 3-19 (Probe 3.4), 3-24 to 3-26 (Probe 3.5), 3-32 to 3-35 (Probe 3.6)

Error-detection activities, 4-11, 4-12 (Box 4.3)

Errors as springboards to inquiry
reader inquiries, 3-32 & 3-33 (Probe 3.6)
teaching tips, 3-36

Estimation, *See also* Benchmarks, numerical
activities, 1-20 (Box 1.6), 7-21 (AF 7.3), 7-32 (AF 7.7)
averaging strategy, 7-23
building on everyday knowledge, 7-19 (Inv 7.7)
checking calculations with a calculator, 7-2 (Inv 7.1)
choosing a strategy, 7-17 (Inv 7.6)
compatible-numbers strategy, 7-23
computation estimation, 7-22, 7-23
decimals, 1-20 (Box 1.6), 11-14, 11-15 (Inv 11.5), 11-20 (Inv 11.7), 11-21 (Inv 11.8), 11-31 (AF 11.3 & 11.4)
definition, 7-3
everyday uses, 7-2 (Inv 7.1)
fractions, 9-11 & 9-12 (text & AF 9.1), 9-14, 9-24, 10-7, 10-9 (Inv 10.1)
front-end strategy, 7-23
instructional resources, 7-29 to 7-31
learning, 7-15, 7-18, 7-22
measurement estimation, 7-32 (AF 7.7), 15-17 (Inv 15.2)
NCTM *Standards*, 7-3, 7-4
number estimation, 7-22
population growth, 7-31 (Box 7.3)
rounding, 7-16 (Pr 7.1), 7-17 (Inv 7.6), 7-21 (AF 7.3), 7-23
teaching tips, 7-18, 7-20, 7-22, 7-23
value of, 7-1 (bulletin board), 7-2 (Inv 7.2)

Euler diagrams, 2-28 & 2-29 (Inv 2.4), 2-31

Everyday Mathematics, 1-37, 5-22 (AF 5.5)

Examples and nonexamples
arithmetic sequence, to clarify the meaning of, 3-17 (Inv 3.2)
best examples, 3-17
critical attributes, discovering, 14-10 & 14-11 (Inv 14.3)
definition, 2-28
diagonals, defining, 14-10 (Inv 14-10)
divisibility rules, discovering, 8-14 & 8-15 (Inv 8.6)
Euler diagram representations of, 2-28 & 2-29 (Inv 2.4)
explicit understanding, role in fostering, 3-16, 3-17 (Inv 3.2)
geometry, 3-17 (Inv 3.2), 14-7, 14-9 (Box 14.1), 14-10 & 14-11 (Inv 14.3), 14-28 (Box 14.2)
rhomboid, to clarify the meaning of, 3-17 (Inv 3.2)
sorting & classifying, 2-30 (AF 2.1 & 2.2)
teaching tips, 3-16
Venn diagrams representations of, 2-30 (AF 2.2)

Exercises, 2-3, 2-5 (Pr 2.1)

Extended projects, *See* Project-based instruction

F

Family involvement
assessment, openness about, 3-22
class newspaper, 17-10
family entertainment night, 17-9
family letters, 1-37, 17-10
Home Connections, 17-7 (Box 17.2), 17-10
investigative approach, explaining, 2-12 (Box 2.2)
open houses, 2-12 (Box 2.12), 2-30 (AF 2.2)
resources, 3-37
student-parent letter, 17-10

Five frames, 4-10 (text & Box 4.2), 7-7 (Box 7.1)

Formal algebra strategies
performing the same operation on both sides, 16-15 & 16-16, 16-17 (Inv 16.3), 16-19 (Box 16.2)
transposing (change sides, change sign), 16-16

Fraction Circles
adding fractions, 10-11 (Pr 10.2), 10-23
assessment, 3-15
comparing fractions, 9-20 & 9-21 (Inv 9.3), 10-23
fraction concepts, 10-23
inquiry-based lessons, 9-27
measure-out meaning of fraction division, 10-17 (Inv 10.2)
part-of-a-whole meaning, 9-24
rediscovering the common-denominator method for fraction division, 10-20 (Pr 10.3)
simplifying fractions, 10-23
subtracting fractions, 10-23

Fractions, *See also* Operations on fractions, Rational numbers
activities, 9-11 & 9-12 (AF 9.1), 9-15 (Box 9.1), 9-25 (AF 9.2)
common fractions, 9-13 to 9-26
comparing fractions, 1-22 & 1-23 (Inv 1.2), 9-20 to 9-23 (Inv 9.3), 9-25 (Fig 9.11, AF 9.2, & Fig 9.12), 11-30 (AF 11.2)
comparison with whole numbers, 9-8 & 9-9 (Pr 9.2)
conceptual basis, 9-4 & 9-5 (Inv 9.1), 9-11 (AF 9.1)
equal partitioning, 9-4 & 9-5 (Inv 9.1), 9-10 (Pr 9.3), 9-18 (Box 9.2)
equivalent fractions, 9-16 & 9-17 (Inv 9.2), 9-20 to 9-23 (Inv 9.3), 9-4 (Fig 9.10)
Egyptian fractions, 9-5
estimation, 9-11 & 9-12 (text & AF 9.1), 9-14, 9-24
fair-sharing, 9-10 (Pr 9.3), 9-12 (Fig 9.4), 9-20 & 9-21 (Inv 9.3), 9-24 (Fig 9.10)
instructional resources, 9-26, 9-27, 12-26
learning, 9-13, 9-14
part-of-a-whole models, 9-16 & 9-17 (Inv 9.2), 9-18 (Fig 9.8)
problems, types of, 9-19 (Fig 9.9)
purposeful instruction of, 9-11 & 9-12 (AF 9.1), 9-15 (Box 9.1)
qualitative reasoning, 9-20 (Inv 9.3)
rectangular cake-cutting analogy, 9-22 & 9-23 (Inv 9.3)
relationship to other real numbers, 8-2 & 8-3 (Pr 8.1)
teaching tips, 9-14, 9-15, 9-18, 9-19, 9-24 to 9-26
writing activities, 9-15 (Box 9.1)

Fraction strips, 9-16 (footnote), 9-18 (Fig 9.8)

comparing numbers, 1-22 & 1-23 (Inv 1.2), 4-13, 4-14 (AF 4.5 & 4.6)
counting, 4-10 to 4-14 (text; AF 4.2, 4.3 & 4.4; Box 4.3; & AF 4.5), 4-25
numeral skills, 4-21 & 4-22 (text & AF 4.7, 4.8, 4.9 & 4.10)
operations on decimals, 1-20 (Box 1.6), 11-31 (AF 11.4)
operations on fractions, 10-7, 10-21 (Box 10.5), 13-3 (Box 13.1)
operations on multidigit whole numbers, 3-40, 6-15 (AF 6.3), 6-21 (Inv 6.4), 15-3 (AF 15.3), 16-20 & 16-21 (Inv 16.5)
operations on single-digit whole numbers, 3-40, 7-30 (AF 7.6), 16-20 & 16-21 (Inv 16.5)

Q

Qualitative reasoning
fraction comparisons, 9-20 (Inv 9.3)
operations on decimals, 11-14, 11-15 (Inv 11.5), 11-21 (Inv 11.8)
operations on fractions, 10-8 & 10-9 (Inv 10.1), 10-10 (Box 10.1)
operations on whole numbers, 7-9 (Inv 7.3), 7-10 & 7-11 (Inv 7.4), 7-30 (AF 7.5)
probability, 13-23, 13-24

Questioning students
effective questioning techniques, 17-8
encouraging student questions, 17-9 (text & Box 17.3)
interviewing children, 3-24 to 3-26 (Pr 3.5)
open-ended, process oriented, 3-26 (Box 3.4)
prompting classroom interaction, 17-7 to 17-9
responding to questions, 17-8, 17-9 (text & Box 17.3)

R

Rational-number meanings, 9-1, 9-8 (Pr 9.2)
operator, 9-6
part of a whole, 9-6, 9-12 (Fig 9.4), 9-16, & 9-17 Inv 9.2)
quotient, 9-2, 9-5 (Inv 9.1), 9-6, 9-12 (Fig 9.4)
ratio, 9-6

Rational numbers, See also Fractions, Rational number meanings
learning, 9-7
role, 9-2
relationships to other real numbers, 8-2 & 8-3 (Pr 8.1)
symbolic representations, 9-6, 9-7, 9-8 & 9-9 (Pr 9.2)
teaching tips, 9-7, 9-11

Ratios
activities, 12-9 (AF 12.1), 12-10 (AF 12.2)
continuous quantities, 12-5 (Pr 12.1)
comparison with fractions, 12-7 (Pr 12.2), 12-8, 12-9
definition, 12-4, 12-6 (Inv 12.2), 12-8
instructional resources, 12-26
teaching tips, 12-9, 12-10, 12-26
uses, 12-4 (text & Box 12.1), 12-5 (Pr 12.1)

Reading numerals, See Numeral skills, Place value

Real numbers, relationships among, 8-2 & 8-3 (Pr 8.1)

Reasoning, See also Classifying and sorting, Conjecturing, Counterexamples, Deductive reasoning, Inductive reasoning, Intuitive reasoning, Proportional reasoning
activities, 2-25 (Pr 2.3), 2-31 (Box 2.8), 2-30 to 2-32 (text, AF 2.1 & 2.2, Box 2.8 to 2.10)
bulletin board, 3-1
concept map of, 3-1
evaluating reasoning, 2-26 to 2-29 (Inv 2.4), 2-30 to 2-32 (text & Box 2.8, 2.9 & 2.10)
limitations and misuses, 2-23, 2-26 (Inv 2.4)
mathematics as, 2-22 to 2-32
NCTM Standards, 2-2
need for, 2-23
reader inquiries, 1-9 & 1-10 (Inv 1.1), 2-24 (Inv 2.3), 2-25 (Probe 2.3), 2-26 to 2-29 (Inv 2.4), 2-38 (Inv 2.5)
teaching tips, 2-23, 2-25, 2-26, 2-30 to 2-32 (text, AF 2.1 & 2.2, & Box 2.8 to 2.10), 2-36, 2-39
types of, 2-24 (Inv 2.3), 2-25 (Pr 2.3)

Reflectas, 14-19, 14-21 (Inv 14.7)

Replacement units
fractions, 10-23, 17-5
geometry, 14-25
multiplication, 5-34
place value, 6-29 & 6-30
statistics, 13-29, 17-5

Roman numerals, 6-4 & 6-6 (Inv 6.1)

Round-robin learning station, 17-11

S

Seeing Fractions: A Unit for Upper Elementary Grades, 10-23, 17-5

Set production
activities, 4-14 (AF 4.5)
definition, 4-4
learning, 4-8

Small-group work, See Cooperative learning

Sorting, See Classifying and sorting

Square tiles
area meaning of fraction division, 10-12 (Pr 10.2)
area meaning of multiplication, 8-17 (Inv 8.8)
even and odd numbers, 8-6 (Inv 8.1)
factors, 1-24 (Inv 1.3)
geometry (definition of rectangles), 1-24 (Inv 1.3)
measurement of area, 1-19 (Box 1.9), 15-19 (AF 15.6)
primes and composites, 8-17 (Inv 8.2)
square numbers and square roots, 8-17 (Inv 8.2)

Statistics, See also Averages, Graphing, Graphs
collecting, organizing, analyzing data, 0-7 & 0-8 (Inv 0.1), 1-20 (Box 1.6 & AF 1.2), 13-1, 13-2, 13-4 (AF 13.1), 13-5 & 13-6 (Inv 13.1), 13-16 to 13-18 (Inv 13.5), 13-27 & 13-28 (Box 13.2), 13-29 (AF 13.2), 15-2 & 15-3 (AF 15.1)
correlations, 13-7, 13-11 & 13-12 (Inv 13.3), 13-13
descriptive statistics, 13-7, 13-13, 13-16 & 13-17 (Inv 13.5)
inferential statistics, 13-13, 13-15, 13-16 & 13-17 (Inv 13.5)
instructional resources, 13-24, 13-29, 13-30
relationships, 13-7, 13-11 & 13-12 (Inv 13.3), 13-13
sampling, 13-13, 13-14 (Inv 13.4), 13-15
spread, 13-7, 13-9 & 13-10 (Pr 13.1), 13-13, 13-16 & 13-17 (Inv 13.5)
teaching tips, 0-7, 13-4, 13-7, 13-13, 13-15, 13-24
types of data, 0-7 & 0-8 (Inv 0.1)
uses, 13-3

APPENDIX E: INDEX OF READER INQUIRIES*

---

*For investigations, ◆ the aims, ◆ grade level, and ◆ intended audience are listed in parentheses.

APPENDIX F:
INDEX OF CHILDREN'S LITERATURE

For books about Children's Literature, see pages 3-39 and 3-40.

BY TITLE

By Topic

APPENDIX G:
TECHNOLOGY INDEX

SOFTWARE, VIDEOS, & LASERDISKS

CALCULATOR APPLICATIONS BY TOPIC

COMPUTER APPLICATIONS BY TOPIC